Not For Tourists Guide to

LONDON

Get more on

notfortourists.com

Keep connected with:

Twitter:
twitter/notfortourists

Facebook:
facebook/notfortourists

iPhone App:
nftiphone.com

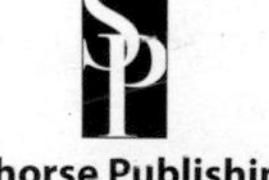

Not For Tourists, Inc

Skyhorse Publishing

designed by:
Not For Tourists, Inc
NFT$_{TM}$—Not For Tourists$_{TM}$ Guide to London
www.notfortourists.com

Publisher
Skyhorse Publishing

Creative Direction & Information Design
Jane Pirone

Director
Stuart Farr

Managing Editor
Scott Sendrow

Production Manager
Aaron Schielke

Writing and Editing
Natalie Ashett
Kate Atwell
Julia Dennison
Adam Kemp
Joseph McCullough
Claire Storrow
Scott Sendrow

Research
Jess Bender

Graphic Design and Production
Aaron Schielke
Sarah Smith

Information Systems Manager
Juan Molinari

Printed in China
ISBN# 978-1-62087-081-5 $18.95 US
ISSN# 2162-7215

5th Edition

Every effort has been made to ensure that the information in this book is as up-to-date as possible at press time. However, many details are liable to change—as we have learned. Not For Tourists cannot accept responsibility for any consequences arising from the use of this book.

Not For Tourists does not solicit individuals, organizations, or businesses for listings inclusion in our guides, nor do we accept payment for inclusion into the editorial portion of our book; the advertising sections, however, are exempt from this policy. We always welcome communications from anyone regarding ANYTHING having to do with our books; please visit us on our website at www.notfortourists.com for appropriate contact information.

www.skyhorsepublishing.com

10 9 8 7 6 5 4 3 2 1

Dear NFT User,

Guess what? It's 2013 and the world didn't end! Yes, we know! Them Mayans, they know nowt! Unlike the team at NFT who know everything that is most important to human beings, namely the best places for quaffing, boogying, spending, and caffeinating ourselves silly in one of the best cities in the world.

Because 2012 really was London's year. We got an extra day's holiday to have a knees-up in honour of Her Maj's Diamond Jubilee. Of course it rained. But all this was just a warm up for the big event: yes, that running-jumping-swimming-cycling-diving event thingummy, the name of which we cannot mention for trademark reasons. Yeah, the Olympics. Just don't print the logo. Or drink Pepsi.

Luckily it all went smashingly, we were ready (eat it Mitt Romney), and Britain's dignity, respectability and credibility remained in tact. Well, there was that moment when Boris got stuck on the zip wire…Oh, and the mix up with the North and South Korean flags…Russell Brand at the Closing Ceremony. But other than that, all good. Well done everyone, jolly good show.

So what of 2013? Well we're going to keep on partying so come, join us, your personal invitation is right here. We've even improved our transport system just for you.

Meanwhile, NASA's rover landed on Mars so if it finds life, there may be a new edition of NFT in the near future.

Jane, Scott & Claire

Central London

West London

North London

East London

Southeast London

Table of Contents

Maps 1–24 • **Central London**

ANGEL
Pentonville Rd
PENTONVILLE
Goswell Rd
City Rd
HOXTON
SHOREDITCH
FINSBURY
Cross Rd
OLD STREET
SPITALFIELDS
Lever St
Calthorpe St
Percival St
Bath St
ST. LUKE'S
Gray's Inn Rd
Rosebery Ave
Farringdon Rd
St. John St
Old St
Bunhill Row
City Rd
Shoreditch High St
CLERKENWELL
Clerkenwell Rd
Aldersgate St
Beech St
Chiswell St
Finsbury Ave
BROADGATE
BRICK LANE
Theobald's Rd
Gray's Inn Gardens
Hatton Gdn
FARRINGDON
BARBICAN
Moorgate
Bishopsgate
Commercial St
Charterhouse St
High Holborn
Holborn
London Wall
Wormwood St
HOLBORN
Chancery Ln
Fetter Ln
Farringdon St
Newgate St
Kingsway
Strand
Fleet St
New Bridge St
Gracechurch St
Minories
COVENT GARDEN
BLACKFRIARS
CITY
Temple Gardens
TEMPLE
Upr Thames St
Lwr Thames St
Tower Hill
Tower Gardens
Tower of London Park
Thames River
Blackfriars Br
Southwark Br
London Br
Tower Br
Waterloo Br
SOUTH BANK
SOUTHWARK
BOROUGH
Jubilee Gardens
NEWINGTON
BERMONDSEY
WATERLOO
Lambeth Palace Garden
ELEPHANT & CASTLE
LAMBETH
WALWORTH
Surrey Square Park
KENNINGTON
Spring Gardens
VAUXHALL
Burgess Park
5
6
7
8
14
15
16
17
18

Map 1 • Marylebone (West)

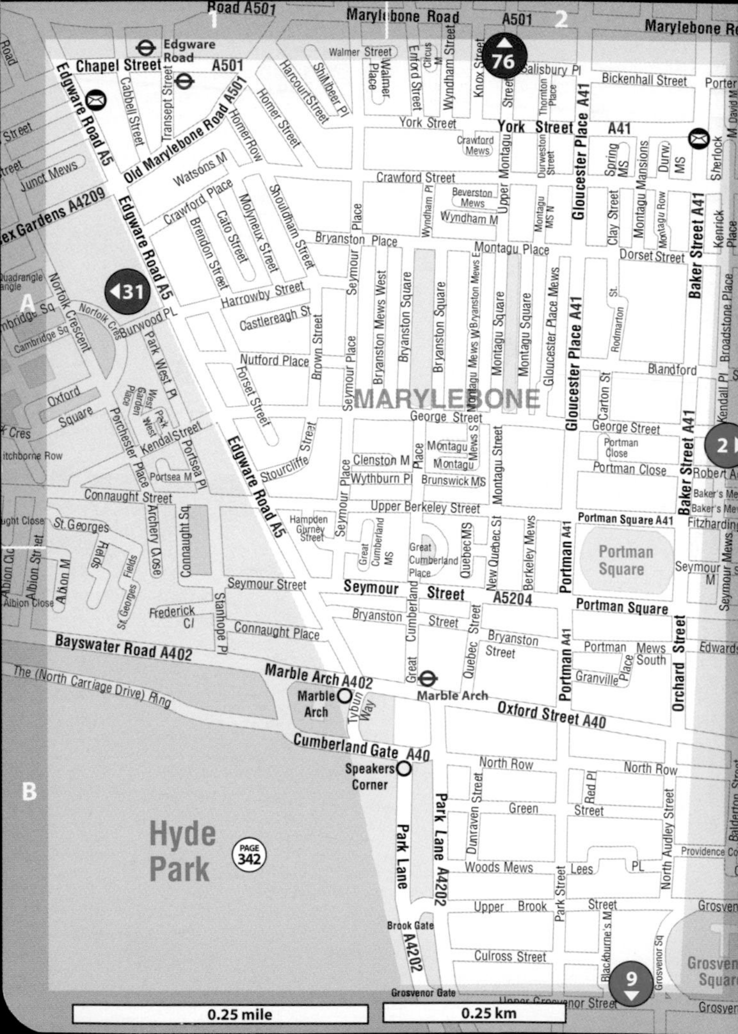

N

Road A501
Marylebone Road
A501
Marylebone Road
1
2
Edgware Road
Chapel Street
A501
Edgware Road A5
Cabbell Street
Transept Street
Old Marylebone Road A501
Homer Row
Homer Street
Harcourt Street
Shillibeer Pl
Walmer Street
Walmer Place
Enford Street
Circus M
Wyndham Street
Knox Street
76
Salisbury Pl
Bickenhall Street
Porter
Street
Thornton Place
Gloucester Place A41
York Street
York Street
A41
Crawford Mews
Upper Montagu
Durweston Street
Spring MS
Montagu Mansions
Durw. MS
Sherlock
Street
Junct Mews
Watsons M
Crawford Street
Beverston Mews
Wyndham Pl
Wyndham M
Montagu MS N
Gloucester Place
Clay Street
Montagu Row
Baker Street A41
Kenrick Place
Sussex Gardens A4209
Crawford Place
Brendon Street
Cato Street
Molyneux Street
Shouldham Street
Bryanston Place
Seymour Place
Montagu Place
Dorset Street
Edgware Road A5
31
Quadrangle
A
Cambridge Sq
Norfolk Crescent
Norfolk Cres
Burwood PL
Harrowby Street
Castlereagh St
Brown Street
Bryanston Mews West
Bryanston Square
Bryanston Square
Montagu Mews W
Bryanston Mews E
Montagu Square
Montagu Square
Gloucester Place Mews
Gloucester Place A41
Rodmarton St.
Broadstone Place
Park West Pl
Nutford Place
Forset Street
Seymour Place
MARYLEBONE
Blandford
Kendall Pl
Oxford Square
West Garden Place
Park West
Porchester Place
Kendal Street
Portsea Pl
Portsea M
George Street
Carton St
George Street
Baker Street A41
2
Stourcliffe Street
Clenston M
Wythburn Pl
Place
Montagu Mews S
Montagu
Montagu
Brunswick MS
Montagu Street
Portman Close
Portman Close
Robert Adam
Hitchborne Row
Connaught Street
Archery Close
Connaught Sq
Edgware Road A5
Upper Berkeley Street
Seymour Place
Hampden Gurney Street
Great Cumberland MS
Great Cumberland Place
Quebec MS
New Quebec St
Berkeley Mews
Portman A41
Portman Square A41
Portman Square
Baker's Mews
Baker's Mews
Fitzhardinge
Seymour M
Seymour Mews
St Georges Fields
Albion Close
Albion Street
Albion M
Albion Close
Seymour Street
Seymour Street A5204
Portman Square
St Georges Fields
Frederick Cl
Stanhope Pl
Connaught Place
Bryanston Street
Cumberland
Quebec Street
Bryanston Street
Portman A41
Portman Mews South
Granville Place
Orchard Street
Edwards
Bayswater Road A402
The (North Carriage Drive) Ring
Marble Arch A402
Marble Arch
Tyburn Way
Great
Marble Arch
Oxford Street A40
Cumberland Gate A40
Speakers Corner
North Row
North Row
B
Dunraven Street
Green
Red Pl
Street
North Audley Street
Balderton Street
Hyde Park
PAGE 342
Park Lane A4202
Park Lane
Woods Mews
Park Street
Lees PL
Providence Co
Upper Brook Street
Grosvenor
Brook Gate
A4202
Culross Street
Blackburne's M
Grosvenor Sq
Grosvenor Square
9
Grosvenor Gate
Upper Grosvenor Street
Grosvenor
0.25 mile
0.25 km

Marylebone (West)

Where the mullah meets the hookah, a stroll down Edgware Road is soundtracked by gurgling shisha pipes and bangin' Arabic pop music. To the east, ostentatiously bejewelled madams patrol Montague Square. They'd turn their noses up at a Shawarma at Beirut Express on the way to the Sequoia Ruby Lo, and probably wouldn't deign to shop at Maroush Deli. Good, more for the rest of us.

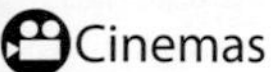

Cinemas

- **Odeon Marble Arch** • 10 Edgware Rd
- **Everyman Baker Street** • 96 Baker St

Coffee

- **Apostrophe** • 19 Baker St
- **Bagel Factory** • 39 Paddington St
- **Caffe Nero** • 184 Edgware Rd
- **Eat.** • 400 Oxford St
- **Eat.** • 114 Baker St
- **Kings Café** • 177 Edgware Rd
- **Palm Cafe Shisha Bar** • 7 Crawford Pl
- **Pret A Manger** • 556 Oxford St
- **Starbucks** • 29 N Audley St
- **Starbucks** • 34 Edgware Rd

Landmarks

- **Marble Arch** • Oxford St & Park Ln
- **Speakers' Corner** • Cumberland Gate & Park Ln

Nightlife

- **Duke of York** • 45 Harrowby St
- **Sequoia Ruby Lounge** • 23 Orchard St

Post Offices

- **Baker St** • 111 Baker St
- **Edgware Rd** • 354 Edgware Rd

Restaurants

- **Beirut Express** • 112 Edgware Rd
- **Locanda Locatelli** • 8 Seymour St
- **Maroush VI Express** • 68 Edgware Rd
- **Nippon Tuk** • 225 Edgware Rd

Shopping

- **Maroush Deli** • 45 Edgware Rd
- **Phil Parker** • 106 Crawford St
- **Primark** • 499 Oxford St
- **Spymaster** • 3 Portman Sq
- **Totally Swedish** • 32 Crawford St

Supermarkets

- **Sainsbury's** • 55 Bryanston St

Map 2 • Marylebone (East)

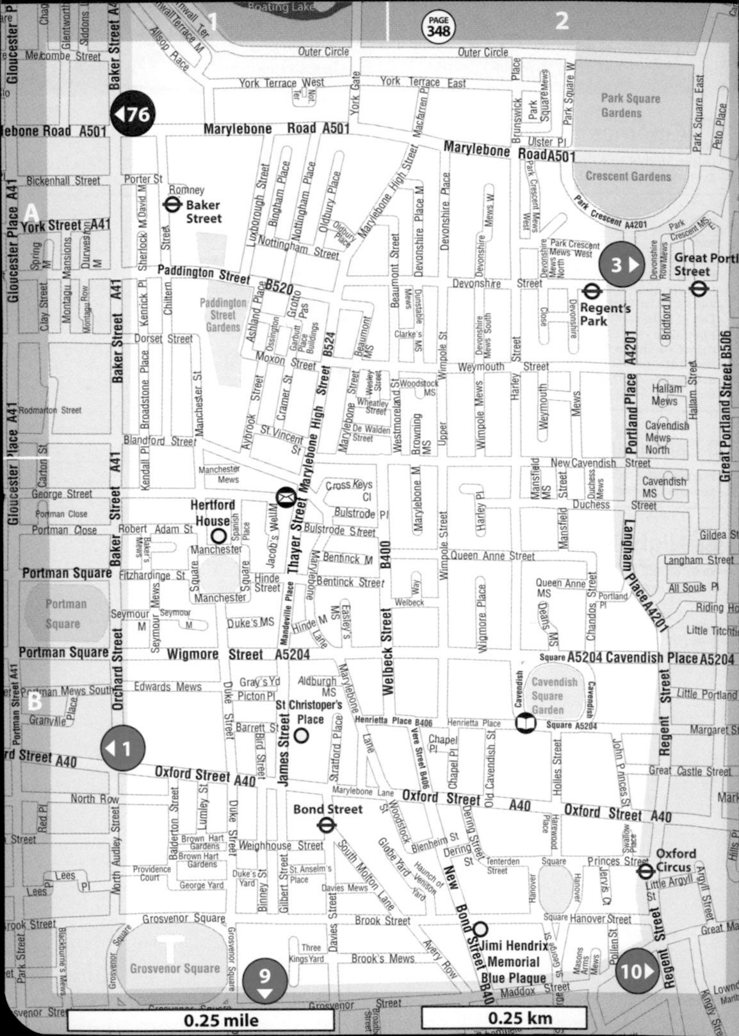

Marylebone (East)

Granted the plush boutiques and old moneyisms of Marylebone are far removed from most Londoners' lives but that's not to say you can't go window shopping, and with VV Rouleaux and the Button Queen nearby, you could even craft your own outfit. Don't forget to stop in at Claridge's to tell Gordon Ramsay to f*** off, then sedate yourself in the beautiful book haven that is Daunt.

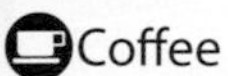

Coffee

- **Apostrophe** • 23 Barrett St
- **Caffe Nero** • 273 Regent St
- **Caffe Nero** • Marylebone Rd
- **Coffee Republic** • 2 S Molton St
- **Costa** • 69 Wigmore St
- **Eat.** • 9 Avery Row
- **Eat.** • 319 Regent St
- **Eat.** • 25 Hanover Sq
- **Eat.** • 92 Wimpole St
- **Eat.** • 214 Oxford St
- **Paul Rothe & Son** • 35 Marylebone Ln
- **Pret A Manger** • 31 Cavendish
- **Pret A Manger** • 1 Ienterden St
- **Pret A Manger** • 18 Hanover St
- **Starbucks** • 22 Princes St
- **Starbucks** • 14 James St
- **Starbucks** • 63 S Molton St

Landmarks

- **Hertford House** • Manchester Sq
- **Jimi Hendrix Memorial Blue Plaque** • 23 Brook St
- **St. Christoper's Place** • 23 Barrett St

Libraries

- **Royal College of Nursing Library** • 20 Cavendish Sq

Nightlife

- **Claridge's Bar** • 55 Brook St
- **Inn 1888** • 21 Devonshire St
- **Moors Bar** • 57 Paddington St
- **The Phoenix** • 37 Cavendish Sq

Post Offices

- **Marylebone** • 24 Thayer St

Restaurants

- **Comptoir Libanais** • 65 Wigmore St
- **Diwan** • 31 Thayer St
- **The Golden Hind** • 73 Marylebone Ln
- **Galvin Bistrot de Luxe** • 66 Baker St
- **Gordon Ramsay at Claridge's** • Brook St
- **Hush Brasserie** • 8 Lancashire Ct
- **La Galette** • 56 Paddington St
- **Meatliquor** • 74 Welbeck St
- **No. 5 Cavendish Square** • 5 Cavendish Sq
- **Patisserie Valerie** • 105 Marylebone High St
- **The Providores** • 109 Marylebone High St
- **Sakura** • 9 Hanover St

Shopping

- **Browns** • 24 S Molton St
- **The Button Queen** • 76 Marylebone Ln
- **Content Beauty/Wellbeing** • 14 Bulstrode Street
- **Daunt Books** • 83 Marylebone High St
- **Divertimenti** • 33 Maryelbone High St
- **The Duffer of St. George** • 268 Oxford St
- **Fenwick** • 63 New Bond St
- **French Sole** • 61 Marylebone Ln
- **Gray's Antique Market** • 58 Davies St
- **John Lewis** • 300 Oxford St
- **La Fromagerie** • 2 Moxon St
- **Marimekko** • 16 St Christopher's Pl
- **Monocle** • 2 George St
- **Niketown** • 236 Oxford St
- **Noa Noa** • 14 Gees Ct
- **Paul Smith** • 38 Marylebone High St
- **Paul Smith Sale Shop** • 23 Avery Row
- **Romanian Charity Shop** • 18 Fitzhardinge St
- **Selfridges & Co.** • 400 Oxford St
- **Skandium** • 86 Marylebone High St
- **VV Rouleaux** • 102 Marylebone Ln
- **The Widescreen Centre** • 47 Dorset St
- **Zara** • 242 Oxford St

Supermarkets

- **Marks & Spencer** • Bond St Station
- **Waitrose** • 98 Marylebone High St

Map 3 • Fitzrovia

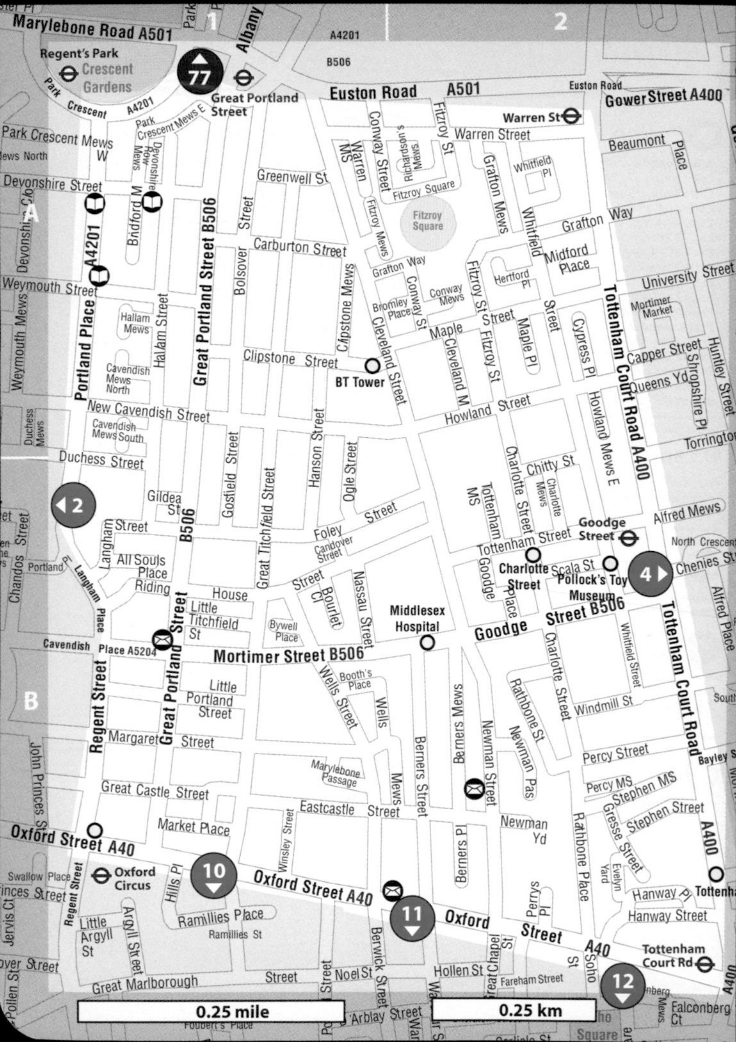

Marylebone Road A501
Regent's Park
Crescent Gardens
Park Crescent
A4201
Great Portland Street
Albany Street
Euston Road A501
A4201
B506
Euston Road
Gower Street A400
Warren St
Warren Street
Park Crescent Mews W
Park Crescent Mews E
Devonshire Row Mews
Devonshire Street
Greenwell St
Conway Street
Richardson's Mews
Fitzroy St
Fitzroy Square
Warren MS
Grafton Mews
Whitfield Pl
Beaumont Place
Bridford M
Great Portland Street B506
Bolsover Street
Carburton Street
Fitzroy Mews
Grafton Way
Whitfield Street
Midford Place
Hertford Pl
University Street
Weymouth Street
Portland Place A4201
Weymouth Mews
Hallam Mews
Hallam Street
Clipstone Mews
Bromley Place
Conway St
Conway Mews
Maple Street
Maple Pl
Cypress Pl
Tottenham Court Road A400
Mortimer Market
Capper Street
Huntley Street
Shropshire Pl
Queens Yd
Cavendish Mews North
Clipstone Street
BT Tower
Cleveland Street
Cleveland M
Fitzroy St
New Cavendish Street
Duchess Mews
Cavendish Mews South
Howland Street
Howland Mews E
Torrington
Duchess Street
Gostield Street
Great Titchfield Street
Hanson Street
Ogle Street
Charlotte Street
Chitty St
Charlotte Mews
Tottenham MS
Alfred Mews
Gildea St
B506
Foley Street
Candover Street
Goodge Street
Tottenham Street
North Crescent
Chenies St
Langham Street
All Souls Place
Riding House Street
Portland Pl
Langham Place
Chandos Street
Charlotte Street
Scala St
Pollock's Toy Museum
Goodge Place
Bourlet Cl
Nassau Street
Middlesex Hospital
Goodge Street B506
Alfred Place
Little Titchfield St
Bywell Place
Cavendish Place A5204
Mortimer Street B506
Whitfield Street
Tottenham Court Road
Regent Street
Great Portland Street
Little Portland Street
Wells Street
Booth's Place
Wells Mews
Berners Mews
Newman Street
Rathbone St
Windmill St
John Princes St
Margaret Street
Berners Street
Newman Pas
Percy Street
Bayley St
Great Castle Street
Marylebone Passage
Percy MS
Stephen MS
Stephen Street
Eastcastle Street
Market Place
Winsley Street
Newman Yd
Gresse Street
Rathbone Place
A400
Oxford Street A40
Oxford Circus
Hills Pl
Berners Pl
Evelyn Yard
Swallow Place
Princes Street
Regent Street
Oxford Street A40
Perrys Pl
Hanway Pl
Hanway Street
Little Argyll St
Argyll Street
Ramillies Place
Ramillies St
Berwick Street
Oxford Street A40
Chapel St
Soho St
Tottenham Court Rd
Great Marlborough Street
Noel St
Hollen St
Fareham Street
Falconberg Ct
Falconberg Mews
Poland St
D'Arblay Street
Foubert's Place
Soho Square
Carlisle St

0.25 mile
0.25 km

Fitzrovia

Map 3

There's a whole recent trend for upmarket Fiztrovians to roam east in return for trendsetting east-enders giving their neighbourhood a bit of cool cred—they're all swapping galleries and premises and god knows what else in some kind of grown-up-exchange programme. Fitrovis has its own history of cool though; you might be lucky enough to see a star or two at the BBC on Great Portland.

Cinemas

- **Odeon Tottenham Court** • 30 Tottenham Ct Rd

Coffee

- **Apostrophe** • 40 Great Castle St
- **Apostrophe** • 216 Tottenham Court Rd
- **BB's Coffee and Muffins** • 120 Oxford St
- **Caffe Nero** • 79 Tottenham Ct Rd
- **Caffe Nero** • 187 Tottenham Ct Rd
- **Caffe Nero** • 2 Charlotte St
- **Caffe Nero** • 48 Oxford St
- **Coffee Republic** • 99 Tottenham Ct Rd
- **Eat.** • 44 Goodge St
- **Eat.** • 68 Oxford St
- **Eat.** • 94 Tottenham Ct Rd
- **Kaffeine** • 66 Great Titchfield St
- **Lantana** • 13 Charlotte Pl
- **Pret A Manger** • 298 Regent St
- **Starbucks** • 203 Oxford St
- **Starbucks** • 51 Goodge St
- **Tapped and Packed** • 114 Tottenham Court Rd

Landmarks

- **BT Tower** • 60 Cleveland St
- **Charlotte Street** • Charlotte St
- **Middlesex Hospital** • Mortimer St & Cleveland St
- **Pollock's Toy Museum** • 1 Scala St
- **Sinner Winner Man** • 216 Oxford St
- **Tottenham Court Road** • Tottenham Ct Rd

Libraries

- **RIBA British Architectural Library** • 66 Portland Pl
- **Institute of Contemporary History and Wiener Library** • 4 Devonshire St
- **Royal Institute of British Architects** • 66 Portland Pl

Nightlife

- **100 Club** • 100 Oxford St
- **The Albany** • 240 Great Portland St
- **Bourne & Hollingsworth** • 28 Rathbone Pl
- **Bradley's Spanish Bar** • 42 Hanway St
- **Bricklayers Arms** • 31 Gresse St
- **Charlotte Street Hotel** • 15 Charlotte St
- **The Cock** • 27 Great Portland St
- **The Fitzroy Tavern** • 16 Charlotte St
- **The Jerusalem Tavern** • 55 Britton St
- **Market Place** • 11 Market Pl
- **The Northumberland Arms** • 43 Goodge St
- **Punk** • 14 Soho St
- **Rising Sun** • 46 Tottenham Ct Rd
- **The Roxy** • 3 Rathbone Pl
- **The Social** • 5 Little Portland St
- **Yorkshire Grey** • 46 Langham St

Post Offices

- **Great Portland St** • 55 Great Portland St
- **Newman St** • 19 Newman St
- **Oxford Street** • 120 Oxford St

Restaurants

- **Archipelago** • 110 Whitfield St
- **Ask** • 48 Grafton Way
- **Beard Papa** • 143 Oxford St
- **Carluccio's** • 8 Market Pl
- **Chutney & Lager** • 43 Great Titchfield St
- **Crazy Bear** • 26 Whitfield St
- **Eagle Bar Diner** • 3 Rathbone Pl
- **Elena's L'Etoile** • 30 Charlotte St
- **Govinda's** • 9 Soho St
- **ICCo** • 46 Goodge St
- **Latium** • 21 Berners St
- **Market Place** • 11 Market Pl
- **Navarro's** • 67 Charlotte St
- **Ragam** • 57 Cleveland St
- **Rasa Express** • 5 Rathbone St
- **Roka** • 37 Charlotte St
- **Salt Yard** • 54 Goodge St
- **Sardo** • 45 Grafton Way
- **Squat & Gobble** • 69 Charlotte St
- **Stef's** • 3 Berners St
- **Thai Metro** • 38 Charlotte St

Shopping

- **Computer Exchange** • 32 Rathbone Pl
- **Chess & Bridge** • 369 Euston Rd
- **Harmony** • 103 Oxford St
- **Hobgoblin Music** • 24 Rathbone Pl
- **Mango** • 225 Oxford St
- **Maplin** • 218 Tottenham Ct Rd
- **Paperchase** • 213 Tottenham Ct Rd
- **R.D. Franks** • 5 Winsley St
- **Scandinavian Kitchen** • 61 Great Titchfield St
- **Stargreen Box Office** • 21 Argyll St
- **Topshop** • 36 Great Castle St
- **Topshop** • 216 Oxford St
- **Urban Outfitters** • 200 Oxford St

Supermarkets

- **Marks & Spencer** • 55 Tottenham Ct Rd
- **Sainsbury's** • 35 Mortimer St
- **Sainsbury's** • 17 Tottenham Ct Rd
- **Sainsbury's** • 145 Tottenham Ct Rd
- **Tesco** • 10 Goodge St

Map 4 • Bloomsbury (West)

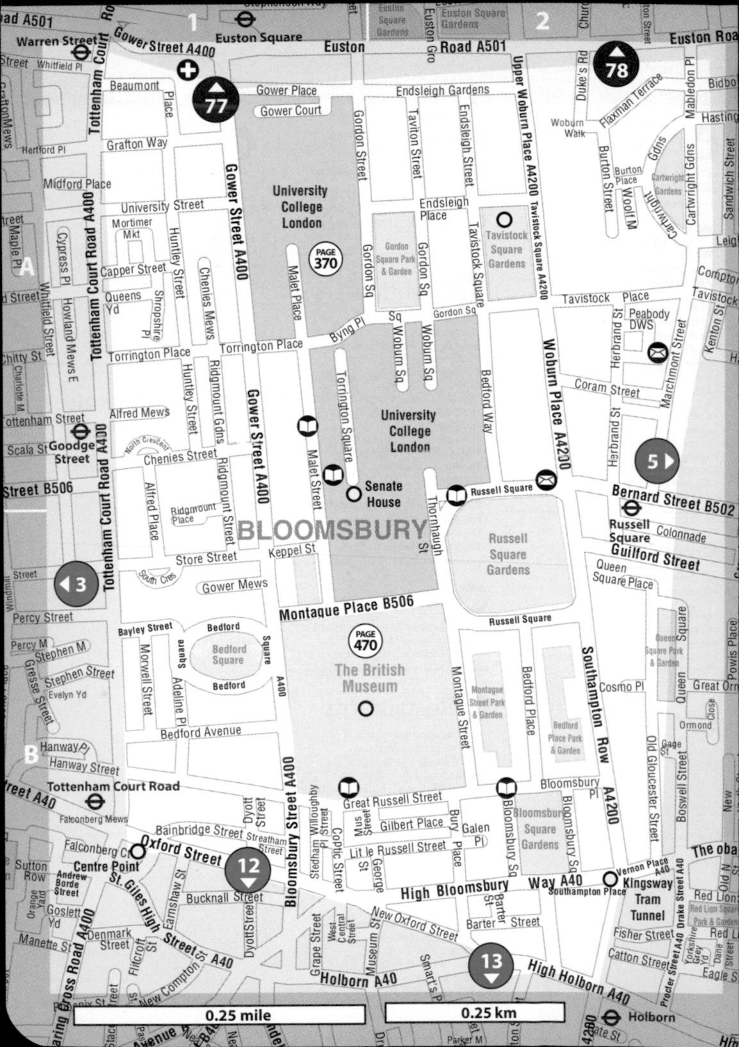

Euston Square
Warren Street
Gower Street A400
Euston Road A501
Euston Square Gardens
Tottenham Court Road A400
Beaumont Place
Gower Place
Gower Court
Endsleigh Gardens
Upper Woburn Place A4200
Duke's Rd
Flaxman Terrace
Woburn Walk
Mabledon Pl
Grafton Way
Midford Place
University Street
University College London
Gordon Street
Taviton Street
Endsleigh Street
Endsleigh Place
Burton Street
Burton Place
Cartwright Gardens
Tavistock Square Gardens
Tavistock Square A4200
Mortimer Mkt
Capper Street
Huntley Street
Chenies Mews
Malet Place
Gordon Square Park & Garden
Gordon Sq
Tavistock Square
Tavistock Place
Queens Yd
Shropshire Pl
Torrington Place
Byng Pl
Woburn Sq
Herbrand St
Peabody DWS
Marchmont Street
Howland Mews E
Whitfield Street
Cypress Pl
Maple Pl
Alfred Mews
Ridgmount Gdns
Torrington Square
Bedford Way
Woburn Place A4200
Coram Street
Goodge Street
North Crescent
Chenies Street
Malet Street
Senate House
Russell Square
Bernard Street B502
Guilford Street
Russell Square Gardens
Colonnade
Alfred Place
Ridgmount Place
Ridgmount Street
BLOOMSBURY
Keppel St
Thornhaugh St
Store Street
South Cres
Gower Mews
Queen Square Place
Montague Place B506
Percy Street
Bayley Street
Bedford Square
Morwell Street
Adeline Pl
The British Museum
Montague Street
Montague Street Park & Garden
Bedford Place
Bedford Place Park & Garden
Southampton Row
Cosmo Pl
Queen Square
Queen Square Park & Garden
Stephen Mews
Stephen Street
Gresse Street
Evelyn Yd
Bedford Avenue
Hanway Pl
Hanway Street
Tottenham Court Road
Great Russell Street
Bloomsbury Pl
Old Gloucester Street
Boswell Street
Gage St
Falconberg Mews
Bainbridge Street
Dyott Street
Streatham Street
Bloomsbury Street A400
Stedham Pl
Willoughby Street
Coptic Street
Museum Street
Gilbert Place
Bury Place
Galen Pl
Bloomsbury Sq
Bloomsbury Square Gardens
Oxford Street
Falconberg Ct
Centre Point
Sutton Row
Andrew Borde Street
St. Giles High Street A40
Earnshaw St
Bucknall Street
Little Russell Street
George St
High Bloomsbury Way A40
Vernon Place A40
Southampton Place
Kingsway Tram Tunnel
Goslett Yd
Charing Cross Road A400
Denmark Street
Manette St
Flitcroft St
New Compton St
Grape Street
West Central Street
New Oxford Street
Barter Street
Fisher Street
Catton Street
Procter Street A40
Drake Street A40
Red Lion Square
Red Lion Square Park & Garden
High Holborn A40
Holborn A40
Smart's Pl
Holborn
Eagle St

PAGE 370
PAGE 470

0.25 mile

0.25 km

Bloomsbury (West)

Bloomsbury didn't incite and excite Britain's most prolific set of literature writers for no good reason. These streets ooze the kind of romanticised idea of London that had Virginia Woolf and E.M Forster zoned in on for inspiration. Clever people have lived here in Bloomsbury and cleverer people still visit. The British Museum's Age of Illumination collection highlights the world's learners.

Cinemas

- **Horse Hospital** • 30 Colonnade
- **Odeon Tottenham Court** • 30 Tottenham Ct Rd

Coffee

- **Café Deco** • 43 Store St
- **Costa** • 44 New Oxford St
- **Costa** • 82 Gower St
- **London Review Cake Shop** • 14 Bury Pl
- **Pret A Manger** • 40 Bernard St
- **Pret A Manger** • 23 Southampton Row
- **Pret A Manger** • 44 New Oxford St
- **Pret A Manger** • 102 Southampton Row
- **Ruskins Cafe** • 41 Museum St
- **Starbucks** • 124 Southampton Row
- **Starbucks** • 112 New Oxford
- **Starbucks** • 425 Oxford St
- **Store Street Espresso** • 40 Store St

Emergency Rooms

- **University College Hospital** • 235 Euston Rd

Landmarks

- **British Museum** • Great Russell St
- **Centre Point** • 101 New Oxford St
- **Kingsway Tram Tunnel** • Theobald's Rd & Southampton Row
- **Senate House** • Malet St & Torrington Sq
- **Tavistock Square** • Tavistock Sq

Libraries

- **Anthropology Library** • Great Russell St
- **Birkbeck College Library** • Malet St
- **German Historical Institute Library London** • 17 Bloomsbury Sq
- **Institute of Advanced Legal Studies Library** • 17 Russell Square
- **University of London, Senate House Library** • Malet St

Nightlife

- **101 Bar** • 101 New Oxford St
- **All Star Lanes** • Victoria House, Bloomsbury Pl
- **Bloomsbury Bowling Lanes** • Bedford Way
- **The Fly** • 36 New Oxford
- **Marquis Cornwallis** • 31 Marchmont St
- **The Old Crown Public House** • 33 New Oxford St
- **The Plough** • 27 Museum St
- **The Princess Louise** • 208 High Holborn
- **ULU** • Malet St

Post Offices

- **Marchmont St** • 33 Marchmont St
- **Russell Square** • 9 Russell Sq

Restaurants

- **Alara** • 58 Marchmont St
- **Bi Won** • 24 Coptic St
- **Savoir Faire** • 42 New Oxford St

Shopping

- **Blade Rubber Stamps** • 12 Bury Pl
- **British Museum shop** • Great Russell St
- **Cinema Bookshop** • 13 Great Russell St
- **Gosh!** • 1 Berwick St
- **James Smith & Sons** • 53 New Oxford St
- **London Review Bookshop** • 14 Bury Pl
- **Maplin** • 218 Tottenham Ct Rd
- **Paperchase** • 213 Tottenham Ct Rd
- **Shepherds Bookbinders** • 76 Southampton Row
- **York Cameras** • 18 Bury Pl

Supermarkets

- **Waitrose** • Brunswick Sq

Map 5 • Bloomsbury (East)

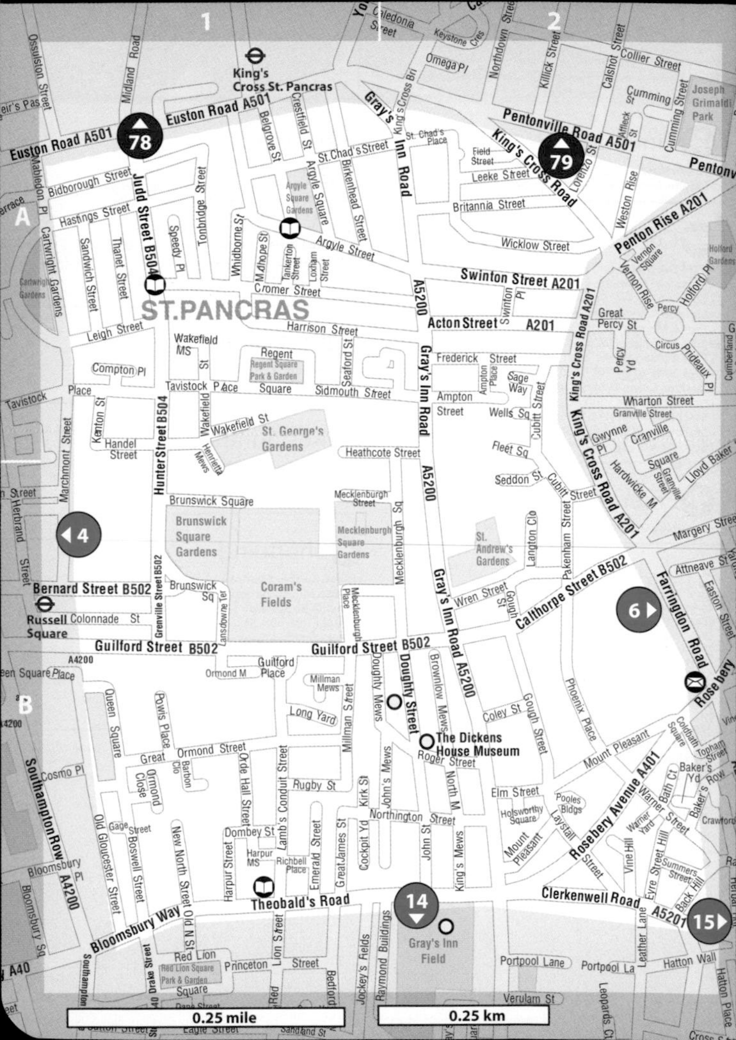

N

1
2
A
B

King's Cross St. Pancras
Euston Road A501
Pentonville Road A501
King's Cross Road
Gray's Inn Road
Caledonia Street
Keystone Cres
Omega Pl
Northdown Street
Killick Street
Calshot Street
Collier Street
Cumming Street
Joseph Grimaldi Park
Affleck St
Lorenzo St
Ossulston Street
Midland Road
Crestfield St
Belgrove St
St. Chad's Street
St. Chad's Place
Field Street
Leeke Street
Britannia Street
Wicklow Street
Weston Rise
Penton Rise A201
Mableton Pl
Bidborough Street
Hastings Street
Judd Street B504
Tonbridge Street
Speedy Pl
Whidborne St
Argyle Square Gardens
Argyle Square
Birkenhead Street
Argyle Street
Midhope St
Tankerton Street
Loxham Street
Cromer Street
Swinton Street A201
Vernon Square
Vernon Rise
Holford Pl
Holford Gardens
Cartwright Gardens
Sandwich Street
Thanet Street
ST. PANCRAS
A5200
Acton Street
Swinton Pl
A201
King's Cross Road A201
Great Percy St
Percy Circus
Prideaux Pl
Cumberland
Leigh Street
Wakefield MS
Regent Square Park & Garden
Regent Square
Harrison Street
Seaford St
Frederick Street
Ampton Place
Sage Way
Compton Pl
Tavistock Place
Tavistock Pl
Sidmouth Street
Ampton Street
Wells Sq
Cubitt Street
Percy Yd
Wharton Street
Granville Street
Gwynne Pl
Granville Square
Kenton St
Marchmont Street
Handel Street
Hunter Street B504
Wakefield St
Henrietta Mews
St. George's Gardens
Heathcote Street
Fleet Sq
Hardwicke M
Lloyd Baker St
Seddon St
Cubitt Street
Brunswick Square
Mecklenburgh Street
Mecklenburgh Sq
Brunswick Square Gardens
Mecklenburgh Square Gardens
St. Andrew's Gardens
Langton Clo
Pakenham Street
Margery Street
Herbrand Street
Attneave St
Bernard Street B502
Grenville Street B502
Brunswick Sq
Lansdowne Ter
Coram's Fields
Mecklenburgh Place
Wren Street
Gough St
Calthorpe Street B502
Farringdon Road
Easton Street
Russell Square
Colonnade St
Guilford Street B502
A4200
Queen Square Place
Guilford Place
Ormond M
Millman Mews
Doughty Mews
Doughty Street
Brownlow Mews
Gray's Inn Road A5200
Phoenix Place
Rosebery
Queen Square
Powis Place
Long Yard
Millman Street
Coley St
Gough Street
Coldbath Square
Topham Street
The Dickens House Museum
Roger Street
Mount Pleasant
Great Ormond Street
Barbon Clo
Orde Hall Street
Lamb's Conduit Street
Rugby St
Kirk St
John's Mews
North M
Elm Street
Pooles Bldgs
Holsworthy Square
Laystall Street
Rosebery Avenue A401
Warner Street
Bath Ct
Baker's Yd
Baker's Row
Crawford
Southampton Row
Cosmo Pl
Ormond Close
Old Gloucester Street
Gage Street
Boswell Street
New North Street
Dombey St
Harpur MS
Richbell Place
Emerald Street
Great James St
Cockpit Yd
Northington Street
John St
King's Mews
Mount Pleasant
Warner Yard
Vine Hill
Eyre Street Hill
Summers Street
Back Hill
Bloomsbury Pl
Bloomsbury Sq
A4200
Harpur Street
Theobald's Road
Clerkenwell Road
A5201
Bloomsbury Way
Old N St
Red Lion
Red Lion Square Park & Garden
Red Lion Square
Princeton Street
Lion Street
Jockey's Fields
Raymond Buildings
Gray's Inn Field
Portpool Lane
Portpool La
Leather Lane
Hatton Wall
Hatton Place
A40
Southampton
Drake Street
Dane Street
Eagle Street
Sandland St
Bedford
Red
Verulam St
Leopards Ct
Cross St

78
79
4
6
14
15

0.25 mile
0.25 km

Bloomsbury (East)

Agog with students, this tract of Bloomsbury is a bustling cultural playground. The brilliant Renoir Cinema resides in the belly of the Brunswick Centre, a Brutalist masterpiece with some posh shops thrown in for good measure. For contrast, stroll over to Lamb's Conduit Street and enjoy some boutique shopping. Indulge in a sit-down cream tea at Bea's or fill up on pizza slices at Malletti.

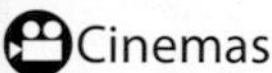

Cinemas

- **Renoir Cinema** • 1 Brunswick Sq

Coffee

- **The Espresso Room** • 31–35 Great Ormond St
- **Pret A Manger** • 15 Theobald's Rd
- **Starbucks** • 57 Theobald's Rd
- **T-HQ** • 55 Gray's Inn Rd

Landmarks

- **Charles Dickens Museum** • 48 Doughty St
- **Gray's Inn Field** • Theobald's Rd
- **Doughty Street** • Doughty St & Guilford St

Libraries

- **Holborn Library** • 32 Theobald's Rd
- **Royal National Institute of the Blind Research Library** • 105 Judd St
- **St Pancras Library** • Argyle St

Nightlife

- **06 St Chad's Place** • 6 St Chad's Pl
- **The Blue Lion** • 133 Grays Inn Rd
- **Calthorpe Arms** • 252 Gray's Inn Rd
- **The Clerk & Well** • 156 Clerkenwell Rd
- **King's Cross Social Club** • 2 Britannia Street
- **The Lamb** • 94 Lamb's Conduit St
- **Monto** • 328 Grays Inn Rd
- **The Perseverance** • 63 Lamb's Conduit St
- **Smithy's** • 15 Leeke St

Post Offices

- **Mount Pleasant** • Farringdon Rd & Rosebery Ave

Restaurants

- **Acorn House** • 69 Swinton St
- **Aki Bistro** • 182 Gray's Inn Rd
- **Bea's of Bloomsbury** • 44 Theobald's Rd
- **Bread and Butter Sandwich Bar** • 100 Judd St
- **Ciao Bella** • 86 Lamb's Conduit St
- **Cigala** • 54 Lamb's Conduit St
- **The Food Bazaar** • 59 Grays Inn Rd
- **Fryer's Delight** • 19 Theobald's Rd
- **Konstam** • 2 Acton St
- **La Provence** • 63 Grays Inn Rd
- **Malletti** • 174 Clerkenwell Rd
- **Mary Ward Centre** • 42 Queen Sq
- **Paolina Thai Snack Bar** • 181 King's Cross Rd
- **The Perseverance** • 63 Lamb's Conduit St
- **Swintons** • 61 Swinton St
- **Thai Candle** • 38 Lamb's Conduit St
- **YouMeSushi** • 180 Grays Inn Rd

Shopping

- **Bibas Hair and Beauty** • 72 Marchmont St
- **The Brunswick** • Hunter St
- **The Flash Centre** • 68 Brunswick Centre
- **Folk** • 49 Lamb's Conduit St
- **International Magic** • 89 Clerkenwell Rd
- **JOY** • 22 Brunswick Centre
- **Magma** • 117 Clerkenwell Rd
- **Something** • 58 Lamb's Conduit St

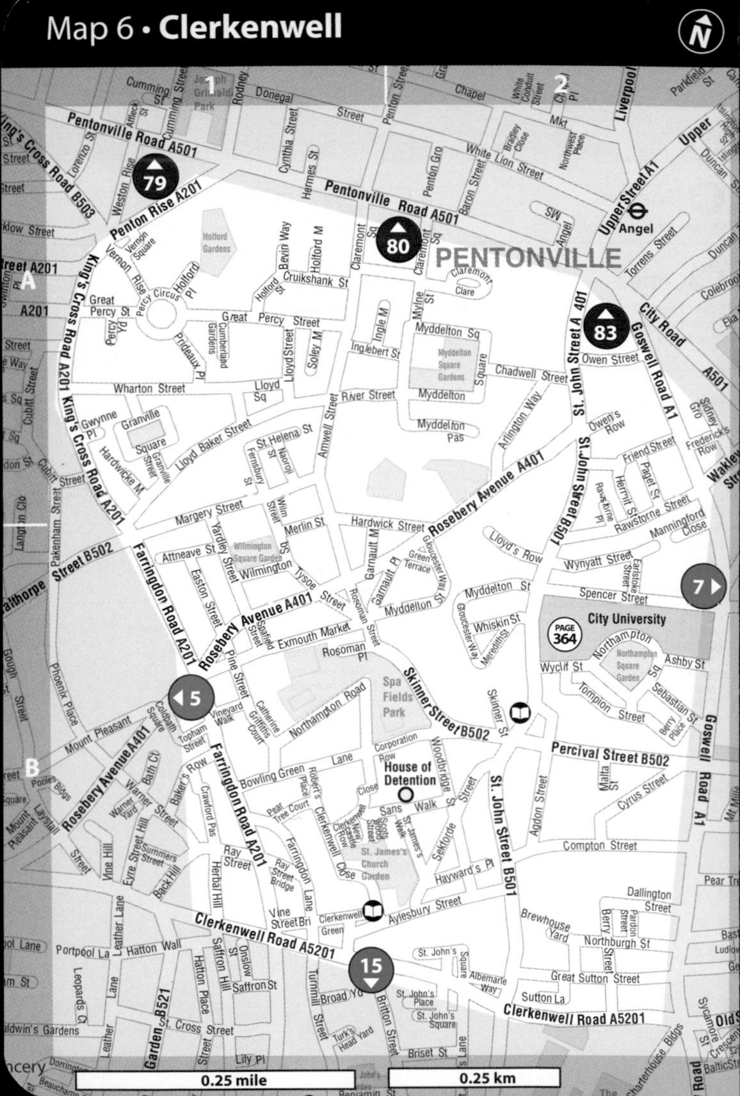

Map 6 • Clerkenwell
N
1
2
A
B
79
80
83
7
5
15
PAGE 364
PENTONVILLE
Angel
City University
House of Detention
Spa Fields Park
Holford Gardens
Myddelton Square Gardens
Wilmington Square Garden
Northampton Square Garden
St. James's Church Garden
Joseph Grimaldi Park
Pentonville Road A501
Penton Rise A201
King's Cross Road A201
King's Cross Road B503
Rosebery Avenue A401
Farringdon Road A201
St. John Street A401
St. John Street B501
Goswell Road A1
Upper Street A1
City Road
Clerkenwell Road A5201
Skinner Street B502
Percival Street B502
Calthorpe Street B502
Chapel Mkt
White Lion Street
Donegal Street
Cumming St
Cynthia Street
Hermes St
Penton Gro
Baron Street
Claremont Sq
Cruikshank St
Bevin Way
Holford M
Great Percy St
Percy Circus
Vernon Rise
Vernon Square
Prideaux Pl
Cumberland Gardens
Lloyd Street
Soley M
Ingle M
Inglebert St
Myddelton Sq
Chadwell Street
Owen Street
Amwell Street
River Street
Myddelton Pas
Arlington Way
Wharton Street
Lloyd Sq
Lloyd Baker Street
Granville Square
Gwynne Pl
Hardwicke M
St. Helena St
Fernsbury St
Margery Street
Wilmington Square
Merlin St
Hardwick Street
Garnault M
Garnault Pl
Green Terrace
Gloucester Way
Lloyd's Row
Wynyatt Street
Spencer Street
Rawstorne Street
Friend Street
Owen's Row
Manningford Close
Attneave St
Yardley Street
Easton Street
Tysoe Street
Rosoman Street
Rosoman Pl
Myddelton St
Whiskin St
Exmouth Market
Pine Street
Northampton Road
Wyclif St
Ashby St
Tompion Street
Sebastian St
Mount Pleasant
Phoenix Place
Coldbath Square
Vineyard Walk
Topham Street
Catherine Griffiths Court
Corporation Row
Bowling Green Lane
Woodbridge St
Baker's Row
Warner Street
Crawford Pas
Ray Street
Sans Walk
Sekforde Street
Agdon Street
Cyrus Street
Compton Street
Hayward's Pl
Herbal Hill
Aylesbury Street
Clerkenwell Green
Vine Street Bri
Brewhouse Yard
Dallington Street
Northburgh St
Great Sutton Street
Sutton La
Hatton Wall
Portpool La
Leather Lane
Saffron Hill
Saffron St
Onslow St
Turnmill Street
Broad Yd
Britton Street
St. John's Square
St. John's Place
Albemarle Way
Briset St
Turk's Head Yard
St. Cross Street
Hatton Place
Lily Pl
Charterhouse Bldgs
Pakenham Street
Cubitt Street
0.25 mile
0.25 km

Clerkenwell

Map 6

A village in the city provides a perfect contrast of a pretty green square separated by only a row of shops from the rest of the corporate world. Modern Pantry is where suits gather for a business power-breakfast, while lunchtimes centre on Exmouth Market. Potter off the main square for back-alley Belgian beers at Dovetail.

Coffee

- **Workshop Coffee Co** • 27 Clerkenwell Rd

Libraries

- **Finsbury Library** • 245 St John St
- **Marx Memorial Library** • 37 Clerkenwell Green

Landmarks

- **The House of Detention** • St. James's Walk

Nightlife

- **1920** • 19 Great Sutton St
- **Bandstand Busking** • Northampton Square
- **The Betsey Trotwood** • 56 Farringdon Rd
- **The Boadicea** • 292 St John St
- **Café Kick** • 43 Exmouth Market
- **Cicada** • 132 St John St
- **Dollar Grills and Martinis** • 2 Exmouth Market
- **The Dovetail** • 9 Jerusalem Passage
- **Filthy McNasty's** • 68 Amwell St
- **Giant Robot** • 45 Clerkenwell Rd
- **The Harlequin** • 27 Arlington Way
- **Old Red Lion** • 418 St. John St
- **The Slaughtered Lamb** • 34 Great Sutton St
- **The Three Kings** • 7 Clerkenwell Close
- **Wilmington Arms** • 69 Rosebery Ave

Restaurants

- **Badabing** • 120 St. John St
- **Caravan** • 11 Exmouth Market
- **Clarks Pie and Mash** • 46 Exmouth Market
- **Dans Le Noir** • 30 Clerkenwell Green
- **The Eagle** • 159 Farringdon Rd
- **Little Bay** • 171 Farringdon Rd
- **The Modern Pantry** • 47 St. Johns Square
- **Moro** • 34 Exmouth Market
- **Pham Sushi** • 159 Whitecross St
- **The Quality Chop House** • 94 Farringdon Rd
- **SandwichMan** • 23 Easton St

Shopping

- **The Black Tulip** • 28 Exmouth Market
- **Bobbin Bicycles** • 397 St. John St
- **EC One Jewellery** • 41 Exmouth Market
- **The Family Business Tattoo Shop** • 58 Exmouth Market
- **London Tattoo** • 332 Goswell Rd
- **M and R Meats** • 399 St. John St
- **Metro Imaging** • 32 Great Sutton St
- **Timorous Beasties** • 46 Amwell St
- **The Wyvern Bindery** • 56 Clerkenwell Rd

Supermarkets

- **Waitrose** • Ayelsbury St & St. John St

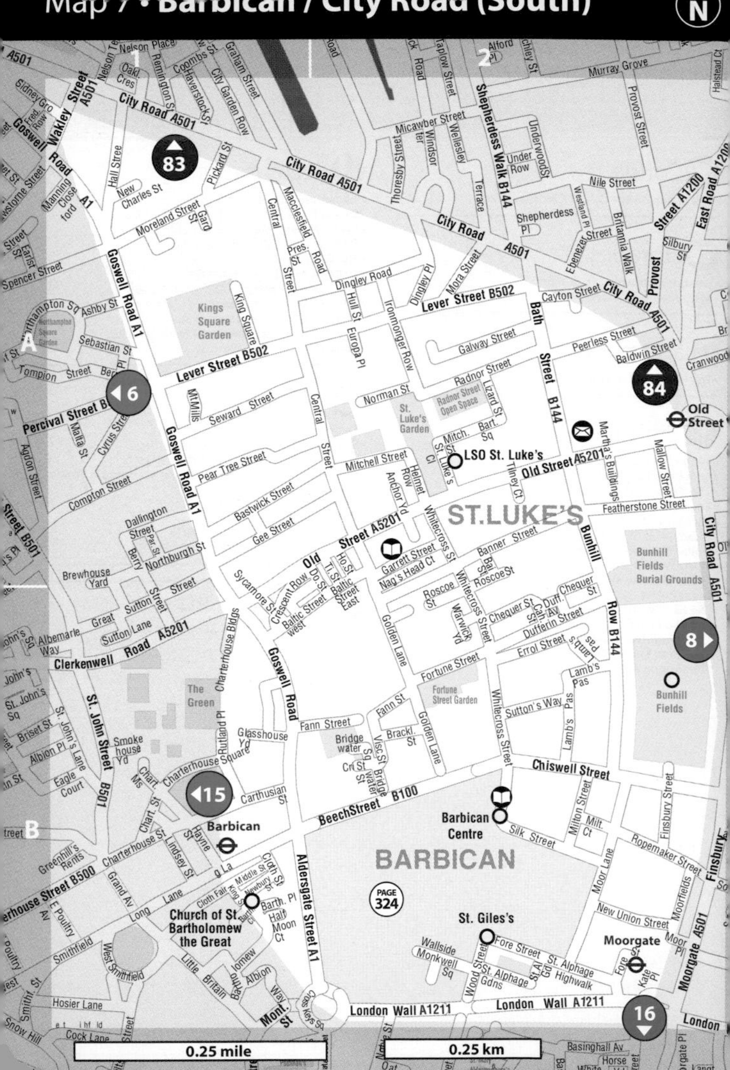
Map 7 • Barbican / City Road (South)
N
City Road A501
Goswell Road A1
Lever Street B502
Old Street A5201
Aldersgate Street A1
London Wall A1211
Beech Street B100
Clerkenwell Road A5201
Charterhouse Street B500
Shepherdess Walk B144
Bath Street B144
Bunhill Row B144
City Road A501
Moorgate A501
Kings Square Garden
St. Luke's Garden
Radnor Street Open Space
Fortune Street Garden
Bunhill Fields Burial Grounds
Bunhill Fields
The Green
ST.LUKE'S
BARBICAN
LSO St. Luke's
Barbican Centre
Church of St. Bartholomew the Great
St. Giles's
Barbican
Old Street
Moorgate
83
84
6
8
15
16
PAGE 324
Nelson Place
Remington St
Coombs St
Haverstock St
City Garden Row
Graham Street
Wakley Street
Hall Street
New Charles St
Pickard St
Moreland Street
Gard St
Macclesfield Road
Central Street
Pres. St
Dingley Road
Dingley Pl
Hull St
Europa Pl
Ironmonger Row
Mora Street
Micawber Street
Thoresby Street
Windsor Ter
Wellesley Terrace
Underwood St
Under Row
Nile Street
Shepherdess Pl
Westland Pl
Ebenezer Street
Britannia Walk
Provost Street
Murray Grove
Silbury St
East Road A1200
Cayton Street
Galway Street
Peerless Street
Baldwin Street
Cranwood
Radnor Street
Norman St
Lizard St
Bart. Sq
Mitch. St
St. Luke's Cl
Martha's Buildings
Mallow Street
Tilney Ct
Featherstone Street
King Square
Ashby St
Sebastian St
Tompion Street
Percival Street
Cyrus Street
Malta St
Agdon Street
Compton Street
Spencer Street
Earlst St
Manning Close
Mt Mills
Seward Street
Pear Tree Street
Bastwick Street
Gee Street
Mitchell Street
Helmet Row
Anchor Yd
Whitecross St
Dallington Street
Berry St
Northburgh St
Brewhouse Yard
Great Sutton Street
Sutton Lane
Albemarle Way
Sycamore St
Crescent Row
Baltic Street West
Baltic Street East
Garrett Street
Nag's Head Ct
Banner Street
Roscoe St
Warwick Yd
Whitecross Street
Chequer St
Dufferin Street
Errol Street
Lamb's Pas
Fortune Street
Golden Lane
Fann Street
Fann St
Brackl. St
Bridgewater Sq
Sutton's Way
Chiswell Street
Charterhouse Bldgs
Rutland Pl
Glasshouse Yd
Charterhouse Square
Carthusian St
Smokehouse Yd
St. John Street B501
St. John's Lane
Briset St
Albion Pl
Eagle Court
Chart. St
Hayne St
Lindsey St
Greenhill's Rents
Grand Av
Long Lane
Cloth St
Middle St
Newbury St
Cloth Fair
Barth. Pl
Half Moon Ct
West Smithfield
Smithfield
Little Britain
Albion Way
Mont. St
Hosier Lane
Cock Lane
Snow Hill
Silk Street
Milton Street
Milt. Ct
Moor Lane
Ropemaker Street
Finsbury Street
Moorfields
New Union Street
Moor Pl
Fore Street
Fore St
Wallside
Monkwell Sq
Wood Street
St. Alphage Gdns
St. Alphage Highwalk
Kate Pl
Basinghall Av
London
Finsbury Sq
0.25 mile
0.25 km

Barbican / City Road (South)

Ugly as the brutalist Barbican might be, its surrounds have happily morphed into one of those areas that thrives on its appalling looks and survives on a generation of media peeps. Where the cool crowds flow, top notch hang-outs will follow. Old Street, or Silicon Roundabout, was designed for those who mainline coffee for survival while Bunhill Fields provides necessary respite.

Cinemas

- **Barbican Centre Cinema** • Silk St & Whitecross St

Coffee

- **Caffe Nero** • 40 City Rd
- **Coffee Republic** • City Rd
- **Costa** • 68 Goswell Rd
- **Costa** • Ropemaker St
- **Eat.** • 143 Moorgate
- **Fix** • 161 Whitecross St
- **Pitch 42** • Whitecross St Market
- **Popular Cafe** • 85 Lever St
- **Pret A Manger** • 9 Goswell Rd
- **Pret A Manger** • Ropemaker St

Landmarks

- **Barbican Centre** • Silk St
- **Bunhill Fields Burial Ground** • 38 City Rd
- **Church of St Bartholomew the Great** • 6 Kinghorn St
- **LSO St Luke's** • 161 Old St
- **St. Giles** • Fore St

Libraries

- **Barbican Library** • Silk St
- **Wandsworth Town Library** • 11 Garrett St

Nightlife

- **Nightjar** • 129 City Rd
- **The Two Brewers** • 121 Whitecross St

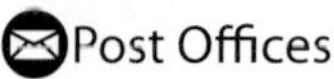

Post Offices

- **Old Street** • 205 Old St

Restaurants

- **Bavarian Beerhouse** • 190 City Rd
- **Carnevale** • 135 Whitecross St
- **De Santis** • 11 Old St
- **Nusa Kitchen** • 9 Old St
- **Original Bagel Bakery** • 22 Goswell Rd

Shopping

- **Bread & Honey** • 205 Whitecross St
- **Red Dot Cameras** • 68 Old St
- **Whitecross Street Market** • Whitecross St

Supermarkets

- **Waitrose** • Whitecross St

Map 8 • Liverpool Street / Broadgate

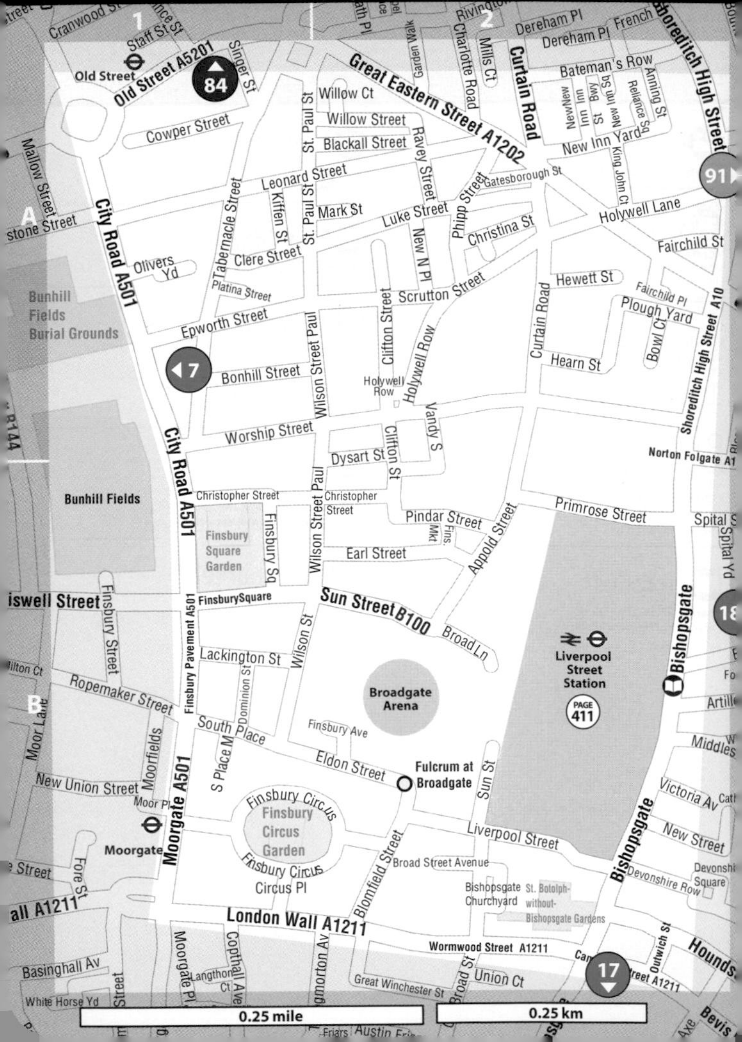

N

1
2
A
B

Old Street
Old Street A5201
84
Cranwood St
Staff St
Singer St
Cowper Street
Mallow Street
City Road A501
Tabernacle Street
Olivers Yd
Bunhill Fields Burial Grounds
Platina Street
Epworth Street
7
Bonhill Street
Worship Street
Bunhill Fields
Christopher Street
Finsbury Square Garden
Finsbury Sq
FinsburySquare
Finsbury Street
Finsbury Pavement A501
Lackington St
Dominion St
Ropemaker Street
South Place
Moor Lane
Moorfields
S Place M
New Union Street
Moor Pl
Moorgate
Moorgate A501
Finsbury Circus
Finsbury Circus Garden
Circus Pl
Fore St
London Wall A1211
Basinghall Av
White Horse Yd
Moorgate Pl
Langthorn Ct
Copthall Ave
Great Eastern Street A1202
Willow Ct
Willow Street
Blackall Street
St. Paul St
Leonard Street
Kiffen St
Mark St
Clere Street
Garden Walk
Ravey Street
Luke Street
New N Pl
Phipp Street
Gatesborough St
Christina St
Scrutton Street
Clifton Street
Holywell Row
Wilson Street
Paul Street
Dysart St
Clifton St
Vandy S
Christopher Street
Pindar Street
Mkt
Fins.
Earl Street
Appold Street
Sun Street B100
Broad Ln
Wilson St
Broadgate Arena
Finsbury Ave
Eldon Street
Fulcrum at Broadgate
Sun St
Liverpool Street
Blomfield Street
Broad Street Avenue
Bishopsgate Churchyard
St. Botolph-without-Bishopsgate Gardens
Wormwood Street A1211
Great Winchester St
Old Broad St
Union Ct
Austin Friars
Charlotte Road
Rivington
Mills Ct
Curtain Road
Dereham Pl
French
Bateman's Row
New Inn Yard
Anning St
Reliance Sq
King John Ct
Shoreditch High Street
91
Holywell Lane
Fairchild St
Hewett St
Fairchild Pl
Plough Yard
Bowl Ct
Hearn St
Shoreditch High Street A10
Norton Folgate A1
Primrose Street
Spital Sq
Spital Yd
Liverpool Street Station
PAGE 411
Bishopsgate
18
Artillery
Middlesex
Victoria Av
New Street
Devonshire Row
Devonshire Square
Outwich St
Camomile Street A1211
17
Houndsditch
Bevis
Axe

0.25 mile
0.25 km

Liverpool Street / Broadgate

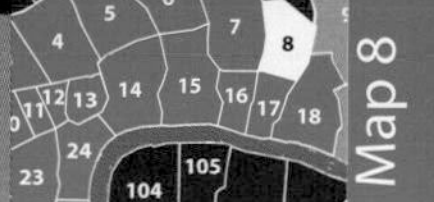

A grimy maw that spews trendos onto Bishopsgate, Liverpool Street is the gateway to the nowness of Brick Lane and Shoreditch. Its arse-end lets out suits and money into the borders of the City. Avoid a 'flash-mob' in the Light after a grease-up in Damascu Bite, but c'mon, you know you're really on your way to an all night rave in Stokey so cut the crap and get on the 149.

Coffee

- **AMT** • Liverpool St & Broadgate Circle
- **Benugo** • 82 City Rd
- **Caffe Nero** • 2 Bishopsgate
- **Caffe Nero** • 40 City Rd
- **Caffe Nero** • 75 London Wall
- **Costa** • 1 Ropemaker St
- **Costa** • 18 Liverpool St
- **Eat.** • 1 City Rd
- **Eat.** • 143 Moorgate
- **Eat.** • 176 Bishopsgate
- **Eat.** • 34 Broadgate Circle
- **Eat.** • 62 London Wall
- **Eat.** • 80 Old Broad St
- **Fab Food Patisserie** • 28 Curtain Rd
- **Starbucks** • Liverpool St Station
- **Starbucks** • 8 Charterhouse Buildings
- **Starbucks** • 28 Broadgate Circle

Landmarks

- **Fulcrum** • Broadgate

Libraries

- **Bishopsgate Library** • 230 Bishopsgate

Nightlife

- **The Book Club** • 100 Leonard St
- **Callooh Callay** • 65 Rivington St
- **The Light Bar** • 233 Shoreditch High St
- **Lounge Bohemia** • 1 Great Eastern St
- **Red Lion** • 1 Eldon St
- **Sosho** • 2 Tabernacle Street
- **Worship Street Whistling Shop** • 63 Worship St
- **XOYO** • 32 Cowper St

Restaurants

- **Damascu Bite** • 21 Shoreditch High St
- **Eyre Brothers** • 70 Leonard St
- **Gaucho Broadgate** • 5 Finsbury Ave
- **Ponti's Caffe** • 176 Bishopsgate
- **The Princess of Shoreditch** • 76 Bishopsgate

Supermarkets

- **Tesco** • 158 Bishopsgate

Map 9 • Mayfair / Green Park

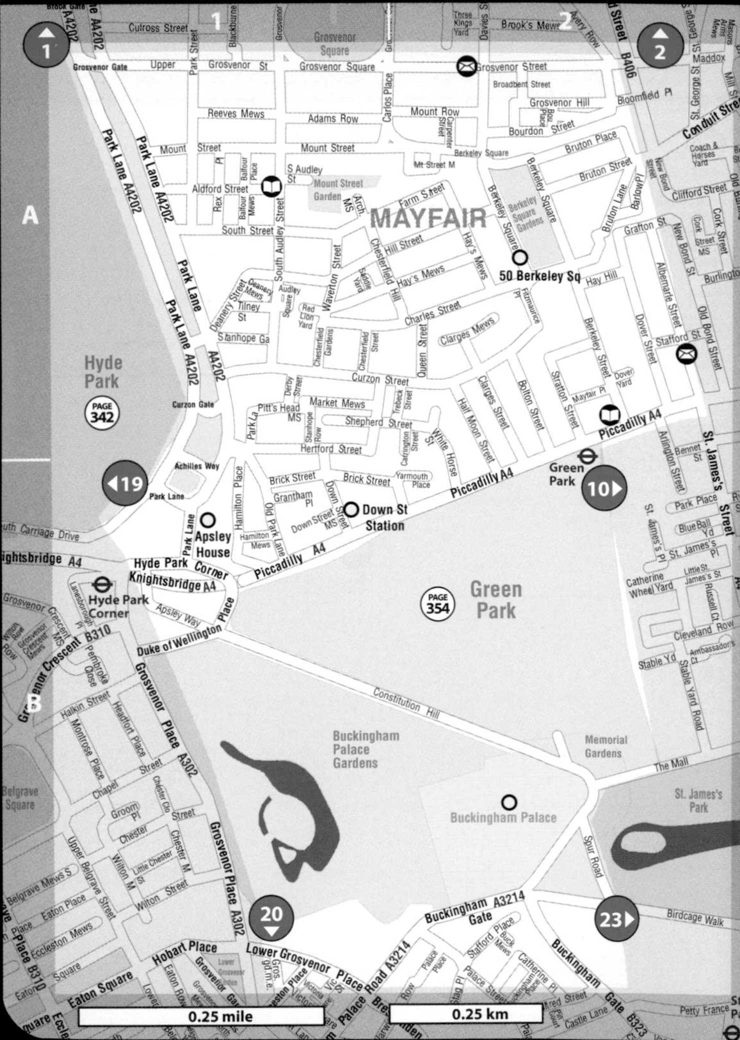

N

1
2
A
B

Brook Gate
A4202
Culross Street
Park Street
Blackburne's
Grosvenor
Grosvenor Square
Three Kings Yard
Davies St
Brook's Mews
Avery Row
Street
B406
George St
Masons Arms Mews
Maddox
Mill St
Grosvenor Gate
Upper Grosvenor St
Grosvenor Square
Grosvenor Street
Broadbent Street
Grosvenor Hill
Bloomfield Pl
St. George St
Conduit Street
Reeves Mews
Adams Row
Carlos Place
Mount Row
Carpenter Street
Bourdon Place
Bourdon Street
Park Lane A4202
Mount Street
Mount Street
Berkeley Square
Bruton Place
Coach & Horses Yard
Rex Pl
Balfour Place
S Audley St
Mount Street Garden
Mt Street M
Bruton Street
New Bond Street
Alford Street
Balfour Mews
South Audley Street
MS
Arch.
Farm Street
Berkeley Square
Berkeley Square Gardens
Bruton Lane
Barlow Pl
Clifford Street
Old Burlington St
MAYFAIR
Grafton St
Cork St
Cork Street MS
South Street
Chesterfield Hill
Hill Street
Hay's Mews
Park Lane
Waverton Street
Saddle Yard
Hay's Mews
50 Berkeley Sq
Hay Hill
New Bond St
Albemarle Street
Burlington
Deanery Street
Deanery Mews
Audley Square
Tilney St
Red Lion Yard
Fitzmaurice Pl
Charles Street
Berkeley Street
Dover Street
Old Bond Street
Stanhope Ga
Chesterfield Gardens
Chesterfield Street
Queen Street
Clarges Mews
Stafford St
Hyde Park
A4202
Curzon Street
Clarges Street
Bolton Street
Stratton Street
Dover Yard
Mayfair Pl
Derby Street
Curzon Gate
Pitt's Head MS
Market Mews
Trebeck Street
Half Moon Street
Park La
Stanhope Row
Shepherd Street
White Horse St
Piccadilly A4
Arlington Street
Bennet St
St. James's Street
Hertford Street
Carrington Street
Achilles Way
Hamilton Place
Brick Street
Brick Street
Yarmouth Place
Piccadilly A4
Green Park
Park Lane
Grantham Pl
Down Street
Down St Station
Park Place
Old Park Lane
Down Street MS
St. James's Pl
Blue Ball Yd
South Carriage Drive
Park Lane
Apsley House
Hamilton Mews
St. James's Pl
Knightsbridge A4
Hyde Park Corner
Piccadilly A4
Catherine Wheel Yard
Little St. James's St
Knightsbridge A4
Russell Ct
Lanesborough Pl
Hyde Park Corner
Green Park
Grosvenor Crescent
Apsley Way
Place
Cleveland Row
Wilton Row
Grosvenor Crescent MS
Grosvenor Crescent Mews
Duke of Wellington
Ambassador's Ct
Grosvenor Crescent B310
Pembroke Close
Stable Yd
Stable Yard Road
Grosvenor Place A302
Constitution Hill
Halkin Street
Headfort Place
Montrose Place
Buckingham Palace Gardens
Memorial Gardens
Chapel Street
Chester Clo
The Mall
Belgrave Square
Groom Pl
Chester Street
Chester M
St. James's Park
Buckingham Palace
Upper Belgrave Street
Wilton M
Little Chester St
Spur Road
Belgrave Mews S
Grosvenor Place A302
Eaton Place
Wilton Street
Buckingham Gate A3214
Birdcage Walk
Eccleston Mews
Place B310
Stafford Place
Buck Mews
Catherine Place
Eaton Square
Hobart Place
Grosvenor Gardens
Lower Grosvenor Gardens
Lower Grosvenor Place
Palace Road A3214
Palace Place
Gros. gd. m.e.
Victoria Sq
Row
Palace Street
Stag Pl
Buckingham Place
Buckingham Gate B323
Petty France
Castle Lane
Eaton Row
Square

1
2
19
10
20
23
PAGE 342
PAGE 354

0.25 mile
0.25 km

Mayfair / Green Park

A taste of Old Money is a decent enough reason to visit Mayfair; splashing out on High Tea at The Ritz is pretty much an investment in one's cultural education. The upside to might-rich neighbourhoods? Art galleries. Ones that give away wine. All the time. Pop down Cork street on an eve to quaff all the free champagne at a private view then know off somewhere far more interesting.

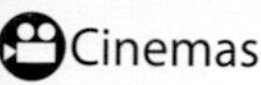

Cinemas

- **Curzon Mayfair** • 38 Curzon St

Coffee

- **Apostrophe** • 10 Grosvenor St
- **Caffe Nero** • 50 Curzon St
- **Caffe Nero** • 70 Piccadilly
- **Costa** • 9 Eldon St
- **Eat.** • 8 Berkeley Sq
- **Eat.** • 55 Stratton St
- **Starbucks** • 52 Berkeley St
- **Starbucks** • 84 Piccadilly
- **Taylor St Baristas** • 22 Brook's Mews

Landmarks

- **50 Berkeley Square** • 50 Berkeley Sq
- **Apsley House** • 149 Piccadilly
- **Buckingham Palace** • The Mall
- **Down Street Station** • Down St & Piccadilly

Libraries

- **Mayfair Library** • 25 South Audley St
- **Royal Society of Chemistry Library and Information Centre** • Piccadilly

Nightlife

- **1707 Wine Bar** • 181 Piccadilly
- **bbar** • 43 Buckingham Palace Rd
- **Funky Buddha** • 15 Berkeley St
- **Mahiki** • 1 Dover St
- **Shepherd's Tavern** • 50 Hertford St
- **Whisky Mist** • 35 Hertford St

Post Offices

- **Albemarle St** • 44 Albemarle St
- **Mayfair** • 32 Grosvenor St

Restaurants

- **Alain Ducasse at The Dorchester** • Park Ln
- **Citrus** • 112 Piccadilly
- **Cookbook Cafe** • 1 Hamilton Pl
- **El Pirata of Mayfair** • 5 Down St
- **The English Tea Room at Brown's** • Albemarle St
- **Galvin at Windows** • Park Ln, 28th Floor
- **Kiplings** • 2 Hill St
- **L'Autre** • 5 Shepherd St
- **Momo Tea Rooms** • 25 Heddon St
- **Nobu** • 19 Old Park Ln
- **The Ritz** • 150 Piccadilly
- **Theo Randall** • 1 Hamilton Pl
- **The Wolseley** • 160 Piccadilly

Shopping

- **A.P.C.** • 35 Dover St
- **Diane Von Furstenberg** • 25 Bruton St
- **Dover Street Market** • 17 Dover St
- **Green Valley** • Berkeley St
- **Marc Jacobs** • 24 Mount St
- **Matthew Williamson** • 28 Bruton St
- **Stella McCartney** • 30 Bruton St

Supermarkets

- **Marks & Spencer** • 78 Piccadilly
- **Sainsbury's** • 38 Stratton St

Map 10 • Piccadilly / Soho (West)

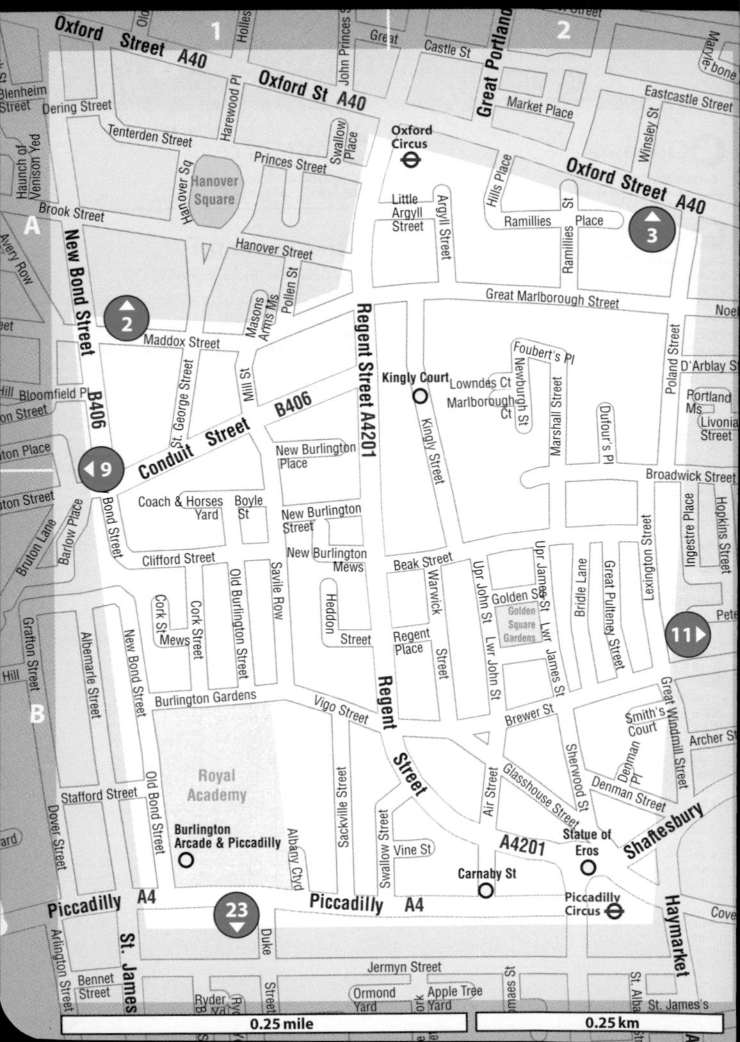

Oxford Street A40
Oxford St A40
Oxford Street A40
Great Castle St
Great Portland
Market Place
Eastcastle Street
Marylebone
Winsley St
Holles
John Princes St
Harewood Pl
Swallow Place
Blenheim Street
Dering Street
Tenterden Street
Haunch of Venison Yed
Princes Street
Hanover Sq
Hanover Square
Oxford Circus
Little Argyll Street
Argyll Street
Hills Place
Ramillies St
Ramillies Place
Brook Street
Avery Row
New Bond Street
Hanover Street
Pollen St
Masons Arms Ms
Great Marlborough Street
Noel
Maddox Street
Regent Street A4201
Kingly Court
Lowndes Ct
Marlborough Ct
Foubert's Pl
Newburgh St
Marshall Street
Poland Street
D'Arblay St
Portland Ms
Livonia Street
Dufour's Pl
Bloomfield Pl
B406
St. George Street
Mill St
B406
Conduit Street
Kingly Street
New Burlington Place
Broadwick Street
Coach & Horses Yard
Boyle St
New Burlington Street
New Burlington Mews
Bond Street
Bruton Lane
Barlow Place
Clifford Street
Beak Street
Warwick Street
Upr John St
Upr James St
Golden Sq
Golden Square Gardens
Bridle Lane
Great Pulteney Street
Lexington Street
Ingestre Place
Hopkins Street
Pete
Grafton Street
Albemarle Street
New Bond Street
Cork St Mews
Cork Street
Old Burlington Street
Savile Row
Heddon Street
Regent Place
Lwr John St
Lwr James St
Burlington Gardens
Vigo Street
Regent Street
Brewer St
Smith's Court
Great Windmill Street
Archer St
Royal Academy
Sackville Street
Air Street
Glasshouse Street
Sherwood St
Denman Pl
Denman Street
Shaftesbury
Stafford Street
Old Bond Street
Dover Street
Burlington Arcade & Piccadilly
Albany Ctyd
Swallow Street
Vine St
A4201
Statue of Eros
Carnaby St
Piccadilly A4
Piccadilly A4
Piccadilly Circus
Haymarket
Coventry
St. James's Street
Duke Street
Arlington Street
Bennet Street
Ryder Yd
Jermyn Street
Ormond Yard
Apple Tree Yard
St. Albans
St. James's
1
2
3
2
9
11
23
A
B

0.25 mile
0.25 km

Piccadilly / Soho (West)

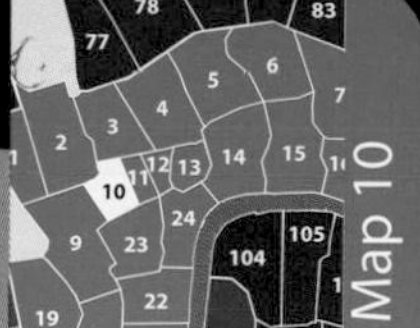

Forget visions of Austin Powers "yeah baby" grooviness, Carnaby Street is a slick study in consumerism with all major streetwear labels present, but the grand dame of department stores, Liberty, retains top marks for a unique shopping experience. Have a coffee in Sacred if you can find a seat or else retreat to the John Snow for a cheeky pint. Polpo restaurant is a winner in the small plates game.

Coffee

- **Caffe Nero** • 62 Brewer St
- **Caffe Nero** • 26 Piccadilly
- **Caffe Nero** • 225 Regent St
- **Costa** • 11 Argyll St
- **Eat.** • 19 Golden Sq
- **Eat.** • 8 Vigo St
- **Fernandez & Wells** • 73 Beak St
- **Pret A Manger** • 298 Regent St
- **Pret A Manger** • 27 Great Marlborough
- **Sacred Cafe** • 13 Ganton St
- **Starbucks** • 16 Picadilly
- **Starbucks** • 171 Picadilly

Landmarks

- **Burlington Arcade** • Piccadilly
- **Carnaby Street** • Carnaby St
- **Kingly Court** • Kingly St & Foubert's Pl
- **Statue of Eros** • Piccadilly Circus

Nightlife

- **22 Below** • 22 Great Marlborough St
- **5th View** • 203 Piccadilly
- **Ain't Nothing But...** • 20 Kingly St
- **Beyond Retro** • 58 Great Marlborough St
- **Cheers Bar** • 72 Regent St
- **Courthouse Bar**• 19 Great Marlborough St
- **John Snow** • 39 Broadwick St
- **Milk and Honey** • 61 Poland St
- **The Pigalle Club** • 215 Piccadilly
- **Red** • 5 Kingly St
- **Strawberry Moons** • 15 Heddon St

Restaurants

- **Atlantic Bar & Grill** • 20 Glasshouse St
- **Bob Bob Ricard** • 1 Upper James St
- **Cecconi's** • 5 Burlington Gardens
- **Cha Cha Moon** • 15 Ganton St
- **Chowki** • 2 Denman St
- **Dehesa** • 25 Ganton St
- **Fernandez & Wells** • 73 Beak St
- **Fernandez & Wells** • 43 Lexington St
- **Kulu Kulu** • 76 Brewer St
- **Le Pain Quotidien** • 18 Great Marlborough St
- **Mildreds Vegetarian** • 45 Lexington St
- **Mosaico** • 13 Albermale St
- **Nordic Bakery** • 14 Golden Sq
- **The Photographers' Gallery** • 16 Ramillies St
- **Ping Pong** • 45 Great Marlborough St
- **Polpo** • 41 Beak St
- **Pure** • 39 Beak St
- **Sartoria** • 20 Saville Row
- **Sketch** • 9 Conduit St
- **Taro** • 61 Brewer St
- **Ten Ten Tei** • 56 Brewer St
- **Tentazioni Restaurant** • 2 Mill St
- **Thanks for Franks** • 26 Fouberts Pl
- **Tibits** • 12 Heddon St
- **Toku @ The Japan Centre** • 14 Regent St
- **Wagamama** • 10 Lexington St
- **Wild Honey** • 12 St George St
- **Yauatcha** • 15 Broadwick St
- **Yoshino** • 3 Piccadilly Pl

Shopping

- **Abercrombie & Fitch** • 7 Burlington Gardens
- **Anthropologie** • 158 Regent St
- **American Apparel** • 3 Carnaby St
- **Apple Store** • 235 Regent Street
- **Arigato** • 48 Brewer St
- **b store** • 21 Kingly St
- **Banana Republic** • 224 Regent St
- **Behave** • 48 Lexington Sreet
- **Beyond Retro** • 58 Great Marlborough St
- **The Black Pearl** • 10 Kingly Ct
- **Burlington Arcade** • Burlington Arcade
- **Cos** • 222 Regent St
- **The European Bookshop** • 5 Warwick St
- **Fortnum & Mason** • 181 Piccadilly
- **Freggo** • 27 Swallow St
- **Hamley's** • 188 Regent St
- **Hatchards Bookshop** • 187 Piccadilly
- **Hoss Intropia** • 211 Regent St
- **Lazy Oaf** • 19 Fouberts Pl
- **Liberty** • 214 Regent St
- **Lillywhites** • 24 Lower Regent St
- **Lucky Voice** • 52 Poland St
- **Mrs. Kibble's Olde Sweet Shoppe** • 57 Brewer St
- **Muji** • 41 Carnaby St
- **Phonica** • 51 Poland St
- **Playlounge** • 19 Beak St
- **Richard James** • 29 Savile Row
- **Rigby & Peller** • 22 Conduit St
- **SKK Lighting** • 34 Lexington St
- **Super Superficial** • 17 Fouberts Pl
- **Twinkled** • 1 Kingly Ct
- **Twosee** • 21 Fouberts
- **The Vin Mag Shop** • 39 Brewer St
- **Whole Foods Market** • 69 Brewer St

Supermarkets

- **Fresh & Wild** • 73 Brewer St
- **Whole Foods Market** • 69 Brewer St

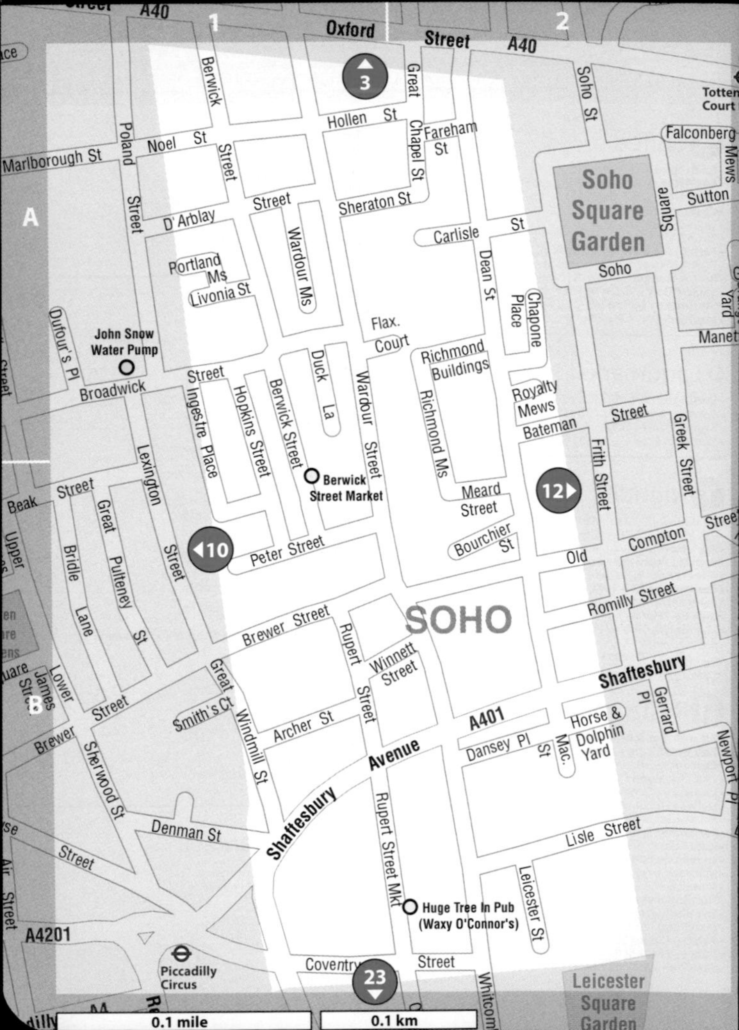

Map 11 • Soho (Central)

N

John Snow Water Pump
Berwick Street Market
Huge Tree In Pub (Waxy O'Connor's)
Piccadilly Circus
Soho Square Garden
Leicester Square Garden
SOHO

Oxford Street A40
Marlborough St
Noel St
Poland Street
Berwick Street
Hollen St
Great Chapel St
Fareham St
Sheraton St
Soho St
Falconberg Mews
Sutton
Soho Square
Carlisle St
Dean St
Chapone Place
D'Arblay Street
Portland Ms
Livonia St
Wardour Ms
Flax. Court
Richmond Buildings
Richmond Ms
Royalty Mews
Bateman Street
Frith Street
Greek Street
Manette
Dufour's Pl
Broadwick Street
Ingestre Place
Hopkins Street
Berwick Street
Duck La
Wardour Street
Meard Street
Bourchier St
Old Compton Street
Romilly Street
Beak Street
Great Pulteney St
Bridle Lane
Lexington Street
Peter Street
Brewer Street
Rupert Street
Winnett Street
Shaftesbury Avenue
A401
Gerrard Pl
Horse & Dolphin Yard
Dansey Pl
Mac. St
Newport Pl
Lower James Street
Great Windmill St
Smith's Ct
Archer St
Brewer Street
Sherwood St
Denman St
Rupert Street Mkt
Lisle Street
Leicester St
Coventry Street
Whitcomb
A4201
Air Street

1
2
A
B
3
10
12
23

0.1 mile
0.1 km

Soho (Central)

By day the turning out of London's new favourite caffeine kick—the flat white courtesy of the Aussies—is relentless at LJ and Milk Bar. All the better to fuel the night's activities: this is still the heart of the red light district, but it's no longer such a sordid affair. Berwick Street is still loved for its record shops and market, and Madame JoJo's doesn't miss a trick.

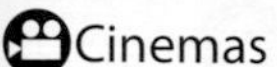

Cinemas

- **Cineworld Shaftesbury Avenue** • 13 Coventry St
- **Curzon Soho** • 99 Shaftesbury Ave
- **Empire Leicester Square** • 5 Leicester Square
- **Prince Charles Cinema** • 7 Leicester Pl

Coffee

- **Coffee Republic** • 7 Coventry St
- **Coffee Republic** • 38 Berwick St
- **Costa** • 62 Shaftesbury Ave
- **Fernandez & Wells Espresso Bar** • 16 St Anne's Ct
- **LJ Coffee House** • 3 Winnett St
- **Milk Bar** • 3 Bateman St
- **Prince Charles Cinema** • 7 Leicester Pl
- **Starbucks** • 60 Wardour St

Landmarks

- **Berwick Street Market** • Berwick St & Rupert St
- **John Snow Water Pump** • Broadwick Street
- **Waxy O'Connor's** • 14 Rupert St

Nightlife

- **Blue Posts** • 22 Berwick St
- **The Blue Posts** • 28 Rupert St
- **Candy Bar** • 4 Carlisle St
- **The Comedy Store** • 1 Oxendon St
- **De Hems** • 11 Macclesfield St
- **The Endurance** • 90 Berwick St
- **Experimental Cocktail Club** • 13 Gerrard St
- **Freedom** • 66 Wardour St
- **The French House** • 49 Dean St
- **LVPO** • 50 Dean St
- **Madame Jojo's** • 8 Brewer St
- **Shadow Lounge** • 5 Brewer St
- **Village** • 81 Wardour St

Restaurants

- **Balans** • 60 Old Compton St
- **Bar Bruno** • 101 Wardour St
- **Beatroot** • 92 Berwick St
- **Bocca di Lupo** • 12 Archer St
- **Busaba Eathai** • 110 Wardour St
- **Cafe Espana** • 63 Old Compton St
- **Grace** • 42 Great Windmill St
- **Hummus Bros** • 88 Wardour St
- **Imli** • 167 Wardour St
- **Italian Graffiti** • 163 Wardour St
- **Leong's Legends** • 4 Macclesfield St
- **Jazz Club** • 10 Dean St
- **Jerk City** • 189 Wardour St
- **Melati** • 30 Peter St
- **Malletti** • 26 Noel St
- **Maoz** • 43 Old Compton St
- **Paul** • 49 Old Compton St
- **Randall & Aubin** • 16 Brewer St
- **Red Veg** • 95 Dean St
- **Snog** • 9 Brewer St
- **St Moritz** • 161 Wardour St
- **Thai Square** • 27 St. Annes Ct
- **Won Kei** • 41 Wardour St
- **Yoshino Delicatessen** • 59 Shaftesbury Ave

Shopping

- **Algerian Coffee Store** • 52 Old Compton St
- **American Retro** • 35 Old Compton St
- **Bang Bang** • 9 Berwick St
- **Calumet Photographic** • 175 Wardour St
- **Chappel of Bond Street** • 152 Wardour St
- **Cheapo Cheapo Records** • 53 Rupert St
- **Cowling & Wilcox** • 26 Broadwick St
- **Gerry's** • 74 Old Compton St
- **I. Camisa & Son** • 61 Old Compton St
- **Revival Records** • 30 Berwick St
- **Sister Ray** • 34 Berwick St
- **Snog** • 9 Brewer St
- **Sounds of the Universe** • 7 Broadwick St

Map 12 • Soho (East)

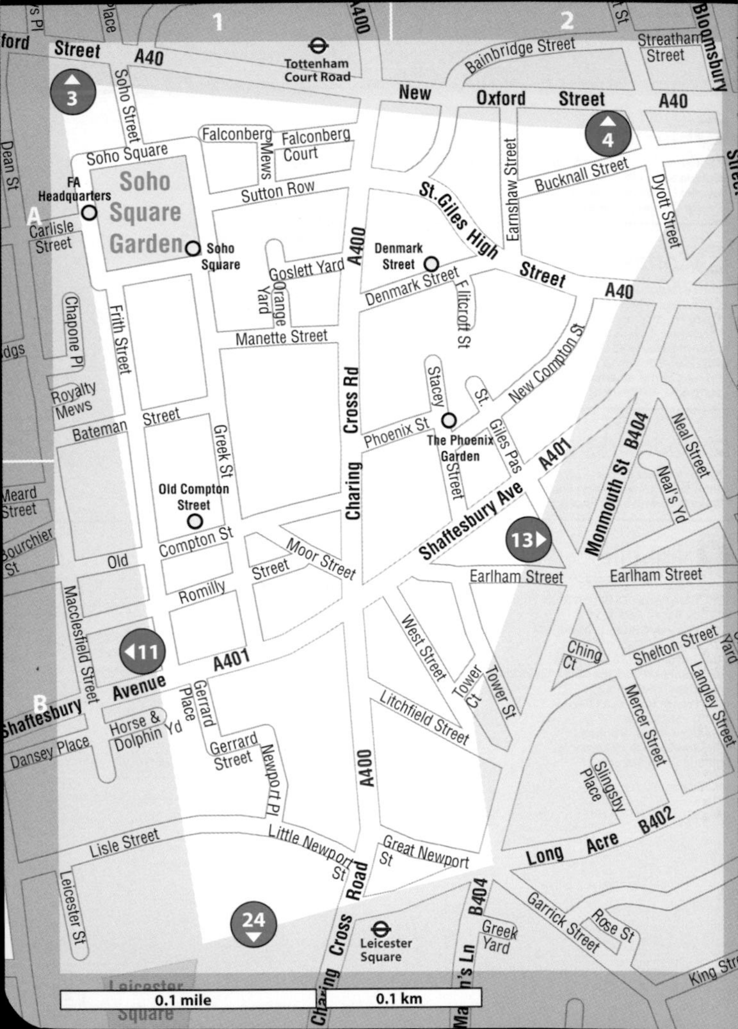

Soho (East)

While The Three Greyhounds (opposite Soho House) might be one of the cheapest pubs in central London, Jazz After Dark on Greek Street certainly isn't but it does have an undeniably attractive ambiance. Blend in with the winos at Soho Square with a shop-bought bottle while G-A-Y and The Village showcase the more colourful side of Soho.

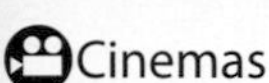

Cinemas

- **Vue West End Cinema** • 3 Cranbourn St

Coffee

- **Caffe Nero** • 32 Cranbourn St
- **Caffe Nero** • 43 Frith St
- **Caffe Nero** • 155 Charing Cross Rd
- **Eat.** • 16 Soho Sq
- **Eat.** • 155 Charing Cross Rd
- **First Out Cafe Bar** • 52 St Giles High St
- **Foyles** • 113 Charing Cross Rd
- **Kaffe Automat** • 62 Frith St
- **Maison Bertaux** • 28 Greek St

Landmarks

- **Denmark Street** • Denmark St
- **FA Headquarters** • 25 Soho Sq
- **Old Compton Street** • Old Compton St
- **The Phoenix Garden** • 21 Stacey St
- **Soho Square** • Soho Sq

Nightlife

- **12 Bar Club** • Denmark St
- **Cafe Boheme** • 13 Old Compton St
- **The Borderline** • Orange Yard
- **Comptons** • 53 Old Compton St
- **The Crobar** • 17 Manette St
- **G-A-Y Bar** • 30 Old Compton St
- **G-A-Y Late** • 5 Goslett Yard
- **Garlic & Shots** • 14 Frith St
- **Green Carnation** • 5 Greek St
- **Jazz After Dark** • 9 Greek St
- **Karaoke Box** • 18 Frith St
- **Ku** • 30 Lisle St
- **LAB Bar** • 12 Old Compton St
- **The Montagu Pyke** • 105 Charing Cross Rd
- **Ronnie Scott's** • 47 Frith St
- **The Royal George** • 133 Charing Cross Rd
- **The Toucan** • 19 Carlisle St

Restaurants

- **Abeno Too** • 17 Great Newport St
- **Arbutus** • 63 Frith St
- **Assa** • 53 St Giles High St
- **Bar Italia** • 22 Frith St
- **Barrafina** • 54 Frith St
- **Bincho Soho** • 16 Old Compton St
- **Boheme Kitchen and Bar** • 19 Old Compton St
- **Café Emm** • 17 Frith St
- **Ceviche** • 17 Frith St
- **Chinese Experience** • 118 Shaftesbury Ave
- **Corean Chilli** • 51 Charing Cross Rd
- **Ed's Easy Diner** • 12 Moor St
- **Friendly Inn** • 47 Gerrard St
- **Gaby's Deli** • 30 Charing Cross Rd
- **Garlic & Shots** • 14 Frith St
- **Gay Hussar** • 2 Greek St
- **Haozhan** • 8 Gerrard St
- **Haozhan** • 8 Gerrard St
- **The Ivy** • 1 West St
- **Koya** • 49 Frith St
- **La Porchetta Pollo Bar** • 20 Old Compton St
- **Le Beaujolais** • 25 Litchfield St
- **Maison Bertaux** • 27 Greek St
- **Malaysia Kopi Tiam** • 67 Charing Cross Rd
- **New World** • 1 Gerrard Pl
- **Soho's Secret Tea Room** • 29 Greek St
- **The Stockpot** • 18 Old Compton St
- **Taro** • 10 Old Compton St
- **The Three Greyhounds** • 25 Greek Street
- **The Village** • 421 Green Lanes

Shopping

- **Angels Fancy Dress Shop** • 119 Shaftesbury Ave
- **Fopp** • 1 Earlham St
- **Forbidden Planet** • 179 Shaftesbury Ave
- **Foyles** • 113 Charing Cross Rd
- **Harmony** • 167 Charing Cross Rd
- **Kokon to Zai** • 57 Greek St
- **Macari's** • 92 Charing Cross Rd
- **Magma** • 8 Earlham St
- **Porselli Dancewear** • 9 West St
- **Rockers** • 5 Denmark St
- **Turnkey** • 114 Charing Cross Rd
- **Wunjo Guitars** • 20 Denmark St

Map 13 • Covent Garden

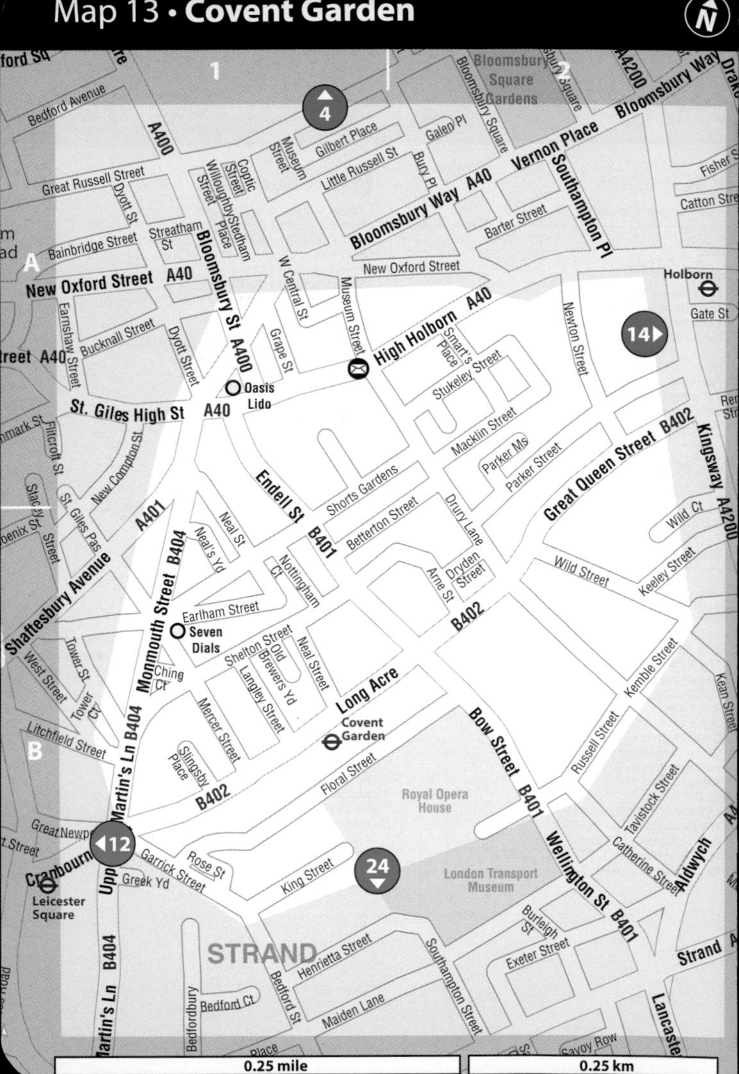

Covent Garden

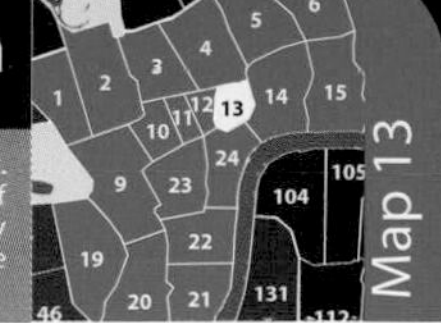

Covent Garden is a shopper's delight, especially on Endell Street and Neal Street. However, such activity will not offer a respite from the Piazza and its hordes of spatially unaware folk. Stop for fish and chips at Rock & Sole Plaice followed by gelato at Scoop. Come the evening, sip cocktails at Freud or convene with the ghost of Bernard Shaw at the Lamb & Flag.

Coffee

- **AMT** • 14 Neal St
- **Bagel Factory** • 18 Endell St
- **Café Metro** • 33 Catherine St
- **Caffe Nero** • 30 Monmouth St
- **Caffe Nero** • 83 Long Acre
- **Pret A Manger** • 65 Long Acre
- **Starbucks** • 10 Russell St
- **Starbucks** • 55 Long Acre

Landmarks

- **Oasis Sports Centre** • 32 Endell St
- **Seven Dials** • Upper St Martin's Ln & Earlham St

Nightlife

- **AKA** • 18 W Central St
- **Bunker** • 41 Earlham St
- **The Cross Keys** • 31 Endell St
- **The End** • 18 W Central St
- **Freud** • 198 Shaftesbury Ave
- **Guanabara** • Parker St
- **Lamb & Flag** • 33 Rose St
- **The Poetry Cafe** • 22 Betterton St

Post Offices

- **High Holborn** • 181 High Holborn

Restaurants

- **Battersea Pie** • Covent Garden Piazza
- **Belgo Centraal** • 50 Earlham St
- **Café Mode** • 57 Endell St
- **Candy Cakes** • 36 Monmouth St
- **Food for Thought** • 31 Neal St
- **Great Queen Street** • 32 Great Queen St
- **Kulu Kulu Sushi** • 51 Shelton St
- **Mon Plaisir** • 21 Monmouth St
- **The Punjab** • 80 Neal St
- **Rock & Sole Plaice** • 47 Endell St
- **Sarastro** • 126 Drury Ln
- **Souk Medina** • 1 Shorts Gardens

Shopping

- **Artbox** • 29 Earlham St
- **The Astrology Shop** • 78 Neal St
- **Beadworks** • 21 Tower St
- **Ben's Cookies** • 13 The Piazza
- **Blackout II** • 51 Endell St
- **Cath Kidston** • 28 Shelton St
- **Coco de Mer** • 23 Monmouth St
- **Cybercandy** • 3 Garrick St
- **David and Goliath** • 4 The Market
- **Ella's Bakehouse** • 20 The Piazza
- **Hope and Greenwood** • 1 Russell St
- **Kiehl's** • 29 Monmouth St
- **Libidex at Liberation** • 49 Shelton St
- **The Loft** • 35 Monmouth St
- **London Graphic Centre** • 16 Shelton St
- **Miss Lala's Boudoir** • 18 Monmouth St
- **Neal's Yard Dairy** • 17 Shorts Gardens
- **Nigel Hall** • 15 Floral St
- **Octopus** • 54 Neal St
- **Orla Kiely** • 31 Monmouth St
- **Poetry Cafe** • 22 Betterton St
- **Pop Boutique** • 6 Monmouth St
- **Rokit** • 42 Shelton St
- **Rossopomodoro** • 50 Monmouth St
- **Scoop** • 40 Shorts Gardens
- **Screenface** • 48 Monmouth St
- **Slam City Skates** • 16 Neal's Yard
- **Stanfords** • 12 Long Acre
- **Superdry** • 24 Earlham St
- **Tabio** • 66 Neal St
- **Urban Outfitters** • 42 Earlham St

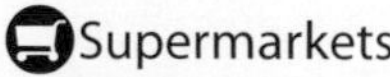

Supermarkets

- **Sainsbury's** • 129 Kingsway

HOLBORN

Sir John Soane's Museum

The Old Curiosity Shop

London School of Economics

Royal Courts of Justice

Site of Sweeney Todd's Barber Shop

BBC Bush House

Somerset House

Aldwych Tube Station

King's College

Inner Temple Gardens

Lincoln's Inn Fields (Fickets Fields)

Gray's Inn Gardens

Hatton Garden

Holborn

Chancery Lane

Temple

River Thames

PAGE 368

PAGE 366

0.25 mile

0.25 km

Holborn / Temple

An essential cog in London's machine, this area is resplendent with curios (Old Curiosity Shop, Sweeney Todd's), public squares full of depressed lawyers and legions of serious-looking people being integrated into The System. The ghosts of Londons past hover around Temple and the Strand, where you'll also find Aldwych Film for brunch and a flick.

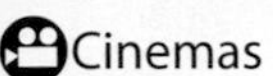

Cinemas

- **Aldwych Film** • 1 Aldwych

Coffee

- **Caffe Nero** • 333 High Holborn
- **Costa** • 15 Chichester Rents
- **Department of Coffee & Social Affairs** • 14–16 Leather Ln
- **Eat.** • 105 Kingsway
- **Eat.** • 239 High Holborn
- **Eat.** • 34 High Holborn
- **Eat.** • 7 Kingsway
- **Eat.** • 77 Chancery Lane
- **Eat.** • 78 Hatton Garden
- **Pret A Manger** • 10 Leather Ln
- **Pret A Manger** • 240 High Holborn
- **Pret A Manger** • 29 Kingsway
- **Prufrock Coffee** • 23–25 Leather Ln
- **Starbucks** • 10 Kingsway
- **Starbucks** • 99 Kingsway

o Landmarks

- **Aldwych Tube Station** • Strand & Surrey St
- **BBC Bush House** • Aldwych & Kingsway
- **Hatton Garden** • Hatton Garden
- **Inner Temple Garden** • Inner Temple
- **Lincoln's Inn Fields** • Newman's Row
- **The Old Curiosity Shop** • 13 Portsmouth St
- **Royal Courts of Justice** • Strand
- **Sir John Soane's Museum** • 13 Lincoln's Inn Fields
- **Sweeney Todd's Barber Shop** • 186 Fleet St
- **Somerset House** • Somerset House Trust, The Strand

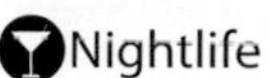

Libraries

- **British Library of Political and Economic Science** • 10 Portugal Street

Nightlife

- **Bar Polski** • 11 Little Turnstile
- **Cittie of Yorke** • 22 High Holborn
- **The Enterprise** • 38 Red Lion St
- **The Seven Stars** • 53 Carey St
- **Temple Bar** • Temple Pl
- **Tutu's** • Surrey St
- **Volupte** • 9 Norwich St

Post Offices

- **Aldwych** • 95 Aldwych
- **Grays Inn** • 19 High Holborn
- **Holborn Circus** • 124 High Holborn

Restaurants

- **Asadal** • 227 High Holborn
- **Casanova's Treats** • 13 Lamb's Conduit Passage
- **Indigo** • 1 Aldwych

Shopping

- **Konditor & Cook** • 46 Grays Inn Rd
- **Topshop** • 60 The Strand

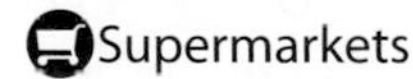

Supermarkets

- **Sainsbury's** • 129 Kingsway
- **Sainsbury's** • 60 Fetter Ln
- **Sainsbury's** • 71 High Holborn

Map 15 • Blackfriars / Farringdon

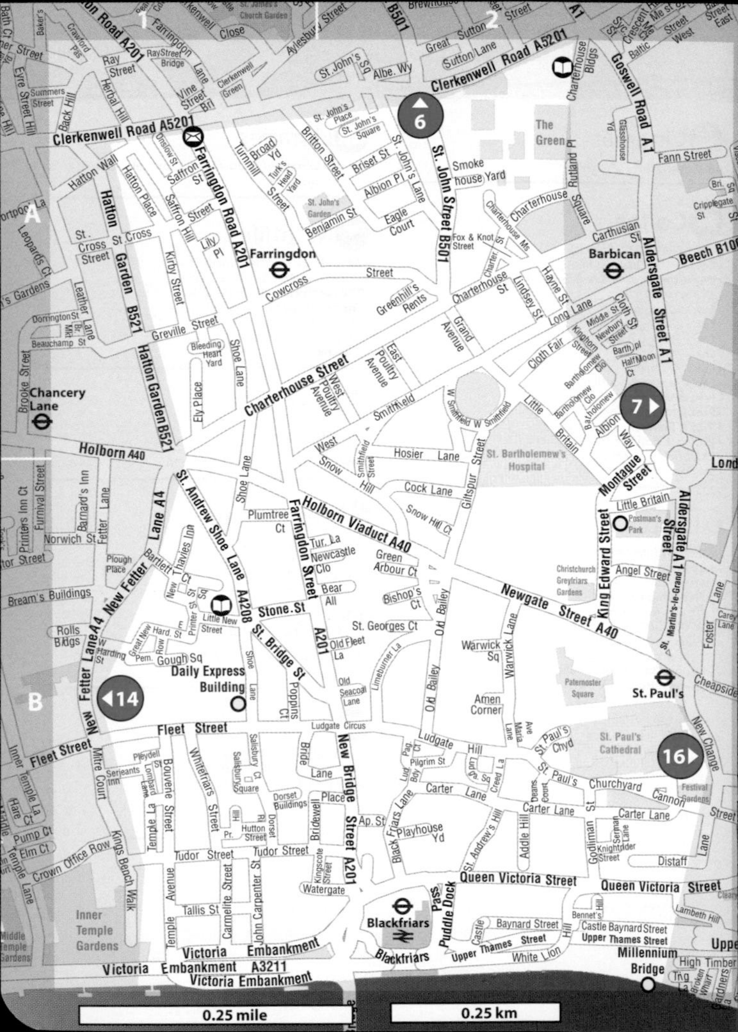

N

Clerkenwell Road A5201
Farringdon Road A201
St. John Street B501
Goswell Road A1
Aldersgate Street A1
Farringdon
Barbican
Chancery Lane
Hatton Garden B521
Charterhouse Street
Charterhouse Square
The Green
Smithfield
St. Bartholemew's Hospital
Long Lane
Cloth Fair
Holborn A40
Holborn Viaduct A40
St. Andrew Shoe Lane A4208
Farringdon Street A201
New Fetter Lane A4
Newgate Street A40
King Edward Street
Postman's Park
Christchurch Greyfriars Gardens
Old Bailey
Warwick Lane
Paternoster Square
St. Paul's
St. Paul's Cathedral
Cheapside
Daily Express Building
Fleet Street
Ludgate Circus
Ludgate Hill
New Bridge Street A201
St. Paul's Churchyard
Carter Lane
Queen Victoria Street
Blackfriars
Inner Temple Gardens
Victoria Embankment A3211
Upper Thames Street
Millennium Bridge
6
7
14
16
A
B
1
2

0.25 mile

0.25 km

Blackfriars / Farringdon

The choices for eating out and drinking in this quarter are myriad, but we recommend getting your chops around a side of cow. Choose from Smithfield Bar & Grill, Smith's or Gaucho. Get a feel for 16th century London with a potter around the old Livery Halls then make like a Dickensian Oliver in the gated Charterhouse Square.

Coffee

- **Apostrophe** • 3 St Bride St
- **Apostrophe** • 10 St. Pauls Churchyard
- **Café Deco** • Charterhouse St & E Poultry Ave
- **Caffe Nero** • Shoe Lane
- **Caffe Nero** • 118 Newgate St
- **Caffe Nero** • Paternoster Sq
- **Costa** • 13 New Bridge St
- **Costa** • 46 Cowcross St
- **Dose** • 69 Long Ln
- **Eat.** • 88 Cowcross St
- **Farm Collective** • 91 Cowcross St
- **Meze Meze** • 95 Turnmill St
- **Pret A Manger** • 101 Turnmill St
- **Pret A Manger** • 5 St John's Sq
- **Pret A Manger** • 19 Ludgate Hill
- **Pret A Manger** • 10 Pasternoster Sq
- **Pret A Manger** • 101 New Bridge St
- **Pret A Manger** • 143 Fleet St
- **Starbucks** • 1 Paternoster Sq
- **Starbucks** • 32 Fleet St
- **Starbucks** • 3 Fleet Pl
- **Starbucks** • 30 New Bridge St
- **Starbucks** • 55 Ludgate Hill
- **Starbucks** • 150 Fleet St

Landmarks

- **Daily Express Building** • 121 Fleet St
- **Millennium Bridge** • Millennium Bridge
- **Postman's Park** • Little Britain

Libraries

- **Shoe Lane Library** • Little New St
- **Society of Genealogists Library** • 14 Charterhouse Buildings [Goswell Road]

Nightlife

- **Corney & Barrow** • 10 Paternoster Sq
- **The Deux Beers** • 3 Hatton Wall
- **Fabric** • 77 Charterhouse St
- **Fox and Anchor** • 115 Charterhouse St
- **The Hat and Tun** • 3 Hatton Wall
- **Smithfield Bar & Grill** • 2 W Smithfield
- **Ye Old Mitre** • 1 Ely Pl
- **Ye Olde Cheshire Cheese** • 145 Fleet St
- **Ye Olde London** • 42 Ludgate Hill

Post Offices

- **Farringdon Road** • 89 Farringdon Rd

Restaurants

- **Beppe's Sandwich Bar** • 23 Wt Smithfield
- **Bleeding Heart** • Bleeding Heart Yard
- **Gaucho Smithfield** • 93 Charterhouse St
- **Hix Oyster And Chop House** • 36 Cowcross St
- **Kurz + Lang** • 1 St. John St
- **The Larder** • 91 St. John St
- **Le Cafe du Marche** • 22 Charterhouse Sq
- **Pho** • 86 St. John St
- **Portal** • 88 St. John St
- **Smiths of Smithfield** • 67 Charterhouse St
- **St Germain** • 89 Turnmill St
- **St John** • 26 St. John St
- **Tinseltown** • 44 St. John St
- **Vivat Bacchus** • 47 Farringdon St
- **Yo! Sushi** • 5 St. Paul's Church Yard

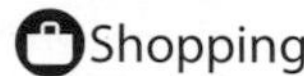

Shopping

- **Pure Groove Records** • 6 West Smithfield

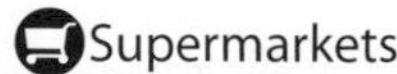

Supermarkets

- **Marks & Spencer** • Ave Maria Lane
- **Sainsbury's** • 23 Farringdon Rd

Map 16 • Square Mile (West)

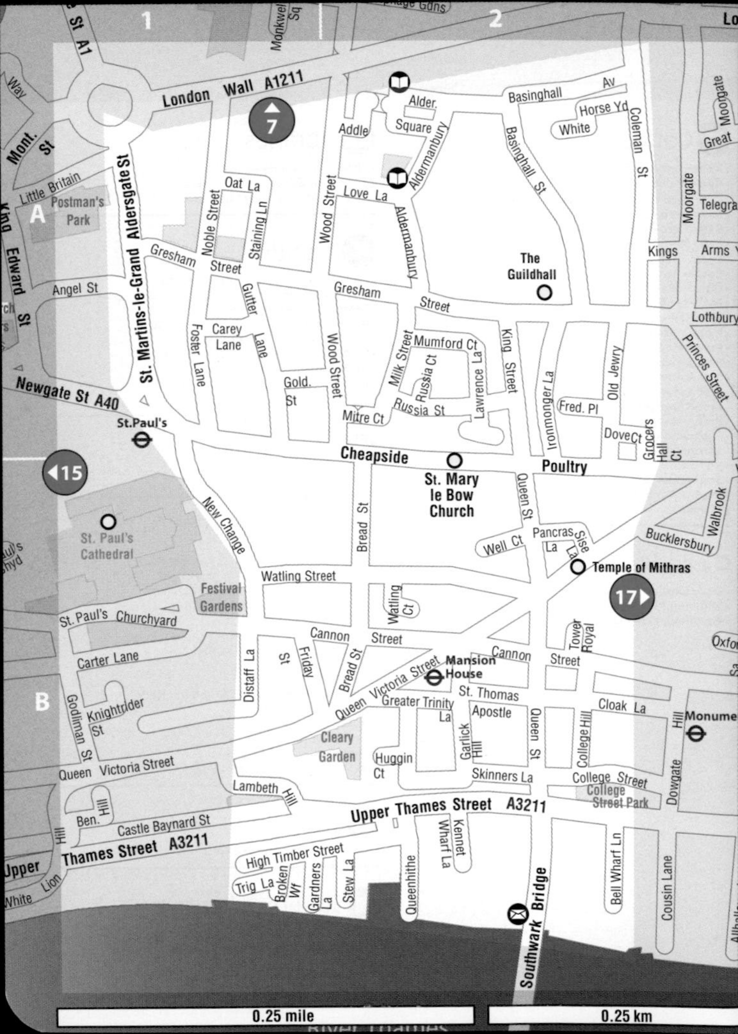

N

1
2
A
B

London Wall A1211
7
Monkwell Sq
Alder. Square
Addle
Basinghall Av
Horse Yd
White
Coleman St
Aldermanbury
Basinghall St
Moorgate
Great
Little Britain
Postman's Park
King Edward St
Mont. St
Aldersgate St
St. Martins-le-Grand
Oat La
Noble Street
Staining Ln
Wood Street
Love La
Aldermanbury
Telegra
Kings Arms
The Guildhall
Gresham Street
Angel St
Gutter Lane
Carey Lane
Foster Lane
Gresham Street
Lothbury
Princes Street
Mumford Ct
Milk Street
Russia Ct
Lawrence La
King Street
Ironmonger La
Old Jewry
Fred. Pl
Gold. St
Wood Street
Mitre Ct
Russia St
Dove Ct
Grocers Hall Ct
Newgate St A40
St.Paul's
Cheapside
St. Mary le Bow Church
Poultry
15
Queen St
Walbrook
New Change
Bread St
St. Paul's Cathedral
Well Ct
Pancras La
Sise La
Bucklersbury
Temple of Mithras
Watling Street
17
Festival Gardens
Watling Ct
St. Paul's Churchyard
Cannon Street
Tower Royal
Oxfo
Carter Lane
Distaff La
Friday St
Bread St
Queen Victoria Street
Mansion House
Cannon Street
St. Thomas Apostle
Godliman St
Knightrider St
Greater Trinity La
Cloak La
Monume
Cleary Garden
Huggin Ct
Garlick Hill
Queen St
College Hill
Dowgate Hill
Queen Victoria Street
Skinners La
College Street
College Street Park
Lambeth Hill
Ben. Hill
Castle Baynard St
Upper Thames Street A3211
Upper Thames Street A3211
White Lion Hill
High Timber Street
Trig La
Broken Wf
Gardners La
Stew La
Queenhithe
Kennet Wharf La
Southwark Bridge
Bell Wharf Ln
Cousin Lane

0.25 mile
0.25 km

Square Mile (West)

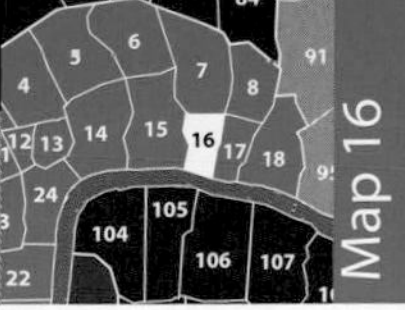

Aah, the City, that faceless square mile at which we direct such disgust and vehemence for the state we're in. Despite meltdowns and protests, the world continues to turn, stocks are traded, and bonuses return. This place has always been empty at the weekends so you can enjoy the caryatids and Doric columns in peace. And of course take in the duomo at San Paulo (so much more romantic don't you think?)

Coffee

- **Coffee Republic** • 32 Coleman St
- **Costa** • 9 Bow Ln
- **Costa** • 99 Gresham St
- **Eat.** • 15 Basinghall St
- **Eat.** • 88 Wood St
- **Eat.** • 143 Cheapside
- **Fab Food Patisserie** • 19 Watling St
- **Fresco Café Bar** • 21 Masons Ave
- **Pret A Manger** • 30 Gresham St
- **Starbucks** • 1 Poultry
- **Starbucks** • 143 Cheapside

Landmarks

- **The Guildhall** • Gresham St
- **St Mary le Bow Church** • Cheapside
- **St. Paul's Cathedral** • St. Paul's Church Yard
- **Temple of Mithras** • Queen Victoria St

Post Offices

- **Southwark** • 136 Southwark Bridge Rd

Libraries

- **City Business Library** • Aldermanbury Square
- **Guildhall Library** • Aldermanbury

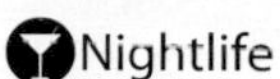

Nightlife

- **The Hatchet** • 28 Garlick Hill
- **The Mansion House** • 44 Cannon St
- **The Samuel Pepys** • Stew Ln
- **Ye Olde Watling** • 29 Watling St

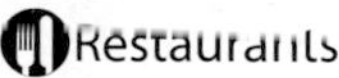

Restaurants

- **Sweetings** • 39 Queen Victoria St

Shopping

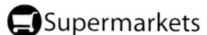

- **Church's** • 90 Cheapside
- **Manucci** • 5 Cheapside
- **Space NK Apothecary** • 145 Cheapside

Supermarkets

- **Marks & Spencer** • Cannon St Station

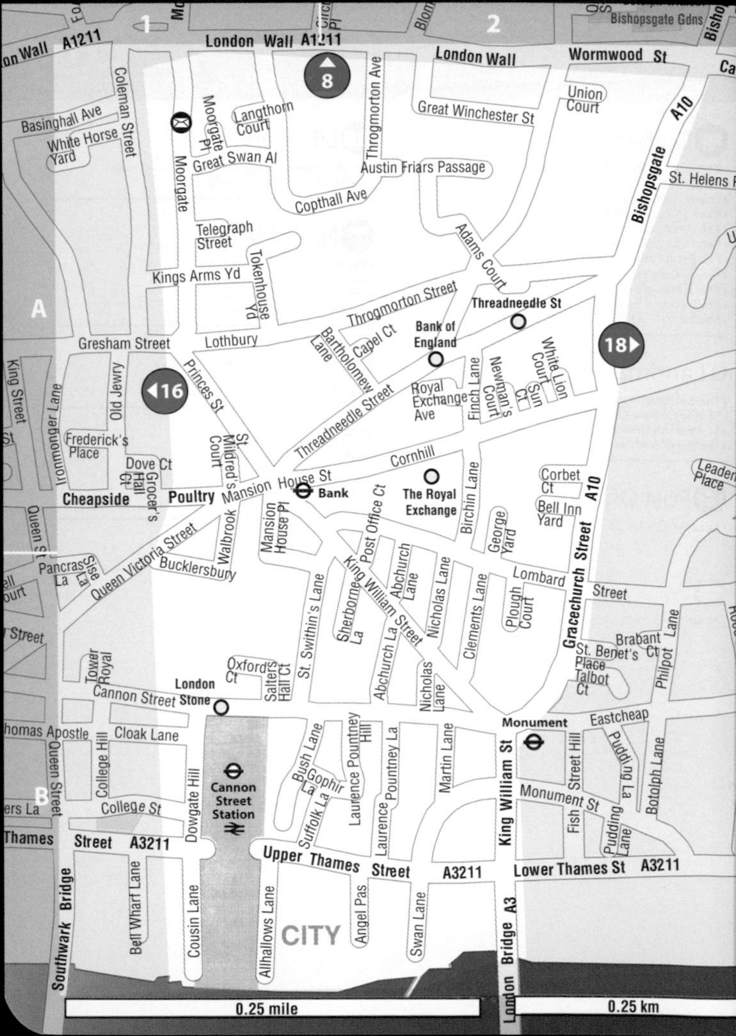

Map 17 • Square Mile (East)

London Wall A1211
Wormwood St
Bishopsgate Gdns
Union Court
Great Winchester St
Langthorn Court
Moorgate Pl
Great Swan Al
Basinghall Ave
White Horse Yard
Coleman Street
Moorgate
Throgmorton Ave
Austin Friars Passage
Copthall Ave
Telegraph Street
Tokenhouse Yd
Kings Arms Yd
Adams Court
Bishopsgate
St. Helens
A10
Throgmorton Street
Threadneedle St
Bank of England
Lothbury
Gresham Street
Bartholomew Lane
Capel Ct
White Lion Court
Sun Ct
Newman's Court
Finch Lane
Royal Exchange Ave
Threadneedle Street
Princes St
King Street
Ironmonger Lane
Old Jewry
Frederick's Place
Dove Ct
Grocer's Hall Ct
St Mildred's Court
Cornhill
Mansion House St
Poultry
Cheapside
Bank
The Royal Exchange
Birchin Lane
Corbet Ct
Bell Inn Yard
Leaden Place
Queen St
Pancras La
Sise La
Queen Victoria Street
Bucklersbury
Walbrook
Mansion House Pl
Post Office Ct
King William Street
Abchurch Lane
Nicholas Lane
Clements Lane
George Yard
Lombard Street
Plough Court
Gracechurch Street
Sherborne La
St. Swithin's Lane
Abchurch La
Brabant Ct
St. Benet's Place
Talbot Ct
Philpot Lane
Tower Royal
Oxford Ct
Salters Hall Ct
London Stone
Cannon Street
Eastcheap
Monument
Thomas Apostle
Cloak Lane
Queen Street
College Hill
Dowgate Hill
Cannon Street Station
Bush Lane
Gophir La
Suffolk La
Laurence Pountney Hill
Laurence Pountney La
Martin Lane
King William St
Street Hill
Pudding La
Botolph Lane
Monument St
Fish St Hill
Pudding Lane
College St
Thames Street A3211
Upper Thames Street A3211
Lower Thames St A3211
Southwark Bridge
Bell Wharf Lane
Cousin Lane
Allhallows Lane
CITY
Angel Pas
Swan Lane
London Bridge A3
0.25 mile
0.25 km

Square Mile (East)

London's most Jekyll-and-Hyde-like hood. By day, the Banking district throbs with suits losing fortunes. They still dig steaks at Gaucho City though perhaps the Michelin-starred Rhodes 24 is out of their price range now. Well, probably not. The Counting House is for after-work beers while the possibility of shopping at the Royal Exchange is laughable, but who says you have to buy? By night, well, just don't go there.

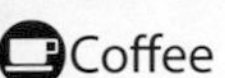

Coffee

- **Bagel Factory** • 59 Moorgate
- **Caffe Nero** • 22 Wormwood Stree
- **Eat.** • 54 Cornhill
- **Eat.** • 123 Cannon St
- **Oi Bagel** • 27 Throgmorton St
- **Pret A Manger** • 43 King William St
- **Starbucks** • 5 Camomile St
- **Starbucks** • 13 Old Broad St
- **Starbucks** • 48 Gracechurch St
- **Starbucks** • 74 Cornhill
- **Starbucks** • 90 Old Broad St

Landmarks

- **Bank of England** • Threadneedle St
- **London Stone** • 111 Cannon St
- **The Royal Exchange** • Cornhill
- **Threadneedle Street** • Threadneedle St

Nightlife

- **The Counting House** • 50 Cornhill
- **Royal Exchange Grand Cafe** • Royal Exchange

Post Offices

- **Moorgate** • 53 Moorgate

Restaurants

- **Gaucho City** • 1 Bell Inn Yard
- **The Mercer** • 34 Threadneedle St
- **Nusa Kitchen** • 2 Adams Ct
- **Rhodes 24** • 25 Old Broad St
- **Wasabi** • 52 Old Broad St

Shopping

- **Paul A Young Fine Chocolates** • 20 Royal Exchange
- **Pretty Ballerinas** • 30 Royal Exchange
- **Sweatshop** • Cousin Lane

Supermarkets

- **Marks & Spencer** • Cannon St Station
- **Sainsbury's** • 10 Lombard St

Map 18 • Tower Hill / Aldgate

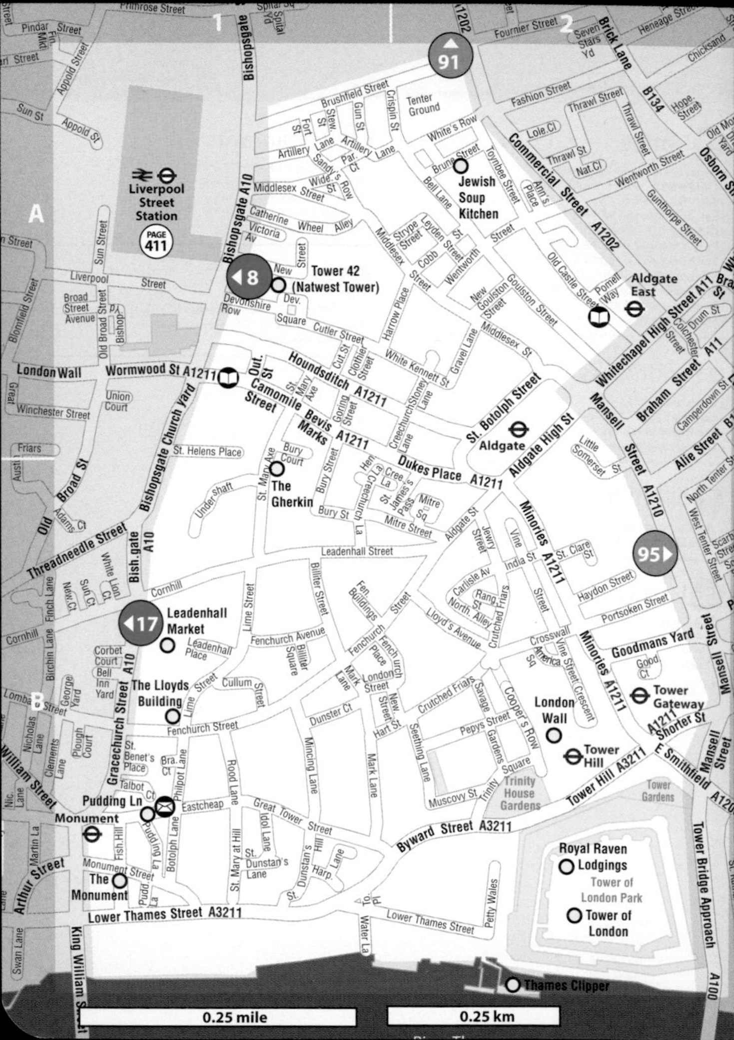

Liverpool Street Station
PAGE 411
Tower 42 (Natwest Tower)
Jewish Soup Kitchen
Aldgate East
Aldgate
The Gherkin
Leadenhall Market
The Lloyds Building
Pudding Ln
Monument
The Monument
London Wall
Tower Hill
Tower Gateway
Trinity House Gardens
Tower Gardens
Royal Raven Lodgings
Tower of London Park
Tower of London
Thames Clipper

91
8
17
95

0.25 mile
0.25 km

Tower Hill / Aldgate

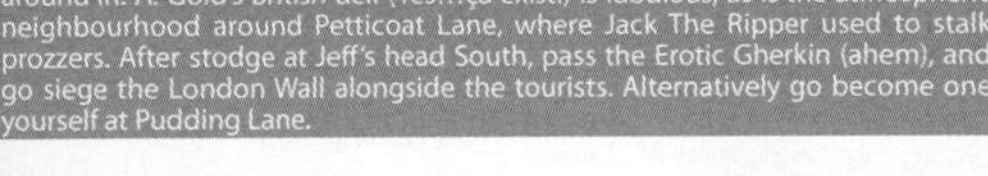

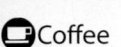

Though on the fringe of the financial cesspit, Aldgate is brilliant to walk and gawp around in. A. Gold's British deli (Yes…ça exist!) is fabulous, as is the atmospheric neighbourhood around Petticoat Lane, where Jack The Ripper used to stalk prozzers. After stodge at Jeff's head South, pass the Erotic Gherkin (ahem), and go siege the London Wall alongside the tourists. Alternatively go become one yourself at Pudding Lane.

Coffee

- **Cafe Cotto** • 12 Mitre St
- **Caffe Nero** • 1 Fenchurch Pl [Coopers Row]
- **Caffe Nero** • 23 Eastcheap
- **Caffe Nero** • 88 Leadenhall St
- **Eat.** • 28 Brushfield St
- **Eat.** • 84 Aldgate High St
- **Eat.** • 2 Eastcheap
- **Eat.** • 155 Fenchurch St
- **Eat.** • 26 Leadenhall St
- **Eat.** • 122 Minories
- **Eat.** • 48 Mark Ln
- **Eat.** • 2 Tower Hill
- **Eat.** • 33 St Mary Axe
- **Market Coffee House** • 52 Brushfield St
- **Pret A Manger** • 3 Cutler St
- **Starbucks** • 8 Brushfield St
- **Starbucks** • 20 Eastcheap
- **Starbucks** • 48 Minories
- **Starbucks** • 66 St Mary Axe

Landmarks

- **The Gherkin** • 30 St Mary Axe
- **Jewish Soup Kitchen** • Brune St & Tenter Ground
- **The Lloyd's Building** • 1 Lime St
- **Leadenhall Market** • Gracechurch St
- **London Wall** • Cooper's Row & Trinity Sq
- **The Monument** • Monument St
- **Pudding Lane** • Pudding Lane
- **The Ravens** • Tower Hill
- **Thames Clippers** • Tower Pier
- **Tower 42** • 25 Old Broad St
- **Tower of London** • Tower Hill

Libraries

- **Camomile Street** • 15 Camomile St
- **The Women's Library** • 25 Old Castle St

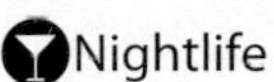

Nightlife

- **Dion** • 52 Leadenhall St
- **Kenza** • 10 Devonshire Sq
- **Mary Janes** • 124 Minories
- **The Minories** • 64 Minories
- **Pepys Bar** • 10 Pepys St
- **Prism** • 147 Leadenhall St
- **Revolution** • 140 Leadenhall St

Post Offices

- **The City of London BO** • 12 Eastcheap

Restaurants

- **Jeff's Cafe** • 14 Brune St
- **La Pietra** • 54 Commercial St
- **S & M Cafe** • 48 Brushfield St

Shopping

- **A. Gold** • 42 Brushfield St
- **Montezuma's** • 51 Brushfield St
- **Petticoat Lane Market** • Middlesex St
- **Precious** • 16 Artillery Passage
- **Sweaty Betty** • 5 Rood Ln

Supermarkets

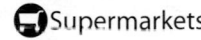

- **Sainsbury's** • 45 Fenchurch St

Map 19 • Belgravia

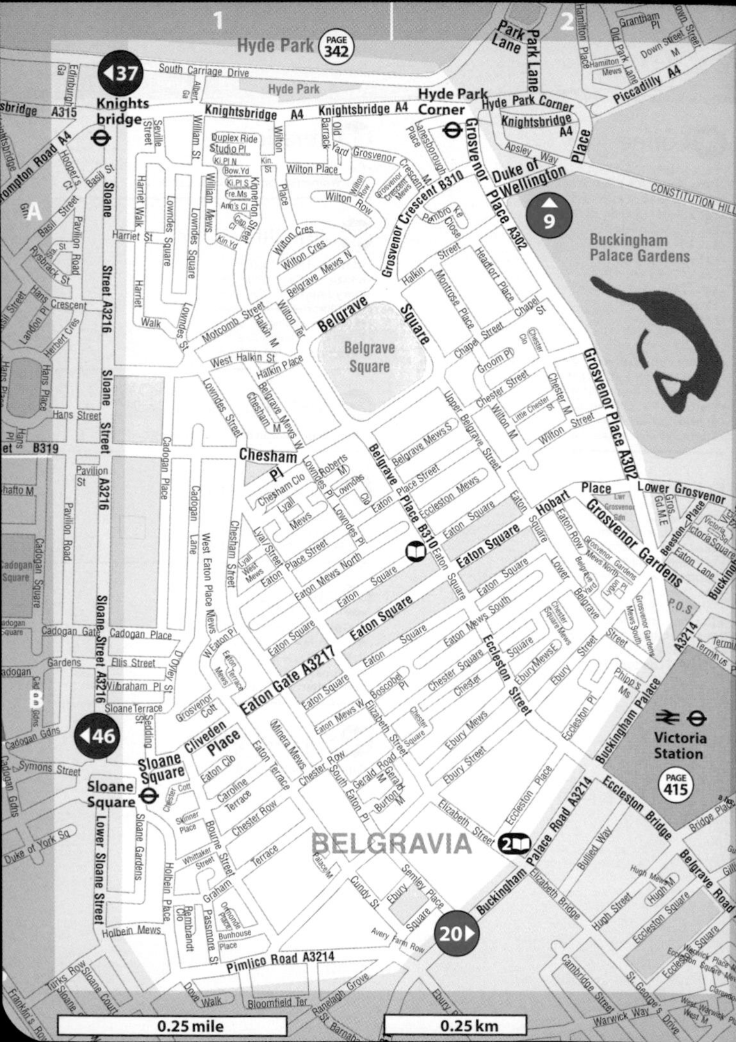

1
2
A
B
Hyde Park
PAGE 342
South Carriage Drive
Knightsbridge A4
Knightsbridge A315
Knights bridge
37
Hyde Park Corner
Park Lane
Hamilton Place
Grantham Pl
Old Park Lane
Down Street
Hamilton Mews
Piccadilly A4
Hyde Park Corner
Knightsbridge A4
Apsley Way
Duke of Wellington Place
Constitution Hill
9
Buckingham Palace Gardens
Grosvenor Place A302
Grosvenor Crescent B310
Grosvenor Crescent Mews
Lanesborough Place
Wilton Place
Wilton Row
Wilton Crescent
Old Barrack Yard
Kinnerton Street
Duplex Ride
Studio Pl
William St
William Mews
Lowndes Square
Harriet Walk
Harriet St
Seville Street
Albert Gate
Sloane Street A3216
Brompton Road A4
Hooper's Ct
Basil Street
Pavilion Road
Rysbrack St
Hans Crescent
Hans Place
Hans Street
Herbert Cres
Pembroke Close
Halkin Street
Montrose Place
Headfort Place
Chapel Street
Belgrave Mews N
Belgrave Square
Motcomb Street
Halkin M
Wilton Ter
West Halkin St
Halkin Place
Belgrave Mews W
Chesham M
Chesham Pl
Chesham Clo
Lyall Mews
Lyall Street
Lowndes Pl
Roberts M
Lowndes Clo
Lowndes Street
Chester Street
Groom Pl
Chester Clo
Chester M
Little Chester St
Wilton M
Wilton Street
Upper Belgrave Street
Belgrave Mews S
Belgrave Place B310
Eaton Place
Eccleston Mews
Eaton Square
Eaton Mews North
Eaton Mews South
Eaton Mews W
Eaton Gate A3217
Hobart Place
Lower Grosvenor Place
Grosvenor Gardens
Beeston Place
Victoria Square
Eaton Lane
Eaton Row
Lower Belgrave Street
Lygon Pl
Chester Square
Chester Square Mews
Ebury Mews
Ebury Mews E
Ebury Street
Eccleston Street
Elizabeth Street
Boscobel Pl
Chester Row
Gerald Road
Gerald M
Burton M
South Eaton Pl
Minera Mews
Eaton Terrace
Eaton Clo
Caroline Terrace
Cliveden Place
Sloane Square
Sloane Terrace
Sedding St
Grosvenor Cott
W Eaton Pl
West Eaton Place Mews
Cadogan Lane
Cadogan Place
Cadogan Gate
Cadogan Square
Cadogan Gardens
Ellis Street
Wilbraham Pl
D'Oyley St
Chesham Street
Pavilion St
Symons Street
46
Lower Sloane Street
Sloane Gardens
Holbein Place
Holbein Mews
Duke of York Sq
Skinner Place
Whittaker Street
Bourne Street
Graham Terrace
Rembrandt Clo
Ormonde Place
Passmore St
Bunhouse Place
Pimlico Road A3214
Turks Row
Sloane Court
Franklin's Row
Dove Walk
Bloomfield Ter
Ranelagh Grove
St Barnabas
Ebury Bridge
Cundy St
Ebury Square
Semley Place
Avery Farm Row
20
BELGRAVIA
Eccleston Place
Buckingham Palace Road A3214
Buckingham Palace Road
Phipp's Ms
Eccleston Pl
Victoria Station
PAGE 415
Eccleston Bridge
Bridge Place
Terminus Pl
Elizabeth Bridge
Bulleid Way
Hugh Mews
Hugh M
Hugh Street
Belgrave Road
Eccleston Square
Cambridge Street
St. George's Drive
Warwick Way
Warwick Place
P.O.S.

0.25 mile
0.25 km

Belgravia

Ugg and Range Rover fetishists are in a constant state of climax around here. It sure is pretty when the sun isn't being blocked by expensively coiffured bouffants, but one suspects the plummy accents and tastless richness would dent anyone's enthusiasm for chic dog clothes (Mungo & Maud) or curry (Amaya). Victoria's Red Cross Charity shop provides opportunities for us to pick over upper class leftovers.

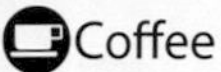

Coffee

- **Starbucks** • 53 Pimlico Rd
- **Tomtom Coffee House** • 114 Ebury St

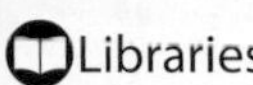

Libraries

- **Instituto Cervantes** • 102 Eaton Square
- **Victoria Library** • 160 Buckingham Palace Rd
- **Westminster Music Library** • 160 Buckingham Palace Rd

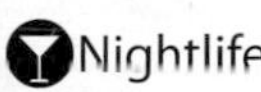

Nightlife

- **The Blue Bar** • The Berkeley Hotel • Wilton Pl
- **Nag's Head** • 53 Kinnerton St
- **The Plumber's Arms** • 14 Lower Belgrave St
- **The Wilton Arms** • 71 Kinnerton St

Restaurants

- **Amaya** • Motcomb St
- **Boisdale** • 15 Eccleston St
- **Noura** • 12 William St
- **One-O-One** • 101 Knightsbridge
- **Yo! Sushi** • 102 Knightsbridge

Shopping

- **British Red Cross** • 85 Ebury St
- **Moyses Flowers** • Peter Jones - Sloane Sq
- **Mungo & Maud** • 79 Elizabeth St
- **Peter Jones** •Sloan Sq

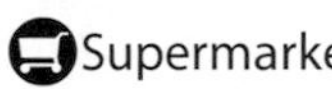

Supermarkets

- **Waitrose** • 27 Motcomb St

Map 20 • Victoria / Pimlico (West)

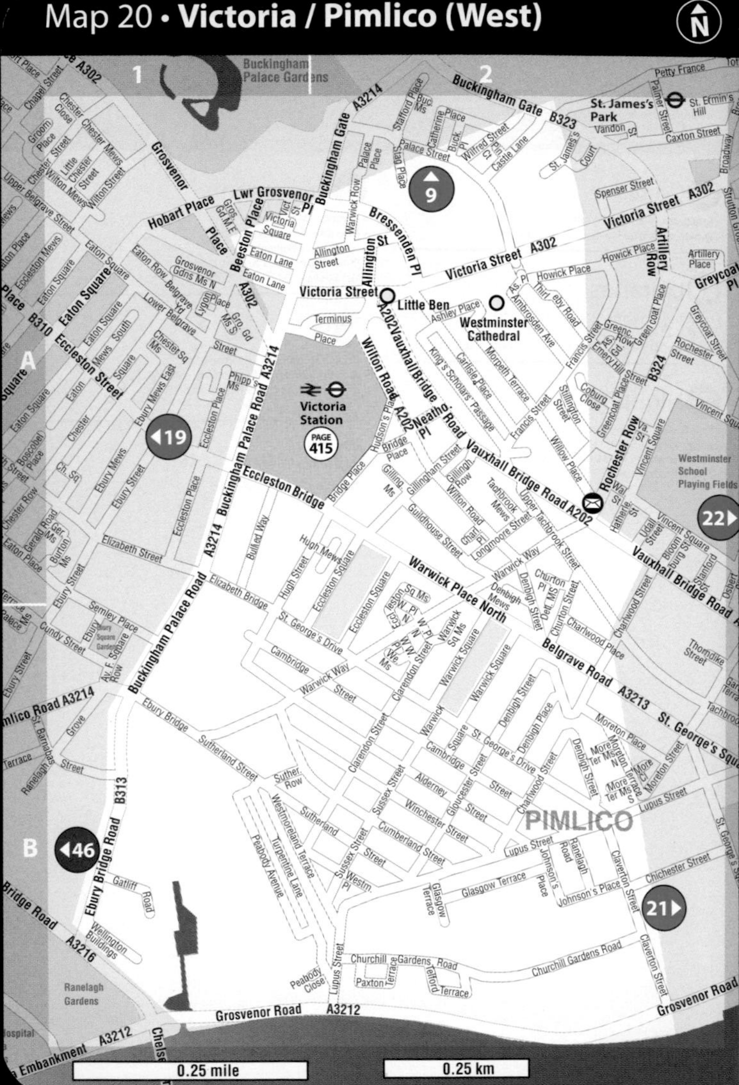

Victoria / Pimlico (West)

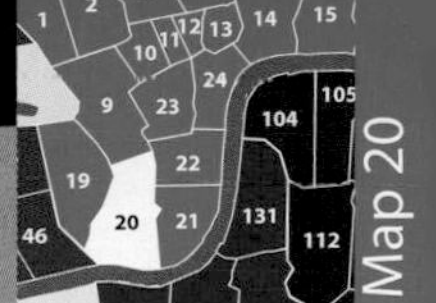

Since the Tower of London closed for business, prisoners have been routinely tortured at weekends in Victoria Station. Surrounding the transit hubs is a dignified 'hood Churchill and Mozart called home. Do a late-night tramp photoshoot on the steps of the magnificent houses of Lupus Street (with a camera from Grays) before heading to The Cask & Glass for a knees-up with your new pals.

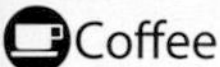

Coffee

- **Bagel Factory** • Victoria Station
- **Bagel Factory** • Victoria Place Shopping Centre • Buckingham Palace Rd
- **Caffe Nero** • 31 Warwick Way
- **Costa** • 3 Cardinal Walk
- **Costa** • 115 Buckingham Palace Rd
- **Eat.** • Cardinal Pl
- **Pret A Manger** • 12 Victoria St
- **Pret A Manger** • 173 Victoria St
- **Pret A Manger** • Unit 36B • Victoria Station
- **Pret A Manger** • 92 Buckingham Palace Rd
- **Starbucks** • 137 Victoria St
- **Starbucks** • Buckingham Palace Rd & Lower Belgrave St

Post Offices

- **Vauxhall Bridge Road** • 167 Vauxhall Bridge Rd

Landmarks

- **Little Ben** • Victoria St & Vauxhall Bridge Rd
- **Westminster Cathedral** • 42 Francis St

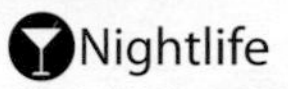

Nightlife

- **The Cask & Glass** • 39 Palace St
- **Windsor Castle** • 23 Francis St

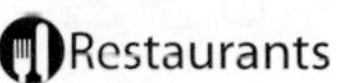

Restaurants

- **Grumbles** • 35 Churton St

Shopping

- **Capital Carboot Sale** • Pimlico Academy, Lupus St
- **Grays of Westminster** • 40 Churton St
- **La Bella Sicilia** • 23 Warwick Way
- **Rippon Cheese Stores** • 26 Upper Tachbrook St
- **Runners Need** • 24 Palace Street
- **Topshop** • 18 Victoria St

Supermarkets

- **Marks & Spencer** • Victoria Mainline Station

Westminster School Playing Fields
St. John's Gardens
Westminster Gardens
Millbank Tower
Tate Britain
Chelsea College of Art & Design
The Shard Building Site
Pimlico
Bessborough Gardens
Riverside Gardens
St. George's Square Garden
Pimlico Gardens
Victoria Tower Gardens
River Thames
Horseferry Road
Vauxhall Bridge Road
Vauxhall Bridge
Millbank
Grosvenor Road
St. George's Square
Rochester Row
Vincent Square

22
20
PAGE 476

0.25 mile
0.25 km

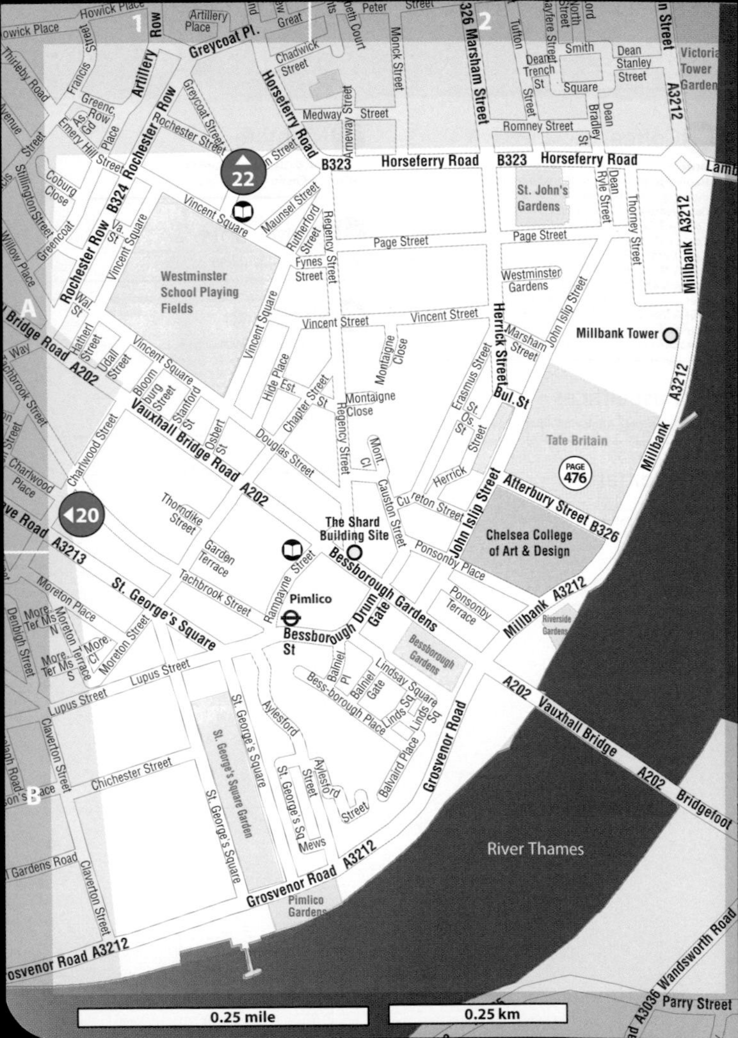

Pimlico (East)

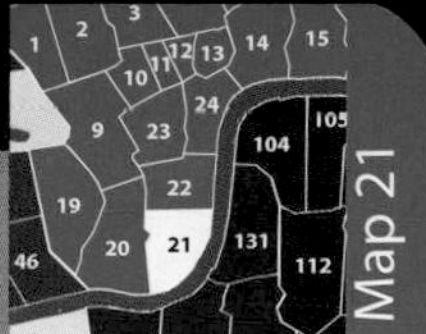

Hugging the curve of the Thames, this princely patch of Pimlico combines the stately Tate with imposing embankment architecture and ancient houses. Check out the old-money splendour of Vincent Street before grabbing lunch at the Regency, a true gem of a caf. Much fun can be had by pretending you acutally live around here, so in this spirit head to the Morpeth as your local.

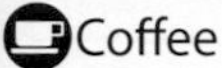

Coffee

• **Starbucks** • 35 Horseferry Rd

Landmarks

• **Millbank Tower** • 21 Millbank
• **The Shard** • 32 Vauxhall Bridge Rd

Libraries

• **Pimlico Library** • Rampayne St
• **Royal Horticultural Society Library** • 80 Vincent Sq

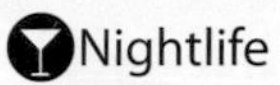

Nightlife

• **Morpeth Arms** • 58 Millibank

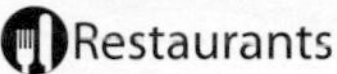

Restaurants

• **The Regency Cafe** • 17 Regency St
• **The Vincent Rooms** • 76 Vincent Square

Shopping

• **Black Rose** • 112 Belgrave Rd

Map 22 • Westminster

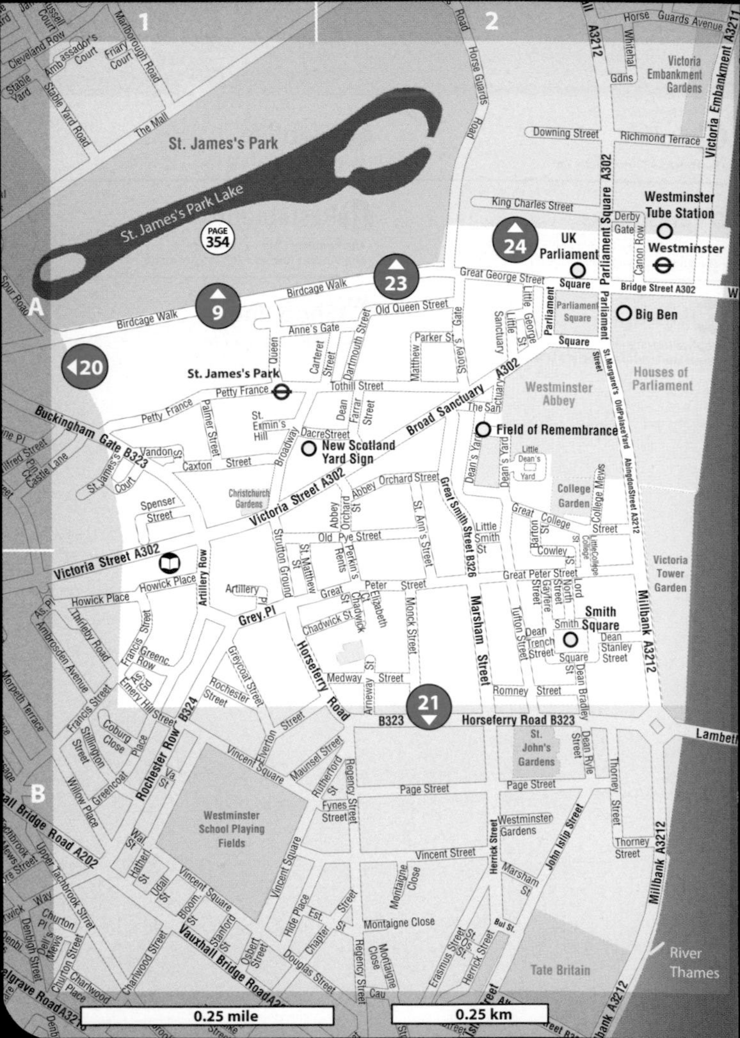

St. James's Park
St. James's Park Lake
PAGE 354
Birdcage Walk
The Mall
Horse Guards Road
Horse Guards Avenue
Whitehall Gdns
Victoria Embankment Gardens
Victoria Embankment
Downing Street
Richmond Terrace
King Charles Street
Westminster Tube Station
Westminster
UK Parliament
Derby Gate
Canon Row
Parliament Square A302
Great George Street
Bridge Street A302
Big Ben
Old Queen Street
Anne's Gate
Parker St
Storey's Gate
Little Sanctuary
Little George St
Parliament Square
Houses of Parliament
Westminster Abbey
St. Margaret's Street
Old Palace Yard
Abingdon Street A3212
St. James's Park
Petty France
Tothill Street
Queen Anne's Gate
Carteret Street
Dartmouth Street
Matthew Parker Street
Dean Farrar Street
Broad Sanctuary A302
The Sanctuary
Field of Remembrance
St. Ermin's Hill
Dacre Street
New Scotland Yard Sign
Broadway
Buckingham Gate B323
Palmer Street
Vandon St
Caxton Street
St. James's Court
Castle Lane
Spenser Street
Christchurch Gardens
Victoria Street A302
Abbey Orchard Street
Dean's Yard
Little Dean's Yard
College Garden
College Mews
Great College Street
Barton St
Cowley St
Little College St
Great Smith Street B326
Little Smith St
St. Ann's Street
Old Pye Street
Strutton Ground
St. Matthew St
Perkin's Rents
Great Peter Street
Victoria Tower Garden
Howick Place
Artillery Row
Artillery Pl
Grey.Pl
Chadwick St
Elizabeth Ct
Monck Street
Marsham Street
Tufton Street
Gayfere Street
North Street
Lord North Street
Smith Square
Dean Trench Street
Dean Stanley Street
Millbank A3212
Thirleby Road
Ambrosden Avenue
Francis Street
Greencoat Row
Emery Hill Street
Greycoat Street
Rochester Street
Horseferry Road
Medway Street
Arneway St
Romney Street
Dean Bradley Street
Horseferry Road B323
Morpeth Terrace
Coburg Close
Stillington Street
Greencoat Place
Willow Place
Rochester Row B324
Vincent Square
Elverton Street
Maunsel Street
Rutherford St
Regency Street
Fynes Street
St. John's Gardens
Dean Ryle Street
Thorney Street
Page Street
Westminster School Playing Fields
Westminster Gardens
Herrick Street
John Islip Street
Vauxhall Bridge Road A202
Upper Tachbrook Street
Hatherley St
Udall St
Bloomburg St
Stanford St
Osbert Street
Vincent Street
Montaigne Close
Marsham St
Hide Place
Chapter St
Douglas Street
Erasmus Street
Herrick Street
Tate Britain
River Thames
Lambeth
Charlwood Street
Churton Street
Charlwood Place
Denbigh Street
Belgrave Road A3213
Cleveland Row
Ambassador's Court
Friary Court
Marlborough Road
Stable Yard
Stable Yard Road
Spur Road

0.25 mile
0.25 km

Westminster

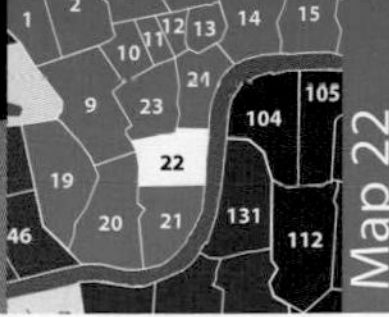

The long shadow of government falls over these parts, beautiful as they are. Protestors and wannabe Guy Fawkeses head to Parliament Square, where they can harangue whichever bunch of jokers are esconced in the Houses of Parliament. Get away from tourists at the tiny St Stephen's Tavern, or grab a classy cocktail at the Cinnamon Club. If you must shop head to Victoria Street.

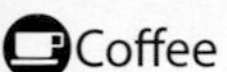

Coffee

- **Caffe Nero** • 1 Bridge St
- **Caffe Nero** • 105 Victoria St
- **Eat.** • 3 Strutton Ground
- **Fresco Cafe Bar** • 11 Tothill St
- **Pret A Manger** • 75 Victoria St
- **Pret A Manger** • 49 Tothill St
- **Puccino's** • 6 Victoria St
- **Starbucks** • 27 Victoria St

Landmarks

- **Big Ben** • Bridge St
- **Field of Remembrance** • Victoria St
- **New Scotland Yard Sign** • 8 Broadway
- **St. John's Smith Square** • Smith Sq
- **UK Parliament** • Victoria St & Abingdon St
- **Westminster Tube Station** • Westminster Bridge Rd

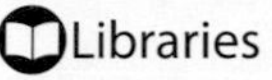

Libraries

- **St James's Library** • 62 Victoria St

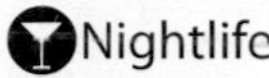

Nightlife

- **The Albert** • 52 Victoria St
- **The Cinnamon Club** • 30 Great Smith St
- **The Speaker** • 46 Great Peter Street
- **Two Chairmen** • 39 Dartmouth St
- **St. Stephen's Tavern** • 10 Bridge St

Shopping

- **Haelen Centre** • 41 Broadway
- **National Map Centre** • 22 Caxton St

Map 23 • St. James's

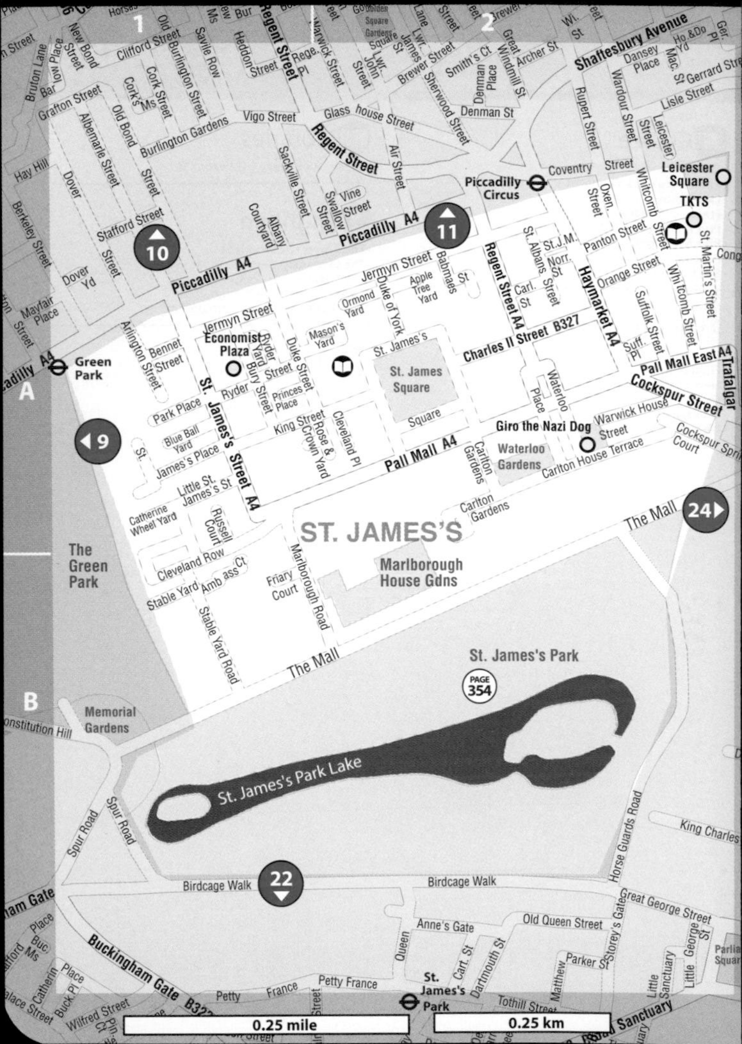

ST. JAMES'S

Piccadilly A4
Regent Street
Jermyn Street
St. James's Street A4
St. James's Square
Pall Mall A4
Haymarket A4
Charles II Street B327
Pall Mall East A4
Cockspur Street
The Mall
Shaftesbury Avenue
Coventry Street
Piccadilly Circus
Leicester Square
TKTS
Green Park
The Green Park
Economist Plaza
Giro the Nazi Dog
Waterloo Gardens
Carlton House Terrace
Marlborough House Gdns
St. James's Park
St. James's Park Lake
Memorial Gardens
Constitution Hill
Spur Road
Birdcage Walk
Horse Guards Road
Great George Street
Old Queen Street
Anne's Gate
Queen Anne's Gate
Petty France
Buckingham Gate B323
St. James's Park
Tothill Street
Broad Sanctuary
Glasshouse Street
Vigo Street
Burlington Gardens
Old Bond Street
Albemarle Street
Dover Street
Berkeley Street
Stafford Street
Sackville Street
Air Street
Duke Street
Bury Street
King Street
Cleveland Row
Stable Yard Road
Marlborough Road
Carlton Gardens
Waterloo Place
Whitcomb Street
St. Martin's Street
Trafalgar

PAGE 354

0.25 mile
0.25 km

St. James's

Dignified, decadent, exclusive, Pall Mall and St. James's Street are where the aristobrats come out to play. With stuffy gentlemen's clubs, bespoke tailors, and the stale scent of a cigar-fuelled colonialist past pervading, you'll want to sweeten up with a macaroon at Laduree. Giro the Nazi dog observes the liberals who get culture fixes at the ICA, but he can't come for scraps at Inn The Park.

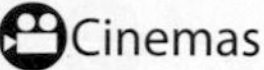

Cinemas

- **Apollo Cinema Piccadily Circus** • 19 Lower Regent St
- **Cineworld Haymarket** • 63 Haymarket
- **ICA Cinema** • The Mall & Horse Guards Rd
- **Odeon Leicester Square** • 24 Leicester Sq
- **Odeon Panton Street** • 11 Panton St
- **Odeon West End Cinema** • 40 Leicester Sq

Coffee

- **Apostrophe** • 16 Regent St
- **Caffe Nero** • 35 Jermyn St
- **Coffee Republic** • 63 Haymarket
- **Eat.** • 18 Regent St
- **Eat.** • 3 Duke of York St
- **Eat.** • 9 Crown Passage
- **ICA Cafe** • The Mall
- **Pret A Manger** • 8 King St

Landmarks

- **Economist Plaza** • 25 St. James's St
- **Giro the Nazi Dog** • 9 Carlton House Terrace
- **Leicester Square** • Leicester Sq
- **TKTS** • Leicester Sq

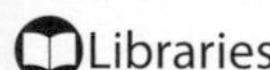

Libraries

- **London Library** • 14 St James's Sq
- **Westminster Reference Library** • 35 St Martin's St

Nightlife

- **Aura** • 48 St James's St
- **Institute of Contemporary Arts** • The Mall
- **The Sports Cafe** • 80 Haymarket

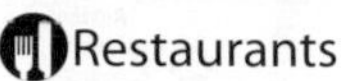

Restaurants

- **Inn The Park** • St James' Park
- **Laduree** • 71 Burlington Arcade
- **The Stockpot** • 38 Panton St

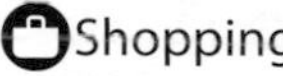

Shopping

- **Partridges Deli** • 2 Duke of York St
- **National Map Centre** • 22-24 Caxton St
- **Richard Caplan** • 25 Bury St

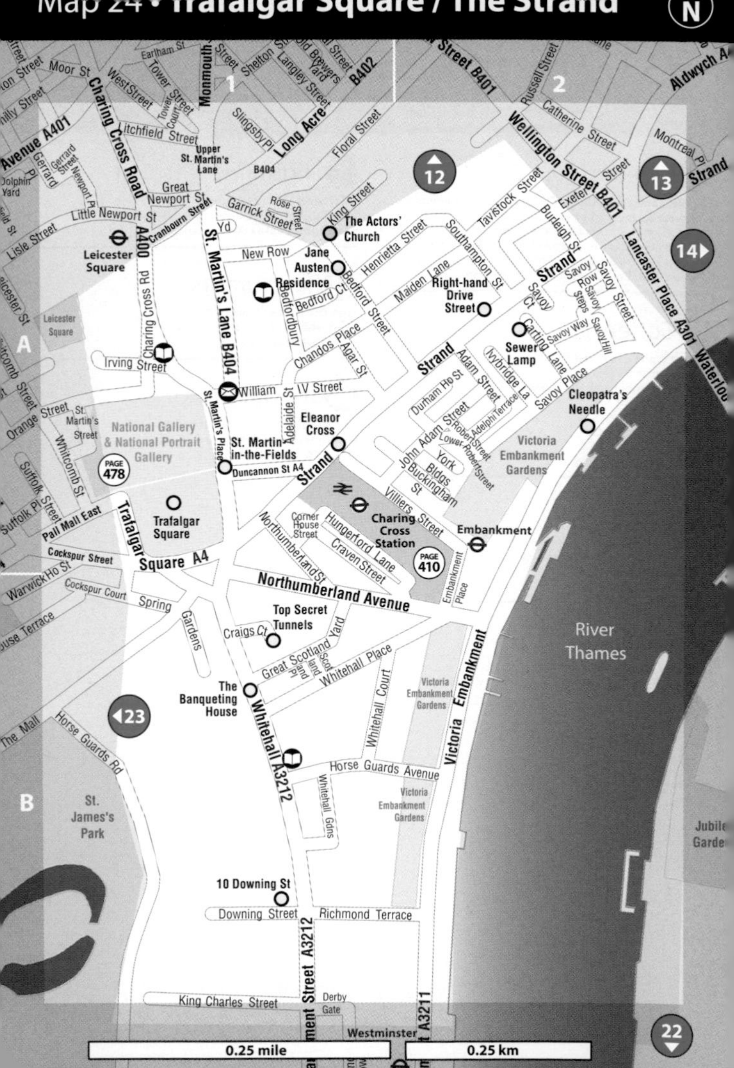

The Actors' Church
Jane Austen Residence
Right-hand Drive Street
Sewer Lamp
Cleopatra's Needle
Eleanor Cross
St. Martin-in-the-Fields
National Gallery & National Portrait Gallery
PAGE 478
Trafalgar Square
Charing Cross Station
PAGE 410
Embankment
Leicester Square
Top Secret Tunnels
The Banqueting House
10 Downing St
St. James's Park
River Thames
Victoria Embankment Gardens
Strand
Northumberland Avenue
Whitehall A3212
Victoria Embankment
Charing Cross Road
St. Martin's Lane B404
Long Acre
Wellington Street B401
Lancaster Place A301
Downing Street
Richmond Terrace
King Charles Street
Horse Guards Avenue
Westminster
0.25 mile
0.25 km

Trafalgar Square / The Strand

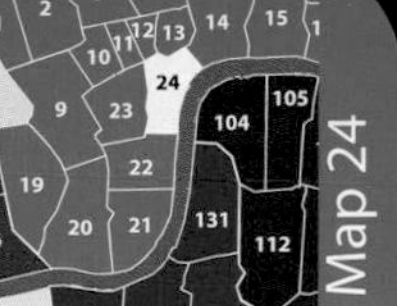

The hawkers came and removed the flying rats and lo! the Square was clean and visible. This ain't Mary Poppins—don't feed the birds you dirty tourists. Instead go to Terroirs and pretend you know a lot about wine. Eat at Wahaca, one of London's few good Mexicans, then walk it off on Waterloo Bridge and watch the sun set over the Thames. Aah. That's why you love London.

Coffee

- **Apostrophe** • 215 Strand
- **Caffe Nero** • 10 Bedford St
- **Caffe Nero** • 181 Strand
- **Caffe Nero** • 125 Strand
- **Caffe Nero** • 36 St Martin's Ln
- **Caffe Nero** • 29 Southampton St
- **Coffee Republic** • 79 Strand
- **Costa** • 17 Embankment Pl
- **Eat.** • 41 Bedford St
- **Eat.** • 39 Villiers St
- **Great American Bagel Factory** • 45 Villiers St
- **Pret A Manger** • 135 Strand
- **Pret A Manger** • 421 Strand
- **Pret A Manger** • 7 St Martin's Ln
- **Scott's Sandwich Bar** • 10 New Row
- **Starbucks** • 355 Strand
- **Starbucks** • 442 Strand
- **Starbucks** • 14 Villiers St
- **Starbucks** • 1 Villiers St

Landmarks

- **10 Downing Street** • 10 Downing St
- **The Actors' Church** • 29 Bedford St
- **Banqueting House** • Whitehall
- **Cleopatra's Needle** • Embankment
- **Eleanor Cross** • Strand
- **Jane Austen Residence** • 10 Henrietta St
- **Right-Hand Drive Street** • Savoy Ct
- **Sewer Lamp** • Carting Lane & Strand
- **St Martin-in-the-Fields** • Trafalgar Sq
- **Top Secret Tunnels** • 6 Craig's Ct
- **Trafalgar Square** • Trafalgar Sqaure

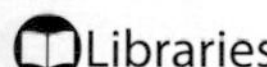

Libraries

- **Charing Cross Library** • 4 Charing Cross Rd
- **Royal United Services Institute Library** • Whitehall

Nightlife

- **Asia de Cuba** • 45 St. Martin's Lane
- **The Chandos** • 29 St Martins Lane
- **The Coal Hole** • 91 Strand
- **Covent Garden Comedy Club** • The Arches
- **Gordon's Wine Bar** • 47 Villiers St
- **Heaven** • The Arches
- **Maple Leaf** • 41 Maiden Ln
- **Punch & Judy** • The Covent Garden Piazza
- **Retro Bar** • 2 George Ct
- **Roadhouse** • 35 The Covent Garden Piazza
- **The Sherlock Holmes** • 10 Northumberland St
- **Terroirs** • 5 William IV St
- **Café Express** • 372 Strand
- **Zoo Bar & Club** • 13 Bear St

Post Offices

- **Trafalgar Square** • 24 William IV St

Restaurants

- **Bistro 1** • 33 Southampton St
- **Cafe in the Crypt** • 6 St Martin's Pl
- **Covent Garden Cafe** • Exeter St
- **Farmer Brown** • 4 New Row
- **Gourmet Burger Kitchen** • 13 Maiden Ln
- **India Club** • 143 Strand
- **J Sheekey** • 28 St Martins Ct
- **Portrait Restaurant & Bar** • St Martin's Pl
- **R.S. Hispaniola** • Victoria Embankment
- **Rules** • 35 Maiden Ln
- **Scott's Sandwich Bar** • 10 New Row
- **Thai Pot** • 1 Bedfordbury
- **Wahaca** • 66 Chandos Pl

Shopping

- **Austin Kaye** • 425 The Strand
- **Australia Shop** • 27 Maiden Ln
- **Gelato Mio** • 45 Villiers St
- **The Italian Bookshop** • 5 Cecil Ct
- **London Camera Exchange** • 98 Strand
- **Motor Books** • 13 Cecil Ct
- **Rohan** • 10 Henrietta St
- **Stanley Gibbons** • 399 Strand

Supermarkets

- **Marks & Spencer** • Charing Cross Station

Maps 25–50 • West London

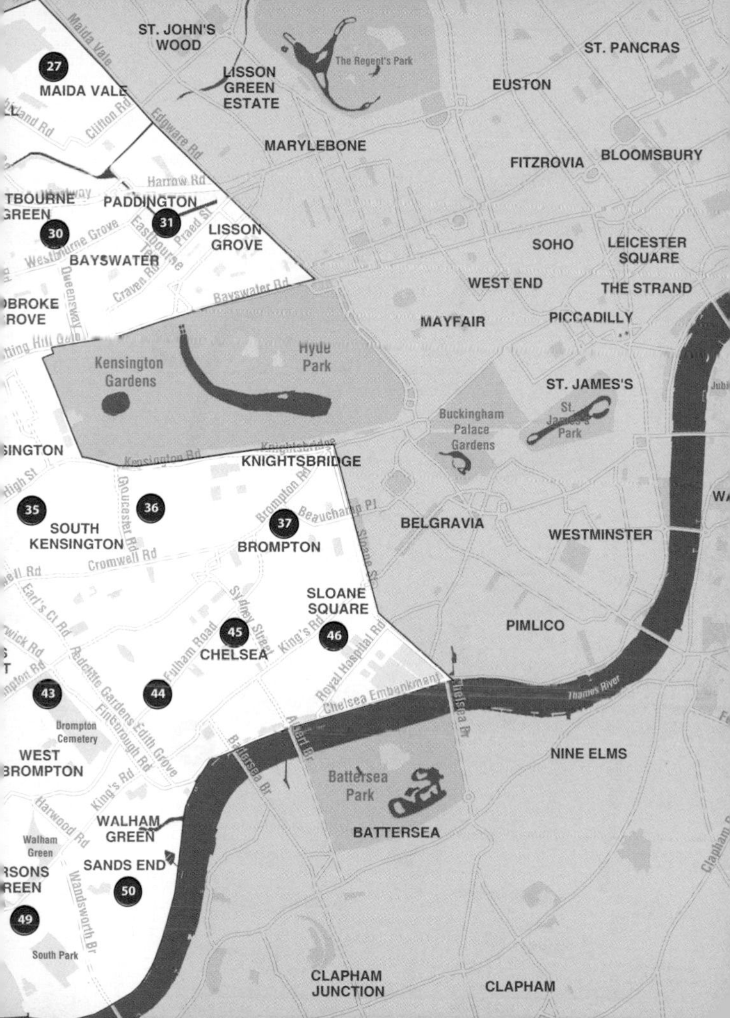

ST. JOHN'S WOOD
Maida Vale
27
MAIDA VALE
Clifton Rd
Edgware Rd
LISSON GREEN ESTATE
The Regent's Park
ST. PANCRAS
EUSTON
MARYLEBONE
FITZROVIA
BLOOMSBURY
Harrow Rd
PADDINGTON
31
30
Westbourne Grove
Eastbourne Terrace
Praed St
LISSON GROVE
BAYSWATER
Queensway
Craven Rd
Bayswater Rd
SOHO
LEICESTER SQUARE
WEST END
THE STRAND
MAYFAIR
PICCADILLY
Kensington Gardens
Hyde Park
ST. JAMES'S
St. James's Park
Buckingham Palace Gardens
Knightsbridge
Kensington Rd
KNIGHTSBRIDGE
High St
35
36
Gloucester Rd
Brompton Rd
37
Beauchamp Pl
SOUTH KENSINGTON
BROMPTON
BELGRAVIA
WESTMINSTER
Sloane St
Cromwell Rd
Earl's Ct Rd
Sydney Street
SLOANE SQUARE
45
46
King's Rd
Royal Hospital Rd
Fulham Road
CHELSEA
PIMLICO
43
44
Redcliffe Gardens
Finborough Rd
Edith Grove
Chelsea Embankment
Chelsea Br
Thames River
Albert Br
Battersea Br
Brompton Cemetery
WEST BROMPTON
NINE ELMS
Battersea Park
King's Rd
Harwood Rd
WALHAM GREEN
BATTERSEA
Walham Green
SANDS END
50
Wandsworth Br
49
South Park
CLAPHAM JUNCTION
CLAPHAM

N
KENSAL TOWN
WEST KILBURN
Grand Union Canal (Paddington Branch)
Harrow Road A404
Queen's Park Public Open Space
Emslie Horniman Pleasance
Athlone Gardens
Meanwhile Gardens
Tavistock Gardens
Trellick Tower
Westbourne Park
Ladbroke Grove
Ladbroke Grove B450
Great Western Road A4207
Westway A40
Kensal Road
Golborne Road
Portobello Road
Wornington Road
Elkstone Road
Southern Row
Manchester Drive
Appleford Road
Bosworth Road
Conlan Street
East Row
Middle Row
West Row
Adair Road
Hazlewood Crescent
Golborne Gardens
Southam Street
Acklam Road
St. Ervans Road
Bevington Road
Blagrove Road
Oxford Gardens
Cambridge Gardens
Bassett Road
St. Charles Square
Bonchurch Road
Faraday Road
Telford Road
Lionel Mews
Treverton Street
Bruce Close
Tavistock Crescent
Tavistock Road
All Saints Road
St. Lukes Road
McGregor Road
Leamington Road Villas
Aldridge Road Villas
Fermoy Road
Hormead Road
Kennet Road
Shirland Road
Bravington Road
Portnall Road
Coomassie Road
Octavia Mews
Caird Street
Second Avenue
Third Avenue
First Avenue
Fourth Avenue
Fifth Avenue
Sixth Avenue
Alperton St
Barfett Street
Enbrook Street
Droop Street
Galton Street
Huxley Street
Ilbert Street
Bruckner St
Lancefield Street
Mozart Street
Ashmore Road
Drayford Close
Portgate Close
Edenham Way
Malvern Close
Orchard Cl
St. Josephs Close
Norfolk Mews
Thorpe Close
St. Lawrence Terrace
St. Michaels Gdns
Golborne Mews
Munro Mews
Swinbrook Road
Canal Close
Kilburn Lane
26
28
29
A
B
1
2
0.25 mile
0.25 km

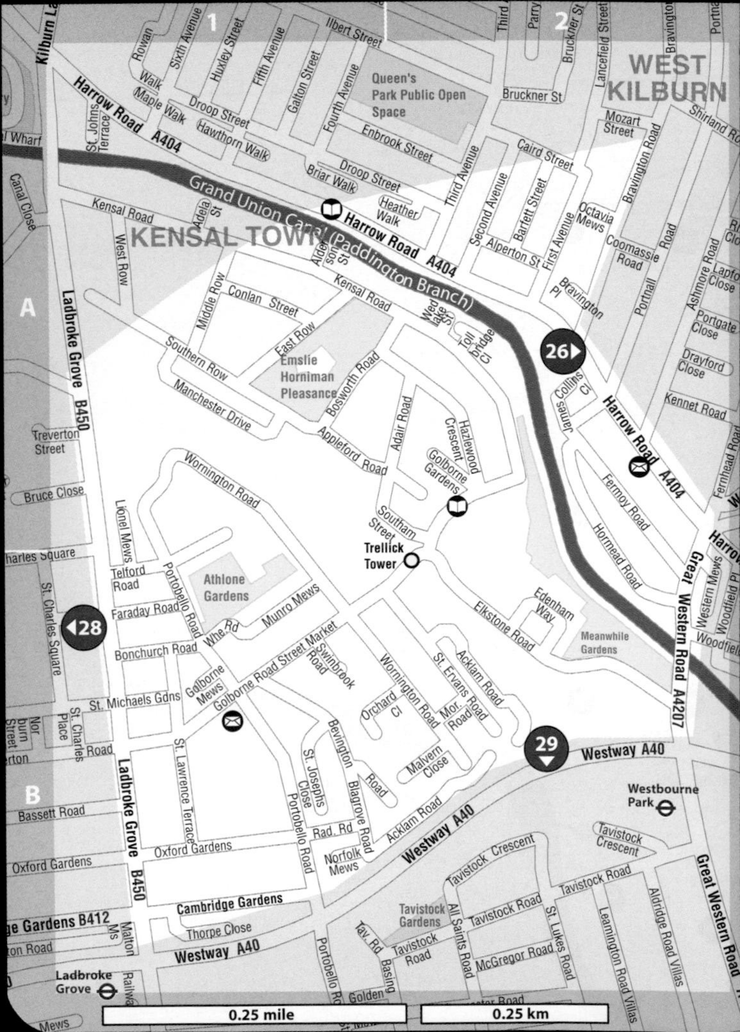

Kensal Town

The "new Notting Hill" label weighs heavily on the Kensals. They look east for inspiration, ignoring the Harlesden yardies at their backs. Thai Rice serves eastern food, while Portobello's Mexican spice shack Santo slings some of the best Mexican in the city and grooves to the Latino cool with regular DJ sets. Prepare for Carnival by visiting What Katie Did for exhibitionist outfits, while Trellick Tower is perfect for real—"I mean it, I'll jump"—attention-seekers.

Landmarks

- **Trellick Tower** • 5 Golborne Rd

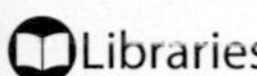

Libraries

- **Kensal Library** • 20 Golborne Rd
- **Queen's Park Library** • 666 Harrow Rd

Post Offices

- **Maida Hill** • 377 Harrow Rd
- **Portobello Road** • 225 Portobello Rd

Restaurants

- **Santo** • 299 Portobello Rd
- **Thai Rice** • 303 Portobello Rd

Shopping

- **Constructive Lives** • 312 Portobello Rd
- **Honest Jon's** • 278 Portobello Rd
- **Rellik** • 8 Golborne Rd
- **What Katie Did** • 281 Portobello Rd

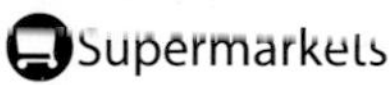

Supermarkets

- **Iceland** • 512 Harrow Rd

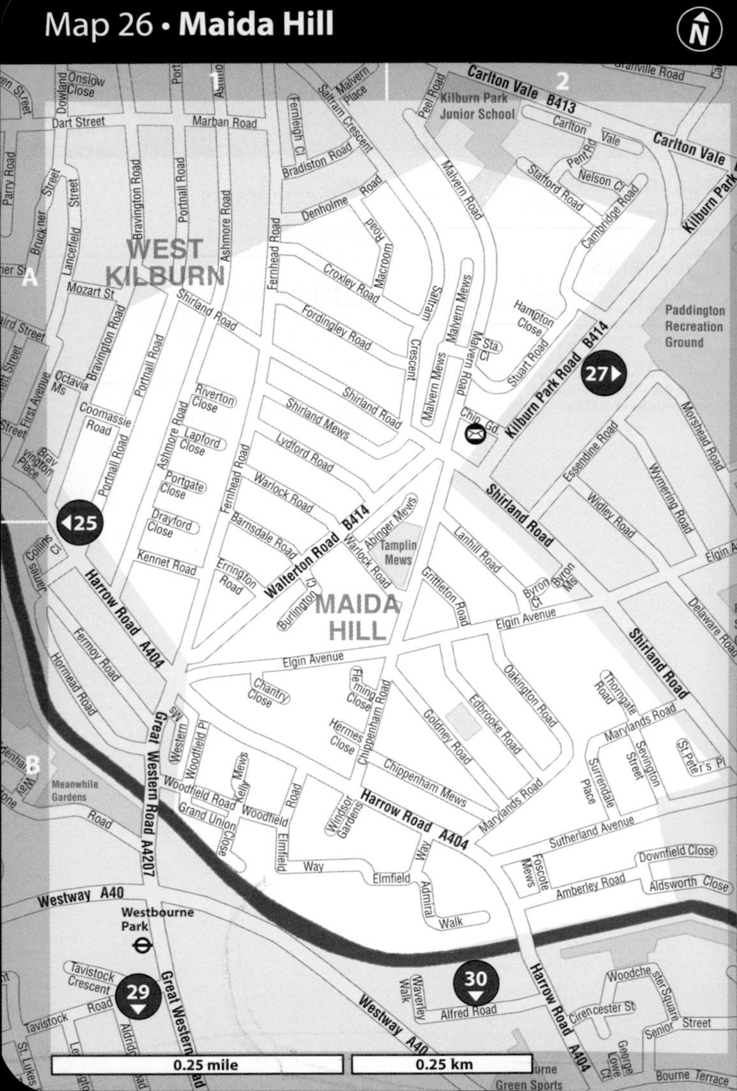

Map 26 • Maida Hill
WEST KILBURN
MAIDA HILL
Kilburn Park Junior School
Paddington Recreation Ground
Tamplin Mews
Meanwhile Gardens
Westbourne Park
Carlton Vale B413
Kilburn Park Road B414
Shirland Road
Walterton Road B414
Harrow Road A404
Great Western Road A4207
Westway A40
Elgin Avenue
Granville Road
Peel Road
Malvern Place
Saltram Crescent
Malvern Road
Malvern Mews
Fernleigh Cl
Bradiston Road
Denholme Road
Macroom Road
Croxley Road
Fordingley Road
Fernhead Road
Shirland Mews
Lydford Road
Warlock Road
Barnsdale Road
Abinger Mews
Errington Road
Burlington Cl
Onslow Close
Dowland Street
Dart Street
Marban Road
Parry Road
Bruckner Street
Lancefield Street
Bravington Road
Portnall Road
Ashmore Road
Mozart St
Octavia Ms
Coomassie Road
First Avenue
Riverton Close
Lapford Close
Portgate Close
Drayford Close
Kennet Road
Collins Ct
James Collins Cl
Fermoy Road
Hormead Road
Pentre Rd
Nelson Cl
Stafford Road
Cambridge Road
Hampton Close
Stuart Road
Sta. Cl
Chip. Gd.
Essendine Road
Widley Road
Morshead Road
Wymering Road
Lanhill Road
Griffleton Road
Byron Ct
Byron Ms
Delaware Road
Chantry Close
Fleming Close
Chippenham Road
Hermes Close
Chippenham Mews
Goldney Road
Edbrooke Road
Oakington Road
Thorngate Road
Marylands Road
Sevington Street
Surrendale Place
St. Peter's Pl
Sutherland Avenue
Western Ms
Woodfield Pl
Kelly Mews
Woodfield Road
Grand Union Close
Woodfield Road
Elmfield Way
Windsor Gardens
Admiral Walk
Foscote Mews
Amberley Road
Downfield Close
Aldsworth Close
Tavistock Crescent
Tavistock Road
Waverley Walk
Alfred Road
Woodchester Square
Cirencester St
Senior Street
George Lowe Ct
Bourne Terrace
25
27
29
30
0.25 mile
0.25 km

Maida Hill

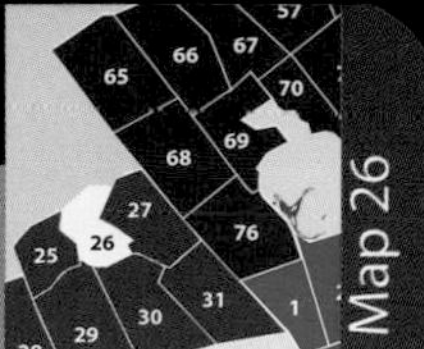

Not as posh as Maida Vale or as cool as Ladbroke Grove, Maida Hill is slightly grubby to the south, not helped by the distinctly unlovely Harrow Road. Things get more upmarket heading north, but the beating heart of the hill can be found Saturdays around Harrow Road's new market. On one of those rare sunny London days get down to the Union Tavern and grab a canal side table.

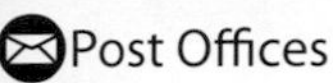

Post Offices

- **Kilburn Park** • 5 Chippenham Gardens

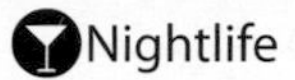

Nightlife

- **Union Tavern** • 45 Woodfield Rd

MAIDA VALE
Paddington Recreation Ground
Essendine Primary School
City of Westminster College
Paddington Sports Club
St Georges RC School
St Josephs RC Primary School
Maida Vale
Warwick Avenue
Kilburn Park Road B414
Carlton Vale
Randolph Gardens
Andover Place
Essendine Road
Widley Road
Wymering Road
Morshead Road
Grantully Road
Elgin Avenue
Shirland Road B413
Delaware Road
Castellain Rd
Lauderdale Road
Biddulph Road
Ashworth Road
Randolph Avenue
Lanark Road
Maida Vale A5
Elgin Mn
Elgin Ms
Marylands Road
Sutherland Avenue
Sutherland Av
Lanark M
Vale Close
Warrington Crescent
Randolph Crescent
Formosa St
Formosa Street
Warwick Avenue
Elnathan Mews
Clearwell Drive
Barnwood Cl
Bristol Gardens
Pindock M
Clifton Gardens B413
Clifton Road
Clifton Villas
Blomfield Road
Warwick Place
Clarendon Gardens
Randolph Mews
Randolph Road
Eliz. Cl
Brown Cl
Robert Cl
Downfield Cl
Aldsworth Clo
Braden St
Byron Ct
Byron M
Thorngate Rd
Savington St
St. Peter's Pl
Surrendale Place
Lanhill Road
Oakington Road
Chippenham Gdns
Stuart Rd
Cambridge Road
Hampton Close
Stafford Close
Malvern Road
Malvern M
Saltram Crescent
Fordingley Road
Kilburn Park Road B414
Harrow Road A404
Westway A40
Royal Oak
Westbourne Green
Chichester Road
Delamere Terrace
Bourne Terr
Blomfield Villas
Desb. Cl
Lord Hills Road
Rowington Clo
Senior Street
Bourne Terr
Aberdeen
St.John's W
Northwick Ter
Clifton Court
0.25 mile
0.25 km
26
68
76
30
31
1
2
A
B

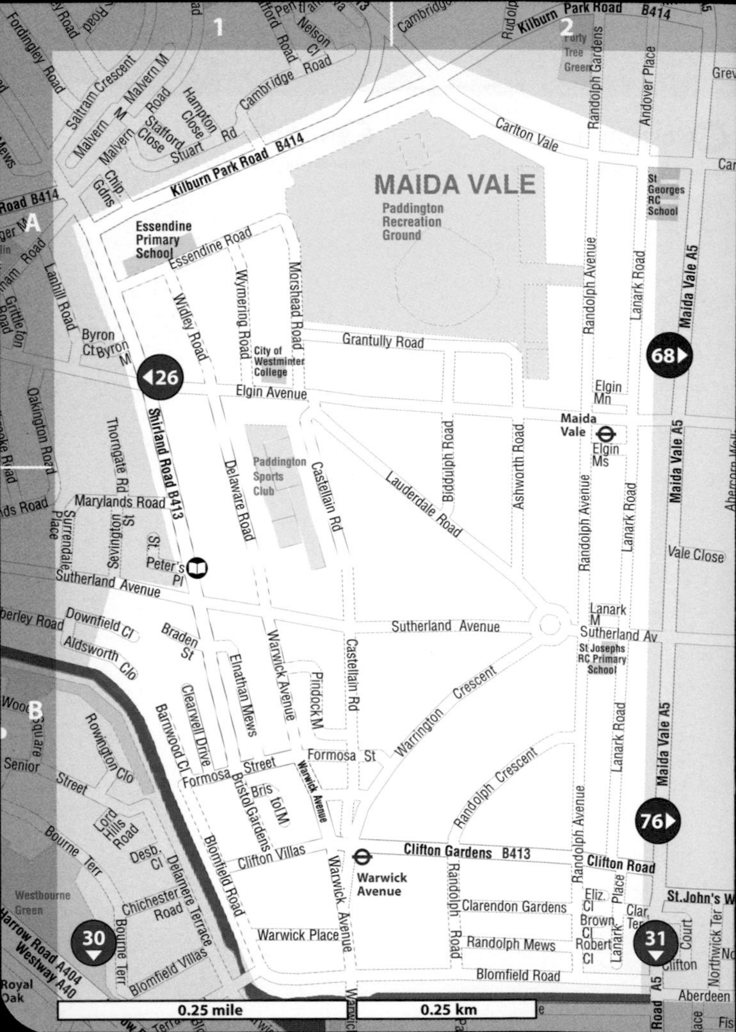

Maida Vale

You don't come to Maida Vale for the nightlife, end of story. Though pretty, canal-side walks are a different matter. Away from 'Little Venice' are endless rows of identical-looking Edwardian mansion blocks on peaceful, tree-lined avenues. It's clean, peaceful, and nice (translation: quite dull).Locals frequent the cafés and eateries around the Maida Vale tube station and on Clifton Road. Head to The Robert Browning for cheap Sam Smith's beer by a roaring fire or the E Bar for basement schmoozing and Spanish tapas.

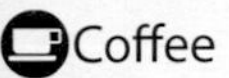Coffee

- **Starbucks** • 168 Randolf Ave

Libraries

- **Maida Vale Library** • Sutherland Ave

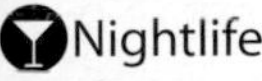Nightlife

- **The Bridge House** • 13 Westbourne Terrace Rd
- **E Bar** • 2 Warrington Crescent
- **The Robert Browning** • 15 Clifton Rd
- **The Warwick Castle** • 6 Warwick Pl
- **The Waterway** • 54 Formosa St

Map 28 • Ladbroke Grove / Notting Hill (West)

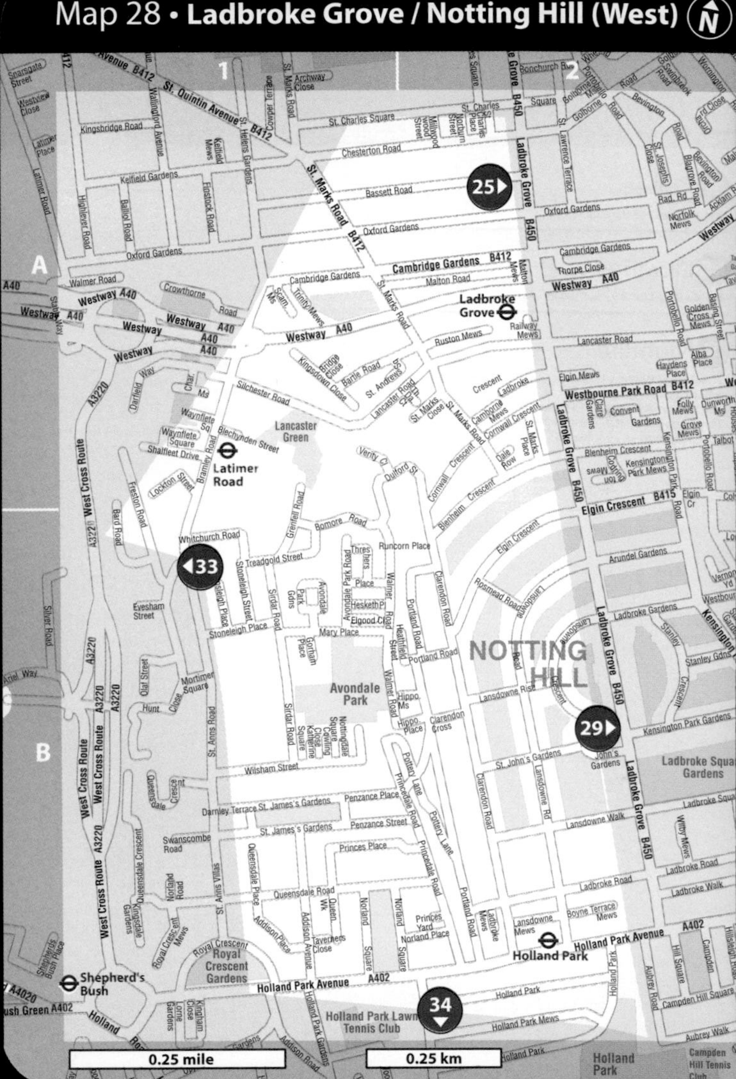

Ladbroke Grove / Notting Hill (West)

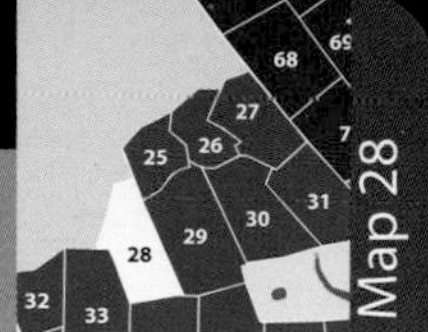

Look at that Westway and tell us you can't hear the opening chords of "London Calling." Maybe Rudie didn't fail but he moved up and moved out. This is the quiet, leafy Notting Hill of gated gardens away from the Hugh Grant-hungry tourists scouring Portobello Road. Head to Clarendon Cross or Portland Road for food and stuff. Grab a bite at Julie's or wander down to Holland Park Avenue for organic treats at Jeroboams Deli.

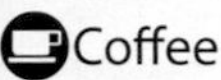

Coffee

• **Starbucks** • 76 Holland Park Ave

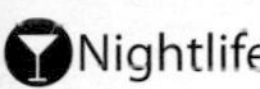

Nightlife

• **Julie's Bar** • 135 Portland Rd

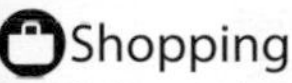

Shopping

• **Cowshed** • 119 Portland Rd
• **The Cross** • 141 Portland Rd
• **Gelato Mio** • 138 Holland Park Ave
• **Jeroboams** • 96 Holland Park Ave
• **Virginia** • 98 Portland Road

Map 29 • Notting Hill Gate

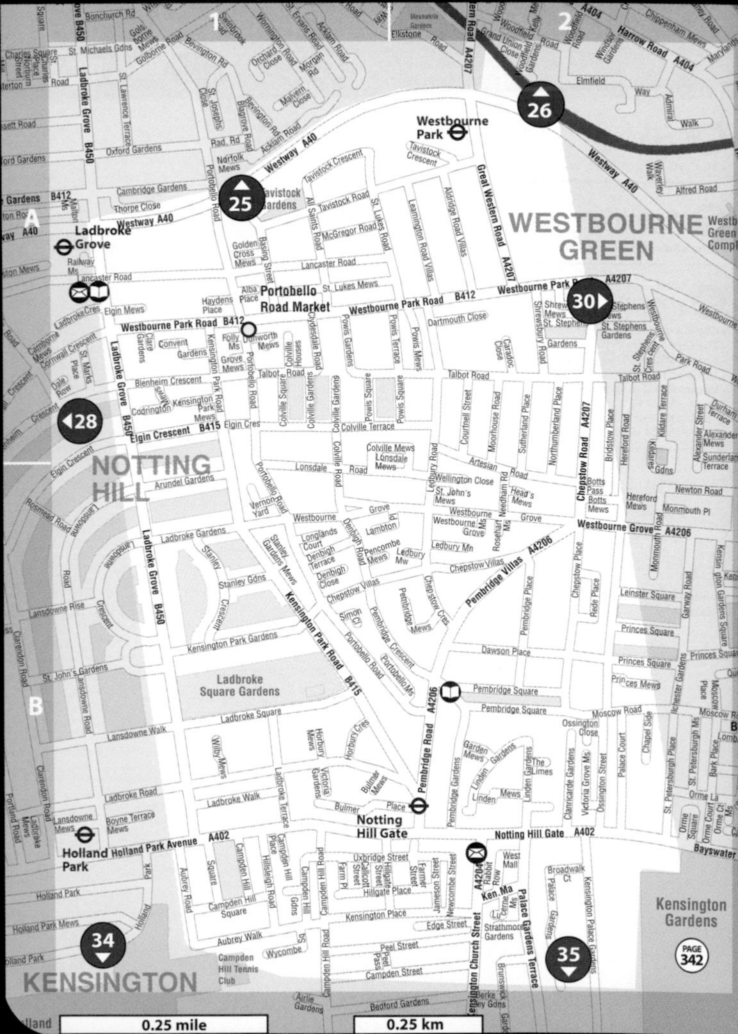
WESTBOURNE
GREEN
NOTTING
HILL
KENSINGTON
Kensington
Gardens
Westbourne
Park
Ladbroke
Grove
Portobello
Road Market
Notting
Hill Gate
Holland
Park
Ladbroke
Square Gardens
Campden
Hill Tennis
Club
Westway A40
Great Western Road A4207
Westbourne Park Road B412
Ladbroke Grove B450
Portobello Road
Kensington Park Road B415
Chepstow Road A4207
Westbourne Grove A4206
Pembridge Villas A4206
Pembridge Road A4206
Notting Hill Gate A402
Holland Park Avenue A402
Kensington Church Street A4204
Palace Gardens Terrace
Kensington Palace Gardens
Elgin Crescent B415
Lancaster Road
Talbot Road
Colville Terrace
Lonsdale Road
Ledbury Road
Artesian Road
Westbourne Park Road A4207
Tavistock Crescent
Tavistock Road
All Saints Road
St. Lukes Road
Cambridge Gardens
Oxford Gardens
Arundel Gardens
Ladbroke Gardens
Stanley Gdns
Kensington Park Gardens
Ladbroke Square
Lansdowne Walk
Ladbroke Road
Ladbroke Walk
Bulmer Place
Pembridge Square
Dawson Place
Princes Square
Leinster Square
Moscow Road
Bayswater
Kensington Place
Edge Street
Peel Street
Campden Street
Bedford Gardens
Aubrey Walk
Holland Park
Holland Park Mews
Clarendon Road
Portland Road
Lansdowne Rise
St. John's Gardens
Harrow Road A404
Elkstone Road
Golborne Road
Bonchurch Rd
St. Michaels Gdns
Bevington Rd
Acklam Road
Alfred Road
Hereford Road
Newton Road
Monmouth Pl
Chepstow Villas
Denbigh Road
Westbourne Grove
1
2
A
B
25
26
28
30
34
35
PAGE
342
0.25 mile
0.25 km

Notting Hill Gate

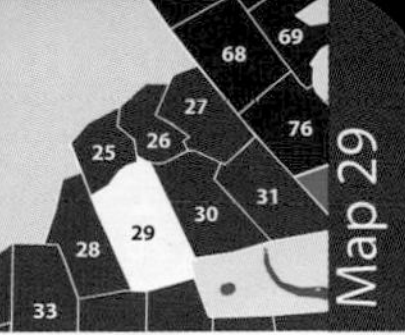

It is hard to believe that until relatively recently this now home of the mega-rich was Kensington's rough bad-boy slum. Traces of the Gate's multicultural past are in the wrinkles of the old eccentrics in the Uxbridge Arms, the lively Portobello Market, and the buzz of the summer Carnival. To feel old and bitter, go scowl at skinny jeans-clad teenagers in the Notting Hill Arts Club. Pig out on some of London's best gelato at Dri Dri, browse the stacks at Rough Trade Records and sit back in leather sofa luxury with a Peroni for a flick at the historic Electric Cinema.

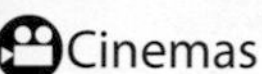

Cinemas

- **The Electric Cinema** • 191 Portobello Rd
- **Gate Picturehouse** • 87 Notting Hill Gate
- **Notting Hill Coronet** • 103 Notting Hill Gate

Coffee

- **Apostrophe** • 138 Notting Hill Gate
- **Caffe Nero** • 113 Westbourne Grove
- **Caffe Nero** • 53 Notting Hill Gate
- **Caffe Nero** • 168 Portobello Rd
- **Coffee Republic** • 214 Portobello Rd
- **Eat.** • 68 Notting Hill Gate
- **Pret A Manger** • 65 Notting Hill Gate
- **Starbucks** • 96 Westbourne Grove
- **Starbucks** • 227 Portobello Rd
- **Starbucks** • 26 Pembridge Rd
- **Starbucks** • 140 Notting Hill Gate
- **Starbucks** • 64 Notting Hill Gate

Landmarks

- **Portobello Road Market** • 223 Portobello Rd

Libraries

- **North Kensington Library** • 108 Ladbroke Grove
- **Notting Hill Gate Library** • 1 Pembridge Sq

Nightlife

- **Mau Mau** • 265 Portobello Rd
- **Montgomery Place** • 31 Kensington Park Rd
- **Notting Hill Arts Club** • 21 Notting Hill Gate
- **Sun in Splendour** • 7 Portobello Rd
- **Trailer Happiness** • 177 Portobello Rd
- **Uxbridge Arms** • 13 Uxbridge St
- **Windsor Castle** • 114 Campden Hill Rd

Post Offices

- **Kensington Church St** • 190 Kensington Church St
- **Ladbroke Grove** • 116 Ladbroke Grove

Restaurants

- **Beach Blanket Babylon** • 45 Ledbury Rd
- **Cafe Diana** • 5 Wellington Terrace
- **Crazy Homies** • 125 Westbourne Park Rd
- **The Electric Brasserie** • 191 Portobello Rd
- **Eve's Market Cafe** • 222 Portobello Rd
- **Geales** • 2 Farmer St
- **Lucky 7** • 127 Westbourne Park Rd
- **Manzara** • 24 Pembridge Rd
- **Osteria Basilico** • 29 Kensington Park Rd
- **Taqueria** • 139 Westbourne Grove

Shopping

- **& Clarke's Bread** • 124 Kensington Church St
- **Bodas** • 38 Ledbury Rd
- **Diane von Furstenberg** • 83 Ledbury Rd
- **Dri Dri Gelato** • 189 Portobello Rd
- **The Grocer on Elgin** • 6 Elgin Crescent
- **The Hummingbird Bakery** • 133 Portobello Rd
- **Melt** • 59 Ledbury Rd
- **Mr Christian's Delicatessen** • 11 Elgin Crescent
- **Music & Video Exchange** • 38 Notting Hill Gate
- **Negozio Classica** • 283 Westbourne Grove
- **Portobello Road Market** • Portobello Rd
- **R Garcia and Sons** • 248 Portobello Rd
- **Retro Man** • 34 Pembridge Rd
- **Retro Woman** • 32 Pembridge Rd
- **Rough Trade** • 130 Talbot Rd
- **Travel Bookshop** • 13 Blenheim Crescent

Map 30 • Bayswater

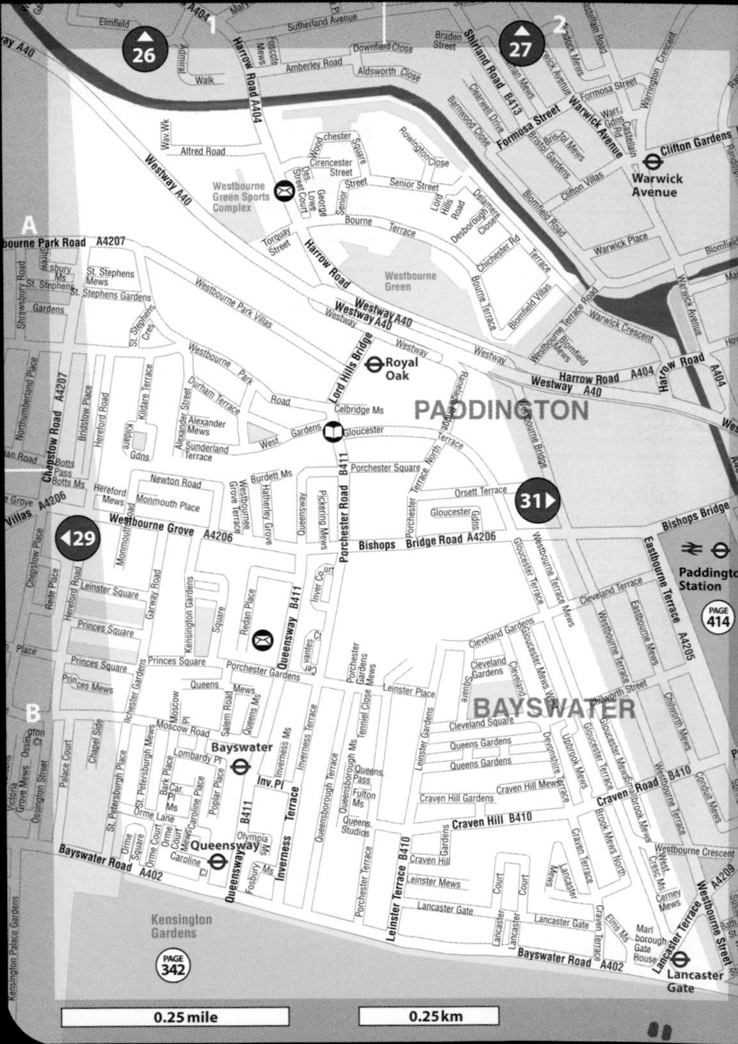

N

PADDINGTON

BAYSWATER

Royal Oak

Warwick Avenue

Bayswater

Queensway

Lancaster Gate

Paddington Station

Westbourne Green

Westbourne Green Sports Complex

Kensington Gardens

26

27

29

31

PAGE 414

PAGE 342

0.25 mile

0.25 km

Bayswater

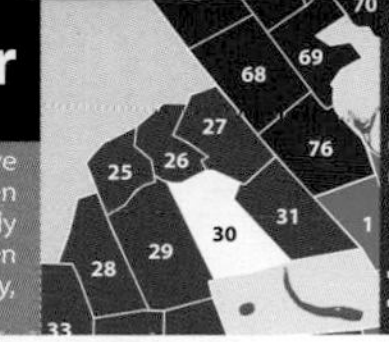

London's unofficial 'Little Beirut' seems to attract both camera-clad tourists (who have strayed too far from Hyde Park) as well as Londoners (who look for food gems on Westbourne Grove). While the place is bustling, beware of the overpriced, and frankly sh***, tourist traps on Queensway. Instead, chill out with a shisha at Berdees, and then be adventurous and try your hand at 1950s-style bowling at All Star Lanes. Alternatively, do it like the Victorians did and get a rub down at Porchester Gate Spa.

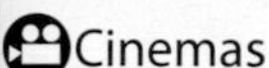

Cinemas

- **Odeon Whiteleys** • Queensway & Porchester Gardens

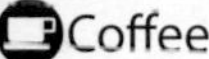

Coffee

- **Berdees Coffee Shop** • 84 Bishop's Bridge Rd
- **Pret A Manger** • 127 Queensway
- **Starbucks** • 49 Queensway

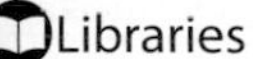

Libraries

- **Paddington Library** • Porchester Rd

Nightlife

- **All Star Lanes** • Bloomsbury Pl & Southampton Row
- **The Cow** • 89 Westbourne Park Rd

Post Offices

- **Harrow Rd** • 272 Harrow Rd
- **Queensway** • 118 Queensway

Restaurants

- **Berdees Coffee Shop** • 84 Bishop's Bridge Rd
- **The Cow** • 89 Westbourne Park Rd
- **Kiasu** • 48 Queensway
- **Royal China** • 13 Queensway
- **Tiroler Hut** • 27 Westbourne Grove

Shopping

- **Al Saqi Books** • 26 Westbourne Grove
- **Planet Organic** • 42 Westbourne Grove
- **Porchester Gate Spa** • Queensway & Porchester Rd
- **SCP** • 87 Westbourne Grove
- **Whiteleys Shopping Centre** • Queensway

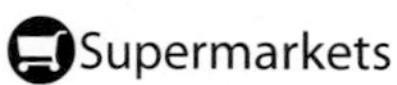

Supermarkets

- **Sainsbury's** • 88 Westbourne Grove
- **Waitrose** • 38 Porchester Sq

Map 31 • Paddington

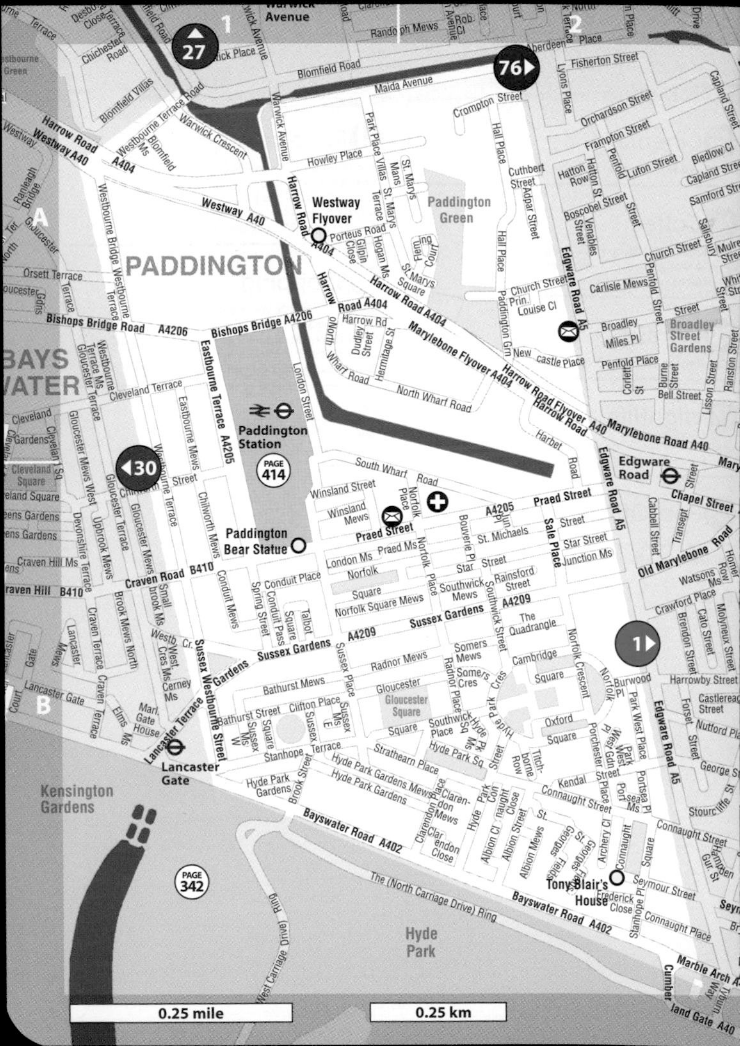

1
2
A
B
27
76
30
1

Warwick Avenue
Randolph Mews
Rob. Cl
Aberdeen Place
Fisherton Street
Lyons Place
Capland Street
Chichester Road
Desborough Close
Westbourne Green
Blomfield Road
Maida Avenue
Crompton Street
Orchardson Street
Frampton Street
Blomfield Villas
Westbourne Terrace Road
Warwick Crescent
Blomfield Ms
Harrow Road
Westway A40
A404
Warwick Avenue
Howley Place
Park Place Villas
St. Marys Mans
Hall Place
Cuthbert Street
Hatton Row
Hatton St
Penfold Street
Luton Street
Bledlow Cl
Capland Street
Samford Street
Ranleagh Bridge
Westbourne Bridge
Westbourne Terrace
Westway A40
Harrow Road
Westway Flyover
Terrace
St. Marys Terrace
Paddington Green
Adpar Street
Boscobel Street
Venables Street
Church Street
Salisbury Street
Gloucester Terrace
PADDINGTON
Porteus Road
Gilpin Close
Hogan Ms
Fleming Court
St Marys Square
Edgware Road A5
Church Street
Carlisle Mews
Penfold Street
Orsett Terrace
Harrow Road A404
Harrow Road A404
Prin. Louise Cl
Paddington Grn
Street
Broadley Street Gardens
Broadley Miles Pl
Bishops Bridge Road A4206
Bishops Bridge A4206
Harrow Rd
North Wharf Road
Dudley Street
Hermitage St
Marylebone Flyover A404
New castle Place
Penfold Place
Corlett St
Burne Street
Bell Street
Lisson Street
Ranston Street
BAYSWATER
Gloucester Terrace
Westbourne Terrace Ms
Cleveland Terrace
Eastbourne Mews
Eastbourne Terrace A4205
London Street
North Wharf Road
Harrow Road Flyover A40
Marylebone Road A40
Cleveland Gardens
Paddington Station
PAGE 414
Harbet Road
Edgware Road A5
Edgware Road
Cleveland Square
Gloucester Mews West
Chilworth Street
Westbourne Terrace
Chilworth Mews
South Wharf Road
Norfolk Place
Praed Street
Chapel Street
Transept Street
Cabbell Street
Devonshire Terrace
Uphrook Mews
Gloucester Terrace
Gloucester Mews
Winsland Street
Winsland Mews
A4205
Bouverie Pl
Junction Pl
St. Michaels Street
Sale Place
Star Street
Junction Ms
Old Marylebone Road
Homer Row
Craven Hill Ms
Paddington Bear Statue
Praed Street
Praed Ms
London Ms
Star Street
Rainsford Street
Watsons Ms
Craven Hill B410
Craven Road B410
Conduit Mews
Conduit Place
Norfolk Square
Norfolk Place
Southwick Mews
Southwick Street
Crawford Place
Cato Street
Molyneux Street
Brendon Street
Brook Mews North
Smallbrook Ms
Spring Street
Conduit Pass
Talbot Square
Norfolk Square Mews
Sussex Gardens A4209
A4209
The Quadrangle
Craven Terrace
Lancaster Mews
Westb. Cr.
West Cres Ms
Sussex Gardens
Sussex Gardens
Sussex Place
Radnor Mews
Somers Mews
Cambridge Square
Norfolk Crescent
Norfolk Pl
Burwood Pl
Harrowby Street
Castlereagh Street
Gate
Lancaster Gate
Cerney Ms
Bathurst Mews
Gloucester Square
Radnor Place
Somers Cres
Hyde Park Cres
Edgware Road A5
Park West Place
Court
Elms Ms
Marlborough Gate House
Lancaster Terrace
Westbourne Street
Bathurst Street
Clifton Place
Sussex Ms E
Sussex Ms W
Sussex Square
Southwick Place
Hyde Pk Sq Ms
Oxford Square
Porchester Place
West Gdn Pl
Park West
Forset Street
Nutford Place
George Street
Lancaster Gate
Stanhope Terrace
Strathearn Place
Hyde Park Sq
Titchborne Row
Kendal Street
Portsea Pl
Port-sea Ms
Stourcliffe St
Kensington Gardens
Hyde Park Gardens
Brook Street
Hyde Park Gardens Mews
Hyde Park Gardens
Clarendon Place
Clarendon Mews
Hyde Park Con
Connaught Close
Connaught Street
Connaught Street
Hampden Gur. St
Bayswater Road A402
Clarendon Close
Albion Cl
Albion Street
Albion Mews
St. Georges Fields
Archery Cl
Connaught Square
PAGE 342
The (North Carriage Drive) Ring
Tony Blair's House
Frederick Close
Stanhope Pl
Seymour Street
Bayswater Road A402
Connaught Place
Hyde Park
West Carriage Drive
Ring
Marble Arch
Tyburn Way
Cumberland Gate A40

0.25 mile
0.25 km

Paddington

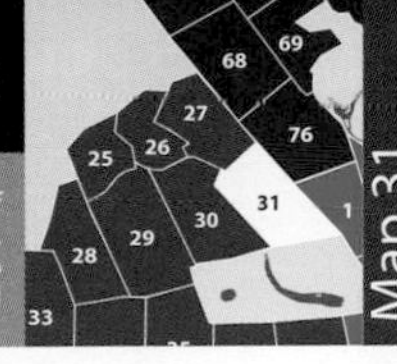

Paddington Bear may not seem so cuddly if he were one of today's commuters hanging around Paddington Station. This area can seem like zombie land, a mass of tired-looking, harassed faces grabbing food from one of the endless chain eateries. It's not all bad news though. Evening boredom can be banished by listening to famous war correspondents' exotic tales over a meal at the Frontline Club. For all other woes solve it with a swift half at 'The Victoria'.

Cinemas

- **Frontline Club** • 13 Norfolk Pl

Coffee

- **Caffe Nero** • 14 Spring St
- **Caffe Nero** • Paddington Station
- **Costa** • 254 Edgware Rd
- **Eat.** • Paddington Station
- **Markus Coffee Company** • 13 Connaught St
- **Pret A Manger** • 9 Sheldon Sq
- **Serpentine Bar & Kitchen** • Serpentine Rd

Emergency Rooms

- **St Mary's Hospital** • Praed St & Winsland St

Landmarks

- **Paddington Bear Statue** • Paddington Station
- **Tony Blair's House** • Connaught Square & Seymour St
- **Westway Flyover** •

Nightlife

- **Frontline Club** • 13 • Norfolk Pl
- **The Royal Exchange** • 26 Sale Pl
- **The Victoria** • 10 Strathearn Pl

Post Offices

- **Edgware Rd** • 354 Edgware Rd
- **Paddington** • 4 Praed St

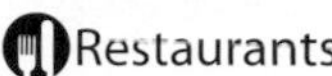

Restaurants

- **Bonne Bouche** •129 Praed St
- **Mandalay** • 444 Edgware Rd

Supermarkets

- **Sainsbury's** • Paddington Station
- **Sainsbury's** • 12 Sheldon Sq

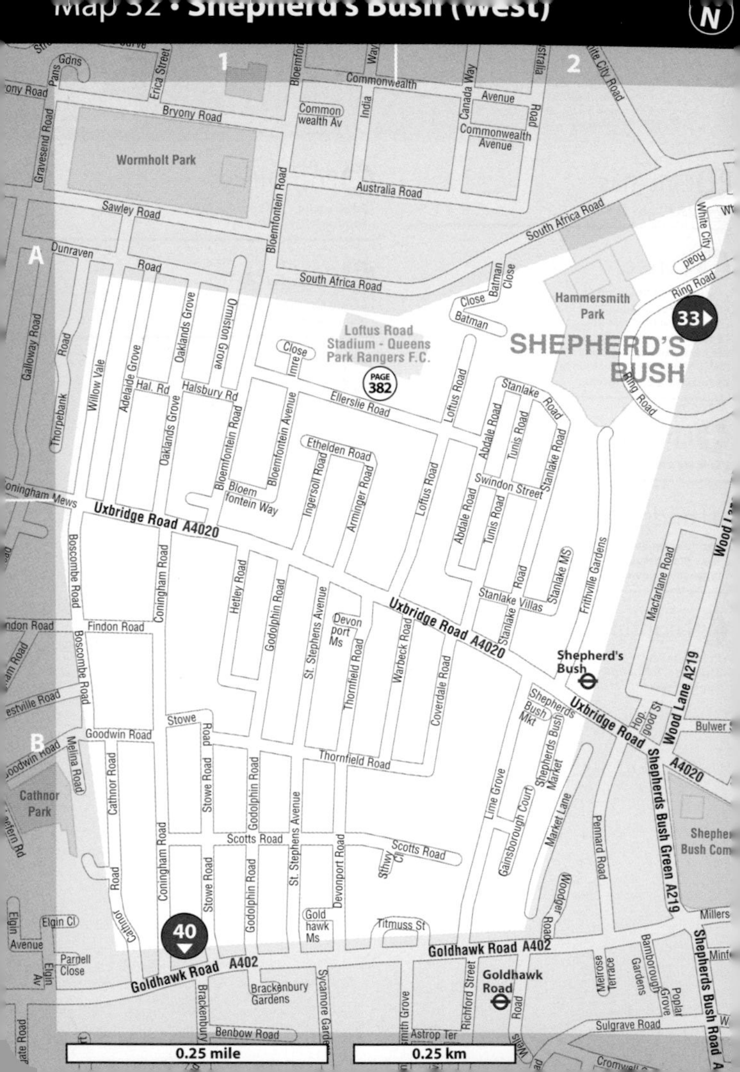

Map 32 • Shepherd's Bush (West)
N
1
2
A
B
Commonwealth
Commonwealth Av
India
Canada Way
Avenue
Australia Road
Commonwealth Avenue
Australia Road
White City Road
Erica Street
Bryony Road
Gdns
Pans
Gravesend Road
Wormholt Park
Bloemfontein Road
Sawley Road
South Africa Road
White City Road
Dunraven Road
Ring Road
South Africa Road
Batman Close
Close Batman
Hammersmith Park
33
SHEPHERD'S BUSH
Ring Road
Loftus Road Stadium - Queens Park Rangers F.C.
PAGE 382
Close
Imre
Galloway Road
Thorpebank Road
Willow Vale
Adelaide Grove
Oaklands Grove
Ormiston Grove
Hal. Rd
Halsbury Rd
Oaklands Grove
Bloemfontein Road
Bloemfontein Avenue
Ellerslie Road
Loftus Road
Stanlake Road
Abdale Road
Tunis Road
Stanlake Road
Ethelden Road
Ingersoll Road
Arminger Road
Loftus Road
Swindon Street
Bloem fontein Way
Coningham Mews
Uxbridge Road A4020
Abdale Road
Tunis Road
Stanlake Ms
Frithville Gardens
Macfarlane Road
Wood Lane
Boscombe Road
Coningham Road
Hetley Road
Godolphin Road
St. Stephens Avenue
Devon port Ms
Thornfield Road
Warbeck Road
Coverdale Road
Stanlake Villas
Stanlake Road
Uxbridge Road A4020
Shepherd's Bush
Findon Road
Findon Road
Boscombe Road
Westville Road
Shepherds Bush Mkt
Shepherds Bush Market
Uxbridge Road
Hopgood St
Wood Lane A219
Bulwer St
A4020
Stowe Road
Goodwin Road
Goodwin Road
Melina Road
Cathnor Park
Cathnor Road
Stowe Road
Godolphin Road
St. Stephens Avenue
Thornfield Road
Lime Grove
Gainsborough Court
Market Lane
Pennard Road
Shepherds Bush Green A219
Shepherds Bush Common
Scotts Road
Scotts Road
Sthwy Cl
Coningham Road
Stowe Road
Godolphin Road
St. Stephens Avenue
Devonport Road
Cathnor Road
Elgin Avenue
Elgin Cl
40
Gold hawk Ms
Titmuss St
Woodger Road
Millers
Parnell Close
Elgin Av
Goldhawk Road A402
Goldhawk Road A402
Goldhawk Road
Melrose Terrace
Bamborough Gardens
Poplar Grove
Shepherds Bush Road
Brackenbury Gardens
Brackenbury
Sycamore Gardens
Richford Street
Wells Road
Benbow Road
Astrop Ter
Sulgrave Road
Cromwell
0.25 mile
0.25 km

Shepherd's Bush (West)

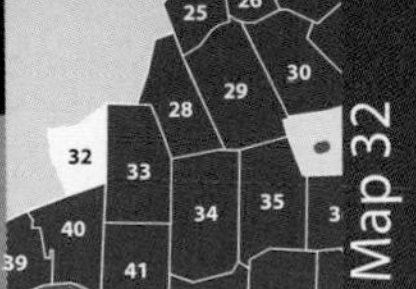

Don't be scared. This part of town won't bite…much. Things may look a bit drab, and indeed you wouldn't want to spend your Friday nights in many of the pubs here, but on Uxbridge Road looks truly can be deceiving. While it's nothing special from the outside, Esarn Kheaw will blow your head off with authentic Thai green curry and leave you begging for more. Have a laid-back beer at 'The Goldhawk' or swoon under the chandeliers to an off the radar act at restored dancehall, 'Bush Hall'.

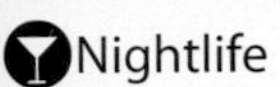

Nightlife

- **Bush Hall** • 310 Uxbridge Rd
- **The Goldhawk** • 122 Goldhawk Rd
- **The Queen Adelaide** • 412 Uxbridge Rd
- **White Horse** • 31 Uxbridge Rd

Restaurants

- **Abu Zaad** • 29 Uxbridge Rd
- **Esarn Kheaw** • 314 Uxbridge Road
- **Vine Leaves Taverna** • 71 Uxbridge Rd

Shopping

- **Nut Case** • 352 Uxbridge Rd

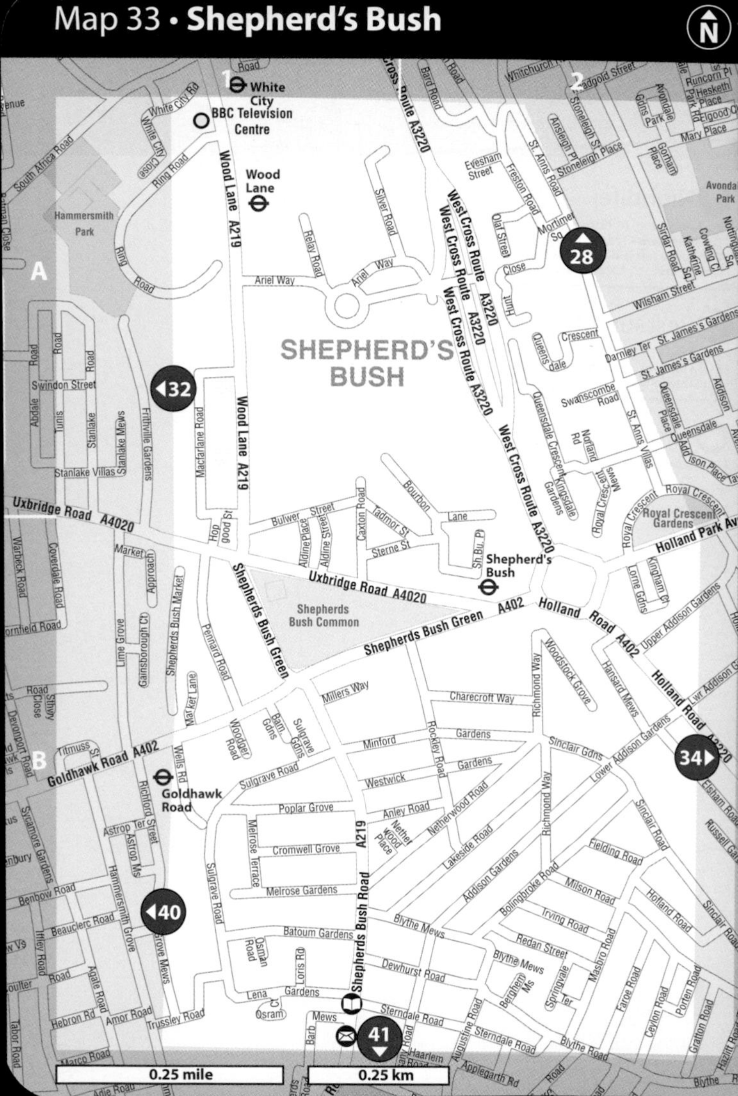

Map 33 • Shepherd's Bush
N
White City
BBC Television Centre
Wood Lane
SHEPHERD'S BUSH
Shepherd's Bush
Goldhawk Road
Hammersmith Park
Shepherds Bush Common
Royal Crescent Gardens
Avondale Park
White City Rd
White City Close
South Africa Road
Ring Road
Wood Lane A219
Ariel Way
Relay Road
Silver Road
West Cross Route A3220
Evesham Street
Freston Road
St. Anns Road
Stoneleigh St
Stoneleigh Place
Ansleigh Pl
Olaf Street
Mortimer Sq
Whitchurch
Bard Road
Avondale Park Gdns
Runcorn Pl
Hesketh Place
Mary Place
Gorham Place
Sirdar Road
Katherine Sq
Cowling Cl
Wilsham Street
St. James's Gardens
Darnley Ter
Queensdale Crescent
Swanscombe Road
Norland Rd
St. Anns Villas
Queensdale Place
Queensdale
Addison Place
Kingsdale Gardens
Royal Crescent
Royal Crescent Mews
Holland Park Av
Swindon Street
Abdale Road
Tunis Road
Stanlake Road
Stanlake Mews
Stanlake Villas
Frithville Gardens
Macfarlane Road
Uxbridge Road A4020
Hop
Wood St
Bulwer Street
Aldine Place
Aldine Street
Caxton Road
Tadmor St
Bourbon Lane
Sterne St
Sh.Bu.Pl
Warbeck Road
Coverdale Road
Cornfield Road
Market Approach
Shepherds Bush Market
Lime Grove
Gainsborough Ct
Pennard Road
Shepherds Bush Green
A402
Holland Road A402
Lorne Gdns
Kingham Cl
Upper Addison Gardens
Hansard Mews
Holland Road A3220
Lwr Addison Gardens
Woodstock Grove
Richmond Way
Charecroft Way
Millers Way
Market Lane
Woodger Road
Bamb. Gdns
Sulgrave Gdns
Minford Gardens
Rockley Road
Westwick Gardens
Sinclair Gdns
Lower Addison Gardens
Goldhawk Road A402
Titmuss St
Wells Rd
Richford Street
Sulgrave Road
Poplar Grove
Anley Road
Netherwood Road
Nether Wood Place
Melrose Terrace
Cromwell Grove
Melrose Gardens
A219
Lakeside Road
Addison Gardens
Sinclair Road
Fielding Road
Devonport Road
Sycamore Gardens
Astrop Ter
Astrop Ms
Hammersmith Grove
Grove Mews
Benbow Road
Beauclerc Road
Iffley Road
Agate Road
Hebron Rd
Amor Road
Trussley Road
Marco Road
Tabor Road
Sulgrave Road
Shepherds Bush Road
Batoum Gardens
Osman Road
Loris Rd
Lena Gardens
Osram
Barb Mews
Blythe Mews
Bolingbroke Road
Milson Road
Irving Road
Redan Street
Masbro Road
Holland Road
Sinclair Road
Dewhurst Road
Berghem Ms
Springvale Ter
Faroe Road
Ceylon Road
Porten Road
Grafton Road
Sterndale Road
Augustine Road
Blythe Road
Haarlem Road
Applegarth Rd
Elsham Road
Russell Gdns
28
32
34
40
41
A
B
1
2
0.25 mile
0.25 km

Shepherd's Bush

'The Bush' has had a bit of a face-lift over the past few years. Once the former grime hub of West London, it now sports one of Europe's biggest shopping centres, Westfield, and with it comes more traffic and more chain shops. Even the Beeb is on its way out. Fear not though, for Shepherds Bush Market still keeps the place decidedly unpretentious, while the Empire continues to attract the best up-and-coming bands. Experience some in-yer-face theatre at 'Bush Theatre' and grab a bonza pie from the Bush's very own Aussie pie shop, 'Jumbucks'.

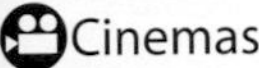

Cinemas

- **Vue Shepherds Bush** • Shepherds Bush Green & Rockley Rd

Coffee

- **BB's Coffee & Muffins** • Richmond Way & Charecroft Way
- **BB's Coffee & Muffins** • 2117 Westfield London Shopping Center
- **Costa** • 72 Uxbridge Rd
- **Starbucks** • 62 Uxbridge Rd

Landmarks

- **BBC Television Centre** • Wood Ln & Ring Rd

Libraries

- **Shepherds Bush Library** • 6 Wood Ln

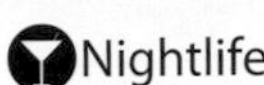

Nightlife

- **Albertine** • 1 Wood Lane
- **Bush Theatre** • 7 Uxbridge Rd
- **The Defectors Weld**• 170 Uxbridge Rd
- **Ginglik** • 1 Shepherd's Bush Green
- **Shepherd's Bush Empire** • Shepherd's Bush Green

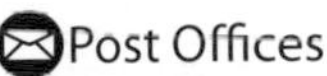

Post Offices

- **Shepherds Bush Road** • 146 Shepherd's Bush Rd

Restaurants

- **Busaba Eathai** • Westfield Shopping Centre
- **Jasmine** • 16 Goldhawk Rd
- **Jumbucks** • 24 Shepherd's Bush Green
- **Le Cinnamon** • 158 Shepherd's Bush Rd
- **Piansu** • 39 Bulwer St
- **Popeseye** • 108 Blythe Rd

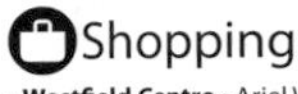

Shopping

- **Westfield Centre** • Ariel Way

Supermarkets

- **Sainsbury's** • 164 Uxbridge Rd

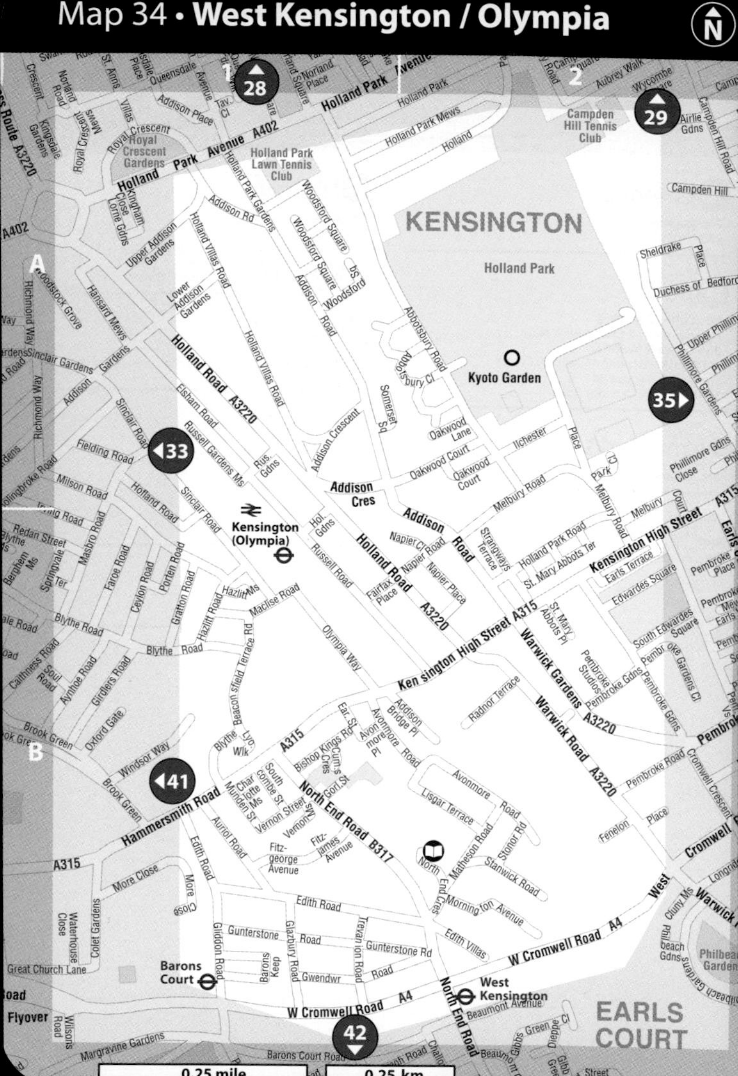
Map 34 • West Kensington / Olympia
N
28
29
33
35
41
42
1
2
A
B
KENSINGTON
Holland Park
Kyoto Garden
Campden Hill Tennis Club
Holland Park Lawn Tennis Club
Royal Crescent Gardens
Kensington (Olympia)
Barons Court
West Kensington
EARLS COURT
Philbeach Gardens
Holland Park Avenue A402
Holland Park
Holland Park Mews
Holland Road A3220
Addison Road
Addison Cres
Addison Crescent
Addison Rd
Addison Place
Upper Addison Gardens
Lower Addison Gardens
Addison Gardens
Addison Bridge Pl
Holland Villas Road
Holland Park Gardens
Woodsford Square
Abbotsbury Road
Abbotsbury Cl
Somerset Sq
Oakwood Lane
Oakwood Court
Ilchester Place
Melbury Road
Melbury Court
Holland Park Road
St. Mary Abbots Ter
St. Mary Abbots Pl
Strangways Terrace
Napier Cl
Napier Road
Napier Place
Fairfax Place
Kensington High Street A315
Warwick Gardens
Warwick Road A3220
Earls Terrace
Edwardes Square
South Edwardes Square
Pembroke Place
Pembroke Road
Pembroke Gdns
Pembroke Studios
Pembroke Gardens Cl
Cromwell Crescent
Cromwell
Radnor Terrace
Avonmore Road
Avonmore Pl
Lisgar Terrace
Matheson Road
Stonor Rd
Stanwick Road
Mornington Avenue
North End Cres
North End Road B317
Edith Villas
Edith Road
W Cromwell Road A4
Beaumont Avenue
Gunterstone Road
Gunterstone Rd
Gwendwr Road
Glazbury Road
Trevanion Road
Gliddon Road
Barons Keep
Barons Court Road
Margravine Gardens
Great Church Lane
Flyover
Wilsons Road
Waterhouse Close
Colet Gardens
More Close
Hammersmith Road
A315
Auriol Road
Fitz-george Avenue
Fitz-james Avenue
Vernon Street
Vernon Ms
Charlotte Ms
Southcombe St
Munden St
Bishop Kings Rd
Cums Cres
Gorl St
Olympia Way
Maclise Road
Hazlitt Road
Hazlitt Ms
Beaconsfield Terrace Rd
Blythe Road
Lyc. Wlk
Russell Road
Russell Gardens Ms
Rus. Gdns
Hol. Gdns
Elsham Road
Sinclair Road
Sinclair Gardens
Fielding Road
Milson Road
Irving Road
Redan Street
Masbro Road
Faroe Road
Ceylon Road
Porten Road
Gratton Road
Springvale Ter
Bergham Ms
Caithness Road
Soul Road
Aynhoe Road
Girdlers Road
Oxford Gate
Brook Green
Windsor Way
Hansard Mews
Woodstock Grove
Richmond Way
Bolingbroke Road
Lorne Gdns
Kingham Close
Royal Crescent
Royal Crescent Mews
Kingsdale Gardens
Norland Road
Norland Place
Queensdale
St. Anns Villas
Tav. Cl
Aubrey Walk
Wycombe Square
Airlie Gdns
Campden Hill Road
Campden Hill
Sheldrake Place
Duchess of Bedford
Upper Phillimore
Phillimore Gardens
Phillimore Gdns Close
Fenelon Place
Cluny Ms
Philbeach Gdns
Warwick
Gibbs Green Cl
Dieppe Cl
0.25 mile
0.25 km

West Kensington / Olympia

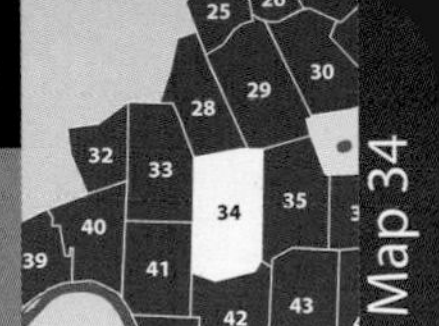

West Ken is a Jekyll-and-Hyde kind of place. The calm, village atmosphere around Holland Park soon gives way to an 'in your face' cluster of kebab shops and grime once you go south of High Street Kensington. While the hordes head to Hyde Park, locals in the know make a beeline to the more intimate Holland Park with its peaceful Kyoto Garden, sublime in autumn. Olympia Exhibition Centre gets that middle class blood boiling - Erotica Show anyone? Near the tube, Café Continente is the place to go for an irresistible stack of blueberry pancakes. The Arab Hall at recently refurbished Leighton House Museum is worth a visit alone.

Coffee

- **Cafe Continente** • 62 N End Rd

Landmarks

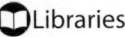

- **Kyoto Garden (Holland Park)** • 100 Holland Park Ave

Libraries

- **Barons Court** • North End Crescent

Nightlife

- **The Cumberland Arms** • 29 N End Rd
- **Famous 3 Kings** • 171 North End Road
- **Plum Bar** • 380 Kensington High St

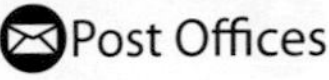

Post Offices

- **Olympia** • 8 North End Road

Restaurants

- **The Belvedere Restaurant** • Abbotsbury Road

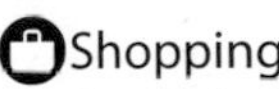

Shopping

- **Homebase** • 195 Warwick Rd

N
1
2
A
B
29
34
36
42
43
PAGE 342
Kensington Palace Gardens
Kensington Gardens
KENSINGTON
Holland Park
Campden Hill Tennis Club
Cricket Ground
High Street Kensington
Kensington High Street
Edwardes Square
EARL'S COURT
Earl's Court
SOUTH KENSINGTON
Cromwell Road A4
Earls Court Road A3220
Warwick Road
Talgarth Road A4
0.25 mile
0.25 km

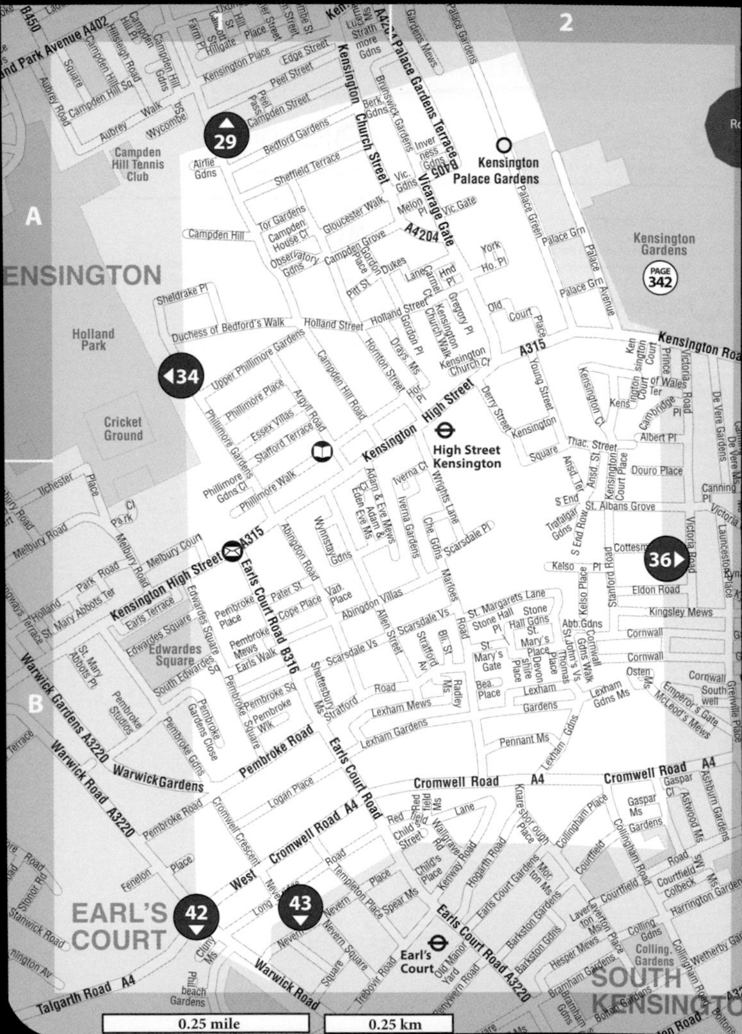

Kensington

Kensington is the London of Disney fantasy – Princesses tip-toeing around grand old homes and taking tea at 3pm. It's the kind of place where a gentile mews cottage will set you a back a cool mill, but if you live here you'll still have some change left over for an SUV and a box of organic veg. You're not going to score any cool points for hanging out here but there's nothing better than frisbee and a picnic (from Whole Foods of course) in Hyde Park on those treasured London summer days. If you've got the cash to splash, High Street Ken has the goods but instead take a detour to The Builders Arms for a not-so-posh pint.

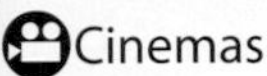

Cinemas

- **Odeon Kensington** • Kensington High St & Edwards Sq

Coffee

- **Caffe Nero** • 160 Kensington High St
- **Caffe Nero** • 1 Wrights Ln
- **Costa** • 149 Cromwell Rd
- **Pret A Manger** • 149 Kensington High St
- **Pret A Manger** • 123 Kensington High St
- **Starbucks** • 25 Kensington High St
- **Starbucks** • 197 Kensington High St

Landmarks

Kensington Palace Gardens • Kensington Palace Gardens

Libraries

- **Kensington Central Library** • Phillimore Walk

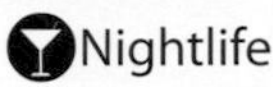

Nightlife

- **Builders Arms** • 1 Kensington Ct Pl
- **The Devonshire Arms** • 37 Marloes Rd
- **Yashin Sushi** • 1 Argyll Rd

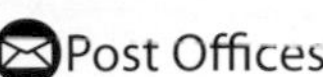

Post Offices

- **Kensington High St** • 257 Kensington High St

Restaurants

Byron • 222 Kensington High St
- **Clarke's** • 124 Kensington Church St
- **Kensington Roof Gardens** • 99 Kensington High St
- **Maggie Jones's** • 6 Old Court Pl
- **Zaika** • 1 Kensington High St

Shopping

- **Ben's Cookies** • 12 Kensington High St
- **Buttercup Cake Shop** • 16 St Albans Grove
- **Notting Hill Housing Trust** • 57 Kensington Church St
- **Trailfinders** • 194 Kensington High St
- **Urban Outfitters** • 36 Kensington High St
- **Whole Foods Market** • 63 Kensington High St

Supermarkets

- **Sainsbury's** • 162 Earl's Ct Rd
- **Tesco** • 100 W Cromwell Rd
- **Waitrose** • 243 Kensington High St

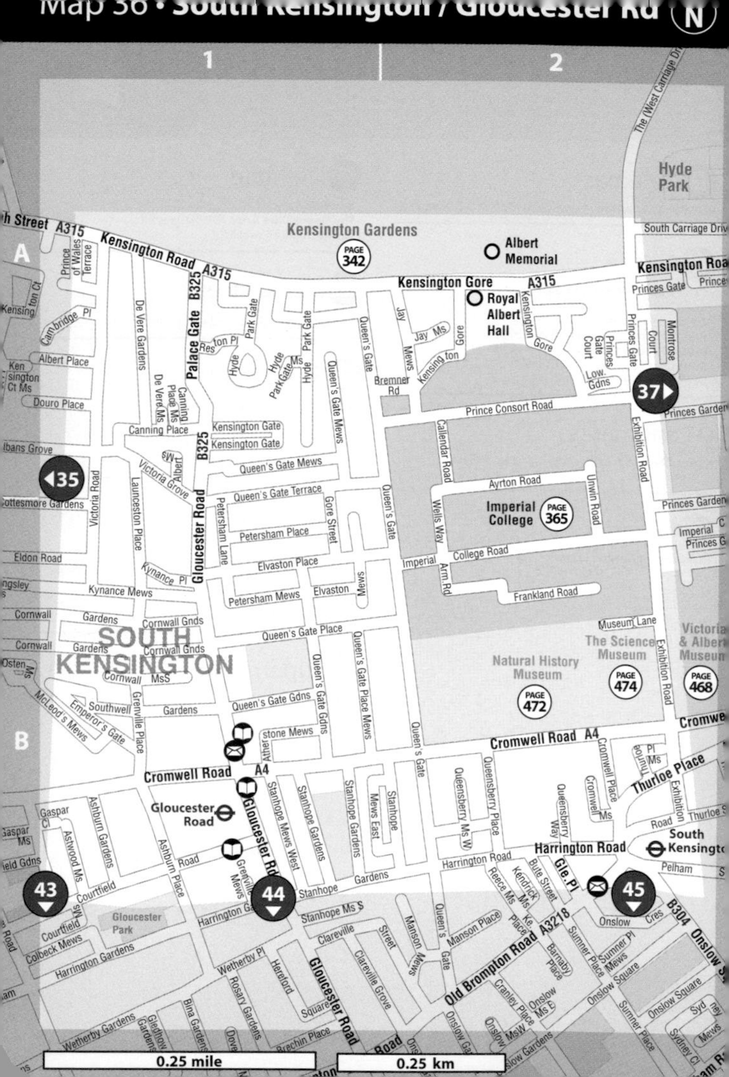

Map 36 • South Kensington / Gloucester Rd
N
1
2
A
B
Hyde Park
The (West Carriage Dr
Kensington Gardens
PAGE 342
Albert Memorial
South Carriage Driv
Kensington Road A315
Kensington Gore
A315
Royal Albert Hall
PAGE 365
Imperial College
Prince Consort Road
Ayrton Road
Imperial College Road
Frankland Road
Natural History Museum
PAGE 472
The Science Museum
PAGE 474
Victoria & Albert Museum
PAGE 468
Cromwell Road A4
Thurloe Place
Harrington Road
South Kensington
Gloucester Road
SOUTH KENSINGTON
Palace Gate
B325
De Vere Gardens
Queen's Gate
Queen's Gate Mews
Queen's Gate Terrace
Queen's Gate Place
Queen's Gate Gdns
Queen's Gate Place Mews
Exhibition Road
Princes Gate
Princes Gardens
Victoria Grove
Victoria Road
Launceston Place
Kynance Mews
Cornwall Gardens
Petersham Place
Petersham Mews
Elvaston Place
Gore Street
Cromwell Place
Queensberry Place
Stanhope Gardens
Stanhope Mews West
Ashburn Gardens
Ashburn Place
Courtfield Gardens
Gloucester Park
Harrington Gardens
Old Brompton Road A3218
Onslow Square
Onslow Gardens
Sumner Place
Bute Street
Manson Place
Clareville Street
Clareville Grove
Rosary Gardens
Hereford Square
Wetherby Gardens
Canning Place
Douro Place
Albert Place
Cambridge Pl
Kensington Gate
Gloucester Road
Grenville Place
Southwell Gardens
Emperor's Gate
McLeod's Mews
35
37
43
44
45
0.25 mile
0.25 km

South Kensington / Gloucester Rd

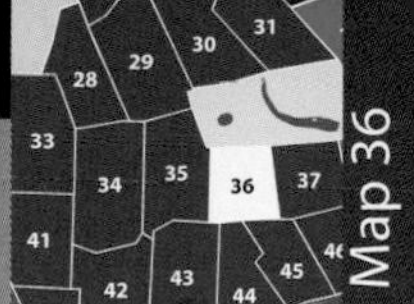

Once known as Albertopolis, this place started out as Prince Albert's playground of learning. These days the museums are the carrot that draws the tourists westwards from the buzzing centre. Free entry to museums mean more money for treats, and if it's treats you're after then fresh gelato at Oddono's or a good wedge of organic brie at the Farmer's Market won't fail to disappoint. If your idea of a good night out consists of more than a few quiet shandies then we suggest checking out another nabe.

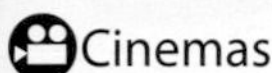

Cinemas

- **Cine Lumiere** • 17 Queensberry Pl

Coffee

- **Café Deco** • 62 Gloucester Rd
- **Pret A Manger** • 99 Gloucester Rd
- **Pret A Manger** • 15 Old Brompton Rd
- **Starbucks** • 17 Gloucester Rd
- **Starbucks** • 83 Gloucester Rd

Landmarks

- **Albert Memorial** • Kensington Gardens
- **Royal Albert Hall** • Kensington Gore

Libraries

- **French Institute Library** • 17 Queensberry Pl
- **National Art Library** • Cromwell Rd
- **Natural History Museum** • Cromwell Rd

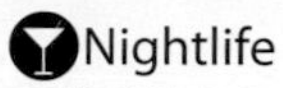

Nightlife

- **Boujis** • 43 Thurloe St

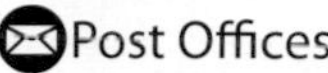

Post Offices

- **Gloucester Road** • 118 Gloucester Rd
- **South Kensington Station** • 41 Old Brompton St

Restaurants

- **Cafe Creperie** • 2 Exhibition Rd
- **Caffe Forum** • 146 Gloucester Rd
- **Da Mario** • 15 Gloucester Rd
- **Jakob's** • 20 Gloucester Rd
- **The Kensington Creperie** • 2 Exhibition Rd
- **Oddono's** • 14 Bute St
- **Pasha** • 1 Gloucester Rd

Shopping

- **Partridges Deli** • 17 Gloucester Rd
- **Snog** • 32 Thurloe Pl

Supermarkets

- **Sainsbury's** • 158 Cromwell Rd
- **Waitrose** • 128 Gloucester Rd

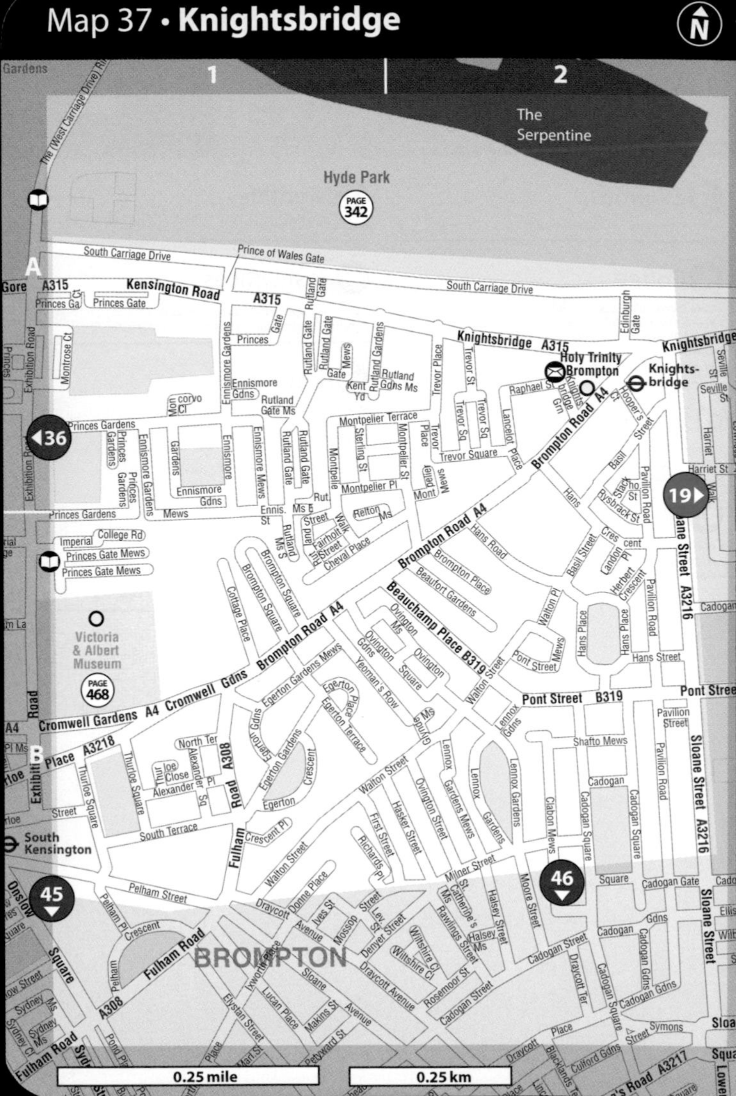

Map 37 • Knightsbridge
N
1
2
The Serpentine
Hyde Park
PAGE 342
South Carriage Drive
Prince of Wales Gate
Kensington Road
A315
Knightsbridge A315
Knightsbridge
Holy Trinity Brompton
Knights-bridge
Princes Gate
Princes Gardens
Ennismore Gardens
Ennismore Mews
Rutland Gate
Rutland Gardens
Montpelier Terrace
Montpelier St
Trevor Place
Trevor Square
Raphael St
Lancelot Place
Hooper's Ct
Brompton Road A4
Hans Road
Hans Crescent
Basil Street
Pavilion Road
Sloane Street A3216
Harriet St
Seville St
Hans Place
Hans Street
Pont Street B319
Beauchamp Place B319
Brompton Square
Cottage Place
Imperial College Rd
Princes Gate Mews
Victoria & Albert Museum
PAGE 468
Cromwell Gardens A4
Cromwell Gdns
Egerton Gardens
Egerton Crescent
Egerton Terrace
Yeoman's Row
Ovington Square
Walton Street
Lennox Gardens
Clabon Mews
Cadogan Square
Cadogan Gate
Milner Street
Moore Street
Thurloe Place A3218
Thurloe Square
South Terrace
Fulham Road A308
South Kensington
Pelham Street
Pelham Crescent
Draycott Avenue
Sloane Avenue
Elystan Street
Cadogan Street
Symons Street
BROMPTON
36
19
45
46
0.25 mile
0.25 km

Knightsbridge

Move on over Z List celebrity, only the truly rich shop here! While you can't move for fur or tourists, Knightsbridge is still a great place to shop. Window shop that is. Harrods and Harvey Nics are the big boys here and if you're after £40 soap you are in the right place. For the rest of us there's the Victoria & Albert Museum—free entry, brilliant cafe to escape the crowds, and multiple naked male sculptures to ogle.

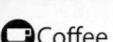

Coffee

- **Bagel Factory** • 102 Brompton Rd
- **Caffe Nero** • 124 Brompton Rd
- **Costa** • 197 Brompton Rd
- **Eat.** • 106 Brompton Rd
- **Pret A Manger** • 132 Brompton Rd
- **Starbucks** • 44 Brompton Rd

Landmarks

- **Holy Trinity Brompton** • Brompton Rd & Knightsbridge
- **Victoria & Albert Museum** • Cromwell Rd & Thurloe Pl

Libraries

- **Goethe-Institut Library** • 50 Princes Gate

Post Offices

- **Knightsbridge** • 6 Raphael St

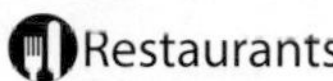

Restaurants

- **Bar Boulud** • 66 Knightsbridge
- **Zuma** • 5 Raphael St

Shopping

- **Burberry** • 2 Brompton Road
- **Divertimenti** • 227 Brompton Rd
- **Harrods** • 87 Brompton Rd
- **Harvey Nichols** • 109 Knightsbridge
- **Rigby & Peller** • 2 Hans Rd
- **Skandium** • 247 Brompton Rd
- **Space NK Apothecary** • 307 Brompton Rd

Supermarkets

- **Marks & Spencer** • 179 Brompton Rd
- **Sainsbury's** • 112 Brompton Rd

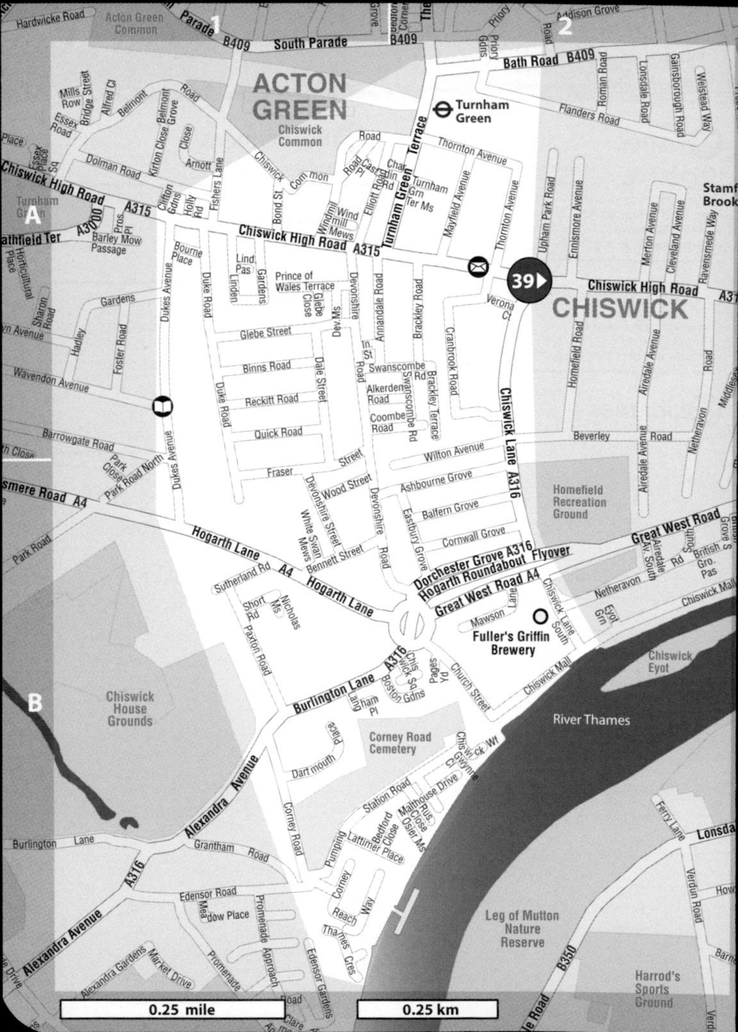

Map 38 • Chiswick

Chiswick

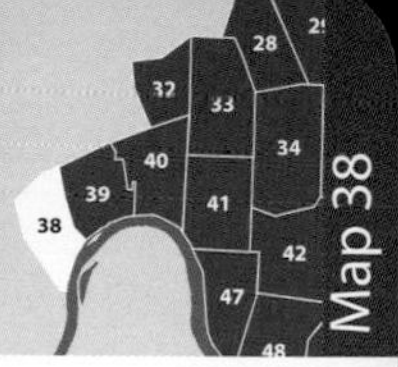

Lean, green and thankfully not so mean. Chiswick's tranquil, leafy, village feel is perhaps what draws families and well-heeled couples with its stacks of laid-back continental style pavement dining and quaint cafes on the High Road. Hit Devonshire Road for boutique shopping, and on sunny days it's all about ice-cream from Foubert's and an afternoon chilling out on Acton Green. The Roebuck serves up a top-notch Sunday roast but the High Road Brasserie still remains the place to be seen.

Coffee

- **Carluccio's** • 342 Chiswick High Rd
- **Starbucks** • 280 Chiswick High Rd

Libraries

- **Chiswick Library** • Duke's Ave

Landmarks

- **Fuller's Griffin Brewery** • Chiswick Lane South

Nightlife

- **Carvosso's** • 210 Chiswick High Rd
- **George IV** • 185 Chiswick High Rd
- **The Packhorse & Talbot** • 145 Chiswick High Rd
- **The Roebuck** • 122 Chiswick High Rd

Post Offices

- **Chiswick High Road** • 110 Chiswick High Rd

Restaurants

- **Boys Authentic Thai** • 95 Chiswick High Rd
- **Chella** • 142 Chiswick High Road
- **Chris' Fish and Chips** • 19 Turnham Green Terrace
- **Foubert's** • 2 Turnham Green Terrace
- **Franco Manca** • 144 Chiswick High Rd
- **High Road Brasserie** • 162 Chiswick High Rd
- **La Trompette** • 5 Devonshire Rd
- **Le Pain Quotidien** • 214 Chiswick High Road
- **Maison Blanc** • 26 Turnham Green Terrace
- **Kalamari** • 4 Chiswick High Rd
- **Turnham Green Cafe** • 57 Turnham Green Terrace
- **Union Jack's** • 217 Chiswick High Rd
- **Zizzi** • 231 Chiswick High Rd

Shopping

- **As Nature Intended** • 201 Chiswick High Rd
- **The Bread Shop** • 296 Chiswick Rd
- **Chiswick Health & Wellness Spa** • 300 Chiswick High Rd
- **Gail's** • 282 Chiswick High Rd
- **Mortimer & Bennett** • 33 Turnham Green Terrace
- **Outsider Tart** • 83 Chiswick High Rd
- **Oxfam Books** • 90 Turnham Green Terrace
- **Theobroma Cacao** • 43 Turnham Green Terrace
- **Something Nice** • 40 Turnham Green Terrace
- **Wheelers Garden Centre** • Turnham Green Terrace

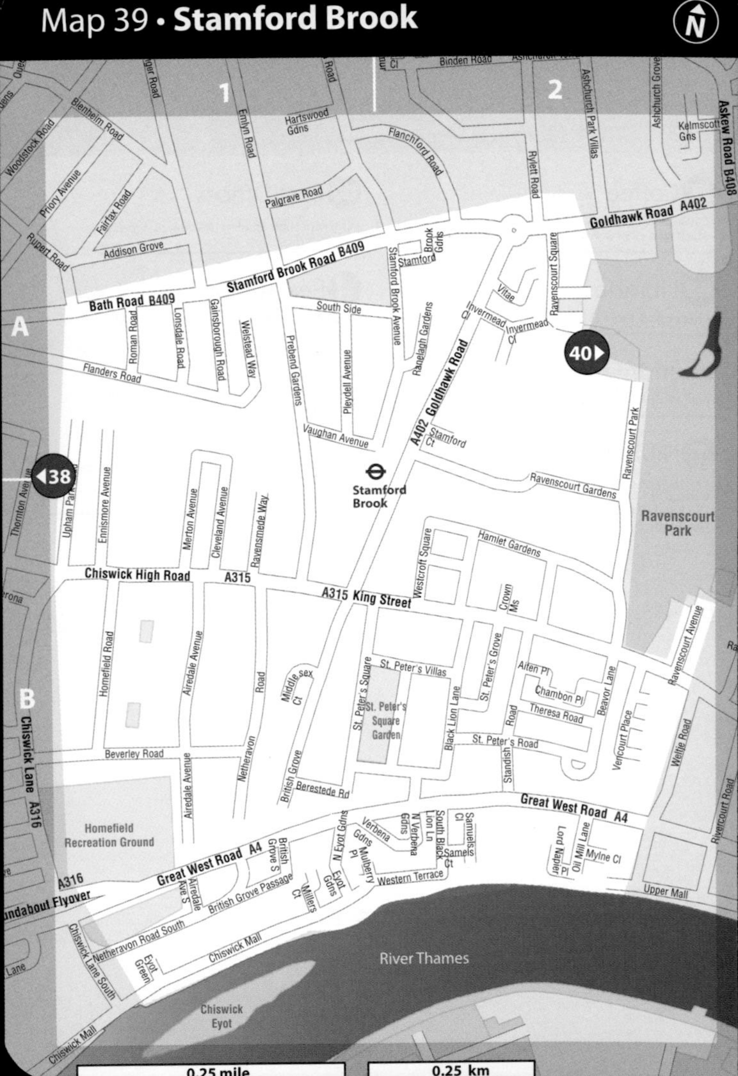

N
1
2
A
B
38
40
Binden Road
Hartswood Gdns
Flanchford Road
Emlyn Road
Ashchurch Park Villas
Ashchurch Grove
Kelmscott Gns
Askew Road B408
Blenheim Road
Woodstock Road
Priory Avenue
Fairfax Road
Rupert Road
Addison Grove
Palgrave Road
Rylett Road
Goldhawk Road A402
Stamford Brook Road B409
Stamford Brook Gdns
Stamford
Stamford Brook Avenue
Ravenscourt Square
Vitae
Invermead Cl
Bath Road B409
South Side
Roman Road
Lonsdale Road
Gainsborough Road
Welstead Way
Prebend Gardens
Pleydell Avenue
Ranelagh Gardens
A402 Goldhawk Road
Flanders Road
Vaughan Avenue
Stamford Ct
Ravenscourt Park
Ravenscourt Gardens
Stamford Brook
Thornton Avenue
Upham Park
Ennismore Avenue
Merton Avenue
Cleveland Avenue
Ravensmede Way
Westcroft Square
Hamlet Gardens
Chiswick High Road
A315
A315 King Street
Crown Ms
Homefield Road
Airedale Avenue
Netheravon Road
Middlesex Ct
St. Peter's Square
St. Peter's Villas
St. Peter's Square Garden
Black Lion Lane
St. Peter's Grove
Aiten Pl
Chambon Pl
Theresa Road
Beavor Lane
Vencourt Place
Ravenscourt Avenue
Weltje Road
Standish Road
St. Peter's Road
Beverley Road
British Grove
Berestede Rd
Great West Road A4
Rivercourt Road
Chiswick Lane A316
Homefield Recreation Ground
Airedale Avenue
N Eyot Gdns
Verbena Gdns
Mulberry Pl
N Verbena Gdns
South Black Lion Ln
Samuels Cl
Samels Ct
Western Terrace
Lord Napier Pl
Oil Mill Lane
Mylne Cl
Upper Mall
A316
Great West Road A4
British Grove S
Airedale Ave S
British Grove Passage
Millers Ct
Eyot Gdns
Roundabout Flyover
Netheravon Road South
Chiswick Lane South
Eyot Green
Chiswick Mall
River Thames
Chiswick Eyot
Chiswick Mall
Lane
0.25 mile
0.25 km

Stamford Brook

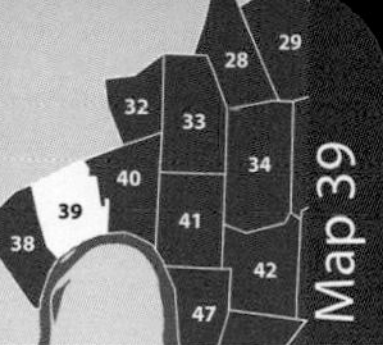

Wedged between Chiswick and Hammersmith, Stamford Brook on the surface may seem like not much more than a tube station and some rather nice, note 'expensive', houses. Brookites, however, know that it's all about that big blue below the A4 – The Thames – for a lazy Sunday stroll or long Saturday brunches at 'Lola and Simon'. Further up King Street, 'Tosa' serves up some authentic Japanese yakitori while thirsty Brookites head to The Carpenter's Arms for oysters and a Guinness in the garden.

Coffee

- **Cafe Ginkgo** • 243 Ravenscourt Park

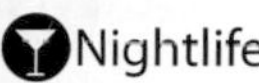

Nightlife

- **The Raven** • 375 Goldhawk Rd

Restaurants

- **Carpenter's Arms** • 89 Black Lion Ln
- **Lola & Simon** • 278 King St
- **Saigon Saigon** • 313 King St
- **Tosa** • 332 Kings St

Supermarkets

- **Sainsbury's** • 120 Chiswick High Rd
- **Tesco** • 327 King St

Shopping

- **Mac's Cameras** • 262 Kings St
- **Thai Smile** • 287 King

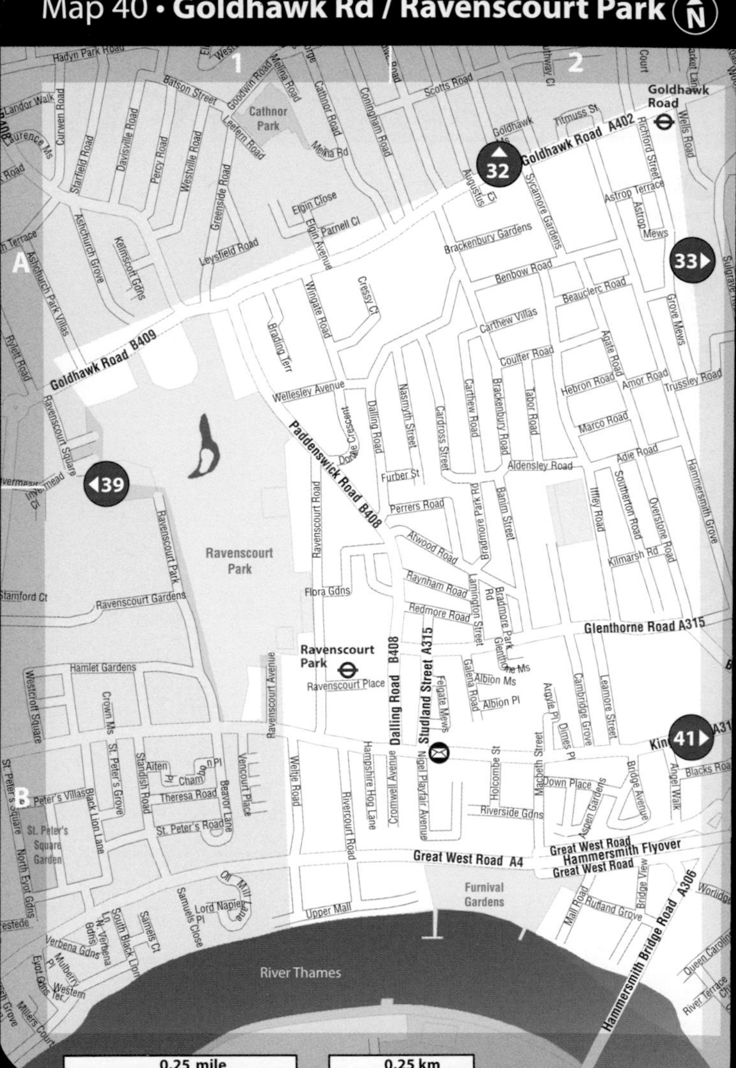

Cathnor Park
Ravenscourt Park
Goldhawk Road
Ravenscourt Park
Furnival Gardens
River Thames
Goldhawk Road B409
Goldhawk Road A402
Paddenswick Road B408
Glenthorne Road A315
Great West Road A4
Hammersmith Flyover
Hammersmith Bridge Road A306
Studland Street A315
Dalling Road B408
32
33
39
41
0.25 mile
0.25 km

Goldhawk Rd / Ravenscourt Park

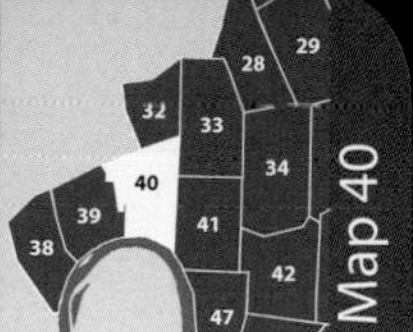

Far enough out on the tube to scare the tourists, this area is a haven for locals who want it all on their doorstep. International flavours colour the Goldhawk Road, Ravenscourt Park offers a calm little slice of green while pretty Thames walks must surely conclude with a visit to the city's most picturesque pub, The Dove. Furnival Gardens is the spot to watch the annual Oxbridge boat race and after get away from it all in Café Ginko, a local secret spot. Life's good in these parts.

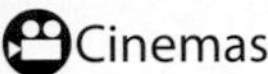

Cinemas

- **Cineworld Hammersmith** • 207 King St

Coffee

- **Caffe Nero** • 1 King St
- **Coffee Republic** • 207 King St
- **Starbucks** • 38 King St

Nightlife

- **The Dove** • 19 Upper Mall
- **Ruby Grand** • 227 King St

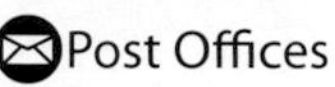

Post Offices

- **King St** • 168 King St

Restaurants

- **A.Cookes** • 48 Goldhawk Rd
- **Blah Blah Blah** • 78 Goldhawk Rd
- **Lowiczanka Polish Cultural Centre** • 238 King Street
- **Mahdi** • 215 King St
- **Sagar** • 157 King St
- **Zippy Diner** • 42 Goldhawk Rd

Shopping

- **Bushwacker Wholefoods** • 132 King St

Supermarkets

- **Iceland** • 111 King St
- **Tesco** • 327 King St

Map 41 • Hammersmith

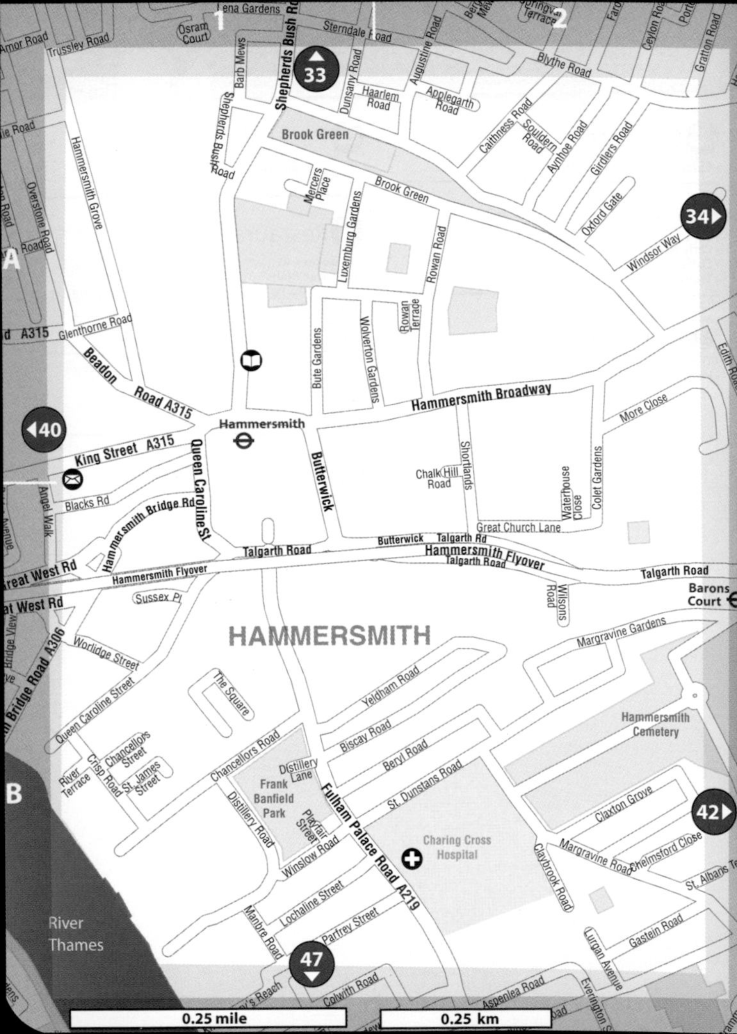

N

Lena Gardens
Shepherds Bush Rd
1
2
Osram Court
Amor Road
Trussley Road
Sterndale Road
Springvale Terrace
Blythe Road
Ceylon Road
Gratton Road
Barb Mews
33
Dunsany Road
Augustine Road
Haarlem Road
Applegarth Road
Shepherds Bush Road
Brook Green
Caithness Road
Souldern Road
Aynhoe Road
Girdlers Road
Hammersmith Grove
Overstone Road
Mercers Place
Luxemburg Gardens
Brook Green
Oxford Gate
34
Windsor Way
Rowan Road
A
Rowan Terrace
Bute Gardens
Wolverton Gardens
A315
Glenthorne Road
Beadon Road A315
Edith Road
Hammersmith Broadway
More Close
40
Hammersmith
King Street A315
Queen Caroline St
Butterwick
Shortlands
Chalk Hill Road
Waterhouse Close
Colet Gardens
Angel Walk
Blacks Rd
Hammersmith Bridge Rd
Great Church Lane
Butterwick
Talgarth Rd
Talgarth Road
Hammersmith Flyover
Talgarth Road
Great West Rd
Hammersmith Flyover
Talgarth Road
Barons Court
Great West Rd
Sussex Pl
Wilsons Road
Bridge View
Hammersmith Bridge Road A306
Worlidge Street
HAMMERSMITH
Margravine Gardens
The Square
Yeldham Road
Queen Caroline Street
Hammersmith Cemetery
Biscay Road
Chancellors Street
Chancellors Road
Beryl Road
River Terrace
Crisp Road
St. James Street
Distillery Lane
Frank Banfield Park
St. Dunstans Road
B
Distillery Road
Playfair Street
Fulham Palace Road A219
Claxton Grove
42
Winslow Road
Charing Cross Hospital
Margravine Road
Chelmsford Close
St. Albans Te
Lochaline Street
Claybrook Road
River Thames
Manbre Road
Parfrey Street
Gastein Road
47
Lurgan Avenue
Colwith Road
Aspenlea Road
Everington St

0.25 mile
0.25 km

Hammersmith

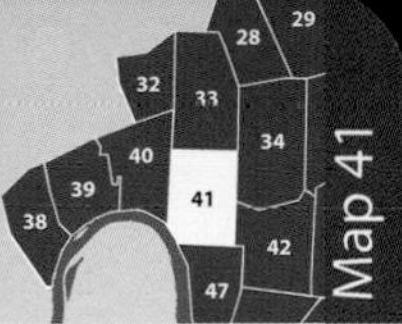

While the shops and pubs on offer along the main drag (King Street) are all pretty drab, Hammersmith has three great venues for the more culturally inclined. The Apollo hosts mainstream bands and big-name comedians; The Lyric is an affordable way to indulge in some modern theatre, and The Riverside Studios offer a satisfying selection of foreign and art house films. London's vegetarians flock to The Gate, with its seriously original and inventive menu.

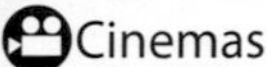

Cinemas

- **Riverside Studios** • Crisp Rd & Queen Caroline St

Coffee

- **Cafe Brera** • Hammersmith Foyer & Roof Garden
- **Cafe Brera** • King St & Angel Walk
- **Costa** • Butterwick
- **Pret A Manger** • Butterwick
- **Starbucks** • 200 Hammersmith Rd

Emergency Rooms

- **Charing Cross Hospital** • Fulham Palace Rd & St Dunstan's Rd

Libraries

- **Hammersmith Library** • Shepherds Bush Rd

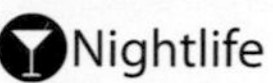

Nightlife

- **Brook Green Hotel** • 170 Shepherd's Bush Rd
- **The Distillers** • 64 Fulham Palace Rd
- **Hammersmith Apollo** • 45 Queen Caroline St
- **The Hampshire Hog** • 227 King St
- **Lyric Hammersmith** • King St

Post Offices

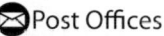

- **Hammersmith** • 16 King's Mall

Restaurants

- **The Gate** • 51 Queen Caroline St

Shopping

- **Bakehaus** • 71 King St

Supermarkets

- **Tesco** • 180 Shepherd's Bush Rd
- **Tesco** • 13 Broadway Ctr

N
1
2
A
B
North End Road B317
Edith Road
Gunterstone Road
Gliddon Road
Barons Keep
Glazbury Road
Trevanion Road
Gwendwr Road
Talgarth Road A4
West Kensington
Barons Court
34
41
43
47
48
Beaumont Avenue
Gibbs Green
Barons Court Road
Comeragh Road
Castletown Road
Charleville Road
Fairholme Road
Challoner Street
Palliser Road
Barton Road
Hammersmith Cemetery
Queen's Club
Gledstanes Road
Vereker Road
Perham Road
Cheesemans Terrace
Star Road
Sun Road
Fane Street
Franklin Square
Aisgill Avenue
Ivatt Place
Mund Street
Earl's Court Exhibition Center
Empress State Building
Marchbank Road
Thaxton Road
Lillie Road A3218
Archel Road
Chesson Road
Turneville Road
Normand Mews
St. Andrews Road
Norfolk Terrace
Field Road
Greyhound Road
Queen's Gardens
Queens Club Gardens
Normand Road
Normand Park
Mulgrave Road
Bramber Road
Sedlescombe Road
Racton Road
Anselm Road
Tasso Road
Kinnoul Road
Musard Road
Humbolt Road
Disbrowe Road
Brecon Road
Moylan Road
Hugh Gaitskell Close
Hugh Dalton Avenue
Barbara Castle Close
Haldane Road
Tournay Road
Delaford Street
Mendora Road
Prothero Road
Estcourt Road
Pellant Road
Chaldon Road
William Close
Rylston Road
St. Thomas's Way
Mirabel Road
Fabian Road
Hartismere Road
Epirus Road
Shorrolds Road
Dawes Road A3219
Munster Road
Strode Road
Hannell Road
Bronsart Road
Aintree Street
Rosaline Road
Sherbrooke Road
Orbain Road
St. Olaf's Road
Kilmaine Road
Varna Road
Parkville Road
Rosaville Road
Brookville Road
Marville Road
Homestead Road
Gironde Road
Burnthwaite Road
Lancaster Court
Darlan Road
Mablethorpe Road
Rowallan Road
Allestree Road
Warwick Road
Philbeach Gardens
Stanwick Road
Mornington Avenue
Edith Villas
Fitzjames Avenue
Chelmsford Close
St. Albans Terrace
Crammond Close
Abbey Gardens
Spencer Mews
Laundry Road
Lampeter Square
Crefeld Close
Purcell Crescent
Lillie Road A3230
0.25 mile
0.25 km

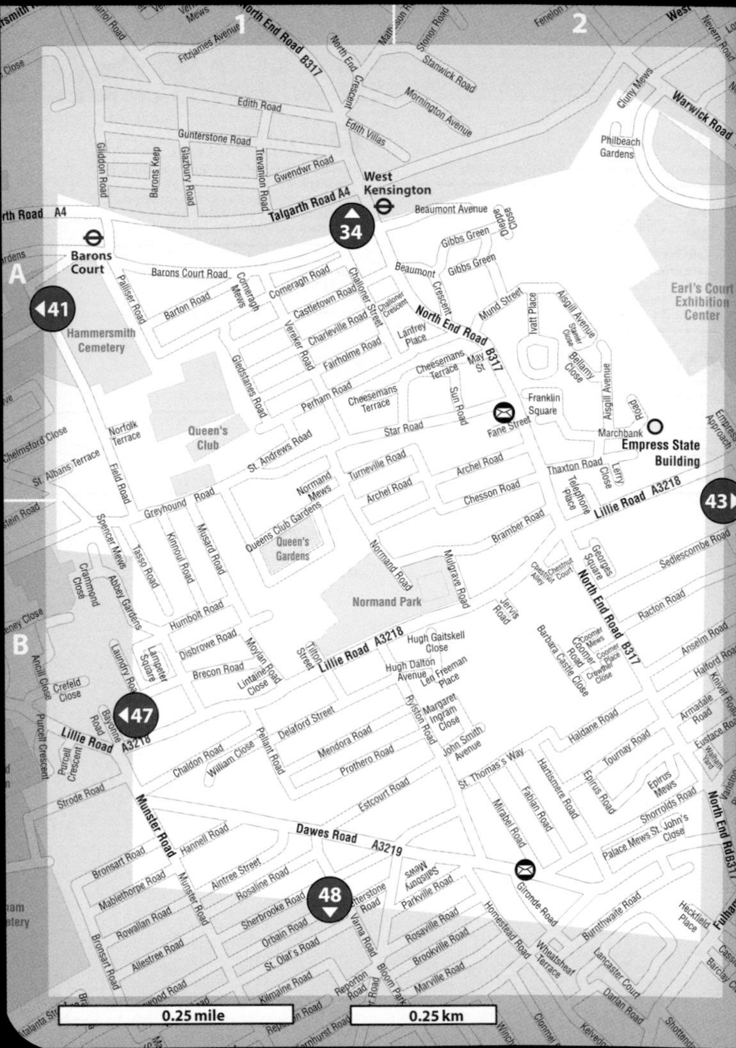

Barons Court

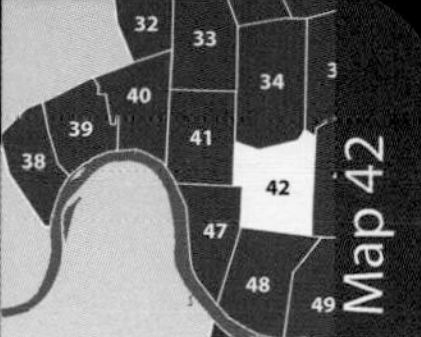

Barons Court doesn't have a scene as such, but it is elegantly lovely. Ignore North End Road—a fried chicken blot among Edwardian mansions—and instead get lost in Lille Road's antique stores. Curtains Up offers intimate theatre in the pub vaults. If you need a change from polished chic, seek the Colton Arms for a jug-pint in its cottage style garden.

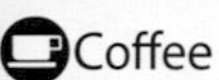

Coffee

- **Café La Cigale** • 353 N End Rd
- **Costa** • 431 North End Rd

Landmarks

- **Empress State Buidling** • Lillie Rd & North End Rd

Nightlife

- **Colton Arms** • 187 Greyhound Road
- **The Curtains Up** • 28 Comeragh Rd
- **The Fulham Mitre** • 81 Dawes Rd
- **Queen's Arms** • 171 Greyhound Rd

Post Offices

- **Dawes Road** • 108 Dawes Rd
- **Olympia** • 8 North End Road

Restaurants

- **Best Mangal** • 104 N End Rd
- **Bombay Bicycle Club** • 352 N End Rd
- **Ta Krai** • 100 North End Rd

Shopping

- **Curious Science** • 319 Lillie Road

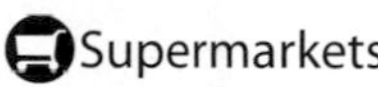

Supermarkets

- **Co-Op** • 88 N End Rd
- **Iceland** • 290 North End Rd
- **Sainsbury's** • 342 N End Rd

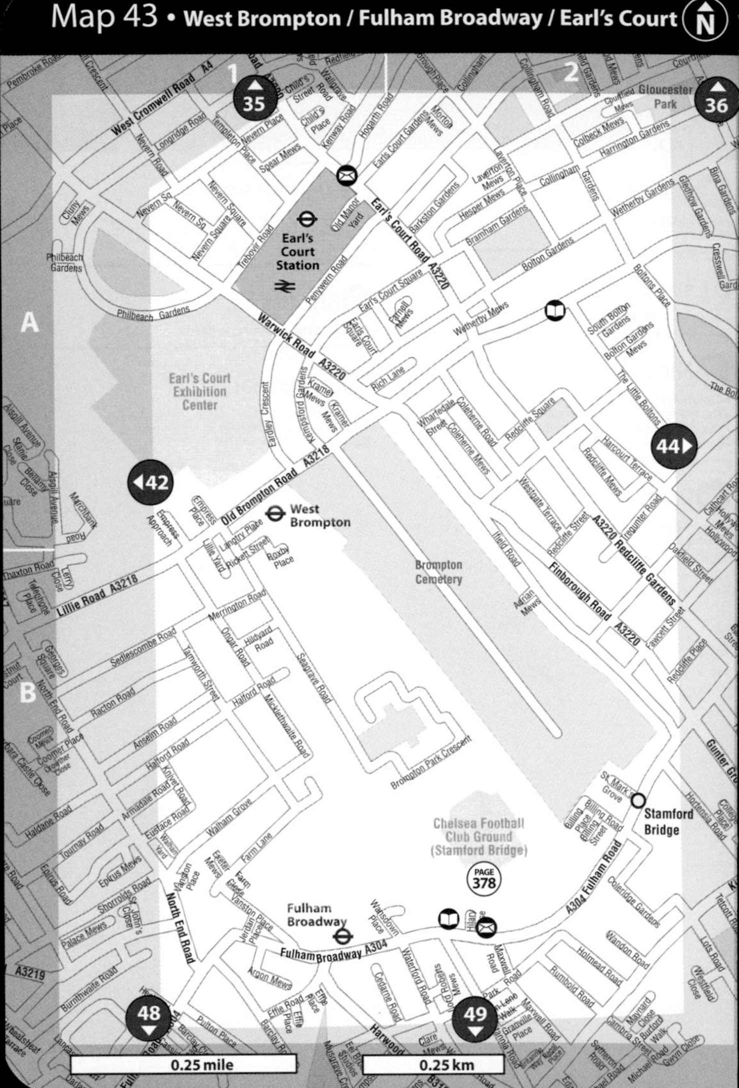
Map 43 • West Brompton / Fulham Broadway / Earl's Court
N
35
36
42
44
48
49
1
2
A
B
Earl's Court Station
West Brompton
Fulham Broadway
Stamford Bridge
Earl's Court Exhibition Center
Brompton Cemetery
Chelsea Football Club Ground (Stamford Bridge)
PAGE 378
Gloucester Park
West Cromwell Road A4
Pembroke Road
Longridge Road
Nevern Road
Nevern Place
Nevern Square
Nevern Sq
Templeton Place
Spear Mews
Trebovir Road
Child's Street
Child's Place
Kenway Road
Hogarth Road
Wallgrave Road
Cluny Mews
Philbeach Gardens
Warwick Road A3220
Earl's Court Road A3220
Old Manor Yard
Penywern Road
Earl's Court Square
Earls Court Gardens
Morton Mews
Collingham Road
Collingham Gardens
Colbeck Mews
Harrington Gardens
Courtfield Mews
Laverton Place
Laverton Mews
Hesper Mews
Barkston Gardens
Bramham Gardens
Bolton Gardens
Wetherby Gardens
Wetherby Mews
Gledhow Gardens
Bina Gardens
Cresswell Gardens
Bolton Place
South Bolton Gardens
Bolton Gardens Mews
The Little Boltons
Farnell Mews
Rich Lane
Eardley Crescent
Kempsford Gardens
Kramer Mews
Old Brompton Road A3218
Wharfedale Street
Coleherne Road
Coleherne Mews
Redcliffe Square
Harcourt Terrace
Redcliffe Mews
Westgate Terrace
Redcliffe Street
A3220 Redcliffe Gardens
Tregunter Road
Finborough Road A3220
Ifield Road
Adrian Mews
Fawcett Street
Redcliffe Place
Oakfield Street
Cathcart Road
Hollywood Mews
Empress Place
Empress Approach
Langtry Place
Lillie Yard
Rickett Street
Roxby Place
Lillie Road A3218
Thaxton Road
Lerry Close
Marchbank Road
Aisgill Avenue
Bellamy Close
Merrington Road
Sedlescombe Road
Tamworth Street
Ongar Road
Hildyard Road
Seagrave Road
Halford Road
Racton Road
Anselm Road
Mickelthwaite Road
Coomer Mews
Coomer Place
Crowther Close
North End Road
Armadale Road
Knivet Road
Eustace Road
Walham Grove
Walham Yard
Farm Lane
Haldane Road
Tournay Road
Epirus Mews
Epirus Road
Shorrolds Road
St John's Close
Palace Mews
Vanston Place
Exeter Mews
Farm Close
Jerdan Place
Brompton Park Crescent
St Mark's Grove
Billing Road
Billing Place
Billing Street
A304 Fulham Road
Coleridge Gardens
Hortensia Road
Gunter Grove
Fulham Broadway A304
Wansdown Place
Waterford Road
Cedarne Road
Maxwell Road
Park Road
Argon Mews
Effie Road
Effie Place
Barclay Road
Pulton Place
Burnthwaite Road
A3219
Harwood Road
Holmead Road
Rumbold Road
Wandon Road
Tetcott Road
Lots Road
Westfield Close
Maynard Close
Burford Walk
Cambria Street
Gwyn Close
Granville Place
0.25 mile
0.25 km

West Brompton / Fulham Broadway / Earl's Court

A lively mix of Aussies, Saffas, rich kids, and sweaty Chelsea fans occupy these neighbourhoods. Fulham Broadway is the focus of the action offering heaving bars and clubs. Earl's Court is slightly more sedate while West Brompton is positively sleepy in comparison. On Brompton Road '60s boho café The Troubadour is still a happening spot for live music and a coffee while Vingt Quatre is a 24-hour institution serving fry-ups to clubbers in the early hours.

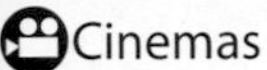

Cinemas

- **Cineworld Fulham Road** • 142 Fulham Rd
- **Vue Fulham** • Fulham Rd & Cedarne Rd

Coffee

- **Caffe Nero** • 480 Fulham Rd
- **Caffe Nero** • 174 Fulham Rd
- **Coffee Republic** • 142 Fulham Rd
- **Pret A Manger** • Fulham Broadway Retail Centre
- **Starbucks** • 259 Old Brompton Rd
- **Starbucks** • 186 Earl's Ct Rd
- **The Troubadour** • 263 Old Brompton Rd

Landmarks

- **Stamford Bridge** • Fulham Road & Moore Park Rd

Libraries

- **Brompton Library** • 210 Old Brompton Rd
- **Institute of Cancer Research Library** • 237 Fulham Rd

Nightlife

- **Onboard Karaoke** • 8 Kenway Rd
- **The Blackbird** • 209 Earl's Court Rd

Post Offices

- **Earls Court** • 185 Earl's Court Rd
- **Fulham Road** • 369 Fulham Rd

Restaurants

- **Bodean's** • 4 Broadway Chambers
- **Chutney Mary** • 535 King's Rd
- **Harwood Arms** • Walham Grove
- **Vingt Quatre** • 325 Fulham Rd
- **Yo! Sushi** • Fulham Road

Shopping

- **Fulham Broadway Centre** • Fulham Road

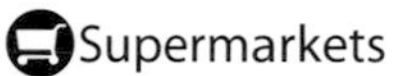

Supermarkets

- **Sainsbury's** • Fulham Rd
- **Tesco** • 459 Fulham Rd
- **Waitrose** • 380 North End Rd

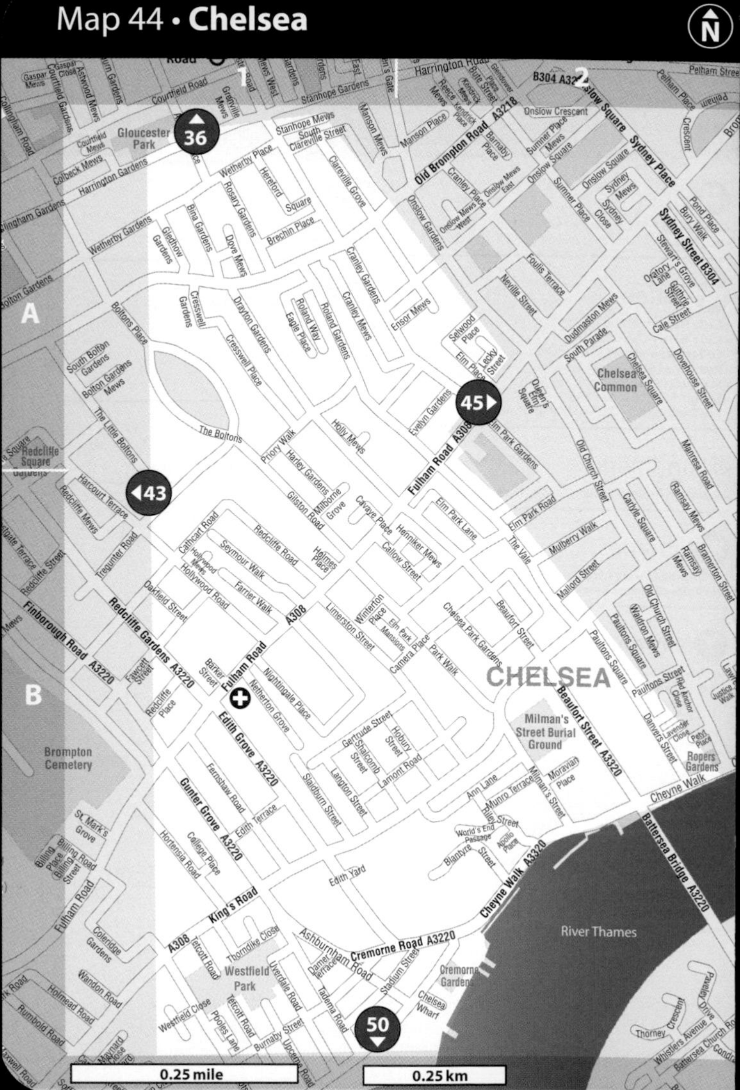

Map 44 • Chelsea
N
1
2
A
B
36
43
45
50
CHELSEA
Gloucester Park
Chelsea Common
Milman's Street Burial Ground
Brompton Cemetery
Westfield Park
Cremorne Gardens
River Thames
Ropers Gardens
Redcliffe Square
Harrington Road
Courtfield Road
Courtfield Gardens
Stanhope Gardens
Stanhope Mews
Harrington Gardens
Colback Mews
Wetherby Place
Wetherby Gardens
Rosary Gardens
Hereford Square
Clareville Grove
Clareville Street
Brechin Place
Manson Mews
Manson Place
Old Brompton Road A3218
Onslow Crescent
Onslow Square
Onslow Gardens
Sumner Place
Sydney Place
Sydney Street B304
Pelham Place
Pelham Street
Cranley Place
Cranley Gardens
Cranley Mews
Foulis Terrace
Neville Street
Gledhow Gardens
Bina Gardens
Dove Mews
Drayton Gardens
Cresswell Place
Cresswell Gardens
Roland Gardens
Roland Way
Eagle Place
Ensor Mews
Selwood Place
Elm Place
Lecky Street
Dudmaston Mews
South Parade
Cale Street
Chelsea Square
Dovehouse Street
Bolton Gardens
Boltons Place
South Bolton Gardens
Bolton Gardens Mews
The Little Boltons
The Boltons
Priory Walk
Harley Gardens
Holly Mews
Evelyn Gardens
Fulham Road A308
Elm Park Gardens
Old Church Street
Manresa Road
Carlyle Square
Ramsay Mews
Elm Park Road
Elm Park Lane
Mulberry Walk
The Vale
Mallord Street
Harcourt Terrace
Redcliffe Mews
Tregunter Road
Redcliffe Street
Finborough Road A3220
Redcliffe Gardens A3220
Cathcart Road
Redcliffe Road
Seymour Walk
Hollywood Road
Farrier Walk
Gilston Road
Milborne Grove
Cavaye Place
Henniker Mews
Callow Street
Holmes Place
Limerston Street
Winterton Place
Camera Place
Park Walk
Chelsea Park Gardens
Beaufort Street A3320
Paultons Square
Paultons Street
Danvers Street
Cheyne Walk
Oakfield Street
Fawcett Street
Redcliffe Place
Barker Street
Fulham Road
Nightingale Place
Netherton Grove
Edith Grove A3220
Gunter Grove A3220
Fernshaw Road
Edith Terrace
Slaidburn Street
Gertrude Street
Shalcomb Street
Hobury Street
Lamont Road
Langton Street
Ann Lane
Munro Terrace
Moravian Place
Milman's Street
World's End Passage
Blantyre Street
Apollo Place
Cheyne Walk A3320
Battersea Bridge A3220
Hortensia Road
College Place
St Mark's Grove
Billing Road
Billing Place
Billing Street
Fulham Road
Coleridge Gardens
King's Road
A308
Tetcott Road
Thorndike Close
Ashburnham Road
Cremorne Road A3220
Edith Yard
Lots Road
Stadium Street
Chelsea Wharf
Dartrey Terrace
Tadema Road
Uverdale Road
Burnaby Street
Poole's Lane
Westfield Close
Wandon Road
Holmead Road
Rumbold Road
Thorney Crescent
Whistlers Avenue
Battersea Church Road
Pavley Drive
0.25 mile
0.25 km

Chelsea

This area drips old money, 4x4s, and people who own rather large things, like, say, Devon. The only way to do Chelsea is to be seen doing it—and if you're paying all that money at least make it worthwhile. Taste Michelin-starred food at Aubergine or perhaps engage in some (super)star-gazing at The Bluebird Café. For a more sedate affair hang out with the locals, property investors 'n all, at local Victorian boozer The Drayton Arms.

Coffee

- **Starbucks** • 388 King's Rd

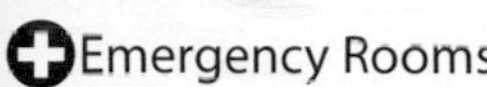

Emergency Rooms

- **Chelsea and Westminster Hospital** • 369 Fulham Rd

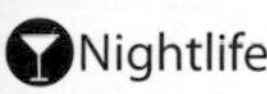

Nightlife

- **Brinkley's** • 47 Hollywood Rd
- **The Drayton Arms** • 153 Old Brompton Rd
- **The Duke of Clarence** • 148 Old Brompton Rd
- **Rumi** • 531 King's Rd

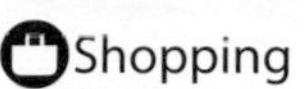

Restaurants

- **Aubergine** • 11 Park Walk
- **Eight Over Eight** • 392 King's Rd
- **The Bluebird** • 350 King's Rd

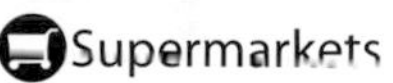

Shopping

- **Furniture Cave** • 533 Kings Rd
- **Richer Sounds** • 258 Fulham Rd
- **The Shop At Bluebird** • 350 King's Rd

Supermarkets

- **Sainsbury's** • 295 Fulham Rd

Map 45 • Chelsea (East)

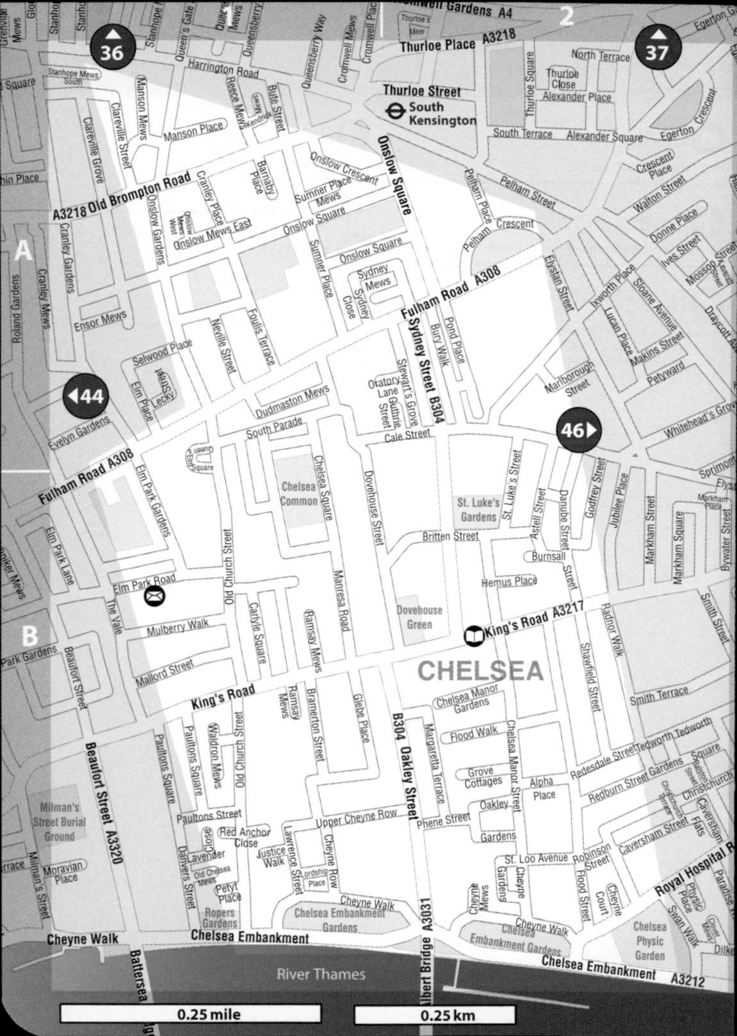

0.25 mile

0.25 km

Chelsea (East)

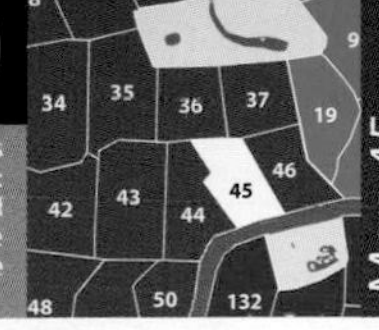

Chelsea East is what Hollywood thinks all of London is like, full of dapper English chaps and potential princesses (who, incidentally, donate their clothes to the Red Cross shop: rummage here for London's best bargains). King's Road buzzes as it did when it spawned the Swinging '60s, and foodies are spoiled around Cale Street. Tom's Kitchen is your place for Sloaney eating without the Sloaney allowance. For a cheaper and sweeter taste of the area get to The Hummingbird Bakery for addictive oh-so-good cupcakes.

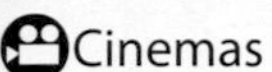

Cinemas

- **Curzon Chelsea** • 206 King's Rd
- **Cineworld Chelsea** • 279 King's Rd

Coffee

- **Cafe de la Paix** • 159 King's Rd
- **Caffe Nero** • 115 King's Rd
- **Caffe Nero** • 201 King's Rd
- **Caffe Nero** • 66 Old Brompton Rd
- **Starbucks** • 123 King's Rd
- **Starbucks** • 72 Old Brompton Rd

Libraries

- **Chelsea Library** • King's Rd

Post Offices

- **Elm Park** • 66 Elm Park Rd

Nightlife

- **The Anglesea Arms** • 15 Selwood Terrace
- **Apartment 195** • 195 Kings Rd
- **Chelsea Potter** • 119 Kings Rd
- **The Pig's Ear** • 35 Old Church St

Restaurants

- **Chelsea Kitchen** • 451 Fulham Rd
- **Four o nine** • 409 Clapham Rd
- **Le Columbier** • 145 Dovehouse St
- **The Hummingbird Bakery** • 47 Old Brompton Rd
- **Made In Italy** • 249 King's Rd
- **My Old Dutch Pancake House** • 221 King's Rd
- **The Pig's Ear** • 35 Old Church St
- **Sushinho** • 312 King's Rd
- **Tom's Kitchen** • 27 Cale St

Shopping

- **British Red Cross Chelsea** • 69 Old Church St
- **Frock Me! Vintage Fashion Fair** • Chelsea Town Hall, Kings Rd
- **Kate Kuba** • 24 Duke of York Sq
- **Nomad Books** • 781 Fulham Rd
- **Sweaty Betty** • 125 King's Rd

Supermarkets

- **Waitrose** • 196 King's Rd

Map 46 • Sloane Square

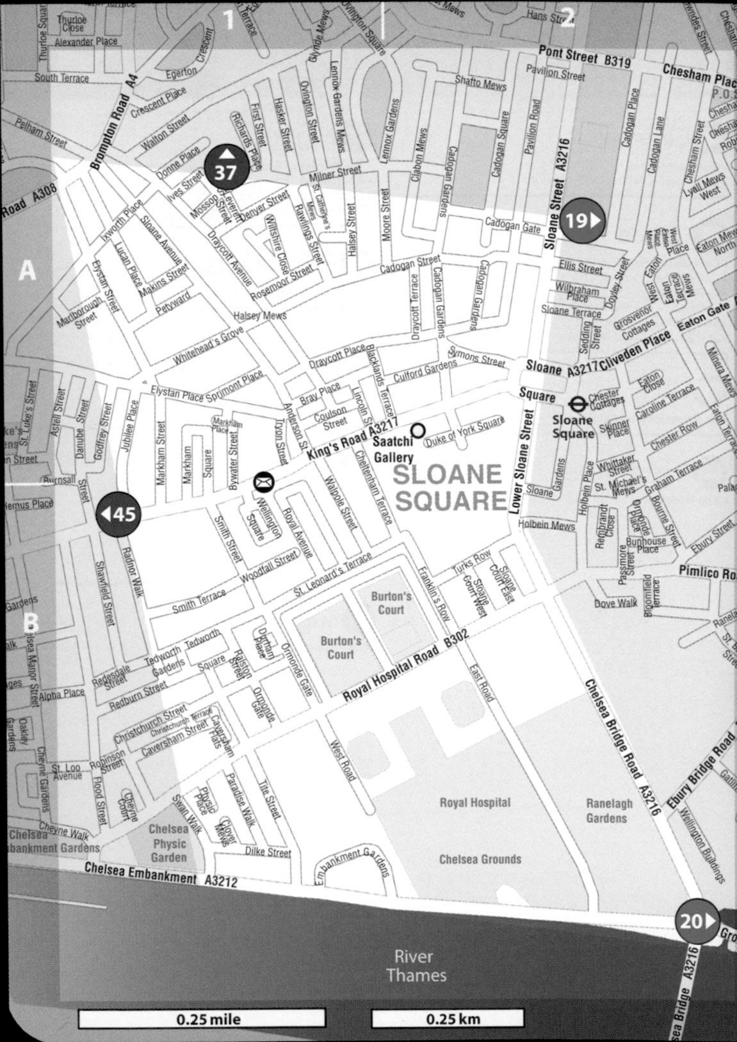

N

1 2 A B

Pont Street B319
Chesham Place
Sloane Street A3216
Brompton Road A4
King's Road A3217
Royal Hospital Road B302
Chelsea Embankment A3212
Chelsea Bridge Road A3216
Ebury Bridge Road
Pimlico Road
Lower Sloane Street
Sloane Square
Cliveden Place
Eaton Gate
Cadogan Gate
Cadogan Street
Milner Street
Sloane Avenue
Draycott Avenue
Pelham Street
Walton Street
Elystan Place
Smith Street
Franklin's Row
Turks Row
Holbein Place
Bourne Street
Ebury Street
Flood Street
Tite Street
West Road
East Road

Saatchi Gallery
SLOANE SQUARE
Sloane Square
Burton's Court
Royal Hospital
Ranelagh Gardens
Chelsea Grounds
Chelsea Physic Garden
River Thames

37
19
45
20

0.25 mile
0.25 km

Sloane Square

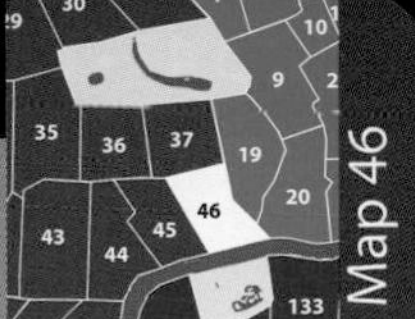

You've got to love a place that spawns an adjective. If you've never met any 'Sloaney' types and are curious as to why the whole of London gets so riled about them, take a walk along the King's Road and observe. Peter Jones stands tall over the square and offers everything you didn't know you wanted. This rather beautiful nabe also hosts some bank-breaking eateries, such as Gordon Ramsay and Bibendum, as well as its fare share of cultural fair—the Saatchi Gallery being the finest example.

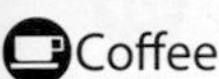

Coffee

- **Eat.** • 82 King's Rd
- **Pret A Manger** • 80 King's Rd
- **Starbucks** • 65 Sloane Ave
- **Starbucks** • 128 King's Rd

Landmarks

- **Saatchi Gallery** • Duke of York HQ, King's Rd

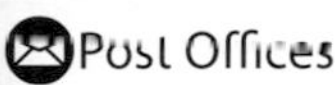

Post Offices

- **Kings Walk** • 122 King's Rd

Restaurants

- **The Admiral Codrington** • 17 Mossop St
- **Bibendum Restaurant & Oyster Bar** • 81 Fulham Rd
- **Blushes Cafe** • 52 King's Rd
- **Foxtrot Oscar** • 79 Royal Hospital Rd
- **Restaurant Gordon Ramsay** • 68 Royal Hospital Rd
- **Le Cercle** • 1 Wilbraham Pl
- **Tom Aikens** • 43 Elystan St

Shopping

- **Partridges** • 2 Duke of York Sq
- **Peter Jones** • Sloane Sq
- **Rigby & Peller** • 13 Kings Rd
- **Space NK Apothecary** • 307 King's Rd

Supermarkets

- **Sainsbury's** • 75 Sloane Ave

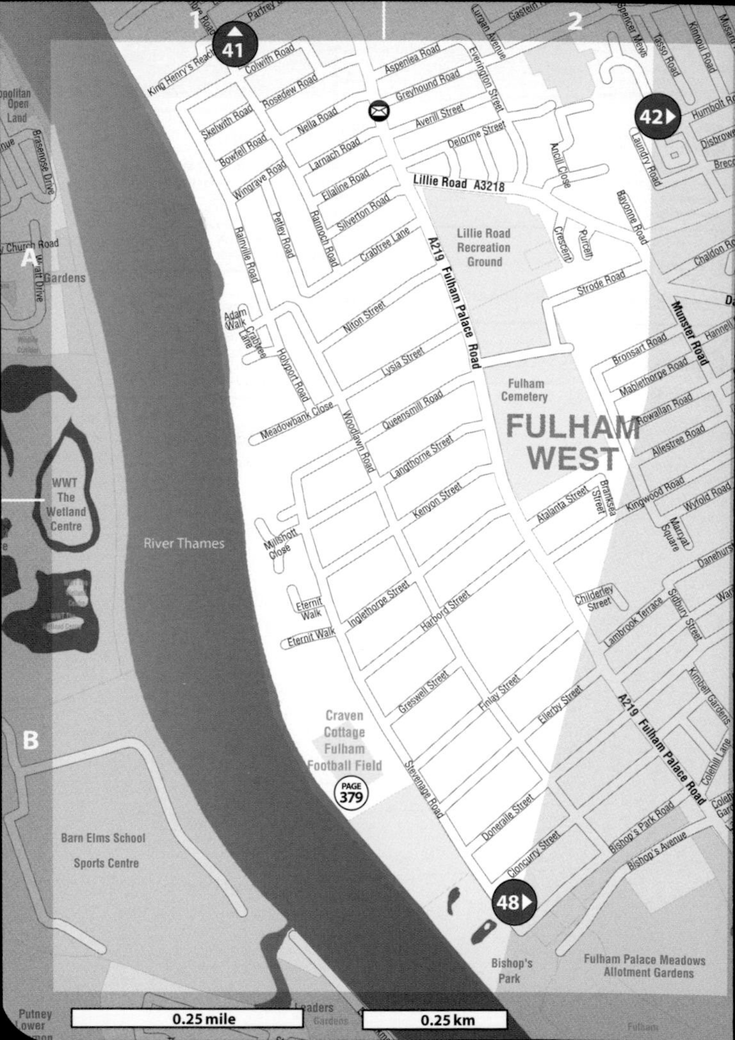

N
1
2
A
B
41
42
48
King Henry's Reach
Colwith Road
Rosedew Road
Skelwith Road
Bowfell Road
Wingrave Road
Nella Road
Larnach Road
Ellaline Road
Silverton Road
Crabtree Lane
Aspenlea Road
Greyhound Road
Averill Street
Delorme Street
Lurgan Avenue
Everington Street
Ancill Close
Lillie Road A3218
Lillie Road Recreation Ground
Crescent
Purcell
Strode Road
Bayonne Road
Laundry Road
Spencer Mews
Tasso Road
Kinnoul Road
Humbolt Road
Rainville Road
Petley Road
Rannoch Road
A219 Fulham Palace Road
Adam Walk
Crabtree Lane
Niton Street
Lysia Street
Holyport Road
Meadowbank Close
Woodlawn Road
Queensmill Road
Langthorne Street
Kenyon Street
Fulham Cemetery
FULHAM WEST
Munster Road
Bronsart Road
Mablethorpe Road
Rowallan Road
Allestree Road
Kingwood Road
Wyfold Road
Atalanta Street
Branksea Street
Marryat Square
Danehurst
Millshott Close
Eternit Walk
Inglethorpe Street
Harbord Street
Childerley Street
Lambrook Terrace
Sidbury Street
Greswell Street
Finlay Street
Ellerby Street
Kimbell Gardens
Colehill Lane
A219 Fulham Palace Road
Craven Cottage Fulham Football Field
PAGE 379
Stevenage Road
Donerale Street
Cloncurry Street
Bishop's Park Road
Bishop's Avenue
Bishop's Park
Fulham Palace Meadows Allotment Gardens
River Thames
WWT The Wetland Centre
Church Road
Gardens
Wyatt Drive
Brasenose Drive
Barn Elms School
Sports Centre
Putney
Leaders Gardens
Chaldon Road
Hannell
Disbrowe
Brecon
0.25 mile
0.25 km

Fulham (West)

This area is an estate agent's wet dream. Leafy, well-heeled, on the river, and made for families. Catch the great English game at Craven Cottage before making the most of the riverside and grabbing a pint at The Crabtree Tavern. Now that you're tipsy, head to The River Café where you'll feel less pained shelling out for top-notch, dead-posh grub.

Coffee

• **Starbucks** • 220 Fulham Palace Rd

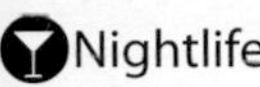

Nightlife

• **The Crabtree Tavern** • Rainville Rd

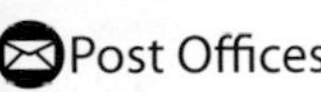

Post Offices

• **Fulham Palace Road** • 185 Fulham Palace Rd

Restaurants

• **The River Café** • Thames Wharf, Rainville Rd

Supermarkets

• **Sainsbury's** • 179 Fulham Palace Rd

Fulham
Parsons Green
Putney Bridge
Putney Bridge Tube Pill Box
Moat Gardens
Fulham Palace Meadows Allotment Gardens
Bishop's Park
Fulham Palace Gardens
Prior Bank Gardens
Hurlingham Club Gardens
Hurlingham Stadium Pitch

Dawes Road A3219
Munster Road
Fulham Road A304
Fulham Palace Road A219
Fulham High Street A219
New Kings Road A308
Fulham Park Road
Fulham Park Gardens
Hurlingham Road
Hurlingham Gardens
Ranelagh Gardens
Heathmans Road
Parsons Green Lane

0.25 mile
0.25 km

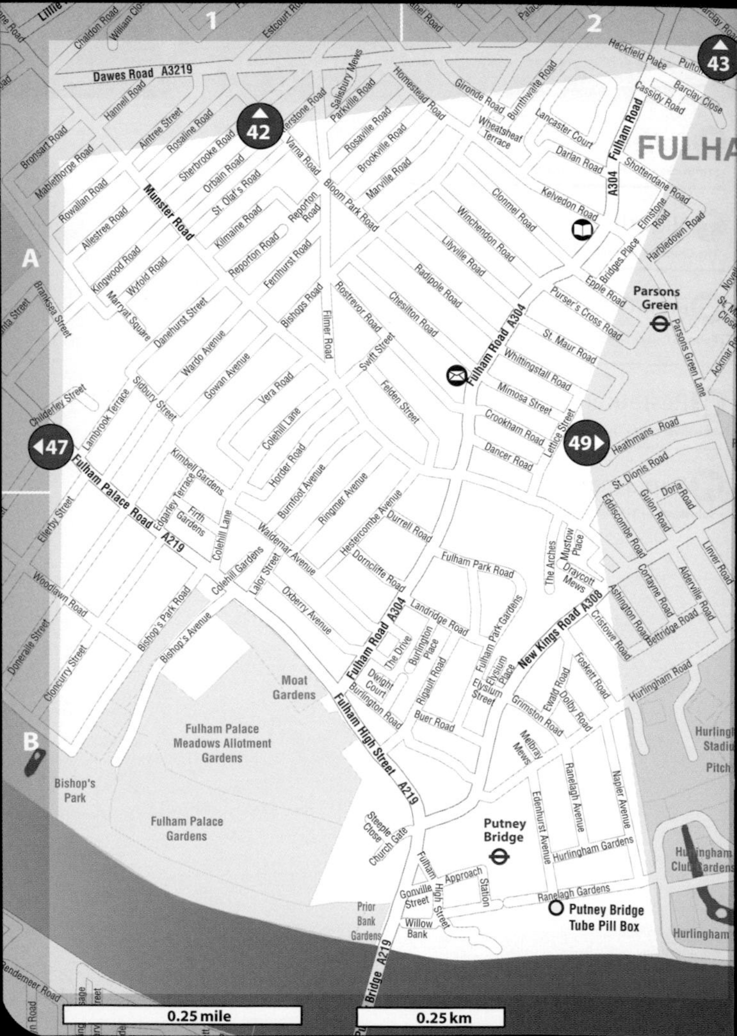

Fulham

This part of town is rather lovely and rather boring in equal measure. Expensive homes belonging to Chelsea FC players sit alongside the often overlooked romantic beauty of Fulham Palace. On the main drag of Fulham High Street is 'Hurlingham Books' with its walls stacked high with texts on anything and everything. With not much else going on away from here we suggest contemplating life while staring out at the mighty Thames in Fulham Palace Gardens. When you're done then warm up in their elegant tearoom, 'The Drawing Room'.

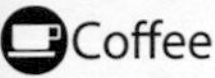

Coffee

- **Caffe Nero** • 717 Fulham Rd
- **Local Hero** • 640 Fulham Rd
- **Starbucks** • 809 Fulham Rd
- **Tinto Coffee** • 411 Fulham Palace Rd

Landmarks

- **Putney Bridge Tube Pill Box** • Putney Bridge Station

Libraries

- **Fulham Library** • 598 Fulham Rd

Nightlife

- **Wheatsheaf** • 582 Fulham Rd

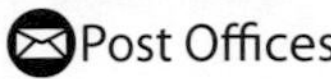

Post Offices

- **Fulham** • 815 Fulham Rd

Restaurants

- **Drawing Room Cafe** • Bishop's Ave
- **Fisher's Chips** • 19 Fulham High St

Shopping

- **Hurlingham Books** • 91 Fulham High St

N

FULHAM

Parsons Green

Eel Brook Common

Parsons Green

William Parnell Park

South Park

Hurlingham Stadium

Hurlingham Club Cricket Ground

Hurlingham Club Grounds

Hurlingham Club Gardens

Fulham Broadway A304

New Kings Road A308

King's Road A308

Harwood Road B318

Wandsworth Bridge Road A217

Fulham Road A304

Carnwath Road

Hurlingham Road

Peterborough Road

Broomhouse Lane

Broughton Road Approach

43

50

48

0.25 mile

0.25 km

River Thames

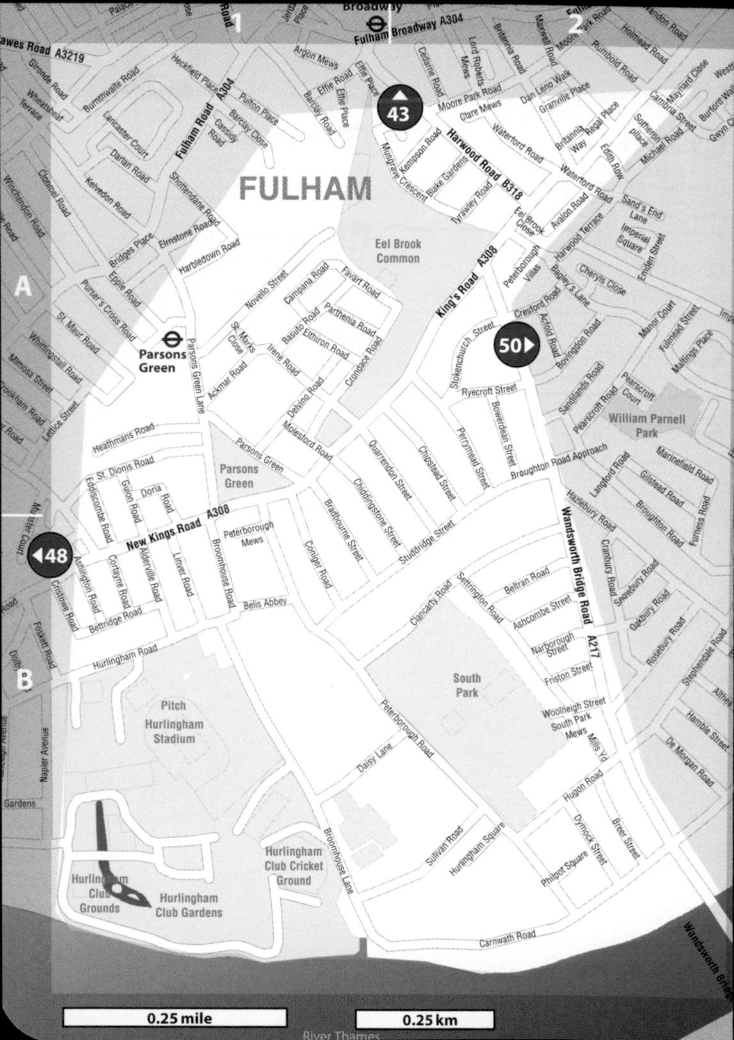

Parson's Green

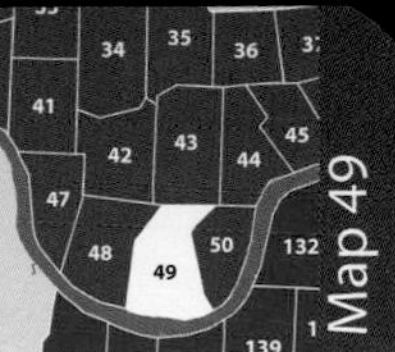

You know you're in a classy neighbourhood when the kebab house ('Kebab Kid') gets people travelling across London. This part of town ain't cheap and unless you're looking for a sedate Sunday lunch you'll most likely not find yourself here. If however, you are looking for a chow down then 'The White Horse' (known locally as the 'Sloany Pony) is the place to be, hands down. Otherwise head to charming 'Duke On The Green' for a pint in style – they even show the footy!

Coffee

- **Caffe Nero** • 142 Wandsworth Bridge Rd
- **Starbucks** • 95 Wandsworth Bridge Rd

Nightlife

- **Amuse Bouche** • 51 Parsons Green Ln
- **The Establishment** • Parsons Green Ln
- **The White Horse** • 1 Parson's Green

Restaurants

- **De Cecco** • 189 New King's Rd
- **Duke on the Green** • 235 New Kings Rd
- **Ghillies** • 271 New King's Rd
- **Kebab Kid** • 90 New Kings Rd
- **Mao Tai** • New King's Rd
- **Tendido Cuatro** • 108 New King's Rd

Supermarkets

- **Tesco** • 601 King's Rd

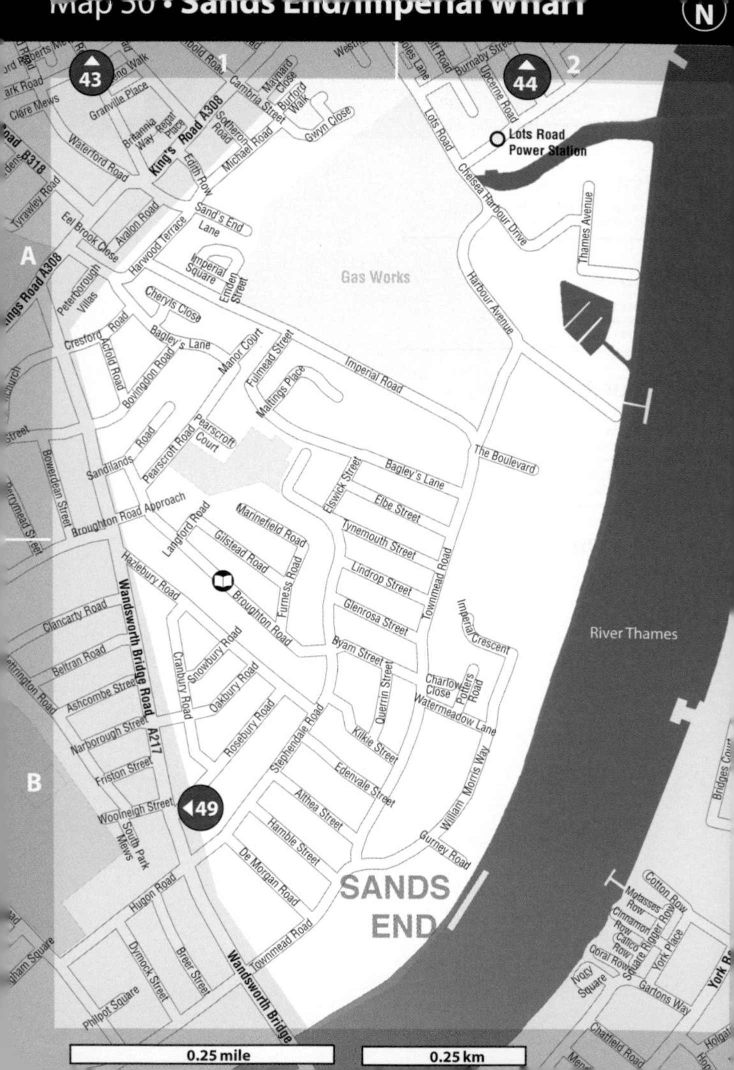
N
43
44
1
2
A
B
49
Lots Road Power Station
Gas Works
River Thames
SANDS END
Clare Mews
Granville Place
Britannia Way
Regal Place
King's Road A308
Sotheron Road
Michael Road
Cambria Street
Maynard Close
Burford Walk
Gwyn Close
Waterford Road
B318
Tyrawley Road
Edith Row
Eel Brook Close
Avalon Road
Sand's End Lane
Harwood Terrace
Imperial Square
Emden Street
Peterborough Villas
Cheryls Close
Bagley's Lane
Cresford Road
Acfold Road
Bovingdon Road
Manor Court
Fulmead Street
Maltings Place
Imperial Road
Sandilands Road
Pearscroft Road
Pearscroft Court
Bowerdean Street
Broughton Road Approach
Langford Road
Gilstead Road
Marinefield Road
Furness Road
Broughton Road
Hazlebury Road
Wandsworth Bridge Road
A217
Clancarty Road
Beltran Road
Ashcombe Street
Narborough Street
Friston Street
Woolneigh Street
South Park Mews
Cranbury Road
Snowbury Road
Oakbury Road
Rosebury Road
Stephendale Road
Elswick Street
Bagley's Lane
Elbe Street
Tynemouth Street
Lindrop Street
Glenrosa Street
Byam Street
Querrin Street
Kilkie Street
Edenvale Street
Althea Street
Hamble Street
De Morgan Road
Townmead Road
Hugon Road
Dymock Street
Breer Street
Philpot Square
Wandsworth Bridge
Lots Road
Upcerne Road
Burnaby Street
Chelsea Harbour Drive
Thames Avenue
Harbour Avenue
The Boulevard
Imperial Crescent
Charlow Close
Potters Road
Watermeadow Lane
William Morris Way
Gurney Road
Cotton Row
Molasses Row
Cinnamon Row
Calico Row
Rigger Row
Square
York Place
Coral Row
Ivory Square
Gartons Way
Chatfield Road
Bridges Court
0.25 mile
0.25 km

Sands End/Imperial Wharf

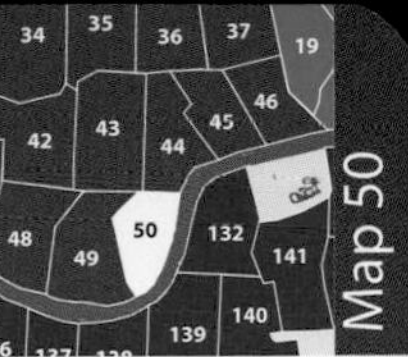

A few years ago if you asked any Londoner where Sands End was you'd receive a blank look and a bemused 'you wot?'. These days the area sees a lot more foot traffic thanks to a newish London Overground stop and the development of Imperial Wharf. Jazz seems to be a major draw to the area with the autumn Jazz Festival and the '606 Club' on Lots Road. When you're all jazzed out pop into 'The Blue Elephant' at its new location for first class Thai food.

Landmarks

- **Lots Road Power Station** • 27 Lots Rd

Libraries

- **Sands End Library** • 59 Broughton Rd

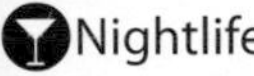

Nightlife

- **606 Club** • 90 Lots Rd

Restaurants

- **Blue Elephant** • The Boulevard
- **Sands End** • 135 Stephendale Rd

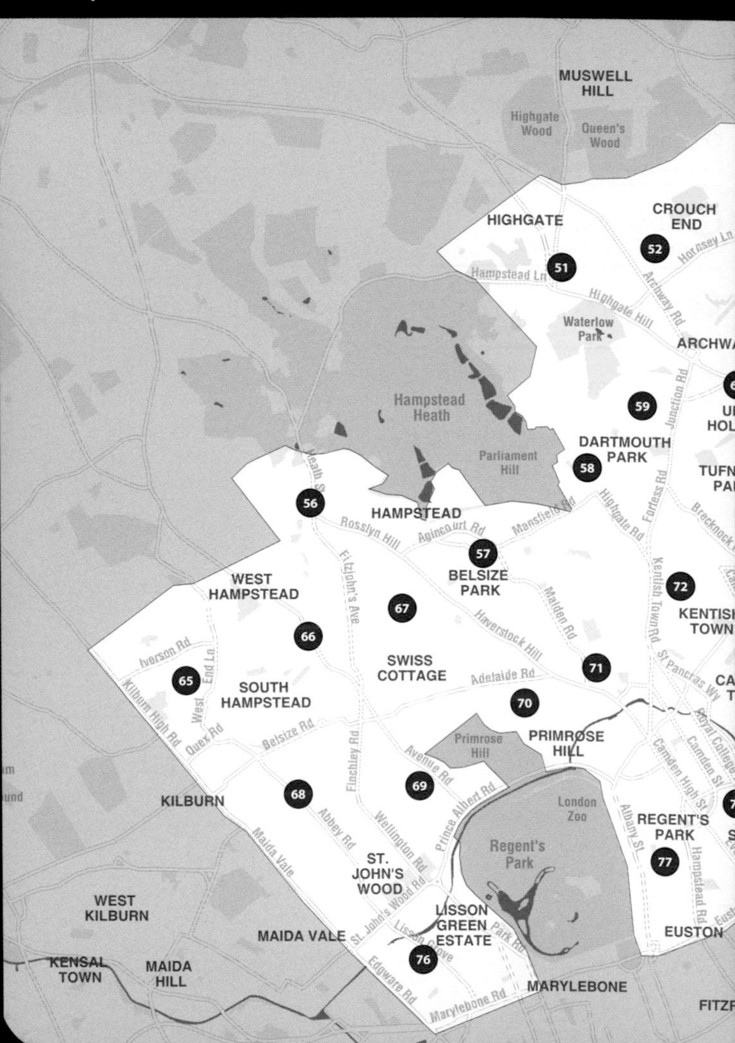
MUSWELL HILL
Highgate Wood
Queen's Wood
HIGHGATE
CROUCH END
Hornsey Ln
Hampstead Ln
Highgate Hill
Archway Rd
Waterlow Park
ARCHWAY
Hampstead Heath
Junction Rd
DARTMOUTH PARK
Parliament Hill
Heath St
HAMPSTEAD
Rosslyn Hill
Agincourt Rd
Mansfield Rd
Highgate Rd
Fortess Rd
Brecknock Rd
BELSIZE PARK
WEST HAMPSTEAD
Fitzjohn's Ave
Malden Rd
Kentish Town Rd
KENTISH TOWN
Haverstock Hill
Iverson Rd
SWISS COTTAGE
West End Ln
Kilburn High Rd
SOUTH HAMPSTEAD
Adelaide Rd
St Pancras Wy
Quex Rd
Belsize Rd
Finchley Rd
Avenue Rd
Primrose Hill
PRIMROSE HILL
Royal College St
Camden High St
Camden St
KILBURN
Abbey Rd
Prince Albert Rd
London Zoo
Albany St
REGENT'S PARK
Maida Vale
Wellington Rd
Regent's Park
ST. JOHN'S WOOD
St. John's Wood Rd
Hampstead Rd
WEST KILBURN
LISSON GREEN ESTATE
Lisson Grove
Park Rd
MAIDA VALE
EUSTON
KENSAL TOWN
MAIDA HILL
Edgware Rd
MARYLEBONE
Marylebone Rd
51
52
56
57
58
59
65
66
67
68
69
70
71
72
76
77

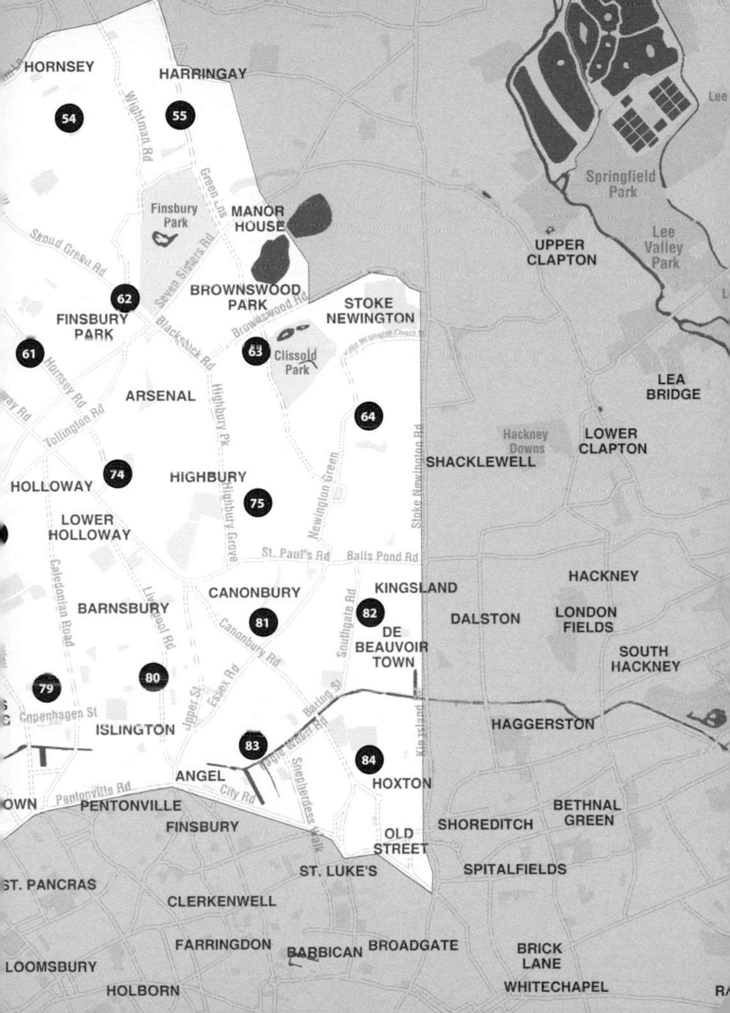

HORNSEY
HARRINGAY
54
55
Wightman Rd
Green Lns
Finsbury Park
MANOR HOUSE
Stroud Green Rd
Seven Sisters Rd
BROWNSWOOD PARK
STOKE NEWINGTON
62
FINSBURY PARK
Blackstock Rd
Brownswood Rd
61
63
Clissold Park
Hornsey Rd
ARSENAL
Highbury Pk
64
Tollington Rd
Stoke Newington Rd
SHACKLEWELL
74
HOLLOWAY
HIGHBURY
Highbury Grove
75
Newington Green
LOWER HOLLOWAY
St. Paul's Rd
Balls Pond Rd
KINGSLAND
CANONBURY
Caledonian Road
BARNSBURY
Liverpool Rd
81
Canonbury Rd
Southgate Rd
82
DE BEAUVOIR TOWN
79
80
Essex Rd
Upper St
Baring St
Copenhagen St
ISLINGTON
Kingsland
83
Eagle Wharf Rd
84
ANGEL
Shepherdess Walk
HOXTON
Pentonville Rd
City Rd
OWN
PENTONVILLE
FINSBURY
OLD STREET
ST. LUKE'S
ST. PANCRAS
CLERKENWELL
FARRINGDON
BARBICAN
BROADGATE
LOOMSBURY
HOLBORN
Lee
Springfield Park
Lee Valley Park
UPPER CLAPTON
LEA BRIDGE
Hackney Downs
LOWER CLAPTON
HACKNEY
DALSTON
LONDON FIELDS
SOUTH HACKNEY
HAGGERSTON
BETHNAL GREEN
SHOREDITCH
SPITALFIELDS
BRICK LANE
WHITECHAPEL

Map 51 • Highgate

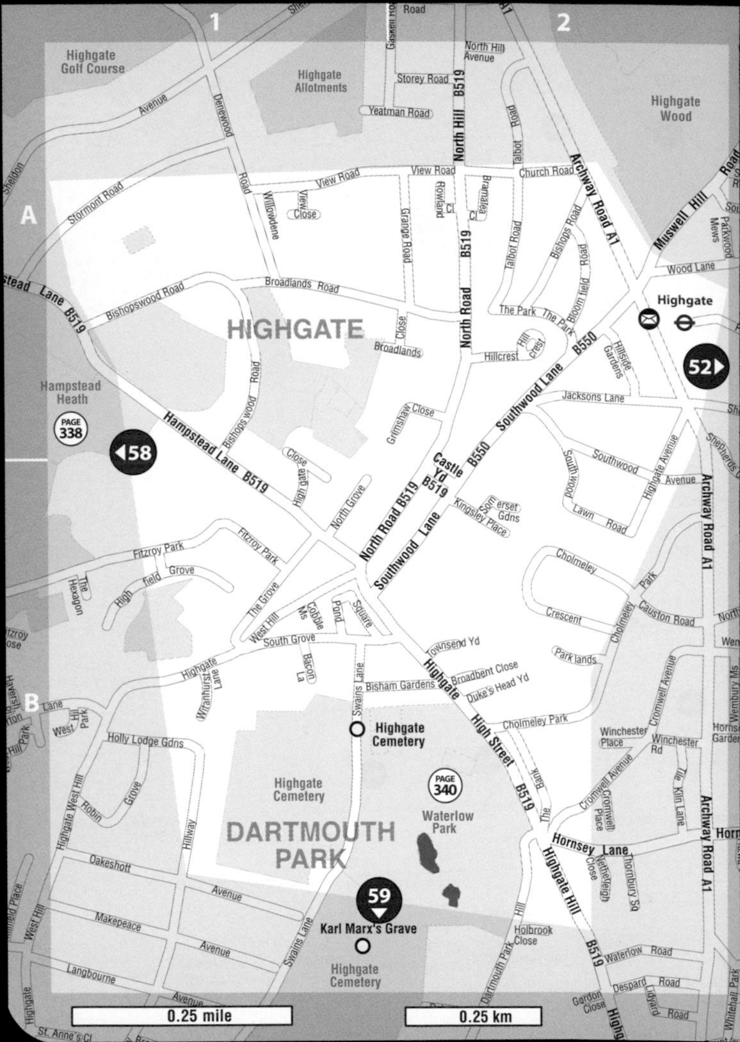

Highgate

On the cusp of north London you'll find the little suburban gem that is Highgate. Hemmed in by parks, woods and a golf course the area is an escapist paradise from the chaos of the city. The residents are well healed and pleasant and you can pop into boutique independent shops like Le Chocolatier before heading over to Highgate Woods with a bottle to enjoy live jazz during the summer.

Coffee

- **Caffe Nero** • 62 Highgate High St
- **Costa** • 66 Highgate High St

Landmarks

- **Highgate Cemetery** • 1 Swain's Lane
- **Karl Marx's Grave** • Highgate Cemetry

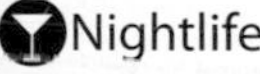

Nightlife

- **The Angel Inn** • 37 Highgate High St
- **The Boogaloo** • 312 Archway Rd
- **The Flask** • 77 Highgate West Hill
- **Prince Of Wales** • 53 Highgate High St
- **The Victoria** • 28 N Hill
- **The Woodman** • 414 Archway Rd
- **The Wrestlers** • 98 North Rd

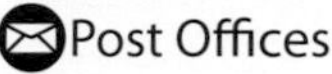

Post Offices

- **Highgate Near Station** • 361 Archway Rd

Restaurants

- **The Bull** • 13 North Hill Ave
- **Cafe Rouge** • 6 South Grove
- **Papa Del's** • 347 Archway Rd
- **Red Lion And Sun** • 25 North Rd

Shopping

- **The Corner Shop** • 88 Highgate High St
- **Dragonfly Wholefoods** • 24 Highgate High Street
- **Highgate Butchers** • 76 Highgate High St
- **Hops N Pops** • 389 Archway Rd
- **Le Chocolatier** • 78 Highgate High St
- **Mind** • 329 Archway Rd
- **Oxfam** • 80 Highgate High St
- **Second Layer Records** • 323 Archway Rd
- **Walter Castellazzo Design** • 84 Highgate High St
- **Wild Guitars** • 393 Archway Road

N

1
2
A
B

Highgate
Priory Gardens
Shepherds Hill
Shepherds Cl
Shepherd's Hill Allotments
Hill Gate Walk
Broughton Gardens
Stanhope Road
CROUCH END
Hurst Avenue
Stanhope Gardens
Wood Lane
Jacksons Lane
Holmesdale Rd
Southwood Avenue
Highgate Avenue
Lawn Road
Archway Road A1
Orchard Mews
Holmesdale Road
Orchard Road
Claremont Road
Coolhurst Lawn Tennis & Squash Rackets Club
Northwood Road
Parkland Walk Nature Reseverve
Cholmeley Crescent
Cholmeley Park
Causton Road
Milton Park
Avenue Road
Wembury Road
Langdon Park Road
Milton Avenue
Milton Road
Parkgate Mews
Maybury Ms
Wychwood End
Wembury Mews
Cromwell Avenue
Parklands
Hornsey Lane Gardens
Tudor Close
Ridgeway Gardens
Roden Court
Winchester Rd
Winchester Place
Tile Kiln Lane
Oldfield Mews
Hornsey Lane Gardens
Ridings Close
Hornsey Lane B540
Ashmount Road
Hazellville Road
Cholmeley Park
Cromwell Pl
Hornsey Lane B540
Suicide Bridge
Fitzwarren Gardens
Gresley Road
Dresden Road
Cressida Road
Highgate High Street B519
The Bank
Hornsey Lane B540
Netherleigh Cl
Thornbury Sq
Park
Whitehall Park
Cheverton Road
Gladsmuir Road
Cardinals Way
Pilgrims Way
Waterlow Park
Highgate Hill B519
Harberton Road
Waterlow Road
Archway Road A1
Hillside Park
Holbrook Close
Despard Road
Lidyard Road
Parolles Road
Prospero Road
Cressida Road
St. Johns Way
Dartmouth Park Hill
Gordon Close
Highgate Hill
Whitehall Park
Pauntley Street
Miranda Road
Lysander Mews
Lysander Grove
Duncombe Road
Mulkern Rd
Calverley Gr

51
53
60

0.25 mile
0.25 km

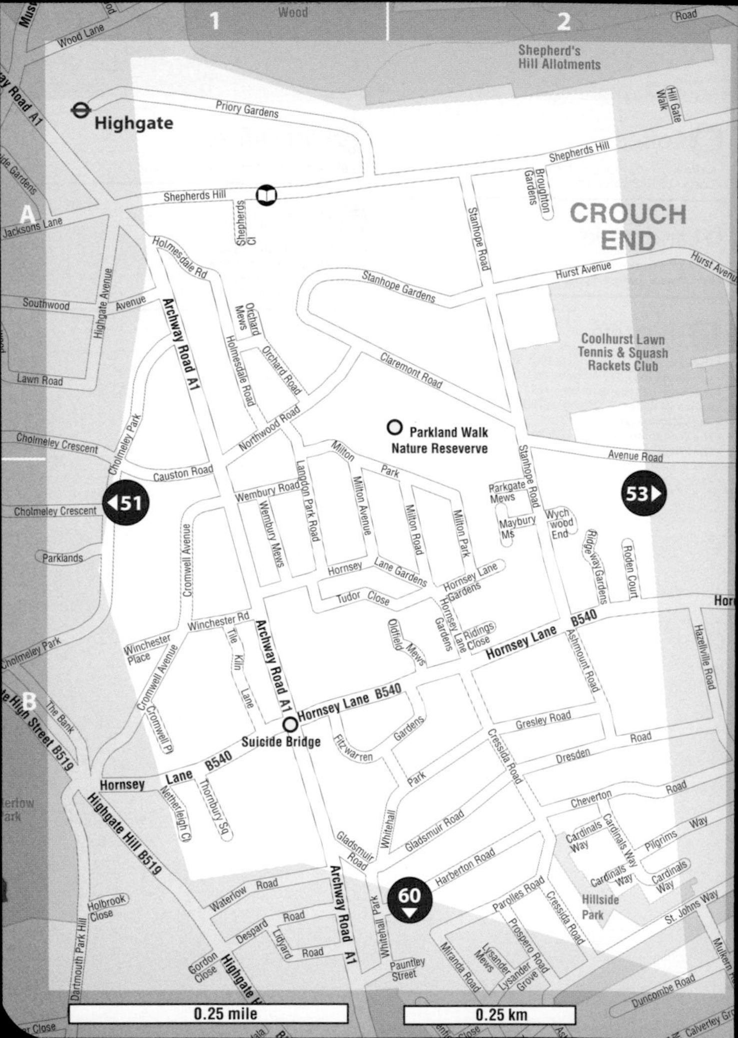

Archway (North)

Something unexpected is happening here. Designer boutiques keep popping up; fashion labels we've never even heard of. Then there's Dean & Hudson, a café so fashionably quirky it should really be in Shoreditch. But real change takes time and at night this becomes even more obvious. The Winchester is still the only decent pub around and The Caipirinha still stays open very, very late.

Landmarks

- **Parkland Walk Nature Reserve** • Parkland Walk
- **Suicide Bridge** • Hornsey Ln & Archway Rd

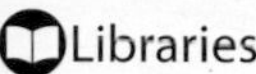

Libraries

- **London Mennonite Centre Library** • 14 Shepherds Hill Heights

Nightlife

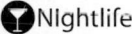

- **Caipirinha Jazz Bar** • 177 Archway Rd
- **The Winchester Pub Hotel** • 206 Archway Rd

Restaurants

- **Bengal Berties** • 172 Archway Rd
- **Dean & Hudson** • 249 Archway Rd
- **Fahrenheit** • 230 Archway Rd
- **The Lighthouse** • 179 Archway Rd

Shopping

- **Archway Cycles** • 183 Archway Rd
- **Archway Video** • 220 Archway Rd
- **The Green Room** • 192 Archway Rd
- **Pax Guns** • 166 Archway Rd
- **Wine of Course** • 216 Archway Rd

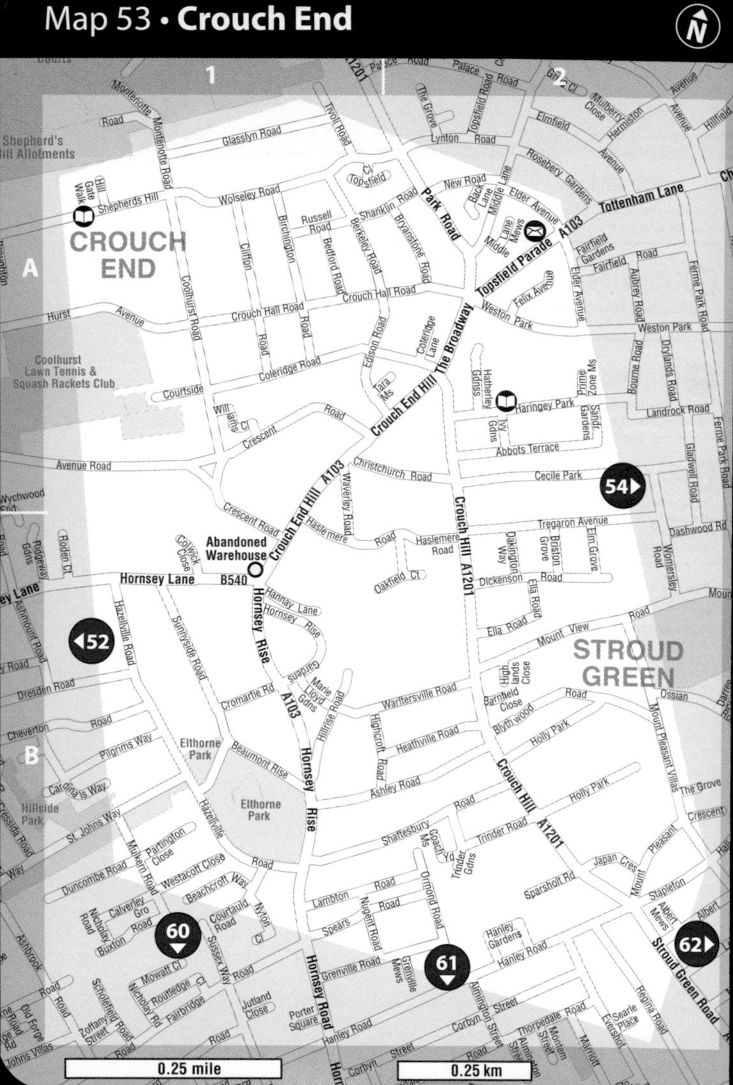
Map 53 • Crouch End
1
2
A
B
CROUCH END
STROUD GREEN
Shepherd's Hill Allotments
Coolhurst Lawn Tennis & Squash Rackets Club
Hillside Park
Elthorne Park
Abandoned Warehouse
Montenotte Road
Glasslyn Road
Tivoli Road
Palace Road
The Grove
Topsfield Road
Lynton Road
Elmfield
Mulberry Close
Hermiston Avenue
Hillfield Avenue
Rosebery Gardens
Hill Gate Walk
Shepherds Hill
Wolseley Road
Topsfield Cl
Russell Road
Shanklin Road
Park Road
New Road
Back Lane
Middle Lane
Middle Lane Mews
Elder Avenue
Tottenham Lane
A103
Topsfield Parade
Fairfield Gardens
Fairfield Road
Clifton Road
Birchington Road
Berkeley Road
Bedford Road
Bryanstone Road
Crouch Hall Road
Felix Avenue
Weston Park
Aubrey Road
Ferme Park Road
Hurst Avenue
Coolhurst Road
Edison Road
Coleridge Lane
Coleridge Road
The Broadway
Crouch End Hill
Tara Ms
Hatherley Gdns
Haringey Park
Ivy Gdns
Prime Zone Ms
Sandr. Gardens
Bourne Road
Drylands Road
Landrock Road
Courtside
Williams Cl
Crescent Road
Abbots Terrace
Avenue Road
Christchurch Road
Cecile Park
Gladwell Road
Waverley Road
Wychwood End
Haslemere Road
Tregaron Avenue
Dashwood Rd
Ridgeway Gdns
Roden Ct
Colwick Close
Crouch Hill A1201
Oakington Way
Briston Grove
Elm Grove
Womersley Road
Hornsey Lane B540
Oakfield Cl
Dickenson Road
Ella Road
Hannay Lane
Hornsey Rise
Hornsey Rise Gardens
Ashmount Road
Hazellville Road
Sunnyside Road
Mount View Road
Highlands Close
Barnfield Close
Dresden Road
Cromartie Rd
Marie Lloyd Gdns
Hillrise Road
Warltersville Road
Ossian Road
Cheverton Road
Pilgrims Way
Beaumont Rise
Highcroft Road
Heathville Road
Blythwood Road
Holly Park
Mount Pleasant Villas
Cardinals Way
Ashley Road
The Grove
Crescent
St. Johns Way
Hazellville Road
Shaftesbury Road
Trinder Road
Coach Yd Ms
Trinder Gdns
Pleasant
Mount Pleasant
Partington Close
Mulkern Road
Duncombe Road
Westacott Close
Beachcroft Way
Japan Cres
Lambton Road
Ormond Road
Sparsholt Rd
Stapleton
Nicholay Road
Calverley Gro
Buxton Road
Courtauld Road
Nyton Cl
Nugent Road
Spears Road
Albert Mews
Albert
Hanley Gardens
Hanley Road
Stroud Green Road
Ashbrook Road
Mowatt Cl
Sussex Way
Grenville Road
Grenville Mews
Almington Street
Scholefield Road
Nicholay Rd
Routledge Ct
Fairbridge Road
Jutland Close
Hornsey Road
Porter Square
Corbyn Street
Thorpedale Road
Montem Street
Evershot Road
Searle Place
Regina Road
Marriott Road
Old Forge Road
Zoffany Street
Johns Villas
52
54
60
61
62
0.25 mile
0.25 km

Crouch End

Map 53

Crouch End gets a bit of a bad rap. It's boring, people say. Just prams and middle-class media types. But, you know—it could be a lot worse. It's safe, with plenty of decent pubs (The King's Head), eateries (Banners) and a great record shop (Flashback). It might be low on the hipster scale, but for plain ol' good livin' it ticks all the boxes.

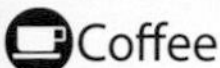

Coffee

- **Spiazzo** • 26 The Broadway
- **Starbucks** • 7 The Broadway

Landmarks

- **Abandoned Warehouse** • Parkland Walk & Crouch End Hill

Libraries

- **Highgate Library** • 1 Shepherds Hill
- **Hornsey Library** • Haringey Park

Nightlife

- **Harringay Arms** • 153 Crouch Hill
- **The King's Head** • 2 Tottenham Ln
- **The Queens Pub & Dining Rooms** • 26 Broadway Parade
- **The Wishing Well** • 22 Topsfield Parade, Tottenham Lane

Post Offices

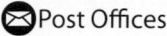

- **Crouch End** • 28 Topsfield Parade

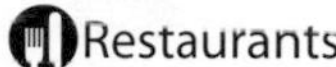

Restaurants

- **Arocaria** • 48 The Broadway
- **Banners** • 21 Park Rd
- **Hot Pepper Jelly** • 11 Broadway Parade
- **Milou's on the Hill** • 83 Hazellville Rd
- **Piya Cafe** • 59 The Broadway
- **Thaitanic** • 66 Crouch End Hill

Shopping

- **Flashback** • 144 Crouch Hill
- **Haelen Centre** • 41 The Broadway
- **Soup Dragon** • 27 Topsfield Parade
- **Walter Purkis And Sons** • 17 The Broadway

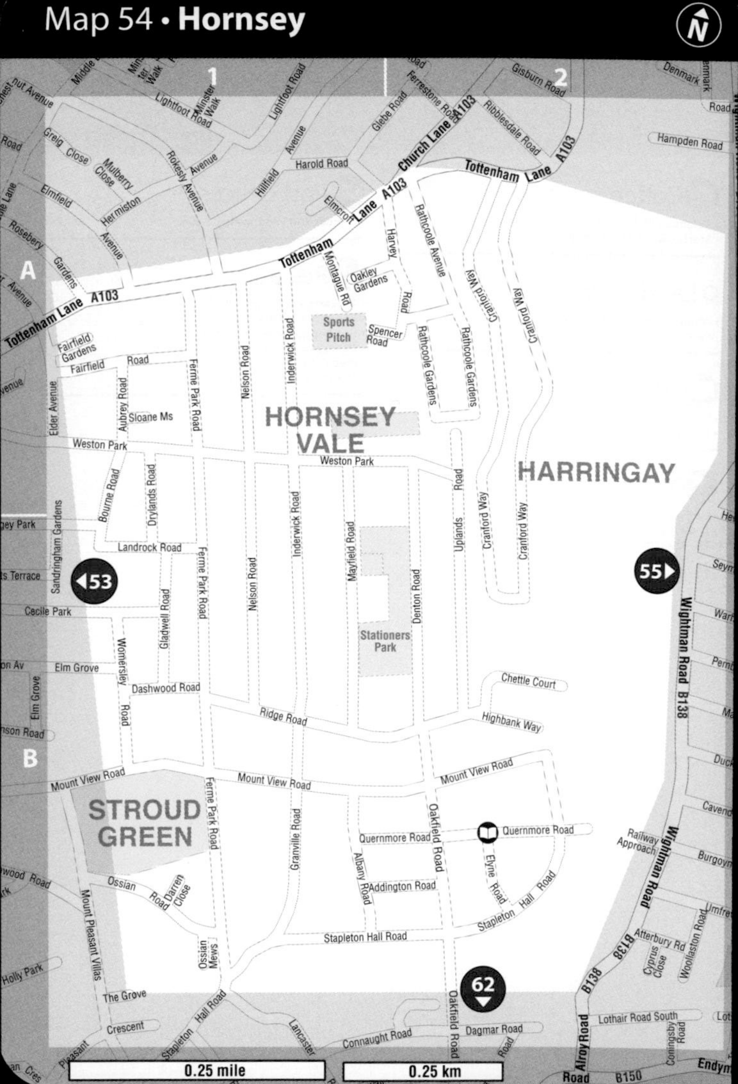
Map 54 • Hornsey
N
1
2
A
B
HORNSEY VALE
HARRINGAY
STROUD GREEN
Sports Pitch
Stationers Park
Tottenham Lane A103
Church Lane A103
Tottenham Lane A103
Lightfoot Road
Minster Walk
Rokesly Avenue
Hillfield Avenue
Harold Road
Elmcroft
Glebe Road
Ferrestone Road
Gisburn Road
Ribblesdale Road
Denmark Road
Hampden Road
Greig Close
Mulberry Close
Elmfield
Hermiston Avenue
Rosebery Gardens
Montague Rd
Oakley Gardens
Harvey Road
Rathcoole Avenue
Spencer Road
Rathcoole Gardens
Cranford Way
Fairfield Gardens
Fairfield Road
Elder Avenue
Aubrey Road
Sloane Ms
Ferme Park Road
Nelson Road
Inderwick Road
Weston Park
Bourne Road
Drylands Road
Landrock Road
Sandringham Gardens
Mayfield Road
Denton Road
Uplands Road
Cecile Park
Gladwell Road
Womersley Road
Elm Grove
Dashwood Road
Chettle Court
Highbank Way
Ridge Road
Mount View Road
Wightman Road B138
Quernmore Road
Granville Road
Albany Road
Oakfield Road
Elyne Road
Addington Road
Railway Approach
Stapleton Hall Road
Ossian Road
Darren Close
Ossian Mews
Mount Pleasant Villas
Holly Park
The Grove
Crescent
Stapleton Hall Road
Lancaster Road
Connaught Road
Dagmar Road
Atterbury Rd
Cyprus Close
Woolaston Road
Lothair Road South
Coningsby Road
Alroy Road
B150
53
55
62
0.25 mile
0.25 km

Hornsey

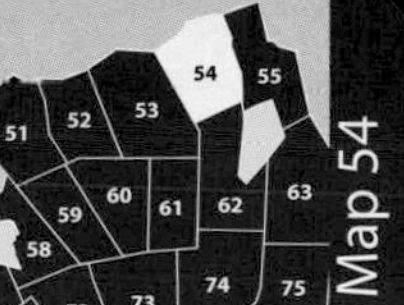

Unless you live in Hornsey, if you're in Hornsey, your bus has probably broken down. In this dystopian residential area you'll be lucky to find a tuft of grass let alone a shop. A modicum of life exist up at Tottenham Lane, but that's pretty much Crouch End. Ridge Cafe is worth a stop for a cup of co ffee and you can watch sport at the unpretentious Hope and Anchor.

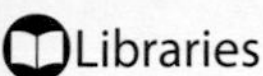

Libraries

• **Stroud Green Library** • Quernmore Rd

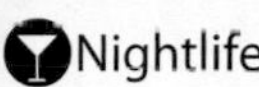

Nightlife

• **The Hope & Anchor** • 128 Tottenham Ln

Restaurants

• **Ridge Cafe** • 97 Tottenham Ln

Map 55 • Harringay

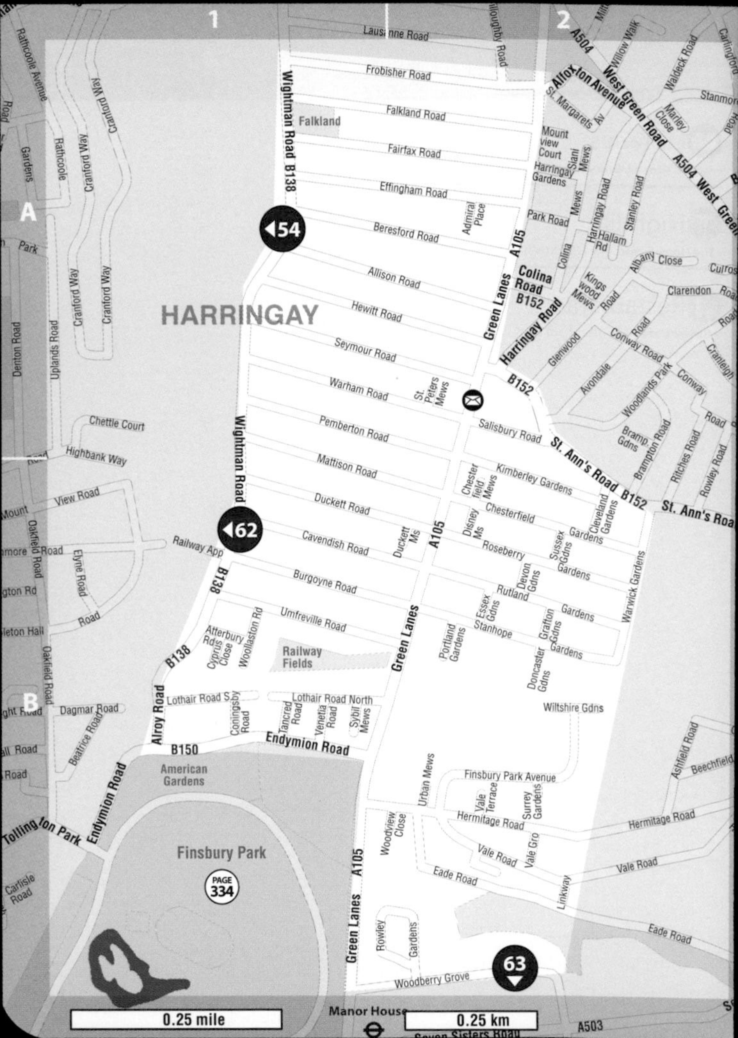

HARRINGAY

1
2
A
B

Lausanne Road
Frobisher Road
Falkland Road
Falkland
Fairfax Road
Effingham Road
Beresford Road
Admiral Place
Allison Road
Hewitt Road
Seymour Road
Warham Road
St. Peters Mews
Pemberton Road
Mattison Road
Duckett Road
Duckett Ms
Cavendish Road
Burgoyne Road
Umfreville Road
Wightman Road B138
Wightman Road
B138
Willoughby Road
A504
Alloxton Avenue
West Green Road
A504 West Green
Willow Walk
Waldeck Road
Carlingford
Stanmore Road
St. Margarets Av
Marley Close
Mount view Court
Harringay Gardens
Siani Mews
Mews
Park Road
Harringay Road
Stanley Road
Hallam Rd
Colina
Colina Road B152
Green Lanes A105
Albany Close
Culross
Clarendon Road
Kings wood Mews
Road
Harringay Road
Glenwood
Avondale
Conway Road
Woodlands Park
Conway Road
Cranleigh
B152
Salisbury Road
St. Ann's Road B152
St. Ann's Road
Bramp. Gdns
Brampton Road
Ritches Road
Rowley Road
Chesterfield Mews
Kimberley Gardens
Chesterfield Gardens
Cleveland Gardens
Disney Ms
Roseberry Gardens
Sussex Gdns
Devon Gdns
Rutland Gardens
Warwick Gardens
Essex Gdns
Stanhope Gardens
Grafton Gdns
Portland Gardens
Doncaster Gdns
Wiltshire Gdns
Green Lanes
Railway Fields
Atterbury Rd
Cyprus Close
Woollaston Rd
Lothair Road South
Lothair Road North
Coningsby Road
Tancred Road
Venetia Road
Sybil Mews
Alroy Road
B150
Endymion Road
American Gardens
Finsbury Park
PAGE 334
Urban Mews
Finsbury Park Avenue
Vale Terrace
Surrey Gardens
Hermitage Road
Woodview Close
Vale Road
Vale Gro
Eade Road
Linkway
Ashfield Road
Beechfield
Green Lanes A105
Rowley Gardens
Woodberry Grove
Manor House
Seven Sisters Road
A503

Rathcoole Avenue
Rathcoole Gardens
Cranford Way
Park
Denton Road
Uplands Road
Chettle Court
Highbank Way
View Road
Mount
Oakfield Road
Elyne Road
Railway App
Road
Dagmar Road
Beatrice Road
Endymion Road
Tollington Park
Carlisle Road

◀54
◀62
63 ▼

0.25 mile
0.25 km

Harringay

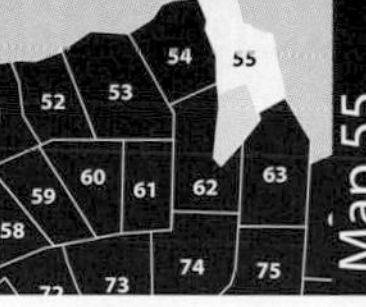

A walk up Green Lanes is a pretty grim experience. Roughly one gazillion kebab places, a bunch of jewellers, a horrid-looking wedding shop and, well, not much else. Eventually, the Garden Ladder provides a glimmer of hope with cheap guest ales and finally, at the very end of the ladder, there's a different culinary option at Muna's, London's premier Sudanese restaurant.

Coffee

- **Cafe Delight** • 351 Green Lanes
- **Mezzo Shisha Lounge** • 64 Grand Parade

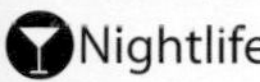

Nightlife

- **The Beaconsfield** • 359 Green Lanes
- **The Garden Ladder** • 501 Green Lanes
- **The Salisbury** • 1 Grand Parade, Green Lanes

Post Offices

- **Harringay** • 509 Green Lanes

Restaurants

- **Muna's** • 599 Green Lanes
- **The Village** • 421 Green Lanes

Supermarkets

- **Sainsbury's** • 4 Williamson Rd

Map 56 • Hampstead Village

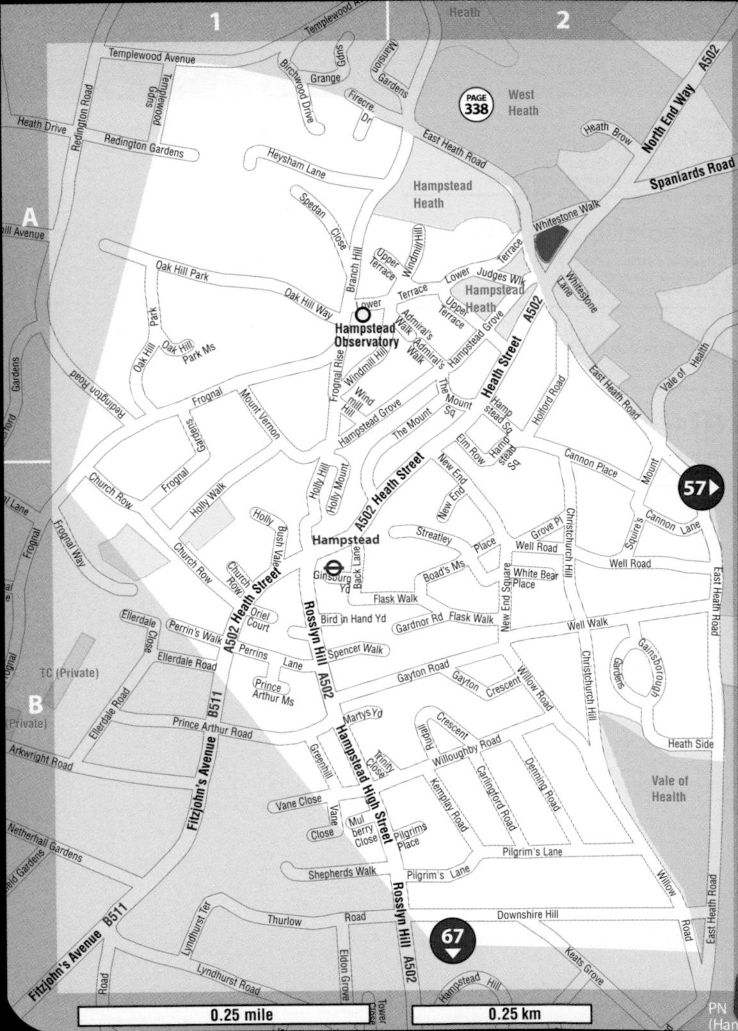

PAGE 338

57

67

0.25 mile

0.25 km

Hampstead Village

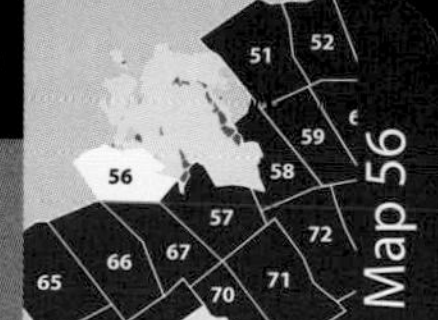

Sure, leafy Hampstead Village defines posh, but there is still some fun to be had. Head to Flask Walk for cute and eccentric local shops and, of course, waffles at Slice of Ice. The Duke of Hamilton is as good a pub you're likely to find anywhere and when they kick you out, much like the bankers kicked out the literary-types from the area there is always Tinsletown.

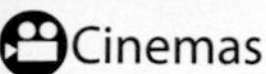

Cinemas

- **Everyman Cinema Club** • 5 Hollybush Vale

Coffee

- **Caffe Nero** • 1 Hampstead High St
- **Ginger & White** • 4 Perrin's Ct

Landmarks

- **Hampstead Observatory** • Lower Terrace & Hampstead Grove

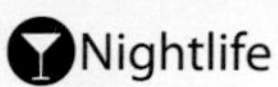

Nightlife

- **The Duke of Hamilton** • 23 New End
- **The Flask** • 14 Flask Walk
- **The Freemasons Arms** • 32 Downshire Hill
- **Holly Bush** • 22 Holly Mount
- **The Rosslyn Arms** • 48 Rosslyn Hill

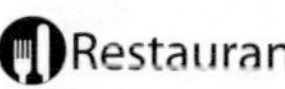

Restaurants

- **Bacchus Greek Taverna** • 37 Heath St
- **Carluccio's** • 34 Rosslyn Hill
- **La Creperie De Hampstead** • 77 Hampstead High St
- **The Louis Patisserie** • 32 Heath St
- **Tinseltown** • 104 Heath St

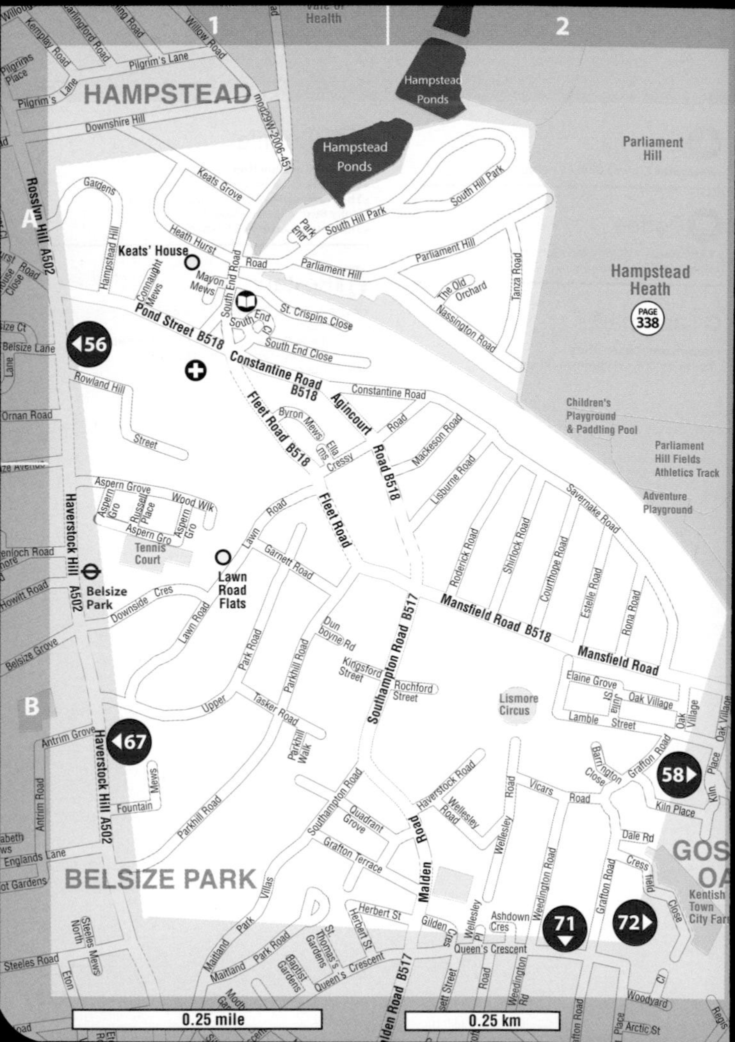
HAMPSTEAD
Hampstead Ponds
Hampstead Ponds
Parliament Hill
Hampstead Heath
PAGE 338
Keats' House
Lawn Road Flats
Belsize Park
Tennis Court
Children's Playground & Paddling Pool
Parliament Hill Fields Athletics Track
Adventure Playground
Lismore Circus
Kentish Town City Farm
BELSIZE PARK
Pilgrim's Lane
Downshire Hill
Keats Grove
Heath Hurst Road
South End Road
Pond Street B518
Constantine Road B518
Fleet Road B518
Agincourt Road B518
Fleet Road
Mansfield Road B518
Mansfield Road
Southampton Road B517
Malden Road
Haverstock Hill A502
Rosslyn Hill A502
South Hill Park
Parliament Hill
Nassington Road
Tanza Road
The Old Orchard
St. Crispins Close
South End Close
Savernake Road
Lisburne Road
Mackeson Road
Roderick Road
Shirlock Road
Courthope Road
Estelle Road
Rona Road
Aspern Grove
Wood Wlk
Garnett Road
Lawn Road
Downside Cres
Park Road
Parkhill Road
Tasker Road
Upper Park Road
Kingsford Street
Rochford Street
Elaine Grove
Oak Village
Lamble Street
Vicars Road
Grafton Road
Haverstock Road
Wellesley Road
Quadrant Grove
Grafton Terrace
Herbert St
Gilden Cres
Queen's Crescent
Weedington Road
Maitland Park Villas
Belsize Grove
Belsize Lane
Rowland Hill Street
Antrim Grove
Fountain Mews
Englands Lane
Steeles Road
0.25 mile
0.25 km
56
67
58
71
72

Hampstead Heath

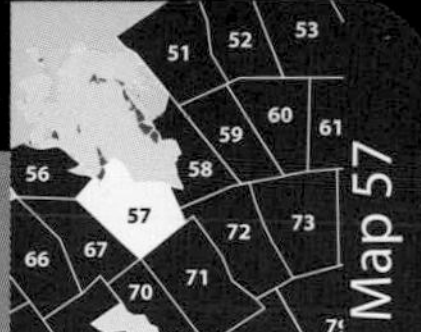

Believed to be the inspiration for CS Lewis's Narnia, Hampstead Heath was absorbed into London proper during the Victoria era but still feels more like one of the Home Counties. With the exception of the blight on the landscape that is the Royal Free Hospital, the area is charming with boutique shops and restaurants on the South End Road, which cater to a refined and heavy wallet type crowd.

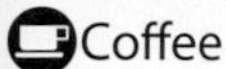

Coffee

- **Starbucks** • 5 South End Rd

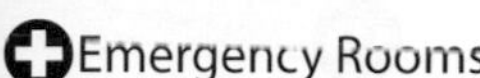

Emergency Rooms

- **Royal Free Hospital** • Pond St & Fleet Rd

Landmarks

- **John Keats House** • 38 Heath Hurst Road
- **Lawn Road Flats** • Lawn Rd & Garnett Rd

Libraries

- **Heath Library** • Keats Grove

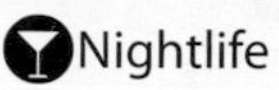

Nightlife

- **The Garden Gate** • 14 S End Rd
- **The Magdala** • 2 South Hill Park
- **Roebuck** • 15 Pond St

Restaurants

- **Hampstead Tea Rooms** • 9 South End Rd
- **Osteria Emilia** • 85 Fleet Rd
- **Paradise** • 49 South End Rd
- **Polly's** • 55 South End Rd

Shopping

- **Daunt Books** • 51 South End Rd
- **Giocobazzi's Delicatessen** • 150 Fleet Rd

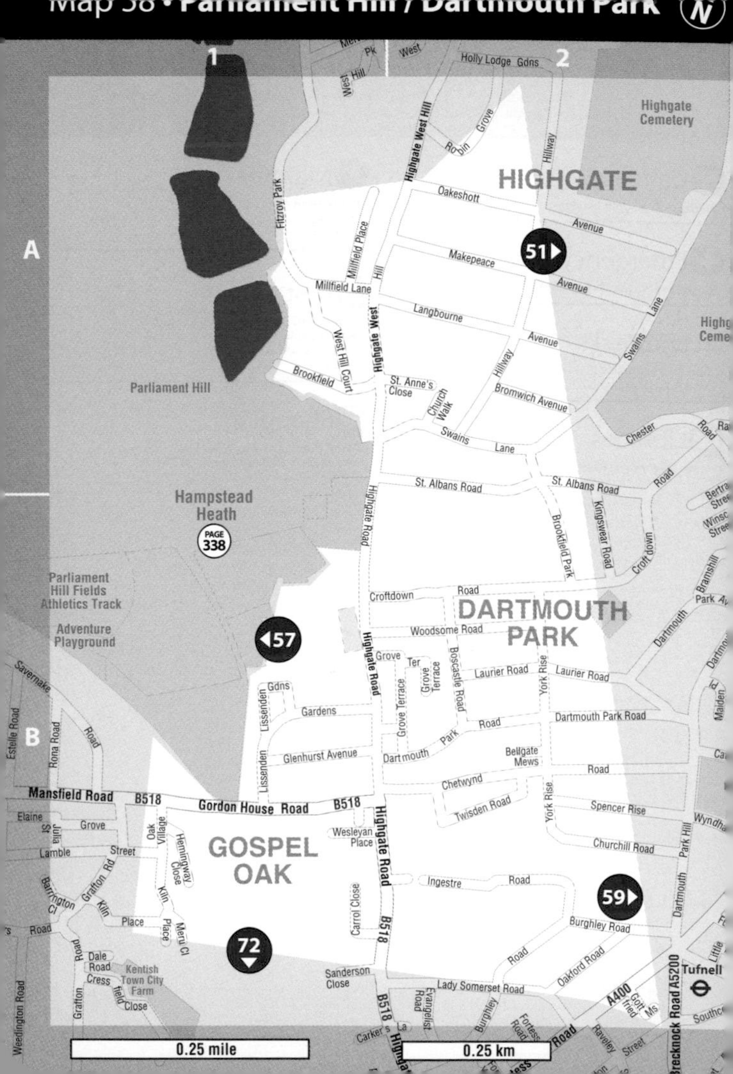

HIGHGATE
Highgate Cemetery
DARTMOUTH PARK
GOSPEL OAK
Hampstead Heath
Parliament Hill
Parliament Hill Fields Athletics Track
Adventure Playground
Kentish Town City Farm
PAGE 338
51
57
59
72
Highgate West Hill
Oakeshott Avenue
Makepeace Avenue
Langbourne Avenue
Millfield Lane
Millfield Place
Fitzroy Park
West Hill Court
Brookfield
St. Anne's Close
Church Walk
Hillway
Bromwich Avenue
Swains Lane
Holly Lodge Gdns
Robin Grove
Chester Road
St. Albans Road
Brookfield Park
Kingswear Road
Croftdown Road
Highgate Road
Woodsome Road
Grove Ter
Grove Terrace
Boscastle Road
York Rise
Laurier Road
Dartmouth Park Road
Lissenden Gdns
Lissenden Gardens
Glenhurst Avenue
Dartmouth Park Road
Bellgate Mews
Chetwynd Road
Twisden Road
Spencer Rise
Churchill Road
Mansfield Road
B518
Gordon House Road
Wesleyan Place
Oak Village
Hemingway Close
Kiln Place
Meru Cl
Grafton Rd
Barrington Cl
Lamble Street
Elaine Grove
Julia St
Savernake Road
Estelle Road
Rona Road
Ingestre Road
Carrol Close
Burghley Road
Oakford Road
Lady Somerset Road
Sanderson Close
Dale Road
Cressfield Close
Grafton Road
Weedington Road
Evangelist Road
Fortess Road
Carker's La
Gotfried Ms
A400
Brecknock Road A5200
Raveley Street
Park Hill
Dartmouth Park Hill
Tufnell
0.25 mile
0.25 km

Parliament Hill / Dartmouth Park

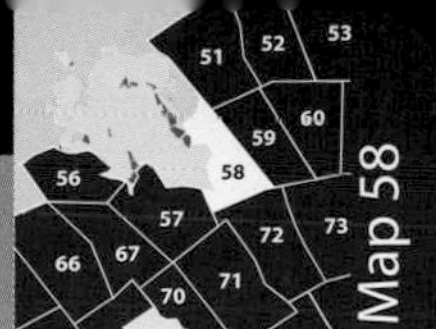

An area you stumble upon by accident, on your way somewhere else, probably Hampstead Heath or Highgate Cemetery. Then you realize how nice it is. Maybe you should try the little restaurants? Soon you find yourself having pizza at Al Parco every week and trekking all across London just to find out what new ales they're serving at the Southampton Arms. You could live here. You really could.

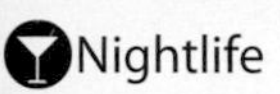

Nightlife

- **Bar Lorca** • 156 Fortress Rd
- **The Bull and Last** • 168 Highgate Rd
- **The Dartmouth Arms** • 35 York Rise
- **Duke of St. Albans** • Highgate Road
- **The Southampton Arms** • 139 Highgate Rd

Restaurants

- **Al Parco** • 2 Highgate West Hill
- **Cafe Mozart** • 17 Swain's Ln
- **The Carob Tree** • 15 Highgate Rd
- **Kalendar** • 15 Swains Lane
- **Stingray Cafe** • 135 Fortess Rd

Shopping

- **Corks** • 9 Swain's Ln

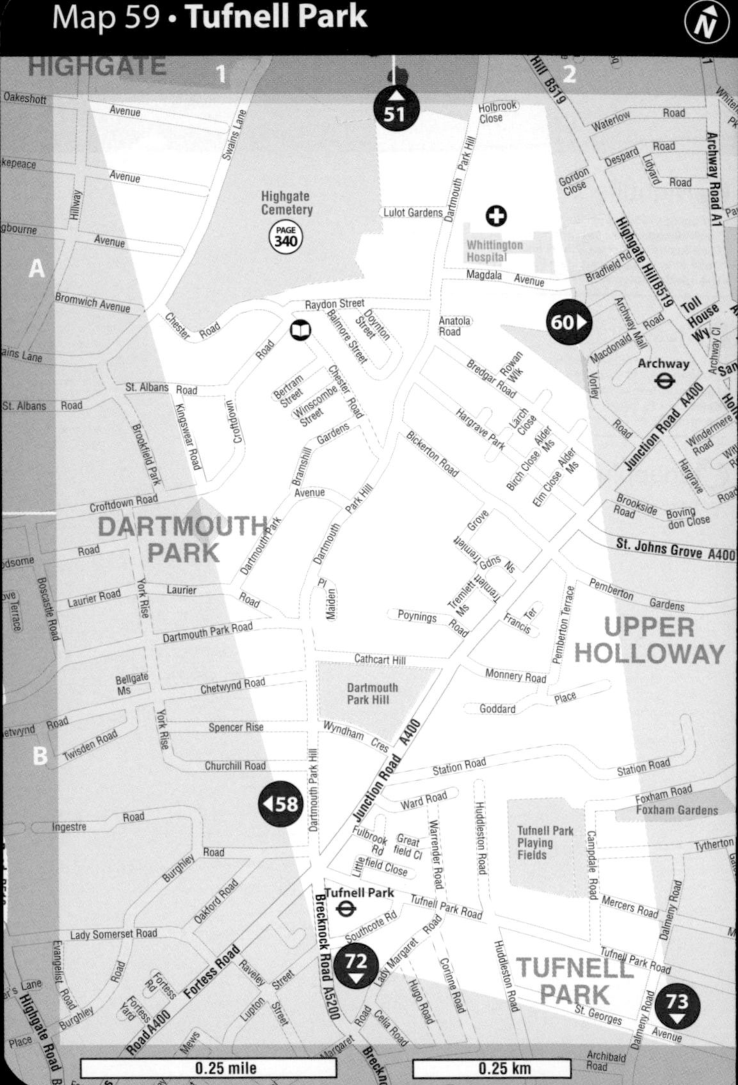
HIGHGATE
1
2
A
B
51
60
58
72
73
Highgate Cemetery
PAGE 340
Whittington Hospital
DARTMOUTH PARK
UPPER HOLLOWAY
TUFNELL PARK
Dartmouth Park Hill
Tufnell Park Playing Fields
Archway
Tufnell Park
Oakeshott Avenue
Swains Lane
Holbrook Close
Highgate Hill B519
Waterlow Road
Despard Road
Lidyard Road
Gordon Close
Archway Road A1
Hillway
Lulot Gardens
Dartmouth Park Hill
Magdala Avenue
Bradfield Rd
Highgate Hill B519
Toll House Wy
Archway Cl
Bromwich Avenue
Chester Road
Raydon Street
Balmore Street
Doynton Street
Anatola Road
Archway Mall
Macdonald Road
Vorley Road
St. Albans Road
Kingswear Road
Croftdown Road
Bertram Street
Winscombe Street
Chester Road
Bredgar Road
Rowan Wlk
Hargrave Park
Larch Close
Birch Close
Alder Ms
Elm Close
Junction Road A400
Windermere Road
Hargrave Road
Brookfield Park
Bramshill Gardens
Bickerton Road
Croftdown Road
Avenue
Park Hill
Dartmouth Park Avenue
Brookside Road
Bovingdon Close
St. Johns Grove A400
Grove
Tremlett Gdns
Tremlett Ms
Tremlett Ns
Road
Laurier Road
Boscastle Road
York Rise
Maiden Pl
Poynings Road
Francis Ter
Pemberton Terrace
Pemberton Gardens
Dartmouth Park Road
Cathcart Hill
Monnery Road
Bellgate Ms
Chetwynd Road
Goddard Place
Twisden Road
Spencer Rise
Wyndham Cres
Churchill Road
Station Road
Ward Road
Huddleston Road
Foxham Road
Foxham Gardens
Ingestre Road
Fulbrook Rd
Greatfield Cl
Littlefield Close
Warrender Road
Campdale Road
Tytherton
Burghley Road
Oakford Road
Tufnell Park Road
Mercers Road
Dalmeny Road
Southcote Rd
Lady Somerset Road
Evangelist Road
Fortess Road
Fortess Rd
Fortess Yard
Road A400
Raveley Street
Lupton Street
Brecknock Road A5200
Lady Margaret Road
Hugo Road
Corinne Road
Celia Road
Huddleston Road
Tufnell Park Road
St. Georges Avenue
Archibald Road
Highgate Road
Mews
0.25 mile
0.25 km

Tufnell Park

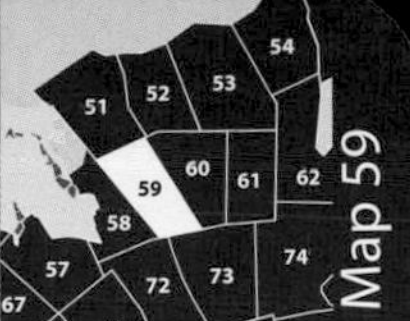

Surrounded by the rougher Archway, Kentish Town, and Holloway and immortalised by Simon Pegg in cult comedies *Spaced* and *Shaun of the Dead*, unassuming Tufnell Park has been quietly fashionable for years. Unwind with a book and a coffee at Rustique, or hit Nuraghe Trattoria for some of the finest Italian food in London. The Dome hosts everything from the latest cutting-edge electronica to seasoned indie rock acts.

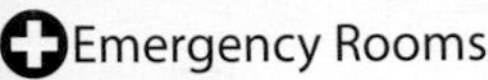

Emergency Rooms

- **Whittington Hospital** • Magdala Ave & Dartmouth Park Hill

Libraries

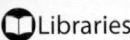

- **Highgate Library** • Chester Rd

Nightlife

- **Boston Arms** • 178 Junction Rd
- **The Dome** • 178 Junction Rd
- **The Hideaway** • 114 Junction Rd
- **The Lord Palmerston** • 33 Dartmouth Park Hill
- **The Star** • 47 Chester Rd

Restaurants

- **Charuwan** • 110 Junction Rd
- **Nuraghe Trattoria** • 12 Dartmouth Park Hill
- **Rustique Cafe** • 142 Fortess Rd
- **Spaghetti House** • 169 Fortess Rd
- **The Spice** • 161 Fortess Rd

Shopping

- **The Blue Carbuncle** • 130 Junction Rd
- **The Hornsey Trust Charity Shop** • 124 Fortess Rd
- **North London Adoption Centre** • 135 Junction Rd

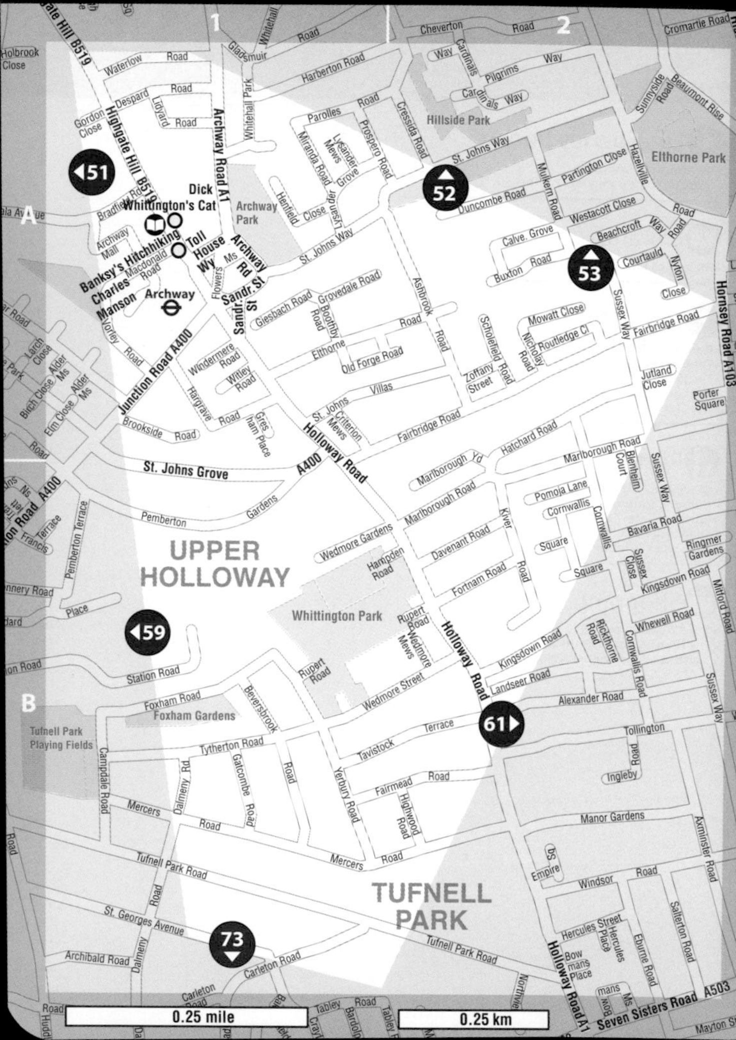

1
2
A
B
51
52
53
59
61
73
Dick Whittington's Cat
Toll House Wy
Banksy's Hitchhiking Charles Manson
Archway
Archway Park
Hillside Park
Elthorne Park
Whittington Park
Foxham Gardens
Tufnell Park Playing Fields
UPPER HOLLOWAY
TUFNELL PARK
Highgate Hill B519
Archway Road A1
Junction Road A400
Holloway Road
A400
Hornsey Road A103
Holloway Road A1
Seven Sisters Road A503
Holbrook Close
Waterlow Road
Despard Road
Lidyard Road
Gordon Close
Whitehall Park
Gladsmuir Road
Harberton Road
Parolles Road
Miranda Road
Lysander Mews
Lysander Grove
Prospero Road
Cressida Road
Cheverton Road
Cardinals Way
Pilgrims Way
St. Johns Way
Duncombe Road
Mulkern Road
Partington Close
Hazellville Road
Westacott Close
Beachcroft Way
Sunnyside Road
Beaumont Rise
Cromartie Road
Calve. Grove
Buxton Road
Courtauld Road
Nyton Close
Sussex Way
Fairbridge Road
Mowatt Close
Routledge Cl
Nicholay Road
Scholefield Road
Zoffany Street
Jutland Close
Porter Square
Hentfield Close
Bradford Rd
Archway Mall
Macdonald Road
Vorley Road
Flowers Ms
Sandr. St
Giesbach Road
Grovedale Road
Boothby Road
Elthorne Road
Old Forge Road
Ashbrook Road
Windermere Road
Wittey Road
Hargrave Road
St. Johns Villas
Criterion Mews
Gresham Place
Brookside Road
St. Johns Grove
Pemberton Gardens
Pemberton Terrace
Francis Terrace
Larch Close
Alder Ms
Birch Close
Elm Close
Hatchard Road
Marlborough Yd
Marlborough Road
Marlborough Court
Blenheim Court
Pomoja Lane
Cornwallis Square
Wedmore Gardens
Hampden Road
Davenant Road
River Road
Fortnam Road
Bavaria Road
Sussex Close
Ringmer Gardens
Kingsdown Road
Mitford Road
Whewell Road
Rickthorne Road
Cornwallis Road
Rupert Road
Wedmore Mews
Wedmore Street
Landseer Road
Alexander Road
Station Road
Foxham Road
Beversbrook Road
Tollington Road
Tavistock Terrace
Tytherton Road
Gatcombe Road
Campdale Road
Dalmeny Rd
Yerbury Road
Fairmead Road
Highwood Road
Ingleby Road
Mercers Road
Manor Gardens
Tufnell Park Road
Empire Sq
Windsor Road
Arminster Road
St. Georges Avenue
Archibald Road
Carleton Road
Hercules Street
Hercules Place
Bowmans Place
Bowmans Ms
Eburne Road
Sallerton Road
Tabley Road
Mayton St
0.25 mile
0.25 km

Archway

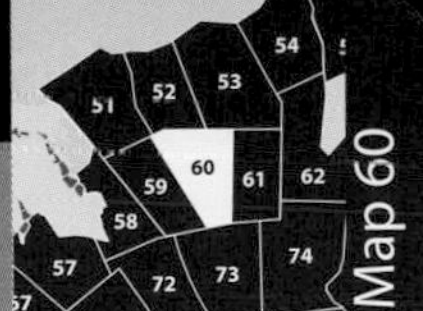

As grey and gritty as ever, Archway could really do with a fresh lick of paint. For a break from the grime try La Voute with their art exhibitions and awesome breakfasts or RRC Thai for something spicier. At night, there are enough old man boozers to keep you busy, but bear in mind, nicer places are only a short bus ride away.

Coffee

- **Cafe Metro** • 4 Junction Rd

Landmarks

- **Banksy's Hitchhiking Charles Manson** • Tally Ho Corner (off Highgate Hill)
- **Dick Whittington's Cat** • 89 Highgate Hill

Libraries

- **Archway Library** • Highgate Hill

Nightlife

- **Archway Tavern** • 1 Archway Close
- **The Mother Red Cap** • 665 Holloway Rd

Restaurants

- **Archgate Café** • 5 Junction Rd
- **Iceland Fish Bar** • 11 Archway Rd
- **Junction Café** • 61 Junction Rd
- **La Voute** • 10 Archway Rd
- **Mosaic Café** • 24 Junction Rd
- **Nid Ting** • 533 Holloway Rd
- **RRC Thai Café** • 36 Highgate Hill
- **St Johns** • 91 Junction Rd
- **The Toll Gate** • 6 Archway Close

Shopping

- **Second Chance** • 7 St John's Way
- **Super Persia** • 621 Holloway Rd

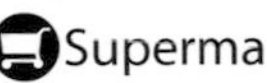

Supermarkets

- **Co-Op** • 11 Junction Rd
- **Sainsbury's** • 643 Holloway Rd

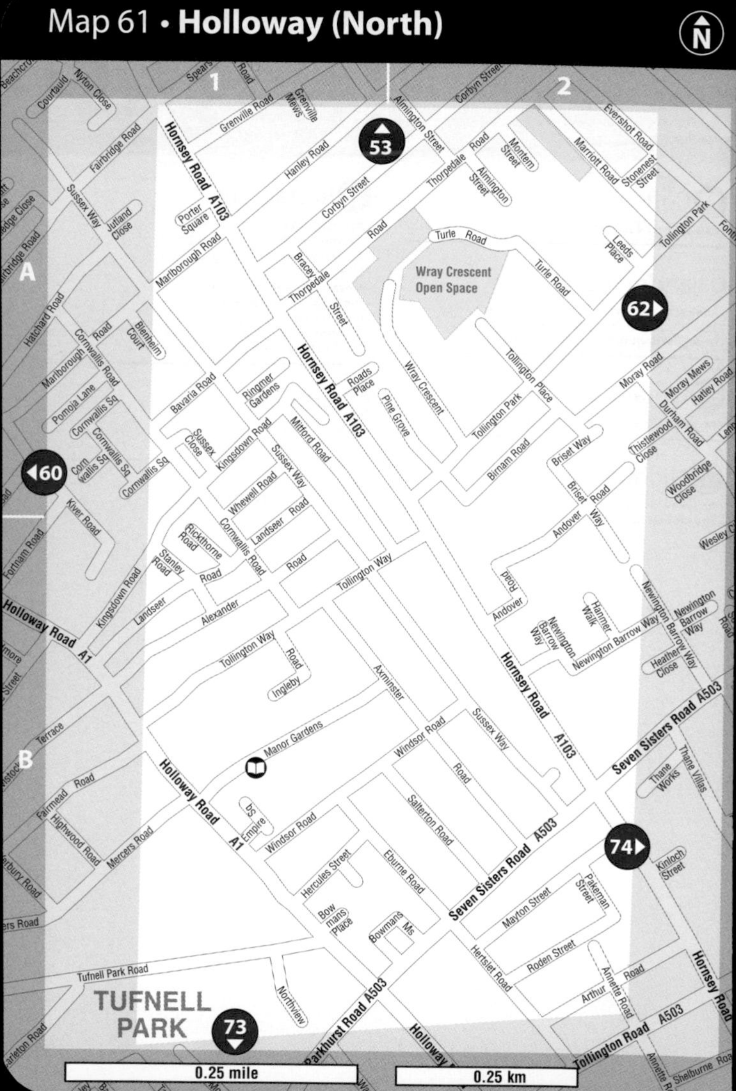
Map 61 • Holloway (North)
N
1
2
A
B
53
62
60
74
73
Nyton Close
Courtauld
Spears Road
Grenville Road
Grenville Mews
Almington Street
Corbyn Street
Evershot Road
Marriott Road
Stonenest Street
Montem Street
Thorpedale Road
Almington Street
Hornsey Road A103
Hanley Road
Fairbridge Road
Sussex Way
Jutland Close
Porter Square
Corbyn Street
Turle Road
Leeds Place
Tollington Park
Marlborough Road
Bracey Street
Thorpedale Road
Wray Crescent Open Space
Turle Road
Hatchard Road
Cornwallis Road
Blenheim Court
Marlborough Road
Pomoja Lane
Cornwallis Sq
Bavaria Road
Ringmer Gardens
Roads Place
Pine Grove
Wray Crescent
Tollington Place
Moray Road
Moray Mews
Hatley Road
Durham Road
Tollington Park
Thistlewood Close
Sussex Close
Kingsdown Road
Mitford Road
Sussex Way
Birnam Road
Briset Way
Briset Road
Briset Way
Woodbridge Close
Cornwallis Sq
Whewell Road
Landseer Road
Andover Road
Wesley Close
River Road
Fortnam Road
Rickthorne Road
Stanley Road
Cornwallis Road
Road
Tollington Way
Road
Hammer Walk
Andover Road
Newington Barrow Way
Newington Barrow Way
Newington Barrow Way
Holloway Road A1
Kingsdown Road
Landseer
Alexander Road
Tollington Way
Ingleby Road
Axminster Road
Hornsey Road A103
Heather Close
Seven Sisters Road A503
Terrace
Manor Gardens
Windsor Road
Sussex Way Road
Thane Works
Thane Villas
Fairmead Road
Highwood Road
Holloway Road A1
Empire Sq
Windsor Road
Salterton Road
Seven Sisters Road A503
Kinloch Street
Mercers Road
Hercules Street
Eburne Road
Pakeman Street
Mayton Street
Bowmans Place
Bowmans Ms
Hertslet Road
Roden Street
Hornsey Road
Tufnell Park Road
Northview
Annette Road
Arthur Road
TUFNELL PARK
Parkhurst Road A503
Holloway
Tollington Road A503
Annette Road
Shelburne Road
0.25 mile
0.25 km

Holloway (North)

The borough of Islington, in which North Holloway sits, is supposed to be either a byword for liberal middle class cosiness or else grim inner city deprivation, depending on who you talk to. This bit has neither, just lots of dull grey streets. The Shaftesbury brightens up Hornsey Road with good pub food and unusual beers, while El Molino (down on Holloway Road) is a great place for tapas.

Coffee

- **Caffe Nero** • 400 Holloway Rd

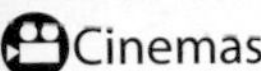

Cinemas

- **Odeon Holloway** • 419 Holloway Rd

Libraries

- **North Library** • Manor Gardens

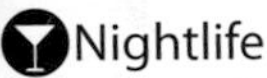

Nightlife

- **The Quays** • 471 Holloway Rd
- **The Swimmer** • 13 Eburne Rd

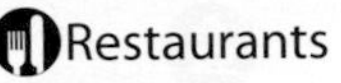

Restaurants

- **El Molino** • 379 Holloway Rd
- **The Landseer** • 37 Landseer Rd
- **North Nineteen** • 194 Sussex Way
- **Orexi** • 236 Hornsey Rd
- **Tagine D' Or** • 92 Seven Sisters Rd

Shopping

- **Michael's Fruiterers** • 56 Seven Sisters Rd

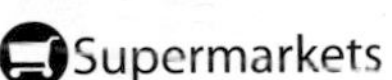

Supermarkets

- **Iceland** • 442 Holloway Rd

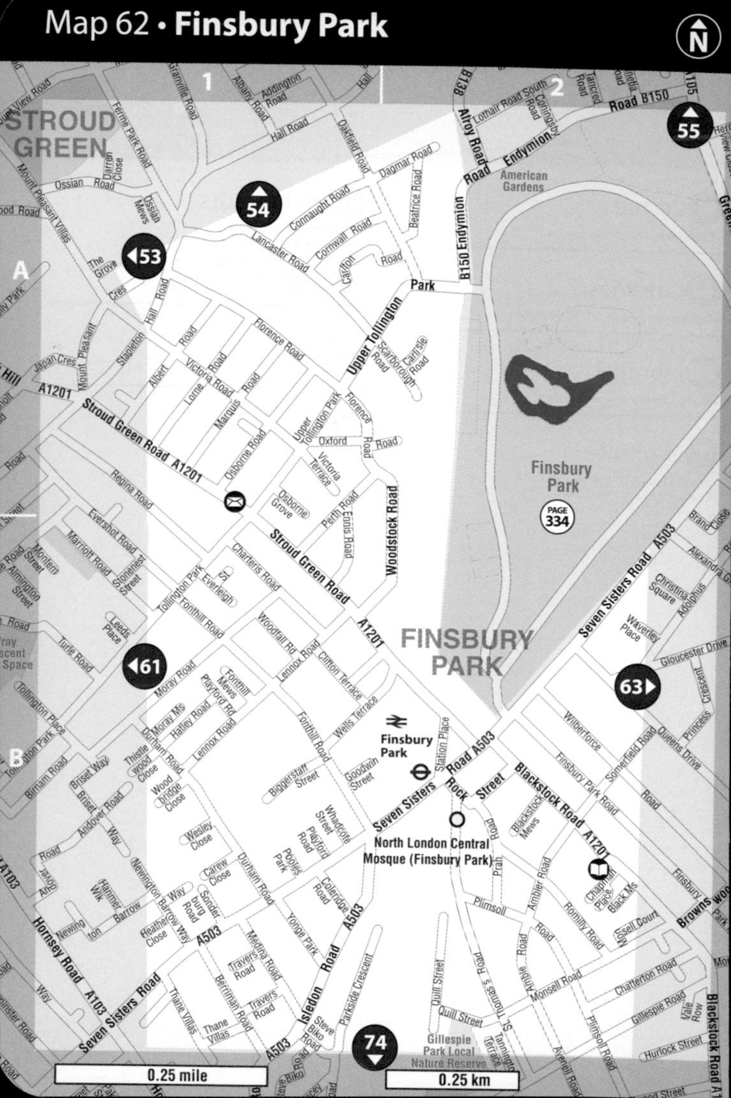

Map 62 • Finsbury Park
N
1
2
A
B
STROUD GREEN
54
53
55
61
63
74
FINSBURY PARK
Finsbury Park
PAGE 334
American Gardens
Finsbury Park
North London Central Mosque (Finsbury Park)
Gillespie Park Local Nature Reserve
Stroud Green Road A1201
Seven Sisters Road A503
Blackstock Road A1201
Hornsey Road A103
Isledon Road A503
Upper Tollington Park
Endymion Road
B150 Endymion Road
Mount Pleasant Villas
Ferme Park Road
Lancaster Road
Florence Road
Victoria Road
Osborne Road
Woodstock Road
Regina Road
Evershot Road
Marriott Road
Tollington Park
Fonthill Road
Charteris Road
Moray Road
Lennox Road
Clifton Terrace
Wells Terrace
Durham Road
Andover Road
Wilberforce
Finsbury Park Road
Somerfield Road
Queens Drive
Princess Crescent
Gloucester Drive
Alexandra Grove
Christina Square
Waverley Place
Brand Close
Romilly Road
Ambler Road
Monsell Road
Chatterton Road
Gillespie Road
Plimsoll Road
Quill Street
St Thomas's Road
Parkside Crescent
Yonge Park
Medina Road
Berriman Road
Thane Villas
Travers Road
Steve Biko Road
Dagmar Road
Connaught Road
Cornwall Road
Oakfield Road
Hall Road
Albany Road
Addington Road
Granville Road
Ossian Road
Ossian Mews
Darren Close
Stapleton Hall Road
Japan Cres
Albert Road
Lorne Road
Marquis Road
Oxford Road
Victoria Terrace
Osborne Grove
Perth Road
Ennis Road
Stonenest Street
Everleigh St
Leeds Place
Turle Road
Tollington Place
Birnam Road
Briset Way
Thistlewood Close
Woodbridge Close
Wesley Close
Carew Close
Hatley Road
Playford Rd
Moray Ms
Fonthill Mews
Bigger staff Street
Goodwin Street
Whadcote Street
Playford Road
Coleridge Road
Station Place
Rock Street
Prah Road
Blackstock Mews
Chapman Place
Black Ms
Monsell Court
Plimsoll
Ambler Road
Amble Road
Hurlock Street
Vale Row
Browns wood Park
Heather Close
Sonderburg Road
Barrow Way
Hammer Wk
Newington Barrow Way
Lothair Road South
Coningsby Road
Alroy Road
Beatrice Road
Carlton Road
Scarborough Road
Carlisle Road
Lennox Road
Woodfall Rd
0.25 mile
0.25 km

Finsbury Park

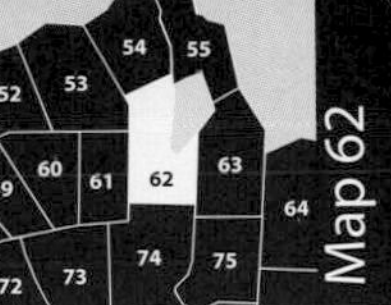

On the surface Finsbury Park has it all, but look closer and you'll find a tube and overground station that are oddly inconvenient, a park that's oddly ugly, and residents that say they live in Angel. However, the area has promise: they've invested £5 million in the park, the North London Mosque does excellent outreach programmes, The Silver Bullet packs atmosphere with its pints, and Dudley's does London's best pancakes.

Landmarks

- **North London Central Mosque (Finsbury Park)** • 7 St Thomas's Rd

Libraries

- **N4 Library** • 26 Blackstock Road

Nightlife

- **The Faltering Fullback** • 19 Perth Rd
- **The Silver Bullet** • 5 Station Pl

Post Offices

- **Stroud Green Rd** • 97 Stroud Green Rd

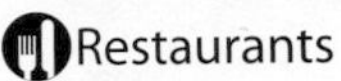

Restaurants

- **Dudley's Pancake House** • 119 Stroud Green Rd
- **Fassika** • 152 Seven Sisters Rd
- **Le Rif** • 172 Seven Sisters Rd
- **Petek** • 96 Stroud Green Rd

Shopping

- **The Happening Bagel Bakery** • 284 Seven Sisters Rd

Supermarkets

- **Tesco** • 105 Stroud Green Rd

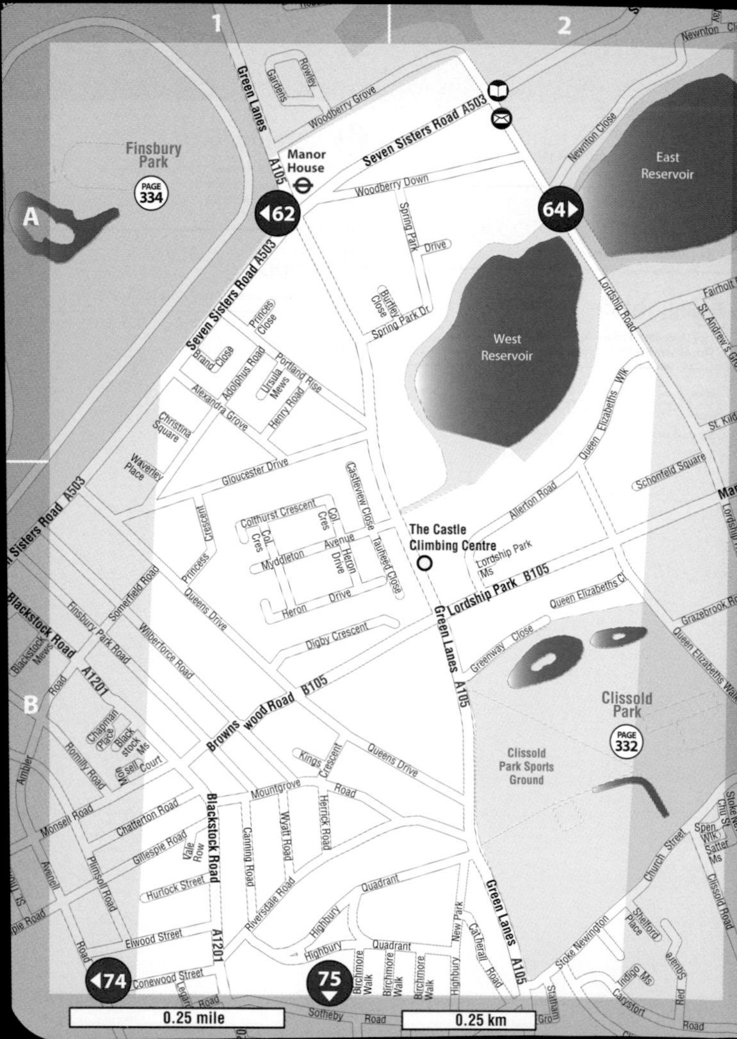

Finsbury Park
PAGE 334
Manor House
Green Lanes A105
Seven Sisters Road A503
Woodberry Grove
Rowley Gardens
Woodberry Down
Newnton Close
East Reservoir
West Reservoir
Spring Park Drive
Burtley Close
Spring Park Dr
Lordship Road
Princes Close
Brand Close
Adolphus Road
Portland Rise
Ursula Mews
Henry Road
Alexandra Grove
Christina Square
Waverley Place
Gloucester Drive
Castleview Close
Queen Elizabeths Wlk
Allerton Road
Schonfeld Square
Colthurst Crescent
Col. Cres
Myddleton Avenue
Heron Drive
Tauheed Close
The Castle Climbing Centre
Lordship Park Ms
Lordship Park B105
Queen Elizabeths Cl
Princess Crescent
Queens Drive
Somerfield Road
Finsbury Park Road
Wilberforce Road
Digby Crescent
Greenway Close
Grazebrook Rd
Queen Elizabeths Walk
Blackstock Road
Blackstock Mews
A1201
Brownswood Road B105
Clissold Park
PAGE 332
Clissold Park Sports Ground
Chapman Place
Blackstock Ms
Romilly Road
Monsell Court
Kings Crescent
Queens Drive
Mountgrove Road
Herrick Road
Wyatt Road
Canning Road
Monsell Road
Chatterton Road
Gillespie Road
Vale Row
Hurlock Street
Plimsoll Road
Avenell Road
Riversdale Road
Highbury Quadrant
Church Street
Stoke Newington Church St
Spenser Wlk
Satter Ms
Clissold Road
Shelford Place
Catherall Road
New Park
Elwood Street
Conewood Street
Legard Road
Birchmore Walk
Highbury
Stoke Newington
Indigo Ms
Carysfort Road
Red Square
Statham Gro
Sotheby Road
Fairholt
St. Andrew's Gro
St. Kilda
Newnton Cl
0.25 mile
0.25 km

◀62
64▶
◀74
75▼

Manor House

Don't hang out near the 'scummy round the edges' station as it can get pretty gruesome at night, particularly round the horrific Manor Club. You might chance upon a warehouse party round here, but walk south, dodge the rats around the reservoir, admire the faux turrets of the Castle Climbing Centre, and head to the New River Café for great fry-ups with views over the leafy oasis of Clissold Park.

Landmarks

- **The Castle Climbing Centre** • Green Lanes & Lordship Park

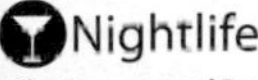

Libraries

- **Woodberry Down Library** • 440 7 Sisters Rd

Nightlife

- **The Brownswood Park Tavern** • 271 Green Lanes
- **The Happy Man** • 89 Woodberry Grove
- **The Manor Club** • 277 Seven Sisters Rd

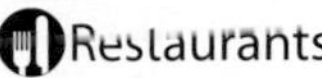

Post Offices

- **Woodberry Grove** • 107 Woodberry Grove

Restaurants

- **Il Bacio** • 178 Blackstock Rd
- **New River Café** • 271 Stoke Newington Church St

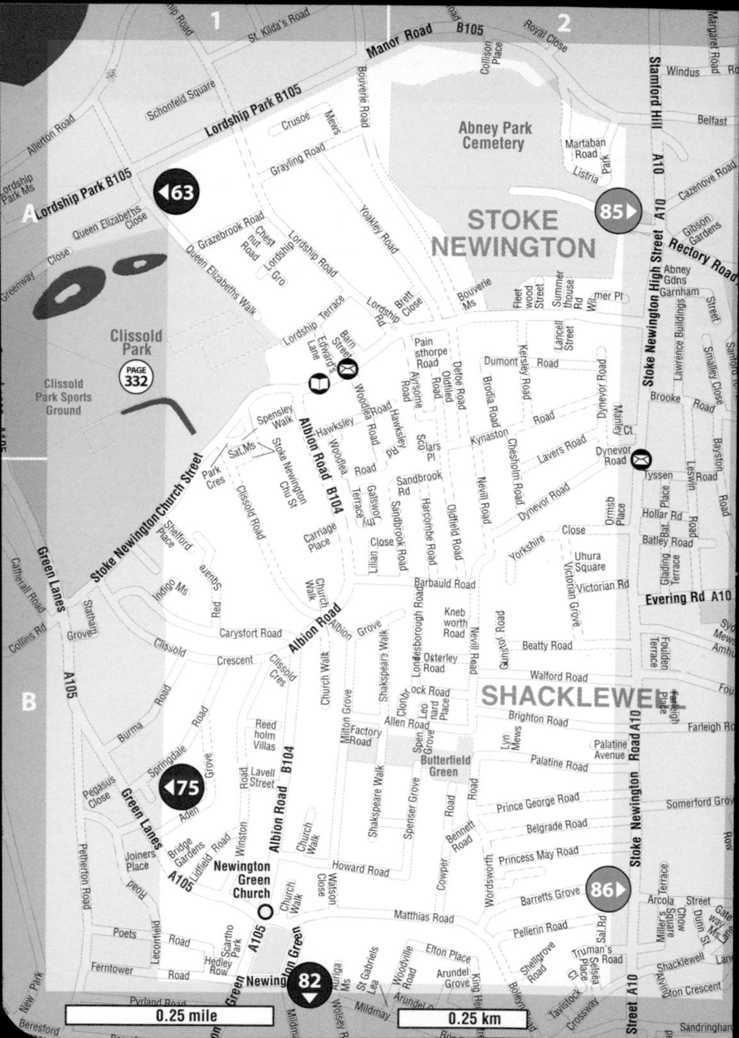

Map 64 • Stoke Newington

N

STOKE NEWINGTON

SHACKLEWELL

Abney Park Cemetery

Clissold Park

PAGE 332

Clissold Park Sports Ground

Newington Green Church

Butterfield Green

63
85
75
86
82

1
2
A
B

Manor Road
B105
Lordship Park B105
St. Kilda's Road
Royal Close
Collison Place
Schonfeld Square
Allerton Road
Lordship Park Ms
Queen Elizabeths Close
Greenway Close
Crusoe Mews
Grayling Road
Bouverie Road
Yoakley Road
Grazebrook Road
Chestnut Road
Lordship Gro
Lordship Road
Queen Elizabeths Walk
Lordship Terrace
Lordship Rd
Brett Close
Bouverie Ms
Barn Street
Edward's Lane
Woodlea Road
Hawksley Road
Hawksley Rd
Spensley Walk
Sat Ms
Stoke Newington Chu St
Albion Road B104
Park Cres
Clissold Road
Stoke Newington Church Street
Shelford Place
Carriage Place
Church Walk
Red Square
Indigo Ms
Green Lanes
Catherall Road
Collins Rd
Statham Grove
Carysfort Road
Clissold Crescent
Clissold Cres
Albion Road
Albion Grove
A105
Burma Road
Springdale Road
Grove
Pegasus Close
Aden
Green Lanes
Bridge Gardens
Lidfield Road
Winston Road
Joiners Place
Petherton Road
A105
Reedholm Villas
Lavell Street
Albion Road B104
Church Walk
Howard Road
Watson Close
Church Walk
Poets Road
Leconfield Road
Scartho Park
Hedley Row
Ferntower Road
Newington Green
Pyrland Road
New Park
Beresford
Martaban Road
Listria Park
Stamford Hill A10
Windus Road
Margaret Road
Belfast
Cazenove Road
Gibson Gardens
Rectory Road
Abney Gdns
Garnham Street
Fleetwood Street
Summerhouse Rd
Wilmer Pl
Lancell Street
Painsthorpe Road
Aysome Road
Oldfield Road
Defoe Road
Dumont Road
Kersley Road
Brodia Road
Dynevor Road
Lawrence Buildings
Smalley Close
Stoke Newington High Street
Brooke Road
Manley Ct
Kynaston Road
Chesholm Road
Lavers Road
Dynevor Road
Tyssen Road
Leswin Road
Bayston Road
Scolars Pl
Sandbrook Rd
Gatsworth Terrace
Harcombe Road
Oldfield Road
Nevill Road
Dynevor Road
Ormsby Place
Hollar Rd
Bat Place
Batley Road
Lillian Close
Sandbrook Road
Yorkshire Close
Uhura Square
Victorian Grove
Victorian Rd
Glading Terrace
Evering Rd A10
Barbauld Road
Londesborough Road
Knebworth Road
Gunstor Road
Beatty Road
Osterley Road
Nevill Road
Walford Road
Shakspeare Walk
Milton Grove
Clonbrock Road
Leonard Place
Allen Road
Spenser Grove
Factory Road
Brighton Road
Lyn Mews
Palatine Avenue
Palatine Road
Farleigh Place
Farleigh Rd
Fouldon Terrace
Stoke Newington Road A10
Shakspeare Walk
Spenser Grove
Bennett Road
Prince George Road
Belgrade Road
Princess May Road
Somerford Grove
Cowper Road
Wordsworth Road
Barretts Grove
Matthias Road
Pellerin Road
Sal Rd
Arcola Street
Terrace
Miller's Square
Chow Square
Dunn St
Gateway Ms
Elton Place
Woodville Road
St Gabriels Lea
Auriga Ms
Arundel Grove
King Henry's Walk
Shellgrove Road
Truman's Road
Selsea Place
Boleyn Road
Tavistock Cl
Crossway
Shacklewell Lane
Alvington Crescent
Mildmay
Wolsey R
Street A10
Sandringham

0.25 mile

0.25 km

Stoke Newington

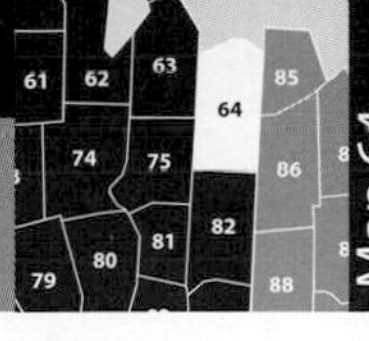

The richer cousin of Dalston, the poorer cousin of Islington, Stoke Newington has an inferiority complex-cum-swagger, which explains why 90% of its inhabitants are creative types. The curvy Church Street is the port of call with its boutique shops (Metal Crumble) and aptly Nietzsche stacked bookshops. Great beer and atmosphere (The Shakespeare), curry (Rasa N16), Sunday roast (Rose and Crown), and check out the butterflies and bats at Park Cemetery.

Landmarks

- **Newington Green Church** • 39 Newington Green

Libraries

- **Stoke Newington Library** • Stoke Newington Church St

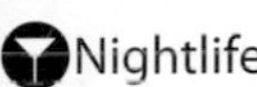

Nightlife

- **The Auld Shillelagh** • 105 Stoke Newington Church St
- **Londesborough** • 36 Barbauld Rd
- **Rose and Crown** • 199 Stoke Newington Church St
- **Ryan's Bar** • 181 Stoke Newington Church St
- **Ruby's** • 76 Stoke Newington Rd
- **The Shakespeare** • 57 Allen Rd
- **White Hart** • 69 Stoke Newington High St

Post Offices

- **Church Street** • 170 Stoke Newington Church St
- **Stoke Newington** • Stoke Newington High St

Restaurants

- **Alistair's Brasserie** • 35 Stoke Newington Church St
- **Anglo Asian** • 60 Stoke Newington Church St
- **Blue Legume** • 101 Stoke Newington Church St
- **Datte Foco** • 10 Stoke Newington Church St
- **Fifty Six** • 56 Newington Green
- **Rasa N16** • 55 Stoke Newington Church St
- **Sariyer Balik** • 56 Green Lanes
- **Yum Yum** • 187 Stoke Newington High St

Shopping

- **Ark** • 161 Stoke Newington Rd
- **The Beaucatcher Salon** • 44 Stoke Newington Church Street
- **Belle Epoque Boulangerie** • 37 Newington Green
- **Bridgewood & Neitzert** • 146 Stoke Newington Church St
- **Church Street Bookshop** • 142 Stoke Newington Church St
- **Metal Crumble** • 13 Stoke Newington Church St
- **Mind** • 11 Stoke Newington Church St
- **Of Cabbages & Kings** • 34 Kersley Rd
- **Pelicans & Parrots** • 81 Stoke Newington Rd
- **Ribbons and Taylor** • 157 Stoke Newington Church St
- **Rosa Lingerie** • 3 Church Walk
- **Route 73 Kids** • 92 Stoke Newington Church St
- **S'graffiti** • 172 Stoke Newington Church St
- **Sacred Art** • 148 Albion Rd
- **The Spence Bakery** • 161 Stoke Newington Church St
- **Stoke Newington Farmers Market** • Stoke Newington Church St & Stoke Newington High St

Supermarkets

- **Whole Foods Market** • 32 Stoke Newington Church St
- **Iceland** • 17 Green Lanes

Kilburn
West Hampstead
Maygrove Peace Park
Kilburn Grange Park

Shoot Up Hill A5
Kilburn High Road A5
West End Lane B510
Iverson Road B520
Abbey Road B507
Belsize Road B509
Maygrove Road
Loveridge Road
Loveridge Mews
Netherwood Street
Palmerston Road
Garlinge Road
Fordwych Road
St. Cuthberts Road
Barlow Road
Brassey Road
Dornfell Street
Glastonbury Street
Ravenshaw Street
Broomsleigh Street
Sumatra Road
Glenbrook Road
Solent Road
Narcissus Road
Holmdale Road
West Cottages
Pandora Road
Inglewood Road
Mill Lane
Denington Park Road
Kingdon Road
Sandwell Cres
Fawley Road
Honeybourne Road
Lymington Road
Liddell Road
Ariel Road
Medley Road
Rowntree Close
Linstead Road
Lowfield Road
Kylemore Road
Gladys Road
Hilltop Road
Sherriff Road
Hemstal Road
Dynham Road
Cotleigh Road
Kingsgate Road
Kingsgate Avenue
Blackburn Road
Exeter Ms
West Hampstead Ms
Broadhurst Gardens
Compayne Gardens
Priory Road
Cleve Road
Woodchurch Road
Smyrna Road
Mazenod Avenue
Kings Gate Place
Kings Gdns
Acol Road
Wavel Mews
Canfield Gardens
Greencroft Gardens
Aberdare Gardens
Goldhurst Terrace
St. Mary's Ms
Abbot's Place
Priory Terrace
Quex Road
Quex Mews
Mutrix Road
Birchington Road
Bransdale Close
West End Lane
Kilburn Pl
Kilburn Vale
Messina Avenue
Gascony Avenue
Grange way
Palmerston Road
Drakes Court yd
Buckley Road
Burton Road
Willesden La
Brondesbury Mews
St. Julian's Road
The Terrace
Victoria Road
Brondesbury Road B451
Brondesbury Villas
Mallard Cl
Fairhazel Gardens
Coleridge Gardens
Lyncroft Gardens
Crown Close
Watling Gardens
Exeter Road
Cavendish Close
Gladstone Ms
Albion Mews
Dunster Gardens
Melaris Ms
Aldred Rd
Finchley Road B510

66
68

0.25 mile
0.25 km

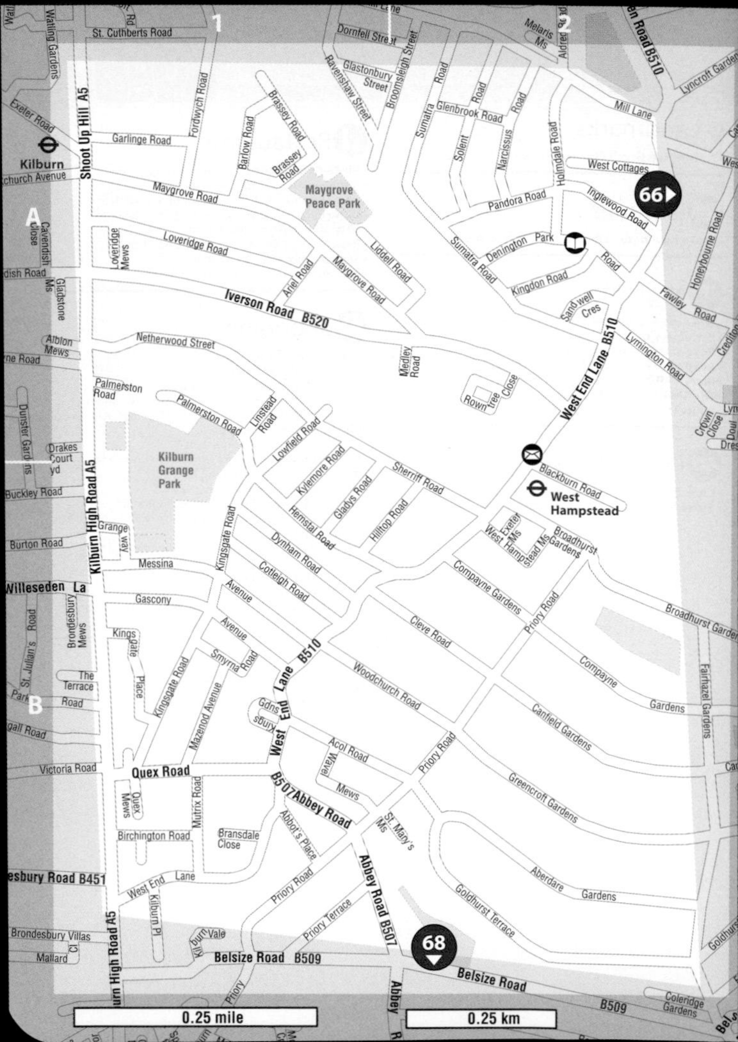

West Hampstead

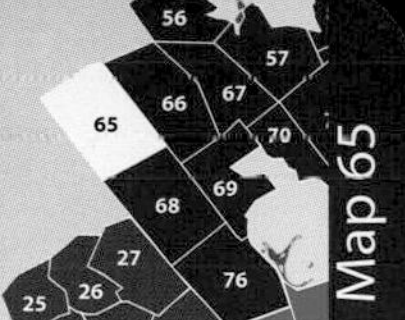

Hampstead's ugly sister, West Hampstead is a leafy suburb that has absorbed some of Kilburn's grittiness. Young urban nomads make up much of the population, as rent is moderate by London standards. Like the rest of London, West Hampstead has its fair share of Caffe Neros and Costa Coffees, but check out the Green Room for atmosphere and The Good Ship for music or comedy.

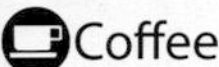

Coffee

- **Caffe Nero** • 101 Kilburn High Rd
- **Costa** • 203 W End Ln
- **Starbucks** • 201 W End Ln

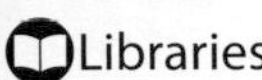

Libraries

- **West Hampstead Library** • Dennington Park Rd

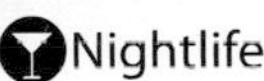

Nightlife

- **The Czech and Slovak Bar** • 74 West End Lane
- **The Good Ship** • 289 Kilburn High Rd
- **The Luminaire** • 311 High Rd

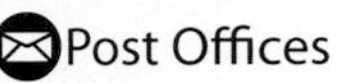

Post Offices

- **West Hampstead** • 128 W End Ln

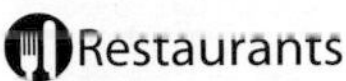

Restaurants

- **The Green Room** • 182 Broadhurst Gardens
- **Small & Beautiful** • 351 Kilburn High Rd

Shopping

- **Party Party** • 206 Kilburn High Rd
- **Primark** • 54 Kilburn High Rd

Supermarkets

- **Sainsbury's** • 88 Kilburn High Rd
- **Sainsbury's** • 377 Kilburn High Rd

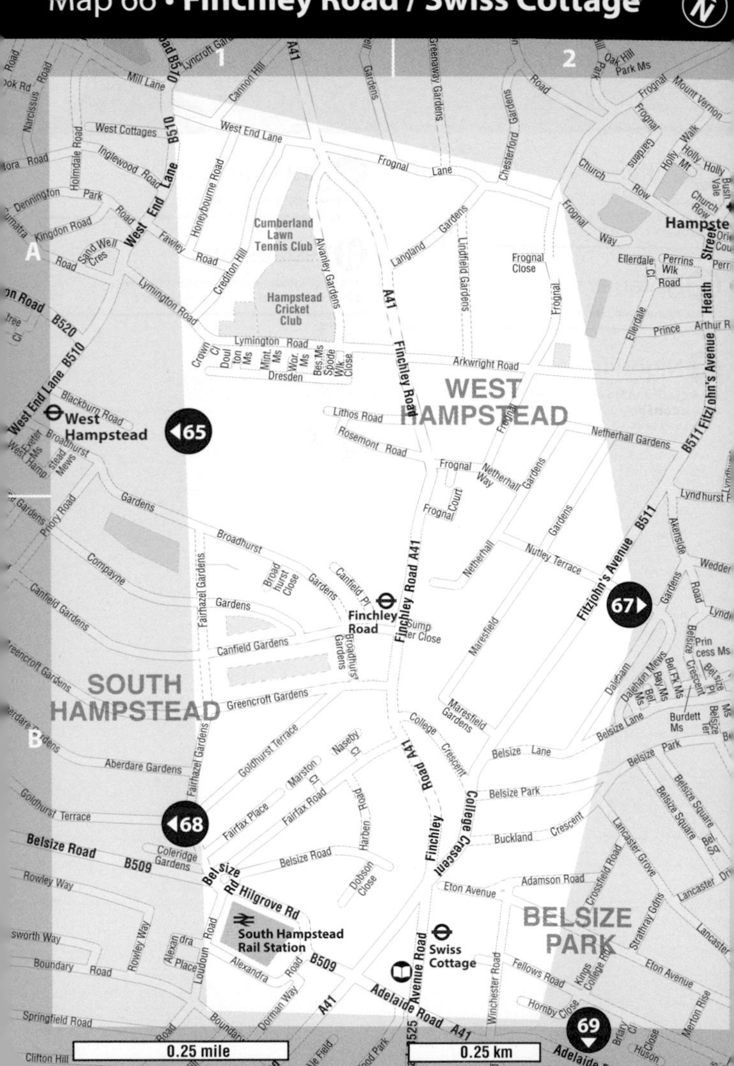
West Hampstead
Finchley Road
South Hampstead Rail Station
Swiss Cottage
WEST HAMPSTEAD
SOUTH HAMPSTEAD
BELSIZE PARK
Cumberland Lawn Tennis Club
Hampstead Cricket Club
Finchley Road A41
West End Lane
Fitzjohn's Avenue
Belsize Road
Adelaide Road
0.25 mile
0.25 km

Finchley Road / Swiss Cottage

With so much promise and surrounded by the likes of West Hampstead, Primrose Hill and Camden the area is still inexplicably in need of resuscitation. A long list of shops not worth mentioning and a few restaurants whose existence defies dignity should not detract from the fact that, The Camden Arts Centre and Freud Museum are jewels in this battered crown and well worth braving the surrounding boredom to visit.

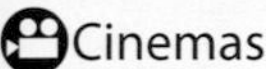

Cinemas

- **Odeon Swiss Cottage** • 96 Finchley Rd
- **Vue Finchley Road** • Finchley Rd & Blackburn Rd

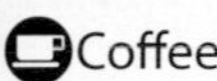

Coffee

- **Cafe Express** • 25 Finchley Rd
- **Costa** • 149 Finchley Rd
- **Starbucks** • 255 Finchley Rd

Libraries

- **Swiss Cottage Library** • 88 Avenue Rd

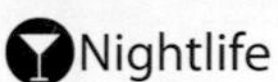

Nightlife

- **Ye Olde Swiss Cottage** • 98 Finchley Rd

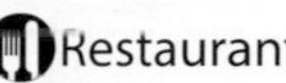

Restaurants

- **Bradleys** • 25 Winchester Rd
- **Camden Arts Centre** • Arkwright Rd
- **Singapore Garden** • 83 Fairfax Rd

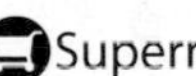

Supermarkets

- **Sainsbury's** • 255 Finchley Rd
- **Waitrose** • 199 Finchley Rd

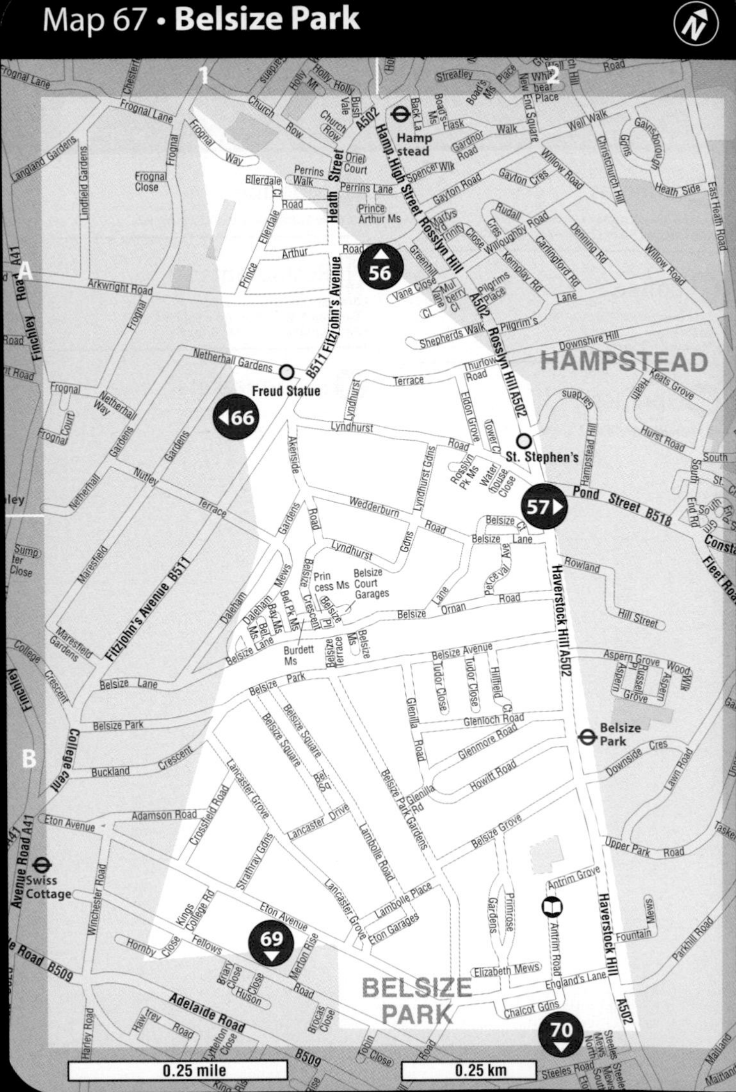

Map 67 • Belsize Park
HAMPSTEAD
BELSIZE PARK
Hampstead
Belsize Park
Swiss Cottage
Freud Statue
St. Stephen's
56
57
66
69
70
0.25 mile
0.25 km
Frognal Lane
Frognal
Frognal Close
Frognal Way
Langland Gardens
Lindfield Gardens
Church Row
Holly Bush Vale
Perrins Walk
Perrins Lane
Oriel Court
Heath Street
Ellerdale Road
Prince Arthur Road
Prince Arthur Ms
Hamp. High Street
Back La
Flask Walk
Well Walk
Gardnor Road
Spencer Wlk
Gayton Road
Gayton Cres
Willow Road
Streatley Place
New End Square
Christchurch Hill
Heath Side
East Heath Road
Rosslyn Hill
Greenhill
Vane Close
Mulberry Cl
Pilgrims Place
Pilgrim's Lane
Rudall Cres
Willoughby Road
Carlingford Rd
Denning Rd
Kemplay Rd
Shepherds Walk
Downshire Hill
Keats Grove
Hurst Road
Arkwright Road
Finchley Road
Netherhall Gardens
Netherhall Way
Frognal Court
Nutley Terrace
Maresfield Gardens
Fitzjohn's Avenue B511
B511 Fitzjohn's Avenue
Lyndhurst Terrace
Lyndhurst Road
Lyndhurst Gdns
Thurlow Road
Eldon Grove
Tower Cl
Rosslyn Pk Ms
Waterhouse Close
Akenside Road
Wedderburn Road
Pond Street B518
Belsize Ct
Belsize Lane
Perceval Ave
Rowland Hill Street
Haverstock Hill A502
Princess Ms
Belsize Court Garages
Belsize Crescent
Belsize Pl
Daleham Gardens
Daleham Mews
Ornan Road
Belsize Avenue
Belsize Terrace
Burdett Ms
Belsize Park
Belsize Park Gardens
Tudor Close
Hillfield Ct
Glenloch Road
Glenmore Road
Glenilla Road
Howitt Road
Aspern Grove
Downside Cres
Lawn Road
College Crescent
Buckland Crescent
Belsize Square
Lancaster Grove
Lancaster Drive
Crossfield Road
Adamson Road
Eton Avenue
Strathray Gdns
Lambolle Road
Lambolle Place
Eton Garages
Belsize Grove
Upper Park Road
Antrim Grove
Antrim Road
Primrose Gardens
Elizabeth Mews
England's Lane
Chalcot Gdns
Haverstock Hill
Fountain Mews
Parkhill Road
Winchester Road
Kings College Rd
Hornby Close
Fellows Road
Merton Rise
Briary Close
Huson Close
Adelaide Road
Hawtrey Road
Lyttelton Close
Brocas Close
Harley Road
Tobin Close
Steeles Road

Belsize Park

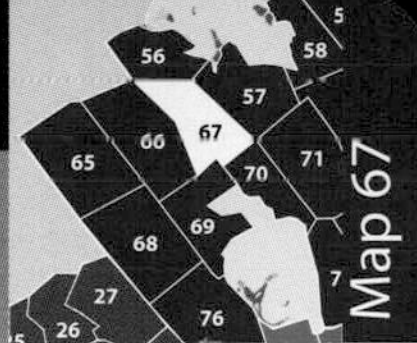

There is a reason that Kate Moss, Jude Law, Chris Martin and Noel Gallagher (to name a few) all live here. It's less pretentious than neighbouring banker filled Hampstead and far enough away from the Primrose set to be artistically elitist. Extraordinarily expensive shops and restaurants reign over the area but in at the celebrity frequented Washington pub there's an excellent atmosphere and food wise Belsize Lane never disappoints.

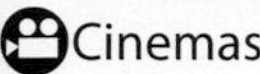

Cinemas

- **Everyman Belsize Park** • 203 Haverstock Hill

Coffee

- **Starbucks** • 57 England's Lane
- **Starbucks** • 202 Haverstock Hill

Landmarks

- **Freud Statue** •
  Fitzjohn's Ave, opposite Maresfield Gardens Junction
- **St Stephen's** • Rosslyn Hill

Libraries

- **Belsize Library** • Antrim Rd

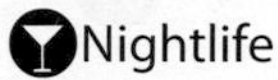

Nightlife

- **The Washington** • 50 England's Ln

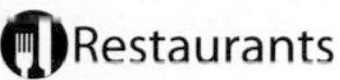

Restaurants

- **Artigiano** • 12 Belsize Terrace
- **Brasserie Gerard** • 215 Haverstock Hill
- **Curry Manjil** • 34 England's Ln
- **Paradiso** • 36 England's Ln
- **Retsina** • 48 Belsize Ln
- **Violette Cafe** • 2 England's Ln

Shopping

- **Belsize Village Delicatessen** • 39 Belsize Ln
- **Lotus and Frog** • 32 England's Ln

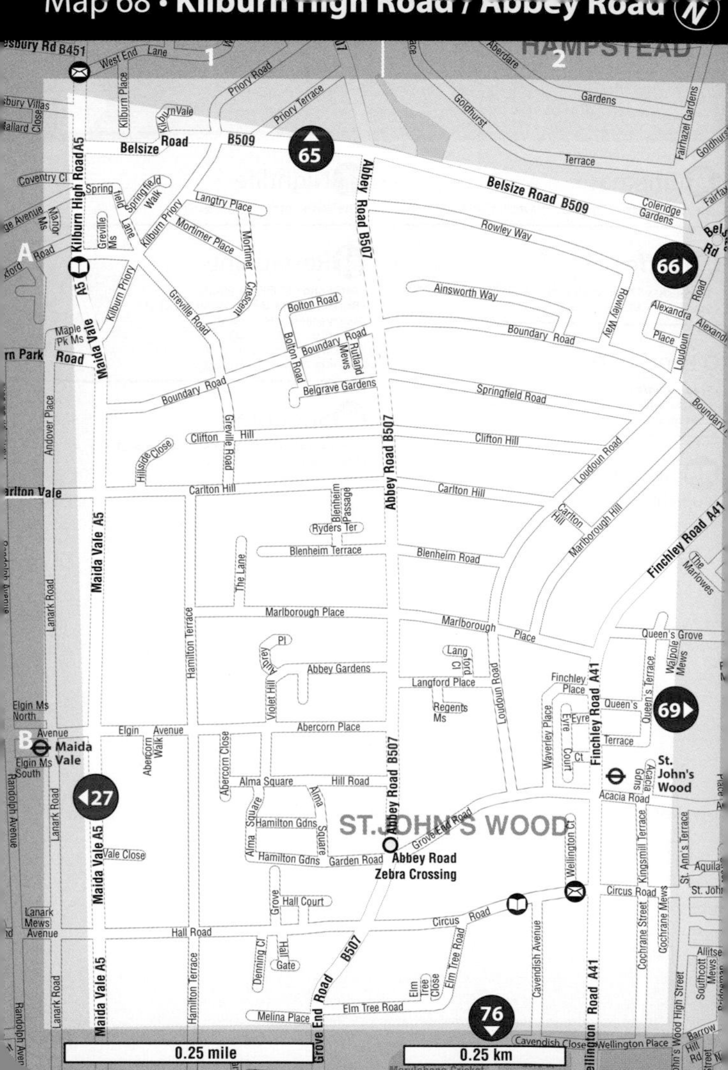

Map 68 • Kilburn High Road / Abbey Road
HAMPSTEAD
1
2
A
B
65
66
69
27
76
Kilburn High Road A5
A5
West End Lane
Kilburn Place
Kilburn Vale
Priory Road
Priory Terrace
Belsize Road B509
Belsize Road B509
Aberdare Gardens
Goldhurst Terrace
Fairhazel Gardens
Coleridge Gardens
Coventry Cl
Springfield Lane
Springfield Walk
Kilburn Priory
Langtry Place
Mortimer Place
Mortimer Crescent
Greville Ms
Greville Road
Manor Ms
Abbey Road B507
Rowley Way
Ainsworth Way
Bolton Road
Boundary Road
Rutland Mews
Belgrave Gardens
Alexandra Place
Loudoun Road
Maple Pk Ms
Maida Vale
Road
Springfield Road
Clifton Hill
Hillside Close
Andover Place
Carlton Hill
Carlton Vale
Loudoun Road
Blenheim Passage
Ryders Ter
Carlton Hill
Marlborough Hill
Finchley Road A41
Blenheim Terrace
Blenheim Road
The Marlowes
Maida Vale A5
Lanark Road
The Lane
Hamilton Terrace
Marlborough Place
Queen's Grove
Walpole Mews
Aubrey Pl
Abbey Gardens
Langford Cl
Langford Place
Finchley Place
Regents Ms
Queen's Terrace
Violet Hill
Waverley Place
Eyre Court
Elgin Ms North
Elgin Avenue
Abercorn Walk
Abercorn Place
Abercorn Close
Maida Vale
Elgin Ms South
Ct
St. John's Wood
Acacia Gdns
Acacia Road
Alma Square
Hill Road
Hamilton Gdns
ST. JOHN'S WOOD
Grove End Road
Wellington Ct
Randolph Avenue
Kingsmill Terrace
St. Ann's Terrace
Vale Close
Abbey Road Zebra Crossing
Garden Road
Aquila
Circus Road
St. John
Grove Hall Court
Lanark Mews
Circus Road
Hall Road
Cochrane Street
Cochrane Mews
Denning Cl
Hall Gate
Elm Tree Road
Elm Tree Close
Cavendish Avenue
Wellington Road A41
Allitsen
Southcott Mews
St John's Wood High Street
Melina Place
Elm Tree Road
Grove End Road
Cavendish Close
Wellington Place
Barrow Hill Rd
0.25 mile
0.25 km

Kilburn High Road / Abbey Road

FFS "Let It Be". While the area's main attraction is a zebra crossing and a dilapidated recording studio, once home to the world's greatest band, the grime and urban decay that surround it hardly make it an "Octopuses Garden". But "Come Together" because "Here Comes The Sun," The Clifton is a cool pub and the delightful Little Bay does excellent food. Don't forget the Art Deco grandeur of the State Building.

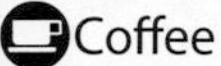

Coffee

- **Starbucks** • 79 St John's Wood High St

Landmarks

- **Abbey Road Zebra Crossing** • 3 Abbey Rd

Libraries

- **Kilburn Library** • 12 Kilburn High Rd
- **St John's Wood Library TEMPORARY LOCATION!** • 20 Circus Rd

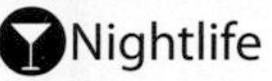

Nightlife

- **The Clifton** • 96 Clifton Hill

Post Offices

- **Kilburn** • 79 Kilburn High Rd
- **St Johns Wood** • 32 Circus Rd

Restaurants

- **Little Bay** • 228 Belsize Rd

Supermarkets

- **Tesco** • 115 Maida Vale

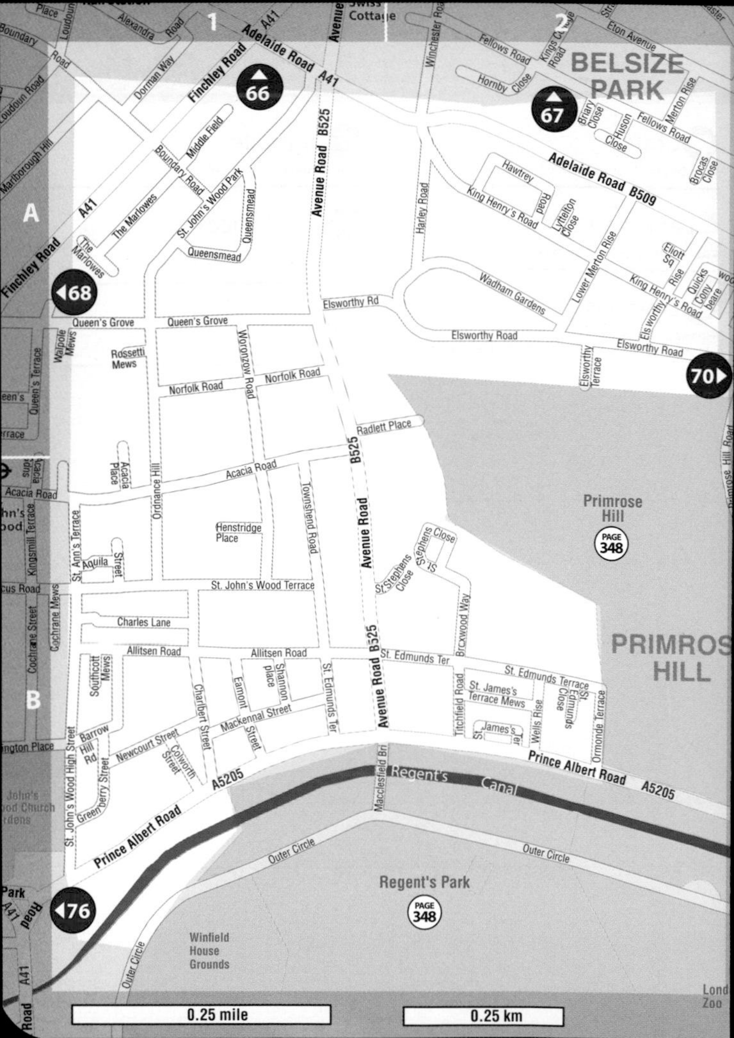

Map 69 • St. John's Wood

1
2
A
B

BELSIZE PARK
PRIMROSE HILL
Primrose Hill
PAGE 348
Regent's Park
PAGE 348
Winfield House Grounds
Swiss Cottage
St. John's Wood
Lond Zoo

66
67
68
70
76

Adelaide Road A41
Adelaide Road B509
Finchley Road
Finchley Road A41
Avenue Road B525
Avenue Road
Alexandra Road
Boundary Road
Loudoun Road
Marlborough Hill
Dorman Way
Middle Field
St. John's Wood Park
Queensmead
The Marlowes
Winchester Road
Fellows Road
Kings College Road
Hornby Close
Eton Avenue
Merton Rise
Briary Close
Huson Close
Brocas Close
Hawtrey Road
King Henry's Road
Lyttelton Close
Harley Road
Lower Merton Rise
Eliott Sq
Elsworthy Rise
Quickswood
Cony beare
Wadham Gardens
Elsworthy Rd
Elsworthy Road
Elsworthy Terrace
Queen's Grove
Walpole Mews
Rossetti Mews
Woronzow Road
Norfolk Road
Queen's Terrace
Radlett Place
Acacia Place
Acacia Road
Ordnance Hill
Townshend Road
Henstridge Place
Kingsmill Terrace
St. Ann's Terrace
Aquila Street
St. Stephens Close
Broxwood Way
St. John's Wood Terrace
Charles Lane
Cochrane Street
Cochrane Mews
Allitsen Road
St. Edmunds Ter
St. Edmunds Terrace
Southcott Mews
Charlbert Street
Earnont Street
Shannon place
Mackennal Street
St. James's Terrace Mews
St. James's Ter
Titchfield Road
Wells Rise
St. Edmunds Close
Ormonde Terrace
Barrow Hill Rd.
Newcourt Street
Colworth Street
St. John's Wood High Street
Greenberry Street
Prince Albert Road A5205
Macclesfield Bri
Regent's Canal
Outer Circle
Primrose Hill Road
Park Road A41

0.25 mile
0.25 km

St. John's Wood

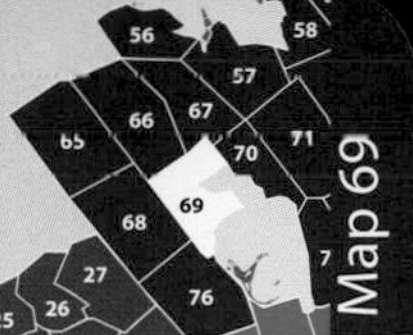

Nouveau riche and bourgeois mix in the is leafy salad of a suburb that, you guessed it, reeks of money. Pinned in between Primrose Hill and Regent's Park, there isn't much to do in this mainly residential area unless you like to gawk at expensive houses. However, the leisure centre on Adelaide Road is pretty swish with its climbing wall and Lord's cricket ground is only a stone's throw away.

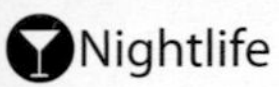

Nightlife

- **The Star** • 38 St. Johns Wood Terrace

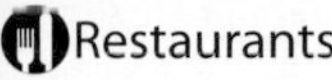

Restaurants

- **Tupelo Honey** • 27 Parkway, Camden

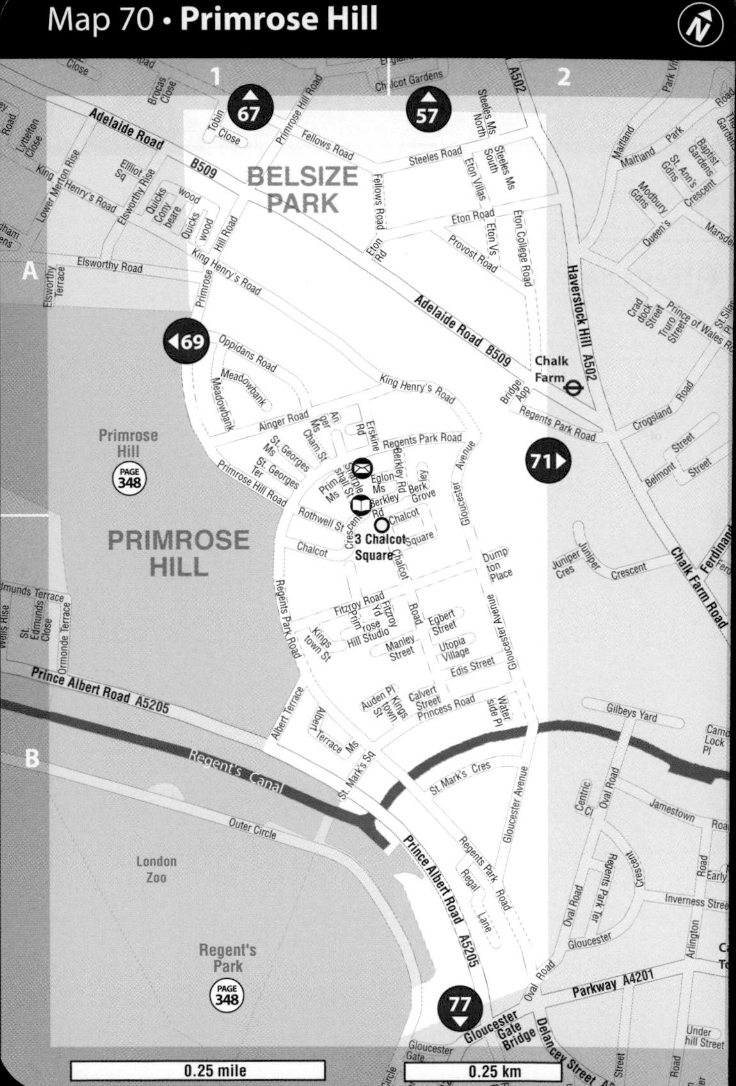
BELSIZE PARK
PRIMROSE HILL
Primrose Hill
PAGE 348
London Zoo
Regent's Park
PAGE 348
67
57
69
71
77
3 Chalcot Square
Chalk Farm
Adelaide Road B509
Haverstock Hill A502
Prince Albert Road A5205
Regent's Canal
Outer Circle
Parkway A4201
Gloucester Gate Bridge
Regents Park Road
King Henry's Road
Primrose Hill Road
Elsworthy Road
Gloucester Avenue
Chalk Farm Road
Fitzroy Road
Chalcot Crescent
Chalcot Square
Eton Road
Provost Road
Steeles Road
Fellows Road
Oppidans Road
Ainger Road
Juniper Crescent
Gilbeys Yard
Oval Road
Delancey Street
0.25 mile
0.25 km

Primrose Hill

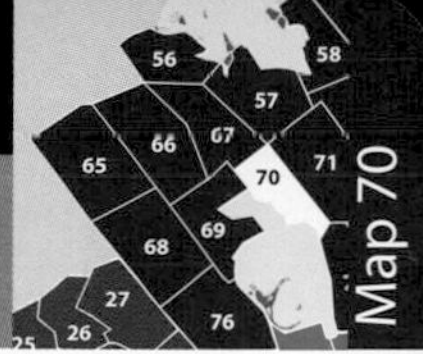

Primrose Hill is factory packed with pretty young things and established actors mixed with models, designers and artistic types in an area that is London's low-key version of Beverly Hills. If you don't stumble across a celebrity or are disinclined to stalk one you can check out the trendy stores, grab a pint in the equally trendy Landsdowne or take in the views of London from the Hill itself.

Landmarks

- **3 Chalcot Square** • 3 Chalcot Sq

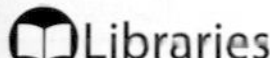

Libraries

- **Chalk Farm Library** • 11 Sharples Hall St

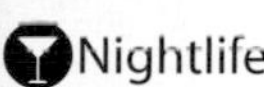

Nightlife

- **The Albert** • 11 Princess Rd
- **Cecil Sharp House** • 2 Regents Park Rd
- **The Engineer** • 65 Gloucester Ave [Princess Road]
- **The Lansdowne** • 90 Gloucester Ave [Regent's Park Road]
- **Princess of Wales** • 22 Chalcot Rd
- **Queens No. 1** • 1 Edis St
- **Sir Richard Steele** • 97 Haverstock Hill

Post Offices

- **Regents Park Road** • 91 Regents Park Road

Restaurants

- **Cafe Seventy Nine** • 79 Regents Park Rd
- **The Hill Bar** • 94 Haverstock Hill
- **J Restaurant** • 148 Regents Park Rd
- **Legal Cafe** • 81 Haverstock Hill
- **Lemonia** • 89 Regents Park Rd
- **Manna** • 4 Erskine Rd [Regent's Park Road]
- **Melrose and Morgan** • 42 Gloucester Ave
- **Odette's** • 130 Regents Park Rd
- **Primrose Bakery** • 69 Gloucester Ave [Edis Street]
- **Trojka** • 101 Regents Park Rd
- **Two Brothers** • 297 Regents Park Rd

Shopping

- **Judith Michael & Daughter** • 73 Regents Park Rd
- **Miss Lala's Boudoir** • 148 Gloucester Ave
- **Nicolas (off licence)** • 67 Regents Park Rd
- **Press** • 3 Erskine Rd
- **Primrose Hill Books** • 134 Regent's Park Rd
- **Primrose Newsagent** • 91 Regents Park Rd
- **Richard Dare** • 93 Regents Park Rd
- **Shepherd Foods** • 59 Regents Park Rd
- **Shikasuki** • 67 Gloucester Ave
- **Sweet Pea** • 77 Gloucester Ave
- **Tann Rokka** • 123 Regent's Park Rd
- **Yeomans Grocers** • 152 Regent's Park Rd

Map 71 • Camden Town / Chalk Farm / Kentish Town (West)

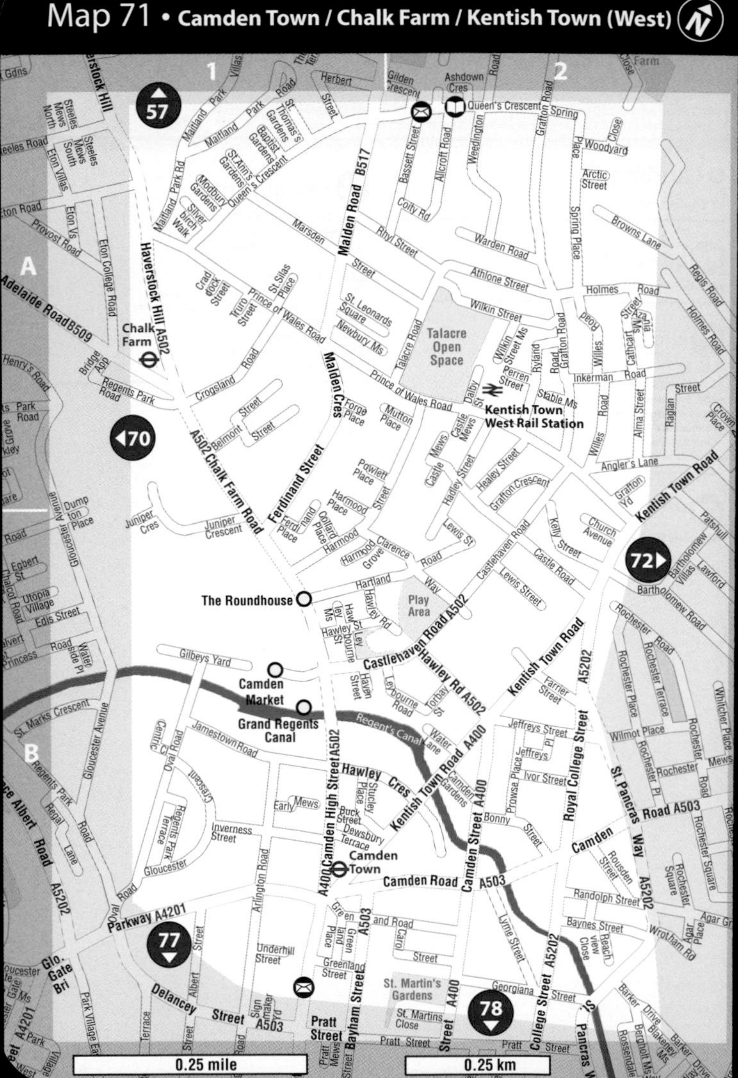

amden Town / Chalk Farm / Kentish Town (West)

Camden is still the musical heartbeat of London and while the ratty-tatty venues of the 60's that solidified this reputation are long gone, or surgically modernized, the pavements still reverberate to a constant beat. The area is crowded during the week and jam-packed during the weekend but the cacophony of wacky stores, the bric-a-brac stalls, and an eclectic selection of culinary treats mean London wouldn't be London without it.

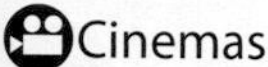

Cinemas

- **Odeon Camden Town** • 14 Parkway

Coffee

- **Cafe La Cigale** • 47 Parkway
- **Cafe Metro** • 178 Camden High St
- **Caffe Nero** • 7 Jamestown Rd
- **Caffe Nero** • 11 Parkway
- **Costa** • 181 Camden High St
- **Eat.** • 185 Camden High St
- **Inhabition** • 15 Chalk Farm Rd
- **Pret A Manger** • 157 Camden High St
- **Pret A Manger** • 261 High St
- **Starbucks** • Parkway Camden & Arlington Rd

Landmarks

- **Camden Market** • Camden Lock Pl
- **Grand Regents Canal** • Grand Regents Canal
- **The Roundhouse** • Chalk Farm Rd & Crogsland Rd

Libraries

- **Queen's Crescent Library** • 165 Queen's Crescent

Nightlife

- **Bar Vinyl** • 6 Inverness St
- **Barfly** • 49 Chalk Farm Rd
- **Bartok** • 78 Chalk Farm Rd
- **The Constitution** • 42 St Pancras Way
- **Dingwalls** • Middle Yard
- **The Dublin Castle** • 94 Parkway
- **Electric Ballroom** • 184 Camden High St
- **The Enterprise** • 2 Haverstock Hill
- **Fiddlers Elbow** • 1 Malden Rd
- **Good Mixer** • 30 Inverness St
- **The Hawley Arms** • 2 Castlehaven Rd
- **Jazz Cafe** • 5 Parkway
- **Koko** • 1 Camden High St
- **The Lock Tavern** • 35 Chalk Farm Rd
- **Monkey Chews** • 2 Queen's Crescent
- **Oxford Arms** • 265 Camden High St
- **Proud Camden** • Chalk Farm Rd
- **Quinn's** • 65 Kentish Town Rd
- **The Underworld** • 174 Camden High St

Post Offices

- **Camden High Street** • 112 Camden High St
- **Queen's Crescent** • 139 Queen's Crescent

Restaurants

- **Andy's Taverna** • 81 Bayham St
- **Bar Gansa** • 2 Inverness St
- **Bar Solo** • 20 Inverness St
- **Bento Cafe** • 9 Parkway
- **Camden Bar And Kitchen** • 102 Camden High St
- **Cotton's** • 55 Chalk Farm Rd
- **Gilgamesh** • The Stables Market, Chalk Farm Rd
- **The Green Note** • 106 Parkway
- **Haché** • 24 Inverness St
- **Kim's Vietnamese Food Hut** • Unit D, Camden Lock Palace
- **Limani** • 154 Regents Park Rd
- **Marathon Cafe** • 87 Chalk Farm Rd
- **Marine Ices** • 8 Haverstock Hill
- **Market** • 438 Parkway
- **Muang Thai** • 71 Chalk Farm Rd
- **My Village** • 37 Chalk Farm Rd
- **Thanh Binh** • 14 Chalk Farm Rd
- **Viet-anh Cafe** • 41 Parkway
- **Woody Grill** • 1 Camden Rd
- **Yumchaa Tea Space** • 91 Upper Walkway, West Yard, Camden Lock Market
- **Zorya Imperial Vodka Room** • 48 Chalk Farm Rd

Shopping

- **Acumedic** • 101 Camden High St
- **Aldo Sale Shop** • 231 Camden High St
- **Arckiv Vintage Eyewear** • Chalk Farm Rd & Castlehaven Rd
- **Black Rose** • The Stables Market, Chalk Farm Rd
- **Cyberdog** • Stables Market, Chalk Farm Rd
- **Episode** • 26 Chalk Farm Rd
- **Escapade** • 45 Chalk Farm Rd
- **Eye Contacts** • 10 Chalk Farm Rd
- **Fresh & Wild, Camden** • 49 Parkway
- **Graham and Green** • 164 Regents Park Rd
- **Metal Militia** • 258 Camden High St
- **Music & Video Exchange** • 208 Camden High St
- **Ray Man Music** • 54 Chalk Farm Rd
- **Rokit** • 225 Camden High St
- **Sounds That Swing** • 46 Inverness St
- **Traid** • 154 Camden High St
- **Up The Video Junction** • Middle Yard, Camden Lock Pl
- **Village Games** • 65 The West Yard
- **Whole Foods Market** • 49 Parkway

Supermarkets

- **Whole Foods Market** • 49 Parkway
- **Sainsbury's** • 77 Chalk Farm Rd
- **Sainsbury's** • 17 Camden Rd
- **Sainsbury's** • 10 Camden Rd

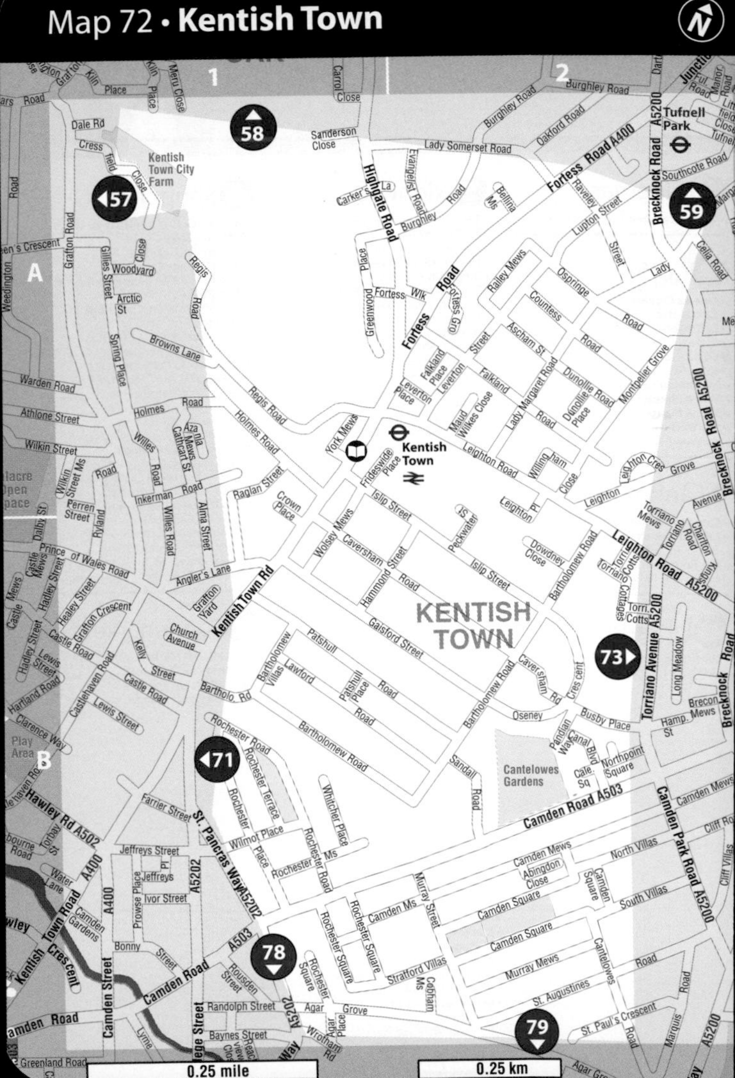
1
2
A
B
58
57
59
73
71
78
79
Kentish Town City Farm
Tufnell Park
Kentish Town
KENTISH TOWN
Cantelowes Gardens
Play Area
Highgate Road
Fortess Road A400
Fortess Road
Brecknock Road A5200
Brecknock Road
Burghley Road
Lady Somerset Road
Oakford Road
Sanderson Close
Carrol Close
Dale Rd
Cressfield Close
Grafton Road
Gillies Street
Woodyard Close
Arctic St
Spring Place
Regis Road
Browns Lane
Warden Road
Athlone Street
Wilkin Street
Wilkin Street Ms
Perren Street
Ryland Road
Holmes Road
Willes Road
Inkerman Road
Alma Street
Azania Mews
Cathcart St
Raglan Street
Crown Place
Prince of Wales Road
Angler's Lane
Grafton Yard
Kentish Town Rd
Castle Road
Castle Mews
Hadley Street
Healey Street
Grafton Crescent
Church Avenue
Kelly Street
Lewis Street
Hartland Road
Castlehaven Road
Clarence Way
Hawley Rd A502
Farrier Street
St. Pancras Way A5202
Jeffreys Street
Jeffreys Pl
Ivor Street
Prowse Place
Bonny Street
Camden Street
Camden Road
Camden Road A503
Randolph Street
Baynes Street
Agar Grove
Agar Place
Wrotham Rd
Rousden Street
Rochester Road
Rochester Terrace
Rochester Place
Rochester Ms
Rochester Square
Wilmot Place
Whitcher Place
Bartholomew Villas
Bartholomew Road
Bartholo. Rd
Lawford Road
Patshull Road
Patshull Place
Gaisford Street
Caversham Road
Caversham Rd
Hammond Street
Wolsey Mews
Islip Street
Frideswide Place
York Mews
Peckwater St
Leighton Road
Leighton Road A5200
Leighton Pl
Leighton Cres
Leighton Grove
Dowdney Close
Torriano Mews
Torriano Cottages
Torriano Avenue A5200
Torri. Cotts
Long Meadow
Brecon Mews
Hamp. St
Busby Place
Oseney Crescent
Sandall Road
Pandian Way
Canal Blvd
Cale. Sq
Northpoint Square
Camden Mews
Camden Park Road A5200
North Villas
South Villas
Cliff Villas
Camden Square
Abingdon Close
Murray Street
Murray Mews
Camden Ms
Stratford Villas
Cobham Ms
Cantelowes Road
St. Augustines Road
St. Paul's Crescent
Marquis Road
Lady Margaret Road
Dunollie Road
Dunollie Place
Maud Wilkes Close
Willingham Close
Falkland Road
Falkland Place
Leverton Street
Leverton Place
Ascham St
Countess Road
Ospringe Road
Railey Mews
Lupton Street
Raveley Street
Montpellier Grove
Celia Road
Southcote Road
Bellina Ms
Evangelist Road
Carker's La
Greenwood Place
Fortess Wlk
Fortess Gro
Charlton Kings Road
Camden Gardens
Water Lane
0.25 mile
0.25 km

Kentish Town

Kentish Town may be Camden's less interesting and less affected neighbour but this isn't necessarily a bad thing. The area is on the up, and between the grubby, horrible collection of pound shops, charity shops, and industrial stores there are new venues springing up that offer some of the most welcoming atmospheres in North London. The Pineapple is a great little pit-stop pub with an infectious atmosphere

Coffee

- **Cafe Metro** • 180 Camden High St

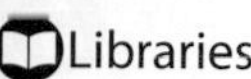

Libraries

- **Kentish Town Library** • 262 Kentish Town Rd

Nightlife

- **The Abbey Tavern** • 124 Kentish Town Rd
- **The Assembly House** • 292 Kentish Town
- **The Bull & Gate** • 389 Kentish Town Rd
- **The Flowerpot** • 147 Kentish Town Rd
- **HMV Forum** • 9 Highgate Rd
- **The Lion and Unicorn** • 42 Gaisford St
- **The Pineapple** • 51 Leverton St
- **Rio's Health Spa** • 239 Kentish Town Rd

Restaurants

- **The Bengal Lancer**• 253 Kentish Town Rd
- **Bintang Cafe** • 93 Kentish Town Rd
- **Cafe Renoir** • 211 Kentish Town Rd
- **Eatzone** • 18 Fortess Rd
- **ITTA** • 225 Kentish Town Rd
- **Le Petit Prince** • 5 Holmes Rd
- **Mario's Cafe** • 6 Kelly St
- **The Oxford** • 256 Kentish Town Rd
- **Pane Vino** • 323 Kentish Town Rd
- **Phoenicia - Mediterranean Food Hall** • 186 Kentish Town Rd

Shopping

- **Blustons** • 213 Kentish Town Rd
- **Dots** • 132 St Pancras Way
- **Fish** • 161 Kentish Town Rd
- **Phoenicia** • 186 Kentish Town Rd
- **Pro Percussion** • 205 Kentish Town Rd

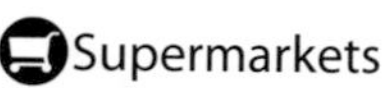

Supermarkets

- **Co-Op** • 250 Kentish Town Rd
- **EARTH natural foods** • 200 Kentish Town Rd
- **Iceland** • 301 Kentish Town Rd
- **Tesco/Esso** • 196 Camden Rd

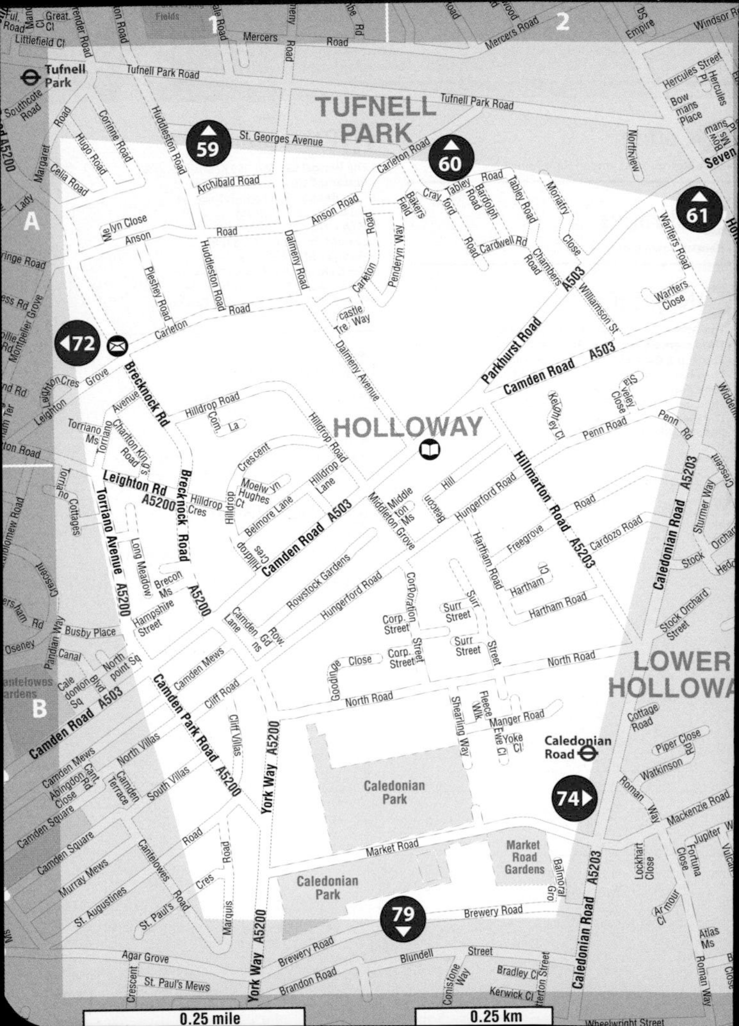

Map 73 • Holloway

N

TUFNELL PARK
HOLLOWAY
LOWER HOLLOWAY

Tufnell Park
Caledonian Road

59
60
61
72
74
79

A
B
1
2

Tufnell Park Road
Mercers Road
St. Georges Avenue
Carleton Road
Archibald Road
Anson Road
Huddleston Road
Dalmeny Road
Dalmeny Avenue
Corinne Road
Hugo Road
Celia Road
Margaret Road
Welyn Close
Pleshey Road
Pendery Way
Bakers Field
Crayford Road
Tabley Road
Bardolph Road
Cardwell Rd
Chambers Road
Moriatry Close
Northview
Warlters Road
Warlters Close
Williamson St
Parkhurst Road
Camden Road A503
Hercules Street
Hercules Pl
Bowmans Place
Bowmans Ms
Castle Tre Way
Brecknock Rd
Leighton Cres
Leighton Grove
Leighton Rd A5200
Hilldrop Road
Hilldrop Com.
Hilldrop La
Hilldrop Crescent
Hilldrop Lane
Hilldrop Cres
Hilldrop Ct
Moelwyn Hughes Ct
Belmore Lane
Torriano Ms
Torriano Avenue A5200
Torriano Cottages
Charlton King's Road
Long Meadow
Brecon Ms
Hampshire Street
Brecknock Road A5200
Middleton Ms
Middleton Grove
Beacon Hill
Hungerford Road
Hillmarton Road A5203
Hartham Road
Hartham Cl
Freegrove Road
Cardozo Road
Penn Road
Penn Rd
Keyworth Cl
Stavely Close
Caledonian Road A5203
Sturmer Way
Stock Orchard Crescent
Stock Orchard Street
Rowstock Gardens
Camden Gdns
Camden Lane
Corporation Street
Corp. Street
Surr Street
North Road
Goodinge Close
Shearling Way
Fleece Wlk
Manger Road
Ewe Cl
Yoke Cl
Cottage Road
Piper Close
Watkinson Rd
Roman Way
Mackenzie Road
Jupiter Way
Fortuna Close
Lockhart Close
Armour Cl
Atlas Ms
Caledonian Park
Market Road
Market Road Gardens
Balmoral Gro
Brewery Road
Blundell Street
Bradley Cl
Kerwick Cl
Lofting Road
Coniston Way
Brandon Road
York Way A5200
Camden Park Road A5200
Camden Mews
Cliff Road
Cliff Villas
North Villas
South Villas
Camden Square
Camden Terrace
Cantelowes Road
Cantelowes Gardens
Murray Mews
St. Augustines Road
St. Paul's Cres
St. Paul's Mews
Marquis Road
Agar Grove
Busby Place
Canal
Caledonian Blvd
North point Sq
Pandian Way
Oseney Crescent
Abingdon Close
Wheelwright Street

0.25 mile
0.25 km

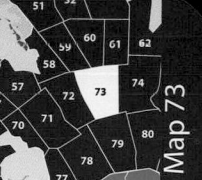

Holloway

Holloway is best known for its women's prison and not much else. To the west of Holloway Road it feels a bit like a sprawling backyard to gentrified Camden, Islington, and King's Cross. Nevertheless, bars like The Lord Stanley and Shillibeers have gone all gastro, so it doesn't quite have the gritty vibe that it once had.

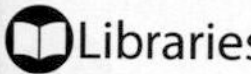

Libraries

- **John Barnes Library** • 275 Camden Rd

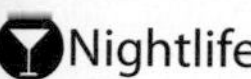

Nightlife

- **The Lord Stanley** • 51 Camden Park Rd
- **Shillibeers** • 1 Carpenter's Mews, North Rd

Post Offices

- **Brecknock Rd** • 20 Brecknock Rd

Shopping

- **Bumblebee Natural Foods** • 33 Brecknock Rd
- **DOC Records** • 5 Cardwell Terrace, Cardwell Rd

Supermarkets

- **Sainsbury's** • 4 Williamson St
- **Tesco/Esso** • 196 Camden Rd

Map 74 • Holloway Road / Arsenal

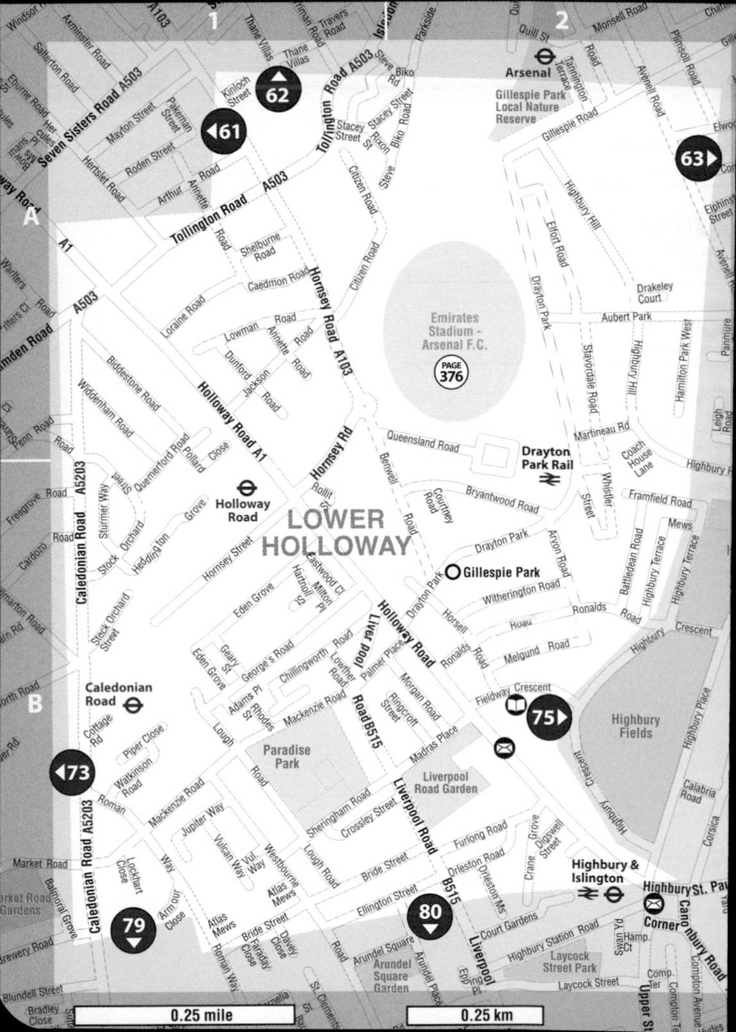

N
1
2
A
B
Arsenal
Gillespie Park Local Nature Reserve
Emirates Stadium - Arsenal F.C.
PAGE 376
Drayton Park Rail
Holloway Road
LOWER HOLLOWAY
Gillespie Park
Caledonian Road
Highbury Fields
Paradise Park
Liverpool Road Garden
Highbury & Islington
Highbury Corner
Laycock Street Park
Arundel Square Garden
62
61
63
73
75
79
80
Seven Sisters Road A503
Tollington Road A503
Tollington Road
Hornsey Road A103
Hornsey Rd
Holloway Road A1
Holloway Road
Caledonian Road A5203
Camden Road
Liverpool Road
Liverpool Road B515
Drayton Park
Gillespie Road
Highbury Hill
Aubert Park
Queensland Road
Benwell Road
Bryantwood Road
Citizen Road
Mayton Street
Roden Street
Hertslet Road
Axminster Road
Salterton Road
Thane Villas
Parkside
Avenell Road
Monsell Road
Quill St
Framfield Road
Martineau Rd
Stavordale Road
Hamilton Park West
Whistler Street
Arvon Road
Witherington Road
Horsell Road
Ronalds Road
Melgund Road
Fieldway Crescent
Highbury Crescent
Highbury Place
Calabria Road
Corsica
Mackenzie Road
Market Road
Brewery Road
Blundell Street
Bride Street
Ellington Street
Furlong Road
Orleston Road
Highbury Station Road
Laycock Street
Court Gardens
Arundel Square
Arundel Place
Canonbury Road
Compton Avenue
Upper St
St. Paul
Westbourne Road
Lough Road
Sheringham Road
Crossley Street
Madras Place
Morgan Road
Ringcroft Street
Chillingworth Road
George's Road
Eden Grove
Hornsey Street
Stock Orchard Street
Piper Close
Watkinson Road
Roman Way
Jupiter Way
Vulcan Way
Lockhart Close
Armour Close
Atlas Mews
Davey Close
Faraday Close
Biddestone Road
Widdenham Road
Quemerford Road
Pollard Close
Penn Road
Freegrove Road
Cardozo Road
Loraine Road
Caedmon Road
Shelburne Road
Lowman Road
Dunford Road
Jackson Road
Annette Road
Drakeley Court
Coach House Lane
Battledean Road
Highbury Terrace
Highbury Terrace Mews
Digswell Street
Crane Grove
Orleston Ms
Swan Yd
Hamp. Ct
Comp. Ter
Balmoral Grove
Market Road Gardens
Bradley Close
St. Clements
Elphinstone Street
Leigh Road
0.25 mile
0.25 km

Holloway Road / Arsenal

Much like the football team the area shares its name with, there is a lot of potential talent here that needs time to come to fruition. On match days the streets make a sardine tin look roomy. This area also includes the grotty stretch of Holloway Road. For something different try House of Harlot for fetish fashion, El Comandante for drinks, and Tbilisi for cheap eastern European eats.

Coffee

- **Cafe Nero** • 348 Holloway Rd
- **Le Peche Mignon** • 6 Ronalds Rd

Landmarks

- **Gillespie Park** • 191 Drayton Park

Libraries

- **Central Library** • 2 Fieldway Crescent

Nightlife

- **The Coronet** • 338 Holloway Rd
- **El Comandante** • 10 Annette Rd
- **Hen and Chicken Theatre Bar** • 109 St Paul's Rd
- **The Horatia** • 98 Holloway Rd
- **The Relentless Garage** • 20 Highbury Corner

Post Offices

- **Highbury** • 5 Highbury Corner
- **Holloway Rd** • 118 Holloway Rd

Restaurants

- **Dastarkhan** • 203 Holloway Rd
- **El Rincon Quiteno** • 235 Holloway Rd
- **Morgan M** • 489 Liverpool Rd
- **Tbilisi** • 91 Holloway Rd

Shopping

- **21st Century Retro** • 162 Holloway Rd
- **Fettered Pleasures** • 90 Holloway Rd
- **House of Harlot** • 90 Holloway Rd
- **Vivien of Holloway** • 294 Holloway Rd

Supermarkets

- **Waitrose** • 366 Holloway Rd

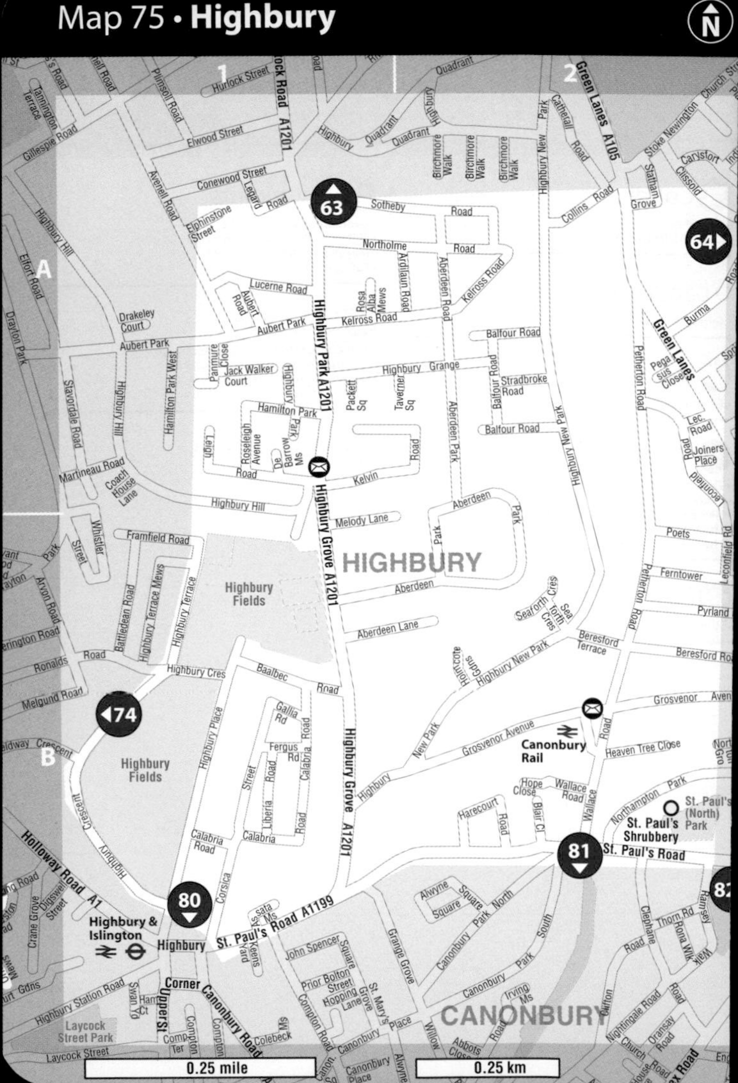
Map 75 • Highbury
N
1
2
A
B
63
64
74
80
81
HIGHBURY
CANONBURY
Highbury Fields
Highbury Fields
Highbury & Islington
Canonbury Rail
Highbury Corner
St. Paul's Shrubbery
St. Paul's (North) Park
Laycock Street Park
Hurlock Street
Elwood Street
Conewood Street
Plimsoll Road
Avenell Road
Legard Road
Elphinstone Street
Tannington Terrace
Gillespie Road
Highbury Hill
Elfort Road
Drayton Park
Drakeley Court
Aubert Park
Aubert Road
Lucerne Road
Highbury Quadrant
Quadrant
Birchmore Walk
Highbury New Park
Sotheby Road
Northolme Road
Ardilaun Road
Rosa Alba Mews
Kelross Road
Aberdeen Road
Balfour Road
Highbury Grange
Stradbroke Road
Collins Road
Cathcart Road
Green Lanes A105
Stoke Newington Church Street
Statham Grove
Carysfort Road
Clissold
Burma
Green Lanes
Pegasus Close
Petherton Road
Lec. Road
Joiners Place
Leconfield Road
Poets
Ferntower
Pyrland
Beresford Terrace
Beresford Road
Grosvenor Avenue
Heaven Tree Close
Northampton Park
St. Paul's Road
Highbury Park A1201
Highbury Grove A1201
Panmure Close
Jack Walker Court
Highbury Hill
Hamilton Park
Packett Sq
Taverner Sq
Leigh Road
Roseleigh Avenue
De Barnow Park Ms
Kelvin Road
Melody Lane
Aberdeen Park
Aberdeen Lane
Seaforth Cres
Sea Forth Cres
Hollycote Gdns
Hamilton Park West
Stavordale Road
Martineau Road
Coach House Lane
Framfield Road
Whistler Street
Battledean Road
Highbury Terrace Mews
Highbury Terrace
Highbury Cres
Baalbec Road
Gallia Rd
Fergus Rd
Calabria Road
Highbury Place
Liberia Road
Corsica Street
Arvon Road
Ronalds Road
Melgund Road
Holloway Road A1
Highbury Crescent
Digswell Street
Crane Grove
Highbury Station Road
Swan Yd
Upper St
Canonbury Road
Compton Ter
Colebeck Ms
Laycock Street
St. Paul's Road A1199
Asesata Ms
Keens Yard
John Spencer Square
Prior Bolton Street
Hopping Lane
St. Mary's Grove
Compton Road
Canonbury Place
Grange Grove
Alwyne Square
Canonbury Park North
Canonbury Park South
Irving Ms
Willow
Abbots Close
Harecourt Road
Hope Close
Wallace Road
Blair Cl
Clephane Road
Thorn Rd
Rona Wlk
Ramsey Walk
Nightingale Road
Oransay Road
Clifton
0.25 mile
0.25 km

Highbury

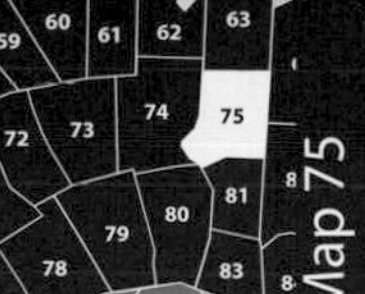

A residential area close enough to Upper Street to keep you entertained and far enough away to keep you grounded. Blessed with Highbury Fields, which during the summer is full of pretty things (in varying states of undress), and London's best music venue (Chapel Union), the area offers a healthy eclectic mix. Bordered by busy St Paul's Road and bustling Green Lanes, you'll never struggle for something to do here.

Landmarks

- **St Paul's Shrubbery** • St Paul's Rd & Northampton Park

Nightlife

- **Alwyne Castle** • 83 St. Pauls Rd
- **Oak Bar** • 79 Green Lanes
- **The Snooty Fox** • 75 Grosvenor Avenue

Post Offices

- **Grosvenor Avenue** • 91 Grosvenor Ave
- **Highbury Park** • 12 Highbury Park

Restaurants

- **Firezza** • 276 St Paul's Rd
- **San Daniele Del Friuli** • 72 Highbury Park
- **Ustun** • 107 Green Lanes

Shopping

- **Cabbies Delight Auto Parts** • 9 Green Lanes
- **La Fromagerie** • 30 Highbury Park
- **Mother Earth** • 282 St Paul's Rd

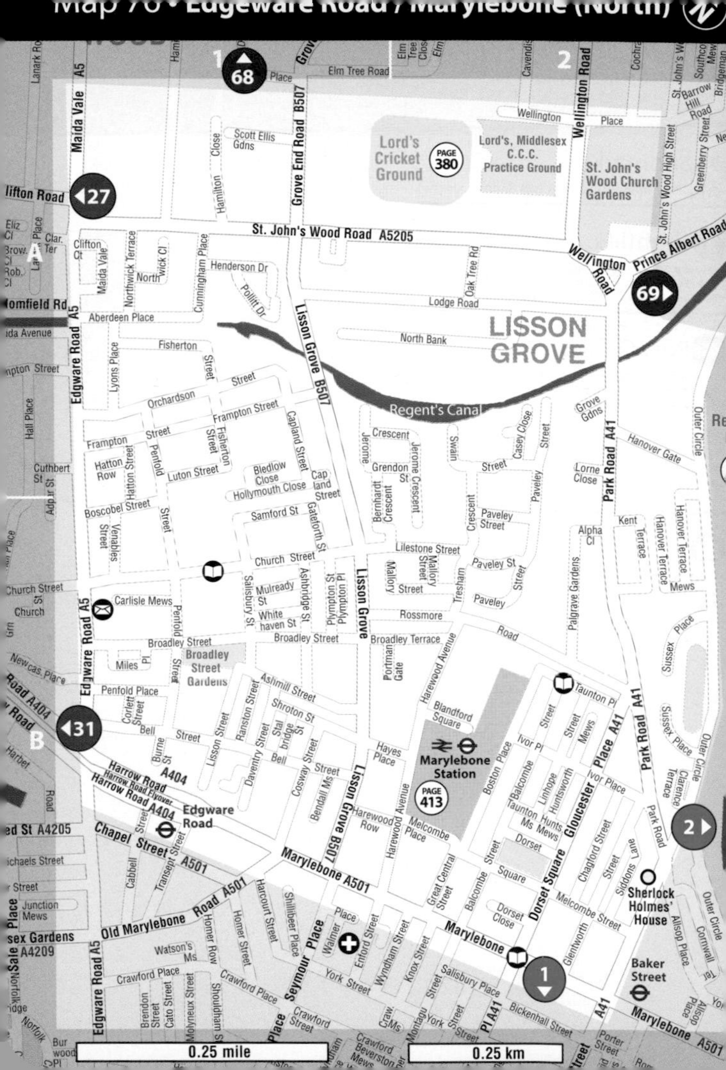
68
Elm Tree Road
Scott Ellis Gdns
Hamilton Close
Grove End Road B507
Lord's Cricket Ground
PAGE 380
Lord's, Middlesex C.C.C. Practice Ground
Wellington Place
Wellington Road
St. John's Wood Church Gardens
St. John's Wood High Street
Greenberry Street
St. Barrow Hill Road
Maida Vale A5
Clifton Road
27
St. John's Wood Road A5205
Wellington Road
Prince Albert Road
69
Clifton Ct
Maida Vale
Northwick Terrace
North wick Cl
Cunningham Place
Henderson Dr
Pollitt Dr
Oak Tree Rd
Lodge Road
Aberdeen Place
North Bank
LISSON GROVE
Lisson Grove B507
Edgware Road A5
Fisherton Street
Lyons Place
Orchardson Street
Frampton Street
Regent's Canal
Capland Street
Frampton Street
Fisherton Street
Penfold Street
Hatton Row
Hatton Street
Luton Street
Bledlow Close
Hollymouth Close
Capland Street
Jerome Crescent
Grendon St
Bernhardt Crescent
Swain Street
Casey Close
Paveley Street
Grove Gdns
Park Road A41
Hanover Gate
Outer Circle
Lorne Close
Boscobel Street
Venables Street
Samford St
Gateforth St
Crescent
Paveley Street
Alpha Cl
Kent Terrace
Hanover Terrace
Hanover Terrace Mews
Church Street
Lilestone Street
Mallory Street
Paveley St
Tresham Street
Salisbury St
Mulready St
Ashbridge St
Plympton St
Plympton Pl
Lisson Grove
Carlisle Mews
White haven St
Paveley Street
Rossmore Road
Palgrave Gardens
Broadley Street
Broadley Terrace
Harewood Avenue
Sussex Place
Broadley Street Gardens
Miles Pl
Portman Gate
Penfold Place
Ashmill Street
Taunton Pl
Shroton St
Blandford Square
Corlett Street
Bell Street
31
Ranston Street
Stalbridge St
Lisson Street
Ivor Pl
Burne St
Daventry Street
Bell Street
Hayes Place
Marylebone Station
Boston Place
Park Road A41
Gloucester Place A41
Clarence Terrace
Harrow Road A404
Harrow Road Flyover
Cosway Street
Bendall Ms
Lisson Grove B507
PAGE 413
Balcombe Street
Linhope Street
Huntsworth Mews
Ivor Place
Edgware Road
Harewood Row
Harewood Avenue
Melcombe Place
Taunton Ms
Hunts Mews
Dorset Square
Chagford Street
Park Road
2
Chapel Street A501
Transept Street
Cabbell Street
Marylebone A501
Great Central Street
Balcombe Street
Dorset Square
Melcombe Street
Siddons Lane
Sherlock Holmes' House
Junction Mews
Old Marylebone Road A501
Harcourt Street
Homer Row
Shillibeer Place
Walmer Place
Enford Street
Dorset Close
Glentworth Street
Allsop Place
Outer Circle
Cornwall
Watson's Ms
Homer Street
Wyndham Street
Knox Street
Marylebone
1
Baker Street
Crawford Place
Edgware Road A5
Brendon Street
Cato Street
Molyneux Street
Shouldham St
Crawford Place
Seymour Place
York Street
Salisbury Place
Montagu Street
Crawford Street
Craw. Ms
York Street
Pl A41
Bickenhall Street
A41
Marylebone A501
Porter Street
Crawford Beverston Mews
0.25 mile
0.25 km

Edgware Road / Marylebone (North)

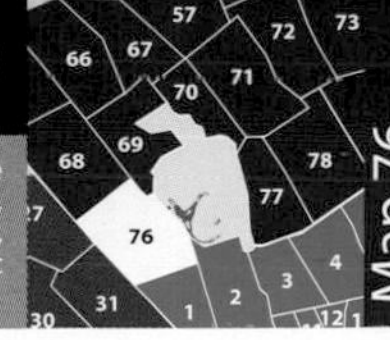

Marylebone Road is noisy enough to have you running for the taps of the twotwentytwo straight away. Things get calmer (meaning duller) further north, but Mandalay's inexpensive Burmese treats save the north end of Edgware Road, while the Sea Shell of Lisson Grove does fine fish. And did we mention the great detective? Baker Street, dear Watson, Baker Street.

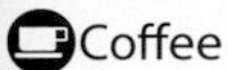

Coffee

- **Pret A Manger** • 120 Baker St

Emergency Rooms

- **Western Eye Hospital** • 173 Marylebone Rd

Landmarks

- **Sherlock Holmes' House** • 221 Baker St

Libraries

- **Church Street Library** • Church St
- **London Business School Library** • 25 Taunton Pl
- **Marylebone Library** • 109 Marylebone Rd

Nightlife

- **twotwentytwo** • 222 Marylebone Road
- **The Perseverance** • 11 Shroton Street
- **Volunteer** • 245 Baker St

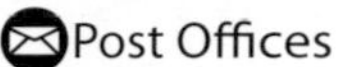

Post Offices

- **Edgware Rd** • 354 Edgware Rd

Restaurants

- **Mandalay** • 444 Edgware Rd
- **Sea Shell of Lisson Grove** • 49 Lisson Grove

Shopping

- **Alfie's Antiques Market** • 25 Church St
- **Archive Secondhand Books & Music** • 83 Bell St
- **Beatles London Store** • 231 Baker St
- **Elvisly Yours** • 233 Baker St
- **Lord's Cricket Shop** • Lord's Cricket Ground, Lisson Grove

Supermarkets

- **Tesco** • 94 Church St

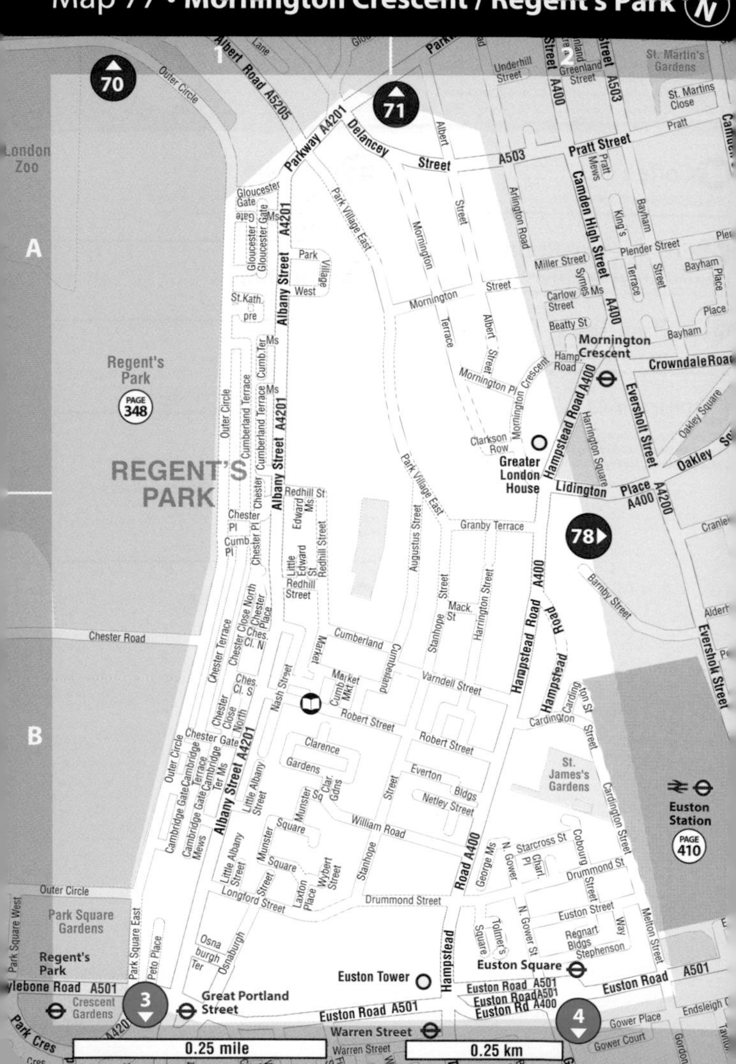

70
71
78
3
4
1
2
A
B
Regent's Park
PAGE 348
REGENT'S PARK
London Zoo
Albert Road A5205
Outer Circle
Parkway A4201
Delancey Street
Albany Street A4201
Park Village East
Park Village West
Gloucester Gate
Mornington Crescent
Mornington Terrace
Camden High Street
Hampstead Road A400
Eversholt Street
Pratt Street
Crowndale Road
Oakley Square
Lidington Place
Greater London House
Granby Terrace
Augustus Street
Harrington Street
Varndell Street
Robert Street
Cumberland Market
Chester Road
Chester Terrace
Cambridge Terrace
Clarence Gardens
Munster Square
William Road
Drummond Street
Stanhope Street
Longford Street
Osnaburgh Street
St. James's Gardens
Cardington Street
Euston Station
PAGE 410
Euston Square
Euston Tower
Euston Road A501
Great Portland Street
Warren Street
Park Square Gardens
Park Square East
Park Square West
Marylebone Road A501
Crescent Gardens
Park Cres
Gower Place
Gower Court
Melton Street
Endsleigh
St. Martin's Gardens
0.25 mile
0.25 km

Mornington Crescent / Regent's Park

Hemmed in by Regent's Park and Euston, this patch combines pretty streets with tower-block thoroughfares. Skip the din of Euston underpass for Drummond Street, Camden's 'little India'—decent dosas in Bhel Poori, Chutneys for veggies, the Crown & Anchor for mugs of Black Sheep ale. Chow on tofu cheesecake with beatnik slam poets in Green Note. Mingle al fresco with Edinboro Castle's yuppier folk.

Landmarks

- **Euston Tower** • 286 Euston Rd
- **Greater London House** • Hampstead Rd

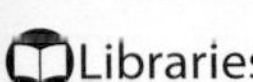

Libraries

- **Regents Park Library** • Robert St [Compton Close]

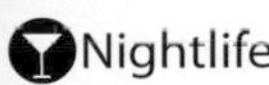

Nightlife

- **Crown & Anchor** • 137 Drummond St
- **Edinboro Castle** • 57 Mornington Terrace
- **Euston Tap** • 190 Euston Rd
- **Queen's Head and Artichoke** • 30 Albany St

Restaurants

- **Chutneys** • 124 Drummond St
- **Diwana Bhel Poori** • 121 Drummond St
- **The Green Note** • 106 Parkway
- **Mestizo** • 103 Hampstead Rd

Shopping

- **Calumet Trading** • 93 Drummond St
- **Chess & Bridge** • 369 Euston Rd
- **Greens and Beans** • 131 Drummond St

Map 78 • **Euston**

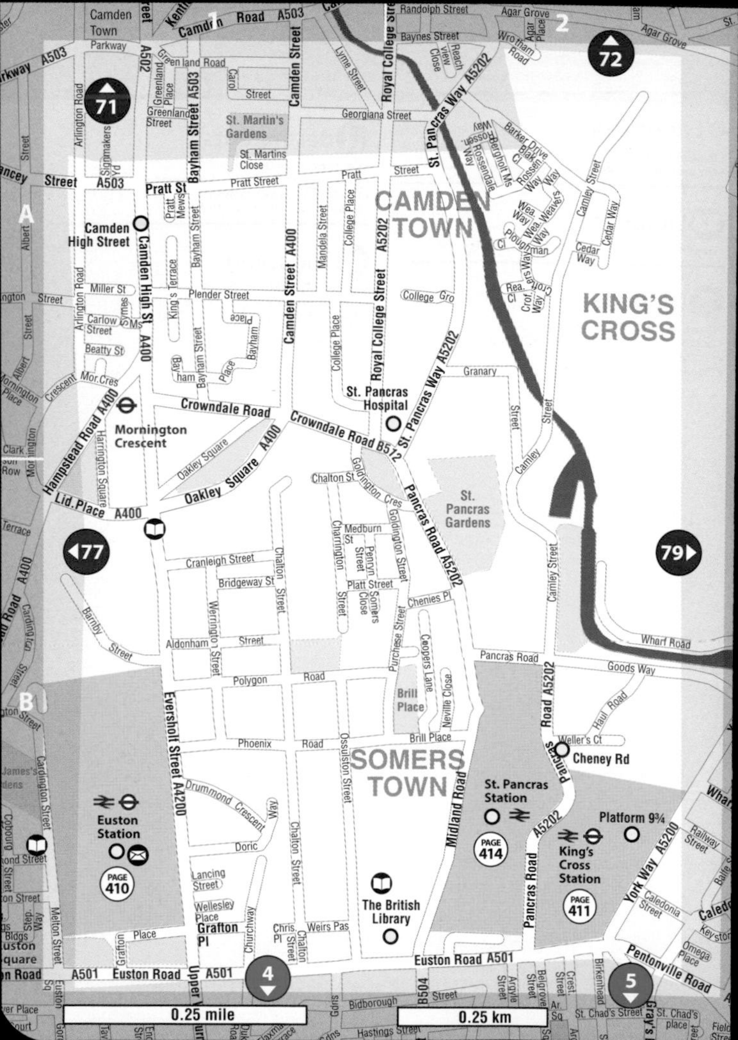

Camden Town
Camden Road A503
Parkway
Parkway A503
A502
Greenland Road
Greenland Place
Greenland Street
Carol Street
Camden Street
Bayham Street A503
St. Martin's Gardens
St. Martins Close
Lyme Street
Royal College Street
Randolph Street
Baynes Street
Reach view Close
Georgiana Street
St. Pancras Way A5202
Agar Grove
Agar Place
Wrotham Road
Arlington Road
Signmakers Yd
Street A503
Pratt St
Pratt Street
Pratt Mews
Street
Rossendale Way
Bergholt Ms
Barker Drive
Blakeney Cl
Rossendale Way
Weavers Way
Wrotham Cl
Ploughman Way
Camley Street
Cedar Way
CAMDEN TOWN
Camden High Street
Camden High St A400
Bayham Street
Mandela Street
College Place
A5202
Camden Street A400
King's Terrace
Plender Street
Miller St
Symes Ms
Carlow Street
Beatty St
Bayham Place
College Gro
Royal College Street
Rea Cl
Crofters Way
KING'S CROSS
Mor. Cres
Crescent
Mornington Place
Crowndale Road
Crowndale Road B572
St. Pancras Hospital
St. Pancras Way A5202
Granary Street
Camley Street
Mornington Crescent
Hampstead Road A400
Harrington Square
Oakley Square
Oakley Square A400
Chalton St
Goldington Cres
Pancras Road A5202
St. Pancras Gardens
Lid. Place A400
Medburn St
Charrington Street
Pennyn Street
Goldington Street
Cranleigh Street
Chalton Street
Bridgeway St
Platt Street
Somers Close
Chenies Pl
Camley Street
77
79
71
72
1
2
A
B
Barnby Street
Werrington Street
Aldenham Street
Purchese Street
Coopers Lane
Wharf Road
Pancras Road
Goods Way
Polygon Road
Brill Place
Neville Close
Road A5202
Haul Road
Eversholt Street A4200
Phoenix Road
Ossulston Street
Brill Place
Weller's Ct
Cheney Rd
SOMERS TOWN
Midland Road
St. Pancras Station
Pancras Road A5202
Drummond Crescent
Doric Way
Platform 9¾
Euston Station
PAGE 410
PAGE 414
PAGE 411
King's Cross Station
York Way A5200
Railway Street
Caledonia Street
Lancing Street
Chalton Street
The British Library
Wellesley Place
Grafton Pl
Churchway
Chris Pl
Weirs Pas
Cardington Street
Melton Street
Grafton Place
Euston Road A501
A501 Euston Road
Upper Woburn Pl
A501
Birkenhead Street
Pentonville Road
Omega Place
Keystone Cres
4
5
B504
Bidborough Street
Argyle Street
Belgrove Street
Crestfield Street
St. Chad's Street
Gray's Inn Road
St. Chad's Place
0.25 mile
0.25 km
Hastings Street

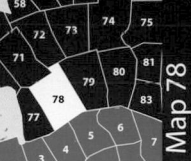

Euston

Euston's the first port of call for thousands of people each day, be it city workers from the Shires or pilgrims to the many erotic bookshops by the railway. Look beyond the station—an ugly grey cube that dominates the area—and you find few gems. Students and bookish types head to the outstanding library (British that is), hipsters to the Wills-Moody Jumble Sale, while beer aficionados head to Euston Tap.

Coffee

- **Bagel Factory** • Euston Station
- **The Espresso Bar** • 96 Euston Rd
- **Pret A Manger** • 296 Pentonville Rd
- **Pret A Manger** • 117 Euston Rd
- **Starbucks** • 296 Pentonville Rd

Landmarks

- **The British Library** • 96 Euston Rd
- **Camden High Street** • Camden High St & Delancey St
- **Cheney Road** • Cheney Rd & Weller's Ct
- **Euston Station** • Eversholt St & Doric Way
- **Platform 9¾** • King's Cross Station
- **St Pancras**• Pancras Rd & Euston Rd
- **St Pancras Hospital** • 4 St Pancras Way

Libraries

- **The British Library** • 96 Euston Rd
- **Camden Town Library** • 218 Eversholt St
- **Wellcome Library** • 183 Euston Rd

Nightlife

- **The Camden Head** • 100 Camden High St
- **The Champagne Bar at St Pancras** • Pancras Rd
- **The Crown & Goose** • 100 Arlington Rd
- **Lincoln Lounge** • 52 York Way
- **Purple Turtle** • 61 Crowndale Rd
- **Scala** • 275 Pentonville Rd

Post Offices

- **Kings Cross** • 21 Euston St

Restaurants

- **Asakusa** • 265 Eversholt St
- **Banger Bros.** • Euston Station
- **Camino** • 3 Varnisher's Yard
- **Chop Chop Noodle Bar** • 1 Euston Rd
- **El Parador** • 245 Eversholt St
- **Great Nepalese** • 48 Eversholt St
- **Kitchin** • 8 Caledonia St
- **Rodon Live** • 7 Pratt St
- **The Somerstown Coffee House** • 60 Chalton St
- **Tony's Natural Foods** • 10 Caledonian Rd

Shopping

- **All Ages Records** • 27 Pratt St
- **Housmans Bookshop** • 5 Caledonian Rd
- **Peyton & Byrne** • Pancras Rd
- **Transformation** • 52 Eversholt St

Supermarkets

- **Sainsbury's** • 10 Camden High St

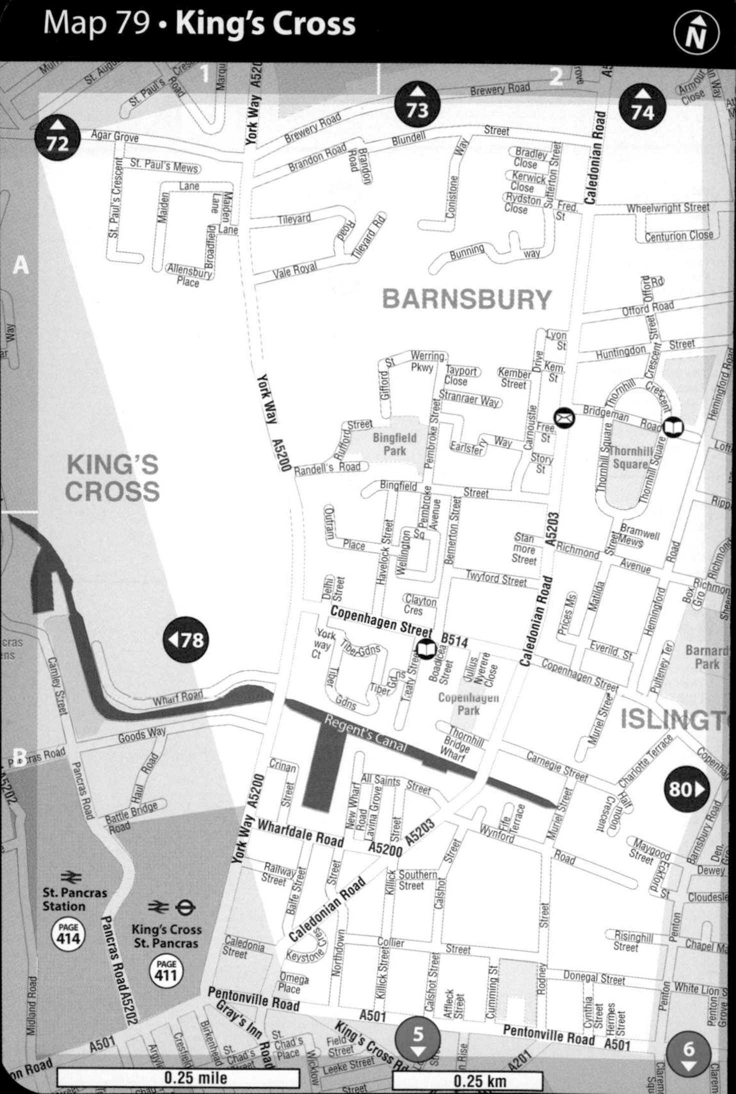

BARNSBURY
KING'S CROSS
ISLINGTON
York Way
Caledonian Road
Pentonville Road
Copenhagen Street
Regent's Canal
Bingfield Park
Thornhill Square
Copenhagen Park
Barnard Park
St. Pancras Station
King's Cross St. Pancras
Pancras Road
Wharfdale Road
Goods Way
Wharf Road
Gray's Inn Road
0.25 mile
0.25 km

King's Cross

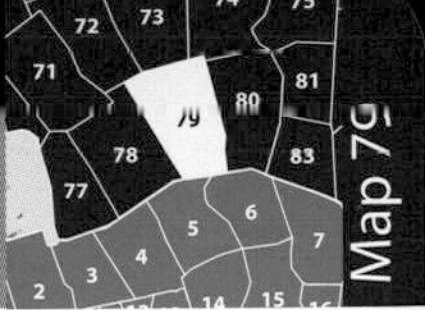

No area in North London benefited more from the Olympic games than this crucial commuter hub. The once tawdry Kings Cross Station has a new face and a modern aura while St Pancras is as glorious a station as you'll find in Europe. Once London's seediest spot the KC is now full of rakish bars and clubs with excellent live music and some tasty eats up Caledonian Road.

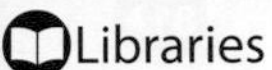

Libraries

- **Lewis Carroll Children's Library** • 166 Copenhagen St
- **West Library** • Bridgeman Road

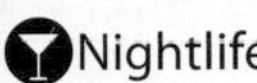

Nightlife

- **The Big Chill House** • 257 Pentonville Rd
- **Canal 125** • 125 Caledonian Rd
- **Central Station** • 37 Wharfdale Rd
- **Cross Kings** • 126 York Way
- **Drink, Shop & Do** • 9 Caledonian Rd
- **EGG** • 200 York Way
- **Hemingford Arms** • 128 Hemingford Rd
- **The Lexington** • 96 Pentonville Rd
- **Lincoln Lounge** • 52 York Way
- **Simmons** • 32 Caledonian Rd
- **Tarmon** • 270 Caledonian Rd

Post Offices

- **Caledonian Road** • 320 Caledonian Rd

Restaurants

- **Addis** • 42 Caledonian Rd
- **Drink, Shop & Do** • 9 Caledonian Rd
- **Dallas Burger Bar** • 257 Caledonian Rd
- **Euro Café** • 299 Caledonian Rd
- **Marathon** • 196 Caledonian Rd
- **Menelik** • 277 Caledonian Rd
- **The New Didar** • 347 Caledonian Rd
- **Oz** • 53 Caledonian Rd
- **Yum Yum** • 48 Caledonian Rd

Shopping

- **Cosmo Cornelio** • 182 Caledonian Rd
- **King's Cross Continental Stores** • 26 Caledonian Rd

Supermarkets

- **Co-Op** • 303 Caledonian Rd
- **Iceland** • 259 Caledonian Rd

Map 80 • Angel / Upper St

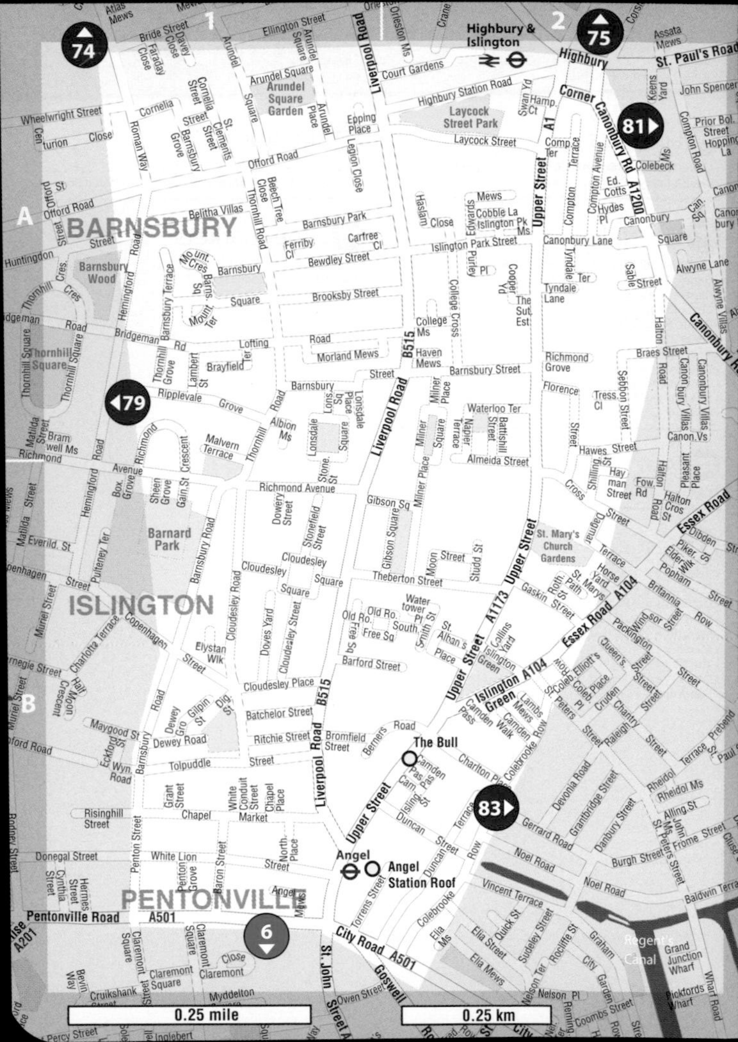

N

74
75
81
79
83
6

Highbury & Islington

Highbury Corner

BARNSBURY

ISLINGTON

PENTONVILLE

Arundel Square Garden

Laycock Street Park

Barnsbury Wood

Thornhill Square

Barnard Park

St. Mary's Church Gardens

Islington Green

The Bull

Angel

Angel Station Roof

Regent's Canal

Grand Junction Wharf

Pickfords Wharf

Upper Street

Liverpool Road

Canonbury Road A1200

Essex Road A104

City Road A501

Pentonville Road A501

Upper Street A1173

Caledonian Road

Barnsbury Street

Richmond Avenue

Cloudesley Road

Copenhagen Street

St. John Street

Goswell Road

0.25 mile

0.25 km

Angel / Upper St

A purpose-built playground for a twenty-something crowd that has to wake up for work in the morning. Whether it's the boutique shops, bars, and restaurants that cater to any and all tastes occupying Upper Street, the antique shops along Camden Passage, or an eclectic and vivid live music and theatre scene (head to the Kings Head Pub for both), Angel has it all, and much more.

Cinemas

- **Everyman Screen on the Green** • 83 Islington Green
- **Vue Islington** • 36 Parkfield St

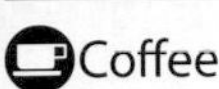

Coffee

- **Estorick Gallery** • 39 Canonbury Sq
- **Euphorium Bakery** • 202 Upper St
- **Pret A Manger** • 27 Islington High St
- **Starbucks** • 71 Upper St
- **Starbucks** • 30 Upper St
- **Starbucks** • 7 Islington High St
- **Tinderbox** • 21 Upper St

Landmarks

- **Angel Station Roof**
- **The Bull** •100 Upper St

Nightlife

- **25 Canonbury** • 25 Canonbury Lane
- **Albert & Pearl** • 181 Upper St
- **The Angel** • 3 Islington High St
- **The Angelic** • 57 Liverpool Rd
- **Buffalo Bar** • 259 Upper St
- **Camden Head** • 2 Camden Walk
- **The Castle** • 54 Pentonville Rd
- **Colebrookes** • 69 Colebrooke Row
- **Compton Arms** • 4 Compton Ave
- **The Crown** • 116 Cloudesley Rd
- **Cuba Libre** • 72 Upper St
- **The Drapers Arms** • 44 Barnsbury St
- **Electrowerkz** • 7 Torrens St
- **The Florence** • 50 Florence St
- **The Garage** • 20 Highbury Corner
- **Hope And Anchor** • 207 Upper St
- **Islington Academy** • 16 Parkfield St
- **The Islington Tap** • 80 Liverpool Rd
- **Jury's Inn** • 60 Pentonville Rd
- **Keston Lodge** • 131 Upper St
- **King's Head Theatre & Pub** • 115 Upper St
- **Lucky Voice** • 173 Upper St
- **Old Red Lion** • 418 St John St
- **Public House** • 54 Islington Park St
- **The Regent** • 201 Liverpool Rd
- **Round Midnight: Jazz and Blues Bar** • 13 Liverpool Rd
- **Slimelight** • 7 Torrens St
- **Union Chapel** • Compton Terrace

Restaurants

- **Afghan Kitchen** • 35 Islington Green
- **The Albion** • 10 Thornhill Rd
- **Alpino** • 97 Chapel Market
- **The Breakfast Club** • 31 Camden Passage
- **Candid Café** • 3 Torrens St
- **Desperados** • 127 Upper St
- **Elk in the Woods** • 39 Camden Passage
- **Fig and Olive** • 151 Upper St
- **Fine Burger Co** • 330 Upper St
- **Fredericks** • Camden Passage
- **Gem** • 265 Upper St
- **House** • 63 Canonbury Rd
- **Indian Veg Bhelpoori House** • 93 Chapel Market
- **Isarn** • 119 Upper St
- **Itsuka** • 54 Islington Park St
- **La Forchetta** • 73 Upper St
- **La Porchetta** • 141 Upper St
- **Le Mercury** • 140 Upper St
- **Masala Zone** • 80 Upper St
- **Mem & Laz** • 8 Theberton St
- **Metrogusto** • 13 Theberton St
- **Olive Grill** • 61 Upper St
- **Ottolenghi** • 287 Upper St
- **Pizzeria Oregano** • 19 St Alban's Pl
- **Pomegranate** • 139 Upper St
- **Rodizo Rico** • 77 Upper St
- **The Seagrass** • 74 Chapel Market
- **Tortilla** • 13 Islington High St
- **Vigata Ristorante** • 70 Liverpool Rd
- **Zaffrani** • 47 Cross St

Shopping

- **A Ferrari Deli** • 48 Cross St
- **After Noah** • 121 Upper St
- **Annie's Vintage Costume and Textiles** • 12 Camden Passage
- **Camden Passage** • Camden Passage
- **Cass Art** • 66 Colebrooke Row
- **Gill Wing Kitchen Shop** • 194 Upper St
- **Little Paris** • 262 Upper St
- **Monte's Deli** • 23 Canonbury Lane
- **Palette London** • 21 Canonbury Ln
- **Paul A Young Fine Chocolates** • 33 Camden Passage
- **Raymond Roe Fishmonger** • 35 Chapel Market
- **Twentytwentyone** • 274 Upper St

Supermarkets

- **Iceland** • 62 Chapel Market

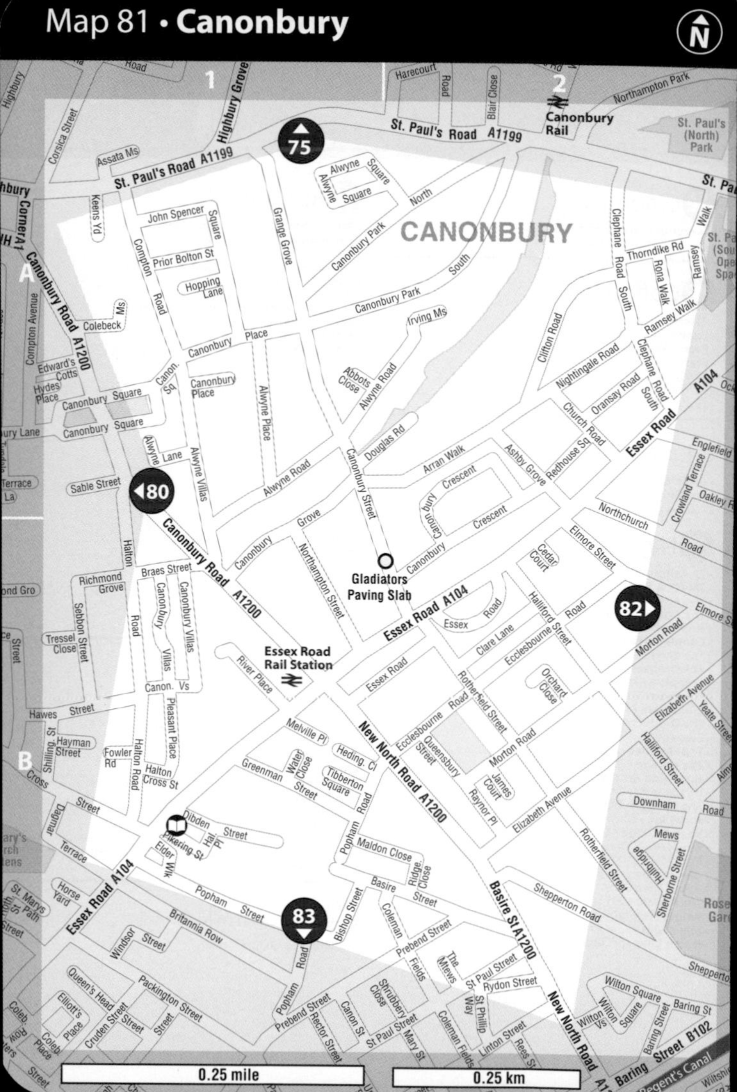
Map 81 • Canonbury
N
1
2
A
B
CANONBURY
75
80
82
83
Canonbury Rail
Essex Road Rail Station
Gladiators Paving Slab
St. Paul's Road A1199
Highbury Grove
Highbury Corner A1
Corsica Street
Assata Ms
Keens Yd
Canonbury Road A1200
Compton Avenue
Colebeck Ms
Edward's Cotts
Hydes Place
Canonbury Square
Canonbury Lane
Sable Street
Compton Road
John Spencer Square
Prior Bolton St
Hopping Lane
Canonbury Place
Canon. Sq
Alwyne Lane
Alwyne Villas
Alwyne Place
Alwyne Road
Alwyne Square
Grange Grove
Canonbury Park North
Canonbury Park South
Irving Ms
Abbots Close
Douglas Rd
Canonbury Street
Canonbury Grove
Northampton Street
Harecourt Road
Blair Close
Northampton Park
St. Paul's (North) Park
Clephane Road South
Clephane Road North
Thorndike Rd
Rona Walk
Ramsey Walk
Clifton Road
Nightingale Road
Oransay Road
Church Road
Redhouse Sq
Ashby Grove
Arran Walk
Canonbury Crescent
Essex Road A104
Englefield Road
Crowland Terrace
Oakley Road
Northchurch Road
Elmore Street
Cedar Court
Halliford Street
Ecclesbourne Road
Clare Lane
Essex Road
Orchard Close
Morton Road
Rotherfield Street
Elizabeth Avenue
Yeate Street
Downham Road
Hullbridge Mews
Sherborne Street
Queensbury Street
James Court
Raynor Pl
Shepperton Road
Halton Road
Richmond Grove
Braes Street
Canonbury Villas
Canon. Vs
Sebbon Street
Tressel Close
River Place
Hawes Street
Pleasant Place
Shillingford St
Hayman Street
Fowler Rd
Halton Cross St
Cross Street
Dagmar Terrace
Melville Pl
Heding. Cl
Water Close
Tibberton Square
Greenman Street
Popham Road
Dibden Street
Hall Pl
Pikering St
Elder Wlk
Maldon Close
Ridge Close
Basire Street
Popham Street
New North Road A1200
Basire St A1200
Horse Yard
St Marys Path
Britannia Row
Windsor Street
Bishop Street
Coleman Fields
Prebend Street
The Mews
St Paul Street
Rydon Street
St Phillip Way
Queen's Head Street
Packington Street
Elliott's Place
Cruden Street
Colebrooke Row
Colebrooke Place
Rector Street
Canon St
Shrubbery Close
Mary St
Linton Street
Rees St
New North Road
Wilton Square
Wilton Vs
Baring Street B102
Regent's Canal
0.25 mile
0.25 km

Canonbury

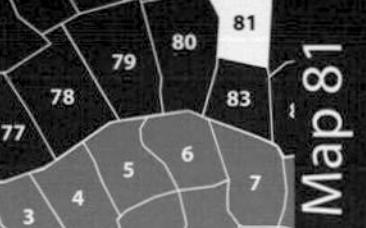

The Cannobury area is a delicious cocktail of diversity with a heady mix of leafy spacious streets, multi-million pound mansions, a dollop of tempered hipster abodes, and some of London's poorest estates. Essex Road has a Banksy and quirky shops, including the notable Get Stuffed for all your taxidermy needs. Foodies are well catered for with real butchers (James Elliot), bakers (Raabís), and great ethnic eateries (Zigni House and Sabor)

Landmarks

- **Gladiators Paving Slab** • 10 Canonbury St

Libraries

- **South Library** • 115 Essex Rd

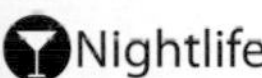

Nightlife

- **Embassy Bar** • 119 Essex Rd
- **Marquess Tavern** • 32 Canonbury St
- **Myddleton Arms** • 52 Canonbury Rd
- **The Green Man** • 144 Essex Rd
- **The Lord Clyde** • 342 Essex Rd

Restaurants

- **Angel Cafe** • 100 Essex Rd
- **Raab's Bakery** • 136 Essex Rd
- **Sabor** • 108 Essex Rd
- **Zigni House** • 330 Essex Rd

Shopping

- **Get Stuffed** • 105 Essex Rd
- **Handmade and Found** • 109 Essex Rd
- **HG Lockey & Sons** • 8 Halton Cross St
- **James Elliot Master Butcher** • 96 Essex Rd
- **Planet Organic** • 64 Essex Rd
- **Raab's The Baker's** • 136 Essex Rd
- **Sew Fantastic** • 107 Essex Rd
- **Steve Hatt** • 88 Essex Rd

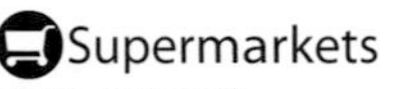

Supermarkets

- **Co-Op** • 132 Essex Rd

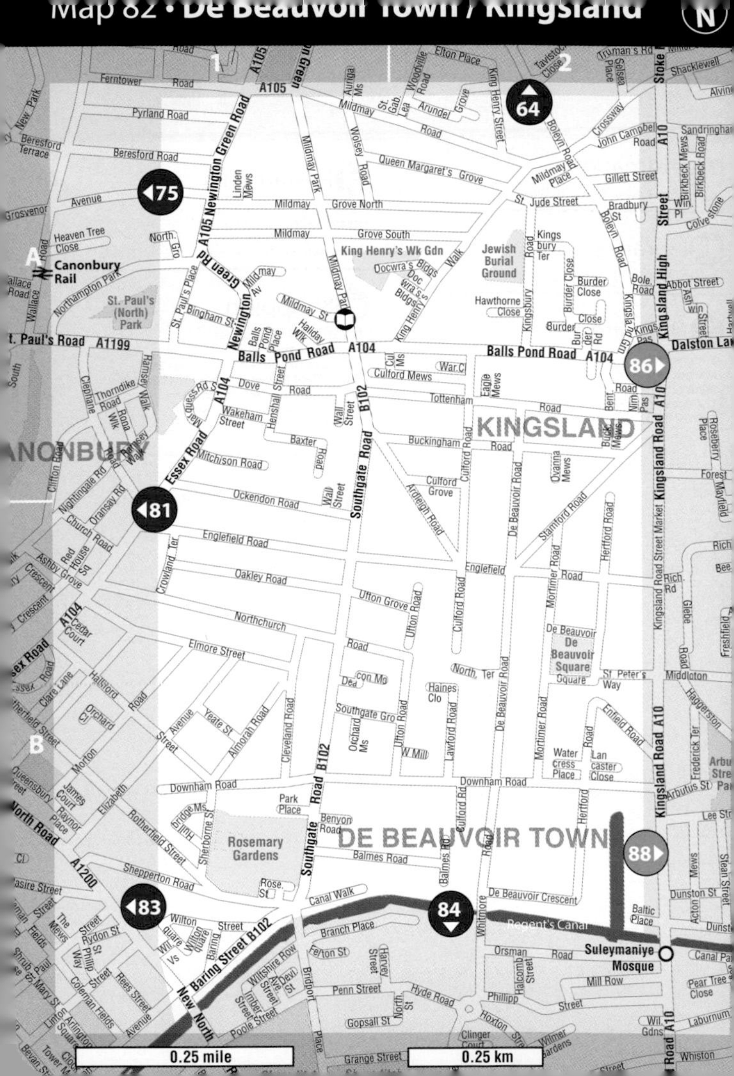

KINGSLAND
DE BEAUVOIR TOWN
CANONBURY
Canonbury Rail
St. Paul's (North) Park
King Henry's Wk Gdn
Jewish Burial Ground
De Beauvoir Square
Rosemary Gardens
Regent's Canal
Suleymaniye Mosque
Balls Pond Road A104
St. Paul's Road A1199
Kingsland Road A10
Southgate Road B102
Essex Road A104
Newington Green Road A105
Baring Street B102
Downham Road
0.25 mile
0.25 km

De Beauvoir Town / Kingsland

De Beauvoir is the buffer zone where swanky Islington meets the erroneous Dalston. As such it's an ideal place to get a reprieve from either side. To the west, are quiet squares and gastro pubs, venture east and you'll be up-till-dawn boozing talking to individuals that comic book writers couldn't dream up. When you're sick of both sit in De Beauvoir Square (with its thousands of palm trees) and ponder life.

Coffee

- **2&4 Gallery** • 4 Southgate Rd
- **Bird Café** • 52 Boleyn Rd
- **Haggerston Espresso Rooms** • 13 Downham Rd
- **Reilly Rocket** • 507 Kingsland Rd
- **Tina, We Salute You** • 47 King Henry's Walk

Landmarks

- **Suleymaniye Mosque** • 212 Kingsland Rd

Libraries

- **Mildmay Library** • 21 Mildmay Park

Nightlife

- **Dalston Boys Club** • 68 Boleyn Rd
- **Dalston Jazz Bar** • 4 Bradbury St
- **Hunter S** • 194 Southgate Rd
- **The Northgate** • 113 Southgate Rd
- **The Orwell** • 382 Essex Rd
- **The Rosemary Branch** • 2 Shepperton Rd
- **The Vortex** • 11 Gillett Sq
- **The Duke of Wellington** • 119 Balls Pond Rd

Restaurants

- **Casaba** • 162 Essex Rd
- **Duke's Brew & Que** • 33 Downham Rd
- **Huong Viet** • 12 Englefield Rd
- **Fuji Fuji** • 122 Balls Pond Rd

Shopping

- **2&4 Gallery** • 4 Southgate Rd
- **North One Garden Centre** • 25 Englefield Rd

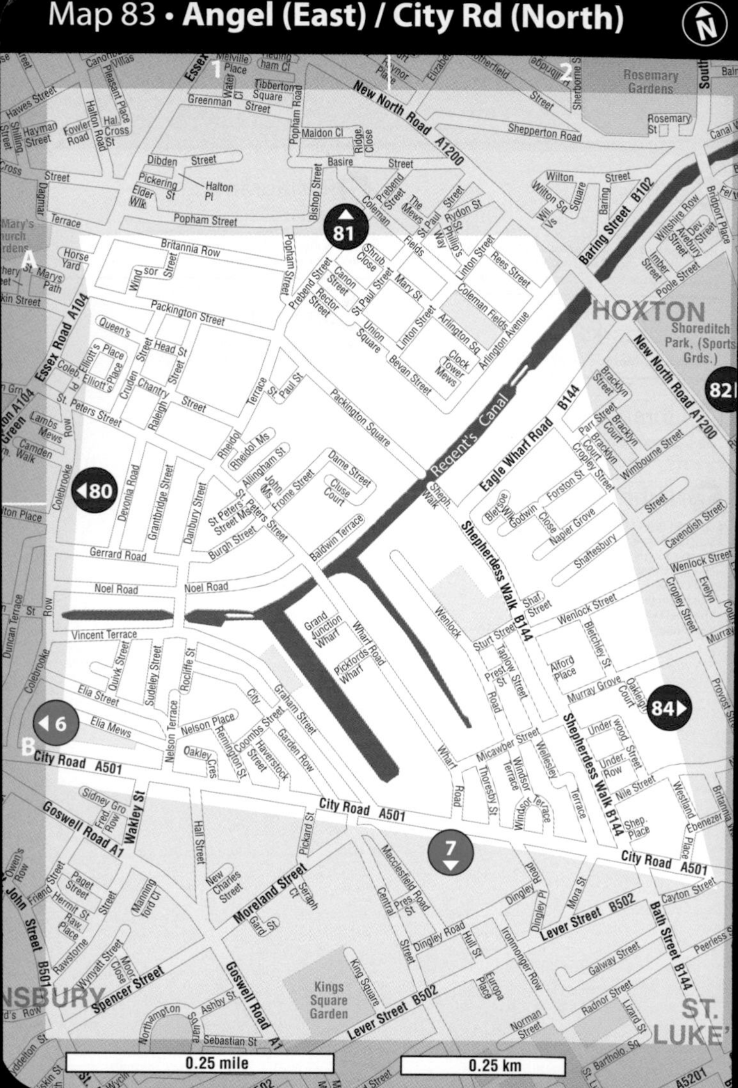

N
Essex Road A104
New North Road A1200
Shepperton Road
Rosemary Gardens
Rosemary St
Canal
Baring Street B102
HOXTON
Shoreditch Park, (Sports Grds.)
New North Road A1200
Regent's Canal
Eagle Wharf Road B144
Shepherdess Walk B144
Wenlock
Wharf Road
Packington Street
Packington Square
Popham Street
Britannia Row
St. Peters Street
Colebrooke Row
Devonia Road
Grantbridge Street
Danbury Street
Gerrard Road
Noel Road
Vincent Terrace
Elia Street
Elia Mews
City Road A501
Goswell Road A1
Wakley St
Hall Street
Moreland Street
Macclesfield Road
Central Street
Dingley Road
Lever Street B502
Bath Street B144
City Road A501
Wenlock Street
Murray Grove
Wimbourne Street
Cavendish Street
Cropley Street
Provost Street
Spencer Street
Kings Square Garden
Goswell Road A1
Ironmonger Row
Galway Street
Radnor Street
ST. LUKE'
0.25 mile
0.25 km
A
B
1
2
81
80
82
84
6
7

Angel (East) / City Rd (North)

If you're bored of the bars on Upper Street or the ironic chic of Hoxton, the streets in between (along Essex Road or by the canal) are a better bet, with a more laid-back atmosphere. The Island Queen (NFT London's official birthplace!) is a cosy local pub and well worth a visit. One day they'll just have to give us one of those blue plaques.

Coffee

- **Food Lab** • 56 Essex Rd

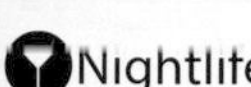

Nightlife

- **Barrio North** • 45 Essex Rd
- **The Charles Lamb** • 16 Elia St
- **The Duke of Cambridge** • 30 St Peter's St
- **Earl of Essex** • 25 Danbury St
- **The Narrow Boat** • 119 St.Peters St
- **Offside Bar and Gallery** • 273 City Rd
- **The Island Queen** • 87 Noel Rd
- **The Mucky Pup** • 39 Queen's Head St
- **The Old Queenís Head** • 44 Essex Rd
- **The Wenlock Arms** • 26 Wenlock Rd

Restaurants

- **The Charles Lamb** • 16 Elia St
- **Shepherdess Cafe** • 221 City Rd
- **William IV** • 7 Shepherdess Walk

Shopping

- **Flashback** • 50 Essex Rd
- **Haggle Vinyl** • 114 Essex Rd
- **Past Caring** • 54 Essex Rd

HOXTON

Shoreditch Park, (Sports Grds.)
Shoreditch Park Garden
Aske Gardens
Hoxton Square
White Cube
Old Street Rail Station
Village Underground
Bunhill Fields Burial Grounds
ST. LUKE'S

Regent's Canal
New North Road A1200
New North Road B101
East Road A1200
City Road A501
Old Street A5201
Old St A10
Kingsland Road A10
Hackney Road A1208
Great Eastern St A1202
Curtain Road A10
Hoxton Street
Pitfield Street B101
Baring Street B102
Calvert Av B122
Bath Street B144

0.25 mile
0.25 km

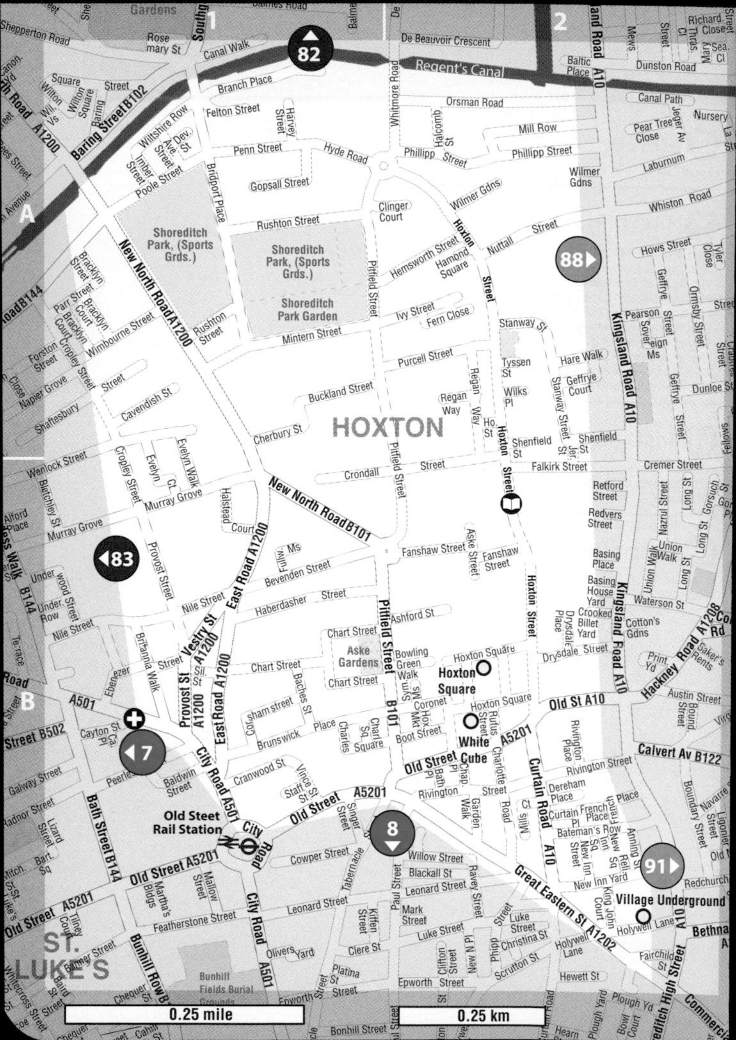

Hoxton

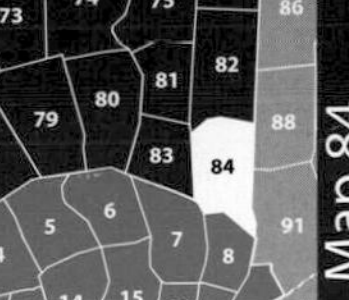

The only constant in Hoxton is change, what passes as monthly rent now, was a deposit on a pad a decade earlier. The vibe is special and the pulse of the area radiates out of Hoxton Square and its bedfellow Curtain Road. Shop at Hoxton Monster Supplies, check modern art at White Cube, drink at Electric Showrooms or Zigfried, eat Thai at Yelo, and finish on the floor at Cargo.

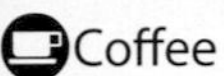

Coffee

- **Apostrophe** • 42 Great Eastern St
- **Eat.** • 59 Great Eastern St

Emergency Rooms

- **Moorfields Eye Hospital** • 162 City Rd

Landmarks

- **Hoxton Square** • Hoxton Sq
- **Village Underground** • 54 Holywell Ln
- **White Cube** • 48 Hoxton Square

Libraries

- **Shoreditch Library** • 80 Hoxton St

Nightlife

- **333 Mother** • 333 Old St
- **Bedroom Bar** • 62 Rivington St
- **The Bricklayer's Arms** • 63 Charlotte Rd
- **Cantaloupe** • 35 Charlotte Rd
- **Cargo** • 83 Rivington St
- **Charlie Wright's International Bar** • 45 Pitfield St
- **Club Aquarium** • 256 Old St
- **Cocomo** • 323 Old St
- **Comedy Cafe** • 66 Rivington St
- **East Village** • 89 Great Eastern St
- **The Elbow Room** • 97 Curtain Rd
- **Electricity Showroom** • 39 Hoxton Sq
- **Favela Chic** • 91 Great Eastern St
- **The Foundry** • 84 Great Eastern St
- **The Griffin** • 93 Leonard St
- **Happiness Forgets** • 9 Hoxton Square
- **Hoxton Square Bar and Kitchen** • 2 Hoxton Sq
- **The Legion** • 348 Old St
- **The Macbeth** • 60 70 Hoxton St
- **The Old Blue Last** • 38 Great Eastern St
- **Plastic People** • 147 Curtain Rd
- **Red Lion** • 41 Hoxton St
- **The Stag's Head** • 55 Orsman Rd
- **Strongroom Bar** • 120 Curtain Rd
- **Troy Bar** • 10 Hoxton St

Restaurants

- **The Bean** • 126 Curtain Rd
- **Big Apple Hot Dogs** • 239 Old St
- **The Diner** • 128 Curtain Rd
- **F. Cooke** • 150 Hoxton St
- **Fifteen** • 15 Westland Pl
- **Rivington Bar and Grill** • 28 Rivington St
- **Shish** • 313 Old St
- **Tramshed** • 32 Rivington St
- **Yelo** • 8 Hoxton Sq

Shopping

- **Good Hood** • 41 Coronet St
- **Hoxton Street Monster Supplies** • 159 Hoxton St
- **SCP** • 135 Curtain Road
- **Sh!** • 57 Hoxton Sq

Supermarkets

- **Co-Op** • 136 New North Rd
- **Iceland** • 209 Hoxton St

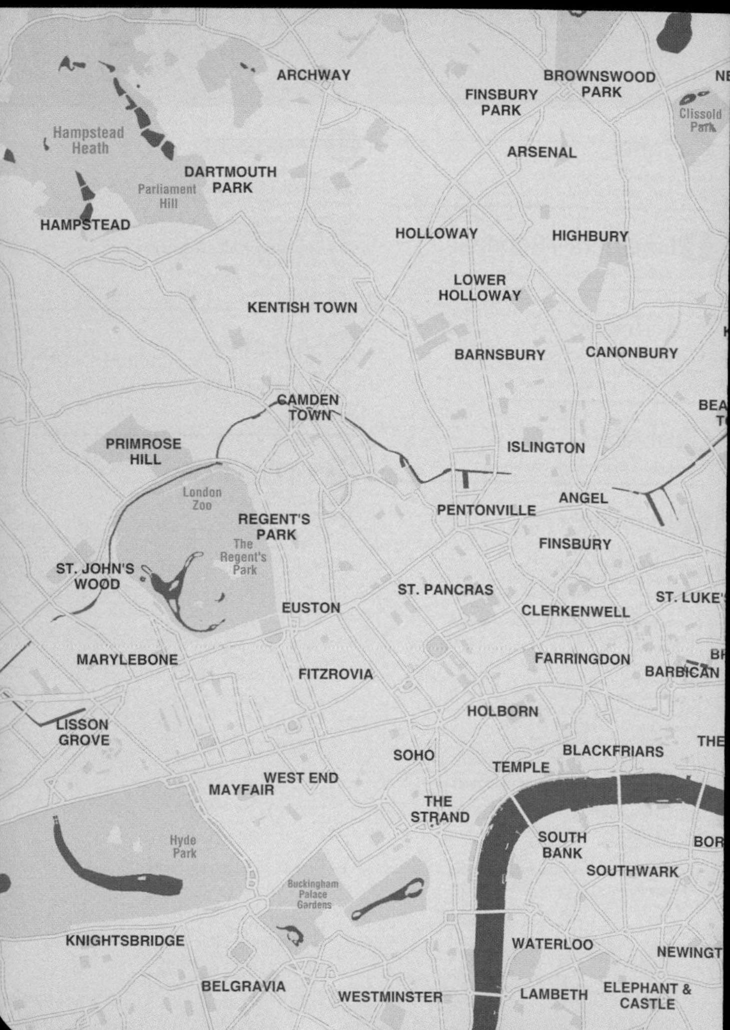
ARCHWAY
BROWNSWOOD PARK
FINSBURY PARK
Clissold Park
Hampstead Heath
ARSENAL
DARTMOUTH PARK
Parliament Hill
HAMPSTEAD
HOLLOWAY
HIGHBURY
LOWER HOLLOWAY
KENTISH TOWN
BARNSBURY
CANONBURY
CAMDEN TOWN
PRIMROSE HILL
ISLINGTON
London Zoo
ANGEL
PENTONVILLE
REGENT'S PARK
The Regent's Park
FINSBURY
ST. JOHN'S WOOD
ST. PANCRAS
EUSTON
CLERKENWELL
MARYLEBONE
FARRINGDON
BARBICAN
FITZROVIA
HOLBORN
LISSON GROVE
BLACKFRIARS
SOHO
TEMPLE
WEST END
MAYFAIR
THE STRAND
SOUTH BANK
Hyde Park
SOUTHWARK
Buckingham Palace Gardens
KNIGHTSBRIDGE
WATERLOO
BELGRAVIA
WESTMINSTER
LAMBETH
ELEPHANT & CASTLE

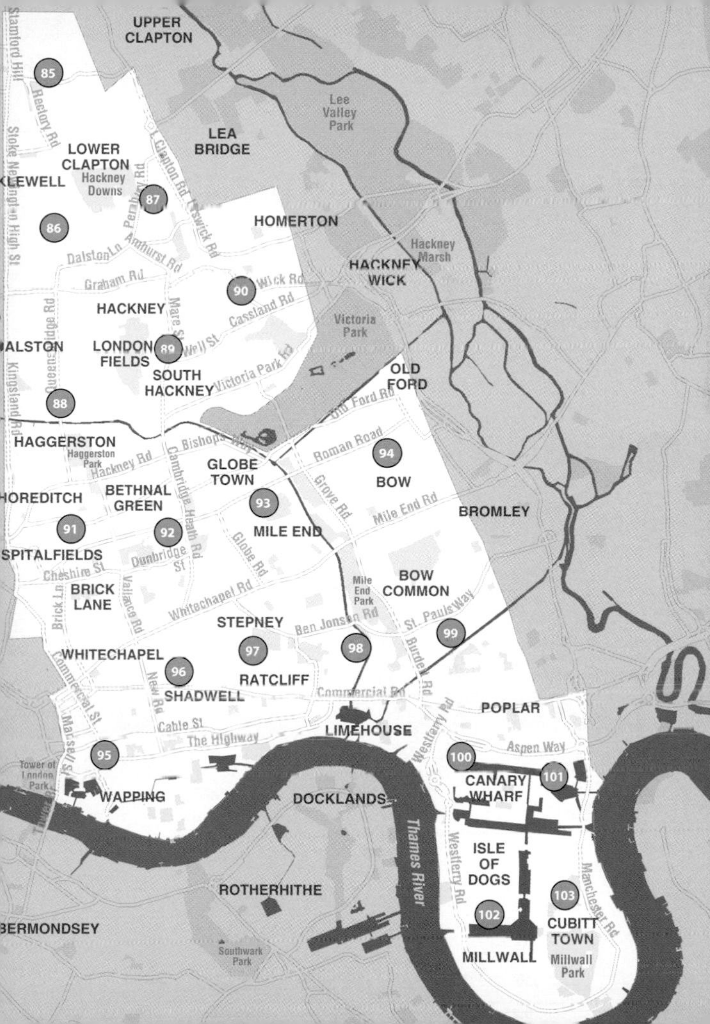
UPPER CLAPTON
LOWER CLAPTON
Hackney Downs
LEA BRIDGE
Lee Valley Park
HOMERTON
Hackney Marsh
HACKNEY WICK
Victoria Park
HACKNEY
LONDON FIELDS
SOUTH HACKNEY
OLD FORD
HAGGERSTON
Haggerston Park
GLOBE TOWN
BOW
BETHNAL GREEN
MILE END
BROMLEY
SPITALFIELDS
BRICK LANE
Mile End Park
BOW COMMON
STEPNEY
WHITECHAPEL
RATCLIFF
SHADWELL
LIMEHOUSE
POPLAR
Tower of London Park
WAPPING
DOCKLANDS
CANARY WHARF
ISLE OF DOGS
ROTHERHITHE
Thames River
CUBITT TOWN
MILLWALL
Millwall Park
Southwark Park
BERMONDSEY
Stamford Hill
Rectory Rd
Stoke Newington High St
Dalston Ln
Amhurst Rd
Graham Rd
Queensbridge Rd
Kingsland Rd
Mare St
Well St
Cassland Rd
Wick Rd
Victoria Park Rd
Old Ford Rd
Bishops Way
Hackney Rd
Cambridge Heath Rd
Roman Road
Grove Rd
Mile End Rd
Globe Rd
Dunbridge St
Cheshire St
Vallance Rd
Brick Ln
Whitechapel Rd
Ben Jonson Rd
St. Pauls Way
Burdett Rd
Commercial St
Commercial Rd
New Rd
Cable St
The Highway
Westferry Rd
Aspen Way
Manchester Rd
85
86
87
88
89
90
91
92
93
94
95
96
97
98
99
100
101
102
103

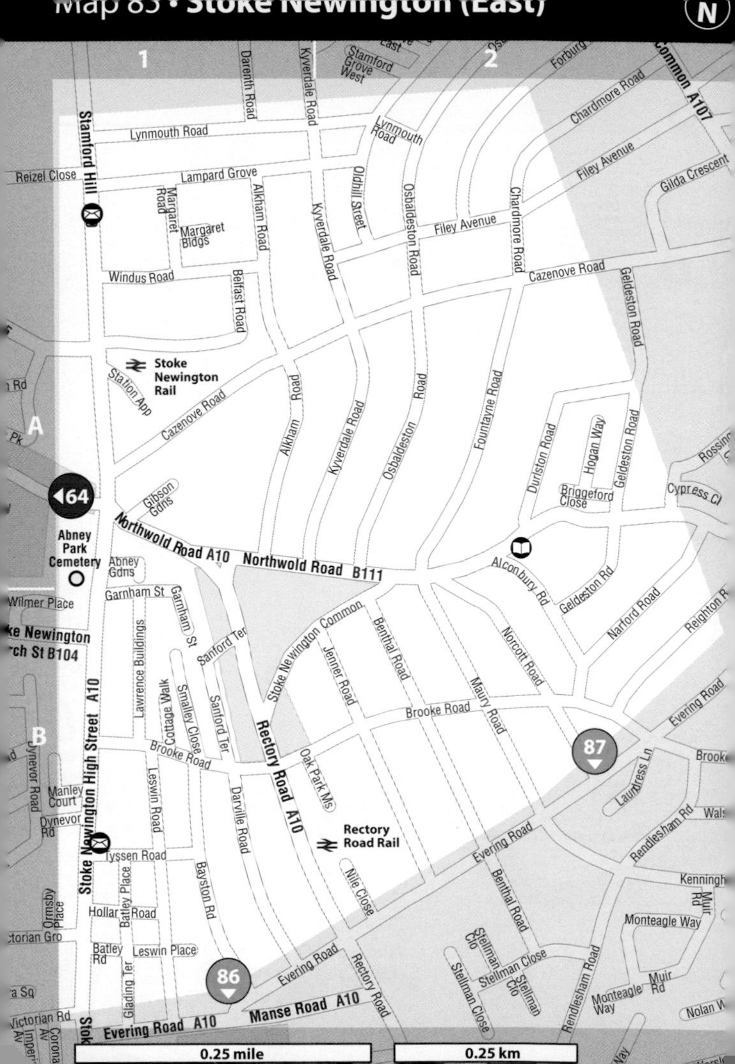

Stamford Grove West
Darenth Road
Kyverdale Road
Lynmouth Road
Stamford Hill
Reizel Close
Lampard Grove
Margaret Road
Margaret Bldgs
Alkham Road
Oldhill Street
Osbaldeston Road
Filey Avenue
Chardmore Road
Common A107
Gilda Crescent
Windus Road
Belfast Road
Cazenove Road
Geldeston Road
Stoke Newington Rail
Station App
Fountayne Road
Durlston Road
Hogan Way
Briggeford Close
Cypress Cl
Gibson Gdns
Northwold Road A10
Northwold Road B111
Abney Park Cemetery
Abney Gdns
Alconbury Rd
Garnham St
Wilmer Place
Stoke Newington Church St B104
Lawrence Buildings
Sanford Ter
Stoke Newington Common
Jenner Road
Benthal Road
Norcott Road
Narford Road
Reighton Rd
Maury Road
Brooke Road
Evering Road
Cottage Walk
Smalley Close
Stoke Newington High Street A10
Rectory Road A10
Oak Park Ms
Laundress Ln
Dynevor Road
Manley Court
Leswin Road
Darville Road
Rendlesham Rd
Dynevor Rd
Rectory Road Rail
Tyssen Road
Bayston Rd
Nile Close
Kenningh
Muir Rd
Ormsby Place
Batley Place
Hollar Road
Monteagle Way
Victorian Gro
Batley Rd
Leswin Place
Stellman Clo
Stellman Close
Rendlesham Road
Glading Ter
Victorian Rd
Manse Road A10
Evering Road A10
Nolan W
Corona
0.25 mile
0.25 km
64
86
87

Stoke Newington (East)

Stokey has turned into something of a Notting Hill of the east with all-terrain buggies taking up the pavement while the MILFs do their organic grocery shopping. It's resplendent in dining options but try Testi first. For paying your respects or cruising, head to Abney Park Cemetery. For a bit of genteel warehouse-partying, check out Stoke Newington International Airport.

Landmarks

- **Abney Park Cemetery** • Stoke Newington High St & Rectory Rd

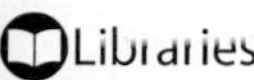

Libraries

- **Clapton Library** • Northwold Road

Nightlife

- **The Birdcage** • 58 Stamford Hill
- **Blush** • 8 Cazenove Rd
- **The Royal Sovereign** • 64 Northwold Rd
- **Stoke Newington International Airport** • 1-15 Leswin Place
- **White Hart** • 69 Stoke Newington High St

Post Offices

- **Stamford Hill** • 82 Stamford Hill
- **Stoke Newington** • 138 Stoke Newington High St

Restaurants

- **19 Numara Bos Cirrik** • 34 Stoke Newington Rd
- **Bagel House** • 2 Stoke Newington High St
- **Café Z Bar** • 58 Stoke Newington High St
- **Testi** • 38 Stoke Newington High St
- **Thai Cafe** • 3 Northwold Rd
- **Three Crowns** • 175 Stoke Newington Church St

Shopping

- **Bargain Bookshop** • 153 Stoke Newington High St
- **Hamdys** • 167 Stoke Newington High St
- **Stoke Newington Bookshop** • 167 Stoke Newington High St
- **Rouge** • 158 Stoke Newington High St

Map 86 • Dalston / Kingsland

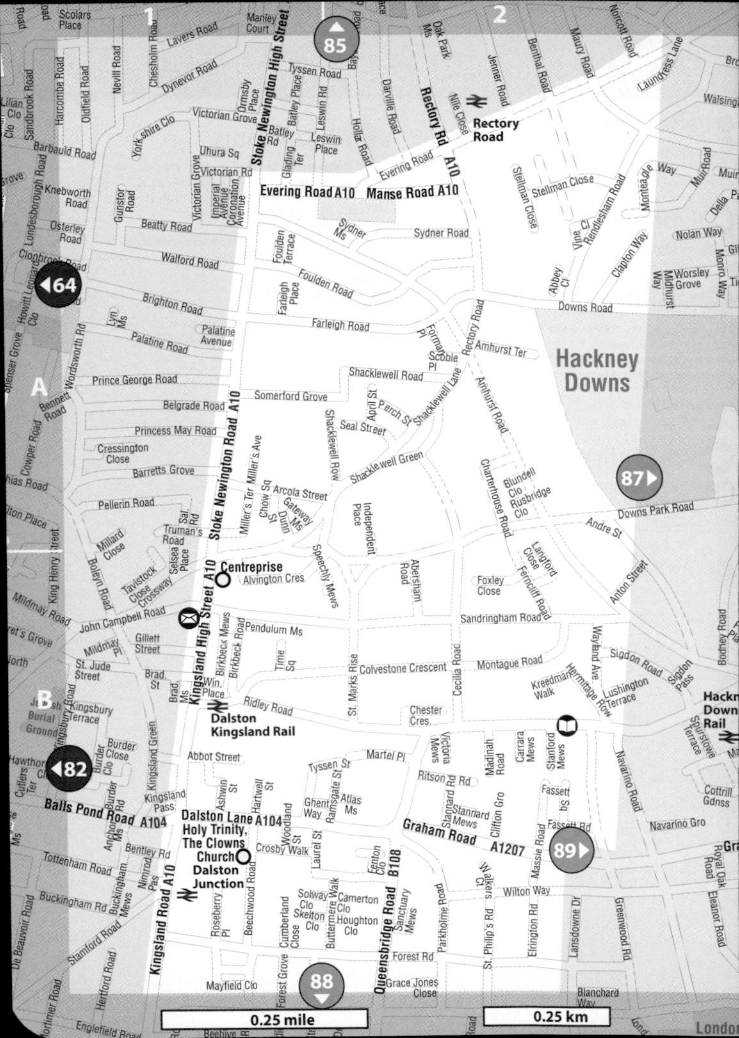

Dalston / Kingsland

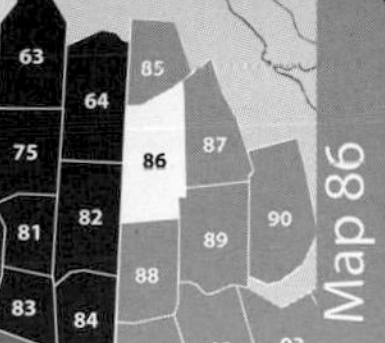

Bustling Ridley Road market is still the beating heart of Dalston, while Kingsland Road is like a Vice mag shoot with Nathan Barleys stalking up and down as though it were a catwalk. With hip bars like Dalston Superstore and Ridley Road Bar, it's no wonder (but we still love the old skool Dalston Jazz Bar, and Cafe Oto is the experimental music cafe de jour).

Cinemas

- **Lux** • 18 Shacklewell Ln
- **Rio Cinema** • 107 Kingsland High St

Coffee

- **Betty's Coffee** • 510 Kingsland Rd
- **Coffee@Ridley's** • 91 Dalston Ln
- **Metolino Cafe** • 162 Stoke Newington Rd
- **Mouse & De Lotz** • 103 Shackwell Ln
- **To The Jungle** • 16 Dalston Ln

Landmarks

- **Centreprise** • 136 Kingsland High St
- **Holy Trinity, The Clowns Church** • Beechwood Rd & Kirkland Walk

Libraries

- **CLR James Library** • 30 Dalston Ln

Nightlife

- **Alibi** • 91 Kingsland High St
- **Bar 23** • 23 Stoke Newington Rd
- **Bardens Boudoir** • 38 Stoke Newington Rd
- **Café Oto** • 18 Ashwin St
- **Dalston Superstore** • 117 Kingsland High St
- **Efes Pool Club & Bar** • 17 Stoke Newington Rd
- **The Haggerston** • 438 Kingsland Rd
- **Marquis of Lansdowne** • 48 Stoke Newington Rd
- **The Moustache Bar** • 58 Stoke Newington Rd
- **Passion** • 251 Amhurst Rd
- **Power Lunches** • 446 Kingsland Rd
- **The Prince George** • 40 Parkholme Rd
- **Ridley Road Market Bar** • 49 Ridley Rd
- **The Shacklewell Arms** • 71 Shacklewell Ln
- **Vogue Fabrics** • 66 Stoke Newington Rd

Post Offices

- **Kingsland High Street** • 118 Kingsland High St

Restaurants

- **The Best Turkish Kebab** • 125 Stoke Newington Rd
- **Dem Cafe** • 18 Stoke Newington Rd
- **Dalston Lane Café** • 170 Dalston Ln
- **Evin Bar and Café** • 115 Kingsland High St
- **LMNT** • 316 Queensbridge Rd
- **A Little Of What You Fancy** • 464 Kingsland Rd
- **Mangal 1** • 10 Arcola St
- **Mangal 2** • 4 Stoke Newington Rd
- **El Panchos** • 176 Stoke Newington Rd
- **Peppers and Spice** • 20 Kingsland High St
- **The Russet** • Amhurst Terrace
- **Shanghai** • 41 Kingsland High St
- **Somine** • 131 Kingsland High St
- **Stone Cave** • 111 Kingsland High St
- **The Tea Rooms** • 155 Stoke Newington Rd

Shopping

- **Centre Supermarket** • 588 Kingsland Rd
- **Dalston Mill Fabrics** • 69 Ridley Rd
- **LN-CC** • 18 Shacklewell Ln
- **Oxfam** • 514 Kingsland Rd
- **Party Party** • 9 Ridley Rd
- **Ridley Road Food Market** • Ridley Rd
- **St Vincent's** • 484 Kingsland Rd
- **Turkish Food Centre** • 89 Ridley Rd

Clapton Rail
Lee Valley Park - North Millfields Recreation Ground
Hackney Downs
Hackney Downs Rail
London Orphan Asylum
The Strand Building
Sutton House

Upper Clapton A107
Lower Clapton Road A102
Lea Bridge Road A104
Downs Rd A104
Cricketfield Road A104
Pembury Road A104
Dalston Lane A107
Dalston Ln A104
Amhurst Rd A107
Lower Clapton Road A107
Urswick Road A102

85
86
89
90

0.25 mile
0.25 km

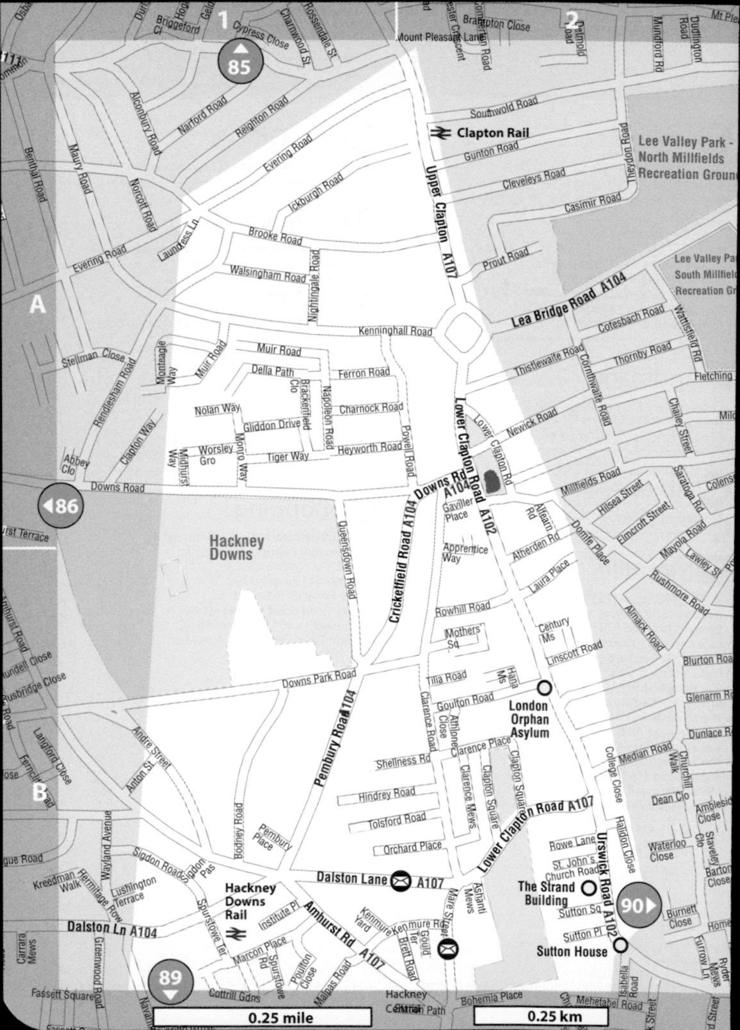

Hackney Downs / Lower Clapton

A few years ago you couldn't move for house gigs and secret raves around the Downs, but these days the area is devolving into the moody gangland it used to be whilst breeding the rioters of tomorrow. Lower Clapton, on the other hand, is ever on the up. Shop at Umit's for rare films and sweets. Food and coffee can be found at vegan punk paradise Pogo or Pacific Social Club.

Coffee

- **Cooper and Wolf** • 145 Chatsworth Road
- **Gulluoglu** • 63 Lower Clapton Rd
- **Organic & Natural** • 191 Lower Clapton Rd
- **Pacific Social Club** • 8 Clarence Rd

Landmarks

- **London Orphan Asylum** • Lower Clapton Rd & Linscott Rd
- **The Strand Building** • 29 Urswick Rd
- **Sutton House** • 2 Homerton High St

Nightlife

- **Biddle Brothers** • 88 Lower Clapton Rd
- **Crooked Billet** • 84 Upper Clapton Rd
- **Hugo's Speaker Palace** • 14 Andre St
- **Pembury Tavern** • 90 Amhurst Rd
- **Riley of Clapton** • 118 Lower Clapton Rd

Post Offices

- **Dalston Lane** • 244 Dalston Ln
- **Hackney** • 382 Mare St

Restaurants

- **Dunya** • 199 Lower Clapton Rd
- **India Gate** • 75 Lower Clapton Rd
- **Mess Café** • 38 Amhurst Rd
- **Parioli** • 90 Lower Clapton Rd
- **Pogo Café** • 76 Clarence Rd

Shopping

- **Palm 2** • 152 Lower Clapton Rd
- **The Pet Shop** • 40 Amhurst Rd
- **Salvation Army Clapton** • 122 Lower Clapton Rd
- **Second Time Around** • 60 Lower Clapton Rd
- **Umit & Son** • 35 Lower Clapton Rd

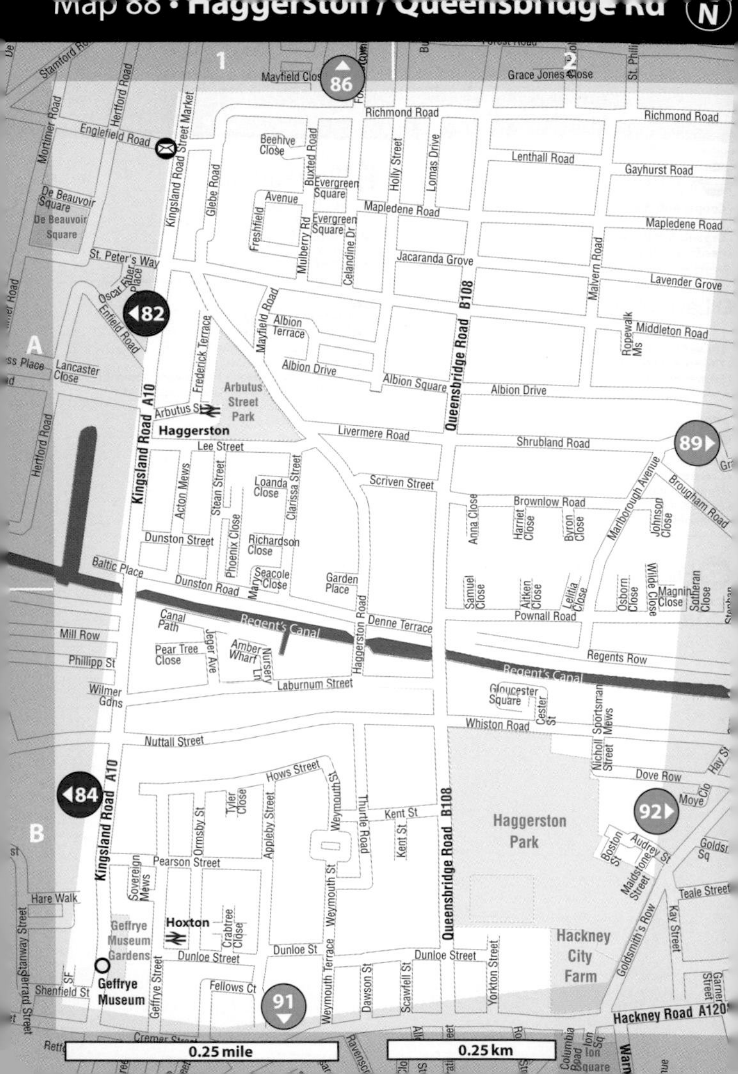

Map 88 • Haggerston / Queensbridge Rd
N
1
2
A
B
86
82
89
84
92
91
Stamford Road
Hertford Road
Mortimer Road
Englefield Road
Kingsland Road Street Market
Mayfield Close
Grace Jones Close
St. Philip
Richmond Road
Beehive Close
Buxted Road
Holly Street
Lomas Drive
Lenthall Road
Gayhurst Road
Glebe Road
Evergreen Square
Avenue
Freshfield
Mulberry Rd
Celandine Dr
Mapledene Road
De Beauvoir Square
Jacaranda Grove
Malvern Road
Lavender Grove
St. Peter's Way
Oscar Faber Place
Enfield Road
Mayfield Road
Albion Terrace
Queensbridge Road B108
Middleton Road
Ropewalk Ms
Frederick Terrace
Albion Drive
Albion Square
Lancaster Close
Arbutus Street Park
Arbutus St
Kingsland Road A10
Haggerston
Livermere Road
Shrubland Road
Hertford Road
Lee Street
Acton Mews
Stean Street
Loanda Close
Clarissa Street
Scriven Street
Brownlow Road
Anna Close
Harriet Close
Byron Close
Marlborough Avenue
Johnson Close
Brougham Road
Dunston Street
Phoenix Close
Richardson Close
Baltic Place
Dunston Road
Mary Seacole Close
Garden Place
Samuel Close
Aitken Close
Lelitia Close
Wilde Close
Osborn Close
Magnin Close
Sotheran Close
Pownall Road
Canal Path
Regent's Canal
Haggerston Road
Denne Terrace
Mill Row
Pear Tree Close
Jeger Ave
Amber Wharf
Nursery Ln
Regents Row
Phillipp St
Laburnum Street
Gloucester Square
Cester St
Wilmer Gdns
Sportsman Mews
Whiston Road
Nuttall Street
Nicholl Street
Hows Street
Dove Row
Hay St
Weymouth St
Moye Clo
Tyler Close
Ormsby St
Appleby Street
Thurtle Road
Kent St
Haggerston Park
Boston St
Audrey St
Goldsmith Sq
Pearson Street
Maidstone Street
Teale Street
Sovereign Mews
Hare Walk
Goldsmith's Row
Kay Street
Stanway Street
Geffrye Museum Gardens
Hoxton
Crabtree Close
Weymouth Terrace
Hackney City Farm
Dunloe St
Dunloe Street
Yorkton Street
Geffrye Museum
Shenfield St
Geffrye Street
Fellows Ct
Dawson St
Scawfell St
Garner Street
Hackney Road A120
Gerrard Street
Cremer Street
0.25 mile
0.25 km
Columbia Road
Ion Square

Haggerston / Queensbridge Rd

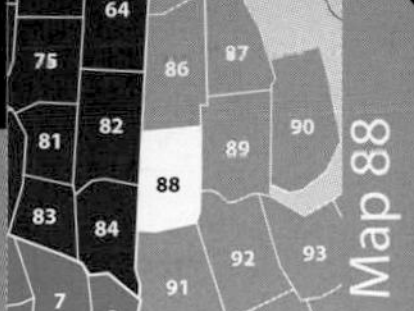

With the opening of Haggerston Station and the Ginger Line, it seems Shoreditch is merging with Dalston to form one sprawling kingdom of hipdom. Where once A10 used to be a dodgy little after-hours place, it's now a regular stop-off. Stroll down to the gardens at the Geffrye Museum or Haggerston Park for some people-watching with a flat white from Long White Cloud.

Coffee

- **Long White Cloud** • 151 Hackney Rd

Landmarks

- **Geffrye Museum** • 136 Kingsland Rd

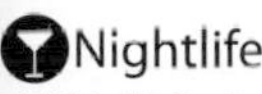

Nightlife

- **A10 (aka The Russian Bar)** • 267 Kingsland Rd
- **The Fox** • 372 Kingsland Rd
- **Passing Clouds** • 440 Kingsland Rd
- **Plaza** • 161 Kingsland Rd

Post Offices

- **Kingsland Road** • 416 Kingsland Rd

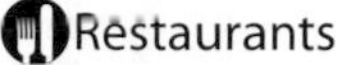

Restaurants

- **Faulkner's** • 424 Kingsland Rd
- **Hackney City Farm** • 1 Goldsmiths Row
- **That Vietnamese Place** • 134 Kingsland Rd
- **Uludag** • 398 Kingsland Rd
- **Usha** • 428 Kingsland Rd
- **Song Que** • 134 Kingsland Rd
- **Viet Hoa Café** • 70 Kingsland Rd

Shopping

- **KTS The Corner** • 415 Kingsland Road

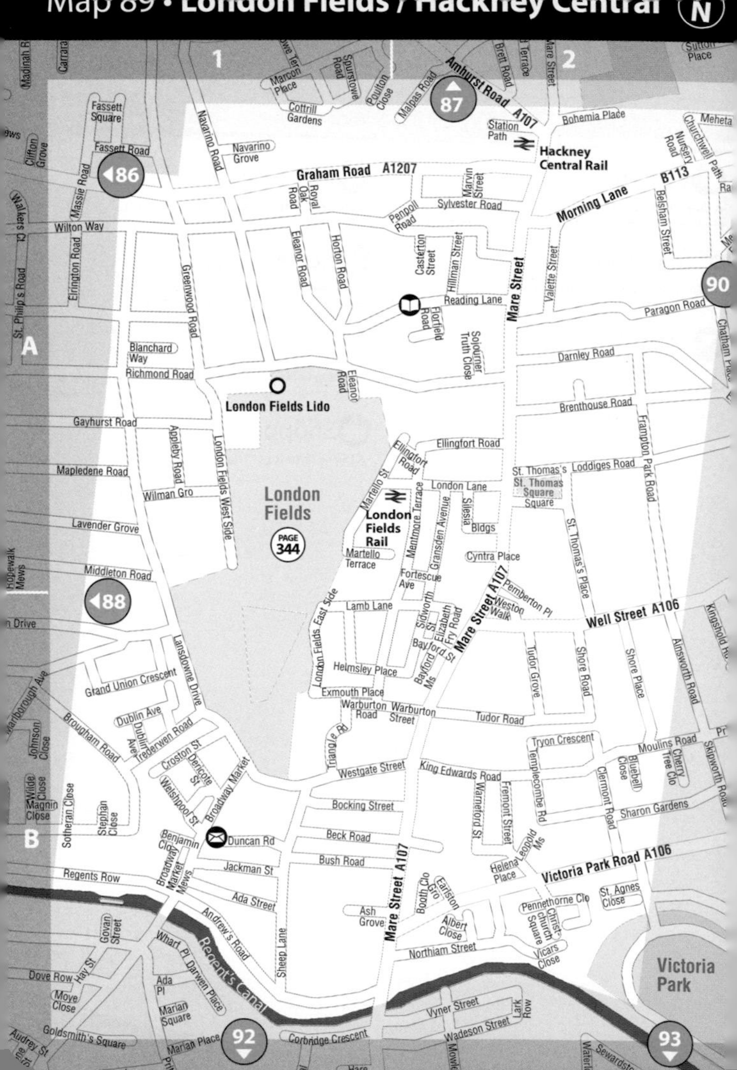
Map 89 • London Fields / Hackney Central
N
1
2
A
B
87
86
88
90
92
93
PAGE 344
Hackney Central Rail
London Fields Rail
London Fields Lido
London Fields
Victoria Park
Regent's Canal
Amhurst Road A107
Graham Road A1207
Morning Lane B113
Mare Street
Mare Street A107
Well Street A106
Victoria Park Road A106
Fassett Square
Fassett Road
Massie Road
Wilton Way
Elrington Road
Navarino Road
Navarino Grove
Marcon Place
Cottrill Gardens
Spurstowe Road
Poulton Close
Malpas Road
Station Path
Bohemia Place
Brett Road
Nursery Road
Churchwell Path
Royal Oak Road
Marvin Street
Sylvester Road
Penpoll Road
Belsham Street
Eleanor Road
Horton Road
Casterton Street
Hillman Street
Valette Street
Reading Lane
Florfield Road
Paragon Road
Greenwood Road
Blanchard Way
Richmond Road
Sojourner Truth Close
Darnley Road
Chatham Place
Brenthouse Road
Gayhurst Road
Appleby Road
London Fields West Side
Ellingfort Road
Frampton Park Road
Mapledene Road
Martello St
London Lane
St. Thomas's Square
Lodiges Road
Wilman Gro
Mentmore Terrace
Gransden Avenue
Silesia Bldgs
Lavender Grove
Martello Terrace
Cyntra Place
St. Thomas's Place
Middleton Road
Fortescue Ave
Pemberton Pl
Weston Walk
Lamb Lane
London Fields East Side
Sidworth St
Elizabeth Fry Road
Bayford St
Bayford Ms
Kingshold Road
Lansdowne Drive
Grand Union Crescent
Helmsley Place
Tudor Grove
Shore Road
Shore Place
Ainsworth Road
Exmouth Place
Warburton Road
Warburton Street
Tudor Road
Dublin Ave
Tredegar Road
Brougham Road
Marlborough Ave
Johnson Close
Triangle Rd
Tryon Crescent
Moulins Road
Cherry Tree Clo
Croston St
Dericote St
Westgate Street
King Edwards Road
Templecombe Rd
Bluebell Close
Clermont Road
Skipworth Road
Welshpool St
Broadway Market
Wilde Close
Magnin Close
Sotheran Close
Stephan Close
Bocking Street
Warneford St
Fremont Street
Sharon Gardens
Benjamin Clo
Duncan Rd
Beck Road
Leopold Ms
Bush Road
Helena Place
Jackman St
Regents Row
Broadway Market Mews
Booth Clo
Earlston Gro
Pennethorne Clo
St. Agnes Close
Ada Street
Andrew's Road
Ash Grove
Albert Close
Christchurch Square
Govan Street
Vicars Close
Northiam Street
Sheep Lane
Wharf Pl
Darwen Place
Dove Row
Hay St
Ada Pl
Moye Close
Marian Square
Vyner Street
Lark Row
Goldsmith's Square
Marian Place
Corbridge Crescent
Wadeson Street
Audrey St
Sewardstone

London Fields / Hackney Central

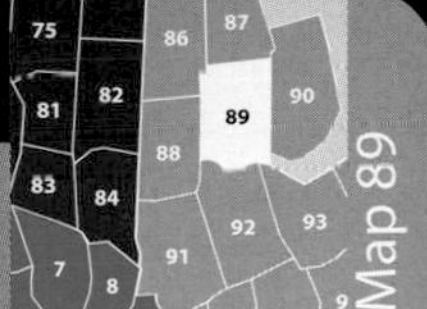

It's quite amusing seeing Chinese tourists waiting at the bus stop opposite Tesco with huge Burberry bags, having been at the Factory shop whilst the rest of us schlep home with our groceries. Skip through London Fields, dip your toe in the Lido, and attempt to make your way through the throngs checking out their reflections in the shop windows on Broadway Market.

Coffee

- **Climpson & Sons** • 67 Broadway Market
- **The Corner Deli** • 121 Mare St
- **Donlon Books** • 77 Broadway Market
- **Hackney Bureau** • 3 Mare St
- **Violet** • 47 Wilton Wy
- **Wilton's** • 63 Wilton Way

Landmarks

- **London Fields Lido** • London Fields Westside

Libraries

- **Hackney Central Library** • 1 Reading Lane

Nightlife

- **Baxter's Court** • 282 Mare St
- **The Dolphin** • 165 Mare St
- **The Dove** • 24 Broadway Market
- **The Old Ship** • 2 Sylvester Path
- **Platform** • 1 Westgate St
- **Pub on the Park** • 19 Martello St

Post Offices

- **London Fields** • 39 Broadway Market

Restaurants

- **Buen Ayre** • 50 Broadway Market
- **Cafe Bohemia** • 2 Bohemia Pl
- **Cat and Mutton** • 76 Broadway Market
- **Corner Deli** • 121 Mare St
- **F. Cooke** • 9 Broadway Market
- **Hai Ha** • 206 Mare St
- **Ombra** • 1 Vyner St
- **The Spurstowe Arms** • 68 Greenwood Rd

Shopping

- **Artvinyl** • 13 Broadway Market
- **Broadway Market** • Broadway Market
- **Burberry Factory Shop** • 29 Chatham Pl
- **Candle Factory** • 184 Mare St
- **E5 Bakehouses** • 395 Mentmore Terrace
- **Lazy Days** • 21 Mare St
- **L'eau a la Bouche** • 49 Broadway Market London
- **Viktor Wynd's Shop of Horrors** • 11 Mare St

Supermarkets

- **Iceland** • 150 Mare St
- **Tesco** • 55 Morning Ln

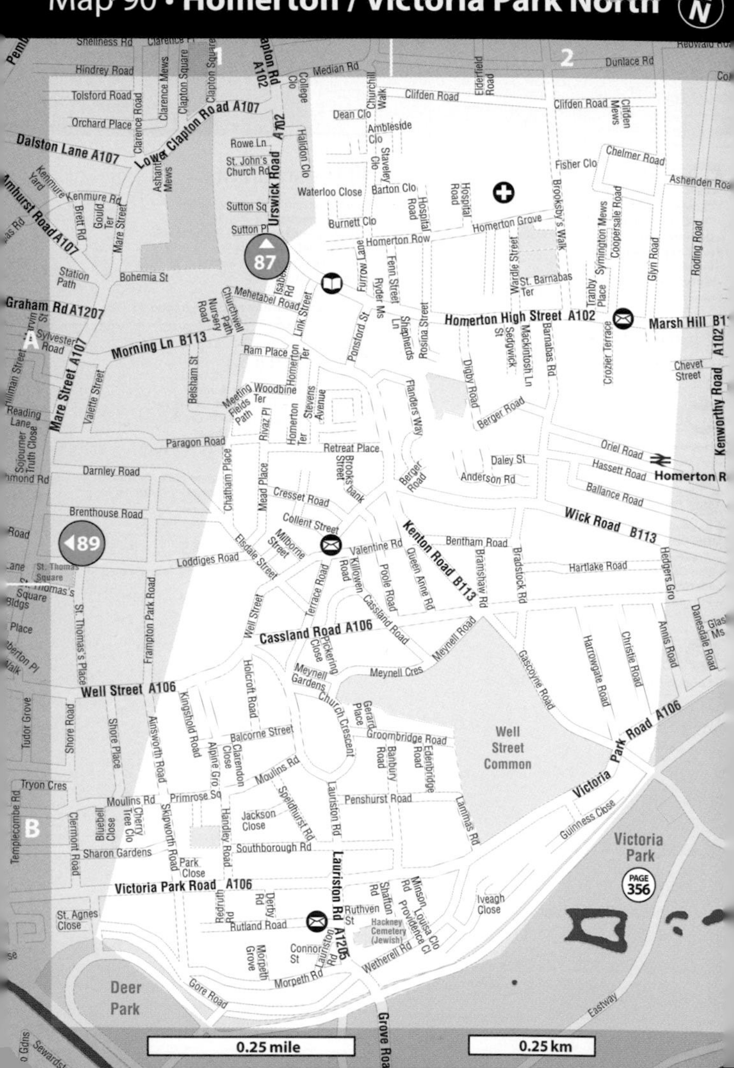
Map 90 • Homerton / Victoria Park North
N
1
2
A
B
Shellness Rd
Clarence Pl
Hindrey Road
Tolsford Road
Orchard Place
Clarence Road
Clarence Mews
Clapton Square
Lower Clapton Road A107
Dalston Lane A107
Kenmure Yard
Kenmure Rd
Amhurst Road A107
Brett Rd
Gould Ter
Mare Street
Ashanti Mews
Station Path
Bohemia St
Graham Rd A1207
Sylvester Road
Morning Ln B113
Mare Street A107
Valette Street
Reading Lane
Sojourner Truth Close
Darnley Road
Brenthouse Road
Paragon Road
Loddiges Road
St. Thomas's Square
St. Thomas's Place
Frampton Park Road
Well Street A106
Tudor Grove
Shore Road
Shore Place
Tryon Cres
Templecombe Rd
Clermont Road
Bluebell Close
Cherry Tree Clo
Moulins Rd
Sharon Gardens
Ainsworth Road
Skipworth Road
Primrose Sq
Park Close
Victoria Park Road A106
St. Agnes Close
Deer Park
Gore Road
Clapton Rd A102
Median Rd
College Clo
Urswick Road A102
Rowe Ln
St. John's Church Rd
Sutton Sq
Sutton Pl
Halidon Clo
87
89
Mehetabel Road
Churchwell Path
Nursery Road
Isabella Rd
Link Street
Ram Place
Belsham St
Meeting Fields Path
Woodbine Ter
Homerton Ter
Stevens Avenue
Rivaz Pl
Chatham Place
Mead Place
Retreat Place
Brooksbank Street
Cresset Road
Collent Street
Milborne Street
Elsdale Street
Valentine Rd
Terrace Road
Killowen Road
Poole Road
Cassland Road
Well Street
Cassland Road A106
Pickering Close
Meynell Gardens
Meynell Cres
Meynell Road
Holcroft Road
Kingshold Road
Balcorne Street
Alpine Gro
Clarendon Close
Moulins Rd
Church Crescent
Gerard Place
Groombridge Road
Banbury Road
Edenbridge Road
Speldhurst Rd
Lauriston Rd
Penshurst Road
Jackson Close
Handley Road
Southborough Rd
Lauriston Rd A1205
Redruth Rd
Derby Rd
Rutland Road
Ruthven St
Connor St
Morpeth Grove
Morpeth Rd
Lauriston Rd
Hackney Cemetery (Jewish)
Shafton Rd
Wetherell Rd
Grove Road
Minson Rd
Providence Cl
Louisa Clo
Ivegah Close
Churchill Walk
Dean Clo
Ambleside Clo
Staveley Clo
Waterloo Close
Barton Clo
Burnett Clo
Hospital Road
Homerton Row
Furrow Lane
Fenn Street
Ryder Ms
Ponsford St
Shepherds Ln
Rosina Street
Clifden Road
Elderfield Road
Homerton Grove
Wardle Street
St. Barnabas Ter
Homerton High Street A102
Sedgwick St
Mackintosh Ln
Barnabas Rd
Digby Road
Flanders Way
Berger Road
Daley St
Anderson Rd
Kenton Road B113
Bentham Road
Bramshaw Rd
Bradstock Rd
Queen Anne Rd
Well Street Common
Gascoyne Road
Lammas Rd
Guinness Close
Victoria Park Road A106
Victoria Park
PAGE 356
Eastway
Dunlace Rd
Redwald Rd
Clifden Road
Clifden Mews
Fisher Clo
Chelmer Road
Brooksby's Walk
Symington Mews
Coopersale Road
Tranby Place
Glyn Road
Roding Road
Ashenden Road
Marsh Hill B113
Crozier Terrace
Chevet Street
Kenworthy Road A102
Oriel Road
Hassett Road
Homerton R
Ballance Road
Wick Road B113
Hartlake Road
Hedgers Gro
Harrowgate Road
Christie Road
Annis Road
Danesdale Road
Glas Ms
0.25 mile
0.25 km
Sewardstone

Homerton / Victoria Park North

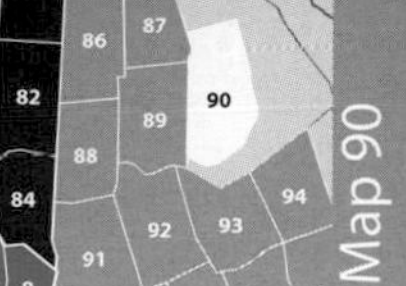

Aah, Hackney Village, leafy Lauriston Road and its surrounds would make a nice retreat from the madding crowd if everyone else didn't have the same idea. Nevermind, have a Sunday Roast at the Royal Inn on The Park. Whereas once one would only be seen in Homerton if one was going to the hospital (or going to the hospital because one was in Homerton), Chatsworth Road (just off map) is now the place du jour.

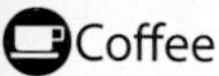

Coffee

- **Railroad Café** • 120 Morning Ln

Emergency Rooms

- **Homerton University Hospital** • Homerton Row

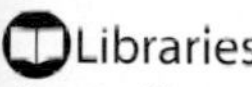

Libraries

- **Homerton Library** • Homerton High St

Nightlife

- **Chats Palace Arts Centre** • 42 Brooksby's Walk
- **The Lauriston** • 162 Victoria Park Rd
- **Royal Inn on the Park** • 111 Lauriston Rd

Post Offices

- **High Street** • 226 Homerton High St
- **Victoria Park** • 112 Lauriston Rd
- **Well Street** • 188 Well St

Restaurants

- **The Empress of India** • 130 Lauriston Rd
- **The Fish House** • 126 Lauriston Rd

Shopping

- **Cheech Miller** • 227 Victoria Park Rd
- **The Ginger Pig** • 99 Lauriston Rd
- **Sublime** • 225 Victoria Park Rd
- **Work Shop** • 77 Lauriston Rd

Supermarkets

- **Tesco** • 180 Well St

Map 91 • Shoreditch / Brick Lane / Spitalfields

Shoreditch High Street
Truman's Brewery
Sweet Toof Graffiti Alley
Dennis Severs' House
Brick Lane
Spitalfields Market
Ten Bells
Christ Church Spitalfields
Brick Lane Mosque
Aldgate East
Aldgate

0.25 mile
0.25 km

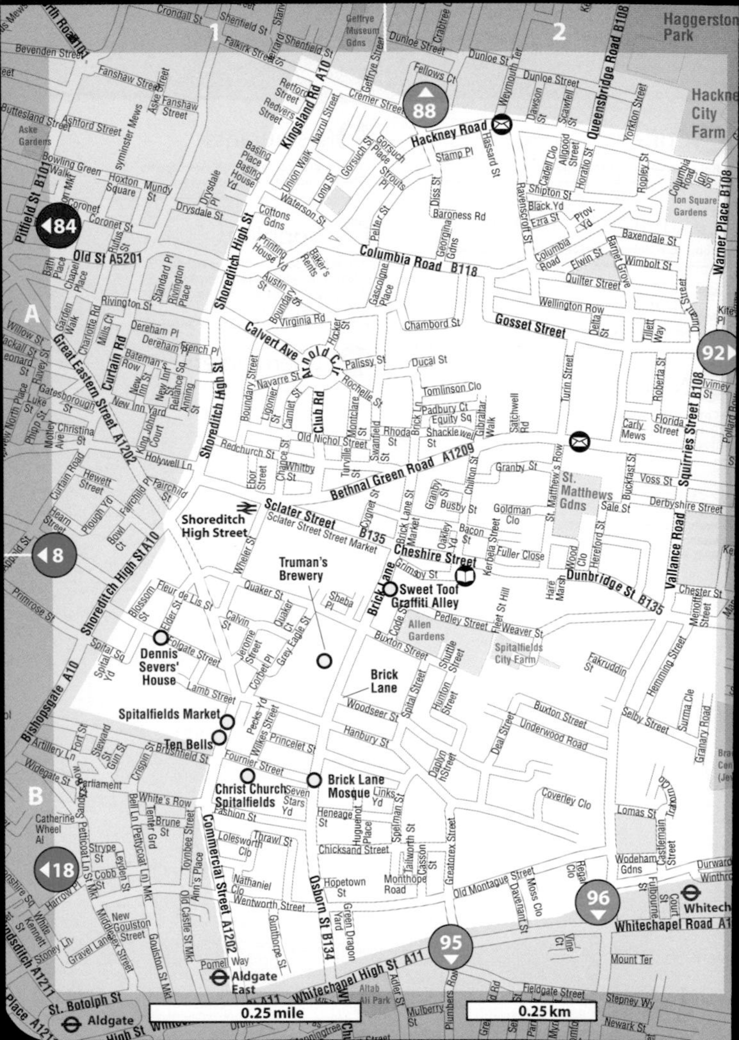

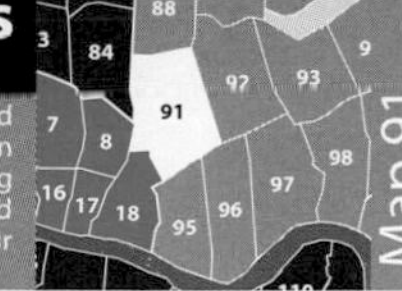

Throbbing with trend-lords on single-speed bikes, great curry houses, and alternative-lifestyle vomit, the trick is to sample Brick Lane and Shoreditch on market days for pure colour and bustle, but to avoid it on weekend eves. Shopping is abundant: Rough Trade, Beyond Retro, and oodles of great little rag shacks. Head towards Jaguar Shoes or Catch for booze. For a dash of authenticity, leave your £1000 bike unlocked and see what happens.

Cinemas

- **Rich Mix Centre** • 34 Bethnal Green Rd
- **Short & Sweet** • 91 Brick Ln

Coffee

- **Cafe 1001** • 91 Brick Ln
- **Coffee@137** • 137 Brick Ln
- **Esoteria** • 276 Hackney Rd
- **Leila's Shop** • 17 Calvert Ave
- **Nude Espresso** • 26 Hanbury St
- **Prufrock** • 140 Shoreditch High St
- **Time For Tea** • 110 Shoreditch High St

Landmarks

- **Brick Lane Mosque** • 59 Brick Ln
- **Christ Church Spitalfields** • 2 Fournier St
- **Dennis Severs' House** • 18 Folgate St
- **Spitalfields Market** • 105 Commercial St
- **Sweet Toof Graffiti Alley** • Pedley St & Brick Ln
- **Ten Bells** • 84 Commercial St
- **Truman's Brewery** • Brick Ln

Libraries

- **Dorset Library** • Ravenscroft St

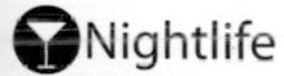

Nightlife

- **93 Feet East** • 150 Brick Ln
- **Anda De Bridge** • 42 Kingsland Rd
- **The Archers** • 42 Osborn St
- **Bar Kick** • 127 Shoreditch High St
- **Bar Music Hall** • 134 Curtain Rd
- **Bedroom Bar** • 62 Rivington St
- **The Birdcage** • 80 Columbia Rd
- **Browns** • 1 Hackney Rd
- **The Big Chill Bar** • Dray Walk off Brick Lane
- **Café 1001** • 91 Brick Lane
- **The Carpenters Arms** • 73 Cheshire St
- **Catch** • 22 Kingsland Rd
- **The Commercial Tavern** • 142 Commercial St
- **Comedy Cafe** • 66 Rivington St
- **Danger of Death** • 202 Brick Ln
- **Ditch Bar** • 145 Shoreditch High St
- **Exit** • 174 Brick Lane
- **The George & Dragon** • Hackney Rd
- **The Golden Heart** • 110 Commercial St
- **The Gramaphone Bar** • 60 Commercial St
- **Mason & Taylor** • 51 Bethnal Green Rd
- **Herbal** • 10 Kingsland Rd
- **Jaguar Shoes** • 32 Kingsland Rd
- **Joiners Arms** • 116 Hackney Rd
- **The Last Days of Decadence** • 145 Shoreditch High St
- **The Love Shake** • 5 Kingsland Rd
- **Short & Sweet** • 91
- **The Old Shoreditch Station** • 1 Kingsland Rd
- **On the Rocks** • 25 Kingsland Rd
- **Owl & Pussycat** • 34 Redchurch St
- **Prague** • 6 Kingsland Rd
- **Pride of Spitalfields** • 3 Heneage St
- **Public Life** • 82 Commercial St
- **The Redchurch** • 107 Redchurch St
- **The Royal Oak** • 73 Columbia Rd
- **Shoreditch House** • Ebor St
- **T Bar** • 18 Houndsditch
- **Vibe Bar** • 91 Brick Ln
- **The Water Poet** • 9 Folgate St
- **Ye Olde Axe** • 69 Hackney Rd

Post Offices

- **Bethnal Green** • 223 Bethnal Green Rd
- **Hackney Road** • 198 Hackney Rd

Restaurants

- **Back in 5 Minutes** • 222 Brick Ln
- **Beigel Bakery** • 155 Brick Ln
- **Boundary** • 2 Boundary St
- **Brawn** • 49 Columbia Rd
- **Brick Lane Clipper Restaurant** • 104 Brick Ln
- **Café Bangla** • 128 Brick Lane
- **Drunken Monkey** • 222 Shoreditch High St
- **Ethiopian Food Stall** • Sunday Upmarket, Truman's Brewery, Brick Ln
- **Frizzante** • 1 Goldsmith's Row
- **Gourmet San** • 261 Bethnal Green Rd
- **Hanoi Cafe** • 98 Kingsland Rd
- **Hawksmoor** • 157 Commercial St
- **Jones Dairy Cafe** • 23 Ezra St
- **Les Trois Garcons** • 1 Club Row
- **Mein Tay** • 122 Kingsland Rd
- **Noodle King** • 185 Bethnal Green Rd
- **Ping Pong** • 3 Steward St
- **The Premises** • 209 Hackney Rd
- **Que Viet** • 102 Kingsland Rd
- **Rootmaster** • Elys Yard
- **Rosa's** • 12 Hanbury St
- **St John Bread and Wine** • 94 Commercial St
- **Story Deli** • 91 Brick Ln
- **Tay Do** • 60 Kingsland Rd
- **Tay Do Cafe** • 65 Kingsland Rd
- **Viet Grill** • 58 Kingsland Rd

Shopping

- **A Butcher of Distinction** • 91 Brick Ln
- **Absolute Vintage** • 15 Hanbury St
- **Bangla City** • 86 Brick Ln
- **Bernstock Speirs** • 234 Brick Ln
- **Beyond Retro** • 112 Cheshire St
- **Blackmans** • 44 Cheshire St
- **Blackman's Shoes** • 42 Cheshire St
- **Brick Lane** • Brick Lane
- **Caravan** • 3 Redchurch St
- **A Child of The Jago** • 10 Great Eastern St
- **Columbia Road Flower Market** • Columbia Rd
- **Columbia Road Market** • Columbia Rd
- **Comfort Station** • 22 Cheshire St
- **Duke of Uke** • 22 Hanbury St
- **FairyGothMother** • 15 Lamb St
- **The Grocery** • 54 Kingsland Rd
- **Hurwundeki** • 98 Commerical St
- **Junky Styling** • 91 Brick Ln
- **The Laden Showrooms** • 103 Brick Ln
- **Lapin & Me** • 14 Ezra St
- **Labour & Wait** • 18 Cheshire St
- **Lily Vanillie** • 6 Ezra St
- **Luna and Curious** • 198 Brick Lne
- **No One** • 1 Kingsland Rd
- **Nudge Records** • 20 Hanbury St
- **Prick Your Finger** • 260 Bethnal Green Rd
- **Rough Trade East** • 91 Brick Ln
- **Ryantown** • 126 Columbia Rd
- **Second Tread** • 261 Hackney Rd
- **Shelf** • 40 Cheshire St
- **Taj Stores** • 112 Brick Ln
- **Tatty Devine** • 236 Brick Ln
- **Taylor Taylor** • 12 Cheshire St
- **Taylor Taylor** • 137 Commercial St
- **Treacle** • 110 Columbia Rd

Map 92 • Bethnal Green

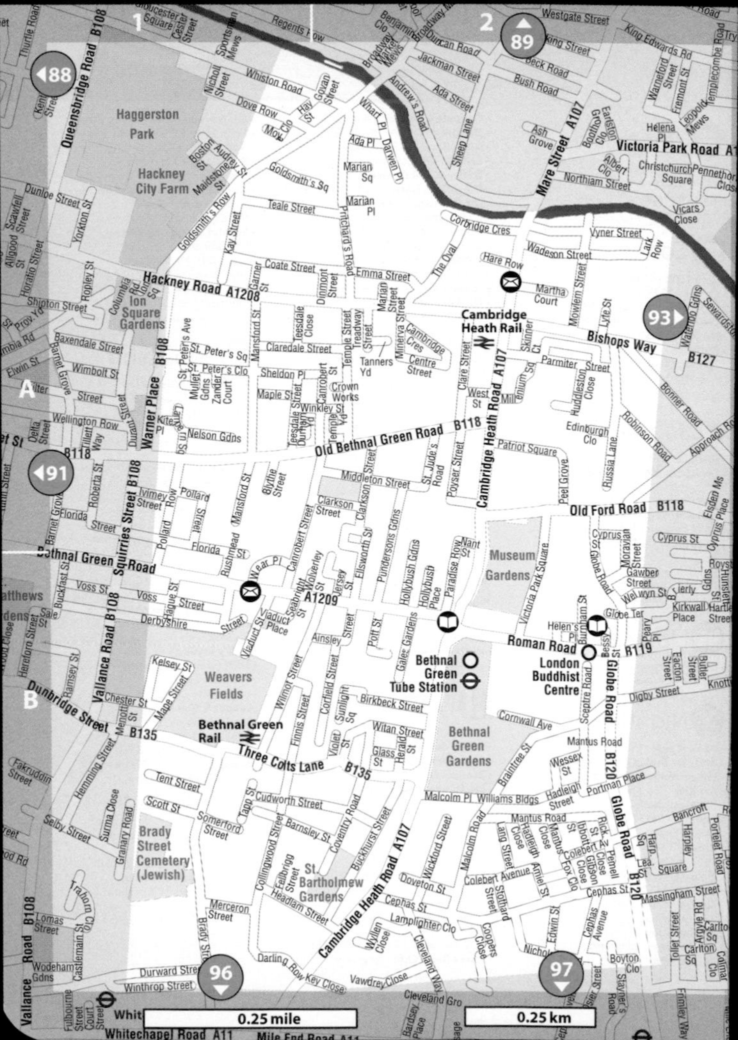
1
2
A
B
88
89
91
93
96
97
Regents Row
Westgate Street
King Street
King Edwards Rd
Broadway Market Mews
Benjamin Clo
Duncan Road
Jackman Street
Beck Road
Bush Road
Ada Street
Andrew's Road
Wharf Pl
Darwen Pl
Ada Pl
Marian Sq
Marian Pl
Sheep Lane
Mare Street A107
Ash Grove
Boothby Rd
Earlston Gro
Warneford Street
Fremont St
Templecombe Road
Leopold Mews
Helena Pl
Victoria Park Road
Albert Clo
Christchurch Square
Pennethorne Close
Northiam Street
Vicars Close
Queensbridge Road B108
Thurtle Road
Nicholl Street
Sportsman Mews
Whiston Road
Dove Row
Govan Street
Hay St
Mow Clo
Haggerston Park
Boston St
Audrey St
Maidstone St
Goldsmith's Sq
Goldsmith's Row
Hackney City Farm
Teale Street
Pritchard's Road
Corbridge Cres
Vyner Street
Wadeson Street
Lark Row
Hare Row
Dunloe Street
Yorkton St
Scawfell Street
Allgood St
Horatio Street
Kay Street
Coate Street
Emma Street
The Oval
Martha Court
Mowlem Street
Hackney Road A1208
Ropley St
Columbia Rd
Ion Sq
Ion Square Gardens
Shipton Street
Prov. Yd
Garner St
Dinmont Street
Mansford St
Teesdale Close
Temple Street
Treadway Street
Marian Street
Minerva Street
Cambridge Cres
Cambridge Heath Rail
Lyte St
Bishops Way
Waterloo Gdns
Sewardstone
B127
Baxendale Street
St. Peter's Ave
St. Peter's Sq
Claredale Street
Tanners Yd
Centre Street
Skinner Ct
Parmiter Street
Barnet Grove
Wimbolt St
Elwin St
St. Peter's Clo
Mullet Gdns
Zander Court
Sheldon Pl
Canrobert St
Crown Works
Clare Street
West St
Mill
Millennium Sq
Huddleston Close
Bonner Road
Alter Street
Maple Street
Winkley St
Teesdale Yd
Durham Yd
Temple Yd
Cambridge Heath Road A107
Warner Place
B108
Wellington Row
Durant Street
Kite Pl
Nelson Gdns
Edinburgh Clo
Robinson Road
Approach Road
Delta Street
Tillett Way
Old Bethnal Green Road B118
Patriot Square
B118
Roberta St
St. Jude's Road
Poyser Street
Peel Grove
Russia Lane
Squirries Street B108
Ivimey Street
Pollard Row
Pollard Street
Blythe Street
Middleton Street
Clarkson Street
Old Ford Road B118
Elsden Ms
Cyprus Place
Florida Street
Clarkson St
Cyprus St
Moravian Street
Bethnal Green Road
Florida St
Rushmead
Wear Pl
Canrobert Street
Wolverley St
Ellsworth St
Pundersons Gdns
Hollybush Gdns
Hollybush Place
Paradise Row
Nant St
Museum Gardens
Victoria Park Square
Globe Road
Gawber Street
Welwyn St
Kirkwall Place
Voss St
Voss Street
Buckfast St
Hague St
Seabright St
Jersey St
A1209
Vallance Road B108
Sale St
Derbyshire Street
Viaduct St
Viaduct Place
Ainsley Street
Pott St
Gales Gardens
Burnham St
Globe Ter
Helen's Pl
Bess St
Roman Road B119
Peary Pl
Hereford Street
Ramsey St
Kelsey St
Mape Street
Weavers Fields
Wilmot Street
Corfield Street
Bethnal Green Tube Station
London Buddhist Centre
Sceptre Road
Globe Road
Fairlop Place
Butler Street
Digby Street
Dunbridge Street
Chester St
Menotti St
Birkbeck Street
Sunlight Sq
Finnis Street
Cornwall Ave
B135
Bethnal Green Rail
Witan Street
Violet St
Bethnal Green Gardens
Mantus Road
Three Colts Lane B135
Glass St
Herald St
Braintree St
Wessex St
Hemming Street
Fakruddin Street
Surma Close
Tent Street
B120
Portman Place
Scott St
Cudworth Street
Tapp St
Malcolm Pl
Williams Bldgs
Hadleigh Street
Bancroft
Granary Road
Selby Street
Brady Street Cemetery (Jewish)
Somerford Street
Barnsley St
Coventry Road
Buckhurst Street
Wickford Street
Malcolm Road
Mantus Road
Lang Street
Hadleigh Close
Mantus Close
Rickman St
Colebert Av
Ibbott St
Gibson Close
Fox Clo
Amiel St
Pemell Close
Harpley Sq
Lea Sq
Square
Portelet Road
Collingwood Street
Fellbrigg Street
St. Bartholmew Gardens
Cambridge Heath Road A107
Doveton St
Colebert Avenue
Stothard Street
Cephas St
Cephas Street
Massingham Street
Trahorn Clo
Lomas Street
Headlam Street
Merceron Street
Lamplighter Clo
Cephas Avenue
Argyle Rd
Carlton Sq
Tollet Street
Brady Street
Wyllen Close
Cleveland Way
Coopers Close
Edwin St
Nicholas
Boyton Clo
Castlemain St
Wodeham Gdns
Durward Street
Darling Row
Key Close
Vawdrey Close
Carlton Sq
Colmar Clo
Winthrop Street
Cleveland Gro
Bardsey Place
Stayner's Road
Frimley Way
Vallance Road
Fulbourne Street
Court Street
Whitechapel Road A11
Mile End Road A11
0.25 mile
0.25 km

Bethnal Green

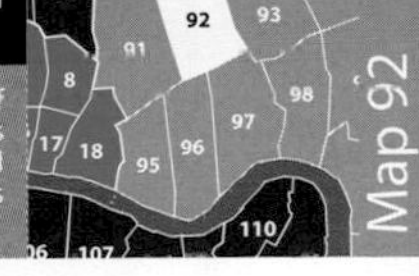

No longer the inner-city ghetto from days of yore, but you can still find some of the gor-blimey-lor-love-a-duck cockney cheekiness that one would expect in this hood. E.Pellicci is one of the oldest remaining greasy spoons in London, so head in for a Full Monty and a cuppa. If a lager and a burger down the Sebright Arms is not your thing, head down to the Buddhist Centre for a bit of instant karma.

Coffee

- **Hurwendeki Cafe** • 299 Cambridge Heath Rd

Landmarks

- **Bethnal Green Tube Station** • Bethnal Green Tube Station
- **London Buddhist Centre** • 51 Roman Rd

Libraries

- **Bethnal Green Library** • Cambridge Heath Rd
- **Idea Store Bow** • Roman Rd

Nightlife

- **The Albion** • 94 Goldsmiths Row
- **The FymFyg Bar** • 231 Cambridge Heath Rd
- **Bethnal Green's Working Men's Club** • 44 Pollard Row
- **The Camel** • 277 Globe Rd
- **Florist** • 255 Globe Rd
- **Images** • 483 Hackney Rd
- **The Star Of Bethnal Green** • 359 Bethnal Green Rd

Post Offices

- **Bethnal Green Road** • 365 Bethnal Green Rd
- **Cambridge Heath** • 481 Cambridge Heath Rd

Restaurants

- **Bistrotheque** • 23 Wadeson St
- **E Pellicci** • 332 Bethnal Green Rd
- **Little Georgia** • 87 Goldsmiths Row
- **Wild Cherry** • 241 Globe Rd

Shopping

- **AP Fitzpatrick** • 142 Cambridge Heath Rd
- **Paul Mark Hatton** • 65 Roman Rd

Supermarkets

- **Tesco** • 361 Bethnal Green Rd

Map 93 • Globe Town / Mile End (North)

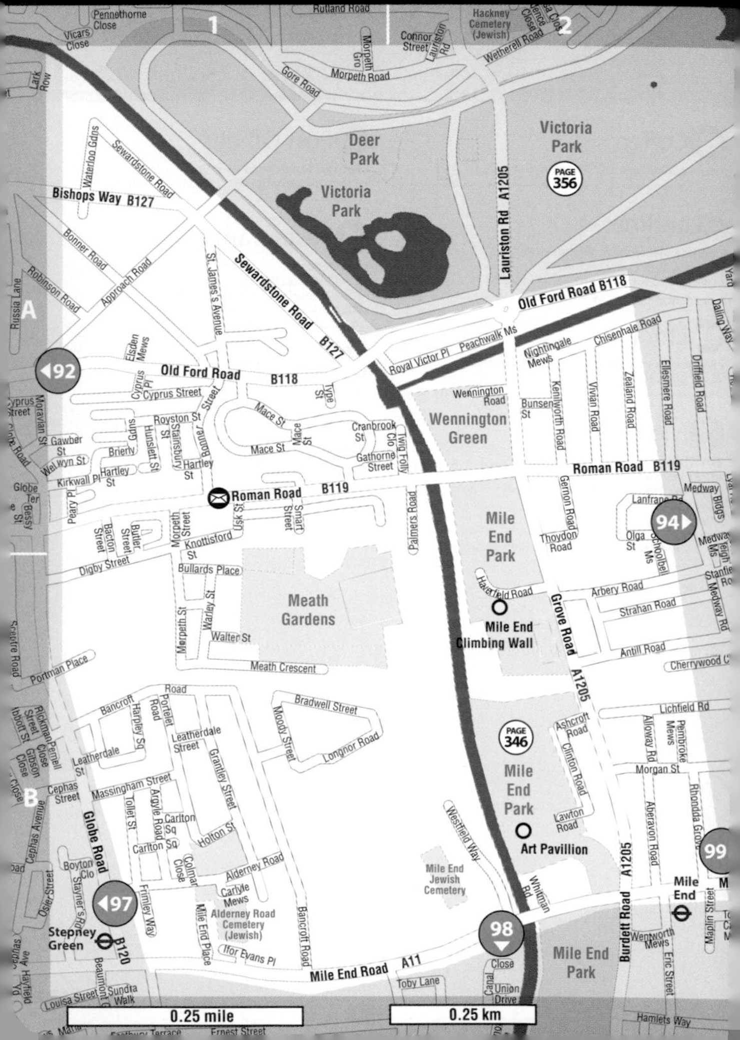

Victoria Park
Deer Park
Victoria Park
Wennington Green
Mile End Park
Meath Gardens
Mile End Park
Mile End Park
Mile End Climbing Wall
Art Pavillion
Mile End Jewish Cemetery
Alderney Road Cemetery (Jewish)
Hackney Cemetery (Jewish)
Old Ford Road B118
Roman Road B119
Sewardstone Road B127
Bishops Way B127
Lauriston Rd A1205
Grove Road A1205
Burdett Road A1205
Mile End Road A11
Globe Road
Stepney Green
Mile End

PAGE 356
PAGE 346
92
94
97
98
99

0.25 mile
0.25 km

Globe Town / Mile End (North)

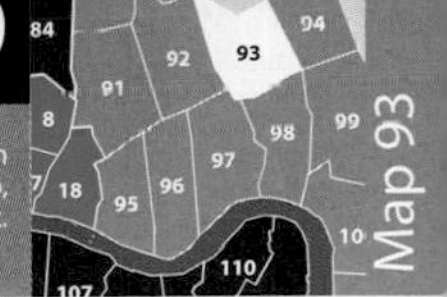

Yeah Victoria Park is nice and all, but it's just a bunch of trees and grass innit? South of all that green sh** is an up-and-coming nabe with so many great little gems. So, The Palm Tree is the best pub in Britain. The Victoria is becoming a brilliant gig spot. Winkles is East End seafood at its best. We'd move here if we had the balls in fact.

Landmarks

- **Art Pavilion** • 221 Grove Rd
- **Mile End Climbing Wall** • Haverfield Rd & Grove Rd

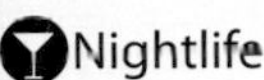

Nightlife

- **The Approach Tavern** • 47 Approach Rd
- **Fat Cat Cafe Bar** • 221 Grove Rd
- **Jongleurs (Bow Wharf)** • 221 Grove Rd
- **The Morgan Arms** • 43 Morgan St
- **Palm Tree** • 1 Haverfield Rd
- **The Victoria** • 110 Grove Rd

Post Offices

- **Roman Road** • 138 Roman Rd

Restaurants

- **Matsu** • 558 Mile End Rd
- **The Morgan Arms** • 43 Morgan St
- **Winkles** • 238 Roman Rd

Victoria Park

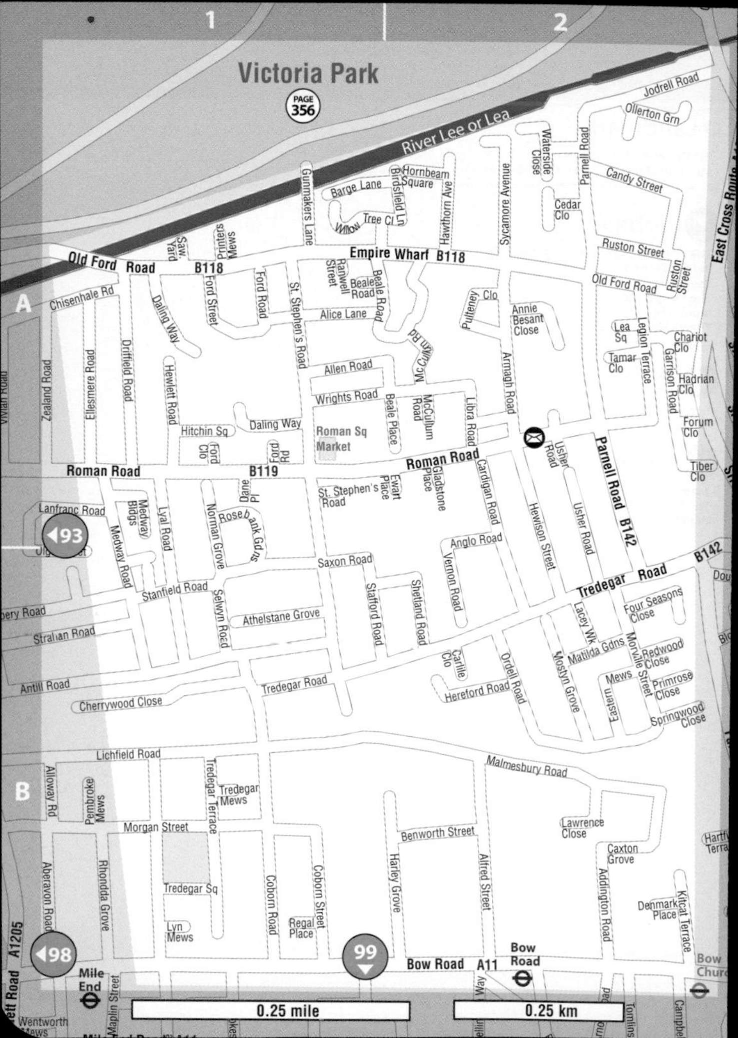

PAGE 356

River Lee or Lea

Old Ford Road B118
Empire Wharf B118
Roman Road B119
Roman Road
Parnell Road B142
Tredegar Road B142
Bow Road A11
Bow Road
Mile End
East Cross Route

Jodrell Road
Ollerton Grn
Waterside Close
Parnell Road
Candy Street
Cedar Clo
Sycamore Avenue
Hawthorn Ave
Hornbeam Square
Birdsfield Ln
Barge Lane
Willow Tree Cl
Gunmakers Lane
Saw. Yard
Printers Mews
Ruston Street
Old Ford Road
Chisenhale Rd
Ford Street
Ford Road
St. Stephen's Road
Ranwell Street
Beale Road
Alice Lane
Pulteney Clo
Annie Besant Close
Lea Sq
Legion Terrace
Chariot Clo
Tamar Clo
Garrison Road
Hadrian Clo
Forum Clo
Tiber Clo
Daling Way
Zealand Road
Ellesmere Road
Driffield Road
Hewlett Road
Allen Road
McCullum Rd
Wrights Road
Beale Place
McCullum Road
Libra Road
Armagh Road
Hitchin Sq
Daling Way
Roman Sq Market
Ford Clo
Ford Rd
Usher Road
Dane Pl
St. Stephen's Road
Ewart Place
Gladstone Place
Cardigan Road
Hewison Street
Usher Road
Lanfranc Road
Medway Bldgs
Lyal Road
Norman Grove
Rosebank Gdns
Medway Road
Anglo Road
Vernon Road
Saxon Road
Stafford Road
Shetland Road
Stanfield Road
Selwyn Road
Athelstane Grove
Lacey Wk
Four Seasons Close
Matilda Gdns
Morville Street
Redwood Close
Mostyn Grove
Eastern Mews
Primrose Close
Springwood Close
Carlile Clo
Ordell Road
Hereford Road
Tredegar Road
Antill Road
Cherrywood Close
Lichfield Road
Malmesbury Road
Alloway Rd
Pembroke Mews
Tredegar Terrace
Tredegar Mews
Morgan Street
Benworth Street
Lawrence Close
Caxton Grove
Tredegar Sq
Lyn Mews
Aberavon Road
Rhondda Grove
Coborn Road
Coborn Street
Regal Place
Harley Grove
Alfred Street
Addington Road
Denmark Place
Kitcat Terrace
A1205
Maplin Street
Wentworth Mews

93
98
99

0.25 mile
0.25 km

Bow

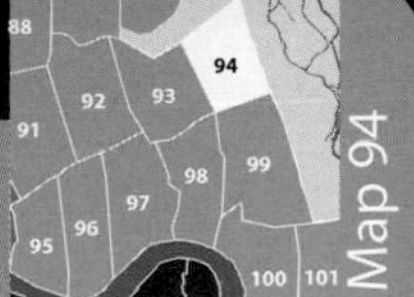

What have the Romans ever done for us? Not much, you might think, walking down Roman Road. But look closer and you'll find not only one of the oldest, most authentically East End jellied eels and mash eateries of the city, but also a market so cheap it'll knock even the most die-hard bargain hunters right out of their Centurion sandals. Pint? The haughty-sounding combo of The Young Prince or The Lord Mopeth.

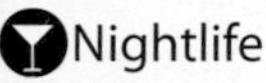

Nightlife

- **The Coborn Arms** • 8 Coborn Rd
- **The Lord Morpeth** • 402 Old Ford Rd
- **The Young Prince** • 448 Roman Rd

Post Offices

- **Roman Road (603)** • 603 Roman Rd

Restaurants

- **Chicchi** • 516 Roman Rd
- **G.Kelly Pie & Mash shop** • 526 Roman Rd
- **Pavilion Victoria Park** • Old Ford Rd
- **The Roman Tandoori** • 432 Roman Rd

Shopping

- **Pure** • 430 Roman Rd
- **Roman Road Market** • Roman Rd
- **Sew Amazing** • 80 St Stephens Rd
- **South Molton Drugstore** • 583 Roman Rd

Map 95 • Whitechapel (West) / St Katharine's Dock

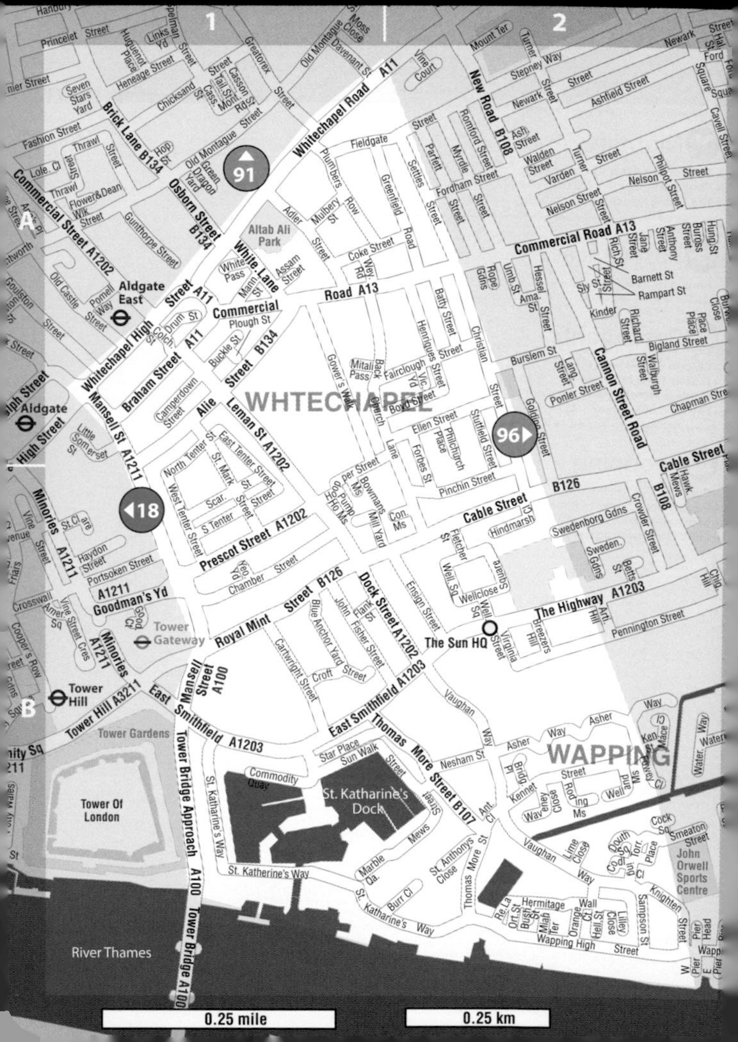

1
2
A
B
N
Hanbury
Princelet Street
Huguenot Place
Links Yd
Spelman Street
Heneage Street
Seven Stars Yard
Chicksand St
Tailworth Street
Cass. St
Casson St
Moni. Rd
Greatorex Street
Old Montague Street
Old Montague Street
Davenant St
Moss Close
Vine Court
Whitechapel Road A11
Brick Lane B134
Fashion Street
Thrawl Street
Lolesworth Cl
Flower&Dean Wlk
Commercial Street A1202
Hopetown St
Green Dragon Yard
Osborn Street B134
Gunthorpe Street
91
Altab Ali Park
Adler Street
Plumbers Row
Mulberry St
Fieldgate Street
Greenfield Road
Settles Street
Parfett Street
Myrdle Street
Romford Street
New Road B108
Mount Ter
Turner Street
Stepney Way
Newark Street
Ashfield Street
Ash Street
Walden Street
Varden Street
Nelson Street
Philpot Street
Fordham Street
Commercial Road A13
Coke Street
Weyhill Rd
White Lane
Whitechurch Pass
Manningtree St
Assam Street
Aldgate East
Old Castle Street
Goulston Street
Pomell Way
Commercial Road A13
Plough St
Drum St
Colchester St
Whitechapel High Street A11
Buckle St
Leman Street B134
Braham Street
Camperdown Street
Alie Street
Gower's Walk
Mitali Pass
Back Church Lane
Fairclough Street
Vic. Yd
Batty Street
Henriques Street
Christian Street
Boyd Street
WHITECHAPEL
Ellen Street
Philchurch Place
Stutfield Street
Forbes St
Goldin Street
96
Aldgate
High Street
Little Somerset St
Mansell St A1211
North Tenter St
East Tenter Street
St. Mark St
Leman St A1202
Hooper Street
Pump Ms
Hooper Ms
Bowmans Ms
Mill Yard
Con. Ms
Pinchin Street
Cable Street
Hindmarsh Cl
B126
18
Minories A1211
Vine Street
St. Clare
Haydon Street
West Tenter Street
Scar.
S Tenter
Prescot Street A1202
Portsoken Street
Yeo. Yd
Chamber Street
Fletcher St
Wellclose Square
Well. Sq
Wellclose Sq
Ensign Street
Dock Street A1202
Royal Mint Street B126
Blue Anchor Yard
John Fisher Street
Flank St
Goodman's Yd
A1211
Crosswall
America Sq
Vine Street Cres
Tower Gateway
Minories A1211
Mansell Street A100
Cartwright Street
Croft Street
The Sun HQ
Virginia Street
Breezers Hill
The Highway A1203
Artichoke Hill
Pennington Street
Tower Hill
Tower Hill A3211
East Smithfield A1203
East Smithfield A1203
Thomas More Street B107
Vaughan Way
Tower Gardens
Trinity Sq
Tower Of London
Tower Bridge Approach A100
St. Katharine's Way
Commodity Quay
Star Place
Sun Walk
St. Katharine's Dock
Nesham St
Asher Way
WAPPING
Marble Quay
Mews
St. Anthonys Close
Thomas More St
Vaughan Way
Lime Close
St. Katherine's Way
Burr Cl
St. Katharine's Way
Hermitage Wall
Wapping High Street
Sampson St
Knighten Street
John Orwell Sports Centre
River Thames
Tower Bridge A100
Burslem St
Lang. Street
Ponler Street
Cannon Street Road
Chapman Street
Cable Street
Hawk. Mews
B108
Crowder Street
Swedenborg Gdns
Sweden. Gdns
Betts St
Bigland Street
Walburgh Street
Richard Street
Kinder
Sly St
Barnett St
Rampart St
Pace Place
Burwell Close
Hessel Street
Umb. St
Rope Gdns
Ama. St
Jane Street
Anthony Street
Buross Street
Hungerford St
Rich St
Cavell Street
Newark Street
Ford Square
0.25 mile
0.25 km

Whitechapel (West) / St Katharine's Dock

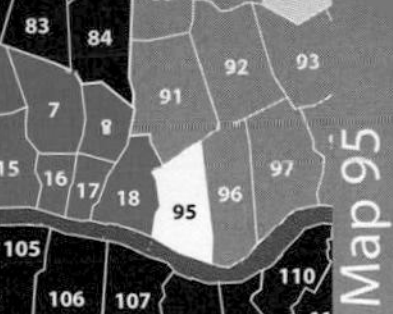

Whitechapel Gallery has reclaimed its place as the jewel in the crown of this 'hood since its renovation. Much like a busty Page 3 girl (see if you can spot one totter out of The Sun's nearby offices) the gallery has burst out of its shackles to reveal something quite magnificent. The Rhythm Factory and The Castle are chaotic boozing dens—or head to Wilton's Music Hall for crumbling decadence and table tennis.

Coffee

- **Oi Bagel** • 45 Commercial Rd
- **Starbucks** • 45 Whitechapel Rd

Landmarks

- **The Sun HQ** • 1 Virginia Street

Nightlife

- **The Castle** • 44 Commercial Rd
- **Dickens Inn** • 1 St. Katherine Docks
- **Prohibition Bar and Grill** • 1 St. Katherine's dock
- **Rhythm Factory** • 16 Whitechapel Rd
- **Wilton's Music Hall** • Graces Alley & Ensign St

Restaurants

- **Cafe Spice Namaste** • 16 Prescot St
- **The Empress** • 141 Leman St

Supermarkets

- **Waitrose** • Thomas More St & Nesham St

Map 96 • Whitechapel (East) / Shadwell (West) / Wapping

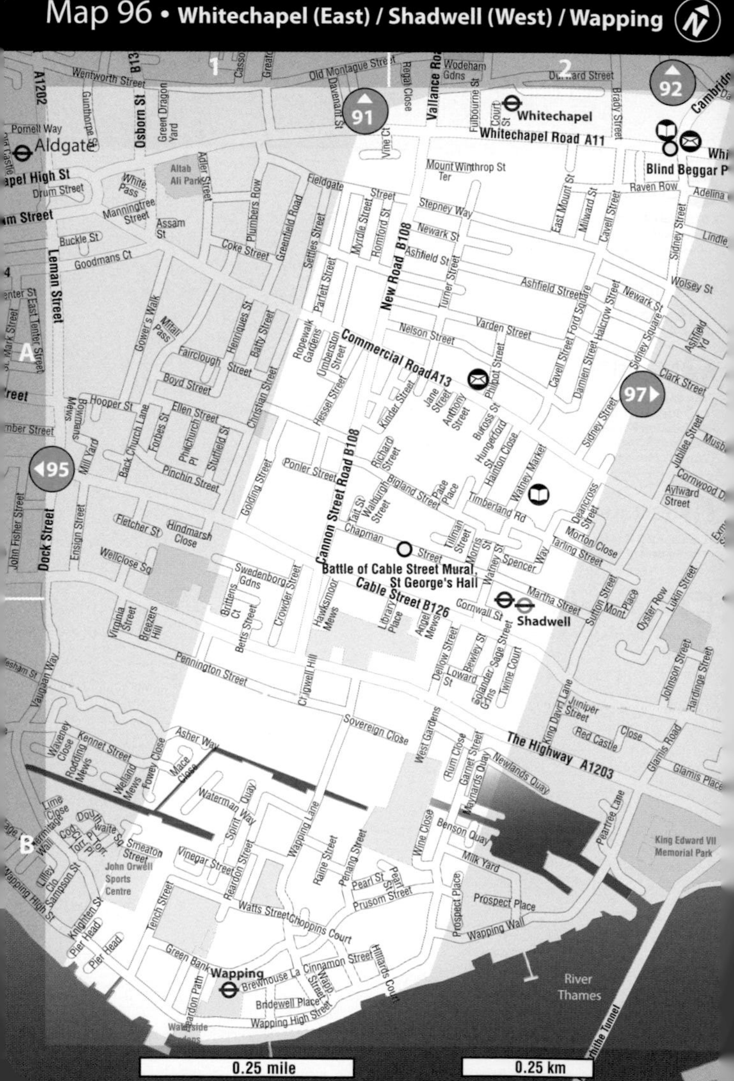

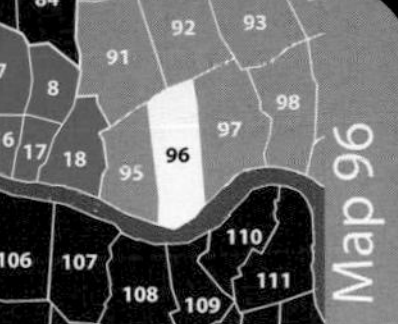

Ex-dockland Wapping now imports yuppies into its converted warehouses, less gleaming Shadwell and Whitechapel keep more of the East End spirit alive. Wapping High Street is mainly residential, Whitechapel Road is more lively. Drink at Indo if you're boho, stick with The Captain Kidd if not. Tayyab's is cracking—stick out the queues, or if curry's not your thing head to Il Bordello.

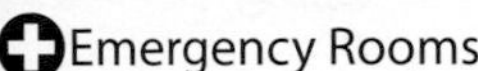

Emergency Rooms

- **Royal London Hospital** • Whitechapel Rd & Vallance Rd

Landmarks

- **Battle of Cable Street Mural, St George's Hall** • 236 Cable St
- **Blind Beggar Pub** • 337 Whitechapel Rd

Libraries

- **Idea Store Whitechapel** • 321 Whitechapel Rd
- **Watney Market Library** • 30 Watney Market

Nightlife

- **The Captain Kidd** • 108 Wapping High St
- **The Caxtons** • 50 The Highway
- **Indo** • 133 Whitechapel Rd
- **Town of Ramsgate** • 62 Wapping High St

Post Offices

- **Eastern** • 206 Whitechapel Rd
- **Philpot Street** • 12 Philpot St

Restaurants

- **Il Bordello** • 81 Wapping High Street
- **Tayyabs** • 83 Fieldgate St

Supermarkets

- **Iceland** • Watney St & Tarling St
- **Sainsbury's** • 1 Cambridge Heath Rd

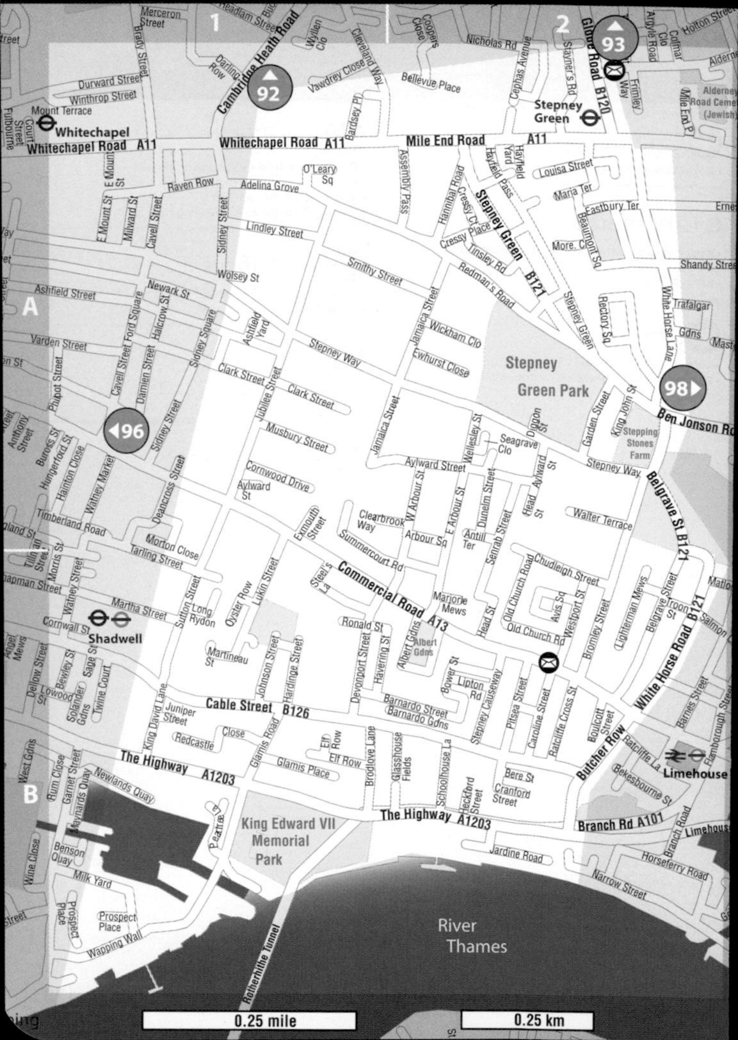
1
2
A
B
92
93
96
98
Merceron Street
Headlam Street
Brady Street
Cambridge Heath Road
Darling Row
Wyllen Clo
Cleveland Way
Coopers Close
Nicholas Rd
Cephas Avenue
Stayner's Rd
Globe Road B120
Frimley Way
Argyle Road
Colmar Clo
Holton Street
Alderney Road Cemetery (Jewish)
Mile End Pl
Durward Street
Winthrop Street
Mount Terrace
Fulbourne Street
Court Street
Whitechapel
Vawdrey Close
Bellevue Place
Bardsey Pl
Stepney Green
Whitechapel Road A11
Mile End Road A11
E Mount St
Raven Row
Adelina Grove
O'Leary Sq
Assembly Pass
Hayfield Yard
Hayfield Pass
Louisa Street
Maria Ter
Eastbury Ter
Beaumont Sq
More. Cl
Shandy Street
Milward St
Cavell Street
E Mount St
Sidney Street
Lindley Street
Hannibal Road
Cressy Ct
Cressy Place
Stepney Green B121
Tinsley Rd
Redman's Road
Smithy Street
Wolsey St
Newark St
Ashfield Street
Ashfield Yard
Jamaica Street
Wickham Clo
Ewhurst Close
Rectory Sq
White Horse Lane
Trafalgar Gdns
Varden Street
Ford Square
Halcrow St
Sidney Square
Stepney Way
Stepney Green Park
Clark Street
Jubilee Street
Cavell Street
Damien Street
Philpot Street
Sidney Street
Musbury Street
Jamaica Street
Wellesley St
Seagrave Clo
Diggon St
Garden Street
King John St
Stepping Stones Farm
Ben Jonson Rd
Anthony Street
Buross St
Hungerford St
Hainton Close
Watney Market
Deancross Street
Cornwood Drive
Aylward St
Aylward Street
W Arbour St
E Arbour St
Dunelm Street
Head St
Stepney Way
Belgrave St B121
Timberland Road
Exmouth Street
Clearbrook Way
Arbour Sq
Antill Ter
Senrab Street
Walter Terrace
Summercourt Rd
Morton Close
Tarling Street
Tillman Street
Morris St
Watney Street
Chapman Street
Steel's La
Commercial Road A13
Lukin Street
Sutton Street
Long Rydon
Oyster Row
Marjorie Mews
Chudleigh Street
Old Church Road
Avis Sq
Westport St
Bromley Street
Lighterman Mews
Belgrave Street
Troon St
White Horse Road B121
Salmon
Martha Street
Cornwall St
Shadwell
Ronald St
Old Church Rd
Angel Mews
Dellow Street
Bewley St
Sage St
Twine Court
Lowood St
Solander Gdns
Martineau St
Johnson Street
Hardinge Street
Devonport Street
Havering St
Albert Gdns
Bower St
Lipton Rd
Stepney Causeway
Pitsea Street
Caroline Street
Ratcliffe Cross St
Boulcott Street
Barnes Street
Flamborough Street
King David Lane
Juniper Street
Cable Street B126
Barnardo Street
Barnardo Gdns
Redcastle Close
Glamis Road
Elf Row
Brodlove Lane
Glasshouse Fields
Schoolhouse La
Butcher Row
Ratcliffe La
Limehouse
The Highway A1203
Glamis Place
Bere St
Cranford Street
Heckford Street
Bekesbourne St
West Gdns
Rum Close
Garnet Street
Maynards Quay
Newlands Quay
Peartree La
King Edward VII Memorial Park
The Highway A1203
Branch Rd A101
Branch Road
Limehouse
Benson Quay
Wine Close
Jardine Road
Horseferry Road
Milk Yard
Narrow Street
Prospect Place
Prospect Place
Wapping Wall
Rotherhithe Tunnel
River Thames
0.25 mile
0.25 km

Stepney / Shadwell (East)

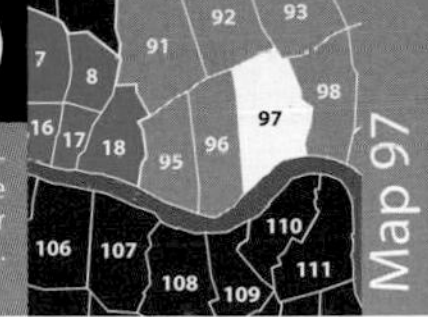

Cockney geezers run into hipsters and smart new developments sit next to run-down estates. No one quite knows where this area is going. We know where we're going, though—to The George Tavern, mainly, for impromptu theatre, blue-collar poetry and other arty madness, or The Prospect of Whitby, if we're feeling nostalgic. Wapping Food, meanwhile, serves great fare inside a century-old power station.

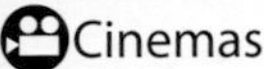

Cinemas

- **Genesis Mile End** • 93 Mile End Rd

Coffee

- **Popular Café** • 536 Commercial Rd

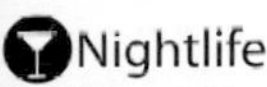

Nightlife

- **Cable Street Studios** • 566 Cable St
- **The George Tavern** • 373 Commercial Rd
- **The Prospect of Whitby** • 57 Wapping Wall
- **Troxy** • 490 Commercial Rd

Post Offices

- **Globe Road** • 34 Globe Rd
- **Stepney** • 502 Commercial Rd

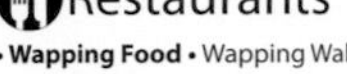

Restaurants

- **Wapping Food** • Wapping Wall

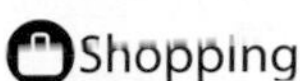

Shopping

- **John Lester Wigmakers** • 32 Globe Rd
- **East End Thrift Store** • 1 Assembly Passage

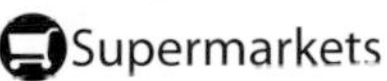

Supermarkets

- **Co-Op** • 193 Mile End Rd

Map 98 • Mile End (South) / Limehouse

1
2
A
B
Stepney Green
Globe Road
Frimley Way
Close Mile End Pl
Alderney Road Cemetery (Jewish)
Bancroft Road
Mile End Road A11
93
94
97
99
100
Mile End
Wentworth Mews
Eric Street
Southern Grove
Louisa Street
Maria Terrace
Eastbury Ter
Beaumont Sq
Ernest Street
Toby Lane
Union Drive
Sandalwood Close
Solebay Street
Emmott Close
Hamlets Way
English Street
Treby Street
Shandy Street
Harford Street
Commodore Street
Mile End Park
PAGE 346
Ropery Street
Bow Common Lane
Stepney Green B121
Redman's Road
Stepney Green
Rectory Sq
White Horse Lane
Trafalgar Gdns
Shandy Park
Bale Road
Essian Street
Regent's Canal
Coppperfield Road
Masters Street
Bohn Road
White Tower Way
Portia Way
Wager Street
Joseph Street
Stepney Green Park
Garden Street
King John St
Duckett Street
Dongola Road
Candle St
Ragged School Museum
Ben Jonson Road
B140
Stepping Stones Farm
White Horse Rd
Our Lady Ben Rd
Rowe Dak Pl
Copley Street
Belgrave Street
Halley Street
Carr Street
Mile End Stadium
Colfman Street
Walter Terrace
Maroon Street
Galsworthy Avenue
Eastfield Street
Jamuna Close
Haven Mews
Revolution Karting
Leopold Street
Baythorne Street
Caudleigh Street
Avis Square
Westport Street
Bromley Street
Lighterman Mews
Belgrave Street
White Horse Road B121
Barnes Street
Aston Street
Hearnshaw Street
Repton Street
Carr Street
Rhodeswell Road
Turners Road
St. Pauls Way
Locksley Street
B140
Booker Close
Clemence Street
Parnham St
Dora Street
A1205
Wallwood Street
Agnes Street
Pitsea Street
Caroline Street
Ratcliffe Cross Street
Boulcott Street
Wakeling St
Flamborough Street
Faby Street
Brenton St
Blount St
Salmon Lane
Yorkshire Road
Norbiton Road
Pixley Street
Southwater Cl
Butcher Row
Ratcliffe Lane
Limehouse
Brunton Pl
Commercial Road A13
Lowell Street
Dal Street
Salmon Street
Salmon Lane
Wil. Pl
Copenhagen Place
Burdett Road
Bekesbourne Street
Branch Road
Basin App
Mill Place
Basin Approach
Limehouse Cut
Dod Street
Tile Yard
Farrance Street
Old School
Pigott St
Branch Road A101
The Highway A1203
Horseferry Road
Norway Pl
Wharf Lane
Island Row
St. Anne Street
Narrow Street
Goodhart Place
Newell Street
St. Anne's Pass
Chusan Place
East India Dock Road
Northey Street
Vicar Place
Limehouse Link
Ropemakers Field
Oak Lane
Three Colt Street
Beccles Street
West India Dock Road
Amoy Place
Birchfield Street
River Thames
Narrow Street
Shoulder of Mutton Alley
Bright Pl
A1203
Rich Street
Grenade St
Stocks Place
Gill Street
Ropemakers Fields
Barleycorn Way
0.25 mile
0.25 km

Mile End (South) / Limehouse

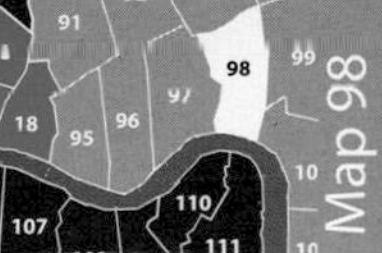

Scary desolate landscapes and urban decay? Cool! Authenticity and Edge go hand-in-hand 'round here until you get to the water, where it livens up and turns into a Foxtons' wank fantasy. Still, The Grapes, The Narrow and La Figa are eats and drinks havens while the Ragged School Museum offers a glimpse of what it was like when it was really grim round 'ere.

Landmarks

- **Ragged School Museum** • 46 Copperfield Rd

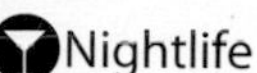

Nightlife

- **The Grapes** • 76 Narrow Street

Post Offices

- **Ben Jonson Road** • 52 Ben Jonson Rd
- **Mile End** • 1 Burdett Rd
- **Salmon Lane** • 127 Salmon Ln

Restaurants

- **La Figa** • 45 Narrow St
- **The Narrow** • 44 Narrow Street
- **Orange Room Café** • 63 Burdett Rd

Map 99 • **Bow Common**

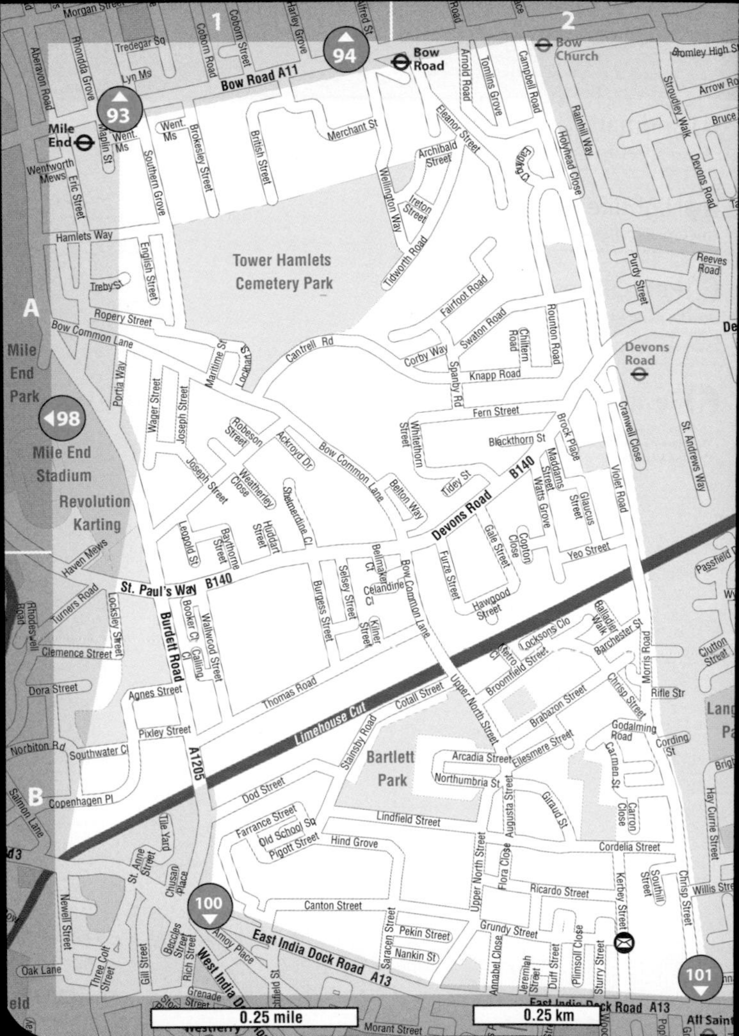
N
1
2
A
B
93
94
98
100
101
Morgan Street
Tredegar Sq
Lyn Ms
Bow Road A11
Bow Road
Bow Church
Bromley High St
Arrow Road
Bruce Road
Aberavon Road
Rhondda Grove
Coborn Road
Coborn Street
Harley Grove
Alfred St
Arnold Road
Tomlins Grove
Campbell Road
Rainhill Way
Stroudley Walk
Devons Road
Mile End
Maplin St
Went. Ms
Wentworth Mews
Eric Street
Southern Grove
Brokesley Street
British Street
Merchant St
Wellington Way
Eleanor Street
Archibald Street
Ireton Street
Ealing Cl
Holyhead Close
Hamlets Way
English Street
Treby St
Tower Hamlets Cemetery Park
Tidworth Road
Fairfoot Road
Purdy Street
Reeves Road
Ropery Street
Bow Common Lane
Maritime St
Lockhart St
Cantrell Rd
Corby Way
Swaton Road
Chiltern Road
Rounton Road
Devons Road
Mile End Park
Portia Way
Wager Street
Joseph Street
Spanby Rd
Knapp Road
Fern Street
Cranwell Close
St. Andrews Way
Mile End Stadium
Revolution Karting
Robeson Street
Ackroyd Dr
Bow Common Lane
Whitethorn Street
Blackthorn St
Brock Place
Maddams Street
Watts Grove
Violet Road
Weatherley Close
Shelmerdine Cl
Belton Way
Tidey St
B140
Devons Road
Glaucus Street
Leopold St
Baythorne Street
Huddart Street
Bellmaker Ct
Gale Street
Copton Close
Yeo Street
Haven Mews
Furze Street
Passfield Dr
St. Paul's Way B140
Celandine Cl
Bow Common Lane
Turners Road
Rhodeswell Road
Locksley Street
Burdett Road
Booker Cl
Wallwood Street
Selsey Street
Burgess Street
Kilner Street
Hawgood Street
Balladier Walk
Barchester St
Locksons Clo
Morris Road
Clutton Street
Clemence Street
Calling Cl
Nero Ct
Broomfield Street
Dora Street
Agnes Street
Thomas Road
Cotall Street
Upper North Street
Brabazon Street
Chrisp Street
Rifle Str
Limehouse Cut
Stainsby Road
Pixley Street
Norbiton Rd
Southwater Cl
A1205
Bartlett Park
Arcadia Street
Ellesmere Street
Godalming Road
Cording St
Northumbria St
Carmen St
Salmon Lane
Copenhagen Pl
Dod Street
Lindfield Street
Augusta Street
Giraud St
Hay Currie Street
Farrance Street
Old School Sq
Pigott Street
Hind Grove
Carron Close
Cordelia Street
Tile Yard
St. Anne Street
Chusan Place
Upper North Street
Flora Close
Southill Street
Chrisp Street
Willis Street
Newell Street
Ricardo Street
Kerbey Street
Canton Street
Amoy Place
Saracen Street
Pekin Street
Grundy Street
East India Dock Road A13
Beccles Street
Rich Street
Nankin St
Three Colt Street
Gill Street
Oak Lane
Annabel Close
Jeremiah Street
Duff Street
Plimsoll Close
Sturry Street
West India Dock Road
Grenade Street
East India Dock Road A13
Morant Street
All Saints
0.25 mile
0.25 km

Bow Common

Desolation Row pretty much. For hardy explorers kitted out with knives and/or chastity belts, the wonderfully overgrown and sh**-your-pants scary Tower Hamlets Cemetery Park is great. In fact, keep the afore-mentioned kit on if you intend creeping through the boarded-up council estates and general doom.

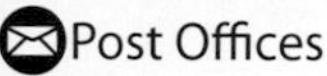

Post Offices

• **Poplar** • 22 Market Sq

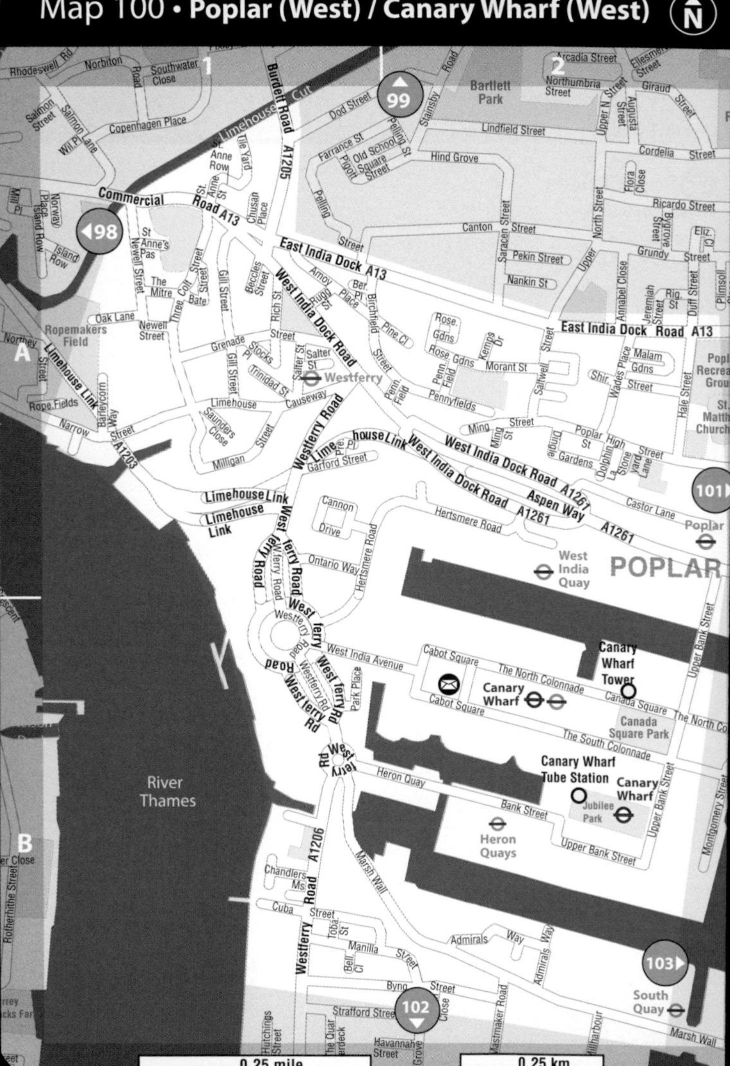
N
River Thames
POPLAR
Canary Wharf Tower
Canary Wharf
Canary Wharf Tube Station
Heron Quays
West India Quay
Westferry
Poplar
South Quay
Canada Square Park
Jubilee Park
Bartlett Park
Ropemakers Field
Limehouse Cut
Commercial Road A13
East India Dock Road A13
West India Dock Road A1261
Aspen Way A1261
Limehouse Link
Westferry Road
Burdett Road A1205
Marsh Wall
Upper Bank Street
Bank Street
Heron Quay
The North Colonnade
The South Colonnade
Cabot Square
West India Avenue
Hertsmere Road
Admirals Way
Montgomery Street
0.25 mile
0.25 km

Poplar (West) / Canary Wharf (West)

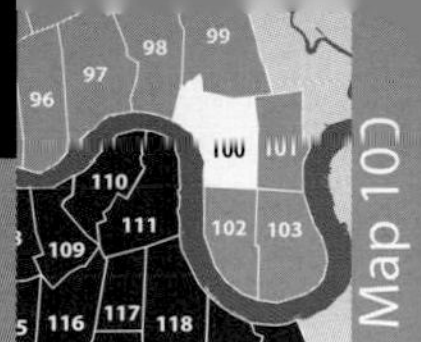

Now that we're officially out of the recession you can wander the wharf marveling at the 'scrapers without pesky ruined bankers landing on you. Ah yes, the smell of money has resurfaced around finance's engine room and the brilliantly futuristic landscape is once again replete with suits shopping at the bland mall under Cabot Square. They never left of course, they just got used to packed lunches like the rest of us.

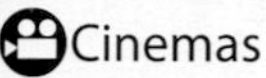

Cinemas

- **Cineworld West India Quay** • 11 Hertsmere Rd

Coffee

- **Bagel Factory** • 7 Westferry Circus
- **Café Brera** • 45 Bank St
- **Café Brera** • 12 Cabot Sq
- **Café Brera** • 31 Westferry Circus
- **Coffee Republic** • 10 Cabot Square
- **Coffee Republic** • Hertsmere Rd
- **Fresco Café Bar** • 15 Cabot Sq
- **Fresco Café Bar** • 22 Canada Sq
- **Starbucks** • 1 Canada Sq
- **Starbucks** • 45 Bank St
- **Starbucks** • 8 Westferry Circus

Landmarks

- **Canary Wharf Tower** • 1 Canada Sq
- **Canary Wharf Tube Station** • Canary Wharf

Nightlife

- **Bar 38** • West India Quay
- **Davy's at Canary Wharf** • 31 Canary Wharf
- **Dion Canary Wharf** • Port East Building, West India Quay
- **Via Fossa**• 18 Hertsmere Rd

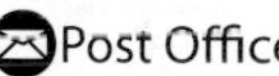

Post Offices

- **Canary Wharf** • 5 Chancellor Passage

Restaurants

- **1802 Bar** • Hertsmere Rd
- **Browns** • Hertsmere Rd
- **Nicolas** • 480 One Canada Sq
- **Plateau** • Canada Pl
- **Tiffin Bites** • 22 Jubilee Place

Supermarkets

- **Tesco** • 15 Cabot Sq
- **Waitrose** • N Colonnade & Canada Sq

Map 101 • Poplar (East) / Canary Wharf (East)

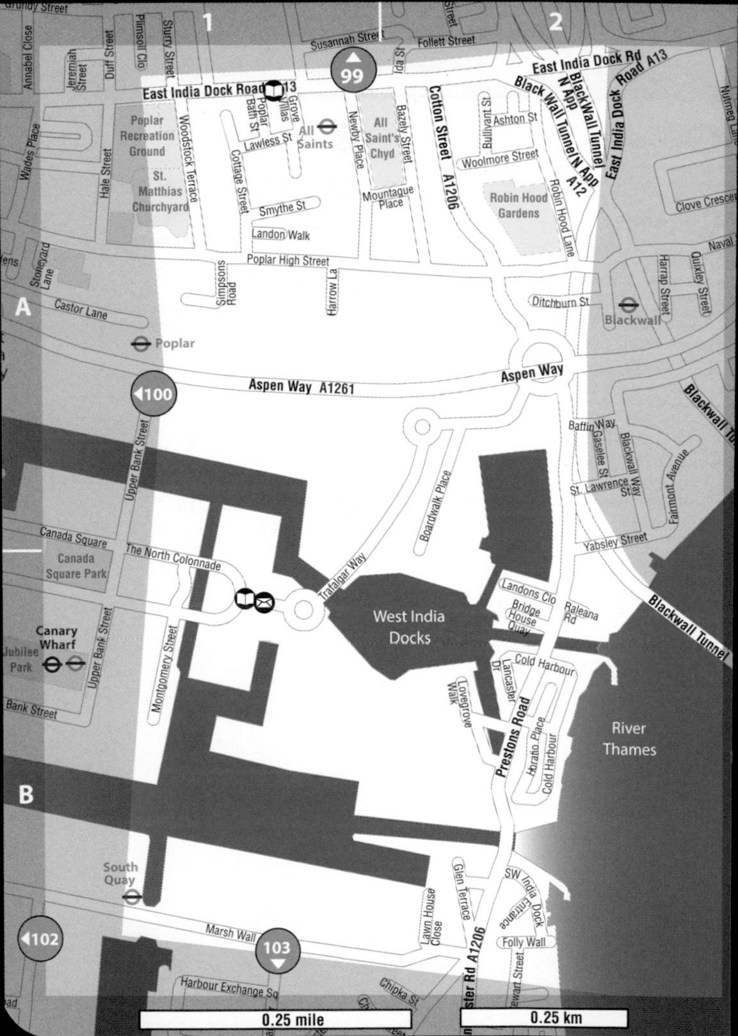

N

1
2
A
B

Susannah Street
Follett Street
Annabel Close
Jeremiah Street
Duff Street
Plimsoll Clo
Sturry Street
East India Dock Road A13
Poplar Bath St
Grove Villas
99
Ida St
Cotton Street A1206
Bullivant St
Ashton St
Black Wall Tunnel N App A12
BlackWall Tunnel N App
East India Dock Rd A13
East India Dock Road A13
Woolmore Street
Robin Hood Gardens
Robin Hood Lane
Clove Crescent
Wades Place
Hale Street
Poplar Recreation Ground
St. Matthias Churchyard
Woodstock Terrace
Cottage Street
Lawless St
All Saints
Newby Place
All Saint's Chyd
Bazely Street
Mountague Place
Smythe St
Landon Walk
Poplar High Street
Simpsons Road
Harrow La
Stoneyard Lane
Castor Lane
Poplar
Ditchburn St
Blackwall
Harrap Street
Quixley Street
Naval
Aspen Way
Aspen Way A1261
100
Upper Bank Street
Boardwalk Place
Baffin Way
Gaselee St
Blackwall Way
Fairmont Avenue
St. Lawrence St
Blackwall Tunnel
Yabsley Street
Canada Square
Canada Square Park
The North Colonnade
Trafalgar Way
West India Docks
Landons Clo
Bridge House Quay
Raleana Rd
Canary Wharf
Jubilee Park
Upper Bank Street
Montgomery Street
Bank Street
Cold Harbour
Lancaster Dr
Lovegrove Walk
Prestons Road
Horatio Place
Cold Harbour
River Thames
South Quay
Glen Terrace
Lawn House Close
SW India Dock Entrance
Folly Wall
Marsh Wall
102
103
Harbour Exchange Sq
Chipka St
Manchester Rd A1206
Stewart Street

0.25 mile
0.25 km

Poplar (East) / Canary Wharf (East)

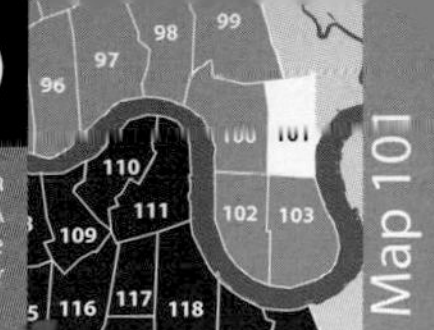

One day NFT lay down in the shadow of the Tower after a few in the Greenwich Pensioner and gazed up at the 'scraper, admiring its Philip K. Dickian splendour. A small plane buzzed by. Well-heeled bankers stuffed with pub grub from Gun strode by us. Then we got pulled up by the dreadlocks by a rozzer and got hoofed out for not reading the Financial Times. Serves us right.

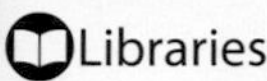

Libraries

- **Idea Store Canary Wharf** • Churchill Pl
- **Idea Store Chrisp Street** • East India Dock Rd • 1 Vesey Path

Nightlife

- **The Greenwich Pensioner** • 28 Bazely Street
- **The Resolute** • 210 Poplar High Street

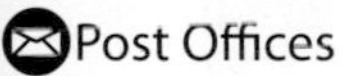

Post Offices

- **Churchill Place** • 2 Churchill Pl

Restaurants

- **Gun** • 27 Coldharbour
- **Jamie's Italian** • 2 Churchill Pl

Map 102 • Millwall

Millwall

Though Millwall has award winning Docklands Sailing Centre and decent community venue The Space (Hubbub Café and Bar), it doesn't really have much else. Bereft of tube, overground, or DLR, it doesn't even have Millwall FC anymore. Despite the potential of Canary Wharf on the doorstep and flush of luxury riverside apartments, it's still tainted with the whiff of BNP and football hooliganism. Buy now.

Landmarks

• **The Docklands Sailing & Watersport Centre** • 235 Westferry Rd

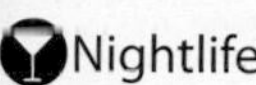

Nightlife

• **Hubbub** • 269 Westferry Rd

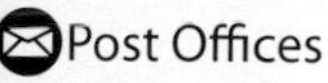

Post Offices

• **Westferry Rd** • 367 Westferry Rd

Map 103 • Cubitt Town / Mudchute

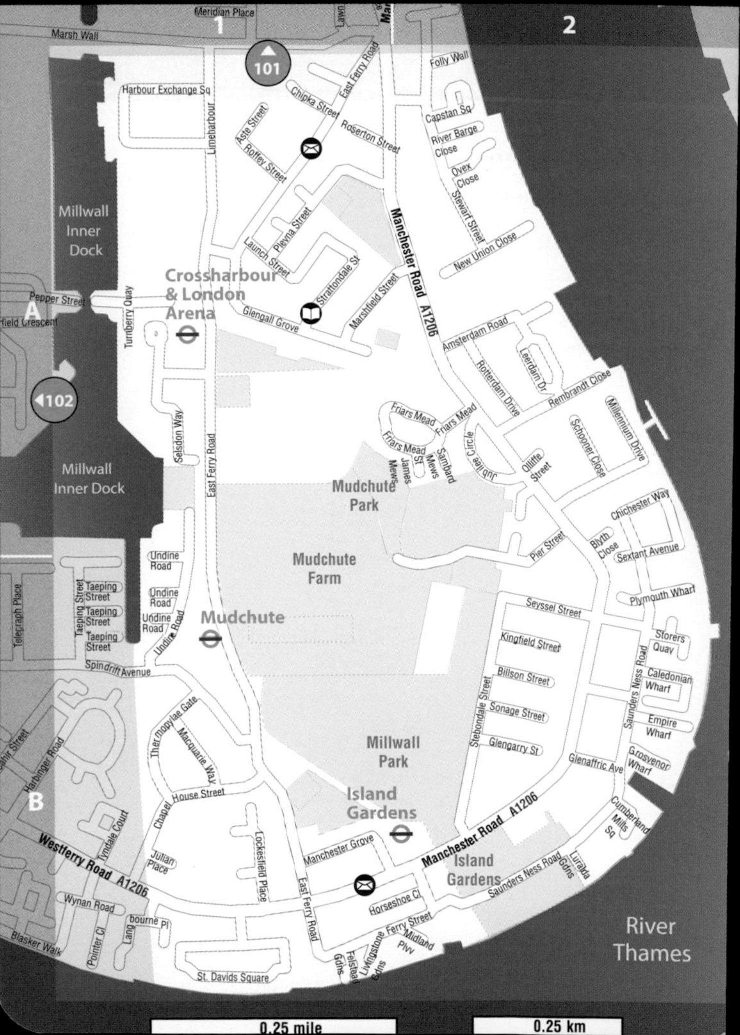

N

Meridian Place
1
2
Marsh Wall
101
Folly Wall
Harbour Exchange Sq
East Ferry Road
Chipka Street
Capstan Sq
Aste Street
Roserton Street
River Barge Close
Limeharbour
Roffey Street
Ovex Close
Millwall Inner Dock
Stewart Street
Manchester Road A1206
Plevna Street
New Union Close
Launch Street
Crossharbour & London Arena
Strattondale St
Marshfield Street
Pepper Street
A
Turnberry Quay
Glengall Grove
field Crescent
Amsterdam Road
Leerdam Dr
Rotterdam Drive
Rembrandt Close
102
Friars Mead
Friars Mead
Friars Mead
Millennium Drive
Schooner Close
Selsdon Way
East Ferry Road
James St
Mews
Mews
Sambard
Jubilee Circle
Olliffe Street
Millwall Inner Dock
Mudchute Park
Chichester Way
Pier Street
Blyth Close
Sextant Avenue
Mudchute Farm
Undine Road
Undine Road
Undine Road
Undine Road
Plymouth Wharf
Taeping Street
Taeping Street
Taeping Street
Taeping Street
Seyssel Street
Telegraph Place
Mudchute
Storers Quay
Kingfield Street
Spindrift Avenue
Billson Street
Saunders Ness Road
Caledonian Wharf
Sonage Street
Stebondale Street
Empire Wharf
Thermopylae Gate
Macquarie Way
Millwall Park
Glengarry St
Glenaffric Ave
Grosvenor Wharf
Harbinger Road
B
House Street
Chapel
Island Gardens
Cumberland Mills Sq
Tyndale Court
Westferry Road A1206
Lockesfield Place
Manchester Grove
Manchester Road A1206
Julian Place
Island Gardens
Saunders Ness Road
Lurada Gdns
East Ferry Road
Wynan Road
Horseshoe Cl
Langbourne Pl
Ferry Street
Midland Plvv
Blasker Walk
Pointer Cl
Felstead Gdns
Livingstone Gdns
River Thames
St. Davids Square

0.25 mile
0.25 km

Cubitt Town / Mudchute

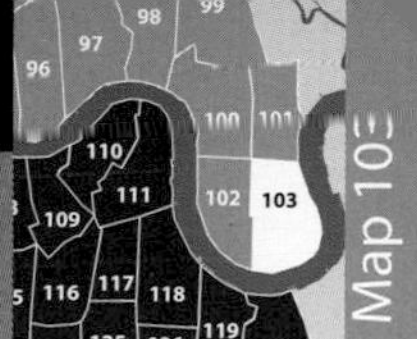

Though shaded by the skyscrapers of Canary Wharf and a rash of luxury developments, this corner of the Island is blessed by the marvellous Mudchute Farm and Park (with the stand out Mudchute Kitchen and equestrian centre), not one, not two, but three DLR stations, and a number of down-to-earth boozers (Lord Nelson, Waterman's Arms). Who let the Isle of Dogs out?

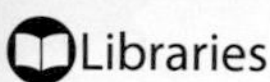

Libraries

- **Cubitt Town Library** • Strattondale St

Nightlife

- **The Ferry House** • 26 Ferry St
- **Lord Nelson** • 1 Manchester Road
- **Waterman's Arms** • 1 Glenaffric Avenue

Post Offices

- **Cubitt Town** • 15 Castalia Sq
- **Isle Of Dogs** • 139 Manchester Rd

Restaurants

- **Mudchute Kitchen** • Pier Street

Supermarkets

- **ASDA** • 151 E Ferry Rd

Maps 104–130 • **Southeast London**

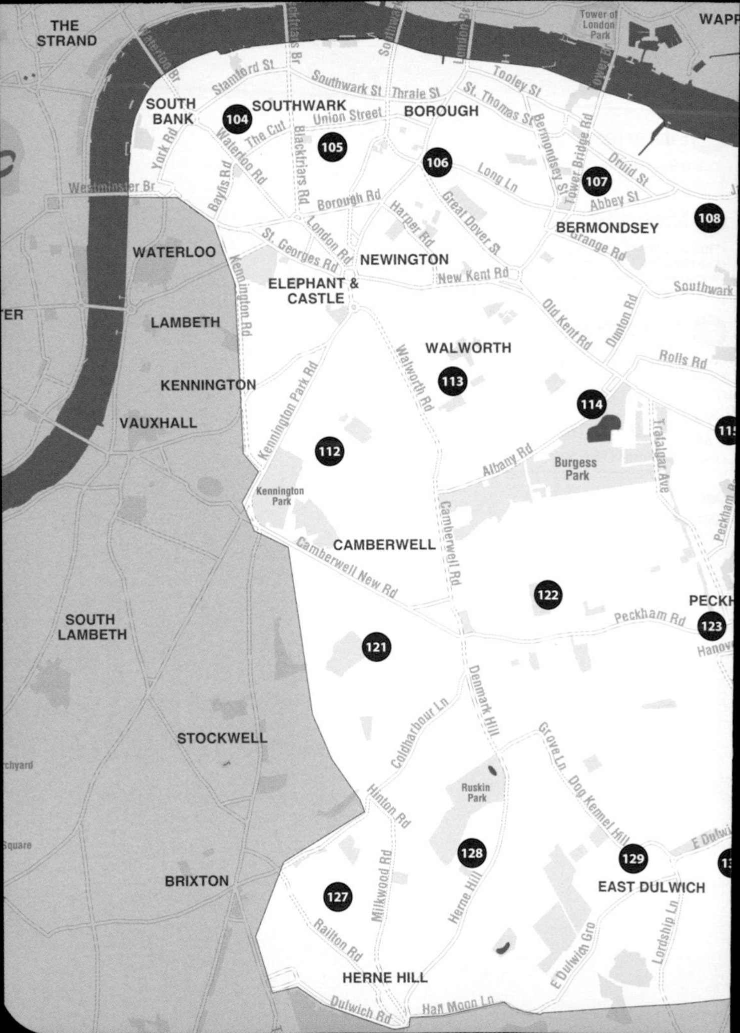

THE STRAND
SOUTH BANK
SOUTHWARK
BOROUGH
BERMONDSEY
WATERLOO
NEWINGTON
ELEPHANT & CASTLE
LAMBETH
WALWORTH
KENNINGTON
VAUXHALL
CAMBERWELL
SOUTH LAMBETH
PECKHAM
STOCKWELL
BRIXTON
EAST DULWICH
HERNE HILL
Tower of London Park
Burgess Park
Kennington Park
Ruskin Park
Waterloo Br
Blackfriars Br
Southwark Br
London Br
Tower Br
Westminster Br
Stamford St
Southwark St
Thrale St
Tooley St
St. Thomas St
Union Street
The Cut
York Rd
Waterloo Rd
Baylis Rd
Blackfriars Rd
Borough Rd
Long Ln
Bermondsey St
Tower Bridge Rd
Druid St
Abbey St
Harper Rd
Great Dover St
Grange Rd
St. Georges Rd
London Rd
New Kent Rd
Kennington Rd
Old Kent Rd
Dunton Rd
Southwark Park Rd
Rolls Rd
Walworth Rd
Kennington Park Rd
Albany Rd
Trafalgar Ave
Peckham Rd
Camberwell Rd
Camberwell New Rd
Hanover
Denmark Hill
Coldharbour Ln
Grove Ln
Dog Kennel Hill
E Dulwich Rd
Hinton Rd
Milkwood Rd
Herne Hill
Railton Rd
E Dulwich Gro
Lordship Ln
Dulwich Rd
Half Moon Ln
104
105
106
107
108
112
113
114
115
121
122
123
127
128
129
130

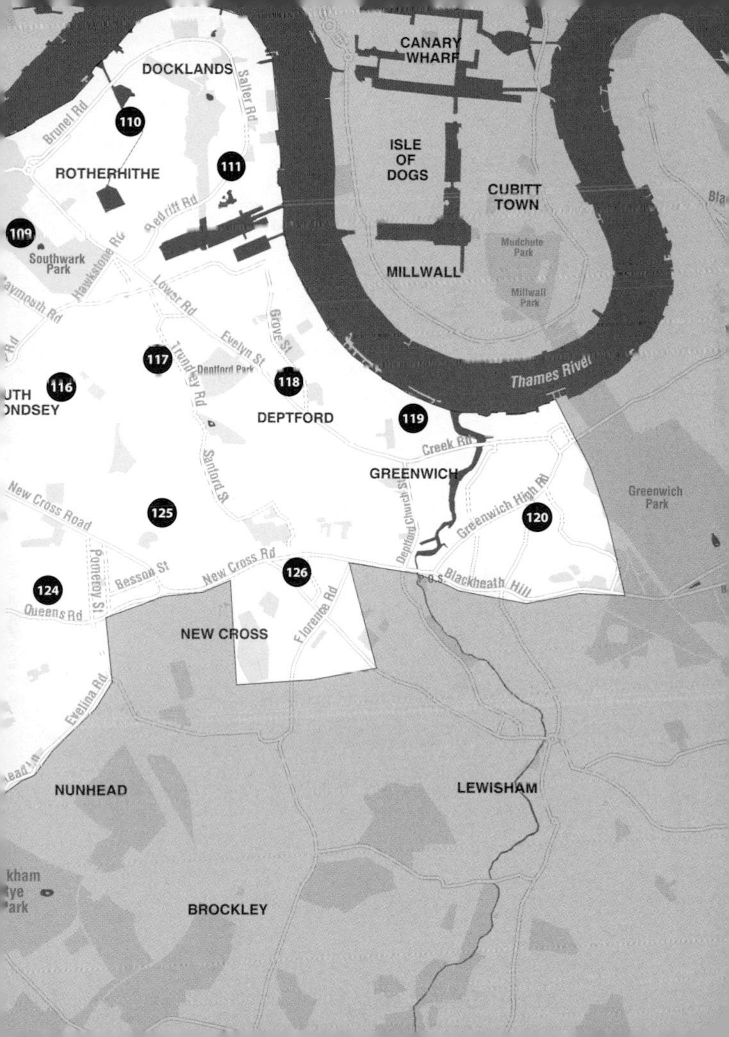

DOCKLANDS
CANARY WHARF
ISLE OF DOGS
CUBITT TOWN
ROTHERHITHE
Brunel Rd
Salter Rd
Redriff Rd
Southwark Park
Hawkstone Rd
Lower Rd
Mudchute Park
Millwall Park
MILLWALL
Grove St
Evelyn St
Trundley Rd
Deptford Park
Thames River
DEPTFORD
GREENWICH
Creek Rd
Sanford St
New Cross Road
Deptford Church St
Greenwich High Rd
Greenwich Park
Pomeroy St
Besson St
New Cross Rd
Blackheath Hill
Queens Rd
NEW CROSS
Florence Rd
Evelina Rd
NUNHEAD
LEWISHAM
BROCKLEY
109
110
111
116
117
118
119
120
124
125
126

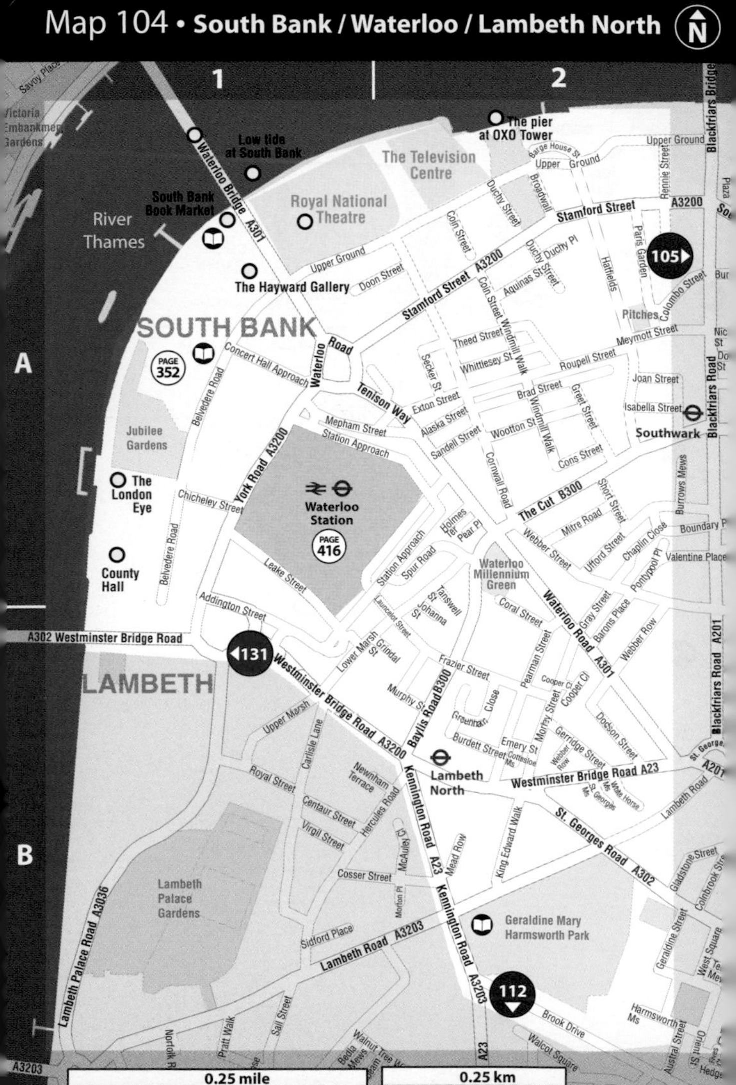
Map 104 • South Bank / Waterloo / Lambeth North
N
1
2
A
B
Savoy Place
Victoria Embankment Gardens
River Thames
Waterloo Bridge A301
Low tide at South Bank
South Bank Book Market
The pier at OXO Tower
The Television Centre
Royal National Theatre
The Hayward Gallery
Upper Ground
Barge House St
Broadwall
Duchy Street
Coin Street
Stamford Street A3200
Stamford Street
A3200
Doon Street
Duchy Pl
Aquinas St
Hatfields
Paris Garden
Rennie Street
Blackfriars Bridge
105
Colombo Street
Pitches
Meymott Street
SOUTH BANK
PAGE 352
Concert Hall Approach
Waterloo Road
Belvedere Road
Tenison Way
Theed Street
Whittlesey St
Windmill Walk
Secker St
Roupell Street
Joan Street
Isabella Street
Southwark
Blackfriars Road
Exton Street
Alaska Street
Brad Street
Greet Street
Mepham Street
Station Approach
Sandell Street
Wootton St
Cons Street
Jubilee Gardens
York Road A3200
Waterloo Station
PAGE 416
Cornwall Road
The London Eye
Chicheley Street
The Cut B300
Short Street
Mitre Road
Burrows Mews
Boundary
Holmes Ter
Pear Pl
Webber Street
Ufford Street
Chaplin Close
Valentine Place
Pontypool Pl
County Hall
Station Approach
Spur Road
Waterloo Millennium Green
Leake Street
Tanswell St
Johanna St
Coral Street
Gray Street
Barons Place
Webber Row
Addington Street
Launcelot Street
A302 Westminster Bridge Road
131
Westminster Bridge Road A3200
Lower Marsh
Grindal St
Frazier Street
Pearman Street
Waterloo Road A301
Blackfriars Road A201
LAMBETH
Murphy St
Baylis Road B300
Greenham Close
Cooper Cl
Morley Street
Dodson Street
Upper Marsh
Carlisle Lane
Burdett Street
Emery St
Cottesloe Ms
Webber Row
Gerridge Street
St. George's
Lambeth North
Royal Street
Newnham Terrace
Kennington Road
Westminster Bridge Road A23
St Georges Ms
White Horse Ms
A201
Centaur Street
Hercules Road
Lambeth Road
Virgil Street
McAuley Cl
Mead Row
King Edward Walk
St. Georges Road A302
Gladstone Street
Colnbrook Street
Cosser Street
Kennington Road A23
Lambeth Palace Gardens
Morton Pl
Geraldine Mary Harmsworth Park
Geraldine Street
West Square
Lambeth Palace Road A3036
Sidford Place
Lambeth Road A3203
Kennington Road A3203
112
Harmsworth Ms
Brook Drive
Walcot Square
Austral Street
Orient St
Norfolk R
Pratt Walk
Sail Street
Walnut Tree W
A23
A3203
0.25 mile
0.25 km

South Bank / Waterloo / Lambeth North

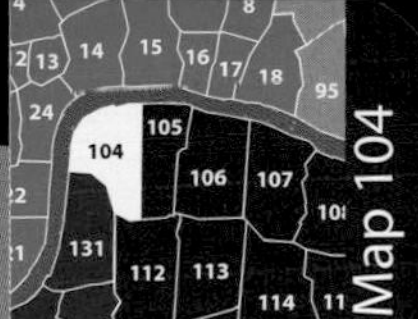

Hug the riverbank and you can culture 'till you puke. But you'll need stamina to survive; with such densely populated institutions your brain will give up long before your body. When it does, head for the cafe by day/bar by night, Concrete, tucked away behind the Southbank Centre, where the art installation du jour promises to have you wetting your pants in no time.

Cinemas

- **BFI London IMAX** • 1 Charlie Chaplin Walk
- **BFI Southbank** • Belverdere Rd & Waterloo Rd

Coffee

- **Bagel Factory** • Waterloo Station
- **Benugo Bar & Kitchen** • Belvedere Rd
- **Eat.** • Belvedere Rd
- **Eat.** • Barge House St
- **ScooterCaffe** • 132 Lower Marsh
- **Starbucks** • 3 Belvedere Rd

Landmarks

- **County Hall** • Westminster Bridge Rd & Belvedere Rd
- **The Hayward Gallery** • Southbank Centre
- **The London Eye** • Westminster Bridge Rd
- **Low Tide at South Bank** • Waterloo Rd & Upper Ground
- **National Theatre** • South Bank
- **The Pier at OXO Tower** • Barge House St & Upper Ground
- **South Bank Book Market** • Under Waterloo Bridge
- **Waterloo Bridge** • Waterloo Bridge

Libraries

- **Imperial War Museum** • Lambeth Road
- **Poetry Library** • Royal Festival Hall
- **Waterloo Library** • 114 Lower Marsh

Nightlife

- **The Anchor & Hope** • 36 The Cut
- **Benugo Bar & Kitchen** • Belvedere Rd
- **Concrete** • Southbank Centre
- **Cubana** • 48 Lower Marsh
- **The Cut Bar** • 66 The Cut
- **Da Vinci's** • 6 Baylis Rd
- **The Fire Station** • 150 Waterloo Rd
- **The Pit Bar at the Old Vic** • The Cut
- **Royal Festival Hall** • Belvedere Rd
- **Skylon** • Belvedere Rd

Restaurants

- **Anchor & Hope** • 32 The Cut
- **Canteen** • Royal Festival Hall, Belvedere Rd
- **Concrete** • Southbank Centre
- **The Cut Bar** • 66 The Cut
- **Emils's Cafe** • 79 Waterloo Rd
- **Giraffe** • Riverside Level 1
- **Livebait** • 45 The Cut
- **Marie's Cafe** • 90 Lower Marsh
- **Oxo Tower Wharf** • Barge House St
- **RSJ** • 33 Coin St
- **Skylon** • Belvedere Rd
- **Studio 6** • 56 Upper Ground
- **Tas Cut** • 33 The Cut

Shopping

- **Calder Bookshop** • 51 The Cut
- **Calder Bookshop - The Bookshop Theater** • 51 The Cut
- **I Knit London** • 106 Lower Marsh
- **Konditor & Cook** • 22 Cornwall Rd
- **Oasis** • 84 Lower Marsh
- **Radio Days** • 87 Lower Marsh
- **ScooterCaffe** • 132 Lower Marsh
- **Silverprint** • 12 Valentine Pl
- **Southbank Book Market** • Under Waterloo Bridge
- **Top Wind** • 2 Lower Marsh
- **Waterloo Camping** • 37 The Cut
- **What The Butler Wore** • 131 Lower Marsh

Supermarkets

- **Iceland** • 112 Lower Marsh
- **Marks & Spencer** • Waterloo Station
- **Sainsbury's** • 101 Waterloo Rd

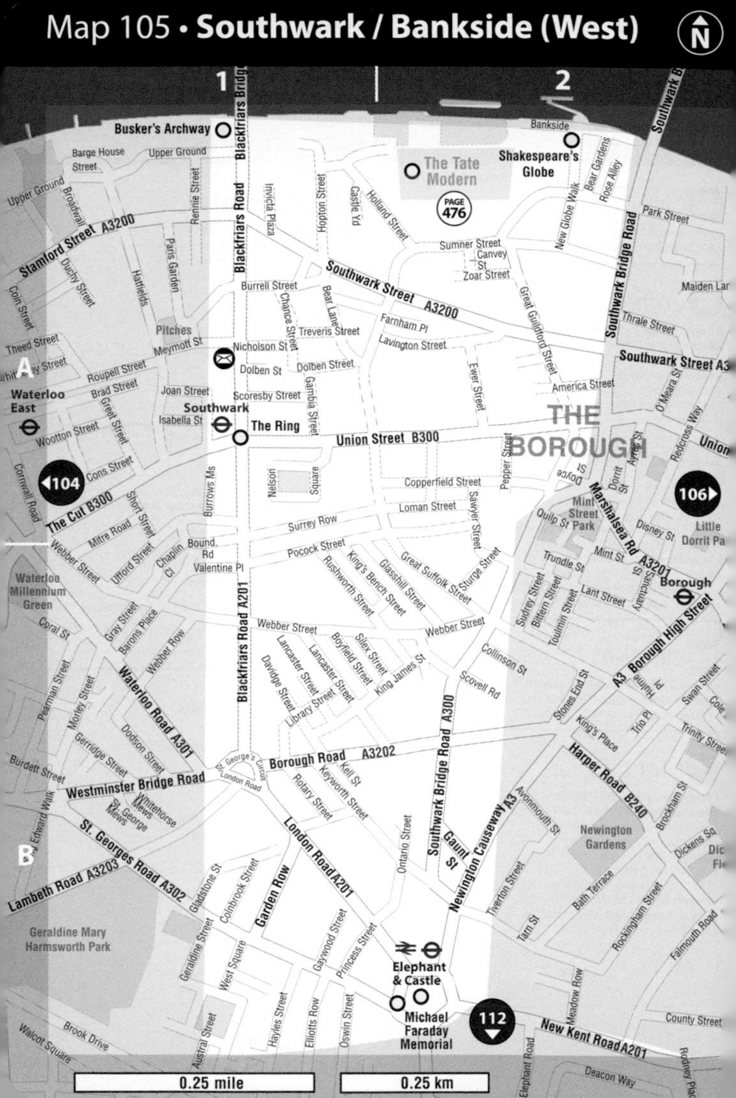

N
1
2
A
B
Busker's Archway
Blackfriars Bridge
Bankside
Shakespeare's Globe
The Tate Modern
PAGE 476
Barge House Street
Upper Ground
Rennie Street
Blackfriars Road
Invicta Plaza
Hopton Street
Castle Yd
Holland Street
Bear Gardens
Rose Alley
New Globe Walk
Park Street
Southwark Bridge Road
Broadwall
Stamford Street A3200
Paris Garden
Sumner Street
Canvey St
Zoar Street
Southwark Street A3200
Duchy Street
Coin Street
Hatfields
Burrell Street
Chance Street
Bear Lane
Great Guildford Street
Maiden Lane
Thrale Street
Pitches
Farnham Pl
Treveris Street
Theed Street
Meymott St
Nicholson St
Lavington Street
Southwark Street A3
Roupell Street
Dolben St
Dolben Street
Ewer Street
Waterloo East
Brad Street
Joan Street
Scoresby Street
America Street
O'Meara St
Great Street
Southwark
Gambia Street
THE BOROUGH
Isabella St
The Ring
Wootton Street
Union Street B300
Redcross Way
Union
Pepper Street
Ayres St
Doyce St
Dorrit St
Cornwall Road
104
Cons Street
Nelson Square
Copperfield Street
106
Burrows Ms
Marshalsea Rd
Mint Street Park
Short Street
Loman Street
Sawyer Street
The Cut B300
Quilp St
Little Dorrit Pa
Mitre Road
Surrey Row
Disney St
Webber Street
Chaplin Cl
Ufford Street
Bound. Rd
Pocock Street
Valentine Pl
Rushworth Street
King's Bench Street
Glasshill Street
Great Suffolk Street
Sturge Street
Trundle St
Mint St
A3201
Borough
Waterloo Millennium Green
Sudrey Street
Bittern Street
Lant Street
St
Sanctuary
Coral St
Gray Street
Barons Place
Toulmin Street
Borough High Street
Webber Street
Webber Street
Webber Row
Lancaster Street
Boyfield Street
Silex Street
King James St
Collinson St
A3
Hulme Pl
Swan Street
Pearman Street
Waterloo Road A301
Davidge Street
Lancaster Street
Scovell Rd
Stones End St
Cole
Morley Street
Blackfriars Road A201
Library Street
Trio Pl
King's Place
Trinity Street
Dodson Street
Southwark Bridge Road A300
Burdett Street
Gerridge Street
St George's Circus
Borough Road A3202
Harper Road B240
London Road
Kell St
Westminster Bridge Road
Rotary Street
Keyworth Street
Whitehorse Mews
St George Mews
Brockham St
Avonmouth St
Newington Gardens
King Edward Walk
St. Georges Road A302
London Road A201
Ontario Street
Gaunt St
Dickens Sq
Newington Causeway A3
Lambeth Road A3203
Gladstone St
Cobbrook Street
Garden Row
Tiverton Street
Bath Terrace
Geraldine Mary Harmsworth Park
Geraldine Street
Gaywood Street
Princess Street
Tarn St
Rockingham Street
Falmouth Road
West Square
Elephant & Castle
Meadow Row
Hayles Street
Elliotts Row
Oswin Street
Michael Faraday Memorial
112
County Street
Brook Drive
Austral Street
New Kent Road A201
Walcot Square
Elephant Road
Deacon Way
Rodney Place
0.25 mile
0.25 km

Southwark / Bankside (West)

The Tate Modern, ladies and gents. It deserves all the praise it gets. And next door there's the reconstruction of Shakespeare's famous playhouse, making this looked-after stretch of the Thames embankment a treasure for those hungry for culture. For those hungry for something else, you're spoilt with quirky options. Try Baltic for Polish Hunters' Stew, The Table for award-winning brunches, or Laughing Gravy for a restaurant named after Laurel & Hardy's dog.

Coffee

- **Eat.** • Bankside
- **Pret A Manger** • 2 Canvey St
- **Starbucks** • Emerson St (Units 1-3 Benbow House)

Landmarks

- **Buskers' Archway** • Southbank
- **Elephant & Castle** • Elephant & Castle
- **Michael Faraday Memorial** • Elephant & Castle
- **The Ring** • 72 Blackfriars Rd
- **Shakespeare's Globe** • 21 New Globe Walk
- **Tate Modern** • Bankside

Nightlife

- **Albert Arms** • 1 Gladstone St
- **Imbibe** • 173 Blackfriars Rd
- **The Lord Nelson** • 243 Union St
- **Ministry of Sound** • 103 Gaunt St
- **The Prince of Wales** • 51 St George's Rd
- **The Wine Theatre** • 206 Union St

Post Offices

- **Blackfriars Road** • 52 Blackfriars Rd

Restaurants

- **Baltic** • 74 Blackfriars Rd
- **Bangkok Kitchen** • 229 Union St
- **Blackfriars Cafe** • 169 Blackfriars Rd
- **El Vergel** • 132 Webber St
- **Laughing Gravy** • 154 Blackfriars Rd
- **The Table** • 83 Southwark St
- **Tate Modern Restaurant** • Bankside
- **Terry's Cafe** • 158 Great Suffolk St

Shopping

- **Elephant & Castle Market** • Elephant & Castle

Supermarkets

- **Tesco** • Elephant & Castle Metro

Map 106 • Bankside (East) / Borough / Newington

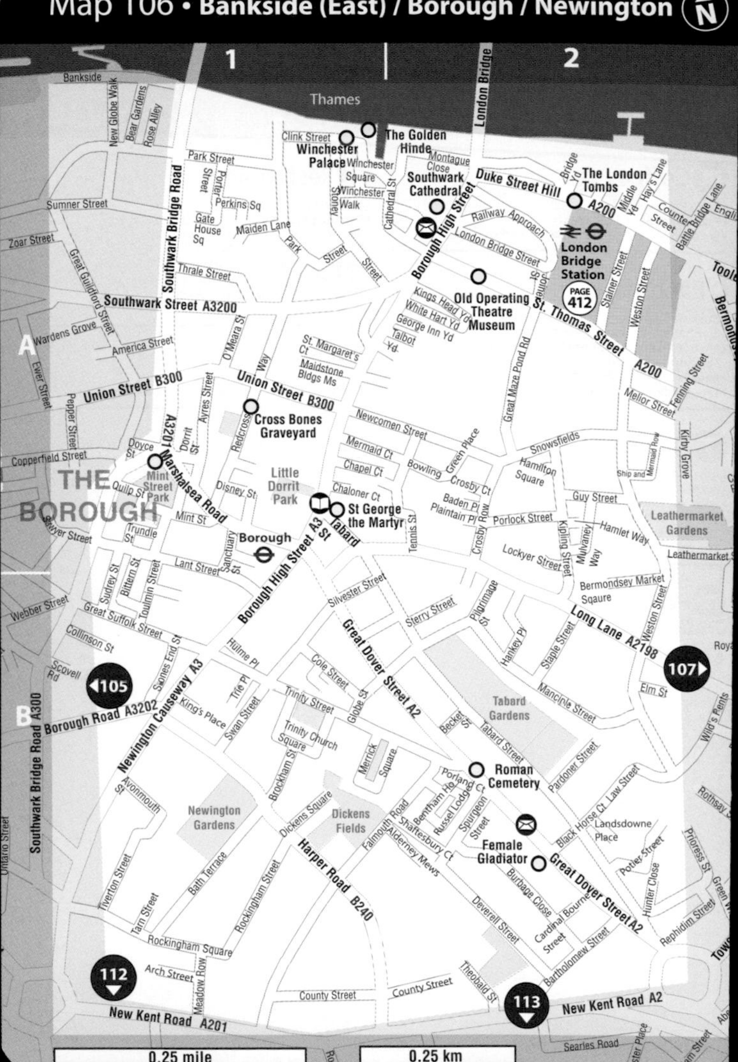

Bankside (East) / Borough / Newington

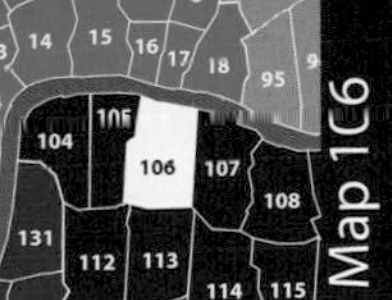

A Shoreditch for grown-ups, these parts have become a bit suitified lately—especially now it's been reborn as 'London Bridge Quarter' under the Shard. Still, there's plenty of fun to be had.

Coffee

- **Bagel Factory** • 12 Joiner St
- **Caffe Nero** • 3 Cathedral St
- **Costa** • 134 Borough High St
- **Patisserie Lila** • 1 Bedale St
- **Pret A Manger** • 8 London Bridge St
- **Pret A Manger** • 49 Tooley St
- **Starbucks** • Clink Wharf, Clink St

Landmarks

- **Cross Bones Graveyard** • Red Cross Way & Union St
- **Female Gladiator** • 159 Great Dover St
- **The Golden Hinde** • Clink St & Stoney St
- **The London Tombs** • 2 Tooley St
- **Mint Street Park** • Southwark Bridge Rd & Marshalsea Rd
- **Old Operating Theatre Museum** • 9 St Thomas St
- **Roman Cemetery** • 165 Great Dover St
- **Southwark Cathedral** • Cathedral St & Montague Close
- **St George the Martyr** • Borough High St & Tabard St
- **Winchester Palace** • Clink St & Storey St

Libraries

- **John Harvard Library** • 211 Borough High St

Nightlife

- **The Anchor** • 34 Park St
- **Belushi's** • 161 Borough High St
- **The Blue-Eyed Maid** • 173 Borough High St
- **Brew Wharf** • Brew Wharf Yard, Stoney St
- **The George Inn** • 77 Borough High St
- **The Globe** • 8 Bedale St
- **La Cave** • 6 Borough High St
- **Number 1 Bar** • 1 Duke St Hill
- **The Market Porter** • 9 Stoney St
- **The Rake** • 14 Winchester Walk
- **The Roebuck** • 50 Great Dover St
- **The Rose** • 123 Snowfields
- **Roxy Bar and Screen** • 128 Borough High St
- **The Royal Oak** • 44 Tabard St
- **Southwark Tavern** • 22 Southwark St
- **Wine Wharf** • Stoney St

Post Offices

- **Great Dover Street** • 159 Great Dover St
- **London Bridge** • 19 Borough High St

Restaurants

- **Amano** • Clink St
- **Boot and Flogger** • 10 Redcross Way
- **Brew Wharf** • Brew Wharf Yard, Stoney St
- **Cantina Vinopolis** • 1 Bank End
- **Champor-Champor** • 62 Weston St
- **Feng Sushi** • 13 Stoney St
- **Fish!** • Cathedral St
- **Hing Loong** • 159 Borough High St
- **Nando's** • 215 Clink St
- **Roast** • The Floral Hall, Stoney St
- **Silka** • Southwark St
- **Tapas Brindisa** • 18 Southwark St
- **Tas Borough High Street** • 72 Borough High St
- **Wright Bros Oyster Bar** • 11 Stoney St

Shopping

- **Borough Market** • 8 Southwark St
- **Brindisa Retail** • Borough Market
- **German Deli** • 8 Southwark St
- **Paul Smith** • 13 Park St
- **Richer Sounds** • 2 London Bridge Walk
- **Vinopolis** • 1 Bank End

Supermarkets

- **Marks & Spencer** • London Bridge Station
- **Sainsbury's** • 116 Borough High St

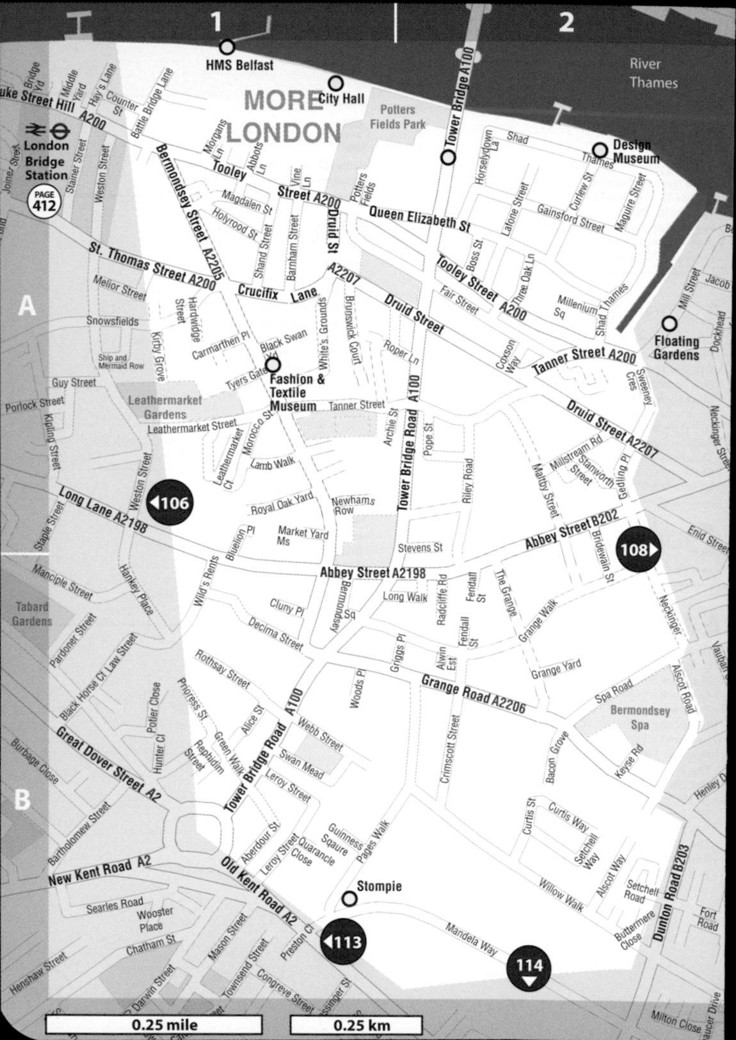

N

1
2
A
B

HMS Belfast
City Hall
MORE LONDON
Potters Fields Park
River Thames
Design Museum
London Bridge Station
PAGE 412
Floating Gardens
Fashion & Textile Museum
Leathermarket Gardens
Tabard Gardens
Bermondsey Spa
Stompie

Duke Street Hill A200
Bridge Yd
Middle Yard
Hay's Lane
Counter St
Battle Bridge Lane
Joiner Street
Stainer Street
Weston Street
Bermondsey Street A2205
Morgans Ln
Abbots Ln
Tooley Street A200
Vine Ln
Potters Fields
Tower Bridge A100
Horselydown La
Shad Thames
Curlew St
Maguire Street
Gainsford Street
Lafone Street
Magdalen St
Holyrood St
Shand Street
Barnham Street
Druid St
Queen Elizabeth St
Boss St
Tooley Street A200
Three Oak Ln
Millenium Sq
Shad Thames
Mill Street
Jacob St
Dockhead
St. Thomas Street A200
Mellor Street
Hardwidge Street
Crucifix Lane
A2207
White's Grounds
Brunswick Court
Druid Street
Fair Street
Snowsfields
Kirby Grove
Carmarthen Pl
Black Swan Yd
Roper Ln
Coxson Way
Tanner Street A200
Sweeney Cres
Ship and Mermaid Row
Guy Street
Tyers Gate
Porlock Street
Kipling Street
Leathermarket Street
Morocco St
Tanner Street
Archie St
Tower Bridge Road A100
Pope St
Druid Street A2207
Neckinger Street
Leathermarket Ct
Lamb Walk
Riley Road
Maltby Street
Millstream Rd
Stanworth Street
Gedling Pl
Weston Street
106
Long Lane A2198
Staple Street
Royal Oak Yard
Newhams Row
Bluelion Pl
Market Yard Ms
Stevens St
Abbey Street B202
Bridewain St
108
Enid Street
Mancinple Street
Hankey Place
Wild's Rents
Abbey Street A2198
Bermondsey Sq
Cluny Pl
Long Walk
Radcliffe Rd
Fendall St
The Grange
Grange Walk
Neckinger
Pardoner Street
Law Street
Decima Street
Griggs Pl
Alwin Est
Fendall St
Grange Yard
Vauban St
Black Horse Ct
Rothsay Street
Potier Close
Prioress St
Alice St
A100
Woods Pl
Grange Road A2206
Spa Road
Alscot Road
Great Dover Street A2
Burbage Close
Hunter Cl
Rephidim Street
Green Walk
Tower Bridge Road
Webb Street
Swan Mead
Crimscott Street
Bacon Grove
Keyse Rd
Henley Dr
Leroy Street
Curtis St
Curtis Way
Setchell Way
Bartholomew Street
New Kent Road A2
Aberdour St
Leroy Street
Quarancle Close
Guinness Saqure
Pages Walk
Alscot Way
Willow Walk
Setchell Road
Dunton Road B203
Old Kent Road A2
Searles Road
Wooster Place
Chatham St
Mason Street
Preston Cl
113
Mandela Way
Buttermere Close
Fort Road
114
Henshaw Street
Darwin Street
Townsend Street
Congreve Street
Milton Close

0.25 mile
0.25 km

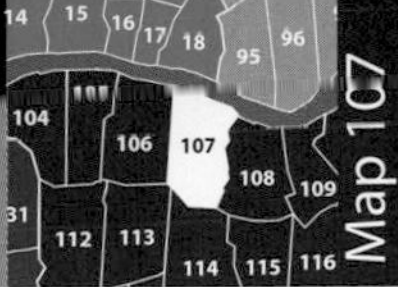

Shad Thames

The elitist's Bermondsey, Shad Thames is home to ultra-hip boutiques, glass balconies, and converted warehouses. No café dares exist without its own gallery. Bermondsey Street blossoms as an epicentre of creatives knocking out their latest bestseller over brunch, while the More London space by the Thames is an invigorating crowd-pleaser. Head to so-new-its-still-burping-formula Shortwave for indie flicks, and The Scoop for top free events.

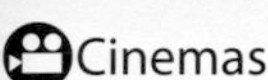

Cinemas

- **Shortwave** • 10 Bermondsey Sq

Coffee

- **Caffe Nero** • 6 More Pl
- **Caphe House** • 114 Bermondsey St
- **Coffee @ Bermondsey** • 163 Bermondsey St
- **SoBo** • 83 Tower Bridge Rd

Landmarks

- **City Hall** • Queen's Walk, More London Development
- **Design Museum** • Shad Thames
- **Fashion and Textile Museum** • 83 Bermondsey St
- **Floating Gardens** • 31 Mill St
- **HMS Belfast** • Morgan's Lane & Tooley St
- **Stompie** • Mandela Way & Page's Walk
- **Tower Bridge** • Tower Bridge Road

Nightlife

- **Cable** • 33 Bermondsey St
- **The Hide** • 39 Bermondsey St
- **Hilton London Tower Bridge** • 5 Tooley St
- **Village East** • 171-173 Bermondsey St
- **The Woolpack** • 98 Bermondsey St

Restaurants

- **Butlers Wharf Chop House** • 36 Shad Thames
- **Delfina** • 50 Bermondsey St
- **Le Pont de la Tour** • 36 Shad Thames
- **M Manze Pie and Mash** • 87 Tower Bridge Rd
- **Magdalen** • 152 Tooley St
- **Village East** • 171-173 Bermondsey St

Shopping

- **Fine Foods** • 218 Long Lane
- **The Design Museum Shop** • 28 Shad Thames
- **Long Lane Deli** • 218 Long Ln
- **Maltby Street Market** • Maltby Street
- **United Nude** • 124 Bermondsey St

Map 108 • Bermondsey

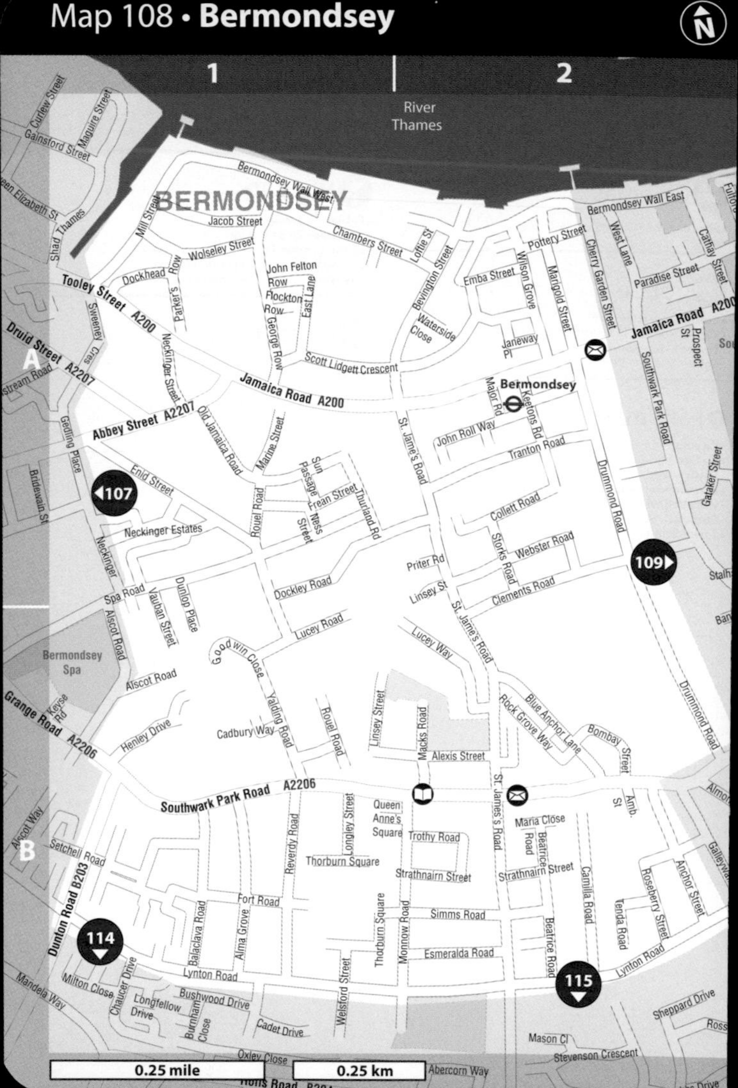

Bermondsey

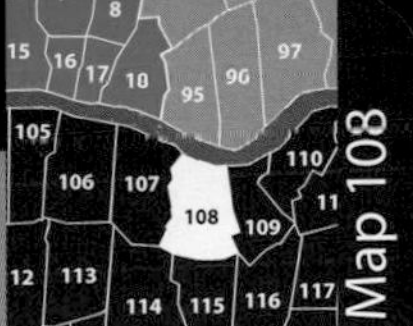

With its mixed bag of winding cobbled streets, council estates, and posh new builds, you can imagine the awkwardness when the new-to-the-neighbourhood clean shirt steps into the the adamantly local Bermondsey boozer. The old-timers are sticking to their guns, and there is a definite dirty side to this on-the-cusp part of town. For quaint Japanese try PoppyHana on Jamaica Road.

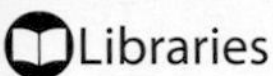

Libraries

- **Blue Anchor Library** • Southwark Park Rd

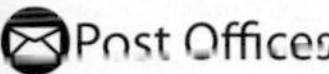

Post Offices

- **Jamaica Road** • 158 Jamaica Rd
- **Southwark Park Road** • 200 Southwark Park Rd

Restaurants

- **Poppy Hana** • 169 Jamaica Rd

Supermarkets

- **Co-Op** • 193 Southwark Park Rd
- **Iceland** • 222 Southwark Park

Map 109 • Southwark Park

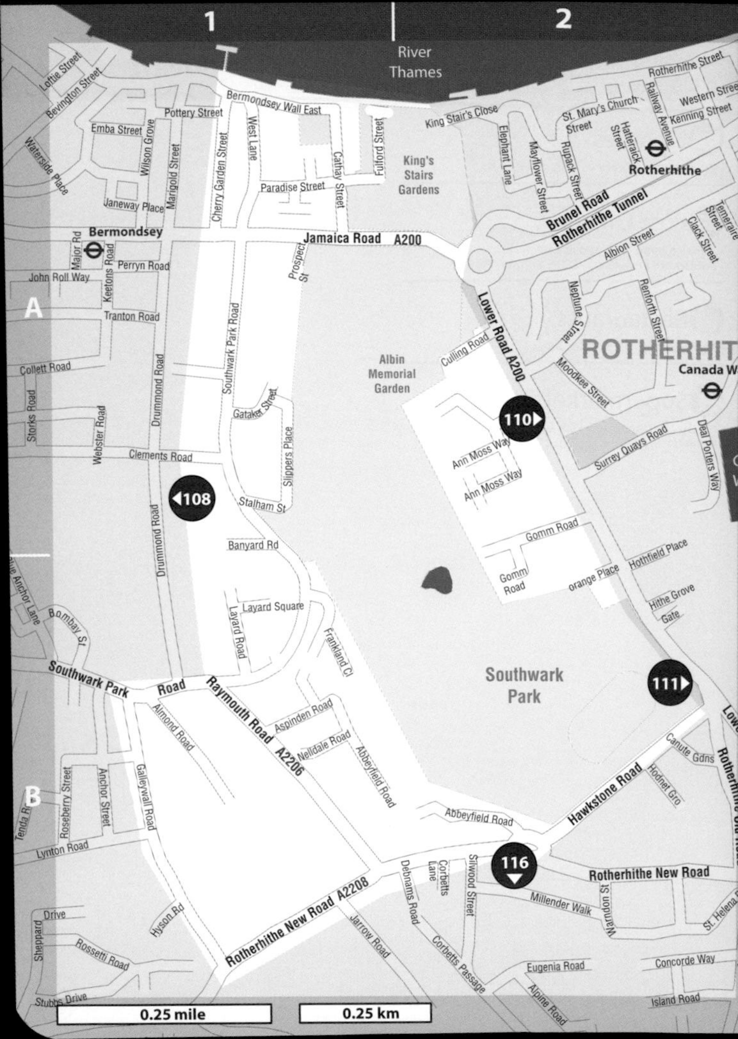

1
2
River Thames
Lottie Street
Bevington Street
Waterside Place
Emba Street
Wilson Grove
Pottery Street
Marigold Street
Janeway Place
Cherry Garden Street
Bermondsey Wall East
West Lane
Paradise Street
Cathay Street
Fulford Street
King's Stairs Gardens
King Stair's Close
Elephant Lane
Mayflower Street
Rupack Street
St. Mary's Church Street
Hatteraick Street
Railway Avenue
Rotherhithe Street
Western Street
Kenning Street
Rotherhithe
Brunel Road
Rotherhithe Tunnel
Temeraire Street
Clack Street
Albion Street
Bermondsey
Major Rd
Keetons Road
Perryn Road
John Roll Way
Jamaica Road A200
Prospect St
A
Tranton Road
Southwark Park Road
Lower Road A200
Neptune Street
Renforth Street
ROTHERHIT
Canada W
Collett Road
Drummond Road
Albin Memorial Garden
Culling Road
Moodkee Street
Storks Road
Webster Road
Gataker Street
Slippers Place
110
Ann Moss Way
Ann Moss Way
Surrey Quays Road
Deal Porters Way
Clements Road
108
Stalham St
Gomm Road
Gomm Road
orange Place
Hothfield Place
Hithe Grove
Gate
Banyard Rd
Drummond Road
Anchor Lane
Bombay St
Layard Square
Layard Road
Frankland Cl
Southwark Park Road
Raymouth Road A2206
Southwark Park
111
Almond Road
Aspinden Road
Nelldale Road
Abbeyfield Road
Canute Gdns
Hodnet Gro
Lower
Rotherhithe Old Road
B
Tenda Rd
Roseberry Street
Anchor Street
Galleywall Road
Abbeyfield Road
Hawkstone Road
Lynton Road
116
Debnams Road
Corbetts Lane
Silwood Street
Rotherhithe New Road
Millender Walk
Warndon St
St. Helena
Sheppard Drive
Hyson Rd
Rotherhithe New Road A2208
Jarrow Road
Corbetts Passage
Rossetti Road
Eugenia Road
Concorde Way
Alpine Road
Island Road
Stubbs Drive
0.25 mile
0.25 km

Southwark Park

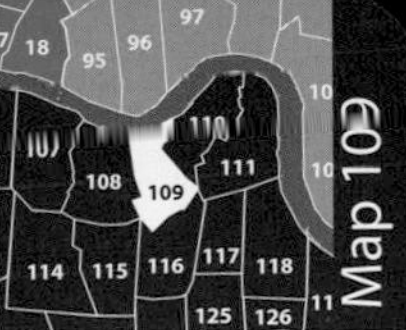

Bordered by tower blocks and the unfortunate [illegible] of a nursing home [illegible], you might toy with taking your picnic elsewhere. But step inside, because it's every bit the oasis that local hero Dr Salter hoped it would be. Well-spent investment has given it a boating lake, rose garden, wildlife area, and the inspired Café Gallery Projects. Nip to the Angel afterwards for cheap beers and river views.

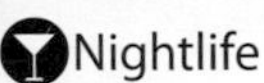

Nightlife

- **Ancient Foresters** • 282 Southwark Park Rd
- **The Angel** • 101 Bermondsey Wall E

Map 110 • Rotherhithe (West) / Canada Water

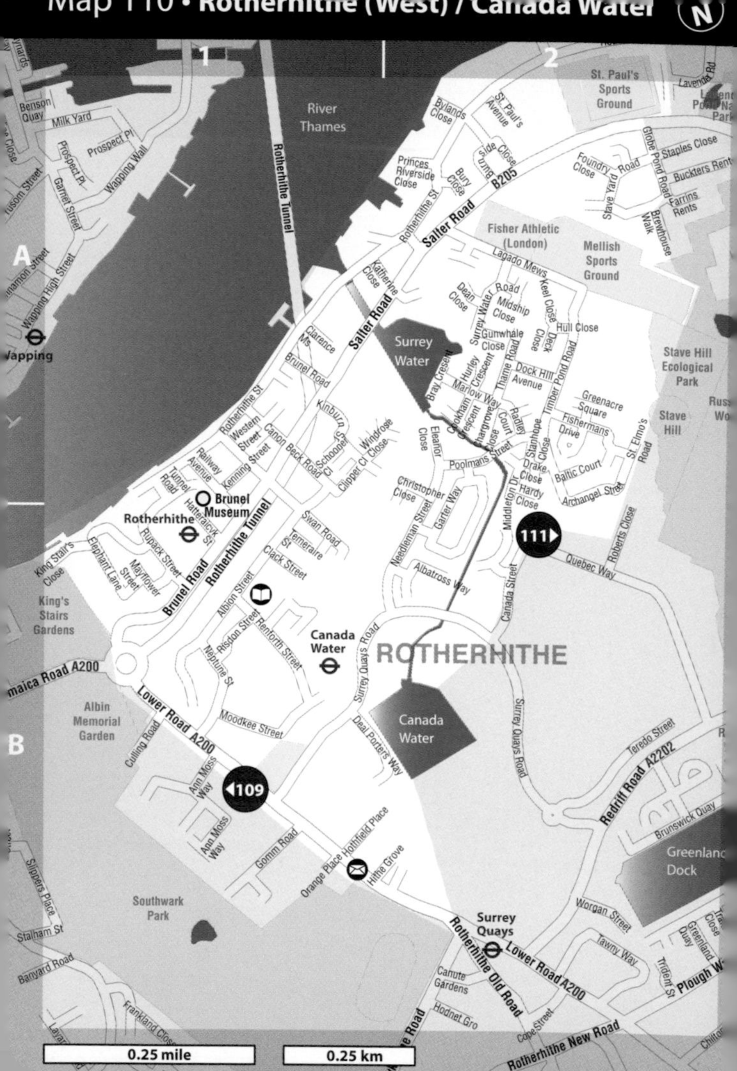

Rotherhithe (West) / Canada Water

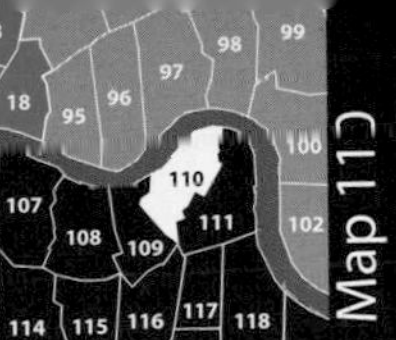

If residential flats are your thing, you'll love Rotherhithe West. Not if bars are your thing though. Or shops. Or life. But among the warren of apartments is the Mayflower, one of the greatest historical pubs in London, with the grave of the Mayflower ship's captain in the churchyard opposite. Entertain your dad at the Brunel Museum, and jog or snog your way along this serene stretch of Thames path.

Coffee

- **Brunel Museum Café** • Railway Ave

Landmarks

- **Brunel Museum** • Railway Ave & Rotherhithe St

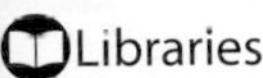

Libraries

- **Rotherhithe Library** • Albion St

Nightlife

- **The Albion** • 20 Albion St
- **The Mayflower** • 117 Rotherhithe St
- **Old Salt Quay** • 163 Rotherhithe St
- **The Ship** • 39 St Marychurch St

Post Offices

- **Lower Road Rotherhithe** • 142 Lower Rd

Restaurants

- **Café Silka** • 30 Albion St
- **Mayflower** • 117 Rotherhithe St
- **The Rainbow** • 33 Brunel Rd
- **Simplicity** • 1 Tunnel Rd

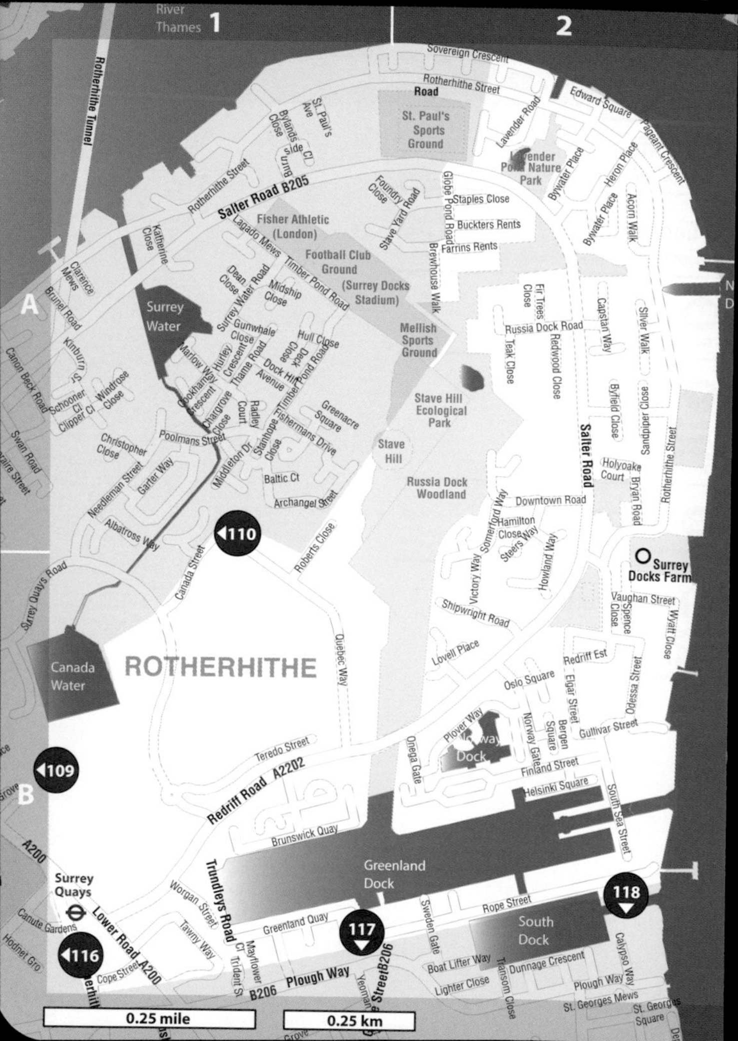

Map 111 • Rotherhithe (East) / Surrey Quays

N

River Thames
1
2
A
B

Rotherhithe Tunnel
Sovereign Crescent
Rotherhithe Street
Road
St. Paul's Sports Ground
Lavender Road
Edward Square
Pageant Crescent
Lavender Pond Nature Park
Bywater Place
Heron Place
Acorn Walk
Bylands Close
St. Paul's Ave
Burnside Cl
Salter Road B205
Foundry Close
Stave Yard Road
Globe Pond Road
Staples Close
Buckters Rents
Farrins Rents
Brewhouse Walk
Katherine Close
Fisher Athletic (London) Football Club Ground (Surrey Docks Stadium)
Lagado Mews
Timber Pond Road
Clarence Mews
Brunel Road
Surrey Water
Dean Close
Surrey Water Road
Midship Close
Gunwhale Close
Hull Close
Dock Close
Mellish Sports Ground
Fir Trees Close
Russia Dock Road
Capstan Way
Silver Walk
Teak Close
Redwood Close
Kinburn St
Canon Beck Road
Marlow Way
Hurley Crescent
Thame Road
Dock Hill Avenue
Timber Pond Road
Windrose Close
Schooner Cl
Clipper Cl
Cookham Crescent
Chargrove Close
Radley Court
Stanhope Close
Fishermans Drive
Greenacre Square
Stave Hill Ecological Park
Byfield Close
Sandpiper Close
Swan Road
Christopher Close
Poolmans Street
Middleton Dr.
Baltic Ct
Stave Hill
Russia Dock Woodland
Salter Road
Holyoake Court
Bryan Road
Rotherhithe Street
Needleman Street
Garter Way
Archangel Street
Somerford Way
Downtown Road
Hamilton Close
Steers Way
Howland Way
Albatross Way
110
Roberts Close
Victory Way
Surrey Docks Farm
Surrey Quays Road
Canada Street
Shipwright Road
Vaughan Street
Spence Close
Wyatt Close
Quebec Way
Lovell Place
Redriff Est
Canada Water
ROTHERHITHE
Oslo Square
Odessa Street
Elgar Street
Plover Way
Norway Dock
Norway Gate
Bergen Square
Gullivar Street
109
Teredo Street
Onega Gate
Finland Street
Redriff Road A2202
Helsinki Square
South Sea Street
Brunswick Quay
A200
Greenland Dock
Surrey Quays
Worgan Street
Trundleys Road
Sweden Gate
Rope Street
118
Canute Gardens
Lower Road A200
Tawny Way
Greenland Quay
117
South Dock
Hodnet Gro
116
Cope Street
Mayflower Ct
Trident St
B206
Plough Way
Yeoman Street B206
Boat Lifter Way
Transom Close
Dunnage Crescent
Lighter Close
Calypso Way
Plough Way
St. Georges Mews
St. Georges Square

0.25 mile
0.25 km

Rotherhithe (East) / Surrey Quays

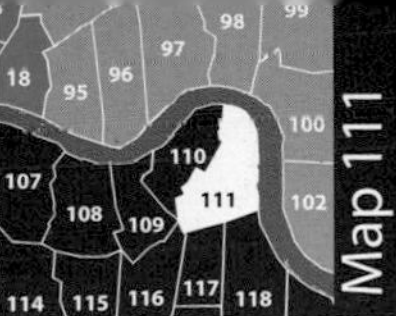

It still has some dodgy estates, but Rotherhithe East is blossoming in a clean-cut city-worker kind of way. The docks are delightful and have resisted the chain bars, instead allowing great little independents like Wibbley Wobbley and Moby Dick to flourish. Trying to be healthy? Enjoy lunch among the goats at wholesome Café Nabo in Surrey Docks Farm, and visit Decathlon for sport equipment paradise.

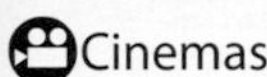

Cinemas

- **Odeon Surrey Quays** • Redriff Rd & Surrey Quays Rd

Landmarks

- **Surrey Docks Farm** • Rotherhithe St

Nightlife

- **Blacksmith's Arms** • 257 Rotherhithe St
- **Moby Dick** • 6 Russell Place, off Greenland Dock
- **Ship & Whale** • 2 Gulliver St
- **Whelan's** • 11 Rotherhithe Old Rd
- **Wibbley Wobbley** • South Dock Marina, Rope St

Restaurants

- **Café East** • 100 Redriff Rw
- **Café Nabo** • Surrey Docks Farm, Rotherhithe St

Shopping

- **Decathlon** • Surrey Quays Road

Supermarkets

- **Tesco** • Redriff Rd

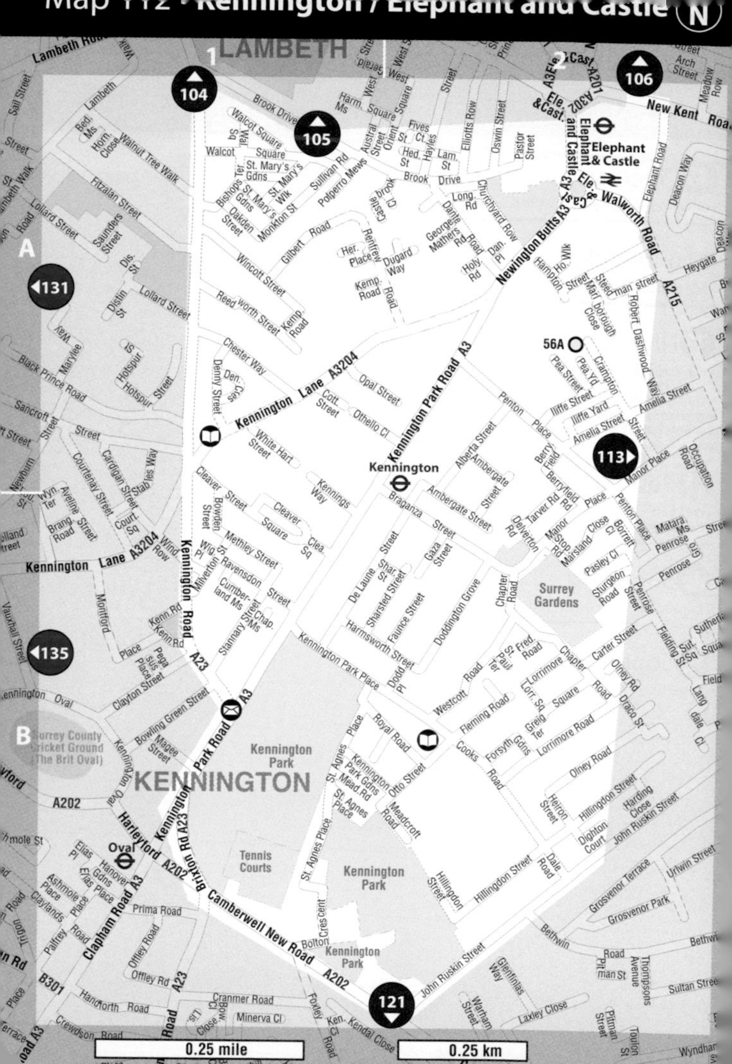
Map 112 · Kennington / Elephant and Castle
N
LAMBETH
1
2
A
B
104
105
106
131
135
113
121
Elephant & Castle
Kennington
Oval
56A
KENNINGTON
Kennington Park
Tennis Courts
Surrey Gardens
Surrey County Cricket Ground (The Brit Oval)
Lambeth Road
Brook Drive
Walcot Square
St. Mary's Gdns
Sullivan Rd
Wincott Street
Reedworth Street
Chester Way
Kennington Lane A3204
Kennington Road A23
Kennington Park Road A3
Newington Butts A3
Walworth Road
New Kent Road
Elephant Road
Heygate
A215
Black Prince Road
Lollard Street
Fitzalan Street
Walnut Tree Walk
Sancroft Street
Cleaver Street
Cleaver Square
Methley Street
Ravensdon Street
Opal Street
Othello Cl
White Hart Street
Kennings Way
Braganza Street
Ambergate Street
Penton Place
Manor Place
Amelia Street
Iliffe Street
Robert Dashwood Way
Crampton
Pea. Yd
De Laune Street
Sharsted Street
Faunce Street
Doddington Grove
Harmsworth Street
Kennington Park Place
Chapter Road
Westcott Road
Fleming Road
Lorrimore Road
Lorrimore Square
Carter Street
Olney Road
Hillingdon Street
John Ruskin Street
Camberwell New Road A202
Brixton Rd A23
Harleyford A202
Clapham Road A3
Kennington Oval
Bowling Green Street
Clayton Street
Vauxhall Street
Montford Place
Cooks Road
Otto Street
Royal Road
Meadcroft Road
St. Agnes Place
Bolton Crescent
Cranmer Road
Minerva Cl
Handforth Road
Crewdson Road
Offley Road
Prima Road
Grosvenor Terrace
Grosvenor Park
Urlwin Street
Bethwin Road
Thompsons Avenue
Sultan Street
Laxley Close
Warham Street
Glenfinlas Way
Ken. Kendal Close
0.25 mile
0.25 km

Kennington / Elephant and Castle

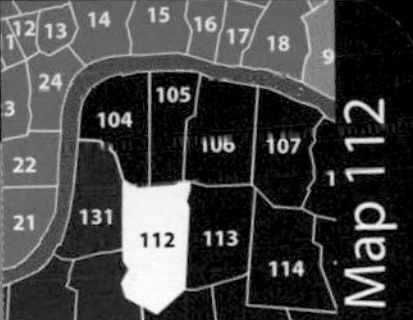

Change is underway in this seedy hub of South East London. But while few will be sad to see the back of the infamous Heygate Estate and the mugger's paradise subway system, there are grumblings in the air that the £1.5 billion redevelopment will do little for the local people. Join the debate at 56A Anarchist infoshop, or take your mind off it with a huge plate of pancakes at Mamuska.

Landmarks

- **56A** • 56 Crampton St

Libraries

- **Brandon Library** • Cooks Rd [Maddock Way]
- **Durning Library** • 167 Kennington Ln

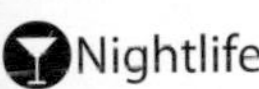

Nightlife

- **Corsica Studios** • 5 Elephant Rd
- **Dog House** • 293 Kennington Rd
- **Prince of Wales** • Cleaver Sq

Post Offices

- **Kennington Park** • 410 Kennington Park Rd

Restaurants

- **Brasserie Tolouse Lautrec** • 140 Newington Bts
- **Dragon Castle** • 114 Walworth Rd
- **Lobster Pot** • 3 Kennington Ln
- **Mamuska** • 233 Elephant and Castle Shopping Centre

Shopping

- **Pricebusters Hardware** • 311 Elephant & Castle Shopping Centre
- **Recycling** • 110 Elephant Rd

Supermarkets

- **Iceland** • 300 Elephant & Castle

Map 113 • Walworth

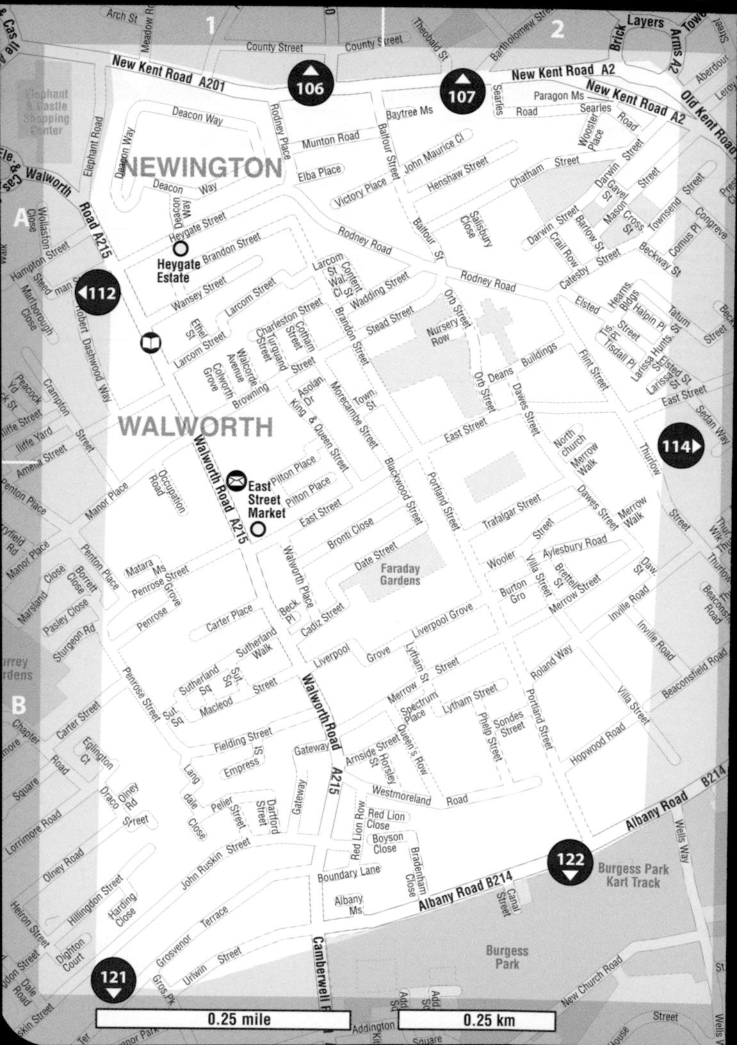

NEWINGTON
WALWORTH
Heygate Estate
East Street Market
Faraday Gardens
Burgess Park
Burgess Park Kart Track
Elephant & Castle Shopping Center
New Kent Road A201
New Kent Road A2
Old Kent Road
Walworth Road A215
Albany Road B214
Camberwell Road
Rodney Road
East Street
Portland Street
Dawes Street
Merrow Street
Liverpool Grove
Westmoreland Road
John Ruskin Street
Heygate Street
Brandon Street
Wansey Street
Larcom Street
Penrose Street
Manor Place
Inville Road
Thurlow Street
Villa Street
Hopwood Road
Trafalgar Street
Aylesbury Road
Chatham Street
Townsend Street
Darwin Street
Balfour Street
Deacon Way
Munton Road
Elba Place
Victory Place
Henshaw Street
Orb Street
Flint Street
Fielding Street
Carter Street
Occupation Road
Wells Way

106
107
112
114
121
122

0.25 mile
0.25 km

Walworth

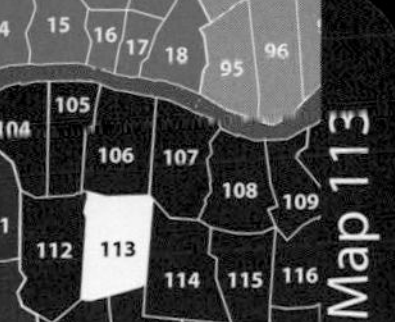

Oh, Walworth. With all this about the Elephant and Castle redevelopment, why do we get the funny feeling you will never change? From the excessive amount of Gregg's bakeries along Walworth Road, to the 'who really buys these things?' tat at East Street Market, Walworth's lack of motivation is somehow endearing. La Luna for pizza is a find, as is the Beehive pub.

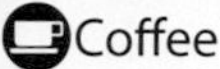

Coffee

- **Ranya Café** • 314 Walworth Rd

Landmarks

- **East Street Market** • Walworth Rd & East St
- **Heygate Estate** • Deacon Way & Heygate St

Libraries

- **Newington Library** • 157 Walworth Rd

Nightlife

- **Banana's Bar** • 374 Walworth Rd
- **The Beehive** • 60 Carter St
- **Red Lion** • 407 Walworth Rd
- **Temple Bar** • 286 Walworth Rd

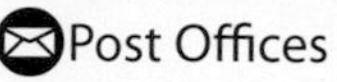

Post Offices

- **Walworth Road** • 234 Walworth Rd

Restaurants

- **La Luna** • 380 Walworth Rd

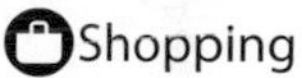

Shopping

- **Mixed Blessings Caribbean Bakery** • 12 Camberwell Rd
- **Threadneedleman Tailors** • 187 Walworth Rd
- **Walworth Surplus Stores** • 211 Walworth Rd

Supermarkets

- **Iceland** • 332 Walworth Rd

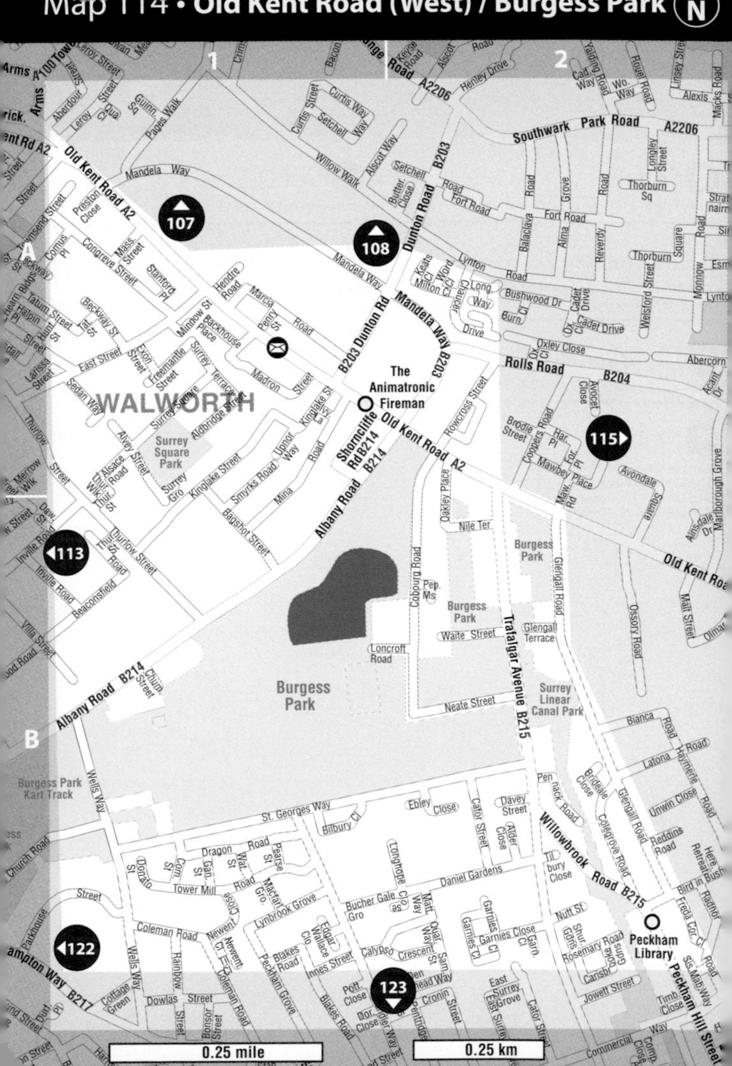
N
WALWORTH
The Animatronic Fireman
Surrey Square Park
Burgess Park
Surrey Linear Canal Park
Burgess Park Kart Track
Peckham Library
Old Kent Road A2
Mandela Way
Dunton Road
Southwark Park Road A2206
Rolls Road B204
Albany Road B214
Trafalgar Avenue B215
Willowbrook Road B215
St. Georges Way
Peckham Hill Street
Glengall Road
Coburg Road
Wells Way
107
108
113
115
122
123
0.25 mile
0.25 km

Old Kent Road (West) / Burgess Park

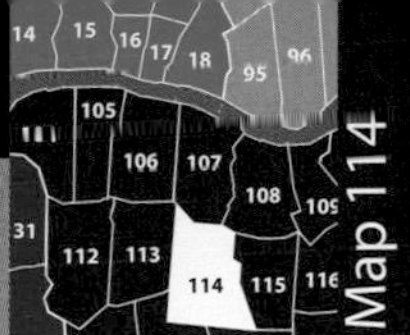

Now that the [illegible] Burgess Park has been given an £8 million facelift (due to tireless community campaigning), locals have good reason to be smug as they enjoy the 30ft water fountains, 5k running track, or any of the other many new additions on their doorstep. For something different entirely, get creeped out by the animatronic fireman above the fireplace shop, or stroll along the old canal and connect with ghosts of Peckham past.

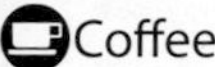

Coffee

- **Chumleigh Gardens Café** • Chumleigh Street

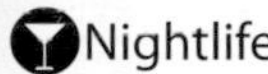

Landmarks

- **The Animatronic Fireman** • Old Kent Road
- **Peckham Library** • 122 Peckham Hill St

Nightlife

- **Auto-Italia South East** • 1 Glengall Rd
- **World Turned Upside Down** • 145 Old Kent Rd

Post Offices

- **Old Kent Road** • 240 Old Kent Rd

Restaurants

- **Pardis** • 280 Old Kent Rd
- **Parrilladas del Sur** • 186 Old Kent Rd

Shopping

- **Old Kent Road Food Centre** • 252 Old Kent Rd

Supermarkets

- **Tesco** • 107 Dunton Rd

Map 115 • Old Kent Road (East)

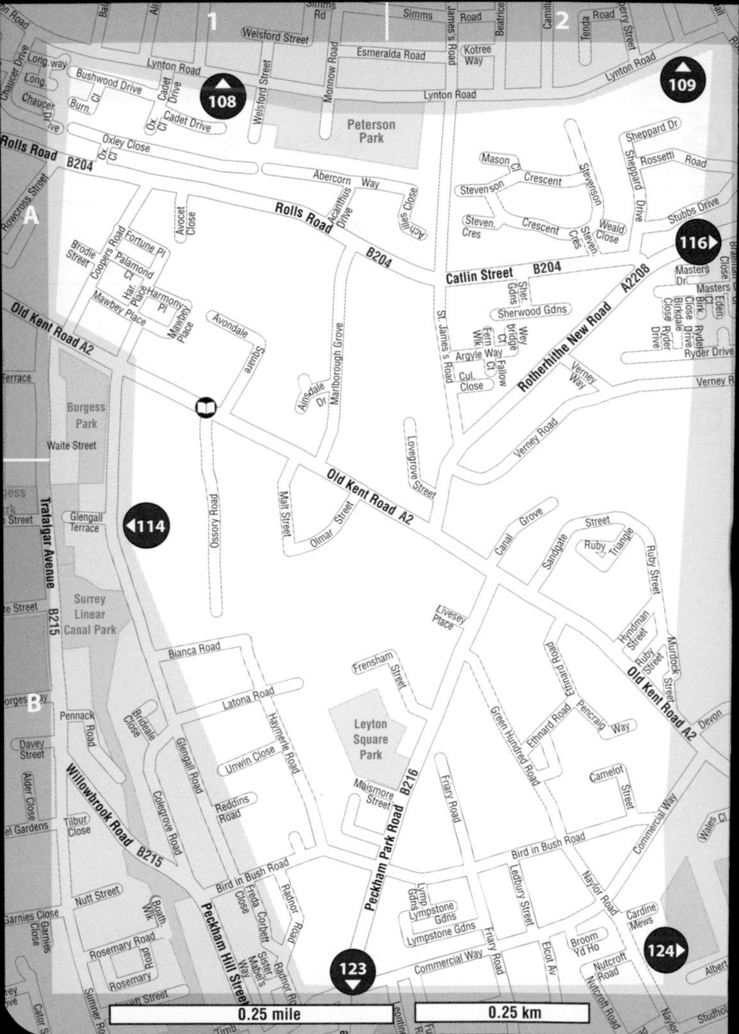
N
1
2
A
B
108
109
116
114
123
124
Welsford Street
Simms Road
Esmeralda Road
James's Road
Kotree Way
Tenda Road
Lynton Road
Bushwood Drive
Cadet Drive
Burn. Cl
Chaucer Drive
Long. way
Welsford Street
Monnow Road
Peterson Park
Oxley Close
Ox. Ct
Rolls Road
B204
Abercorn Way
Acanthus Drive
Achilles Close
Avocet Close
Mason Ct
Stevenson Crescent
Steven. Cres
Weald Close
Sheppard Dr
Sheppard Drive
Rossetti Road
Stubbs Drive
Rowcross Street
Brodie Street
Coopers Road
Fortune Pl
Palamond Ct
Har. Place
Harmony Pl
Mawbey Place
Avondale Square
Marlborough Grove
Ainsdale Dr
Catlin Street
Sherwood Gdns
Weybridge Ct
Fern Wlk
Argyle Way
Fallow Ct
Cul. Close
St. James's Road
Rotherhithe New Road
A2208
Masters Dr
Masters
Birkdale Close
Ryder Drive
Verney Way
Verney Road
Old Kent Road A2
Terrace
Burgess Park
Waite Street
Glengall Terrace
Trafalgar Avenue
B215
Ossory Road
Lovegrove Street
Malt Street
Olmar Street
Canal Grove
Sandgate Street
Ruby Triangle
Ruby Street
Surrey Linear Canal Park
Livesey Place
Hyndman Street
Murdock Street
Ethnard Road
Pencraig Way
Devon
Bianca Road
Latona Road
Frensham Street
Leyton Square Park
Pennack Road
Davey Street
Brideale Close
Glengall Road
Unwin Close
Haymerle Road
Reddins Road
Maismore Street
Green Hundred Road
Camelot Street
Commercial Way
Wales Cl
Alder Close
Tilbury Close
Willowbrook Road B215
Colegrove Road
Peckham Park Road
B216
Friary Road
Bird in Bush Road
Nutt Street
Boath. Wlk
Freda Corbett Close
Radnor Road
Lympstone Gdns
Ledbury Street
Naylor Road
Cardine Mews
Garnies Close
Rosemary Road
Peckham Hill Street
Sister Mabel's Way
Commercial Way
Elcot Av
Broom Yd Ho
Nutcroft Road
Albert
Sumner Road
Cator St
0.25 mile
0.25 km

Old Kent Road (East)

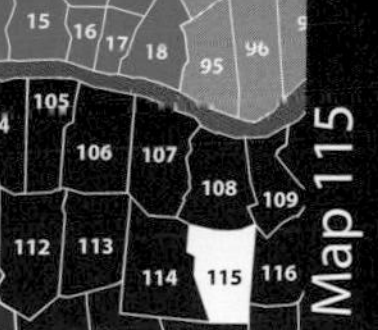

There must be something to this portion of Old Kent Road, as the Pearly Kings and Queens won't shut up about the whole thing. As far as we can tell, it's not that much more than a giant Asda. Walk along Bird In Bush Road to laugh at its name and over to Peckham Park Road for a damn good fry-up at Roma Café.

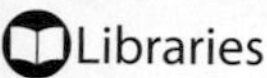

Libraries

- **East Street Library** • 168 Old Kent Rd

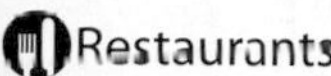

Restaurants

- **Roma Café** • 21 Peckham Park Rd

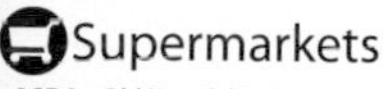

Supermarkets

- **ASDA** • Old Kent Rd & Ossory Rd

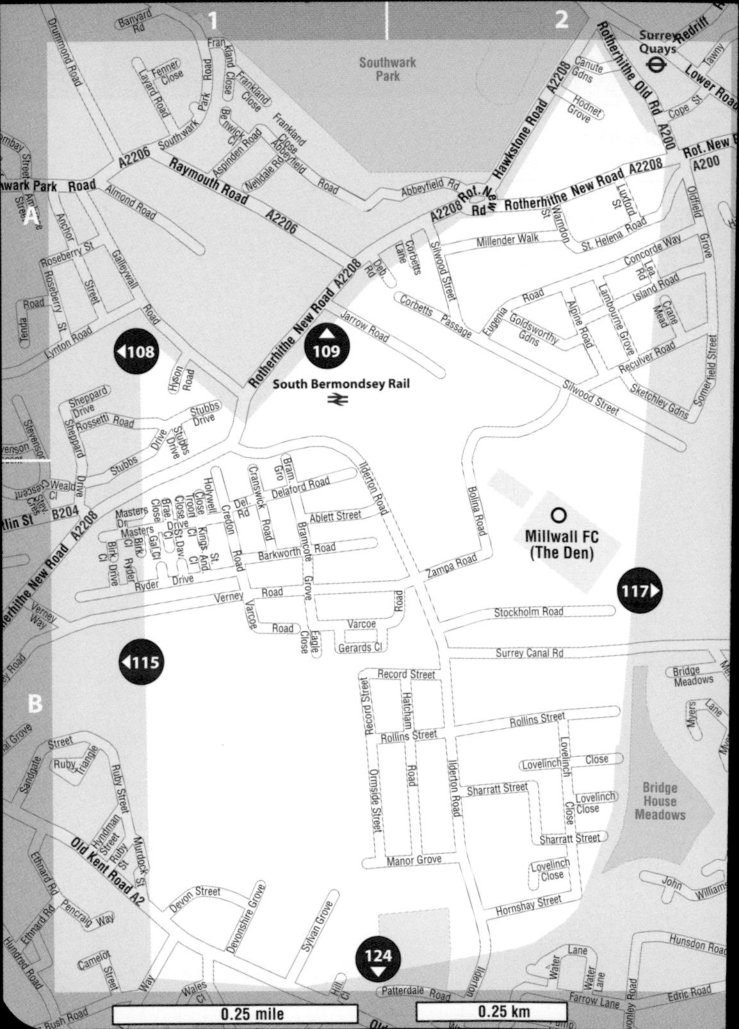

Map 116 • South Bermondsey

108
109
115
117
124

South Bermondsey

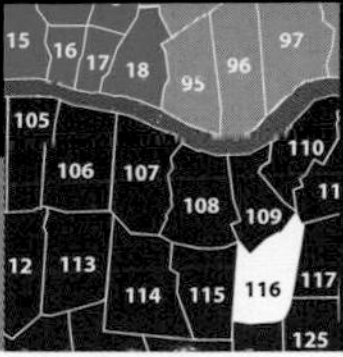

There may be more to this area than we've listed, but the fact is: we like you. We want to see you live to enjoy our favourite picks among these pages. If you make the wrong kind of eye contact as you tremble past the Millwall flags fluttering menacingly from the balconies, then we're worried we'll lose a much-loved reader. Swallow your valuables and back slowly away.

○ Landmarks

- **Millwall FC Stadium** • Zampa Road & Bolina Rd

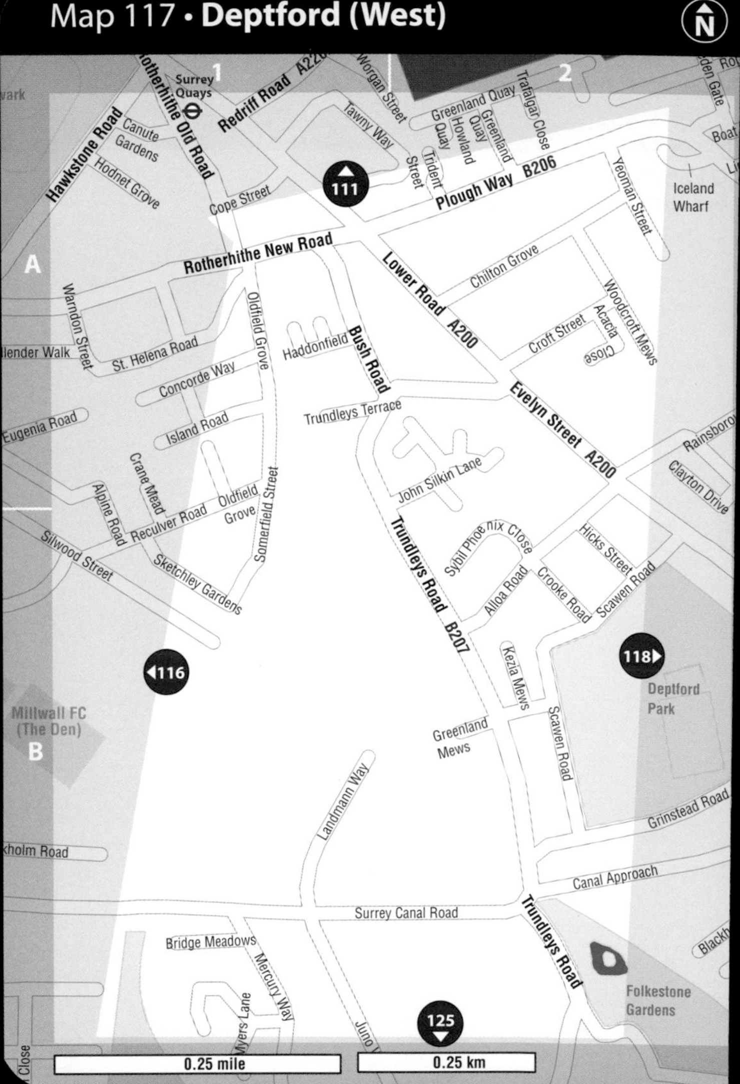
N
1
2
A
B
Surrey Quays
Rotherhithe Old Road
Redriff Road A2208
Worgan Street
Tawny Way
Greenland Quay
Trafalgar Close
Greenland Quay
Howland Quay
Trident Street
Plough Way B206
Yeoman Street
Iceland Wharf
Hawkstone Road
Canute Gardens
Hodnet Grove
Cope Street
111
Rotherhithe New Road
Lower Road A200
Chilton Grove
Woodcroft Mews
Acacia Close
Croft Street
Warndon Street
St. Helena Road
Oldfield Grove
Haddonfield
Bush Road
Concorde Way
Island Road
Trundleys Terrace
Evelyn Street A200
Eugenia Road
Crane Mead
Alpine Road
Reculver Road
Oldfield Grove
Somerfield Street
John Silkin Lane
Rainsborough
Clayton Drive
Silwood Street
Sketchley Gardens
Trundleys Road B207
Sybil Phoenix Close
Hicks Street
Alloa Road
Crooke Road
Scawen Road
116
118
Kezia Mews
Deptford Park
Millwall FC (The Den)
Greenland Mews
Scawen Road
Landmann Way
Grinstead Road
Canal Approach
Surrey Canal Road
Trundleys Road
Bridge Meadows
Mercury Way
Myers Lane
Juno Way
125
Folkestone Gardens
0.25 mile
0.25 km

Deptford (West)

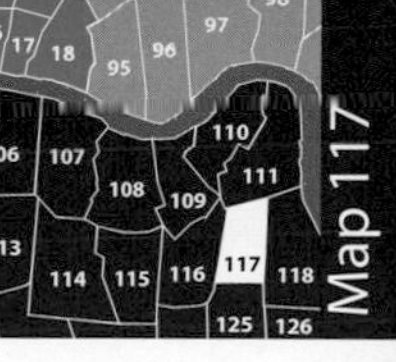

Apparently, developers have their eye on Deptford West. You've really got to hope so. The Blitz did its best, but the area came back with hastily built and charmless '60s tower blocks. Still, like the rest of Deptford it's going through a gradual regeneration as young buyers move in to make their money stretch. The Yellow House offers salvation for eating out.

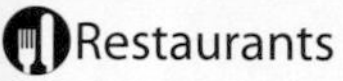

Restaurants

• **Yellow House** • 37 Plough Way

Map 118 • Deptford (Central)

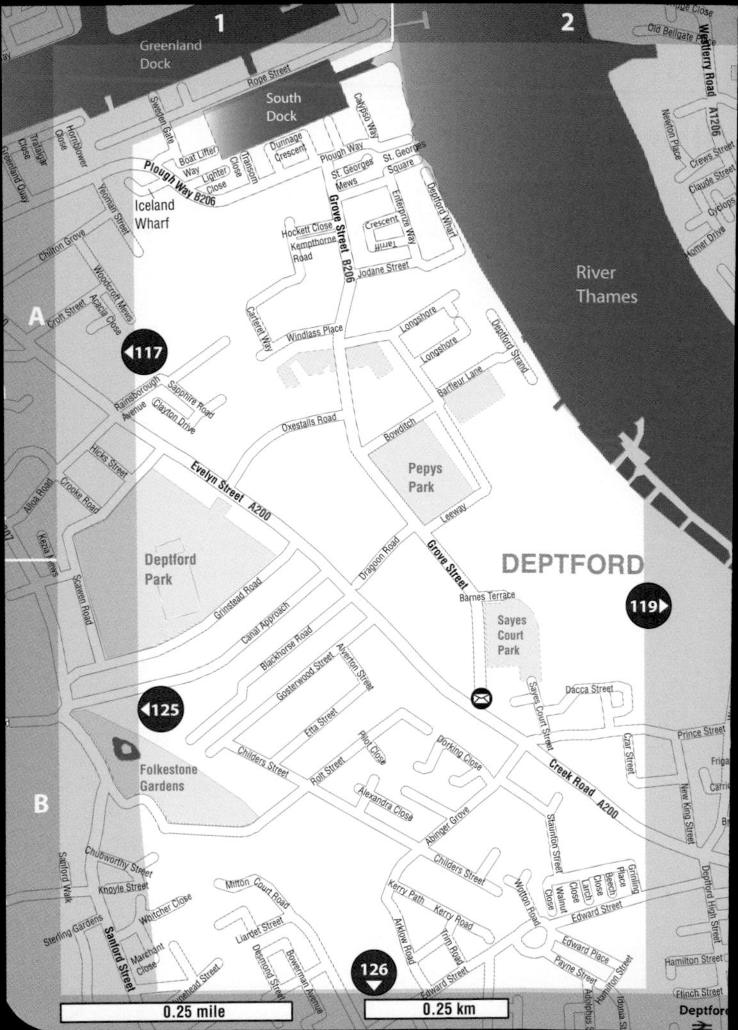

N

1
2
A
B

Greenland Dock
South Dock
River Thames
Iceland Wharf
Pepys Park
Deptford Park
Sayes Court Park
Folkestone Gardens
DEPTFORD

Rope Street
Sweden Gate
Boat Lifter Way
Lighter Close
Transom Close
Dunnage Crescent
Calypso Way
Plough Way
Plough Way B206
St. Georges Mews
St. Georges Square
Hornblower Close
Trafalgar Close
Greenland Quay
Yeoman Street
Chilton Grove
Woodcroft Mews
Croft Street
Acacia Close
Hockett Close
Kempthorne Road
Grove Street B206
Crescent
Tarfiff
Enterprize Way
Deptford Wharf
Jodane Street
Carteret Way
Windlass Place
Longshore
Deptford Strand
Bartleur Lane
Rainsborough Avenue
Sapphire Road
Clayton Drive
Oxestalls Road
Bowditch
Leeway
Hicks Street
Evelyn Street A200
Alloa Road
Crooke Road
Kezia Mews
Scawen Road
Grinstead Road
Dragoon Road
Grove Street
Barnes Terrace
Canal Approach
Blackhorse Road
Gosterwood Street
Alverton Street
Sayes Court Street
Dacca Street
Etta Street
Pilot Close
Childers Street
Rolt Street
Dorking Close
Alexandra Close
Abinger Grove
Creek Road A200
Czar Street
Staunton Street
Childers Street
Kerry Path
Kerry Road
Wotton Road
Grinling Place
Beech Close
Larch Close
Walnut Close
Edward Street
Edward Place
Payne Street
Hamilton Street
Arklow Road
Trim Road
Edward Street
Chubworthy Street
Sanford Walk
Knoyle Street
Whitcher Close
Milton Court Road
Sterling Gardens
Sanford Street
Marchant Close
Liardet Street
Desmond Street
Bowerman Avenue
Adolphus Street
Old Bellgate Place
Westferry Road
Newton Place
A1206
Crews Street
Claude Street
Cyclops
Homer Drive
Prince Street
New King Street
Deptford High Street
Hamilton Street
Flinch Street
Deptford

117
119
125
126

0.25 mile
0.25 km

Deptford (Central)

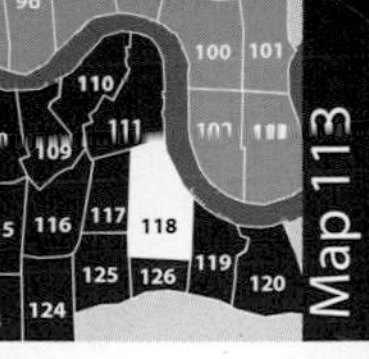

When Christopher Marlowe was murdered in a Deptford tavern, Deptford hit its nightlife peak. That was 1593. Today, while the rest of London turns everything into a pub, Deptford turns its pubs into churches. Without beer, you may want to drown your sorrows in the Thames, but even that is thwarted: here the Thames path breaks to take you through neglected residential areas instead. Escape!

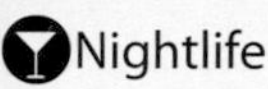

Nightlife

- **The Lord Palmerston** • 81 Childers Street

Post Offices

- **Evelyn Street** • 301 Evelyn St

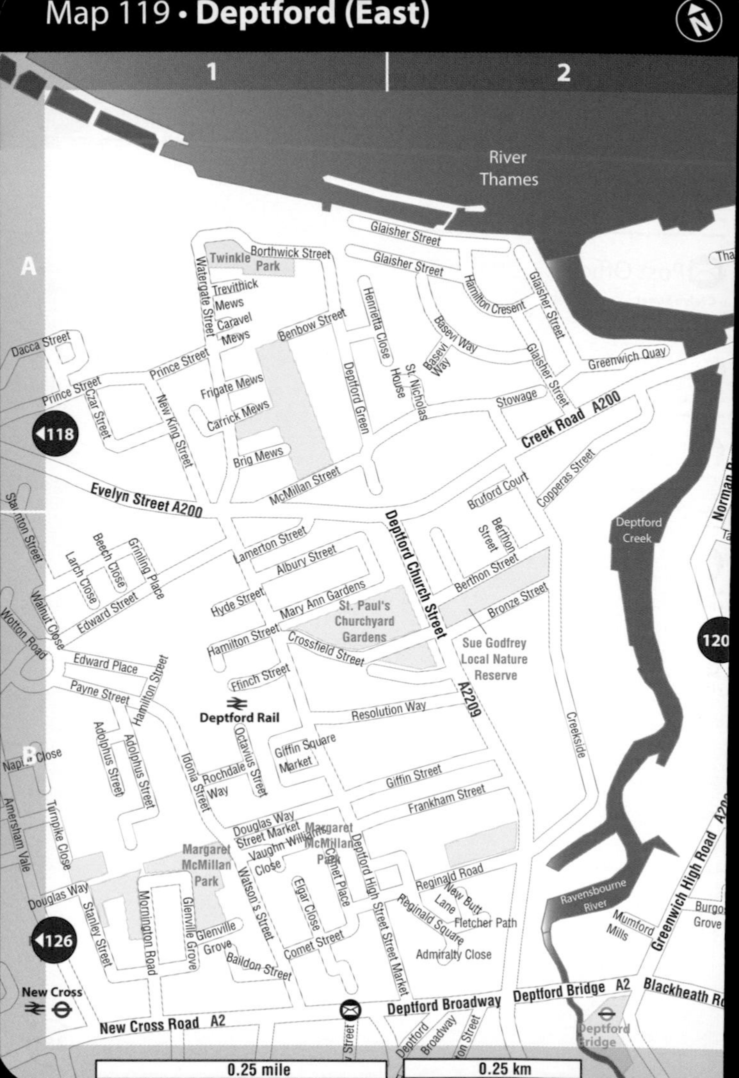
1
2
A
B
River Thames
Glaisher Street
Glaisher Street
Glaisher Street
Glaisher Street
Hamilton Cresent
Twinkle Park
Borthwick Street
Watergate Street
Trevithick Mews
Caravel Mews
Benbow Street
Henrietta Close
Basevi Way
Basevi Way
Greenwich Quay
Dacca Street
Prince Street
Prince Street
Czar Street
New King Street
Frigate Mews
Carrick Mews
Brig Mews
Deptford Green
House
St. Nicholas
Stowage
Creek Road A200
118
Evelyn Street A200
McMillan Street
Bruford Court
Copperas Street
Berthon Street
Deptford Creek
Staunton Street
Beech Close
Grinling Place
Larch Close
Lamerton Street
Albury Street
Deptford Church Street
Berthon Street
Walnut Close
Edward Street
Hyde Street
Mary Ann Gardens
St. Paul's Churchyard Gardens
Bronze Street
Wotton Road
Hamilton Street
Crossfield Street
Sue Godfrey Local Nature Reserve
120
Edward Place
Hamilton Street
Ffinch Street
Payne Street
Deptford Rail
A2209
Resolution Way
Adolphus Street
Adolphus Street
Giffin Square Market
Creekside
Close
Idonia Street
Rochdale Way
Octavius Street
Giffin Street
Amersham Vale
Turnpike Close
Frankham Street
Douglas Way Street Market
Margaret McMillan Park
Vaughn Williams Close
Margaret McMillan Park
Deptford High Street Street Market
Comet Place
Douglas Way
Stanley Street
Mornington Road
Glenville Grove
Glenville Grove
Watson's Street
Elgar Close
Reginald Road
New Butt Lane
Reginald Square
Fletcher Path
Admiralty Close
Ravensbourne River
Mumford Mills
Greenwich High Road
Burgos Grove
126
Baildon Street
Comet Street
New Cross
New Cross Road A2
Deptford Broadway
Deptford Bridge A2
Blackheath Rd
Deptford Bridge
Deptford Broadway
0.25 mile
0.25 km

Deptford (East)

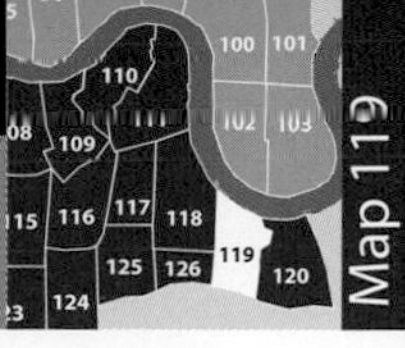

If you're one for a bargain, then this is your place. Browse the charity shops for dresses rumored to be donated by local prostitutes, pick up all manner of junk from the market or visit one of the many fishmongers, who have been known to sell live eels and sharks. And if you want to fit in with the countless old punks drinking cider get yourself a face tattoo on Church Street.

Coffee

- **The Deptford Project** • 121 Deptford High St

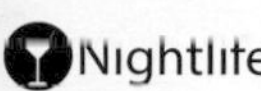

Nightlife

- **The Bird's Nest** • 32 Deptford Church St
- **Dog & Bell** • 116 Prince Street

Post Offices

- **New Cross** • 500 New Cross Rd

Restaurants

- **Chaconia Roti** • 26 Deptford High St
- **Kaya House** • 37 Deptford Broadway
- **Manzes** • 204 Deptford High St

Shopping

- **Deptford Market** • Deptford High St
- **Rag N Bone** • 140 Deptford High St

Supermarkets

- **Iceland** • 112 Deptford High St

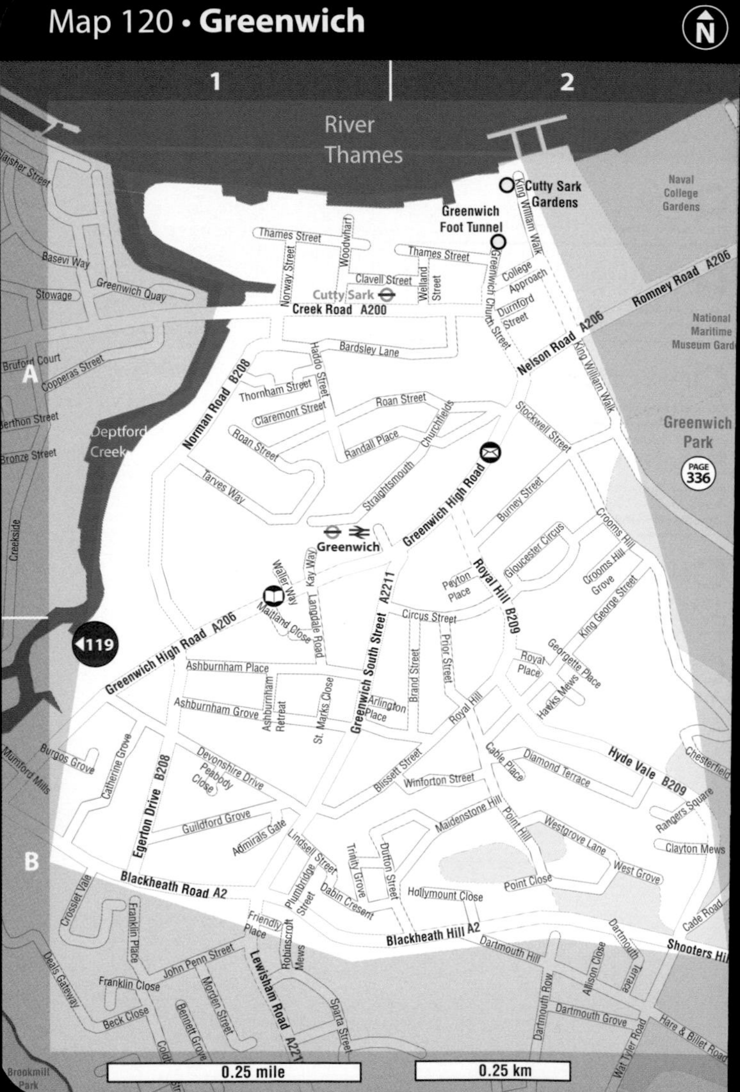

Map 120 • Greenwich
N
1
2
A
B
River Thames
Cutty Sark Gardens
Greenwich Foot Tunnel
King William Walk
Naval College Gardens
Thames Street
Woodwharf
Norway Street
Clavell Street
Welland Street
Cutty Sark
Creek Road A200
Greenwich Church Street
College Approach
Durnford Street
Romney Road A206
Nelson Road A206
National Maritime Museum Gard
Glaisher Street
Basevi Way
Greenwich Quay
Stowage
Bardsley Lane
Haddo Street
Bruford Court
Copperas Street
Norman Road B208
Thornham Street
Claremont Street
Roan Street
Berthon Street
Deptford Creek
Bronze Street
Randall Place
Churchfields
Stockwell Street
Greenwich Park
PAGE 336
Tarves Way
Straightsmouth
Greenwich High Road
Burney Street
Creekside
Greenwich
Crooms Hill
Gloucester Circus
Waller Way
Kay Way
Peyton Place
Royal Hill B209
Crooms Hill Grove
Maitland Close
Langdale Road
Greenwich South Street A2211
Circus Street
King George Street
119
Greenwich High Road A206
Prior Street
Royal Place
Georgette Place
Ashburnham Place
Brand Street
Hawks Mews
Ashburnham Grove
Ashburnham Retreat
St. Marks Close
Arlington Place
Royal Hill
Mumford Mills
Burgos Grove
Catherine Grove
Egerton Drive B208
Devonshire Drive
Peabody Close
Bissett Street
Cable Place
Diamond Terrace
Hyde Vale B209
Chesterfield
Winforton Street
Maidenstone Hill
Point Hill
Westgrove Lane
Rangers Square
Guildford Grove
Admirals Gate
Lindsell Street
Trinity Grove
Dutton Street
Clayton Mews
West Grove
Blackheath Road A2
Crossley Vale
Plumbridge Street
Dabin Cresent
Hollymount Close
Point Close
Cade Road
Friendly Place
Robinscroft Mews
Blackheath Hill A2
Dartmouth Hill
Dartmouth Terrace
Shooters Hi
Franklin Place
John Penn Street
Lewisham Road A21
Allison Close
Deals Gateway
Franklin Close
Morden Street
Dartmouth Row
Dartmouth Grove
Beck Close
Bennett Grove
Sparta Street
Hare & Billet Road
Wat Tyler Road
Brookmill Park
0.25 mile
0.25 km

Greenwich

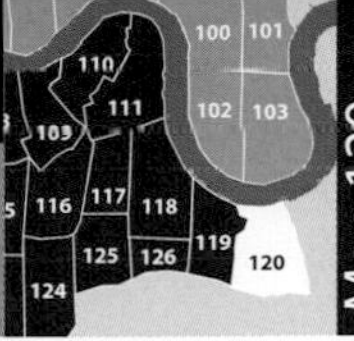

With the Cutty Sark magnificently restored and Greenwich's status as an Olympic Borough, the area has been given a new, touristy lease of life recently. There's still plenty of quirky pubs and shops to let you escape the crowds though, from dusty vinyl at The Beehive to artisan beer at Greenwich Union. And anyway, if you do want to do some proper sightseeing, what better place to do it.

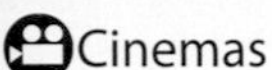

Cinemas

- **Greenwich Picturehouse** • 180 Greenwich High Rd

Coffee

- **Rhodes Bakery** • 37 King William Walk
- **Starbucks** • 54 Greenwich Church St

Landmarks

- **Cutty Sark Gardens** • King William Walk & Romney Rd
- **Greenwich Foot Tunnel** • Greenwich Church St & Thames St

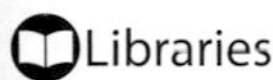

Libraries

- **West Greenwich Library** • Greenwich High Rd

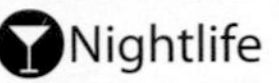

Nightlife

- **Bar du Musee** • 17 Nelson Rd
- **The Beehive** • 60 Carter St
- **The Greenwich Union** • 56 Royal Hill
- **O2** • O2 Arena
- **Up The Creek** • 302 Creek Rd

Post Offices

- **Greenwich** • 261 Greenwich High Rd

Restaurants

- **Goddard's Pie Shop Booth** • Fountain Court (off Greenwich Church Street)
- **Greenwich Park Bar & Grill** • 1 King William Walk
- **The Hill** • 89 Royal Hill
- **Inside** • 19 Greenwich South St
- **Piano Restaurant** • 131 Greenwich High Rd
- **Rivington Grill** • 178 Greenwich High Rd

Shopping

- **Belle** • 20 College Approach
- **Bullfrogs** • 22 Greenwich Church St
- **Cheeseboard** • 26 Royal Hill
- **Compendia** • 10 The Market
- **Emma Nissim** • 10 Greenwich Market
- **Johnny Rocket** • 10 College Approach
- **Meet Bernard** • 23 Nelson Rd
- **Mr Humbug** • Greenwich Market
- **Music And Video Exchange** • 23 Greenwich Church St

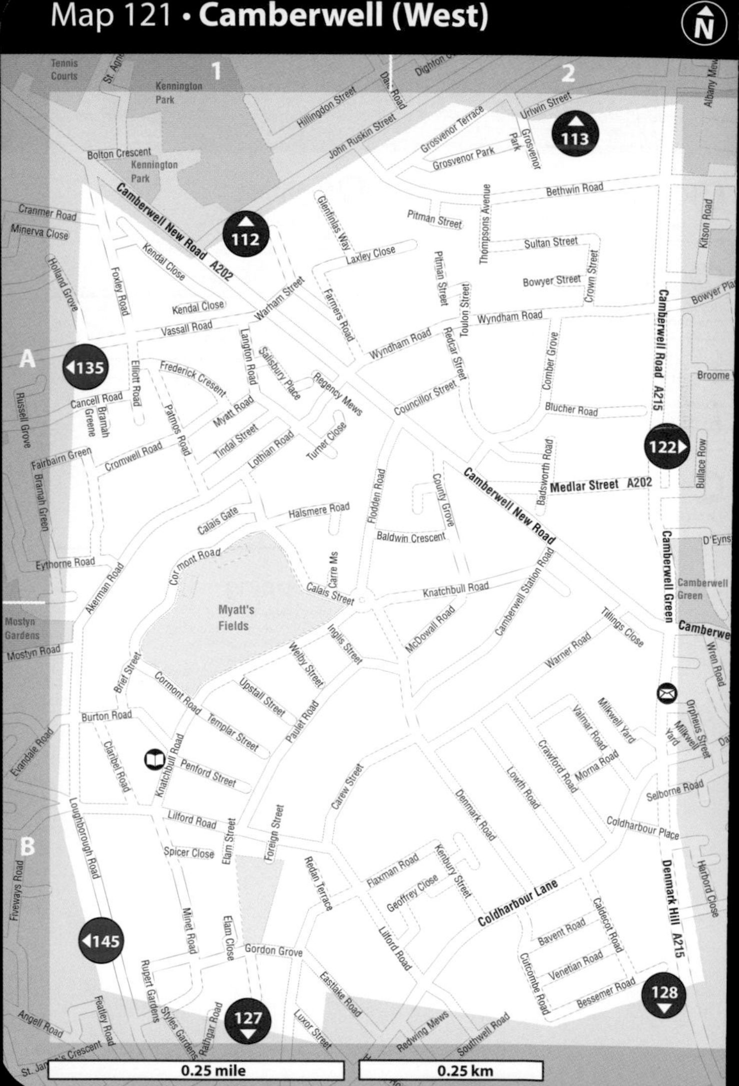
Map 121 • Camberwell (West)
N
1
2
A
B
Tennis Courts
Kennington Park
Bolton Crescent
Kennington Park
Hillingdon Street
John Ruskin Street
Grosvenor Terrace
Urlwin Street
Grosvenor Park
Grosvenor Park
113
Bethwin Road
Cranmer Road
Minerva Close
Camberwell New Road A202
112
Glenfinlas Way
Pitman Street
Thompsons Avenue
Sultan Street
Laxley Close
Holland Grove
Foxley Road
Kendal Close
Kendal Close
Warham Street
Farmers Road
Pitman Street
Toulon Street
Bowyer Street
Crown Street
Kitson Road
Bowyer Place
Vassall Road
Wyndham Road
Wyndham Road
Redcar Street
Comber Grove
Camberwell Road A215
135
Elliott Road
Frederick Crescent
Langton Road
Salisbury Place
Regency Mews
Councillor Street
Blucher Road
Broome
Cancell Road
Bramah Greene
Russell Grove
Patmos Road
Myatt Road
Tindal Street
Lothian Road
Turner Close
122
Badsworth Road
Bullace Row
Fairbairn Green
Cromwell Road
Bramah Green
Flodden Road
County Grove
Camberwell New Road
Medlar Street A202
Halsmere Road
Calais Gate
Baldwin Crescent
Camberwell Green
D'Eyns
Eythorne Road
Cormont Road
Carre Ms
Akerman Road
Myatt's Fields
Calais Street
Knatchbull Road
Camberwell Station Road
Camberwell Green
Mostyn Gardens
Mostyn Road
Brief Street
Inglis Street
Welby Street
McDowall Road
Tillings Close
Camberwe
Wren Road
Warner Road
Cormont Road
Upstall Street
Burton Road
Templar Street
Paulet Road
Valmar Road
Milkwell Yard
Orpheus Street
Milkwell Yard
Evandale Road
Claribel Road
Knatchbull Road
Penford Street
Crawford Road
Morna Road
Lowth Road
Carew Street
Denmark Road
Selborne Road
Loughborough Road
Lilford Road
Foreign Street
Coldharbour Place
Elam Street
Spicer Close
Redan Terrace
Flaxman Road
Kenbury Street
Denmark Hill A215
Harbord Close
Fiveways Road
Geoffrey Close
Coldharbour Lane
Caldecot Road
Minet Road
Elam Close
Bavent Road
145
Lilford Road
Gordon Grove
Cutcombe Road
Venetian Road
Rupert Gardens
Eastlake Road
Bessemer Road
128
Angell Road
Featley Road
Styles Gardens
Rathgar Road
127
Luxor Street
Redwing Mews
Southwell Road
0.25 mile
0.25 km

Camberwell (West)

This slowly reviving segment of Camberwell brings together a minority of polite arty types in the crumbling-yet-quaint town houses of Camberwell New Road with take-no-prisoners urbanites as seen in the chaos of Denmark Hill and its pointless Butterfly Shopping Centre (why?). The neighbourhood good stuff includes music bargains (Rat Records), killer Indian (New Dewaniam), and the unpronounceable Central Asian eatery at the Pasha Hotel: Kazakh Kyrgyz Restaurant.

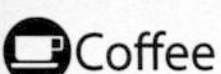

Coffee

- **Kings Cafe** • 120 Denmark Hill

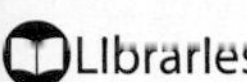

Libraries

- **Minet Library** • 52 Knatchbull Rd

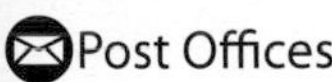

Post Offices

- **Camberwell Green** • 25 Denmark Hill

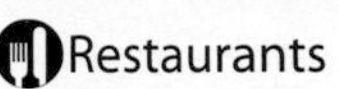

Restaurants

- **Kazakh Kyrgyz Restaurant** • 158 Camberwell Rd
- **New Dewaniam** • 225 Camberwell New Rd
- **Rock Steady Eddie's** • 2 Coldharbour Ln
- **Su-Thai** • 16 Coldharbour Ln
- **Viet Cafe** • 75 Denmark Hill

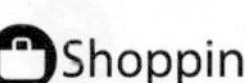

Shopping

- **Butterfly Walk Shopping Centre** • Denmark Hill
- **Men's Traditional Shoes** • 171 Camberwell Rd
- **Rat Records** • 348 New Camberwell Rd

Supermarkets

- **Co-Op** • 177 Camberwell New Rd
- **Iceland** • 120 Camberwell Rd
- **Kazakh Kyrgyz Restaurant** • 158

Map 122 • Camberwell (East)

Camberwell (East)

Maybe it was Kevin Spacey moving to the Grove, maybe something else entirely, but this area of Camberwell, in particular Church Street, has become something of an eating and drinking mecca in recent years. Work through the mammoth selection of craft beers in Stormbird before soaking it up with excellent kebabs from FM Mangal, high-end tapas from Angels & Gypsies, or regional Chinese from Silk Road.

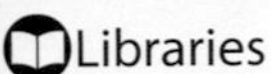

Libraries

- **Camberwell Library** • 17 Camberwell Church St

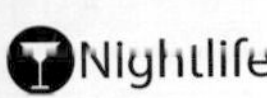

Nightlife

- **Bunker Club** • 46 Deptford Broadway
- **The Castle** • 65 Camberwell Church St
- **The Flying Dutchman** • 156 Wells Wy
- **Hermit's Cave** • 28 Camberwell Church St
- **Stormbird** • 25 Camberwell Church St

Post Offices

- **Southampton Way** • 156 Southampton Way

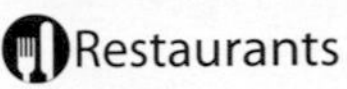

Restaurants

- **Angels & Gypsies** • 29 Camberwell Church St
- **Caravaggio's** • 47 Camberwell Church St
- **Falafel** • 27 Camberwell Church St
- **FM Mangal** • 54 Camberwell Church St
- **Silk Road** • 49 Camberwell Church St

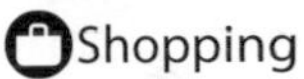

Shopping

- **Architectural Rescue** • 1–3 Southampton Way

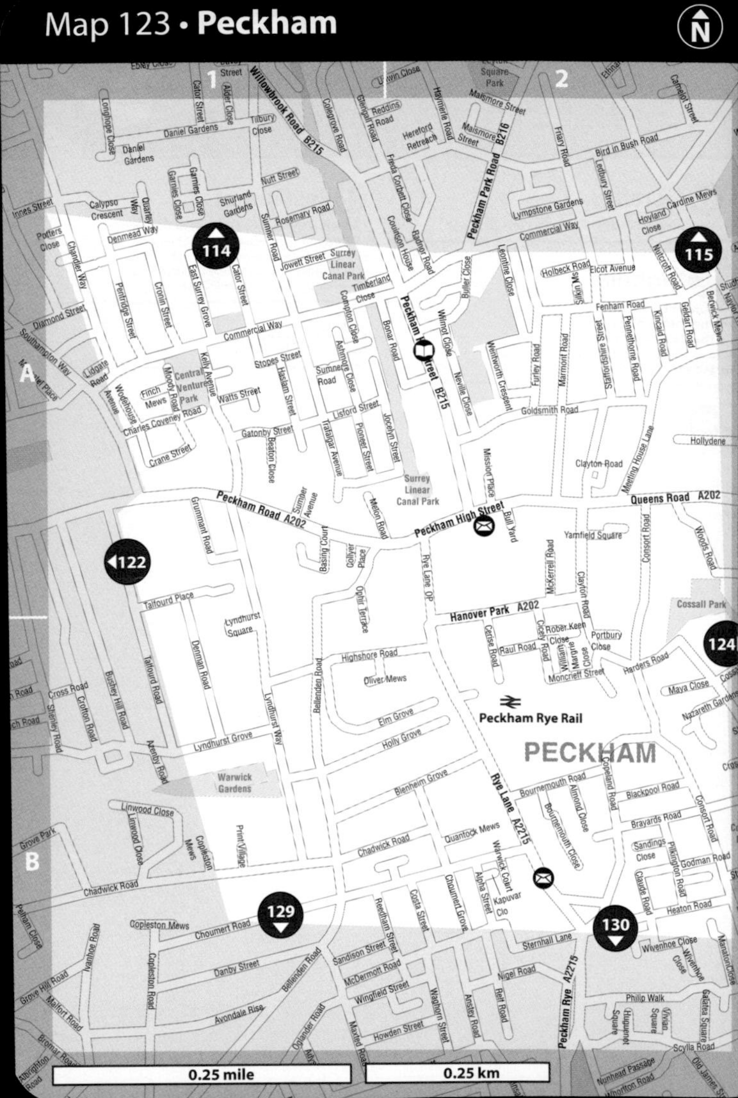
Map 123 • Peckham
N
1
2
A
B
Street
Willowbrook Road B215
Unwin Close
Square Park
Maismore Street
Cator Street
Alder Close
Longhope Close
Daniel Gardens
Tilbury Close
Colegrove Road
Glengall Road
Reddins Road
Hereford Retreach
Haymerle Road
Maismore Street
B216
Friary Road
Camelot Street
Bird in Bush Road
Ledbury Street
Lympstone Gardens
Hoyland Close
Cardine Mews
Commercial Way
Peckham Park Road
Freda Corbett Close
Coulston House
Radnor Road
Nutt Street
Garnies Close
Quarley Way
Shurland Gardens
Rosemary Road
Calypso Crescent
Innes Street
Potters Close
Denmead Way
Chandler Way
114
115
Sumner Road
Jowett Street
Surrey Linear Canal Park
Timberland Close
East Surrey Grove
Cator Street
Cronin Street
Penfridge Street
Diamond Street
Southampton Way
Commercial Way
Compton Close
Ashmore Close
Bonar Road
Peckham High Street B215
Wilmot Close
Buller Close
Leontine Close
Holbeck Road
Sumner Mews
Elcot Avenue
Fenham Road
Nutcroft Road
Berwick Mews
Geldart Road
Kincaid Road
Pennethorne Road
Staffordshire Street
Marmont Road
Furley Road
Wentworth Crescent
Neville Close
Lidgate Road
Wodehouse Avenue
Finch Mews
Moody Road
Central Venture Park
Kelly Avenue
Watts Street
Stopes Street
Haslam Street
Sumner Road
Lisford Street
Charles Coveney Road
Crane Street
Gatonby Street
Beaton Close
Trafalgar Avenue
Pioneer Street
Jocelyn Street
Goldsmith Road
Mission Place
Clayton Road
Meeting House Lane
Hollydene
Queens Road A202
Surrey Linear Canal Park
Peckham Road A202
Grummant Road
Sumner Avenue
Melon Road
Peckham High Street
Bull Yard
Yarnfield Square
Consort Road
Woods Road
122
Basing Court
Collyer Place
Rye Lane
McKerrell Road
Clayton Road
Cossall Park
Talfourd Place
Lyndhurst Square
Ophir Terrace
Hanover Park A202
Cerise Road
Raul Road
Cicely Road
Robert Keen Close
William Margrie Close
Portbury Close
Moncrieff Street
Harders Road
124
Maya Close
Nazareth Gardens
Highshore Road
Oliver Mews
Bellenden Road
Denman Road
Talfourd Road
Bushey Hill Road
Crofton Road
Cross Road
Sterling Road
Lyndhurst Way
Elm Grove
Holly Grove
Peckham Rye Rail
PECKHAM
Lyndhurst Grove
Azenby Road
Warwick Gardens
Blenheim Grove
Rye Lane A2215
Bournemouth Road
Almond Close
Copeland Road
Blackpool Road
Bournemouth Close
Brayards Road
Consort Road
Sandings Close
Pilkington Road
Godman Road
Linwood Close
Grove Park
Copleston Mews
Print Village
Chadwick Road
Quantock Mews
Warwick Court
Alpha Street
Kapuvar Clo
Claude Road
Heaton Road
Chadwick Road
Pelham Close
129
130
Copleston Mews
Choumert Road
Reedham Street
Costa Street
Choumert Grove
Sternhall Lane
Wivenhoe Close
Manaton Close
Ivanhoe Road
Copleston Road
Danby Street
Bellenden Road
Sandison Street
McDermott Road
Nigel Road
Grove Hill Road
Malfort Road
Avondale Rise
Wingfield Street
Waghorn Street
Anstey Road
Rein Road
Peckham Rye A2215
Philip Walk
Huguenot Square
Vivian Square
Galatea Square
Oglander Road
Maxted Road
Howden Street
Scylla Road
Bromar Road
Albrighton Road
Nunhead Passage
Old James Street
0.25 mile
0.25 km

As old pubs, pool halls, telephone boxes, and coal bunkers are converted into galleries faster than you can say "fixed gear bicycle", it's safe to say Peckham is the epicenter of the new(ish) South London art scene. But don't be scared off—get the cheapest lunch for miles at Manze's or pay a visit to the art/ music/ religion/ theatre behemoth that is The Bussey Building.

Coffee

- **Petitou** • 63 Choumert Rd

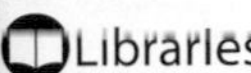

Libraries

- **Peckham Library** • 122 Peckham Hill St

Movie Theaters

- **Peckham Multiplex** • 95 Rye Ln

Nightlife

- **Bar Story** • 213 Blenheim Grove
- **The Bussey Building** • 133 Rye Ln
- **Canavan's Peckham Pool Club** • 188 Rye Ln
- **Frank's Cafe and Campari Bar** • 95 Rye Ln

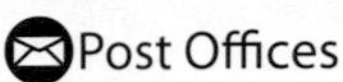

Post Offices

- **Peckham** • 121 Peckham High St
- **Rye Lane** • 199 Rye Ln

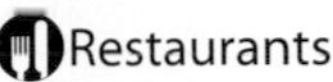

Restaurants

- **Agrobeso African Cuisine** • 139 Peckham High St
- **Bellenden Brasserie** • 168 Bellenden Rd
- **Manze's** • 105 Peckham High St
- **Obalende Suya Express** • 43 Peckham High St

Shopping

- **Curious Science** • 5 Commercial Waya
- **Persepolis** • 30 Peckham High St
- **Primark** • 51 Rye Ln

Supermarkets

- **Iceland** • 74 Rye Ln

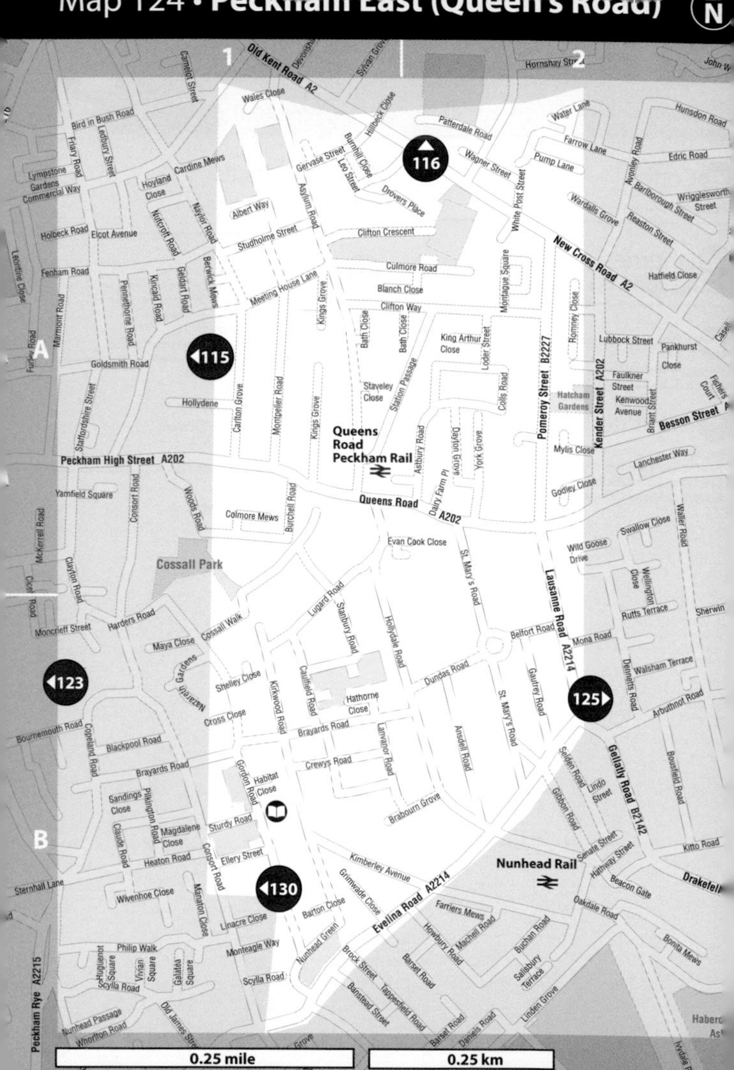
N
1
2
A
B
116
115
123
125
130
Old Kent Road A2
Camelot Street
Wales Close
Sylvan Grove
Hornshay Street
John Williams
Bird in Bush Road
Ledbury Street
Friary Road
Lympstone Gardens
Commercial Way
Cardine Mews
Hoyland Close
Hillbeck Close
Burnhill Close
Gervase Street
Leo Street
Patterdale Road
Water Lane
Farrow Lane
Pump Lane
Wagner Street
Hunsdon Road
Edric Road
Avonley Road
Barlborough Street
Wrigglesworth Street
Wardalls Grove
Reaston Street
Drovers Place
Albert Way
Asylum Road
Clifton Crescent
White Post Street
Holbeck Road
Elcot Avenue
Nutcroft Road
Naylor Road
Studholme Street
New Cross Road A2
Hatfield Close
Leontine Close
Fenham Road
Berwick Mews
Geldart Road
Kincaid Road
Pennethorne Road
Marmont Road
Meeting House Lane
Kings Grove
Culmore Road
Blanch Close
Clifton Way
Montague Square
Romney Close
Bath Close
King Arthur Close
Loder Street
Pomeroy Street B2227
Lubbock Street
Pankhurst Close
Furley Road
Goldsmith Road
Station Passage
Staveley Close
Colls Road
Hatcham Gardens
Kender Street A202
Faulkner Street
Kenwood Avenue
Briant Street
Fishers Court
Besson Street
Staffordshire Street
Hollydene
Carlton Grove
Montpelier Road
Queens Road Peckham Rail
Astbury Road
Dayton Grove
York Grove
Mylis Close
Lanchester Way
Peckham High Street A202
Yamfield Square
Consort Road
Woods Road
Burchell Road
Dairy Farm Pl
Queens Road
A202
Godley Close
Waller Road
Colmore Mews
Evan Cook Close
Swallow Close
Wild Goose Drive
McKerrell Road
Cossall Park
Clayton Road
St. Mary's Road
Lausanne Road A2214
Wellington Close
Cicely Road
Lugard Road
Stanbury Road
Hollydale Road
Rutts Terrace
Sherwin
Moncrieff Street
Harders Road
Cossall Walk
Belfort Road
Mona Road
Maya Close
Nazareth Gardens
Shelley Close
Kirkwood Road
Caulfield Road
Dundas Road
Gautrey Road
Dennetts Road
Walsham Terrace
Hathorne Close
Arbuthnot Road
Bournemouth Road
Copeland Road
Blackpool Road
Cross Close
Brayards Road
Lanvanor Road
Ansdell Road
Selden Road
Gellatly Road B2142
Bousfield Road
Brayards Road
Crewys Road
Gordon Road
Habitat Close
Lindo Street
Sandings Close
Pilkington Road
Magdalene Close
Sturdy Road
Brabourn Grove
Gibbon Road
Senate Street
Kitto Road
Claude Road
Heaton Road
Consort Road
Ellery Street
Nunhead Rail
Hathway Street
Drakefell
Sternhall Lane
Kimberley Avenue
Grimwade Close
Evelina Road A2214
Beacon Gate
Wivenhoe Close
Manaton Close
Barton Close
Farriers Mews
Oakdale Road
Linacre Close
Machell Road
Buchan Road
Howbury Road
Bonita Mews
Philip Walk
Monteagle Way
Nunhead Green
Brock Street
Barset Road
Salisbury Terrace
Huguenot Square
Vivian Square
Galatea Square
Scylla Road
Scylla Road
Tappesfield Road
Linden Grove
Banstead Street
Nunhead Passage
Whorlton Road
Old James Street
Barset Road
Daniels Road
Peckham Rye A2215
0.25 mile
0.25 km

Peckham East (Queen's Road)

Although the local half way house ensures the streets are filled with beggars, and the buses passing through en route to the continent make you wish you were some where else, this small pocket of Peckham isn't really so bad. Head for great African food at 805 Bar Restaurant or take a short walk to the incredible Victorian Nunhead Cemetery.

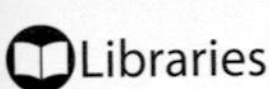

Libraries

- **Nunhead Library** • Gordon Rd

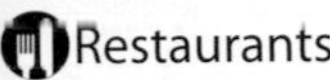

Restaurants

- **805 Bar Restaurant** • 805 Old Kent Rd
- **Tops Carribean Takeaway** • 173 Queens Rd

Map 125 • New Cross Gate

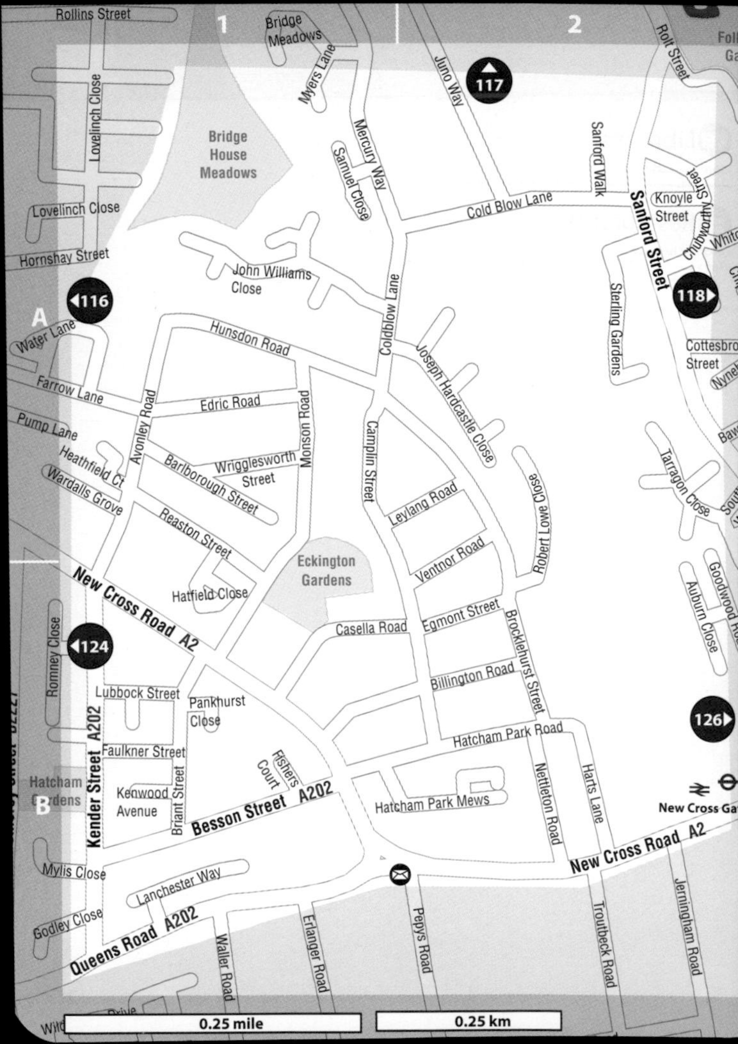

New Cross Gate

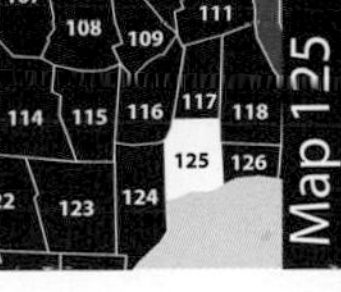

Since the sad demise of the Montague Arms this strip has become even more of a no man's land—not quite New Cross but not quite Peckham. Apart from a semi-decent junk shop and a not-so-great retail park, there's not much to see. Do yourself a favor and stroll on into one of the aforementioned neighborhoods—or jump on the brilliant London Overground and be in Dalston in no time.

Post Offices

- **New Cross Gate** • 199 New Cross Rd

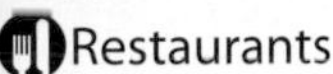

Restaurants

- **Hong Kong City** • 43 New Cross Rd

Map 126 • New Cross

N
1
2
A
B
118
119
125
Sanford Street
Nynehead Street
Desmond Street
Bowerman Avenue
Milton Court Road
Edward Place
Payne Street
Hamilton Street
Bawtree Road
Ludwick Mews
Alexandra St
Primrose Walk
Edward Street B207
Amersham Gr
Napier Close
Adolphus Street
Idonia Street
Rochdale Way
Octavius Street
Tarragon Close
Southerngate Way
Clifton Rise
Angus Street
Pagnell Street
Royal Naval Place
Amersham Vale
Turnpike Cl
Auburn Close
Goodwood Road
Southerngate Way
Pear Cl
Childeric Road
Fordham Park
Douglas Way
Stanley Street
Mornington Rd
Glenville Grove
Margaret McMillan Park
Watson's Street
Achilles Street
Exeter Way
New Cross Rail
Batavia Road
Clifton Rise
Baildon Street
Comet St
New Cross Gate Rail
Batavia Mews
Ben Pimlott Building
New Cross Road A2
New Cross Road A2
Laurie Grove
Parkfield Rd
Amersham Rd A20
Dixon Road
St. James's
Loring Road
Goldsmiths College
Lewisham Way A20
Mulberry Mews
Alpha Road
Florence Road B218
Heald Street
Florence Terrace
Omega Street
Heston Street
St. Donatts Road
Chestnut Close
Tanners Hill
Brindley St
Thornville Street
Alexandra Cottages
St. Donatts Road
Luxmore Street
Tanners Mews
New Cross Gate Cutting Nature Reserve
Malpas Road
Luxmore Gardens
Friendly Gardens
Rokeby Road
Upper Brockley Road
Oscar Street
Cheshire Close
Shardeloes Road
Barriedale
Sandbourne Road
Malpas Road B218
Vulcan Road
Vesta Road
Vesta Road
Wickham Road

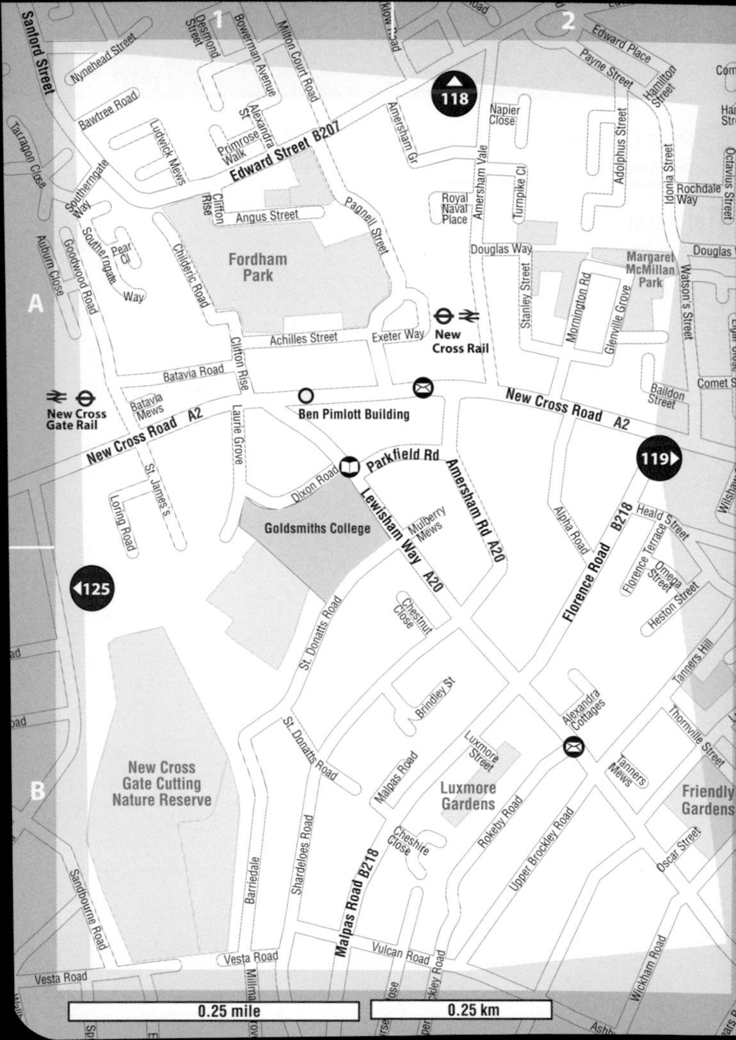

0.25 mile

0.25 km

New Cross

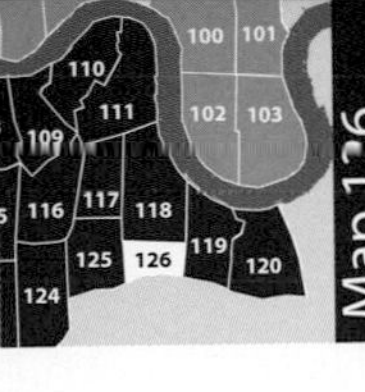

Once hailed as the new Shoreditch, this corner of Lewisham has managed to provide us with all the good stuff about hipsterville, while avoiding everything bad. So while there's regularly excellent live music at New Cross Inn, your still guaranteed a smack around the chops off some bloke in the Hobgoblin if you try and explain why the blank sheets of paper you stuck on the wall really have a deeper meaning.

Landmarks

- **Ben Pimlott Building** • University of London, New Cross

Libraries

- **Goldsmiths Library** • Lewisham Wy

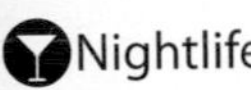

Nightlife

- **Amersham Arms** • 388 New Cross Rd
- **Hobgoblin** • 272 New Cross Rd
- **New Cross Inn** • 323 New Cross Rd

Post Offices

- **Lewisham Way** • 150 Lewisham Way
- **New Cross Road** • 500 New Cross Rd

Restaurants

- **Manzes**• 204 Deptford High St
- **Sirius Fish And Chips**• 397 New Cross Rd

Supermarkets

- **Iceland** • 277 New Cross Rd
- **Sainsbury's** • 263 New Cross Rd

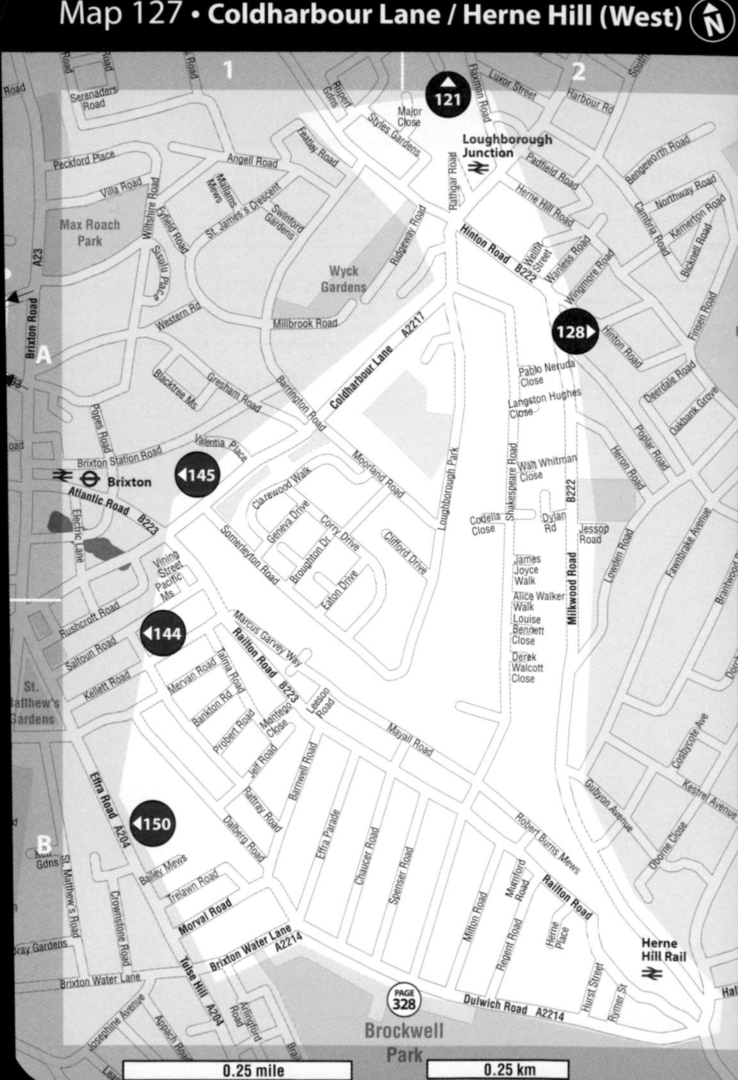

Loughborough Junction
Brixton
Herne Hill Rail
Max Roach Park
Wyck Gardens
Brockwell Park
Coldharbour Lane A2217
Railton Road B223
Milkwood Road B222
Hinton Road B222
Brixton Water Lane A2214
Dulwich Road A2214
Effra Road A204
Tulse Hill A204
Atlantic Road B223
Brixton Road
Loughborough Park
Shakespeare Road
Mayall Road
0.25 mile
0.25 km

Coldharbour Lane / Herne Hill (West)

There don't seem to be as many shootings on Coldharbour Lane as there used to be. Maybe the crack dealers are just quietly selling the stuff, as somebody on *The Wire* once sensibly advised. Or maybe they've all been converted by the pleasant conservatory at The Florence, invigorating swims at the Brockwell Lido (p 328), and handmade jams from the Blackbird Bakery. Yes, that's probably it.

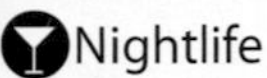

Nightlife

- **The Commercial** • 210 Railton Rd
- **Escape Bar and Art** • 214 Railton Rd
- **The Florence** • 133 Dulwich Rd
- **Prince Regent** • 69 Dulwich Rd

Restaurants

- **Café Prov** • 2 Half Moon Ln
- **Ichiban Sushi** • 58 Atlantic Rd
- **New Fujiyama** • 5 Vining St

Shopping

- **Blackbird Bakery** • 208 Railton Rd

Coffee

- **Pullens** • 293 Railton Rd

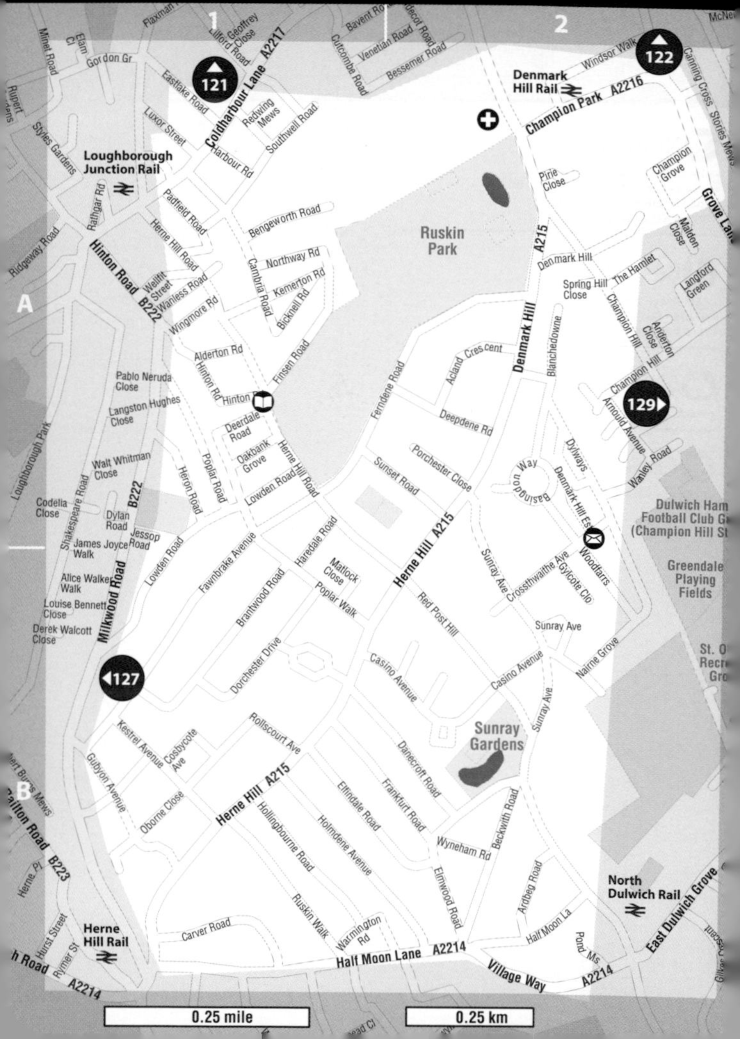

Map 128 • Denmark Hill / Herne Hill (East)

Ruskin Park
Sunray Gardens
Loughborough Junction Rail
Denmark Hill Rail
Herne Hill Rail
North Dulwich Rail
Dulwich Hamlet Football Club Ground (Champion Hill Stadium)
Greendale Playing Fields
Coldharbour Lane A2217
Champion Park A2216
Denmark Hill A215
Herne Hill A215
Half Moon Lane A2214
Village Way A2214
Milkwood Road
Hinton Road B222
East Dulwich Grove

0.25 mile
0.25 km

Denmark Hill / Herne Hill (East)

There's something quaintly grounded about the leafy Victorian suburb of Herne Hill, where funky neo-hippies settle into dreadlocked nuclear families. Denmark Hill sits at its top, with its imposing Salvation Army training grounds, following on to Ruskin Park for ornamental ponds and Edwardian ruins. Half Moon Lane plays main drag—get lost in a book at Tales on Moon Lane and lost in a bowl of noodles at Lombok.

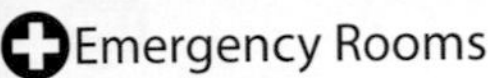

Emergency Rooms

- **King's College Hospital** • Denmark Hill & Champion Park

Libraries

- **Carnegie Library** • 188 Herne Hill Rd

Post Offices

- **Crossthwaite Avenue** • 6 Crossthwaite Ave

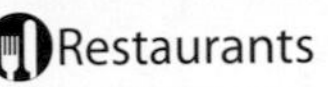

Restaurants

- **Lombok** • 17 Half Moon Ln
- **Number 22** • 22 Half Moon Ln

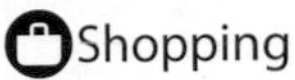

Shopping

- **Tales on Moon Lane** • 25 Half Moon Ln

Supermarkets

- **Sainsbury's** • 132 Herne Hill

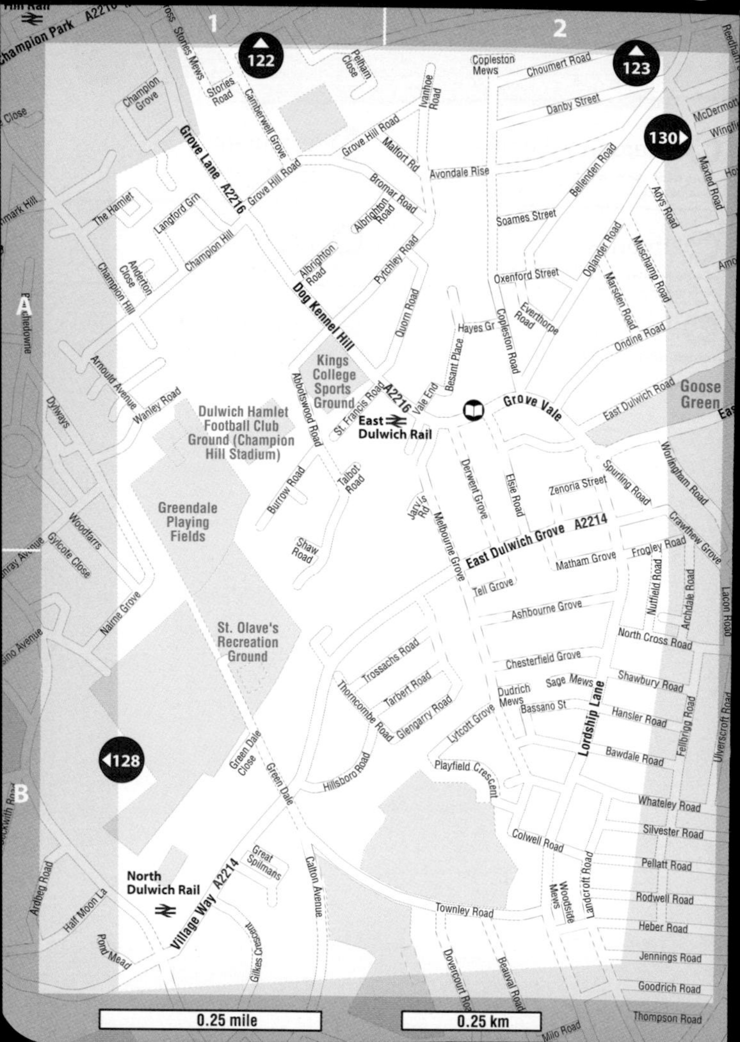

Map 129 • East Dulwich

East Dulwich

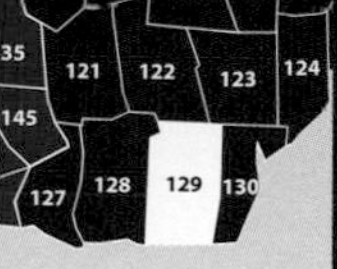

East Dulwich is where your ex-flatmate finally settled down and now won't shut up about taramasalata, babies, and how he's only fifteen minutes from London Bridge by train over perfect cocktails at Black Cherry. Dodge baguettes, pushchairs, and delis along Lordship Lane, just don't get sucked in. Try the Sea Cow for fish & chips, a pint at the Palmerston, and a night out at Liquorish.

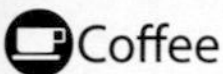

Coffee

- **Caffe Nero** • 8 Lordship Ln

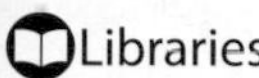

Libraries

- **Grove Vale library** • 25 Grove Vale

Nightlife

- **Black Cherry** • 21 Lordship Ln
- **liquorish** • 123 Lordship Ln

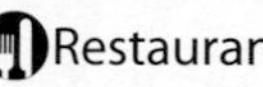

Restaurants

- **The Palmerston** • 91 Lordship Ln
- **Sea Cow** • 37 Lordship Ln

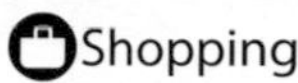

Shopping

- **The Cheeseblock** • 69 Lordship Ln

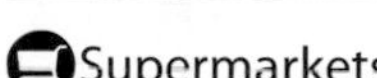

Supermarkets

- **Iceland** • 84 Lordship Ln
- **Sainsbury's** • 80 Dog Kennel Hill

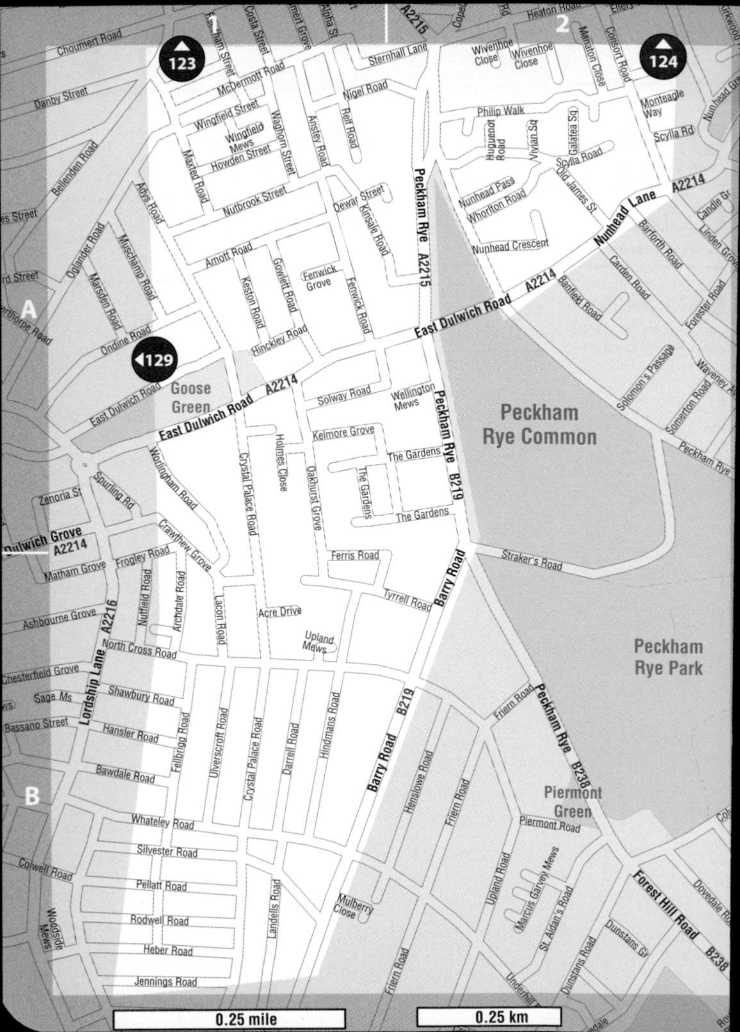

Map 130 • Peckham Rye

Peckham Rye

A noticeboard on Peckham Rye Common alleges that ancient British Queen Boudicca was finally defeated by the Romans here. Anyone suggesting that the very middle class streets around North Cross Road—with its market, twee sweets at Hope and Greenwood, and lazy Sunday lunches at The Rye—have anything to do with Peckham as we know it might get the same treatment.

Coffee

- **Blue Mountain Café** • 18 N Cross Rd

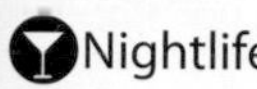

Nightlife

- **The Rye** • 31 Peckham Rye

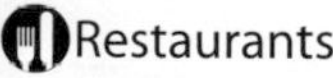

Restaurants

- **Thai Corner Cafe** • 44 Northcross Rd
- **The Rye** • 31 Peckham Rye

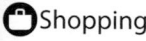

Shopping

- **Hope And Greenwood** • 20 North Cross Rd

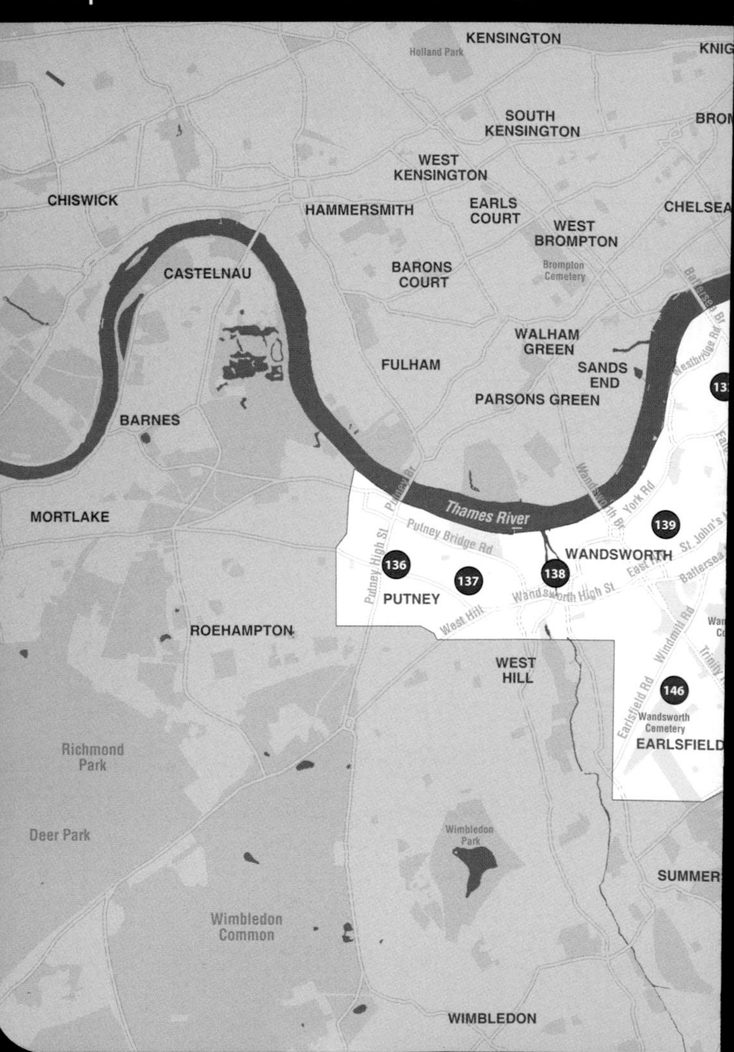
KENSINGTON
Holland Park
KNIG
SOUTH KENSINGTON
BROM
WEST KENSINGTON
CHISWICK
HAMMERSMITH
EARLS COURT
CHELSEA
WEST BROMPTON
CASTELNAU
BARONS COURT
Brompton Cemetery
Battersea Br
WALHAM GREEN
Battersea Bridge Rd
Westbridge Rd
FULHAM
SANDS END
PARSONS GREEN
BARNES
Putney Br
Wandsworth Br
York Rd
Thames River
MORTLAKE
Putney Bridge Rd
Putney High St
139
St. John's
WANDSWORTH
136
137
138
East Hill
Battersea
Wandsworth High St
PUTNEY
West Hill
ROEHAMPTON
Windmill Rd
WEST HILL
Trinity
Earlsfield Rd
146
Wandsworth Cemetery
EARLSFIELD
Richmond Park
Deer Park
Wimbledon Park
SUMMER
Wimbledon Common
WIMBLEDON

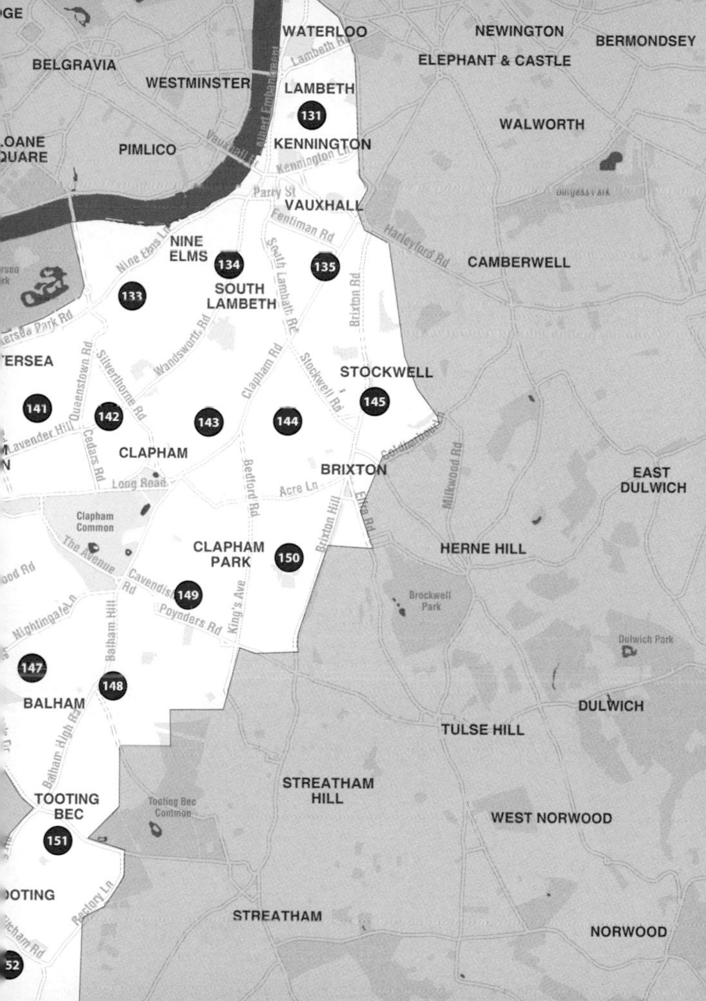
WATERLOO
NEWINGTON
BERMONDSEY
BELGRAVIA
ELEPHANT & CASTLE
WESTMINSTER
LAMBETH
Lambeth Rd
Albert Embankment
131
WALWORTH
KENNINGTON
PIMLICO
Vauxhall Br
Kennington Ln
Parry St
VAUXHALL
Fentiman Rd
Harleyford Rd
NINE ELMS
Nine Elms Ln
134
135
CAMBERWELL
133
SOUTH LAMBETH
South Lambeth Rd
Brixton Rd
Wandsworth Rd
Clapham Rd
Stockwell Rd
Silverthorne Rd
Queenstown Rd
STOCKWELL
145
141
142
143
144
Lavender Hill
Cedars Rd
CLAPHAM
Coldharbour Ln
Milkwood Rd
BRIXTON
EAST DULWICH
Long Road
Acre Ln
Bedford Rd
Effra Rd
Brixton Hill
Clapham Common
The Avenue
CLAPHAM PARK
150
HERNE HILL
Cavendish Rd
149
Brockwell Park
Nightingale Ln
Poynders Rd
King's Ave
Balham Hill
Dulwich Park
147
148
BALHAM
DULWICH
TULSE HILL
Balham High Rd
STREATHAM HILL
TOOTING BEC
Tooting Bec Common
WEST NORWOOD
151
Rectory Ln
STREATHAM
NORWOOD

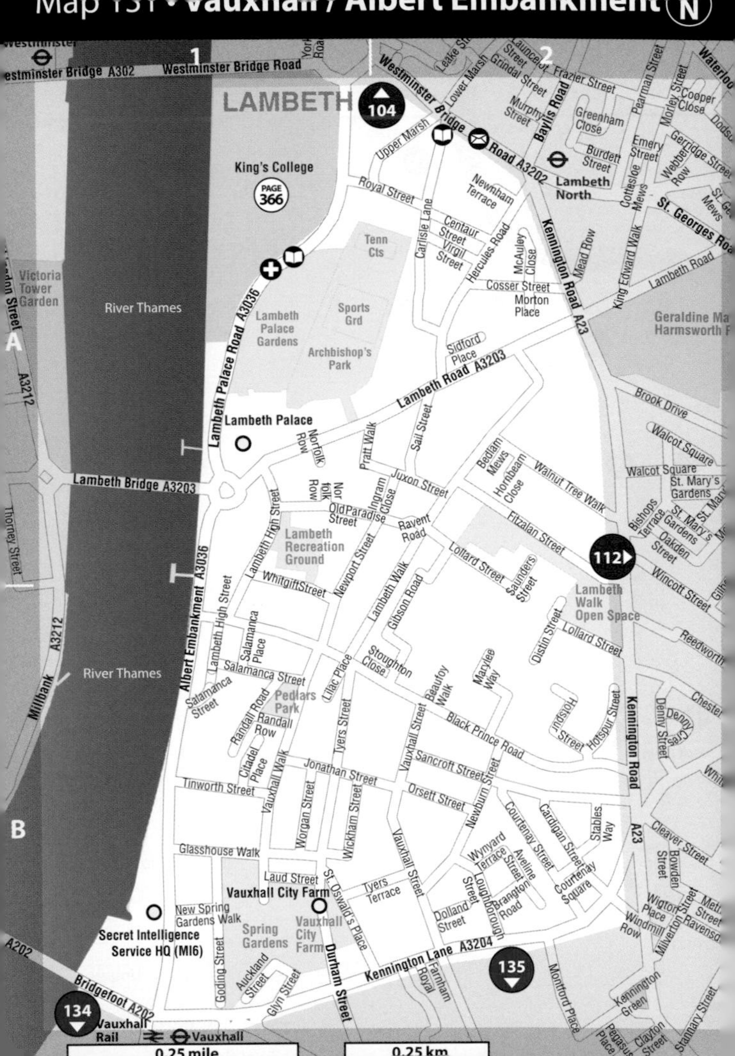
N
1
2
A
B
Westminster Bridge A302
Westminster Bridge Road
York Road
LAMBETH
104
Westminster Bridge Road A3202
Leake Street
Lower Marsh
Launcelot Street
Grindal Street
Frazier Street
Murphy Street
Baylis Road
Greenham Close
Pearman Street
Morley Street
Cooper Close
Waterloo
Upper Marsh
Burdett Street
Emery Street
Gerridge Street
Webber Row
Lambeth North
King's College
PAGE 366
Royal Street
Newnham Terrace
Cottesloe Mews
St. Georges Road
Centaur Street
Virgil Street
Carlisle Lane
Hercules Road
McAuley Close
Kennington Road A23
Mead Row
King Edward Walk
Lambeth Road
Tenn Cts
Sports Grd
Cosser Street
Morton Place
Victoria Tower Garden
River Thames
Lambeth Palace Road A3036
Lambeth Palace Gardens
Archbishop's Park
Sidford Place
Lambeth Road A3203
Geraldine Mary Harmsworth Park
A3212
Brook Drive
Walcot Square
Lambeth Palace
Norfolk Row
Pratt Walk
Sail Street
Bedlam Mews
Hornbeam Close
Walnut Tree Walk
St. Mary's Gardens
Lambeth Bridge A3203
Juxon Street
Thorney Street
Lambeth High Street
Old Paradise Street
Ingram Close
Ravent Road
Fitzalan Street
Bishops Terrace
Oakden Street
112
Lambeth Recreation Ground
Newport Street
Lollard Street
Saunders Street
Wincott Street
Whitgift Street
Lambeth Walk
Gibson Road
Lambeth Walk Open Space
Albert Embankment A3036
Salamanca Place
Distin Street
Reedworth
Stoughton Close
Marylee Way
Millbank
Salamanca Street
Lilac Place
Beaufoy Walk
Hotspur Street
Chester
Pedlars Park
Randall Road
Randall Row
Tyers Street
Vauxhall Street
Black Prince Road
Denny Street
Denny Cres
Kennington Road
Citadel Place
Vauxhall Walk
Jonathan Street
Sancroft Street
Newburn Street
Tinworth Street
Orsett Street
Courtenay Street
Cardigan Street
Stables Way
A23
Cleaver Street
Bowden Street
Worgan Street
Wickham Street
Glasshouse Walk
Wynyard Terrace
Aveline Street
Courtenay Square
Laud Street
Vauxhall City Farm
St. Oswald's Place
Tyers Terrace
Loughborough Street
Brangton Road
Wigton Place
Milverton Street
Ravensdon Street
Windmill Row
New Spring Gardens Walk
Spring Gardens
Dolland Street
Secret Intelligence Service HQ (MI6)
A202
Durham Street
Kennington Lane A3204
Farnham Royal
135
Montford Place
Goding Street
Auckland Street
Glyn Street
Kennington Green
Bridgefoot A202
134
Vauxhall Rail
Vauxhall
Pegasus Place
Clayton Street
Stannary Street
0.25 mile
0.25 km

Vauxhall / Albert Embankment

Map 131

Feel like doin' the Lambeth Walk? You can. Right here. On Lambeth Walk, incidentally. Though nowadays 'doing the Lambeth Walk' is likely to have an entirely less innocent connotation if some of the area's kinkier gay clubs are anything to go by. This part of Vauxhall, under the watchful eye of MI6, is slightly less that way inclined, but maintains its share of hot spots like the now popular Hidden (foiled!). If you're after a sausage fest of another kind, get stuffed at Zeitgeist at the Jolly Gardeners.

Emergency Rooms

- **St Thomas' Hospital** • Westminster Bridge Rd & Lambeth Palace Rd

Landmarks

- **Lambeth Palace** • Lambeth Palace Rd & Lambeth Rd
- **Secret Intelligence Service HQ (MI6)** • 85 Vauxhall Cross
- **Vauxhall City Farm** • 165 Tyers St

Libraries

- **CILT Resources Library** • 111 Vauxhall Bridge Rd
- **Lambeth Palace Library** • Lambeth Palace Rd

Nightlife

- **Area** • 67 Albert Embankment
- **Eagle London** • 349 Kennington Ln
- **Hidden** • 100 Tinworth St
- **The Lavender** • 112 Vauxhall Walk
- **The Royal Vauxhall Tavern** • 372 Kennington Ln
- **Zeitgeist at the Jolly Gardeners** • 49–51 Black Prince Rd

Post Offices

- **Westminster Bridge Road** • 125 Westminster Bridge Rd

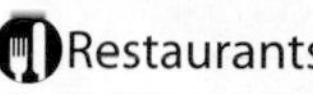

Restaurants

- **Thai Pavillion East** • 78 Kennington Rd

Supermarkets

- **Tesco** • Kennington Ln

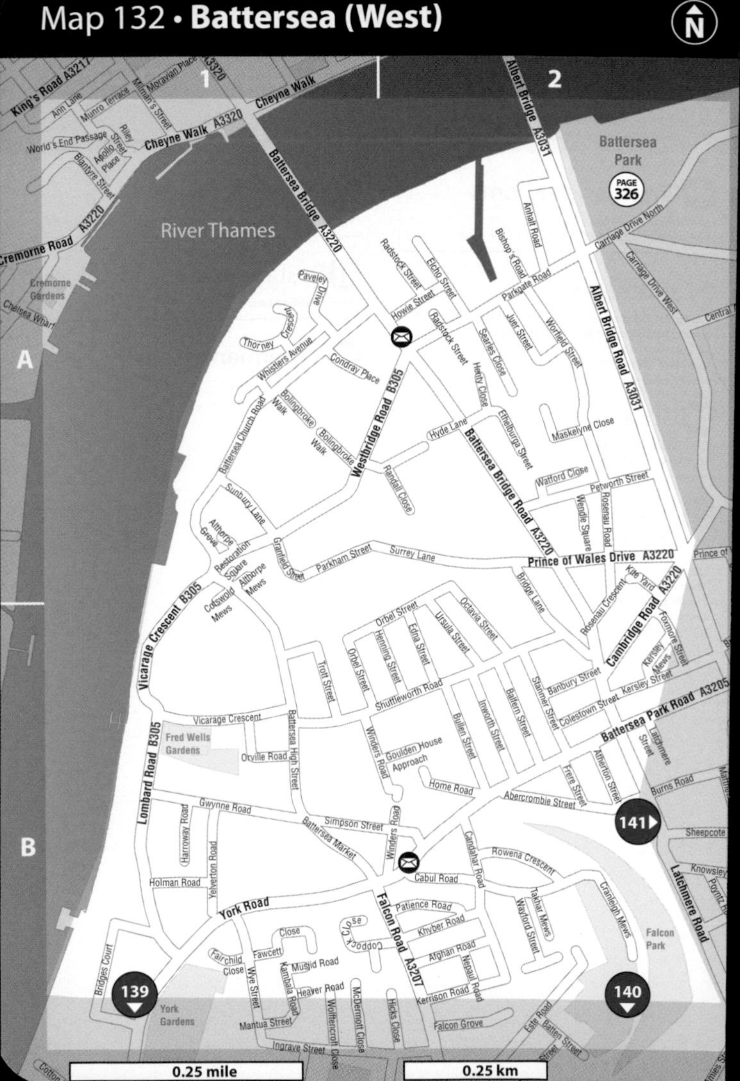

River Thames
Battersea Park
PAGE 326
Cheyne Walk
Cheyne Walk A3320
King's Road A3217
Moravian Place
Milman's Street
Munro Terrace
Ann Lane
World's End Passage
Riley Street
Apollo Place
Blantyre Street
Cremorne Road A3220
Cremorne Gardens
Chelsea Wharf
Battersea Bridge A3220
Albert Bridge A3031
Albert Bridge Road A3031
Carriage Drive North
Carriage Drive West
Central
Anhalt Road
Bishop's Road
Parkgate Road
Radstock Street
Elcho Street
Howie Street
Paveley Drive
Thorney Crescent
Whistlers Avenue
Condray Place
Westbridge Road B305
Searles Close
Juer Street
Worfield Street
Hearty Close
Ethelburga Street
Maskelyne Close
Hyde Lane
Battersea Bridge Road A3220
Battersea Church Road
Bolingbroke Walk
Randall Close
Watford Close
Petworth Street
Wendle Square
Rosenau Road
Sunbury Lane
Althorpe Grove
Restoration Square
Granfield Street
Parkham Street
Surrey Lane
Prince of Wales Drive A3220
Prince of
Kite Yard
Bridge Lane
Rosenau Crescent
Cambridge Road A3220
Foxmore Street
Kersley Mews
Kersley Street
Vicarage Crescent B305
Cotswold Mews
Althorpe Mews
Orbel Street
Octavia Street
Ursula Street
Edna Street
Henning Street
Trott Street
Shuttleworth Road
Stanmer Street
Banbury Street
Colestown Street
Battersea Park Road A3205
Balfern Street
Inworth Street
Bullen Street
Vicarage Crescent
Fred Wells Gardens
Orville Road
Battersea High Street
Winders Road
Goulden House Approach
Home Road
Atherton Street
Frere Street
Latchmere Street
Burns Road
Abercrombie Street
Sheepcote
Lombard Road B305
Gwynne Road
Harroway Road
Simpson Street
Battersea Market
Winders Road
Candahar Road
Rowena Crescent
Knowsley
Poyntz
Latchmere Road
Holman Road
Yelverton Road
Cabul Road
York Road
Patience Road
Khyber Road
Falcon Road A3207
Takhar Mews
Wayford Street
Cranleigh Mews
Falcon Park
Coppock Close
Afghan Road
Nepaul Road
Close
Fawcett
Fairchild Close
Musjid Road
Kambala Road
Heaver Road
Bridges Court
Wye Street
York Gardens
Mantua Street
Wolftencroft Close
McDermott Close
Hicks Close
Kerrison Road
Falcon Grove
Este Road
Batten Street
Ingrave Street
Cotton
0.25 mile
0.25 km
1
2
A
B
139
140
141

Battersea (West)

With no tubes or trains to attract the hoi polloi, Battersea West sits smugly hugging the River Thames, happily cut off from the hustle and bustle of the rest of London. However, with the Imperial Wharf Overground not far away, the commute isn't as bad as it used to be (thanks also to Mr Coffee) and the masses flock -- mostly for the spacious floor-to-ceiling glass apartments with killer river views. Take in a Sunday lunch at the Prince Albert or cook your own with meat from The Butcher and Grill.

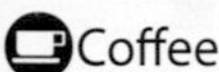

Coffee

- **Mr Coffee** • Hester Rd

Nightlife

- **Barrio** • 14 Battersea Sq
- **The Draft House Westbridge** • 74 Battersea Bridge Road
- **The Greyhound** • 136 Battersea High St
- **Le QuecumBar** • 42 Battersea High St
- **The Prince Albert** • 85 Albert Bridge Rd
- **The Woodman** • 60 Battersea High St

Post Offices

- **Battersea Bridge Road** • 72 Battersea Bridge Rd
- **York Road** • 583 Battersea Park Rd

Restaurants

- **The Greyhound** • 136 Battersea High St
- **Ransom's Dock** • 35 Parkgate Rd

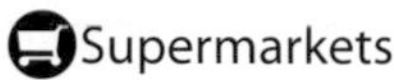

Supermarkets

- **Sainsbury's** • 326 Battersea Park Rd

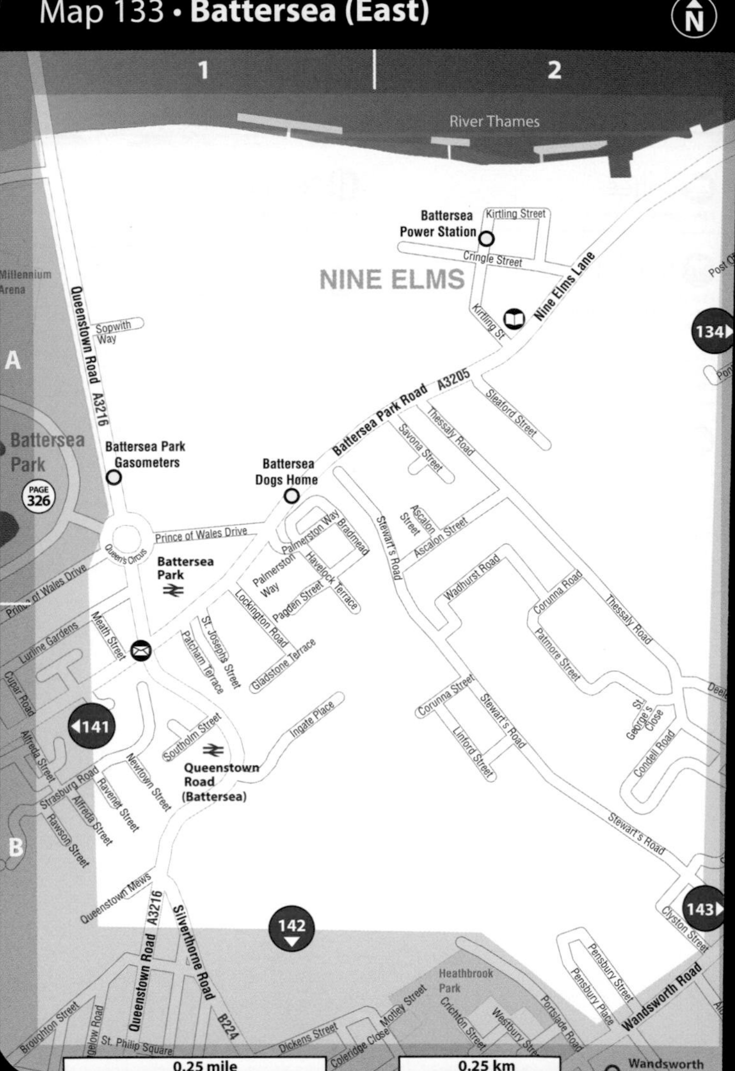

N
1
2
A
B
River Thames
Battersea
Power Station
Kirtling Street
Cringle Street
NINE ELMS
Nine Elms Lane
Kirtling St
Post O
134
Millennium
Arena
Queenstown Road
A3216
Sopwith
Way
Battersea Park Road
A3205
Sleaford Street
Thessaly Road
Savona Street
Battersea
Park
PAGE
326
Battersea Park
Gasometers
Battersea
Dogs Home
Prince of Wales Drive
Queen's Circus
Battersea
Park
Palmerston Way
Bradmead
Stewart's Road
Ascalon
Street
Ascalon Street
Palmerston
Way
Havelock Terrace
Pagden Street
Lockington Road
St. Josephs Street
Patcham Terrace
Gladstone Terrace
Meath Street
Lurline Gardens
Cupar Road
Wadhurst Road
Corunna Road
Thessaly Road
Patmore Street
Corunna Street
Stewart's Road
Linford Street
St George's Close
Condell Road
Deeley
141
Alfreda Street
Southolm Street
Ingate Place
Queenstown
Road
(Battersea)
Newtown Street
Strasburg Road
Ravenet Street
Alfreda Street
Rawson Street
Stewart's Road
143
Clyston Street
Queenstown Mews
A3216
Queenstown Road
Silverthorne Road
142
Heathbrook
Park
Motley Street
Crichton Street
Westbury Street
Portslade Road
Pensbury Street
Pensbury Place
Wandsworth Road
Broughton Street
St. Philip Square
B224
Dickens Street
Coleridge Close
0.25 mile
0.25 km
Wandsworth
Road

Battersea (East)

An odd slice of post-industrial London dominated by the derelict Battersea Power Station, there's naff-all here until someone decides what to do with the old hulk and its surrounding domain. In the meantime, try registering for a new pooch at the Dogs' Home, buying veg at New Covent Garden Market or cycling around nearby Battersea Park. The Mason's Arms serves a decent beer.

Landmarks

- **Battersea Dogs' Home** • 4 Battersea Park Rd
- **Battersea Park Gasometers** • Queenstown Rd & Prince of Wales Dr
- **Battersea Power Station** • 188 Kirtling St

Libraries

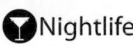

- **Battersea Park Library** • 309 Battersea Park Rd

Nightlife

- **Mason's Arms** • 169 Battersea Park Rd

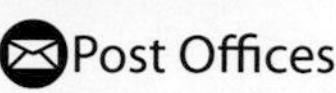

Post Offices

- **Battersea Park Road** • 20 Battersea Park Rd

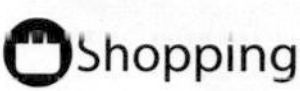

Shopping

- **London Recumbents** • Battersea Park

Supermarkets

- **Sainsbury's** • 326 Queenstown Rd

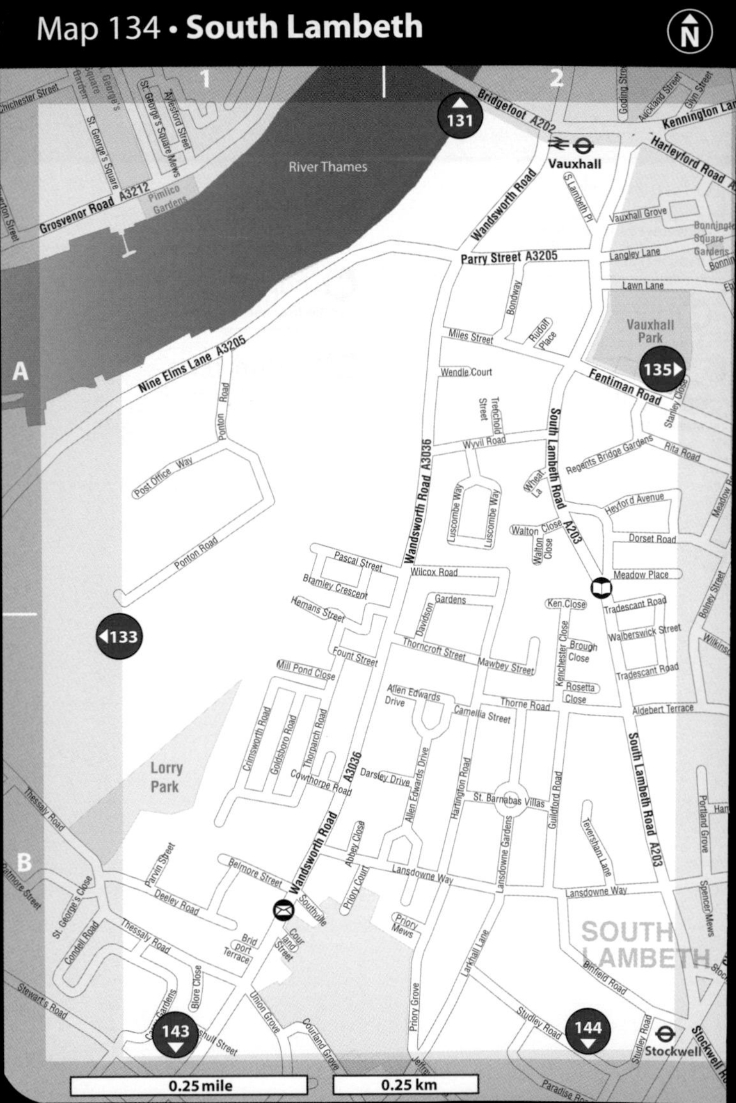

N
1
2
A
B
131
133
135
143
144
River Thames
Vauxhall
Bridgefoot A202
Kennington Lane
Harleyford Road
Grosvenor Road A3212
Pimlico Gardens
Chichester Street
St. George's Square
Aylesford Street
St. George's Square Mews
Wandsworth Road
S Lambeth Pl
Vauxhall Grove
Bonnington Square Gardens
Parry Street A3205
Langley Lane
Lawn Lane
Vauxhall Park
Bondway
Rudolf Place
Miles Street
Wendle Court
Fentiman Road
Stanley Close
Nine Elms Lane A3205
Ponton Road
Trenchold Street
Wyvil Road
South Lambeth Road
Regents Bridge Gardens
Rita Road
Post Office Way
Luscombe Way
Wheat La
Heyford Avenue
Walton Close
A203
Dorset Road
Wandsworth Road A3036
Pascal Street
Wilcox Road
Meadow Place
Bramley Crescent
Gardens
Davidson
Ken. Close
Tradescant Road
Hemans Street
Walberswick Street
Bolney Street
Thorncroft Street
Brough Close
Fount Street
Mawbey Street
Kenchester Close
Mill Pond Close
Rosetta Close
Allen Edwards Drive
Thorne Road
Camellia Street
Aldebert Terrace
Crimsworth Road
Goldsboro Road
Thorparch Road
Lorry Park
Cowthorpe Road
A3036
Darsley Drive
Hartington Road
St. Barnabas Villas
Guildford Road
Portland Grove
Thessaly Road
Abbey Close
Teversham Lane
Parvin Street
Belmore Street
Lansdowne Way
Lansdowne Gardens
Spencer Mews
Deeley Road
Priory Court
St. George's Close
Southville
Priory Mews
Condell Road
Courland Street
Bridport Terrace
Larkhall Lane
SOUTH LAMBETH
Binfield Road
Stewart's Road
Blore Close
Union Grove
Priory Grove
Studley Road
Courland Grove
Stockwell
Stockwell Road
Paradise Road
0.25 mile
0.25 km

South Lambeth

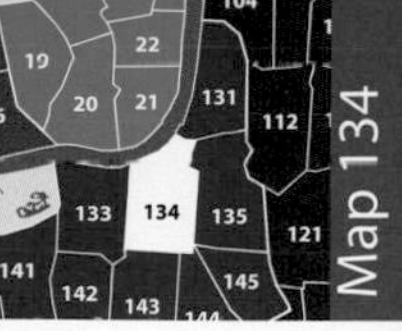

With an overground, tube, and extensive bus station, Vauxhall's southern counterpart is remarkably well connected. But it offers a mixed bag. Gritty backwater estates intermix with middle class townhouses and no-nonsense gay clubs. For pastel de nata like nobody's business, hit up Little Portugal on South London Road. Get into industrial fetish at Club Colosseum's Club Antichrist. Bite into a fois gras toastie at the Canton Arms and wash it down with beer and amateur comedy at The Cavendish Arms.

Coffee

- **Starbucks** • 2 South Lambeth Rd

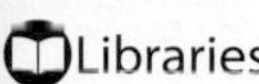

Libraries

- **South Lambeth Library** • 180 S Lambeth Rd

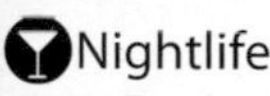

Nightlife

- **Bar Estrella** • 115 Old South Lambeth Rd
- **The Battersea Barge** • Nine Elms Ln
- **Club Colosseum** • 1 Nine Elms Ln
- **The Cavendish Arms** • 128 Hartington Rd
- **Fire** • 38 Parry St
- **Hoist** • 47 S Lambeth Rd
- **The Vauxhall Griffin** • 8 Wyvil Rd
- **Roller Disco @ Renaissance Rooms** • 126 S Lambeth Rd

Post Offices

- **South Lambeth** • 347 Wandsworth Rd

Restaurants

- **Bar Estrella** • 115 Old South Lambeth Rd
- **Canton Arms** • 177 S Lambeth Rd
- **Hot Stuff** • 19 Wilcox Rd

Shopping

- **Lassco House & Garden** • 30 Wandsworth Rd
- **New Covent Garden Market** • Nine Elms Lane

Supermarkets

- **Sainsbury's** • 62 Wandsworth Rd

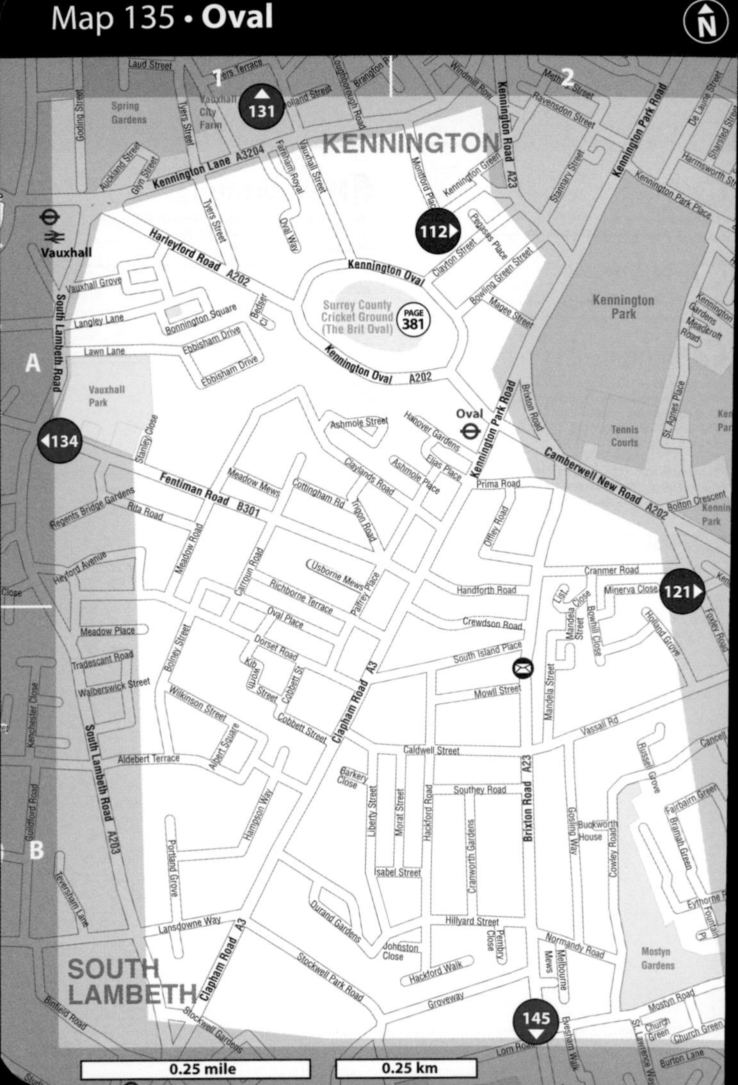
Map 135 • Oval
N
KENNINGTON
SOUTH LAMBETH
131
112
134
121
145
PAGE 381
Surrey County Cricket Ground (The Brit Oval)
Kennington Park
Tennis Courts
Vauxhall Park
Spring Gardens
Vauxhall City Farm
Mostyn Gardens
Vauxhall
Oval
Laud Street
Tyers Terrace
Holland Street
Loughborough Road
Brangton Road
Windmill Row
Kennington Road A23
Methley Street
Ravensdon Street
Kennington Park Road
De Laune Street
Sharsted Street
Harmsworth Street
Kennington Park Place
Goding Street
Tyers Street
Auckland Street
Glyn Street
Kennington Lane A3204
Farnham Royal
Vauxhall Street
Montford Place
Kennington Green
Stannary Street
Oval Way
Pegasus Place
Clayton Street
Bowling Green Street
Magee Street
Kennington Oval
Kennington Oval A202
Harleyford Road A202
Vauxhall Grove
South Lambeth Road
Langley Lane
Bonnington Square
Bedser Cl
Ebbisham Drive
Lawn Lane
Kennington Gardens
Meadcroft Road
St. Agnes Place
Brixton Road
Camberwell New Road A202
Bolton Crescent
Stanley Close
Ashmole Street
Hanover Gardens
Elias Place
Ashmole Place
Claylands Road
Meadow Mews
Cottingham Rd
Trigon Road
Fentiman Road B301
Regents Bridge Gardens
Rita Road
Meadow Road
Prima Road
Offley Road
Heyford Avenue
Carroun Road
Usborne Mews
Palfrey Place
Richborne Terrace
Oval Place
Cranmer Road
Handforth Road
Crewdson Road
Minerva Close
List
Mandela Close
Mandela Street
Bowhill Close
Holland Grove
Foxley Road
Meadow Place
Tradescant Road
Walberswick Street
Bolney Street
Dorset Road
Kibworth Street
Cobbett St
South Island Place
Mowll Street
Clapham Road A3
Kenchester Close
Wilkinson Street
Cobbett Street
Vassall Rd
Cancell
Albert Square
Aldebert Terrace
Caldwell Street
Russell Grove
Barkery Close
Southey Road
Guildford Road
South Lambeth Road A203
Hampson Way
Liberty Street
Morat Street
Hackford Road
Cranworth Gardens
Brixton Road A23
Gosling Way
Buckworth House
Cowley Road
Fairbairn Green
Bramah Green
Eythorne
Fountain Pl
Portland Grove
Teversham Lane
Isabel Street
Durand Gardens
Hillyard Street
Pembry Close
Lansdowne Way
Johnston Close
Normandy Road
Mews
Melbourne
Hackford Walk
Stockwell Park Road
Groveway
Binfield Road
Stockwell Gardens
Mostyn Road
Evesham Walk
St. Lawrence Way
Church Green
Burton Lane
Lorn Road
0.25 mile
0.25 km

Oval

Posh town houses rub shoulders somewhat uneasily with housing estates here, and there's no denying the walk from Oval Station can be dodgy, but if you're a fan of cricket, the presence of the Oval cricket ground more than makes up for it. When there's a match on, the area fills to the brim, but normally it's a modest and unimposing neighbourhood. Organic foodies delight in the Oval Farmers' Market and vegan ex-squat The Bonnington Café.

Coffee

- **Bonnington Cafe** • 11 Vauxhall Grove

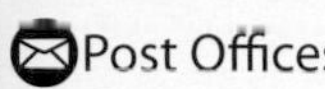

Post Offices

- **Brixton Road** • 82 Brixton Rd

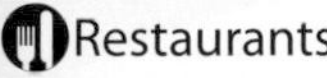

Restaurants

- **Adulis** • 44 Brixton Rd
- **The Bonnington Café** • 11 Vauxhall Grove
- **Kebab and Hamburger Bar** • 32 Clapham Rd

Nightlife

- **The Brown Derby** • 336 Kennington Park Rd
- **Fentiman Arms** • 64 Fentiman Rd
- **South London Pacific** • 340 Kennington Rd

Map 136 • Putney

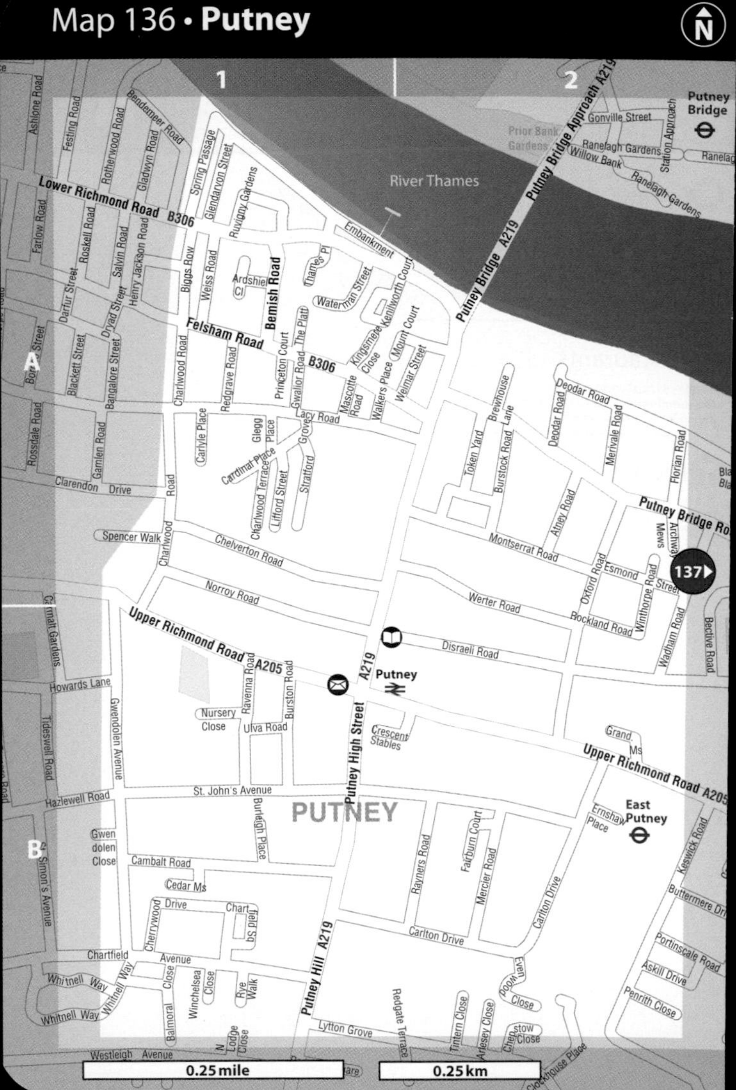

Putney

Putney has a bit of a bipolar personality disorder. On the one side, it's suburban middle England with its rugby and rowing types, on the other, it's increasingly vibrant and hip. The High Street's a bit genteel by day and young-and-up-for-it at night. Try Olé Restaurant and Bar or La Mancha for excellent Spanish, and Ma Goa for authentic Goan cuisine. For fab brunch head to celebrity chef's Wallace & Co or Moomba Bar & Kitchen.

Coffee

- **BB's Coffee and Muffins** • Putney High St & Chelverton Rd
- **Caffe Nero** • 95 Putney High St
- **Caffe Nero** • 112 Upper Richmond Rd
- **Costa** • 132 Putney High St
- **Pret A Manger** • 121 Putney High St
- **Starbucks** • 117 Putney High St

Libraries

- **Putney Library** • 5 Disraeli Rd

Movie Theaters

- **Odeon Putney** • 26 Putney High St

Nightlife

- **The Boathouse** • Brewhouse Lane
- **Duke's Head** • 8 Lower Richmond Rd
- **Jolly Gardeners** • 61 Lacy Rd
- **Star & Garter** • 4 Lower Richmond Rd

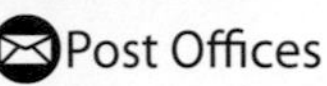

Post Offices

- **Putney** • 214 Upper Richmond Rd

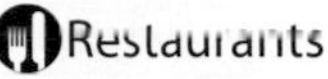

Restaurants

- **Chakalaka** • 136 Upper Richmond Rd
- **La Mancha 32** • Putney High St
- **Ma Goa** • 242 Upper Richmond Rd
- **Moomba Bar & Kitchen** • 5 Lacy Rd
- **Olé Restaurant and Bar** • 240 Upper Richmond Rd
- **Talad Thai** • 320 Upper Richmond Rd
- **Wallace & Co** • 146 Upper Richmond Rd

Supermarkets

- **Sainsbury's** • 2 Werter Rd
- **Waitrose** • Putney High St & Lacy Rd

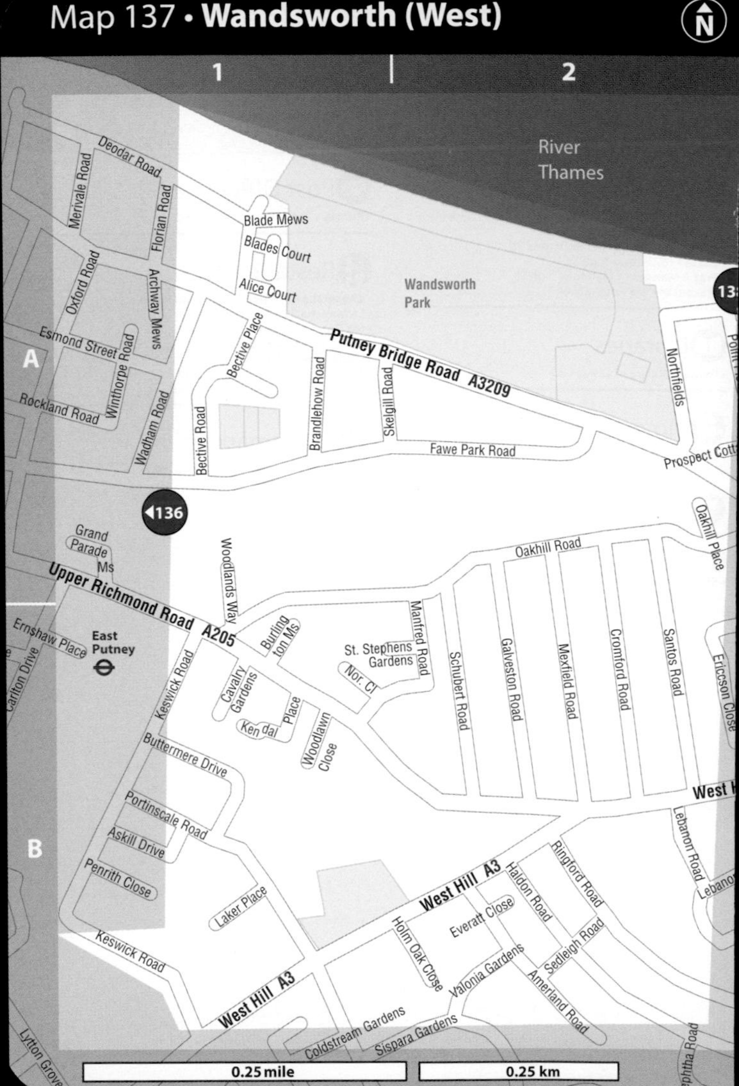
N
1
2
A
B
River Thames
Wandsworth Park
Deodar Road
Merivale Road
Florian Road
Blade Mews
Blades Court
Alice Court
Oxford Road
Archway Mews
Esmond Street
Winthorpe Road
Bective Place
Putney Bridge Road A3209
Brandlehow Road
Skelgill Road
Northfields
Rockland Road
Wadham Road
Bective Road
Fawe Park Road
Prospect Cott
136
Grand Parade Ms
Woodlands Way
Oakhill Road
Oakhill Place
Upper Richmond Road A205
East Putney
Ernshaw Place
Carlton Drive
Burlington Ms
St. Stephens Gardens
Manfred Road
Nor. Cl
Schubert Road
Galveston Road
Mexfield Road
Cromford Road
Santos Road
Ericcson Close
Keswick Road
Cavalry Gardens
Kendal Place
Woodlawn Close
Buttermere Drive
West H
Portinscale Road
Askill Drive
Penrith Close
Lebanon Road
Lebanon
Laker Place
West Hill A3
Haldon Road
Ringford Road
Everatt Close
Holm Oak Close
Keswick Road
Valonia Gardens
Sedleigh Road
Amerland Road
West Hill A3
Coldstream Gardens
Sispara Gardens
Lytton Grove
Nephtha Road
0.25 mile
0.25 km

Wandsworth (West)

Dissected by the busy Upper and Lower Richmond Roads, this bit of Wandsworth is a bit lifeless though pleasant enough. The pretty, riverside Wandsworth Park is a huge plus and heaves with locals with the first sniff of sunshine. Head to The Upper Lounge for a spot of liquid refreshment after a hard day's Frisbee chucking.

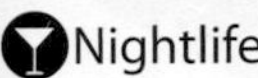

Nightlife

- **The Upper Lounge** • 26 Upper Richmond Rd

Restaurants

- **Miraj** • 123 Putney Bridge Road
- **Yia Mas** • 40 Upper Richmond Rd

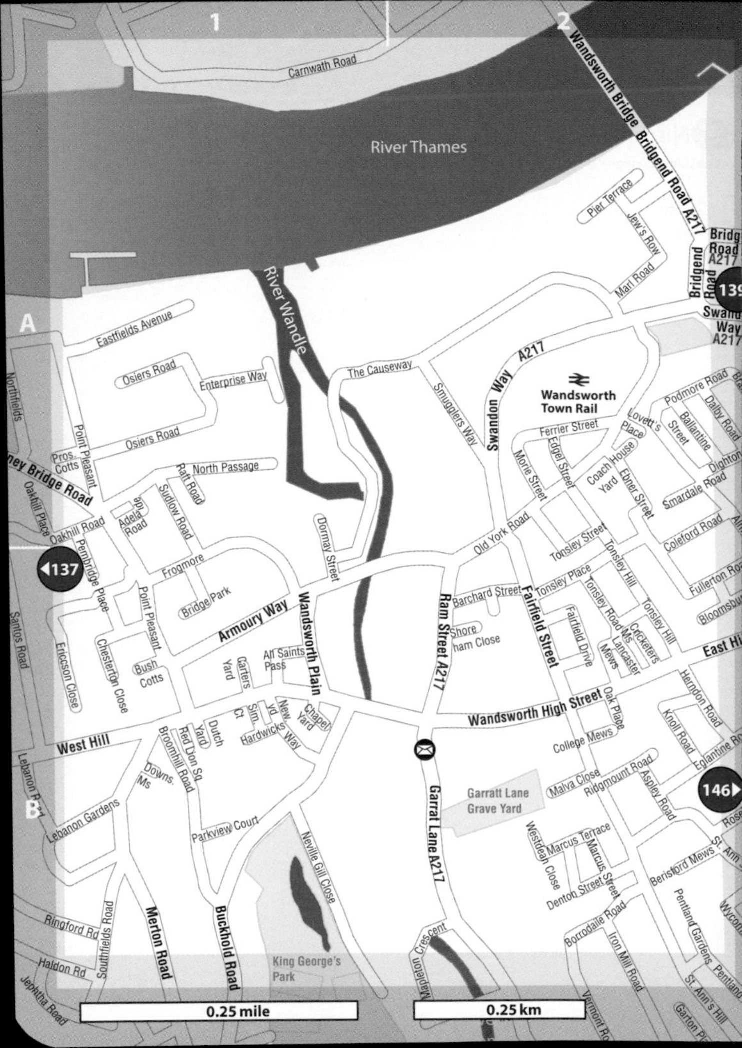

N

1
2
A
B

River Thames
River Wandle
Carnwath Road
Wandsworth Bridge
Bridgend Road A217
Bridgend Road A217
Bridgend Road
Swandon Way A217
Pier Terrace
Jew's Row
Marl Road
Swandon Way A217
Wandsworth Town Rail
Eastfields Avenue
Osiers Road
Enterprise Way
Osiers Road
Point Pleasant
Pros. Cotts
North Passage
Ratt Road
The Causeway
Smugglers Way
Ferrier Street
Lovett's Place
Podmore Road
Dalby Road
Ballantine Street
Dighton
Edgel Street
Morie Street
Coach House Yard
Ebner Street
Smardale Road
Coleford Road
Fullerton Ro
Bloomsbu
Wandsworth Bridge Road
Oakhill Place
Oakhill Road
Adela Road
Ide
Sudlow Road
Dormay Street
Old York Road
Tonsley Street
Tonsley Hill
Tonsley Place
Tonsley Road
Tonsley Hill
Pembridge Place
Frogmore
Bridge Park
Point Pleasant
Armoury Way
Wandsworth Plain
Ram Street A217
Barchard Street
Shore
ham Close
Fairfield Street
Fairfield Drive
Ms
Mews
Lancaster
Cricketers
East Hi
Santos Road
Ericsson Close
Chesterton Close
Bush Cotts
Carters Yard
All Saints Pass
Wandsworth High Street
Oak Place
Herndon Road
Knoll Road
Eglantine Ro
West Hill
Broomhill Road
Red Lion Sq
Yard
Dutch Yard
Sim. Ct
Yd
New Way
Hardwicks
Chapel Yard
College Mews
Malva Close
Ridgmount Road
Aspley Road
Garratt Lane Grave Yard
Garrat Lane A217
Lebanon Road
Downs. Ms
Lebanon Gardens
Parkview Court
Neville Gill Close
Westdean Close
Marcus Terrace
Marcus Street
Denton Street
Borrodaile Road
Iron Mill Road
Beristord Mews
Pentland Gardens
St. Ann
Rose
Wycom
Pentland
St. Ann's Hill
Garton Pl
Vermont Ro
Ringford Rd
Southfields Road
Haldon Rd
Jephtha Road
Merton Road
Buckhold Road
King George's Park
Mapleton Crescent

137
139
146

0.25 mile
0.25 km

Wandsworth (Central)

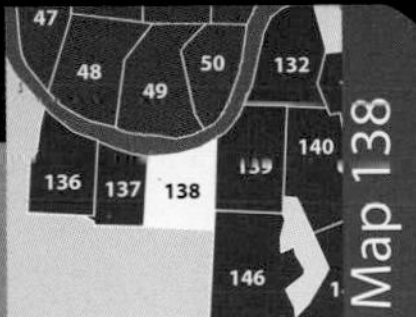

This is East Wandsworth's poorer, uglier cousin—and you've got to feel sorry for it. It's got a drab shopping centre and a four-lane traffic system brings noise and air pollution. On the plus side, plenty of chain stores (Gap, Uniqlo etc.) and a Cineworld make life a little easier. To get away from it all, hibernate in the Old York Road. For the best Nepalese food in London, hit Kathmandu Valley.

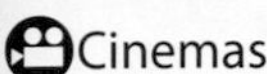

Cinemas

- **Cineworld Wandsworth** • Wandsworth High St & Ram St

Coffee

- **Caffe Nero** • Southside Shopping Centre
- **Coffee Republic** • Wandsworth High St

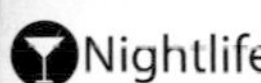

Nightlife

- **The Cat's Back** • 88 Point Pleasant
- **GJ's** • 89 Garratt Lane
- **The Queen Adelaide** • 35 Putney Bridge Rd

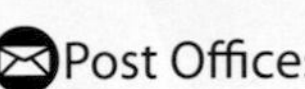

Post Offices

- **Wandsworth** • 1 Arndale Walk

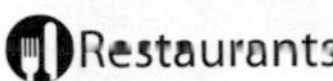

Restaurants

- **Brady's** • 513 Old York Rd
- **Kathmandu Valley** • 5 West Hill

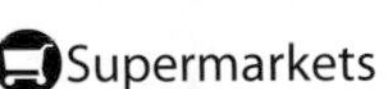

Supermarkets

- **Iceland** • Wandsworth High St & Buckhold Rd
- **Sainsbury's** • 45 Garratt Ln
- **Waitrose** • 66 Wandsworth High St

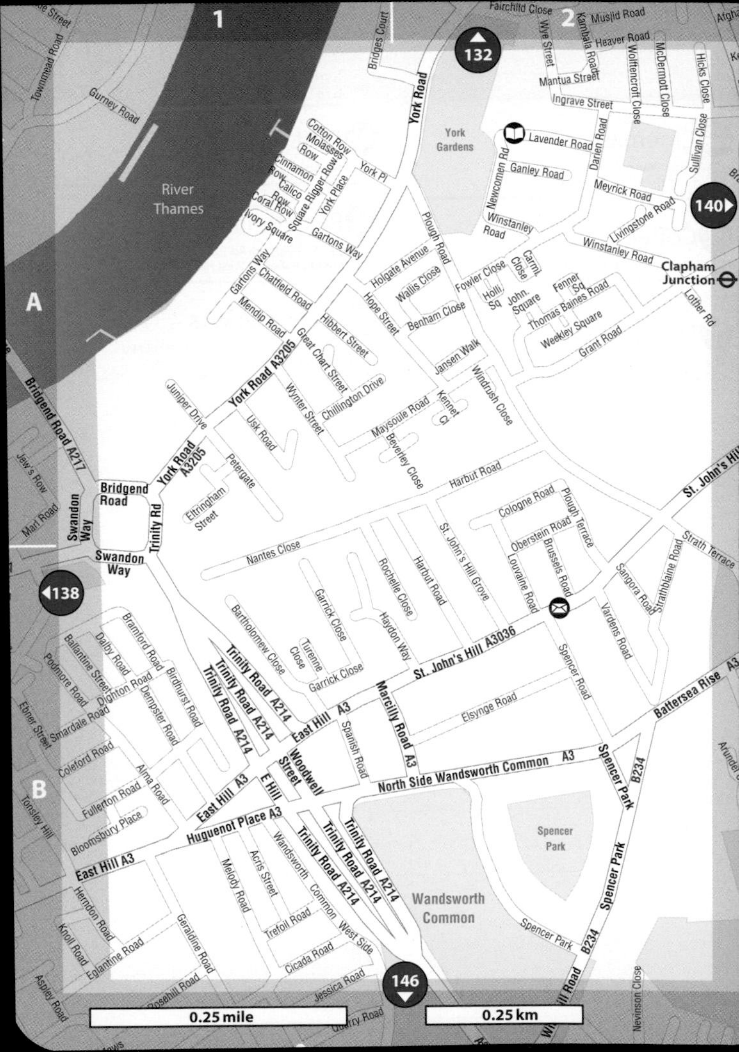

Map 139 • Wandsworth (East)

Wandsworth (East)

With London's new Overground network and Clapham Junction on its doorstep, this corner of Wandsworth, including what locals call 'the Toast Rack' on East Hill, is becoming more gentrified everyday. You'll hear your share of 'rah's at Powder Keg Diplomacy, with its upscale gastro fare and nod to colonial Britain, while yummy mummies stuff their cake holes at Cake Boy and practice their French at Gazette. Stay true to the neighbourhood's roots with a less than picturesque view of the Thames at The Waterfront.

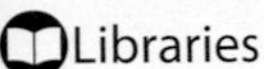

Libraries

- **York Gardens Library** • 34 Lavender Rd

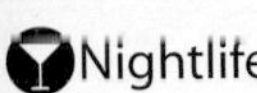

Nightlife

- **The Cat's Back** • 88 Point Pleasant
- **GJ's** • 89 Garratt Lane
- **Powder Keg Diplomacy** • 147 St Johns Hill
- **The Waterfront** • Juniper Dr

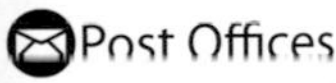

Post Offices

- **St Johns Hill** • 7 St John's Hill

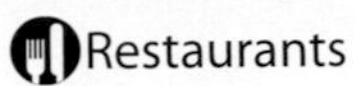

Restaurants

- **The Fish Club** • 189 St John's Hill
- **Gazette** • 79 Chatfield Rd
- **Steam** • 55 E Hill

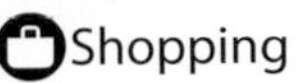

Shopping

- **Cake Boy** • 2 Kingfisher House, Battersea Reach

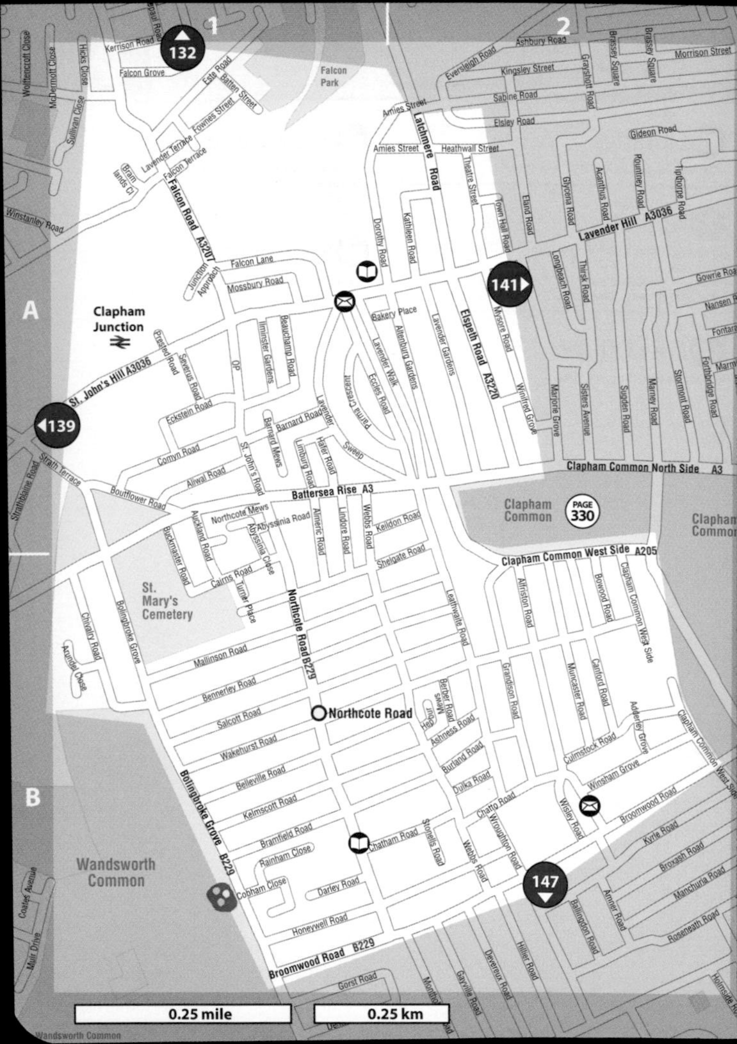

N
132
141
139
147
PAGE 330
Clapham Junction
Falcon Park
Clapham Common
St. Mary's Cemetery
Wandsworth Common
Northcote Road
Battersea Rise A3
St. John's Hill A3036
Falcon Road A3207
Lavender Hill A3036
Clapham Common North Side A3
Clapham Common West Side A205
Northcote Road B229
Bolingbroke Grove B229
Broomwood Road B229
Latchmere Road
Elspeth Road A3220
0.25 mile
0.25 km

Clapham Junction / Northcote Rd

We have a newfound sense of respect for Clapham Junction after it rose like a determined phoenix from the ashes of the summer 2011 riots. Suffering extensive devastation from looters, the neighbourhood dusted itself off with help of volunteers from across the capital and was back in business almost instantly. Seeing the Party Superstores open again after nearly burning to the ground is a particular sight for sore eyes. All fancy dress party goers can breathe a sigh of relief.

Coffee

- **Caffe Nero** • 20 St John's Rd
- **Caffe Nero** • 21 Battersea Rise
- **Starbucks** • 33 Northcote Rd

Landmarks

- **Northcote Road** • Northcote Rd

Libraries

- **Battersea Library** • 265 Lavender Hill
- **Northcote Library** • 155 Northcote Rd

Nightlife

- **adventure bar and lounge** • 91 Battersea Rise
- **B@1** • 85 Battersea Rise
- **Jongleurs (Battersea)** • 49 Lavender Gardens
- **The Peacock** • 148 Falcon Rd

Post Offices

- **Alfriston Road** • 99 Alfriston Rd
- **Battersea** • 202 Lavender Hill

Restaurants

- **Cafe Parisienne** • 225 Lavender Hill
- **I Sapori di Stefano Cavallini** • 146 Northcote Rd

Shopping

- **Anita's Vintage Fashion Fair** • Battersea Arts Centre, Lavender Hill
- **Dub Vendor** • 274 Lavender Hill
- **EF Russ** • 101 Battersea Rise
- **Huttons** • 29 Northcote Rd
- **Kiehls** • 20 Northcote Rd
- **Party Superstores** • 268 Lavender Hill
- **QT Toys and Games** • 90 Northcote Rd
- **Space NK Apothecary** • 46 Northcote Rd
- **Sweaty Betty** • 136 Northcote Rd
- **TK Maxx** • St John's Rd & Barnard Rd
- **Traid** • 28 St John's Rd
- **Vintage Market Place** • Battersea Arts Centre
- **Whole Foods Market** • 305 Lavender Hill

Supermarkets

- **ASDA** • 204 Lavender Hill
- **Whole Foods Market** • 305 Lavender Hill
- **Sainsbury's** • Clapham Junction Shopping Ctr

Map 141 • Battersea (South)
N
1
2
Battersea Park
PAGE 326
133
142
132
140
A
B
Battersea Park Boating Lake
Queen's Circus
Battersea Park
Queenstown Road (Battersea)
Falcon Park
Prince of Wales Drive A3220
Prince of Wales Drive
Carriage Drive South
Albert Bridge Road A3031
Maskelyne Close
Watford Close
Petworth Street
Wendle Square
Rosenau Road
A3220
Kite Yard
Rosenau Crescent
Cambridge Road A3220
Foxmore Street
Kersley Mews
Kersley Street
Banbury Street
Colestown Street
Latchmere Street
A3205
Atherton Street
Frere Street
Soudan Road
Kassala Road
Cyril Mansions
Beechmore Road
Warriner Gardens
Brynmaer Road
Battersea Park Road
Alexandra Avenue
Forfar Road
Macduff Road
Cupar Road
Lurline Gardens
Elmwood Court
Meath Street
Newtown Street
Rawson Street
Alfreda Street
Strasburg Road
Ravenet Street
Roydon Street
Chesney Street
Parkside Road
Harpsden Street
Charlotte Despard Avenue
Francis Chichester Way
Austin Road
Dagnall Street
Millgrove St
Kennard St
Anerley St
Orkney St
Blondel Street
Astle Street
Henley Street
Longhedge Street
Culvert Road
Rowditch Lane
Queenstown Mews
St James Grove
Burns Road
Matthews Street
Joubert Street
Odger Street
Freedom Street
Reform Street
Sheepcote Lane
Knowsley Road
Poyntz Road
Shellwood Road
Cranleigh Mews
Latchmere Road
Culvert Place
Broughton Street
St. Philip Square
Eversleigh Road
Wycliffe Road
Caroline Place
Stanley Grove
Emu Road
Prairie Street
Ingelow Road
Queenstown Road A3216
St. Philip Street
Tennyson Street
Montefiore Street
Thackeray Road
Bewick Street
Wickersley Road
Birley Street
Tyneham Road
Holden Street
Ashbury Road
Grayshott Road
Brassey Square
Morrison Street
Kingsley Street
Sabine Road
Elsley Road
Evesham Way
Dunston Road
Ashley Crescent
Robertson Street
Keith Connor Close
Heather Close
Bev Callender Close
Willard Street
Wandsworth Road
Amies Street
Heathwall Street
Theatre Street
Town Hall Road
Eland Road
Glycena Road
Acanthus Road
Pountney Road
Gideon Road
Shirley Grove
Woodmere Close
Basnett Road
Audley Close
Abberley Mews
Turnchapel Mews
Marmion Mews
Craven Mews
Crosland Place
Garfield Road
Garfield Mews
Lavender Hill A3036
Tipthorpe Road
Rush Hill Road
Rush Hill Mews
Taybridge Road
Freke Road
Victoria Rise
Cedars Road A3216
Dorothy Road
Kathleen Road
Longbeach Road
Thirsk Road
Gowrie Road
Nansen Road
Fontarabia Road
Marmion Road
Wix's Lane
Bakery Pl
Elspeth Road A3220
Mysore Road
Lavender Gardens
Altenburg Gardens
Lavender Walk
Eccles Road
Parma Crescent
Lavender Sweep
Beauchamp Road
Ilminster Gardens
Barnard Rd
Barnard Mews
Limburg Road
Hafer Road
Winifred Gro
Marjorie Grove
Sisters Avenue
Sugden Road
Marney Road
Stormont Road
Forthbridge Road
Meteor Street
Tregarvon Road
Jedburgh Street
Lyncott Crescent
Willoughby Mews
Cedars Mews
Victoria Mews
Wilderness
Clapham Common North Side A3
Battersea Rise A3
A205
0.25 mile
0.25 km

Battersea (South)

Apart from the occasional house party, few have reason to go to Battersea South. You either live there, congratulating yourself on your nice Victorian conversion, or you pass through on the way to Clapham or one of the livelier bits of Battersea. The 'action' happens around Lavender Hill. Lost Angel is an eccentrically fabulous boozer that would rather be a mile east or west. Have a Coffee Affair to remember near Queenstown Road Station.

Coffee

- **Captain Corelli** • 132 Battersea Park Rd

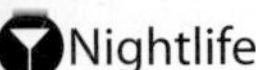

Nightlife

- **Halo** • 317 Battersea Park Rd
- **The Lost Angel** • 339 Battersea Park Rd

Restaurants

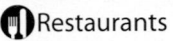

- **The Lavender** • 171 Lavender Hill

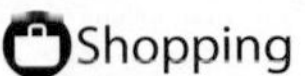

Shopping

- **Avalon Comics** • 143 Lavender Hill
- **Battersea Car Boot Sale** • 401 Battersea Park Rd
- **Comet Miniatures** • 44 Lavender Hill

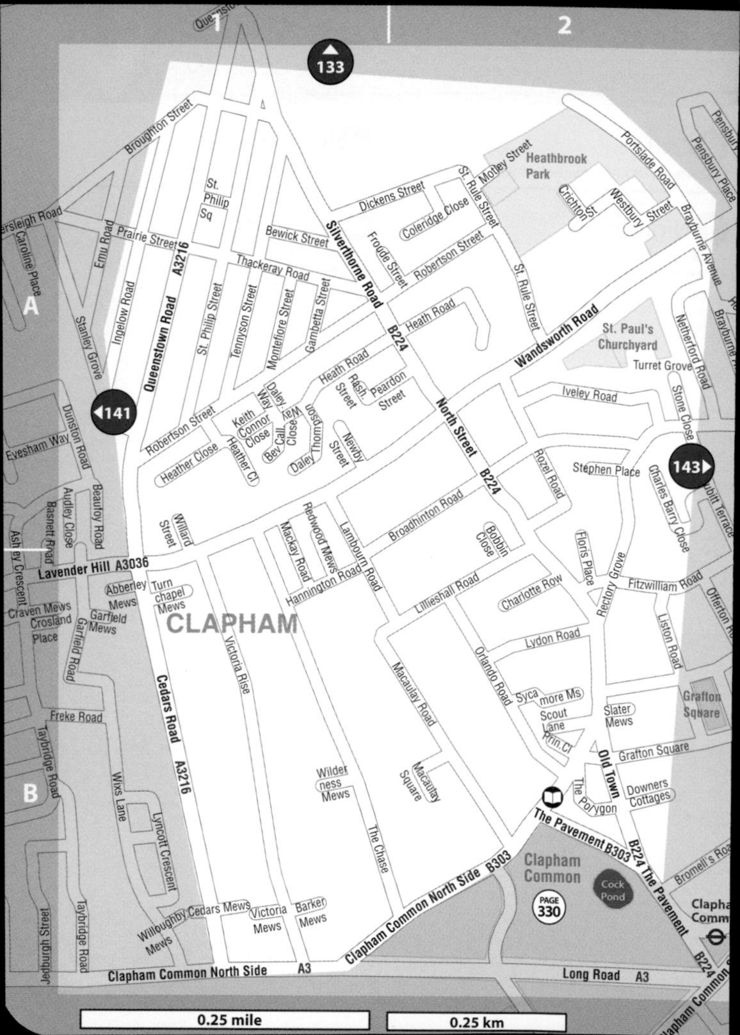
N
1
2
A
B
133
141
143
CLAPHAM
Queenstown Road A3216
Broughton Street
Prairie Street
Emu Road
Caroline Place
Stanley Grove
Ingelow Road
St. Philip Sq
St. Philip Street
Tennyson Street
Montefiore Street
Gambetta Street
Thackeray Road
Bewick Street
Silverthorne Road
B224
Dickens Street
Froude Street
Coleridge Close
Robertson Street
St. Rule Street
Motley Street
Heathbrook Park
Crichton St
Westbury Street
Portslade Road
Pensbury Place
Brayburne Avenue
Heath Road
Wandsworth Road
St. Paul's Churchyard
Turret Grove
Netherford Road
Iveley Road
Stone Close
Stephen Place
Charles Barry Close
North Street
B224
Rozel Road
Rash. Street
Peardon Street
Daley Way
Keith Connor Close
Way Close
Bev Call. Close
Daley Thompson
Newby Street
Robertson Street
Heather Close
Heather Cl
Evesham Way
Dunston Road
Audley Close
Beaufoy Road
Basnett Road
Ashley Crescent
Willard Street
Lavender Hill A3036
Redwood Mews
Mackay Road
Lambourn Road
Hannington Road
Broadhinton Road
Bobbin Close
Floris Place
Rectory Grove
Fitzwilliam Road
Offerton Road
Cubitt Terrace
Abberley Mews
Turn chapel Mews
Craven Mews
Crosland Place
Garfield Mews
Garfield Road
Lillieshall Road
Charlotte Row
Lydon Road
Liston Road
Orlando Road
Sycamore Ms
Scout Lane
Prin.Cl
Slater Mews
Grafton Square
Victoria Rise
Macaulay Road
Macaulay Square
Cedars Road A3216
Freke Road
Taybridge Road
Wixs Lane
Lyncott Crescent
Wilderness Mews
The Chase
Old Town
The Polygon
Downers Cottages
The Pavement B303
B224 The Pavement
Clapham Common
Cock Pond
PAGE 330
Bromell's Road
Clapham Common North Side B303
Willoughby Mews
Cedars Mews
Victoria Mews
Barker Mews
Jedburgh Street
Clapham Common North Side A3
Long Road A3
B224
0.25 mile
0.25 km

Clapham Old Town

The more genteel side of Clapham, Old Town hosts some fine restaurants (Trinity, Mooli), good watering-holes (The Prince of Wales, Frog and Forget-Me-Not), and one of London's best butchers (Moen's), all bordered by the green of Clapham Common. If you need more, and can resist fish & chips with free banter (Benny's), head to Queenstown Road for further classy dining establishments.

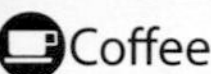

Coffee

- **The Roastery** • 789 Wandsworth Rd
- **Starbucks** • 40 Old Town

Libraries

- **Clapham Library** • 1 Clapham Common North Side

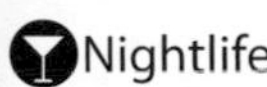

Nightlife

- **Frog and Forget-Me-Not** • 32 The Pavement
- **Lost Society** • 697 Wandsworth Rd
- **Prince of Wales** • 38 Clapham Old Town
- **Rose & Crown** • 2 The Polygon
- **The Sun** • 47 Old Town

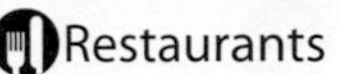

Restaurants

- **Benny's** • 30 North St
- **Mooli** • 36 Old Town
- **Tom Ilic** • 123 Queenstown Rd
- **Trinity** • 4 The Polygon

Shopping

- **M. Moen & Sons** • 24 The Pavement
- **Puppet Planet** • 787 Wandsworth Rd

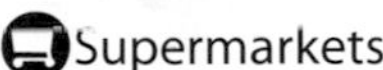

Supermarkets

- **Sainsbury's** • 646 Wandsworth Rd

Map 143 • Clapham High Street

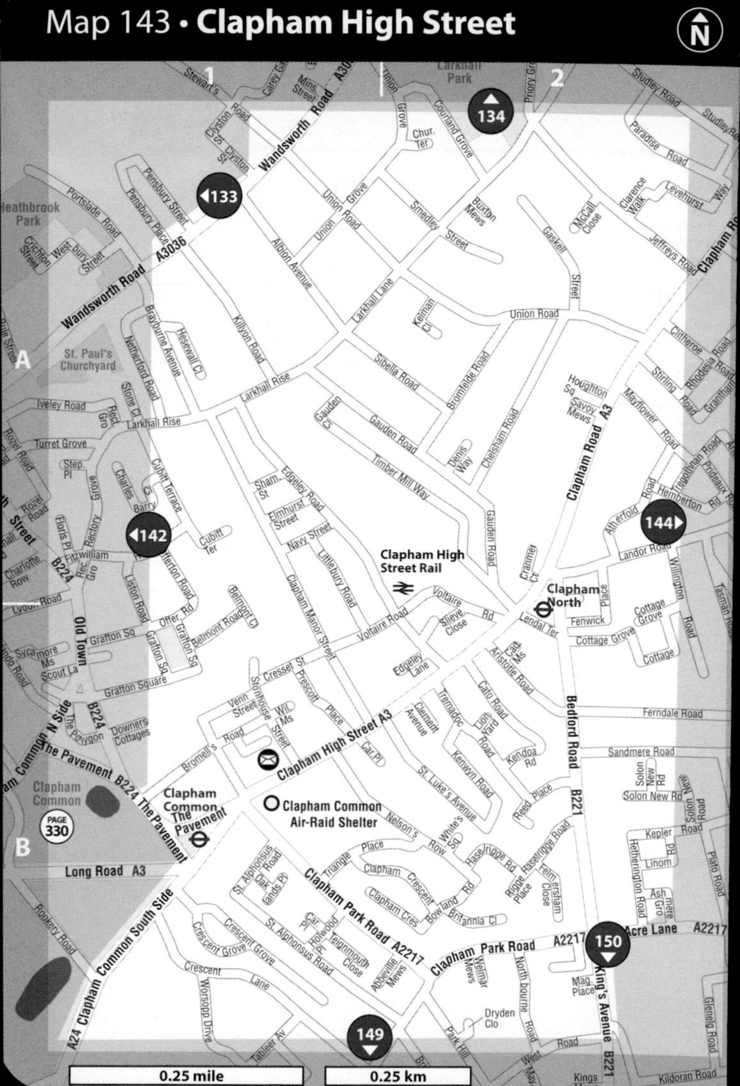

134
133
142
144
150
149
PAGE 330

Clapham High Street

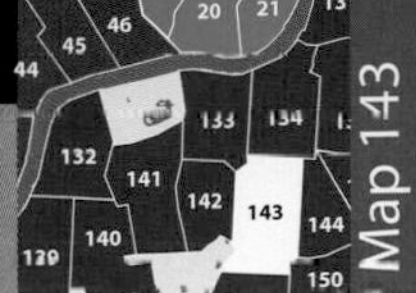

Clapham is a microcosm of Cath Kidston mummies and their token gay best friends—watch them jog and brunch around the common in all weather. Stock up on al fresco goodies at Esca, neck a mojito at Buena Vista, and gorge on sushi at Tsunami or pizza at San Marco. Whatever you do, do not—we repeat, DO NOT—set foot in Infernos. We will find out and we will judge you.

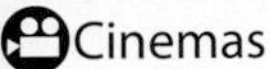

Cinemas

- **Clapham Picturehouse** • 76 Venn St

Coffee

- **Café Delight** • 19 Clapham High St
- **Caffe Nero** • 186 Clapham High St

Landmarks

- **Clapham Common Air-Raid Shelter** • Clapham High St

Nightlife

- **The Alexandra** • 14 Clapham Common South Side
- **Bread & Roses** • 68 Clapham Manor St
- **Buena Vista** • 19 Landor Rd
- **The Clapham North** • 409 Clapham Rd
- **The Falcon** • 33 Bedford Rd
- **Green & Blue** • 20 Bedford Rd
- **Infernos** • 146 Clapham High St
- **Inn Clapham** • 15 The Pavement
- **The Loft** • 67 Clapham High St
- **The Railway** • 18 Clapham High St
- **Two Brewers** • 114 Clapham High St
- **The White House** • 65 Clapham Park Rd

Post Offices

- **Clapham Common** • 161 Clapham High St

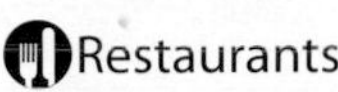

Restaurants

- **Alba Pizzeria** • 3 Bedford Rd
- **Café Wanda** • 153 Clapham High St
- **The Fish Club** • 57 Clapham High St
- **Gastro** • 67 Venn St
- **The Pepper Tree** • 19 Clapham Common South Side
- **The Rapscallion** • 75 Venn St
- **San Marco Pizzeria** • 126 Clapham High St
- **Tsunami** • 5 Voltaire Rd

Shopping

- **Apex Cycles** • 40 Clapham High St
- **Esca** • 160 Clapham High St
- **M. Moen & Sons** • 24 The Pavement
- **Paws** • 62 Clapham High St
- **Today's Living Health Store** • 92 Clapham High St

Supermarkets

- **Iceland** • 4 The Pavement
- **Sainsbury's** • 133 Clapham High St
- **Sainsbury's** • 33 Clapham High St

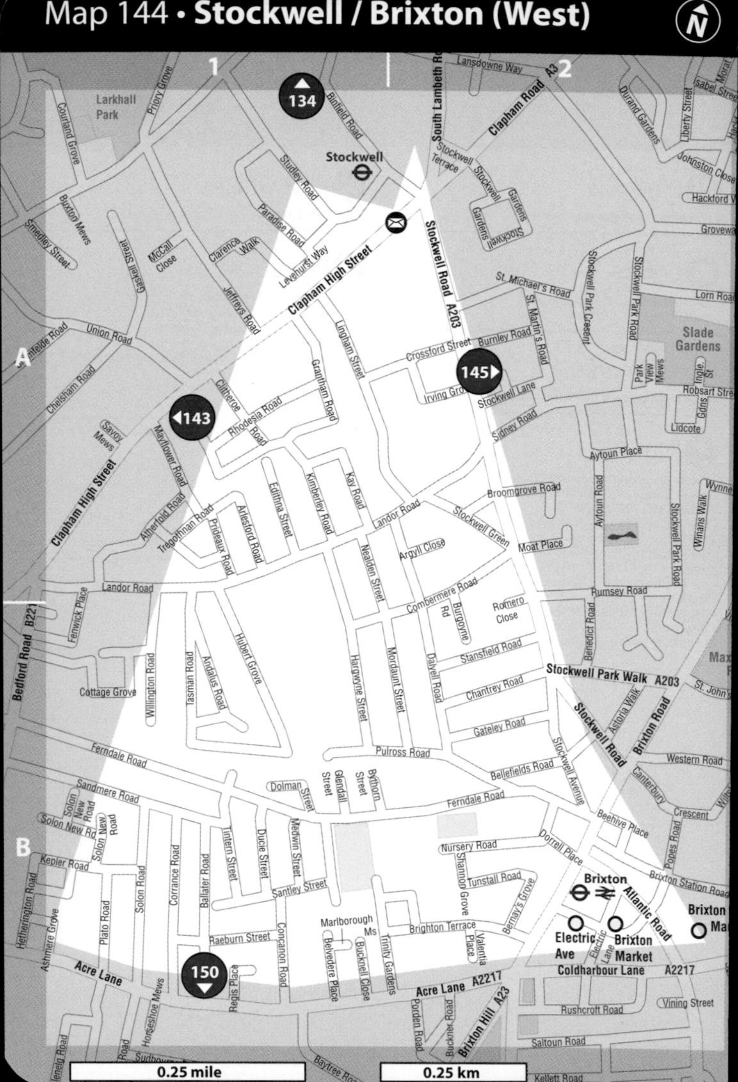

Map 144 • Stockwell / Brixton (West)
N
1
2
A
B
134
143
145
150
Larkhall Park
Courland Grove
Priory Grove
Binfield Road
Stockwell
Studley Road
Paradise Road
Levehurst Way
Clarence Walk
McCall Close
Gaskell Street
Buxton Mews
Smedley Street
Jeffreys Road
Clapham High Street
Union Road
Chelsham Road
Savoy Mews
Mayflower Road
Clitheroe Road
Rhodesia Road
Grantham Road
Lingham Street
South Lambeth Rd
Lansdowne Way
A3
Clapham Road
Stockwell Terrace
Stockwell Gardens
Stockwell Road A203
St. Michael's Road
St. Martin's Road
Crossford Street
Burnley Road
Irving Gro
Stockwell Lane
Sidney Road
Durand Gardens
Liberty Street
Isabel Street
Johnston Close
Hackford
Stockwell Park Crescent
Stockwell Park Road
Lorn Road
Slade Gardens
Park View Mews
Ingle. St
Robsart Street
Lidcote Gdns
Aytoun Place
Aytoun Road
Broomgrove Road
Stockwell Green
Moat Place
Winans Walk
Wynne
Landor Road
Edithna Street
Kimberley Road
Kay Road
Arlesford Road
Prideaux Road
Tregothnan Road
Atherfold Road
Argyll Close
Nealden Street
Combermere Road
Burgoyne Rd
Romero Close
Rumsey Road
Benedict Road
Stansfield Road
Stockwell Park Walk A203
Chantrey Road
Gateley Road
Astoria Walk
Brixton Road
Stockwell Road
St. John's
Western Road
Canterbury Crescent
Fenwick Place
Bedford Road B221
Cottage Grove
Willington Road
Tasman Road
Andalus Road
Hubert Grove
Hargwyne Street
Mordaunt Street
Dalyell Road
Pulross Road
Bellefields Road
Stockwell Avenue
Ferndale Road
Dolman Street
Glendall Street
Bythorn Street
Beehive Place
Popes Road
Sandmere Road
Solon New Road
Solon New Rd
Kepler Road
Tintern Street
Ducie Street
Medwin Street
Santley Street
Nursery Road
Shannon Grove
Tunstall Road
Dorrell Place
Bernay's Grove
Brixton
Atlantic Road
Brixton Station Road
Hetherington Road
Ashmere Grove
Plato Road
Solon Road
Corrance Road
Ballater Road
Raeburn Street
Concanon Road
Marlborough Ms
Belvedere Place
Bucknell Close
Trinity Gardens
Brighton Terrace
Valentia Place
Electric Ave
Electric Lane
Brixton Market
Coldharbour Lane A2217
Acre Lane
Acre Lane A2217
Regis Place
Horseshoe Mews
Porden Road
Buckner Road
Brixton Hill A23
Vining Street
Rushcroft Road
Saltoun Road
Kellett Road
Glenelg Road
Baytree Road
0.25 mile
0.25 km

Stockwell / Brixton (West)

Lift up the roof of Brixton Village Market on Thursday, Friday, and Saturday nights and underneath you will find rows of arcades teaming with all species of hipster. After years of almost being cool, this microcosmic neighbourhood beneath the train tracks has officially earned Brixton the title of hippest place in town. With so much to do, no two nights out are the same. Binge on pizza at Franco Manco; dumplings at Mama Lan; take in some live music at Agile Rabbit; gelato at Lab G, and cocktails at Seven at Brixton.

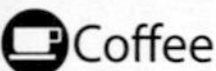

Coffee

- **Federation Coffee** • 77–78 Brixton Village Market
- **Rosie's Deli Cafe** • 14 Market Row

Landmarks

- **Brixton Market** • Electric Ave & Electric Ln
- **Brixton Village Market** • Coldharbour Ln
- **Electric Avenue** • Electric Ave

Nightlife

- **Duke of Edinburgh** • 204 Ferndale Rd
- **Plan B** • 410 Brixton Rd
- **The Prince** • 469 Brixton Rd
- **The Rest Is Noise** • 442 Brixton Rd
- **Seven at Brixton** • 7 Market Row
- **The Swan** • 215 Clapham Rd

Post Offices

- **Stockwell** • 225 Clapham Rd

Restaurants

- **Agile Rabbit** • 24–25 Coldharbour Ln
- **Bellantoni's** • 81 Granville Arcade
- **Breads Etcetera** • 88 Brixton Village Market
- **Brixton Cornercopia** • 65 Coldharbour Ln
- **Casa Morita** • 9 Market Row
- **Franco Manca** • 4 Electric Ln
- **Honest Burgers** • 12 Brixton Village
- **Mama Lan** • 18 Brixton Village Market
- **Speedy Noodle** • 506 Brixton Rd
- **SW9 Bar Cafe** • 11 Dorrell Pl

Shopping

- **A&C Co Continental Grocers** • 3 Atlantic Rd
- **Brixi** • 7 Second Ave
- **Funchal Bakery** • 141–143 Stockwell Rd
- **Lisa Stickley London** • 74 Landor Rd
- **The Old Post Office Bakery** • 76 Landor Rd

Supermarkets

- **Iceland** • 441 Brixton Rd
- **Iceland** • 314 Clapham Rd
- **Sainsbury's** • 425 Brixton Rd
- **Tesco** • 330 Brixton Rd

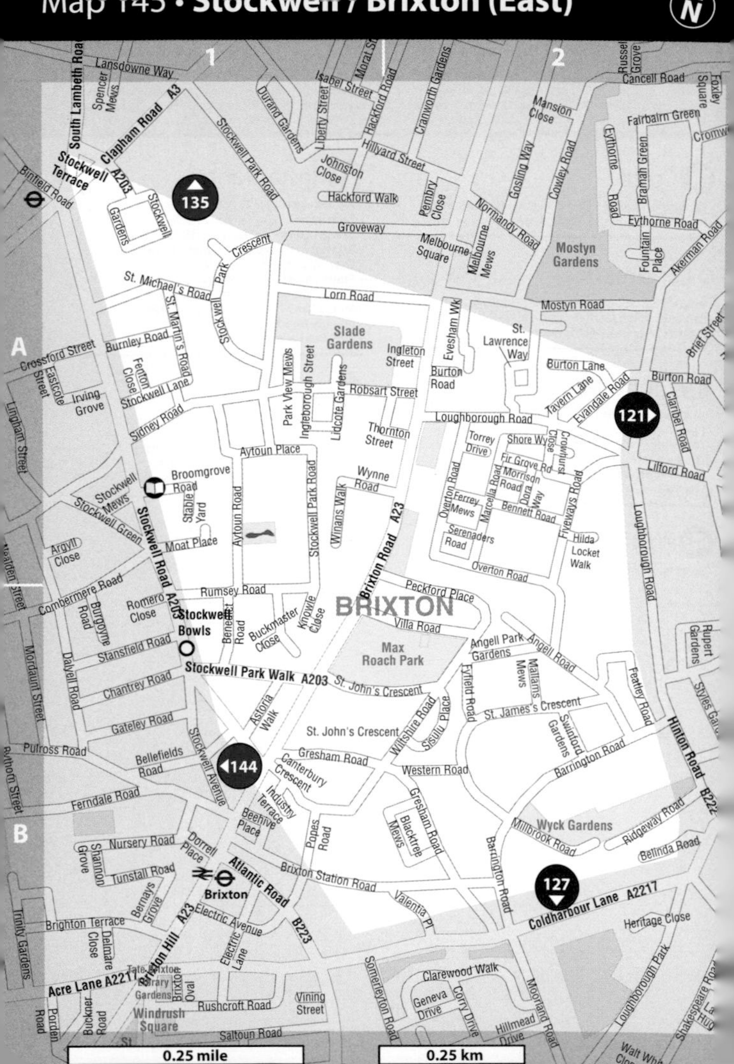

Map 145 • Stockwell / Brixton (East)
N
1
2
A
B
135
121
144
127
BRIXTON
South Lambeth Road
Lansdowne Way
Spencer Mews
Clapham Road A3
Stockwell Terrace
A203
Binfield Road
Stockwell Gardens
Stockwell Park Road
Durand Gardens
Isabel Street
Liberty Street
Morat St
Hackford Road
Cranworth Gardens
Hillyard Street
Johnston Close
Hackford Walk
Pembry Close
Groveway
Melbourne Square
Melbourne Mews
Normandy Road
Gosling Way
Cowley Road
Mansion Close
Russell Grove
Cancell Road
Foxley Square
Fairbairn Green
Cromwell
Eythorne Road
Bramah Green
Fountain Place
Akerman Road
Mostyn Gardens
Mostyn Road
Stockwell Park Crescent
St. Michael's Road
St. Martin's Road
Lorn Road
Slade Gardens
Ingleton Street
Evesham Wk
St. Lawrence Way
Burton Road
Burton Lane
Tavern Lane
Evandale Road
Burton Road
Brief Street
Crossford Street
Eastcote Street
Burnley Road
Fenton Close
Stockwell Lane
Irving Grove
Lingham Street
Sidney Road
Park View Mews
Ingleborough Street
Lidcote Gardens
Robsart Street
Thornton Street
Loughborough Road
Torrey Drive
Shore Wy
Crowhurst Close
Claribel Road
Aytoun Place
Wynne Road
Fir Grove Rd
Morrison Road
Dora Way
Fiveways Road
Lilford Road
Broomgrove Road
Stockwell Mews
Stockwell Green
Stable Yard
Aytoun Road
Stockwell Park Road
Winans Walk
A23
Overton Road
Ferrey Mews
Marcella Road
Bennett Road
Serenaders Road
Hilda Locket Walk
Loughborough Road
Argyll Close
Moat Place
Brixton Road
Overton Road
Stockwell Road
Combermere Road
Rumsey Road
Peckford Place
Burgoyne Road
Romero Close
Stockwell Bowls
Benedict Road
Buckmaster Close
Knowle Close
Villa Road
Max Roach Park
Angell Park Gardens
Angell Road
Mallams Mews
Rupert Gardens
Stansfield Road
Dalyell Road
Mordaunt Street
Stockwell Park Walk A203
St. John's Crescent
Fyfield Road
Featley Road
Styles Gardens
Chantrey Road
Gateley Road
Astoria Walk
Wiltshire Road
Sisulu Place
St. James's Crescent
Swinford Gardens
Hinton Road
St. John's Crescent
Pulross Road
Bellefields Road
Stockwell Avenue
Gresham Road
Canterbury Crescent
Western Road
Barrington Road
Rythorn Street
Ferndale Road
Industry Terrace
Beehive Place
Popes Road
Gresham Road
Blacktree Mews
Wyck Gardens
Millbrook Road
Ridgeway Road
B222
Shannon Grove
Nursery Road
Dorrell Place
Belinda Road
Tunstall Road
Atlantic Road
Brixton Station Road
Barrington Road
Brixton
Bernays Grove
Valentia Pl
Coldharbour Lane A2217
Heritage Close
Brighton Terrace
Trinity Gardens
Delmare Close
Electric Avenue
B223
Brixton Hill
Electric Lane
Somerleyton Road
Clarewood Walk
Loughborough Park
Shakespeare Road
Acre Lane A2217
Tate Brixton Library Gardens
Brixton Oval
Geneva Drive
Corry Drive
Moorland Road
Porden Road
Buckner Road
Windrush Square
Rushcroft Road
Vining Street
Hillmead Drive
Saltoun Road
Walt Whitman Close
0.25 mile
0.25 km

Stockwell / Brixton (East)

Things have changed a bit since The Clash sang 'The Guns of Brixton' in '79 and race riots were a regular occurrence. While the middle classes have infiltrated most parts of Brixton, this neighbourhood still retains a defiant edge. Community spirit and close-knit neighbourhoods take precedence over trendy bars and pricey restaurants. Live music rules here; the legendary Brixton Academy still draws the hordes, while Jamm offers an eclectic and worthy alternative.

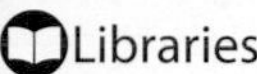

Landmarks

- **Stockwell Bowls** • Stockwell Rd & Stockwell Park Walk

Libraries

- **Anti-Slavery International Library** • Broomgrove Rd

Nightlife

- **Brixton Academy** • 211 Stockwell Rd
- **The Grosvenor** • 17 Sidney Rd
- **Jamm** • 261 Brixton Rd

Map 146 • Earlsfield

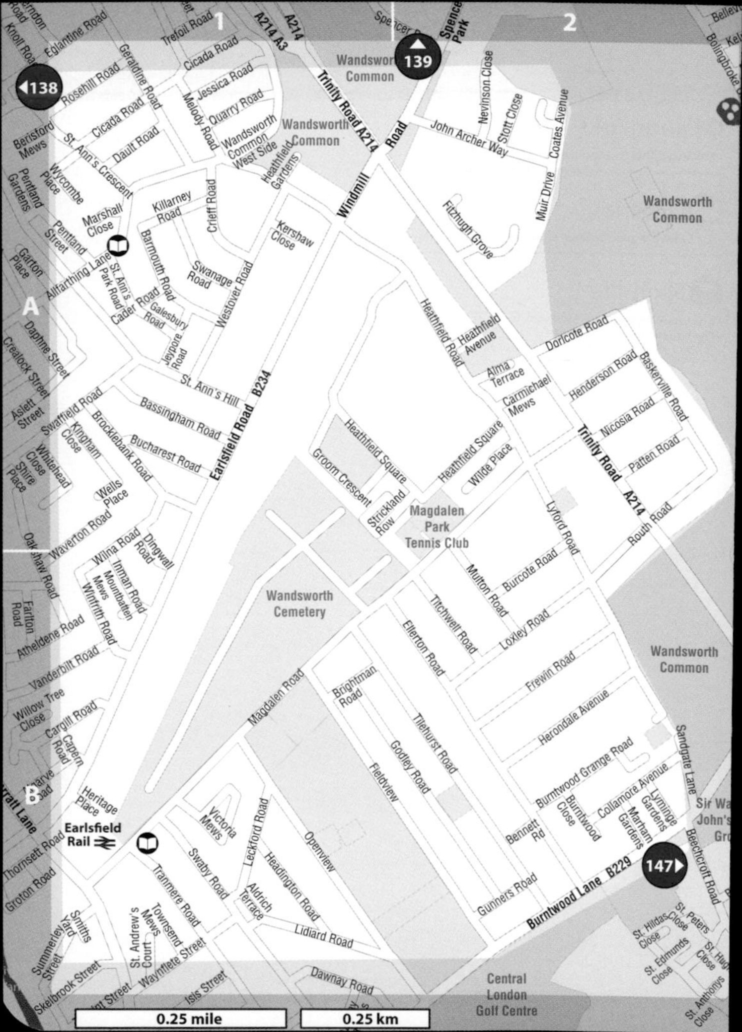

Earlsfield

Sleepy little Earlsfield tends to mind its own business. It's a pretty sedate kind of place, slightly cut off by the lack of a tube stop. The well-heeled locals seem happy enough and make the most of what's on offer. Try Amaranth for great noodles before moving on to Bar 366 a few doors down for some chilled boozing.

Coffee

- **Caffe Nero** • 529 Garratt Ln
- **Refuel** • 515 Garratt Ln

Libraries

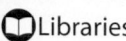

- **Alvering Library** • 2 Allfarthing Lane
- **Earlsfield Library** • 276 Magdalen Rd

Nightlife

- **Bar 366** • 366 Garratt Ln
- **Baraza** • 561 Garratt Ln
- **Halfway House** • 521 Garratt Ln
- **Le Gothique** • Windmill Rd & John Archer Wy

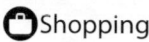

Restaurants

- **Amaranth Cafe & Noodle Bar** • 346 Garratt Ln
- **Carluccio's** • 537 Garratt Ln

Shopping

- **The Earlsfield Bookshop** • 513 Garratt Ln

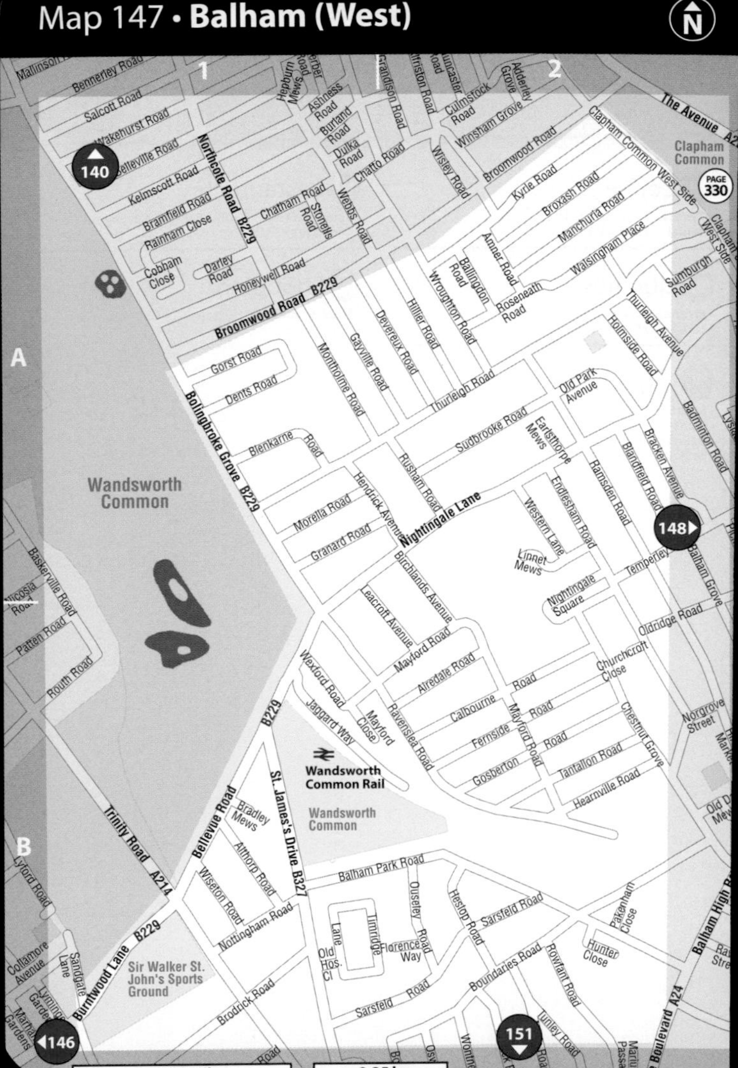

N
1
2
A
B
140
148
146
151
PAGE 330
Clapham Common
Wandsworth Common
Wandsworth Common Rail
Sir Walker St. John's Sports Ground
Northcote Road B229
Broomwood Road B229
Bolingbroke Grove B229
Nightingale Lane
Trinity Road A214
Burntwood Lane B229
St. James's Drive B327
Bellevue Road
Clapham Common West Side
The Avenue A2
Balham Grove
Balham High R
Boulevard A24
Thurleigh Road
Sudbrooke Road
Honeywell Road
Balham Park Road
Boundaries Road
Sarsfeld Road
Oldridge Road
Chestnut Grove
Badminton Road
Temperley
0.25 mile
0.25 km

Balham (West)

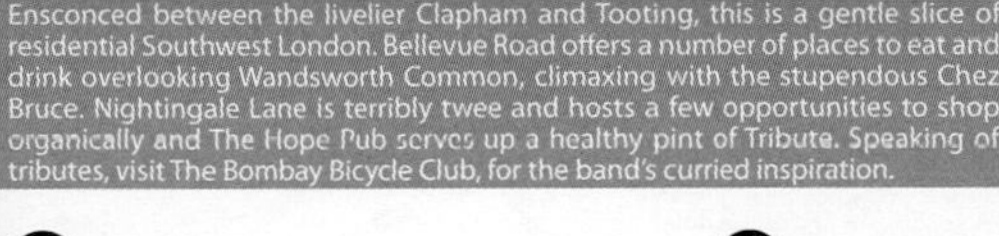

Ensconced between the livelier Clapham and Tooting, this is a gentle slice of residential Southwest London. Bellevue Road offers a number of places to eat and drink overlooking Wandsworth Common, climaxing with the stupendous Chez Bruce. Nightingale Lane is terribly twee and hosts a few opportunities to shop organically and The Hope Pub serves up a healthy pint of Tribute. Speaking of tributes, visit The Bombay Bicycle Club, for the band's curried inspiration.

Coffee

- **Caffe Nero** • 137 Balham High Rde

Nightlife

- **The Nightingale** • 97 Nightingale Lane

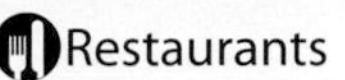

Restaurants

- **The Bombay Bicycle Club** • 95 Nightingale Lane
- **Chez Bruce** • 2 Bellevue Rd

Shopping

- **Bon Vivant** • 59 Nightingale Lane

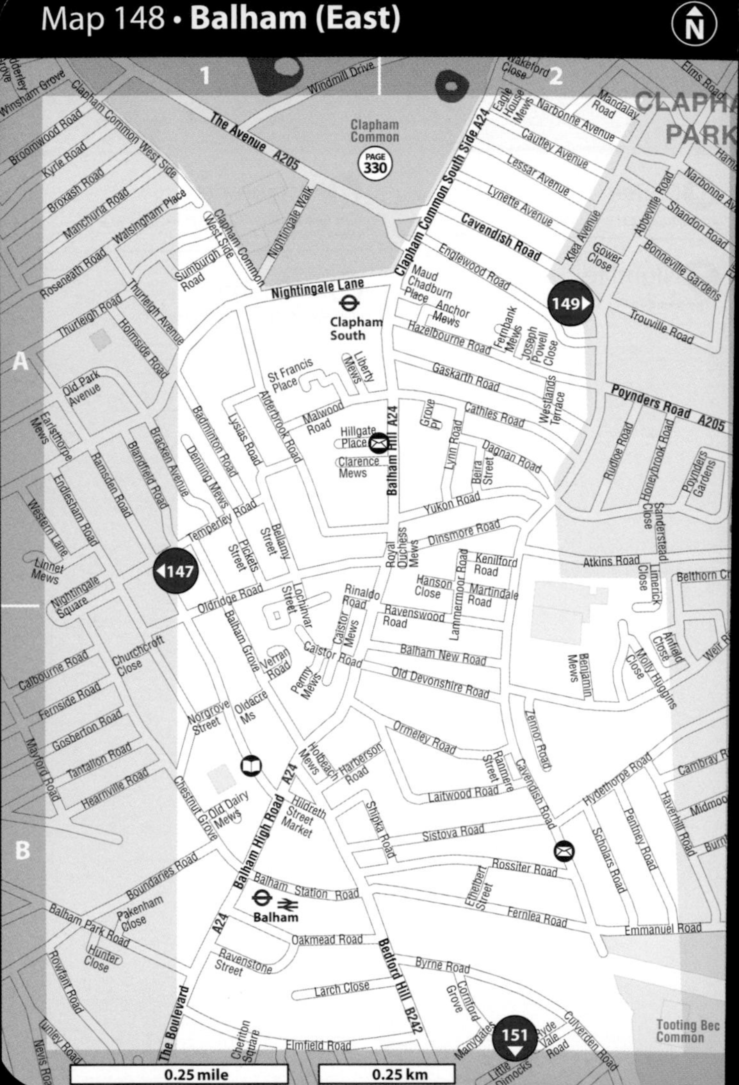
N
1
2
A
B
Windmill Drive
Wakeford Close
Clapham Common
PAGE 330
The Avenue A205
Clapham Common West Side
Winsham Grove
Broomwood Road
Kyrle Road
Broxash Road
Manchuria Road
Walsingham Place
Roseneath Road
Thurleigh Road
Thurleigh Avenue
Holmside Road
Old Park Avenue
Nightingale Walk
Clapham Common West Side
Sumburgh Road
Nightingale Lane
Clapham South
Clapham Common South Side A24
Eagle House Mews
Narbonne Avenue
Cautley Avenue
Lessar Avenue
Lynette Avenue
Cavendish Road
Englewood Road
Mandalay Road
Elms Road
CLAPHAM PARK
Narbonne Avenue
Abbeville Road
Shandon Road
Klea Avenue
Gower Close
Bonneville Gardens
149
Trouville Road
Maud Chadburn Place
Anchor Mews
Hazelbourne Road
Fernbank Mews
Joseph Powell Close
Liberty Mews
St Francis Place
Gaskarth Road
Westlands Terrace
Poynders Road A205
Rudloe Road
Honeybrook Road
Poynders Gardens
Cathles Road
Grove Pl
Malwood Road
Hillgate Place
Clarence Mews
Balham Hill A24
Lynn Road
Beira Street
Dagnan Road
Alderbrook Road
Lysias Road
Badminton Road
Denning Mews
Bracken Avenue
Blandfield Road
Ramsden Road
Earlsthorpe Mews
Endlesham Road
Western Lane
Linnet Mews
Yukon Road
Dinsmore Road
Honeybrook Close
Sanderstead Close
Temperley Road
Bellamy Street
Pickets Street
Royal Duchess Mews
Kenilford Road
Atkins Road
Limerick Close
Belthorn Cr
147
Nightingale Square
Oldridge Road
Lochinvar Street
Rinaldo Road
Hanson Close
Martindale Road
Lammermoor Road
Balham Grove
Caistor Mews
Ravenswood Road
Anfield Close
Weir R
Churchcroft Close
Calbourne Road
Fernside Road
Verran Road
Caistor Road
Penny Mews
Balham New Road
Benjamin Mews
Molly Huggins Close
Old Devonshire Road
Norgrove Street
Oldacre Ms
Gosberton Road
Tantallon Road
Mayford Road
Hearnville Road
Holbeach Mews
Harberson Road
Ormeley Road
Zennor Road
Rainmere Street
Cavendish Road
Hydethorpe Road
Cambray R
Chestnut Grove
Old Dairy Mews
A24
Balham High Road
Hildreth Street Market
Shipka Road
Laitwood Road
Haverhill Road
Midmoor
Scholars Road
Penthey Road
Burn
Sistova Road
Rossiter Road
Boundaries Road
Balham Station Road
Balham
Ethelbert Street
Fernlea Road
Emmanuel Road
Pakenham Close
Balham Park Road
Hunter Close
Rowfant Road
A24
Oakmead Road
Ravenstone Street
Bedford Hill B242
Byrne Road
Larch Close
Cornford Grove
Culverden Road
Tooting Bec Common
The Boulevard
Cheriton Square
Elmfield Road
Manygates
151
Ryde Vale Road
Little Dimocks
Lumley Road
Nevis Road
0.25 mile
0.25 km

Balham (East)

Balham is growing up to become the cooler, decidedly more understated little brother to nearby Clapham. Although it still oozes its own sense of character, evident in quirky mainstays like the Balham Bowls Club, the polished wood of Harrison's and draw of its Waitrose risks losing its hip factor. The happy hour at Iacuba Bar soon makes up for it. But if we have to go to another friend's 30th at The Avalon, we might have to up sticks and go elsewhere.

Coffee

- **Starbucks** • 41 Bedford Hill

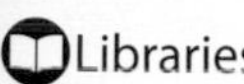

Libraries

- **Balham Library** • 16 Ramsden Rd

Nightlife

- **The Avalon** • 16 Balham Hill
- **Balham Bowls Club** • 7 Ramsden Rd
- **The Bedford** • 77 Bedford Hill
- **The Exhibit** • 12 Balham Station Rd
- **Iacuba Bar** • 10 Bedford Hill

Post Offices

- **Balham Hill** • 92 Balham Hill
- **Cavendish Road** • 273 Cavendish Rd

Restaurants

- **Dish Dash** • 11 Bedford Hill
- **The Exhibit** • 12 Balham Station Rd
- **Harrison's** • 15 Bedford Hill

Shopping

- **Moxon's** • Westbury Parade

Supermarkets

- **Sainsbury's** • 149 Balham High Rd
- **Sainsbury's** • 21 Balham Hill
- **Waitrose** • Balham High Rd & Ramsden Rd

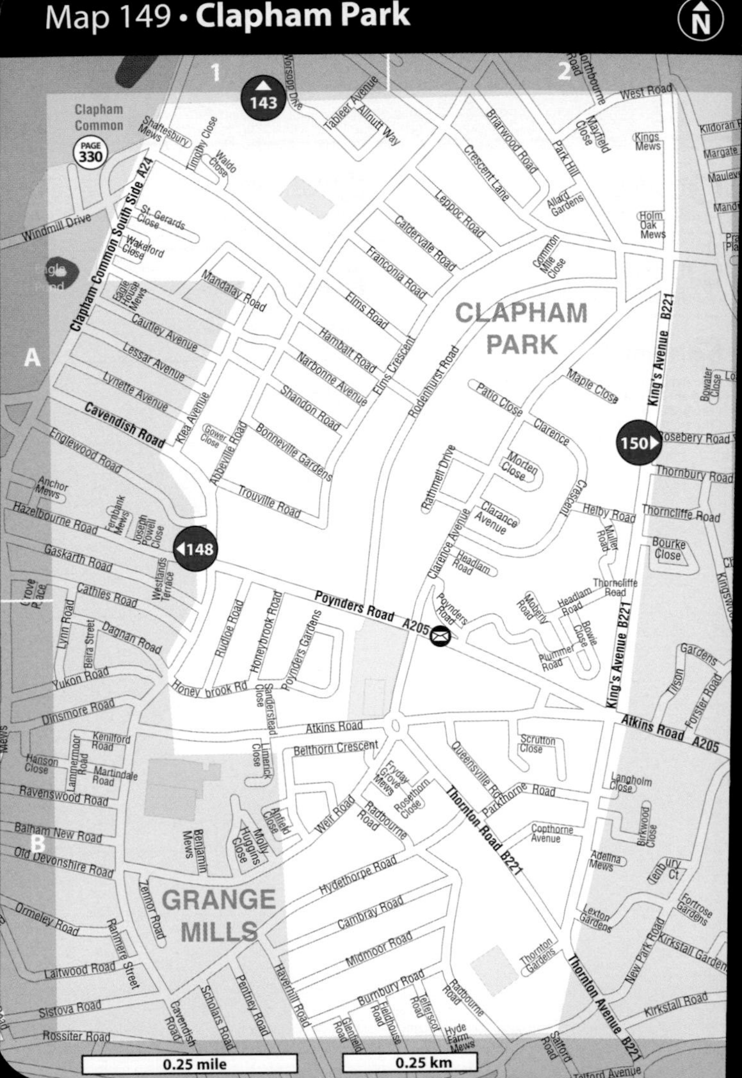
CLAPHAM
PARK
GRANGE
MILLS
Clapham Common
PAGE 330
143
148
150
Clapham Common South Side A24
Windmill Drive
Cavendish Road
Poynders Road A205
Atkins Road A205
King's Avenue B221
Thornton Road B221
Thornton Avenue B221
Rodenhurst Road
Elms Crescent
Crescent Lane
Briarwood Road
Park Hill
West Road
Kings Avenue
0.25 mile
0.25 km

Clapham Park

This is where all the Claphamites settle down, have kids, move into their dream town house, and one-up their friends with dinner parties and barbecues every other weekend. All this domesticity has left the locals' only restaurant options north on Clapham High Street or south in Balham. Still, you need fodder for your friends, so gourmet food shopping is where it's at at MacFarlenes and the Clapham Farmers' Market.

• **Starbucks** • 39 Abbeville Rd

• **Clapham Park** • 49 Poynders Rd

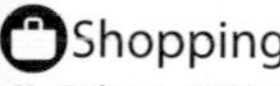

• **MacFarlanes** • 48 Abbeville Rd

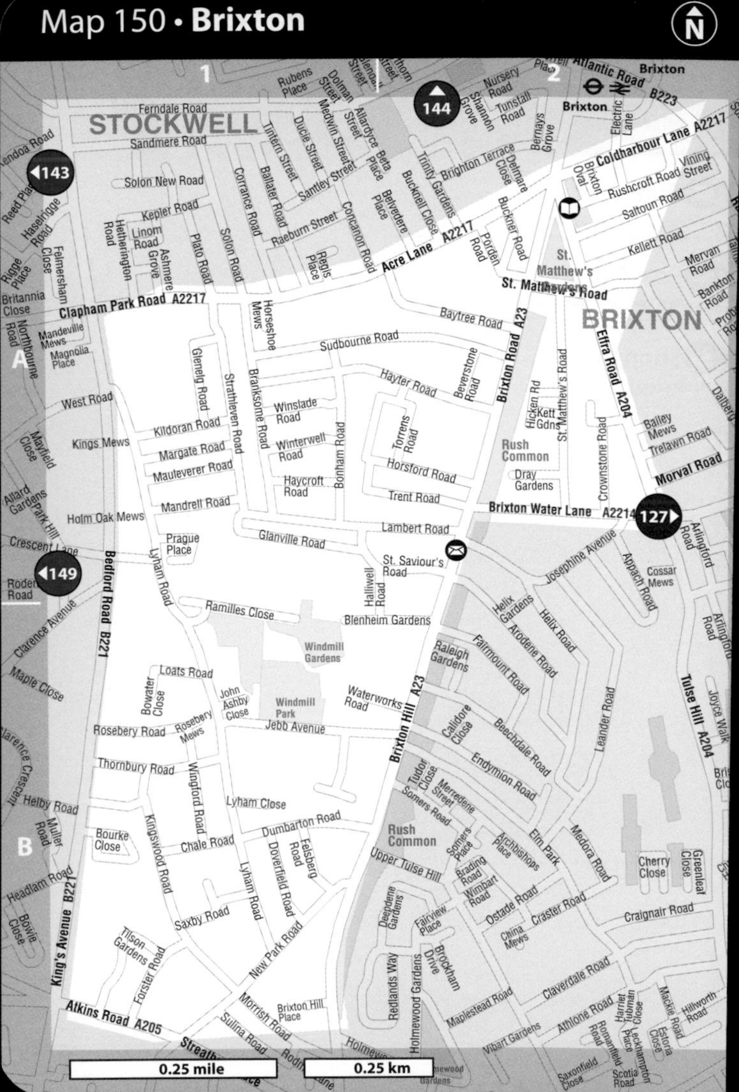
Map 150 • Brixton
N
1
2
A
B
143
144
149
127
STOCKWELL
BRIXTON
Brixton
Atlantic Road
B223
Rubens Place
Dolman Street
Medwin Street
Allardyce Street
Nursery Road
Shannon Grove
Tunstall Road
Bermays Grove
Electric Lane
Coldharbour Lane A2217
Vining Street
Rushcroft Road
Saltoun Road
Kellett Road
Mervan Road
Bankton Road
Brixton Oval
Ferndale Road
Sandmere Road
Solon New Road
Kepler Road
Linom Road
Hetherington Road
Ashmere Grove
Plato Road
Solon Road
Corrance Road
Tintern Street
Ballater Road
Ducie Street
Santley Street
Beta Place
Raeburn Street
Concanon Road
Regis Place
Belvedere Place
Bucknell Close
Trinity Gardens
Brighton Terrace
Delmare Close
Buckner Road
Porden Road
Acre Lane A2217
St. Matthew's Gardens
St. Matthew's Road
Haselrigge Road
Felmersham Close
Rigge Place
Britannia Close
Clapham Park Road A2217
Northbourne Road
Mandeville Mews
Magnolia Place
Horseshoe Mews
Baytree Road
Sudbourne Road
Gleneig Road
Strathleven Road
Branksome Road
Hayter Road
Beverstone Road
Brixton Road A23
Hicken Rd
Kett Gdns
St. Matthew's Road
Effra Road A204
West Road
Winslade Road
Winterwell Road
Bonham Road
Torrens Road
Kildoran Road
Margate Road
Mauleverer Road
Kings Mews
Mayfield Close
Haycroft Road
Horsford Road
Trent Road
Rush Common
Dray Gardens
Crownstone Road
Bailey Mews
Trelawn Road
Morval Road
Allard Gardens
Park Hill
Holm Oak Mews
Mandrell Road
Brixton Water Lane A2214
Lambert Road
Glanville Road
Prague Place
Crescent Lane
Bedford Road B221
Lyham Road
St. Saviour's Road
Halliwell Road
Josephine Avenue
Arlingford Road
Appach Road
Cossar Mews
Roden Road
Clarence Avenue
Ramilles Close
Blenheim Gardens
Windmill Gardens
Helix Gardens
Helix Road
Arodene Road
Raleigh Gardens
Fairmount Road
Maple Close
Loats Road
Bowater Close
John Ashby Close
Windmill Park
Waterworks Road
Brixton Hill A23
Calidore Close
Leander Road
Tulse Hill A204
Joyce Walk
Rosebery Road
Rosebery Mews
Jebb Avenue
Beechdale Road
Thornbury Road
Wingford Road
Endymion Road
Tudor Close
Merredene Street
Somers Road
Clarence Crescent
Helby Road
Lyham Close
Kingswood Road
Dumbarton Road
Elm Park
Medora Road
Muller Road
Bourke Close
Chale Road
Doverfield Road
Felsberg Road
Rush Common
Somers Place
Archbishops Place
Upper Tulse Hill
Brading Road
Wimbart Road
Cherry Close
Greenleaf Close
Headlam Road
King's Avenue B221
Saxby Road
Deepdene Gardens
Fairview Place
Ostade Road
Craster Road
Craignair Road
Bowie Close
Tilson Gardens
Forster Road
New Park Road
China Mews
Brockham Drive
Redlands Way
Holmewood Gardens
Claverdale Road
Atkins Road A205
Morrish Road
Brixton Hill Place
Sulina Road
Maplestead Road
Athlone Road
Harriet Tubman Close
Mackie Road
Hillworth Road
Vibart Gardens
Romanfield Road
Leckhampton Place
Estoria Close
Saxonfield Close
Scotia Road
0.25 mile
0.25 km

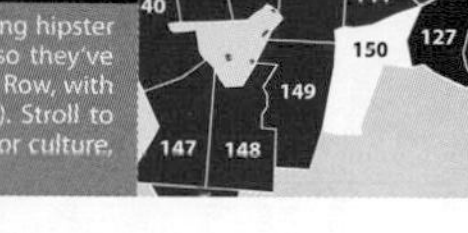

Brixton is where it's at. Shoreditch: old news. Dalston: yawn. Any self-respecting hipster wouldn't be caught dead around these hot spots (too many hipsters) and so they've gravitated south of the river. For Brixton Village's other half, check out Market Row, with its killer katsu (Curry Ono) and flavourful vegan baked goods (Ms Cupcake). Stroll to Coldharbour Lane for homemade ginger beer and brunch (Duck Egg Cafe). For culture, take in an exhibition at Photofusion and a flick at stalwart The Ritzy.

Cinemas

- **Ritzy Picturehouse** • Coldharbour Ln & Brixton Oval

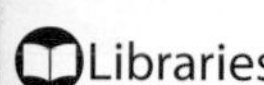

Libraries

- **Brixton Library** • Brixton Oval

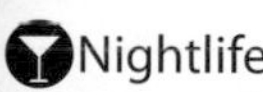

Nightlife

- **The Dogstar** • 389 Coldharbour Ln
- **The Effra** • 38 Kellet Rd
- **Fridge Bar** • 1 Town Hall Parade, Brixton Hill
- **Grand Union** • 123 Acre Ln
- **Hootananny Brixton** • 95 Effra Rd
- **Mango Landin'** • 40 St Matthew's Rd
- **Mass** • Brixton Hill
- **Prince Albert** • 418 Coldharbour Ln
- **Upstairs at the Ritzy** • Ritzy Picturehouse • Brixton Oval, Coldharbour Lane
- **Satay** • 447 Coldharbour Ln
- **St Matthews Church** • Brixton Hill
- **The Windmill** • 22 Blenheim Gardens

Post Offices

- **Brixton Hill** • 104 Brixton Hill

Restaurants

- **Asmara** • 386 Coldharbour Ln
- **Curry Ono** • 14 Market Row
- **Duck Egg Cafe** • 424 Coldharbour Ln
- **Elephant** • 55 Granville Arcade
- **Franco Manca** • 4 Market Row
- **KaoSarn** • Coldharbour Ln
- **Khan's** • 24 Brixton Water Lane
- **The Lounge** • 56 Atlantic Rd
- **Negril** • 132 Brixton Hill
- **Opus Café** • 89 Acre Ln
- **Upstairs Bar and Restaurant** • 89 Acre Ln
- **Yum-D** • 14 Market Row

Shopping

- **Lab G** • 6 Granville Arcade
- **Ms Cupcake** • 408 Coldharbour Ln
- **Traid** • 2 Acre Ln

Supermarkets

- **Iceland** • 13 Winslade Rd

Map 151 • Tooting Bec

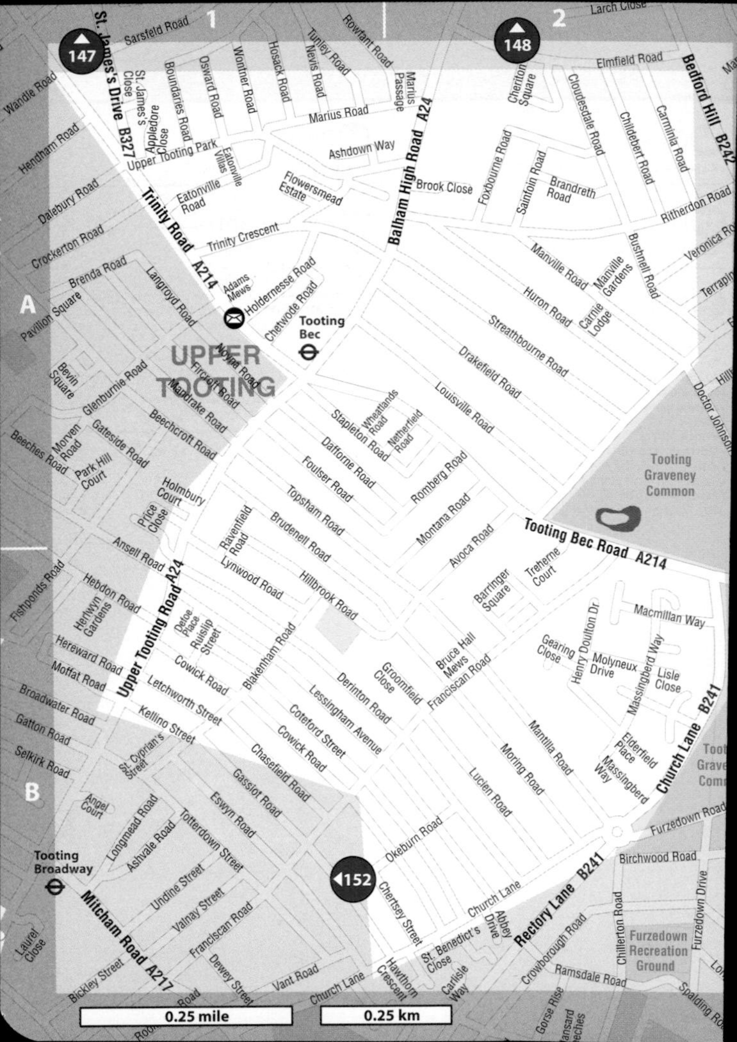

Tooting Bec

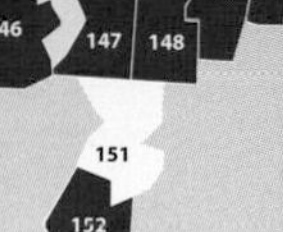

Not quite the Bec of beyond, this Tooting is the home of Europe's largest lido and has a plethora of Asian grill bars for post-pub munchies. The best of the curry houses has to be Al Mirage, despite a popular following at Mirch Masala. For fairy cakes head to Bertie and Boo (we boo the name) and cocktails stop at Smoke. So what, you say? Sew buttons at the London Sewing Machine Museum no less.

Coffee

- **Bertie and Boo** • 162 Balham High Rd
- **Caffe Moka** • 243 Balham High Rd

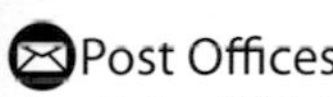

Nightlife

- **The Bec Bar** • 26 Tooting Bec Rd
- **King's Head** • 84 Upper Tooting Rd
- **Smoke Bar** • 14 Trinity Rd

Post Offices

- **Upper Tooting** • 63 Trinity Rd

Restaurants

- **Al Mirage** • 215 Upper Tooting Rd
- **Masaledar Kitchen** • 121 Upper Tooting Rd
- **Mirch Masala** • 213 Upper Tooting Rd
- **Spice Village** • 32 Upper Tooting Rd

Shopping

- **Russell's Hardware & DIY** • 46 Upper Tooting Rd
- **Wandsworth Oasis HIV/AIDs Charity Shop** • 40 Trinity Rd

Map 152 • Tooting Broadway

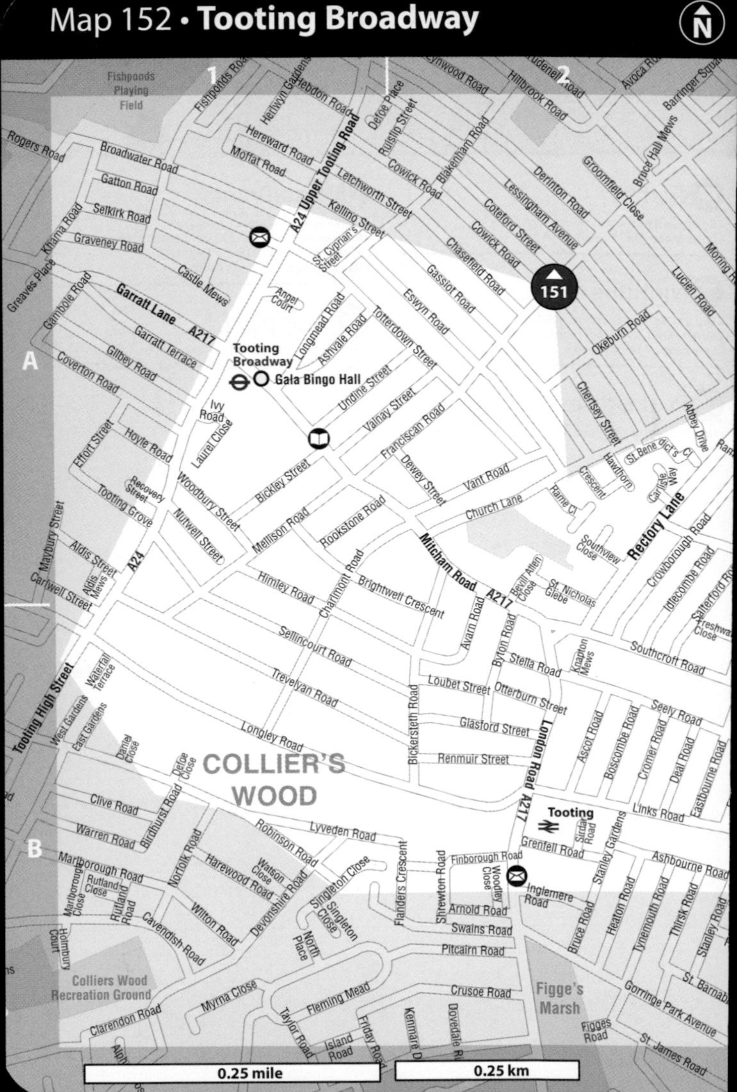

Tooting Broadway

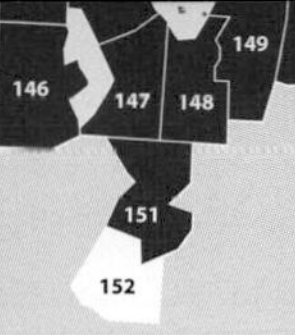

Decent rent, a Northern Line station and a grade one listed bingo hall: there's a lot here to like. Hit the High Street for curries and halal it all. Need anything else? Mitcham Road has the ticket. Local eat treats include Radha Krishna Bhavan, Sette Bello and Rick's Café, while Garden House and Tram & Social show that trendy pubs can indeed survive this far south.

Coffee

- **Cafee Manal** • 984 Garratt Ln
- **Urban Coffee** • 74 Tooting High St

Landmarks

- **Gala Bingo Hall** • 50 Mitcham Road

Libraries

- **Tooting Library** • 75 Mitcham Rd

Nightlife

- **Garden House** • 196 Tooting High St
- **Ramble Inn** • 223 Mitcham Rd
- **Tooting Tram and Social** • 46 Mitcham Rd

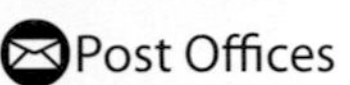

Post Offices

- **London Road** • 47 London Rd
- **Tooting** • 2 Gatton Rd

Restaurants

- **Jaffna House** • 90 Tooting High St
- **Radha Krishna Bhavan** • 86 Tooting High St
- **Rick's Cafe** • 122 Mitcham Rd
- **Sette Bello** • 8 Amen Corner
- **Urban Coffee** • 74 Tooting High St

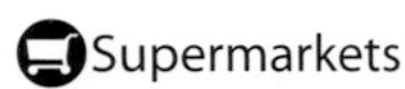

Shopping

- **Tooting Market** • 21 Tooting High St

Supermarkets

- **Iceland** • 27 Tooting High St

General Information

Website: www.alexandrapalace.com
Phone: 020 8365 2121

Overview

If you fancy panoramic London views, exemplary Victorian architecture and an unrelenting stiff breeze to the face, the heights of Alexandra Park could be your cup of tea. With a fraction of the visitors of North London neighbours Hampstead Heath and Primrose Hill, Alexandra Park is nonetheless home to Ally Pally – Alexander Mackenzie's magnificent 1873 exhibition centre once renowned as the home of television after the BBC used it to broadcast the world's first high def transmissions in '36. It also boasts 196 acres of pristine, Green Flag-winning parkland, a two-hectare conservation area, and a fully functioning ice rink to boot.

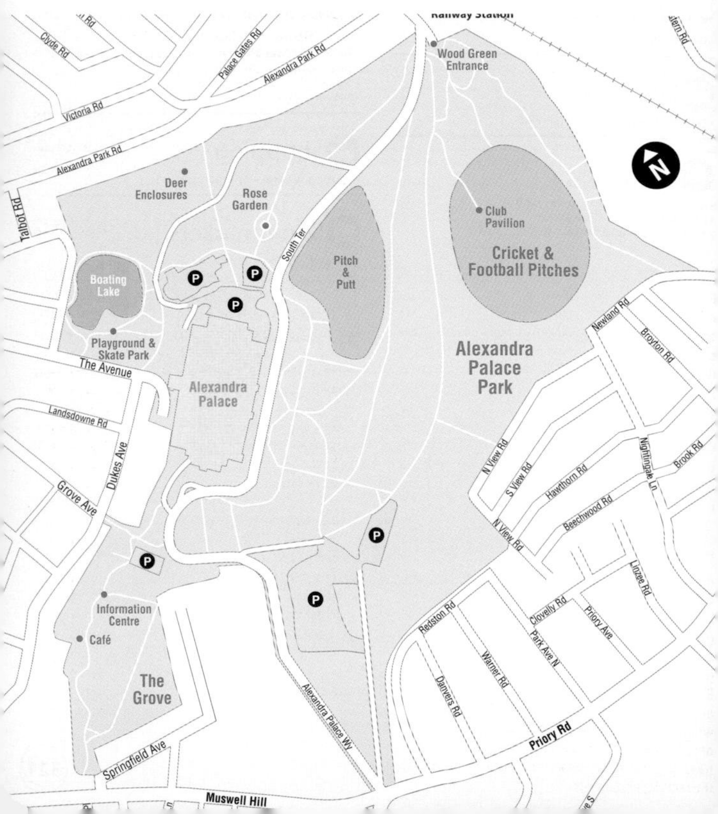

Practicalities

Alexandra Park is well served by public transport: Alexandra Palace railway station is a short ride from King's Cross and Moorgate and sits directly next to the park's Wood Green entrance. You can also take the underground to Wood Green, catch the W3 direct to Ally Pally from just outside. You could also take advantage of the 2000 free parking spaces in the park itself if driving, though it's only a short walk from Muswell Hill town centre.

Nature

No doubt tempted by the reservoirs, 155 species of birds have been spotted in the park over the last 30 years. Nature fetishists should take in the two-hectare conservation area, which includes a wide array of animals including deer, donkeys, foxes and rabbits. In 1998, there was even a rare water vole sighting. There he was, large as life, like he owned the bloody place.

Architecture

For most Alexandra Park visitors it's all about the Palace, these days a thriving hub for exhibitions, concerts, farmer's markets and, uh, world darts tournaments. The Palace building itself was ravaged by fire in the 80s and has since been restored to its former glory, though nearby banqueting venue Blandford Hall succumbed to the same fate in 1971 and was completely destroyed. No matter: Ally Pally remains an impressive, domineering building well worth a nose-around. For the less active, admiring the view from sedentary perspective from the underrated Phoenix Bar (located in the south wing) is just as good.

Open Spaces

It's safe to say that Alexandra Park has more than enough grass to keep Cheech & Chong happy, being typified by the diverse range of landscaped grounds that can be found within. The Grove Garden actually pre-dates the park itself and there's also a good little café here if you fancy a quick bite. The Rose Garden is to the east side of the Palace and is even more aesthetically pleasing. Many newer small woodlands have been developing over the last few decades owing to the planting of large numbers of trees, producing an environment pleasing to both the rambler and runner.

Performance

The park often plays host to funfairs and circuses, but the Palace itself will usually be used at night for concerts. Its revival over recent years as a gig venue has led to the likes of the Arctic Monkeys and Paul Weller playing there, with its capacity being around 8,500, making it ideal for bands who've outgrown the Brixton Academy. Other parts of the Palace, such as the Great Hall, are used for classical music recitals.

More recently 'The Secret Cinema' took over the Palace for a screening of Lawrence of Arabia, attracting thousands of filmgoers clad in Bedouin attire. Some even brought a camel.

The Palace also houses a theatre, which was dormant for over sixty-five years until a performance took place in 2004. It is still being restored and should be re-opened to the public for performances in the near future.

Check out Ally Pally's informative website (listed above) for a full calendar of upcoming events.

Sports

An indoor ice rink is housed within the Palace with a capacity of 1,250, with all manner of ice sports catered for (you can get further information by ringing 020 8365 4386). There is also a large boating lake with its own islands and fishing area (and even a smaller area for kids to boat on their own), with pedalos and rowing boats available for hire; being a seasonal facility, it's best to ring the operators Bluebird Boats Ltd. (020 7262 1330) beforehand. The boating pond is adjacent to a children's playground as well. For those who like golf with a view, the popular ten-hole pitch and putt course was recently revamped with an injection of Heritage Fund money: for prices and booking info see www.pitchnputt.co.uk or call 01245 257682. Alexandra Palace Park is also popular with cyclists, with the Parkland Walk a particular favourite, being a disused railway line that links up with Finsbury Park. In summertime the park is also a great place to get embroiled in countless spontaneous games of football and Frisbee, or to gawp/hurl insults at joggers

General information

NFT Map: 7
Address: Barbican Centre, Silk St, London, EC2Y 8DS.
Phone: Box Office & Membership: 020 7638 8891 (9 am-8 pm daily); Switchboard: 020 7638 4141
Centre opening times: Mon-Sat: 9 am-11 pm; Sun & Public Holidays: 12 pm-11 pm (although different parts of the centre may open at different times)
Website: www.barbican.org.uk

Overview

As terrifying as it is impressive, the Barbican Centre is a one-stop shop for all things cultural. At its best, the Barbican is utterly brilliant: a rambling collection of cinemas, galleries, bars, theatres, even a housing estate and a school. But stay after dark, when the culture vultures have left, and you can find yourself alone and lost in this city-within-a-city.

That the centre is brutally ugly makes what's inside even more splendid. The gallery space hosts world-class exhibitions and the cinemas show both mainstream and arthouse films. There's a world, classical and jazz music programme catering for everyone from scruffy backpackers to bearded professors. Most are sensible enough to leave before it gets too spooky. But plan your exit route in advance just in case.

Music

The heart of the Barbican monster is its music hall. A mecca for lovers of cerebral music, the centre's resident band is the London Symphony Orchestra: classical heavyweights who play year-round. The BBC Symphony Orchestra also has a base here, and the stage attracts biggies from around the world, including performances from Yo-Yo Ma, the Vienna Philharmonic and Cesaria Evora. But you don't need a high brow to find something to like: a flick through their listings—which last year included Sufjan Stevens, Sparks,

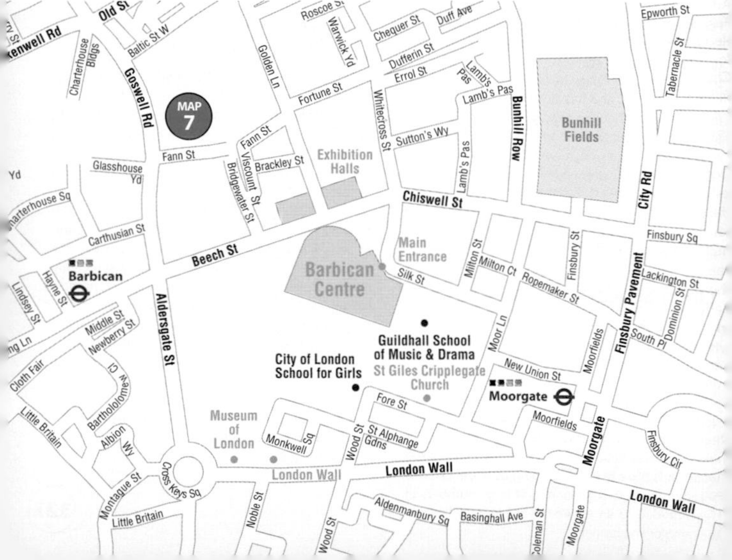

The Africa Express and Micachu—will soon have you clicking Book Now.

Festivals are another key draw: not the pot-and-portacabin type, but impassioned celebrations. The Mostly Mozart festival reaches sci-fi convention levels of fanaticism; the Great Performers Festival is an orgy of some of the world's most spectacular musicians; and the Jazz Festival will have you feeling über hip (then perhaps a bit perplexed. And then, if you're 100% honest, rather wishing it was over). African, Latin, Contemporary and Opera festivals also sell out the near-2000 capacity venue.

Film

The programme has an arty bias but is so diverse that you're bound to find something inviting on one of the three screens. Rule of thumb: silent films, in. J Lo, out. Subtitles, in. Mighty Duck trilogy, out. But they do offer the screens for private hire, so if you really want you can stick it to 'em and have your own showing of Snakes on a Plane. The Barbican also hosts the annual Australian Film and London Children's Film Festivals, and runs constantly changing series. Recent favourites include the Bad Film Club for fans of the most reviled films, and Second Chance Sunday so you can see on the big screen films which you missed first time around.

Theatre and Dance

Don't be fooled by the Barbican's hulking exterior—the centre dabbles in the more delicate arts rather well. Its two theatres cater for both ends of the performance spectrum. The main room, a shared home for acting and dance, seats over 1,000 punters and attracts some of the biggest names in high culture. Deep in the Barbican's bowels the smaller Pit theatre is home to experimental and new acts. But be warned: with just 200 seats the Pit is small enough for anyone dozing off to be highly visible.

Art

Nowhere else at the Barbican is the idea of making culture accessible for all more apparent than their art spaces. The main gallery hosts temporary exhibitions, mixing all types of art into one cultural hot pot. In 2007, under the umbrella of Art and Sex from Antiquity to Now, erotic Roman cutlery—that's right: erotic cutlery—shared a stage with impressionist paintings and an 11-minute film of someone's face as she was, ahem, attended to. Every first Thursday of the month the gallery opens for a nocturnal viewing, with talks, performances—burlesque dancers for the art and sex exhibition—and a themed bar. A second space, The Curve, winds its way round the ground floor where the exhibitions are generally free.

The Library

Libraries often get a bad press. They've got stuck with an image of frumpy, middle-aged women peering down their spectacles and telling youths to be quiet. But this couldn't be further removed from the reality of the Barbican Library. Alongside a decent array of books, there's a dazzling collection of live musical recordings. Some of these tracks are so rare that they can't be heard anywhere else in the world. Put some headphones on and rock out. Just don't get carried away and smash up the children's section.

How To Get There

By car: Parking is pricey with two hours costing £6.50 and each hour thereafter costing two or three quid more, though there's a flat weekend fee of £7.50 per day

By bus: The 153 (which runs from Liverpool Street to Finsbury Park) stops directly outside the Barbican at Silk Street; the following buses run nearby: 8, 11, 23, 26, 35, 42, 43, 47, 48, 55, 56, 76, 78, 100, 133, 141, 149, 172, 214, 242, 243, 271, 344 (seven days a week); 4, (Mon-Sat); 21, 25, 521 (Mon-Fri). If none of these buses can take you home then consider yourself extremely unlucky. By tube: Barbican stations runs on the Circle, District and Hammersmith & City lines. Other stations nearby are Moorgate, St Paul's, Bank, Liverpool Street and Mansion House.

By train: The nearest overland stations are Liverpool Street, Farringdon and Blackfriars. City Thameslink services run through Barbican, Moorgate and Cannon Street.

Practical Information

NFT Map: 132, 133, & 141

Official opening time is 8 am, although the gates are usually unlocked a little earlier than this. The park closes at dusk.

Friends of Battersea Park:
www.batterseapark.org

Zoo: www.batterseaparkzoo.co.uk

Local council: www.wandsworth.gov.uk (see also for information on the Pump House Gallery)

Cycle hire:
www.londonrecumbents.co.uk

BlueBird boat hire:
www.bluebirdboats.co.uk

Overview

Opened in 1858 with the aim of giving the Victorian working classes something to do other than drinking gin, Battersea Park has developed to become one of London's prettiest, most popular and most usable parks. Squeezing a range of gardens, cafes, animals, sports, cultural facilities and even a peace pagoda into its diminutive 200 acres, the park is popular with everyone from hordes of snotty little kids to wandering dog-walkers. It is also centrally located enough to be easy to get to but still far enough from Central London to retain a local feel.

The park is about two miles southwest from Westminster and occupies the spot on the south bank of the Thames between Albert and Chelsea bridges. Originally used for duelling, the Duke of Wellington famously discharged upon the Earl of Winchelsea on the site in 1829. Rather than the vast open and flat spaces that many London parks offer, Battersea is neatly divided into a number of features and sections, making it feel much larger than it is.

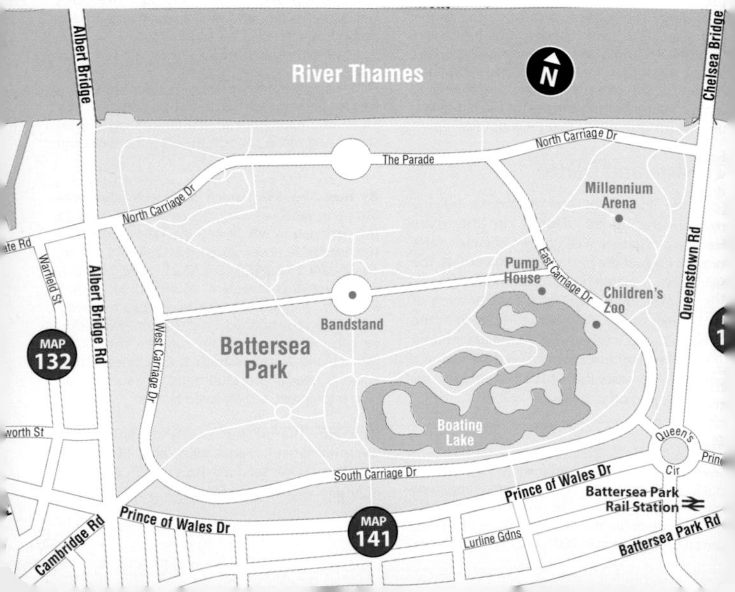

Sporting Activities

Battersea has an incredibly good array of sporting facilities. The 'Millennium Arena' is a 400m 8-lane running track situated in the northeast corner of the park; it hosts athletic meets and training sessions and it benefited from an expensive overhaul in, you guessed it, 1999. Next to the arena are ten tennis courts and an all-weather football pitch whilst there are further all-weather astro-turf pitches in the southeast corner of the park marked for both hockey and football. The park also boasts cricket pitches and practice nets, a bowling green, smooth wide paths for skating and enough open spaces to invite impromptu sessions of pretty much any other sport. If you consider attacking fish a sport, and have a permit and rod licence, the park's lake offers fishing for nine months of the year. Rowing boats and pedaloes can also be taken out on to the lake during July and August (adults £4.50/hour, children £2). Bicycles can be hired from the London Recumbents shop, which is next to the Millennium Arena on the park's East Carriage Drive—but be warned: bikes can only be used in the park itself, and as it takes just 15 minutes for a leisurely pedal around the parameter, an hour's hire can become a little Groundhog Day.

Art

Battersea has fostered a creative relationship with the arts and has a number of sculptures dotted about, its own public gallery and a biannual art fair. Taking pride of place next to the lake are two large Henry Moore and Barbara Hepworth sculptures, both of which are well worth rooting out. The Pumphouse Gallery is a grade II-listed building, originally used to power the park's water works, which has been restored and converted into a gallery and information centre with six exhibitions throughout the year. The Gallery, located northeast of the lake, is also available for private hire and even has a licence to hold civil weddings. The park has hosted the Affordable Art Fair since 1999, which has become a leading showcase for art priced under £3,000.

Performance

In summer music aficionados should head down to La Gondola al Parco, the café by the lake, for free live concerts every Tuesday and Friday from 7 pm. Entrance is free and there's also a BBQ and refreshments aplenty.

Nature and Children's Zoo

Battersea's varied landscapes ensure you stand a decent chance of seeing more than a rat or a pigeon while you saunter round. Squirrels, ducks and Canada geese are all too plentiful. More interesting potential sightings include woodpeckers, cormorants, Peregrine falcons, terrapins and, according to the RSPB, Pochards (whatever they are). If you don't come across any interesting wildlife, your only option is to cheat and visit the park's zoo. A five-minute stroll from the Chelsea Gate entrance, the zoo is aimed at children and has a cool collection of small mammals, including lemurs, as well as small farm animals and some excitingly named birds, such as some 'Peach-faced Love birds'. In case you do fall in love with any of the zoo's inhabitants, most are available for adoption. Mice start at £10 for six months, pay-up and claim it's for your kid. The zoo is open throughout the year and entry costs £7.95 for adults, £6.50 for children.

How To Get There

By tube: Sloane Square (on the Circle and District lines) is the nearest Underground station at just under a mile away. From the station walk down Lower Sloane Street, which becomes Chelsea Bridge Road and leads to the Thames. Walk over Chelsea Bridge and you will see the park on your right. Alternatively take bus no 319.

By bus: From central London, buses run to the park from Liverpool Street (number 344), Notting Hill (452), Oxford Circus (137), Sloane Square (319, 137), Victoria Station (44) and Vauxhall (344).

By train: Battersea Park station is within sight of the park, trains run to both Clapham Junction and Victoria at high frequency. Queenstown Road is around 300m from the park. Trains from this station run to Waterloo and Clapham Junction and depart less often than from Battersea Park.

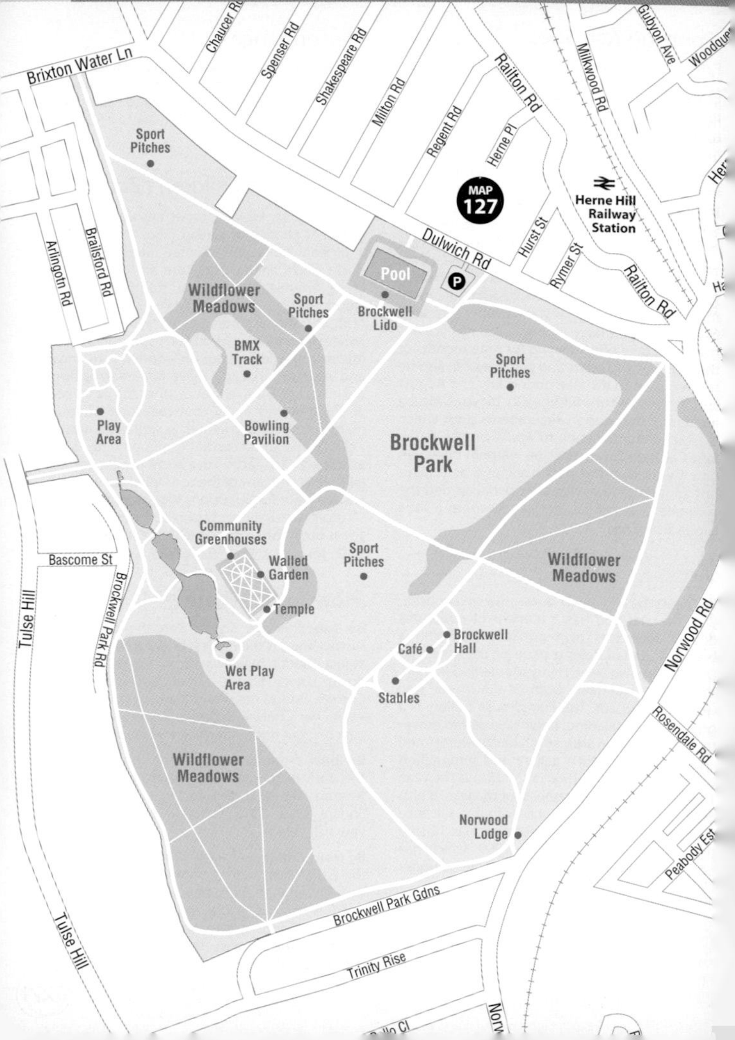

Brixton Water Ln
Chaucer Rd
Spenser Rd
Shakespeare Rd
Milton Rd
Regent Rd
Railton Rd
Herne Pl
Milkwood Rd
Gubyon Ave
MAP 127
Herne Hill Railway Station
Dulwich Rd
Hurst St
Rymer St
Railton Rd
Sport Pitches
Brailsford Rd
Arlingotn Rd
Wildflower Meadows
Sport Pitches
Pool
Brockwell Lido
BMX Track
Sport Pitches
Play Area
Bowling Pavilion
Brockwell Park
Community Greenhouses
Walled Garden
Sport Pitches
Temple
Wildflower Meadows
Bascome St
Brockwell Park Rd
Tulse Hill
Wet Play Area
Brockwell Hall
Café
Stables
Norwood Rd
Rosendale Rd
Wildflower Meadows
Norwood Lodge
Peabody Est
Brockwell Park Gdns
Tulse Hill
Trinity Rise

General Information

NFT Map: 127
Brockwell Park: www.brockwellpark.com
Brockwell Park Lido: www.brockwelllido.com
020 7274 3088

Overview

Brockwell Park may not be a household name when it comes to London Parks but for many South Londoners – not least residents of neighbouring Herne Hill – it's the pick of the bunch, all the loveller for its unconventionality, tattiness and relative anonymity. It's eclectic, it's quirky, and it's impossible not to fall in love with.

History

By the end of the 19th century the local population was large, growing and in need of a serious park. Brockwell was secured for use by the public after MP Thomas Bristowe got wind of a private country estate that seemed just the ticket. Still, he might have over-exerted himself in the process: having taken a Bill through Parliament to convert the land, led a committee to negotiate the price, and raised funds from across the community, Bristowe himself promptly collapsed and died on the steps of Brockwell Hall, moments after the opening ceremony in 1892.

Café

If that doesn't put you off your scones, nowadays, the ground floor of Brockwell Hall is a café where refreshments have been served ever since. Located at the top of the hill, it's a great place to stop for inexpensive cake, drinks etc. after some…

Activities!

There's heaps to do. A BMX track, tennis courts, bowling green, football and cricket pitches, basketball courts, outdoor theatre club, a children's play area and a paddling pool. Or you could chill by the ponds, in the walled garden, under the clock tower, at the picnic area, near the flower gardens, etc.

Brockwell Lido and Greenhouses

Built in 1937, Brockwell Lido is essentially an (unattractive) art deco building that replaced an old bathing pond. After experiencing financial difficulty it was restored and reopened in 2007. As well as a large outdoor pool, there is a gym and classes are held in yoga, pilates, tai-chi and meditation. For the under 5s, Whippersnappers have everything from acrobatics to puppets and African drumming. A Miniature Railway runs between Herne Hill Gate and the Lido. Run by a local enthusiast on a not-for-profit basis; it's only £1 for a round trip. May–Sept, Sat–Sun, 11am–5pm.

Brockwell also boasts a superb community greenhouse project open to volunteers. The greenhouses are open Sunday afternoons and give Londoners a rare chance to get green fingers and grow their own produce. Contact the greenhouse secretary on bpcgsecretary@gmail.com to get involved.

Annual Events

July: Lambeth Country Show is always good fun and involves medieval jousting, farm animals, live reggae/dub and rides, and there are homemade cake and jam contests, too. The Alternative Vegetable Animal Competition requires fruit and veg be crafted into a famous person or building with a very entertaining adult category.
September: The annual Urban Green Fair helps teach London to become more sustainable.
November: The big fireworks show on Guy Fawkes Night is worth braving the cold for.

How to Get There

By rail/tube/foot: The park is a short walk from the following overland and underground stations:

Herne Hill Rail Station—5 mins
Tulse Hill Rail Station —15 mins
Brixton Tube —20 mins
Clapham North Tube —30 mins

By bus: The following all stop at Brockwell Park—2, 3, 37, 68, 196, 322, 468, P15

Overview

Lively and happening; youngish, professional, and trendy (in a safe way). Clapham Common reflects the area well.

Popular all year round, the Common truly comes alive in summer. On a warm weekend you'll find the park overflowing with picnickers sipping champagne and just plain lookin' good. It's a lovely scene made better by the relaxed, friendly atmosphere. And, when the sun finally sets, you're left with a seriously impressive choice of bars close by.

As well as drawing the usual funky sophisticates, the park is also family-friendly with lots of little ones enjoying the space.

Plenty of organised (or not) sport, kite flying, model boating, Ultimate Frisbee, and even fishing happens here too, but while the common is safe as houses during the day, at night time it is best avoided.

History

Clapham began as a Saxon village. Back then it was called Clopp Ham, meaning the village (ham) by the short hill (clopp). The common was used by villagers to graze their livestock and as a source of firewood.

In the late 17th century the population began to grow as refugees arrived from the Great Plague of London (1665) and the fire of 1666. During this time, the rich gentry of London built a number of fine country houses around the common. When the railways were developed there was a sudden influx of commuters, driving the upper class away to somewhere less, um, common.

Today, the surrounding area is one of the more expensive in South London, partly because of its excellent transport links.

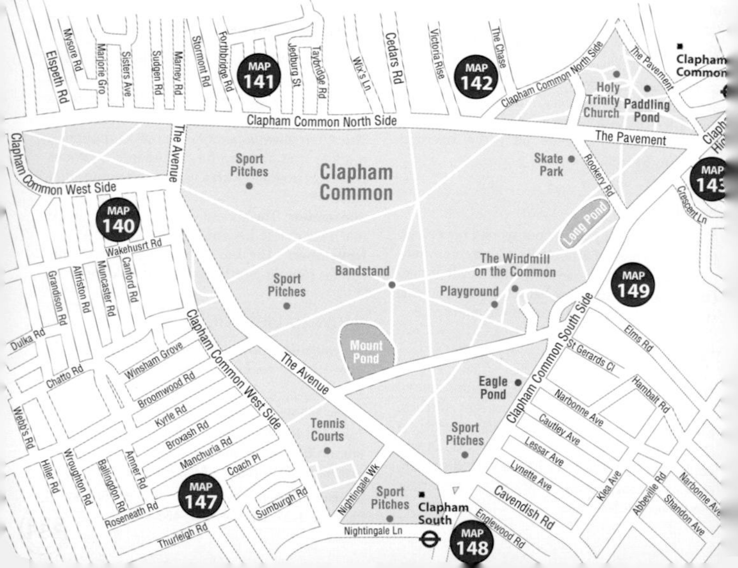

Clapham Sect

On the common is the Holy Trinity Church. This was a meeting place of the Clapham Sect, a group of 19th-century Evangelical Anglicans who fought for social reform. "Ugh" you say, but wait…

The Clapham Sect played a significant part in the abolition of slavery in England. They didn't stop there, going on to campaign for the eradication of slavery worldwide. They also fought for reform in the penal system, focusing on unjust sentencing and the dire prison conditions of the time.

Eateries

Cicero's on the Common (vegetarian)
2 Rookery Road, SW49QN, 020 7498 0770

Cafe Des Res (English/ Carribean)
8 The Pavement, SW4 0HY, 020 7622 6602

The Bowling Green Café (sandwiches, pasta etc)
Clapham Common West Side, SW4 9AN, 020 7801 0904

Three ponds

Mount Pond – is a fishing park pond about three acres in size. It contains carp, roach, gudgeon and eels. Suggested baits include pellet, maggot, meat, and boilies, it says here.

Eagle Pond – Is a smaller pond with a little island. This one is also fishable. Stocks include carp, tench, bream, roach, rudd, perch, chub and gudgeon. Best baits are bread, pellet, maggot, hemp and castor, it goes without saying.

Long Pond – has a century-old tradition of use for model boating.

Activities

These days there are still some nice leafy pathways lined by mature trees left for the strollers to enjoy.

Sporty types can go for the football, rugby, cricket, softball, tennis, basketball, Aussie rules football, croquet (!) or bowling.

Events

Some of the annual highlights include:

Race For Life— Throughout the year: Race For Life – The girls take on the common in pink to raise awareness of cancer. One of the biggest Race For Life running events.

July: Ben 'n Jerry's Sundae On The Common—also goes down well. If it sounds horribly corporate, it's worth noting that a full restoration of the bandstand in '05/'06 was partly funded by proceeds from this festival. Or, just think of the free ice-cream…

August: The Clapham Common Metro Weekender—Two successful, quality festivals have joined forces. South West Four (progressive house, trance, and breaks) and Get Loaded In the Park (indie/dance) now happen side by side at the end of August.

November: The Bonfire Night Fireworks—it's as good as it gets here.

How to Get There

By train: Wandsworth Road Station (12 minutes), Clapham High Street Station (12 minutes)

By tube: Clapham Common (4 minutes), Clapham South (13 minutes)

By bus: 4, 35, 37, 88, 137, 155, 255, 345, 355, 417, G1

Overview

A lot is packed into this 54-acre park—mostly people. On a sunny day Clissold throngs with Stokenewingtonites; yummy mummies and three-wheeled buggies; gaggles of youths, with or without hoods; lads playing football; and assorted dog walkers. Visitors can see deer and goats in the animal enclosure, diamond doves and love birds in the aviary, and coots and moorhens in the nature ponds. Parents take little ones to the paddling pool (summer months only), toddlers group at the One O'clock Club or the well-equipped children's playground. The park hosts the usual hodgepodge of circuses and steam fairs as well as the famous arts festival, StokeFest, in the summer. On grey days, chilly days, or in the early hours, peace can be found - in the rose garden perhaps, or underneath one of the ancient trees.

Clissold Park Café

Phone: 0207 923 9797
Email: info@clissoldparkcafe.com
Website: www.clissoldparkcafe.com
Hours: 9 am–5.30 pm (winter)
7.30 pm (summer)
Admission: FREE

Clissold Mansion, the Grade II listed building just visible from Stoke Newington Church Street, is home to a large, child-friendly cafe. Herbal tea drinkers jostle with dripping ice-cream cone lickers on the sun trap front veranda and circular lawn. The large inside rooms are best avoided if you find children's chatter grating, but otherwise a lively spot to tuck into a plate of egg and chips. The building was constructed in the late 18th century on behalf of a Quaker family whose daughter was courted by a local reverend—Augustus Clissold. He wooed, then married her, and swiftly changed the name of the estate to Clissold Place. Where is Catherine Cookson when you need her?

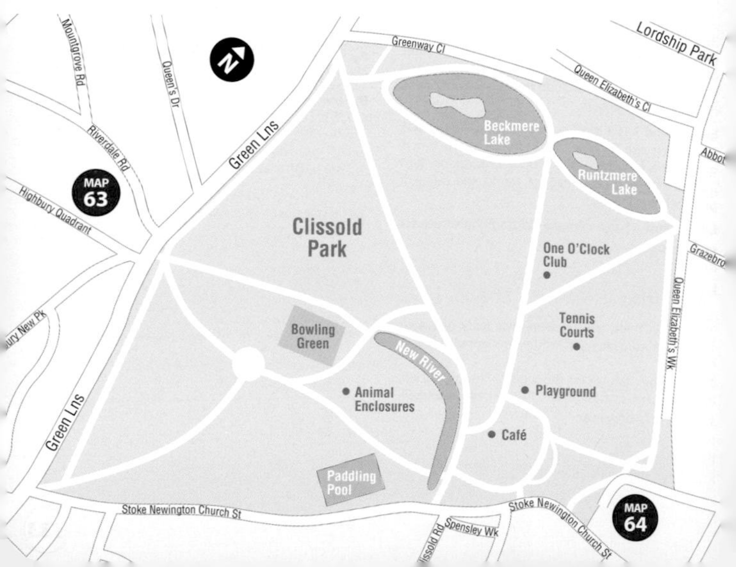

A hundred years later when the land was up for redevelopment, two influential campaigners persuaded the Metropolitan Board of Works to create a public space, and Clissold Park was born on 24 July 1889. Now run by the London Borough of Hackney, Clissold is kept in check by the Clissold Park User Group, who recently secured a multi-million pound lottery bid to spruce the place up a bit and return it to its former 19th century splendour.

Sport in the Park

Year round you can hear the yells of football players churning up mud, the whine of iPods as joggers run in ever decreasing circles, the thwack of cricket ball against cricket bat, and the crunch of misthrown Frisbees hitting the litter bins. There is a basketball court and 10 tennis courts (two kiddies' sized) which are bookable by contacting the Park rangers (020 7254 4235) though they are impossible to get your hands on around Wimbledon—and they say TV doesn't affect our behaviour.

But one of the delights of this park is the more unusual sport that takes place. On misty mornings you can watch cotton-clad figures practice tai chi, and on warm weekends you can nearly always spot a group of hotties from the London School of Capoeira circling around each other. Then there is the occasional father/ daughter pair practising Taekwondo, or two dreadlocked crusties slinging up a line to get some tightrope practice in. Most recent addition to watchable sports in the park is run by 'Pushy Mothers' - groups of mums exercising with buggies. The buggy, with child on board, is pushed hither and thither by the panting parent. It's the ultimate in resistance training.

Nature and The Ponds

Hackney is one of the greenest inner-city boroughs and though relatively small, Clissold Park is still an important green, shady and watery spot for local wildlife, particularly waterfowl. The two nature ponds are named Beckmere and the Runtzmere in honour of the two principal founders (Beck and Runtz, in case you were wondering). The third pond in front of the cafe is more of a 'canalette' and actually used to be part of the New River built in the early 1600s to supply drinking water to London.

The animal enclosure with its fuzzy-nosed deer, fluffy rabbits and bearded mini-goats are popular with visitors who stand stuffing chips and handfuls of poisonous leaves from nearby bushes through the fence directly under the signs saying: 'Please don't feed the animals—it will make them ill.'

Note: the paddling pool is not a nature pond and though you still can't let your dog in, hours spent gazing at its inhabitants are not looked on kindly.

How to Get There

By car: Don't. There isn't much in the way of parking. But if you really need to, from Newington Green head north along Green Lanes until you see a large green space with trees on your right. Or from the A10 turn left onto Stoke Newington Church St past all the cute shops and inviting pubs, until you get to the large church on your left. The park is on your right.

By tube: From Manor House, take exit 4 and walk south down Green Lanes for 10 minutes. The park is on your left.

By train: From Stoke Newington station, head south down the High St and turn right up Stoke Newington Church St, walk for 10 minutes until you see the park on your left just past Stoke Newington Town Hall.

By bus: The 341, 141, 73, 393, and 476 all stop at various entrances to the park

Additional Information

London Borough of Hackney
www.hackney.gov.uk/cp-community-park.htm

Clissold Park User Group
www.clissoldpark.com

Stokefest
www.stokefest.co.uk

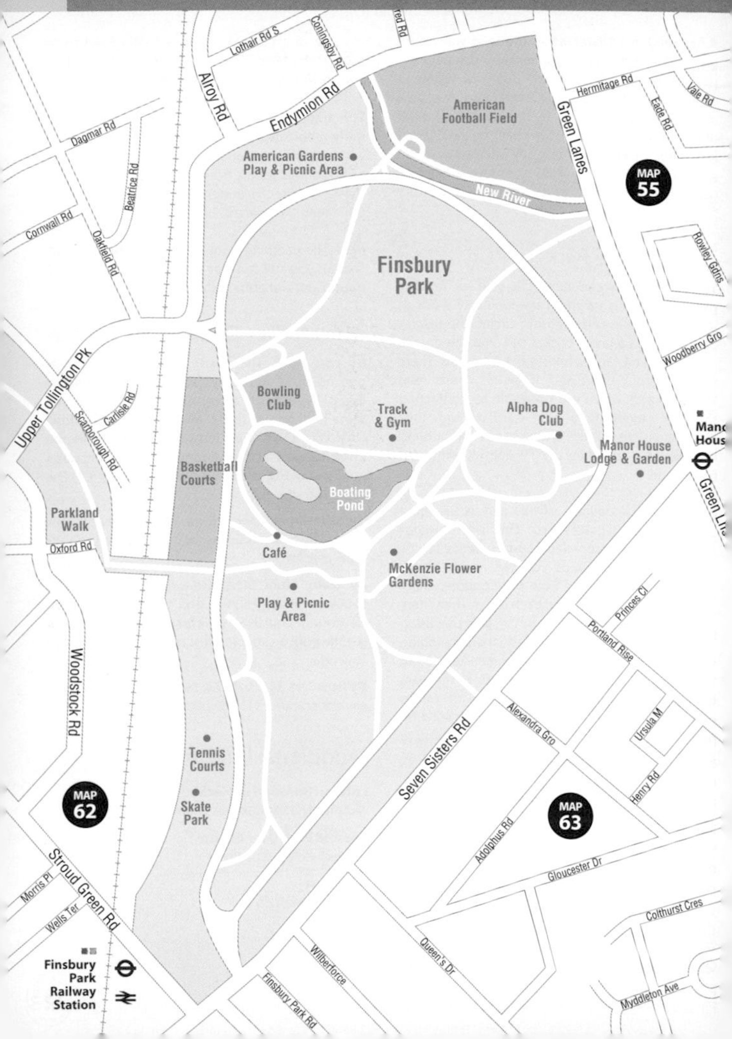
Lothair Rd S
Coningsby Rd
Alroy Rd
Endymion Rd
American Football Field
Hermitage Rd
Vale Rd
Eade Rd
Green Lanes
MAP 55
Dagmar Rd
Beatrice Rd
American Gardens Play & Picnic Area
New River
Cornwall Rd
Oakfield Rd
Finsbury Park
Rowley Gdns
Woodberry Gro
Upper Tollington Pk
Carlisle Rd
Scarborough Rd
Bowling Club
Track & Gym
Alpha Dog Club
Manor House Lodge & Garden
Basketball Courts
Boating Pond
Parkland Walk
Oxford Rd
Café
McKenzie Flower Gardens
Play & Picnic Area
Princes Cl
Portland Rise
Woodstock Rd
Alexandra Gro
Ursula M
Seven Sisters Rd
Tennis Courts
Skate Park
Henry Rd
MAP 62
MAP 63
Adolphus Rd
Gloucester Dr
Stroud Green Rd
Morris Pl
Wells Ter
Colthurst Cres
Wilberforce
Queen's Dr
Finsbury Park Railway Station
Finsbury Park Rd
Myddleton Ave

General Information

NFT Map: 55, 62, & 63
Website: www.haringey.gov.uk/finsbury_park_leaflet.pdf

Overview

Sculpted from what was once a large woodland area on the fringes of London, Finsbury Park was baptized officially in the mid 19th century as a green escape for increasingly urbanized North Londoners. Today's Finsbury Park has been revamped to the tune of £5 million in an attempt to shake off the cloak of urban grime which descended during the 1970s. Though it certainly has cleaned up its act, the park is still a barren tundra-esque plain compared to Hyde or Regent's Park. More of a green scab on the city landscape that surrounds it, the sparse shrubbery and token trees are more suitable for football or running away from Staffordshire Terriers. Delve a little deeper, however and there are quaint eccentricities and little gems dotted around.

Practicalities

You can enter this veritable urban Oz at Endymion Road, Seven Sisters Road, Green Lanes and Stroud Green Road. Two tube stops serve Finsbury Park: Manor House and the eponymous Finsbury Park. There are also overland trains at Harringey Green Lanes (grab an opulent Turkish meal on the way) and at Finsbury Park Stroud Green Road. Buses 4, 19, N19, 29, N29, 106, N106, 253, N253, 254, N279, W3 and W7 all touch the park at some point. Bear in mind that if you wish to travel in the area during an Arsenal match day you'd better take a stun gun and a red scarf to navigate the crowds!

Attractions

Quaint Englishness and sweaty sporting pursuits abound within the perimeters of Finsbury Park. There are many activities you can partake in from tennis (seven courts are available on a turn up and play basis) to running in the Heathside Athletics Club (020 8802 9139). There are even two American Football pitches. For a more twee time stroll up to the tiny boating pond and spend an hour in a beat-up boat circling the aviary island—home to exotic birds like ducks, some swans and, uh, ducks again. The kidz are catered for in the form of a skate park. Best of all is the amazing Parkland Walk, which snakes out from Finsbury Park to Alexandra Palace via Highgate.

Nature

The Arboretum and the Avenue of Mature Trees are the two main spots for tree watching. Granted, experienced botanists may find little to fire them up here, but on a mild Autumn day there are plenty of rich colours and textures that enrich any stroll through the park. There are no real 'wild' areas in the park, unlike Hampstead Heath, but there are some lovely quiet spots in the American Gardens which have been landscaped according to the original 19th century plans, with added kiddie play areas. There are some shrubs planted around the boating pond which Harringey Council calls the 'McKenzie Flower Garden' with capital letters which are barely merited.

Festivals

Recently the vast open spaces of the park have been used for music festivals and various other fairs. The Rise, Fleadh, and FinFest festivals are all fairly regular events. The park is also a popular venue for one off special music events—both the Sex Pistols and Morrissey have played controversial shows here. The steam and fun fairs are also worth going to for nostalgic or regressive fun.

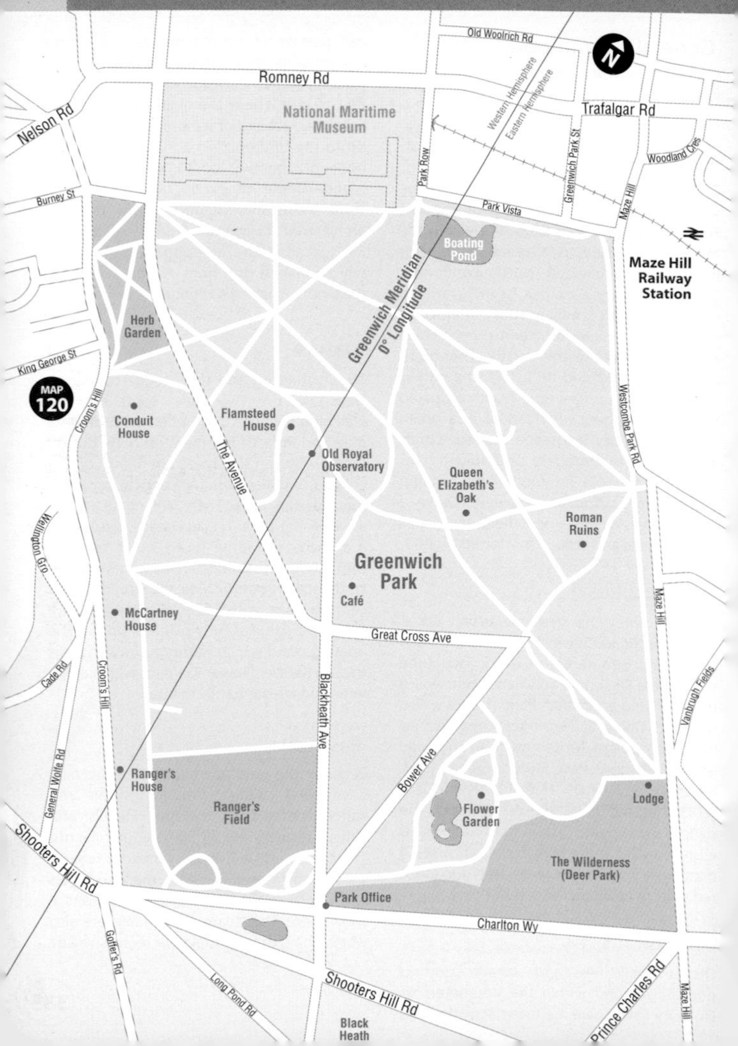
Old Woolrich Rd
Romney Rd
Nelson Rd
National Maritime Museum
Western Hemisphere
Eastern Hemisphere
Trafalgar Rd
Woodland Cres
Park Row
Greenwich Park St
Maze Hill
Burney St
Park Vista
Boating Pond
Maze Hill Railway Station
Greenwich Meridian 0° Longitude
Herb Garden
King George St
MAP 120
Croom's Hill
Conduit House
Flamsteed House
Old Royal Observatory
The Avenue
Westcombe Park Rd
Queen Elizabeth's Oak
Roman Ruins
Wellington Gro
Greenwich Park
Café
McCartney House
Great Cross Ave
Maze Hill
Cade Rd
Croom's Hill
Blackheath Ave
Vanbrugh Fields
Bower Ave
General Wolfe Rd
Ranger's House
Ranger's Field
Flower Garden
Lodge
Shooters Hill Rd
The Wilderness (Deer Park)
Park Office
Charlton Wy
Goffers Rd
Long Pond Rd
Shooters Hill Rd
Prince Charles Rd
Maze Hill
Black Heath

Overview

Greenwich Park is the oldest enclosed Royal Park in Britain and has been an integral part of London life for centuries. Saxons built mounds here; Romans worshipped here; King Henry VIII and Anne Boleyn flirted here, and Charles II even built an observatory here. Then the modern day caught up and 2012 brought it to the world as an Olympic venue. It's now a playground for ageing eccentrics escaping London, yuppie families with new puppies, and heaps of tourists trekking up the staggeringly steep hill towards the iconic Royal Observatory.

And it's worth the trek. The sweeping views from the highest point are spectacular and beat the London Eye hands down. London is revealed in all its glory, from the jutting skyline of Canary Wharf, to the sinuous turns of the Thames and the seemed-like-a-good-idea-at-the-time Millennium Dome. All in stark contrast with the neoclassical architecture of the Old Royal Observatory, Royal Naval College, National Maritime Museum and the Queen's House in the immediate foreground.

A well sought-after spot throughout history, the park has belonged to the Royal Family since 1427, and in the early 1600s, under James I, the park was given a makeover in the French style, which gave it its well-groomed tree-lined pathways. He then had Inigo Jones build the missus the stately Queen's House.

The Royal Observatory and Flamsteed House

Address:	Greenwich Royal Park, Greenwich, London SE10
Phone:	020 8858 4422
Website:	www.nmm.ac.uk
Hours:	10 am-5 pm daily
Admission:	Flamsteed House & Meridian Courtyard - £7.00 adults, £2.00 Children

Time begins, rather arbitrarily, here—on the Prime Meridian of the World, or Longitude 0°. Time all over the earth is based on a place's distance east or west from this imaginary line, outlined in metal so throngs of tourists can gawp at it. Thanks to Charles II's interest in science, Sir Christopher Wren was commissioned to build the Royal Observatory and Flamsteed House, the living quarters for the first Royal Astronomer. Time your visit to catch a workshop, talk, exhibition or planetarium show, which seek to give visitors a richer experience than simply straddling the Meridian with thumbs up.

Also notable is the Camera Obscura, which sits in a small building next to Flamsteed House. A predecessor to the modern camera, this small dark room displays a live image of the distant National Maritime Museum, projected using only a small hole in the roof.

National Maritime Museum

Address:	Greenwich, London SE10 9NF
Phone:	020 8858 4422
Website:	www.nmm.ac.uk
Hours:	10 am-5 pm daily
Admission:	Free

Adjacent to the park's boundaries, this is a museum dedicated to all things nautical. It comprises the Royal Observatory, as well as the Queen's House, but its main components are the Maritime Galleries. Highlights include a collection of ships' figureheads, navigational charts, maps, medals, flags and models. They also host relics from Sir John Franklin's ill-fated Northwest Passage expedition (1845-1848) including a pair of his very old-school sunglasses.

Nature

Amongst the well-mowed green are trees of infinite varieties. The scented herb garden is best enjoyed in the summer time. The fallen remains of the 900 year-old Queen Elizabeth Oak can still be viewed and lie as proof of Henry VIII's passion for these grounds, he was said to have danced around the younger tree with Anne Boleyn (before he had her executed, obviously).

How to Get There

The nearest DLR station is Cutty Sark. It's fun too: push the excitable children out the way so you can sit in the front and pretend to be the driver – always a winner with the ladies. By bus, the 53, 177, 180, 188, 199 and 286 will all get you to points of suitable proximity.

You can also take the Greenwich foot tunnel from the Isle of Dogs, which runs beneath the Thames and is open 24 hours a day. Ignore the ominous drips: it's been sturdy for over 110 years, and even if it does at last succumb to the pressure of 50 ft of river above it, then you'll not have time to worry about it. So relax and enjoy!

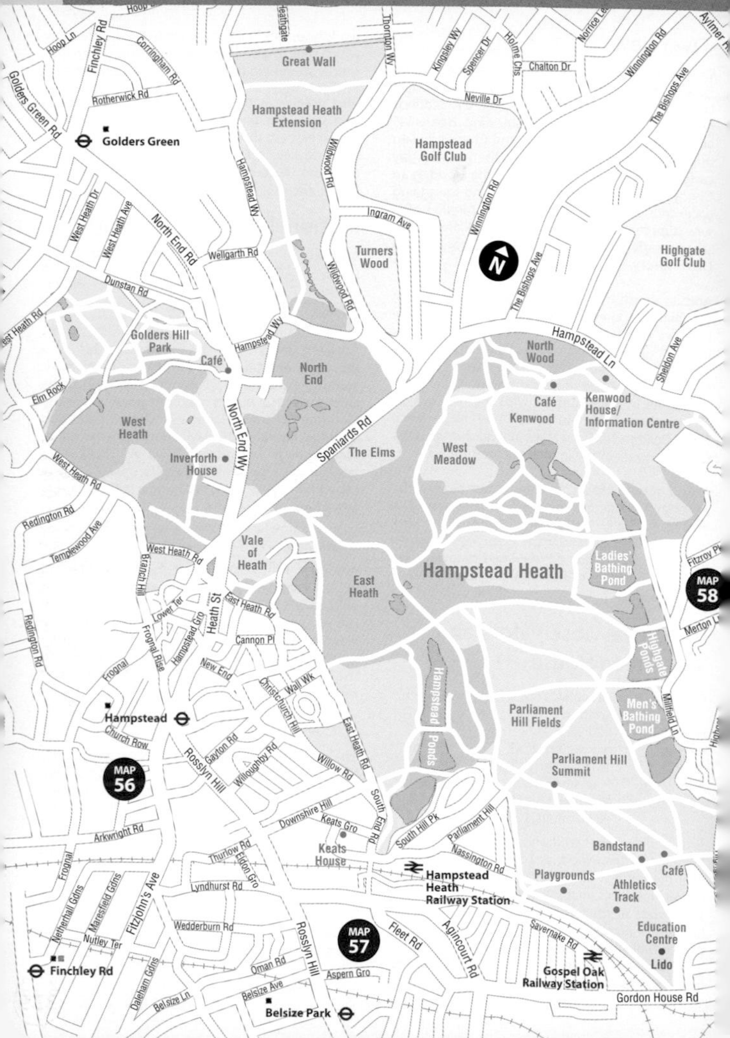
Great Wall
Hampstead Heath Extension
Hampstead Golf Club
Golders Green
Turners Wood
Highgate Golf Club
Golders Hill Park
Café
North End
North Wood
Café
Kenwood
Kenwood House/ Information Centre
West Heath
Inverforth House
The Elms
West Meadow
Vale of Heath
East Heath
Hampstead Heath
Ladies' Bathing Pond
Highgate Ponds
Men's Bathing Pond
Hampstead Ponds
Parliament Hill Fields
Parliament Hill Summit
Hampstead
Keats House
Hampstead Heath Railway Station
Bandstand
Café
Playgrounds
Athletics Track
Education Centre
Lido
Gospel Oak Railway Station
Finchley Rd
Belsize Park
MAP 56
MAP 57
MAP 58
Hoop Ln
Finchley Rd
Corringham Rd
Rotherwick Rd
Golders Green Rd
Heathgate
Thornton Wy
Kingsley Wy
Spencer Dr
Holme Chs
Norrice Lea
Chalton Dr
Winnington Rd
Aylmer Rd
Neville Dr
The Bishops Ave
Hampstead Wy
Wildwood Rd
Ingram Ave
Winnington Rd
West Heath Dr
West Heath Ave
North End Rd
Wellgarth Rd
Dunstan Rd
West Heath Rd
Hampstead Ln
Sheldon Ave
Elm Rock
North End Wy
Spaniards Rd
Redington Rd
Templewood Ave
West Heath Rd
Branch Hill
Lower Ter
Heath St
East Heath Rd
Fitzroy Pk
Merton Ln
Redington Rd
Frognal Rise
Hampstead Gro
Cannon Pl
New End
Frognal
Wall Wk
Christchurch Hill
East Heath Rd
Millfield Ln
Church Row
Gayton Rd
Willoughby Rd
Willow Rd
Rosslyn Hill
South End Rd
Downshire Hill
Keats Gro
South Hill Pk
Parliament Hill
Arkwright Rd
Thurlow Rd
Eldon Gro
Nassington Rd
Frognal
Lyndhurst Rd
Netherhall Gdns
Maresfield Gdns
Fitzjohn's Ave
Wedderburn Rd
Rosslyn Hill
Fleet Rd
Agincourt Rd
Savernake Rd
Nutley Ter
Daleham Gdns
Oman Rd
Aspern Gro
Belsize Ave
Belsize Ln
Gordon House Rd

Overview

Hampstead Heath is 791 acres of rambling woods and idyllic meadows worthy of much frolicking. It's the fact that its wilderness seems so, well, wild that makes this London park deceptive. You can be merrily re-enacting the Brothers Grimm, only to be spat out rather rudely onto Parliament Hill and confronted with gob-smacking views of St Paul's and the Gherkin. The Heath is truly nothing short of heaven—until you stumble over George Michael up to no good in the bushes. You can swim naked in its ponds, stroll amongst its tall grasses without seeing another living soul for twenty minutes or more and engage in a little sex scandal amongst the greenery. The park's common theme is one of a hidden countryside retreat right in the middle of it all.

Most likely because it *is* countryside. It's just the rest of London that's gone all urban around it. Long-established hedgerows and ancient trees attest to its lengthy history. The range of wildlife on show is impressive—kingfishers, parakeets, 300 species of fungi and several types of bat, to name a few. All sorts of famous people have enjoyed its leafy company through the years. Boudicca's Mound near the men's bathing pond (hmm... sounds dirty), is said to mark the ancient queen's burial chamber. Karl Marx and his family had a picnic here every Sunday while he lived in London and writer Wilkie Collins used the park as a backdrop for The Woman in White. All in all, the Heath has been a much-loved place of social gathering and strolling for centuries, a place of peace and perspective amongst the greater hustle and bustle of the Big Smoke.

Ponds, Ponds and... Oh Yeah, More Ponds…

It might be argued that losing your Heath virginity consists of swimming in one of its famous outdoor bathing ponds. These are open throughout the year and attract throngs of dedicated swimming fans. On the eastern side—closer to Highgate—are a series of eight 17th and 18th century reservoirs dotted between Parliament Hill Fields and Kenwood House. Amongst these is one swimming pond for guys, another for gals, a toy boat pond, a wildlife reserve pond, and a lake for fishing. On the western side of the Heath are three more, including the 'mixed pond', where you can have some underwater flirtations, should you wish.

Kenwood House

Kenwood House is closed for refurbishment until Autumn 2013. However, the Brewhouse Café remains open and can be visited between 9am-5pm. Kenwood House, a 17th century manor in the middle of the park, adds very nicely to the Heath's countryside effect. Its striking classically white walls and landscaped grounds play backdrop to summer jazz festivals as well as a few scenes in the movie Notting Hill. Purchased by brewing magnate Edward Cecil Guinness in 1925, Kenwood House is more than just a pretty façade. Thanks to Guinness's fortune and interest in art, the manor house is also a very noteworthy art gallery featuring works by the likes of Rembrandt, Turner and Gainsborough.

Golders Hill Park

Golders Hill Park is the younger brother to the bigger Hampstead Heath, adjoining it on the western side. Where the latter is an icon of epic proportions, the former is more of a good ol' neighbourhood park. Its large expanse of grass was created rather suddenly when a house that stood on the grounds was bombed during the Blitz. It has a lot to offer for its size though, with a formal flower garden, a deer park and a small zoo (with alpacas no less). If you're feeling sporty, there are tennis courts, putting greens and plenty of jogging paths.

How to Get There

The closest tube stations are Hampstead, Golder's Green and Archway on the Northern Line. Nearby overland stations include Hampstead Heath and Gospel Oak. Bus numbers running to the park are the 168, 268 and 210, which cuts through on Spaniard's Road (where you may want to stop for a pint at the historic Spaniard's Inn).

Additional Information

City of London
www.cityoflondon.gov.uk

Information and booking tickets for swimming:
020 7485 5757

Heath and Hampstead Society:
www.heathandhampsteadsociety.org.uk

Highgate Cemetery General Info

NFT Map: 51 & 59
Web: www.highgate-cemetery.org
Phone: 020 8340 1834

West Cemetery

The West Cemetery opened in 1839 and most of the original pathways and structures still exist. This part of the cemetery is a wild wonderland of creeping vines and eerie Victorian tombs. On weekdays, tours take place daily at 2 pm from March to November. There's a limit of 15 people so you'll need to book in advance on the number above. The weekends are a free-for-all with tours taking place hourly from 11 am until 4 pm April to November and until 3 pm December to March.

East Cemetery

The newer East Cemetery is located on the opposite side of the road to the West entrance. This side is open daily and for three pounds you get to roam unsupervised for as long as you please. It may not be as impressive as the West side, but it's still a place of breathtaking beauty. Although there are some well-trodden paths and proper walkways, large parts of the cemetery are almost completely overgrown, making it a wonderful place to go for a stroll.

Opening Hours
1st April to 31st October
Mon-Fri: 10 am-5 pm
Sat-Sun: 11 am-5 pm

1st November to 31st March
Mon-Fri: 10 am-4 pm
Sat-Sun: 11 am-4 pm

Famous Occupants

Quite a few notable people are buried here. The caretakers will be more than willing to inform you of the whereabouts of the following graves and plenty of others.

Douglas Adams, author. Most famous for the *Hitchhiker's Guide To The Galaxy* series of books.

George Eliot, English author and poet; also actually a woman.

Christina Rossetti, English poet.

Karl Marx. Philosopher; considered the father of communism.

Alexander Litvinenko, Russian ex-spy, famously murdered by radiation poisoning in a Soho sushi restaurant in 2006. A whole load of Charles Dickens' clan but not the man himself.

The Highgate Vampire

There have been numerous accounts of shapes, ghosts and supernatural figures seen on the cemetery grounds, and in the early 70s the media picked up on a theory involving a vampire and the legend of The Highgate Vampire was born. It caused quite a stir and soon mobs of 'vampire hunters' descended on the place (imagine something like the Thriller video, but with flares and tank tops). Finally, Sean Manchester, president and founder of the Vampire Research Society, claimed to have killed the fiend in 1973, when he tracked it to a nearby house. Manchester was also, in his spare time, patron of the Yorkshire Robin Hood society, and remains, in this publication's estimation, the single most compelling reason not to wander around Highgate Cemetery after dark.

Waterlow Park

Overview

Waterlow Park is a beautifully landscaped park located just next to the cemetery, making it a perfect spot for a pre- or post-gravespotting picnic. Often overlooked and overshadowed by nearby Hampstead Heath it is a charming and peaceful alternative. You can feed the ducks in one of the three ponds, hire tennis courts by the hour, admire the awesome view of London, wander in the rose garden, or just go and look at the cool hollow tree at the bottom of the park.

Lauderdale House

Address: Highgate Hill, Waterlow Park
London N6 5HG
Tel: 020 8348 8716
Web: www.lauderdalehouse.co.uk

Lauderdale House operates independently from the park, but is located on its grounds. The original house was built in 1582, but has gone through major alterations and restorations since then. In 1963 a major fire destroyed much of the old building and it was left untouched and unoccupied for 15 years. In 1978 it was finally repaired and reopened in its current incarnation. The house runs classes, concerts and exhibitions by local artists. There's also a small café. The House and the galleries are usually open Tue-Fri 11 am-4 pm, Sat 1.30 pm-5 pm & Sun 12 pm-5 pm, but you can always phone in advance to avoid disappointment.

How to Get There

Nearest tube station is Archway. Exit the station and turn left up Highgate Hill. Waterlow Park is about five minutes walk on your left hand side. To get to the cemetery, cross the park down to the Swain's Lane exit, which is adjacent to the East Cemetery gates.

General Information

Website:	www.royalparks.org.uk/parks/hyde_park
Phone:	020 7298 2000

Overview

For over 370 years Hyde Park has been the 'Lungs of London' - the place to go for oxygen-starved Londoners to take a breath of fresh air. his park remains an essential part of the beating heart of London. For over 370 years it has been *the* place to go for oxygen-starved Londoners to take a breath of fresh air. As the city's grown, so has the desire to preserve this 350-acre mass of parkland and thankfully, Hyde Park has never been in better shape.

Eating

Perambulating through the park is bound to get that metabolism going, so stop off at one of the numerous food stalls to quench your thirst or down a plasticky hot-dog. Yum. For a more civilised affair check out one of the park's seated joints: the **Lido Café** (which also has a paddling pool) or **The Serpentine Bar & Kitchen**.

Nature, Architecture & Sculpture

The Serpentine Lake attracts the usual assortment of ducks as well as some exotic additions, such as Egyptian Geese. **The Lookout Education Centre** holds informative talks about the park's wildlife. **The Grand Entrance** at Hyde Park Corner is an awe-inspiring arched construction of Greek influence, whilst the **Albert Memorial**, erected by Queen Victoria after her husband's death, is a true show of love. The **Diana, Princess of Wales Memorial Fountain**, remains one of the most visited areas in Hyde Park and is worth a look to satisfy curiosity, as is the **Peter Pan Memorial**. And pause to reflect at the heartbreaking 7 July Memorial, which pays tribute to each of the victims of the 2005 London Bombings.

Performance

The park attracts big musical events, and by big we mean Live 8 big. It's only the musical deities that get their own special Hyde Park treatment— Bruce Springsteen, Paul McCartney and Blur, but summer means festival time and the annual 02 Wireless Festival and Hyde Park Calling. Brass band concerts are held throughout the summer at **The Bandstand**. **Speakers' Corner** is guaranteed to entertain. Since 1872 it's been the site of a verbal free-for-all stemming from the activities of the Reform League who marched for manhood suffrage in 1866. These days the topics aren't quite as revolutionary. Heather Mills sounded off here recently…ah, the injustice of having too much cash.

Sports

There are ample jogging paths, designated bike routes (see www.companioncycling.org.uk) and great paths for roller-blading and walking. Even more fun is boating on **The Serpentine Lake** from March to October. Informal games of rugby, football or cricket can be played on the **'Sports Field'** while **Hyde Park Tennis & Sports Centre** does exactly what it says on the tin. There's also a bowling green and horse riding at the **Manege.**

Kensington Gardens

The 111 hectares west of the Western Carriage Drive are known as Kensington Gardens. Annexed from the main park in 1689, the area retains a slightly more formal air, with regular tree-lined avenues to stroll down and less spaces for rambunctious sporting displays. This makes the Gardens an ideal spot for a picnic or a quiet ponder. Kensington Gardens also boasts the **Serpentine Gallery** (in between the Diana Fountain and the Albert Memorial), a toy-sized venue for renowned modern and contemporary art exhibitions, and the rather stunning **Kensington Palace**. Still a royal residence, the palace majestically overlooks some of the most well ordered green spaces London has to offer.

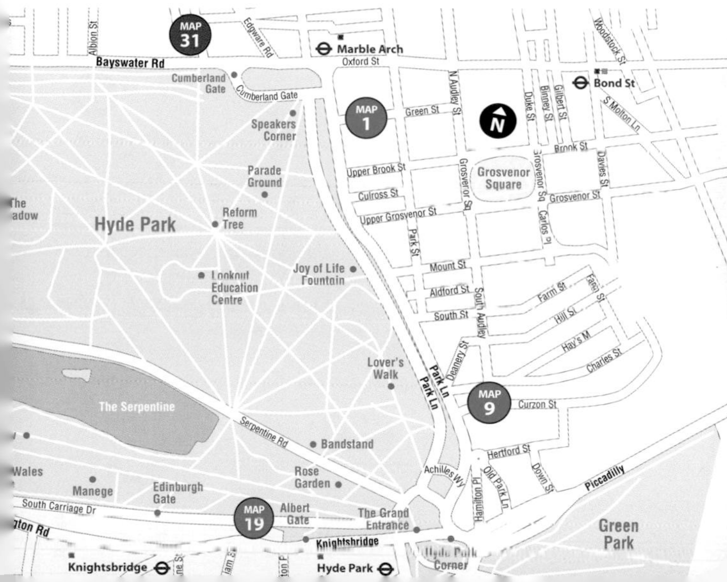

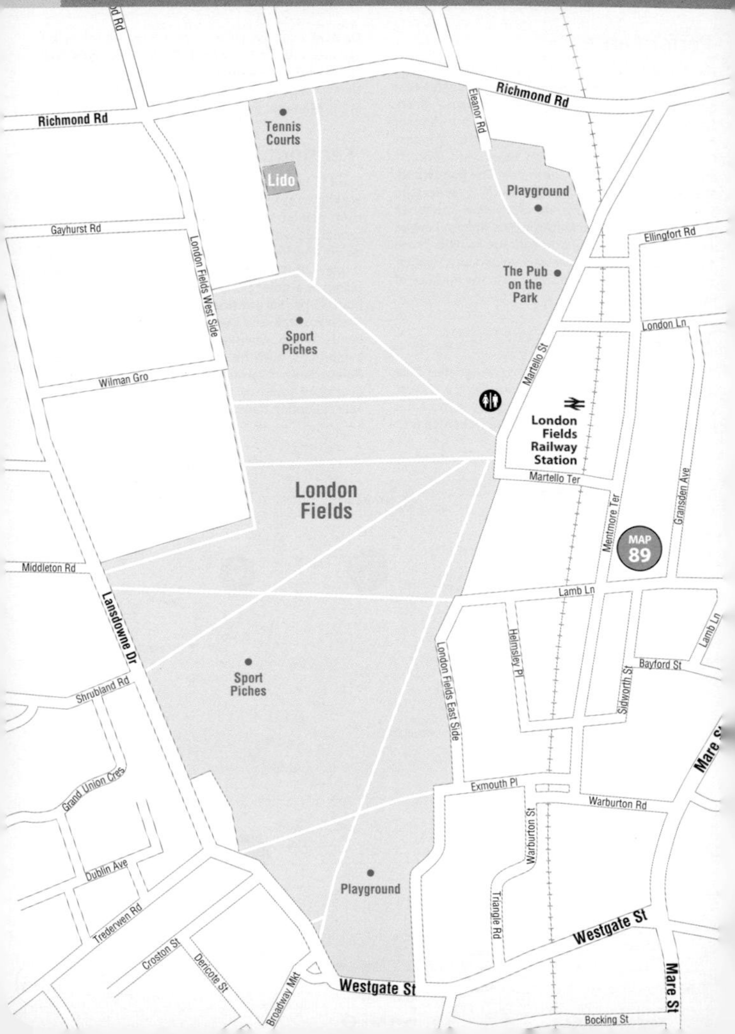

Richmond Rd
Richmond Rd
Tennis Courts
Lido
Eleanor Rd
Playground
Ellingfort Rd
Gayhurst Rd
London Fields West Side
The Pub on the Park
London Ln
Sport Piches
Martello St
Wilman Gro
London Fields Railway Station
Martello Ter
London Fields
Gransden Ave
Mentmore Ter
MAP 89
Middleton Rd
Lamb Ln
Lansdowne Dr
Lamb Ln
Helmsley Pl
London Fields East Side
Bayford St
Shrubland Rd
Sport Piches
Sidworth St
Mare St
Grand Union Cres
Exmouth Pl
Warburton Rd
Warburton St
Dublin Ave
Playground
Triangle Rd
Tederwen Rd
Westgate St
Croston St
Dericote St
Broadway Mkt
Westgate St
Mare St
Bocking St

Overview

Best green space of the northeast? Victoria Park might still bag the accolade, but this relaxed, mid-sized park in the middle of Hackney is catching up. And quickly. It's lush and it's spacious and its latest addition, a smashing 50-metres Lido (see below), is hard to beat. Just off busy Mare Street and minutes from Regent's Canal, the park is easily reachable and easily manageable. There are two tennis courts, football, basketball and cricket pitches, and two well-equipped and well-maintained playgrounds, if you have kids in tow. London Fields does a nice job of attracting a pleasantly diverse mix of people, from Hoxton refugee artists and rollie-smoking would-be philosophers, to pram-pushing mums and East End qeezers with no teeth and big dogs. The architecture framing the tree-studded space is just as varied: bland high rises, pretty Victorians, depressing brick estates and fancy new developments, all modern Hackney is there.

The park's own drinking spot, imaginatively called Pub on the Park, is good for a relaxed outside pint, simple pub food or the footie. If you're after a slightly more refined meal, check the gastropub-ish Cat and Mutton at the park's bottom. This is also where Broadway Market begins, a traditional East End market street, now brimming with nice little shops, several pubs and original eateries. If the red wine you shared with your painter friends on their picnic blanket got you into serious party mood, head to the close-by (and late-night) Dolphin on Mare Street. Or just fall asleep in the shadows of those massive oak trees. Chances are, one of the dogs will lick you back to reality.

London Fields Lido

Address: London Fields Westside, London E8 3EU
Phone: 020 7254 9038
Website: http://www.hackney.gov.uk/c-londonfields-lido.htm
Hours: Mon-Fri 6.45 am-6 pm; Sat-Sun 8 am-5 pm
Admission: £4.50 for adults, £2.70 for kids

You might say that in a city where, essentially, you have the choice between stomach-turningly grotty leisure centre pools and hopelessly overpriced member gym versions, any new public swimming basin would be a winner. Fair enough. But WHAT a winner. Having mouldered closed for almost two decades, a £2.5m effort has restored this art deco gem to its former glory. In fact, it's probably better than ever: the 50-metre basin is nicely heated all year round (25C when we last checked), the changing rooms are modern and clean, admission's okay. Come during the week for a few pre-work lanes, when steam mysteriously hangs over the water, or jump in on the weekend, followed by a Sunday roast in one of the pubs close-by or a picnic in the park. Sounds nice? We know.

Sports

There's no shortage of things to do. The park's two tennis courts can be booked for hourly slots (open 8.30 am-dusk; £5.50/h during peak times, £2.50/h off-peak; call 020 7254 4235 for more info). The Hackney Tennis Club (www.hackneycitytennisclub.co.uk) also offers classes and joint sessions. The football pitch (just come and play) is located in the middle, the basketball space (ditto) towards the south. Follow the sound of children for the playgrounds, one in the north, one in the south. If cricket is your cup of tea, get in touch with the London Fields Cricket Club (londonfieldscc@gmail.com), who keep the park's long-standing tradition as a cricket pitch alive (which, incidentally, is said to go back to 1800).

How to Get There

By bus: Most buses stop on Mare Street (get off at the London Fields stop), a few minutes walk from the actual park. From Liverpool Street Station, take 48 and 55, from Mile End or Bethnal Green grab the D6. The 106 takes you here from Finsbury Park, the 277 from Highbury & Islington. Two buses stop directly at the bottom of the park: the 236 (connecting to Dalston, Newington Green, Finsbury Park) and the 394 (Hackney Central, Homerton Hospital, Hoxton, Angel).

By train: The train is a great option, since London Fields station is located right next to the park. Train operator National Express East Anglia (formerly known as One Railway) serves the central Liverpool Street Station (via Cambridge Heath and Bethnal Green) and connects the Victoria Line tube stations Seven Sisters and Tottenham Hale further north. You can travel using your Oyster Card, for timetables check www.nationalexpresseastanglia.com.

Victoria Park
Old Ford Rd
Hertford Union Canal
Grove Rd
Garmon Rd
Vivian Rd
Zealand Rd
Ellesmere Rd
Driffield Rd
Hewlett Rd
Roman Rd
St Stephen's Rd
Cardigan Rd
Vernon Rd
Shetland Rd
Stafford Rd
Tredegar Rd
Mace St
Twig Folly Cl
Lanfranc Rd
Medway Rd
Lyal Rd
Norman Gro
Saxon Rd
Athelstane Gro
Selwyn Rd
Roman Rd
Grand Union Canal
Arbery Rd
Strahan Rd
Antill Rd
Malmesbury Rd
Cherrywood Cl
Grove Rd
Mile End Park
Meath Gardens
Morpeth St
Lichfield Rd
Merchant St
Harley Gro
Ashcroft Rd
Morgan St
Coborn Rd
Coborn St
Tredegar Sq
Tredegar Sq
Meath Crescent
Clinton Rd
Bradwell St
Longnor Rd
MAP 93
Aberavon Rd
Rhondda Gro
Mile End Rd
Lawton Rd
"The Banana"
Moody St
Grantley St
W Field Wy
Bancroft Rd
Mile End
Southern Grove
Brokersly St
British St
Grove Rd
Eric St
Alderney Rd
Hamlets Wy
English St
Tower Hamlets Cemetery
Stepney Green
Mile End Rd
Mossford St
Eric St
Treby St
Solebay St
Mile End Park
Canal Rd
Ropery St
Ropery St
Bow Common Ln
Ernest St
Commodore St
Shandy St
Hartford St
Ragged School Museum
Burdett Rd
Wager St
Joseph St
White Horse Ln
Essian St
Beaumont Sq
Duckett St
Copperfield Rd
Bale Rd
Stadium
Bohn Rd
MAP 98
Ackroyd Dr
Dongola Rd
Rectory Sq
Stepney Green
Rhodeswell Rd
Leopold St
Timothy Rd
Burdett Rd
Ben Jonson Rd
Halley St
Stepney Green
Garden St
Stepney High St
Whitehorse Rd
Alston St
Carr St
Rhodeswell
St Paul's Wy
Turner's Rd
Locksley
Stepney Wy

Overview

Bordered at the north by the chain-ridden fake-a-rama, Bow Wharf, to the east and south by rat runs, and to the west by the dank waters of the Regent's Canal, this strange elongated park doesn't appear to have a lot going for it. However, this 32-hectare wiggle of green is more a string of mini parks—divided up by roads and railway lines—and each segment has hidden treasures worth digging for. There is an adventure playground, an arts pavilion with weird orange-and-white sculptural seats by Leona Matuszczak, an ecology park with moths and all sorts, a terraced garden and a sheltered children's playground. Clever landscaping and inventive use of space creates pockets of peace, and when the sun comes out, sparkling on the canal, bouncing off of the reflective jackets of the cyclists bombing past or laying its beams on giggling young couples, the park of many parks comes into its own.

It was created following the Second World War after the area was destroyed in the Blitz. The idea of Lord Abercombie, who envisioned a creepy-sounding 'finger of green' in amongst the rubble, Mile End really came into being in 1999 with Millennium Commission funding providing new areas, strange metal cross signage and an amazing green bridge—known by locals as the Banana. It actually has grass and shrubs taking walkers and cyclists over Mile End Road.

The remains of the Victorian terraces sit on the west side of the park, and one resilient pub, The Palm Tree, squats alone in the middle of a grey car park, a testament to the rows of two-up-two-downs which no longer flank the pub. This great local boozer is filled most nights with a mix of climbers and locals tucking into doorstep sandwiches and draft beer.

For those who want a bit more local history, The Ragged School Museum (www.raggedschoolmuseum.org.uk) on Copperfield St overlooks the southern tip of the park: a canal side slum that was transformed into a school for the local urchins by philanthropist Dr Barnado. It now has a mocked-up Victorian classroom and clunky little cafe. Only open Wednesday and Thursday and the occassional Sunday—check before you go.

Sports in the Park

The southern end of the park is a haven for sporty types with a refurbished stadium and ten all-weather pitches made from recycled car tyres, a go-kart track and the large Ikea-like Mile End Leisure Centre with all the usual sauna, gym, pool and verruca-infested changing rooms.
Mile End Climbing Wall is housed in an old pipe engineering works in the middle of the park, and is one of London's 'big three' (The Castle and the Westway are the others). It was opened in the 80s and some of its users seem unaware of time's passage, judging by their fetching leggings.

How to Get There

By tube: Turn left out of Mile End station, cross Grove Rd and you'll find yourself at one of the entrances to the middle section of the park.

By car: The park can be easily accessed from Bow Road, Grove Rd, or Mile End Rd, though according to London Borough of Tower Hamlets, 'The local streets operate a resident's parking permit system and are regularly patrolled by traffic wardens. Limited parking is available at Bow Wharf.'

By bus: The, D6, D7, 25, 205, 277, 323, 339 and all take you to various entrances around the park.

Additional Information

London Borough of Tower Hamlets
www.towerhamlets.gov.uk/data/discover/data/parks/mile-end/the-park-map.cfm

Mile End Climbing Wall
www.mileendwall.org.uk

General Information

Website:	www.royalparks.org.uk/parks/regents_park
Park Tel:	020 7486 7905
London Zoo:	www.zsl.org
Open Air Theatre:	www.openairtheatre.org

Overview

Whenever your quaint and backward country-dwelling friends are telling you the virtues of rural life, you can silence them with two words: Regent's Park. Let the yokels have their cleaner lungs, their maypoles and their children running barefoot and feral, because London may have its city drawbacks but it knows how to do a good park. When you stroll in Regent's Park, you're strolling on nothing less than Property of the Crown—you can see tigers and gorillas, play on the largest outdoor sports area in London, take in some Shakespeare, or, on a very good day, watch girls playing volleyball in bikinis. With 410 acres of parkland, you will always find a spot away from the (many thousands of) fellow visitors. It is the perfect space to take stock, step back and refresh, to sit in a deckchair with a good book, picnic with friends, breathe better air. Moreover, the same obnoxious people who wouldn't move down the tube to let you on or

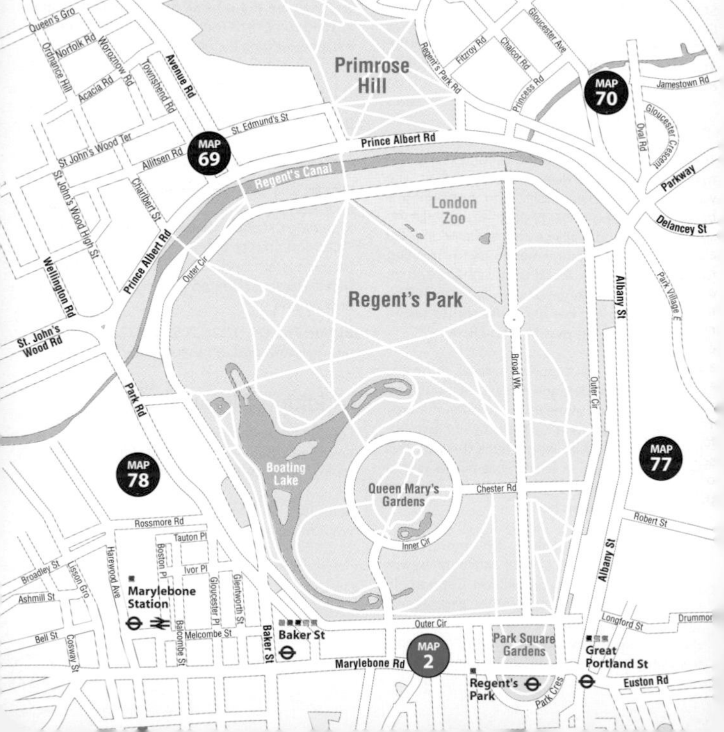

who pushed in the sandwich queue, are here relaxing with their families, lazing over a paper in a patch of sun, falling in love, throwing a Frisbee: it can be just what you need to re-bond with London when you're becoming jaded, and to get away from it all without leaving Zone One.

How to Get There

By tube:
Regent's Park – Bakerloo.
Great Portland St – Hammersmith & City, Circle, Metropolitan.
Baker St – Hammersmith & City, Jubilee, Metropolitan, Bakerloo.
St John's Wood – Jubilee.
Camden Town – Northern.

The Park is served by bus routes 2, 13, 18, 27, 30, 74, 82, 113, 139, 189, 274, 453 and C2.

Nature

The Park is a haven for the city's wildlife, thanks to a biodiversity which includes grassland, woodland, wetland, lakes and scrubs, as well as beautifully tended and fragrant gardens. Over 200 species of birds have been spotted in the Park, along with favourite garden mammals such as hedgehogs, squirrels and foxes. But if that's all just a bit too Beatrix Potter, you can get your fix of the more badass species at London Zoo in the Park's north-east end, where in addition to the normal enclosures, visitors can get closer to some of the animals with events like "Meet the Monkeys" or even help as a volunteer.

The Park's size and calm makes it a choice hangout for celebrities (not strictly nature, but dandelion schmandelion: spotting A-LIsters doing tai chi in oversized sunglasses will impress more down the pub, and can there be a nobler calling?).

Performances and Events

The Park's permanent outdoor theatre is an absolute treat. The shows have a Shakespearian bias, but the venue also puts on non-bard performances, comedy nights and concerts. It is the experience more than the performance which will likely stay in your memory. Among the atmospheric trees of the park in the evening, with a bottle of wine and a blanket to snuggle up in (it is Britain after all—how many other theatres have an official "weather policy"?), it is a magical way to spend an evening. Outdoor does not mean free however: prices range from £10–£50 (Saturdays are the most expensive), and you pay theatre prices for food and drink. Cheaper to bring a picnic to enjoy in front of the theatre before the performance.

Regent's Park also hosts a number of big outdoor events. Notable regulars include Taste of London, the Innocent Smoothies Festival, and the Frieze art show. Check the website for one-off listings.

Primrose Hill

To the north of Regent's Park sits Primrose Hill, which is a rather large hill, boasting corking views of much of Central and East London. It's also surrounded by some rather lovely eateries.

The former hunting ground for playboy king Henry VIII has a murky history, becoming the scene of a political feud in 1678, when magistrate Edmund Berry Godfrey was found dead there after being implicated in a plot to kill Charles II. In later generations Primrose Hill became the setting for duels: London lovers fought there over their ladies, while fops found it a good place to settle literary disagreements ("I say Dryden is naught but a one-trick satirist sir!" "Well then I say you are a cad and a scoundrel! Die you maggot!").

Celebrity voyeurs should keep 'em peeled for the likes of Kates Moss and old bumbles himself Mr Boris Johnson, writer Alan Bennett, while Primrose Hill in winter is the ideal spot to check out panoramic views of fireworks across the city on Guy Fawkes' night (5 November).

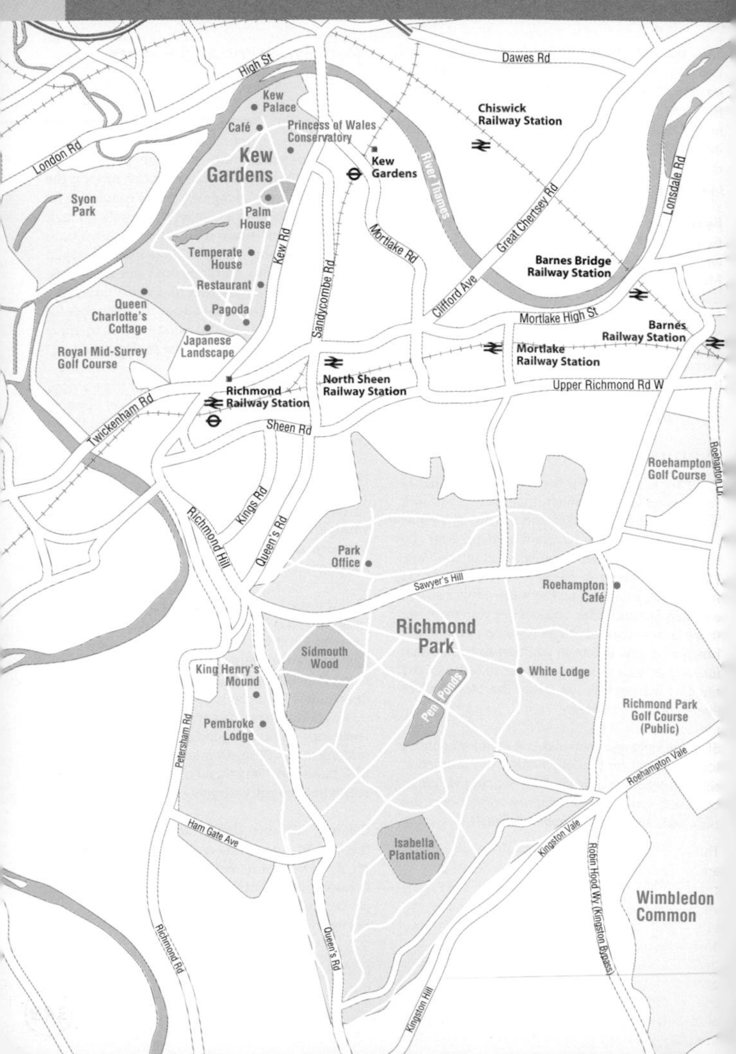
High St
Dawes Rd
Kew Palace
Café
Princess of Wales Conservatory
Kew Gardens
Kew Gardens
River Thames
Chiswick Railway Station
London Rd
Syon Park
Palm House
Temperate House
Restaurant
Pagoda
Kew Rd
Sandycombe Rd
Mortlake Rd
Great Chertsey Rd
Lonsdale Rd
Barnes Bridge Railway Station
Clifford Ave
Queen Charlotte's Cottage
Japanese Landscape
Royal Mid-Surrey Golf Course
Mortlake High St
Barnes Railway Station
Mortlake Railway Station
North Sheen Railway Station
Richmond Railway Station
Upper Richmond Rd W
Twickenham Rd
Sheen Rd
Roehampton Golf Course
Roehampton Ln
Kings Rd
Richmond Hill
Queen's Rd
Park Office
Sawyer's Hill
Roehampton Café
Richmond Park
Sidmouth Wood
King Henry's Mound
White Lodge
Pen Ponds
Pembroke Lodge
Richmond Park Golf Course (Public)
Petersham Rd
Roehampton Vale
Ham Gate Ave
Kingston Vale
Isabella Plantation
Robin Hood Wy (Kingston Bypass)
Wimbledon Common
Richmond Rd
Queen's Rd
Kingston Hill

Overview

In 1625 Charles I brought his court to Richmond. He subsequently, with quite heroic selfishness, built a wall 'round a large expanse of open grassland, and created Richmond Park. These days the park is thankfully accessible to the public, opening at 7 am (or 7.30 in the winter) and closing at dusk every day. It's the biggest of the Royal Parks in London, and is an obvious choice for long bike rides, picnics, informal sports and other wholesome pursuits for your golden, happy days of youth. Oh, and there's deer.

Attractions

The park has a number of gardens and wooded areas, the most beautiful of which is probably the Isabella Plantation, an organic woodland garden that blooms with azaleas and rhododendrons. The Pen Ponds is another popular feature, as is Pembroke Lodge, the park's Georgian mansion, which can be rented out for weddings and conferences (www.pembroke-lodge.co.uk or call 020 8940 8207). The adjacent café also does a mean cream team.

Sports

There are three rugby pitches near the Roehampton Gate that are available for rental on weekdays during winter (contact the Rosslyn Park Rugby Club at 020 8948 3209), and two eighteen hole, pay and play golf courses (call 020 8876 1795 for info. and booking). Between 16 June and 14 March you can purchase a fishing permit for the Pen Ponds (call 020 8948 3209 for information). Or for more extreme park-goers there is the option of Power Kiting, whatever the hell that is (www.kitevibe.com), and military-led Boot Camps to shape you up fast and mercilessly.

Kew

The Royal Botanic Gardens at Kew, begun in 1660, are not only easy on the eyes but an important centre for horticultural research and a UNESCO world heritage site Guaranteed to take place every year though are the summer festival 'Kew The Music' (July) and Ice-skating (Nov-Feb). The gardens are still going strong, with record amounts of visitors. The Gardens are a hugely popular day trip destination for schoolchildren and adults alike and contain such a surplus of sights and attractions that repeat visits are always surprising.

Attractions

Of course the main attractions here are the Gardens themselves. Between the formal gardens, smaller themed collections of plants and wildlife and conservation areas, there is enough walking and cooing to be done to justify any length of cake and sandwich sessions at one of the Gardens' eateries. There are also 39 Grade I and II listed buildings, all of which have some kind of historic significance. The 17th century Kew Palace (www.hrp.org.uk), is one of the most interesting of these, having previously been home to the notoriously 'mad' King George III. Other buildings in the gardens include the Chinese Pagoda of 1762, a traditional Japanese 'Minka' house and a number of museums. Decimus Burton's glasshouses (The Palm House and the Temperate) are iconic examples of this quintessentially Victorian architectural theme, and an essential part of any visit to Kew.

Events

Kew Gardens is run with great enthusiasm and has a packed programme of events throughout the year. These occur and change frequently so it's best to check the Kew website, which has comprehensive listings of everything that is going on in the Gardens, down to the blooming or blossoming of individual plant species: www.kew.org.

Several of the historic buildings, most spectacularly the Temperate Glasshouse, are available to rent for corporate and private parties.

How to Get There

Richmond station (overland trains, District Line) is a 20 minute walk from Richmond Park, or buses 371 and 65 both go from the station to the pedestrian gate at Petersham. Kew Gardens is (surprisingly) the closest station for Kew Gardens, London Overground trains stop here from across North and North West London. Trains from Waterloo stop at Kew Bridge station, a ten- minute walk from the gardens.

A large number of buses go from Hammersmith, Fulham, Clapham Junction, Wandsworth and Ealing to Richmond Park and to Kew Gardens.

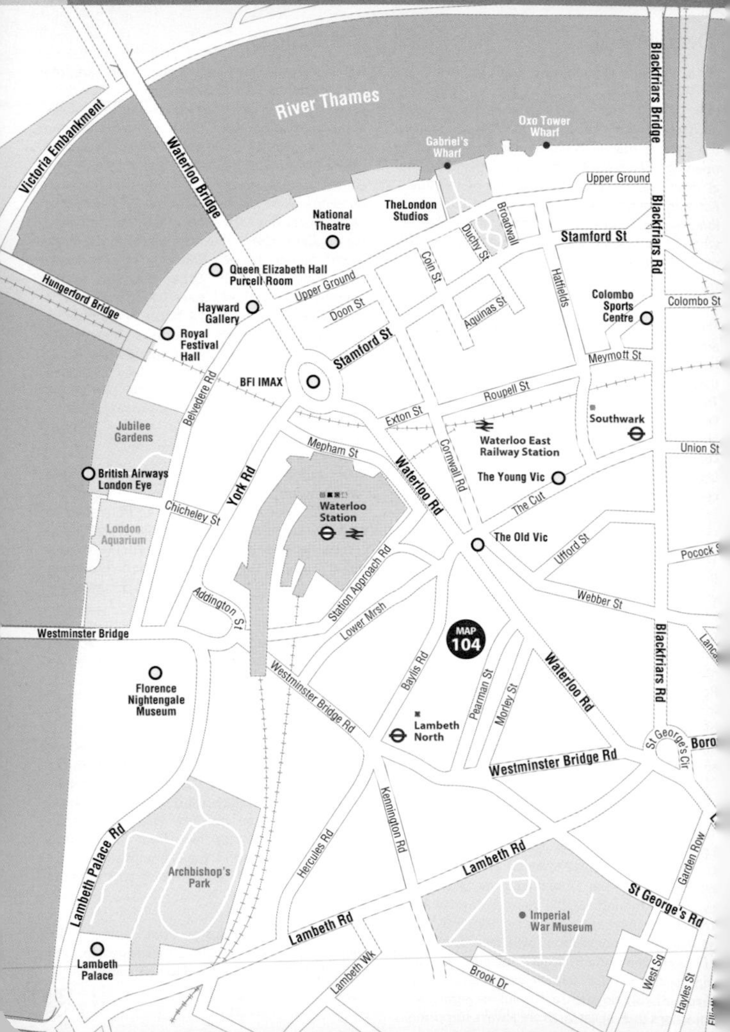
River Thames
Victoria Embankment
Waterloo Bridge
Hungerford Bridge
Blackfriars Bridge
Oxo Tower Wharf
Gabriel's Wharf
Upper Ground
National Theatre
TheLondon Studios
Broadwall
Duchy St
Stamford St
Blackfriars Rd
Coin St
Hatfields
Queen Elizabeth Hall
Purcell Room
Upper Ground
Doon St
Aquinas St
Colombo Sports Centre
Colombo St
Hayward Gallery
Royal Festival Hall
Stamford St
Meymott St
BFI IMAX
Belvedere Rd
Roupell St
Exton St
Southwark
Jubilee Gardens
Union St
Mepham St
Cornwall Rd
Waterloo East Railway Station
British Airways London Eye
York Rd
Waterloo Rd
The Young Vic
Chicheley St
Waterloo Station
The Cut
London Aquarium
The Old Vic
Station Approach Rd
Ufford St
Pocock S
Addington St
Lower Mrsh
Webber St
Westminster Bridge
MAP 104
Baylis Rd
Pearman St
Morley St
Waterloo Rd
Florence Nightengale Museum
Westminster Bridge Rd
Lambeth North
St George's Cir
Boro
Westminster Bridge Rd
Kennington Rd
Lambeth Palace Rd
Hercules Rd
Lambeth Rd
Garden Row
Archbishop's Park
Imperial War Museum
St George's Rd
Lambeth Rd
Lambeth Palace
Lambeth Wk
Brook Dr
West Sq
Hayles St

Overview

A pedestrianised quarter formed of venues for theatre, music, cinema, art and various other artistically orientated entities, the South Bank is the realisation of a post-war dream of an arts-for-all hub in London. The area has its roots in 1951's Festival of Britain, a technicoloured marvel designed to showcase an optimistic future for Britons used to coal, Spitfires and fake mashed potato. The legacy of the Festival ensured that the surrounding area went on to grow into the playground that it has become today.

The South Bank Centre

The actual 'South Bank Centre' is officially formed of the Royal Festival Hall, the Queen Elizabeth Hall, the Purcell Room, the Hayward Gallery and the Saison Poetry Library, which are all concentrated in the centre of the South Bank. The Royal Festival Hall hosts a variety of musical and dance performances from its auditorium, whilst the Hall's foyer is an enormous and relaxed open-plan area with a bar, performance spaces and shop. The Queen Elizabeth Hall and Purcell Room offer further stages for musical recitals whilst the Saison Poetry Library houses a vast collection of poetry dating from 1912 onwards. The Hayward Gallery has an exterior of frightening ugliness, which shields a surprisingly spacious interior, devoted to exhibitions of the visual arts.

The National Theatre

The National Theatre is next-door to the South Bank Centre complex and is another gaping example of uncompromising architecture. Opened in 1963, it still looks slightly unhinged. The building consists of three theatres and puts on a range of productions from the established to the experimental. It also features an inviting foyer, and in the open spirit of the South Bank, offers back-stage tours, workshops, talks and costume and prop hire to Joe Schmo.

British Film Institute and IMAX

Nestling under Waterloo Bridge, the BFI promotes film and television through its archives, cinema screens, talks and festivals. It's a great alternative to the disgustingly over-priced and sticky-floored chain cinemas of central London and promotes an all-encompassing program from its three screens. The Film Café and Benugo Bar & Kitchen do good pre- and post-flick munch. The BFI IMAX is the separate, rotund glass building situated around 200m south of the BFI. It shows films on Britain's biggest cinema screen accompanied by sound pumped from a gargantuan 11,600-watt sound system.

Everything Else

Beyond its theatres, music halls, galleries and cinemas, the South Bank has spawned a number of other attractions. The London Eye is an enormous Ferris wheel built in 2000 on the banks of the Thames adjacent to Westminster Bridge, It revolves at a leisurely 0.5 mph and offers brilliant views from its 135m-high peak. The London Aquarium is just opposite but with ticket prices roughly similar to the Eye, seeing big fish in small tanks starts to look a distinctly lame option. Less expensive attractions around South Bank include the open-air book market tucked under Waterloo Bridge and Gabriel's Wharf, a dinky enclave of small shops, bars and restaurants that offer succour to those cultured-out Or you can ogle at the cool kids doing half pipes at the South Bank Skate Park..

Getting There

By tube: Nearest stations are Waterloo (Northern, Bakerloo, Jubilee and Waterloo & City lines) and Embankment (Circle, District, Northern & Bakerloo lines). From Waterloo, head 50m towards the river. Embankment station is at the northern foot of Hungerford footbridge.

By train: Nearest stations are Waterloo & Charing Cross. For directions from Waterloo, see 'By Tube'. From Charing Cross, walk 100m down Villiers Street towards the river and then walk across the Hungerford footbridge.

By bus: The South Bank is on numerous bus routes. Buses stop on nearby Waterloo Bridge, York Road, Belvedere Road, Stamford Street and Waterloo Station. Most coming from the North get to South Bank via Holborn, The Strand or Victoria. From the South they come via Elephant and Castle or Lambeth North.

By boat: Festival Pier is adjacent to the London Eye. Pleasure boats dock here on cruises, as do riverboat services which sail west as far as Tate Britain and east as far as Woolwich Arsenal.

General Information

NFT Maps: 9 & 23
Website: www.royalparks.org.uk/parks/st_james_park
www.royalparks.org.uk/parks/green_park
Free guided walks: 020 7930 1793
Inn the Park Café and Restaurant (St. James's Park): 020 7451 9999

Overview

With Trafalgar Square at one end and Buck Palace at the other, both St. James's and Green Park are slap-bang in the heart of picture-postcard London. When the belching fumes of the Hackney cab and hordes of Oxford Street shoppers threaten both health and sanity, there's only one place to go. Zip past the crowds and pigeons in Trafalgar Square and head under the grand curve of Admiralty Arch into the stately calm of St. James's Park. Stand yourself on the bridge that crosses the lake, take a deep breath and marvel at the history surrounding you in the city's oldest Royal Park, dating back to the days of Henry VIII.

The views: fairytale Buckingham Palace to the west, Downing Street, the seat of Parliament and Big Ben jutting out over Horse Guards' Parade to the east and the towers of Westminster Abbey to the south. There ain't nowhere else in London where you can view the icons of Church, State and Monarchy in one quick spin on your heels. Impressive. And when you're done marvelling, join the families, office workers, joggers and tourists in taking a stroll round the lake for pelican-spotting, duck-feeding, lunching and romancing.

A hop across the Mall and you'll find yourself in the rolling green of, yup, Green Park. Flowerbed free, this 53-acre patch of park with its aged plane trees is the more meditative of the two. A refuge from the noisy thoroughfare of Piccadilly and Hyde Park corner, its grounds soon fill with picnicking office-workers at the slightest suggestion of sun while the tree-lined Mall is the nearest you'll get to a Parisian boulevard.

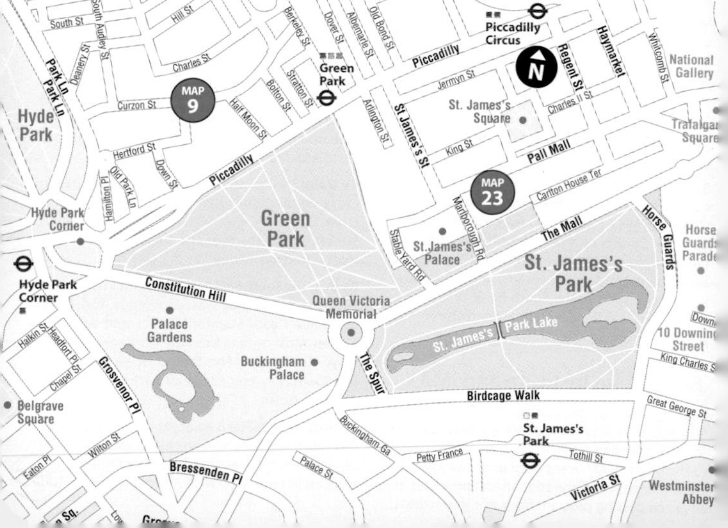

Nature

The curving lake of St. James's park runs the length of the grounds and is perfect for indulging in some casual bird-spotting. Ever since the days of James I, the park has been home to an exotic menagerie, once including elephants, camels and even crocs.

While the crocs and ellies might be long gone, both Duck Island and the smaller West Island remain home to an impressive array of water birds. Beyond the humble duck and gulls, there are suitably stately black swans, rare golden eyes and the rather less illustrious sounding shovelers, a close relative of the time-starved office-worker on lunch, we believe. But, with their gentlemanly swagger and mighty beaks, the five resident pelicans unquestionably steal the show. A gift from the Russian Ambassador in 1664, feeding time is worth a gander at 3pm daily. Known for their entertaining antics—like flying to Regent's Park Zoo on fish-stealing sprees—one caused a media storm when, clearly lusting after a menu change, it swallowed a live pigeon whole, flapping feathers 'n' all.

Take some old bread and the park's tame, tubby squirrels will feast from your hand. Hang around 'til dusk and the bats come out to play.

Architecture & Sculpture

As if housing ol' Queenie's Buckingham Palace wasn't enough, the parks are surrounded by two more palaces—Westminster, now the Houses of Parliament, and St. James's. From the Regency elegance of the Mall's Carlton House, home to the Institute of Contemporary Arts (ICA), to the impressive frontage of Horse Guard's Parade, the parks are hemmed in by grandeur.

Once a swampy wasteland for grazing pigs, it's a tale with humble beginnings for London's most royal park. While each passing King and Queen slowly improved St. James's Park, it was Charles II that really put the work in, getting trees planted, lawns laid and then opening it up for the first time to us commoners.

Sobering war memorials in St. James's Park abound, including world war icons Mountbatten and Kitchener in Horse Guards' Parade, and an overblown marble statue of Queen Victoria complete with glitter and gates. Oh, and that grand old Duke of York, best-known for marching his men up and down some hill? He's here too, in bronze atop a mighty pillar by the ICA.

The Parks in Season

St. James's in spring is carpeted with crocuses and daffodils. Come summer, they're quickly replaced with a carpet of sun-starved Tom, Dick and Sallys, laid bare as they dare to catch some rays. For an instant upgrade from the rabble, head to Green Park by the tube and hire a stripy deck-chair at £1.50 a pop from April to September.

Between May and August, add a dash of high-brow culture to your day with free concerts at the bandstand every lunchtime and early evening.

Autumn days might be chilly but clear skies make for impressive sunsets while wintry strolls are all the more head-clearing, especially after a night on the Soho tiles.

Sports

With cycling and ball-games banned—*entirely inappropriate in such stately surrounds!*—jogging, morning tai chi, leisurely strolls and pigeon chasing are as energetic as it gets. Sundays are best for strolling when Constitution Hill is closed to traffic.

The Mall and Constitution Hill are cycle-friendly and make a pleasant cut through the West End. Join the Serpentine running club for regular jaunts through St. James's. (www.serpentine.org.uk).

Enjoy the sedate pace with free lunch-time guided walks twice a month, discussing anything from horticulture to royalty (booking line: 020 7930 1793).

General info

NFT Map: 90, 93, & 94
Website: http://www.towerhamlets.gov.uk/lgsl/451-500/461_parks_and_open_spaces/victoria_park.aspx
Information: 020 8985 1957

Overview

Look at all the joggers, skaters, cricketers and picnickers swarming in Victoria Park on any given weekend, and it seems hard to continue calling this 218-acres green space one of London's best-kept secrets. Yet, to many Londoners not living east, it still is. Lined by Regent's Canal in the south, London's third-largest cultivated green space is a nice blend of Regent's Park's beauty and the wilderness found in Hampstead Heath. It's also far enough off the Central London map to stay virtually tourist-free, while, at the same time, feeling reassuringly inner city urban, with the Gherkin and Canary Wharf's skyscrapers all in sight.

Divided into two handy bits by Grove Road, Victoria Park has much of what makes a park more than just grass and trees: excellent sporting facilities, ranging from athletics to rugby, several lakes, a deer enclosure, a secret garden—and plenty of decent drinking holes nearby. Designed in the 1840s to bring much needed greenery and breathing space to a soul-destroyingly grim East End, the "people's park" can also look back on an intriguing past of dissent, non-conformist rallying and all sorts of political mischief-making. And it's home to the oldest model boat racing club in the country. Come now, before the Olympics do. Once the squirrels start digging out amphetamines, the secret will be gone forever.

Nature

Ducks, swans, birds and god knows what else live around The Lake in the west, while deer and goats graze slightly further north. You're allowed to fish in the Old Lake, although we're not at all sure that there are really many fish in there. Pretty oak trees and hawthorns stud the whole place; colourful flowers and perfectly-groomed shrubs grow in the Old English Garden. It's a beautifully landscaped gem of a garden and one of this city's most peaceful spots—if you don't mind the odd greying philosopher, mumbling to himself.

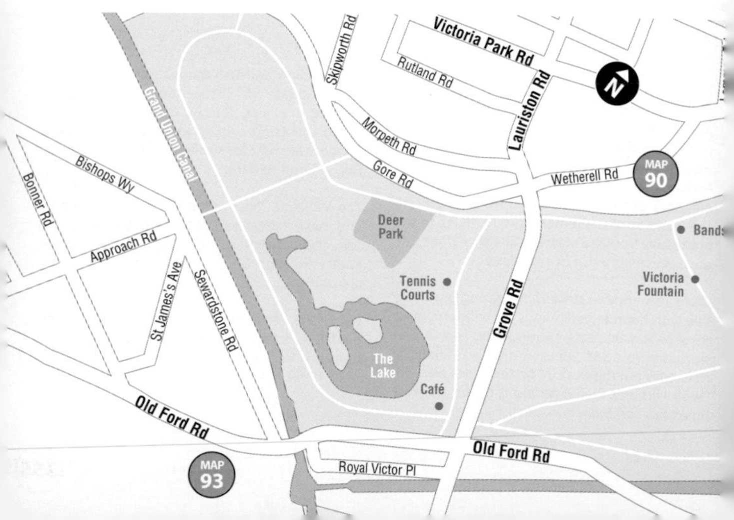

Sports

Jogging and skating are popular and, thanks to wide pathways, possible throughout the park. There's a rugby pitch, a large dedicated football area, four tennis courts (call 020 8986 5182) and three all-weather cricket pitches, run by the esteemed Victoria Park Community Cricket League (www.vpccl.co.uk). The children's playgrounds are decent enough, and the athletic field is excellent. Get in touch with the park's own athletics association (www.vphthac.org.uk) for access to changing rooms, showers and its indoor training hall.

Architecture & sculpture

Rising in the middle of the park is a Grade-II listed drinking fountain erected by Baroness Angela Burdett-Coutts (England's wealthiest woman at some point, we're told), adorned by several half-naked marble boys, smiling cheekily. The Hackney Wick Great War Memorial, in the east part of the park, is a reminder that this part of London was hit especially hard by the bombings of the Second World War. Close-by, you'll find two alcove-type fragments that survived the demolition of the old London Bridge Station. Fairly unremarkable, but good shelter when it's raining. Let's face it, no one comes here for architecture.

Festivals

The hazy days when The Clash whipped up a beer-can-throwing frenzy in the park—heralding a new era called punk along the way—might be over, but Victoria Park has kept its musical tradition alive. Slightly more tamed and organised, the festivals taking place these days range from the trendy, village-feel Field Day to the indie-and-electro-blending Lovebox Weekender, while big names (Radiohead for one) have also discovered a liking for the park's scenery and music-appreciating attitude.

Eat & drink

The park's café, next to The Lake, is tiny, but the organic cakes are a tasty lot. That aside, you have to venture to the park's fringes for food and drink, but fear not: a tap is never far. Leave behind the bog-standard, soulless pub that is The Victoria and opt for the East End earthiness of the Top of the Morning instead, near the Cadogan Gate. Good Ales, a real fireplace, and up-marketish pub food make The Royal Inn on the Park, near the Royal Gates, the usually busy favourite. The Fat Cat, a few minutes south of the park along Grove Road, is more restaurant than pub, a bit pricey but a good choice for high-quality pasta, burgers and steaks.

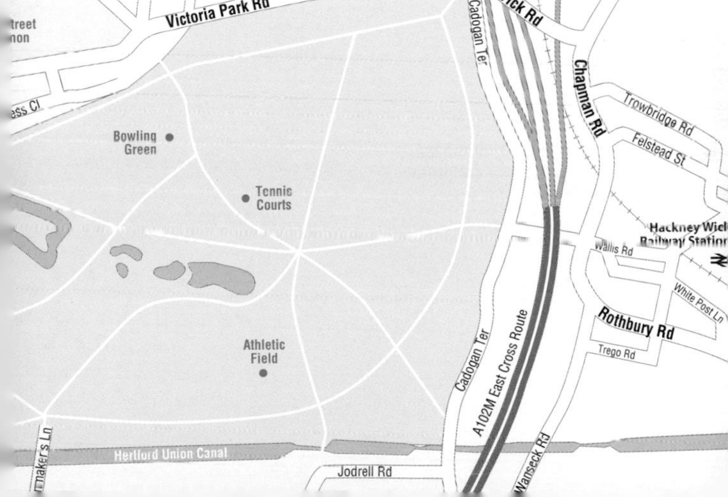

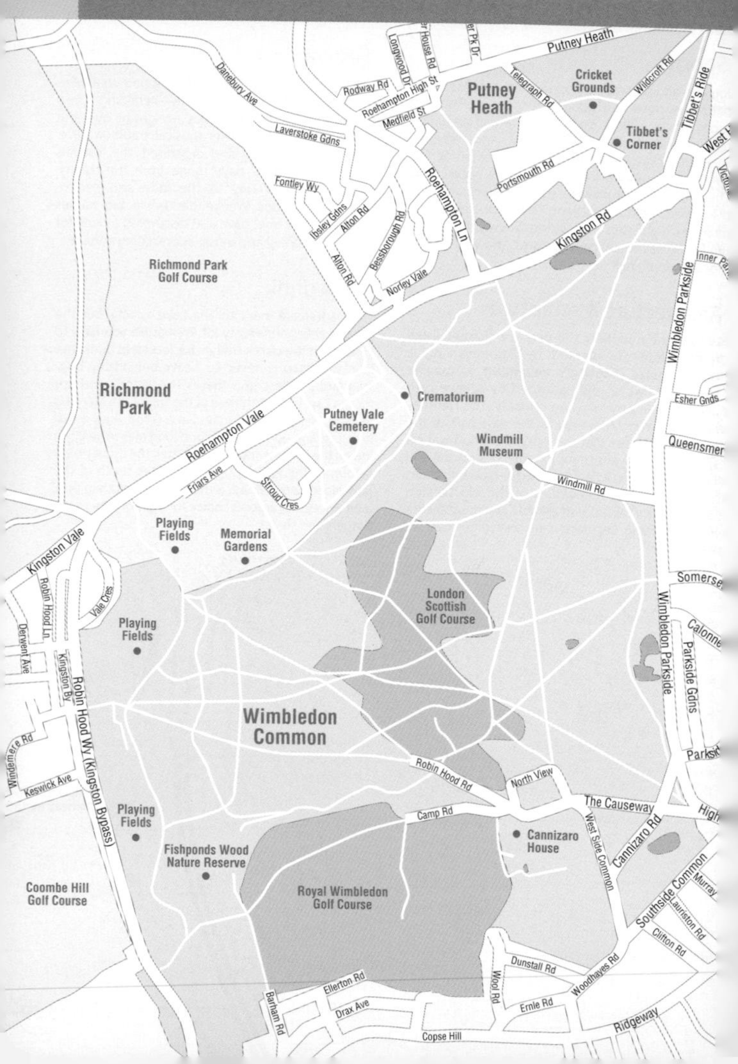
Putney Heath
Longwood Dr
House Rd
Pk Dr
Danebury Ave
Rodway Rd
Roehampton High St
Medfield St
Laverstoke Gdns
Putney Heath
Telegraph Rd
Cricket Grounds
Wildcroft Rd
Tibbet's Ride
Tibbet's Corner
West H
Portsmouth Rd
Roehampton Ln
Fontley Wy
Ibsley Gdns
Alton Rd
Bessborough Rd
Kingston Rd
Richmond Park Golf Course
Alton Rd
Norley Vale
Inner Park
Wimbledon Parkside
Richmond Park
Roehampton Vale
Crematorium
Putney Vale Cemetery
Esher Gnds
Windmill Museum
Queensmer
Friars Ave
Stroud Cres
Windmill Rd
Kingston Vale
Playing Fields
Memorial Gardens
Robin Hood Ln
Vale Cres
London Scottish Golf Course
Somerse
Playing Fields
Derwent Ave
Kingston By
Robin Hood Wy (Kingston Bypass)
Wimbledon Parkside
Calonne
Parkside Gdns
Wimbledon Common
Windemere Rd
Keswick Ave
Robin Hood Rd
North View
Parksid
The Causeway
High
Playing Fields
Camp Rd
Cannizaro House
West Side Common
Cannizaro Rd
Fishponds Wood Nature Reserve
Southside Common
Murray
Coombe Hill Golf Course
Royal Wimbledon Golf Course
Lauriston Rd
Clifton Rd
Dunstall Rd
Wool Rd
Woodhayes Rd
Ellerton Rd
Barham Rd
Drax Ave
Ernle Rd
Ridgeway
Copse Hill

General Information

www.wpcc.org.uk

Overview

If London life starts to get you down, but trekking to the countryside is too much hassle, then Wimbledon Common provides the best of both worlds. Incorporating Putney Heath to the north, Wimbledon Common offers over 1000 acres of wild woodland, scrubland, heathland, ponds and well-tended, mown areas for sports and recreation. Bordered by the urban sprawls of Wimbledon, Putney and Richmond, the common has offered Londoners an escape from city life for centuries. Although thousands visit every weekend, the scale of the place is so vast that you can easily find a private haven for reading a book or a romantic picnic.

Unlike the micro-managed and perfectly structured central London parks, Wimbledon feels much more natural and random. Paths are unpaved and often little more than a muddy track leading off in unlikely directions. The untamed beauty of the common and the lack of traffic noise, or any noise for that matter, make it hard to believe you are still in London.

After a hard day of outdoor activity, or sunbathing, there are plenty of historic pubs to retire to in Wimbledon village. If you prefer your nature tamed or don't want to get your shoes dirty, head to the southeast corner of the common for Cannizaro House and gardens, a grand mansion converted into a boutique hotel and restaurant, with elegantly manicured gardens open to the public. In the summer, the friendly hotel bar opens onto a patio overlooking the grounds and makes a good spot for a sun-downer as you imagine being Lord or Lady of the Manor for the day.

Nature

The common is home to many animals including bats, badgers, and muntjac deer. It's also an important breeding ground for dragonflies and damselflies. For anyone wanting to find out more about the flora and fauna, the London Bat Group organises 'bat walks' while the London Wildlife Trust organises guided walks. You can also take a self-guided wander along The Windmill Nature Trail. 800 metres long, the trail has been created with accessibility in mind and begins right next to the Windmill car park. The visitors' centre behind the Windmill has wildlife exhibits and also tells the history of the common. It also sells maps and booklets giving the low down on the nature on offer.

Recreation

There is loads of space on the common for pick-up games of rugby, football, Frisbee and cricket. If you fancy a 'real game', you can hire tennis courts by the hour, cricket pitches by the day (from as little as £100) or enjoy a round of golf on the two available courses. The common is very popular with runners and steeplechase events have been held here since 1867. Various running clubs such as the South London Harriers and Hercules Wimbledon use the Common. If you've ever fancied trying horse riding, there are a number of stables that make use of the 16 miles of trails—or bring your own nag with you.

Golf
www.wcgc.co.uk
www.londonscottishgolfclub.co.uk

Horse Riding
Wimbledon Village Stables: 020 8946 8579
Ridgway Stables: 020 8946 7400

Rugby, Football and Cricket Pitch Hire
020 8788 7655

How to Get There

By public transport:
The Northern Line goes to South Wimbledon where you can take a bus to central Wimbledon then change or walk to the village and common. Wimbledon station is much closer. Take the District Line from central London or over ground trains from Waterloo or London Bridge. If you are feeling fit, a ten-minute walk up Wimbledon Hill takes you to Wimbledon village and beyond that, the edge of the common. Regular buses serve the village. Alternatively, you can access Putney Heath which joins up with Wimbledon Common. To do this, take the District Line to Putney Bridge or East Putney overground to Putney mainline station and take a bus up Putney Hill.

It's likely that at some point during your London residence, you've been seized with the romantic notion of floating your way round a London market—savouring the smells, laughing with a vendor, flirting your way to some freebies. If you have, then your attempts to live that dream almost certainly resulted in you silently fuming as you crawled among a crowd of thousands, trekking for a cashpoint because you forgot that stalls don't accept cards, and getting crapped on by a pigeon. Don't be put off!

At the markets you can buy some of the most unique, quirky, fresh, stylish, grungy, exquisite, unusual items in London. Sometimes you'll get brilliant bargains, sometimes you'll pay high for something you fall in love with. And sometimes, yes, you'll be driven near to homicidal rampage. But they're one of London's great strengths: use them while you can, because the developers have their evil, dollar-signed eyes on them.

For groceries

The food in markets isn't necessarily locally grown, but you get a much more tempting choice than in most supermarkets. Expect fruit, veg, breads, cheeses, meats, spices and pastries, as well as stalls concocting irresistible snacks from around the world.

Borough (Map 106)
You don't come here for bargains: you come for ambiance, exquisite international foods, and to impress the person you woke up with. If you're rich and like the finer things in life, then here your weekly shop can consist of some of the freshest vegetables, plumpest fruit, sweetest patisseries and sockiest cheeses in London. If you're poor and just fancy a change from Saturday morning repeats of *Friends*, then head here for a hearty hog roast sandwich and to snaffle some free samples.

Broadway (Map 89)
As gorgeous as Borough, for a third of the price and a fifth of the crowds. It's a pain to get to, stuck in one of the city's remaining quaintly retro spots not closely served by the tube (London Fields), but you'll want to move here by the end of your visit.

Ridley Road (Map 86)
If the gourmet markets are too poncey for you, with their Bavarian organic rye bread and Malaysian honey from breast-fed bees, then get down the Ridley Road. Here, in a market which is bright, chaotic, grubby and bouncing to reggae, you can pick up an incredible array of Jamaican, Turkish, African, Indian and Chinese foodstuffs (and possibly e-coli).

For market-chic

You won't necessarily pay less than at the high street, but you will have a choice of original and irresistible items sold with passion and knowledge. Expect to leave these markets with a lighter pocket (though try to make sure it's not because of the pickpockets…).

Spitalfields (Map 91)
Mecca for anyone looking for ethnic-hip and well-priced clothes, bags and jewellery. Here you can often chat to the maker of the clothes you're eyeing up and learn the story behind their designs. Which is all very inspiring, until you try on their beloved creations, realise you're too fat for it, and reject it having slightly stretched it. Because then it's just awkward.

Greenwich (Map 120)
Craft-tastic: a great place to go for beautiful handmade gifts which people love to receive and then put in a cupboard for the rest of their useful life. Here you'll find a gorgeous range of items for home and lifestyle: pictures, antiques, candles, pottery, soft furnishings and clothes, as well as some great food stalls, and an above-average number of beautiful rich people than at most markets.

Portobello Road (Map 29)

Although famed for being the World's Largest Antiques Market, Portobello Road seems to sell *everything*. You'll need patience to work around its sprawling size and the crowds, but just about anything you're looking for is there somewhere or can be sourced by speaking to the right vendor. Stalls include clothes (from classy-vintage to student-cheap), jewellery, fabric, food, as well as 1500 antique stalls selling maps, medals, silverware, and things you never thought you needed (and which, after you've got them home, you realise you didn't).

Camden (Map 71)

Camden is actually home to six markets, though "chic" doesn't do any of them justice. Here you'll find a purse-emptying range of alternative fashions, vintage clothes, accessories, gifts, t-shirts, comedy hot water bottle covers, tie-dyed hippies, teeny-punks and chaps asking if you'd care for a nice bit of crack. Anything goes, and this open, free atmosphere makes it a major and exciting draw. Hit Camden Stables for brilliant international food stalls.

Fer findin a bit o Laaandon prop'a.

If you're a Londoner who "just adores the city! But oh dear *no,* wouldn't *dream* of bringing kids up here", then chances are you don't mingle much with the Prop'a Laandoner. This hardy breed whose family history is a Dickensian yarn of blitzes, TB and chimney sweeps are the core of this city, and the gradual nudging out of their jellied eels and pub sing-songs is tantamount to ethnic cleansing. Find them at London's Propa Markets before they vanish.

Smithfield (Map 15)

Smithfield Market is in full swing at 4 am, which makes it the perfect place to stumble into on your way home from clubbing. Unless you're vegetarian, because while frying bacon may have you yearning for looser morals, the smell of this 800 year old meat market will have you retching over your recycled sandals. It's the best place in London to pick up any meat you could hope for, including, in the 1500s, a barbecued Protestant or a topside of William Wallace, this being the site of hundreds of executions in its time. Some of the local pubs hold special early licenses, so on your way to the office you can swing in for breakfast over a pint with some of the meat porters: they'd just *love* it if you did.

Columbia Road (Map 91)

There's something deeply touching about an exquisite flower market being manned by some of the burliest Cockneys you'll see outside a Guy Ritchie film. Get there first thing on Sundays for the best choice, or in a low-cut top for the best bargains. And if the crowds and cries of the "daffs, dahlin'?" become too much, just slip into the enchanting boutiques lining Columbia Road.

Billingsgate (Map 101)

For the largest selection of fish in London, outside the London Aquarium (where they frown on you if you try to fry the fish. Bloody bureaucracy.), head to Billingsgate. People were buying their fish here long before London went all yuppie, and much the same stock is available—winkles, cockles, potted shrimp and things which smell ungodly. Today you'll find alongside them almost any fish you could hope for (though don't ask for goldfish), as well as poultry, oils and snacks.

General info

Address: Southampton Row, London, WC1B 4AP
Phone: 020 7514 7022
Website: www.csm.arts.ac.uk

Overview

Though hyped to infinity, and often lazily editorialised as the one vital source of all things up-and-coming in London, Central St Martins nevertheless has an undeniable history of producing graduates that tend to rocket to international fame upon leaving. The frequently cited list of alumni reads like a Who's Who of European art-and-design talent, and includes past superstars such as Alexander McQueen, Gilbert and George, and Anthony Gormley, as well as recent fashion darlings Christopher Kane, Gareth Pugh and Kim Jones, to name a few.

The school as it is today was formed in 1989 through the amalgamation of two prestigious 19th century institutions, the Central School of Arts and Crafts and St Martins School of Art. Since then it has annexed the Byam Shaw School of Art in Archway, and as a result offers a huge range of courses covering most areas of the visual and performing arts. St Martins has a particularly formidable reputation for fashion design—it is the only university to show student collections as part of London Fashion Week—but it is well respected in all departments for its hyper-progressive ethos (expect to hear words like 'challenging,' and 'risk-taking' liberally thrown around on open days). The college has recently moved to a swish new building in Kings Cross where student activity will be centralised and everyone will no doubt be even more fabulous than before. Consequently, whether you find the whole thing pretentious and overrated or are waiting in breathless anticipation for the next St Martins wunderkind, it's going to be very difficult to ignore the place in the coming years.

Campuses

Kings Cross

The new Kings Cross campus should help with the rejuvenation of an area that has always been one of transience rather than permanence due to its transport links (and its whores and junkies). In fact, the CSM website claims the "new 39,000 square-metre campus is the centrepiece of the redevelopment of King's Cross". But more importantly, students of art, fashion, design, and drama will now be in one location, able to interact cross-discipline, and form more of a united front rather than being scattered across the capital. Anyone who has walked the corridors of the old Charing Cross Road building will tell you that however charming the decaying archaic halls of academia may be, a brand spanking new building with technology to match is more than welcome. Occupying the Grade II listed Granary

Building, architects Stanton Williams have integrated such wonders as an internal street, a Performance Centre, and an open-air terrace.

Byam Shaw
The Byam Shaw School of Art in Archway is a fairly recent addition (2003) to Central St Martins, the 'Central' tag here being somewhat misleading as it's a good 20 minutes by tube from the other sites. Devoted solely to fine art, it runs a BA and a more skills-based 2 year FdA as well as a variety of short and post-graduate courses.

College Culture

As is the case with most London institutions, the university community is massively subsumed by the bright lights of the city itself, but this is no bad thing. Though the college puts on frequent exhibitions, talks and events, there is no independent bar or central hub—students will instead inevitably find themselves taking advantage of the central location (which is, after all, a short walk from the National Gallery and ICA). The Student Union is not particular to Central St Martins but provides services for and represents all the art colleges in London (University of the Arts London) as a whole, and various services and societies (such as sports clubs) are run at this level. As far as the education part goes, it's not always easy being in the midst of the constant search for the next-big-thing, but at the same time the idiosyncratic slant of the teaching makes for a unique experience, and the generally high talent level of the students fosters a fantastic creative and social atmosphere.

Tuition

Fees for 2012/2013 are £9,000 a year for UK/EU applicants taking an undergraduate or Foundation level degree. Some courses require payment of an additional course fee for materials. International students can expect to pay between £9,300 and £12,250 depending upon the type of course taken. International students can expect to pay between £9, 300 and £13,300 depending upon the type of course taken.

Short Courses

Central St Martins also runs a large number of short courses for all aspirational (and rich) non-students wanting a piece of the action. Prices are high but the courses very popular, partly because of the college's reputation and partly because there are many interesting options to choose from. The courses run in evenings, weekends, or can be taken intensively as a Summer, Easter or Christmas school. Information: www.csm.arts.ac.uk or call 020 7514 7015.

Phone Numbers:

Charing Cross Road site: 020 7514 7190

Southampton Row site: 020 7514 7037

Drama Centre: 020 7514 8778

Byam Shaw School of Art: 020 7281 4111

Admissions—degree courses:
020 7514 7023

Admissions—short courses: 020 7514 7015

International Office: 020 7514 7027

Charing Cross Road Shop: 020 7514 7612

Southampton Row Shop: 020 7514 7017

Back Hill Shop: 020 7514 6851

University of the Arts Students' Union:
020 7514 6270

General info

Address: Northampton Square, London, EC1V 0HB
Phone: 020 7040 5060
Website: www.city.ac.uk

Overview

In London, a place rich with academia, City University often gets overlooked. Unlike King's or LSE it has no grand halls, secret-handshakes or old-boys' networks. Its facilities are modest and its library short on fusty books. But it's carved out a reputation as a supplier of professionals, cementing its place in the top five for graduate employment in recent years.

Located on a pretty park on the edge of the City of London—the 'Square Mile' that's fast becoming the centre of the global economy—the university is overwhelmingly diverse. Ethnicities make up over half the student body, with young Chinese and wealthy Russians flocking to the business school. It's that section of the university that churns out workers for the finance industry—students who are so hell-bent on business success that they go to school in suits.

The university's first incarnation came in 1894 as an industrial college for the working classes. The on-site swimming pool was used when London hosted the 1908 Olympics, although it wasn't until 1966 that it gained full university status. It's maintained strong links with industry, with alumni including the founding father of budget Euro-travel, easyJet's Stelios (like Sting and Madonna he chooses to use only one name). Students at City may be lined up for good jobs when they graduate; but it comes at the cost of having to explain what their less well-known university is whenever they mention it.

Tuition

2012/13 fees are £9K. Maintenance and bursaries will remain at 2009/10 levels due to negative inflation in the economy. International undergraduate student fees range from between £11,000 - £12,500. Postgraduate professional courses range form £12, 500 (Legal Practice Course) to £16, 500 (Bar Professional Training Course) for UK/EU students. From 2012 the A-Level performance based' Lord Mayor of London Scholarship' of up to £3,000 will be available to eligible students. Students from England may be eligible for a means tested maintenance grant of £3,250.

Culture

Culture in the traditional sense is a little thin on the ground. There are no museums or galleries to speak of, although one department did exhibit photos of prisoners at work last year. But as it included a con making sandwiches for 16p an hour this could've just been to get the wayward students to knuckle down.

Instead, the uni hosts some heavyweight lectures. The Students' Union offers limited clubs and societies with all the usual fare – tennis, chess, Christian Union. The Saddlers Wells Sport Centre is also home to the intramural team sports. 'Ten' (10 Northampton Square) is where the kids hang out, the social hub of City.

Departments

Admissions office (undergrad and postgrad): 020 7040 8716
Library 020 7040 8191
Saddler's Sports Centre 020 7040 5656
Student Union 020 7040 5600

General info

Address: Imperial College London
South Kensington Campus
London SW7 2AZ
Phone: 020 7589 5111
Website: www3.imperial.ac.uk

Overview

Imperial College really did have imperial beginnings with Prince Albert setting up the college as a research and learning centre of science, maths, medicine and engineering to enhance the image of the British Empire in 1887. In the Victorian age, and to this day, the college attracted the most enquiring of minds and was the central feature of what was once Prince Albert's successful push to create a centre of culture and learning, encompassing the nearby museums, Royal College of Music, Royal Geographical Society and the Royal Albert Hall. The university remains one of the best in the world, ranked 8th in 2012, and as such remains one of the most selective institutions in the UK with the application to admissions ratio being 7:1. Famous alumni include clever clogs Brian May (Queen), HG Wells and Alexander Fleming. In 2007 Imperial College became independent from the University of London and now awards its own degrees.

Departments

The pride and soul of the college are three faculties, each headed by a principal: engineering, medicine and natural sciences. The Tanaka Business School doesn't offer undergraduate degrees, but does allow undergraduate students to study management modules towards their degrees. The main purpose of the Humanities department is to provide elective subjects and language courses for the science students. For medical students Imperial is also associated with various London hospitals including St Mary's Hospital and Charing Cross Hospital.

Campus Culture

Imperial may have a 'heads down' atmosphere but there is still that unwritten rule that if you work hard you play hard. Imperial College Union (ICU) offers numerous clubs and societies from Bellydancing to Wakeboarding to Backgammon. The Union bar is also well used, and is particularly lively on an afternoon when a football or rugby match is screened. The free student paper, Felix (http://felixonline.co.uk/), is a popular and useful resource for keeping up to date with campus life and aims to be independent from the College itself. Imperial also has its own student TV station, Stoic, and radio station ICRadio (1134 AM or www.icradio.com). There are also regular public lectures on a variety of subjects.

Facilities

Imperial's main campus in South Kensington is surrounded by many of London's best museums including the Natural History Museum, Science Museum and Victoria & Albert Museum. Being in the thick of it also means a close proximity to the shops and cafes of South Ken and High Street Kensington and being a stone's throw from Hyde Park.

The main campus boats some of the best facilities of the London universities. As well as the usual on-campus shops (including bookshop, cafes, travel agents and bank) there are some impressive sports facilities on offer. The recently built ETHOS centre contains not only a fully equipped gym but also an inside climbing wall, swimming pool, squash courts, sports hall and a treatment room offering massages and physiotherapy. On top of that there's a boathouse and a 60-acre athletic ground. Naturally, there's a well-stocked central library and various smaller departmental libraries.

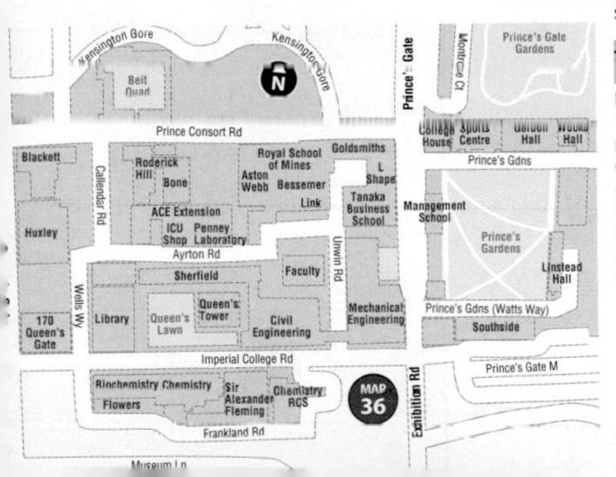

Tuition

Home students' (UK/EU) annual fees for 2012/13 are £9,000 for undergraduate programmes. International students can expect to pay the whopping amount of between £15, 500 and £24, 500 depending upon the subject studied. Students from England may be eligible for a means tested maintenance grant of £3,250.

General Information

Address: King's College London
Strand
London
WC2R 2LS
Phone: 020 7836 5454
Website: www. kcl.ac.uk

Overview

Kings College is one of the 19 colleges that make up the colossus that is the University of London. King's (or KCL, as otherwise known) has nearly 20,000 students and five campuses—the Strand, Guy's, Waterloo, St. Thomas' and Denmark Hill. In 2011 the school of law moved into the East Wing of the magnificent Somerset House. It has an excellent academic reputation and ranks in the top ten UK universities. Unlike some of the other University of London colleges, King's is equally well known for its arts and science courses.

Its religious affiliation is now less central, but back in 1829 King's was founded as a Church of England institution to counter University College London, or "the godless college in Gower Street." The beautifully designed chapel at the Strand campus testifies to its pious beginnings, though few students would consider it a motivation for attending the college. The student body is diverse, as the societies list reflects—it includes a Catholic society, a Christian Union, a Krishna Consciousness group, and a Nomads society, amongst a myriad of others.

King's boasts a number of famous alumni. Keats studied apothecary there (he didn't like it much), and Florence Nightingale set up the world's first school of nursing at St. Thomas' Hospital, now the Florence Nightingale School of Nursing and Midwifery. In the 1960s, Archbishop Desmond Tutu spent time in its halls. The KCL student union nightclub, Tutu's—a pretty grungy place but one of the few open past 2 am in the Strand on a Saturday—is named after him.

London prices may take their toll on the student purse, but King's students at least benefit from

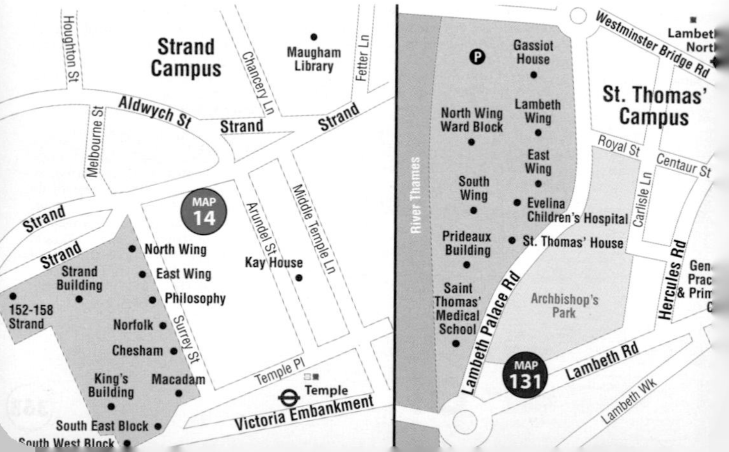

a prime location. As well as the nightclub, the college has two bars, one at Guy's Campus and one at the Strand. The Waterfront bar at the Strand looks directly onto the Thames, giving a view of everything from Westminster to the Oxo Tower. It's also a great gig venue—Alanis Morissette, Richard Ashcroft, and Beth Orton have all played there.

Sports

The college's sports facilities are impressive. It caters to almost anything—it has a swimming pool, gym, and even rifle range. Although King's cannot rival the Oxbridge rowing tradition, its sports do have a history—two of the men's rugby clubs, Guy's and St. Thomas', are the oldest in the world. To access the sports grounds students must leave Zone 1; the grounds are in Dulwich, Surrey, and South London.

Culture

Kings has numerous dramatic societies where amateur thespians can hone their skills, especially with the recent acquisition of the Grade I listed Anatomy Theatre and Museum.More unusually, its classics department stages a play in ancient Greek every year, and is the only classics department in the UK to do so. The college's religious origins are evident in its wonderful choral music. 25 choral scholars uphold this tradition.

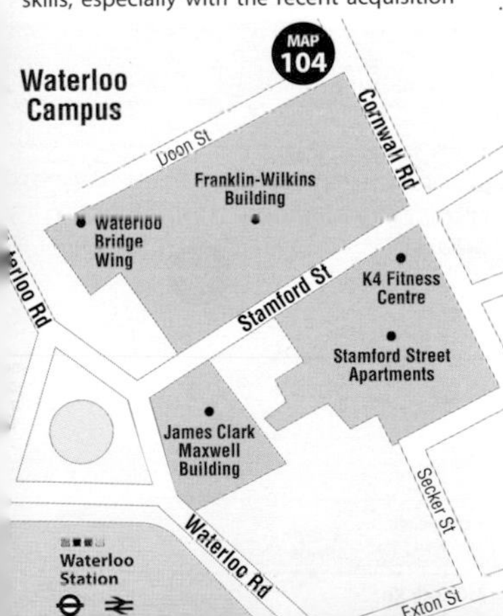

Tuition

2012/13 fees are £9K; Postgrad fees range between £1200 and £6085 depending upon the subject.

Contact details

General Enquiries 020 7836 5454
Social Science and Public Policy .020 7848 1495
Physical Sciences and Engineering 020 7848 2267/2268
Nursing and Midwifery 020 7848 4698
Medicine 020 7848 6501
Law. 020 7836 5454
Institute of Psychiatry 020 7836 5454
Humanities 020 7848 2350
Dental Institute . . . .020 7848 6512 (undergrad), ...020 7848 6703 (postgrad)
Biomedical and Health Sciences. . . . . 020 7848 6400 (Guy's)
. . . . .020 7848 4172 (Waterloo)

Libraries:

Maughan Chancery Lane. . . .020 7848 2430
Waterloo. 020 7848 3000
St. Thomas. 020 7188 3740
Guy's 020 7848 6900
Denmark Hill 020 7848 5740
Student Union 020 7848 1588

General Information

Address: Houghton Street,
London WC2A 2AE
Phone: 020 7405 7686
Website: www.lse.ac.uk

Overview

The London School of Economics and Political Science, or LSE as it is commonly known, is a single faculty college focused on the social sciences; world-renowned for its highly prestigious programmes and distinguished alumni. Located amidst a hub of academic activity with UCL, Kings College, SOAS and Birkbeck nearby, the college is affiliated with the University of London and stands apart due to its high proportion of postgraduate students. LSE was founded in 1895 by the intellectual socialist movement, the Fabian Society, with the aim of bettering society through the education of Britain's business and political elite. Today it remains a strongly political institution, with considerable influence in government through both its research programmes and campaigns. Its alumni are also highly represented in business and law spheres. While best known for its economics and politics degrees, the broad range of social science programmes offered complements the international ethos of the school and it remains at the cutting edge in terms of research.

The college enrolls around 8,000 students who represent over 140 different countries; over half of these are postgraduates who

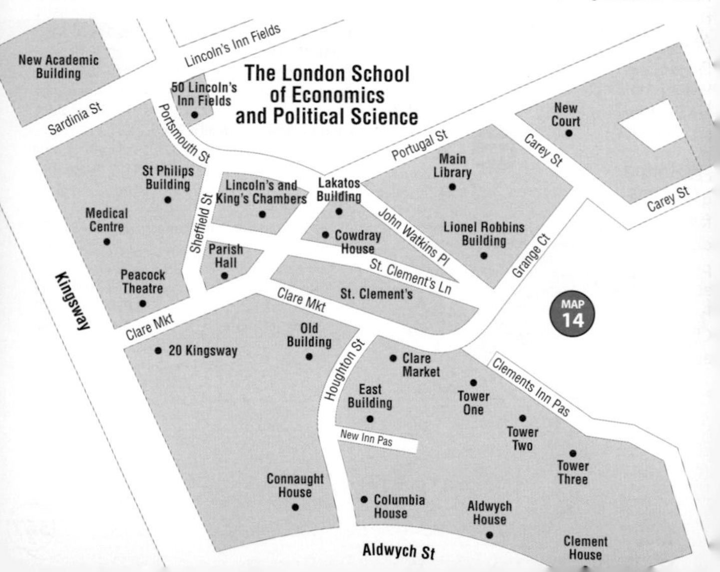

rarely leave the library unless attending high-brow seminars on globalization and inequality. Its starry alumni includes Nobel laureates, international Heads of State, outstanding academics, and a notable proportion of British MP's. And of course Mick Jagger.

Culture On Campus

Despite its reputation for academic excellence, LSE's social activities are mainly fuelled by a lively undergraduate population who also know how to enjoy themselves. With over 170 eclectic student societies, ranging from 'Catalan' to 'Taiwanese'; from 'United Nations' to 'Anti-Authoritarian' and from 'Maths&Stats' to good old fashioned 'Lager&Real Ale', the broad international and diverse facets of the student population is encompassed. An atmosphere of work hard/play hard prevails and nightly events lure the undergraduates from the libraries and keep the campus buzzing. The large postgraduate population tends to shuffle by however, books in hand; the days of cheesy music, luminous drinks in shot glasses and ill-conceived experimental fashions behind them while they actually do some work. LSE also hosts numerous public lectures with acclaimed speakers at the forefront of the subject discussed. Past speakers have included Noam Chomsky, Kofi Annan, David Cameron and architect Richard Rogers.

Sports

Not to be let down by its central, and somewhat geographically limited campus, LSE manages to maintain a thriving sports culture through the Athletics Union. Football and rugby seem to top the bill, with provision for some of the less mainstream athletic pursuits such as capoeira and Ultimate Frisbee. The college makes use of its affiliation with the University of London Union, which broadens the scope for sports participation alongside students of other universities.

Tuition

2012/13 fees are £8,500; International fees between £15,168 and £23,928.

Departments

Undergraduate Admissions Office ....
.... 020 7955 7125
.... 020 7955 7757
Graduate Admissions Office ....
.... 020 7955 7160
Library....................... 020 7955 6733
Students' Union............. 020 7955 7158

General Information

Address: Gower Street
London WC1E 6BT
Phone: 020 7679 2000
Website: www.ucl.ac.uk

Overview

UCL, a constituent college of the University of London, has been a place of diversity from the word go—living very much up to its status as London's Global University. University College London was founded in 1826 by Jeremy Bentham as a progressive alternative to Oxford and Cambridge's social exclusivity and religious restrictions. Thus, it was the first university in England to admit students of any race, class or religion and welcome women on equal standing with men. International students have been a part of the college's fabric since day one and it was the first English university to offer the systematic teaching of law, architecture and medicine. Bentham even requested in his will that his body be preserved in the name of science and stored in a wooden cabinet, which is on display to this day in the main building of the College. Creepy.

UCL consistently ranks among the top five universities in Britain and is currently in the top twenty universities globally. To this day, the science, law and medical departments are still some of its strongest. 20 Nobel prizes have been awarded to UCL academics and students, ten of which were in Physiology & Medicine alone. However, UCL degrees in anthropology, history and the arts are also very highly regarded in their fields.

UCL's many networks of libraries are impressive and an easy place to get lost. The Main Library, designed by William Wilkins, who also designed the similar National

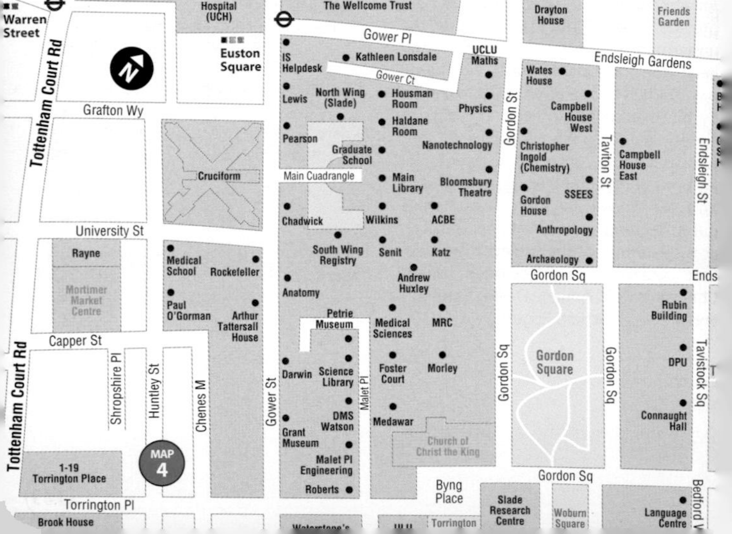

Gallery building, focuses on arts and humanities, history, economics, public policy and law. The Special Collections include medieval manuscripts and first editions of works by George Orwell, James Joyce's *Ulysses*, Newton's *Principia* and Darwin's *Origin of the Species*.

There's no such thing as a typical UCL student, as it's such a diverse place. The only thing students have in common is their intelligence and London. Because it's a university with great academics right In the heart of Bloomsbury, it makes for some pretty interesting alums. Where else can you have such diverse graduates as Alexander Graham Bell, Mahatma Gandhi, Ricky Gervais, and all four members of Coldplay?

Tuition

Undergraduate home students (UK/EU) fees are £9,000 per year while International students should expect to pay between pay £14,000 - £18,500 depending upon the subject studied. Postgraduate study fees range from £3, 350 to £11, 250 depending upon subject and level studied.

UCL is one of the few London universities who charge only one rate of tuition fee regardless of whether the student is studying for an equivalent or lower qualification than they have already achieved. UCL offer numerous bursaries and scholarships for all types of students.

Sports

UCL's sports are as diverse as its students—everything from hockey, rowing and women's rugby to Kung Fu, skateboarding and water polo. The UCLU (University College London Union) is your one-stop shop for campus sports teams and clubs.

If you're looking for football, The 90-acre UCL sports ground at Shenley, Hertfordshire, has very high quality pitches. Watford football club even train there. The Union gym (Bloomsbury Fitness) offers facilities for activities such as basketball and personal fitness programmes.

Culture

Being right in the centre of London means that you're never short of something cultural to do. However, UCL stands up quite well. It even has its own museum—the Petrie Museum of Egyptian Archaeology—accessible from the Science Library. Here you're even given your own torch to explore the collection of over 80,000 rare objects DIY (or Indiana Jones) style. UCL also has its own West End theatre, the UCL Bloomsbury, wedged into the maze of main buildings. It's a must-stop for top comedian tours. Jimmy Carr and Ricky Gervais have been known to shoot their stand-up DVDs there. The UCL Union has access to the theatre for at least ten weeks a year, where it is dedicated to student drama and music society performances. Although neither drama, music nor dance are formally taught at UCL, this does not stop the Union's drama club from making it to the Edinburgh Fringe Festival. At UCL, despite the fact that students can really go out just about anywhere in London, many stay loyal to the bars within the Union, and it's usually a great place to meet before a bigger night out.

Departments

Undergraduate & Postgraduate Admissions
. . . . 020 7679 7742
Student Information Centre . 020 7679 3000
UCL Union 020 7387 3611
UCL Bloomsbury Theatre 020 7388 8822
Petrie Museum. 020 7679 2884

General Information

Address: Thornhaugh Street, Russell Square, London WC1H 0XG
Phone: 020 7637 2388
Website: www.soas.ac.uk

Overview

The School of African and Oriental Studies is a specialist college which focuses on the languages, cultures, law and social studies of Africa, Asia, and the Near and Middle East. SOAS, as it is commonly known, is part of the University of London and is the only institution of its kind in the United Kingdom. It has an excellent reputation as one of the leading authorities on African and Asian studies in the world and ranks highly in university charts on the strength of its programmes Originally founded in 1916 to educate and inform British citizens bound for overseas postings, the school began with an Oriental studies' focus and later incorporated African studies. SOAS is nestled in the corner of Russell Square, with another campus up close to King's Cross; its diversity complements the hotbed of academic activity that makes up this part of London.

The college enrolls over 4,000 students and nearly half of the postgraduates are from countries outside of the UK or the EU. They are often seen sitting in Russell Square eating their organic lunch, and chatting (in Swahili or Taiwanese) about their UNICEF internships. SOAS's alumni include members of parliament and royalty of a range of countries from Ghana to Burma. The Crown Princess of Norway went here. Well of course she did. The Norwegians are so PC. Except for whale hunting.

Culture On Campus

One thing to be said about SOAS students is: they are serious. The Students Union has a reputation of leaning heavily to the left and is very politically active. SOAS students have been a notable presence at anti-war protests, and they are also now rather concerned with environmental causes—campaigning for the reduction of carbon footprints, among other issues. Societies at the college, unsurprisingly, have a very international, 'right-on' flavour, and include the obvious 'Amnesty International Society', 'Campaign for Human Rights in the Philippines Society', 'Model United Nations' and of course the 'Natural Remedies Society' for when these guys need to let their hair down and knock back an entire bottle of Echinacea.

Tuition

2012/13 fees are £9K; Postgrad fees range between £6,360 and £13,230; International students can expect to pay around £13,890 per year.

Departments

Undergraduate Admissions Office
020 7898 4301/ 4306

Graduate Admissions office
020 7898 4300/ 4311/ 4322/ 4361

Library
020 7898 4197

Students Welfare Office
020 7074 5014

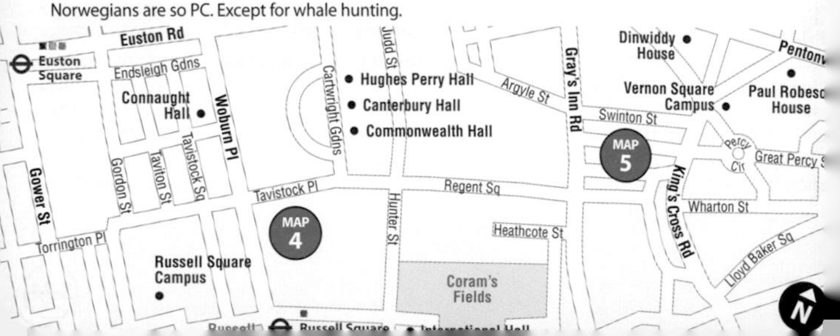

General Information

University of London Students Union (ULU),
Malet Street, WC1E 7HY
www.ulu.co.uk
www.thebarflyclub.com/ulu (The Venue)

Overview

Students are the same the world over and in London they ain't no different. In amongst the banter over Bronte and misunderstandings about Marx stands beer, boogying and burgers. Luckily, for over 100,000 of the University of London's students there's a central place to go to make your university years active and sociable—ULU.

You will need to be a member of ULU to get into some of the events, although grabbing a cheeky cheap sarnie in the café shouldn't pose too much of a problem for clued-up Londoners. There are 20 University of London colleges that are eligible for ULU membership including Kings College and UCL. If you are a student at one of the lucky 20 then you've got it made. If not, use your powers of persuasion to get the gold dust of cheap beer and food.

Practicalities

You cannot really get more central. There is a plethora of tube stations and lines within a 5–10 minute walk, not to mention Oxford Street. The nearest tube, however, is Russell Square (Piccadilly Line) or Goodge Street (Northern Line).

Clubs & Societies (non-sport)

The range of clubs and societies on offer at ULU change more often than Europe's borders. Reason being the turnover of students and the lure from students' own colleges – all the more reason to get down there and sign up now! You've got the usual suspects such as Drama club but it would not be Londontown without a few obscure offerings – Revelation Rock Gospel Choir anyone? Hell, yeah.

Sports

ULU has to cater for thousands of students, but also attract students away from sports clubs in their particular college. Sports, and the bar afterward, is the place to mix with students from the other colleges. Sportswise there's the usual fare – tennis, football, swimming and martial arts – may come in handy for students living in Severn Sisters. There's also Energybase which contains a gym and pool. Amongst other things take your pick from salsa, breakdancing, fencing or rifle club. Now there's one for the CV…

Food & Bars

Lunch Box is ULU's coffee shop, perfectly located on the ground floor for those who want to grab a quick (Fair Trade) coffee or a bargain meal deal—you even get fruit—how healthy. The aptly named **Duck 'n Dive** bar is, erm, a bit of a dive in that usual charming student way, but does have a lively atmosphere and loads of events. There's also **The Gallery Bar** which, despite the rather odd sheets hanging from the ceiling, serves up some wallet and taste bud satisfying treats until 11pm.

Facilities

The **Student Print Centre** will resolve all your reprographics and binding troubles. Wander into the **Student Union Shop** with a clear conscience to grab a Fair Trade snack or a recycled notepad. Open until 7pm on weekdays.

Events

You'll never be without events at ULU. You've got the **Duck 'n Dive** for regular events but there's also live music at **The Venue** hosting up and coming unsigned bands as well as the odd better-known act. For gigs enter ULU on Byng Place.

Learning in the capital has a long and venerable history. University College London (UCL) was the third university founded in England after Cambridge and Oxford and the first to admit students of any race or religion. Now there are hundreds of universities, colleges and adult education centres offering a mind-boggling array of courses.

The first port of call for those with a lust for learning or even an empty Tuesday night to fill is Floodlight (www.floodlight.co.uk), which lists 40,000 courses. Fancy brushing up your motorbike maintenance skills at Hackney Community College, getting an NVQ in sugar modelling at the National Bakery School, learning how to create the ultimate kitchen garden at the English Gardening School or studying the nonsense verse of Lear and Carroll at City Lit? The sky is your oyster.

Continuing Education and Professional Development

University College London
Gower Street, WC1E 6BT
020 7679 2000
www.ucl.ac.uk

City University
Northampton Square, EC1V 0HB
020 7040 5060
www.city.ac.uk

London South Bank University
103 Borough Road, SE22 0HU
020 7815 7815
www.lsbu.ac.uk

London Metropolitan University
31 Jewry Street, EC3N 2EY
020 7423 0000
www.londonmet.ac.uk

University of East London
4 University Way, E16 2RD
020 8223 2420
www.uel.ac.uk

University of Greenwich
Park Row, SE10 9LS
020 8331 8000
www.gre.ac.uk

A Little Bit of Everything…

Birkbeck
26 Russell Square, WC1B 5DQ
0845 601 0174
www.bbk.ac.uk/ce/aboutus

Open University
Your home
0845 300 60 90
www.open.ac.uk

Bishopsgate Institute
230 Bishopsgate, EC2M 4QH
020 7392 9200
www.bishopsgate.org.uk

Arts and Lifestyle

University of the Arts London
65 Davies Street, W1K 5DA
020 7514 6000
www.arts.ac.uk

Leiths School of Food and Wine
16-20 Wendell Road, W12 9RT
020 8749 6400
www.leiths.com

The London School of Journalism
126 Shirland Road, W9 2BT
020 7289 7777
www.lsj.org

Glass Blowing Courses
15 Forest Trading Estate, E17 6AL
020 8418 5900
www.glassblowingcourses.co.uk

English Gardening School
66 Royal Hospital Road, SW3 4HS
020 7352 4347
www.englishgardeningschool.co.uk/

London School Of Beauty & Make-Up
47-50 Margaret Street, W1W 8SB
020 7636 1893
www.lond-est.com

Institute Francais
17 Queensbury Place SW7 2DT
020 7073 1350
www.institut-francais.org.uk

London Buddhist Centre
51 Roman Road, E2 0HU
084 5458 4716
www.lbc.org.uk

The School of Life
70 Marchmont Street
WC1N 1AB
020 7833 1010
www.theschooloflife.com

Athletics and Dance

Circus Space
Coronet Street, London, N1 6HD
020 7613 4141
www.thecircusspace.co.uk

Tokei Martial Arts
28 Magdalen Street, SE1 2EN
020 7403 5979
www.tokeicentre.org

Jump and Dance
400 York Way, N7 9LR
020 7700 7722
www.jumpanddance.com

Regents Canoe Club
Regents Canal, Graham Street, N1
www.regentscanoeclub.co.uk

Docklands Sailing & Watersport Centre
235a Westferry Road, E14 3QS
020 7537 2626
www.dswc.org

London School of Capoeira
1 & 2 Leeds Place, N4 3RF
020 7281 2020
www.londonschoolofcapoeira.co.uk

General Information

NFT Map: 74
Website: www.arsenal.com
Phone: 020 7704 4000
Box office: 020 7704 4040
Location: Highbury House, 75 Drayton Park, London N5 1BU

Overview

Seven long years have passed since Arsenal last stuffed another piece of silverware into their rather dusty, albeit full, trophy cabinet. Arsene Wenger continues to avoid splashing the cash on top names; building a young thriving team out of foreign talent and an exciting new crop of home-grown kids. The problem with this is that during the start of every new season at the Emirates it is inevitable that a pundit will proclaim this will be the year Arsenals young side realize their full potential, but just as equally inevitable, a big money club will breeze in and buy out marquee players adding to the fans dismay and Wegner's greys. However, Arsenal is historically London's greatest club and holds numerous national records with a trophy room packed with more silver than any other, save Manchester United and Liverpool. T'was not always thus of course. From humble beginnings south of the river, Arsenal built themselves up from roots level, with glory years seeming to come in waves. The mid 80s saw the instatement of George Graham, a hugely popular former player, who begat a powerful, muscular side captained by local hero Tony Adams. Wenger brought a continental flavour to the team and an invigorating playing style—the once "boring, boring Arsenal" started playing "sexy football" which reached its zenith with the 2003-04 "Invincibles" who went the entire season without losing a game. Following Arsenal is not always an easy ride. It's surprising that so many people still flock to the new Emirates stadium in Holloway given the stupendous ticket prices (anywhere between £51 and £120+), and that's if you can even get one, given the six year Membership waiting list. If you're lucky enough to have the £1000s needed for a decent season ticket then you get to sit in a huge, soulless stadium named after an airline company to watch what are ostensibly a bunch of bloody foreigners. On the plus side, those bloody foreigners play some of the most dazzling football in Europe and you never know, this just could be the year Arsenal's young team realizes their full potential (groan).

How to Get There

By Car: The Arsenal website states: 'Supporters are strongly advised not to drive to Emirates Stadium. The ground is situated in a mainly residential area with an extensive Event Day Parking Scheme in operation. Only car owners with resident's permits will be allowed to park on-street in the designated areas and any cars parked illegally will be towed away'. In other words, don't bother bringing a car.

By Public Transport: Arsenal (Piccadilly Line) is the nearest tube station, around three minutes walk from the ground. Finsbury Park (Victoria, Piccadilly Lines and Great Northern rail) and Highbury & Islington (Victoria Line, North London Line and Great Northern rail) stations are around a 10-minute walk - these should be slightly less crowded.

How to Get Tickets

As Arsenal play some damn sexy football, tickets are not easy to come by. However, in the new, swanky Emirates stadium there is always going to be one or two no-shows or corporate tickets that have slipped into the wrong hands. Members have first dibs on tickets and snap them up but the less scrupulous ones sell them on to make a fast buck. Try Gumtree or matchday touts if you really must. To be honest, it's probably one of the rare instances where it really is worth the hassle.

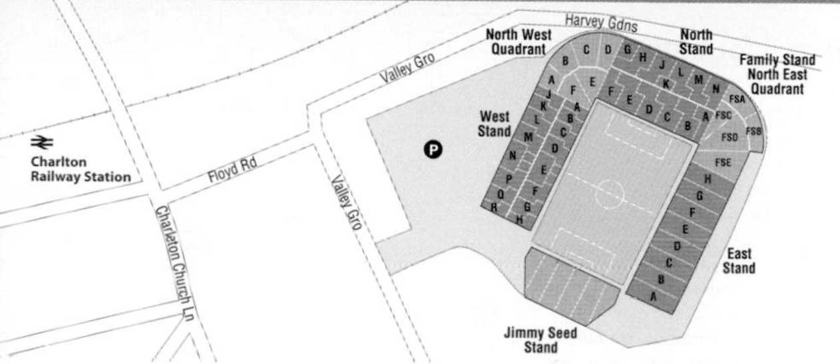

General Information

Phone: (0)20-8333 4000
Website: www.cafc.co.uk
Location: The Valley, Floyd Road, Charlton, London SE7 8BL

Overview

Supporting Charlton is like being a drug addict without a healthy bank balance, the highs are amazing (when they come) but the lows are dark and lonely days. Back in 2007, The Addicks were mixing it with the big boys in the Premier League. But after several seasons in freefall, Charlton found themselves in football's third tier. During the dark days football's ugliest man, Iain Dowie took control and drunkenly drove the team off a bridge. He played a brand of football, which matched his grotesque looks, and got the boot (no, not to his face, that's just how he looks). Inexplicably, Les Reed got the job next – a man with no managerial experience. He lasted a month. That year they went down to the Championship. And guess what? They were relegated again, and finished 13th in League 1 (Third Division). In 2009 Phil Parkinson took over and things remained more or less the same. But during 2010 new ownership meant big changes, the effective but unremarkable Parkinson was given the boot in place of Charlton legend Chris Powell. After the 2010-11 season ended with mixed results the team had a spring clean, literally, Powell bought 19 new players and 2011-12 season ended with Charlton winning the Third Division and earning promotion to the Championship. With the clubs recent turn in fortune 2013 should see the darkness lifted from the club and the ground should reflect Charlton's reputation as a family club, rather than a stadium full of recovering addicts.

How to Get There

By Car: You can leave the M25 at Junction 2 in order to access the A2, heading towards London. When the A2 becomes the A102 (M), take the right hand exit at the roundabout into the A206 Woolwich Road. After passing the major set of traffic lights at the junction of Anchor and Hope Lane and Charlton Church Lane, turn right at the second roundabout into Charlton Lane. Go over the railway crossing then take the first right into Harvey Gardens, with the road leading to the ground. From central London, travel along the A13 until it becomes the East India Dock Road, then take the A102 through the Blackwall Tunnel. Come off at the second junction and take the first exit at the roundabout, then go along the A206 Woolwich Road into Charlton Lane as detailed above. Thanks to the local residents' parking scheme, you'll be hard pushed to find a parking space; try Westmoor Street, Eastmoor Street, Warspite Road and Ruston Road.

By Public Transport: The ground is within walking distance of Charlton railway station, with the Southeastern line running services from mainline stations Charing Cross and London Bridge and services from Cannon Street on Saturdays. You can also take the Jubilee Line to North Greenwich, and then take a short ride on buses 161, 472 or 486 to get to the Valley. Moderate masochists can walk from the tube station.

How to Get Tickets

In recent years Charlton couldn't give their tickets away, but with the teams turn in fortunes, seeing a match in 2013 may be a little more tricky, but certainly not impossible. Tickets can be ordered by phone from the Box Office, via the internet at the club's website or in person at The Valley.

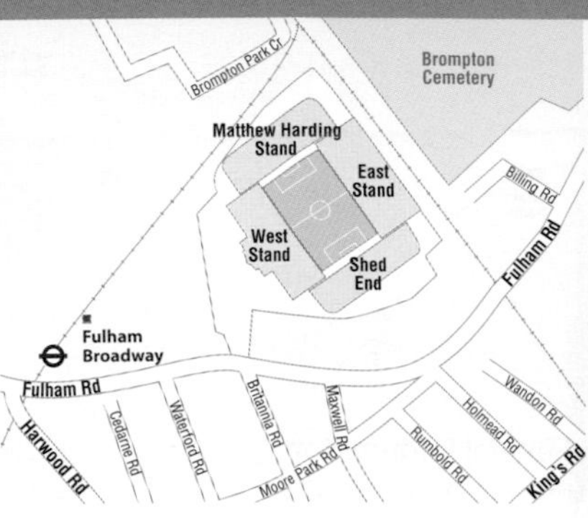

General Information

NFT Map: 43
Phone: 0871 984 1905
Website: www.chelseafc.com
Location: Stamford Bridge,
Fulham Road,
London, SW6 1HS

Overview

Stamford Bridge, home to one of the Premiership's 'big four' clubs, is now one of Europe's most glamorous stadiums. However, 'The Bridge' was once an unappealing and daunting shit-hole more used to hosting pitch invasions and fighting hooligans than the well-heeled city types and Russian oligarchs of today. In the '70s and '80s, it was the violent 'headhunters' that made the club unpopular, but as 'The Blues' never won anything, no one took much notice. In recent years, Chelsea have succeeded in wrestling the mantle of most-hated team in England away from Manchester United, largely due to winning things with the never-ending supply of money from Roman Abramovich. The hooligans have all but gone, either priced out or grown up, but the antics of Prima Donna players and their sitcom private lives have been placing cement shoes on the club's image of late. While Chelsea's coffers have meant they've been able to import expensive foreign players, leading to back-to-back title wins in 2004-2006, their homegrown players have spent more time on tabloid front covers than on football pitches. John Terry and Ashley Cole's bed-hopping adventures will make a great airport novel one day but they've left a lot of fans disappointed in the meantime. These are troubling times indeed for the Blues; after the departure of celebrated manager Mourinho the top position has seen its own share of turbulence. With superstar coach Scolari sacked and the silverware drying up it seems money can't buy you everything. However, after two seasons of relative anonymity (especially for a club with the highest wage bill in the country) and a parade of failed managers, unlikely hero Roberto Di Matteo took over the reins of the club during 2012 and managed to win both the FA Cup and owner Abramovich's perverted wet-dream - the Champions League final. The result was a blow to Tottenham and to decency but another boom for the boys at the bridge, who have made their intentions for 2013 clear by spending over £70 million on new talent during the summer of 2012.

How to Get There

By Car: It is possible to drive to Stamford Bridge on match days but it's pretty pointless to do so. Traffic snarls up badly and the effects are felt throughout Southwest London. If you do brave the traffic, remember that Fulham Road is closed off on match days. Parking is a nightmare with most zones given over to residents. Gangs of eager traffic wardens are on hand to make your Saturday afternoon miserable.

By Public Transport: Stamford Bridge is a two-minute stroll from Fulham Broadway tube station. Regular district line underground trains deliver the hordes from central London in a matter of minutes. If the idea of a packed train full of sweaty football fans isn't your idea of heaven, many fans descend at Ealing Broadway and take the ten-minute walk to the stadium instead.

How to Get Tickets

With so many competitions and cups, getting tickets is easier than you might think. The 'big' fixtures—London derby's, Man U, Liverpool and the later cup stages are either impossible to get or crazily priced but tickets for the less glamorous ties can be picked up from the Chelsea website or box office. Otherwise cheeky geezers will be on hand to fleece you on match day. You will probably end up in the new West Stand alongside Japanese and American tourists but that might be preferable to a fat skinhead in the 'Shed.'

General Information

NFT Map: 47
Tickets: 0870 442 1222
Website: www.fulhamfc.com
Location: Craven Cottage, Stevenage Road, London SW6 6HH

Overview

Fulham like to think of themselves as a family club. They have a quaint little stadium by the Thames; their manager is a pleasant Dutchman and they play In Fulham for God's sake. Overlook their sexually charged nickname—The Cottagers—and all seems hunky dory.

That, in part, is why their recent recovery has been so lovely. When Roy Hodgson took the reins in 2008 they were doomed. But he rescued The Cottagers—seriously. That is easily the most X-rated nickname in football —from relegation and, in 2009, guided them into Europe, before taking over football's worst job (England manager) in 2012. Mark Hughes took over the team and inexplicably quit before the season finished which, tossed Fulham into turmoil, until the steady hand of Martin Jol took control and ensured business as usual.

The club's sugadaddy is barmy passport-chaser Mohamed Al-Fayed. That's the same Mo who used to own Harrods, and whose son died with Princess Diana.

That aside, Craven Cottage is still one of the nicest grounds In London and tickets are relatively easy to come by. Just be wary of that hole in the gents.

How to Get There

By Car: Craven Cottage sits in a leafy, riverside suburb of Fulham. Parking is relatively easy around the ground with plenty of parking meters, although reaching the ground could be difficult as weekend traffic in London is never fun to negotiate.

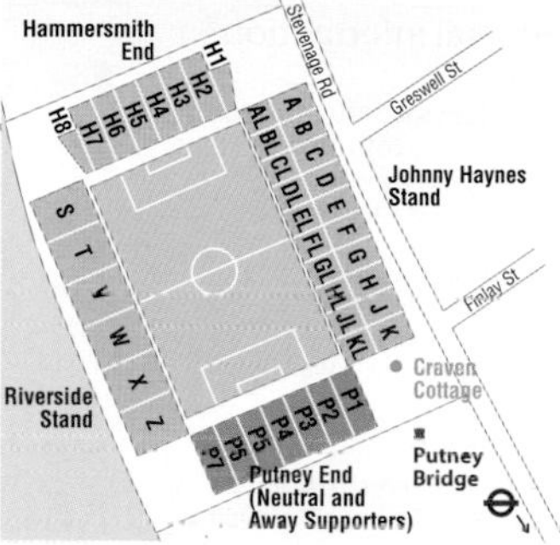

By Public Transport: Putney Bridge on the District Line is your best bet. Putney also has a mainline station with connections from Clapham Junction and direct trains from Waterloo. Cross the road opposite Putney station and hop on any passing bus. Alternatively, a ten-minute walk down the high street and over the river will get you to the ground.

How to Get Tickets

One of the 'joys' of watching Fulham is that tickets are easy to get your hands on. Many games are available on general sale through the club website. For the biggest matches, priority is given to members but persevere and you should be rewarded. If you can't get a ticket legitimately, you can always take your chance with a tout on match day. Try haggling; due to Fulham's fortunes, you could get lucky.

General Information

NFT Map: 76
Main switchboard: 020 7616 8500
Ticketline: 020 7616 8700
Lord's website: www.lords.org
England Cricket Board website: www.ecb.co.uk
Middlesex CCC website: www.middlesexccc.com
Location: St John's Wood, London, NW8 8QN.

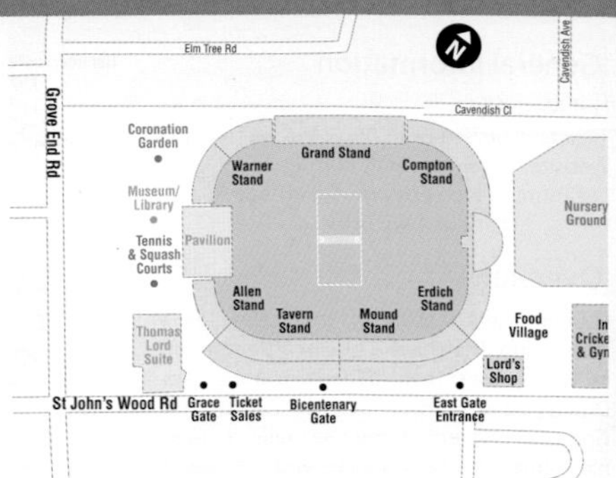

Overview

Even if you know nothing about cricket, don't be put off coming to Lord's. Yes, some games last for five days, and yes, it can still be a draw at the end of it. But as much as anything else Lord's is a fabulous place to come and have a drink. On a hot day the ground is paradise. The sunburnt crowd get slowly boozed up and by the time the players break for tea—yes, tea—few people are concerned at what's going on in the middle. With the polite hum of chatter building up to full-blown drunken singing, it's worth going to Lord's for the atmosphere alone. But when the rabble have calmed down, Lord's is a very genteel place. It's widely seen as the Home of Cricket, and used to house the international governing body. It hosts a heap of England games every year and it's the home ground of county side Middlesex. There's also a year-round gym—you don't even have to be posh to use it—and an indoor training centre. There's even a museum to amuse you when rain stops play. And, rest assured, at some point rain WILL stop play. At the moment Lords holds two Test matches (the marathon international five-dayers) and a handful of England one-day games. These are the ground's showpiece events, where the crowd are at their most boisterous. Middlesex games rarely attract many spectators, and unless you're an old man or a dog you may be in a minority.

How to Get There

By Car: There's little parking around Lord's so, as you'll be parked up all day, public transport will always be cheaper. If you must drive, the ground is off the A4, which turns into the M4.

By Public Transport: The nearest station is St John's Wood (Jubilee Line). Marylebone (Bakerloo) and Baker Street (Bakerloo, Jubilee, Hammersmith and City, Metropolitan and Circle) are both nearby. Marylebone mainline station serves the north and west of the country. London Paddington is a short bus ride away. Dozens of buses run to Baker Street, many of which stop right outside the ground: 13, 82, 113, 139, 189, 755, 757, 758, 768, 771, 772, 773, 797

How to Get Tickets

Getting your hands on England tickets can be tricky. The first few days of a Test match tend to sell out months in advance, though tickets for the last day never go on pre-sale (as the game could be over by then). Similarly, One Day Internationals are normally sell-outs, so it does take a little planning to get in. Check the website over the preceding winter and you might get lucky. If there are less than ten overs in a day due to rain, or if the game's already over, you can claim the full ticket price back. If the weather limits play to between 10.1-24.5 overs (in English, that's up to 149 balls played) you get a 50 per cent refund. Any more than that and you're deemed to have got your money's worth. Middlesex games rarely sell out, however, so you can just rock up on the day, beers in hand, and enjoy the Lord's village.

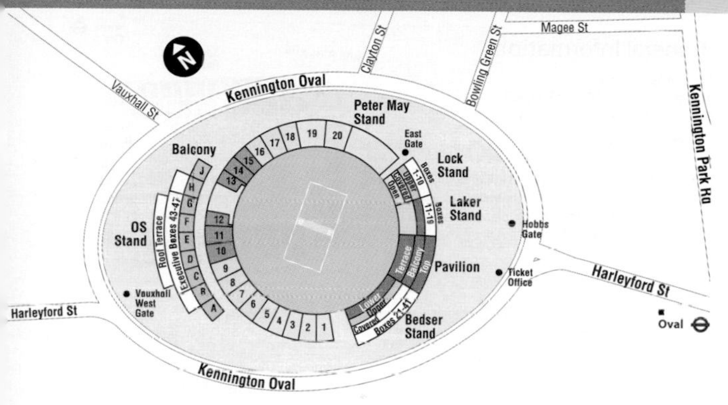

General Information

FT Map: 135
elephone: 020 7582 6660
Vebsite: www.surreycricket.com
the-brit-oval
ocation: The Brit Oval, Kennington,
London, SE11 5SS

Overview

/hat better way to while away a sunny summer's ay than at The Oval cricket ground, typically ongside hundreds of other shirkers who also alled in sick? The Oval is one of London's twin ons of the game, alongside Lord's in North ondon, and boasts a rich history stretching all ie way back to 1846, when it was converted from abbage patch to cricket pitch. It now plays host Surrey County and international test matches, cluding the biennial England-Australia slugfest The Ashes." Live international cricket remains a oozy, good natured affair with English fanbase he Barmy Army' typically belting out salty chants id cheering occasional streakers. County cricket a mellower, no less enjoyable event, with readily ailable tickets and a good portion of the crowd ore interested in today's paper than the action in ont of them. Taxing it ain't.

How to Get There

By Car: Driving to the Oval is not ideal, because parking is near impossible. Should you be willing to risk it, it's situated on the A202, near the junction with the A3 and A24, south of Vauxhall Bridge. As ever with London driving, you'll need your A to Z and nerves of steel.

By Public Transport: The Oval boasts its own, eponymous tube stop on the Northern Line, from which the stadium is a few hundred yards walk. Determinedly overground travellers should alight at Vauxhall, from which Oval is a ten minute jaunt, tops. Buses 36, 185 and 436 stop right outside the ground too.

How to Get Tickets

Tickets for Surrey county matches are relatively easy to get hold of, though seats for some fixtures can only be bought on site on the day of the match. Check www.surreycricket.com/tickets/domestic for a list of fixtures and availability. International matches tend to sell out very quickly indeed—touts or online sales sites like eBay and Gumtree are usually the best option, at a price. Check out www.surreycricket.com/tickets/international for more info. Ticketmaster also offers tickets to all Oval fixtures at www.ticketmaster.co.uk/venue/147862.

General Information

NFT Map: 32
Telephone: 020 8743 0262
Ticket hotline: 08444 777 007
Website: www.qpr.premiumtv.co.uk
Location: Loftus Road Stadium, South Africa Road, Shepherds Bush, W12 7PA

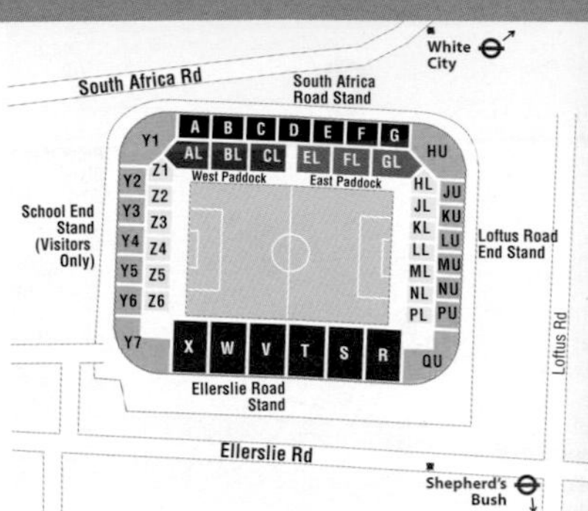

Overview

Once-itinerant football club Queen's Park Rangers have called Loftus Road—based, confusingly, in Shepherd's Bush—home since 1917, give or take a few seasons. Their footballing fortunes have yo-yoed through the decades: once a whisker away from winning Division One in the years before it became the Premiership; they finished last season just above the relegation zone, but gave us what undoubtedly was the game of the season after losing a 2 – 0 lead in stoppage time to gift moneybags Man City the Premier League title. New ownership, including pint-sized F1 oligarch Bernie Eccleston, injected some much needed glamour into the club (prior to the takeover, Pete Doherty was the Hoop's most famous fan). But, amid wacky boasts of Euro domination, Bernie was cut down to size. The years following the sacking of their Italian boss De Canio has seen the Hoops' top spot resemble a revolving door in a busy brothel. Nine different managers and caretakers have come and gone in three years resulting in turmoil on the pitch, and off it too. They're still in the Premiership though thanks to Mark Hughes who looks set to stay, at least for a few months. The erratic QPR are definitely and defiantly worth watching live, especially during the brief periods their philosophical and slightly psycho captain Joey Barton remains out of prison. They're still in the Championship though thanks to Neil Warnock who looks to stay, at least for this year.

How to Get There

By Car: Whether you're approaching Loftu Road from the North (from the M1 through the A406 and A40), East (via the A40(M)) South (from the A3 and A219) or West (up the M4 via the A315 and A402 on a wing and a prayer), all routes lead through White City Once there, turn right off Wood Lane into South Africa Road. Don't even set off withou your NFT London, or emergency rations For the brave, full details of all journey are available at QPR's official website liste above.

By Public Transport: The majority of QPR fan are local and rely either on nearby tube stop (White City on the Central Line, Shepherd Bush on the the Hammersmith and Ci Line), any of buses 72, 95, or 220 to Whit City Station, or overground train to Acto Central, followed by a quick bus ride.

How to Get Tickets

Getting tickets for a QPR game is harde than you might expect. The team has loyal fan base and is quickly becoming guilty pleasure (due mainly to moments madness) for casual spectators. Howeve getting tickets for a run of the mill midseaso game should be a cinch, either via th Rangers' ticket website (eticketing.co.u qpr) or phone numbers listed above. You ca also visit the Loftus Road box office on matc days. Tickets are around £35 per person.

General Information

Ticketline: 0844 499 5000
Website: www.spurs.co.uk
Location: Bill Nicholson Way,
748 High Road,
London, N17 OAP

Overview

The times they are a-changin at Tottenham, the blaggers at Stamford Bridge robbed them of a deserved Champion's League place and the countries favourite tax dodger Harry Redknapp didn't get the England job and then, to add insult to injury, was let go by the club. Chelsea failure Andre Villas-Boas is set to take over control in 2013 and it s likely that he will lose at least one, if not a few, of his best players. The scruffy but (for some reason) adored century old White Hart Lane is on its last legs and 2013 could be the ast full season played in the iconic stadium. This isn't a bad thing, because nostalgia aside, few grounds in the capital are located further from a tube stop and closer to a corner of London where even police dogs walk in pairs. More than most fans, the Spurs faithful have a tight grasp of history (which could be because there's been no league title there since 1961). And it shows at the stadium—supporters even chant about what a grand old team Spurs are. But that song only gets sporadic outings. Most of the chants that ring around White Hart Lane are about how much the fans hate Arsenal. It's a rivalry that's as intense as any in football—and as Arsenal started out in the south of the city, only moving across the river in 1913, Spurs claim of being Kings of North London isn't such a wild one. This division grew deeper during Arsenal's years of success, their American ownership, snooty fans, and their new corporate-branded Emirates Stadium just added fuel to the fire. But Spurs are contenders now, they have a new stadium of their own in the pipeline and the days of old ladies selling bagels inside the ground will soon be replaced by £400 million hotel-cum-shopping-centre-cum-football-ground.The days of the "Old Team" are ending but during 2013 Tottenham will be a team to watch.

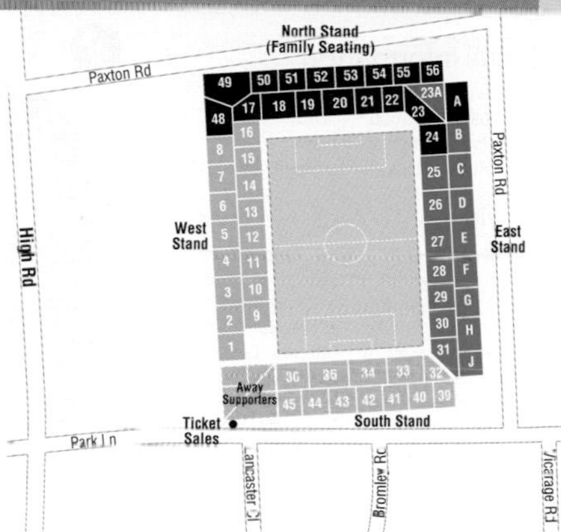

How to Get There

By Car: The area's congested at the best of times; on match days, traffic can grind to a standstill. But if you don't mind a bit of gridlock, White Hart Lane is on the Tottenham High Road (A1010) a mile south of the North Circular (A406). This is easily accessible from junction 25 of the M25, in itself a temple to traffic.

By Public Transport: The nearest tube is Seven Sisters (Victoria Line), which is a 25 minute walk away. But at least if you work up a hunger from all that walking there's hundreds of kebab shops en route. White Hart Lane overland station, which runs from Liverpool Street through Seven Sisters, is a five-minute walk from the ground. Bus routes 279, 349, 149, 259 run closest to the stadium, but many more pass nearby.

How to Get Tickets

Although home games normally sell out, tickets are fairly easy to get hold of. Club members get first refusal at tickets (it costs £47 to join), ten days before going on sale to the public. This costs £62; but as the club's fortunes are on the rise, the wait could be some time. To get on the season ticket waiting list, you have to become a One Hotspur Bronze Member. This costs £47; but as the club's fortunes are on the rise, the wait could be some time.

General Information

Website: www.rfu.com
Phone: 0870 405 2000
Location: Twickenham Stadium,
Rugby Road, Twickenham, TW1 1DZ

Overview

The home of English rugby, Twickenham is a behemoth of a stadium. An ugly chunk of concrete seemingly dumped from a great height onto a quiet London suburb, Twickenham lacks the charm and character of Ireland's Landsdowne Road and Scotland's Murrayfield, and has been all but pushed to the sidelines by the magnificent Millennium Stadium in Wales. However, the stadium has largely remained a fortress when it comes to England Internationals. Cheered on by 82,000 well-spoken, white-shirted fans booming out 'Swing Low Sweet Chariot' probably helps. Maybe the England players absorb the unfussy and uncompromising nature of their surroundings into their psyche on match days. Critics would argue that their style of rugby is as ugly and bland as the stadium they play in. This would be harsh if England hadn't consistently under-performed after carrying off the Rugby World Cup in 2003. Twickenham also hosts a series of Rugby tournaments and exhibition matches, including the famous 'Sevens', in addition to the occasional Premiership fixture. Outside the Rugby season, the stadium is given over to rock concerts for international bands like Bon Jovi and R.E.M.

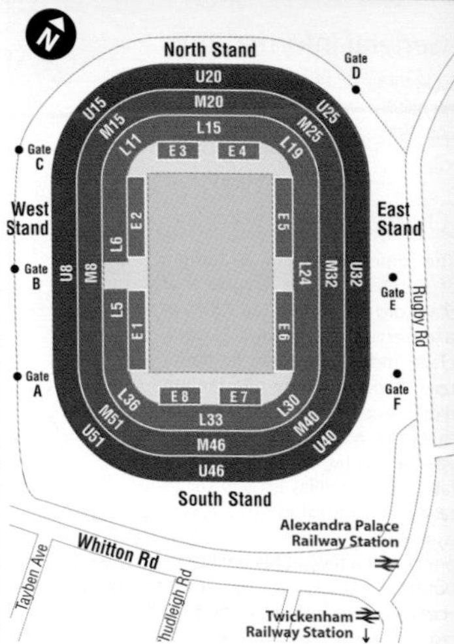

How to Get There

By Car: Twickenham is very accessible by road - if you live in the South. The M3 motorway turns into the A316 that passes the stadium, carrying on into central London. Certain roads get closed down on match days so drivers should allow plenty of time. Parking at the stadium is extremely limited and should be booked in advance. Resident permits are helpfully required for all roads bordering the stadium so the best thing to do is park in the general vicinity and walk the rest of the way.

By Public Transport: Mainline trains run to Twickenham station from Waterloo and Reading. London Underground runs to Richmond on the District Line where shuttle buses will take fans to the stadium (50p outbound. Free return). Hounslow is an alternative Underground station but shuttle buses only run from Twickenham to Hounslow station so you will have to make it to the stadium under your own steam. Bus numbers 281, 267 and H22 all have regular services passing close to the stadium.

How to Get Tickets

England rugby tickets are hot property commanding higher prices than top football games. As competition games are relatively infrequent, tickets sell out well in advance so keep checking the website for updates on ticket releases. Premiership tickets and friendly matches are easier to come by but will generally sell out. If you don't get lucky in advance, rugby touts (slightly less aggressive than their football cousins) will happily make your wallet lighter for you. Ticketmaster is the best option for concerts or Gumtree and Craigslist for re-sales and swaps.

General Information

Website: www.whufc.com
Phone: 020 8548 2794
Location: Boleyn Ground,
Green Street,
London E13 9AZ

Overview

When bald biscuit king Eggert Magnusson bought the Hammers everything looked rosy. But then the world went tits up. The recession meant Icelander Eggert's companies were suddenly worth nothing. He went bankrupt—and West Ham became a Scandinavian IOU. While boss Gianfranco Zola was leading a revolution on the pitch—shepherding a young team to the brinks of Europe—there were real dangers the club would fold.

Currently, West Ham is owned by a consortium that seized the club off Magnusson—made up of, er, Icelandic banks. Not really where you want your money right now. But if they survive, the Irons are on the way up. If you can find the ground in deepest East London they're well worth a look.

Over the years, West Ham has been unfairly tainted by association with the ICF hooligan firm. Largely active in the '70s and '80s, a 2005 film, 'Green Street' did its best to rekindle unwanted memories. The drama was undermined slightly by giving the lead role to a hobbit. They finished the 2011 season at the bottom of the Premiership and were relegated—but during 2012 they proved they were too good for the Championship and will be back with the big boys in 2013, where we hope they have an excellent season, we don't want to give them any excuse to get angry. They finished last season bottom of the Premiership and were relegated—let's hope they do better in 2012, we don't want to give them any excuse to get angry.

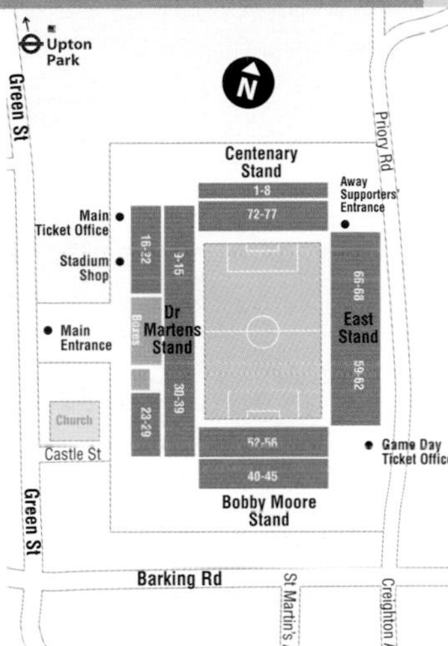

How to Get There

By Car: Driving in London is a waste of time even on the best of days, but try it on match days and you are asking for trouble. East London is a warren of one way streets, dead ends and no through roads. You are likely to either miss kick-off or get a parking ticket or both.

By Public Transport: The district line will 'whisk' you from central London to Upton Park in half an hour or so. The Boleyn Ground is 5 minutes walk from the underground station.

How to Get Tickets

Unless you want to pay through the nose for tickets against the big clubs, you should be able to find spares for the smaller fixtures. West Ham is a relatively small ground with a dedicated, hardcore following. Being less glamorous than Chelsea et al means that casual fans have a better chance of watching a game for a decent price.

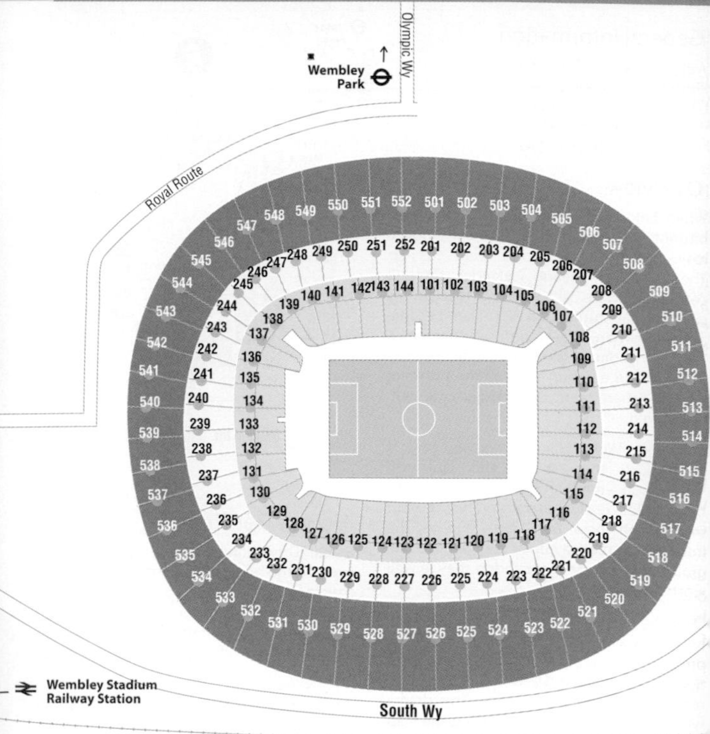

General Information

Phone: 0844 980 8001
Website: www.wembleystadium.com
Location: Wembley Stadium, Wembley HA9 0WS

Overview

Wembley Stadium enjoys a strange position in the British psyche. For football fans it's most significant as the scene of England's only World Cup win back in 1966, as well as numerous pitch invasions by angry / jubilant Scottish fans whenever their national team came down to play. Plus, a generation of British bands have grown up dreaming of the day they'd bellow: "hello Wem-ber-ley, are you ready to rock?!!" to tens of thousands of people who've just paid a fiver for a chewy patty of minced spleen 'n' testicles in a dry bun. For these sentimental reasons, then, very few people complained that the National Stadium was a bit of a crap-hole stuck in an inaccessible suburb of West London. By the late '90s the place was looking a bit battered, so they knocked it down and then very, very slowly, and at tremendous, tabloid-scandalising expense, built a replacement on the same site. The result is, just about, worth it. There are none of the blind spots for spectators that the old stadium used to have, plus it has far greater leg-room for 90-thousand-plus people and much more comfortable seating. It also looks fantastically imposing as you walk out of Wembley Park tube with its massive arch curving into the sky. A trip here might not make your knees go "all trembly" as fans used to sing but for football lovers it's one of the world's great venues. They also have a special removable running track for athletics and, to the disgust of "soccer" purists, they've even let American "football" teams play here, too.

How to Get There

By Car: Short of hiring snipers to pick drivers off as they approach the mighty arch, the Stadium could hardly do more to discourage visitors from driving. "Wembley Stadium is a public transport destination. Please leave your car behind," the website primly advises. However, if you are some kind of die-hard, planet-raping petrol-head you'll see signs pointing to the stadium from Great Central Way onwards. There are very few parking spaces at the Stadium itself and these need to be booked in advance for £25 or £12 for disabled users and, despite the prices, they often sell out. On match days, or when there's anything else happening, the local area becomes residents' parking only, too. Yes, they really don't want you to bring your car.

By Public Transport: The nearest Tube is Wembley Park on the Metropolitan and Jubilee line. Wembley Central (on the Bakerloo line) is about 10–15 minutes walk and there's also Wembley Stadium mainline train station with links all over the country. If you're travelling from outside London there are National Express coaches from 43 different towns and cities.

How to Get Tickets

Easier said than done. 'Club Wembley' have kindly created a 'ten year seat licence'—no doubt to re-coup the massive overspend that accompanied completion of the stadium. These licences give owners access to all major events hosted at Wembley and its worth going on the website to laugh at the ridiculous prices. A 'one-off licence fee' costs from £1,440 to £16,943. Annual season tickets are on top of that. Cloud Cuckoo Land. 'Normal' people can buy tickets to England games through the FA (you need to be a member), for football and rugby cup games through the respective clubs and tickets for one off events and shows through Ticketmaster. It's always worth checking Gumtree.com as you never know who might be flogging off a golden ticket to the highest bidder.

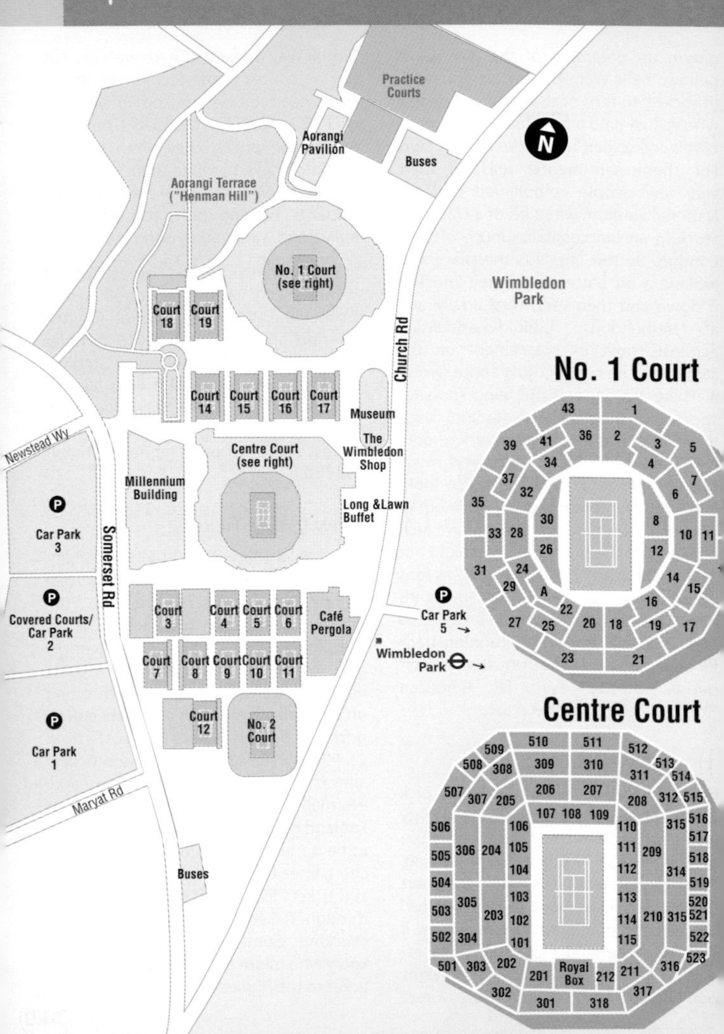
Practice Courts
Aorangi Pavilion
Buses
Aorangi Terrace ("Henman Hill")
No. 1 Court (see right)
Court 18
Court 19
Court 14
Court 15
Court 16
Court 17
Museum
Church Rd
Wimbledon Park
Newstead Wy
Centre Court (see right)
The Wimbledon Shop
Millennium Building
Long &Lawn Buffet
Car Park 3
Somerset Rd
Covered Courts/ Car Park 2
Court 3
Court 4
Court 5
Court 6
Café Pergola
Car Park 5
Wimbledon Park
Court 7
Court 8
Court 9
Court 10
Court 11
Court 12
No. 2 Court
Car Park 1
Maryat Rd
Buses
No. 1 Court
Centre Court
Royal Box

General Information

Telephone: 020 8944 1066
Website: www.wimbledon.org
Location: The All England Lawn Tennis and Croquet Club, Church Road, Wimbledon, SW19 5AE

Overview

New balls please! If it's not pissing it down—which is a big if—Wimbledon's All England Tennis and Croquet Club is the place to witness the world's finest tennis players do battle on rye grass courts, home as it is to the oldest major Championship in the game each June/July. But this is also a place to be seen and to be merry—sure, it's about the tennis, but it's also about strawberries and cream (of which 62,000 pounds and 1,540 gallons worth are sold each year respectively), the free flowing champagne, the celebrity crowd, and the Ralph Lauren-designed ballboy and ballgirl outfits. If you can't actually get a ticket for the tournament—the All England Club makes approximately 1,500 of them available each day, and more importantly, if you're not prepared to camp out overnight in the queue—you can always sit yourself on Murray Mound (formerly Henman Hill) at the northern end of the complex, where a vast television screen allows you to watch British players systematically eliminated in typically heartbreaking fashion. Really, we should stick to darts.

How to Get There

By Car: During the tournament, traffic and parking are nightmarish propositions, and you're better off using public transport. Nonetheless, the determined will need to take the A219 from the A3, and turn off left onto Church Road once in Wimbledon itself.

By Public Transport: Wimbledon railway station is a short journey from both Waterloo and Clapham Junction, and is otherwise serviced (Vicar!) by trains from towns right across the South of England. From here, board the London General shuttle bus straight to the grounds; they depart every five minutes or so during the tournament. Tube users should head for Southfields on the District Line, from where a London General shuttle also operates. Those who prefer to saunter can mosey on down Wimbledon Park Road heading south for ten minutes or so, and you can also walk it from Wimbledon Park tube station, heading north-west.

How to Get Tickets

You can (legally) come by tickets to Wimbledon in two ways—one, apply in advance to the public 'ballot', via the website above, in the hope you are selected at random to purchase tickets (closing date end of December). Two, join the serpentine, overnight queues for on-the-day tickets, of which five hundred are usually made available for each of Centre, Number One and Number Two Courts. Then, of course, there are all the other methods of which you're already no doubt aware.

Overview

Any bowling buff will tell you that there are two types of bowling in this country. Ten-pin bowling, the ghastly Americanized import, is by far the most popular among Londoners and the generally disrespectful 'Youth Of Today. Crown Green Bowling is a far more serene, (elderly) gentlemanly pursuit complete with its own rules and rituals. London's ten-pin bowlers are spoiled rotten.

London's ten pin bowlers are spoiled rotten. As it's now a trendy pastime shot through with irony, there are plenty of old, large basements converted into pristine bowling alleys designed to look retro. There's no chavs in tracksuits on speed around here: the All Star Lanes franchises are heaving with immaculately dressed trendos and hen/stag nights drunkenly bowling and singing in the karaoke booths. However, at a peak rate of £8.75 per person per game (your average game is a mere 10 minutes) and an off peak rate of a laughably similar £7.75 per game, you'll have to access whether it's worth blowing the rent money on one night of fun. Bloomsbury Bowling Lanes does the American chic thing a bit better and its lanes are £39 an hour, which works out cheaper in a group. They also host cool gigs and DJs occasionally.

For families and the penniless, London has plenty of more 'traditional' British bowling lanes. By this, of course, we mean cavernous warehouses with pumping chart music, scary underage drinkers and sticky air hockey tables. Try the classic Rowans (Finsbury Park) which at its priciest is a mere £4.70 per person per game or Queens (Bayswater) which has also has an ice rink to cool off those skittle blues.

And what of Green Bowling? Well, being an outdoor pursuit in Britain, it's safe to say it is primarily a Summer affair. When the sun is out you'll find bowling greens in all the major parks; Hyde Park offers a set of woods for £5 (with no time limit) May till October.

After suffering at the hands of boho and cheapo ten-pin bowling facilities you may find that there can be no better way to waste an afternoon than to sit around a bowling green in Finsbury Park with a beer in hand, laughing at your idiot friends' attempts to hit the 'jack.' Maybe those elderly gentlemen are on to something...

Bowling	*Address*	*Phone*	*Map*
All Star Lanes	95 Brick Ln	020 7426 9200	91
All Star Lanes	Victoria House, Bloomsbury Pl	020 7025 2676	4
All Star Lanes	6 Porchester Gardens	020 7313 8363	30
Bloomsbury Bowling Lanes	Bedford Way	020 7183 1979	4
Hyde Park	Hyde Park	020 7262 3474	n/a
Queens	17 Queensway	020 7229 0172	30
Rowans	10 Stroud Green Rd	020 8800 1950	62

Overview

Nothing combines relaxation and hypertension quite like golf, nor indeed knee-length socks, spats and flat caps. For golfing Londoners, opportunities to play must be sought towards the outskirts of the capital, where the city shore is lapped once more by greenery and open space. You can, of course, take your one wood out onto London's pavements and practise your fade drive there, but you're odds on to be arrested if you do.

You'll be better received moving clockwise around London from the North, at establishments such as the Highgate Golf Club and Muswell Hill Golf Club. Both are highbrow member institutions with epic fairways, open nonetheless to the public, as long as that public is wearing a decent shirt. Eighteen holes at each are in the £30-40 range, which is also the case at the Hampstead Golf Club, home of one of England's toughest front nines. Nearby Finchley Golf Club is similarly priced for visitors but also offers some neat specials such as winter green fees in the £25 range and knockdown prices for twelve holes of 'twilight golf'. A little further north, Mill Hill Golf Club is a shade cheaper though no less satisfying.

In the south-east, the Royal Blackheath Golf Club positions itself as the oldest in the world, which might be why playing eighteen holes as a visitor requires a small trust fund, at £50 during summer weekdays. Moving further west, the Central London Golf Centre is a no-nonsense 'pay-and-play' establishment offering nine full-length holes to golfers of all standards for little more than a tenner. The Wimbledon Park Golf Club is another quality members club open to visitors, while nearby Royal Wimbledon Golf Club terms itself a 'very private' club—visitors are welcome but will be required to apply in writing, prove handicap and, in all likelihood, undergo some kind of permanently scarring initiation ritual. Access to each of these Wimbledon clubs kicks off at a chokingly high £70 for eighteen holes. You could buy a second hand Playstation for that. The London Scottish Golf Club on Wimbledon Common is much more like it, at £20 a round, though a pillar-box red top is compulsory for all. Out west, Dukes Meadows Golf Club in Chiswick offers nine three-par holes, a driving range and function rooms, all at a reasonable price.

For golfers who really are determined not to leave Zone One, there is one option after all. Urban Golf, with venues in Soho (W1) and Smithfield (EC1), is the last word in golf simulation, with the chance to play, virtual-style, some of the world's top courses. It also boasts well-stocked bars and chic lounge areas. You just know the purists will loathe it.

Golf Clubs	*Address*	*Phone*	*Map*
Central London Golf Centre	Burntwood Ln	020 8871 2468	n/a
Dukes Meadows Golf Club	Dukes Meadow	020 8995 0537	n/a
Finchley	Frith Ln	020 8346 1133	n/a
Hampstead Golf Club	82 Winnington Rd	020 8455 0203	n/a
Highgate Golf Club	Denewood Rd	020 8340 3745	n/a
Holland Park	Ilchester Pl	020 7602 2226	34
London Scottish Golf Club	Windmill Rd	020 8788 0135	n/a
Mill Hill Golf Club	100 Barnet Way	020 8959 2339	n/a
Muswell Hill Golf Club	Rhodes Ave	020 8888 1764	n/a
Royal Blackheath Golf Club	Court Rd	020 8550 1795	n/a
Urban Golf	33 Great Pulteney St	020 7434 4300	10
Urban Golf	12 Smithfield St	020 7248 8600	15
Wilbledon Park Golf Club	Home Park Rd	020 8946 1250	n/a

Overview

Remember the Levi's ad in the pool hall? The one which had The Clash's *Should I Stay Or Should I Go?* as the soundtrack? Yeah, that one. It conjured up a pretty cool image, right? Unfortunately London's pool halls have not had the retro revamp (is that an oxymoron?) that bowling is currently enjoying (All Star Lanes, Bloomsbury Bowling) so it's rare to actually find a place where you can stand around looking like James Dean, kissing your teeth, chewing on a tooth pick, and generally inviting any hustler to take you on without like, really being taken on by someone from the Russian/Turkish mafia. The Islington Elbow Room experienced a couple of shootings, making it one of the areas only establishments for unsavoury types so naturally they moved their business down to Shoreditch. The Islington Elbow Room has experienced a couple of shootings of the gun variety in recent years, so try not to spill your pint on anyone as you go from bar to pool table. The Shoreditch Elbow Room has a ping pong table in the summer. Why it is a seasonal attraction is uncertain but us Brits tend to associate sports according to weather it seems. We also inextricably link shooting some pool with having a drink or two, but it is often the lesser red and yellow-balled "pub" pool table (funnily enough) rather than the greater spotted (and striped) genuine American pool table which is found within the confines of the few remaining non-chain traditional pubs in London.The Westbury Bar in Kilburn however, has three American pool tables in a rather swank environment of leather Chesterfields, parquet flooring and red lampshades. Food is pan-Asian and roasts are served on Sundays, adding to a pub vibe. 19:20 in Clerkenwell has more of a pool hall feel with media types taking their game a little more seriously at the end of the working day. If you do fancy something a little more louche, there are many a pool and snooker hall to be found on the edges of central London which can offer a grittier atmosphere. EFES used to be a bit of a no-go for white middle-class hipster kids until the owners realised that they were sitting on a goldmine what with having a long-standing late licence and being slap bang in the middle of the action. Now the place hosts gigs and is a regular fixture for anyone doing a Kingsland crawl. Oh yeah, and has pool tables.

Pool & Snooker	*Address*	*Phone*	*Map*
19:20	20 Great Sutton St	020 7253 1920	6
Efes Pool Club & Bar	17 Stoke Newington Rd	020 7249 6040	86
The Elbow Room	97 Curtain Rd	020 7613 1316	84
The Elbow Room	89 Chapel Market	020 7278 3244	80
The Elbow Room	103 Westbourne Grove	020 7221 5211	30
Number 1 Bar	1 Duke Street Hill	020 7407 6420	106
Riley's	638 Wandsworth Rd	020 7498 0432	142
Riley's	16 Semley Pl	020 7824 8261	19
Rowans	10 Stroud Green Rd	020 8800 1950	62
The Westbury	34 Kilburn High Rd	020 7625 7500	68

Tennis

Ah…the other beautiful game, beloved of park fence jumpers and upper class grunters alike. Like many popular sports, tennis may have originated in Britain, but we're pretty consistent in our ineptitude at it. This is not for the lack of trying: the country's capital is packed full of tennis clubs, outdoor park courts and large sports complexes.

Tennis is certainly not as exclusive as it once was, with an hour's playing a lot cheaper than ten-pin bowling, for example. You can mince about amidst leafy surroundings in Hyde Park (Hyde Park Sports Centre, 020 7262 3474), flail in the dark depths of Finsbury Park on a turn-up-and-play basis, or in the luxury of the historic Queens Club (www.queensclub.co.uk, 020 7386 3429 for membership information). Also commendable are the Paddington Sports Club (020 7286 8448) in Maida Vale and the courts in Regent's Park: go to www.tennisintheparks.co.uk for information on, uh, playing tennis in parks. Indicative of the new equalitarian nature of the game are Tennis London International (www.tennislondon.com) who take pride in being 'the largest gay and lesbian tennis group in the UK.' But it's not all democratic: there's always Wimbledon (www.wimbledon.org, which due to the jaw dropping ticket prices, still is as exclusive as it's always been. If you still want to get caught up in the annual tennis frenzy, head to Henman Hill, or Murray Mound, or whatever it's called these days. Essentially a hill outside Centre Court, here you can sit on the grass and watch the action on video screens with all the other poor proles who don't have any kidneys left to trade for a ticket.

Squash

Like some weird secret society, squash players spend their time locked indoors, organised into little private clubs and engaged in an activity which will eventually mess them up. Squash is hard—just ask your poor knees. The squash court is a high-octane containment tank swimming in adrenalin, which explains why Londoners have taken to it with such gusto. A court at Sobell Center (020 7609 2166) in Finsbury Park for example, is near impossible to book at peak times. In Shepherd's Bush, there's the exclusive squash club New Grampians (020 7603 4255) which is lush, but there are sizeable membership fees to match. Be warned—a lot of sports centres don't have squash facilities, but somewhere like the Oasis Sports Centre (0207 831 1804) in Tottenham Court Road is a church to all things sweaty and squashy…and you can go for an outdoor swim afterwards too. For a quirkier court try Maiden Lane (020-7267 9586)—a community centre in a housing estate, which has one beat-up court for £6 an hour. If there isn't a yoga class in progress, that is.

Badminton/Table Tennis

They may be worlds apart in many ways, but badminton and table tennis are usually offered in the same place, and both are 'genteel' sports in which it is almost acceptable to be beaten by the opposite sex (whichever sex you are). Badminton is especially popular across the board, with almost all sizeable sports centres offering courts and equipment. However, if you've any experience in attempting to book a court at most public sports complexes you'll know of the often depressing amount of phone wrangling and frustration that arises from these exchanges. Chief perpetrator is Kings Hall Sports Centre (020 8985 2158) in Lower Clapton, who will test your patience to inhumane limits. The Brixton Recreation Centre (020 7926 9779) caters for badminton and squash players but always sound like they can't wait to get you off the phone; their rates are around £7 for badminton, which is pretty competitive. The Sobell Centre, as mentioned above, also caters for table tennis (doesn't ping pong sound nicer?) and badminton. The best strategy is to phone your local centre to ascertain which racquet sports they cater for and then prepare yourself to be either double-booked, misinformed or given a free session depending on the ability of the desk assistant!

Overview

As the nascent city of 'Londinium' was being named by the Romans in AD 43, in Asia the practice of yoga was entering its third or fourth millennium. Nineteen hundred years on, at last it found its way out west, and London's yoga establishments have flourished ever since. Essentially, the capital's schools can be divided into those concerned primarily with physical fitness—often the larger institutions offering a range of styles—and those with a more spiritual bent. Of the former, Go Yoga in Shepherd's Bush is a fine example, offering yoga and pilates for adults and kids alike, while the popular Triyoga centres in Primrose Hill and Covent Garden are one-stop holistic shops for the upwardly mobile set. More specialised centres include Bikram Yoga College of India in Kentish Town, and its partner Bikram Yoga City—bring water and a towel for hard wearing, specially heated sessions—and the Iyengar Yoga Institute in Maida Vale, which offers a free introductory class. Special mention also goes to Fulham Yogashala, a newish venture offering all sorts including, unnervingly, 'power yoga'. Still, entering the peaceful surroundings of Yogashala is, according to one client, like getting a hug. Those more spiritual schools include the wonderful Sivanada Yoga Centre, an oasis of serenity in the midst of Putney boasting resident yogi teachers, and the Satyananda Yoga Centre in Clapham with its deep focus on yoga-meditation techniques. Shanti Sadam, out west, is also more concerned with inner stillness than downward dogs. And hidden away in Archway, the Kriya Centre runs a series of kundalini yoga classes in humble but hospitable surroundings—Ohm tastic!

Yoga Centers	*Address*	*Phone*	*Website*	*Map*
Alchemy	Stables Market	020 7267 6188	www.alchemythecentre.co.uk	71
Battersea Yoga	152 Northcote Rd	020 7978 7995	www.batterseayoga.com	140
Bikram Yoga City	6 Vestry St	020 7336 6330	www.bikramyoga.co.uk/studio_city.html	84
Bikram's Yoga College Of India	173 Queen's Crescent	020 7692 6900	www.bikramyoga.co.uk/studio_north.html	71
Fulham Yogashala	11 Lettice St	079 5609 1696	www.fulhamyogashala.co.uk	48
Go Yoga	140 Percy Rd	020 8740 1989	www.go-yoga.co.uk	n/a
The Hidden Space	93 Falkland Rd	020 8347 3400	www.thehiddenspace.co.uk	55
Islington Yoga	357 City Rd	020 7704 6796	www.islingtonyoga.com	83
Iyengar Yoga Institute	223 Randolph Ave	020 7624 3080	www.iyi.org.uk	27
Jamyang Buddhist Centre	43 Renfrew Rd	020 7820 8787	www.jamyang.co.uk	112
The Kriya Centre	25 Bickerton Rd	020 7272 5811	www.karamkriya.co.uk	59
The Lotus Exchange	Black Prince Rd	020 7463 2234	www.lotusexchange.com	131
North London Buddhist Centre	72 Holloway Rd	020 7700 1177	www.northlondonbuddhistcentre.com	74
Satyananda Yoga Centre	70 Thurleigh Rd	020 8673 4869	www.syclondon.com	147
The Shala	26 Voltaire Rd	020 8670 0925	www.theshala.co.uk	143
Shanti Sadan Yoga Centre	29 Chepstow Villas	020 7727 7846	www.shantisadan.org	29
Shoreditch Studio	49 Curtain Rd	020 7012 1238	www.shoreditchstudio.co.uk	8
Siddha Yoga Sangham Of Europe	63 Collier St	020 7278 0567		79
Sivananda Yoga	51 Felsham Rd	020 8426 9795	www.sivananda.co.uk	136
Surya Yoga Studio	9 Park Hill	020 7622 4257	www.suryayoga.co.uk	149
Synchronicity	157 Hubert Grove	07956 945 417	www.synchronicitylondon.com	144
Templeton House Yoga Studio,	34 Chiswell St	020 7074 6000	www.templetonhouse.co.uk	7
Triyoga	6 Erskine Road	020 7483 3344	www.triyoga.co.uk	70
Urban Bikram	24 Shacklewell Ln	020 7254 3060		86
Yoga Place	449 Bethnal Green Rd	020 7739 5195	www.yogaplace.co.uk	92
Yoga Therapy Center	92 Pentonville Rd	020 7689 3040	www.yogatherapy.org	80

There's nothing quite like an obesity epidemic to make a city sporty. We're constantly being told that we're swelling to huge new levels. The message is worrying: buck up fatties, or you won't even fit into your own coffin. Unlike the majority of celebrations that take place in the capital, the 2012 Olympic Games didn't leave us dry mouthed and heaving on the floor with a national hangover. Instead the summer games littered our fair city with a legacy of leading sports venues, and lower-level sport has benefited the most with increased involvement citywide. And in the hope that we won't all be housebound when the Olympics rolls into town, lower-level sport is seeing increased investment. London's sizeable ethnic communities have also brought weird and wonderful games with them (American Football? In London? Not in our lifetimes). Dozens of leagues, in dozens of sports, gather every evening to try and beat the bulge.

General tips

A good starting point is the Gumtree website (www.gumtree.com). Their sports and community section is full of ads trying to fills gaps in sports teams. And as it was started by born-to-sweat Aussies, it never lets up in sheer quantity of athletic opportunities. The local press is also a decent bet. All London boroughs have their own newspapers, who cover amateur sports with as much enthusiasm as the professionals. You may never make it in the big leagues, but at least you can be a hero in Camden. But one area where London struggles is with the concept of pick-up games. Perhaps it's part of our reserved nature, but it's unusual to just rock up at a park and challenge whoever's there. By all means try, but you may get rebuked by a stiff upper lip.

Football

Sunday league football in London used to have a reputation of being rough. For many years it was the preserve of hungover builders, who wanted ninety minutes letting off steam by kicking people around. But it's moved on slightly from those days, with a more general acceptance of skill and less emphasis placed on pain. The spiritual home of recreational football is Hackney Marshes. The east London site has a whopping 87 pitches—so many leagues and teams play there that it's worth just turning up and asking around. If you draw a blank there, then the FA website (www.thefa.com) has a club locator search. Regardless of where you live, you'll get a mammoth list of clubs. The hardest part of finding a team in London is narrowing down who it is you want to play for. Five-a-side football is also booming in London. In the city centre, where space is at a premium, it's often the only way of getting in a game. Powerleague (www.powerleague.co.uk) organise leagues around the capital, though these can be pricey. A cheaper option is to head to a leisure centre with a five-a-side pitch. They often run leagues and are less profit-driven than the private companies. Lists of leisure centres can be found on specific borough's website (such as Islington's www. [illegible]).

Rugby

Don't mind drinking pints of your team-mates' urine? Enjoy a good eye-gouging? Then you must be a rugby fan! The Rugby in London website (www.rugbyinlondon.co.uk) is a Bible for lovers of casual violence, as it lists hundreds of clubs, contact details and even training venues and times. Female fans of egg chasing are also well represented. Most teams play around Southwest London, though there's a few more dotted around the city. A full list is on the RFU Women's website (www.rfuwlonse.co.uk). If you don't fancy the full-on ear-biting code of the sport there's a flourishing touch rugby scene in London. In this form of the game tackling is represented by tagging your opponent. It's an altogether less bloody type of rugby, although you're still allowed to indulge in the booze-fuelled rituals that the contact players enjoy. In2Touch (www.in2touch.com) lists a few of these leagues.

Cricket

As a sport that takes up plenty of space, you have to head to the leafier parts of London such as Hampstead, Putney, and Dulwich to find cricket clubs at play. But with more green space than any other London borough, Hackney has embraced the gentleman's game, and the thwack of leather on willow can oft be heard on London Fields during the summer months where the North East London Cricket League (www.nelcl.teamopolis.com) has established itself. Victoria Park also has a Community Cricket League (www.vpccl.co.uk). The Play-Cricket website (www.play-cricket.com) has a full rundown on London clubs.

Athletics and the London Marathon

Every spring, London's runners dust down their gorilla costumes and tackle the London Marathon. If you feel up to it then you have to plan ahead; places are limited and dished out via a ballot. If you need a helping hand in the run up to the race, there's a list of jogging and road-running clubs at www.onesite.co.uk/find/running. As well as getting you in shape, so you don't die after 20 miles, they can help you get a spot in the starting line-up. And if you catch the bug of competitive athletics, there are six clubs who compete in the London Inter Club Challenge (www.licc.co.uk).

Miscellaneous

For fans of all things Irish, there's the London Gaelic Sports Association (www.londongaa.org); American footballers can get their fix with the British American Football League (www.bafl.org.uk); and if tight shorts and sleeveless shirts are your thing there's the British Aussie Rules Association (www.barfl.co.uk; or you could just join the navy).

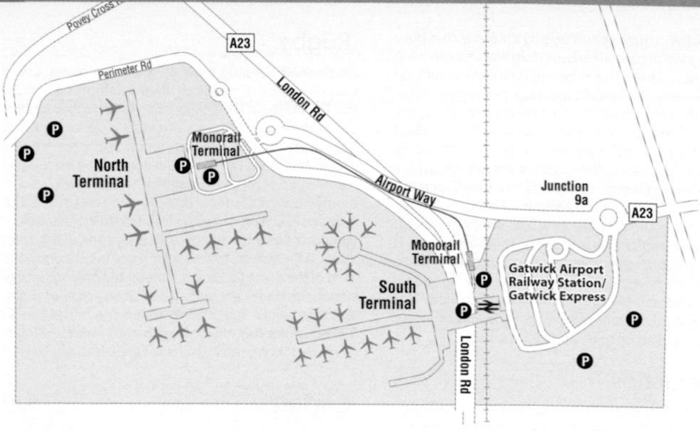

Airline	Terminal	Phone Number
Adria Airways	North	020 8099 7254
Aer Lingus	South	0871 521 2772
Afriqiyah	South	0870 040 5040
Air Algerie	South	0870 111 1111
Air Baltic	South	0870 190 0737
Air Comet	North	0870 111 1111
Air Europa	South	0844 493 0787
Air Malta	South	0844 493 0787
Air Namibia	North	0870 066 1472
Air Southwest	North	0870 111 1111
Air Transat	South	0870 190 0737
Air Zimbabwe	South	0870 040 5040
Atlas Blue	North	0870 111 1111
Aurigny	South	0870 190 0737
Azerbaijan Airlines	South	0870 190 0737
Belavia Belarusian Airlines	South	020 7752 0445
BH Air (Balkan Holidays)	South	0845 600 0950
bmi	South	0870 066 1472
British Airways	North	0870 574 7747
British Jet	South	0800 091 4444
Brussels Airlines	North	0870 190 0737
Bulgaria Air	South	0870 111 1111
Cimber Sterling	South	0870 111 1111
Clickair	North	0870 190 0737
Croatia Airlines	South	0870 066 1472
Cubana	South	0844 493 0787
Daallo Airlines	North	0870 243 2222
Delta Air Lines	North	0870 876 5000
easyJet	North & South	0870 111 1111
Emirates	North	0870 040 5040
Estonian Air	South	0870 111 1111
Eurocypria	South	0870 190 0737
Flybe	South	0870 111 1111
flyglobespan	South	0870 190 0737
flyLAL Lithuanian Airlines	North	01293 579 900

Airline	Terminal	Phone Number
Flystar Astraeus	North	01293 819 800
Ghana International Airlines	South	0870 60 70 555
Iceland Express	South	0870 066 1472
Karthago	South	0870 111 1111
Kibris Turkish Airlines	North	0870 190 0737
Malev	North	0871 737 8155
Meridiana Airlines	South	01293 596 609
Mexicana	South	0870 574 7747
Monarch Airlines	South	0870 876 5000
Montenegro Airlines	South	0870 040 5040
norwegian.no	South	0870 190 0737
Olympic Airlines	South	0870 111 1111
Onur Air	South	0870 190 0737
Pakistan International Airlines	South	0800 587 1023
Qatar Airways	North	0870 190 0737
Rossiya Airlines	South	0844 493 0787
Ryanair	South	0870 876 5000
SAS	South	020 7393 1201
SATA International	South	0870 066 1472
TAP Air Portugal	South	0845 601 0932
Tarom	North	0870 111 1111
Thomas Cook	South	0870 190 0737
Thomson Airways	North	0844 493 0787
Ukraine International Airlines	South	0870 190 0737
US Airways	South	0844 493 0787
Viking Airlines	South	0844 493 0787
Virgin Atlantic Airways	South	0870 876 5000
Virgin Nigeria	North	0844 412 1788
Wizz Air	South	+48 22 351 9499
XL Airways	South	0870 169 0169
Zoom Airlines	South	0870 240 0055

General Information

West Sussex
RH6 0NP
General enquiries: 0844 892 0322
Lost property: 01293 503 162
www.gatwickairport.com

Overview

"Gatwick is the busiest single-runway airport in the world." No shit. And they say that like it's a good thing. Basically if you've ever had to go to Spain in high summer, you know the reasons why you shouldn't go to Gatwick: it's not on the Tube and, more importantly, the check-in zone is a sweat-filled free-for-all. Realistically, if being in an airport really was some kind of holiday, you wouldn't need to fly out of the place. Gatwick, though clunkier than some of the bigger, flashier airports, is not so bad to deal with if you have patience. There's light at the end of the world's largest air passenger bridge however as BAA sold the airport to Global Infrastructure Partners (of London City Airport fame). GIP have promised a billion-pound overhaul of the airport and its services (don't they all) and speculation in the financial world is that the owners' connections and experience will lead to more flights and airlines using the airport once it's been done up. In even-more-layman's terms, things can only get better innit?

As far as amenities go, the usual suspects are all present, with convivial times available at Britain's premier diluting station, J.D. Wetherspoons, and the glamour of Knightsbridge miraculously squeezed into one of those little airport branches of Harrods—just in case you feel the need to inflict one of their god-awful teddy bears on another country. As far as eating's concerned, you could try something apart from McDonald's but then again why pretend to yourself that you're having a nice time when it's clearly not on the cards for the next few hours?

Which Terminal?

Trains arrive at the South Terminal, and there are more shops here - but if your flight is from the North Terminal, a free automated train will take you on the five minute transfer.

Getting There

A refreshingly good train service—the creatively-titled Gatwick Express (www.gatwickexpress.com) — runs from Victoria at 3.30, 4.30 then every fifteen minutes thereafter with the last trains being at 00.01 and 00.32. It takes 30 minutes and if you're near the rail hubs it is by far the most pleasant way to get there—though a single journey is going to set you back around £16. First Capital Connect run trains to Gatwick from St Pancras International and London Bridge which costs closer to £8 and take only about 45 minutes. Easybus coaches from Victoria Coach Station get to Gatwick in 40 minutes, and cost around £5-8 for a single.

To drive to Gatwick from the M25 you need to leave at Junction 7 and carry on southwards along the M23, following the signs. Leave the M23 at junction 9 and again, follow those handy signs to get to the appropriate terminal.

Parking

The short stay car park is recommended for up to five hours at a time, and is incremented every 15 minutes then every hour, with a maximum charge of £33.80 per 24 hours. For long stays there are several parks located 5-15 minutes away (via bus transfers) from the airport. These are best booked in advance. For the official Gatwick car park, charges are £13 per day for drive-up, but much cheaper if you book online.

Car Hire

All the big names are represented, or you can try generic websites such as www.travelsupermarket.com/carhire.

Shops

There is the usual wide range of shops ranging from chemists to food/drink to fashion. Retail stores include Harrods, Monsoon, Nike, Quiksilver, Ray Ban, and Yo! Sushi.

Hotels

Alexander House
Arora International
Cambridge Hotel
Clarion Hotel
Copthorne Hotel
Corner House Hotel
Effingham Park Hotel
Europa Hotel
Express
Felbridge Hotel
George Hotel
Hilton
Holiday Inn
Ibis Hotel
Langshott Manor
Moathouse Hotel
Premier Travel Inn
Ramada Plaza
Renaissance Hotel
Russ Hill
Skylane Hotel
Sofitel Hotel
Thistle
Travelodge
Whitehouse
Worth Hotel

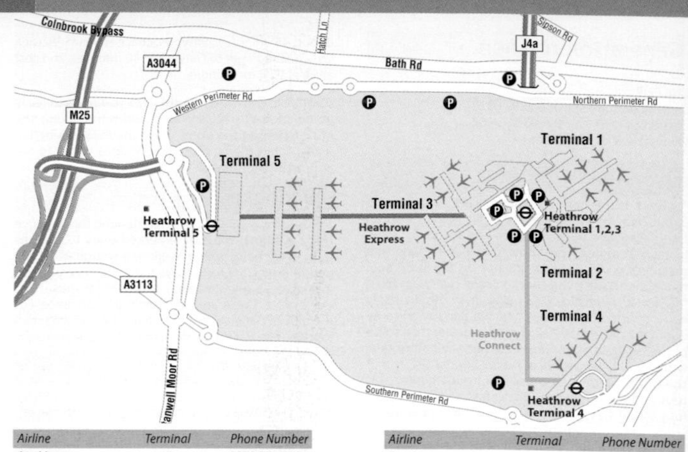

Airline	Terminal	Phone Number
Aer Lingus	1	0870 876 5000
Aeroflot	2	020 7355 2233
Air Algerie	2	020 8750 3300
Air Astana	2	01293 596 622
Air Canada	3	0871 220 1111
Air China	3	020 8745 4624
Air France	2	0870 142 4343
Air India	3	020 8560 9996
Air Malta	4	0906 103 0012
Air Mauritius	3	020 7434 4375
Air New Zealand	1	0800 028 4149
Air Seychelles	2	01293 596 656
Air Transat	2	020 7616 9187
Alitalia	2	0870 544 8259
All Nippon Airways	3	+44 (0)870 837 8811
American Airlines	3	+44 (0)20 7365 0777
Arik Air	2	08444 822324
Asiana Airlines	1	020 7304 9900
Atlas Blue	2	020 7307 5803
Austrian Airlines	2	020 7766 0300
Azerbaijan Airlines	2	0870 760 5757
Bellview Airlines	2	020 7372 3770
Biman Bangladesh Airlines	3	020 7629 0252
Blue1 (SAS Group)	3	0906 294 2016
bmi	1	0870 60 70 555
bmi	1	0870 60 70 555
British Airways	3 & 4 but mainly 5	0844 493 0787
Bulgaria Air	2	020 7637 7637
Cathay Pacific Airways	3	020 8834 8888
China Eastern	2	020 7935 2676
Clickair	3	00 800 25425247
Croatia Airlines	2	020 8563 0022
CSA Czech Airlines	2	0870 444 3747
Cyprus Airways	1	020 8359 1333
Delta Air Lines	4	0845 600 0950
Egypt Air	3	020 8759 3635
El Al Israel Airlines	1	020 7957 4100
Emirates	3	0870 243 2222
Ethiopian Airlines	3	020 8745 4235
Etihad Airways	3	0870 241 7121

Airline	Terminal	Phone Number
Eva Air	3	020 7380 8300
Finnair	3	0870 241 4411
Gulf Air	3	0870 777 1717
Iberia	3	0870 609 0500
Icelandair	1	0870 787 4020
Iran Air	3	020 8759 0921
Japan Airlines	3	0845 774 7700
JAT Airways	2	020 8745 0899
Jet Airways	3	0808 101 1199
Kenya Airways	4	020 8283 1818
Kibris Turkish Airlines	3	020 7930 4851
Kingfisher Airlines	4	0800 047 0810
KLM Royal Dutch Airlines	4	0870 507 4074
Korean Air	3	0800 413 000
Kuwait Airways	3	020 8745 7772
Libyan Arab Airlines	2	020 8750 4066
LOT Polish Airlines	1	0845 601 0949
Lufthansa	1	0871 945 9747
Malaysia Airlines System	3	0870 607 9090
MEA Middle East Airlines	3	020 7467 8000
Northwest Airlines	4	0870 507 4074
Pakistan International Airlines	3	0800 587 1023
Qantas	4	0845 774 7767
Qatar Airways	3	020 7896 3636
Singapore Airlines	3	0844 800 2380
South African Airways	1	0870 747 1111
Sri Lankan Airlines	4	020 8538 2000
Swiss International Airlines	2	0845 601 0956
Syrianair	2	020 7493 2851
Transaero Airlines	1	0870 850 7767
Tunisair	2	020 7734 7644
Turkish Airlines	3	0844 800 6666
Turkmenistan Airlines	3	020 8577 2211
United Airlines	1	0845 844 4777
US Airways	1	0845 600 3300
Uzbekistan Airways	2	020 7935 4775
Virgin Atlantic Airways	3	0870 574 7747
Yemenia Yemen Airways	2	0870 732 3213

General Information

234 Bath Road, Hayes, Middlesex, UB3 5AP
General enquiries: 0844 335 1801
Lost property: 0844 824 3115
www.heathrowairport.com

Overview

We all *love* airports, especially Heathrow. You can play all those xenophobic guessing games with the nationalities of the passengers and mix in a bit of class snobbery concerning which airline they're taking. Then there's all the anticipation and fervour in the air, the relaxed vibes in arrivals department. Yes, we're being sarcastic. Heathrow is resplendent in all the main offenders: infinite queues, bad food, draconian security and the acrid scent of 'the British on holiday.' which should fill every Briton with fear and dismay It's way overcrowded and has tiresome security checks; delays; queues; overpriced shops; terrible food and a tendency to lose baggage. Even our ex-mayor Ken Livingstone has accused Heathrow of keeping people "prisoner" in its "ghastly shopping mall." There does seem to be slow, gradual improvement but it's still a long way from what it should be, and gives a poor first impression of the UK.

For years Heathrow has been stretched beyond its capacity but is currently in mid-transformation. Terminals 1 and 2 are being turned into something called Heathrow East while Terminal 5 has picked up the baton following a chaotic opening a few years and tears ago. The new terminal has taken the annual passenger count to 90 million, placing the airport in contention for busiest in the world. Talking of new terminals there's yet another on the cards along with a controversial third runway. The local residents might not like it but at least they don't have to suffer an hour on the tube to catch a flight. On a positive note the transport services have been vastly improved: new motorway access, a terminal 5 stop on the tube and, uh, well that's it for now.

Which Terminal?

Heathrow is in a seemingly constant state of flux, so confirm before you travel.

Terminal 1 is due to be demolished in a few years but currently deals with domestic flights, UK airline flights to Europe, EL AL, South Afrian and United. **Terminal 2** has retired in the corner, waiting to be demolished. **Terminal 3** is the long haul terminal for Asian and Asia Pacific airlines, US and South American, plus most African and Middle Eastern carriers. **Terminal 4** deals with North African, European airlines and miscellaneous other rogue airlines. **Terminal 5** is pretty much the throne of British Airways.

Terminals 1-3 are within walking distance of each other (up to 15 minutes) so just follow the signs. You can transfer (for free) to T4 on the Heathrow Connect train and T5 on the Heathrow Express. There is also a free bus which connects T4 and T5, every 6 minutes and tube journeys between terminals are free using an oyster card.

Getting There

The London Underground's Piccadilly Line can get you to central London in less than an hour for only about £4. The wait time for a train is generally no more than 10 minutes. Heathrow has three underground stations; one servicing terminal 1, 2 & 3, and one each for terminals 4&5.

Heathrow Express is a non-stop train between the airport and Paddington station, "In 15 minutes—every 15 minutes" for pretty much half the price of the Express though, it's worth the added few minutes. It stops at Heathrow Central Station (T1-3) and the new T5. £18 one way and £34 for a return if bought online (£18 from ticket machine; £23 purchased on board); £32 return (£37 on board).

Heathrow Connect follows the same route into west London, but serves intermediate stations making its journey time 25 minutes. Trains depart Paddington every 30 minutes from Platform 12, stopping at Heathrow Central (Terminal 1,2,3) and Terminal 4. £7.90 one way. Passengers arriving at T5 may catch the Heathrow Express free of charge to Central station if they wish to use Heathrow Connect into town.

Both these trains run between approx 5 am–12 am. There are also three tube stations—a cheaper and slower option. Roughly £4 for an hour's journey to central London. During rush hour it gets packed with commuters.

National Express run a bargain bus from London Victoria station which only costs £6 one way. It takes anywhere from 45-75 minutes and drops you off at Heathrow Central bus terminal (T1,2,3)

Driving from Central London takes about 45-60 minutes—well anything really—depending on traffic. When leaving Terminals 1-3, follow exit signs to the access/exit tunnel. Then follow signs to the M4 motorway, which will eventually bring you into London. A taxi to central London takes 45-60 minutes and costs £35+.

Car Parking

There are short-term and long-term car parks, both are expensive. An hour at the short stay is £4.70, 48 hours is £103.60. The long stay car park is about 10 minutes away by courtesy bus and the drive-up price is £17.90 per day.

General Information:

Royal Docks,
London, E16 2PX
General Enquiries: 020 7646 0000/88
www.londoncityairport.com

Overview

With its one wee runway squeezed over the water between the old George V and Royal Albert Docks, City is London's smallest and most central airport (6 miles from the City of London). Where once stevedores ate pie and mash, stockbrokers are now whisked off to lunchtime meetings on dinky short take-off jets. Primarily used by business types, its small size and short runway means city serves mainly European destinations, with BA's New York service (including a stop off) being the one exception. Still, this means much faster check-in times and fewer delays than at the comparative behemoths of Heathrow and Gatwick.

Getting There

In 2005 someone, somewhere, saw the light and extended the DLR (Docklands Light Railway) to City. The airport now couldn't be simpler to get to by public transport: get on the DLR at Bank; make sure you take a train destined for the King George V branch (these are marked "via City Airport"); and you'll arrive at the airport's station in 25 minutes. A slightly quicker route is to take the Jubilee Underground line to Canning Town and take the DLR a mere three stops westbound from there. There is a taxi rank directly outside the terminal exit, expect to pay at least £35 for a black cab to go to or from the West End. Don't expect the journey to be much faster than on the DLR/Underground. Pre-booked cabs should be a little cheaper, try Airport Executive (020 8838 3333) or the trusty Addison Lee (020 7387 8888).

If you're driving—given its central location—there's no obvious route to City. A useful general rule is to point your wheels at the eastern end of Central London and then keep going that way from Tower Hill on the A1203 (East Smithfield/The Highway). The airport is signposted from this road. If you're getting there from the South East, head through the Blackwall tunnel and follow signs once you emerge into the daylight. If you're near the M25 and like traffic jams, crawl your way to junction 30 and take the Thames Gateway to the airport from there.

Parking

Short stay is directly next to the terminal and rates start at £10 for one hour going up to £90 for 48 hours.

You can also have your car valet-parked for no extra cost (apart from having to tip the man entrusted with not scratching your pride and joy).

The long stay carpark is a short walk from the terminal and will relieve you of £16 for up to four hours, £22 for 8-12 hours, £35 from 12-25 hours, or £35 for the first day and £40 thereafter.

So parking is expensive. If you still feel the need to park and can book in advance, get in touch with BCP airport parking for a (slightly) cheaper option at www.parkbcp.co.uk.

Car Hire

Avis 084 4544 6030
Europcar................. 087 1384 1087
Hertz 087 0599 6699

Hotels

Etap Hotel London City Airport,
North Woolwich Road, Silverstown,
London, E16 2EE
020 7474 9106

Custom House Hotel Excel Docklands,
272-283 Victoria Dock Road, London,
E16 3BY
020 7474 0011

Premier Travel Inn
Excel East, Royal Victoria Docks, Canning
Town, E16 1SL
0870 238 3322

Novotel London Excel
7 Western Gateway Royal Victoria Dock,
London, E16 1AA
020 7540 9700

Ibis London Excel
9 Western Gateway, London, E16 1AB
020 7055 2300

Sunborn Yacht Hotel
1 Royal Victoria Dock, London, E16 1SL
020 70599100

Holiday Inn Express
1 Silvertown Way, Docklands, London,
E16 1EA
020 75404040

Travelodge London City Airport Hotel
Hartmann Road, Silvertown, London
E16 2BZ
0871 9846290

Airlines:

Aer Arann

British Airways

CityJet

KLM

Lufthansa

Luxair

SAS

SunAir

Swiss International Air Lines

VLM Airlines

General Information

London Luton Airport
Navigation House
Airport Way
Luton, Bedfordshire LU2 9LY
General enquiries including lost property: 01582 405100
www.london-luton.co.uk

Overview

To call Luton Airport a 'London' airport is surely one HUGE marketing scam. In fact, calling Luton Airport an 'Airport' is pushing it: the reality is it's one huge shit pit that airplanes depart and arrive from occasionally. The same tragedy happens everyday: the unsuspecting traveller smugly enters their credit card details as they book their £2.99 easyJet flight to some godforsaken club 18-30 resort on the Spanish coast, thinking they got the best deal *ever*. One big problem. The flight's from Luton Airport—which should stop any celebrating London traveller dead. Unless you live in North London, getting to and from Luton by public transport is awful. It consists of taking an unreliable half-hour train service from St Pancras or London Bridge to Luton Parkway. After your train journey, if you're lucky, you'll be met at Luton Parkway by a shuttle bus. Be sure to purchase your rail tickets with London Luton Airport as your final destination. If your plane is delayed past midnight, which most budget airlines tend to be, God help you. Where's the Luton Express you might wonder? Ha ha. Good question…

Once you get to the one-terminal airport, your travelling companions will be the kind of people who hunt down the absolute cheapest airfares for their raucous stag or hen nights. Inside security, the few shops and cafés of the Pret a Manger and Dixons variety, will be teeming with these unsavoury characters. So next time you select 'all London airports' when booking your weekend getaway—think carefully!

Getting There

This can be extremely tricky and there's really no easy way. What with a Tube journey to St Pancras or London Bridge station, a train journey, and finally a shuttle bus, you better pack light. Also, you really don't want to get stuck sleeping in the airport when the shuttle bus stops at midnight.

Coach services, such as the 757 Greenline (collaborating with Terravision), easyBus and National Express are good alternatives that will at least get you home if your flight comes in late. Greenline & Terravision are probably your best bet (0990 747 777) with pick-up and drop-off points on Buckingham Palace Road, Marble Arch and Baker Street. Prices are from £15 and it takes about an hour, but it runs pretty regularly through the

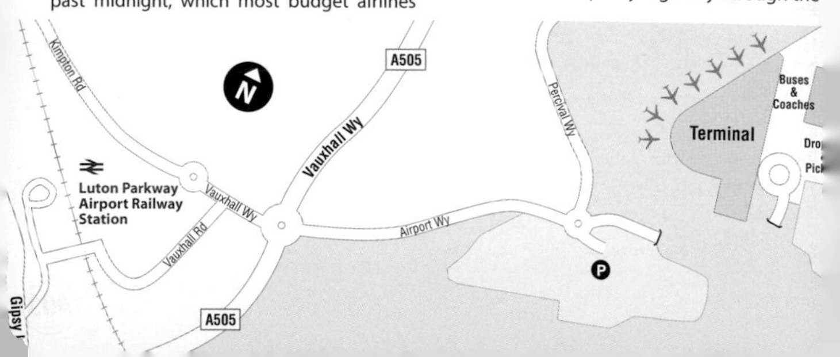

night. The National Express (08705 80 80 80) service 421 also operates between Luton, Heathrow Airport and London Victoria.

London Luton Airport is somewhat accessible from both the M1 and M25. If you have a choice, go for the M1, as the airport is only about five minutes from junction 10. Without traffic, it can take c. 45 minutes from central London. This can sometimes be longer when there are extensive road works, which tends to be always. When using Sat Nav systems, use the postcode LU2 9QT.

How To Get There – Really

Seriously. You've paid next to nothing for your airfare, splash out on a private cab. If you book a licensed mini-cab ahead of time, the service is often cheaper than the equivalent black cab fare and definitely easier, as they'll meet you at the arrivals hall. A consistently cheap company is Simply Airports (020 7701 4321) which is usually under £55, but you may want to get a quote from your own local company. If you leave it to the last minute, and must take a black cab, get ready to shell out at least £85 (with their meters, this can increase with traffic) plus a meeting fee if you want them to wait for you. Cab rides from central London usually take about an hour.

Parking

Short Term Parking is pricier but situated closest to the terminal, with prices ranging from £3.80 for 30 minutes or £36 per day drive-up. Mid-term is ideal for stays of around five days and is about a five-minute transfer by bus. Mid term is £19.50 per day drive-up or £27.99 for 5 days if booked well in advance. Long-term parking is about 10 minutes from the terminal by bus, and can be as cheap as £6 per day if booked well in advance online (www.ncp.co.uk) to save money. Prices range from £12.50 per day for up to four days to £90 for eight days. NCP can be reached on 01582 395484 (9 am–4 pm) and 07734 595560 in an emergency.

Rental Cars

Hertz Rent A Car 087 0846 0012
Avis Rent A Car Ltd 087 0608 6348
Thrifty Car Rental 015 8241 6222
National Car Rental.......... 087 0607 5000
Enterprise 015 8239 0969

Shops

Luton has a small selection of shops and is slowly getting better, but don't expect too much. There is a Boots (chemist/drugstore), a newsagent, and somewhere to eat/drink.

Hotels

Chiltern Hotel Luton
73 Beechwood Road; 01582 575911

Days Hotel Luton
Regent Street; 01582 878 090

Express by Holiday Inn Hotel
2 Percival Way; 01582 589 100

Holiday Inn Luton South
London Road; 0870 443171

Menzies Strathmore Hotel Luton
The Luton Arndale Centre; 01582 734199

Airlines

Aer Arann
Blue Air
easyJet
El Al
Flybe
Monarch
Ryanair
SkyEurope
Thomson
transavia.com
Wizz Air

General Information

Address: Stansted Airport,
Essex CM24 1QW
General enquiries: 0 8443 351 803
Lost property: 0 1279 663 293
Left luggage: 0 1279 663 213
Police: 0 1245 452 450
Website: www.stanstedairport.com

Overview

It might be tucked away in the middle of the dull Essex countryside, but Stansted Airport has one thing going for it—it's amazingly simple. One terminal (and quite a nice one too, Norman Foster saluted), one check-in area, one security gate. Take that, Heathrow. Around 20 airlines, most of them budget, fly more than 20 million passengers from here to a growing list of mainly domestic and short-haul destinations. If you're budget-crazy enough to fly in the middle of the night, there are several breakfast opportunities. Eating options are generally better before security—unless you like tiny, overpriced ciabatta baguettes or the sugar-drenched fare offered by the big coffee chains. But once through, you can settle for a few surprisingly average-priced pints at Est Bar Est and grab a sandwich on the run once you hear your name being called for the third time. On the downside, the ridiculously long walk to your gate is often obstructed by screaming children or singing hen-night crowds. And the queue at border control is, at most times, long enough to make you reconsider the whole affair and just run back to your plane.

Getting There

Public Transport

Stansted might seem a long way from London, but getting there by public transport is surprisingly easy. All you have to do is choose between the train (fast) and the bus (cheap). Several train operators serve the airport from Liverpool Street Station. But before you start struggling with too many timetables for trains that stop at too many stops, opt for the dedicated Stansted Express (www.stanstedexpress.com; 0 8456 007 245). The service runs every 15 minutes and takes you to the airport in 45 minutes straight. Tickets start at £21.50 online or £22.50 from the machine. Buses will take an hour to take you to the airport, and longer if there's a lot of traffic, but single tickets start at £5. A number of operators fight for your custom, the main ones are: Terravision (01279 680 028; www.terravision.eu) leaves from Liverpool Street Station and Victoria Station. The slightly more expensive National Express (08705 747 777; www.nationalexpress.com) connects to the same stations but some buses also stop in Stratford and Golders Green. Easybus (www.easybus.co.uk) gives you the intimacy of a small mini-van, stopping in Baker Street and Victoria

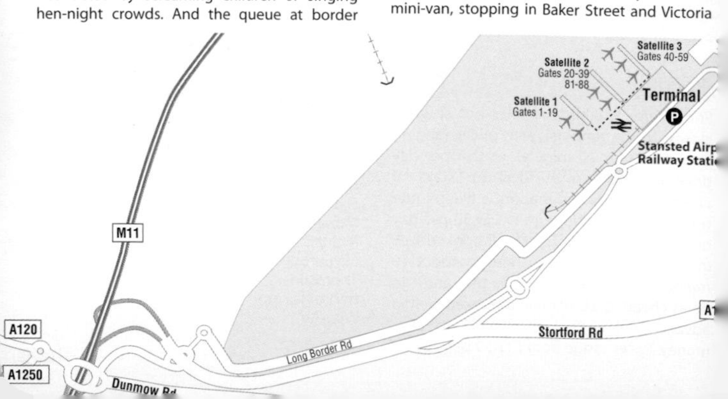

Station. If you're traveling during the rush hour, take a book. Whitechapel Road is one of London's most bustling streets, but it will get boring at some point.

Driving

If you're fortunate enough to have a car, or managed to convince your dad-in-law to lend you his, find your way out of the city via Stratford and hit the M11. It's a straight drive from here and amid Essex' greenery, the airport is hard to miss. Cab drivers will know how to get you to the airport, but will probably charge you a small fortune for it.

Parking

Daily parking rates start at £2.80 for the first 25 minutes and rise in steps to £36 for 24 hours. Long-term parking, in the intriguingly christened Pink Elephant car park, will cost you £10 a day if booked ahead. If you're in for a weekend trip, opt for the mid-stay car park, which is closer to the terminal than the Elephant and charges £16.50/day drive-up. The airport recently introduced valet parking, which can be pre-booked on 08708 502 825. Once there, drop your car at the end of Set Down Lane; the pick-up point is next to the Fast Track car park. For discounts on all Stansted parking options, call BAA Advance on 0121 410 5228 and book your parking lot before you head off.

Car Rental

Alamo.................................0 1279 506 534
Hertz, Check-In Concourse............0 8708 460 005
Budget, Check-In Concourse..........0 1279 681 396
Avis, Check-In Concourse 0 1279 663 030
Europcar, Check-In Concourse 0 1279 506 534
National, International Arrivals Concourse ....
....0 1279 506 534
Thrifty..................................0 1279 655 368

Shops

Stansted has the usual selection of 'small airport shops', more aimed at passing the time than serious purchases.

Hotels

Hilton National Hotel, Enterprise House, Bassingbourne Road, Essex CM24 1QW , 0 08700 000 303

Radisson SAS Hotel, Waltham Close, London Stansted Airport, Essex CM24 1PP, 0 1279 661 012

Express by Holiday Inn, Thremhall Avenue, Stansted, Essex CM24 1PY, 0 1279 680 015

Airlines

Aegean Airlines
Air Arabia Maroc
Air Berlin
Air Malta
Air Moldova
Air Asia X
Atlantic Airways
Aurigny
Blue Air
Cyprus Airways
easyJet
El Al Israel Airlines
Esprit Ski
Germanwings
Kibris Turkish Airlines
norwegian.no
Pakistan International
Pegasus Airlines
Ryanair
Snowjet
Turkish Airlines
(There's only one terminal)

Overview

If the Underground had a motto it wouldn't be "Mind the gap" but "Sorry for any inconvenience caused." But as we grumble and ponder if anyone is ever actually sorry for squeezing you 30m below the surface, in a sweat-box held together by dust, rust and expensive fares, the magnificence of the 'Tube' network should really be appreciated. Across its 250-odd miles of track the Underground will take you to 275 stations spread the length and breadth of London (although with disproportionately few lines reaching into south London). The system is well integrated with the bus and overground train networks and—with the advent of the Oyster card—most of these share a common ticketing system.

When fully functioning, the Underground will get you across town quicker than the bus and without the complicated timetables and schedules of overground trains. When it is struck by signal failures and breakdowns, which is very often, it can be excruciatingly slow and get very overcrowded, very quickly. In conclusion: the Underground won't necessarily get you anywhere on time, in style or in comfort, but it will (eventually) get you pretty much anywhere.

Fares

The vast majority of the network is divided into concentric fare rings or zones (1-6). Zone 1 covers central London, zone 6 covers the outskirts of London. Fares are dependent on how many zones your journey includes and there's a premium for travelling in zone 1. Peak fares (Monday to Friday from 4.30-9.30 am and 4-7 pm) are from 50p to a few pounds more than off-peak, although journeys limited to zone 1 do not benefit from the off-peak discount. Your best bet is to get an Oyster Card—lowest single fare is £2 instead of £4.30 if you pay by cash. Oyster cards are available for just £5 from vending machines. It's a total no-brainer. The total amount that can be deducted from your Oyster card is also capped over a 24-hour period to match the equivalent cost of a one day travel card.

So the fare system is complicated, but if you take £2 (which will get you a single journey within zone 1 with an Oyster card) as a base rate, and add to this the further out of zone 1 you travel, things become clearer. If you feel the need to marvel at the full intricacy of the fares and ticketing system, give yourself eye-strain at Transport for London's website www.tfl.gov.uk.

Frequency and Quality of Service

The vast majority of centrally-located stations will have a train at least every three minutes most of the day. At the very beginning and end of the day service frequency tails-off and can get as low as eight minutes between trains. Trains are also much less frequent at the further reaches of some lines—the Metropolitan line has trains only every 20 minutes from its most north-western stations, even during peak times. Almost all lines have a reduced frequency on Sundays. First trains are 05:00-05:30, last trains are between midnight and 12.30. Last trains are generally safe; expect a slightly raucous mix of pickled after-workers and overly obsequious rough-sleepers rather than any real troublemakers. Mayor Boris Johnson's initially controversial booze ban seems to have been accepted now. The whole network has now had £5bn thrown at it for the Olympics, but the only noticeable improvement has been increased cleanliness in many of the stations.

Lines

Bakerloo: (Brown coloured on maps) Runs from Harrow & Wealdstone in the north west to Elephant & Castle in the south east.

Central: (Red) Runs from West Ruislip in the west to Epping in the far north east. The central section is buried under Oxford Street and has four stops on the street, the quietest usually being Bond Street.

Circle: (Yellow) Notoriously slow, unreliable, and not strictly a circle—even more so now that a tail reaches down to Hammersmith. For this reason Edgeware Road is now the end of the line. Shares almost all of its track and stations with other lines so don't necessarily bother waiting specifically for a dedicated Circle Line train. Look out for the 'Platform for Art' as you pass Gloucester Road station.

District: (Green) One of the few lines to serve deepest south London, branches run into Richmond and Wimbledon in the southwest and also to Ealing. The line continues up to Upminster in the northeast. Almost all of the branches of this fragmented line come together at Earls Court station into an infuriating mess, so plan ahead if changing there.

Hammersmith & City: (Pink) Starts at Hammersmith in the west of the city before heading north to Paddington and continuing east to Barking. Take it to Ladbroke Grove if heading to the Portobello market.

Jubilee: (Silver) Silver coloured as it opened in the year of the Queen's Silver Jubilee in 1977, the line serves northwest, central and east London, including the Canary Wharf business district. The section east of Green Park is the most recent addition to the network (it opened in 1999) and has a number of architecturally exemplary stations.

Metropolitan: (Dark Purple) The oldest of all the lines, this granddaddy of metropolitan underground railways strikes far out in the suburbs and countryside northwest of the city from its central root at Aldgate.

Northern: (Black) Presumably given black as its colour to reflect the dark mood of anyone unlucky enough to have to commute on it, the Northern line is the overcrowded spine of London, covering vast swathes of the city centre, the north and the south.

Piccadilly: (Dark Blue) From Cockfosters in the far northeast this line trundles all the way to Heathrow airport, with some of the most popular tourist spots in between. It's a very cheap way to the airport but is also the slowest. Southgate and Arnos Grove stations are both 1930s modernist brilliance.

Victoria: (Light Blue) Runs from Walthamstow in the north to Brixton in the south. This musty line is currently undergoing refurbishment and will feature new trains and track by 2011. In the meantime, check for early closing and shutdowns, particularly during weekends.

Waterloo & City: (Turquoise) No-one has ever met anyone who has been on this line. Erm, it has two stations, Waterloo and Bank, and is designed for suited and booted commuters coming in by train from Waterloo. No trains on Sundays.

London Overground: (Orange) TfL took over part of the overground rail network, notably the somewhat shabby and North London Line which runs from Richmond to Stratford This has now been merged with what was the East London Line, which connects East, Southeast and Northeast London. Just think of it as an extension to the tube network.

Bicycles

Bicycles are generally only allowed on the tube outside peak hours and only from stations outside central London. They are not permitted on the Victoria or Waterloo and City lines at all. Folding bicycles can be taken on all sections of the Tube free of charge.

General Info

Website: www.tfl.gov.uk/dlr
Phone: 020 7363 9700
Lost property: 020 7363 9550

Overview

Not quite a tram, tube or train, it's simply the Docklands Light Railway, a nifty little thing that makes getting to places like Greenwich Village and City Airport easy and cheap. Launched in 1987 with a modest 11 trains and only 15 stations, the regeneration of the Docklands area has seen it grow to 94 trains covering 38 stations and counting. Serving the east and Southeast of the city, it is pretty much as pleasant as London public transport gets. It's reliable, less noisy than the tube, generally less crowded and it's pretty well air-conditioned. The DLR is also fully-automated and most of the time there is no driver, meaning that you can take the front seat and pretend that you're actually driving the thing.

The DLR provides a key service for London's suits, with the Bank to Canary Wharf journey taking just over ten minutes. For normal people, Canary Wharf also makes an interesting/unusual weekend destination. Almost completely deserted, a stroll amongst the abandoned skyscrapers is a strangely satisfying way to spend a Sunday afternoon.

Fares

As on the rest of London's public transport you're best off with an Oyster card. One thing to remember is that there are no barriers at DLR stations and instead Oyster readers are located at station exits and entrances. To avoid getting slapped with a fine and to ensure you're charged the right amount, remember to touch in and out correctly. The prices are similar to the tube, so cash works out more expensive; though not as expensive as the tube with its £4 cash single.

Hours

The DLR runs 5.30 am–12.30 am, with train frequencies depending on the time of day. During peak hours, there's usually a train every three minutes or so, but even on Sundays you shouldn't have to wait more than 10 minutes.

General Information

National Rail Enquiries 08457 48 49 50
Tickets...................... www.thetrainline.com;
.............also websites of individual franchisees
Eurostar ....08705 186 186 or
..................................0 1233 617 575
.... www.eurostar.com

Overview

The railways are one of the great British inventions but, unfortunately, the Victorians who built the network in this country did slightly too good a job. Every generation since has taken one look at the massively expensive task of modernising them and scuttled back into their Ford Fiestas. So, while France, Germany and Japan got on with building super-speed bullet trains Britain was stuck with an uneasy compromise between the technologies of 1950 and 1850. This doesn't mean that you shouldn't use trains. It just means that it's probably best to avoid them at peak times. That's when London plays a cruel trick on people who choose to live in places with names like 'Gravesend' and 'Slough' by making them lurch home slowly with less personal space than the legal minimum for cattle. During off-peak times train travel can, in contrast, be positively pleasant. It's a great way to see the countryside, every city and major town in the country is connected, and, if you book far enough in advance and shop around on sites like www.megatrain.com it can be less expensive than you'd think. In London itself, the Thameslink improvement programme will help a little; Crossrail will (eventually) arrive; and pay as you go Oyster will be grudgingly accepted by all train operators.

Stations

Broadly speaking, Euston and King's Cross stations serve the north of the country, Liverpool Street the east, Victoria the south, Paddington and Marylebone the west.

Eurostar

The King's Cross area is also home to the splendid St Pancras—the terminal for the Eurostar train service which connects Britain with the rest of Europe. Since November 2007 it's been possible to get from here to Paris or Brussels in around two hours—with connecting trains to Siberia and beyond.

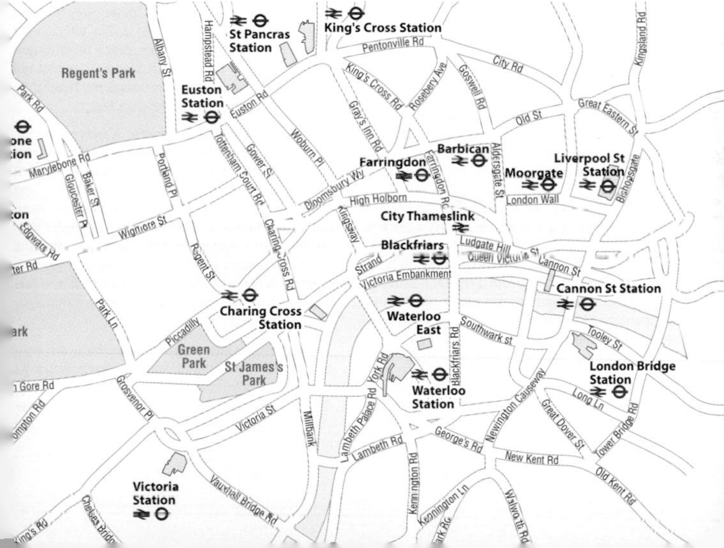

Charing Cross Station

NFT Map:	24
Address:	12-30 The Strand, London WC2N 6RQ
General enquiries:	020 7839 2576
South Eastern Trains:	0 8450 002 222
Southern Trains:	0 8451 272 920

Overview

Perched at the top of the Strand amidst popular tourist attractions such as Trafalgar Square and with the majestic 1865 Charing Cross Hotel being part of the station, you may presume that a cornucopia of ornate delights lies within. Well, it's a dump; the chances of "Brief Encounter" being remade here are pretty slim. But your chances of being barged by a curmudgeonly office worker are very good, what with it being the fifth busiest rail terminal in London. Still, can you blame them for wanting to get out of the place so quickly?

With services to south London and Kent, even the pigeons give the concourse here a wide berth. It's also home to possibly the worst station pub in the country; "The Boadicea" excels in the areas of soullessness and morbidity, likely to satisfy only the hardened alcoholic on their third liver and with a preference for pubs that reek of urine. If only Dante had been able to sample this place…

Tickets

There is a small ticket office open some 20 hours per day, and three banks of ticket machines on or around the concourse.

Services

If you're in need of a quick bite, there's a decent variety of food outlets to cater for all tastes, whether burger-lover (Burger King) or health food freak (Cranberry). Indulge your Schadenfreude by watching the beleaguered information guy having to dispense a plethora of poor excuses as to why the 17.34 to Margate was cancelled. And those kinky souls with a tie fetish will love Tie Rack.

Natwest and Bank of Scotland cash machines can be found on the concourse, as well as a Barclays in the front entrance.

Public Transport

The station is easily accessible by Charing Cross station (Northern & Bakerloo lines) and also the adjoining Embankment station (Circle & District lines). The nearby Trafalgar Square is a major hub for buses—especially night buses for post-West End madness—which inch their way out to places as far apart as Harrow and Crystal Palace.

Euston Station

NFT Map:	78
Address:	Euston Road NW1 2RT
General enquiries:	020 7922 6482
Lost property:	0207 387 8699
First Scotrail:	0845 601 5929
London Midland:	0844 811 0133
Virgin Trains :	0871 977 9222

Overview

Easily the ugliest station in London, Euston creeps up as you nervously edge along Euston Road. The first inter-city terminal built in London, it was originally constructed in 1837, but the lovely original was demolished to make way for the monstrous concrete-and-glass coffin which now squats next to the mail depot. Since privatisation the interior has become an identi-kit British rail station with more chain businesses per head than is morally decent. Thanks Network Rail.

It's not all doom and gloom, however. Within this architectural eyesore you'll find a scarily concise summation of human nature. Like most busy stations, there's plenty of eccentricity and electricity here: abandoned Tube tunnels; stressed-out coffee guzzling power-commuters; fresh-faced backpackers sprawled out on the floor ; and the infamous beggar who — to the delight of football lovers everywhere except in Manchester — was arrested for punching Manchester Utd manager Sir Alex Ferguson.

The station is London's gateway to the north west of England and Scotland, and also North Wales. As such it is the point of entry for Scousers, Mancunians, Glaswegians and more. Virgin trains (www.virgintrains.co.uk) to Glasgow can take as little as 4 hrs 10 mins.

Tickets

The ticket cashiers may have the glazed look of Kafka-esque zombies but the cleaning staff are often more helpful. Just use the Fasttrack machines!

Services

There's plenty of eating and drinking options, all of the 'chain' variety. Of this motley crew Paul and Upper Crust are as good as it gets. If you're determined to hang around, check out the Doric Arch (1 Eversholt St; 020 7388 2221) which is a shoddy little boozer with a cool 'end of the world' vibe. The left luggage office is at the top of the ramp to platforms 16–18 and is open between 7 am–11 pm.

Public Transport

As an actual railway station it is adequate. Served by two Tube lines and nine bus routes, it's nothing if not convenient.

King's Cross Station

NFT Map:	78
Address:	Euston Rd & Pancras Rd N1 9AP
General enquiries:	0 2079 224 902
Lost property:	0 2072 783 310
National Express East Coast:	0 8457 225 225
First Capital Connect:	0 8450 264 700

Overview

Previously a dingy playground for prostitutes, drug dealers, and all sorts of similarly bad kids, King's Cross Station has scrubbed up a bit in recent years, thanks to lots of chin scratching and typically panicked spending on the government's part. Built in 1852 on the site of a former smallpox hospital, it is one of the busiest and most well-connected stations in the country: running trains to Edinburgh; Newcastle; the East coast; as well as six Tube lines. Zany trivia about the station includes the fact that it is supposedly built on top of legendary Fembot-Queen Boudicea's grave (most probably a total lie) and that it has a tacky little shrine to Harry Potter at what has been designated 'Platform 9 3⁄4' (oh God).

Nearly all long distance train services leave from the overground platforms under the arches straight ahead of you as you enter from Euston Road. The Tube is also accessible from steps at this entrance and at what used to be the Thameslink station next to the Scala on Pentonville Road. From the main Tube entrance there is a pedestrian subway that comes up on the other side of Euston road just outside Macdonald's. This is handy for crossing the road at busy times, and of course for getting chips.

Tickets

Tube tickets, including Oyster top ups and season tickets, can be purchased from the machines in front of the Tube entry gates, located just at the bottom of both sets of stairs at the station. For railcard discounts and more specific enquiries you'll have to queue at the manned ticket desks next to the machines. For all other tickets go to the upstairs ticket hall which is to the left of the main Euston Road entrance.

Services

With the renovations finally complete, the quality of services has significantly improved. But with the excellent Eat St literally round the corner, ditch the station completely and sample the wares of London's best street food traders. And for the basics, the trusty newspaper kiosk underneath the awning is still going strong.

Public Transport

King's Cross crosses more Tube lines (six) than any other station, and is serviced by at least twice as many buses, many of which run all night. For full details of bus routes look at the bus maps for Camden on the Transport for London website: http://www.tfl.gov.uk/tfl/gettingaround/maps/buses/.

Liverpool Street Station

NFT Map:	8
Address:	EC2M 7QH
General enquiries:	020 7295 2789
Lost property:	020 7247 4297

Natl Express East Anglia Railway 0845 6007245

Overview

Scene of drunken anarchy at the infamous Facebook party that preceded Boris's booze ban, it's not that Liverpool Street is particularly ugly, but if it's architectural beauty you're after, you're much better off heading to Paddington or the newly re-opened St. Pancras International. In comparison to these two icons of British station design, Liverpool Street is extremely modest, boring even. Clean, modern and easy to navigate around, it is simply a good train station. With the markets, bars and restaurants of Spitalfields and Brick Lane just around the corner, the station is the perfect starting point to explore east London. First opened to the public in 1874, it is now the second-busiest station in London (after Waterloo) with an estimated 123m visitors each year. With 18 platforms, the station mainly serves destinations in the east of England, including daytrip favourites such as Cambridge and Southend on Sea.

It is also the home of the Stansted Express, providing easy airport access with departures every 15 minutes. If you're travelling with a group of people a taxi might work out slightly cheaper, but the train is much quicker and more reliable. The Tube station, with its main entrance centrally located on the main concourse, makes all of London easily accessible with the Central, Hammersmith & City, Circle and Metropolitan lines all passing through. Being the fifth busiest station on the underground network, rush hour can get nasty and is best avoided.

Tickets

The ticket office is located on the main concourse, on your left hand side if entering from Bishopsgate. Ticket windows are open for immediate travel 24/7 with advance ticket purchases available between 7.30 am–7.30 pm. There are also several express ticket machines scattered throughout the station. Tickets for the Stansted Express can be purchased from designated ticket machines opposite platforms 5-6. A cluster of cash machines can be found by the stairs leading up to the Old Broad Street exit. There are payphones on both levels and most are located on the Bishopsgate side of the station.

Services

With Brick Lane just around the corner, eating, drinking and shopping here should really be a last resort. The regular big-chain fast food joints are scattered (some of them repeatedly) throughout the station with the usual selection of coffee, burgers, sandwiches and sweets. The main shopping area is on the lower level around the Broadgate and Exchange Square exits, offering everything from toiletries and birthday cards to Italian silk ties and double-glazed windows.

Passengers are invited to wait for their trains in the so-called "food court," which really isn't much more than a few cramped tables between Burger King and The Wren, one of the station's two shitty pubs. There's a small but nicer waiting lounge located adjacent to platform 10. Here you also find the left luggage, a bureau de change, a less busy cash machine and access to the main taxi rank. Smoking is prohibited at all times throughout the station.

Public Transport

The main bus station is located on the upper level of the station (Broadgate end), and provides a large number of services to destinations throughout London. Plenty of buses also stop on the street just outside the Bishopsgate exit.

London Bridge Station

NFT Map:	106
Address:	Station Approach SE1 9SP
General enquiries:	0 207 234 1068
Lost property:	0 845 127 2920
Southern Trains:	0 845 127 2920
South East Trains:	0 845 000 2222
First Capital Connect:	0 845 026 4700
South Eastern disabled contact:	0 800 783 4524

Overview

Around in one form or other since 1836, when steam trains filled the air with smoke, London Bridge is the city's oldest station. Sounds romantic? It's anything but. Even with redevelopment now close to finishing, the station is still pretty drab and the Shard is much better viewed from afar. Jump on a train and do just that.

It's a good starting point for weekend trips to Kent's countryside or days on Brighton's beach. Operators Southeastern and Southern cover the south east, while First Capital Connect operates (little known) connections to the airports Gatwick and Luton. The station couldn't be better connected to public transport, with two Tube lines and a plethora of buses at the doorstep. The catacombs underneath the station—said to be haunted—have been turned into the museum-cum-gore-fes

London Bridge Experience, adding to the spooky entertainment already provided by the London Dungeon next door—just in case a cancelled or delayed train leaves you with too much time on your hands. Does happen, we're told.

Tickets

The main office is located next to the main entrance (London Bridge Street) or there are machines situated throughout the station. Jump the queues by booking online at www.nationalrail.co.uk.

Services

The main concourse is lined with eating and shopping options. Grab Cornish pasties, sandwiches, donuts; and the usual burgers from the usual chains, with Borough Market just over the road though, you'd be mad to waste your money on these. Bodyshop, M&S and WH Smith lead the list of practical, but terribly unexciting shop names. There are toilets on platforms 1-2 and 5-6. The caverns connecting the Underground station with the national trains is teeming with better food options however - some even non-chain.

Public Transport

Connections are excellent. London Bridge Station is served by the Jubilee Line and the Bank branch of the Northern Line. Escalators take you down from the main concourse. Step outside the main entrance for the massive bus station, where buses leave in all directions of the city, except its far western reaches.

Marylebone Train Station

NFT Map:	76
Address:	Great Central House Melcombe Place NW1 6JJ
Central number:	08456 005165

Overview

Despite Monopoly-board notoriety, Marylebone railway station fell into neglect in the mid to late-twentieth century, spurned as a rundown piggy-in-the-middle wedged haplessly between neighbours Paddington and Euston. But it's an aimless drifter no more. A refurb' in the 90s and again in 2006 saw Marylebone reinvigorated, with a thorough sprucing up and two new platforms. Servicing the Midlands, it now threads as far as Birmingham, Shakespeare's Stratford-Upon-Avon, Leamington Spa, Aylesbury, and High Wycombe, amongst others. It remains the runt of the London train station litter, but is a popular location for television filming (Doctor Who; Magnum PI; Green Wing; Peep Show) at a mere £500 per hour—half the price of King's Cross. In its bowels, Bakerloo Line trains rumble through an underground station of the same name.

Tickets

Rail ticket windows are to the north of Marylebone's relatively petite concourse and open Monday-Saturday 06.30–22:10 or Sunday 07.30–21.30. As with all mainline train stations, self-service ticket machines are in abundance should ticket offices be closed or queues too long. Sturdy padded-barriers ensure buying tickets on board the train, or getting away without them, is not an option. Underground tickets can be purchased from windows or machines alike within the Tube station itself.

Services

The usual plethora of railway station chains are on hand: newsagent WH Smith, baguette bakers Upper Crust, supermarket Marks & Spencer, and pasty purveyors the West Cornwall Company among them. More individually, Marylebone also hosts AMT Coffee, a café with a seating area at the centre of the concourse, the nifty Chiltern Flowers on the south wall, and The V&A free house in the west passageway—an old man's boozer in the classic, wood panelled style. Cash points and payphones are in this same walkway, and toilets are situated on the south wall.

Public Transport

Marylebone underground station lies directly beneath Marylebone overground, and is serviced (Matron!) by the Bakerloo Line, while buses 2, 205 and 453 stop directly outside the main entrance. A taxi stand is also situated out front. Baker Street and Edgware tube stations are a short walk away.

Paddington Station

NFT Map:	31
Address:	Paddington, London, W2 1HQ
General enquiries:	020 7922 6793
Lost property:	020 7247 4297
First Great Western:	084 5700 0125
Heathrow Express:	084 5600 1515
Chiltern Railways:	084 5600 5165

Overview

If you're in that small minority of people who love stations, then Paddington's paradise. Designed by engineering legend Isambard Kingdom Brunel—his middle name is Kingdom for God's sake, of course his work's going to be magnificent—this barn-like structure harks back to an era when train travel retained a little glamour. If it wasn't for the on-site Burger King you could easily imagine tearful ladies waving silk handkerchiefs at dapper gents.

The station also occupies a unique place in literary heritage. Every British child in the last half-century knows the tales of Paddington Bear. From "deepest darkest Peru", he was left unattended at the station; but a kind family picked him up, took him in, and named him after it. No other station name can inspire such genuine warmth. It certainly wouldn't have worked if he'd been found at Clapham Junction.

Heathrow Express

The super-fast link to Heathrow runs from Paddington. Be warned, though; it's far from cheap. At £34 return it could end up being more than your flight. Ouch.

Tickets

A ticket office and machines are located near platforms 9-10, and there are other machines and an information point near the Eastbourne Terrace entrance and also underneath the mezzanine.

Services

If you have any money left from your ticket—unlikely at today's prices—there are plenty of sharks who can take it off you. Burger King and Upper Crust will overcharge you for burgers or baguettes and there's an 'offie' (off-license) for expensive booze. There's also a pub that resembles a building site (Portakabin). If you find yourself drinking in there you've got some serious questions to ask yourself.

There are other ways of staying amused; as it's the main portal for commuters entering London from the west and Wales) there's WiFi, a supermarket, a bookshop and curiously, a lingerie shop. Just what sort of a job do you have if you get to the station and realise: "Bollocks! No suspenders!"? Certainly not one compatible with Paddington's place in children's lit, that's for sure.

Public Transport

The Bakerloo, Circle, District, and Hammersmith & City Tube lines all stop at Paddington. Buses serve west and north west London.

St Pancras International

NFT Map:	78
Address:	Pancras Road, London, NW1 2QP
Central number:	020 7843 4250
Eurostar:	084 3218 6186
Midland Mainline:	084 5712 5678

Overview

The newly souped-up St Pancras station has been generating waves of breathless excitement ever since its opening ceremony in 2007, which was by all accounts a pretty histrionic affair. This "Cathedral of Transport" situated next door to King's Cross station, is now home to the Eurostar international train service and has domestic connections (via First Capital Connect's Thameslink trains) to Luton Airport, Bedford and Brighton; as well as Midland Mainline connections to places like Leicester and Sheffield. As the first major project of a huge scheme to redevelop the area, St Pancras has been marketed as so-much-more-than-a-station. Alongside its rail platforms it features Europe's longest Champagne bar, a farmers market, and an arcade of pointedly-classy shops. All this is housed within beautiful listed buildings dating from 1868, with an extension for the long Eurostar trains designed by British starchitect Norman Foster—presumably on time out from his usual business of making pleasure domes for the world's nastiest totalitarian governments.

Tickets

The Eurostar ticket office and travel centre is located at the Euston Road end of the long arcade, while self-service machines (for collecting pre-booked tickets) can be found outside the Eurostar departure lounge further along the arcade and to the right. Opening times for the Eurostar ticket office are 4.30 am–20.00 pm (Mon and Fri), 4.45 am–20.00 pm (Tues-Thurs) 5.30 am–20.00 pm (Sat) and 6.45-20.30 (Sun). For National Rail services, you will need to buy tickets from machines, or a manned ticket desk at the designated area at the far end of the Arcade, next to that horrific kissing statue.

Services

At St Pancras International there are more than 40 places to eat, drink and shop, with a fair number of chain stores as well as some exclusives, such as the Champagne Bar and Gastro Pub. Best of all is the Booking Office bar, which serves some of the best cocktails in the city. The station has its own dedicated shopping arcade with branches of classic London stores Hamleys and Foyles, as well as a market area and another brace of shops at the north end of the station ('The Circle'). Everything is shiny, new and upmarket, so expect your money to vanish pretty damn quickly. The Betjeman Arms pub – named after the famous poet whose petition saved the listed buildings from the same fate as Euston's arch – hosts beer festivals and music/literature events.

Public Transport

St Pancras can be reached by Tube (via adjacent King's Cross station) on the Victoria, Hammersmith & City, Circle, Piccadilly, Northern and Metropolitan Lines. A large number of buses also stop along Euston Road day and night. For route details check the bus maps for Camden borough at www.tfl.gov.uk/tfl/gettingaround/maps/buses/.

Victoria Station

LFT Map:	20
Address:	Buckingham Palace Road SW1V 1JU
General enquiries:	020 7922 6214
Lost property:	020 7963 0957
Gatwick Express:	0845 850 1530
Southern:	0845 127 2920
Southeastern:	0845 000 2222

Overview

80 million people use London Victoria per year, making it one of the UK's busiest stations. Hit it at rush hour and it will feel like those 80 million are all there with you. Built a century ago for a less populous, less rushed and less demanding city, it struggles with crowds of commuters who jostle for platform space. Now it enforces crowd-control measures at peak times: prepare to be patient. Nevertheless, it is well laid-out with services clearly sign-posted, and a major upgrade is planned to improve its capacity.

Victoria's main train operators are Southeastern, Southern and Gatwick Express, who between them will whisk you to Brighton, Portsmouth, Hastings and Gatwick, among other Southeastern towns. Or if you're looking for a romantic break and the Victoria route to Bognor Regis is just a little too obvious for you, you can earn yourself brownie points and a hefty overdraft by taking the Orient Express from this station.

The building itself is impressive: look above the modern shop fascias to enjoy century-old architecture. But if that is all a little too high-brow, look up anyway, as the entrance to the South East building sports four caryatids: columns shaped like women, whose tunics saucily hang open so a gratuitous nipple can pop out to cheer the commuters. Rule Britannia!

Tickets

If you haven't booked in advance (why? Why?!), then head for the 24 hour ticket office in the central concourse, where you will queue for anything up to a year to buy your journey for much more money than you'd have paid online a week earlier. If you don't require assistance from a ticket officer, use the automated machines dotted round the concourse: their queues always move faster (unless the person in front of you is a newbie who can't figure out the buttons, which is guaranteed if you have less than five minutes to catch your train). Keep your ticket handy as all platforms are guarded by ticket barriers, and add a few extra minutes to reach platforms 15–19.

Services

All the predictable station fare is available in the main concourse for your journey's usual sandwich, loofah and tie needs. Food options have mercifully diversified so in addition to the obligatory artery-cloggers you can now grab sushi from the Wasabi stand or maintain your body's temple-status at the Camden Food Co. If it's a meal you're after and you must remain at the station, head up to the food court via Victoria Place for a choice of what could charitably be described as restaurants. Victoria Place itself boasts the ubiquitous high street shops to help you kill time or for any last minute gifts (as long as you don't really like the person you're buying for). Station loos are 30p—even up in the food court you can't pee for free—and showers are available if you're getting a bit ripe. Victoria also has a left luggage service, WiFi (charged) and photo booths.

Public Transport

Victoria is on the Victoria, Circle and District lines: entrance to the underground is opposite platform 7. The bus terminus is just outside the main entrance. It is also next door to London's national bus depot for cheapo travel to/from other parts of the UK. The main taxi rank is outside the main entrance, but if it has a heart-sinking queue then head up to the Plaza exit for an alternative rank.

Waterloo Station

NFT Map:	104
Address:	Waterloo, London, SE1 8H
Train company:	South West Trains
General enquiries:	020 7922 2545
Lost property:	020 7401 7861
Website:	www.southwesttrains.co.uk

Overview

Until 2007, Waterloo was the first port of call for 'Europeans' arriving by train. Thousands of chic foreigners, clutching manbags and sporting huge sunglasses, would arrive at the station every week. But not any more. Nearly 200 years after the British triumphed in the first battle of Waterloo—a town in Belgium—the French got their revenge. Last November Eurostar gave the two fingers to the British Waterloo and promiscuously buggered off to St Pancras. Rumour has it that ex-PM Margaret Thatcher had specifically ordered that Eurostar terminate at a station named after a famous French defeat; but things have moved on a little since the "Iron Lady" left office. We're all Europeans now…

In truth, perhaps it's not that bad a thing. Even though no other British station covers as much space, Waterloo feels like it's at bursting point. Even without the Eurostar it has a whopping 19 platforms—in almost constant use—and four Tube lines. It's calmed down slightly since the international terminal was put out to stud, but it's still pretty manic.

The station services London's south western suburbs (as can be seen by the swathes of well dressed commuters) and, further afield, the towns south west of the capital.

Waterloo East

NFT Map:	104
Address:	Sandell St, SE8 8H
Central number:	0 800 405 040

Overview

If the south west isn't your bag, you can disappear to England's south east—Kent, Sussex and SE London—from Waterloo East. There's an escalator next to Burger King, opposite platform 12, that makes a trip to the south east look far more alluring than it really is.

Tickets

The main office is opposite platforms 16–17. And it's open 24 hours—so why not charm them into giving you a free ticket after a few drinks? They can't have heard it before, right?

Services

A delay is just unplanned "me time", so make the most of it by buying a newspaper, eating your own weight in overpriced pasties and cookies; then wash it down with a few pints of generic football-sponsor lager in Bonaparte's pub before buying your loved-one a novelty tie/'cute' socks to make for up being late. And drunk. And flatulent. And tasteless. There's a left luggage office between platforms 11-12.

Public Transportation

Waterloo is served by four underground lines: Bakerloo, Jubilee, Northern, Waterloo & City; and approximately 20 bus routes. See tfl.gov.uk for details.

Overview

f there's one thing that screams London, it's big ed buses—loads of 'em—preferably passing eneath Big Ben for maximum iconic impact. here was an almighty roar from Londoners vhen the Routemaster was scrapped: panoramas iewed from the Oxo tower were dotted with ists clutching rolled-up Time Outs shaking at he mayoral offices. The accordion buses which eplaced them were met with similar anger but ney've now been phased out: one can only uess at the amount of revenue lost by fare odgers.

Vhatever you think of the death of the bendy us and Boris' reinvention of the Routemaster which is apparently to feature a glass roof) one ning is certain: you're going to spend a lot of me on buses, around them, dodging them or noaning about them. Let's have a quick run-own of things to drop in a London bus convo:)rivers take pleasure in driving off just as you et to the stop,'Why do they always drive so fast/ ow?' 'They're earning up to £500 a week? Why e they so grumpy all the time?' ad infinitum. s a Londoner, your list of hobbies and interests ow includes transport: deal with it.

rmer mayor Ken Livingstone always had a ing for buses and we make 6m journeys every y. There are a variety of different operating mpanies, but to us they're all the same, all the ay out to the frontiers of Zone 6. Get on at the ont, get off at the middle.

big red bus featured in the Beijing Olympics osing ceremony, as the world looked to ndon 2012. And Thomas Heatherwick's all-w Routemaster is set to be launched in Spring 12. Just like the old one there is an open rear atform for hopping on and hopping off. A duction in those nasty diesel particulates has o been specified, as excuses for capital car ivers become ever weaker.

Fares

In an effort to make the city more efficient and to cut down on theft-based attacks on drivers, Transport for London (TfL) introduced the Oyster card. Now people only beat up drivers for fun. The Oyster ("The world's your..."—geddit?) is an electronic swipe card that can be bought at all 275 Tube stations and some 4,000 other outlets such as newsagents.

The card can carry a mixture of travel passes (often referred to as travelcards in a nod to the pre-electronic age of cardboard); and pay-as-you-go cash value. Note that if you choose pay-as-you-go, and you end up making more journeys than you anticipated; once it reaches the equivalent cost of a one-day travelcard, it will cap itself so you don't spend more.

Unless you are making a small number of journeys it usually works out cheaper to get a travelcard. In a further move towards the cashless society, coins are still accepted—but you will pay more for a journey. A single ticket costs £1.30 with Oyster or £2.20 with cash. On some bus routes you will not be allowed to purchase a ticket on the bus, but instead there will be a roadside ticket machine. Believe us, Oyster's just easier...

When you get on, don't forget to push your card against the scanner by the drivers' window. Sure, you're on camera 300 times per day, and every journey you make is recorded. But if you're paranoid, try another city, because they *are* watching you here.

You can buy a bus and tram pass (£10.00 p/w), or you can buy a bus/tube travelcard (prices vary by zones). If you don't work or socialise in the centre, and you only buy, let's say a Zone 2-3 bus travelcard, you can still use this on all buses in Zones 1-6. Which is nice. An Oyster card costs £5 to get, but you'll soon recoup that. Concessions are also available for the unemployed and for full-time students.

24-Hour Services

You'll not hear London referred to as "the other city which never sleeps". Partly because it's unwieldy, but mostly because it's not true. After a hard night's binge-drinking and fighting in taxi ranks, we like our kip.

But for those of you that are hardcore no-sleep-till-Brockley types, there is a network of 24-hour services. There are also a large number of night buses. They're just like day buses, except the route number is prefixed by a large 'N' and the view is less interesting.

Information

TfL's website (tfl.gov.uk) is an essential reference. Fare information and travel updates are available, plus PDFs of routes and timetables. As you get closer to central London, many routes operate on a frequency-basis rather than at fixed times.

The main reason to visit TfL's site is the Journey Planner. Enter your start and end points and it will (usually) calculate the best options. A word of warning though, computers are fallible and some route maps are schematics—so do check your own map and use common sense. Like those idiots that follow their GPS even when it tells them to drive into a river, it's frustrating to take three buses in a big circuit then realise you could have walked it in five minutes…

If you do want to live out your 1940s film fantasies, you can still catch the quaint old Routemasters doddering along 'Heritage Routes' 9 and 15. If you're wondering who this guy is that keeps bugging you at the door-less rear step, it's the conductor and he only wants your money. It's the silent guy in the corner who wants your soul that you have to watch out for…

Safety

Like all big cities, London has its fair sha of oddballs and criminals. And then a fe institution-loads more in case things ev get boring. But CCTV in every bus and th creation of Safer Transport teams is havir an effect—and not just on the share price video camera manufacturers. TfL claimed a 11% reduction in reported crime at the er of 2007 and a ratio of 15 crimes per millic journeys. Also, bus crime is concentrated particular areas on particular routes. An you'll soon get to know the 'usual suspects' s don't worry. Night buses can get a bit lairy, s follow a few tips below to make sure the on stress you suffer is traffic-related. Gangste may wish to laugh at the following; Moth Theresas may wish to tattoo it on the insic of their eyelids:

Avoid the top deck when possible. Sit on th left so the driver can see you (he has a radi link to base). Don't fall asleep. Use the sam stop at night and know your surroundings s you can be confident. Keep your belongings close to you and be switched on. Get to kno the 'hot spots' so you can be aware.

For more info, see our fabulous fold out bu map.

Overview

Coaches are traditionally associated with the grimier side of travel. But London's biggest coach company, National Express, are desperately trying to shake their image as a purveyor of seedy transport. They're rebranding themselves as quick, comfortable and green. Their fleet of coaches are shiny and the drivers slightly less grumpy than they used to be.

National Express' nemesis is the Megabus. There's a few misconceptions about these guys and they are: that all their fares are £1 and that they're shoddy scum buckets on wheels. Their advertising screams the £1 thing but they release only a handful of these tickets for each journey and then the fare rises the closer you get to your preferred date. However, they're not as bad as they used to be: the coaches are now pretty much as good as National Express. In addition, National Express have started a super cheap ticket campaign: pretty soon both companies will merge in holy matrimony and we won't need to choose between them anymore. What you have to bear in mind is that if you use coaches in general you will be showered with sick by cold turkey junkies at the back and you will have to take a gas mask if you're sat within 3 coach lengths of the portal of hell that is the toilet. Just sit back, for an additional 4 hours, and think of the £10 you've spent on not taking the train.

The main coach hub is near Victoria train station. You can buy tickets for both Megabus and National Express—the two main operators who run from Victoria Coach Station—from the same booths just inside the station. But, like plane tickets, (only without that last shred of glamour that air travel still has) if you buy in advance, you can get some super-cheap prices. National Express has an office on the road between the train and bus stations.

London's other main hub is Golder's Green. This is the last stop for services heading north (or the first stop for buses coming down into London). If you live in north London, it's worth jumping off here, as it's on the Northern Line and can shave an hour off the trip.

There's also a healthy trade in coaches to Oxford. The Oxford Tube competes with National Express on the route from Victoria; travelling via Marble Arch, Notting Hill and Shepherd's Bush. Tickets normally cost about £14 and you can buy on board. They also run through the night—so if you get drunk and have the urge to go on an impromptu holiday—well, Oxford it is.

Beyond Tooting, Croydon's trams will take you from places like Wimbledon to shop – lemming-like with the locals – at the Ampere Way IKEA. The trams accept Oyster and use a similar charging scale to buses. Once you get back on the map, your flatpacked sideboard will win admiring glances but few friends as you trail home on busy tubes.

National Express

Unit 6/7 Collonades Walk
123 Buckingham Palace Road, SW1W 1SH
08717 818181
www.nationalexpress.com

Megabus
0900 160 0900
www.megabus.co.uk

Oxford Tube
01865 772250
www.oxfordtube.com

There's a war going on out there, one with real casualties and collateral damage. When Tory leader David Cameron was spotted going through a red light on his bicycle, it threw into sharp relief a low level conflict which has been going on for decades. Bikes v. Cars: with hapless pedestrians caught in the middle.

Cycling around London is not for the faint-hearted, but recent improvements, like Boris' cycling revolution campaigning and the hard work of the London Cycling Campaign (www.lcc.org.uk), are encouraging people to drop their Oyster cards and jump on their bikes. Indeed, the Tory mayor has now completed 4 of the 12 planned 'Cycle superhighways'. 2 of the 12 proposed 'Cycle Superhighways' and has already introduced the city cycle-hire program: a brilliant system based on European models in which users pick up a bike and then drop it off when finished at a suitable point in the city. Some of the routes highlighted in the brilliant (and free) maps produced by LCC and Transport for London have become so popular, cycling along them is like taking part in the Tour de France (albeit slower and with slightly fewer drugs). Talking of France, the 'Boris Bike' which was inspired by the Velib' communal bike scheme is enormously successful, so much so that the haughty Parisians have had to concede that, "oui, c'est tres chic". Another design victory for London.

But cycling does hold some risks. As well as the nightmare of walking around all day with 'helmet hair' you've got accidents and theft. LCC's website has details of road-confidence training and lists local cycling groups who run social events and cycle maintenance classes. They will sometimes cycle your new route to work with you to help you negotiate the difficult bits. Aren't they nice?

For those new to cycling on London's roads, basic rules include: stay a door length (or stride) away from the pavement or parked cars; watch out for distracted office drones leaping into the road and into black cabs; don't undertake bendy-buses or HGVs; don't use your phone while moving; and if in doubt on a tricky junction, transform yourself into a pedestrian—get off and push your bike wherever you need to go. For debates around riding on pavements, wearing helmets and jumping red lights check out www.cyclechat.co.uk/forums.

Bolt-cutting 'tea-leaves' steal thousands of bikes every year. You have three options to reduce this particular risk. One, buy a rubbish bike that no-one would want to steal and lock it with one lock. Two, get a decent bike, carry around a D-lock and two other locks and spend 20 mins each time you stop. Three, get a shit-hot bike and never take it out.

Where to Ride Bikes

There are plenty of great rides around town and a happy cyclist is one who has been able to incorporate one into their commute. The cycling maps mentioned above give colour-coded help, look for the brown routes (separate from the traffic) or even better the green routes (separate from the traffic and passing through parks, beside canals or rivers.)

Good options are the short but scenic Parkland Walk Nature Reserve, which links Finsbury Park to Highgate via an abandoned railway line; a Saturday morning cycle takes you to one of Highgate's wonderful pubs for lunch and a lazy pint. The City, normally snarled with cabs, buses and kamikaze pedestrians, is a dream on a Sunday morning.

Though not continuous, the path along the Regent's Canal linking Paddington with Canary Wharf takes cyclists away from traffic and along some surprisingly gorgeous stretches of canal (which also sport some top notch graffiti)—as well as some godawful, festering dumps. A useful section of the canal links the west side of Regent's Park with Paddington via Lisson Grove and Warwick Avenue. Watch out for super-fast cyclists determined to slice a second off their PB, especially where the path narrows under bridges or around ramps. Also recent yellow crime signs around London Fields spoke of a gang of youths pushing cyclists into the canal for fun. Watch out for them too.

A jaunt through any of the capital's great parks seems an obvious choice, but beware, some parks (notably Hampstead Heath) ban bikes on almost all paths, thanks to selfish cyclists of the past who went too fast and frightened the jumpy pedestrians.

The new anarchic FreeWheel Event is a real highlight, where great swathes of normally packed roads along the Embankment and up to St James's Park are closed to all but cyclists every September (we fervently hope this will remain forever). And the London Critical Mass meet at 6 pm on the last Friday of the month by the National Film Theatre, if you can't wait that long.

www.londonfreewheel.com
www.criticalmasslondon.org.uk

Bike Shops	*Address*	*Phone*
Apex Cycles	40-42 Clapham High St, SW4 7UR	020 7622 1334
Archway Cycles	183 Archway Rd	020 8340 9696
Bicycle Magic	6 Greatorex St, E1 5NF	020 7375 2993
Bikefix	48 Lamb's Conduit St, WC1N 3LJ	020 7405 1218
Brick Lane Bikes	118 Bethnal Green Rd, E2 6DG	020 7033 9053
Bobbin Bicycles	397 St John St	020 7837 3370
Brixton Cycles	145 Stockwell Rd, SW9 9TN	020 7733 6055
Cheech Miller	227 Victoria Park Rd	020 8985 9900
Condor Cycles	51 Gray's Inn Rd, WC1X 8PP	020 7269 6820
Decathlon	Surrey Quays Rd	020 7394 2000
Evans (Spitalfields)	The Cavern, 1 Market St, E1 6AA	020 7426 0391
Holloway Cycles	290 Holloway Rd, N7 6NJ	020 7700 6611
London Fields Cycles	281 Mare St, E8 1PJ	020 8525 0077
London Recumbents	Battersea Park	020 7498 6543
Mosquito	123 Essex Rd, N1 2SN	020 7226 8765
ReCycling	110 Elephant Rd, SE17 1LB	020 7703 7001

To consider taking a taxi in London you either need (a) a trust fund, or (b) to be drunk. If you are both, congratulations: prepare to be taken for a ride in more ways than one.

Dating back to the mid-17th Century (kind of), London's 'black cabs' (www.londonblackcabs.co.uk), or 'Hackneys', are the world's oldest taxi service and are as representative of London as Routemasters, Big Ben and robbery. They are the most visible, the most iconic and probably the most expensive taxi service in London. While this flag-down option is great (they are the only company licensed to pick up on the street) budgeting for a black cab is tricky. Their prices are designed to confuse passengers into parting with huge wads for what often feels like a round-the-block trip. A whole range of metaphysical problems contribute to that huge sum waiting to be paid at jouney's end; all fares start at £2.20 and then go up according to the time of day, speed, and the time spent in the cab. There's also an airport surcharge and the 'puke charge' of £40. Keep it in!

Black cabs are operated by many different companies who are all regulated and licensed by the Public Carriage Office (PCO). Generally speaking, the service you receive doesn't vary much from company to company, though some boast little add-ons to capture your fare. Big, well organized companies like Dial-A-Cab (www.dialacab.co.uk; 020 7253 5000) and Radio Taxis (www.radiotaxis.co.uk; 020 7272 0272) offer online booking, carbon neutral trips, and friendly service. All black cab drivers must pass 'The Knowledge' test to get their license, so every driver will have a labyrinthine understanding of London and most will not be shy in sharing this with you.

Though a cheaper option, going private can be a minefield. Since 2001 all taxi services in London are required by law to be licensed by the PCO: this includes the city's thousands of private-hire minicabs. Private hire companies are everywhere you look and often take the form of nicotine-stained, shoddily-built little offices with lots of bored men milling about. Every neighbourhood has plenty of local services and it's really trial and error to find one that doesn't rip you off or drive barely roadworthy chariots of rust. The drivers of these little companies can be pretty eccentric—you can be regaled by tales of times past, given essential life advice or simply receive the disdainful silent treatment. The website www.taxinumber.com offers a list of local minicabs for every postcode in the UK.

The 'private taxi sector' does do upmarket however. By far the most efficient and elegant service is that offered by Addison Lee, (www.addisonlee.com; 020 7387 8888) who text you twice, have huge gleaming six-seaters, and perfectly-manicured drivers. Fares are pretty cheap over longer distances but the minimum is around £10. E-London Cars are almost as good (www.elondoncars.co.uk; 020 7494 4004). Of course, you can also sup from the cup of bad taste by ordering a stretch hummer or pink limo at Book A Limo (www.booklimo.co.uk; 020 8965 1724).

A word of warning: London is awash with rogue taxi-drivers who are not licensed and who will attempt to pick you up from outside a club or theatre. These guys will either charge you more than you agreed upon, not know where they are going, or they will be driving beat-up death-traps. There are also many stories of attacks on women, so if in doubt, don't get in!

Helicopter Services

Westland Heliport
020 7228 0181 www.helipad.co.uk

SW11's very own heliport! Aerial tours of London can be made online with Helipad running from Westland Heliport in Battersea, Elstree and London City Airport. The nearest tube is Clapham Junction.

EBG Helicopters
01737 823 282 www.ebghelipcopters.co.uk

Running helicopter tours of London and charter flights from Redhill Airport in Surrey, 10 minutes by car from Gatwick Airport. £140 will get you 35 minutes over London, the only downside is getting to Surrey. Flights are between 10-4pm. Also offers charters for weddings and corporate events. Flying from Heathrow? Take a 20 minute sky ride for a cool £1,200.

Helicopter Days
0 844 815 0952 www.helicopterdays.co.uk

Operating out of Biggin Hill, 30-minute flights over Canary Wharf and Westminster start at £125 per person and you can cram up to 5 friends in with you. Lessons are available for less than £200. For drivers the helipad's close to M25 or you can be picked up by a helicopter from another location!

Elstree Aerodrome
020 8953 7480 londonelstreeareodrome.com

A variety of charters operate out of Elstree offering sky tours, as well as flight academies for those who want to take the wheel. On site is The Elstree Bar & Café, plus it's close to M1.

Ferries/Boat Tours, Rentals & Charters

London River Services (LRS)
020 7941 2400
www.tfl.gov.uk/gettingaround

Provides commuter river transportation on the Thames. This runs in the East from Masthouse Terrace Pier to Savoy Pier at Embankment. In peak hours services run to Woolwich Arsenal with a further service from Blackfriars Millenium Pier in the City to Putney Pier in the west costing £15 return. WiFi is available on boats serving Woolwich. Services run every 20 minutes. All are wheelchair friendly.

Thames Clippers
0870 7815049
www.thamesclippers.com

London's answer to the NYC water taxis, primarily serving the O2 stadium from Waterloo, Embankment and Tower Bridge. Conveniently runs later than the Tube meaning you can actually stay right to the end of a show without the worry of being stranded on the south side of the river. Single tickets cost between £3-5 with Oyster Card holders getting 1/3 off. Boats leave every 15 minutes.

Bateux London
020 7695 1800
www.bateuxlondon.com.

Dinner, lunch and charter cruises from Embankment Pier. Yes, there's even a jazz cruise.

Westminster Passenger Services Association
020 7930 2062
www.wpsa.co.uk

One of the only popular charters to offer services upriver to Kew, Richmond and Hampton Court.

City Cruises
020 7488 0344
www.citycruises.com.

Hop on hop off services primarily aimed at tourists and with tourist prices. Tickets start from £11 return for adults from Greenwich to Westminster/Waterloo Pier.

Heritage Boat Charters
01932 224 800
www.heritageboatcharters.com

For something different, try messing about on the river in one of these historic wooden numbers. On offer are skippered cruises down the Thames starting at £825. Formal dinner on board is available.

Silver Fleet Woods River Cruises
020 7759 1900
www.silverfleet.co.uk

Luxury chartered boats. Particularly good at putting on top-notch corporate events.

Thames Cruises
020 7928 9009
www.thamescruises.com

Two words—disco cruise. Hot pants are not required for dinner cruises.

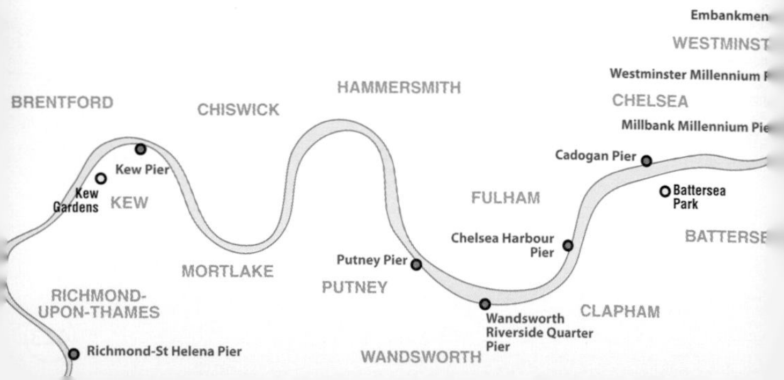

Marinas/Passenger Ship Terminal

Chelsea Marina
07770 542 783
www.chelseaharbourmarina.com

Despite being in upmarket Chelsea, the prices for mooring your boat here are incredibly generous—£2 per metre a night or £300 a year with space for 60 boats. Secure subterranean parking also available.

Chiswick Quay Marina
020 8994 8743
www.chiswickquay.com/marina

Great, secluded spot for West Londoners near Chiswick Bridge. A little far from a tube station, yet Chiswick overland station is within walking distance with services to Waterloo. Prices are on an annual basis at £162 per metre including a resident harbourmaster, shower block, mains water and electricity.

Gallions Point Marina
020 7476 7054
www.gallionspointmarina.co.uk

In London's Docklands and therefore perfect for those working in the city.

St Katharine Haven
020 7264 5312
skdocks.co.uk

One of London's best marinas. Great location by Tower Bridge, close to the quayside bars and restaurants and reasonable London prices—£3.60 per metre, per day.

Welcome Floating Terminal in Greenwich
01474 562 200
www.portoflondon.co.uk

Built in 2004 and believed to be the world's first floating terminal. Welcome has on-site immigration and custom services for cruise ship passengers entering or leaving London.

London Cruise Terminal at Tilbury
01375 852 360
www.londoncruiseterminal.com

The most popular regional departure point for passenger liners is 25 miles from Central London in Essex. Its close proximity to the M25 makes it easy for Londoners to get to. Current destinations from here include Scandinavia and continental Europe.

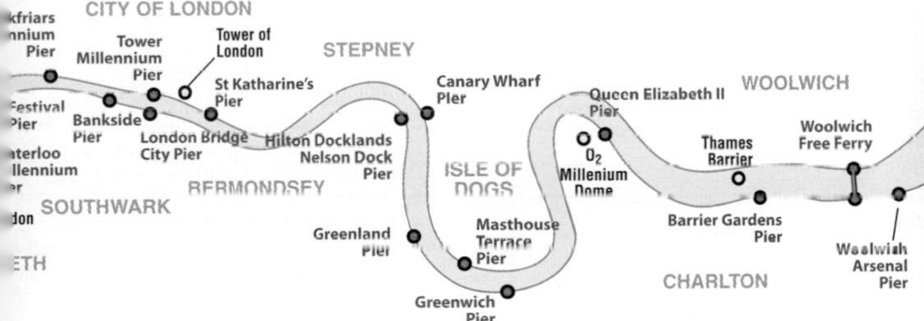

With London's Congestion Charge, Low Emission Zone, pricey parking, kamikaze bus drivers, dreaded speed bumps, speed cameras and a road layout that would give Spock the night terrors—*"it's so illogical Captain"*—driving around town is something to be avoided. Combine this with over 7.5 million people who just want to get from A to B without anyone getting in their frickin' way, and you can see where problems arise.

But, there are times when a four-wheeler is the only option, and for those times here are some things to watch out for:

Pedestrians love to stride purposefully into the road with nary a thought for their safety. Keep a weather eye out, one foot over the brake and one hand over the horn.

Cyclists are ever-increasing in number—give them plenty of space and remember for the one speedhound jumping the lights there are hundreds of law abiders that you just don't notice. Try to focus on them.

Motorbikes and Scooters are not all ridden by leather clad Hells Angels or Jamie Oliver clones; most just want to get about and avoid the Congestion Charge. As with cyclists, give plenty of space and check your blind spots.

Black Cabs, these roving London landmarks have been known, on occasion, to pull up to the curb, do a 'U-ie' and even advertise the FT without sufficient warning.

Traffic Wardens A.K.A. 'council revenue generating units'. Make sure you avoid illegal parking—unless you are an ambassador.

Driving Statistics

Speed Limit: **30 mph**

Average speed in rush hour: **6 mph** (estimates vary)

Amount stolen from Westminster parking meters: **Over £50,000 a week**

Increase in congestion predicted by 2015: **25%**

Amount of UK Carbon emissions coming from road traffic: **21%**

Worst day of the week for accidents: **Friday**

Ways to make it bearable

Most of the stress caused by driving in London, apart from the sheer volume of traffic, is caused by lack of consideration for others—usually as drivers are running late. So make sure you leave PLENTY of time for your journey, try not to block junctions, and let people out if you have a chance.

Get a tiny car that you can park sideways. Ha! That'll show 'em.

Join a car club like Street Car or WhizzGo– then you can drive whenever you want at a fraction of the cost of owning a car.

Try and avoid rush hour. Morning rush lasts from 7 am to 10.30 am, lunch rush from 11 am to 2.30 pm, school run rush from 2.45 pm to 4.15 pm and afternoon rush from 4.30 pm to 8.45 pm. Bonne chance…

Driving in the Congestion Charge Zone and the Low Emission Zone

The Congestion Zone, introduced in 2003, meant the centre of town was remarkably less congested—for about twenty minutes if the Daily Mail is to be believed. The charge is currently £10 (£9 with autopay) if you enter the zone between 07:00 and 18:00, Monday to Friday. Bank Holidays don't count. You have until midnight the next day to pay the charge after which you're liable for a £120 penalty charge (reduced to £60 if paid within 14 days). After that, hefty fines apply. Huge red Cs in circles alert drivers to the start of the zone, if you miss them you should consider a swift visit to your optician. Check the website for exemptions. There is ongoing debate over the actual impact of the charge, and whether the zone will expand, or be removed altogether.

The Low Emission Zone (LEZ) was introduced in February 2008 to deter large lorries, buses, coaches and vans from dragging their belching exhausts through town. It covers a much larger area than the Congestion Charge: almost all of London within the M25 and applies 24/7. The charge varies between £100 and £200. A DAY.

Key Roads

A1

Running straight north from St Paul's Cathedral in the City through Islington, Archway, Highgate and beyond, this old Roman Road has some freer stretches allowing the frustrated drive to accelerate to 43 mph for 3 seconds, get a speeding ticket and then slam on the brakes. Ends (eventually) in Princes Street, Edinburgh, Scotland.

North Circular/South Circular (A406)

This is the M25's angrier and twisted little brother. Circling Outer London it has some of the busiest stretches of road in London and even includes a ferry across the river at Woolwich. The way dwindles to one exhausted lane in certain sections, causing great clots of traffic every day in rush hour. See left for rush hour times.

Euston Rd/Marylebone Road (A501)

Running east-west past King's Cross and Euston, this wide road skirts the northern edge of the congestion zone. It gets very crowded, because it's a feeder road to the relatively breezy start of the A40 heading out of London.

Embankment

The view as you drive along the Embankment along the north bank of the Thames is breathtaking. It needs to be to keep you occupied as you inch forward for hours. Runs from Chelsea (A4) to Tower Bridge.

Vauxhall Bridge Rd/Grovesnor Place/Park Lane/Edgware Rd (A5)

Running roughly north-west from Vauxhall Bridge Rd, around Victoria, past Hyde Park Corner and Marble Arch and out to join the A40, this route is a free corridor through the Congestion zone – free from charge rather than free from traffic. Be prepared—it's rammed.

Old Kent Rd / New Cross Rd / Lewisham Way / etc. (A2/A20)

Running south-west from The Bricklayers Arms roundabout and eventually down to Dover, where you catch the ferry to France; the Old Kent Rd, despite being the cheapest Monopoly property, is totally free from traffic at all times. No wait—that can't be right.

A3

Starting at London Bridge, this road eventually ends up in Portsmouth, but you have to struggle past Elephant and Castle, Clapham Common and Wimbledon Common along with everyone else trying to get to Guildford.

Traffic Hot Spots

Angel, Elephant and Castle, Hanger Lane Gyratory, Vauxhall Gyratory, Trafalgar Square, Parliament Square, Hammersmith Gyratory, everywhere else.

Useful links

TfL Interactive Traffic Map:
trafficalerts.tfl.gov.uk/microsite

Capital FM for traffic news from the Flying Eye 95.8 FM

Parking for Cars
www.park-up.com

Parking for Motorbikes and Scooters:
www.parkingforbikes.com

Route Planner:
www.theaa.com/travelwatch/planner_main.jsp

Congestion Charge:
www.tfl.gov.uk/roadusers/congestioncharging

Parking Ticket Appeals:
www.ticketbusters.co.uk

The great thing about being a Londoner is there's really no need to have a car. Except on those few occasions where you're cursing yourself for hauling a flat-packed Ikea coffee table on the shitty Croydon tram service. This is where joining a membership-based carsharing company, such as such as Streetcar + Zipcar (now one entity) www.streetcar.co.uk; 0203 004 7811, City Car Club (www.citycarclub.co.uk; 0845 330 1234), or fledgling Connect by Hertz (www.connectbyhertz.com; 08708 45 45 45) comes in handy.

Streetcar and Zipcar are your best bet, as they offer self-service cars and vans to members, billable by the hour, day, week or month. The beauty of this service is there's probably either a Zipcar or Streetcar parked around the corner from wherever you are in central London, which means you don't have to hike to a car rental centre, stand in a queue or deal with annoying upselling at a counter. Plus, if you get thrown out of your girlfriend's flat at 2 am and need a ride, you're in luck. Both offer a 24/7, 365 day a year self-service. For a membership fee of £59.50 a year, all you have to do is unlock the car with your Streetcard, grab the keys from the glovebox and away you go.

On top of the membership fee, cars cost from £5.25 per hour depending on what car or van you choose from a fleet of fuel efficient VWs and BMWs with iPod and SatNav connections as standard. You can also join Streetvan which gives you access to all the vans at £19.50 per year if you only need to transport stuff occasionally like uh, for the band (www.streetvan.co.uk).

If you must go the conventional route, there are, of course, Hertz, National, and Avis centres aplenty, but for a smart Londoner who only wants a car sometimes—go for a carshare.

Company	*Address*	*Phone*	*Map*
Avis	8 Balderton St	0870 153 9104	2
Avis	88 Eversholt St	0840 010 7967	78
Avis	20 Seagrave Rd	0870 010 7968	43
Avis	86 St Katharines Wy	0207 423 8875	95
Avis	33 York Rd	0870 608 6369	104
Easy Car	Elms Mews	0871 0500 444	30
Easy Car	20 Seagrave Rd	0871 0500 444	43
Easy Car	88 Eversholt St	0871 0500 444	78
Easy Car	77 Britannia Rd	0871 0500 444	43
Easy Car	37 Munster Rd	0871 0500 444	48
Easy Car	68 Clapham Rd	0871 0500 444	135
Easy Car	136 Pentonville Rd	0871 0500 444	79
Easy Car	1 Brewery Rd	0871 0500 444	73
Easy Car	7 Bryanston St	0871 0500 444	1
Easy Car	171 Battersea Park Rd	0871 0500 444	133
Easy Car	43 York Rd	0871 0500 444	104
Easy Car	131 Belsize Rd	0871 0500 444	68
Easy Car	8 Balderton St	0871 0500 444	2
Easy Car	12 Semley Pl	0871 0500 444	19
Easy Car	33 York Rd	0871 0500 444	104
Easy Car	245 Warwick Rd	0871 0500 444	34
Enterprise	145 Bow Rd	02089805600	94
Enterprise	131 Belsize Rd	02073280200	68
Enterprise	200 King St	02085637400	40
Enterprise	59 Royal Mint St	02076809944	95
Enterprise	202 Ilderton Rd	02077323838	116
Enterprise	49 Woburn Pl	02076314700	94
Hertz	156 Southampton Row	087 0850 2664	4
Hertz	200 Buckingham Palace Rd	0870 8460002	20
Hertz	35 Edgware Rd	0870 8460011	1
Hertz	79 Clapham Rd	0207 582 5775	135
Hertz	713 Old Kent Rd	020 76392121	116
National	68 Clapham Rd	44 207 8200202	135
National	150 Pentonville Rd	44 20 72782273	79
National	7 Bryanston St	44 207 4081255	1
National	12 Semley Pl	44 207 2 59 16 00	19
National	43 York Rd	44 207 9282725	104
Thrifty	131 Belsize Rd	44 20 76253556	68
Thrifty	Sloane Ave	44 02072622223	46
Thrifty	178 Tower Bridge Rd	44 02074033458	107

Transport • **Petrol Stations**

Petrol Stations	Address	Map
Total	170 Marylebone Rd	2
Jet	30 Clipstone St	3
BP	Russell Ct & Woburn Pl	4
Shell	198 Old St	7
BP	Park Ln & Mount St	9
BP	Vauxhall Bridge Rd & Udall St	21
Esso	115 Sutherland Ave	27
Shell	104 Bayswater Rd	30
Texaco	383 Edgware Rd	31
BP	383 Edgware Rd	31
BP	1 Westwick Gardens	33
BP	Shepherds Bush Green & Rockley Rd	33
Total	137 Chiswick High Rd	38
Total	372 Goldhawk Rd	39
BP	Great West Rd & Oil Mill Ln	39
BP	372 Goldhawk Rd	39
Jet	182 Goldhawk Rd	40
BP	Talgarth Rd & Gliddon Rd	41
Tesco	459 Fulham Rd	43
Shell	49 Tadema Rd	44
Shell	106 Old Brompton Rd	45
Tesco	601 King's Rd	49
Total	31 N Rd	51
Shell	89 Hornsey Rise	53
Sainsbury's	4 Williamson Rd	55
Esso	640 Holloway Rd	60
Texaco	73 Stapleton Hall Rd	62
Jet	314 7 Sisters Rd	63
Total	409 Kilburn High Rd	65
BP	Finchley Rd & College Crescent	66
BP	Haverstock Hill & Oman Rd	67
BP	Wellington Rd & Wellington Pl	68
Tesco	115 Maida Vale	68
Esso	33 Chalk Farm Rd	71
BP	142 Camden Rd	72
Tesco	196 Camden Rd	72
Sainsbury's	4 Williamson St	73
Total	109 York Wy	73
Shell	104 Holloway Rd	74
BP	Hampstead Rd & Cardington St	77
BP	Goodsway & Camley St	78
Shell	276 Upper St	80
Jet	43 Stamford Hill	83
BP	144 Stoke Newington Rd	86
Texaco	168 Shoreditch High St	91
Total	112 Vallance Rd	91
BP	Cambridge Heath Rd & Paradise Row	92
Sainsbury's	1 Cambridge Heath Rd	92
Texaco	51 Grove Rd	93
Texaco	127 Bow Rd	94
Texaco	77 The Highway	95
Texaco	102 The Hwy	96
Shell	139 Whitechapel Rd	96
ASDA	151 E Ferry Rd	103
Shell	101 Southwark Bridge Rd	106
Shell	137 Walworth Rd	113
BP	New Kent Rd & Balfour St	113
Total	234 Old Kent Rd	114
Tesco	107 Dunton Rd	114
Total	272 St James Rd	115
Jet	747 Old Kent Rd	116
Shell	101 Evelyn St	118
Jet	179 Creek Rd	119
Jet	25 Greenwich High Rd	120
BP	Camberwell Rd & Albany Rd	121
BP	Peckham Rd & Southampton Wy	122
Total	38 Peckham Rd	122
BP	New Cross Rd & Pomeroy St	125
Sainsbury's	263 New Cross Rd	125
Jet	42 Hinton Rd	127
Jet	13 E Dulwich Rd	130
Texaco	213 Kennington Rd	131
BP	238 Kennington Ln	131
Shell	326 Queenstown Rd	133
Esso	2 Battersea Park Rd	133
Esso	54 Wandsworth Rd	134
Sainsbury's	62 Wandsworth Rd	134
Esso	77 Clapham Rd	135
Total	257 Upper Richmond Rd	136
BP	Swandon Wy & Smugglers Wy	138
Texaco	474 Wandsworth Rd	142
Tesco	330 Brixton Rd	144
Esso	243 Brixton Rd	145
Total	39 Nightingale Ln	147
Total	40 Balham Hill	148
BP	124 Brixton Hill	150
BP	Marius Rd & Rowfant Rd	151

January

- **New Year's Day Parade** • Big Ben to Piccadilly Circus • Marching band and thousands of kids. How better to cure a hangover?
- **London Boat Show** • ExCel Exhibition Centre • Like we always say: you can never have too many yachts.
- **Russian Winter Festival** • Trafalgar Square • Magical Russian Winterland replaces the normal Pigeon-Crap Land.
- **London Art Fair** • Over 100 galleries and thousands of artists under one roof.
- **The London Bike Show** • ExCel Exhibition Centre • The best of the best of modern cycling equipment pandering to over-indulged cyclists.
- **London International Mime Festival** • Southbank Centre • Even weirder when you see it for real.
- **The London Outdoors Show** • ExCel Exhibition Centre • The country's biggest collection of outdoor goods—ironically hosted indoors.
- **Charles I Commemoration Ceremony** • Trafalgar Sq • St James' Palace • Thousands of uniformed Cavaliers confuse the tourists.
- **TNA Wrestling** • Wembley Arena • Strange men in spandex faux-fighting in front of drunken man-children.
- **Walking with Dinosaurs** • The O2 • Get your prehistoric freak on with twenty life-size dinosaurs (not literally) freaks!

February

- **British Academy Film Awards (BAFTA)** • Royal Opera House • Britain's finest film and television talent take a bow.
- **Chinese New Year** • West End • Party like it's 4707.
- **Destinations: Holiday and Travel Show** • Earls Court Exhibition Centre • Chase away the Winter Blues.
- **Live Tudor Cookery** • Hampton Court Palace • Glutinous Tudor food prepared in classic Tudor fashion. It's OK the New Year's resolutions will be long dead by now.
- **London Fashion Week** • Somerset House• Far Too Thin.
- **National Wedding Show** • Olympia • Perfect day out for a first date.
- **Professional Beauty** • ExCel Exhibition Centre • Pay to get pretty with the latest developments in modern cosmetics.
- **Lifted** • Harrods • A bizarre annual exhibition inside Harrod's lifts.
- **The Great Spitalfields Pancake Race** • Old Truman Brewery • Pancake race in wacky clothes. No, London. Just, no.
- **Blessing the Throats** • St Ethelreda's Church, Ely Place • Lemsip not working? Sore throats cured by holy candle.
- **Clowns' Service** • Holy Trinity, Dalston • Because God likes clowns too.
- **Kinetica Art Fair**• P3• Carnivorous lampshades and pole-dancing robots? We're there.
- **BAFTAs** • London Palladium • Ten points per autograph.

March

- **Affordable Art Fair** • The Marquee, Battersea Park • Now even The Great Unwashed can buy art!
- **Affordable Art Fair** • The Marquee, Battersea Park • Now even The Great Unwashed can buy art!
- **Easter Egg Hunt** • Kew Garden's • Delightful Easter affair, perfect for the kids, don't forget to check out the animal farm.
- **Ideal Home Show** • Earls Court Exhibition Centre • Make your home ideal (or a bit less grotty).
- **St Patrick's Day Parade** • Park Lane • Shamrocks, river-dancing, big fluffy Guinness hats: true Irish tradition.
- **London Drinker Beer & Cider Festival** • The Camden Centre • Get rat-arsed on Pressed Rat & Warthog.
- **La Dolce Vita** • Business Design Centre • Get your sampling face on
- **Men's Afternoon Tea** • Mandeville Hotel • Because nothing is manlier than an exclusive tea, champagne and cake afternoon.
- **Move It** • Olympia • Put on your dancing shoes.
- **The International Food & Drink Event** • Olympia • This gorge-fest happens biannually, so start starving yourself now.
- **The Country Living Spring Fair** • Business Design Centre • For those with time for wooden chicken eggs
- **JobServe Live!** • Olympia • Career ideas and thousands of vacancies.

April

- **Cake International** • ExCel Exhibition Centre • Decorate and glutinously devour delicious cakes.
- **Oxford & Cambridge Boat Race** • River Thames • Hole up in a pub by the river and cheer over a beer.
- **Virgin London Marathon** • Greenwich – The Mall • 35,000 pairs of bleeding nipples.
- **London Book Fair** • Earl's Court • The publishing industry's main event. Occasionally stuff for free.
- **Alternative Fashion Week** • Old Spitalfields Market • Huge range of cutting edge fashion. And fetishwear.
- **Queen's Birthday Gun Salute** • Hyde Park • Who said the monarchy is archaic?
- **St George's Day** • Covent Garden / Cenotaph / Shakespeare's Globe • Brush up your Morris dancing skills.
- **The Real Food Festival** • Earl's Court Exhibition Centre • Real Food: much nicer than fake food.
- **Hot Cross Bun Service** • St Bartholomew-the-Great, Smithfield • Widows get a free hot cross bun. Worth losing the husband.
- **London Independent Film Festival** • Various West and Central Cinemas • Cool celebration of cinematographic indieness without The Man. Or something.

May

- **Freedom of the City** • Central London • Frequently awesome improv and experimental festival attracting top names.
- **Baishakhi Mela** • Brick Lane • Celebrate the Bengali New Year in the British tradition: vindaloo.
- **Bathing the Buddha** • Leicester Square • Buddha gets a birthday bath.
- **Mind, Body, Spirit Festival** • Royal Horticultural Halls • Make up for all the time in the pub.
- **Camden Crawl** • Throughout Camden • If you're not crawling by the end, you haven't done it right.
- **Chelsea Flower Show** • Royal Hospital Chelsea • You'll go for the flowers. You'll stay for the Pimms.
- **Chelsea Flower Show** • Royal Hospital Chelsea • You'll go for the flowers. You'll stay for the Pimms.
- **Greenwich Beer & Jazz Festival** • Old Royal Naval College • An odd paring that somehow works.
- **London Pet Show** • Earls Court Two – The cute, odd, scary and weird bring their pets and show them off.
- **Sci-Fi Festival** • London Apollo • The UK's only Sci-Fi Festival. Thank god.
- **Interiors London** • ExCel Centre • For those rich enough to treat their homes like art.
- **The Drag Olympics** • The Way Out Club • Drag Queens are put through their pedicured, high heeled paces.

June

- **City of London Festival** • The City • Bringing High Culture to a bunch of bankers.
- **Field Day** • Victoria Park • A pseudo hippy music festival with a lighthearted vibe.
- **Start of Open Air Theatre season** • Regent's Park • Ignore the climate and take in an outdoor play.
- **Taste of London** • Regent's Park • The best picnic in the world.
- **Wimbledon** • All England Lawn Tennis and Croquet Club • Short skirts and grunting. Marvellous.
- **Trooping the Colour** • Horse Guard's Parade • Hundreds of chaps in uniforms. Ohhhhh yes.
- **Meltdown Festival** • Southbank Centre • Eclectic music festival curated by major musicians.
- **Royal Academy Summer Exhibition** • Royal Academy • Lots and lots and LOTS of art.
- **Arts Festival Chelsea** • Chelsea • The artists formerly known as 'The Chelsea Festival'.
- **Naked Bike Ride** • Hyde Park • Don't think about the bums on seats.
- **Polo in the Park** • Hurlingham Park • Its turbo-rah dahhling, pass the Pimms.
- **Shakespeare Globe Season** • Bankside • To go, or not to go, that is the question.

July

- **Dogget's Coat & Badge Race** • Thames: London Bridge to Chelsea • Intense boat race to win a badge. Hardly seems worth it.
- **Pimms Urban Regatta** • Finsbury Square • People full of Pimms race on land in bottomless boats. Bloody Ozzies.
- **Pride London** • Trafalgar Square • One of Britain's biggest, funnest street parties.
- **The British 10k London Run** • Hyde Park • Whitehall • Work off the pies.
- **Hampton Court Palace Show** • Hampton Court • Stock up your garden / flowerpot / imagination.
- **The Chap Olympiad** • Bedford Square Gardens • Olympics for gentleman—no sportswear please.
- **Uprise Festival** • Islington • Celebrating the best of multicultural London, for free.
- **Swan Upping** • River Thames • Census of swans. For goodness sake.
- **Opening of Buckingham Palace** • Buckingham Palace • The Plebeians allowed in to see how their taxes (and steep entrance fees) are spent.
- **Wireless Festival** • Hyde Park • Big names vibrate the Serpentine.
- **Shoreditch Festival** • Shoreditch. • Because you can never have too many local festivals. Apparently.

August

- **Innocent Smoothies Festival** • Regent's Park • You wouldn't think fun could be this wholesome.
- **Great British Beer Festival** • Earls Court Exhibition Centre • A festival that puts the Great in Britain.
- **Trafalgar Square Festival** • Trafalgar Square • 3 weeks of music, theatre, dance and art.
- **Carnaval del Pueblo** • Royal Victoria Docks • Thousands of Latino lovelies. That's all you need to know, right?
- **Camden Fringe** • Camden People's Theatre • Wonderfully weird, hilariously funny and light on the wallet.
- **London Triathlon** • Docklands • Marathons are for pussies.
- **London Mela** • Gunnersbury Park • Partaaaay, Asia-style.
- **Metro Weekender** • Clapham Common • Dance music Saturday, bands on Sunday, chilled all weekend.
- **Notting Hill Carnival** • Ladbroke Grove • Party till your wallet gets nicked.
- **Parliament Tour Season** • Westminster • Go see first hand where it all goes so wrong.
- **Kids Week** • West End • West End shows free for kids. Soooo unfaaaaiiiiir.
- **Tiger Beer Singapore Chilli Crab Festival** • Truman Brewery • Cold beer, hot food and cool sounds.

September

- **The Great British Duck Race** • The Thames • Like the Oxbridge boat race. But with 165,000 rubber ducks.
- **Horseman's Sunday** • Hyde Park Crescent • London's horses say their Hail Maries. Yes, really.

- **Oyster & Seafood Fair** • Hays Galleria • The romance of oysters with the unholy stink of kippers.
- **Thames Festival** • Tower Bridge • Westminster • Fireworks, costumes, river races, carnivals. Kids like it.
- **Last Night of the Proms** • Royal Albert Hall • Camp overnight if you want tickets.
- **London Duathlon** • Richmond Park • It's like a triathlon… for people who can't swim.
- **London Tattoo Convention** • Old Truman Brewery • Who cares if it looks crap when you're 80?
- **Spitalfields Show & Green Fair** • Buxton Street • Who has the biggest marrow?
- **Open House Weekend** • Various around London • Over 600 architectural landmarks open for a nosey.
- **Fashion Week** • Summerset House • the September instalment of the famous frockfest.
- **Great Gorilla Run** • Start at London Underwriting Centre • Raise £400 for the Gorilla Organisation and the costume's yours.
- **Vintage Fashion Fair** • Primrose Hill • For those with a passion for vintage fashion.

October

- **The Big Draw** • Museum of Childhood • Pencils, not guns. Unfortunately.
- **Down Under Live** • Olympia • For those contemplating emigrating to warmer climes.
- **'Original Pearly Kings & Queens Association Harvest Festival** • Church of St Martin-in-the-Fields Affordable Art Fair.
- **International Halloween Festival** • Queen Mary College • Witches, druids and shamans unite for Europe's biggest Pagan festival.
- **Halloween** • London Dungeon • Trick Or Treating is for pussies.
- **Frieze Art Fair** • Regent's Park • Air kisses all round.
- **London Film Festival** • BFI Southbank • Two weeks of the best new films and lectures from A-Listers.
- **Metro Ski & Snowboard Show** • Olympia • London hosts the world's biggest winter sport show. Naturally.
- **Veolia Entertainment Wildlife Photographer of the Year (exhibition opens, for 6mths)** • Natural History Museum Puts your arty market photos to shame.
- **The Yoga Show** • Olympia • Bendy people upon bendy people. Literally.
- **Turner Prize Exhibition** • Tate Britain • Get to know the next Hirst or Emin.

November

- **London's Christmas Ice Rinks** • Venues across London • Much more romantic in your head than in reality.
- **Brighton Veteran Car Run** • Starts Hyde Park • Century-old bangers potter their way to Brighton.
- **Erotica Show** • Olympia • 31,000 horny adults pretend they're just browsing.
- **Barclays ATP World Tour Finals** • O2 Arena • Very rich tennis players make more money at this entertaining but unimportant tournament.
- **Bonfire Night** • Venues across London • Hundreds of thousands of pounds go pop.
- **Country Living Christmas Fair** • Business Design Centre • For those dreaming of a posh Christmas.
- **Royal British Legion Festival of Remembrance** • Royal Albert Hall • Take tissues.
- **Lord Mayor's Show** • Central London • Running for over 800 years and yet still a bit crap.
- **London Jazz Festival** • South Bank Centre • Start practising your jazz hands.
- **Winter Wonderland** • Hyde Park Grottos and Glühweins galore.

December

- **Satan's Grotto** • London Dungeon • Tortured elves and spit-roasting robins.
- **Trafalgar Square Christmas Tree** • Trafalgar Square • The only thing everyone knows about Oslo.
- **Aegon Masters Tennis** • Royal Albert Hall • Former World No.1s wheeze their way through a tournament.
- **Peter Pan Cup** • Serpentine Lido, Hyde Park • Freeze your nipples off on Christmas morning.
- **Great Christmas Pudding Race** • Covent Garden • We're mad, us! What are we like? Crazy!
- **Christmas Carol Sing-along** • Royal Albert Hall • Belt out your favourites and get in the mood.
- **Christmas Carol Sing-along** • Royal Albert Hall • Belt out your favourites and get in the mood.
- **Taste of Christmas** • ExCel Exhibition Centre • Tasty tips for making Christmas that little merrier.
- **Midnight Mass at St Paul's** • St Paul's • Eats the other Midnight Masses for breakfast.
- **New Year's Eve Fireworks** • Jubilee Gardens • Oooooh. And, of course, aaaaaaah.

Tactics

Finding somewhere to live in London is a ruthless and cutthroat business. Make sure you have plenty of red bull, cigarettes and patience. However, places go in the blink of an eye so it's important to move quick. Take a week off and hire a driver, if you can.

Ok, so these precautions aren't completely necessary, but you will have to work in mysterious and multifarious ways if you don't want to spend the next six months paying through your gullible nose for mice and verrucas. A good place to start by harassing your friends, your friends' friends, and your friends' friends' friends. Send out a group email and hope it gets passed around, and make sure you Tweet like mad about it. Twitter is a great place to get your request passed around. Who knows? Stephen Fry might have a room to let. Estate agents (see below for a list) will invariably try and rip you off but, then again, so will everyone else, so it's worth registering with all the big ones, as well as any whose office you see in the street, or you spot in newspapers, on TV or the internet. After uncovering a fair few completely brazen lies in the property listings on www.gumtree.com you will find that many of the smaller businesses place adverts for (sometimes fake) properties here. Don't be put off by the lies though, because this can be a good way of finding an agent (or getting in direct contact with a landlord) who is keen to make a deal with you, or who will try and match the prices advertised, even if they have nothing that fits the bill at the exact moment of lying. Of course, some of these listings are also genuine, and a good way to find rooms/apartments at lower than usual rates. Just bare in mind that a LOT of people use this site.

General sites

www.gumtree.com
www.findaproperty.co.uk
www.craigslist.org
www.rightmove.co.uk
www.propertyfinder.com
www.roombuddies.com

Estate Agents

There are hundreds of Estate Agents and Letting Agents across the city, some of the larger players (good and bad) include:

www.foxtons.co.uk - Offices all over London.
www.keatons.co.uk - Bow, Hackney, Harringey, Kentish Town, Stratford.
www.black-katz.com - Lettings only agency, numerous offices.
www.fjlord.co.uk - Numerous offices, specialise in uncooperative staff.
www.nelsonslettings.com - South and central London.
www.atkinsonmcleod.com - City and Docklands.

If you do end up using an agent, they will of course want to charge you an additional fee beyond any deposits or advance rent required by the landlord. But, as many of the agents in central London are close together, it's possible that they may be competing with each other to sell/rent the same properties. This will enable you to get a better deal. So shop around, be devious, and backstab as much as possible.

Council Tax

Council Tax is an annoying hidden cost that always comes as a bit of a surprise. It is worked out by your local council and is based on the value of your house/flat, which the council will already have placed in to one of 8 tax bands (bands are A–G, G covering the most valuable properties).There are several ways to determine the value of a property, but the easiest is probably to go to the website of the valuation office at www.voa.gov.uk. Having done that, it's possible to weigh up the benefits of different areas by comparing the council tax in equivalent bands charged by different local councils. It's fairly laborious, but worth it in the long run, if you can be bothered.

Because council tax is based on the property, not the people inside it, the rate is constant no matter how many people live in the house. This means that it's much cheaper to live in a big house with lots of people to split the tax with, than on your own, when you are liable for the full amount. Students do not have to pay council tax at all, but if they are sharing with one or more non-students then there will still be council tax to pay. A single non-student in a house full of students receives a 25% discount on his/her council tax bill, but if there is more than one non-student then all non-students are liable to pay full whack.

Deposit Information

The deposit is the necessary bank drain of every new tendency agreement. Typically deposits range from one – three months rent in advance, but if you pay over a two-month deposit you are entitled to special privileges including the right to sublet your space. If you can't afford the financial outlay there are other options available to you; it is possible to get involved with the Deposit Guarantee Scheme (you will need to contact your local council for more information), or independent agencies offer a similar service for a 10% - 20% fee. While not all landlords in London are Ebenezer Scrooge pre hallucination-esque you'll still hear your fair share of horror stories. Make sure you use the Deposit Protection Scheme (DPS) www.depositprotection.com to protect your cash. For a comprehensive overview on deposit information and your rights visit the Direct Gov website www.direct.gov.uk.

Alternative Options

In a city where house prices have been soaring through the roof for some time now (although it's calmed down somewhat recently), of course people do things like squat, have dreadlocks and go vegan. If you're not willing to go the whole way but fancy an adventure, or simply don't have much money, then it might be worth taking a look at being a guardian for Camelot. This company aims to fill vacant properties with responsible people who will prevent them from being abused. You must have good references, a job, and be over eighteen, as well as be ok with sharing with an indeterminate number of strangers, but the benefits are the unusual properties (e.g. schools, disused churches), the often large spaces and the ridiculously cheap rent (£25–60 pw inclusive of all bills). Of course loads of people want to do this and properties in London are not always available, but it's nevertheless a good idea to keep an eye on their site if the idea excites you: www.camelotproperty.co.uk.

WAREHOUSES

As with Starbucks and obesity, us Brits have finally caught on to the American craze for warehouse 'live/work' spaces. Okay we may have had the likes of Tracey Emin and other artists living in old carpet factories since the YBA days, but recently a whole crop of established estate agents have been refurbishing lofts and factories for letting at a premium. Any established warehouser will tell you the way to go is independent, through enthusiastic urban explorers who renovate and convert these old buildings for love and enjoyment. Often the only way into this secret brotherhood of the leaky roof is by simply ending up at a huge party at 4am in one of these spaces and asking the residents politely. The freedom of living in these places can be exhilirating if you've spent years toeing the line with grumpy neighbours and grumpier landlords.

CANAL-BOATS

If all this land lubbing is bringing you down, there's always the option of dropping anchor at Little Venice or the Lea Valley Harbour and sampling London's canal networks. More and more skint artsy fartsy folk are squeezing their possessions into canal boats and living a romantic life on the water. A casual stroll down Regent's Canal may convince you this is the way to live, but bare in mind the hidden cons of London nautical life: mooring fees, fuel, unlit walks down leafy paths frequented by degenerates...Don't say we didn't warn you!

The best of the best

London is full of interactive children's pursuits, and nothing beats discovering all the joys that the city has to offer to the little ones, so we thought we'd give you some inside tips on what there is!

- **Best Rainy Day Activity:** The Science Museum (Exhibition Road, SW7 2DD, 0870 870 4868) is great fun and one of London's most interactive museums. Don't miss the Launchpad gallery, which is full of hands-on exhibits to tinker with, simulators and a face morphing machine. The museum's occasional Science Nights are activity filled, with overnight camping in the building included. Entry is free. Open 7 days a week from 10am to 6pm.
- **Coolest Cinema:** The BFI London IMAX Cinema (1 Charlie Chaplin Walk, SE1 8XR, 020 7902 1234) has the largest screen (20 metres) in the country, as well as an 11,600-watt digital surround sound system with which to deafen your children. With most of the cinema's 3D programming dedicated to children's films, they'll be spoilt rotten by the whole experience; even the entrance to the place is cool, with futuristic blue lighting paving your way through the tunnels.
- **Goriest Tourist Haunt:** The London Dungeon (28-34 Tooley Street, SE1 2SZ, 020 7403 7221) specialises in the darker side of English history and has a preponderance of gruesome waxworks, theme rides and costumed staff to scare the bejesus out of your children, which they'll love (unless you've brought them up to be soft). Open all week from 11am to 5pm.
- **Best Tour For Budding Media Moguls:** The BBC Television Centre Tour (Wood Lane, W12 7RJ, 0870 603 0304) provides a chance for children 9 and over to take a behind the scenes look at the world of TV, as well as a chance to play in an interactive studio. A separate tour (ages 7 and over) entitled "The CBBC Experience" is based on the BBC's kids' channel and offers visitors the chance to roam around the Blue Peter garden, amongst other things. Regular tours are conducted every day except Sunday.
- **Best Ice Cream:** It's no secret that kids love ice cream, but the plethora of dodgy "Mr Whippy" vans selling their frozen wares in London can be improved upon. For outstanding homemade gourmet sorbets and exotic ice cream cones, there is no better place than the kiosk to the side of Golders Hill Park Refreshment House (North End Road, NW3 7HD, 020 8455 8010); prices are very reasonable and the park is a gorgeous setting within which to consume such tasty delights.
- **Best Inner City Farm:** Hackney City Farm (1a Goldsmiths Row, E2 8QA, 020 7729 6381). You don't want your child to be the one hiding on the bus on their first fieldtrip because they've never seen a cow. Hackney City Farm gives children and adults alike the chance to experience farming first-hand, interact with the animals and understand sustainable living, all of this in the heart of Hackney.
- **Best For Halloween Costumes:** Escapade (45-46 Chalk Farm Road, NW1 8AJ, 020 7485 7384) has been kitting kids out in all manner of costumes since 1982, and offers wigs (maybe one for Dad?), hats, masks, make-up, jokes and magic tricks. Perfect for trick or treat, or for those already bored of their child's ugly face.
- **Best Eatery For Families:** Maxwell's (8-9 James Street, WC2E 8BH) lies deep in the heart of Covent Garden and specialises in burgers (does any child not like burgers?) which won't break parents' banks. A kids' menu is provided, as well as activities and games.

Rainy day activities

Especially for when the infamous London weather puts a dampener on outdoor activities...

- **Cartoon Museum** (35 Little Russell Street, WC1A 2HH, 020 7580 8155) This fascinating place archives the development of cartoon art in Britain, from the 18th century through to the present day; best of all, the Young Artists' Gallery lets children try their hands at animation and claymation.
- **London Aquarium** (County Hall, Westminster Bridge Road, SE1 7PB, 020 7967 8000) One of the largest aquariums in the world, over 400 species of aquatic life (including the only zebra sharks in the U.K.) can be found within this building. With three floors, piranhas, and pools where you can prod things, there's more than enough to keep even the most jaded parent happy.

- **London Eye** (Jubilee Gardens, South Bank, SE1 7PB, 0870 500 0600) This 135-metre high riverside Ferris wheel offers breathtaking views of London in up to 25 miles in each direction, all from the vantage point of an air-conditioned glass pod. Book online to beat the queues.
- **Natural History Museum** (Cromwell Road, SW7 5BD, 020 7942 5000) Ever wanted to see a replica skeleton of a 26-metre long Diplodocus dinosaur? It's one of the 70 million items housed within this excellent museum, which also includes the Darwin Centre, a must for any budding paleontologists; non-nerds should love it too.
- **Madame Tussaud's** (Marylebone Road, NW1 5LR, 0870 999 0046) Infamous exhibition of waxworks, with recently introduced interactive exhibits giving you the chance to score a goal for England or sing with Britney Spears (she'll be the one lip-syncing). Worth booking online to avoid the often long queues.
- **Museum Of London** (150 London Wall, EC2Y 5HN, 0870 444 3852, some galleries undergoing renovation and due to re-open late 2009) Explains the history of London in vivid detail; the innovative layout consists of a chain of chronological galleries (no skipping to 1945, OK?) Also has fragments of the old London Wall in the grounds.
- **Peter Harrison Planetarium** (Royal Observatory Greenwich, Greenwich Park, SE10 9NF, 020 8312 8565) Open since 2007 and the only planetarium in London seats 120 and uses the latest technology to take you on an armchair tour of the universe. Children aged 4 and under will not be admitted.
- **Queens Ice And Bowl** (17 Queensway, W2 4QP, 020 7229 0172) An ice rink, ten pin bowling alleys and a pizza restaurant, it's the perfect opportunity for kids to stuff their faces whilst watching their Dad break a bone on the rink. Children's skating classes available.
- **Topsy Turvy World** (Brent Cross Shopping Centre, Prince Charles Drive, NW4 3FP, 020 8359 9920) A huge indoor playground in the middle of one of London's busiest shopping centres. There's more to this place than just bouncy things and over-excitement, it also offers baking activities (might as well get your children cooking for you early) and various classes.
- **Tower Of London** (Tower Hill, EC3N 4AB, 0870 756 7070) A cornucopia of royal history and English culture lies within the Tower's ancient walls, with royal jewels aplenty. Good for the whole family, and under 5s get in free. Avoid the queues by booking ahead.
- **The V&A Museum Of Childhood** (Cambridge Heath Road, E2 9PA, 020 8983 5200) This lesser known gem of the Victoria & Albert Museum houses the national childhood collection, which basically means it's full of toys, games, dolls, dollhouses, nursery antiques and children's costumes. There's no shortage of activities and events going on here to keep your kids occupied, and it's free.

Classes

A recent resurgence in the amount of out of school programmes being implemented in the capital means that there's more for your kids to do than ever before.

- **Art Club** (Orleans House Gallery, Riverside, TW1 3DJ, 020 8831 6000) A rare opportunity for 5-10 year olds to work with practicing artists and explore new techniques and materials. Every Wednesday and Thursday from 3.45-5pm.
- **Barnsbury One O'Clock Club** (Barnard Park, Hemingford Road, N1 0JU, 020 7278 9494) Fun and games for the under 5s.
- **Brixton Recreation Centre** (27 Brixton Station Road, SW9 8QQ, 020 7926 9779) Recently refurbished, this centre includes The Energy Zone (ages 5-15) for ball games and The Fitness Zone (ages 8-15) with SHOKK fitness equipment specifically designed for the younger body builder/steroid abuser.
- **Camden Square Play Centre** (Camden Square, NW1 9RE, 020 7485 6827) After school (and school holiday) centre with fun activities for children aged 4-12.
- **Camden Swiss Cottage Swimming Club** (Swiss Cottage Leisure Centre, Winchester Road, NW3 3NR, 020 7974 5440) Swimming lessons for children aged 4 and upward.
- **Chang's Hapkido Academy** (Topnotch Health Club, 3 Tudor Street, EC4Y 0AH, 07951 535876) Martial arts school with classes for ages 12 and upward.

- **The Circus Space** (Coronet Street, N1 6HD, 020 7613 4141) Prepare your children for a life in the circus with The Circus Space's variety of classes and workshops for all ages.
- **Crazee Kids** (Jackson Lane Community Centre, Archway Road, N6 5AA, Tuesdays), (Union Church & Community Centre, Weston Park, N8 9TA, Saturdays) 020 8444 5333, Weekly term-time dance, drama and music classes. Summer workshops.
- **Harringay Club** (Hornsey YMCA, 50 Tottenham Lane, N8 7EE, 020 8348 2124) A range of things to do for those aged up to 15, including a pre-school programme, gymnastics, ballet, street dance and kickboxing.
- **The Kids' Cookery School** (107 Gunnersbury Len W3 8HQ, 020 8992 8882) Get your kids cooking at this fine venue which offers classes and workshops for those aged 3 and upwards.
- **Kite Art Studios** (Priory Mews, 2B Bassein Park Road, W12 9RY, 020 8576 6278) Courses and workshops on painting, pottery and jewellery making amongst other fun activities for kids of all ages. Mother and toddler sessions too.
- **London Irish Centre** (50-52 Camden Square, NW1 9XB, 020 7916 7222) Irish dancing classes for beginners upwards, every Monday at 6pm, courtesy of the Barrett Semple-Morris School.
- **The Little Angel Theatre** (14 Dagmar Passage, Cross Street, N1 2DN, 020 7226 1787) Children's theatre offering after-school courses in puppet making, the art of puppetry performance and a Saturday Puppet Club.
- **The Little Gym** (Compass House, Riverside West, Smugglers Way, SW18 1DB, 020 8874 6567) Gymnastics and skills development within a relaxed environment for children aged up to 12.
- **Music House For Children** (Bush Hall, 310 Uxbridge Road, W12 7LJ, 020 8932 2652) Whether it's instrumental or singing lessons, this wonderful place can provide individual and group tuition and even caters for 1 year olds!
- **Painted Earth** (Arch 65, The Catacombs, Stables Market, NW1 8AH, 020 7424 8983) Ceramic arts classes supervised by staff. Children can make their own mugs and plates.
- **Pirate Castle** (Oval Road, NW1 7EA, 020 7267 6605) Kids can canoe or Kayak around Camden's only castle at this outdoor adventure club, which moonlights as a school and youth services centre.
- **Richmond Junior Chess Club** (ETNA Community Centre, 13 Rosslyn Road, TW1 2AR, 07720 716336) Chess classes with a mixture of instruction and play for those up to the age of 18.
- **Sobell Leisure Centre** (Hornsey Road, N7 7NY, 020 7609 2166) No need to book, just turn up for coached sessions in basketball, badminton, football and ice hockey amongst other sports. Children aged 7 and under must be accompanied by an adult.
- **Tricycle Theatre** (269 Kilburn High Road, NW6 7JR, 020 7328 1000) Not just a theatre/cinema/gallery, the Tricycle also runs term-time workshops in drama, storytelling and music.
- **Triyoga** (6 Erskine Road, NW3 3AJ, 020 7483 3344) Let the kids get their Zen on at after school yoga classes for ages 5 and over.
- **Westway Stables** (20 Stable Way, Latimer Road, W11 6QX, 020 8964 2140) Horse riding lessons for the over 5s in the heart of Notting Hill.

Babysitting/nanny/services

- **Nannies Unlimited** 11 Chelveton Road, SW15 1RN, 020 8788 9640
- **Nanny Search** 1st Floor, 1 Shepherds Hill, N6 5QJ, 020 8348 4111
- **Sleeptight Nannies** 20 Nursery Road, N14 5QB, 020 8292 2618
- **Top Notch Nannies** 49 Harrington Gardens, SW7 4JU, 020 7259 2626

Where to go for more info

www.kidslovelondon.com

www.dayoutwiththekids.co.uk

Shopping essentials

- **Baby Dior** 6 Harriet Street, SW1X 9JW, 020 7823 2039 – Encourage label envy as soon as possible.
- **Baby Munchkins** 186 Hoxton Street, N1 5LH, 020 7684 5994 – Baby wear.
- **Balloonland** 12 Hale Lane, NW7 3NX, 020 8906 3302 – Balloons and party supplies.
- **Benjamin Pollock's Toyshop** 44 The Piazza, Covent Garden WC2E 8RF, 020 7379 7866 – Toys.
- **Biff** 43 Dulwich Village, SE21 7BN, 020 8299 0911 – Designer and street brands.

- **Boomerang** 69 Blythe Road, W14 0HP, 020 7610 5232 – Clothes and necessities for tots.
- **Bonpoint** Chic clothes.
  17 Victoria Grove, W8 5RW – 020 7584 5131
  197 Westbourne Grove, W11 2SE – 020 7792 2515
  256 Brompton Road, SW3 2AS – 020 3263 5057
  35B Sloane Street, SW1X 9LP – 020 7235 1441
  38 Old Bond Street, W1S 4QW – 020 7495 1680
- **Burberry** 21-23 New Bond Street, W1S 2RE, 020 7839 5222 – Clothes.
- **Caramel** 291 Brompton Road, SW3 2DY, 020 7589 7001 – Cool clothes.
- **Catamini** – Babies and children's clothes. 33C King's Road, SW3 4LX – 020 7824 8897, 52 South Molton Street, W1Y 1HF – 020 7629 8099
- **Cheeky Monkeys** – Mainly wooden toys. 202 Kensington Park Road, W11 1NR – 020 7792 9022, 94 Kings Road, SW6 4UL – 020 7731 3037
- **Children's Book Centre** 237 Kensington High Street, W8 6SA, 020 7937 7497 – Books.
- **Coco Children's Boutique** 27A Devonshire Street, W1G 6PN, 020 7935 3554 – Children's boutique (fancy that!).
- **D2 Leisure** 201-203 Roman Road, E2 0QY, 020 8980 4966 – Bicycle shop.
- **Daisy & Tom** 181 King's Road, SW3 5EB, 020 7352 5000 – Clothes, toys and a carousel.
- **Davenports Magic Shop** 7 Adelaide Street, WC2N 4HZ, 020 7836 0408 – Magic shop.
- **Early Learning Centre** 36 King's Road, SW3 4UD, 020 7581 5764 – Educational toyshop.
- **Disney Store** – Disney merchandise.
  Unit 10, The Piazza, WC2E 8HD – 020 7836 5037
  22A & 26 The Broadway Shopping Centre, W6 9YD – 020 8748 8886
  360-366 Oxford Street, W1N 9HA – 020 7491 9136
- **Eric Snook's Toyshop** 32 Covent Garden Market, WC1 8RE, 020 7379 7681 – Toys and teddies.
- **Escapade** 45-46 Chalk Farm Road, NW1 8AJ, 020 7485 7384 – Costumes and masks.
- **The Farmyard** 63 Barnes High Street, SW13 9LF, 020 8878 7338 – Toys for younger children and babies.
- **GapKids/Baby Gap**
  35 Hampstead High Street, NW3 1QE – 020 7794 9182
  146-148 Regent Street, W1B 5SH – 020 7287 5095
  Brent Cross Shopping Centre, NW4 3FB – 020 8203 9696
  122 King's Road, SW3 4TR – 020 7823 7272
  4 Queens Road, SW19 8YE- 020 8947 9074
  101-111 Kensington High Street, W8 5SA – 020 7368 2900
  260-262 Chiswick High Road, W4 1PD – 020 8995 3255
  47-49 St John's Wood High Street, NW8 7NJ – 020 7586 6123
  151 Queensway, W2 4YL – 020 7221 8039
  330-340 Cabot Place East, E14 4QT – 020 7513 0241
  121-123 Long Acre, WC2E 9PA – 020 7836 0646
- **Green Rabbit** 20 Briston Grove, N8 9EX, 020 8348 3770 – Contemporary kids' wear.
- **Hamley's** 188-196 Regent Street, W1B 5BT, 020 7153 9000 – Toys galore, tourists galore.
- **Happy Returns** 36 Rosslyn Hill, NW3 1NH, 020 7435 2431 – Toys again!
- **Honeyjam** 267 Portobello Road, W11 1LR, 020 7243 0449 – Retro and vintage toys and rocking horses.
- **Igloo Kids** Wide range of kids' clothes. 300 Upper Street, N1 2TU – 020 7354 7300, 80 St John's Wood, NW8 7SH – 020 7483 2332
- **Infantasia Unit 103** Wood Green Shopping City, N22 6YA, 020 8889 1494 – Furniture and bedding.
- **International Magic** 89 Clerkenwell Road, EC1R 5BX, 020 7405 7324 – Magic shop.
- **Joujou & Lucy** 32 Clifton Road, W9 1ST, 020 7289 0866 – Children's boutique.
- **Kent & Carey** 154 Wandsworth Bridge Road, SW6 2UH, 020 7736 5554 – Classic children's clothes.
- **Little Stinkies** 15 Victoria Grove, W8 5RW, 020 7052 0077 – Dolls' houses, toys and puppet theatres.
- **Marie Chantal** 148 Walton Street, SW3 2JJ, 020 7838 1111 – Children's fashion.
- **MIMMO** 602 Fulham Road, SW6 5PA, 020 7731 4706 – Designer duds.
- **Mothercare** – The leading chain for baby stuff in the UK; will sell you everything but the baby.
  Brent Cross Shopping Centre, NW4 3FD – 020 8202 5377
  416 Brixton Road, SW9 7AY – 020 7733 1494
  Unit 7, The Waterglade Centre, 1-8 The Broadway, W5 2ND – 0208 579 6181

Ravenside Retail Park, Angel Road, N18 3HA – 020 8807 5518

146 High Street, SE9 1BJ – 020 8859 7957

4 Palace Gardens, EN2 6SN – 020 8367 1188

316 North End Road, SW6 1NG – 020 7381 6387

Kings Mall Shopping Centre, W6 0PZ – 020 8600 2860

448 Holloway Road, N7 6QA – 020 7607 0915

112 High Street, TW3 1NA – 020 8577 1767

Unit 1A, Richmond Retail Park, Mortlake Road, Kew – 020 8878 3758

41 Riverdale High Street, SE13 7EP – 020 8852 2167

526-528 Oxford Street, W1C 1LW – 0845 365 0515

Unit 2, Aylesham Centre, Rye Lane, SE15 5EW – 020 7358 0093

33-34 The Mall, E15 1XD – 020 8534 5714

BHS Surrey Quays Shopping Centre, Redriff Road, SE16 7LL – 020 7237 2025

Unit 59, Southside Shopping Centre, SW18 4TF – 020 8877 4180

Unit Lsu4, Centre Court, SW19 8YA – 020 8944 5296

38-40 High Road, N22 6BX – 020 8888 6920

62 Powis Street, SE18 1LQ – 020 8854 3540

- **Never Never Land** 3 Mildhurst Parade, Fortis Green, N10 3EJ, 020 883 3997 – Toys and dolls.
- **Olive Loves Alfie** 84 Stoke Newington Church Street, N16 0AP, 020 7241 4212 – Children's lifestyle boutique.
- **Patrick's Toys & Models** 107 Lillie Road, SW6 7SX, 020 7385 9864 – Outdoor games and equipment.
- **Patrizia Wigan** 19 Walton Street, SW3 2HX, 020 7823 7080 – Clothing boutique.
- **Petit Bateau** 62 South Molton Street, W1K 5SR, 020 7491 4498 – Luxurious baby wear.
- **Petite Ange** 6 Harriet Street, SW1X 9JW, 020 7235 7737 – Exclusive clothing.
- **Please Mum** 85 Knightsbridge, SW1X 7RB, 020 7486 1380 – Expensive clothing.
- **Pom D'Api** 3 Blenheim Crescent, W11 2EE, 020 7243 0535 – Classy shoes.
- **QT Toys** 90 Northcote Road, SW11 6QN, 020 7223 8637 – Toys, games and gifts.
- **Rachel Riley** 14 Pont Street, SW1X 9EN, 020 7935 7007 – Clothes.
- **Rainbow** 253 Archway Road, N6 5BS, 020 8340 9700 – Toys, games and clothes.
- **Showroom** 64 Titchfield Street, W1W 7QH, 020 7636 2501 – Funky children's clothes.
- **Soup Dragon** 27 Topsfield Parade, Tottenham Lane, N8 8PT, 020 8348 0224 – Toys and clothes.
- **The Shoe Station** 3 Station Approach, Kew Gardens, TW9 3QB, 020 8940 9905 – Shoes and footwear.
- **Their Nibs** 214 Kensington Park Road, W11 1NR, 020 7221 4263 – Designer clothes and bedding.
- **Tots** 39 Turnham Green Terrace, W4 1RG, 020 8995 0520 – Clothes boutique.
- **Toys R Us** - Toys, toys, toys.

Tilling Road (opposite Brent Cross Shopping Centre), NW2 1LW – 020 8209 0019

Great Cambridge Road, EN1 3RN – 020 8364 6600

Hayes Road, UB2 5LN – 020 8561 4681

760 Old Kent Road, SE15 1NJ – 020 7732 7322

- **Traditional Toys** Chelsea Green, 53 Godfrey Street, SW3 3SX, 020 7352 1718 – Timeless toys.
- **The Little White Company** 261 Pavillion Road, SW1X 0BP, 020 7881 0783 – Clothing, bed linen and furniture.

For many, the Internet is *the* key to the city. Before the dawning of the Internet, we Dickensian scamps had to scurry around in the filth foraging for information in 'books' and by talking to actual 'people'. Now that the future is here, Londoners can navigate their city's streets, explore its dark history, organise a debauched weekend in Chiswick or, as is more likely, peer over the shoulder of men in raincoats in Internet Cafes.

Internet Cafes are *everywhere*. In fact you probably live in one. They can range from the dimly lit 'Money Transfer' shacks that have an air of illegality, to the over-orange **Easyeverything** chain that dominated the market before home internet use skyrocketed in the late 90s. You can escape the grim D.I.Y. flea pits in chic coffee outlets like **Coffee** @ (155 Brick Lane 020 7247 6735) but sharpen your elbows as space is tight. **Cyberia Cafe** near Goodge Street (39 Whitfield Street Tel No – 020 7209 0984) claims to have been the first Internet Cafe in the world and is still very plush. To be fair, internet use in these places is usually criminally cheap : as low as 50p per hour in the non-tourist areas. For a large list of London internet cafes check out http://www.allinlondon.co.uk/directory/1166.php.

London was recently crowned WiFi capital of the world, owing to its astronomical rate of increase in WiFi networks. It is becoming more and more difficult to move in your local cafe without catching the sharp edge of a laptop. The **Apostrophe Cafe** chain is efficient, expensive and has WiFi as standard. Like many WiFi-compatible eateries, wireless access is limited to an hour and they give out passwords to paying customers only. If you wish to cook your internal organs with your PowerBook you can do so in hundreds of cafes in London; for a decent online map of WiFi locations check out http://londonist.com/2007/05/free_wifi_in_lo.php. Of course there is always the pirate option—dodging the Community Officers and fiendishly stealing a neighbours connection. Beware however, in 2007 a man was arrested in what was the first case of WiFi theft—he was balancing his laptop on his garden wall!

A legal alternative is available to those of you who have joined the growing legion of smartphone users. If you "need" to be connected at all times via a data plan and don't want the commitment of a long-term contract try Gifgaff (www.giffgaff.com). For £10 you can get 250 minutes, unlimited texts and unlimited data for a month with no additional cost incurred. They offer a best in business rate for the Internet addicts among you.

Useful And/Or Fun London Links:

www.notfortourists.com/London.aspx
www.fedbybirds.com
www.royalparks.org.uk
www.tfl.gov.uk
www.londonist.com
www.londonfreelist.com
www.davehill.typepad.com
www.shadyoldlady.com
www.derelictlondon.com
www.walk-london.blogspot.com
www.hiddenlondon.com
www.londonbloggers.iamcal.com
www.london-underground.blogspot.com
www.fancyapint.com
www.dailycandy.com/london
www.gumtree.com
www.timeout.com
www.brickads.blogspot.com
www. wildinlondon.blogspot.com
www. westlondonblogger.blogspot.com
www. dalstonoxfamshop.blogspot.com
www.viewlondon.co.uk
www.lecool.com/cities/london
www.deadcafesociety.org.uk
www.londonreviewofbreakfasts.blogspot.com
www.beerintheevening.com
www.london-se1.co.uk
www.talkonthetube.com
www.london.thewayweseeit.org
londoncabby.blogspot.com

The doom-sayers have less cause to complain about the decline of Gayhood in London recently, what with **Heaven** (London's self-proclaimed most famous gay club) hanging on and new nights popping up everywhere. Yes, popular Indie discos **Popstarz** and **Rebel Rebel** have relocated but **Girl's Action** at Ghetto promises great things and we are so in love with 'polysexual' club **Dalston Supermarket** at the moment. Of course every time one door (read: gay club) closes another one opens, and let's face it, the latter will probably open later and sell you even cheaper Red Bull and vodka.

One of the most exciting developments in the past few years has been the advent of what has been dubbed London's new 'Gay Village'—the cluster of clubs, saunas and after-hours hangover incubators that have sprung up in Vauxhall. Now it's possible, though still just as inadvisable, to party from Thursday through to Tuesday without stopping to reapply deodorant, or think about the consequences of what you're doing—hooray. The small outcrop of gay and 'polysexual' nights in the East End, is still thriving, and offers another refreshing alternative to Soho for those in search of an aggressive fashion consciousness and a less cruisy atmosphere. This said, if you can handle bright lights, pop music, tight t-shirts and a lot of hair gel, you'll still have massive amounts of fun around Soho and Old Compton Street, the traditional central London gay epicentre. This area is always buzzing, day and night, and is a great place to sit back and do some people watching as well as to go out and, y'know, go crazy.

For girls there is still room for improvement, with options fewer and less centralised, but **The Minorics'** new Girls' night is a blast and the continuing women-only nights at **Village** and **Element** are cause for celebration. Many mixed and polysexual nights (such as Motherfucker at **Garden's Boudoir**) also draw large female crowds, and though dedicated lesbian bars and clubs are few and far between, there is enough going on in the city to make any day of the week a possible night out.

Websites

www.dirtydirtydancing.com - Super-airbrushed photos from many of the trendier Soho and east London nights.

http://scene-out.com - Comprehensive mainstream scene guide.

www.gingerbeer.co.uk - Lesbian guide to London.

www.girlguidelondon.co.uk - Does what it says on the tin.

www.gmfa.org.uk - Gay men's health charity.

www.patroc.com/london/clubs.html-Great source for upcoming gay events.

www.pinkdate.com - Speed dating events for gay men and women in central London.

Publications

The following are all free listings/scene magazines that can be found in most gay shops and venues (anywhere on Old Compton Street should have some copies lying around):

Boyz Magazine - Weekly scene news and listings, out Thursdays. www.boyz.co.uk

G3 Magazine - Lesbian scene, monthly. www.g3mag.co.uk

Out in the City Mag - Monthly London lifestyle magazine for gay men. www.outmag.co.uk

Qx Magazine - Gay men's mag. www.qxmagazine.com

Shops

Gay's the Word, 66 Marchmont Street, WC1N 1AB, 020 7278 7654, http://freespace.virgin.net/gays.theword/, The only dedicated Gay and Lesbian Bookshop in London, recently threatened by rising rent. Visit whilst it's still there!

Prowler, 5–7 Brewer Street, W1F 0RF, 020 7734 4031, The ultimate gay men's shop, stocking everything from (skimpy) clothes to sex toys plus mountains of lube, pornography, and the other usual suspects.

Sh! Women's Erotic Emporium, 57 Hoxton Square N1 6PD, 020 7697 9072, http://www.sh-womenstore.com/, London's only female-orientated sex shop, run by women, for women.

Sexual Health

A comprehensive list of London clinics that offer same day HIV testing and PEP treatments for gay/bisexual men is available at www.gmfa.org.uk/londonservices/clinics. CLASH, below, is particularly recommended.

CLASH (Central London Action on Street Health), 11 Warwick Street, W1B 5NA, 020 7734 1794, Friday night clinic for gay men, with incredibly friendly staff who will offer comfort and advice. Same day (often instant) HIV testing, PEP treatment. Fridays, 5 - 8.30pm, call for an appointment.

Support Organizations

Again, a more comprehensive list can be found at the GMFA website: www.gmfa.org.uk/londonservices/support-groups/index

Stonewall, Tower Building, York Road, SE1 7NX, www.stonewall.org.uk, Gay rights charity and lobbying group.

PACE Youthwork Service, 34 Hartham Road, N7 9LJ, 020 7700 1323, www.outzone.org, Support organization for gay and lesbian youths under 25. Organizes regular social events and offers one to one consultations with advisors: phone or visit the website to get involved.

London Friend, 86 Caledonian Road, N1 9DN, 020 7833 1674, www.londonfriend.org.uk, Voluntary organization which runs several helplines, group workshops and social events, as well as offering advice on reporting hate crime.

London Lesbian and Gay Switchboard, 020 7837 7324 (helpline), 020 7689 8501 (Volunteers), Counselling and information service.

Kairos in Soho, Unit 10, 10-11 Archer Street, W1D 7AZ, 020 7437 6063, www.kairosinsoho.org.uk, Gay and lesbian charity which organises a variety of recreational events to promote the health, well being and development of the LGBT community.

Naz Project London, Palingswick House, 241 King Street, W6 9LP, 020 8741 1879 www.naz.org.uk, Charity that organizes support and sexual health services for black and ethnic minority communities in London. Various services, including free one-on-one counselling and support groups are available, phone or check website for details.

GALOP, PO Box 32810, N1 3ZD, 020 7704 6767, www.galop.org.uk, Charity specialising in advice about reporting hate crime.

Annual Events

Pride London, www.pridelondon.org, Large pride festival, takes place every July.

GFEST – www.gaywisefestival.org.uk, London's premier cross-arts festival, GFEST features a variety of established and new LBG&T artists. The festival promotes the queer arts scene while keeping LBGT human rights the underlying focus of proceedings.

London Lesbian and Gay Film Festival, www.bfi.org.uk/llgff, Film festival at the BFI on South Bank, March–April.

London LGBT History Month, www.lgbthistorymonth.co.uk, Nationwide awareness month, with various talks and events staged in London, every February.

Gay/mixed venues

Soho:

79CXR, 79 Charing Cross Road, WC2H 0NE, 020 7734 0769, Dingy bar with middle aged crowd.

The Admiral Duncan, 54 Old Compton Street, W1D 4UB, 020 7437 5300

Barcode Soho, 3-4 Archer Street W1D 7AT, 020 7734 3342

Box, 32–34 Monmouth Street, WC2H 9HA, 020 7240 5828, Civilised bar and eatery.

Comptons, 53–57 Old Compton Street, W1D 6HN, 020 7479 7961, Crammed gay pub.

Duke of Wellington, 77 Wardour Street, W1D 6QA

The Edge, 11 Soho Square, W1D 3QF, 020 7439 1313

G-A-Y Bar, 30 Old Compton Street, W1D 5JX, 020 7494 2756, Poptastic bunker. Video walls and cheap drinks.

G-A-Y Late, 5 Goslett Yard, WC2H 0ER, 020 7734 9858, Cheap drinks and pop videos wipe out brain functions 'til 3am.

Ghetto, Falconberg Court, W1D 3AB, 020 7287 3726, Loud electro at this busy gay club. Thursday is ladies night.

Halfway to Heaven, 7 Duncannon Street, WC2N 4JF, 020 7321 2791.

Heaven, Under the Arches, Villiers Street, WC2N 6NG, 020 7930 2020, Legendary gay club. An institution.

Ku Bar, 30 Lisle Street, WC2H 7BA, 020 7437 4303, Newly relocated bar for the young and clueless.

Kudos, 10 Adelaide Street, WC2N 4HZ, 020 7379 4573

Profile, 56–57 Frith Street, W1D 3JG, 020 7734 8300

Shadow Lounge, 5 Brewer Street, W1F, 020 7439 4089, Supposed to be a shi-shi cocktail lounge. Hmmmm.

Soho Revue Bar, 11 Walkers Court, Brewer Street, W1F 0ED, Cabaret acts followed by dancing 'til late.
The Village, 81 Wardour Street, W1D 6QD, 020 7434 2124, Tacky, flirtatious bar spread across two floors.
Trash Palace, 11 Wardour Street, W1D 6PG, 020 7734 0522, Bratty queer indie bar.

North:
Cosmo Lounge, 43 Essex Road, N1 2SF, 020 7688 0051, Subdued bar, normally full of regulars.
Central Station, 37 Wharfdale Road, N1 9SD, 020 7278 3294. Pub/club with ominously blacked out windows.
The Green, 74 Upper Street N1 0NY, 0871 971 4097, Innocuous gay bar/restaurant frequented by many unsuspecting straight couples.
King Edward VI Pub, 25 Bromfield Street, N1 0PZ
The Black Cap, 171 Camden High Street, NW1 7JY, 020 7428 2721, Slightly crummy gay pub.

East:
Bistrotheque, 23–27 Wadeson Street, E2 9DR, Jonny Woo's restaurant, great food and drag acts.
The Black Horse, 168 Mile End Road, E1 4LJ, 020 7790 1684
George and Dragon, 2 Hackney Road, E2 7NS, Small, atmospheric pub full of trendy boys and girls.
Joiners Arms, 116–118, Hackney Road, E2 7Q, Late opening free-for-all with a wonderfully mixed crowd. ('til 2/3am most nights)

South:
Area, 67–68 Albert Embankment, SE1 7TP
Barcode Vauxhall, 69 Albert Embankment, 020 7582 4180
The Two Brewers, 114 Clapham High Street, SW4 7UJ, 020 7498 4971
Depot, 66 Albert Embankment, SE11 7TP, Sister club of Area, with a more cruisy vibe.
Fire, South Lambeth Road, SW8 1RT, 020 7434 1113, The quintessential Vauxhall club. Open pretty much forever, bulging muscles everywhere.
The Fort, 131 Grange Road, Bermondsey, SE1 3AL - Themed cruising/fetish/sex bar.
Kazbar Clapham, 50 Clapham High Street, SW4 7UL, 020 7622 0070
Little Apple Bar, 98 Kennington Lane, SE11 4XD Mixed/lesbian bar.
The Powder Monkey, 22 King William Walk, SE10 PHU, 020 8293 5928, thepowdermonkey.net
Royal Vauxhall Tavern, 372 Kennington Lane, SE11 5HY, 020 7820 1222
South Central, 349 Kennington Lane, SE11 5QY, 020 7793 0903
Substation South, 9 Brighton Terrace, SW9 8DJ, 020 7737 2095
XXL, 51–53 Southwark Street, SE1 1TE, www.fatsandsmalls.com, Busy bear club.

West:
Bromptons, 294 Old Brompton Road, SW5 9JF, 020 77370 1344
The Coleherne, 261 Old Brompton Road, SW5 9JA020 7244 5951

Recommended Nights

Club Motherfucker, second Saturdays @ Barden's Boudoir, 38 Stoke Newington Road, Dalston, N16 7XJ, Polysexual band night. Sweaty, noisy, very much about the music.
Circus, Fridays @ Soho Revue Bar, 11 Walkers Court, Brewer Street, W1F 0ED, Drag Queen Jodie Harsh's long running night attracts its fair share of celebrities from both on and off the scene. Get there early or be prepared to queue.
DTPM, www.myspace.com/dtpm, Legendary event, no longer with a fixed location. See site for details of upcoming parties.
For3ign, Saturdays @ Bar Music Hall, 134 Curtain Road, EC2A 3AR, 020 7613 5951, Outlandish costumes and, of course, thumping electro.
Horsemeat Disco, Sundays @ South Central, Italo and 70s Disco bring all sorts to this fantastic night, originally a bear love club.
Icon, Sundays @ Essence, 562a Mile End Road, E3 4PU, 0208 980 6427, mob 07813 110 113 (weekly), New night in the East End. Yet to prove itself.
Issue, monthly (check site for details) @ Electricity Showrooms, 39a Hoxton Square, N1 6NN, Issueclub.blogspot.com. Polysexual parties to coincide with the launch of this scene/fashion magazine.
Matinee, monthly (check site) @ Fabric, 77a Charterhouse Street, EC1M 3HN, 020 7335 8898, www.matineelondon.com, Irregular gay night at this enormous club in Farringdon.
Popstarz, Fridays @ Sin, 144 Charing Cross Road, WC2H 0LB, 020 7240 1900, Gay indie institution, recently relocated.

Trailer Trash, Fridays @ On the Rocks, 25 Kingsland Road, E2 8AA, 020 7688 0339, The dirtiest electro and the drunkest you've ever been. Crammed with sweating fashionistas.

Wet Yourself, Sundays @ Aquarium, 256–264 Old Street, EC1V 9DD, 020 7251 6136, This used to be the place to be after Boombox. It's lost only a little of its charm since (mixed polysexual crowd).

Lesbian Venues

Blush Bar, 8 Cazenove Road, Stoke Newington N16, 020 7923 9202, www.blushbar.co.uk

Candy Bar, 23-24 Bateman Street, W1V 5HR, 020 7437 1977, The reluctant epicentre of the Lesbian scene in Soho.

First Out Café Bar, Soho - 52 St Giles High St, WC2H 8LH, 020 7240 8042, Cafe with nightly events. All girls on Friday.

Oak Bar, 79 Green Lanes, N16, www.oakbar.co.uk, 020 7354 2791,

The Star At Night, 22 Great Chapel Street, Soho, W1 8FR, 020 7434 3749, Mixed cocktail bar with a predominantly female crowd.

Recommended Nights

100% Babe, Bank Holiday Sundays @ The Roxy, 3 Rathbone Place, W1P 1DA, 020 7636 1598, Irregular party for fans of funky house, R&B, old skool and electropop.

Blue Light, last Saturdays @ Bar Med, Triton Court, 14 Finsbury Square, EC2, 020 7588 3056

Club Wotever, first Saturday of the month @ The Masters Club, 12 Denman Street, Piccadilly, W1D 7HH, 020 7734 4243, Draggy night with a large 'King' quota.

Code, irregular night @ the Enclave, 25–27 Brewer Street, W1F 0RR, www.club-code.net - check website for details.

Girls on Girls, Wednesdays @ Village, 81 Wardour Street, W1D 6QD, 020 7434 2124

Lounge, second Thursdays @ Vertigo, 1 Leicester Square, WC2H 7NA, 020 7734 0900, Relaxed cocktail night at this swish Leicester Square club.

Miss Shapes, Thursdays @ Ghetto, Falconberg Court, W1D 3AB, 020 7287 3726, Popular girls-only indie night.

Pink, Wednesdays @ Element, 4-5 Greek Street, W1D 4DD, 020 7434 3323.

Play, irregular night @ Bar Rumba, 35 Shaftesbury Ave, W1D 7EP, 020 7287 2715, www.myspace.com/_clubplay

Rumours, last Saturday of the month @ 64–73 Minories, EC3, 07949 477 804

Smack, irregular night @ various venues, check website, www.myspace.com/smackclub

Wish, first Saturdays @ Gramophone, 60–62 Commercial Street, E1 6LT, Style conscious night for young techno-heads and indie girls.

Women's Anarchist Nuisance Cafe, Penultimate wednesdays @ the RampART Creative Centre and Social Space, Rampart St, Aldgate, E1 2LA, Social group and cooperative vegan women's cafe.

Stickier Options

Club Fukk, second Fridays @ Central Station, 37 Wharfdale Road, N1 9SD, 020 7278 3294, www.centralstation.co.uk or www.woteverworld.com/id12.html, Predominantly Lesbian fetish/play club. One of many sex/cruising nights at the venue – check site for details.

Chariots, www.gaysauna.co.uk, Popular chain of gay saunas, with branches at the following locations: *Shoreditch*: 1 Fairchild Street, EC2A 3NS, *Waterloo*: 101 Lower Marsh, SE1 7AB, 020 7401 8484, *Limehouse*: 574 Commercial Road, E14 7JD, 020 7791 2808, *Streatham*: 292 [rear of] Streatham High Road SW16 6HG, 020 8696 0929, *Farringdon*: 57 Cowcross Street, EC1M 6BX, 020 7251 5553, *Vauxhall*: 63-64 Albert Embankment, SE1, 020 7247 5333

The Fort,131 Grange Road, Bermondsey, SE1 3AL Themed cruising/fetish/sex bar.

Hard On, monthly @ Hidden, 100 Tinworth Street SE11 5EQ, www.hardonclub.co.uk, Rubber and fetish sex club for gay and bisexual men and women.

The Hoist, Arch 47b & 47c, South Lambeth Road SW8 1RH, 020 7735 9972, www.thehoist.co.uk Fetish sex club with strict dress codes, check website for details.

Nudity, first Fridays @ Hidden, 100 Tinworth Street SE11 5EQ, Nude men's dance/play club.

Purrrr, 87 Fortess Road, Kentish Town NW5, www.purrrr.co.uk, Monthly S&M play club for Lesbians.

London Timeline

A timeline of significant events in London's history.

50: The Romans found Londinium, building the first London Bridge.

61: Queen Boudicca burns Londinium down.

100: Londinium becomes the capital of Roman Britain.

200: The Romans build the London Wall.

410: Roman occupation ends and Londinium is largely abandoned for many years.

604: King Aethelbert of Kent completes the first St Paul's Cathedral.

700: The Saxons build Lundenwic a mile to the west of old Londinium.

851: The Vikings burn Lundenwic down (starting to see a pattern, here?)

878: Alfred The Great defeats the Vikings and establishes a new settlement within the Roman Walls.

1013: The Viking King Canute besieges London.

1066: William The Conqueror becomes the first king to be crowned at Westminster Abbey.

1088: William The Conqueror builds the Tower Of London.

1097: William Rufus builds Westminster Hall—later part of the Houses Of Parliament.

1176: The wooden London Bridge is replaced by a stone structure.

1343: 'The Canterbury Tales' author Geoffrey Chaucer is born in London.

1348: The Black Death wipes out between a third and half of London's population in 18 months.

1381: Peasants revolt, storming the Tower Of London.

1599: William Shakespeare's theatre company The Chamberlain's Men build the Globe Theatre.

1605: Guy Fawkes' Gunpowder Plot fails to blow up the Palace Of Westminster.

1635: Hyde Park opens to the public.

1649: King Charles I is beheaded at Whitehall.

1665: The Great Plague kills a fifth of London's population (starting to see another pattern, here?)

1666: The Fire of London destroys 60% of the city, including St Paul's Cathedral, but wipes out the plague. This really must have been a great year.

1708: The new St Paul's Cathedral is completed by Sir Christopher Wren.

1732: Downing Street becomes the home of the Prime Minister.

1750: Westminster Bridge is built.

1814: Lord's Cricket Ground is opened.

1829: Robert Peel establishes the Metropolitan Police force, policemen known as 'Bobbies' or 'Peelers'

1831: London becomes the world's biggest city.

1834: The Houses Of Parliament are built.

1843: Nelson's Column Is completed in Trafalgar Square.

1851: Six million people gawp at newfangled technology and design at The Great Exhibition.

1858: The Great Stink inspires the 19th century's biggest civil engineering project—London's sewerage system.

London Timeline

1863: The first London Underground line is built.

1876: The Albert Memorial to Queen Victoria's husband Prince Albert is completed.

1877: The first Wimbledon Championship takes place. A Brit wins, but only Brit's are playing.

1884: An imaginary line through Greenwich Royal Observatory is internationally accepted as the Prime Meridian. Except by the French.

1887: Arthur Conan Doyle publishes the first Sherlock Holmes story 'A Study In Scarlet.'

1888: Jack The Ripper's first victim, Mary Ann Nichols, is murdered.

1908: London hosts the Olympics for the first time.

1915: German Zeppelin airships launch first air raids on London, ultimately killing over 700 people.

1923: Wembley Stadium is built in 300 days, costing £750,000.

1940: The Blitz begins—German bombs kill over 30,000 Londoners by the end of WW2 and destroy large areas of the city.

1946: Heathrow Airport opens for commercial flights.

1948: The second London Olympics is held.

1951: The Royal Festival Hall is built as part of the Festival Of Britain.

1952: The Great Smog, caused by a combination of fog and coal smoke, kills 4000 people in five days.

1956: The Clean Air Act puts an end to London's smog problems.

1965: The Notting Hill Carnival is established by West London's Caribbean community

1966: England win the FIFA World Cup at Wembley stadium, better still, against Germany.

1969: The Beatles play their last ever gig on the roof of the Apple building.

1976: The Sex Pistols play at the first 'International Punk Festival' at the 100 Club on Oxford Street.

1981: The first London Marathon.

1983: Six people are killed when the IRA bombs Harrods.

1991: London's tallest building, One Canada Square (better known as Canary Wharf), is completed.

2000: Ken Livingstone becomes London's first directly-elected Mayor.

2005: 52 people are killed by four suicide bombers on Underground trains and a bus.

2007: The rebuilt Wembley Stadium is completed after four years, costing £778 million.

2008: Boris Johnson defeats Red Ken in the London Mayoral Election with a promise to re-instate the Routemaster.

2011: Royal Wedding mania.

2012: London's third Olympics held; Danny Boyle adapts NHS as West End spectacular.

2012: Queen Elizabeth II celebrates her Diamond Jubilee with a rainy-day boat show.

London is an egotist—it just *loves* to talk about itself. As you might expect, there's a vast array of print and online publications, not to mention radio stations, designed to let the city do exactly that. Single-handedly forcing the environmental movement back twenty years are freebie dailies **The Metro** and the more fiscally orientated **City A.M.** Free weeklies to look out for include **Stylist** on Wednesday's for girls, **ShortList** on Thursday's for boys and **Sport** on Friday's for, well, sports enthusiast. The Aussies are pushing **TNT** at tube stations on Monday, but it lacks the wider appeal. The new addition to the freesheet line-up is now the substantial **Evening Standard**, which went free in January of last year and is the preferred news-roundup du jour of suburbanites and city types alike, if only for the sudoku and quick crossword puzzles. Online, **www.thisislocallondon.co.uk** condenses forty local newspapers into 'one online voice'. On the wireless, **Capital Radio** broadcasts an irksome parade of popular hits and frenetic DJs, whilst **Heart** and **Magic** corner the market on lip-trembling power ballads, mid-paced chart rock and wacky quizzes. All of the British Broadcasting Corporation's national radio stations—including the snazzy, young(ish) **Radio 1** and ovaltine-drinkers' choice **Radio 2**—are based in London, as is (surprisingly) **BBC London**, a decent option for weekend sports coverage. Cooler, urban types are more likely to be tuning into **Kiss FM** (dance, hip hop), **Smooth FM** (jazz, soul) or **Choice** (dancehall, roots), while alternative rockers tune their dials anguishedly to **XFM**, and the talkative indulge in unreserved subjectivity over at **LBC.** Of course, the undisputed king of alternative London broadcasting is **Resonance FM**, a 'community run' station which has just been granted a permanent licence: expect everything from 'Calling All Pensioners' to live psycho-geographic wanders around city's warped dark streets. Un-licensed and illegal pirate radio stations offer a slightly un-hinged ear into the fringes of London's musical society. Twiddle your dials around the extreme ends of the FM spectrum for pirate stalwarts **Rude FM** and **Kool FM**. On the telly-box, the latest news is spoon-fed to you on ITV's **London Tonight** show and delivered in short slots at the end of the BBC and ITV national news programs. For those actually risking going outside, **Time Out** remains the socialite's sacred text.

Print

The Evening Standard Northcliffe House, 2 Derry Street, W8 5TT, 020 7938 6000, Newly reinstated as a freesheet, it continues to be London's favourite journey home read.

Metro Northcliffe House, 2 Derry Street, W8 5TT, 020 7651 5200, Free underground daily from same stable.

City AM New London Bridge House, 25 London Bridge St, SE1 9SG, 020 7015 1200, Free morning business bulletin for city-goers.

Sport Third Floor, Courtyard Building, 11 Curtain Road, EC2A 3LT, 0207 375 3175 Free sports overview every Friday.

TimeOut London 251-255 Tottenham Court Road, Universal House, W1T 7AB, 0207 813 3000, Listings & reviews across the city. Pretty damned comprehensive.

London Gazette PO Box 7923, SE1 5ZH, 020 7394 4517, Capital's oldest paper—official journals record of the government.

London Literary Review 44 Lexington Street, W1 0LW, 020 7437 9392, Fortnightly publication for the bookish.

The London Magazine 32 Addison Grove, W4 1ER, 020 8400 5882, Bi-monthly Arts reviews.

TNT London 14-15 Childs Place, Earls Court, SW5 9RX, 020 7373 3377, Info and opinion for the antipodean set.

Loot 31 John Street, WC1N 2AT, 0871 222 5000, Classifieds: flats, bought/sold and lonely hearts.

The Voice GV Media Group Ltd, Northern & Shell Tower, 6th Floor, 4 Selsdon Way, E14 9GL, 020 7510 0340, African-British national.

London Bichitra Bangalink Media, 272 Holton Road, Barry, CF63 4HU, Bengali monthly.

Polish Express 603 Cumberland House, 80 Scrubs Lane, NW10 6RF, 020 8964 4488 , News and info for the Polish community.

Reflect Magazine 130 Stroud Green Road, N4 3RZ, 020 7272 8502, For 'thinking, young Muslims'.

Live Listings Magazine Keith Villa (House), 102 Mallinson Rd, SW11 1BN, 020 7207 2734 Guide to what's on in multicultural London.

ShortList 6 Emerald Street, London, WC1N 3QA, 020 7242 5873, A Thursday freebie for metrosexuals.

Sport 18 Hatfields, London SE1 8DJ, 020 7959 7800, A free Friday magazine dedicated to, you guessed it, sports.

Stylist 6 Emerald Street, London, WC1N 3QA, 020 7242 5873, London's first free women's glossy. Handed out on Wednesdays.

Public Radio

FM

89.1 BBC Radio Two: Middle-aged music and chat.
91.3 BBC Radio Three: Classical.
93.5 BBC Radio Four: Current affairs, comfort listening.
94.9 BBC London: Chat, sport.
95.8 Capital FM: Chart, capers.
96.9 Choice FM: Hip Hop, R&B.
97.3 LBC: Phone in, chat.
98.8 BBC Radio 1: Pop, rock, more pop.
100.0 Kiss FM: Dance, urban.
100.9 Classic FM: Classical.
102.2 Smooth FM: Jazz, soul.
102.6 Essex FM: Audible in East London.
103.3 London Greek Radio: Um, Greek.
103.5 BBC Essex: Audible out East.
104.4 Resonance FM: Always bizzare, always brilliant.
104.9 Xfm: Alternative, rock.
105.4 Magic: Pop, slush.
105.8 Virgin Radio: Pop, rock.
106.2 Heart: Chart, pop.
106.6 Time: West London only.
107.3 Time: South East London only.

AM

252 Atlantic: Rock.
558 Spectrum International: Multi-ethnic.
648 BBC World Service: Global.
720 BBC Radio Four: Spoken word.
909 BBC Radio Five Live: Sport, phone in.
963 Liberty Radio: 70s, 80s pop.
1035 Ritz: Country.
1089 talkSPORT: Sports phone in.
1152 LBC News: News, weather.
1215 Virgin Radio: Pop, rock.
1305 Premier Radio: Christian.
1458 Sunrise: Asian.
1548 Capital Gold: Rock 'gold', sport.
1584 London Turkish Radio: Turkish community.

Essential London Books

The Diary of Samuel Pepys (1825): Samuel Pepys: eyewitness accounts of the Restoration, Great Plague and Fire of London from noted sixteenth century scribbler.

Oliver Twist; Hard Times; Great Expectations (1837, 1854, 1860): Charles Dickens: any Dickens novel paints Victorian London at its most exacting.

The Strange Case of Dr. Jekyll and Mr. Hyde (1886): Robert Louis Stevenson: the book that enthralled a city unnerved by Jack the Ripper.

The Adventures of Sherlock Holmes; The Hound of the Baskervilles (1892): Arthur Conan Doyle: classic whodunits featuring Holmes and Watson.

The Inimitable Jeeves (1923): P.G. Wodehouse: prewar upper-class tomfoolery in London Town.

Mrs Dalloway (1925): Virginia Woolf If you know London, you can follow Clarissa Dalloway every step of the way – in real time.

Londinium: London in the Roman Empire, John Morris (1982): London's rise from a Roman outpost into a debauched medieval mecca.

V For Vendetta (1982-1989): Alan Moore, The world's greatest comic writer blows up London in a fit of Anarchist fantasies.

London Fields (1989): Martin Amis: post-modern jaunt through London at the end of the millennium.

London – The Biography, and ***Illustrated London*** (2000): Peter Ackroyd: definitive, eight hundred page mother lode of remarkable city history, and lavish pictorial version.

London's Disused Underground Stations (2001): JE Connor: documenting forgotten, ghostly tube stations beneath the pavements.

London Orbital and Hackney That Rose Red Empire (2002): Iain Sinclair: London's premier scribe continues to fill our brains with joy despite being ripped off by devotee Peter Ackroyd.

The Clerkenwell Tales (2003): Peter Ackroyd: corking murder mystery set in the time of Chaucer.

Brick Lane (2003): Monica Ali: award winning coming-of-age tale centred on Brick Lane's Muslim community.

Art Deco London (2003): Colin Michael Hines: Wistful but enjoyable stroll around London's Art Deco heritage.

Intimate Adventures of a London Call Girl (2005): Belle de Jour: steamy, real-life shenanigans ahoy.

From Here to Here (2005): Simmons, Taylor, Lynham, Rich: 31 top notch short stories about Circle Line destinations, includes Simon Armitage.

Secret London: Exploring the Hidden City, with Original Walks and Unusual Places to Visit (2006): Andrew Duncan: an explorer's dream.

The London Bombings: An Independent Inquiry (2006): Nafeez Mosaddeq Ahmed: balanced, subtle overview of 2005 Underground bombings.

Around London with Kids – 68 Great Things to See and Do (3rd edition; 2006): Eugene Fodor: should keep the little rascals from breaking into cars.

I Never Knew That About London (2007): Christopher Winn: Well, did you?

The London Encyclopaedia (2008): Ben Weinreb and Christopher Hibbert: London's history and culture documented in minutest detail

Derelict London (2008): Paul Talling: The urban explorers' bible!

Essential London Songs

Lambeth Walk, Noel Gay/Douglas Furber (1937): All together! *Doing the Lambeth Walk! Oi!*

A Nightingale Sang in Berkeley Square, Judy Campbell (1940): Wartime cheer made famous by Vera Lynn.

London Pride, Sir Noel Coward (1941): Written during the Blitz, this sensational ballad gave comfort to Londoners being bombed nightly.

Maybe It's Because I'm a Londoner, Hubert Gregg (1944): Pearly Queen favourite crammed with WWII spirit.

A Foggy Day (In London Town), Ella Fitzgerald (1956): Definitive recording of Gershwin classic.

Waterloo Sunset, The Kinks (1967): Timeless paean to the nation's capital.

Consider Yourself, Lionel Bart (1968): Oliver Twist hoodwinked into a life of crime by the Artful Dodger, the rascal.

Primrose Hill, John and Beverly Martyn (1970). Folk rock's second couple never had to deal with Katie Frost and Kate Moss when they were watching the sun set, did they?

Streets Of London, Ralph McTell (1974). Cool folk dude destroys credibility forever with international monster hit.

Baker Street, Gerry Rafferty (1978): Feel that sax line, air that guitar.

London Calling, The Clash (1979): Joe Strummer paints an apocalyptic vision of a city in post-punk transition.

Electric Avenue, Eddy Grant (1983): Roots-rock champion name checks 80s Brixton scene.

London, The Smiths (1983): Morrissey lugubriously debates a trip south. Miserable shite.

West End Girls, Pet Shop Boys (1986): East London working class meets West London affluence in electro-pop classic.

Pump Up London, Mr. Lee (1988). Squelchy Chicago House dude makes London sound amazing whilst name checking every British town he can think of: Leeds! Manchester! Scatland!

Parklife, Blur (1994): Home counties-boys get cockney makeover while eyeing London's jogging scene.

Sunny Goodge Street, Donovan (2002). Folk crooner sings of a hippy London goneby.

The London Underground Song, Amateur Transplants (2005): Sweary, infectiously catchy and a comical ballad to the tube, rings painfully true.

Sheila, Jamie T (2006): Mr. T delivers an excellent poetic diatribe on what being young and hopeless in London is like.

Hometown Glory, Adele (2007): This song will make you fall in love with the city all over again.

Essential London Films

The 39 Steps (1935): Hitchcock adaptation of John Buchan novel.

Pygmalion (1938): Leslie Howard as Henry Higgins and Wendy Hiller as Eliza Doolittle prove Shaw's classic comedy does very well without music.

Great Expectations (1946): Rare Richard Attenborough acting outing in classic Dickens adaptation.

The Ladykillers (1955): Superb black comedy from the Ealing canon, with pre-Obi Wan Alec Guinness.

One Hundred and One Dalmations (1961): Innocent pelt-seeker tortured by 101 belligerent pups. For shame.

Mary Poppins (1964): Notable for Dick Van Dyke's confounding, lanky turn as cockney chimney sweep.

A Hard Day's Night (1964): Classic, swinging 60s' comedy from the Fab Four.

Alfie (1966): Caine in much-lauded role as audience-addressing lothario.

Carry On Doctor (1967): Critically-panned, guilty-pleasure raunchfest from Pinewood Studios.

The London Nobody Knows (1967): The greatest film about London ever. Period.

Oliver! (1968): Sprightly musical adaptation of Dickens classic.

A Clockwork Orange (1971) Kubrick's dystopian masterpiece was set in Thamesmead, which is still, "Feeling a bit shagged and fagged and fashed."

The Elephant Man (1980): John Merrick 'accepted' by London's polite Victorian-era society in David Lynch masterpiece.

An American Werewolf in London (1981): US student attacked on moors; gets haunted; romps with Jenny Agutter; becomes werewolf; slaughters innocents; is shot in alley; credits roll.

My Beautiful Launderette (1985): Hanif Kureishi's controversial depiction of cross-culture, same-gender love in the Thatcher-era.

Muppet Christmas Carol (1992): That Michael Caine, he sure can act. But he sure can't sing.

London (1994): Patrick Kellier's abstract ramble through 'the most unsociable and reactionary of cities.'

Lock, Stock and Two Smoking Barrels (1998): East End crime capers from Madonna's (not from the East End) husband.

Notting Hill (1999): Hugh Grant as mumbling, bumbling, lovesick fop.

Bridget Jones's Diary (2001): Rene Zellweger goes Sloane in adaptation of Helen Fielding novel.

28 Days Later (2002): Us Londoners finally erupt in pandemic rage at how slow tourists are on the tube.

Love Actually (2003): Expansive Richard Curtis romcom with Grant in slightly-less mumbly, slightly-more bumbly form.

Shaun of the Dead (2003): Fighting off zombies at the local pub. Hilarious.

The Kings Speech (2010): A stuttering King finds his voice and wins a few Academy Awards for his efforts.

There can't be anything worse than the inconvenience of trying to find a convenience when nature takes an unexpected hold of your nether regions; you may choose to follow the lead of many a Saturday evening reveller and use a public doorway, but is it really worth the £80 fine that will be levied if caught in the act (and let's face it, it's hard to conceal the evidence)?

Unfortunately, London has seen a recent decline in the provision of public toilet facilities, as local councils seem to have decided that they are under no obligation to provide such a service; you'll also be hard pushed to find a toilet attendant manning a lavatory these days, and the dubious goings-on in some loos may not be quite what you had in mind, unless your name has a "Michael" in it. Most surviving public toilets seem also to emit their own particular aroma of…well, you don't really have to use your imagination. But don't get down in the dumps!

The most obvious place to go to when in need is McDonald's. Despite what some may say about their food, their outlets are the place to go when caught short and not wishing to pay to pee. Usually maintained and cleaned throughout opening hours, they can also be used inconspicuously and without purchasing anything; and let's face it, you can't move without the glow of those golden arches following you across London. It's also a safe bet to use Starbucks, Caffe Nero and Costa Coffee bars, although they often have a policy of access to toilets by key only, which can be a bit of a bummer (groan).

It may seem like a good idea to visit pubs or bars solely for their toilets, but you might find yourself being hauled out by an irked landlord mid-act. Furthermore, don't expect luxury; pub toilets are usually fairly scummy and often not furnished with toilet paper. It's also unlikely to find a men's cubicle that will have a working lock in it; do you really wish to have an unwanted visitor whilst on the throne? Exceptions are the Wetherspoon's chain, which prides itself on having toilets cleaned on the hour, and the nicest of gastro pubs, which can offer commodious and clean facilities (at least during the day). Otherwise, if desperate, at least go for a pub or bar that's busy.

Also bear in mind that if you find yourself in need in the City of Westminster, you can use a toilet text service from your mobile phone! Known as SatLav, texting the word 'Toilet' to 80097 will result in a message being sent to your phone informing you of the nearest public convenience. It may prove to be the most relieving 25p you'll ever spend in London…

A good and extensive list of London public toilets can be found at www.lastrounds.co.uk/public_toilets.html.

If none of the afore-mentioned places are available, there are other options:

Other street public toilets—yes, those bizarre futuristic looking structures on some of London's central streets are toilets. Known as sanisettes or "superloos", there is a charge to use them and once in, you've got 15 minutes before the door automatically opens (don't get extended stage-fright). They're self-cleaning, which usually means that they're in a right state, and are also quite popular with junkies and prostitutes, so best saved for when extremely desperate.

There are also a few pop up toilettes which, although intended for the right use, unfortunately stink like hell and fortunately return back there during the day. These are only suitable for (drunk) men and rise to the challenge of channelling away an evening's excesses from 7pm to 6am. Located at notorious 'wet spots' in the West End, they are linked to the main sewerage system; taking the piss, indeed…

Stations—including almost all large railway stations and a few central London tube stations. There will usually be a cost for these facilities though (around 30p).

Department Stores—All the large ones, including John Lewis, Selfridges, Debenhams and Harrods. Smaller shops rarely have toilets for public use.

Supermarkets—many larger branches of Sainsbury's and Marks & Spencer.

Museums—the majority of London's large museums and galleries are free to enter (erm, and have toilets).

Libraries—most libraries will have an area of salvation for the needy.

Universities and Colleges—and you get to pass yourself off as a student or lecturer (in need of the loo).

Hospitals—you can also drop in on that relative that you always meant to visit, or maybe leave a stool sample; just try not to leave with a superbug.

Parks—not on the grass, please.

Hotels—larger hotels shouldn't pose a problem.

London has some of the finest hospitals in the world, attracting top-notch specialists who carry-out state-of-the-art procedures—the trick is, getting in to see one of them. An appointment at a specific hospital, or with a specialist, requires a referral from your GP and plenty of patience. In an emergency go to your nearest A&E—bring a book and some earplugs. On the weekends after eleven, waiting times for non-urgent problems can be measured in aeons, but rest assured, if something is seriously wrong you'll be seen very quickly—lucky ol' you. For non serious injuries or illnesses, find your nearest Minor Injuries Unit or Walk-in Centre on www.nhs.uk. You'll spend less time hanging around and free up A&E for critical cases and over-cidered teens needing stomach pumps. The ever-friendly 24 hr NHS Direct 0845 4647 is also always available for advice.

If you have the money, numerous private sector hospitals and clinics are available to cure what ails you, or to pander to your hypochondriacal needs. You won't necessarily get better treatment, but there'll be less waiting, more pampering and more grapes by your bedside. For information, start at www.privatehealth.co.uk.

A & E	*Address*	*Phone*	*Map*
Charing Cross Hospital	Fulham Palace Rd & St Dunstan's Rd	020 3311 1234	41
Chelsea and Westminster Hospital	369 Fulham Rd	020 8746 8000	43
Homerton University Hospital	Homerton Row	020 8510 5555	90
King's College Hospital	Denmark Hill & Champion Park	020 3299 9000	128
Moorfields Eye Hospital	162 City Rd	020 7253 3411	84
Royal Free Hospital	Pond St & Fleet Rd	020 7794 0500	57
Royal London Hospital	Whitechapel Rd & Vallance Rd	020 7377 7000	96
St Mary's Hospital	Praed St & Winsland St	020 3312 6666	31
St Thomas' Hospital	Westminster Bridge Rd & Lambeth Palace Rd	020 7188 7188	131
University College Hospital	235 Euston Rd	0845 155 5000	4
Western Eye Hospital	173 Marylebone Rd	020 7886 6666	2
Whittington Hospital	Magdala Ave	020 7272 3070	59

Other Hospitals	*Address*	*Phone*	*Map*
Bupa Cromwell Hospital	162 Cromwell Rd	020 7460 2000	35
Capio Chelsea	1 Radnor Walk	020 7351 7098	45
Capio Eye	114 Harley St	020 7034 1030	2
Capio Nightingale Hospital	11 Lisson Grove	020 7535 7700	76
Charing Cross Hospital	Fulham Palace Rd & St Dunstan's Rd	020 3311 1234	41
Chelsea and Westminster Hospital	369 Fulham Rd	020 8746 8000	43
Eastman Dental Hospital	256 Gray's Inn Rd	020 7915 1000	5
Elizabeth Garrett Anderson Hospital	Huntley St	0845 155 5000	4
Gordon Hospital	Bloomburg St & Vauxhall Bridge Rd	020 8746 8733	21
Great Ormond St Children's Hospital	34 Great Ormond St	020 7405 9200	5
Guy's Hospital	Great Maze Pond & St Thomas St	020 7188 7188	106
Heart Hospital	16 Westmoreland St	020 7573 8888	2
Highgate Private Hospital	17 View Rd	020 8341 4182	51
Homerton University Hospital	Homerton Row	020 8510 5555	90

Other Hospitals	*Address*	*Phone*	*Map*
Hospital For Tropical Diseases	Martimer Market & Capper St	0845 155 5000	4
Hospital of St John and St Elizabeth	60 Grove End Rd	020 7806 4000	68
King Edward VII Hospital For Officers	5 Beaumont St	020 7486 4411	2
King's College Hospital	Denmark Hill & Champion Park	020 3299 9000	128
Lambeth Hospital	108 Landor Rd	020 3228 6000	144
Lister Hospital	Chelsea Bridge Rd	020 7730 7733	20
London Bridge Hospital	27 Tooley St	020 7407 3100	106
London Chest Hospital	Bonner Rd & Approach Rd	020 7377 7000	93
London Independent Hospital	1 Beaumont Sq	020 7780 2400	97
London Welbeck Hospital	25 Welbeck St	020 7224 2242	2
Mildmay Mission Hospital	Hackney Rd & Columbia Rd	020 7613 6309	91
Mile End Hospital	Bancroft Rd & Alderney Rd	020 7377 7000	93
Moorfields Eye Hospital	162 City Rd	020 7253 3411	84
National Hospital for Neorology and Neurosciences	Queen Sq & Great Ormond St	0845 155 5000	5
Portland Hospital For women and Children	209 Great Portland St	020 7580 4400	3
Princess Grace Hospital	42 Nottingham Pl	020 7486 1234	2
The Rosenheim Building	25 Grafton Way	0845 155 5000	4
Royal Brompton Hospital	Sydney St & Cale St	020 7352 8121	45
Royal Free Hospital	Pond St & Fleet Rd	020 7794 0500	57
Royal London Homeopathic Hospital	60 Great Ormond St	020 7391 8888	5
Royal London Hospital	Whitechapel Rd & Vallance Rd	020 7377 7000	96
Royal Marsden Hospital	Fulham Rd & Sydney Close	020 7352 8171	45
Royal National Orthopaedic Hospital	51 Bolsover St	020 8954 2300	3
Royal National Throat, Nose and Ear Hospital	330 Gray's Inn Rd	020 7915 1300	5
St Bartholomew's	West Smithfield & Hosier Ln	020 7377 7000	15
Fitzroy Square Hospital	14 Fitzroy Sq	020 7388 4954	3
St Mary's Hospital	Praed St & Winsland St	020 3312 6666	31
St Pancras Hospital	4 St Pancras Way	020 7530 3500	78
St Thomas' Hospital	Westminster Bridge Rd & Lambeth Palace Rd	020 7188 7188	131
University College Hospital	235 Euston Rd	0845 155 5000	4
Wellington Hospital	8 Wellington Pl	020 7586 5959	76
Western Eye Hospital	173 Marylebone Rd	020 3312 6666	2
Whittington Hospital	Magdala Ave & Dartmouth Park Hill	020 7272 3070	59

Overview

Librarians love nothing more than a warm cardigan and a complex cataloguing system, nevertheless, they've done themselves proud with London's libraries. London boasts an enormous, if somewhat eccentric and confusing, network of over 360 libraries. NFT have tried to make things a little clearer with a starter guide below, but check www.londonlibraries.org for a great searchable database to match your needs with the right library. In 2009 the Chief Librarians initiative passed and 4,000 libraries in England, Wales and Northern Ireland can now be easily accessed and used for all library services including checking out books, as long as you have an existing library card and proof of address. This excludes the elite British institutions (see below) and all books must be returned to a library in the same area.

London's libraries vary enormously in subject, range and facilities, with some accessible for free, some for a fee, some with an appointment and some only if you are very very nice and give the curator a chocolate digestive. But the treat of such a large network, apart from the world-class breadth, depth and quality of collections, is that many of the libraries have a unique personality to make them a treasured part of London. For example, £10 will get you a day's membership to the **London Library (Map 23)**, an atmospheric labyrinth where you can browse alongside ghosts of past members including Dickens, Tennyson and Darwin, and feel several IQ points higher than before you went in. In Tower Hamlets, libraries are now **"Ideas Stores" (Map 92, 101, 96)**, because Tower Hamlets is, like, cool. In addition to the books, magazines, music and internet facilities which are available at most public libraries, these superb spaces also offer activities such as free PopLaw legal advice clinics, homework clubs and jazz classes. The borough has built four of these wonders; find them in Bow, Whitechapel, Canary Wharf and on East India Dock Road. London linguists are spoiled with the excellent **French Institute (Map 36)**, **Instituto Cervantes (Map 19)** and the **Goethe Institut (Map 37)**, while more cunning linguists may prefer the eye-opening gynaecological collection among the 2.5 million medical-related works in the **Wellcome Library (Map 4)**. Poets should meander their way to the **Saison Poetry Library (Map 104)**, ensconced within the South Bank Centre, for a little inspiration. Artists will enjoy the **National Art Library (Map 36)**, which nestles within the V&A Museum. You can use many of London's academic and specialist libraries through the Inspire London scheme, which grants one-day reference access to collections throughout London; ask your local library to refer you.

However, the Daddy of them all is the **British Library (Map 78)**. This behemoth receives a copy of every publication printed in the UK and Ireland, and requires 625km of shelving space to accommodate its 150million items. But it's just such a tease. You cannot borrow books, and to even access the collections you need to obtain a Reader Pass, via an introductory discussion to establish why you need it and whether you're likely to doodle on the books. This requires two forms of ID, no compromise: refer to www.bl.uk for the latest guidelines. Once you have your pass you can access the Reading Rooms, albeit with your personal belongings in a clear plastic bag (or stored in a locker). But if you just fancy seeing the Magna Carta, Shakespeare in Quarto or some Beatles manuscripts, you can access the book-free visitor areas without appointment and still gain an impressive look at one of the world's greatest information resources.

General Information

Important phone numbers:
All emergencies: 999
Non-emergencies: 101
Anti-terrorism hotline: 0800 789 321
Crime Stoppers: 0800 555 111
Neighbourhood Watch: 020 79934709
Missing Persons: 0500 700 700
Complaints: 08453 002 002
Websites:
www.met.police.uk
www.cityoflondon.police.uk (Separate police force specifically covering the Square Mile).
www.btp.police.uk (Separate police force specifically covering public transport).

Statistics* (Greater London)

	2008/09	2009/10	2010/2011
Murder	146	113	124
Rapes	2,177	2,839	3279
GBH	11,212	10,525	8374
Burglary (res)	59,176	60,909	60803

* all sourced from the MPS Crime Website http://content.met.police.uk

Police Stations

Police Stations	Address	Phone	Map
Albany Street Police Station	60 Albany St	030 0123 1212	77
Battersea Police Station	112 Battersea Bridge	030 0123 1212	132
Belgravia Police Station	202 Buckingham Palace Rd	030 0123 1212	20
Brixton Police Station	367 Brixton Rd	030 0123 1212	144
Camberwell Police Station	22 Camberwell Church St	030 0123 1212	122
Cavendish Road Police Station	47 Cavendish Parade	030 0123 1212	149
Charing Cross Police Station	Agar St & Strand	030 0123 1212	24
Chelsea Police Station	2 Lucan Pl	030 0123 1212	46
Chiswick Police Station	209 Chiswick High Rd	030 0123 1212	38
Deptford Police Station	114 Amersham Vale	020 8297 1212	126
East Dulwich Police Station	173 Lordship Ln	030 0123 1212	129
Greenwich Police Station	31 Royal Hill	030 0123 1212	120
Hampstead Police Station	26 Rosslyn Hill	030 0123 1212	56
Harrow Road Police Station	325 Harrow Rd	030 0123 1212	26
Holborn Police Station	10 Lamb's Conduit St	030 0123 1212	5
Holloway Police Station	284 Hornsey Rd	030 0123 1212	61
Hornsey Police Station	98 Tottenham Ln	030 0123 1212	54
Islington Police Station	2 Tolpuddle St	030 0123 1212	80
Kennington Police Station	49 Kennington Rd	030 0123 1212	104
Kensington Police Station	72 Earl's Court Rd	030 0123 1212	35
Kentish Town Police	12 Holmes Rd	030 0123 1212	72
Lavender Hill Police Station	176 Lavender Hill	030 0123 1212	140
Marylebone Police Station	1 Seymour St	030 0123 1212	1
Notting Hill Police Station	100 Ladbroke Grove	030 0123 1212	28
Paddington Green Police Station	2 Harrow Rd	030 0123 1212	31
Peckham Police Station	177 Peckham High St	030 0123 1212	123
Rotherhithe Police Station	99 Lower Rd	020 7378 1212	110
Southwark Police Station	323 Borough High St	030 0123 1212	106
St John's Wood Police Station	20 Newcourt St	030 0123 1212	69
Tooting Police Station	251 Mitcham Rd	030 0123 1212	152
Walworth Police Station	12 Manor Pl	030 0123 1212	113
Wandsworth Police Station	146 Wandsworth High St	030 0123 1212	138
West End Central Police Station	27 Savile Row	030 0123 1212	10

N8
N15
N6
N4
N19
N16
E5
NW3
NW5
N7
N5
E8
E9
NW6
N1
NW8
NW1
E2
E3
W9
WC1
EC1
W10
EC2
W1
E1
W2
WC2
EC4
EC3
W11
W12
W8
SE1
E14
SW7
SW1
SE16
W14
SW5
SE11
SE17
SE8
W4
SW3
SW10
SE10
SW13
SW8
SE5
SE14
SW6
SE15
SW11
SW9
SW4
SE24
SE22
SW15
SW18
SW2
SW12
SW17

Overview

London hotels can be sources of hopelessly romantic creativity. In 1899 Claude Monet painted the Houses of Parliament from his balcony at the Savoy hotel. About 100 years later, Fay Weldon moved in with her typewriter as writer in residence. If you've got visitors in town, fancy giving Claude a run for his money, or just can't face going back to your dump of a flat, you'll need the services of a hotel. When choosing your hotel, think carefully about what kind of London you're looking to experience and whom the room is for. We've identified a few of the usual suspects for whom you may find yourself booking a hotel room, and heartily offer you our best suggestions for each. Just don't expect to emerge from any of them clutching a masterpiece penned overnight.

Only the best, Daah-ling

So you need to find a hotel for a VIP client who will accept nothing but the best. Where to start? Since you don't have to cover the bill yourself, here is where you can really dig into London hospitality at its most deluxe. Start by trying to book **The Ritz (Map 9)**, with its amazing views of Green Park, Rococo detailing and killer high tea. **Brown's (Map 9)** is a stunning five-star and was the first hotel in London to have a lift. There is also the **Dorchester (Map 9)**, and its neighbour the **Hilton Park Lane (Map 9)**, where you may see a celebrity stumbling back to their quarters at four in the morning, if you're very, very lucky. **The Landmark (Map 76)** is a wonderfully Victorian retreat in the centre of ritzy Marylebone and has a rather fine atrium. But the granddaddy of luxury London must be the **Savoy (Map 24)**. This elegant old-timer stunk of old money until its temporary closure in 2007 for a £100 million spruce-up. It was built on the location of the Savoy Palace, which burned down during the Peasants' Revolt in 1381. We say let them eat cake (and tea).

A Dirty Weekend

This can be any weekend where a Londoner decides booze-goggled sex and/or quick-to-bed access after a night of clubbing is worthy of dishing out the dosh on an über-chic central hotel. It's one (giant) step up from splurging on a taxi and is the realm of the London boutique hotel where location is everything. **Hazlitt's (Map 12)** is right in the middle of Soho yet still wonderfully intimate. **Andaz Hotel (Map 8) (formerly Great Eastern Hotel)** is in the heart of the City, with funky Shoreditch on its doorstep, whilst the 'modern English' style of the **Charlotte Street Hotel (Map 3)** is painfully hip and sophisticated.

The Tea-and-Crumpet Tourist

Then there's the hotel for your sweetly naïve cousin that sees London through rose-tinted Ray Bans: full of scones, Mary Poppins and the chimes of Big Ben. You wouldn't want to burst her cute little bubble, would you? Not to worry, there are plenty of hotels to satisfy the Harrods tourist. **San Domenico House London (Map 46)** is a Chelsea boutique hotel that is about as warm and cuddly as a cup of sugary tea. **The Rookery (Map 15)**, built amongst a row of once derelict Georgian townhouses in Clerkenwell, is cluttered with museum-worthy furniture, open fires and ye oldey worldey frippery. Or, if she can't bear to be too far away from Buckingham Palace, there's the nearby **Windermere (Map 20)**.

Parents in Town?

If your parents have spent their nest egg on bailing you out of your London-induced debt, they will probably want to get the most out of London for the least money possible. But if the hotel you pick for their stay is anything short of perfect, you'll never hear the end of it. If they have loyalty cards with any of the bigger hotel chains, now is a good time to use them. **The London Bridge Hotel (Map 22)** is an independent four-star that usually has good deals and is conveniently close to Borough Market and London Bridge station. Gower Street has a wealth of small family run hotels at reasonable prices, including the **Cavendish (Map 23)**, within stumbling distance of the British Museum. There's also the nearby **Crescent Hotel (Map 4)**, next to Russell Square. If you miss home cooking, get your 'rents a serviced apartment with a kitchenette. Marlin Apartments and Think London have a few different properties, often ripe for the celeb sighting as pop stars are known to hitch up their wagons there during drawn-out tours.

In Lieu of a Couch to Crash On

Then you get your university friend still in strong denial of the real world, who refuses to get a real job. The amount of times this sponger has crashed on your sofa has been enough to send your might-be-the-one girl/boyfriend packing. Instead of blaming him/her for your future life of loneliness, banish them from the flat and call in the services of one of London's cheapies. They do exist, you just have to look hard. The **Hoxton Hotel (Map 84)**, an urban cheap boutique founded by the owner of Pret a Manger, is famous for its £1 hotel room sales. Cheap but cheerful chain Premier Inn (multiple locations) boasts rooms from £29 a night. Sometimes short-term rental companies, like **Airbnb** (www.airbnb.com), offer shared facility flats at very cheap prices. This is perfect if a guest is wishing to stay for a week or more. Airbnb has over 9,000 listings in London, which start as low as £10 a night. This can be a necessary and friendly alternative to endless weeks of friends imposing on your hospitality.

Where to Stick Your Best Friend From School

(And Her Husband, Two Perfect Kids and a Dog)

Unfortunately, for some people visiting London, a dodgy guesthouse isn't going to cut it. You want to show them how your city can be just as perfect as their countryside home and how not jealous you are of them! Of course, they don't see the point in paying tons either. This is where the few and far between bed and breakfasts come out of the woodwork. Most of these are small, so book in advance. London's best is the warm and welcoming **Bay Tree House and Annex B&B (Out of coverage)**. Great for families or singletons alike, it's in New Southgate (about 25 minutes by tube from central London) but can be a relaxing retreat. **Barclay House (Map 43)** is a hidden gem in Fulham Broadway (make sure you write down the address as it's not signposted and can blend in). **Aster House (Map 45)** is a bit pricier but close enough to posh High Street Kensington to give a glimpse of how the other half live.

With all these hotels, compare prices online, ask for their best rate and/or call for last minute deals, you may be surprised at the reductions available. Good offers mean you can pay less than you'd think for the best, and London does really have the best.

As you might expect from a site constantly inhabited since the Roman invasion of Britain, and probably before, London has managed to assemble a vast array of good, bad and ugly landmarks. The city is, in fact, stuffed with them, and the following is a slightly subjective rumination on a small proportion of some of the most noteworthy.

Historical

London gracefully bears a massive weight of history, and many of its landmarks reflect this. One of the oldest is the remains of the **Temple of Mithras (Map 16)** on Walbrook, built by the Romans when London was Londinium. Parts of the **London Wall (Map 18)**, also originally built by the Romans, still exist, the best fragments are around Tower Hill station. In Medieval times London became a bustling place; celebrate one of its most beautiful churches by visiting the oddly named **St Giles' Cripplegate (Map 7)**, which is ensconced within the brutal **Barbican Centre (Map 7)**, a landmark itself. By the 1600s, London was bustling so hard it got the plague and then some idiot burnt the entire city down in 1666. Celebrate three days of the Great Fire by climbing to the top of the 202 feet high **Monument (Map 18)**, before visiting post-fire architect Christopher Wren's masterpiece, **St Paul's Cathedral (Map 16)**. Into the 18th century, things became a little more sophisticated and some of London's prettiest domestic architecture bloomed. Stroll down Bloomsbury's **Doughty Street (Map 5)**, stopping at Charles Dickens' House, for perfectly proportioned Georgian elegance. The Victorians had a huge impact on London, with whole tracts of the city bearing the stamp of the starched times of chimney sweeps and empire bashing. For the lighter side of Victorian London, poke about the museums quarter from the **Victoria & Albert Museum (Map 37)** up to the **Albert Memorial (Map 36)**. For the darker, dodge the elderly at the **St Pancras Hospital (Map 78)**, an ex-workhouse.

Tourist Bait

London has a host of over-exposed landmarks that are honey to the swarms of tourist worker-bees but over-rated in the eyes of many Londoners. We don't necessarily share this view, but if you want to venture beyond the crowds at **Big Ben (Map 22)**, try some of the following. The aforementioned **St Paul's Cathedral (Map 16)** is an absolute wonder, although try the smaller **Southwark Cathedral (Map 106)** for a more intimate option. **The British Museum (Map 4)** is a beauty made fairer by its recent courtyard renovation; peruse the library to see where Marx pondered upon 'Das Kapital'. **The Burlington Arcade (Map 10)** is how shopping should be. The crypt under **St Mary-le-Bow Church (Map 16)** is 11th century weirdness complete with its own vegetarian restaurant. The Thames is long enough to provide you with your own spot of riverside tranquillity. If you're scared of bridges, burrow under the river at the **Greenwich Foot Tunnel (Map 120)**, or chug across it on the free Woolwich Ferry. For a weekend mooch, try the **Grand Regent's Canal (Map 71)**.

Modern Landmarks

The 20th century blessed the city with some opinion splitting contributions. **The Hayward Gallery (Map 104)** and **National Theatre (Map 104)** are both concrete frighteners which we are learning to love. Despite originally housing a power station, **Tate Modern (Map 105)** has been more graciously received. Meanwhile further down the river, long abandoned **Battersea Power Station (Map 133)** will be undergoing major developments in 2013, at the time of writing it will either be converted into the new Chelsea football stadium or a collection of soulless expensive office blocks and flats, either way a nostalgic blight will be replaced by some form of flashy money-without-substance monstrosity, so make sure you nod goodbye to it in 2013. The **BT Tower (Map 3)** is like a 1960s lighthouse for central London drunks. **The Lloyds Building (Map 18)** and **Tower 42 (Map 18)** are both absorbing odes to the banker and glare menacingly at new rival **One Canada Square (or Canary Wharf Tower) (Map 100)**. A more recent contribution to the city is the **Canary Wharf Underground Station (Map 100)**. Until at least 2014 the 150-year squabble over what to put in **Trafalgar Square's (Map 24)** fourth and only empty plinth rages on. Expect modern, classic and performance art in this space for the time being, at least, until they add a statue of Britain's future supreme commander Rupert Murdoch strangling Lady Justice in 2014.

Lowbrow

In these clean times of starchitects, steel and glass, a few minutes spent gawping at **Elephant and Castle (Map 105)** shopping centre is enough to remind anyone how awry a landmark can go. Even a quick squizz at the nearby **Faraday Memorial (Map 105)** may not lift your gloom, largely as it now forms the body of a clogged roundabout. However, London can do lowbrow with the best of them, starting with the **Westway Flyover (Map 31)**: a noisy, dusty shard of concrete to remind you that the car is still king. The disused **Kingsway Tram Tunnel (Map 4)** is a forgotten piece of prime underground real estate and **Centre Point (Map 4)** and **Millbank Tower (Map 21)** are good examples of dodgy skyscrapers that no-one needed. **Battersea Park Gasometers (Map 133)** are imposing monsters, whereas **Lots Road Power Station (Map 50)** is fast becoming London's trendiest disused power station. If you must jump upon band wagons, keep your eyes peeled around east London for art left on walls by Banksy. Mobile lowbrow starts with a trip on a Routemaster, despite the buses being withdrawn in 2005, two heritage routes are still running. Lowbrow (along with logic, aesthetic quality and planning) finishes with **Euston Station (Map 78)**, which is, simply, disgusting.

Map 1 • Marylebone (West)

Marble Arch	Oxford St & Park Ln	Randomly plonked gateway to nowhere.
Speakers' Corner	Cumberland Gate & Park Ln	It's easy—stand on the corner and listen to the 'speeches.'

Map 2 • Marylebone (East)

Hertford House	Manchester Sq & Hinde St	Terribly twee home of the Wallace Collection.
Jimi Hendrix Memorial Blue Plaque	23 Brook St	Jimi lived here. Some bloke called Handel lived next door.

Map 3 • Fitzrovia

BT Tower	60 Cleveland St	A 574 foot tall official government secret until 1993.
Charlotte Street	Charlotte St	Restaurant strip for the advertising in-crowd.
Middlesex Hospital	Mortimer St & Cleveland St	Closed-down and spooky-looking.
Pollock's Toy Museum	1 Scala St	Brimming with delightful, traditional toys and Dickensian atmosphere.
Sinner Winner Man	216 Oxford St	Are you a sinner? Or a winner? London's top preacher's patch.
Tottenham Court Road	Tottenham Ct Rd	Buy your electronics 'ere, innit?

Map 4 • Bloomsbury (West)

The British Museum	Great Russell St & Museum St	Newly-covered Great Court is architectural manna.
Centre Point	101 New Oxford St	Ugly skyscraper looking kinda out of place.
Kingsway Tram Tunnel	Theobalds Rd & Southampton Row	Spooky remnant of London's defunct Tram network.
Senate House	Malet St & Torrington Sq	Ominous art deco building; Orwell's Ministry of Truth.
Tavistock Square	Tavistock Sq	Has a statue of Gandhi looking as cool as ever.

Map 5 • Bloomsbury (East)

The Dickens House Museum	48 Doughty St	Unassuming from the outside, mecca for Dickens' fans on the inside.
Doughty Street	Doughty St & Guilford St	Exquisite Georgian street in heart of literary land.
Gray's Inn Field	Theobald's Rd	Holborn Hideaway.

Map 7 • Barbican / City Road (South)

Barbican Centre	Silk St & Whitecross St	An architectural eyesore. Bloody good events though.
Bunhill Fields	38 City Rd	120 thousand dead people, including William Blake. All buried, luckily.
Church of Saint Bartholomew	6 Kinghorn St	Stroll in for your daily dose of frankincense and choir song.
LSO St Luke's	161 Old St	Home to the London Symphony Orchestra. Peaceful gardens for relaxation.
St. Giles-without-Cripplegate	Fore St & Wood St	Medieval church which defied the Blitz. Catch an organ recital.

Map 8 • Liverpool Street / Broadgate

Fulcrum at Broadgate	Broadgate	Richard Serra's overwhelming steel megalith.

Map 9 • Mayfair / Green Park

50 Berkeley Square	50 Berkeley Sq	The most haunted house in all of London town!
Apsley House	149 Piccadilly	"Number One, London"—former hip address of Duke of Wellington.
Buckingham Palace	The Mall	Unofficial HQ for Fathers For Justice.
Down Street Station	Down St & Piccadily	Bricked-up Underground station. The Turtles didn't live here.

Map 10 • Piccadilly / Soho (West)

Burlington Arcade	Burlington Arcade & Piccadilly	Welcoming shoppers since 1819.
Carnaby Street	Carnaby St	Will anything innovative ever come from here again?
Kingly Court	Kingly St & Foubert's Pl	Flash the cash to cut a dash.
Statue of Eros	Piccadilly Circus	God of Love, smothered in pigeon crap: a cautionary tale.

Map 11 • Soho (Central)

Huge Tree In Pub (Waxy O'Connor's)	14 Rupert St	No, you're not drunk, it really is a tree.
John Snow Water Pump	Broadwick Street	Source of 1854 Cholera outbreak identified by Snow.
Berwick Street Market	Berwick St & Rupert St	Arrive early for traditional Cockney trader songs / off-duty hookers.

Map 12 • Soho (East)

Denmark Street	Denmark St & Charing Cross Rd	Guitar land. 'Enter Sandman' forbidden in most stores.
FA Headquarters	25 Soho Sq	Home of English football's top brass.
Old Compton Street	Old Compton St	Dubious gay hub.
The Phoenix Garden	21 Stacey St	A beautiful green mini-oasis in the middle of the city.
Soho Square	Soho Sq	Great atmosphere on hot summer days.

Map 13 • Covent Garden

Oasis Lido	32 Endell St	A lido in central London! In a 50s housing estate!
Seven Dials	Upper St Martin's Ln & Earlham St	Slum area in the past. Now great for shopping!

Map 14 • Holborn / Temple

Aldwych tube station	Strand & Surrey St	Creepy abandoned tube station. With a photo booth... of doom?
BBC Bush House	Aldwych & Kingsway	London calling the world, since 1940.
Hatton Garden	Hatton Garden	Historic jewelry and diamond district
Inner Temple Garden	Inner Temple	So peaceful even the lawyers look relaxed.
Lincoln's Inn Fields	High Holborn & Chancery Ln	Largest public square in London.
The Old Curiosity Shop	13 Portsmouth St	The oldest shop in London is truly Dickensesque.
Royal Courts of Justice	Strand & Bell Yard	Witness justice meted out to all, even the McCartneys.
Sir John Soane's Museum	13 Lincoln's Inn Fields	Spooky museum dedicated to the great 18th century architect.
Site of Sweeny Todd's Barber Shop	186 Fleet St	Swing by for a demon haircut and lovely pie.
Somerset House	Strand	10th century palace, beautiful fountains, has various modern functions.

Map 15 • Blackfriars / Farringdon

Daily Express Building	121 Fleet St	Art Deco sleeper.
Millennium Bridge	Millennium Bridge	Footbridge famous for wobbling alarmingly when it was opened.
Postman's Park	King Edward St & Little Britain	Tile memorial for 'average' people who did really cool things.

Map 16 • Square Mile (West)

The Guildhall	Gresham St & Basinghall St	Big, posh, old... Like Prince Phillip but less entertaining.
St Mary le Bow Church	Cheapside & Bow Ln	A historic place for City tycoons to save their souls.
St. Paul's Cathedral	St. Paul's Church Yard & Cannon St	Magnificence since 604AD.
Temple of Mithras	Queen Victoria St & Queen St	3rd century Roman temple foundations. Discovered 1954 and moved here.

Map 17 • Square Mile (East)

Bank of England	Threadneedle St	The 'Old Lady' still churns out the pounds.
London Stone	111 Cannon St	Possibly used by Romans to measure all distances in Britannia.
Threadneedle Street	Threadneedle St & Prince's St	London's original Grope Cunt Lane. Seriously, it's a true story.

Map 18 • Tower Hill / Aldgate

The Gherkin	30 St Mary Axe	Phwoar.
Leadenhall Market	Leadenhall Market	Designed by Horace Jones (Billingsgate and Smithfield Markets)
The Lloyds Building	1 Lime St	Dystopia's nicer side.
London Wall	Cooper's Row & Trinity Sq	Ruins, should be re-built to keep Northerners out.
The Monument	Monument St & Fish St Hill	Climb 311 coronary-inducing steps for unique, unsung London views.
Pudding Lane	Pudding Ln	Starting point for Great Fire of 1666. No smoking.
Royal Raven Lodgings	Wakefield Tower	Want to upgrade your pokey flat? Become a raven.
Soup Kitchen for the Jewish Poor	Brune St & Tenter Ground	The kitchen's gone; the stunning ornate façade is still there.
Thames Clipper	Tower Pier	
Tower 42 (Natwest Tower)	25 Old Broad St	One of London's skyscrapers. Great view (and restaurant) at top.
Tower of London	The Tower of London	Kings and Queens. Surprisingly insightful, annoyingly expensive.

Map 20 • Victoria / Pimlico (West)

Little Ben	Victoria St & Vauxhall Bridge Rd	Big Ben's runty kid brother.
Westminster Cathedral	42 Francis St	Yep, impressive.

Map 21 • Pimlico (East)

Millbank Tower	21 Millbank	Ugly sore thumb. And Labour Party HQ!
The Shard Building Site	32 Vauxhall Bridge Rd	Site of the super tall skyscraper to be.

Map 22 • Westminster

Big Ben	House of Commons	The world's most famous clock and pretty damn cool.
Bolan Rock Shrine	Queen's Ride, Putney	Memorial shrine where 70s rock star Marc Bolan died.
Field of Remembrance	Victoria St & Dean's Yard	Sea of crosses and poppies to honour veterans.
New Scotland Yard Sign	8 Broadway	It spins!! Just like on the telly!!
Smith Square	Smith Sq	Square with great concert venue--watch out for MPs.
UK Parliament	Victoria St & Abingdon St	Parliament buildings where you can watch government debates.
Westminster Tube Station	Bridge St & Victoria Embankment	A daunting, soulless, engineering playground. Good and bad both extinct here...

Map 23 • St. James's

Economist Plaza	25 St James's St	Rotating sculpture installations from bratty young artists.
Giro the Nazi Dog	9 Carlton House Terrace	London's sole Nazi memorial. You'd think there'd be more…
Leicester Square	Leicester Sq	Tragic, tacky, always inexplicably heaving. Avoid.
TKTS	Leicester Square & St Martin's St	Cheapo tickets to sometimes worth-seeing shows.

Map 24 • Trafalgar Square / The Strand

10 Downing Street	10 Downing St	The Prime Minister's house.
The Actors' Church	29 Bedford St	Somewhat hidden and unique church long-associated with thesps.
The Banqueting House	Whitehall & Horse Guards Ave	Unsullied Renaissance cum-shot. Still does private parties.
Cleopatra's Needle	Embankment	Ancient-Egyptian Empire esoterica, with additional Luftwaffe-era 'distressed' styling.
Eleanor Cross	Charing Cross Station, The Strand	A mourning King's tribute to his expired Queen.
Jane Austen Residence	10 Henrietta St	The first Bridget Jones' bachelorette crashed here for a time.
Right-hand Drive Street	Savoy Ct	Britain's only right-hand-drive street. Like being on holiday! (Ish)
Sewer Lamp	Carting Lane & Strand	Lit by the power of your bowels.
St Martin-in-the-Fields	St Martin's Pl & Duncannon St	Was indeed surrounded by fields once. Just TRY to imagine!
Top Secret Tunnels	6 Craig's Ct	Government's WWII tunnels, 100ft below London. But shhh: top secret.
Trafalgar Square	Trafalgar Sq	Hardly an oasis but space to sit, look and think.

Map 25 • Kensal Town

Trellick Tower	5 Golborne Rd	Grade II listed 1960s council estate inspiring love/hate reactions.

Map 29 • Notting Hill Gate

Portobello Road Market	223 Portobello Rd	Antiques, clothes, food and more. A London institution.

Map 31 • Paddington

Paddington Bear Statue	Paddington Station	The statue's pleasant. But they're milking it with the crap shop.
Tony Blair's house	Connaught Square & Seymour St	Promise not to do anything naughty now.
Westway Flyover		Coolest car route into London

Map 33 • Shepherd's Bush

BBC Television Centre	Wood Ln & Ring Rd	Treasure it before the BBC moves out in 2013.

Map 34 • West Kensington / Olympia

Kyoto Garden (Holland Park)	100 Holland Park Ave	Traditional Japanese Garden in Holland Park offering peace and tranquility.

Map 35 • Kensington

Kensington Palace Gardens	Kensington Palace Gardens	Billionaire's Row. Stunning street to amble down and gawp at the mansions.

Map 36 • South Kensington / Gloucester Rd

Albert Memorial	Kensington Gardens	The shiniest balding head in town.
Royal Albert Hall	Kensington Gore	One stunner of a music hall, inside and out.

Map 37 • Knightsbridge

Holy Trinity Brompton	Brompton Rd & Knightsbridge	Historic HTB is home to the Alpha course. Even Guy Ritchie's been!
Victoria & Albert Museum	Cromwell Rd & Thurloe Pl	Victorian treasure trove, building a beauty itself.

Map 42 • Baron's Court

Empress State Buidling	Lillie Rd & North End Rd	Awesome Art Deco building now a scary cult center.

Map 43 • West Brompton / Fulham Broadway / Earl's Court

Stamford Bridge	Fulham Road & Moore Park Rd	That's not sweat you smell but money at Chelsea FC's HQ.

Map 46 • Sloane Square

Saatchi Gallery	Duke of York HQ, King's Rd	See rich dude's great art collection, for free.

Map 48 • Fulham

Putney Bridge Tube Pill Box	Putney Bridge Station	"We will fight them on the platforms!"

Map 50 • Sand's End

Lots Road Power Station	27 Lots Rd	Pint-sized power station, now disused.

Map 51 • Highgate

Highgate Cemetery	1 Swain's Ln	Eerily gothic home to Karl Marx and The Highgate Vampire.
Karl Marx's grave	Highgate Cemetry	Exactly what it says on the tin.

Map 52 • Archway (North)

Parkland Walk Nature Reserve	Parkland Walk	Hedgehogs and graffiti to be spotted along this abandoned railway.
Suicide Bridge	Hornsey Ln & Archway Rd	Former London entry point, now very much an exit point.

Map 53 • Crouch End

Abandoned Warehouse	Parkland Walk & Crouch End Hill	Dereliction galore along one of the best walks in London.

Map 56 • Hampstead Village

Hampstead Observatory	Lower Terrace & Hampstead Grove	The highest point in London, and open to the public!

Map 57 • Hampstead Heath

Keats' House	Keats Grove	Beautiful buildin' where some bloke wrote some poem. Innit.
Lawn Road Flats	Lawn Rd & Garnett Rd	c.1934 modern living. Learn to love concrete.

Map 60 • Archway

Banksy's Hitchhiking Charles Manson	Tally Ho Corner (off Highgate Hill)	Early stencil by internationally renowned graff artist.
Dick Whittington's Cat	89 Highgate Hill	Small stone statue of obscure Mayor's cat.

Map 62 • Finsbury Park

North London Central Mosque (Finsbury Park)	7 St Thomas's Rd	New name, ethos for once controversial, now myth-dispelling, mosque.

Map 63 • Manor House

The Castle Climbing Centre	Green Lanes & Lordship Park	Fake castle, real climbers.

Map 64 • Stoke Newington

Newington Green Church	39 Newington Green	'ERECTED 1708, ENLARGED 1860'...well, it made us laugh.

Map 67 • Belsize Park

Freud Statue	Fitzjohn's Ave, opposite Maresfiend Gardens Junction	Statue by Oscar Nemon near the psychoanalyst's Hampstead home.
St Stephen's	Rosslyn Hill	Gothic awesomeness. Currently being restored to its former glory.

Map 68 • Kilburn High Road / Abbey Road

Abbey Road Zebra Crossing	3 Abbey Rd	Go on. Take THAT photo. You know you want to.

Map 70 • Primrose Hill

3 Chalcot Square	3 Chalcot Sq	Home of poet Sylvia Plath, 1960-61.

Map 71 • Camden Town / Chalk Farm / Kentish Town (West)

Camden Market	Camden Lock Pl	Shop, hang, drink, listen, pose, watch, chill, rock, laugh.
Grand Regents Canal	Grand Regents Canal	London's best bike lane. Or canoe to Birmingham.
The Roundhouse	Chalk Farm Rd & Crogsland Rd	Prominent round building and historic performance venue.

Map 74 • Holloway Road / Arsenal

Gillespie Park	191 Drayton Park	Weird and wonderful nature park along the train tracks.

Map 75 • Highbury

St Paul's Shrubbery	St Paul's Rd & Northampton Park	All Monty Python jokes welcome, in fact, positively encouraged.

Map 76 • Edgeware Road / Marylebone (North)

Sherlock Holmes' House	221 Baker St	It's elementary my dear Watson!

Map 77 • Mornington Crescent / Regent's Park

Euston Tower	286 Euston Rd	Quite an impressive erection.
Greater London House	180 Hampstead Rd	Crazy Art Deco building.

Map 78 • Euston

The British Library	96 Euston Rd	Prestigious research library with unmatched collection.
Camden High Street	Camden High St & Delancey St	'Alternative' tourist mecca.
Cheney Road	Cheney Rd & Weller's Ct	"Chaplin, "Alfie" and many more were filmed on these cobbles.
Euston Station	Eversholt St & Doric Way	So ugly it's oogly.
Platform 9¾	King's Cross Station	This Harry Potter thing has gone way too f'ing far.
St Pancras Station	St Pancras Way	Listed Gothic frontage, massive modern Eurostar hangar behind.
St Pancras	Pancras Rd & Euston Rd	Ex-Victorian workhouse turned superbug den.

Map 80 • Angel / Upper St

Angel Station Roof	Angel	You can get on the roof here, you epic teens.
The Bull	100 Upper St	Hands up: who loves beer?

Map 81 • Canonbury

Gladiators Paving Slab	10 Canonbury St	Logo of fighty telly show built into pavement. Me neither.

Map 82 • De Beauvoir Town / Kingsland

Suleymaniye Mosque	212 Kingsland Rd	Striking minaret silhouetted against Shoreditch Church spire and Broadgate Tower.

Map 84 • Hoxton

Hoxton Square	Hoxton Sq	Great in summer. Buy some cans and join the hipsters.

Village Underground	54 Holywell Ln	How did they get the trains up there?
White Cube	48 Hoxton Sq	Jay Jopling's homage to modern art

Map 85 • Stoke Newington (East)

Abney Park Cemetery	Stoke Newington High St & Rectory Rd	Egyptian revival-style, spooky nature reserve.

Map 86 • Dalston / Kingsland

Centreprise	136 Kingsland High St	Multi-cultural art centre, cafe, bookshop and venue.
Holy Trinity, The Clowns Church	Beechwood Rd & Kirkland Walk	Every Feb, clowns mourn Grimaldi. In full costume.

Map 87 • Hackney Downs / Lower Clapton

London Orphan Asylum	Lower Clapton Rd & Linscott Rd	Grandiose remains of historic site now beloved of enviornmental artists.
The Strand Building	29 Urswick Rd	Beautiful Art Deco building, NOT the subject of Roxy Music song.
Sutton House	2 Homerton High St	Music and arts in the oldest house in East London.

Map 88 • Haggerston / Queensbridge Rd

Geffrye Museum	136 Kingsland Rd	English interior design from 1600 to today.

Map 89 • London Fields / Hackney Central

London Fields Lido	London Fields Westside	Open-air swimming for hardy Hackney folk.

Map 91 • Shoreditch / Brick Lane / Spitalfields

Brick Lane Mosque	59 Brick Ln	The area's changes reflect on the building – once a synagogue, now a mosque.
Christ Church Spitalfields	2 Fournier St	Star architect Nicholas Hawksmoor's pretty masterpiece
Dennis Severs' House	18 Folgate St	Candle-lit cellar, parlour, smoking room - step 300 years back in time.
Spitalfields Market	105 Commercial St	No bargains but certainly one-of-a-kind fashions.
Sweet Toof Graffiti Alley	Pedley St & Brick Ln	Signature sweeties and skulls – just off Brick Lane.
Ten Bells	84 Commercial St	Where Jack the Ripper got his victims.
Truman's Brewery	91 Brick Lane	Beautiful old building now a hip weekend market. That's progress...

Map 92 • Bethnal Green

Bethnal Green Tube Station	Bethnal Green Tube Station	Scene of the worst civilian loss of the Second World War.
London Buddhist Centre	51 Roman Rd	Get your freak om.

Map 93 • Globe Town / Mile End (North)

Art Pavilllion	221 Grove Rd	Arts center seemingly designed by the Teletubbies.
Mile End Climbing Wall	Haverfield Rd & Grove Rd	Classic climbing centre - one of London's big three.

Map 95 • De Beauvoir Town / Kingsland

The Sun HQ	1 Virginia Street	It's probably not legal to stake out Page 3 girls.

Map 96 • Whitechapel (East) / Shadwell (West) / Wapping

Battle of Cable Street Mural, St George's Hall	236 Cable St	Celebrating an almighty multi-faith bashing of a 1930s fascist march.
Blind Beggar Pub	337 Whitechapel Rd	A killing here finally led to Ronnie Kray doing porridge.

Map 98 • Mile End (South) / Limehouse

Ragged School Museum	46 Copperfield Rd	Barnado's school 'for the deserving poor' turned East End museum.

Map 100 • Poplar (West) / Canary Wharf (West)

Canary Wharf Tower	1 Canada Sq	You can smell the money yards away. Look, don't touch.
Canary Wharf Tube Station	Canary Wharf	Norman Foster's Jewel in the Jubilee Line Extension.

Map 102 • Millwall

The Docklands Sailing & Watersport Centre	235 Westferry Rd	Award-winning sailing centre.

Map 104 • South Bank / Waterloo / Lambeth North

County Hall	Westminster Bridge Rd & Belvedere Rd	One of London's most historical and vast buildings.
The Hayward Gallery	Southbank Centre	Revered and reviled bruiser.
The London Eye	Westminster Bridge Rd	Two words: Tourist. Trap. Nice view though.
Low Tide at South Bank	South Bank	Go for a walk on the exposed riverbed.
National Theatre	Waterloo Rd & Upper Ground	South Bank centre-piece, looked like it was from 2050 in 1960.
The Pier at OXO Tower	Barge House St & Upper Ground	Screw OXO! Have a picnic on the pier instead.
South Bank Book Market	Under Waterloo Bridge	Little-known outdoor market; heaps of vintage and second-hand reads.
Waterloo Bridge	Waterloo Bridge	When tired with London, come here and watch the sunset.

Map 105 • Southwark / Bankside (West)

Buskers' Archway	Southbank	Excellent acoustics make the decorated tunnel a coveted buskers' spot.
Elephant & Castle	Elephant & Castle	Everything that was wrong with 60s town planning. Concrete hell.
Michael Faraday Memorial	Elephant & Castle	He gave us electromagnetism, we gave him a roundabout.
The Ring	72 Blackfriars Rd	London's first boxing ring was here; now a characterful pub.
Shakespeare's Globe	21 New Globe Walk	The Bard's famous playhouse reconstructed.
Tate Modern	Bankside	Herzog and de Meuron dazzler.

Map 106 • Bankside (East) / Borough / Newington

Borough Market	8 Southwark St	London's best food market. Enjoy the free samples.
Cross Bones Graveyard	Redcross Way & Union St	Medieval resting place for London's ladies of the night.
Female Gladiator	159 Great Dover St	1st centruy AD grave of London's very own Xena.
The Golden Hinde	Clink St & Stoney St	Amazing replica of Francis Drake's Tudor war ship.
The London Tombs	2 Tooley St	Lesser known Tower experience—beware the plague pits.
Mint Street Park	Southwark Bridge Rd & Marshalsea Rd	Open space on the site of the old Evelina Children's Hospital.
Old Operating Theatre Museum	9 St Thomas St	Macabre ancient operating theatre, with gallery for eager spectators.
Southwark Cathedral	Cathedral St & Montague Close	Worth the diversion to see Chaucer and Shakespeare's stomping grounds.
St George the Martyr	Borough High St & Tabard St	Look for the homage to Dickens.
Winchester Palace	Clink St & Storey St	Random 13th century ruins with remarkable rose window.

Map 107 • Shad Thames

City Hall	Queen's Walk, More London	Dubbed 'The Testicle' by Mayor Ken Livingston. Nice.
Design Museum	Shad Thames	Fairly unsatisfying shows - drool-worthy bookshop.
Fashion and Textile Museum	83 Bermondsey St	DAH-ling, it's just fabulous!
Floating Gardens	31 Mill St	Gardens. Mad tramps. On Boats. What else do you want?
HMS Belfast	Morgan's Lane & Tooley St	Floating WW2 killing machine, much beloved of children.
Stompie	Mandela Way & Page's Walk	Sounds like a baby elephant. But it's a Soviet tank.
Tower Bridge	Tower Bridge Road	Messing about on the water.

Map 110 • Rotherhithe (West) / Canada Water

Brunel Museum	Railway Ave & Rotherhithe St	Where engineering geeks can seek refuge from being picked on.

Map 111 • Rotherhithe (East) Surrey Quays

Surrey Docks Farm	Rotherhithe St & Salter Rd	Show the kids what their bacon used to look like.

Map 113 • Walworth

East Street Market	Walworth Rd & East St	Gloriously useless stuff.
Heygate Estate	Deacon Way & Heygate St	A testament to urban planning gone horribly wrong.

Map 114 • Old Kent Road (West) / Burgess Park

The Animatronic Fireman	Old Kent Rd	Be afraid. Be very afraid.
Peckham Library	122 Peckham Hill St	Groundbreaking modern architecture or huge, carelessly

		dropped Tetris block?

Map 116 • South Bermondsey

Millwall FC Stadium	Zampa Road & Bolina Rd	A football mecca for somebody?

Map 120 • Greenwich

Cutty Sark Gardens	King William Walk & Romney Rd	Where the Archbishop of Canterbury was murdered in 1012.
Greenwich Foot Tunnel	Greenwich Church St & Thames St	Walk/crawl/skip/limp under the Thames.

Map 126 • New Cross

Ben Pimlott Building	University of London, New Cross	A building of cheerful, dreary, warped, modern fascist fun.

Map 131 • Vauxhall / Albert Embankment

Lambeth Palace	Lambeth Palace Rd & Lambeth Rd	Where the Archbishop of Canterbury lives; no, not in Canterbury, stupid.
Secret Intelligence Service HQ (MI6)	85 Vauxhall Cross	Real life James Bonds in a not-so-secret location.
Vauxhall City Farm	165 Tyers St	So that's where an egg comes from.

Map 133 • Battersea (East)

Battersea Dogs' Home	4 Battersea Park Rd	Re-house a pooch. Now does cats too.
Battersea Park Gasometers	Queenstown Rd & Prince of Wales Dr	Rusting monsters.
Battersea Power Station	188 Kirtling St	The world's most beautiful power station, surely.

Map 140 • Clapham Junction / Northcote Rd

Northcote Road	Northcote Rd	Middle-class marketing-types mecca.

Map 143 • Clapham High Street

Clapham Common Air-Raid Shelter	Clapham High St	The depths of government paranoia.

Map 144 • Stockwell / Brixton (West)

Brixton Market	Electric Ave & Electric Ln	Caribbean flavours, smells and sounds.
Electric Avenue	Electric Ave & Brixton Rd	First shopping area in Britain lit by electricity, in 1880.

Map 145 • Stockwell / Brixton (East)

Stockwell Bowls	Stockwell Rd & Stockwell Park Walk	70's concrete skatepark, take quads and get beaten-up.

Map 152 • Tooting Broadway

Gala Bingo Hall	50 Mitcham Rd	Bingo hall with Grade One listed interior.

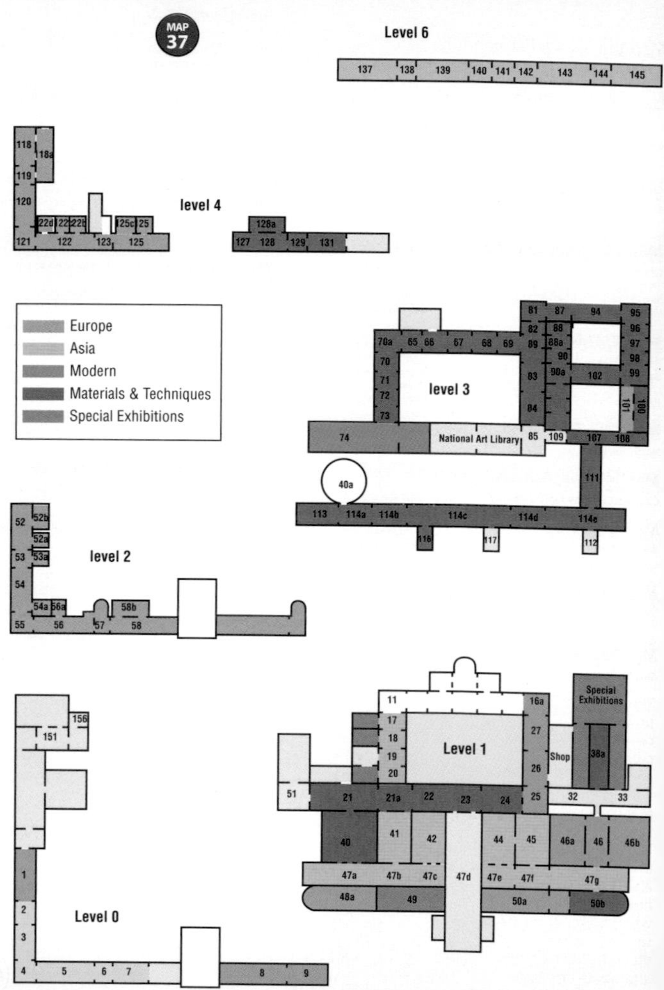
MAP 37
Level 6
137
138
139
140
141
142
143
144
145
level 4
118
118a
119
120
121
122d
122
122b
122
123
125c
125
125
128a
127
128
129
131
Europe
Asia
Modern
Materials & Techniques
Special Exhibitions
level 3
81
87
94
95
82
88
96
70a
65
66
67
68
69
89
88a
97
90
98
70
83
90a
102
99
71
72
101
100
84
73
74
National Art Library
85
109
107
108
40a
111
113
114a
114b
114c
114d
114e
116
117
112
52
52b
52a
53
53a
level 2
54
54a
56a
58b
55
56
57
58
11
16a
Special Exhibitions
156
17
27
151
18
Level 1
Shop
38a
19
26
20
51
21
21a
22
23
24
25
32
33
40
41
42
44
45
46a
46
46b
1
47a
47b
47c
47d
47e
47f
47g
48a
49
50a
50b
2
Level 0
3
4
5
6
7
8
9

General Information

NFT Map: 37
Address: Cromwell Road
London SW7 2RL
Phone: 020 7942 2000
Website: www.vam.ac.uk
Hours: 10am- 5.45pm daily. Select areas open until 10pm every Friday. National Art Library open 10am-5.30pm daily and 6.30 on Fridays. Check website for areas/ activities that require booking. Closed 24th, 25th and 26th of December.

Admission: Free to the permanent collection. There is a charge for temporary exhibitions. Tickets have an allotted time slot and although they can be purchased on the day, it is recommended you book ahead of= time by phone or online, especially with the more popular exhibitions.

Overview

The Victoria and Albert Museum, or the V&A, calls itself the world's greatest museum of art and design and nowhere has there ever been such an eclectic collection of objects inducing so many 'oooohs', 'aaaaahs' and 'holy shits!'. With a permanent collection of over 4.5 million objects, pretty much all on display in the 145 galleries, you can go everyday for a lifetime and be blown over by something you hadn't noticed before. For the tourist and non-tourist alike, the V&A is a wonderful maze of cultural ramblings. You'll get lost, overwhelmed and flustered, but we promise you won't get bored.

The V&A is a cabinet of curiosities of gargantuan proportions, boasting 5000 years of art and design, in every medium imaginable (from wax dioramas to a little black dress made of bras), spread over seven levels and organised by five themes—Asia, Europe, Materials & Techniques, Modern and Exhibitions. The trouble is where to start. You'll no doubt spend the first 10 minutes mesmerised by the glass Chihuly chandelier over the information booth, but what you do afterwards depends on how much time you have. Got hours? Avoid structure and just wander. Got an hour? Take a look at the map, see what strikes your fancy and head straight there. Just don't forget to hit up the gift shop afterwards—it's killer.

The Greatest Hits

There's no real method to the V&A's madness. Despite their best efforts to categorise everything, Vivienne Westwood gowns are just a stumble away from 1000 year-old Buddhas. But this is a great thing. The best advice is really to ditch the guidebook and go with your instincts. To make sure you take in the best stuff, start in the basement (having arrived through the Tunnel Entrance from the tube station), where you'll find the 17th century **Cabinet of Curiosities**—predecessors to the modern museum—which will get you in the right mind set. Weaving past bits and pieces of **Versailles**, you emerge onto the ground floor (Level 1) which covers fashion, Asia and both Medieval and Renaissance Europe. Highlights of which include the **cast courts**, which boast a life size replica of **Trajan's Column** in plaster, then onto ancient **samurai swords** and spectacular **kimonos** in Asia, the **Ardabil Carpet**—the largest and most amazing Islamic carpets in existence dating from 1539 (lit up on the hour and half-hour), an extensive costume room covering everything from **18th century crinolines** to **Juicy Couture** worthy of Paris Hilton, and lastly, **Raphael's cartoons**—massive sketches for a 1515 commission of tapestries that now hang in the Vatican. Before heading on, stop for a tea in the **Morris, Gamble & Poynter Rooms** café for teacakes in 1860s arts and crafts surroundings. Level 2 consists of the tucked away **British Galleries**, including the **Great Bed of Ware** as well as the endearing **Lord and Lady Clapham** dolls bedecked in miniature turn-of-the-18th century outfits. Up again on Level 3, you'll find the Materials & Techniques rooms, with its vast collections of **silver, ironwork and musical instruments**, as well as some dynamite paintings. Don't miss **Rossetti's The Daydream** and then **Ron Arad's Chair** in the modern rooms. This floor also houses the **National Art Library**—an art history student's research dream (you have to get a reading pass to study here though). Level 4 has a wonderfully tactile display of **glasswork**, as well as **architecture** and more **British Galleries from 1760-1900**. If you've made it this far, you deserve a knighthood.

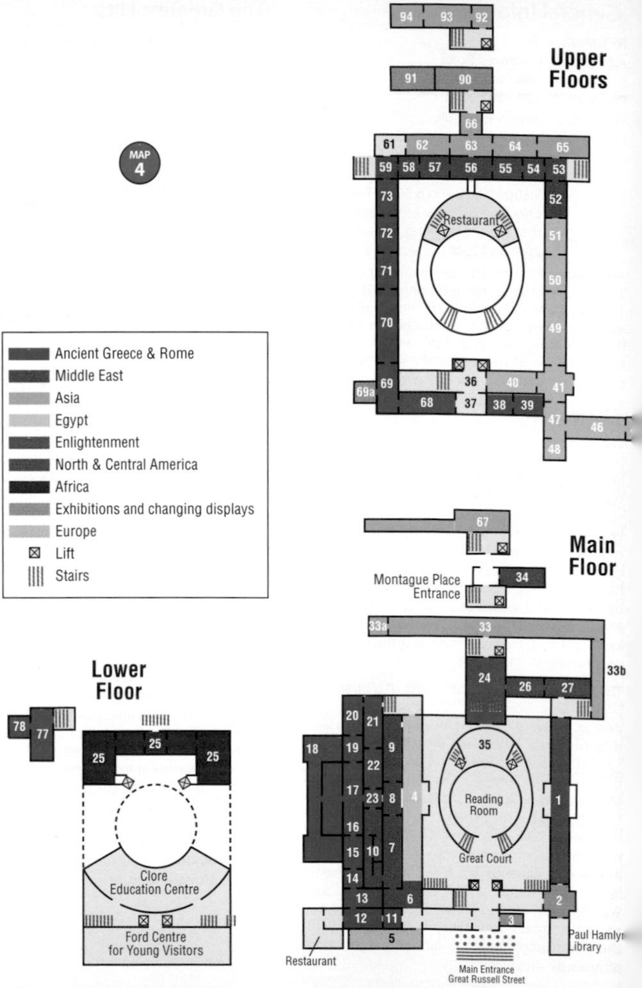

Upper Floors

94 93 92
91 90
66
61 62 63 64 65
59 58 57 56 55 54 53
73 52
Restaurant
72 51
71 50
70 49
69 36 40 41
69a 68 37 38 39
47 46
48

Main Floor

67
Montague Place Entrance
34
33a 33
33b
24 26 27
20 21
18 19 9
22 35
17 23 8 4 Reading Room 1
16
15 10 7 Great Court
14
13 6 2
12 11 3
5
Restaurant
Main Entrance Great Russell Street
Paul Hamlyn Library

Lower Floor

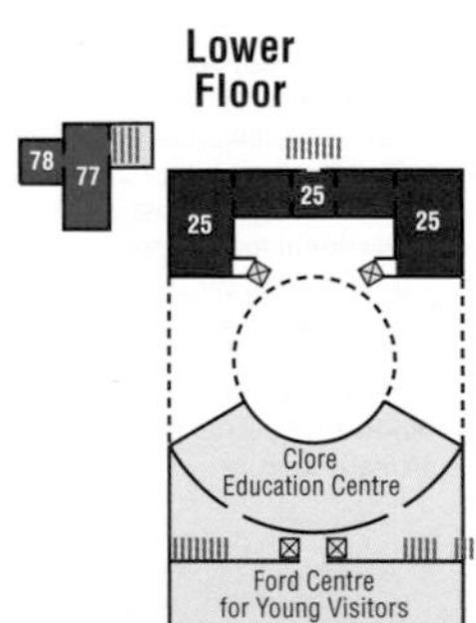

General Information

NFT Map: 4

Address: Great Russell Street, WC1B 3DG

Phone: 020 7323 8299 (information) or 020 7323 8181 (exhibition tickets)

Website: www.britishmuseum.org

Hours: The galleries open daily 10am-5.30pm and until 8.30pm on Fridays (except from good Friday). The Great Court is open 9am- 6pm and 8.30pm on Fridays. Check website for planned maintenance causing gallery closures. Closed 1st of January and 24th, 25th and 26th of December.

Admission: Free, with a charge for some special exhibitions.

Overview

Unless you're Indiana Jones, combining archaeological expertise with the swashbuckling energy to defeat obnoxious school groups, then do not attempt to cover the British Museum in a day. With 13 million items covering two million years of human history in almost 100 permanent and temporary galleries, you are better off treating yourself to different sections when the mood takes you—a perk of having one of the world's largest museums on your doorstep and open for free.

At 250 years, it is also the oldest museum in the world, but forget preconceptions of dusty urns and endless Roman coins—they're there if that's your bag, but this is a very modern organisation. The permanent displays include some of the world's most fascinating treasures, while the temporary exhibitions bring London a chance to break and lose artefacts which have seen some of the greatest moments of history, such as the recent display of drawings by Michelangelo, Raphael, Leonardo, and some other Renaissance scribblers who didn't make Ninja Turtle status.

However, while preserving artefacts to inspire its visitors, the Museum can also be seen as a testament to the great British pastime of looting. Some of the shining lights of its collection were acquired under the shadiest of circumstances, and the countries which were plundered so that snotty kids could chortle at the genitalia of their sculptures are increasingly vocal about getting the items back. For example the Elgin Marbles, rechristened with their pleasantly playful English name after the earl who helped himself to them, are huge slabs hacked from the 2500 year old Athenian Parthenon (albeit Elgin's entire nose later rotted off due to syphilis: a gratifying example of one-upmanship by nature). The legality of this move is hotly debated, but apart from the damage to the Parthenon, the Marbles undeniably suffered when they were cut into smaller pieces for transport to Britain, and when rowdy schoolboys bopped the leg off a centaur in 1961. The Museum holds firm that returning debated items would empty the museums of the world, but it has extended the occasional olive branch to ease the controversy; compensation was paid for the display of drawings stolen by Nazis, and they returned the Tasmanian Ashes (aboriginal human remains) to Australia after a 20-year battle.

The Greatest Hits

The **Great Court** is not just a Greatest Hit of the Museum, but of London as a whole. Being "the world's largest covered public square" may sound too niche an accolade to be impressive, but it really is stunning. The 150 year old **Reading Room** at its centre is a delight, both for the excellent library and for the wall-mounted list of major historical figures who have sought inspiration within its round walls. Whatever your ethics on plunder, some of the most morally-dubious exhibits are among the absolute must-sees: the **Elgin Marbles** in Room 18 are remarkable, while the **Rosetta Stone** in Room 4 gives you the irresistible buzz of seeing something so legendary up close, or as close at the backpacked hordes will allow, in your own town. A whole **Moai Statue** from Easter Island is in Room 24, the **Lewis Chessmen** set is in Room 42, and the **Mausoleum of Halikarnassos** exhibition displays some of the last remaining fragments of one of the Seven Wonders of the World. However, it is the stories of heartache, adventure, mystery and passion behind the items which bring them to life. Asking the steward of Rooms 62-3 how the **mummies** came to be in the museum, or seeing the pages from **The Book of the Dead** which recorded lives of the deceased, is a fascinating way to gain insight to people around the world and throughout time. And if that's a bit too deep, just head to one of the four **shops** for a mummy-shaped pencil case or replica Rosetta Stone.

General Information

NFT Map:	36
Address:	Cromwell Road, SW7 5BD
Phone:	020 7942 5000
Website:	www.nhm.ac.uk
Hours:	Daily 10 am–5.50 pm (Last admission 17.30) "After Hours" events run on the last Friday of each month during Nov–Apr. 24–26 Dec: closed.
Admission:	Free access to most of the Museum. Fee charged for some special exhibitions (free to Members).

Overview

Visiting the Natural History Museum is like reading National Geographic, if it was edited by JK Rowling. As imagination-tingling to adults as it is to kids, you can mull over serious questions about genetic modification and the environmental cost of modern life, while walking inside a termite mound or knocking on a petrified tree.

With more than 70 million specimens in their collection, you simply won't see it all at once, or for most of us—ever. But with free entry, regularly refreshed exhibits and unforgettable special exhibitions, it's worth dropping in when you have the opportunity. Grab a free map at the entrance to work out your route, which is colour-coded for a

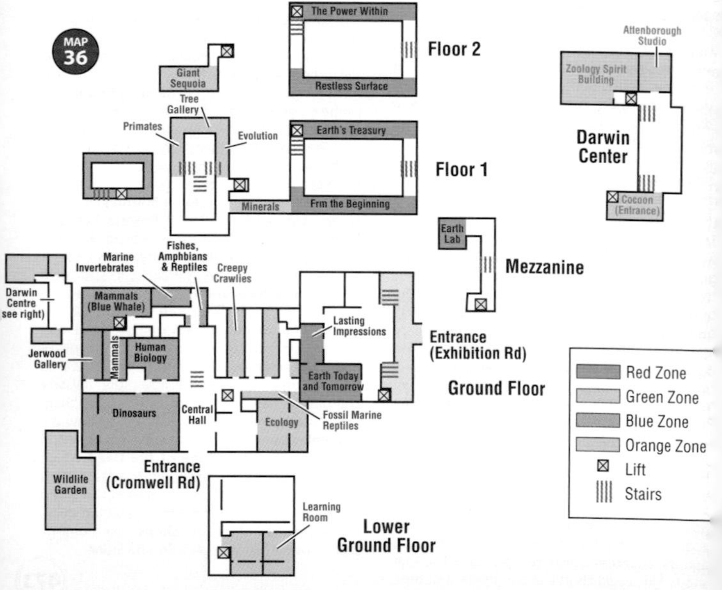

(slightly) easier life: Red Zone for the planet and forces of nature; Green for ecology and the environment; Blue for dinosaurs, mammals and biology; and Orange for the Wildlife Garden and behind-the-scenes peeks.

Weekends are inevitably heaving with hyperactive button-pressing families, spellbound tourists and Londoners trying to rebuild the brain cells they killed off with the night before's drinking; weekdays are amok with school groups. But don't let this put you off. If there's a queue outside the main entrance on Cromwell Road, and you don't fancy killing time by spotting all the different creatures carved around the entrance arch, pop 'round the side to Exhibition Road entrance and you'll fast-track yourself in. You can go early or late for fewer crowds, or stick with the permanent exhibitions, which are superb but not as sexy as the world-class special exhibitions which draw in the masses. Or, if all else fails, just shove the kids out the way: they're smaller than you and the buttons are *so much fun* to press.

The Greatest Hits

Anyone who didn't see the **Dinosaur Exhibition** as a child really missed out: run here and rectify the situation immediately if you haven't been, or revisit and enjoy the modernised exhibits if you have. The **Mammals Exhibition** will get you wondering exactly *how* someone stuffs a giraffe, and gives you a chance to get close to the gaping jaws of a hippo. For a different perspective on this room, go up to the balcony around it: watching people stare agog at the brilliantly-displayed **blue whale** is as entertaining as the exhibits themselves. For proof that even history geeks can make the earth move for you, visit the **Power Within** exhibition which recreates an earthquake (though don't expect a Universal Studios experience. The will is there, bless, but the budget just isn't…). Watch blushing parents introduce their kids to the birds and the bees in the **Human Biology** section, where an 8-times-life sized model of a **foetus** will put you off pregnancy forever. The **Wildlife Garden** is an oasis of serenity open from April–October, or you can impress a date (or not, depending on your coordination) by **ice-skating** next to the stunning Victorian building from November–January.

The Museum's Special Exhibitions are superb—check the website for current information. The annual **Veolia Wildlife Photographer of the Year**, October–April, is utterly inspirational, while a varying daily programme of events includes **lectures, behind the scenes tours** of the botany department, and **fossil workshops** for kids. Due to the success of the children's version, the museum is now running Dino Snores sleepovers for adults, which includes a three course meal, life drawing classes and an all night monster movie marathon. So if you fancy yourself as Ben Stiller in Night at The Museum start saving, as the stay will cost you a whopping £175.

"Like the creatures it displays (except for the Dodo—you'll find one in the Green Zone), the museum keeps evolving. Aptly, the latest major development is the Darwin Centre, where you can stoke your nightmares by checking out the giant tarantulas, experience life in a cocoon (like life in a London flat, but more spacious), and watch scientists at work. You might not think that watching scientists analysing and cataloguing bits of plant would be much of a spectator sport, but an hour in the centre will whiz by and leave you bursting with new knowledge to irritate your mates with.

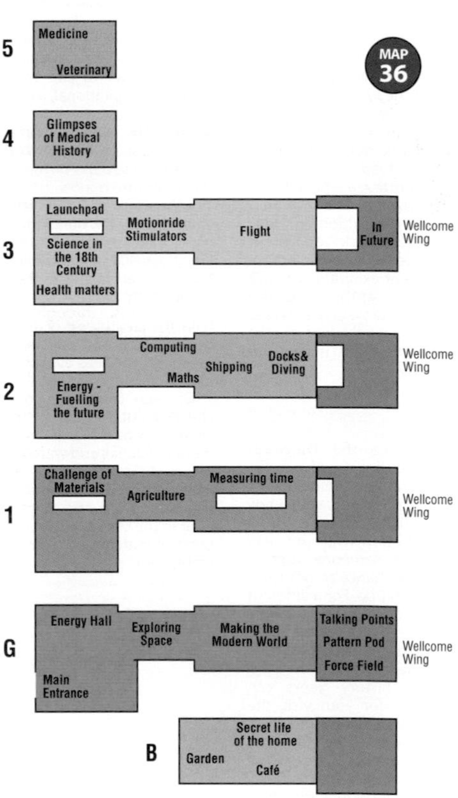
MAP
36
5
Medicine
Veterinary
4
Glimpses of Medical History
3
Launchpad
Science in the 18th Century
Health matters
Motionride Stimulators
Flight
In Future
Wellcome Wing
2
Energy - Fuelling the future
Computing
Maths
Shipping
Docks& Diving
Wellcome Wing
1
Challenge of Materials
Agriculture
Measuring time
Wellcome Wing
G
Energy Hall
Main Entrance
Exploring Space
Making the Modern World
Talking Points
Pattern Pod
Force Field
Wellcome Wing
B
Secret life of the home
Garden
Café

General Information

NFT Map:	36
Address:	Exhibition Road, South Kensington, London SW7 2DD.
Phone:	0870 870 4868
Website:	www.sciencemuseum.org.uk
Hours:	Open 10 am–6 pm every day except 24 to 26 December. check website for special school holiday and summer opening hours.
Admission:	Free, but charges apply to IMAX 3D Cinema, simulators & a few special exhibitions.

Overview

Museum and Science. Two words known to strike fear into the heart of many a child. And many a grown-up, come to that. But the Science Museum is one of the most visited museums in London. How so? Perhaps it's the heady mix of mildly erotic pistons and shafts; 60s room-sized computers and Bakelite ashtrays; special affects simulators and the mighty IMAX theatre? Or maybe it is the multitude of buttons; red and blue and green actual buttons, as well as Minority Report-style touch screens? We know they're aimed at kids, but we like. Oh and levers, did we mention levers?

The museum has its origins in the popular Great Exhibition of 1851. Prince Albert (no laughing in the back please) suggested the extra cash made by the Exhibition be used to found a number of educational establishments. Following a number of building moves and expansions the Science Museum as we know and love it opened in 1885.

The Greatest Hits

The museum's 300,000 gidgets, gadgets and gizmos attract 2.5 million visitors a minute or something, but venture above the third floor, to the **medical floors**, and you will have the place almost to yourself. The most popular area is the main drag along the ground floor which includes **Exploring Space** hung with real life space probes and other relics that look like they've come from the Doctor Who costume and props department, and **Making of the Modern World** featuring **Stephenson's Rocket**, to titillate your dormant trainspotter.

The third floor's **Launchpad** area has as many interactive displays as an 8-year-old could ever want. Parents hope their little darlings are actually learning something as they race from exhibit to exhibit whirling wheels, spinning liquids in plastic tubes and grimacing through head-sized lenses till tiredness or RSI sets in. For younger kids the tactile **Pattern Pod** on the ground floor makes up for its lack of buttons by its immensely pleasing shape.

The museum has its own Imax to impress the grown-ups and to make whimpering children cower as 3D Rexes loom into their faces. Don't even think about going in with a hangover. A huge silver hoop joins the **Energy exhibition** on the second to the ground floor. Answer a question on a nearby monitor, (don't worry they are easy) and watch your initials and age whiz around the inside of the ring. But what's that BUZZ? Like a huge electric fly killer? It's the inspired **'don't touch' display**—irresistible for the naughtiest in the class, one small electric shock later, the rest of the lemmings race over for a turn. Hilarious.

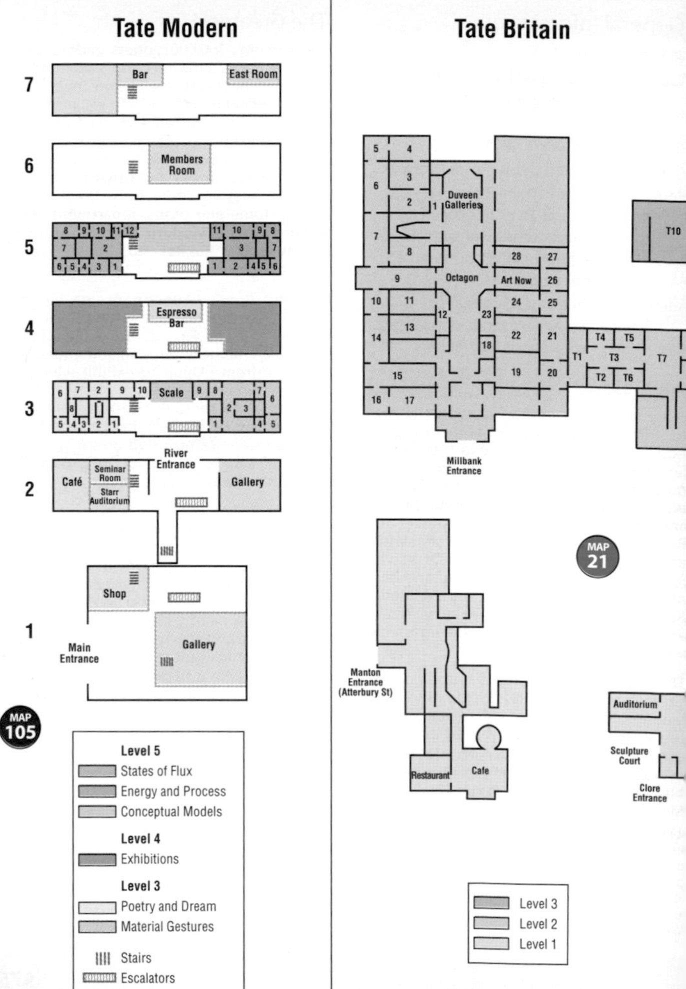
Tate Modern
7
Bar
East Room
6
Members Room
5
4
Espresso Bar
3
Scale
2
River Entrance
Café
Seminar Room
Starr Auditorium
Gallery
1
Shop
Main Entrance
Gallery
MAP 105
Level 5
States of Flux
Energy and Process
Conceptual Models
Level 4
Exhibitions
Level 3
Poetry and Dream
Material Gestures
Stairs
Escalators
Tate Britain
Duveen Galleries
Octagon
Art Now
Millbank Entrance
T10
MAP 21
Manton Entrance (Atterbury St)
Restaurant
Cafe
Auditorium
Sculpture Court
Clore Entrance
Level 3
Level 2
Level 1

General Information

Tate Britain:

NFT Map:	21
Address:	London SW1P 4RG
Phone:	020 7887 8888
Website:	www.tate.org.uk/britain
Hours:	Open 10am- 6pm Saturday to Thursday, and until 10pm on Fridays. Last admission to special exhibitions is 45 minutes before closing time.

Tate Modern:

NFT Map:	105
Address:	London SE1 9TG
Phone:	020 7887 8888
Website:	www.tate.org.uk/modern
Hours:	Sunday–Thursday 10 am–6 pm, Friday and Saturday 10 am 10 pm. Last admission into exhibitions is 5.15 pm (Friday and Saturday 8.15 pm).

Overview

In a city renowned for its galleries and museums, London's Tate galleries shine from the banks of the Thames. The first Tate was founded in 1897 as the National Gallery of British Art, but was renamed soon afterwards after its main patron Henry Tate—he of Tate and Lyle and the sugar cube. Originally on the site of the former Milbank Prison (where Tate Britain remains), the gallery gradually expanded and divided its collection over the four sites, two in London, one in Liverpool and the last in St Ives. In London, Tate Britain houses British art dating from 1500 to the present day, while Tate Modern was created to house—yes you've guessed it—more modern work from 1900 to the present day, and is reportedly the most visited modern art gallery in the world.

The two Tates carry the same trendy Tate logo and the shops contain much of the same avant-garde merchandise with a great range of children's stuff available in both. But while the more traditional Tate Britain more closely resembles the National Gallery in architectural and artistic flavour, Tate Modern has a very hip feel and draws a slightly broader audience, in part due to its location on the increasingly buzzy South Bank.

Both museums have popular restaurants and cafes, but to encourage those without a membership to sign up, each offers an exclusive members' room. These provide the best views, nicest toilets, designated staff and ever so slightly self-important customers, and are always a safe bet to impress a date.

Tate Modern

Based in the former Bankside Power Station, Tate Modern has proved to be an extremely popular attraction for tourists and Londoners alike since its opening in 2000. It houses the national collection of modern art, so expect plenty of inspirational and challenging works alongside exhibits that look like your cat sicked them up. The temporary art installations of the five-storey tall Turbine Hall provide much of the draw to the gallery. This huge space displays specially commissioned works from October to April of each year—a programme which was intended to run for only five years, but was extended due to its popularity. Quirky exhibitions fill the vast Turbine Hall, like Olafur Eliasson's 'Weather Project' which encouraged visitors to lie back on the floor in their thousands, gazing at the shadows cast by the synthetic sun. Ai Wei Wei's Sunflower Seeds, in 2010/11, was probably his most ambitious and attention-grabbing work before going MIA—ironically and probably due to the unwanted exposure it brought to the Chinese government. That and the fact punters had to be forbidden from walking on the seeds due to the fine dust the porcelain they were made from produced which could have been inhaled and damage the lungs. Again, ironically. In 2013, we await with baited breath who will fill the Turbine Hall and with what. If it all seems like you could have created better art yourself, then try one of the gallery's excellent workshops or courses and give it a go.

Tate Britain

The Tate Britain boasts the most comprehensive collection of British art in the world, and is home to the annual and unmissable Turner Prize show. Stone steps lead up to the portico and once inside, the Duveen Galleries' ethereal sculptures lie straight ahead, giving the first taste of a breathtaking collection of artwork. Tate Britain's collection is divided chronologically and dedicates space exclusively to notable artists, such as Turner, Blake and Constable. The gallery also includes significant works by William Hogarth, Stanley Spencer and Francis Bacon. While lacking the hip ambience of its sister gallery down the river, Tate Britain has been attempting to trend-ify itself with 'Late at Tate Britain' between 6pm and 10pm on the first Friday of every month, which aims to lure young'uns from the pub for some after-hours art-appreciation with exhibitions, performances, music, talks and films.

Look out for the themed guides to suit your mood, such as "The I've Just Split Up", "The I'm In A Hurry" and "The I Haven't Been Here For Ages" collections: a highly endearing way ease you through the 500 years of exhibits.

General Information

NFT Map: 24
Address: Trafalgar Square
London WC2N 5DN
Phone: 020 7747 2885
Website: www.nationalgallery.org.uk
Hours: 10 am–6 pm daily,
Fridays until 9 pm.

Admission: Free to the permanent collection and temporary exhibitions in the Sunley Room, Room 1 and The Space on Level 2. There is a charge for temporary exhibitions held on Level 2 in the Sainsbury Wing. Tickets have an allotted time slot and although they can be purchased on the day, it is recommended you book them ahead of time online, especially with the more popular exhibitions.

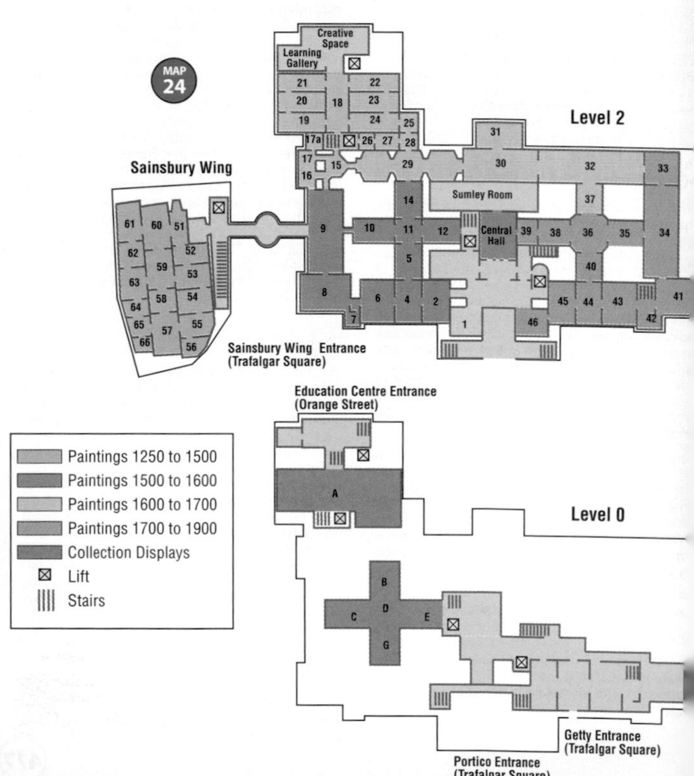

Overview

The National Gallery is home to one of the best and largest collections of Western European painting in the world, coming in at around 2100 paintings on display at any one time. An emphasis on *Western* and *painting* is needed. If you're looking for Roman antiquities or Persian miniatures, head for the British Musuem or the V&A—this is not where you're going to get it. Furthermore, if you're into anything post-impressionist, make an about face for the Tate Britain. This is a celebration of the arts of Europe in all their old-school occidental glory. Taking the surprisingly manageable tour around the galleries (most of which are on one floor) will leave you wowed by how many works of art you will recognise. This is a collection that has been branded deep into your subconscious—with its oh-yeah-that-one Turners, Hogarths, Rembrandts and Leonardos. Bring a date and even the most culturally challenged will be able to impress.

The collection came into being in 1824 when the House of Commons paid £57,000 for 38 paintings belonging to a banker, using his Pall Mall home as the exhibition space. Compared to the Louvre, calling a few paintings in some guy's house the National Gallery was a little too embarrassing for the British public. So the great and the good demanded the Government pull their finger out and get to work on a purpose-built gallery worthy of a national art collection. In 1832, architect William Wilkins was given the job, constructing the recognisable porticoed façade in an up-and-coming area known as Trafalgar Square, called by one trustee 'the very gangway of London'. The most recent addition to the gallery is the Sainsbury Wing, designed in 1991 by leading contemporary architects Robert Venturi and Scott Brown after much controversy. Prince Charles, notoriously fussy when it comes to architecture, dismissed one suggested design as "a monstrous carbuncle on the face of a much-loved and elegant friend".

The National Gallery can be tackled in one exhausting afternoon, if you put your mind to it. Take advantage of the fancy benches, as many of the more epic paintings are best viewed from a distance. Be sure to get lost in the many smaller galleries, which house some dynamite, lesser-known, works. If you're feeling hungry, the National Dining Rooms is a critically acclaimed (read: expensive) restaurant, serving up the best in British fare. If you're feeling like a little culinary nationalism, the more casual National Café serves a very good cream tea.

The Greatest Hits

Starting with the Sainsbury Wing, the collection snakes around, covering European painting in chronological order from 1250 to 1900. There are a lot of paintings and it can get slightly overwhelming, so if you're pressed for time and want to make sure you've 'done' the National Gallery, try one of their 60 minute taster tours or pick up their guide to the 30 must-see paintings. Don't miss the **Arnolfini Portrait** (signed with 'Van Eyck was here' above the mirror—hilarious), **Botticelli's Venus and Mars**, **The Wilton Diptych**, and **Uccello's The Battle of San Romano**. Moving onto the 1500-1600 range, you'll recognise **Leonardo's cartoon of The Virgin and Child with St Anne and St John the Baptist**, **'The Ambassadors'** by Hans Holbein the younger (the one where you have to crouch to see the skull), the still-hilarious portrait of **A Grotesque Old Woman** by Quinten Massys (a 1664 example of the classic conundrum—a 64 year-old trying desperately to look 16) and **Titian's Bacchus and Ariadne**. Moving on, the collection houses a rather large collection of Dutch masters, including **Rembrandt, Rubens and van Dyck**. If you're sick of 2-D, a rather cool contraption is **Samuel von Hoogstraten's peepshow**. Peer through the peep hole in this painted box for an eye-popping view of the interior of a Dutch house. Very cool. A trip to the museum is never complete without viewing a **Gainsborough, Turner and Hogarth**, all of which are housed in the 1700-1900 galleries. Do not miss Hogarth's **Marriage a la Mode** a comical rendition of an 18th century arranged marriage—in a series of six paintings. Last but not least, onto the juxtaposition of three epic 19th century history paintings depicting corporal punishment with chilling realism—**Manet's Execution of Maximillian, Delaroche's Lady Jane Gray and Puvis de Chavanne's Beheading of St John the Baptist.** What a way to end it all, quite literally.

General Information

Address:	Peninsula Square, London, SE10 0DX
Website:	www.theO2.co.uk
General Information:	020 8463 2000
Tickets:	0871 984 0002

Overview

Exactly how the Millennium Dome transformed itself from national embarrassment and vortex for millions of taxpayers' money to the slick new home of groovy events is a bit of a mystery. Or maybe it's blindingly obvious—suits are better than politicians at this kind of thing. Anyway, on the outside it looks the same—the oversized lovechild of a jellyfish and hedgehog. Inside, gone are the attractions and concepts of 1999, aimed at celebrating all things British, so visionary that visitors stayed away in droves. Instead, the contents of an above-average high street have been stuffed inside—generic bistro food and wine bars, a multi-screen cinema. Whoope-doo you might think. But hold on—people come for the music. No really, they do.

Enter the O2 Arena or its little sis, the IndigO2 (see what they did there?) and be very impressed. The Arena has been engineered to provide sight lines that older venues can only dream of. The air conditioning—usually a rarity at London gigs, actually works. The acoustics have to be heard to be believed. It might not be a destination venue for mosh-loving purists and those who like the sweat and beer to fly, but if you like your music with a bit of comfort and luxury, you know, like toilets that work and don't stink of piss (548 of them!) then the 02 is well worth a look. Wheelchair users are catered for with fully accessible facilities. London seems to have its first venue that feels like some real thought has gone into its creation. If the organisers get their act together and diversify the bands appearing, including more that veer away from mainstream bands then it could become unstoppable.

How to Get There—Driving

Driving to the O2 isn't as daft as it might sounc considering its location—previously un-chartered industrial wastelands of south east London. 2,00C parking spaces can be reserved in advance. With decent road links, traveling after rush hour should be bearable. The A102 linking north and south London runs through the Blackwall Tunnel, righ next to the venue.

How to Get There—Mass Transit

In theory, the O2 has excellent transport links nc matter how you travel. In practice, there's a gooc chance that your gig coincides with engineers digging up the precise bit of track you need to trave on. Check www.tfl.gov.uk before you travel. Bu when everything is working, then the Jubilee line at nearby North Greenwich connects directly with Waterloo and London Bridge. The Docklands Ligh Railway is one stop away and several bus routes dro off right outside. But the best way to arrive has t be by boat— the high speed Thames Clipper run every 20-30 minutes. from several piers includin Greenwich, Embankment and Waterloo. It's not onl relaxing, but you get to see London at its best o the trip.

How to Get Tickets

Ticketmaster. Naturally. Try Gumtree and Craigslis for swaps, unwanted tickets and scum-of-the-eart touts.

Life in London can sometimes seem like one continuous, eventful film, but if you like your plots to take place on screen then the city has a lot to offer. Going to catch a flick in London can often unravel like some kind of Indiana Jones-esque adventure—the Holy Grail being a reasonably-priced ticket in a clean, comfortable theatre, that can only be sought after battling hundreds of tourists and fellow Londoners all with the same thought. Every year 164 million people visit London's cinemas; now that's a fair few ticket stubs.Thankfully, by leaving The Twilight Zone (a.k.a. the tourist trap of the West End) there are plenty of cinematic treasures to be plundered. Whatever genre of film takes your fancy, whatever time of night and whether you want a velour seat and popcorn or a leather chair and glass of champagne, you are sure to find it in the nation's capital.

For those who are desperate to catch Spielberg's latest offering, and are crazy enough to stick it out in the West End, chain cinemas abound. You'll find **Odeon (Maps 1, 4, 23, 30, 35, 61, 66, 71, 111 & 136)**, **Vue (Maps 12, 33, 43, 66 & 80)** and **Cineworld (Maps 11, 23, 40, 43, 45, 100 & 138)** theatres all over London. If you're brave, or just fancy seeing a star or two at one of the regular premiers, **Odeon Leicester Square (Map 23)** (made up of two separate theatres) could be for you. Another monster on the square is the historic **Empire (Map 11)**, seating an impressive 1,300 patrons is a landmark in itself, although she is a slightly faded leading lady these days. Beware though. While the price of a cinema ticket in the big smoke is normally enough to make you choke on your Butterkist, wandering into any of the theatres in Leicester Square may force you to re-mortgage with prices as high as £22.50 a ticket at peak times. **Apollo West End Multiplex (Map 23)** on Lower Regent Street was formerly the home of Paramount Pictures in the UK but now houses five small, luxurious theatres showing the latest flicks on general release.

It's not hard to find cinemas offering art house and independent films in London. Finding a good one, however, can be more of a challenge. **The Barbican (Map 7)** is always a good bet, and you can take in an exhibition before your film to really beef up your grey matter. We highly recommend the **Curzon Soho (Map 11)** offering not only a wide range of cinematic gems but also a plush bar to loosen you up for that three hour Kurasawa number. Remember if the queue is snaking along the pavement, tickets can be bought at the bar downstairs too. Check out the cinema's cousin in **Mayfair (Map 9)** as well as the slightly shabby **Renoir (Map 5)** in Brunswick Square. **Cineworld Chelsea (Map 45)** on the lustrous King's Road is one of London's premier art houses with two-seaters available for the perfect smooching experience. **The Gate (Map 29)** in Notting Hill was created from a restaurant in 1911 and now offers independent releases in a luxurious setting. **BFI Southbank (Map 104)** specializes in film through the ages as well as hosting frequent events. Who would have thought old Charlie would help us save our pennies? **The Prince Charles Cinema (Map 11)** off Leicester Square sits in a perfect location and offers revivals, cult and foreign language films for as low as £1.50. Now that's a bloody bargain. For those with a penchant for 'le cine' courtesy of our French neighbours visit **Cine Lumiere (Map 36)** in South Kensington. Uber-cool Clapham has an equally trendy art house cinema, the **Clapham Picturehouse (Map 143),** Dalston's Art Deco gem the **Rio Cinema (Map 86)** is worth a look, while Bloomsbury offers up **The Horse Hospital (Map 4)**—the name's almost as avant-garde as the films they show. Just leave Dobbin behind.

There are some wonderful cinematic experiences to be had too. **BFI IMAX (Map 104)** is housed in a curious circular building, south of Waterloo Bridge, with the biggest screen in the UK—the size of five double-decker buses. Then there are those three magic words—**The Electric Cinema (Map 29)** on Portobello Road. Grab a Pinot Grigio, rest your derriere on a soft leather seat and munch away at home-made ice cream all the way from sunny Hampshire while catching the latest Polish release. We now have the first British cinema to be opened in the 21st century: **Shortwave (Map 107)**, popped up in 2009 in the stylish Bermondsey Square, and among its 50 seats are some which were shrewdly rehoused from the Electric Cinema. And treat your mates to another round and a packet of crisps, because there are increasing numbers of mini-cinemas in pubs and bars such as **The Garrison (Map 107)** and **The Roxy (Map 106)**.

Remember Londoners! Those on the Orange phone network get 2 for 1 on Wednesday nights—an ideal opportunity to save some precious pounds.

Cinemas	*Address*	*Phone*	*Map*
Aldwych Film	1 Aldwych	020 7300 1000	14
Apollo Cinema Piccadily Circus	19 Lower Regent St	0871 2233 444	23
Barbican Centre Cinema	Silk St & Whitecross St	020 7638 4141	7
BFI London IMAX	1 Charlie Chaplin Walk	0870 787 2525	104
BFI Southbank	Belverdere Rd & Waterloo Rd	020 7928 3232	104
Cine Lumiere	17 Queensberry Pl	020 7073 1350	36
Cineworld Chelsea	279 King's Rd	0871 200 2000	45
Cineworld Fulham Road	142 Fulham Rd	0871 200 2000	43
Cineworld Hammersmith	207 King St	0871 200 2000	40
Cineworld Haymarket	63 Haymarket	0871 200 2000	23
Cineworld Shaftesbury Avenue	13 Coventry St	0871 200 2000	11
Cineworld Wandsworth	Wandsworth High St & Ram St	0871 220 8000	138
Cineworld West India Quay	11 Hertsmere Rd	0871 200 2000	100
Clapham Picturehouse	76 Venn St	020 7498 2242	143
Curzon Chelsea	206 King's Rd	020 7351 3742	45
Curzon Mayfair	38 Curzon St	020 7495 0501	9
Curzon Soho	99 Shaftesbury Ave	020 7292 1686	11
The Electric Cinema	191 Portobello Rd	020 7908 9696	29
Empire Leicester Square	5 Leicester Square	020 7437 9011	11
Everyman Baker Street	96 Baker St	020 3145 0565	1
Everyman Belsize Park	203 Haverstock Hill	020 3145 0520	67
Everyman Hampstead	5 Hollybush Vale	0870 066 4777	56
Everyman Screen on the Green	83 Islington Green	020 3145 0525	80
Frontline Club	13 Norfolk Pl	020 7479 8950	31
Gate Picturehouse	87 Notting Hill Gate	020 7727 4043	29
Genesis Mile End	93 Mile End Rd	020 7780 2000	97
Greenwich Picturehouse	180 Greenwich High Rd	087 0755 0065	120
Horse Hospital	30 Colonnade	020 7833 3644	4
ICA Cinema	The Mall & Horse Guards Rd	020 7930 3647	23
Lux	18 Shacklewell Ln	020 7503 3980	86
Notting Hill Coronet	103 Notting Hill Gate	020 7727 6705	29
Odeon Camden Town	14 Parkway	020 7482 4576	71
Odeon Holloway	419 Holloway Rd	0871 22 44 007	61
Odeon Kensington	Kensington High St & Edwards Sq	0871 22 44 007	35
Odeon Leicester Square	24 Leicester Sq	0871 22 44 007	23
Odeon Marble Arch	10 Edgware Rd	0871 22 44 007	1
Odeon Panton Street	11 Panton St	0871 22 44 007	23
Odeon Putney	26 Putney High St	0871 22 44 007	136
Odeon Surrey Quays	Redriff Rd & Surrey Quays Rd	0871 22 44 007	111
Odeon Swiss Cottage	96 Finchley Rd	0871 22 44 007	66
Odeon Tottenham Court	30 Tottenham Ct Rd	0871 22 44 007	4
Odeon West End Cinema	40 Leicester Sq	0871 22 44 007	23
Odeon Whiteleys	Queensway & Porchester Gardens	0871 22 44 007	30
Peckham Multiplex	95 Rye Ln	0870 0420 299	123
Phoenix Cinema	52 High Rd	020 8444 6789	na
Prince Charles Cinema	7 Leicester Pl	020 7494 3654	11
Renoir Cinema	1 Brunswick Sq	0870 0420 299	5
Rich Mix Centre	34 Bethnal Green Rd	020 7613 7490	91
Rio Cinema	107 Kingsland High St	020 7241 9410	82
Ritzy Picturehouse	Coldharbour Ln & Brixton Oval	020 7733 2229	150
Riverside Studios	Crisp Rd & Queen Caroline St	020 8237 1111	41
Short & Sweet	91 Brick Ln	020 7247 6166	91
Shortwave	10 Bermondsey Square	0207 357 6845	107
Vue Finchley Road	Finchley Rd & Blackburn Rd	08712 240 240	66
Vue Fulham	Fulham Rd & Cedarne Rd	08712 240240	43
Vue Islington	36 Parkfield St	08712 240240	80
Vue Shepherds Bush	Shepherds Bush Green & Rockley Rd	08712 240 240	33
Vue West End Cinema	3 Cranbourn St	08712 240 240	12

It seems that every pub, bench and bridge in London has a tale to tell of past literary greats mulling over their troubles, weeping over lovers lost or launching themselves into the Thames. Ours is a city saturated in literary history and literature-lovers, with an abundance of bookshops and diversity of readers. While so many other retailers are homogenising, our independent bookshops—with their knowledgeable staffs and their often narrow focus—remain as eclectic and enthusiastic as ever. As well as a great selection of specialist independent stores, London is also home to dozens of second-hand bookshops, book markets, a literature festival, a major international book trade fair, and Europe's largest bookshop.

General

The **Foyles** flagship store on Charing Cross Road **(Map 12)** is a London institution, with a history as eccentric as its stock. Along with mainstream books and best-sellers, it offers a good range of second hand and out-of-print books, as well as a specialist Antiquarian department and a chilled jazz café. Venerable **Hatchard's (Map 10)** has been hawking books for over 200 years, making it London's oldest bookstore. The **London Review Bookshop (Map 4)** offers a huge range of constantly updated books with an intellectual bent and intellectual staff. **Metropolitan Books (Map 6)** is small but perfectly stocked, and Phil the owner makes time for any customer seeking advice or a friendly chat. Kids can find a bookshop wonderland in **Tales on Moon Lane (Map 128)** while parents can find the books they grew up with at **Ripping Yarns (Map 51).** The excellence of the independent stores has meant the chains have had to up their game—and loath though we are to say it, some, such as **Borders (Maps 10, 12, 43 & 80)** and academic specialists **Blackwells (Maps 4, 12 & 74)** have got it very right indeed. In particular, **Waterstone's** in Piccadilly **(Map 23)** attracts all sorts of excitable superlatives, being the largest bookshop in Europe, running a range of literary activities to complement their stock, and even hosting a bar with some of the finest views of London.

Second Hand

Sadly, the world-renowned status Charing Cross Road used to command as the Mecca of second-hand bookstores is fading, and those who go looking for the genteel expertise immortalised in Helene Hanff's bestseller *84 Charing Cross Road* will find a "Med Kitchen" (shudder) at number 84. Many shops still cling to their ideals however, such as **Any Amount of Books (Map 12)** selling titles from as little £1 and offering a leather-binding service so your books can furnish your room as well as your mind. Good places to start if you are scouting for quality second-hand bookshops are: the tardis-like **The Bookshop (Map 129)** staffed by bookworms who have read *everything* (or so it seems) and can always help you find a gem; **John Sandoe (Map 46)** for true bookshop charm (rickety staircases, passionate staff, enchanting atmosphere); and the **Trinity Hospice (Map 136)** and **Oxfam Bookshops (Maps 38, 51, 86)**—not only an astonishingly cheap and broad collection of works, but all for charidee.

Specialist

Finding a bookshop devoted to your passion is like finding a club of old friends, and London caters for all tastes. Bored of cheese toasties? **Books for Cooks (Map 29)** smells as good as the recipes look, as they're tested in their kitchen first, while in-store cooking workshops teach new skills to avid customers. Sci-Fi nerds will be in their element at **Forbidden Planet (Map 179)**. **Gekoski (Map 4)** stocks a good range of modern first editions, or for older and rarer first editions try **Henry Sotheran (Map 10)**: a unique, but pricey, treat for any enthusiast. Head to **Atlantis (Map 4)** for all your occult needs (though no doubt the Spirits had already tipped you off on that one). Arty types are extensively catered for: **The Photographers' Gallery (Map 3)**, a treat in itself, has a substantial shop stocking photography titles, artists' monographs and unusual cameras; the **ICA Bookshop (Map 23)** is a great destination for art and film fans, and you can take in an exhibition while you're there; **Travis & Emery (Map 24)** stocks a vast range of music books and scores; comic geeks can get their fix at **Gosh! (Map 4)**. And for those with a passion for passion, pop along to the book section of **Coco de Mer (Map 13)**. Head to **Artwords (Map 84)** for books on—nope, I'll see if you can guess. Or to **Chappell (Map 11)** to supplement your Abba Hits keyboard book with some of their 50,000 music titles. **Motor Books (Map 24)**, surprisingly London's only shop dedicated to motoring, rail, aviation and military books, is the ideal repository for your menfolk when you need some peace.

Travel

Feeling lethargic? Head to one of the city's superb travel bookshops to have your energy restored. **Stanford's (Map 13)** has been inspiring London for 150 years, with its enormous collection of travel books and maps. A bookshop for travellers who like to read, **Daunt Books (Maps 2, 28, 57 & 67)** arranges all its books by geographical location, so even its fiction, cookbooks and history are shelved by country. Or to learn any of over 150 languages, head to **Grant & Cutler (Map 10),** the UK's largest foreign-language specialist.

Politics

Bookmarks (Map 4) stocks left-leaning works on a huge range of issues and takes a lively role in political activism, giving it a real and infectious sense of purpose. Also hugely right-on, both representing and driving several lefty social movements, is **Housmans (Map 78)**. Or for a more balanced approach with political works across the parties and even the odd Minister browsing for ideas, try **Westminster Bookshop (Map 22).**

Talks and events

Publishing is a cut-throat business, and many writers have to sell their soul to get noticed. For them, it means an endless round of book signings and talks; for us, it means a fabulous chance to hobnob with our favourite authors. Most bookshops host occasional signings, but for regular events from the most celebrated authors, the big boys predictably have all the clout. **Foyles (Maps 12, 33, 78, 104)** and **Waterstone's (see p.489)** attract huge names: recent guests have included JK Rowling, Louis de Bernières, Salman Rushdie and AS Byatt. **Stanford's (Map 13)** offers opportunities to hear well-known travel editors, writers and photographers for an inspirational and sometimes career-changing evening. For intellectually stimulating debates and literary discussions, check out the **London Review Bookshop (Map 4)** and **Bookmarks (Map 4)**. Some events are free, some as much as a theatre ticket, but all should be booked in advance to ensure a place.

Bookshops	*Address*	*Phone*	*Map*
Any Amount of Books	56 Charing Cross Rd	020 7836 3697	12
Artwords	65 Rivington St	020 7729 2000	84
Atlantis	49 Museum St	020 7405 2120	4
Bargain Bookshop	153 Stoke Newington High Street	020 7249 8983	85
Bertram Rota	31 Long Acre	020 7836 0723	13
Blackwell	119 London Road	020 7928 5378	105
Blackwell Business + Law Bookshop	243 High Holborn	020 7831 9501	14
Blackwell Medical Bookshop	St Thomas Street	020 7403 5259	106
Blackwells	183 Euston Road	020 7611 2160	4
Blackwells	100 Charing Cross Rd	020 7292 5100	12
Blackwells	158 Holloway Road	020 7700 4786	74
Bookmarks	1 Bloomsbury St	020 7637 1848	4
Bolingbroke Bookshop	147 Northcote Rd	020 7223 9344	140
Books etc.	30 Broadgate Circle	020 7628 8944	8
Books etc.	115 Buckingham Plalace Road	020 7630 6244	20
Books etc.	66 Victoria St	020 7931 0677	22
Books etc.	Queensway	020 7229 3865	30
Books etc.	28 Broadway shopping centre	020 8764 3912	41
Books etc.	Cabot Place East	020 7513 0060	100
Books etc.	Southside Shopping Centre	020 8874 4587	138
Books for Cooks	4 Blenheim Crescent	020 7221 1992	29
The Bookshop	1 Calton Ave	020 8693 2808	129
Chappell of Bond St	152 Wardour St	020 7432 4400	11
Coco de Mer	23 Monmouth St	020 7836 8882	13
Daunt Books	83 Marylebone High St	020 7224 2295	2

Bookshops	*Address*	*Phone*	*Map*
Daunt Books	193 Haverstock Hill	020 7794 4006	67
Daunt Books	51 S End Rd	020 7794 8206	57
Daunt Books	112 Holland Park Ave	020 7727 7022	28
Donlon Books	77 Broadway Market	020 7684 5698	89
The Dover Bookshop	18 Earlham St	020 7836 2111	12
Forbidden Planet	179 Shaftesbury Ave	020 7420 3666	12
Foyles	113 Charing Cross Rd	020 7437 5660	12
Foyles	Upper Ground	020 7440 3212	104
Foyles	Pancras Road	020 3206 2650	78
Foyles	Westfield	020 3206 2656	33
Gosh! Comics	39 Great Russell St	020 7636 1011	4
Grant & Cutler	57 Great Marlborough Street	020 7734 2012	10
Hatchard's	187 Piccadilly	020 7439 9921	10
Henry Sotheran	2 Sackville St	020 7439 6151	10
Highgate Bookshop	9 Highgate Highstreet	020 8348 8202	n/a
Housmans Bookshop	5 Caledonian Rd	020 7837 4473	78
ICA Bookshop	The Mall	020 7766 1452	23
John Sandoe	10 Blacklands Terrace	020 7589 9473	46
The Lion and Unicorn Bookshop	19 King Street	020 8940 0483	n/a
London Review Bookshop	14 Bury Pl	020 7269 9030	4
Magma	8 Earlham St	020 7240 8498	12
Metropolitan Books	64 Exmouth Market	020 7278 6900	6
Motor Books	13 Cecil Court	020 7836 5376	24
Oxfam	80 Highgate High St	020 8340 3888	51
Owl Books	209 Kentish Town Rd	020 7485 7793	72
Pages of Hackney	70 Lower Clapton Rd	020 8525 1452	87
The Photographers' Gallery	16 Ramillies St	020 7831 1772	10
Quinto	72 Charing Cross Rd	020 7379 7669	12
R. A. Gekoski	15 Bloomsbury Square	020 7706 2735	4
Ripping Yarns	355 Archway Rd	020 8341 6111	51
Southbank Book Market	Under Waterloo Bridge	0871 663 2501	104
Stanford's	Long Acre	020 7836 1321	13
Stoke Newington Bookshop	159 Stoke Newington High Street	020 7249 2808	85
Tales on Moon Lane	25 Half Moon Ln	020 7274 5759	128
Travis & Emery	17 Cecil Ct	020 7240 2129	24
Trinity Hospice Bookshop	208 Upper Richmond Rd	020 8780 0737	136
Village Books	1 Calton Ave	020 8693 2808	129
Waterstone's	421 Oxford St	020 7495 8507	2
Waterstone's	82 Gower St	020 7636 1577	4
Waterstone's	Spencer Street	020 7608 0706	6
Waterstone's	9 Garrick St	020 7836 6757	13
Waterstone's	176 Fleet St	020 7353 5939	14
Waterstone's	Ludgate Circus	020 7236 5858	15
Waterstone's	54 London Wall	020 7628 9708	17
Waterstone's	1 Whittington Ave	020 7220 7882	18
Waterstone's	206 Piccadilly	020 7851 2400	23
Waterstone's	Trafalgar Square	020 7839 4411	24
Waterstone's	Exhibition Rd	020 7942 4481	36
Waterstone's	87 Brompton Rd	020 7730 1234	37
Waterstone's	151 King's Rd	020 7351 2023	45
Waterstone's	255 Finchley Road	020 7433 3299	66
Waterstone's	128 Camden High Street	020 7284 4948	78
Waterstone's	45 Bank Street	020 7719 0688	100
Waterstone's Economists' Bookshop	Clare Market	020 7405 5531	14
Westminster Bookshop	8 Artillery Row	020 7802 0018	22
WHSmith	124 High Holborn	020 7242 0535	14
WHSmith	Cannon Street Station	020 7626 5643	16
WHSmith	Fenchurch Street Station	020 7480 7295	18
WHSmith	Surrey Quays Shopping Centre	020 7237 5235	111
WHSmith	Elephant and Castle Shopping Centre	020 7703 8525	112

Yep you've heard the news. Theatre in the capital is all commercial. Predictable. Repetitive. Uncontroversial. If you believe the whingers, it's all boring stuff. Don't, because it's not. Yes, the West End, that heartland of commercial theatre around Shaftesbury Avenue, is filled with tourist-grabbing, crowd-pleasing musicals. Yes, there are more star-dominated, tried-and-tested plays than ever. Yes, the Mousetrap is still taking up the space at St Martin's after 58 years of we-bloody-well-know-whodunit.

But all that's only half the story. To find the other half, look beyond the glittering billboard signs to find the daring, small West End theatres, such as the **Donmar Warehouse (Map 13)**, bringing the innovative and unusual to Theatreland. There are the Off-West End theatres that proudly fly the flag for new writers, unafraid of being political, controversial and in-yer-face: **The Royal Court (Map 19)**, **The Soho (Map 11)**, **The Bush (Map 33)**. There are the unconventional, anarchic ensemble companies, such as PunchDrunk, shaking up things all the way from the fringe to the West End, while innovative short-play evenings are popping up at pubs across the city (see below).

But let's not forget the cracking double-whammy of the **National Theatre (Map 104)** and **The Old Vic (Map 104)**, two artistic powerhouses currently going from strength to strength. At the National, the unstoppable Nicholas Hytner brings original works to this Southbank concrete colossus (coupled with a £10-tickets offer), while down the road, Hollywood-star-turned-theatre-connoisseur Kevin Spacey is returning the Old Vic into its former glory. The refurbished **Young Vic (Map 104)**, meanwhile, is one of the best places to see fresh, new theatre (and get drunk afterwards). And, whatever you do, you're never far from a good Shakespeare production.

Keeping It Real In The West End

The Donmar Warehouse (Map 13), the West End's smallest theatre, has gained a reputation for being one of Theatreland's most innovative, yet still crowd-pleasing houses. It's quite common for good new plays that have successfully kicked off at a fringe or Off-West End venue to transfer to the West End, such as Tom Stoppard's guitars-meet-politics cracker Rock'n'Roll. **Dean Street's Soho Theatre (Map 11)** hunts out some of the most original, fearless or hilarious theatre around, while the **Comedy Theatre (Map 23)** may play it a little more safe but packs its shows with jaw-dropping casts. The West End is also a great place to catch up on those classics you always wanted to see but never got round to: from Beckett to Shakespeare.

Off-West End & The Fringe – The Best

The underground-led, breakneck guerrilla heyday might be over, but theatre outside the West End is in rude health. Head to rough-around-the-edges Dalston, where the **Arcola Theatre (Map 86)** continues to thrive in its scruffy ex-factory home, thanks to eclectic programming, an early-fringe-days feel and heaps of creative energy. The tiny **Bush Theatre (Map 33)** has long been a fierce champion of new work, and after being rescued by a star-studded tantrum in the face of funding cuts in 2008 it will doubtless continue to discover exciting new talent. So will **The Royal Court (Map 19)** on Sloane Square, which is one of London's finest. For new, innovative work, also keep your eyes on the **Battersea Arts Centre (Map 140)**, to watch what others will pay £50 to see next year (such as its premiere of Jerry Springer The Opera while other theatres nervously wrung their hands).

Theatre can't change society? Try telling that to the conviction-led crew of Kilburn's **The Tricycle (Map 65)**—easily London's most radical and most dedicated, political theatre. Islington's **Almeida (Map 80)** is far more conventional, but pretty—and that's got to count for something. If you're up for a laugh, check **The Hackney Empire (Map 87)**, a turn-of-the-century music hall, hosting some of London's best variety shows. **The Old Red Lion (Map 80)**, home inside an Islington pub, stubbornly clings to its unconventional, ale-fuelled fringe attitude, while **Battersea's Theatre 503 (Map 132)** is as provocative as ever. Be surprised.

If the thought of being in a theatre at all is too bourgeois for you, then you're still well catered for. London thesps it up wherever it can so you're never too far from a performance and its sometimes unwitting audience. Recent outings have included an opera about domesticity and flatpack furniture in the Wembley Ikea, and a thriller performed in an office while the audience watch with binoculars and audiophones from the terrace opposite. Or if it's sunny, squeeze among the crowds and their bottles of rosé for the occasional performances at **The Scoop**.

Tickets

If you know what you're after, check the theatre's website—they will either have their own system, a link to a ticket selling site, or provide a phone number. If not, check www.officiallondontheatre.co.uk, which lists shows by name, theatre and genre. The site also displays shows that are just opening, or just closing, and links straight to the appropriate ticketing website, once you have made your mind up. There's a handy map of all West End venues, too.

Fancy a bargain? The iconic TKTS ticket booth on Leicester Square sells on-the-day tickets for most big shows, half price. The queue can be mind-boggling, so go early. There's a £2.50 booking fee, but it's included in the price shown. Many theatres also have their own discount schemes. If you don't mind standing, you can get Royal Court tickets for as little as 50p. Yes, that's 50p. Just show up between 6 pm and 6.30 pm on the day of the performance. The National has £5 standing tickets for all shows, but the view ain't always great.

Exciting & New

Enter the ensemble. They are multi-skilled, imaginative and are shaking the cosy, venue-obsessed Theatreland with a vengeance. Ensemble companies like PunchDrunk and Kneehigh are touring their way through London's venues in vigorously anarchic fashion. The result is increasingly physical, increasingly unconventional—and increasingly exciting theatre, which you'd be mad to miss.

PunchDrunk (www.punchdrunk.org.uk) have gained a reputation for site-specific productions, inviting the audience to walk around and follow actors and themes as they please. Their 2006 treatment of Goethe's Faust at the National Theatre was widely hailed as one of the best things to have happened to British theatre in years. Kneehigh (www.kneehigh.co.uk) enjoy setting their nightmarish productions in outside mystical locations, but aren't afraid of West End constraints either. The award-winning Cheek by Jowl (www.cheekbyjowl.com), which have been producing Shakespeare and European classics since 1982, keep discovering hot talent—and ways to innovate.

If that's not grassroots enough, visit one of the themed short-play evenings that are popping up across town. Bringing together writers, actors and directors for twenty-minutes-or-so mini-shows, they have become a popular theatre alternative. Take your pick: Established organisers Nabokov (www.nabokov-online.com) have found a West End home at the **Trafalgar Studios (Map 24)**, SourFeast (www.sourfeast.co.uk) are based at Brixton's **Dogstar Pub (Map 150)**, and relative newcomers DryWrite have made Whitechapel's **The George Tavern (Map 97)** their own. The message is spreading. What you thought was a boozer, really is a stage. The possibilities are endless.

Contemporary Dance

From small company shows to big stage spectacles, contemporary dance is having one hell of a ride. **Sadlers Wells (Map 6)** (www.sadlerswells.com), the grand old lady of dance venues, is still doing a fine job bringing some of the world's best dance to London. Check their Sadler's Wells Sampled programme, showcasing dazzling future talent for as little as £10. **The Barbican (Map 7)** (www.barbican.org.uk) has established itself as a reliable source of powerful dance performances, while the **Royal Festival Hall (Map 104)** attracts increasingly bold and interesting works to its refurbished riverside location. For London's most innovative dance performances, check **The Place (Map 4)**, a stylish venue that combines performance, training and dance education (www.theplace.org.uk).

Theatres	*Address*	*Phone*	*Type*	*Map*
Adelphi Theatre	The Strand	087 0403 0303	West End	24
Aldwych Theatre	49 Aldwych	0870 4000 805	West End	14
Almeida Theatre	Almeida St	020 7359 4404	Fringe	80
Ambassadors Theatre	West St	084 4811 2334	West End	12
Apollo Theatre	Shaftesbury Ave	084 4579 1971	West End	11
Apollo Victoria Theatre	17 Wilton Rd	020 7834 6318	West End	20
Arcola Theatre	27 Arcola St	020 7503 1646	Fringe	86
Arts Theatre	6 Great Newport St	084 5017 5584	West End	12
Barbican Centre	Silk St & Whitecross St	020 7638 4141	Performing Arts	7
Barons Court Theatre	28 Comeragh Rd	020 8932 4747	Fringe	42
Battersea Arts Centre	Lavender Hill & Theatre St	020 7223 2223	Fringe	140
Bloomsbury Theatre	15 Gordon St	020 7388 8822	Fringe	4
Brixton Academy	211 Stockwell Rd	020 7771 3000	Performing Arts	145
Bush Theatre	2 Shepherd's Bush Rd	020 8743 3584	Fringe	33
Cadogan Hall	5 Sloane Terrace	020 7730 4500	Performing Arts	19
Cambridge Theatre	Earlham St	084 4412 4652	West End	13
Chats Palace Arts Centre	42 Brooksby's Walk	020 8533 0227	Performing Arts	90
Comedy Theatre	Panton St	087 1297 5454	West End	23
Criterion Theatre	218 Piccadilly	087 0060 2313	West End	10
The Dogstar	389 Coldharbour Ln	020 7733 7515	Fringe	150
Dominion Theatre	268 Tottenham Court Rd	020 7413 3546	West End	4
Donmar Warehouse Theatre	41 Earlham St	020 7438 9200	West End	13
The Drill Hall	16 Chenies St	020 7307 5060	Fringe	4
Duchess Theatre	Catherine St	084 5434 9290	West End	14
Duke of York's Theatre	St Martin's Ln	087 0060 6623	West End	24
Etcetera	265 Camden High St	020 7482 4857	Fringe	71
Fortune Theatre	Russell St	020 7369 1737	West End	13
Garrick Theatre	Charing Cross Rd	020 7520 5690	West End	24
Gate Theatre	11 Pembridge Rd	020 7229 0706	Fringe	29
The George Tavern	373 Commercial Rd	020 7790 7335	Fringe	97
Gielgud Theatre	Shaftesbury Ave	084 4482 5130	West End	11
Greenwich Theatre	Crooms Hill & Nevada St	020 8858 7755	Fringe	120
Hackney Empire	291 Mare St	020 8985 2424	Fringe	89
Hampstead Theatre	Eton Ave	020 7722 9301	Fringe	66
Her Majesty's Theatre	Haymarket	0844 412 2707	West End	23
Indigo2	Millenium Way	020 8463 2000	Performing Arts	na
Jermyn Street Theatre	16 Jermyn St	020 7287 2875	Fringe	23
King's Head Theatre & Pub	115 Upper St	020 7226 1916	Fringe	80
Koko	1 Camden High St	087 0432 5527	Performing Arts	71
Leicester Square Theatre	5 Leicester Pl	020 7534 1740	West End	11
Hammersmith Apollo Theatre	Queen Caroline St	020 8563 3800	West End	41
Her Majesty's Theatre	Haymarket	084 4412 4653	West End	23
HMV Forum	9 Highgate Rd	020 7428 4099	Performing Arts	72
Little Angel Theatre	14 Dagmar Passage	020 7226 1787	Performing Arts	80
London Palladium	Argyll St	020 7494 5020	West End	10
Lyceum Theatre	21 Wellington St	020 7432 4220	West End	14
Lyric Theatre	29 Shaftesbury Ave	020 7494 5045	West End	11
National Theatre	South Bank	020 7452 3400	West End	104
New London Theatre	Drury Ln	0870 890 0141	West End	13
Noël Coward Theatre	St Martin's Ln	084 4482 5140	West End	24
Novello Theatre	Aldwych	084 4482 5170	West End	14

Theatres	*Address*	*Phone*	*Type*	*Map*
Old Red Lion	418 St John St	020 7837 7816	Fringe	6
The Old Vic Theatre	103 The Cut	084 4871 7628	West End	104
Palace Theatre	Shaftesbury Ave	087 0890 0142	West End	12
Phoenix Theatre	Charing Cross Rd	087 0060 6629	West End	12
Piccadilly Theatre	16 Denman St	020 7478 8800	West End	10
The Place	17 Duke's Rd	020 7121 1000	Performing Arts	4
Playhouse Theatre	Northumberland Ave	084 4871 7631	West End	24
Prince Edward Theatre	28 Old Compton St	084 4482 5151	West End	12
Prince of Wales Theatre	Coventry St	084 4482 5115	West End	11
Queen Elizabeth Hall	South Bank Centre	020 7960 4200	Performing Arts	104
Queen's Theatre	Shaftesbury Ave	084 4482 5160	West End	11
Riverside Studios	Crisp Rd & Queen Caroline St	020 8237 1111	Fringe	41
Ronnie Scott's	47 Frith St	020 7439 0747	Performing Arts	12
The Roundhouse	Chalk Farm Rd & Crogsland Rd	020 7424 9991	Performing Arts	71
Royal Albert Hall	Kensington Gore	020 7589 8212	Performing Arts	36
Royal Court Theatre	Sloane Sq	020 7565 5000	West End	19
Royal Festival Hall	Belvedere Rd	084 4875 0073	Performing Arts	104
Royal Opera House	Bow St	020 7304 4000	Performing Arts	13
Sadler's Wells	Rosebery Ave	084 4412 4300	Performing Arts	6
Savoy Theatre	The Strand	0870 164 8787	West End	24
Scala	275 Pentonville Rd	020 7833 2022	Performing Arts	78
The Scoop	The Queen's Walk	020 7403 4866	Performing Arts	107
Shaftesbury Theatre	210 Shaftesbury Ave	020 7379 5399	West End	13
Shakespeare's Globe	21 New Globe Walk	020 7902 1400	West End	105
Shepherd's Bush Empire	56 Shepherd's Bush Green	084 4477 2000	Performing Arts	33
Soho Theatre	21 Dean St	020 7478 0100	Fringe	11
The Space	269 Westferry Rd	020 7515 7799	Fringe, Performing Arts	na
St John's	Smith Square	020 7222 1061	Performing Arts	22
St Martin's Theatre	West St	020 7836 1443	West End	12
Sutton House	2 Homerton High St	020 8986 2264	Performing Arts	87
Theatre 503	503 Battersea Park Rd	020 7978 7040	Fringe	132
Theatre Royal Drury Lane	Catherine St	087 0890 6002	West End	13
Theatre Royal Haymarket	Haymarket	020 7930 8890	West End	23
Toynbee Studios	28 Commercial St	020 7650 2350	Fringe	91
Trafalgar Studios	14 Whitehall	087 0060 6632	West End	24
The Tricycle Theatre	259 Kilburn High Rd	020 7372 6611	Fringe	65
Vaudeville Theatre	404 Strand	087 0890 0511	West End	24
Victoria Palace Theatre	Victoria St	084 4248 5000	West End	20
Wembley Stadium	Wembley Hill Rd	084 4980 8001	Performing Arts	na
Wigmore Hall	36 Wigmore St	020 7935 2141	Performing Arts	2
Wilton's Music Hall	Graces Alley & Ensign St	020 7702 2789	Fringe	95
Wyndham's Theatre	32 Charing Cross Rd	084 4482 5120	West End	12
The Young Vic Theatre	66 The Cut	020 7922 2922	West End	104

There are many great things about London's vibrant art world. The best? It's free. Granted, if you want to see some of the big show-stopping exhibitions that pass through the **Tates (Maps 21 & 105)**, **British Museum (Map 4)**, **National Gallery (Map 23)** and **Royal Academy (Map 2)** you'll have to pay quite a hefty sum, but overall, you can experience visual arts throughout the capital without coughing up much dough. This might be a contributing factor to London's sprawling art scene, as it is so easy to duck in and out of the capital's 300+ museums and galleries on a lunch break.

Of course, there are concentrations of art in locations around Piccadilly and Bond Street (check out Cork Street for its galleries, such as **Messum (Map 10)** and the **Adam Gallery (Map 10)**, running parallel with Savile Row), the East End (funkier affair and an artistic hipster breeding ground—check out Vyner Street in Bethnal Green), South Kensington/ Chelsea (a major culture scene as a result of the Great Exhibition of 1851) and various institutions dotted along the Thames (as seen from the Tate to Tate boat service). If your feeling really adventurous/ bored pretend you're really in the know and head to the New Cross, Peckham and Camberwell areas of South London where artists and galleries are pushing new boundaries in creativity/ pretentiousness. Great art is all over the this city, so get out your Oyster Card, and get ready to cover a lot of ground.

Starting with London's modern art, the **Tate Modern (Map 105)**, with its massive smoke stack, has become a major London landmark. This is despite it only existing as a separate entity from the **Tate Britain (Map 21)** since 2000. Check out its spacious turbine hall, with often spectacular installations.

It's not surprising that the Tate Modern is often the London tourist's first stop these days, as the city has become well-known for contemporary art. Due in part to the too-cool-for-school London art scene of the 1990s, which saw the establishment of Turner Prizers Tracy Emin, Rachel Whiteread and Damien Hirst, and made a major mark under Saatchi's guiding light. This light has faded somewhat, as the movement's personalities have slowly sold out a little (Emin designing for Longchamp is a case and point). But certain London galleries remain as monuments to this explosion of counter-culture, and, in addition to the **Saatchi Gallery (Map 46)**, these include the **Serpentine Gallery (Map 30)**, **Haunch of Venison (Map 10)**, and **Victoria Miro (Map 31)**. Other inspiring alternatives include the **Riflemaker (Map 10)**, **South London Gallery (Map 122)**, **Camden Arts Centre (Map 66)**, the **White Cube** at Mason's Yard **(Map 23)**, Hoxton Square **(Map 84)**, and Bermondsey **(Map 107)**.

London is a city with a lot on offer, and if you're looking for something a bit more traditional, start with the **National Gallery (Map 24)** in Trafalgar Square, moving onto the **National Portrait Gallery (Map 24)** next door, which presents you with a who's who of British culture past and present. Stroll up Charing Cross Road to the awesome **British Museum (Map 4)** with its jaw-dropping two acre roof over the Great Court (yet another example of Norman Foster's obsession with glass and geometry). Be sure to take in the Parthenon Marbles, aka Elgin Marbles, before the Greek government makes any attempt to get them back. Then over to the not-nearly-praised-enough **Wallace Collection (Map 2)** behind Selfridge's for some tea and Watteau action. A traditional art-lover's tour of London is not over without a trip to the **Royal Academy (Map 2)** with its epic exhibitions and finally to the **Tate Britain (Map 21)**, where the Pre-Raphaelites reign supreme.

Feeling a little non-conformist? London has a brilliant array of cultural institutions that offer more than just marble and canvas. From ceramics to dolls houses, kimonos to plaster casts of just about every great sculpture in the world—the V&A has it all (not to mention an awesome gift shop). Other alternatives to the mainstream include **The Photographers' Gallery (Map 13)** by Leicester Square, which not only squeezes in the best photographic exhibitions in town, but also boasts the best bookshop on the subject. Odd in its own way is the **Museum of London (Map 7)**, which walks you through the history of the city from prehistoric times to the present day. Recent London museum gems also include the newly renovated **London Transport Museum (Map 24)**, **Fashion and Textile Museum (Map 107)**, **Museum of Brands, Packaging and Advertising (Map 29)** and the **Design Museum (Map 107)**, with cars and video games in case you're stuck entertaining your nephew. Or check out one of London's hidden glories, from the The Vault at The Hard Rock Café (Map 9) by Hyde Park, or the mind blowing Hunterian Museum (Map 14) for fans of fetuses in jars and other macabre wonders (although be warned, do not go suffering from a weak stomach). The Horniman (*snigger*) Museum is a legacy of Victorian curiosity, starring an overstuffed walrus whose taxidermist didn't realise that walruses are supposed to have wrinkles.

The **Geffreye Museum (Map 88)** is a good one to check out when you're in Shoreditch and tired of being hip. Just up Kingsland Road from **Flowers (Map 91)** (a good British contemporary art gallery), this museum of domestic interiors runs through the history of Britain one living room at a time. Somewhat forgotten are the weird and wonderful **Sir John Soane's Museum (Map 14)**, **Leighton House (Map 35)** and **Dennis Severs' House (Map 91)**—but we'll let you discover these gems for yourself.

So forget Pret a Manger—feed your soul in one of London's many museums and galleries. They certainly have more to offer than one of those crappy no bread sandwiches, anyway.

Museums & Galleries	*Address*	*Phone*	*Map*
2 Willow Road	2 Willow Road	020 7435 6166	56
19 Princelet Street - Museum of Immigration and Diversity	19 Princelet St	020 7247 5352	91
7 Hammersmith Terrace	7 Hammersmith Terrace	0208 741 4104	39
Adam Gallery	24 Cork St	020 7439 6633	10
Apsley House	149 Piccadilly	020 7499 5676	9
Arsenal Museum and Stadium Tour	Drayton Park	020 7704 4504	74
Bank of England Museum	Threadneedle Street	020 7601 5545	17
The Banqueting House	Whitehall & Horse Guards Ave	020 3166 6000	24
Benjamin Franklin House	36 Craven St	020 7839 2006	24
The Bramah Museum of Tea and Coffee	40 Southwark Street	020 7403 5650	106
Britain At War Experience	66 Tooley Street	020 7403 3171	107
The British Library	96 Euston Rd	084 3208 1144	78
The British Museum	Great Russell St & Museum St	020 7323 8299	4
Brunel Museum	Railway Ave & Rotherhithe St	020 7231 3840	110
Brunswick House	30 Wandsworth Rd	020 7394 2100	134
Camden Arts Centre	Arkwright Rd	020 7472 5500	66
Cartoon Museum	35 Little Russell St	020 7580 8155	4
Chelsea FC Museum and Stadium Tour	Stamford Bridge	087 1984 1955	43
Chelsea Physic Garden	66 Royal Hospital Rd	020 7352 5646	45
Churchill Museum and Cabinet War Rooms	King Charles Street	020 7930 6961	24
Clink Prison Museum	1 Clink St	020 7403 0900	106
Clockmakers' Museum	Aldermanbury	020 7332 1868	16
Cuming Museum	151 Walworth Rd	020 7525 2332	113
Dennis Severs' House	18 Folgate St	020 7247 4013	91
Design Museum	Shad Thames	020 7403 6933	107
The Dickens House Museum	48 Doughty St	020 7405 2127	5
Dr Johnson's House	17 Gough Square	020 7353 3745	15
Fan Museum	12 Croom's Hill	020 8305 1441	120
Fashion and Textile Museum	83 Bermondsey St	020 7407 8664	107
Florence Nightingale Museum	2 Lambeth Palace Rd	020 7620 0374	131
Flowers	82 Kingsland Rd	020 7920 7777	91
Foundling Museum	40 Brunswick Square	020 7841 3600	5
Freud Museum	20 Maresfield Gardens	020 7435 2002	66
Geffrye Museum	136 Kingsland Rd	020 7739 9893	88
Grant Museum of Zoology	Malet Place	020 7679 2647	4
Guards Museum	Birdcage Walk	020 7414 3428	22
Hampstead Museum	New End Square	020 7431 0144	56
Handel House Museum	25 Brook St	020 7495 1685	2
Haunch of Venison	6 Burlington Gardens	020 7495 5050	10
Hayward Gallery	Belvedere Rd	0871 663 2501	104
Horniman Museum & Gardens	100 London Rd	020 8699 1872	n/a
Hunterian Museum	35 Lincoln's Inn Fields	020 7869 6560	14
Imperial War Museum	Lambeth Road	020 7416 5000	104
Jewish Museum	129 Albert St	020 7284 7384	71
King's Place Gallery	90 York Way	020 7520 1485	79
Kirkaldy Testing Museum	99 Southwark St	013 2233 2195	105
Leighton House Museum	12 Holland Park Rd	020 7602 3316	34
The Library and Museum of Freemasonry	60 Great Queen St	020 7395 9251	13
Linley Sambourne House	18 Stafford Terrace	020 7602 3316	35
London Canal Museum	12 New Wharf Rd	020 7713 0836	79
London Dungeon	29 Tooley St	020 7403 7221	106
London Fire Brigade Museum	94 Southwark Bridge Rd	020 8555 1200	106

Museums & Galleries	*Address*	*Phone*	*Map*
London Sewing Machine Museum	293 Balham High Rd	020 8767 4724	151
London Transport Museum	Covent Garden Piazza	020 7379 6344	24
Marylebone Cricket Club Museum	St John's Wood Rd	020 7616 8656	76
Messum	8 Cork St	020 7437 5545	10
Museum in Docklands	Hertsmere Road	020 7001 9844	100
Museum of Brands, Packaging and Advertising	2 Colville Mews	020 7908 0880	29
Museum Of Childhood	Cambridge Heath Road	020 8983 5200	92
Museum of Fulham Palace	Bishops Avenue	020 7736 3233	48
Museum of Garden History	Lambeth Palace Road	020 7401 8865	131
Museum of London	150 London Wall	020 7001 9844	7
Museum of Methodism & Wesley's Chapel	49 City Rd	020 7253 2262	7
Museum of the Order of St John	26 St John's Ln	020 7324 4005	15
Museum of the Royal Pharmaceutical Society	1 Lambeth High St	020 7572 2210	131
National Army Museum	Royal Hospital Road	020 7881 2455	46
National Gallery	Trafalgar Square	020 7747 2885	24
National Maritime Museum	Park Row	020 8312 6565	n/a
National Portrait Gallery	St Martin's Place	020 7306 0055	24
Natural History Museum	Cromwell Rd	020 7942 5460	36
The Old Operating Theatre, Museum & Herb Garret Venue	9 St Thomas St	020 7188 2679	106
Petrie Museum of Egyptian Archaeology	Gower St	020 7679 2884	4
Pollock's Toy Museum	1 Scala St	020 7636 3452	3
Ragged School Museum	46 Copperfield Rd	020 8980 6405	98
Riflemaker Gallery	74 Beak St	020 7439 0000	10
Rootstein Hopkins Parade Ground	16 John Islip St	020 7514 8514	21
Rotherhithe Picture Research Library	82 Marychurch St	020 7237 2010	109
Royal Academy of Music Museum	Marylebone Rd	020 7873 7373	2
Saatchi Gallery	King's Road	020 7823 2332	46
Science Museum	Exhibition Rd	087 0870 4868	36
Serpentine Gallery	Kensington Gardens	020 7402 6075	30
Sherlock Holmes Museum	221 Baker St	020 7224 3688	76
Sikorski Museum	20 Princes Gate	020 7589 9249	37
Sir John Soane's Museum	13 Lincoln's Inn Fields	020 7440 4263	14
Smythson Stationery Museum	40 New Bond St	020 7629 8558	10
South London Gallery	65 Peckham Rd	020 7703 6120	122
Spencer House	27 St James's Pl	020 7499 8620	23
St Bartholomew's Hospital Museum	West Smithfield	020 7601 8152	15
Tate Britain	Millbank	020 7887 8888	21
Tate Modern	Bankside	020 7887 8888	105
Tower Bridge Exhibition	Tower Bridge	020 7403 3761	107
Victoria & Albert Museum	Cromwell Rd & Thurloe Pl	020 7942 2000	37
Victoria Miro Gallery	16 S Wharf Rd	020 7336 8109	31
Wallace Collection	Manchester Square	020 7563 9500	2
Wellcome Collection	183 Euston Rd	020 7611 2222	4
Westminster Abbey	Parliament Square	020 7222 5152	22
White Cube	26 Mason's Yard	020 7930 5373	23
White Cube	48 Hoxton Square	020 7930 5373	84
White Cube	144 Bermondsey St	020 7930 5373	107

Overview

Stumbling out teary-eyed into the light, pallid skin wrecked by long hours in darkness and surrounded by strangers, it's hard to believe that this time last year we were counting out our coppers and begging our friends to buy us another drink. Okay, so we're not completely in the red and London's cash registers may not be overflowing with moolah as they once were but we've managed to open new bars, forget about old ones, sing ourselves raw in amateur karaoke sessions, break a few bones dancing in scary clubs we shouldn't be in - you know, the usual. What is scary though is how fast the night-time landscape is changing around us. These days walking around Soho is like picking your way through a war zone; with The Astoria and its surrounding area now bulldozed, it sometimes feels the heart of London's soul has been ripped out by greedy developers. Maybe it has, but we're not dwelling on all those bad vibes: we're too busy digging amateur folk in Stokey, or quaffing luxurious cocktails in the depths of Old Street, or down the front at some dingy gig hellhole in the depths of Brixton having the time of our sorry little lives. As you may have gathered by now, London's options are as endlessly varied as her tastes. And being children of the post-modern age (or is that post-post-modern age?) we've given up caring about tribalism and consistency and have dived head-first into everything at once. Economy, what economy?

Local Pubs For Local People

North to South, East to West, whether in Zone 1 or Zone 6 the London 'local' encapsulates the city itself. That calm beating heart of the old geezer talking of times gone by in Limehouse or the adrenaline fuelled racing heart of the City's next 'big thing' in Farringdon - all echoing around a city that tells its stories, shares its woes and gets itself together over a pint of 'Pride' in the local boozer. The cavernous bowels of Dickens' favourite local **Ye Olde Cheshire Cheese (Map 15)** now provide tourist-free shelter for City folk. Borough's **George Inn (Map 106)**, with a dazzling selection of ales, is as ancient as they get. **The Lamb (Map 14)** is where to go after your office job if you want to pretend you're a writer, while the Grade-II-listed **Princess Louise (Map 4)** is sparkling with old man-ness but in the heart of London. In Hampstead, it's got to be the pretty, and pretty hidden, **Holly Bush (Map 56)**. And while it's been gentrified since it was run by the Kray's mum, **The Carpenter's Arms (Map 91)**, is still a great, tiny little foreign beer-heaven. Modern rot has yet to set in at Highgate's old-school **The Winchester (Map 52)** and you can eyeball woodworm in the brilliant **The Compton Arms (Map 80)**. The old-timers in Rotherhithe's dream-of-your-dad **The Mayflower (Map 109)**, and Brixton's **The Effra (Map 150)** will have never heard of the 'Interweb', never mind Facebook. Way out west, **The Dove (Map 40)** draws the local collective with its cosy fire, relaxed chatter and river spectacular.

Keep it Real Ale

The Carling brigade can take a hike, this town takes Price (sic) in its real brews. **The Wenlock Arms (Map 83)** proves we can do down-to-earth ale-enthusiast and **The Jerusalem Tavern (Map 3)** shows we can do fake ye olde times with amazing beer selection as well as any Lancashire local. Borough's **Market Porter (Map 106)** has a great selection, and is full of market traders counting their cash. Lovers of the Belgian stuff (and trendy Hackney-ites) will feel at home in **The Dove (Map 89)** and those after an even greater selection of European ales without the pretentiousness should head to **Quinns (Map 71)** in Camden. Too fancy? For great ale selections, there's **The Royal Oak (Map 106)** also in Borough, where the taps come courtesy of the Harveys brewery. Pitfield, Freedom and St Peter's, meanwhile, supply Islington's **Duke of Cambridge (Map 83)** with organic beer, if you like that kind of stuff. In Parson's Green **The White Horse (Map 49)** is a Victorian gem and the **Roebuck (Map 38)** provides Chiswick with an ever changing selection of local and national brews.

Good Mixers

While our ale keeps us down to earth, it's the lure of the cocktail that causes us to show off. Shaken or stirred, it doesn't matter. It's all about looking good with a long glass of the colourful sugary stuff dressed to the nines, glace cherry 'n all. For aesthetic hedonism we love **Loungelover (Map 91)** and **Lounge Bohemia (Map 8)** but for tequilas head to **Green & Red (Map 91)**.

Martinis? You'll find us at the **Charlotte Street Hotel (Map 3)**. At **5th View (Map 9)** there's vistas of Big Ben with your Kir Royal and the secretive speak-easy mood of **Milk & Honey (Map 10)** comes with eight handy house rules, including "no star fucking". We like Soho's **22 Below (Map 10)** for its down-to-earth attitude, and the plush Art Deco heaven that is **Claridge's Bar (Map 2)** for the opposite. **Montgomery Place (Map 29)** serves Notting Hill a bit of old world cool. If you find yourself on Clapham High Street then you could do a lot worse than heading to **The Loft (143)**--a modern, lush escape.One can feel studious while nursing a punch bowl at **The Cinnamon Club (Map 22)**, nestled perfectly inside the old serenity of the Old Westminster Library. On the contrary, vivacious **Buena Vista (Map 143)** brings a bit of Havana to the streets of Clapham and is the perfect spot for a mojito.

Weirdos

Let's face it, sometimes the booze just isn't enough to keep you entertained. Destroying your internal organs with the stuff is just sometimes a little boring, right? Well just walk past the New Cross Inn and head to the **Montague Arms (Map 125)** for some pirate-themed taxidermy action. **The Foundry (Map 84)** is pretty weird with an outsider art chic, and **Public Life (Map 91)**, a refurbished toilet, is literally a shithole. **Stoke Newington Airport (Map 85)** and **Jamboree at Cable Street Studios (Map 97)** are artist-run warehouse spaces that do mannered bohemian and hipster rave-offs respectively. **The Windmill (Map 150)** of Brixton is a handmade weirdo magnet and **The Battersea Barge (Map 134)** is a friendly old pub. On a very thin barge. **The Coronet (Map 74)** in Holloway has a desolate, nostalgic charm as does perhaps the weirdest pub of them all, the **Palm Tree (Map 93)**, a celebration of British antiquity with crooners of a certain age most nights.

Smoker-Friendly

If the merciless prohibition regime of 2007 hasn't resulted in reluctant surrender, don't despair: from provisionally erected patios to all-year beer gardens to secret backdoors, London's ban-bashing creativity knows no boundaries. Great fag spots include the terrace at **Proud (Map 71)**, overlooking Camden's roofs, the barbeque-and-beer-can courtyard of 93 **Feet East (Map 91)** and the tree-shaded garden of the **Edinboro Castle (Map 77)**. Hang out in front of Highgate favourite **The Flask (Map 51)** or combine a late-night pint with a rollie in the backyard of the **The Dolphin (Map 89)**. For clubbing, consider **Egg (Map 79)**, where you're allowed to smoke in the massive garden. **The Owl & Pussycat (Map 91)** is not just a surprisingly pleasant pub in Shoreditch, it's also got a surprisingly nice garden, where smoking is not just allowed, dear friends, but encouraged.

We're Raving We're Raving

While the fierce bass from the basement at **Plastic People (Map 84)** reverberates around Shoreditch, over at superclub **Fabric (Map 15)** the cool kid of the capital are bringing down the house with...er, a bit of House music. For the groovier seeking a smaller joint try **Guanabara (Map 13)** or the swanky **Images (Map 92)**. The ever-so-eclectic **Notting Hill Arts Club (Map 29)** continues to come up with exhilerating and inventive nights, as does Brick Lane's **93 Feet East (Map 91)** and **333 (Map 84)**. **Cargo (Map 84)** is for those who like a deep seated couch with their DJ while **Madame Jojo's (Map 11)** provides exactly the kind of decadence we demand from Soho clubbing. As long as lip fuzz is still trendy there's always the **Moustache Bar (Map 86)** and for quirky, artsy fartsery head to **Passing Clouds (Map 88)**, both in Dalston, natch. For serious rockabilly, find **Ye Olde Axe (Map 91)** gentlemen's club on Hackney Road, where the rock 'n' roll starts as soon as the last naked girl has disappeared behind the big-mirrored wall.

Great Bars

George Orwell's ideal pub was all about "draught stout, open fires, cheap meals, motherly barmaids and no radio." These days we'd maybe add music straight from a blog, handmade decor and a dangerous vibe. For some if not all of these try up-beat **Jaguar Shoes (Map 91)**. **Freud (Map 13)** or the **French House (Map 11)** in the

West End are also solid contenders for boho shlock. But there's so much more: crawl from **Barrio North's (Map 80)** caravan to the country-house of **Lost Society (Map 142)**, from the **Island Queen (Map 83)** to the Moijto-fuelled **Mau Mau (Map 29)**. We like standing next to (would-be) artists at the **ICA Bar (Map 23)** and actor types on the terrace of **The Cut Bar (Map 104)**. Or in front of a movie screen, at **Roxy Bar and Screen (Map 106)**. Later on, you'll find us nibbling cheese in Dalston's **Jazz Bar (Map 82)**, dancing to trashy music at **Da Vinci's (Map 104)**.

Best Of The Rest

Want to feel exclusive? Members-only clubs are not only becoming ever more popular, but also ever more accessible. So there. Escape Shoreditch's terrifying hordes to the rooftop swimming pool of **Shoreditch House (Map 91)** or the boredom of Shepherd's Bush to the underground ex-toilets that have become **Ginglik (Map 33)**. Of course, most of those in the know will drag you to the various warehouse raves that fire up every weekend. People like **Real Gold** (http://wearerealgold.com) are a good place to start if you fancy some of this awfulness. Remember it's not who you know but, oh wait, it is who you know.

To create your own entertainment and/or embarrass yourself **Lucky Voice (Maps 10, 80)** is one of many joints offering private karaoke booths for you and some people who will most probably cease to be your friends after they hear you massacre 'Time After Time.' Shoreditch's exposed brick joint **The Book Club (Map 8)** has a bit of 'Social Athletics' on the bill - ping pong, old chap? If relying on that notoriously joke-cracking ex-friend of a friend for your evening's amusement sounds a bit risky, consider these alternatives: The standard-setting **Comedy Store (Map 11)** (book in advance), Bethnal Green's **FymFyg Bar (Map 92)** and **Covent Garden Comedy Club (Map 24)**, or, at the pub end of things, **The Bedford (Map 148)** and **the Camden Head (Map 78)**. If you think that YOU should in fact provide the evening's amusement, well, the **Poetry Café (Map 13)** gives you the stage. Or stay at home and talk to yourself; it's cheaper.

Music, Sweet Music

London's veins are pumped by its mellifluous melodies, the driving sound of grime, the sneers of angry young men and the coos of sweet maidens. Whether you're dub-stepping in the dark or jamming along at folk night there'll be something to hear at any given time of the week.

Strummin' Mental

This city's music scene is in a constant state of flux with bands, venues and styles falling in and out of cool lists quicker than a Ramones song. What never changes though is that there always is a scene and with that scene comes the venue. The good news is that there are so many great places to do this in. Yes we've got our share of corporate megaliths (that means you O2) but for every church of Carling there are two or three brilliant dives like the punky **Grosvenor (Map 145)** or the ever-mobbed **Stag's Head (Map 84)**.

For the sweatily inclined there are infinite choices. Bethnal Green's **Star of Bethnal Green (Map 92)** (formerly the Pleasure Unit), Highgate's **Buffalo Bar (Map 80)** and Angel's **Lexington (Map 79)** are as pant-wettingly indie as they come but if you like harder or weirder stuff the **Camden Underworld (Map 71)** and **Slimlight (Map 80)** does all the metals while **Cafe Oto (Map 86)** handles experimental and improv. **The MacBeth (Map 84)** is very popular yet somehow suffers from a fun bypass but **Monto Water Rats (Map 5)** is an unshakeable legend. The refurbished **Old Blue Last (Map 84)** or Vice Magazine party HQ has surfed to the crest of the trend wave fueled by young kids attempting to be sexually harassed by older men like in their favourite adverts for American Apparel. Mid-sized venues for mid-fame bands?The **Scala (Map 78)** is a brilliant converted cinema, **The Luminaire (Map 65)** is a great venue, but **The Dome (Map 59)** is fast becoming our favourite school hall-like venue. The now legal **Barden's Boudoir (Map 86)** has come a long way since it was a dingy dive run by gangsters and of course the **ICA (Map 23)** is the 'art-space' par excellence for all artistes who insist on that 'e' at the end of 'artist.' The **Amersham Arms (Map 126)** and **The Rest Is Noise (Map 144)** are owned by the same hipster morons but they're good places to watch some twonks you've been told to like by Dazed. The city's electronic music scene generally piggy-backs the guitars, but new places like **Cable (Map 107)** and **Lightbox (Map 134)**.

As for the classics, the **Shepherd's Bush Empire (Map 33)** and the breathtakingly beautiful **Bush Hall (Map 32)** remain west London's finest, while Camden stalwart **Koko (Map 71)** keeps rocking in the free world. The north London show is being stolen by **The Roundhouse (Map 71)**, though, boasts a healthy "I am legend"-attitude and some bloody horrible Anthony Gormley statues waiting to jump from the top. **Brixton Academy (Map 145)** might be slightly overrated, but its sky-like ceiling remains awesome. If you have to do stadium-size, do stadium-size in style and get your seat in the **Royal Albert Hall (Map 36)**, which is increasingly luring good non-classical acts. The refurbishment of the **Royal Festival Hall (Map 104)**, meanwhile, has kick-started more pop-oriented programming on the South Bank.

A World of Jazz And Blues

Camden's intimate **Jazz Café (Map 71)** seems to have no intention of stopping its relentless stream of first-rate jazz performances, getting in more soul, funk and pop at the same time, while **Ronnie Scott's Jazz Club (Map 12)**, London's undisputed grandaddy of jazz originalcontinue to offer up an eclectic programme of past an present. For some of the freshest jazz, alongsid great contemporary folk and world music, hea to Dalston, where the plush **Vortex (Map 8** is a-buzz with free-spirited legends. On th other side of town, Fulham's small but perfect formed **606 Club (Map 50)** sets the tone wit crammed, small tables within slobberin distance from the saxes. Catch excellent blue and singer/songwriter stuff every night c the week at **Ain't Nothing But The Blues Ba (Map 10)**, or Denmark Street's **12 Bar Clu (Map 12)**. Latin jazz breezes through the air a Archway's **Caipirinha Jazz Bar (Map 52)**. Fc world music, the **Barbican Centre (Map 7)** lead the pack, but is easily beaten in atmospher stakes by the **Union Chapel (Map 80)**, a Islington church doubling as one of London most beautiful venues and in scummy stakes b **Dingwalls (Map 71)** who continue to expan their programming. The home of folk is th brilliant **Cecil Sharp House (Map 70)**. If classica music floats your boat, look beyond the obviou venues and settle amid the great acoustics o Chelsea's **Cadogan Hall (Map 19)**, the historica brilliance of Hackney's **Sutton House (Map 87** or the magnificent **Wigmore Hall (Map 2)**, ir Mayfair.

Map 1 • Marylebone (West)

Ruby Lo	23 Orchard St	020 7486 3671	Dimly-lit, sexy bar with kick ass Mojitos.

Map 2 • Marylebone (East)

Claridge's Bar	55 Brook St	020 7629 8860	Posh and plush and Art Deco. More champagne!
Inn 1888 East	21 Devonshire St	020 7486 7420	Quiet pint perfection.
Moors Bar	57Paddington St	020 8348 4161	Hub for well-off media types with films, music and booze.
The Phoenix	37 Cavendish Sq	020 7493 8003	A quirky gem amidst an ocean of crappy chain bars.

Map 3 • Fitzrovia

100 Club	100 Oxford St	020 7636 0933	Ancient club that's seen off Nazi bombs and Sex Pistols.
The Albany	240 Great Portland St	020 7387 0221	Swanky, but nice. And the music's good.
Bourne & Hollingsworth	28 Rathbone Pl	020 7636 8228	Fine Fitzrovian basement boutique.
Bradleys Spanish Bar	42 Hanway St	020 7636 0359	60's rock joint with awesome jukebox and disgusting toilets.
Bricklayers Arms	31 Gresse St	020 7636 5593	Advertising types fake no-nonsense boozing.
Charlotte Street Hotel	15 Charlotte St	020 7806 2000	Dirty gossip over dirty martinis.
The Fitzroy Tavern	16 Charlotte St	020 7580 3714	Sam Smith's, anyone?
Hakkasan	8 Hanway Pl	020 7927 7000	Sleek, blue-lit boutique. For saketinis and rose petal martinis.
The Jerusalem Tavern	55 Britton St	020 7490 4281	A tiny old wooden gem of a pub. And organic ale.
Market Place	11 Market Pl	020 7079 2020	Warm buzz. Hot crowd. Cool prices.
Northumberland Arms	43 Goodge St	020 7637 3806	Cosy, old-style bar with a local feel.
Punk	14 Soho St	084 5094 5195	Starf***er central. But kinda fun.
The Rising Sun	46 Tottenham Ct Rd	020 7636 6530	Bordering studentland and Fitzrovia; pretty name, less pretty pub.
The Roxy	3 Rathbone Pl	020 7255 1098	Hip subterranean hangout. More chicks than dicks.
The Social	5 Little Portland St	020 7636 4992	Fab music, nonchalant surroundings and plenty of trendsters.
The Yorkshire Grey	46 Langham St	020 7636 4788	Upstairs is perfect when Oxford Street's pissing you off.

Map 4 • Bloomsbury (West)

All Star Lanes	Victoria House, Bloomsbury Pl	020 7025 2676	You'll be bowled over. Oh yes you will.

Bloomsbury Bowling Lanes	Bedford Way	020 7183 1979	As cool as bowling gets.
The Fly	36 New Oxford	020 7688 8994	For your quick indie fix on New Oxford.
Marquis of Cornwallis	31 Marchmont St	020 7278 8355	Chilled couches.
Old Crown	33 New Oxford St	020 7836 9121	After-work bar that takes itself very seriously.
The Plough	27 Museum St	020 7636 7964	Fancy a bite? Vampyre Society meetings held here monthly.
Point 101	101 New Oxford St	020 7379 3112	Even mass murderers on day-release get in here.
The Princess Louise	208 High Holborn	020 7405 8816	Victorian gin palace now serving cheap but good lager.
ULU	1 Malet St	020 7664 2000	Student union, student prices, student bands.

Map 5 • Bloomsbury (East)

06 St Chad's Place	6 St Chad's Pl	020 7278 3355	Stylish wine bar with plastic chairs? SOOO avant-garde, dahhhling!
The Blue Lion	13 Gray's Inn Rd	020 7405 4422	Pool table!
Calthorpe Arms	25 Gray's Inn Rd	020 7278 4732	Impressive old man pub.
Duke of York	156 Clerkenwell Rd	020 7837 8548	You and a hundred cycle couriers.
King's Cross Social Club	2 Brittania Street	020 7278 4252	Where to go and be social in King's Cross apparently
Monto Water Rats	328 Gray's Inn Rd	020 7837 4412	No rats here, only the best up-and-coming bands.
The Perseverance	63 Lamb's Conduit St	020 7405 8278	Bustling, young and semi-trendy.
Smithy's	15 Leeke St	020 7278 5949	Our lunchtime to late-night-wind-down friend.

Map 6 • Clerkenwell

Bandstand Busking	Northampton Sq		Free acoustic gigs in summer. Dreamy.
The Betsey Trotwood	56 Farringdon Rd	020 7253 4285	Thoroughly likable Shepherd Neame pub renowned for live music.
The Boadicea	292 St John St	020 7354 9993	Full of students paying their lecturers off with pints.
Café Kick	43 Exmouth Market	020 7837 8077	Creaky, Latin American table football cafe.
Cicada	132 St John St	020 7608 1550	Gorgeous Art Deco interior, original and classic cocktails.
Dollar Grills and Martinis	2 Exmouth Market	020 7278 0077	Forget the grills, go with the martinis.
The Dovetail	9 Jerusalem Passage	020 7490 7321	Small, but perfectly formed Clerkenwell sister to Broadway Market's The Dove.
Filthy McNasty's	68 Amwell St	020 7837 6067	Disappointingly un-filthy or nasty. Sigh.
The Harlequin	27 Arlington Way	079 7565 2669	Livingroom boozer.
Old Red Lion	418 St John St	020 7837 7816	Theatre pub legend.
The Slaughtered Lamb	34 Great Sutton St	020 7253 1516	Dimly-lit pub that's still packing in the Clerkenwell crowd.
The Three Kings	7 Clerkenwell Close	020 7253 0483	Quirky pub that dies on weekends.
The Wilmington Arms	69 Rosebery Ave	020 7837 1384	Staff have 'arsehole' tattooed on their foreheads. .

Map 8 • Liverpool Street / Broadgate

The Light	233 Shoreditch High St	020 7247 8989	Light at the end of the tunnel for city revellers.
Lounge Bohemia	1 Great Eastern St	077 2070 7000	Vintage martinis make up for neo-avant-garde pretenses.
The Red Lion	1 Eldon St	020 7247 5381	Drinkers near Moorgate can't be choosers. So there.
Sosho	2 Tabernacle St	020 7920 0701	It's so Sosho darhling.

Map 9 • Mayfair / Green Park

1707 Wine Bar	181 Piccadilly	020 7734 8040	Empty Fortnum & Mason's wine cellar.
bbar	43 Buckingham Palace Rd	020 7958 7000	Get drunk behind Elizabeth's back.
Funky Buddah	15 Berkeley St	020 7495 2596	Overpriced, overrated, tacky Z-list haunt. Apart from that, it's great!
Mahiki	1 Dover St	020 7493 9529	Crushingly tropical cocktail bar. Pineapples a-go-go.
Shepherd's Tavern	50 Hertford St	020 7499 3017	For drinking within Shepherd's Market.

Map 10 • Piccadilly / Soho (West)

22 Below	22 Great Marlborough St	020 7437 4106	Table-service cocktail lounge - without being snooty. We love it.
5th View	203 Piccadilly	020 7851 2433	Spill Bloody Marys over books in full view of Big Ben.
Ain't Nothing But The Blues Bar	20 Kingly St	020 7287 0514	Bracingly raw music in a tiny frontroom.
Cheers Bar	72 Regent St	020 7494 3322	Sitcom-themed Americana: wags shouting 'Norm!' at regular intervals.
Courthouse Bar	19 Great Marlborough St	020 7297 5555	Drink where Oscar Wilde was in the clink.
Green and Red	51 Bethnal Green Rd	020 7749 9670	Tequila bar worth its post-shot salt - you're spoilt for choice.
John Snow	39 Broadwick St	020 7437 1344	Soho drinkers! Sam Smith's full range and a relaxed upstairs!
Lucky Voice	52 Poland St	020 7439 3660	Why is this London's best karaoke bar? The dress up box.
Milk & Honey	61 Poland St	020 7065 6840	The promised land of after-hours cocktails. Members club, so join.
The Pigalle Club	215 Piccadilly	020 7644 1420	Ladies and gentleman, welcome to the 40s.
Red	5 Kingly St	020 7434 3417	Soho cocktail madness. Plush, sexy and red.
Strawberry Moons	15 Heddon St	020 7437 7300	Dig the cheese, with your new squeeze.

Map 11 • Soho (Central)

Blue Posts	22 Berwick St	020 7437 5008	Unreformed, scuzzy boozer.
The Blue Posts	28 Rupert St	020 7437 1415	Hey, a decent pub in Soho.
Cafe Boheme	13Old Compton St	020 7734 0623	Beautiful bar to prop up and people watch.
Candy Bar	4 Carlisle St	020 7287 5041	Soho's premier all-girl venue.
The Comedy Store	1 Oxendon St	084 4847 1728	It ain't world famous for no reason, chuckles.

De Hems	11 Macclesfield St	020 7437 2494	Dutch bar with brain-cell-annihilatingly strong beer. Hic!
The Endurance	90 Berwick St	020 7437 2944	Hang-out for loud media twats.
Freedom	66 Wardour St	020 7734 0071	Neon green cocktail kitsch.
The French House	49 Dean St	020 7437 2799	Boho Soho hang-out for eccentrics.
LVPO	50 Dean St	020 7317 9260	A labyrinth of candlelit corners and sophisticated conversation.
Madame Jojo's	8 Brewer St	020 7734 3040	Unpretentious club where you won't remain single for too long.
Shadow Lounge	5 Brewer St	020 7317 9270	Gay chi chi lounge.
Village	81 Wardour St	020 7478 0530	Tacky, flirtatious Soho gay bar.

Map 12 • Soho (East)

12 Bar Club	22 Denmark St	020 7240 2622	Ludicrously tiny live club with singer/songwriter focus.
The Borderline	16 Manette St	020 7734 5547	Cool basement club, bizarrely got up in Tex-Mex decor.
Comptons	53 Old Compton St	020 7479 7961	Crammed gay pub.
Crobar	17 Manette St	020 7439 0831	Heavy metal and cheap bourbon. Be a man for once.
G-A-Y Bar	30 Old Compton St	020 7494 2756	Poptastic gay bunker.
G-A-Y Late	5 Goslett Yard	020 7734 9858	Cheap drinks and pop videos wipe out brain functions 'til 3 am.
Garlic & Shots	14 Frith St	020 7734 9505	Drunken vampires beware.
Green Carnation	5 Greek St	020 7434 3323	Sexy, Oscar Wilde-inspired lounge that Oscar would have approved of.
Jazz After Dark	9 Greek St	020 7734 0545	Tunes and cheap drinks, until LATE.
Karaoke Box	18 Frith St	020 7494 3878	A bit gritty but one of London's cheaper karaoke bars.
Ku Bar	30 Lisle St	020 7437 4303	Newly relocated gay bar for the young and clueless.
Lab	12 Old Compton St	020 7437 7820	London Academy of Bartending - they know how to make martinis.
Montagu Pyke	105 Charing Cross Rd	020 7287 6039	Cheap beer - in the West End.
Ronnie Scott's Jazz Club	47 Frith St	020 7439 0747	Original, and still the best.
The Royal George	133 Charing Cross Rd, Goslett Yard	020 7734 8837	Busy, but the crowd's nice. Board games and food.
The Toucan	19 Carlisle St	020 7437 4123	Small and snug central bolthole for Guinness.

Map 13 • Covent Garden

AKA	18 W Central St	020 7836 0110	Proper drinks and proper DJs. And pizza for in-between.
Bunker	41 Earlham St	020 7240 0606	Beer brewed in front of your eyes.
The Cross Keys	31 Endell St	020 7836 5185	Tiny old-school boozer.
The End	18 W Central St	020 7419 9199	The beginning is the end is the beginning. This pioneering club's still rockin' it.
Freud	198 Shaftesbury Ave	020 7240 9933	Intimate basement bar that used to be Alex of Blur's living room. Literally.
Guanabara	Parker St	020 7242 8600	Brasil. But in Holborn.
The Lamb and Flag	33 Rose St	020 7497 9504	Cobbled lane leads to a crowded but gloriously timeless inn.
Poetry Cafe	22 Betterton St	020 7420 9887	Eat, drink, write, listen or, yes, PERFORM!

Map 14 • Holborn / Temple

Cittie of Yorke	22 High Holborn	020 7242 7670	Soe olde it's name has extra e's. A marvellouse pube.
The Enterprise	38 Red Lion St	020 7269 5901	More Captain Cook than Captain Kirk.
The Lamb	92 Lamb's Conduit St	020 7405 0713	Legendary little place with Victorian touches.
Na Zdrowie The Polish Bar	11 Little Turnstile	020 7831 9679	With 50 types of vodka, even beetroot soup tastes good.
The Seven Stars	53 Carey St	020 7242 8521	Tiny, slightly dusty bar frequented by barristers.
Temple Bar Bar	Temple Pl	020 7836 3555	A touch of Bertie Wooster open to all.
Tutu's	Surrey St	020 7848 1588	King's College students' very own nightclub.
Volupte	9 Norwich St	020 7831 1622	They call it burlesque, we call it strippers with tassles.

Map 15 • Blackfriars / Farringdon

Corney & Barrow	10 Paternoster Sq	020 7618 9520	Champagne breakfast, anyone?
The Deux Beers	3 Hatton Wall	020 7405 9777	Home of the original politically incorrect 100 shooter list.
Fabric	77 Charterhouse St	020 7336 8898	Debauched club mecca for gurners of all persuasions.
Fox and Anchor	115 Charterhouse St	020 7012 3702	Amazing interior and the tankards make up for the wankers.
The Hat and Tun	3 Hatton Wall	020 7242 4747	Home of the original politically incorrect 100 shooter list.
Smithfield Bar & Grill	2 W Smithfield	020 7246 0900	Suits, suits, suits. And chandeliers, jazz and cocktails. And suits.
Ye Olde Cheshire Cheese	154 Fleet St	020 7353 6170	Get tanked up where Dickens used to. Historic.
Ye Olde London	42 Ludgate Hill	020 7248 1852	It ain't Olde, really, but it sells beer.
Ye Olde Mitre	1 Ely Ct	020 7405 4751	Elizabeth I used to dance here, don't you know?!

Map 16 • Square Mile (West)

Hatchet	28 Garlick Hill	020 7236 0720	Lost in the City? Escape here.
The Mansion House	44 Cannon St	020 7248 1700	Out of the tube, into the House.
The Samuel Pepys	48 Upper Thames St	020 7489 1871	Find it and be rewarded with Thames views.
Ye Olde Watling	29 Watling St	020 7653 9971	Squeeze in.

Map 17 • Square Mile (East)

The Counting House	50 Cornhill	020 7283 7123	A truly magnificent (former) bank. That sells beer now.
Grand Cafe & Bar	The Ctyard, Royal Exchange	020 7618 2480	The courtyard of the Royal Exchange. Fancy, eh?

Map 18 • Tower Hill / Aldgate

Dion City	52 Leadenhall St	020 7702 9111	Veuve Clicquot La Grande Dame Rose, anyone?
Kenza	10 Devonshire Sq	020 7929 5533	Belly-dancers, cocktails & couscous.
Mary Janes	64 Minories	020 7481 8195	Inconspicuous perspex floor catches out the knickerless.
The Minories	64-73 Minories	020 7702 1658	Cavernous boozer by day, thumping disco by night.
Pepys Bar at the Novotel Hotel	10 Pepys St	020 7265 6000	Get on the Kir Royales and kiss tomorrow goodbye.
Prism	147 Leadenhall St	020 7256 3875	Cocktails underneath the former Bank of New York.
Revolution	140 Leadenhall St	020 7929 4233	Vodka-drenched, vault-like DJ bar that couldn't care less about the revolution.
T Bar	18 Houndsditch	020 7729 2973	Does cool well.

Map 19 • Belgravia

The Blue Bar	The Berkeley Hotel, Wilton Pl	020 7235 6000	It's blue. Mindboggingly so.
Nag's Head	53 Kinnerton St	020 7235 1135	No mobiles allowed. Says it all.
The Plumber's Arms	14 Lower Belgrave St	020 7730 4067	Tradesman's pub from days of yore. Ask about Lord Lucan.
Wilton Arms	71 Kinnerton St	020 7235 4854	A Shepherd Neame pub? In Belgravia?

Map 20 • Victoria / Pimlico (West)

The Cardinal	23 Francis St	020 7834 7260	Easier to like than to find.
Cask & Glass	39 Palace St	020 7834 7630	Teeny tiny, English country garden-esque drinking hole. Flower-festoned frontage, real ale.

Map 21 • Pimlico (East)

Morpeth Arms	58 Millbank	020 7834 6442	Where Millbank prisoners used to escape to.

Map 22 • Westminster

The Albert	52 Victoria St	020 7222 5577	Distinguished, well-preserved period pub. Tourist haunt but rightly so.
The Cinnamon Club	30 Great Smith St	020 7222 2555	Cocktail classiness inside the Old Westminster Library. Try finding it.
The Speaker	46 Great Peter St	020 7222 1749	Good after-worker with guest ales.
St. Stephen's Tavern	10 Bridge St	020 7925 2286	Tiny pub with character, despite being on tourist trail.
Two Chairmen	39 Dartmouth St	020 7222 8694	Public servants galore! Decent pub for this area though.

Map 23 • St. James's

Aura	48 St James's St	020 7499 9999	If you ain't on the list, you ain't coming in. Seriously.
ICA	The Mall	020 7930 3647	Cutting edge arts complex/bar, weirdly stuck on the upper-crust Mall.
The Sports Cafe	80 Haymarket	020 7766 4687	Umpteen screens of international sport distract from appalling service/grub.

Map 24 • Trafalgar Square / The Strand

Asia de Cuba	45 St Martin's Lane	020 7300 5588	For rum-drinking with the jet set.
The Chandos	29 St Martins Lane	020 7836 1401	All Trafalgar Square pubs are tourist traps? Think again.
The Coal Hole	91 Strand	020 7379 9883	Genuine old style.
Covent Garden Comedy Club	The Arches, Off Villiers St	079 6007 1340	Good acts play to a friendly crowd drinking awful beer.
Gordon's Wine Bar	47 Villiers St	020 7930 1408	Candle-lit vaults. Romantic perfection.
Heaven	Under the Arches, off Villiers St	020 7930 2020	Epicentre of London's late night gay scene.
Maple Leaf	41 Maiden Ln	020 7240 2843	Just don't ask which State they're from.
Punch & Judy	The Covent Garden Piazza	020 7379 0923	Naff, naff, naff. 'Nuff said?
Retro Bar	2 George Ct	020 7321 2811	Chilled gay bar, hiding from Charing Cross in a small alley.
Roadhouse	35 The Piazza	020 7240 6001	"You're the one that I want, ooh-ooh-ooh"
The Sherlock Holmes	10 Northumberland St	020 7930 2644	Unintentionally sinister, must-see Holmes waxwork upstairs. Expect bad dreams.
The Ship and Shovell	1 Craven Passage	020 7839 1311	A pub made of two pubs, both obsessed with Sherlock Holmes.
Terroirs	5 William IV St	020 7036 0660	Non-pretentious wine bar with good eats too.
Zoo Bar & Club	13 Bear St	020 7839 4188	Wake up with someone new.

Map 26 • Maida Hill

The Skiddaw	46 Chippenham Rd	020 7286 7815	West London trendy hang out. Great Sunday roast.

Map 27 • Maida Vale

The Bridge House	13 Westbourne Terrace Rd	020 7266 4326	Canal views and comedy. Lovely.
E Bar	2 Warrington Crescent	020 7432 8455	Basement lounge for a quiet drink.
Robert Browning	15 Clifton Rd	020 7286 2732	Cheapo boozer in posh surroundings.
The Warwick Castle	6 Warwick Pl	020 7266 0921	Down-to-earth drinking in Maida Vale. Indeed.
The Waterway	54 Formosa St	020 7266 3557	Try not to fall into the canal.

Map 28 • Ladbroke Grove / Notting Hill (West)

Julie's Bar	135 Portland Rd	020 7229 8331	Pleasantly posh wine bar full of pleasantly posh ladies.

Map 29 • Notting Hill Gate

Black Cherry	21 Lordship Ln	020 8299 8877	Oh ya, only the boutique-iest of cocktails here.
Mau Mau	265 Portobello Rd	020 7229 8528	Ace mojitos and Thursdays open-mic. Wear your dancing shoes.
Montgomery Place	31 Kensington Park Rd	020 7792 3921	The mixers rock. And they know it.
Notting Hill Arts Club	21 Notting Hill Gate	020 7460 4459	Indie cave with bands, lurid projections and teenagers.
Sun in Splendour	7 Portobello Rd	020 7792 0914	Notting Hill denizens' choice.
Uxbridge Arms	13 Uxbridge St	020 7727 7326	Warm little place full of eccentric old toffs.
Windsor Castle	114 Campden Hill Rd	020 7243 8797	A wood-panelled piece of pub history.

Map 30 • Bayswater

The Cow	89 Westbourne Park Rd	020 7221 0021	Lovely pub. Let down by braying trustafarians.

Map 31 • Paddington

The Royal Exchange	26 Sale Pl	020 7723 3781	Irish boozer; amazing homemade pies

Map 32 • Shepherd's Bush (West)

Bush Hall	310 Uxbridge Rd	020 8222 6955	The red carpet, the ornate walls…the sheer beauty!
The Goldhawk	122 Goldhawk Rd	020 8576 6921	A pub, ladies and gentleman.
The Queen Adelaide	412 Uxbridge Rd	020 8746 2573	Chic gastropub serving the West Bush.
White Horse	31 Uxbridge Rd	020 8723 4531	Did you call my pint a slag? Outside, now!

Map 33 • Shepherd's Bush

Albertine	1 Wood Lane	020 8743 9593	Drink wine with the Beep set.
Ginglik	1 Shepherd's Bush Green	020 7348 8968	Members-only underground ex-toilets. Join free on the door.
Shepherd's Bush Empire	Shepherd's Bush Green	020 8354 3300	Still among London venueland's finest.

Map 34 • West Kensington / Olympia

The Cumberland Arms	29 N End Rd	020 7371 6806	Where long hard days become good again.
Famous 3 Kings	171 North End Rd	020 7603 6071	Brilliant atmosphere for big matches, especially rugby. Pool tables too.
Plum Bar	380 Kensington High St	020 7603 3333	Dying for a drink in Kensington? Well there.

Map 35 • Kensington

Builders Arms	1 Kensington Ct Pl	020 7937 6213	Boozy haven from High Street Kensington's shopping madness.

Map 36 • South Kensington / Gloucester Rd

Boujis	43 Thurloe St	020 7584 2000	If you want to see the two princes drunk. And only then.

Map 38 • Chiswick

Carvosso's	210 Chiswick High Rd	020 8995 9121	For a glass of wine before dinner.
George IV	185 Chiswick High Rd	020 8994 4624	Fullers pies, real ale and a comedy club on the High Road? Sweet.
The Packhorse & Talbot	145 Chiswick High Rd	020 8994 0360	A Chiswick institution. Proper British pub…with live jazz?! Truly.

Map 39 • Stamford Brook

The Raven	375 Goldhawk Rd	020 8748 6977	A bit grubby on the outside but £4 handmade pies are part of the appeal.

Map 40 • Goldhawk Rd / Ravenscourt Park

The Dove	19 Upper Mall	020 8748 9474	So perfect for dates that Charles II brought Nell Gwynne here.
Ruby Grand	227 King St	020 8748 3391	Self-proclaimed purveyor of elegance.

Map 41 • Hammersmith

Brook Green Hotel	170 Shepherd's Bush Rd	020 7603 2516	Lost between Hammersmith and Shepherd's Bush? Fear not.
The Distillers	64Fulham Palace Rd	020 8748 2834	Chandelier clad pub-bar with ace live music and comedy in The Regal Room.
Hammersmith Apollo	45 Queen Caroline St	084 4844 4748	Still West London's best music venue
Lyric Hammersmith	King St	087 1221 1729	Hammersmith's hottest home of hentertainment..

Map 42 • Baron's Court

Colton Arms	187 Greyhound Road	020 7385 6956	If you're not already a regular, you'll wish you were.
The Curtains Up	28 Comeragh Rd	020 7386 7543	Pub which keeps actors in the basement.
The Fulham Mitre	81 Dawes Rd	020 7386 8877	Young, trendy Fulhamites like it. We don't.
Queen's Arms	171 Greyhound Rd	020 7386 5078	Relaxed and comfy local boozer with tip top Sunday roasts.

Map 44 • Chelsea

Brinkley's	47 Hollywood Rd	020 7351 1683	Enter the cougar's lair.
The Duke of Clarence	148 Old Brompton Rd	020 7373 1285	All leather seats and wooden floors. Cool spot for a drink after work.
Rumi	531 Kings Rd	020 7823 3362	Fulham's secret, chic and cosy jewel.

Map 45 • Chelsea (East)

The Anglesea Arms	15 Selwood Terrace	020 7373 7960	4th Best Pub in the UK, says The Morning Advertiser Industry.
Apartment 195	195 Kings Rd	020 7349 4468	Hire your personal Kings Road party apartment.
Chelsea Potter	119 Kings Rd	020 7352 9479	Chelsea old school.
The Drayton Arms	153 Old Brompton Rd	020 7835 2301	Low-lit Victorian pub with mismatched chairs and a great beer selection.
The Pig's Ear	35 Old Church St	020 7352 2908	Quirky, restored boozer. Deep fried pigs ear anyone? Seriously.

Map 47 • Fulham (West)

The Crabtree Tavern	Rainville Rd	020 7385 3929	Great riverside location. So-so pub.

Map 48 • Fulham

Wheatsheaf	582 Fulham Rd	020 7384 1444	Slouch sofas and soft lighting with great food. Quiz on Thursday evenings.

Map 49 • Parson's Green

Amuse Bouche	51 Parsons Green Lane	020 7371 8517	Fizzy fun.
Duke on the Green	235 New Kings Road	020 7736 2777	If only all pub food was this good (but half the price).
The Establishment	45-47 Parsons Green Ln	020 7384 2418	British favourites meet retro cool. Pie and…Pimms anyone?
The White Horse	1 Parson's Green	020 7736 2115	Victorian pub and a beer drinker's heaven. Book a table.

Map 50 • Sand's End

606 Club	90 Lots Rd	020 7352 5953	Great jazz venue. If you like ten minute sax solos.

Map 51 • Highgate

The Angel Inn	37 Highgate High St	020 8341 5913	Lively local with board games and unusual beers.
The Boogaloo	312 Archway Rd	020 8340 2928	Not as cool as it thinks it is.
The Flask	77 Highgate West Hill	020 8348 7346	Great beers, great food, great place. Really, it is.
Prince Of Wales	53 Highgate High St	020 8340 0445	Friendly local for posh Highgaters and their even posher dogs.
The Victoria	28 N Hill	020 8340 6091	Try to catch the Sunday sing-along sessions.
The Woodman	414 Archway Rd	020 8340 3016	Reformed fight club with gastropub intentions.
The Wrestlers	98 North Rd	020 8340 4297	Branded "best pub in Highgate" by residents.

Map 52 • Archway (North)

Caipirinha Jazz Bar	177 Archway Rd	020 8342 8146	Cosiness! Cocktails! Latin jazz! Sherpa required to find it!
The Winchester Pub Hotel	206 Archway Rd	020 8374 1690	Wonky-floored palace of boozy delight.

Map 53 • Crouch End

Harringay Arms	153 Crouch Hill	020 8340 4243	No music, plenty of beer.
The Hope & Anchor	128 Tottenham Ln	020 8340 3051	Proper local.
The King's Head	2 Tottenham Ln	020 8340 102	Plenty of funny business.
The Queens Pub & Dining Rooms	26 Broadway Parade	020 8340 2031	God save the Queens.
The Wishing Well	22 Topsfield Parade, Tottenham Lane	020 8340 1096	Goodbye Crouch End gastropub, hello Hornsey cheap boozer.

Map 55 • Harringay

The Beaconsfield	359 Green Lanes	020 8800 2153	Friendly local. The footy's always on!
The Garden Ladder	501 Green Lanes	020 8348 8553	Relaxed place with interesting guest ales.
The Salisbury	1 Grand Parade, Green Lanes	020 8800 9617	A local's secret…no longer! Exceptional.

Map 56 • Hampstead Village

The Flask	14 Flask Walk	020 7435 4580	Hampstead alleyway classic that's been refitted. But nicely so.
The Freemasons Arms	32 Downshire Hill	020 7433 6811	Lovely beer garden.
Holly Bush	22 Holly Mount	020 7435 2892	It's hidden. It's a gem. Really.

Map 57 • Hampstead Heath

The Garden Gate	14S End Rd	020 7435 4938	Nice pub with garden for those sunny days. (yeah right)
The Magdala	2 South Hill Park	020 7435 2503	Gastropub and site of Ruth Ellis's infamous shooting of husband outside the joint.
Roebuck	15 Pond St	020 7433 6871	Somewhere between cosy pub and stylish bar. And good at it.
The White Horse	154 Fleet Rd	020 7485 2112	Yet another pub on the Thai food bandwagon.

Map 58 • Parliament Hill / Dartmouth Park

Bar Lorca	156 Fortress Rd	020 7485 1314	Spanish beer. Spanish tapas.
The Bull and Last	168 Highgate Rd	020 7267 3641	Good place for a post-Heath pint.
The Dartmouth Arms	35 York Rise	020 7485 3267	A fire. Dogs. Old gits. The perfect local.
Duke of St. Albans	Highgate Road	020 7209 0385	Pretty dodgy at times, but also the only pub around.

Map 59 • Tufnell Park

Boston Arms	178 Junction Rd	020 7272 8153	Ferociously scruffy but friendly Irish pub, with rock pit attached.
The Dome	178 Junction Rd	020 7272 8153	Fast becoming our favourite venue!
The Hideaway	114 Junction Rd	020 7561 0779	Beer, pizza, dancing. What else do you need?
The Lord Palmerston	33 Dartmouth Park Hill	020 7485 1578	Gone a bit plastic, but still worth it.
The Star	47 Chester Rd	020 7263 9067	It's a star.

Map 60 • Archway

Archway Tavern	1 Archway Close	020 7272 2840	Cheap beer, plentiful fisticuffs.
The Mother Red Cap	665 Holloway Rd	020 7263 7082	Begorra! Bejesus! Be better off going to another boozer!

Map 61 • Holloway (North)

The Quays	471 Holloway Rd	020 7272 3634	Into bad U2 cover bands? Then you'll love it here.
The Swimmer	13 Eburne Rd	020 7281 4632	No running, diving in the shallow end, or heavy petting.

Map 62 • Finsbury Park

The Faltering Fullback	19 Perth Rd	020 7272 5834	Tardis-like local. Avoid match nights unless you're a Gooner.

Map 63 • Manor House

The Brownswood Park Tavern	271 Green Lanes	020 8809 2846	Enter, before Manor House drives you mad.
The Manor Club	277 Seven Sisters Rd	078 2823 2869	Once a historic pub, now a strip club. No brainer.

Map 64 • Stoke Newington

The Auld Shillelagh	105 Stoke Newington Church St	020 7249 5951	The best Guinness in London; you won't leave standing up.
Londesborough	36 Barbauld Rd	020 7254 5865	Stokey trendies on leather sofas.
Rose and Crown	199 Stoke Newington Church St	020 7254 7497	Sunday roasts to die for and step-back-in-time décor.
Ryan's Bar	Stoke Newington Church S	020 7275 7807	Boho cafe and venue with a noise limiter! Pussies.
The Shakespeare	57 Allen Rd	020 7254 4190	The Bard would be proud.
White Hart	69 Stoke Newington High St	020 7254 6626	Huge pub, huge beer garden—really it's huge.

Map 65 • West Hampstead

The Czech and Slovak Bar	74 West End Lane	020 7372 0131	Go Czech.
The Good Ship	289 Kilburn High Rd	079 4900 8253	Where Kilburn takes music seriously.
The Luminaire	311 High Rd	020 7372 7123	Regular winner of "best live venue" awards, despite the weird decor.

Map 66 • Finchley Road / Swiss Cottage

Ye Olde Swiss Cottage	98 Finchley Rd	020 7722 3487	What can we say.

Map 67 • Belsize Park

The Washington	50 England's Ln	020 7722 8842	Monday night is pub quiz night.

Map 68 • Kilburn High Road / Abbey Road

The Clifton	96 Clifton Hill	020 7372 3427	Not as secret as they want you to believe. But very nice.

Map 69 • St. John's Wood

The Star	38 St. Johns Wood Terrace	020 7722 1051	Drink face-to-face with a huge Highland Terrier.

Map 70 • Primrose Hill

The Albert	11 Princess Rd	020 7722 1886	A local. Cosy and relaxed.
Cecil Sharp House	2 Regents Park Rd	020 7485 2206	Sword dancing and Olde Stuffe.
The Engineer	65 Gloucester Ave	020 7722 0950	The classy chandeliers say it all.
The Lansdowne	90 Gloucester Ave	020 7483 0409	Home of the beautiful people.
Princess of Wales	22 Chalcot Rd	020 7722 0354	Traditional pub with occasional jazz performances.
Queens No. 1	1 Edis St	020 7586 3049	Comfy, quiet local.
Sir Richard Steele	97 Haverstock Hill	020 7483 1261	Friendly local with quirky decor.

Map 71 • Camden Town / Chalk Farm / Kentish Town (West)

Bar Vinyl	6 Inverness St	020 7482 5545	DJ Bar. And good coffee.
Bartok	78 Chalk Farm Rd	020 7916 0595	Hip, late-night bar with chilled-out sofa feel.
The Constitution	42 St Pancras Way	020 7387 4805	Proper boozer away from the madness of Camden Taaahn.
Dingwalls	Middle Yard	019 2082 3098	Camden Lock's guitar-smashing heartland.
The Dublin Castle	94 Parkway	020 7485 1773	Famous, small, LOUD.
Electric Ballroom	184 Camden High St	020 7485 9006	Scruffy but essential rock haunt, perennially threatened by developers.
The Enterprise	2 Haverstock Hill	020 7485 2659	Literary Irish pub with tiny indie venue upstairs.
Fiddlers Elbow	1 Malden Rd	020 7485 3269	Live music venue pub sans pretention.
Good Mixer	30 Inverness St	020 7916 7929	Ah, remember those halcyon days of Britpop?
The Hawley Arms	2 Castlehaven Rd	020 7428 5979	The Hawley will rise from the ashes. Camden needs it.
Jazz Cafe	5 Parkway	020 7485 6834	A relentless stream of excellent gigs.
Koko	1 Camden High St	087 0432 5527	From Charlie Chaplin to Lenny Kravitz, playing Koko still kicks ass.
The Lock Tavern	35 Chalk Farm Rd	020 7482 7163	Great gigs, Sunday roasts and (unpainfully) hip clientele.
Monkey Chews	2 Queen's Crescent	020 7267 6406	Dark and intimate bar and music venue.
Oxford Arms	265 Camden High St	020 7267 4945	Theatre pub where you may stumble upon Amy Winehouse, stumbling.
Proud Camden	Chalk Farm Rd	020 7482 3867	Oh-so-casual, trendy little bar. Fairy lights and arty types.
Quinn's	65 Kentish Town Rd	020 7267 8240	More German beer than you can pronounce.
The Underworld	174 Camden High St	020 7482 1932	Throbbing pit of angry rock and even angrier metal.

Map 72 • Kentish Town

The Abbey Tavern	124 Kentish Town Rd	020 7267 9449	Fairy lit, casual beer garden with talented DJs on Saturdays.
The Assembly House	292 Kentish Town Rd	020 7485 2031	Massive pub with friendly atmosphere.
The Bull & Gate	389 Kentish Town Rd	020 8826 5000	A gigging institution.
HMV Forum	9 Highgate Rd	020 7428 4099	Good venue for medium-sized bands.
The Pineapple	51 Leverton St	020 7284 4631	Backstreet Victorian with good beers and Thai grub.
Rio's Health Spa	239 Kentish Town Rd	020 7485 0607	Bored of your wife? Swap her here.

Map 73 • Holloway

The Lord Stanley	51 Camden Park Rd	020 7428 9488	Dark wood, Edwardian interior, fireplace and secret walled garden.
Shilibeers	1 Carpenter's Mews, North Rd	020 7700 1858	For relaxed drinking on comfy couches.

Map 74 • Holloway Road / Arsenal

The Coronet	338 Holloway Rd	020 7609 5014	The smell of old men's piss is abound, but it's cheap!
El Comandante	10 Annette Rd	020 7607 3961	South American vibe in a Victorian pub.
The Garage	20 Highbury Corner	020 7619 6720	Bad sound and a guaranteed black hole in your evening.
Hen and Chickens Theatre Bar	109 St. Paul's Rd	020 7704 2001	All the best pubs have theatres. Fact.

Map 75 • Highbury

Alwyne Castle	83 St Pauls Rd	020 7359 7351	Alright for a pint.

Oak Bar	79 Green Lanes	020 7354 2791	Eclectic programme of events at this mixed/lesbian venue.
The Snooty Fox	75 Grosvenor Avenue	020 7354 9532	Strangely empty - shame for such a great pub.

Map 76 • Edgeware Road / Marylebone (North)

The Perseverance	11 Shroton St	020 7723 7469	Perseverance in finding it will be rewarded.
twotwentytwo	222 Marylebone Rd	020 7631 8000	Grand is the word.
The Volunteer	245 Baker St	020 7486 4091	Grand old Victorian taphouse great for a lively post-work pint.

Map 77 • Mornington Crescent / Regent's Park

The Crown & Anchor	137 Drummond St	020 7383 2681	A pub makeover masterpiece.
Edinboro Castle	57 Mornington Terrace	020 7255 9651	Huge outdoors bit, great BBQ on summer weekends.
Queen's Head & Artichoke	30 Albany St	020 7916 6206	The pinchos are addictive. We have warned, friends.

Map 78 • Euston

The Champagne Bar at St Pancras	Pancras Rd	020 7870 9900	Miss your train!
The Crown & Goose	100 Arlington Rd	020 7485 8008	Delightfully old-fashioned pub with good grub and an open fire.
Lincoln Lounge	52 York Way	020 7837 9339	Arty, quirky and cool. Does King's Cross proud.
Purple Turtle	61 Crowndale Rd	020 7383 4976	Rock club that looks like a wacky goth spaceship.
Scala	275 Pentonville Rd	020 7833 2022	Historic venue with plush edges. If these walls could talk…

Map 79 • King's Cross

The Big Chill House	257 Pentonville Rd	020 7427 2540	Allow staff 28 working days to process your drinks order.
Canal 125	125 Caledonian Rd	020 7837 1924	Upmarket local bar that draws a swanky crowd.
Central Station	37 Wharfdale Rd	020 7278 3294	Ominous looking cabaret bar-cum-cruise emporium. Check site first.
Cross Kings	126 York Way	020 7278 8318	Nice little place that tries but usually fails to be 'edgy.'
Drink, Shop & Do		0203 343 9138	Perfect cocktails, art to buy, and lovely atmosphere.
EGG	200 York Way	020 7609 8364	Big club, big garden, big night out.
Hemingford Arms	128 Hemingford Rd	020 7607 3303	Full of local aleheads.
The Lexington	96 Pentonville Rd	020 7837 5371	Come and support your boyfriend's shit band.
Tarmon	270 Caledonian Rd	020 7607 3242	Character. Lots of character.

Map 80 • Angel / Upper St

25 Canonbury	25 Canonbury Ln	020 7226 0955	You'll never love it as much as it loves itself.
Albert and Pearl	181 Upper St	020 7354 9993	Classy when dark. Garish when lit.
The Angel	3 Islington High St	020 7837 2218	Students. The elderly. The unemployed.
The Angelic	57 Liverpool Rd	020 7278 8433	A sophisticated local.
Buffalo Bar	259 Upper St	020 7359 6191	Sweaty, small venue. You'll see them here first.
Camden Head	2 Camden Walk	020 7359 0851	Comedians debut new gags upstairs. Cheap—and mostly cheerful.
The Castle	54 Pentonville Rd	020 7713 1858	Needs breaking in.
Compton Arms	4 Compton Ave	020 7359 6883	Islington's only real pub—or so they say.
The Crown	116 Cloudesley Rd	020 7837 7107	Jovial spot for a quiet pint and Sunday roasts.
Cuba Libre	72 Upper St	020 7354 9998	Tank up with mojitos. Salsa with the barman.
The Drapers Arms	44 Bransbury St	020 7619 0348	Celeb backlash against new CCTV. Big Brother really is watching.
Electrowerkz	7 Torrens St	020 7837 6419	Crumbling rave labyrinth.
Embassy Bar	119 Essex Rd	020 7226 7901	Wannabe DJs' last real hope.
The Florence	50 Florence St	020 7354 5633	Refurbed, warm Georgian boozer.
The Green Man	144 Essex Rd	020 7226 2692	Eerie inside, scary punters.
Hope And Anchor	207 Upper St	020 7704 2689	Scuzzy pub with even scuzzier bands in the basement.
Islington Academy	16 Parkfield St	020 7288 4400	Grubby live music. Slap on some skinny jeans first.
Islington Tap	80 Liverpool Rd	020 7354 5111	Vast, ornate ceilings and over-priced beer.
Jury's Inn	60 Pentonville Rd	020 7282 5500	Really? Why did you even buy this book?
Keston Lodge	131 Upper St	020 7354 9535	Just the right side of poncy.
King's Head Theatre & Pub	115 Upper St	020 7226 8561	Proper, good-time boozer.
The Lord Clyde	342 Essex Rd	020 7288 9850	Like boozing in Land of Leather.
Lucky Voice	173 Upper St	020 7354 6280	Singing in private? Like a bathroom with beer.
Marquess Tavern	32 Canonbury St	020 7354 2975	Scruffy locals live on despite gastro revolution.
Myddleton Arms	52 Canonbury Rd	020 7226 4595	Don't those people have, y'know, jobs?
Old Red Lion	418 St John St	020 7837 7816	Theatre pub legend.
The Regent	201 Liverpool Rd	020 7700 2725	Good news: it's finally starting to fray.
Round Midnight: Jazz and Blues Bar	13 Liverpool Rd		Great music and a good atmosphere.
Union Chapel	Compton Terrace	020 7226 3750	God's favourite music venue. Hell, everyone's.

Map 81 • Canonbury

Marquess Tavern	32 Canonbury St	020 7354 2975	Scruffy locals live on, despite gastro revolution.

Map 82 • De Beauvoir Town / Kingsland

Dalston Boys Club	68 Boleyn Road	no phone	Keep your eyes peeled for gigs at this place.
Jazz Bar	4 Bradbury St	020 7254 9728	Funk and free cheese. Until 5. Need we say more?
The Northgate	113 Southgate Rd	020 7359 7392	Reliable local despite being—gasp!—a gastro.
The Orwell	382 Essex Rd	020 7288 1914	Drinking in the day. George would be proud.
The Rosemary Branch	2 Shepperton Rd	020 7704 2730	Theatre pub with great selection of ales and hearty fare.
The Vortex	11 Gillett Sq	020 7254 4097	Dalston's only real jazz bar.
The Duke of Wellington	119 Balls Pond Rd	020 7275 7640	Nice little boozer, as they say.

Map 83 • Angel (East) / City Rd (North)

Barrio North	45 Essex Rd	020 7688 2882	Groovy little bar with friendly international vibe. And a caravan!
The Charles Lamb	16 Elia St	020 7837 5040	It's not big, but It's clever.
The Duke of Cambridge	30 St Peter's St	020 7359 3066	Feel self-righteous in the world's first organic pub.
Earl of Essex	25 Danbury St	020 7226 3608	For drinking in the day. In the dark.
The Island Queen	87 Noel Rd	020 7354 8741	Where NFT planned the London guide. Sweet.
The Mucky Pup	39 Queen's Head St	020 7226 2572	The dog's bollocks.
The Narrow Boat	119 St Peters St	020 7288 0572	Cheerful canal-side pub for lazy pints and people-watching.
Offside Bar and Gallery	273 City Rd	020 7253 3306	Like a football stadium, but without anyone pissing in the sinks.
The Old Queen's Head	44 Essex Rd	020 7354 9993	Trendier than the name suggests.
The Wenlock Arms	26 Wenlock Rd	020 7608 3406	Threadbare, battered old boozer with a magnificent range of real ales.

Map 84 • Hoxton

333	333 Old St	020 7739 5949	The Shoreditch grandfather.
The Bricklayer's Arms	63 Charlotte Rd	087 2148 3675	Double bypass heart of 90s Britart scene. Barely still beating.
Cantaloupe	35 Charlotte Rd	020 7729 5566	Of course YOU'RE not a corporate whore.
Cargo	83 Rivington St	020 7739 3440	Cavernous, sterile hole with bad sound but good gigs. Natch.
Charlie Wright's International Bar	45 Pitfield St	020 7490 8345	Does anyone turn up here sober?
Club Aquarium	256 Old St	020 7253 3558	After-hours swimming pool scuzzfest.
Cocomo	323 Old St	020 7613 0315	Cocktail bar with cakes, comfy sofas and scrumptious staff.
East Village	89 Great Eastern St	020 7739 5173	Shoreditch clubbing novice where the DJ is king.
The Elbow Room	97 Curtain Rd	020 7613 1316	Pricey, mildly funky pool joint.
Electricity Showroom	39 Hoxton Sq	020 7739 3939	Shark-infested waters.
Favela Chic	91 Great Eastern St	020 7613 4228	Caipirinha-lovin', shabby-chic bar full of clothes-swapping kwaziness.
The Foundry	84 Great Eastern St	020 7739 6900	Like a pretentious art student's dream bar. In a good way.
The Griffin	93 Leonard St	020 7739 6719	NOT the strip bar of the same name…
Hoxton Square Bar & Kitchen	2 Hoxton Sq	020 7613 0709	Snotty bands and doormen. Wear something uber.
The Legion	348 Old St	020 7729 4441	Free jukebox, quality DJs, cheap beer. Happy times.
The Macbeth	60 70 Hoxton St	020 7749 0600	Hot new bands love it. And so do we.
The Old Blue Last	38 Great Eastern St	020 7739 7033	Until the bass drum WILL bring down that pub ceiling.
Plastic People	147 Curtain Rd	020 7739 6471	Tiny, pitch black musical adventure.
Red Lion	41 Hoxton St	020 7729 7920	Stay forever if you bag the chaise lounge…
The Stag's Head	55 Orsman Rd	020 7739 6741	Run down boozer currently being used for hip gigs.
Strongroom Bar	120 Curtain Rd	020 7426 5103	Shoreditch's last stronghold of unpretentiousness?
Troy Bar	10 Hoxton St	020 7739 6695	A semi-hidden gem with soul and funk music most nights.

Map 85 • Stoke Newington (East)

The Birdcage	58 Stamford Hill	020 8806 6740	High-ceilinged pub with squishy sofas and lived-in feel.
Blush	8 Cazenove Rd	020 7923 9202	Pink pint-parlour with poker and personable patrons (oh please!)
The Royal Sovereign	64 Northwold Rd	020 8806 2449	Drink with the locals.
Stoke Newington Int'l Airport	1-15Leswin Place	079 7128 4912	Eclectic live entertainment is always on the menu.

Map 86 • Dalston / Kingsland

Alibi	91 Kingsland High St	020 7249 2733	The kids like it.
Bar 23	23 Stoke Newington Rd	020 7241 2060	A slice of weirdness with wacked out DJing and drinking.
Bardens Boudoir	38 Stoke Newington Rd	020 7249 9557	Anything can happen in this basement. The beating heart of Dalston's music shenanigans.
Cafe Oto	18 Ashwin St	020 7923 1231	Mysterious new venue importing music from the hinterlands of psychedelia.
Dalston Superstore	117 Kingsland High St	020 7254 2273	Uber hip polysexual squelch-a-thon.
Efes Pool Club & Bar	17 Stoke Newington Rd	020 7249 6040	Down some pints at this great spot to play pool.
The Haggerston	438 Kingsland Rd	020 7923 3206	Artist-run flea pit. Chaotic crowd surfing most nights.

Marquis of Lansdowne	48 Stoke Newington Rd	020 7254 1104	Pleases long-standing locals and hip Hackneyites alike.
The Moustache Bar	58 Stoke Newington Rd	075 0715 2047	Follow the moustache (sticker) trail to this trendy/grimy subterranean bar.
Passion	251 Amhurst Rd	020 7254 3667	Tiny basement venue that hosts massive all-nighters.
The Prince George	40 Parkholme Rd	087 1934 1384	Buzzing local favourite. Renowned Monday quiz night, great jukebox.
Vogue Fabrics	66 Stoke Newington Rd	no phone	The latest place to Vogue.

Map 87 • Hackney Downs / Lower Clapton

Biddle Brothers	88 Lower Clapton Rd	020 8985 7052	Almost trendy oasis for the trendy in an eccentric neighbourhood.
Crooked Billet	84 Upper Clapton Rd	020 8806 2747	Proof that Clapton can still be f***ing terrifying.
Hugo's Speaker Palace	14 Andre St	020 8968 5704	Clandestine speaker cemetery. Very hush-hush and very cool.
Pembury Tavern	90 Amhurst Rd	020 8986 8597	Large selection of microbrews.

Map 88 • Haggerston / Queensbridge Rd

A10 (aka The Russian Bar)	267 Kingsland Rd	n/a	It's hell and it's heaven and we can't make our f'ing minds up.
The Fox	372 Kingsland Rd	020 3215 2093	Half-way stop for Shoreditch-to-Dalston pub crawls.
Passing Clouds	440 Kingsland Rd	020 7168 7146	Back alley arts collective and live venue.
Plaza	161 Kingsland Rd	020 7613 1319	Sometime gig venue, all-the-time scary East End boozer.

Map 89 • London Fields / Hackney Central

Baxter's Court	282 Mare St	020 8525 9010	A chain pub, okay, okay. But check the ladies' toilets!
The Dolphin	165 Mare St	020 8985 3727	Pathos-sodden karaoke occasionally ruined by post-opening art people.
The Dove	24 Broadway Market	020 7275 7617	Belgian beer paradise.
Pub on the Park	19 Martello St	020 7275 9586	Tap for London Fields.
The Old Ship	2 Sylvester Path	020 8986 1641	Nicely refurbed ex-dive.

Map 90 • Homerton / Victoria Park North

Chats Palace Arts Centre	42 Brooksby's Walk	020 8533 0227	Fantastic community arts venue—Hackney classic.
The Lauriston	162 Victoria Park Rd	020 8985 5404	As vamped up as its would-be-village surroundings.
Royal Inn on the Park	111 Lauriston Rd	020 8985 3321	Victoria Park's prime boozer.

Map 91 • Shoreditch / Brick Lane / Spitalfields

93 Feet East	150 Brick Ln	020 7247 3293	Enthusiastic, trendy club (to impress out-of-towners).
Anda De Bridge	42 Kingsland Rd	020 7503 9651	Cocktail party, Caribbean-style.
The Archers	42 Osborn St	020 7247 3826	Nice ole pub that's resisted Shoreditchification. Perfect for pre-curry pints.
Bar Kick	127 Shoreditch High St	020 7739 8700	Lemon-yellow table football gaff.
Bar Music Hall	134 Curtain Rd	020 7613 5951	Nice wallpaper, free music. Who's complaining?
Bedroom Bar	62 Rivington St	020 7613 5637	Saturday's DJ 'n' sax players mean dancing til dawn.
Bethnal Green Working Men's Club	44 Pollard Row	020 7739 7170	Saucy amateur burlesque that still confuses the resident Working Men.
The Big Chill Bar	Dray Walk off Brick Lane	020 7392 9180	Still among Brick Lane's better drinking spots.
Browns	1 Hackney Rd	020 7739 4653	Now really. What would your mother say?
Café 1001	91 Brick Ln`	020 7247 6166	Like a house party. But one where cans cost £3.
The Carpenter's Arms	73 Cheshire St	020 7739 6342	No longer run by the Kray twins' mother, still felonious fun.
Catch	22 Kingsland Rd	020 7729 6097	Reliable active dancefloor, reliable silly hats, reliable good fun.
Comedy Cafe	66 Rivington St	020 7739 5706	Fun venue, but invariably a dud in the line-up.
The Commercial Tavern	142 Commercial St	020 7247 1888	Trusty Shoreditch traditional.
Ditch Bar	145 Shoreditch High St	020 7739 4018	Noisy electro bar/scrum.
Exit	174 Brick Lane	020 7377 2088	Sit in a row with fellow Brick Lane trendies.
The George & Dragon	2 Blackheath Hill	020 8691 3764	Witness the E2 gay clique rev up for imminent carnage.
The Golden Heart	110 Commercial St	020 7247 2158	Has it all: fires, pints and a lazy resident dog.
The Gramaphone Bar	60 Commercial St	020 7377 5332	Dark basement venue.
Herbal	10 Kingsland Rd	020 7613 4462	It's small enough to shout at the DJ. And groovy.
Jaguar Shoes	32 Kingsland Rd	020 7729 5830	Happy hipsters behind wide windows.
Joiners Arms	116 Hackney Rd	020 7739 9397	Popular gay pub that knows how to have fun.
Loungelover	1 Whiteby St	020 7012 1234	Kitsch-colonial glitter-ball of a cocktail bar.
Mason & Taylor	51 Bethnal Green Rd	020 7749 9670	Purveyors of traditional beer and real ale.
The Old Shoreditch Station	1 Kingsland Rd	020 7729 5188	Used to be cool. When it was a train station.
On the Rocks	25 Kingsland Rd	020 7688 0339	Come face to face with oblivion every Friday.
Owl & Pussycat	34 Redchurch St	020 7613 3628	Crooked little place, tucked in the folds of Shoreditch's blubber.
Prague	6 Kingsland Rd	020 7739 9110	The closest you'll ever get to a romantic bar in Shoreditch.
Pride of Spitalfields	3 Heneage St	020 7247 8933	The only East End boozer left on Brick Lane.
Public Life	82 Commercial St	020 7375 1631	Used to be a toilet. Kinda still is. Moronic fun.
The Redchurch	107 Redchurch St	020 7729 8333	Late, loud DJ box.

The Royal Oak	73 Columbia Rd	020 7729 2220	Gentrifying, gentrifying… gentrified.
Shoreditch House	Ebor St	020 7739 5040	Last one in the rooftop pool buys the drinks!
Vibe Bar	91 Brick Ln	020 7247 3479	Bar in a brewery. Feel the vibe?
The Water Poet	9 Folgate St	020 7426 0495	Mismatched chairs, over-stuffed sofas, philosophy and beer.
Ye Olde Axe	69 Hackney Rd	020 7729 5137	Rockabilly-only weekends. That's right: rockabilly-only. Occasional gentleman's club.

Map 92 • Bethnal Green

The Albion	94 Goldsmiths Row	020 7739 0185	Friendly, footy-mad local. All welcome.
Bethnal Green Working Men's Club	44 Pollard Row	020 7739 7170	Saucy amateur burlesque that still confuses the resident Working Men.
The Camel	277 Globe Rd	020 8983 9888	Bethnal Green's best kept secret… D'oh!
Florist	255 Globe Rd	020 8981 1100	The Camel's naughty little sister.
The FymFyg Bar	231 Cambridge Heath Rd	020 7613 1057	The comedian's comedy house: this one knows what it's doing.
Images	483 Hackney Rd	020 7739 5213	When the lapdancing's over, the clubbing madness begins.
The Star of Bethnal Green	359 Bethnal Green Rd	020 7729 0167	Formerly the Pleasure Unit. Still Bethnal Green's live music best.

Map 93 • Globe Town / Mile End (North)

The Approach Tavern	47 Approach Rd	0208 983 3878	Great if you can tolerate the ironic haircuts crew.
The Fat Cat Cafe Bar	221 Grove Rd	020 8983 4353	No fat cats, but a good mix of locals and trendies.
Jongleurs (Bow Wharf)	221 Grove Rd	0844 499 4062	Blandard comedy chain.
The Morgan Arms	43 Morgan St	020 8980 6389	Grab a pint with some gourmet food.
Palm Tree	1 Haverfield Rd	020 8980 2918	Brass walls and retired crooners! Amazingly old-fashioned boozer.
The Victoria	110 Grove Rd	020 8980 6609	Coolified old man's boozer turned hipster joint.

Map 94 • Bow

The Coborn Arms	8 Coborn Rd	020 8980 3793	Nice ales, nice beer garden.
The Young Prince	448 Roman Rd	020 8980 1292	If on Roman Road…

Map 95 • Whitechapel (West) / St Katharine's Dock

The Castle	44 Commercial Rd	020 7481 2361	East End fortress holding it against the City.
Dickens Inn	St Katharine's Way	020 7488 2208	Proof that an awesome location can conquer all.
Prohibition Bar & Grill	1 St. Katherine's Docks	020 7702 4210	Gormless bar.
Rhythm Factory	16 Whitechapel Rd	020 7375 3774	The Libertines' old haunt, with all the grimy 'chic' that implies.

Map 96 • Whitechapel (East) / Shadwell (West) / Wapping

The Captain Kidd	108 Wapping High St	020 7480 5759	Pub with nice Thames-side beer garden.
The Caxton	50 The Highway	020 7481 2961	Opens weekdays at 4am. Depressing, but come here to kick-on.
Indo	133 Whitechapel Rd	020 7247 4926	Very narrow and everything but narrow-minded.
Town of Ramsgate	62 Wapping High St	020 7481 8000	Get nautical.

Map 97 • Stepney / Shadwell (East)

Cable Street Studios	56 Cable St	020 7790 1309	'Artists.' 'Warehouse studios.' 'Parties.' It'll never work.
The George Tavern	373 Commercial Rd	020 7790 7335	Old men, hipsters and blue-collar poets in imperfect harmony.
The Prospect of Whitby	57 Wapping Wall	020 7481 1095	Ye olde pub(e) on ye Thames(e).
Roxy	400 Commercial Rd	020 7790 9000	Glorious art deco palace.

Map 98 • Mile End (South) / Limehouse

The Grapes	76 Narrow St	020 7987 4396	True to its roots East End boozer—natural survivor.

Map 100 • Poplar (West) / Canary Wharf (West)

Bar 38	West India Quay	020 7515 8361	Great inside and out.
Davy's at Canary Wharf	31 Canary Wharf	020 7363 6633	Traditional-style with fine ales, wine and food.
Dion Canary Wharf	Port East Building, West India Quay	020 7987 0001	Docklands warehouse-turned-champagne heaven.
Via Fossa	18 Hertsmere Rd	020 7515 8549	Three floors of bankers…

Map 101 • Poplar (East) / Canary Wharf (East)

The Greenwich Pensioner	28 Bazely St	020 7987 4414	No pensioners and not in Greenwich.
The Resolute	210 Poplar High St	020 7987 1429	In Poplar? Desperate for a drink?

Map 102 • Millwall

Hubbub	269 Westferry Rd	020 7515 5577	Oasis in Docklands desert.

Map 103 • Cubitt Town / Mudchute

The Ferry House	26 Ferry St	020 7537 9587	Beer-drenched docks time capsule.
Lord Nelson	1 Manchester Rd	020 7987 1970	Can I have a half, Nelson?
Waterman's Arms	1 Glenaffric Ave	020 7093 2885	Proper boozer on the Island.

Map 104 • South Bank / Waterloo / Lambeth North

The Anchor & Hope	36 The Cut	020 7928 9898	For that intellectual pre-theatre/dinner chat.
Benugo Bar & Kitchen	Belvedere Rd	020 7401 9000	Cheerily mismatched armchairs welcome students and film buffs alike.
Concrete	Southbank Centre	020 7928 4123	Restaurant/bar features Russian beer, food, absinthe.
Cubana	48 Lower Marsh	020 7928 8778	Still riding the mojito trend. But good at them.
The Cut Bar	66 The Cut	020 7928 4400	Enjoy the outdoor terrace with trendy media types and thesps.
Da Vinci's	6 Baylis Rd	020 7928 8099	Cheesy and bizarre late-night fun.
The Fire Station	150 Waterloo Rd	020 7620 2226	Only fun when you're desperate.
The Pit Bar at The Old Vic	The Cut	020 7928 2975	Guzzle champagne with Kevin Spacey and friends.
Royal Festival Hall	Belvedere Rd	084 4875 0073	Increasingly exciting programming amid nicely refurbished surroundings.
Skylon	Belvedere Rd	020 7654 7800	Impress someone with the view, then split the bill.

Map 105 • Southwark / Bankside (West)

Albert Arms	1 Gladstone St	020 7928 6517	Where yuppies meet students meet blow-ins meet locals.
Imbibe	173 Blackfriars Rd	020 7928 3693	Studenty feel, mid-week. Shouty after-workers, otherwise.
The Lord Nelson	243 Union St	020 7207 2701	Like a student union.
Ministry of Sound	103 Gaunt St	087 0060 0010	The sound really IS amazing.
The Prince of Wales	51 St George's Rd	020 7582 9696	Cheap local with downright scary karaoke.
The White Theatre	206 Union St	020 7261 0209	Free aperitvo food excuses their 'TWT' abbreviation.

Map 106 • Bankside (East) / Borough / Newington

The Anchor	34 Park St	020 7407 1577	Did Samuel Johnson have to battle this many tourists?
Belushi's	161 Borough High St	020 7939 9700	Drunk Antipodeans. Karaoke. General carnage.
The Blue-Eyed Maid	173 Borough High St	020 7378 8259	It's never too late for a last drink in Borough.
Brew Wharf	Brew Wharf Yard, Stoney St	020 7378 6601	Beer lovers' heaven.
The George Inn	77 Borough High St	020 7407 2056	Grab a home brew in the dazzlingly ancient George Inn.
The Globe	8 Bedale St	020 7407 0043	Bridget Jones' home? Do we care?
La Cave	6 Borough High St	020 7378 0788	So delightful you'll even start liking the French. Briefly.
The Market Porter	9 Stoney St	020 7407 2495	Market traders and suits neck real ale. Smell the testosterone.
Number 1 Bar	1 Duke Street Hill	020 7407 6420	One stop party: booze, pool and karaoke.
The Rake	14 Winchester Walk	020 7407 0557	Tiny place with a hundred different beers. Honestly, a hundred.
The Roebuck	50 Great Dover St	020 7357 7324	Cool but calm drinkerie for a pre-night-out drink.
The Rose	123 Snowfields	020 7378 6660	Superb backstreet boozer full of human oddities.
Roxy Bar and Screen	128 Borough High St	020 7407 4057	Mingle with baby yuppies at the Roxy Bar & Screen.
The Royal Oak	44 Tabard St	020 7357 7173	Possibly the friendliest landlords in London.
SeOne	Weston St	020 7407 1617	Loud music & louder people.
Southwark Tavern	22 Southwark St	020 7403 0257	Traditional ambience and ordinary fare in ye olde Southwark Tavern.
Wine Wharf	Stoney St	087 0899 8856	If you're as crazy about wine as they are.

Map 107 • Shad Thames

Cable	33 Bermondsey St	020 7403 7730	Get messed up in a dark tunnel. Again.
The Hide	39 Bermondsey St	020 7403 6655	Slightly odd vibe, but cracking drinks.
Hilton London Tower Bridge	5 Tooley St	020 3002 4300	Super-chilled, low-lit relaxation zone for the wealthy.
The Woolpack	98 Bermondsey St	020 7357 9269	Filling lunches, comfy sofas, great garden. Job done.

Map 109 • Southwark Park

Ancient Foresters	282 Southwark Park Rd	020 7394 1633	Surprise charmer in an otherwise grimy area.
The Angel	101 Bermondsey Wall E	020 7394 3214	Sam Smith pub with great views across the river
The Mayflower	117 Rotherhithe St	020 7237 4088	Used to be The Shippe from whenst the Mayflower departed
The Ship	39 St Marychurch St	020 7237 4103	Sunny day? Settle in with a beer and a sarnie.

Map 110 • Rotherhithe (West) / Canada Water

The Albion	20 Albion St	020 72370182	Only if three generations of your family drank here first.
old Salt Quay	163 Rotherhithe St	020 7394 7108	Pub-by-numbers, but the riverside patio of dreams.

Map 111 • Rotherhithe (East) Surrey Quays

Blacksmith's Arms	257 Rotherhithe St	020 7237 1349	Good enough for the Queen Mum: good enough for us.
Moby Dick	6 Russell Pl, off Greenland Dock	020 7231 6719	Once here, it's hard to leave. Because it's really far from the tube.
Ship & Whale	2 Gulliver St	020 7237 7072	So good we even come for breakfast.
Whelan's	11 Rotherhithe Old Rd	020 7237 9425	Looks rough around the edges, but you could do worse.
Wibbley Wobbley	South Dock Marina, Rope St	020 7232 2320	Great dinky boat-bar, for short people.

Map 112 • Kennington / Elephant and Castle

Corsica Studios	5 Elephant Rd	020 7703 4760	Sweaty music venue with 'home-made' vibe.
Dog House	293 Kennington Rd	020 7820 9310	Like your scruffy, unpretentious younger brother. Made for chill-axing.
Prince of Wales	43 Cleaver Sq	020 7735 9916	Stuart's favourite pub in Kennington.

Map 113 • Walworth

Temple Bar	286 Walworth Rd	020 7703 4117	Only when you really, REALLY need a drink.
The Beehive	60 Carter St	020 7703 4992	The local bit of nice.

Map 114 • Old Kent Road (West) / Burgess Park

World Turned Upside Down	145 Old Kent Rd	020 7237 4181	Original headquarters of the Pearly Kings & Queens.

Map 118 • Deptford (Central)

The Lord Palmerston	81 Childers St	020 8692 1575	Fewer brawls than your average Deptford pub.

Map 119 • Deptford (East)

The Bird's Nest	32 Deptford Church St	020 8694 1852	Hilarious 'locals vs. trendies' vibe. Go for monthly Flesh Dunce!
Dog & Bell	116 Prince St	020 8692 5664	Now why can't ALL pubs in Deptford be like this?

Map 120 • Greenwich

Bar du Musee	17 Nelson Rd	020 8858 4710	"You have beautiful eyes, you know that?"
The Greenwich Union	56 Royal Hill	020 8692 6258	Beers galore.
Up The Creek	30 Creek Rd	0208 858 4581	Comedy club (plus comedy dancing at the disco)

Map 122 • Camberwell (East)

The Castle	65 Camberwell Church St	020 7277 2601	Locals, board games and disco.

Map 123 • Peckham

Frank's Cafe and Campari Bar	95 Rye Ln	07943 379 726	Cheap Campari cocktails in a multi-story car park. Pure class.

Map 125 • New Cross Gate

The Montague Arms	289 Queen's Rd	020 7639 4923	Semi-legendary, bizarrely decorated local, staffed by the world's oldest barmen and women.

Map 126 • New Cross *Address*

Amersham Arms	388 New Cross Rd	020 8469 1499	Art school hipdom in grimy New Cross's coolest venue.
Hobgoblin	272 New Cross Rd	020 8692 3193	Get drunk with the Goldsmiths crowd.
New Cross Inn	323 New Cross Rd	020 8691 7222	Someone's gotta keep "the scene" going.

Map 127 • Coldharbour Lane / Herne Hill (West)

The Commercial	210 Railton Rd	020 7733 8783	Roaring fire and mulled wine in winter. Fits like a glove.
Escape Bar and Art	214 Railton Rd	020 7737 0333	The bar's alright, the art's excellent.
The Florence	133 Dulwich Rd	020 7326 4987	Microbrewery on premises.
Prince Regent	69 Dulwich Rd	020 7274 1567	Life drawing on Wednesdays to titillate posh diners.

Map 129 • East Dulwich

Liquorish	123 Lordship Ln	020 8693 7744	Good things happen here.

Map 130 • Peckham Rye

The Rye	31 Peckham Rye	020 7639 5397	For lazy lunches on summer Sundays. A pocket of delicious East Dulwich swank Peckham-side.

Map 131 • Vauxhall / Albert Embankment

Area	67 Albert Embankment	020 3242 0040	Another massive Vauxhall rave hole. Serious gay clientele.
Eagle London	349 Kennington Ln	020 7793 0903	Fur on tap throughout the week. Sundays recommended.
The Lavender	112 Vauxhall Walk	020 7735 4440	Just popping to the Lav.
The Royal Vauxhall Tavern	372 Kennington Ln	020 7820 1222	Fun gay pub with trashy cabaret.

Map 132 • Battersea (West)

Barrio	14 Battersea Sq	020 7801 9548	What balmy Sunday evenings were made for.
The Draft House Westbridge	74 Battersea Bridge Road	020 7228 6482	A great pub well worth the trek.
The Greyhound	136 Battersea High St	020 7978 7021	1000-bottle wine list? Not your normal pub.
Le QuecumBar	42 Battersea High St	020 7787 2227	Gypsy jazz, honkytonk and frogs legs in bygone Parisian chic.
The Woodman	60 Battersea High St	020 7228 2968	A nice fire. Pint of Badger. Luverleee.

Map 134 • South Lambeth

Bar Estrela	115 Old South Lambeth Rd	020 7793 1051	Like mama used to make. Probably.
The Battersea Barge	Nine Elms Ln	020 7498 0004	Bouncy, buoyant, thrilled to see you—the Labrador puppy of venues.
Fire	38 Parry St	020 7820 0550	Legendary gay terrordrome with LED ceiling.
Hoist	47 S Lambeth Rd	020 7735 9972	Slap on some leather and get hoisted up.
The Lightbox	6S Lambeth Pl	075 0066 7874	15,000 LED lights. Enough to give us all seizures.
Roller Disco @ Renaissance Rooms	126 S Lambeth Rd	084 4736 5375	Roller skates, alcohol, and a very nervous Health & Safety officer.
The Vauxhall Griffin	8 Wyvil Rd	020 7622 0222	Theme nights to knock your socks off

Map 135 • Oval

Fentiman Arms	64 Fentiman Rd	020 7793 9796	The staff believe that smiles kill kittens.

Map 136 • Putney

The Boathouse	Brewhouse Ln	020 8789 0476	Riverside pub with loadsa outdoor space.
Duke's Head	8 Lower Richmond Rd	020 8788 2552	Typical gastro pub upstairs. Dark DJ bar downstairs.
Jolly Gardeners	61 Lacy Rd	020 8789 2539	Like all good pubs. And sock monkey classes on Wednesdays.
Star & Garter	4 Lower Richmond Rd	020 8788 0345	Upscale Saturday night hotspot on the Thames.

Map 137 • Wandsworth (West)

The Upper Lounge	26 Upper Richmond Rd	020 8875 0269	Utterly likeable. Except Thursdays when it heaves with excitable Saffas.

Map 138 • Wandsworth (Central)

The Cat's Back	88 Point Pleasant	020 8877 0818	Atmospheric and busy with loadsa obscure decoration.
GJ's	89 Garratt Ln	020 8874 2271	Party with snow bunnies.
The Upper Lounge	35 Putney Bridge Rd	020 8874 1695	Good beer selection. Mixed crowd. Decent Sunday Roast.

Map 139 • Wandsworth (East)

Adventure Bar and Lounge	91 Battersea Rise	020 7223 1700	Laid back lounging. Friendly crowd. Poncey cocktails.

Map 140 • Clapham Junction / Northcote Rd

B@1	85 Battersea Rise	020 7978 6595	Be at one with a cocktail menu the size of a book.
Jongleurs (Battersea)	49 Lavender Gardens	0844 499 4060	Lots and lots of laughs. Turns into a scary club.
The Peacock	148 Falcon Rd	020 7223 9633	Burlesque off the beaten track

Map 141 • Battersea (South)

Halo	317 Battersea Park Rd	020 7801 8683	A halo isn't enough. Give this bar a sainthood.
The Lost Angel	339 Battersea Park Rd	020 7622 2112	Put this in your pipe and smoke it, Shoreditch.

Map 142 • Clapham Old Town

Frog and Forget-Me-Not	32 The Pavement	020 7622 5230	A first floor terrace that's just made for summer.
Lost Society	697 Wandsworth Rd	020 7652 6526	Country-house drinking, in Clapham.
Prince of Wales	38 Old Town	020 7622 3530	Eccentric, friendly. Run by a magpie.
Rose & Crown	2 The Polygon	020 7720 8265	For the CAMRA purists.
The Sun	47 Clapham Old Town	020 7622 4980	Nice pub. Ruined by surfeit of twats.

Map 143 • Clapham High Street

The Alexandra	14 Clapham Common South Side	020 7627 5102	Join an up-for-it crowd as multinational as the sport here.
Bread and Roses	68 Clapham Manor St	020 7498 1779	Surprisingly pleasant socialist boozer. Without Clapham tossers.
The Clapham North	409 Clapham Rd	020 7274 2472	A bit 'Clapham', but pretty likable really.
The Falcon	33 Bedford Rd	020 7274 2428	"I told Daddy, I've nowhere to even PARK a GTi!"
Green & Blue	20 Bedford Rd	020 7498 9648	For the finest wine. Because you're worth it.
nfernos	146 Clapham High St	020 7720 7633	Oh God no.
nn Clapham	15 The Pavement	020 7652 2948	Charmingly tatty and full of French people.
The Loft	67 Clapham High St	020 7627 0792	A welcome oasis from Clapham High Street.
The Railway	18 Clapham High St	020 7622 4077	Half-trendy, half-local, three-quarters cool.
Two Brewers	114 Clapham High St	020 7819 9539	Club nights, gay cabaret, lots of fu-un!
The White House	65 Clapham Park Rd	020 7498 3388	Manhattan in Clapham? Erm, O.K.

Map 144 • Stockwell / Brixton (West)

Duke of Edinburgh	204 Ferndale Rd	020 7924 0509	Warm, traditional pub with massive beer garden.
Plan B	418 Brixton Rd	087 0116 5421	Has made a name for itself, but pretty lame really.
The Prince	469 Brixton Rd	020 7326 4455	Behind dealers chanting skunk lies a nothin' special pub.
The Rest Is Noise	44 Brixton Rd	[illegible]	New hip wank-a-thon frequented by your worst nightmare.
The Swan	215 Clapham Rd	020 7978 9778	Don't worry about spitting on the floor.

Map 145 • Stockwell / Brixton (East)

Brixton Academy	211 Stockwell Rd	020 7771 3000	Overrated, but still a tad awesome.
The Grosvenor	17 Sidney Rd	020 7733 1799	Rough n' ready local with amazing crust/noise/punk gigs.
amm	261 Brixton Rd	020 7274 5537	The real deal a little way out.

Map 146 • Earlsfield

ar 366	366 Garratt Ln	020 8944 9591	Chilled, lounge-type bar.
araza	561 Garratt Ln	020 8944 9009	Teeny, funky bar with cocktails-a-go-go.
alfway House	521 Garratt Ln	020 8946 2788	Slinky, chardonnay-swilling pub with terrific terrace.
e Gothique	Windmill Rd & John Archer Wy	020 8870 6567	The answer to: "Open a bar! What could go wrong?"

Map 147 • Balham (West)

he Nightingale	97 Nightingale Ln	020 8673 1637	Untrendified local. Long may it stay so.

Map 148 • Balham (East)

alham Bowls Club	7 Ramsden Rd	020 8673 4700	A pub. In a bowling club circa 1950. Genius.
he Bedford	77 Bedford Hill	020 8682 8940	Music and comedy pub with great bands but crappy beer.
he Exhibit	12 Balham Station Rd	020 8772 6556	Cool, up-market venue. Friendly, laid back vibe.

Map 150 • Brixton

he Dogstar	389 Coldharbour Ln	020 7733 7515	The burritos are great, but leave before the tunes get cheesy.
he Effra	38 Kellet Rd	020 7274 4180	A slice of the real Brixton.
idge Bar	1 Town Hall Parade	020 7326 5100	Techno, trance, hardcore venue avec occasional stabbing.
rand Union	123 Acre Ln	020 7274 8794	Come for the tiki shacks and burgers.
ootananny Brixton	95 Effra Rd	020 7737 7273	Great gigs - many for free
ango Landin'	40 St Matthew's Rd	020 7737 3044	Reggae-tinged alternative bar.
ass	Brixton Hill	020 7738 7875	Drum and Bass + Hard House + Fetish Nights – Hedonist Heaven
ince Albert	418 Coldharbour Ln	020 7274 3771	It's charming, trust us. In a not too obvious kindaway.
atay	447 Coldharbour Ln	020 7326 5001	Cocktails to suit the snobbiest of drinks connoisseurs
he Windmill	22 Blenheim Gardens	020 8671 0700	Rough-edged weirdo magnet. Unique and brilliant.
pstairs at the Ritzy	Brixton Oval, Coldharbour Lane (above Ritzy cinema)	020 7733 2229	Where Brixton sparkles. Cinema, bar, café and free live music.

Map 151 • Tooting Bec

he Bec Bar	26 Tooting Bec Rd	020 8672 7722	Pleasant enough. Go for sport.
ng's Head	84 Upper Tooting Rd	020 8767 6708	Former gin palace brings yesteryear flair to the wasteland.
moke Bar	14 Trinity Rd	020 8767 3902	Standard, compact DJ bar.

Map 152 • Tooting Broadway

arden House	196 Tooting High St	020 8767 6582	Revived Victorian local. Live music and log fire.
amble Inn	223 Mitcham Rd	020 8767 4040	Irish/locals bullcrap-free boozer.
ooting Tram and Social	46 Mitcham Rd	020 8767 0278	Cavernous, funky and cool without trying.

British food and British chefs had a pretty bad reputation until fairly recently; greasy piles of stodge topped off with gravy was the general consensus for what to expect in a London restaurant. A couple of years back France's premier chef Alain Ducasse upped the ante for the London dining scene by declaring it the 'restaurant capital of the world.' While there are still numerous naff cafes around they're far outnumbered by brilliant bistros, bountiful brunch places, bodacious BBQs and boatloads of other badass eateries.

As one of the most multicultural cities in the world, London is packed with cuisine from around the world, with some areas dedicated to a signature cuisine. We've got Jewish, Indian, Peruvian, Mexican, Vietnamese, Moroccan, hell even Mongolian. Visitors don't even have to look at a Yorkshire pudding, roast beef, a full English, or fish & chips if there're not so inclined but anyone would be a fool to miss out on some of the better English places.

Foodie trends come and go in this dusty old town so if you really want be down with the urban gourmands you'll need to know what's hot right now. It would be terribly embarrassing to be caught nibbling on sushi when munching on king ribs is the in thing. Then there's the staple and stable cool places that manage to keep the hungry masses happy no matter what's cool.

What you spend on food is as flexible as British weather too; street food provides some of London's most famed snacks while places like Hix's Tramshed dishes out minimalist done well, and old English favourites like The Ritz stick to the traditional-type menu its customers expect. For everyone else in between there's everything else in between. London even does Vegetarian, apparently.

Eating For Britain

In a country whose national dish is reportedly a Chicken Tikka Masala, pin-pointing what British cuisine actually is doesn't come easy. Taking a traditional approach we've got those archetypal dishes like the Sunday Roast, Full English, Fish & Chips, and Jellied Eels; if visitors believed every stereotypical image of the British it would stand to reason that these dishes make up our standard diet, along with bucket loads of builder's tea, of course.

Delve a little deeper though and you'll find a revolutionised British menu brought about by the demand of a newly sophisticated palate. We still do the soggy seaside favourite but you're just as likely to find grilled mackerel with potato salad on a chip-chop menu as you are a battered saveloy which is what you'll see at **Poppie's** in Spittalfields. We still do Sunday lunch but you're more likely to be served the rarest of beef, a whole Poisson, or tenderloin pork than a leathery piece of gravied meat. Breakfast is a class of its own and though we're still to see a food revolution hit the East End pie shops, some things are best left as they are like the centuries old **F.Cooke (Map 89)** on Broadway Market.

We're partial to a fusion too; it's not unusual to see British tapas on a pub menu – expect things like mini toad-in-the-hole, bite sized beef wellington, and pork belly squares served with apple sauce. We're seeing things like whole Indian menus that are made entirely of British ingredients to keep the eco-warriors happy, and we're munching on American style pulled pork that is smoked over English craft ales.

Our adopted second cuisine award goes to the Indian sub-continent whose spicy dishes us Brits consider to be synonymous with a night out on the tiles or a night in front of the telly. Samosas as a snack, bhajis on the way home from work, and a five course special of a Sunday eve; it's all good

Hold the Pesticides

You'd think that with all the smog the city creates and the pollution that's pumped around this place that Londoners would have come to accept the pesticides and chemicals often found in food you would, of course, be wrong. London loves a good farmer's market and all organic café, and a good serving of local produce and meat. Weekly farmer's markets like those in **Islington (Map 80)**, London Fields and **Borough (Map 106)** are credited with starting the trend for street food in London, a few years back. The vendors would cook each other's produce to sell to hungry shoppers which in turn created a demand for top end, tasty, chemical free food.

Any café worth its salt uses free-range eggs, bacon from British pigs, lamb from Wales) not New Zealand), apples from Somerset orchards and oysters from Whitstable. There's certainly no crime in sticking to produce form British soils, serving misshapen tomatoes, and purple carrots, just be aware that more than a handful of 'organic' places like to charge over the odds for the pleasure of non-tainted meals. Find and add some Organic Restaurants.

Breakfast & Lunch – Brunch

Any good Londoner values their weekend days off like a dog loves his bone. The working week leaves time for no more than coffee and a croissant at breakfast time which is why we revel so much in a weekend brunch date. Be it with a lover, a group of rowdy friends, or visiting family members, we're developed the act of brunching into an art form in its own right.

You'll still see the off greasy spoon around, serving lukewarm baked beans, fatty bacon, and pebbly scrambled eggs but chances are that the dove grey (or Victorian green) painted shop two doors down will be packed to the proverbial rafters with a convivial young crowd of foodies and hipsters. There's a lot to be said for the Full English' it's a world famous classic, and done well, it's the breakfast of kings. We've even branched out into providing grease-free breakfasts for the more delicate morning palate.

Nothing beats the Veggie Breakfast at the **Counter Café (Map 94)** in Hackney Wick, and **Pavilion Café (Map 93)** in Victoria Park is a close contender for feeding the east's foodies – kippers with potato cakes and poached eggs is a fantastic Irish classic. **Caravan (Map 6)** has enjoyed its time at the top for a City brunch and it looks set to stay in the number one spot for some time; the chefs here are renowned for mixing up exotic flavour and creating elixical hangover cures. For American treats **The Breakfast Club (Map 80)** is a firm favourite and with three locations there's a seat for everyone. **Dukes Brew and Que (Map 82)** is a sneaky new American brekkie place vying for the winner's ribbon and Scandinavian influenced **Victor and Wolf (Map 87)** has some wholesome northern European options on offer for the more health conscious.

Street is Sweet

Eating on the street might mean using a plastic fork and sitting on a kerb but it certainly doesn't mean dissecting your way through a soggy sarnie or pulling half-eaten burgers out of the bin. It does mean queuing for a while to eat at the nest places, trying to decide which of the tempting street stalls to eat from, and possibly dripping mustard down your best top.

You can literally find everything on the streets of London; from cockroaches to sleeping people, dog shit and hypodermics. Quite delightfully you can also find the much more attractive options of food from all over the world – we've got Peruvian, Polish, Vietnamese, Mexican, French, and pretty much everything else you can think of.

The humble burger has enjoyed huge acclaim over the past year with stalls like **Lucky Chip** reinventing the British BBQ classic to resemble something much more palatable. **Bahn Mi** is a travelling Vietnamese baguette specialist that keeps chiming in reward for serving the best pork rolls in town, and the East.St collective have a permanent spot at Kings Cross where they present the baying public with things like **The Wild Game Co (Map 11)**, and Engine with its haute-gourmet Hot Dogs. Even city centre workers have taken the bait for their bait though there is a heavy lean towards superfood salads and sushi in the city, the current bento leader is also perfectly positioned for visitors; right outside of Liverpool Street Station, **Wasabi** has a stall where you can pick up a salad, a couple of bits of sushi, and a delicious miso soup for less than a fiver.

Camden Market food used to be famous for all the wrong reasons; overcooked noodles, oily fried chicken, watery curry and cardboard pizzas, there's still plenty of that around but a newer set of stalls also caters to more refined tastes. What's on offer can be interchangeable but there are a few stalwarts that are worth a go. There's a French stall that does mushrooms and sauté potatoes in a Roquefort sauce and there's no exceptions made just because the chefs are serving from a stall instead of inside a restaurant; these things are literally sit-down-white-table-cloth standard.

The absolute upside to street food stalls, which we've cleverly held back til last, is the ability to enjoy top-notch, amazing food for a fraction of the price that a restaurant would charge for the same dish. We're talking £5-6 a go for a main meal that might be paella, Moroccan tagine, Goan curry, or an Argentinian steak. A little cake for afters should knock you back a couple of quid and will round off your stand-up meal quite nicely – **Violet's (Map 89)** lemon drizzle cake makes the proverbial icing on your day.

Doffing Hats to a Trend

The London food scene can be a fickle thing. One day it's Gin and Venison that's the reigning king of the food world and the next it's knocked off its perch by a BBQ rib and a craft beer. See, once the masses have caught onto a top secret food trend, the gourmands move on to new pastures where The Guardian is yet to report, and a license is yet to be passed.

2012 has been the crux of some foodie revolutions, the death of others, and the birthing of a few. While the burger has surely enjoyed its time, one of the new kids on the block, Peruvian, is sticking around for a while, and crawling across the city like a drunk crab – the **Last Days of Pisco** pops up in venues across the city which can be a bit pesky if you turn up the day after it has moved on but their ceviche is possibly one of London's best new additions. Out in the West, the aptly named **Ceviche (Map 12)** does more of the fish-cooked-with-citrus thing and complements each dish with lashing of Peruvian firewater, Pisco which comes on its own, in dessert, and as a range of cocktails.

Onto another trend which is set to stay; the French have hors d'oeuvres the Spanish have tapas, the Swedish have smorgasbord and now the British have small plates, and we love them. Russell Norman's **Polpo (Map 10)** restaurants will remain as popular as ever to serve up shareable small plates in a New York diner style setting. Expect to see things like Anchovy & Chickpea Crostini, Spicy Pork & Fennel Meatballs, and Rabbit & Chicory Salad, all made in perfect proportions whether you're planning to take a couple for yourself or share a load with friends.

Yauatcha (Map 10) is Soho's answer to the small plate influx where head chef Tong Chee Whee is renowned for combining complicated flavours and adding delicate notes to create things like Venison Puffs. **Brawn (Map 91)** on Columbia Road is in a class of its own when it comes to creating meaty feasts; the restaurant shamelessly rejoices in all things pig and waives any requests for a veggie option. The menu is dependent on season and on what the chefs feel like cooking; you might find salted ox tongue, pork scratching, or pickled wild boar here and it will all be delicious and meaty.

Pop-up, Pop-Down

Providing a location for these pop up restaurants and supper clubs can be a challenge, mainly because the very nature of them means that most don't stay in the same place for too long, instead choosing to change venues every 3-6 months, allowing each little part of insular London to enjoy the experience.

Some of the more business-inclines places choose to pop in the same place, say, once a month, which makes it easier to pinpoint them but harder to actually get a table. Other that started as a travelling-circus version of a restaurant have settled into grown-up, permanent accommodation, or at least rented a kitchen to become semi-perm tenants. **The Seagrass (Map 80)** in Islington is one of the second type – started as a pop-up and matured to a mainstay; they take over a pie & mash shop three nights a week to serve up a menu heavy on game and fish, you're also invited to bring your own booze.

Disappearing Dining Club follows a similar vein. Having started as a pop-up group offering tea dances and three course dinners, it recently moved out of its student digs into a parently home on Brick Lane where they're operating under the name of **Back in Five Minutes (Map 91)**. It's hidden behind a clothes shop, limited to thirty guests, and operates from Thursday to Sunday.

Pay for What You Eat

It seems only sensible and fair that you should only pay for what you eat, right? Think about how much of your evening dining bill is often down to the sheer amount of booze you've put away though. Now imagine that you don't have to pay for that portion of the bill..

London has its fair share of bring your own bottle

restaurants and the best part is that they're not all of one vein i.e Oriental, dingy, or in one place; even high-end Mayfair has BYOB bottle restaurants. There does seem to be a higher than normal number of BYOB eateries in the east but that's just because hipsters are skint, preferring to spend their cash on purple leggings and (il) legal highs.

By day **Hurwendeki (Map 92)** is a standard little coffee shop, tucked in a railway arch with a unique terrace, by night it is a Korean restaurant with perfect ambiance a brilliant, affordable menu and a BYOB policy. **Little Georgia (Map 92)** is a darling of a place; pretty pale green with a warm, inviting basement, and hearty portions of Georgian food is what to expect here. Kingsland Road is scattered with Vietnamese places where u can BYOB and while they're all fairly good **Mein Tay (Map 91)** is always packed out.

Key: £ : Under £10 / ££ : £10–£20 / £££ : £20–£30 / ££££ : £30–£40 / £££££: £40+
** : Does not accept credit cards./ † : Accepts only American Express / ††: Accepts only Visa and Mastercard*
Time listed refers to kitchen closing time on weekend nights

Map 1 • Marylebone (West)

Abu Ali Cafe	136 George St	020 7724 6338	£		Good cheap 'n chearful Lebanese joint among many similar in the area!
Beirut Express	112 Edgware Rd	020 7724 2700	££	2 am	Chaotic, rude and the best Lebanese in town.
Maroush IV	68 Edgware Rd	020 7724 9339	££	12 am	Wax philosophical while smoking a hookah out front.
Locanda Locatelli	8 Seymour St	020 7935 9088	££££	11.30 pm	Outstanding Italian food.
Nippon Tuk	225 Edgware Rd	020 7616 6496	££££	11.15 pm	One to avoid for vertigo sufferers—astounding, 23rd floor views.

Map 2 • Marylebone (East)

Comptoir Libanais	65 Wigmore St	020 7935 1110	£	8 pm	Uncompromisingly cheap and cheerful mezes.
Diwan	31 Thayer St	020 7935 2445	££	11 pm	Lebanese gorge spot.
Galvin Bistrot de Luxe	66 Baker Street	020 7935 4007	£££	11 pm	Veloutés, ballatines, tartares and escargots. Delicieux? Mais oui.
The Golden Hind	73 Marylebone Ln	020 7486 3644	££	10 pm	Fish and chips from the top-drawer. Can do BYOB.
Gordon Ramsay at Claridge's	Brook St	020 7499 0099	£££££	11 pm	A rich perfectionist's culinary art deco dream.
Hush Brasserie	8 Lancashire Ct	020 7659 1500	££££	11 pm	European food al fresco. Go on a lunch hour holiday.
No. 5 Cavendish Square	5 Cavendish Square	087 1223 5000	£££	11 pm	A No. 5 desperately trying to be as opulent as Chanel's.
Patisserie Valerie	105 Marylebone High St	020 7935 6240	£	9 pm	Boho coffee and pastry.
The Providores	109 Marylebone High St	020 7935 6175	££	11 pm	Sip Rioja and gorge on tapas for the cognoscenti.
Sakura	9 Hanover St	020 7629 2961	££	10 pm	Authentic Japanese queue. Worth it for the food.

Map 3 • Fitzrovia

Archipelago	110 Whitfield St	020 7383 3346	£££££	10.30 pm	London's best, alright only, chocolate-covered scorpions and crocodile steaks
Ask	48 Grafton Way	020 7388 8108	£	11.30 pm	…for pizza.
Carluccio's	8 Market Pl	020 7636 2228	£££	11 pm	Pretty good for a chain. Have the espresso and ice cream.
Chutney & Lager	43 Great Titchfield St	0207 636 5737	££	11 pm	Indian tapas restaurant and lounge bar.
Crazy Bear	26 Whitfield St	020 7631 0088	££££	10.30 pm	Thai deluxe. Where the media world feeds its clients.
Eagle Bar Diner	3 Rathbone Pl	020 7637 1418	££	11 pm	Trendy modern American diner; two words: Crocodile Burger.
Elena's L'Etoile	30 Charlotte St	020 7636 7189	£££££	11 pm	Old school French sophistication, politicians and journos.
Govinda's	9 Soho St	020 7437 4928	£*	8 pm	Cheap Krishna food. You know the deal.
Hakkasan	8 Hanway Pl	020 7927 7000	££££	12 am	Soho's sexiest subterranean Chinese. China-chic dining for the beautiful people.
Icco Pizza	46 Goodge St	020 7580 9250	£	11 pm	Zen it is not—but who cares at £3.50 a pizza?
Latium	21 Berners St	020 7323 9123	£££	10.30 pm	Romantic (and pricey) first date place.

Key: £ : Under £10 / ££ : £10–£20 / £££ : £20–£30 / ££££ : £30–£40 / £££££: £40+
** : Does not accept credit cards./ † : Accepts only American Express / ††: Accepts only Visa and Mastercard*
Time listed refers to kitchen closing time on weekend nights

Market Place	11 Market Pl	020 7079 2020	£	1 am	Warm buzz all day/night. Hot clientele/tepid prices.
Navarro's	67 Charlotte St	020 7637 7713	£££	10 pm	Delicioso! Smells like Seville, tastes like Seville.
Ragam	57 Cleveland St	020 7636 9098	££	10.45 pm	Can't dis these dosas (potato crepes) at very decent prices.
Rasa Express	5 Rathbone St	020 7637 0222	£	11 pm	Take-away-priced Indian lunch boxes, seating included.
Roka	37 Charlotte St	020 7580 6464	£££	11 pm	Dazzling Izakaya concept Japanese.
Salt Yard	54 Goodge St	020 7637 0657	£££	11 pm	Intimate and sexy. Take a date. Get laid. Possibly.
Sardo	45 Grafton Way	020 7387 2521	££	10 pm	Hit after hit. Try the crab pasta.
Squat & Gobble	69 Charlotte St	020 7580 5338	£	4.30 pm	Scrumptious, cheap, tiny. Just squat and, um, gobble.
Stef's	3 Berners St	020 3073 1041	££	11 pm	You can't knock the gnocchi.
Thai Metro	36 Charlotte St	020 7436 4201	££	11 pm	Thai food, cooked well, served well, job done.

Map 4 • Bloomsbury (West)

Alara	58 Marchmont St	020 7837 1172	£££	7 pm	Hardcore veggie/vegan mecca, surprisingly good.
Bi Won	24 Coptic St	020 7580 2660	£	10 pm	Manhandling staff but great food.
Savoir Faire	42 New Oxford St	020 7436 0707	££	10.30 pm	Sweet little rustic restaurant, a stroll from Soho.

Map 5 • Bloomsbury (East)

Acorn House	69 Swinton St	020 7812 1842	£££	10.30 pm	Eco-chic: the Gwyneth Paltrow of restaurants.
Aki Bistro	182 Gray's Inn Rd	020 7837 9281	££	11 pm	Almost too Japanese Japanese.
Beas of Bloomsbury	44 Theobald's Rd	020 7242 8330	£	6 pm	You can watch the chefs create artisan cupcake masterpieces here.
Bread and Butter Sandwich Bar	100 Judd St	020 7713 7767	£*	9 pm	Notable for its very cheap al fresco fry-ups.
Ciao Bella	86 Lamb's Conduit St	020 7242 4119	££	11 pm	Authentic, rustic feel Italian complete with piano.
Cigala	54 Lamb's Conduit St	020 7405 1717	££	10.45pm	Great service and gorgeous salty Spanish bread.
The Food Bazaar	59 Gray's Inn Rd	020 7242 6578	£*	9 pm	Casual and friendly with great hot food selection.
Fryer's Delight	19 Theobald's Rd	020 7405 4114	£*	10 pm	No frills chippie; big portions of chunky, salty, greasy tastiness.
Konstam	2 Acton St	020 7833 5040	££	10 pm	All food sourced within London. Should be grim—actually delicious.
La Provence	63 Gray's Inn Rd	020 7404 4920	£	10 pm	Super-friendly staff and a generous hot food deal.
Malletti	174 Clerkenwell Rd	020 7713 8665	£	4.30 pm	Pizza served al taglio like in Italia.
Mary Ward Centre	42 Queen Sq	020 7269 6000	£*	5 pm	Hippy educational centre with a great organic cafe.
Paolina Thai Snack Bar	181 King's Cross Rd	020 7278 8176	£*	10 pm	Grotty exterior disguises this diamond of cheerful authentic Thai.
The Perseverance	63 Lamb's Conduit St	020 7405 8278	££	10.30pm	Good quality gastropub food.
Swintons	61 Swinton St	020 7837 3995	££	9.30 pm	If Heaven made fishfinger sandwiches, they'd use Swintons' recipe.
Thai Candle	38 Lamb's Conduit St	020 7430 2472	£££	10 pm	Cosy, cheerful with a nice lunchtime meal deal.

Map 6 • Clerkenwell

Bada Bing!	120 St John St	020 7253 3723	£	4 pm	Excellent lunch joint. The toasted ciabattas are divine.
Clarks Pie and Mash	46 Exmouth Market	020 7837 1974	£*	5.30 pm	A last bastion of a lost London.
Dans Le Noir	30 Clerkenwell Green	020 7253 1100	££££	9 pm	Blind waiters serve in pitch darkness: don't wear white.
The Eagle	159 Farringdon Rd	020 7837 1353	££	10.30 pm	London's first gastro pub—just look what they started.
Little Bay	171 Farringdon Rd	020 7278 1234	££	12 am	Posh-people food at pikey-people prices.
Moro	34 Exmouth Market	020 7833 8336	££££	11 pm	DO believe the hype.
The Quality Chop House	94 Farringdon Rd	020 7837 5093	££	10.45pm	OMG it's so BRITISH. Meat and potatoes like nowhere else.
Sandwichman	23 Easton St	020 7833 9001	£*	2.30 pm	Office delivery returns. Gourmet—and just 65p. Best lunch in London.

Map 7 • Barbican / City Road (South)

Bavarian Beerhouse	190 City Rd	0844 330 2005	££	11 pm	Unlace your lederhausen for some serious schnitzel madness.
Carnevale	135 Whitecross St	020 7250 3452	££	11.00 pm	Veggie on the cheap.
De Santis	11 Old St	020 7689 5626	££	9.30 pm	Like being in Milan; owner Enzo takes care of you
NUSA Kitchen	9 Old St	020 7253 3135	£*	5 pm	People queuing? For ages? For soup? Now I've seen everything.

Map 8 • Liverpool Street / Broadgate

Damascu Bite Kebab	21 Shoreditch High St	020 7247 0207	£*	1 am	It's the way they grill them from the outside.
Eyre Brothers	70 Leonard St	020 7613 5346	££	10.45 pm	Great place run by the Eyre brothers—Jane no relation.
Gaucho Broadgate	5 Finsbury Ave	020 7256 6077	££££	11 pm	Divine, ohmigod, melt-in-your-mouth steak. Oops, drooling!
Ponti's Caffe	176 Bishopsgate	020 7283 4889	£	24 hrs	24 hour cafe for the inebriated insomniac.
Rivington Bar and Grill	28 Rivington St	020 7729 7053	££	11 pm	Emin on the walls, meat in the buns.

Map 9 • Mayfair / Green Park

Alain Ducasse at The Dorchester	Park Ln	020 7629 8866	££££	10 pm	Better known for its extortionate prices than Michelin-starred food.
El Pirata of Mayfair	5 Down St	020 7491 3810	£££	11.30 pm	Don't be put off by stuffy location—these are f'ing good tapas.
The English Tea Room at Browns	Albemarle Street	020 7518 4155	££££	11 pm	Ah, so that's what a £48 cup of tea tastes like.
Galvin at Windows	28th Floor, Hilton Park Lane	020 7208 4021	£££££	11 pm	Art Deco French overlooking Buckingham Palace. We're not worthy!
Kiplings	2 Hill St	020 8340 1719	££	11.30 pm	Swanky curry joint boasts Raffles Hotel stylings including resident pianist.
L'Autre	5 Shepherd St	020 7499 4680	££££	11 pm	Polish meets Mexican. Surprisingly well.
Nobu	19 Old Park Ln	020 7447 4747	£££££	12 am	Rob a bank on the way as it's bloody expensive!
The Ritz	150 Piccadilly	020 7300 8765	£££££	10 pm	High tea amidst ornaments and swank - resist temptation to swipe towels.
Theo Randall at the InterContinental	1 Hamilton Pl	020 7318 8747	£££££	11 pm	Sincere and stylish cuisine unfortunately hidden behind a hotel façade.
The Wolseley	160 Piccadilly	020 7499 6996	££££	12 am	Over-hyped. There. We said it.

Map 10 • Piccadilly / Soho (West)

Bob Bob Ricard	1 Upper James St	020 3145 1000	£££	11.30 pm	Proper posh British diner serving Cornish crab cake and…Ribena.
Cecconi's	5 Burlington Gardens	020 7434 1500	££££	11.15 pm	All-day menu for the spoilt. Delicious breakfasts.
Cha Cha Moon	15 Ganton St	020 7297 9800	££	11 pm	Like Wagamamas but for Chinese.
Chowki	2 Denman St	020 7439 1330	£££	11.30 pm	Rotating regional cuisines of India; brilliant.
Dehesa	25 Ganton St	020 7494 4170	£££	11 pm	Faux-rustic protein-rich tapas, sweetie.
Fernandez and Wells Coffee Bar	73 Beak St	020 7287 8124	££	6 pm	Perfect pasteis de nata and locally made ice-cream. Delightfully friendly!
Kulu Kulu	76 Brewer St	020 7734 7316	£	10 pm	Great, fresh, fast sushi for people on the go. Sit down is 45 minutes only.
Le Pain Quotidien	18 Great Marlborough St	020 7486 6154	£	10 pm	Feel like a right old tartine.
Mildred's	45 Lexington St	020 7494 1634	££	10.30 pm	Great food, sometimes crap service. Get the sweet potato curry to takeaway!
Mosaico	13 Albermale St	020 7409 1011	£££	11 pm	Stylish Italian. Prices more for the Mayfair Mamas.
Nordic Bakery	14 Golden Sq	020 3230 1077	£	7 pm	Authentic sticky cinnamon buns, Karelian pies and smoked Moomin.
The Photographers' Gallery	16 Ramillies St	020 7831 1772	£*	6 pm	Artsy coffee spot with photos on view.
Ping Pong	45 Great Marlborough St	020 7851 6969	££	11 pm	Don't leave without trying a char sui bun!
Pure California	39 Beak St	020 7287 3708	£	6 pm	As pure a salad/juice as you'd find in the Sunshine State all made to order.
Sartoria	20 Saville Row	020 7534 7000	£££££	11 pm	The pick of the Conran restaurants.
Sketch	9 Conduit St	020 7659 4500	£££	1 am	Colossally trendy kitsch palace.
Taro	61 Brewer St	020 7734 5826	£££	10.30 pm	Where London's Japanese locals eat sushi.
Ten Ten Tei	56 Brewer St	020 7287 1738	£££££	10 pm	The Japanese restaurant Japanese people love.
Tentazioni Restaurant	2 Mill St	0207 237 1100	££	10.45 pm	Stunningly sophisticated for a neighbourhood eaterie.
Thanks for Franks	26 Fouberts Pl	020 7494 2434	£*	6 pm	Good sandwiches.

Key: £ : Under £10 / ££ : £10–£20 / £££ : £20–£30 / ££££ : £30–£40 / £££££: £40+
** : Does not accept credit cards./ † : Accepts only American Express / ††: Accepts only Visa and Mastercard*
Time listed refers to kitchen closing time on weekend nights

Tibits	12 Heddon St	020 7758 4110	££		Buffet: sans meat, sold by weight. Genius!
Toku @ The Japan Centre	212 Piccadilly	020 7255 8255	££	10 pm	The best gyoza outside of Tokyo.
Wagamama	10 Lexington St	020 7292 0990	£	11 pm	Reliable, speedy noodle chain.
Wild Honey	12 St George St	020 7758 9160	£££	10.30 pm	This Michelin star's got skillz (and a damn good tête-de-veau).
Yauatcha	15 Broadwick St	020 7494 8888	£££££	11.45 pm	Traditional Chinese tea-house meets star-spangled media haunt.
Yoshino	3 Piccadilly place	020 7287 6622	££	10 pm	Back alley bentos so good you'll pretend they were your discovery.

Map 11 • Soho (Central)

Balans	60 Old Compton St	020 7439 2183	££	3 am	Share a 4am breakfast with the likes of Amy Winehouse.
Bar Bruno	101 Wardour St	020 7734 3750	£*	10 pm	Hidden Italian cafe gem. Authentically loud and friendly.
Beetroot	92 Berwick St	020 7437 8591	£	10 pm	Awesome veggie/vegan place.
Bocca di Lupo	12 Archer St	020 7734 2223	£££	12 am	Italian for 'break a leg'; authentic fare gets your bocca watering.
Busaba Eathai	110 Wardour St	020 7255 8686	£££	11 pm	Never mind the shared benches, the food's too yummy.
Cafe Espana	63 Old Compton St	020 7494 1271	££	11 pm	Highly recommended. 10% off for eating with castanets (possibly).
Grace	42 Great Windmill St	020 7851 0800	££££	10.30 pm	Wannabe a WAG? Get in 'ere!
Hummus Bros	88 Wardour St	020 7734 1311	££	11 pm	Where hummus is the main dish.
Imli	167 Wardour St	020 7287 4243	£	11 pm	Tapas + curry. Fusion gone insane but somehow works.
Italian Graffiti	163 Wardour St	020 7439 4668	£££	11 pm	Less 'street' than the name suggest. Nice though.
Jerk City	189 Wardour St	020 7287 2878	£	10 pm	Jamaican fast food. In doubt? Go for ackee and saltfish.
Leong's Legends	4 Macclesfield St	020 7287 0288	££	11 pm	A Taiwanese Chinatown legend.
Malletti	26 Noel St	020 7439 4096	£*	3 pm	Amazing! Use your mobile and you won't get served.
Maoz	43 Old Compton St	020 7851 1586	£*	1 am	Falafeltastic!
Melati	30 Peter St	020 7437 2011	£	11.30 pm	Enthusiastic staff and greased up curry/noodle hybrids.
Paul	49 Old Compton St	020 7287 6261	£	10 pm	French cafe/bakery chain. Amazing baguettes!
Pizza Express Jazz Club	10 Dean St	020 7439 8722	£	11 pm	Surprisingly, jazz takes the mediocre chain up a notch.
Randall & Aubin	16 Brewer St	020 7287 4447	£££	11 pm	Over-indulgently carnal seafood delights which only call for champagne.
Red Veg	95 Dean St	020 7437 3109	£*	10 pm	Veggie fast food joint.
Snog	9 Brewer St	020 7494 3301	£*	12 am	If they had yoghurt and not milk in Clockwork Orange.
Soho Thai	27 St. Annes Ct	020 7287 2000	££	11 pm	Thai with a good range. In set meals: go for starter NOT dessert.
St Moritz	161 Wardour St	020 7734 3324	££££	11.30 pm	Swiss cheese heaven.
Won Kei	41 Wardour St	020 7437 8408	££	10 pm	AKA Wonky's: institutionally rude service, cheap fast Chinese.
Yoshino Delicatessen	59 Shaftesbury Ave	020 7434 3610	£	10 pm	Cheap as chips but with sushi.

Map 12 • Soho (East)

Abeno Too	17 Great Newport St	020 7379 1160	££	11 pm	Addictive Okonomiyaki (pancakes) flipped and fried on the table.
Arbutus	63 Frith St	020 7734 4545	£££	11 pm	Chocolate soup! Worth it for that alone.
Assa	53 St Giles High St	020 7240 8256	££	12 am	Cheerful eager-to-please Korean cafe
Bar Italia	22 Frith St	020 7437 4520	££	4.30 am	Soho institution; perfect for people watching at any hour.
Barrafina	54 Frith St	020 7813 8016	£££	11 pm	Seriously, the best (and hippest) place for tapas.
Bincho Soho	16 Old Compton St	020 7287 9111	££	11.30 pm	Save on skewers every Tuesday
Boheme Kitchen and Bar	19 Old Compton St	020 7734 5656	£££	11.45 pm	You want frites with that? Deliciously snobby comfort food.
Café Emm	17 Frith St	020 7437 0723	£££	10.30 pm	Double-take cheap prices and wholesome fare. Wins popular vote.
Chinese Experience	118 Shaftesbury Ave	020 7437 0377	£££	11 pm	Popular for a reason. Overwhelmed? Go for the always-great set menu.

Corean Chilli	51 Charing Cross Rd	020 7734 6737	££	12 am	Karaoke and stir-fries with the Korean cool kids.
Ed's Easy Diner	12 Moor St	020 7434 4439	££	11 pm	It's like, you know? Soooo, like, American? You know?
Friendly Inn	47 Gerrard St	020 7437 4170	£	1 am	Where Londoners go for Chinese in Soho.
Gaby's	30 Charing Cross Rd	020 7836 4233	££	10 pm	High on tradition, low on frills. Authentically spartan.
Garlic & Shots	14 Frith St	020 7734 9505	££££	1 am	Garlic, garlic and more garlic. No-go zone for vampires.
Gay Hussar	2 Greek St	020 7437 0973	££	10.45 pm	Everything from strudel to cherry soup at this old-school Hungarian.
Haozhan	8 Gerrard St	020 7434 3838	£££	11 pm	Can't pick? This is the one.
Kettners	29 Romilly St	020 7734 6112	£££££	12 am	Sit and sup with the champagne set.
La Porchetta Pollo Bar	20 Old Compton St	020 7494 9368	£££	12 am	Cheap and cheerful Italian. In the West End? Well, exactly.
Le Beaujolais	25 Litchfield St	020 7836 2277	££	10 pm	Get insulted by a Frenchman here in London—Mai oui!
Maison Bertaux	27 Greek St	056 0115 1584	££*	5 pm	Heavenly cakes, art gallery, boutique downstairs, what's not to like?
Malaysia Kopi Tiam	67 Charing Cross Rd	020 7287 1113	£	11 pm	A beef rendang-infused oasis away from the West End's clatter.
New World	1 Gerrard Pl	020 7734 0396	£	11.45 pm	Crispy duck, Dim Sum, custard dumplings… bring it on!
Stockpot	18 Old Compton St	020 7287 1066	££*	12 am	Fantastically cheap stodge.
Taro	10 Old Compton St	020 7439 2275	££	10.30 pm	Like Taro Brewer Street. But gayer, obviously.

Map 13 • Covent Garden

Battersea Pie Station	Covent Garden Piazza	020 7240 9566	£	6 pm	Who ate all the pies?
Café Mode	57 Endell St	020 7240 8085	££	11.30 pm	Pizza, pasta, salad. No fuss.
Belgo Centraal	29 Shelton St	020 7813 2233	£££	11pm	Thoroughly enjoyable moules et frites. And beer… mmm… beer.
Candy Cakes	36 Monmouth St	020 7497 8979	£	8 pm	Cupcakes almost too beautiful to eat. But eat them anyway.
Food for Thought	31 Neal St	020 7836 9072	£	8.30 pm	Queues this long mean they've got cheap, veg food right.
Great Queen Street	32 Great Queen St	020 7242 0622	£££	11 pm	Affordable, and might be London's best gastropub.
Kulu Kulu	51 Shelton St	020 7240 5687	££	10 pm	Tiny conveyor belt sushi joint. Bang on the money.
Mon Plaisir	21 Monmouth St	020 7836 7243	£££	11.15 pm	Not up to typical Paris standards, but still tres bon!
The Punjab	80 Neal St	020 7836 9787	£££	11.30 pm	Relive the days of the Raj in this old-school curry house.
Rock & Sole Plaice	47 Endell St	020 7836 3785	£££	11 pm	London's oldest chippie. Est. 1871. On-street, fairy-lit picnic benches. Huge portions.
Rossopomodoro	50 Monmouth Street	020 7240 9095	£	12am	Chain Italian with very tasty pies. Cutlery prohibited!
Sarastro	126 Drury Ln	020 7836 0101	££	11.30 pm	Hilarious over-the-top decor; includes fornicating cherubs.
Souk Medina	1 Shorts Gardens	020 7240 1796	££	11 pm	Atmospheric Morrocan joint. Free refills on mouthwatering £20 set menu.

Map 14 • Holborn / Temple

Asadal	227 High Holborn	020 7430 9005	£££	10.30 pm	Go on, venture down those stairs—it's worth it.
Indigo @ OneAldwych	1 Aldwych	020 7300 0400	£££	11 pm	Sunday brunch and a movie—all in the same place!

Map 15 • Blackfriars / Farringdon

Beppe's	23 West Smithfield	020 7236 7822	££	3 pm	As classically Italian as oversized sunglasses. Only much, much better.
The Bleeding Heart	Bleeding Heart Yard, off Greville St	020 7242 2056	£££	10.30 pm	Historic, hard to find, eccentric beauty.
Cafe du Marche	22 Charterhouse Sq	020 7608 1609	£££	11 pm	Wonderful French cuisine in delightful venue. Tucked away in Charterhouse Square.
Gaucho Smithfield	93 Charterhouse St	020 7490 1676	££	11 pm	Where cows would choose to be eaten.
Hix Oyster And Chop House	36 Cowcross St	020 7017 1930	£££	10.45 pm	Never tried beef and oyster pie?
Kurz + Lang	1 St John St	020 7993 2923	£	11.30 pm	Ze German Bratwurst sausage at its zizzling best.

Key: £ : Under £10 / ££ : £10–£20 / £££ : £20–£30 / ££££ : £30–£40 / £££££: £40+
** : Does not accept credit cards./ † : Accepts only American Express / ††: Accepts only Visa and Mastercard*
Time listed refers to kitchen closing time on weekend nights

The Larder	91 St John St	020 7608 1558	£££	10.30 pm	Fresh, seasonal food, good breakfast menu and takeaway sarnies.
Pho	86 St John St	020 7253 7624	£	10.30 pm	Steaming bowlfuls for hungry Clerkenwell workers. Specialises in street food.
Portal	88 St John St	020 7253 6950	££££	10.15 pm	Astoundingly good Portuguese. Swanky but not stuffy.
Smiths of Smithfield	67 Charterhouse St	020 7251 7950	£££	10.45 pm	Overflowing with yuppies and trendy types; pricey but tasty.
St Germain	89 Turnmill St	020 7336 0949	£££	11 pm	Sleek, chic. Bon Appetit.
St John's Smithfield	26 St John St	020 7251 0848	£££	11 pm	This place is ALL about the offal.
Tinseltown	44 St. John St	020 7689 2424	£	24 hrs	Funky diner serving great late-night milkshakes.
Vivat Bacchus	47 Farringdon St	020 7353 2648	£££	9.30 pm	Three wine cellars and a cheeseroom. A ROOM of cheese.
Yo! Sushi	5 St Paul's	020 7248 8726	£	11 pm	Sushi in Paul's shadow.

Map 16 • Square Mile (West)

Sweetings	39 Queen Victoria St	020 7248 3062	£££	4 pm	Old fashioned institution for nostalgia trips. Lunch only.

Map 17 • Square Mile (East)

Gaucho City	1 Bell Inn Yard	020 7626 5180	££££	11 pm	The best steakhouse in the city. Located in former gold vaults.
The Mercer	34 Threadneedle St	020 7628 0001	££	9.30 pm	Proper British grub in a light contemporary atmosphere.
Nusa Kitchen	2 Adams Ct	020 7628 1149	£	4 pm	Fresh soup made daily.
Rhodes 24	25 Old Broad St	020 7877 7703	£££££	8.30 pm	Anyone for Gherkin (building) with your Michelin star?
Wasabi	52 Old Broad St	020 7374 8337	£*	10 pm	Delicious sushi and bento for those in a rush.

Map 18 • Tower Hill / Aldgate

Jeff's Café	14 Brune St	020 7375 2230	£*	10 pm	Cheap as chips (which they serve here, incidentally).
S & M Café	48 Brushfield St	020 7247 2252	££	10 pm	Not what you think it is, perverts. Sausages and mash!

Map 19 • Belgravia

Amaya	Halkin Arcade, Motcomb St	020 7823 1166	££££	11.30 pm	Where the trendies go for their curry fix.
Boisdale, Victoria	15 Eccleston St	020 7730 6922	£££££	11 pm	Posh Scottish nosh. No deep-fried Mars Bars, sadly.
Noura	12 William St	020 7235 5900	££	11 pm	Frequently orgiastic Lebanese pig-outs, habibi.
One-O-One	101 Knightsbridge	020 7290 7101	££££	10 pm	One man's fish is another man's pleasure.
Yo! Sushi	102 Knightsbridge	020 7235 5000	££	10 pm	A London institution—we dream in sashimi on conveyor belts.

Map 20 • Victoria / Pimlico (West)

Grumbles	35 Churton St	020 7834 0149	££	11 pm	Unfashionably unfussy Brit/French home-cooking. Gorgeous pies, no grumbles.

Map 21 • Pimlico (East)

The Regency Café	17 Regency St	020 7821 6596	£*	7 pm	Proper British fry-ups and atmosphere in this 1940's café.
Vincent Rooms	76 Vincent Sq	020 7802 8391	£££	7 pm	Brilliant food served by awkward catering students.

Map 23 • St. James's

Inn The Park	St James' Park	020 7451 9999	££££	7.30 pm	Watch the ducks watching you as you eat.
Stockpot	38 Panton St	020 7839 5142	££*	10.45 pm	Treacle pud & custard. Bish bash bosh.
The Wolsey	160 Piccadilly	020 7499 6996	££	12 am	Step back in time for an elegant afternoon tea for under 20 quid.

Map 24 • Trafalgar Square / The Strand

Bistro 1	33 Southampton St	020 7379 7585	££	11.30 pm	Posh kebabs etc at bargain prices.
Cafe in the Crypt	6 St Martin's Pl	020 7839 4342	££	10 pm	Spooky sandwiches and fruit crumble.
Covent Garden Market Café	Covent Garden	020 7240 4844	£*	10 pm	Cheap egg 'n' chips in heart of tourist London.
Farmer Brown	4 New Row	020 7240 0230	££*	8 pm	Cheap and very cheerful. Great lunches.
Gourmet Burger Kitchen	13 Maiden Ln	020 7240 9617	££	11 pm	Go for the Kiwiburger. Don't question the ingredients. Trust us.
India Club	143 Strand (Second floor, Strand Continental Hotel)	020 7836 0650	£	11 pm	Quirky run-down BYOB eaterie; more character than Brick Lane equivalents.
J Sheekey	28 St Martin's Ct	020 7240 2565	££££	11 pm	Old-fashioned seafood haven that the celebs still love.
RS Hispaniola	Victoria Embankment	020 7839 3011	£££	10 pm	Feel the bloat, on a boat.
Rules	35 Maiden Ln	020 7836 5314	£££££	10.30 pm	London's oldest restaurant with old-fashioned comfort food to match.
Scott's Sandwich Bar	10 New Row	020 7240 0340	£	4 pm	Gets very busy at lunch mainly for the salt beef.
Thai Pot	1 Bedfordbury	020 7379 4580	££	11 pm	Busy but fast with fresh and generous helpings. Delicious Massaman curry.
Wahaca	66 Chandos Pl	020 7240 1883	£££	11 pm	Tasty Mexican market food/tapas. Always busy.

Map 25 • Kensal Town

Santo	299 Portobello Rd	020 8968 4590	££	11.30 pm	Fresh, frisky Mexican. Too bad about the resentful waiters.
Thai Rice	303 Portobello Rd	020 8968 2001	££	10.30 pm	Jaw-dropping food in sterile, bland environment.

Map 29 • Notting Hill Gate

Beach Blanket Babylon	45 Ledbury Rd	020 7229 2907	££££	12 am	Maze of baroque nooks and crannies where celebs nibble discreetly.
Cafe Diana	5 Wellington Terrace	020 7792 9606	£	10.30 pm	Creepy, kitsch shrine to Princess Diana with so-so food.
Costas	14 Hillgate St	020 7229 3794	££	10.30 pm	Heavenly, Cypriot-run fish and chips. Hellish Notting Hill prices.
Crazy Homies	125 Westbourne Park Rd	020 7727 6771	££	10.15 pm	Avoid first date awkwardness over quality Mexican at this lively get-up.
The Electric Brasserie	191 Portobello Rd	020 7908 9696	££	10 pm	Uber-trendy, worth a visit for the eggs benedict alone.
Eve's Market Cafe	222 Portobello Rd	020 7221 2633	£		Traditional greasy caff with vintage nicotine stains.
Geales	2 Farmer St	020 7727 7528	£££	10.30 pm	Feels ever-so-slightly like a front to appease visiting Americans.
Lucky 7	127 Westbourne Park Rd	020 7727 6771	£££	10.30 pm	Atmospheric diner for wistful yuppies.
Manzara	24 Pembridge Road	020 7727 3062	£	10 pm	Burek Obama for president! Arf.
Negozio Classica	283 Westbourne Grove	020 7034 0005			Half bar, half store selling high-end Italian kitchen goods.
Osteria Basilico	29 Kensington Park Rd	020 7727 9372	£££	11.30 pm	Quaint, buzzing and full of Italian rustic charm. A local hot spot.
Ruby & Sequoia	6 All Saints' Rd	0207 243 6363	££££	12am	On the razzle at the Ruby.
Taquerla	139 Westbourne Grove	020 7229 4734	££	11 pm	Wash down these fresh mini-tacos with a good tequila.

Map 30 • Bayswater

Berdees Coffee Shop	84 Bishop's Bridge Rd	020 7727 0033	£*	9 pm	Hubbly Bubbly Jubbly. Chubbly?
The Cow	89 Westbourne Park Rd	020 7221 0021	£££	9.45pm	Top end bar food. Smart restaurant upstairs.
Kiasu	48 Queensway	020 7727 8810	£	11 pm	The best budget Indonesian/Malaysian cuisine. Mmmm…. Char Kway Teow…
Royal China	13 Queensway	020 7221 2535	£££	11.15 pm	Keep the Cantonese dim sum comin'!
Tiroler Hut	27 Westbourne Grove	020 7727 3981	££££	12 am	Dementedly kitsch Austrian madhouse with lederhosen-clad waiters.

Map 31 • Paddington

Bonne Bouche	129 Praed St	020 7724 5784	£	4.30 pm	Deli counter is popular with local workers for sandwiches.
Mandalay	444 Edgware Rd	020 7258 3696	£	10.30 pm	Cheap treats await, despite the God awful situation.

Key: £ : Under £10 / ££ : £10–£20 / £££ : £20–£30 / ££££ : £30–£40 / £££££: £40+
** : Does not accept credit cards./ † : Accepts only American Express / ††: Accepts only Visa and Mastercard*
Time listed refers to kitchen closing time on weekend nights

Map 32 • Shepherd's Bush (West)

Abu Zaad	29 Uxbridge Rd	020 8749 5107	£	11 pm	A colourful Syrian welcome. Posh Kebabs.
Esarn Kheaw	314 Uxbridge Road	020 8743 8930	£	11.30 pm	Outstanding Thai. Transport your taste buds to Bangkok.
Vine Leaves Taverna	71 Uxbridge Rd	020 8749 0325	£	1 am	Friendly staff, traditional grub, huge portions.

Map 33 • Shepherd's Bush

Jasmine	16 Goldhawk Rd	020 8743 7920	££	11 pm	Awesome Thai.
Jumbucks	24 Shepherd's Bush Green	020 8811 8111	£	1 am	Proper Aussie pies and heaps of Cherry Ripes served by smily peeps.Streuth!
Le Cinnamon	158 Shepherd's Bush Rd	020 7602 8899	££	11.30 pm	Great for dates. Intimate and a biryani to win over any girl (or guy!).
Popeseye	108 Blythe Rd	020 7610 4578	££££	10.30 pm	London's ONLY member of the Aberdeen Angus Society.

Map 34 • West Kensington / Olympia

The Belvedere Restaurant	Abbotsbury Road	020 7602 1238	£££	11 pm	Sublime setting—the same cannot always be said for the service.

Map 35 • Kensington

Byron	222 Kensington High St	020 7361 1717	££	10 pm	London's best burger? Locals in the know say so.
Clarke's	124 Kensington Church St	020 7221 9225	££	10 pm	Elegant, English fine dining. Perfect brunch spot if feeling refined.
Kensington Roof Gardens	99 Kensington High St	020 7937 7994	££££	1 am	Truly spectacular roof gardens and devine restaurant 100 foot above HS Ken.
Maggie Jones's	6 Old Court Pl	020 7937 6462	£££	10.30 pm	A British culinary time warp, but we like it anyway.
Zaika	1 Kensington High St	020 7795 6533	££	10.45 pm	If you can afford to treat yourself this is the place. Starters at £12.95!

Map 36 • South Kensington / Gloucester Rd

Cafe Creperie	2 Exhibition Rd	020 7589 8947	£	11.30 pm	Parisian crepe haven a stones throw from the museums.
Caffe Forum	146 Gloucester Rd	020 7259 2322	£*	11 pm	Strange proverbs about cows on the wall and £3.75 pizza. Student digs.
Da Mario	15 Gloucester Rd	020 7584 9078	£££	11.30 pm	Apparently Princess Di's local Italian Pizzeria. Affordable and A+ pizza.
Jacobs	20 Gloucester Rd	020 7581 9292	££	10 pm	Brave the slow service for delicious veggie dishes and fresh juices.
The Kensington Creperie	2 Exhibition Rd	020 7589 8947	£*	11 pm	The best sweet and savoury crepes in London.
Little Japan	32 Thurloe St	020 7591 0207	£*	11.30 pm	Wowzers: bento for a fiver? Suspicious and delicious.
Oddono's	14 Bute St	020 7052 0732	£	11 pm	Gelato fix for homesick Italians and ice-cream freaks alike.
Pasha	1 Gloucester Rd	020 7589 7969	££££	11.30 pm	Cozy, intimate cubby holes, A+ service and delicious, yet pricey, set menus.

Map 37 • Knightsbridge

Bar Boulud	66 Knightsbridge	020 7201 3899	££	12 am	Best burger in town.
Zuma	5 Raphael St	020 7584 1010	£££	12 am	If your gal likes sushi, ideal for a romantic night out.

Map 38 • Chiswick

Boys Authentic Thai	95 Chiswick High Rd	020 8995 7991	££	10.30 pm	The staff are as funky and fresh as the food.
Chris' Fish and Chips	19 Turnham Green Terrace	020 8995 2367	£*	12 am	It's all British-ness wrapped in warm, greasy paper.
The Devonshire	126 Devonshire Rd	020 7592 7962	£££	11 pm	A more affordable version of Ramsay.
Fish Hook	6 Elliot Rd	020 8742 0766	££	10.30 pm	Get hooked on seafood.
Foubert's	2 Turnham Green Terrace	020 8994 5202	£	11 pm	Little Italian owned cafe. Excellent ice gream and gelato.
Franco Manca	144 Chiswick High Rd	020 8747 4822	££	10 pm	London's best pizza with longer opening hours.

High Road Brasserie	162 Chiswick High Rd	020 8742 7474	££	11 pm	As good as it looks. The continent comes to the High Road.
Kalamari	4 Chiswick High Rd	020 8994 4727	££	12 am	For those with a feta fetish.
La Trompette	5 Devonshire Rd	020 8747 1836	£££	10.30 pm	Unpretentious French restaurant with excellent service and set menus.
Maison Blanc	26 Turnham Green Terrace	020 8995 7220	£		The cupcakes look devine from the window. Just wait until you get inside.
Turnham Green Cafe	57 Turnham Green Terrace	020 8994 3839	££		Looks can be deceiving. Serves up good thai in a small space.
Zizzi	231 Chiswick High Rd	020 8747 9400	££	11.30 pm	Skip the mains—cut straight to the heavenly Apple Crumble.

Map 39 • Stamford Brook

Carpenter's Arms	89 Black Lion Ln	020 8741 8386	£££	11 pm	As gastropub as it gets.
Tosa	332 King St	020 8748 0002	£	10 pm	Low-key authentic yakitori (fried skewered meat) joint. Easy on the wallet.

Map 40 • Goldhawk Rd / Ravenscourt Park

Blah Blah Blah	78 Goldhawk Rd	020 8746 1337	££*	10.30 pm	Eccentric, worldly vegetarian. Kinda like your ex, only cooler.
Lowiczanka Polish Cultural Centre	238 King Street	020 8741 3225	££	10 pm	Stodgy grub, hard drink, concrete block. So Polish you'll need a passport.
Mahdi	215 King St	020 8563 7007	££	12 am	Truly authentic, unpretentious Iranian place -menu in Arabic 'n all. Tasty!
Sagar	157 King St	020 8741 8563	££	11 pm	Yummy South Indian veggie food at a great price.

Map 41 • Hammersmith

The Gate	51 Queen Caroline St	020 8748 6932	££££	10 pm	Light and airy by day, cosy at night. Lovely food.

Map 42 • Baron's Court

Best Mangal	104 N End Rd	020 7610 1050	££	1 am	Proper good kebabs with heeeeaps of nosh. Can sit in too - a rarity.
Bombay Bicycle Club	352 North End Rd	08454788205	£££	11pm	Lighter, brighter, more expensive, less authentic Indian restaurant. Still yum.
Ta Krai	100 North End Rd	020 7386 5375	££	10 pm	Decent, cheap food. Interior as tacky as its name suggests.

Map 43 • West Brompton / Fulham Broadway / Earls Court

The Blue Elephant	4 Fulham Broadway	020 7385 6595	££££	11.30 pm	Disney's version of Bangkok—grandiose, expensive, but oh, so good.
Bodean's	4 Broadway Chambers	020 7610 0440	£££	11 pm	Stuff yourself on BBQ pulled-pork sandwiches. Yee haw!
Chutney Mary	535 King's Rd	020 7351 3113	££££	11.30 pm	Get coddled over a curry (at a price).
Pizza@Home	350 Old Brompton Rd	020 7244 8080	£*	10 pm	Maybe London's most authentic Italian pizza. Fast and cheap as chips!!
Vingt Quatre	325 Fulham Rd	020 7376 7224	£	24-hrs	24 hour booze! Incidentally, the food is very good.
Yo! Sushi	Fulham Road	[illegible]	££	11 pm	Japanese conveyor belt sushi for [illegible]

Map 44 • Chelsea

Aubergine	11 Park Walk	020 7352 3449	££££	11 pm	Foie gras, lobster and truffles. Need we say more?
The Bluebird	350 King's Rd	020 7559 1000	£££	10.30 pm	So it seems you can get a bacon butty and look cool on the Kings Road.
Eight Over Eight	392 King's Rd	020 7349 9934	££££	11 pm	Exotic and dripping with celebs.

Map 45 • Chelsea (East)

Chelsea Kitchen	451 Fulham Rd	020 3055 0088	£	11 pm	New place, same affordable stodge. A Winner.
Four o nine	409 Clapham Rd	020 7737 0722	££££	10.30 pm	Inviting and intimate, it's nice.
Le Columbier	145 Dovehouse St	020 7351 1155	£££	11 pm	Vive le Bistro!
Made In Italy	249 King's Rd	020 7352 1880	££	11 pm	"Food Mama used to Make." Unless you're not Italian, obviously.

Key: £ : Under £10 / ££ : £10–£20 / £££ : £20–£30 / ££££ : £30–£40 / £££££: £40+
** : Does not accept credit cards./ † : Accepts only American Express / ††: Accepts only Visa and Mastercard*
Time listed refers to kitchen closing time on weekend nights

My Old Dutch Pancake House	221 King's Rd	020 7376 5650	£	11.30 pm	Sweet or savory pancakey goodness in the heart of Chelsea.
The Pig's Ear	35 Old Church St	020 7352 2908	££	10pm	Quirky, restored boozer. Deep fried pigs ear anyone? Seriously.
Sushinho	312 King's Rd	020 7349 7496	£££	10.30 pm	Sushi pizza anyone? They have it here.
Tom's Kitchen	27 Cale St	020 7349 0202	££££	11 pm	Crush-worthy (maybe just us?) Tom Aiken's British brasserie masterpiece.
Tom's Place	1 Cale St	020 7351 1806	£££	11 pm	Posh chippie.

Map 46 • Sloane Square

The Admiral Codrington	17 Mossop St	020 7581 0005	£££	10.30 pm	Go for simplicity here. Even the chips they get exactly right.
Bibendum Restaurant & Oyster Bar	81 Fulham Rd	020 7581 5817	£££££	11 pm	French institution with a cool (literally) oyster bar.
Blushes Cafe	52 King's Rd	020 7589 6640	£	1.30 am	Always reliable, always packed. C'est La Vie.
Foxtrot Oscar	79 Royal Hospital Rd	020 7352 4448	££	10 pm	Tango Alpha Sierra Tango Yankee.
Le Cercle	1 Wilbraham Pl	020 7901 9999	££££	12 am	Tapas-sized French yumminess. Pears with caramel popcorn, anyone?
Tom Aikens	43 Elystan St	020 7584 2003	£££££	11 pm	Artistic approach to just about everything.
Restaurant Gordon Ramsay	68 Royal Hospital Rd	020 7352 4441	£££££	11 pm	Mmmmmm… debt…

Map 47 • Fulham (West)

The River Café	Thames Wharf, Rainville Rd	020 7386 4200	£££	11 pm	Fine dining by the Thames for champagne socialists.

Map 48 • Fulham

Drawing Room Cafe	Bishop's Ave	020 7736 3233	£	5 pm	A historical and elegant spot for a cup of Earl Grey and a scone.
Fisher's Chips	19 Fulham High St	020 7610 9808	£	10 pm	Quality chips AND quality punning. It's why Britain's Great.

Map 49 • Parson's Green

De Cecco	189 New King's Rd	020 7736 1145	££	11 pm	Belissimo! Spaghetti a'll Aragosta is the signature dish and it's goood!
Ghillies	271 New King's Rd	020 7610 9675	££	10.30pm	Chic, relaxed continental eatery.
Kebab Kid	90 New Kings Road	020 7731 0427	£*	10 pm	Kebabs so impressive you could bring your gran here.
Mao Tai	58 New King's Rd	020 7731 2520	££	1 am	Modern, chic and pricey-but-delectable Pan-Asian menu in Parsons Green.
Tendido Cuatro	108 New King's Rd	020 7371 5147	£££		Perfecto! Mouth watering iberico jamon, buzzing and friendly Spanish staff.

Map 50 • Sand's End

Deep	The Boulevard, Imperial Wharf	020 7736 3337	££££	11 pm	Set for Gordon Ramsay's F-word. F-ing good itself.
Sands End	135 Stephendale Rd	020 7731 7823	£££		Hearty, rustic Irish fare. Nowt much else around but makes the grade.

Map 51 • Highgate

The Bull	13 North Hill Ave	0845 456 5033	£££	12 am	Chic eatery with perfectly positioned front terrace.
Cafe Rouge	6 South Grove	020 8342 9797	££	11 pm	Decent French restaurant and cafe chain
Papa Del's	347 Archway Rd	020 8347 9797	££	11 pm	Nice place. Good cookies. £3 pizzas after 9pm!
Red Lion And Sun	25 N Rd	020 8340 1780	££££	10 pm	Excellent Sunday roasts.

Map 52 • Archway (North)

Bengal Berties	172 Archway Rd	020 8348 1648	££	11 pm	Spit and sawdust venue with excellent nosh.
Dean & Hudson	249 Archway Rd	020 8340 1698	£		Amazing cakes and sweets for twee sugar junkies.
Fahrenheit	230 Archway Rd	020 8347 0333	££	11 pm	Corking Caribbean food with a broad smile.
The Lighthouse	179 Archway Rd	020 8348 3121	££	11 pm	Outstanding fresh fish joint flies beneath radar.

Map 53 • Crouch End

Arocaria	48 The Broadway	020 8340 0580	£££		Uber cute and relaxed Greek place.
Banners	21 Park Rd	020 8348 2930	££££	11.30 pm	Notoriously child-friendly but the breakfasts make up for that.
Hot Pepper Jelly	11 Broadway Parade	020 8340 4318	££*	5 pm	Pepperphobes probably shouldn't come to this culinary wonder.
Milou's on the Hill	83 Hazellville Rd	020 7272 1188	£*	9 pm	Go there for the hilltop terrace and homemade smoothies.
Piya Cafe	59 The Broadway	020 8347 8861	££	12 am	Great cheap and friendly Mediterranean grub.
Thaitanic	66 Crouch End Hill	020 8341 6100	£	11 pm	Groanworthy name, moanworthy food!

Map 54 • Hornsey

Ridge Cafe	97 Tottenham Ln	£££	£		Good place for quick lunch or just a caffeine boost.

Map 55 • Harringay

Muna's	599 Green Lanes	020 8340 8411	£££	1 am	Extremely slow service, but at least the food is good.
The Village	421 Green Lanes	077 8518 7715	££	2 am	Mountains of lovely, stodgy food.

Map 56 • Hampstead Village

Bacchus Greek Taverna	37 Heath St	020 7435 1855	£	11 pm	Lovely little place that has been here an age.
Carluccio's	34 Rosslyn Hill	020 7794 2184	£££	11 pm	Deli by day, diner by night.
La Creperie De Hampstead	77 Hampstead High St	020 7372 0081	£*	11 pm	No crap crepes at this sublime French street stall.
The Louis Patisserie	32 Heath St	020 7435 9908	£	6 pm	Tea and gorgeous cakes beloved of elderly Eastern European gentlemen.
Tinseltown	104 Heath St	020 7435 2396	£	3 am	Welcome to milkshake heaven!

Map 57 • Hamstead Heath

Hampstead Tea Rooms	9 S End Rd	020 7435 9563	£££	6.30 pm	Slooooooow service…but the breakfast is worth the wait.
Osteria Emilia	85 Fleet Rd	020 7433 3317	££££	11.30 pm	Sure, it's pricey but the locals can afford it.
Paradise	49 S End Rd	020 7794 6314	£££		Excellent Indian with a modern twist.
Polly's	55 S End Rd	020 7431 7947	£	5 pm	Sometimes you just fancy a sarnie and a cuppa.

Map 58 • Parliament Hill / Dartmouth Park

Al Parco	2 Highgate West Hill	020 8340 5900	£	10 pm	Probably the best pizza in London.
Bistro Laz	1 Highgate West Hill	020 8342 8355	£	11 pm	Lovely meze. Or order in pizza if next door's full.
Cafe Mozart	17 Swain's Ln	020 8348 1384	££	10 pm	Great place for lunch on a sunny day.
The Carob Tree	15 Highgate Rd	020 7267 9880	£££	11 pm	Swanky Greek place with nice terrace in summer.
Indian Spice Lounge	13 Swain's Ln	020 8340 7818	££	11 pm	Curry and cocktails. No really.
Kalendar	15 Swains Lane	020 8348 8300	££	11 pm	Pre-Heath brekkie, mid-Heath lunch or post-Heath dinner. All good!
Stingray Cafe	135 Fortess Rd	020 7482 4855	£	11 pm	Another reason why Tufnell Park rocks: great place!

Map 59 • Tufnell Park

Charuwan	110 Junction Rd	020 7263 1410	£££	10 pm	Friendly, quiet, tasty, cheap. Yup, it's pretty awesome.
Rustique Cafe	142 Fortess Rd	020 7692 5590	££	8 pm	Damn those tasty tasty cookies for being so small.
Spaghetti House	169 Fortess Rd	020 7485 7984	££	10 pm	Just like mama used to make it.
The Spice	161 Fortess Rd	020 7482 2700	££	11.30 pm	Top-notch curries

Map 60 • Archway

Archgate Café	5 Junction Rd	020 7272 2575	£	10 pm	Lovely English breakfasts face-off against equally ace Turkish food.
Iceland Fish Bar	11 Archway Rd	020 7272 6606	£	10 pm	Proper old-school chippie.
Junction Café	61 Junction Rd	020 7263 2036	£*	10 pm	Greasy. Spoon.
La Voute	10 Archway Rd	020 7281 7314	£	4.30 pm	Ace brekkies and lunches in this snazzy caff.
Mosaic Café	24 Junction Rd	020 7272 3509	££	10.30 pm	Head for the back garden sun-trap in Summer.

Key: £ : Under £10 / ££ : £10–£20 / £££ : £20–£30 / ££££ : £30–£40 / £££££: £40+
** : Does not accept credit cards./ † : Accepts only American Express / ††: Accepts only Visa and Mastercard*
Time listed refers to kitchen closing time on weekend nights

Nid Ting	533 Holloway Rd	020 7263 0506	£££	11.15 pm	Bigger, meatier portions than most Thai Restaurants.
RRC Thai Cafe	36 Highgate Hill	020 7561 0421	£	10.30 pm	Cheap, tasty and beautifully presented Thai food.
St Johns	91 Junction Rd	020 7272 1587	££££	11 pm	Gastro pub oasis stranded among the pound-shops of Archway.
The Toll Gate	6 Archway Close	020 7687 2066	££	11 pm	On with the pince-nez for slightly self-satisfied veggie venue.

Map 61 • Holloway (North)

The Landseer	37 Landseer Rd	020 7263 4658	££	9.30 pm	Gastropub extraordinaire.
Orexi	236 Hornsey Rd	020 7607 7098	££		Amazing: unchanged since elderly couple opened 30 yrs ago.
Tagine D' Or	92 Seven Sisters Rd	020 7700 7666	£		Tiny, weird and criminally cheap. Like the NFT!

Map 62 • Finsbury Park

Fassika	152 Seven Sisters Rd	020 7272 7572	££	12 am	Intimate with lovely food. Distinctly flirty waitresses though...
Le Rif	172 Seven Sisters Rd	020 7263 1891	£*	10 pm	Essential for all your banter and microwaved Tagine needs.
Petek	96 Stroud Green Rd	020 7619 3933	£	10.45 pm	Classy but cheap Turkish.

Map 63 • Manor House

Il Bacio	178 Blackstock Rd	020 7226 3339	££	11 pm	Friendly, reliable and huge portions.
New River Cafe	271 Stoke Newington Church St	020 7923 9842	£	11 pm	Steamy windows and top hangover cure fry-ups.

Map 64 • Stoke Newington

Alistair's Brasserie	35 Stoke Newington Church St	020 7249 2782	££££	10 pm	Luxurious food with gobshite, luddite customers. Mmmmm.
Anglo Asian	60 Stoke Newington Church St	020 7254 3633	££	11.30 pm	Classic curry house right down to the free sherry.
Blue Legume	101 Stoke Newington Church St	020 7923 1303	£	11 pm	Dreamy eggs benedict, served under a giant aubergine.
Datte Foco	10 Stoke Newington Church St	020 7254 6055	££	11 pm	Mouth watering pizza sold by the weight.
Fifty Six	56 Newington Green	020 7359 6377	££	11.30 pm	Bring a date.
Rasa N16	55 Stoke Newington Church St	020 7249 0344	££	11.30 pm	Vegetarian-style Indian cooking at its mouth-watering best.
Sariyer Balik	56 Green Lanes	020 7275 7681	£££	12 am	Turkish Seafood.
Yum Yum	187 Stoke Newington High St	020 7254 6751	£££	11 pm	Tasty tasty, Thai Thai. Go for the Kang Massuman.

Map 65 • West Hampstead

The Green Room	182 Broadhurst Gardens	020 7372 8188	££	11 pm	West Hampstead's newest joint brimming with charm. Nice risotto.
Small & Beautiful	351 Kilburn High Rd	020 7328 2637	£		Small and beautiful indeed, as is the bill.

Map 66 • Finchley Road / Swiss Cottage

Bradleys	25 Winchester Rd	020 7722 3457	£££	11 pm	Your friendly face in the neighbourhood that loves wine.
Camden Arts Centre	Arkwright Rd	020 7472 5500	£	6 pm	Excellent food in buzzing artistic setting.
Singapore Garden	83 Fairfax Rd	020 7328 5314	££	11 pm	Surprising flavours make a welcome alternative on a night out.

Map 67 • Belsize Park

Artigiano	12 Belsize Terrace	020 7794 4288	£££	11 pm	Fancy some fancy pasta?
Brasserie Gerard	215 Haverstock Hill	020 7431 8101	£££	11 pm	Bon jour. Une burger with fromage, merci please.
Curry Manjil	34 England's Ln	020 7722 9101	££	12 am	Local fave still going strong after 40 years.
Paradiso	36 England's Ln	020 7586 9001	££	11.30 pm	For those on a carbs, cheese and cream diet.
Retsina	48 Belsize Ln	020 7431 5855	£££	11 pm	Lively Greek - grilled meat galore!
Violette Cafe	2 England's Ln	020 7586 4326	££	6.30 pm	Cakey goodness.

Map 68 • Kilburn High Road / Abbey Road

Little Bay	228 Belsize Rd	020 7372 4699	££*	11 pm	Crazy cheap. Crazy cute!

Map 69 • St. John's Wood

Tupelo Honey	27 Parkway, Camden	020 7284 2989	££	11 pm	A coffee-shop, wine bar and restaurant combined.

Map 70 • Primrose Hill

Cafe Seventy Nine	79 Regents Park Rd	020 7586 8012	£	6 pm	Excellent veggie fare, though you might have to wait.
The Hill Bar	94 Haverstock Hill	020 7267 0033	£££	11 pm	The Hill is an ideal place to meet friends before heading off to a show.
J Restaurant	148 Regents Park Rd	020 7586 9100	££	11 pm	Excellent food, especially brunch. Tempestuous service.
Legal Cafe	81 Haverstock Hill	020 7586 7412	£	6 pm	Great coffee, good food and wifi: a pleasant working environment.
Lemonia	89 Regents Park Rd	020 7586 7454	£££	11.30 pm	Fancy a real Greek meal?
Manna	4 Erskine Rd	020 7722 8028	££	11.30 pm	Aesthetically gorgeous veggie restaurant, serving scrumptious food.
Melrose and Morgan	42 Gloucester Ave	020 7722 0011	£	8 pm	Scrumptious food and coffee. Good for solo snacks.
Odette's	130 Regents Park Rd	020 7586 8569	£££	1 am	Delectably dainty restaurant, high-class service.
Primrose Bakery	69 Gloucester Ave	020 7483 4222	£	6 pm	A delectably dinky bakery. These cakes can't be missed.
Trojka	101 Regents Park Rd	020 7483 3765	££	10 pm	Authentically spartan but colourful decor. Nice 'n' quirky.
Two Brothers	297 Regents Park Rd	020 8346 0469	££	10 pm	Middle class fish & chips.

Map 71 • Camden Town / Chalk Farm / Kentish Town (West)

Andy's Taverna	81 Bayham St	020 7485 9718	££	11 pm	Big Greek restaurant with a garden.
Bar Gansa	2 Inverness St	020 7267 8909	££	12 am	More buzzing and pleasurable than a rampant rabbit.
Bar Solo	20 Inverness St	020 7482 4611	££	1 am	Where'd they find the waitresses? On the set of Clueless?
Bento Café	9 Parkway	020 7482 3990	££	11pm	Exquisite Japanese food at very reasonable prices.
Camden Bar and Kitchen	102 Camden High St	020 7485 2744	££	11 pm	Great burgers at this bohemian gem; sorry, McDonalds!
Cotton's	55 Chalk Farm Rd	020 7485 8388	££	10 pm	No hustle and bustle, just chill Jamaican-style.
Gilgamesh	The Stables Market, Chalk Farm Rd	020 7428 4922	£££*	12 am	Awesome surroundings will confuse the hell out of future archaeologists.
The Green Note	106 Parkway	020 7485 9899	££	11 pm	Excellent veggie tapas with a side of bongo drums.
Haché	24 Inverness St	020 7485 9100	££	10.30 pm	Burger heaven for both vegetarians and carnivores.
Kim's Vietnamese Food Hut some	Unit D, Camden Lock Palace	N/A	£*	11 pm	Once you pass the Spanish Inqusition, excellent slop.
Limani	154 Regents Park Rd	020 7483 4492	£££	11 pm	Greek-Cypriot fare in a sophisticated environment. Friendly service.
Marathon Cafe	87 Chalk Farm Rd	020 7485 3814	£*	4 am	Legendary late-night venue serving kebabs, chips and beer.
Marine Ices	8 Haverstock Hill	020 7482 9003	£	11 pm	Fantastic ice cream restaurant with '70s decor and autographed photos.
Market	438 Parkway	020 7267 9700	£££	11 pm	The only restaurant in Camden deserving of the name.
Muang Thai	71 Chalk Farm Rd	020 7916 0653	£	11 pm	Quiet vibe, tinkly music, reliably decent food.
My Village	37 Chalk Farm Rd	020 7485 4996	£	9pm	Cute ethnic organic shop serving food, tea and coffee.
Thanh Binh	14 Chalk Farm Rd	020 7267 9820	£	10 pm	Excellent Vietnamese with very friendly and chatty staff.
Viet-anh Cafe	41 Parkway	020 7284 4082	£	11 pm	Surly service, cheap plentiful food. Would it hurt to smile?
Woody Grill	1 Camden Rd	020 7485 7774	£*	12 am	Late night post-alcohol food without salmonella poisoning.
Yumchaa Tea Space	91 Upper Walkway, West Yard, Camden Lock Market	020 7209 9641	£*	6 pm	The carrot cake… oh mama!
Zorya Imperial Vodka Room	48 Chalk Farm Rd	020 7485 8484	££	12 am	Vodka, vodka and more vodka. Oh… and gorgeous food too.

Key: £ : Under £10 / ££ : £10–£20 / £££ : £20–£30 / ££££ : £30–£40 / £££££: £40+
** : Does not accept credit cards./ † : Accepts only American Express / ††: Accepts only Visa and Mastercard*
Time listed refers to kitchen closing time on weekend nights

Map 72 • Kentish Town

Bintang Cafe	93 Kentish Town Rd	020 7813 3393	££	11 pm	Good for eating copiously in a gaudy shack.
The Bengal Lancer	253 Kentish Town Rd	020 7485 6688	£££		The best (and priciest) indian in the area.
Eatzone	18 Fortess Rd	020 7485 0152	£*	11 pm	Quick and delicious, with roughly 1 gazillion choices. Addictive.
Le Petit Prince	5 Holmes Rd	020 7267 3789	££	11 pm	Adorable homage to French cartoon character with excellent merguez.
Mario's Cafe	6 Kelly St	020 7284 2066	£*	10 pm	Saint Etienne's local greasy spoon.
The Oxford	256 Kentish Town Rd	020 7485 3521	££	9.45 pm	Smug comfort eating.
Pane Vino	323 Kentish Town Rd	020 7267 3879	££	10.30 pm	Staff can be Italian. Food can be fantastic.
Phoenicia - Mediterranean Food Hall	186 Kentish Town Rd	020 7267 1267	£	10 pm	Coffee n' baclava, falafel, meze. All a steal.

Map 74 • Holloway Road / Arsenal

Dastarkhan	203 Holloway Rd	075 4521 1010	££	2 am	Frankly bizarre Khazak place. Entertaining, but so so nosh.
Morgan M	489 Liverpool Rd	020 7609 3560	£££££	11 pm	Divine Frenchie. Mais zut alors! £1200 bottles of wine!
Tbilisi	91 Holloway Rd	020 7607 2536	££££	11 pm	Get your Georgian on.

Map 75 • Highbury

San Daniele Del Friuli	72 Highbury Park	020 7226 1609	£££	12 am	Like mama used to make—well someone had to say it.
Ustun	107 Green Lanes		£	10 pm	Very nice lamachun.

Map 76 • Edgeware Road / Marylebone (North)

Sea Shell Of Lisson Grove	49 Lisson Grove	020 7224 9000	££	10.30 pm	Pescatarians will love this place—sorry, carnivores!

Map 77 • Mornington Crescent / Regent's Park

Chutneys	124 Drummond St	020 7388 0604	££	11.30 pm	Flavoursome, no-frills, fill-yer-boots affair. Bargainous buffet colossal.
Diwana Bhelpoori	121 Drummond St	020 7387 5556	££	11 pm	South-Indian veggie with tasty dosai and puris.
Mestizo	103 Hampstead Rd	020 7387 4064	£££	11 pm	Great. The margarita is made by the devil himself.
York & Albany	127 Parkway	020 7388 3344	£££	11 pm	Gordo on a budget.

Map 78 • Euston

Asakusa	265 Eversholt St	020 7388 8399	£££	11.30 pm	Authentic Japanese.
Banger Bros.	Euston Station	020 7387 6958	£	7.30 pm	Sing it: It's a small world (of sausages) after all!
Camino	3 Varnisher's Yard	020 7841 7331	£££	12 am	Sophisticated Spanish restaurant in Kings Cross. Seems wrong, somehow.
Chop Chop Noodle Bar	1 Euston Rd	020 7833 1773	£	11 pm	Great for a quick and cheap meal. Massive portions.
El Parador	245 Eversholt St	020 7387 2789	££	11 pm	Great tapas. A little ray of sunshine in your mouth.
Great Nepalese	48 Eversholt St	020 7388 6737	££	11 pm	Really the only option in the area.
Kitchin	8 Caledonia St	020 7713 8777	££	11 pm	Round-the-world all-you-can-eat. Vile and great.
Rodon Live	7 Pratt St	020 7267 8088	££	11 pm	Friendly rotund owner masks just above average food.
The Somerstown Coffee House	60 Chalton St	020 7691 9136	££	10 pm	Bistro food in grade II listed pub. Excellent set menu.
Tony's Natural Foods	10 Caledonian Rd	020 7837 5223	£	11 pm	Vegan salad bar with peaceout garden, man.

Map 79 • King's Cross

Addis	42 Caledonian Rd	020 7278 0679	££	11 pm	Lovely food with convivial sloth-like service.
Dallas Burger Bar	257 Caledonian Rd	020 7278 4955	£*	9 pm	JR smiles down as you destroy your arteries. Hilarious.
Euro Café	299 Caledonian Rd	020 7607 5362	£	10 pm	Loveable caff with some unusual specials.
Marathon	196 Caledonian Rd	020 7837 4499	££	12 am	Raw meat, ritualistic coffee and crazed dancing.

Menelik	277 Caledonian Rd	020 7700 7774	££	12 am	If only more places let you eat with your hands.
The New Didar	347 Caledonian Rd	020 7700 3496	£	12 am	Friendly staff willing to strike deals. Haggling gets you everywhere.
Oz	53 Caledonian Rd	020 7278 9650	£*	10 pm	Unusually well-kempt greasy spoon.
Yum Yum	48 Caledonian Rd	020 7278 4737	£	11 pm	Super-cheap Chinese that may even remain in your stomach.

Map 80 • Angel / Upper St

Afghan Kitchen	35 Islington Green	020 7359 8019	£££*	10.45 pm	Only a few tables; Islington's smallest—and biggest— Afghan place.
The Albion	10 Thornhill Rd	020 7607 7450	££	10 pm	How many places offer whole suckling pigs? Not enough.
Alpino	97 Chapel Market	020 7837 8330	£	4 pm	This, guv'nor, is a proper tea'n'two slices caff. Alright?
The Breakfast Club	31 Camden Passage	020 7226 5454	££	9.30 pm	Not just breakfast, not a club. But just so gooood.
Candid Café	3 Torrens St	020 7837 4237	£	10 pm	Laid-back, arty cafe for dreamy types. Candle-lit. Perfect for lingering.
Desperados	127 Upper St	[illegible]	££	11.30 pm	Garish. More like the Mexico of MTV than the real world.
Elk in the Woods	39 Camden Passage	020 7226 3535	££	10.30 pm	Laid-back, hunting-themed eatery.
Fig and Olive	151 Upper St	020 7354 2605	££	11 pm	Incredibly busy at weekends which can affect service and quality.
Fine Burger Co	330 Upper St	020 7359 3026	£	10 pm	For when you've grown out of McDonalds.
Fredericks	Camden Passage	020 7359 2888	££		Swanky Euro-flash bistro.
Gem	265 Upper St	020 7359 0405	£££	11 pm	A good vibe is precious.
House	63 Canonbury Rd	020 7704 7410	£££	10.30 pm	Gastro bar-restaurant where seasonal food's served with flair. For those feeling flush.
Indian Veg Bhelpoori House	93 Chapel Market	020 7833 1167	£	10 pm	Honest all-you-can-eat Indian. Veggie propaganda on walls.
Isarn	119 Upper St	020 7424 5153	££	11 pm	Pretty, flower-adorned food, green curry cooked to perfection. Candle-lit courtyard.
Itsuka	54 Islington Park St	020 7354 5717	£	12 am	Cheap set menus and heartfelt J-Pop.
La Forchetta	73 Upper St	020 7226 6879	££	11.30 pm	Unpretentious, cheap pizza. Eat fast, then leg it.
La Porchetta	141 Upper St	020 7288 2488	£££	11 pm	This little pig says yes to good cheap pizza.
Le Mercury	140 Upper St	020 7354 4088	££	1 am	This place will seduce you AND your mother.
Masala Zone	80 Upper St	020 7359 3399	££	11 pm	Cheap, good thalis served on metal trays.
Mem & Laz	8 Theberton St	020 7704 9089	££	11 pm	Mediterranean chaos by candlelight.
Metrogusto	13 Theberton St	020 7226 9400	££	10.30 pm	Try not to let the menacing art put you off the amazing pasta.
Olive Grill	61 Upper St	020 7226 9002	£*	10 pm	The falafels are so good you may quit kebabs. Forever.
Ottolenghi	287 Upper St	020 7288 1454	££	10 pm	Staff you'll want to take home to meet your mum.
Pizzeria Oregano	19 St Alban's Pl	020 7288 1123	££	11 pm	Great pizza and lentil soup. Delicious odd couple.
Pomegranate	139 Upper St	020 7704 1002	££	12 am	Bright. And not in a clever way.
Rodizo Rico	77 Upper St	020 7354 1076	£££	11 pm	Meat. And lots of it.
Tortilla	13 Islington High St	020 7833 3103	££	10 pm	Damn good burritos!
Vigata Ristorante	70 Liverpool Rd	020 7226 1475	££	10 pm	Sardonic about Sicilian? This lobster linguine will soon fix that.
Zaffrani	47 Cross St	020 7226 5522	££	11 pm	Thinking man's curry.

Map 81 • Canonbury

Angel Cafe	100 Essex Rd	020 7704 6866	£	11 pm	Blue collar fusion cuisine: Brit greasy spoon serving Turkish boreks.
Raab's Bakery	136 Essex Rd	020 7226 2830	£	6 pm	Use your loaf sunshine.
Sabor	108 Essex Rd	020 7226 5551	££££	11 pm	Latin American; even the tables are tropical.
Zigni House	330 Essex Rd	020 7226 7418	£	12 am	Hearty East African eatery with boho, raffish charm.

Map 82 • De Beauvoir Town / Kingsland

Casaba	162 Essex Rd	020 7288 1223	££	7 pm	Fresh spin on Turkish meze and shisha bar.
Huong Viet	12 Englefield Rd	020 7249 0877	££	11 pm	A crumbling old bath house? Look again.
Puji Puji	122 Balls Pond Rd	020 7923 2112	££	10 pm	Malaysian Malaysian.

Key: £ : Under £10 / ££ : £10–£20 / £££ : £20–£30 / ££££ : £30–£40 / £££££: £40+
** : Does not accept credit cards./ † : Accepts only American Express / ††: Accepts only Visa and Mastercard*
Time listed refers to kitchen closing time on weekend nights

Map 83 • Angel (East) / City Rd (North)

The Charles Lamb	16 Elia St	020 7837 5040	££	9.30pm	Chilled-out Sunday lunch perfection.
Shepherdess Cafe	221 City Rd	020 7253 2463	£	5pm	Cafe offering no-frills traditional English far
William IV	7 Shepherdess Walk	020 3119 3010	££	12am	Lovely gastropub, off the beaten track and with delicious food.

Map 84 • Hoxton

The Bean	126 Curtain Rd	020 7739 7829	£*	8 pm	Decent coffee! It's hard to find, you know.
The Diner	128 Curtain Rd	020 7729 4452	£££	10.30 pm	Door-stopper burgers that should come wi health warnings.
F.Cooke	150 Hoxton St	020 7729 7718	££	8 pm	Pies, Liquor, Eels… British culinary retardation at it's finest.
Fifteen	15 Westland Pl	020 3375 1515	£££££	10 pm	Lots of Jamie Oliver. Lots of great, expensiv food.
Shish	313 Old Street	020 7749 0990	££	10 pm	Great kebabs in surroundings devoid of authenticity.
Yelo	8 Hoxton Sq	020 7729 4626	£	11 pm	Suspiciously quick service, but cheap and tasty so who cares?

Map 85 • Stoke Newington (East)

19 Numara Bos Cirrik	34 Stoke Newington Rd	020 7249 0400	££	10 pm	Meat, meat, meat—oh and onion, pomegranate and turnip salad.
Bagel House	2 Stoke Newington High St queues.	020 7249 3908	£*	10 pm	Bagels to rival Brick Lane and without the queues.
Cafe Z Bar	58 Stoke Newington High St	020 7275 7523	£*	11 pm	Popular grease-shop/hangover center for Stokey Lefties.
Testi	38 Stoke Newington High St	020 7249 7151	£££	12 am	Yes, it's named after bollocks. No, it's really not bollocks.
Thai Cafe	3 Northwold Rd	020 7249 2618	££		Deceptively pokey, unimaginatively named yet brilliant.
Three Crowns	175 Stoke Newington Church St	020 7241 5511	££	9.30 pm	Impressive Victorian pub that's undergone gastropubification.

Map 86 • Dalston / Kingsland

The Best Turkish Kebab	125 Stoke Newington Rd	020 7254 7642	£*	12 am	Feed your soul. Always buzzing.
Dalston Lane Café	170 Dalston Ln	020 7254 4704	£	5pm	French toast with bacon and maple: an alchemical combination of savoury and sweet.
Dem Cafe	18 Stoke Newington Rd	020 7254 6364	££		For when Zed Bar's too full.
El Panchos	176 Stoke Newington Rd	020 7923 9588	£	11 pm	Cheesoid mexican with decent cocktails.
Evin Bar and Cafe	115 Kingsland High St	020 7254 5634	££	11 pm	Fantastic Turkish place without the grease factor. Speciality is gozleme.
LMNT	316 Queensbridge Rd	020 7249 6727	£££	10.45 pm	Eat inside an urn or by a sphinx's paws.
A Little Of What You Fancy	464 Kingsland Rd	020 7275 0060	££	12 am	A bit like being in a friend's kitchen/dining room.
Mangal 1	10 Arcola St	020 7275 8981	£*	12 am	May the grill's smoke guide you, meat-lovin friends.
Mangal 2	4 Stoke Newington Rd	020 7254 7888	££	12 am	Gilbert & George aren't the only ones loving this one.
Peppers and Spice	20 Kingsland High St	020 7275 9818	£*	10.30 pm.	The real deal: jerk, oxtail, festival, plantain, ackee. Everyting irie.
Shanghai	41 Kingsland High St	020 7254 2878	££	10.30 pm	Tasty, good-value Chinese hiding behind th facade of a dingy old Kaff.
Somine	131 Kingsland High St	020 7254 7384	£*	24 hrs	Reanimating red lentil soup, Turkish style. Around the clock.
Stone Cave	111 Kingsland High St	020 7241 4911	££	12 am	Cave look and cave feel. Up-scale(ish) Turkis And great.
The Tea Rooms	155 Stoke Newington Rd	020 7923 1870	£	10 pm	Stokey in a tea-cup. Pleasant…

Map 87 • Hackney Downs / Lower Clapton

Dunya	199 Lower Clapton Rd	020 8985 7989	£	2 am	Cuz you can't diet all the time. Or any time.
India Gate	75 Lower Clapton Rd	020 8986 0505	£*	11 pm	Very, very cheap, pretty cheerful and a little rank.
Mess Café	38 Amhurst Rd	020 8985 3194	£	5pm	All manner of breakfast all the time.
Parioli	90 Lower Clapton Rd	020 7502 3288	£	9 pm	Best food of any kind in Clapton.
Pogo Cafe	76 Clarence Rd	020 8533 1214	£*	9 pm	Vegan co-op community caff. Real food for thought.

Map 88 • Haggerston / Queensbridge Rd

Faulkner's	424 Kingsland Rd	020 7254 6152	£££	10 pm	Legendary and traditional with traditional opening times
That Vietnamese Place	134 Kingsland Rd	020 7729 4843	££	10 pm	Not as memorable as the name would have you believe.
Uludag	398 Kingsland Rd	020 7241 1923	£		Great falafels and a bit of a nutter hub to boot.
Usha	428 Kingsland Rd	020 7241 0836	£	11 pm	One of few curry houses in the area. Consistently good.
Viet Hoa Café	70 Kingsland Rd	020 7729 8293	£	11.30 pm	Bland looking cafe hides gorgeous delicacies.

Map 89 • London Fields / Hackney Central

Buen Ayre	50 Broadway Market	020 7275 9900	££££	10.30 pm	Vegetarians take note—run for the hills.
Cafe Bohemia	2 Bohemia Pl	020 8986 4352	£	11 pm	Feeling Bohemian? Quirky cafe with live blues/jazz/world Saturday nights.
Cat and Mutton	76 Broadway Market	020 7254 5599	££	10 pm	Gastropub without the gastropub nastiness.
Corner Deli	121 Mare St	020 8986 0031	£	9 pm	Nice spot for brunch away from the bustle of Broadway Market.
Hai Ha	206 Mare St	020 8985 5388	££*	11 pm	Brilliant BYO Vietnamese cafe.
R Cooke and Sons	9 Broadway Market	020 7254 6458	£*	8 pm	Lor' love a duck! Pie n' mash shop—liquor an' all!
The Spurstowe Arms	68 Greenwood Rd	020 7254 4316	££	11 pm	Suntrap beer garden, good wine selection and gamey menu. Marvellous.

Map 90 • Homerton / Victoria Park North

The Empress of India	130 Lauriston Rd	020 8533 5123	£££	10 pm	Spiffy menu from brekkie through to dinner in Hackney Village.
The Fish House	126 Lauriston Rd	020 8533 3327	££	9.45 pm	Not as cheap as chips but still very good.

Map 91 • Shoreditch / Brick Lane / Spitalfields

Beigel Shop	155 Brick Lane	020 7729 0826	£*	24 hrs	For 3am cravings; salted beef bagel from the Beigel Shop.
Brick Lane Clipper Restaurant	104 Brick Ln	020 7377 0022	££	12 am	For less spice-oriented connoisseurs, Bengali Clipper's exceptional lamb korma.
Boundary	2 Boundary St	020 7729 1051	£££	10.30 pm	Warehouse conversion, great view, some major boxes being ticked here.
Cafe Bangla	128 Brick Lane	020 7247 7885	££	12 am	Popular Bangladeshi adorned with psychedelic and surreal fantasy art.
Drunken Monkey	222 Shoreditch High St	020 7392 9606	££	12 am	Debauched, dimly-lit dim-sum drinking hole. Chinese lanterns and lethal mojitos.
Ethiopian Food Stall	Sunday Upmarket, Truman's Brewery, Brick Lane	N/A	£*	N/A	One of many great food stalls, get Brazilian dessert after!
Frizzante	1A Goldsmith's Row	020 7739 2266	££	4 pm	All the Italians go to Agriturismo night (Thursday)—just sayin'.
Gourmet San	261 Bethnal Green Rd	020 7729 8388	£	11pm	Whole crabs and minimal English.
Hackney City Farm	1 Goldsmiths Row	020 7729 6381	££	4.30 pm	Animals! In Hackney! And some overpriced fry-up.
Hanoi Cafe	98 Kingsland Rd	020 7729 5610	££	11 pm	Cosy Viet joint, where the whole family's around.
Hawksmoor	157 Commercial St	020 7247 7392	£££	10.30 pm	France and America forget their differences for some serious steakage.
Jones Dairy Café	23 Ezra St	020 7739 5372	£*	3 pm	Sit back and watch the world go by at Columbia Road.
Les Trois Garcons	1 Club Row	020 7613 1924	££££	11 pm	Kitch décor/slick service/fantastic grub.
Noodle King	185 Bethnal Green Rd	020 7613 3050	£*	11.30 pm	Half the normal price; double the normal portions. Come hungry.
Ping Pong	3 Steward St	020 7422 7650	££	11 pm	Serviceable dim sum in a frantic shitstorm.
The Premises	209 Hackney Rd	020 7684 2230	££	11 pm	Bistro swarming with musicians thanks to next door's recording studio.
Que Viet	102 Kingsland Rd	020 7033 0588	££	11 pm	So du jour—even Marc Jacobs munches noodles here.
Rootmaster	Elys Yard	079 1238 9314	££	10 pm	Eat on a bus without looking homeless.
Rosa's	12 Hanbury St	020 7247 1093	££		Quirky, warm little Thai place.
Song Que	134 Kingsland Rd	020 7613 3222	££	11 pm	Still Little Vietnam's queen. An authentic, no-nonsense affair.
St John Bread and Wine	94 Commercial St	020 7251 0848	£££	11 pm	Minimalist and meaty. Anyone for deep-fried pig's head?
Story Deli	91 Brick Ln	020 7247 3137	£	9 pm	Lo-tech pizza joint. Think hipster Pizza Express.

Key: £ : Under £10 / ££ : £10–£20 / £££ : £20–£30 / ££££ : £30–£40 / £££££: £40+
** : Does not accept credit cards./ † : Accepts only American Express / ††: Accepts only Visa and Mastercard*
Time listed refers to kitchen closing time on weekend nights

Tay Do	60 Kingsland Rd	020 7739 0966	£	11 pm	Squish 'em in, feed 'em quick variety of chea & filling Vietnamese cuisine.
Tay Do Cafe	65 Kingsland Rd	020 7729 7223	£££	12 am	Hectic and noisy. Just like Vietnam, then.
Viet Grill	58 Kingsland Rd	020 7739 6686	££	11 pm	Eccentric but tasty. Non-edible tropical fish decor…

Map 92 • Bethnal Green

Bistrotheque	23 Wadeson St	020 8983 7900	££	11 pm	Brunch, burlesque and pianist playing Smel Like Teen Spirit. Fabulous.
E Pellicci	332 Bethnal Green Rd	020 7739 4873	£	4.30 pm	Challenge your hangover to survive their fry-ups.
Little Georgia	87 Goldsmiths Row	020 7739 8154	££	10 pm	Hearty fayre from the former Soviet State. N drinks licence.
Wild Cherry	241 Globe Rd	020 8980 6678	££	4 pm	Buddhist staff serve yummy breakfasts to hungover partiers. Instant karma.

Map 93 • Globe Town / Mile End (North)

Matsu	558 Mile End Rd	020 8983 3528	££	11 pm	Japanese food? In Mile End? You're 'avin a giraffe aintcha?
The Morgan Arms	43 Morgan St	020 8980 6389	£££	12 am	Which joker invented the term "gastropub"? This is one of them.

Map 94 • Bow

Chicchi	516 Roman Rd	020 8141 4190	£*	7 pm	The Italians reclaim Roman Road.
G.Kelly Pie & Mash shop	526 Roman Rd	020 8980 3165	£	7 pm	Servin' 'ot 'ome-made pies, jellied eels 'n mash since 1937.
The Roman Tandoori	432 Roman Road	020 8980 1390	££	10 pm	If you can't stand eels, 'ave a curry instead.

Map 95 • Whitechapel (West) / St Katharine's Dock

Cafe Spice Namaste	16 Prescot St	020 7488 9242	££	10.30 pm	Open-minded Indian that strays far from rur of the mill.
The Empress	141 Leman St	020 7265 0745	£	11.45 pm	Forget Brick Lane. This is where it's at.

Map 96 • Whitechapel (East) / Shadwell (West) / Wapping

Il Bordello	81 Wapping High St	020 7481 9950	£££	10 pm	Upscale neighbourhood Italian.
Tayyabs	83 Fieldgate St	020 7247 6400	£	12 am	Lipsmacking seekh kebabs alone are worth the queues.

Map 97 • Stepney / Shadwell (East)

Wapping Food	Wapping Wall	020 7680 2080	£££	11 pm	Stunning dining in 100 year old powerstation/ art gallery. Go!

Map 98 • Mile End (South) / Limehouse

La Figa	45 Narrow St	020 7790 0077	££	11 pm	Tasty Italian in courtyard setting.
The Narrow	44 Narrow St	020 7592 7950	£££	11 pm	Gordon Ramsay's nod to gastropubs—cracking views.
Orange Room Cafe	63 Burdett Rd	020 8980 7336	£££	11.30 pm	Tasty, fresh Lebanese food in a wasteland of stodgy takeaways.

Map 100 • Poplar (West) / Canary Wharf (West)

1802 Bar	Hertsmere Rd	020 7538 2702	££	11 pm	Dine inside the warehouse built by Napoleonic prisoners.
Browns	Hertsmere Rd	020 7987 9777	£££	11 pm	Always reliable.
Nicolas	480 One Canada Sq	020 7512 9092	££	10.30 pm	Micro French restaurant and vintners in one.
Plateau	Canada Pl	020 7715 7100	££££	10.30 pm	Striking views and truffle gnocchi.
Tiffin Bites	22 Jubilee Place	020 7719 0333	££	10 pm	Eat curry, watch Bollywood films.

Map 101 • Poplar (East) / Canary Wharf (East)

Gun	27 Coldharbour	020 7515 5222	£££	11 pm	Enjoyed by 18th century dockers and city workers alike.
Jamie's Italian	2 Churchill Pl	020 3002 5252	£££	11 pm	Bang-on Jamie O on the cheap.

Map 103 • Cubitt Town / Mudchute

Mudchute Kitchen	Pier St	020 7515 5901	££	5 pm	Food companion to the farm bit. Chi chi children.

Map 104 • South Bank / Waterloo / Lambeth North

Anchor & Hope	36 The Cut	020 7928 9898	££££	10.30 pm	A British gastro-pub obsession, long waits though.
Canteen	Royal Festival Hall, Belvedere Rd	084 5686 1122	££	10.30 pm	A menu that sums up the best of British food with aplomb.
Concrete	Southbank Centre	020 7928 4123	£	1 am	Restaurant/bar features Russian beer, food, absinthe.
The Cut Bar	66 The Cut	020 7928 4400	£££	11 pm	Brilliant chips. A cut above the rest.
Enis's Cafe	79 Waterloo Rd	N/A	£	11 pm	You wouldn't believe me if I told you. Just go.
Giraffe	Riverside Level 1	020 7928 2004	££	10.45pm	Good crowd pleaser. Though too much world music and balloons.
Livebait	45 The Cut	020 7928 7211	£££	11 pm	Very fishy, in a very good way.
Marie's Café	90 Lower Marsh	020 7928 1050	£	10.30 pm	Greasy spoon by day, a no-frills, super-yum BYO Thai by night.
Oxo Tower Wharf	Barge House St	020 7803 3888	££££	11 pm	You might have to rob a bank, but the view's amazing.
RSJ	33 Coin St	0207 928 4554	££	11 pm	Forget about those crappy South Bank chains. Go here.
Skylon	Belvedere Rd	020 7654 7800	££££	10.45 pm	Expensive, but staffs' uniforms and view make up for it.
Studio 6	56 Upper Ground	020 7928 6243	££	11 pm	Service with a reluctant grunt doesn't stop the crowds.
Tas Cut	33 The Cut	020 7928 2111	££	11.30 pm	Blink and you'll miss it. Buzzing Turkish cafe—best hummous in London.

Map 105 • Southwark / Bankside (West)

Baltic	74 Blackfriars Rd	020 7928 1111	££££	10.30 pm	Try Polish Hunter's stew: made with real Polish Hunters. Probably.
Blackfriars Cafe	169 Blackfriars Rd	020 7928 4034	£*	10 pm	Old-school, family-run greasy spoon; amazing fry-ups.
El Vergel	132 Webber St	020 7401 2308	£*	10 pm	Its Latin breakfast: Oh. My. God. Soooooo good.
Laughing Gravy	154 Blackfriars Rd	020 7721 7055	££	12 am	Ropey exterior. Sounds odd. Bugger to get to.
The Table	83 Southwark St	020 7401 2760	£*	10.30 pm	Go and find out why we're all obsessed.
Tate Modern Restaurant	Bankside	020 7887 8888	££	6 pm	Stunning views, crap food, clueless staff.

Map 106 • Bankside (East) / Borough / Newington

Amano	Clink St	020 7234 0000	££	10 pm	Trust Amano for stone-baked pizza and freshly-made flatbreads. We do.
Boot and Flogger	10 Redcross Way	020 7407 1184	££	8 pm	Splendidly gentleman's club-esque—all savile row suits and chesterfield sofas
Brew Wharf	Brew Wharf Yard, Stoney St	020 7378 6601	££	11 pm	Unusual comfort food and tasty home brews.
Cantina Vinopolis	1 Bank End	087 0899 8856	££££	10.30 pm	Gourmet food and wine at a bad museum? Believe it.
Champor-Champor	62 Weston St	020 7403 4600	£££	10.15pm	Jaw-droppingly inspired high-end Malaysian cuisine. Totally impressive.
Feng Sushi	13 Stoney St	020 7407 8744	££	10 pm	The best sushi in London and available to takeaway. Dangerous!
Fish!	Cathedral St	020 7407 3803	££	10.30 pm	Great fish. Simple. Let it have its exclamation mark.
Hing Loong	159 Borough High St	020 7378 8100	£	11 pm	Stupidly cheap. Very cheerful. The duck rocks.
Nando's	215 Clink St	020 7357 8662	££	11 pm	Peri-peri madness underneath the arches.
Roast	The Floral Hall, Stoney St	084 5034 7300	££	9.30 pm	Meat, glorious meat. High-end food. Fab location.
ilka	Southwark St	020 7378 6161	£££	11.30 pm	Curry house that won't damage your arse in the morning.
Tapas Brindisa	18 Southwark St	020 7357 8880	££	11 pm	If you can bear the crowds, lovely market-bordering eaterie.
Tas Borough High Street	72 Borough High St	020 7403 7200	££	11 pm	Reduce your carbon footprint: come here and feel 1000 miles away.
Wright Bros Oyster Bar	11 Stoney St	020 7403 9554	£££	10.30 pm	Tastebuds say no, but libido says YES.

Key: £ : Under £10 / ££ : £10–£20 / £££ : £20–£30 / ££££ : £30–£40 / £££££: £40+
** : Does not accept credit cards./ † : Accepts only American Express / ††: Accepts only Visa and Mastercard*
Time listed refers to kitchen closing time on weekend nights

Map 107 • Shad Thames

Butlers Wharf Chop House	36 Shad Thames	020 7403 3403	£££	11 pm	What better place for British best than under Tower Bridge?
Delfina	50 Bermondsey St	020 7357 0244	££££	11 pm	Gallery/restaurant offering works of art on your plate.
Le Pont de la Tour	36 Shad Thames	020 7403 8403	£££££	11 pm	Blair & Clinton's rendezvous. Posh but gosh!
M Manze Pie and Mash	87 Tower Bridge Rd	020 7407 2985	£	2.30 pm	As English as it gets. Try it once.
Magdalen	152 Tooley St	020 7403 1342	££££	10.30 pm	Forever fascinating Franco-Spanish cuisine.
Village East	171 Bermondsey St	020 7357 6082	£££	11 pm	Superior food. Slick surroundings.

Map 108 • Bermondsey

Poppy Hana	169 Jamaica Rd	020 7237 9416	£	11 pm	Cute as a button Japanese. Don't be put off by the food sculptures.

Map 109 • Southwark Park

Mayflower	117 Rotherhithe St	020 7237 4088	£££	9.30 pm	The pub Sunday Lunch was invented for.

Map 110 • Park Rotherhithe (West) / Canada Water

Simplicity	1 Tunnel Rd	020 7232 5174	££	10.30 pm	Boldly goes where no restaurant has gone before: Rotherhithe.
Café Silka	30 Albion St	020 7237 2122	££		Wishes it were somewhere else, but nicely done.
The Rainbow	33 Brunel Rd	020 7231 0028	£££	11 pm	Will make you happily plump.

Map 111 • Rotherhithe (East) Surrey Quays

Café Nabo	Surrey Docks Farm, Rotherhithe St	020 7231 1010	££	10 pm	Rid the toxins with a healthy farmyard lunch.

Map 112 • Kennington / Elephant and Castle

Dragon Castle	114 Walworth Rd	020 7277 3300	££	11 pm	Odd locale for such a curious pocket of culinary authenticity.
Lobster Pot	3 Kennington Ln	020 7582 5556	£££	10.30 pm	Dine to a soundtrack of seagull caws. We don't kid.

Map 113 • Walworth

La Luna	380 Walworth Rd	020 7277 1991	££	11 pm	Ignore exterior. It's the garlic bread inside that counts.

Map 115 • Old Kent Road (East)

Roma Café	21 Peckham Park Rd	020 7639 7730	£	10 pm	Escape Peckham and enjoy a good fry-up here.

Map 117 • Deptford (West)

Yellow House	37 Plough Way	020 7231 8777	£££	10.30 pm	The food stands out as much as the yellow building.

Map 119 • Deptford (East)

Kaya House	37 Deptford Broadway	020 8692 1749	££	10.45 pm	Tiny but excellent. Toilet is in the kitchen!

Map 120 • Greenwich

Goddard's Pie Shop Booth	Fountain Court (off Greenwich Church Street)	080 0862 0400	£	6pm	Pie n' mash n' eels. Only at the weekend.
Greenwich Park Bar & Grill	1 King William Walk	020 8853 7860	£££	10 pm	Kobe steak burgers. Nuff said.
The Hill	89 Royal Hill	020 8691 3626	£££	10 pm	Bistro food. Local favourite.
Inside	19 Greenwich South St	020 8265 5060	£££	11 pm	Surprisingly sophisticated worldly foods for a modest local.
Piano Restaurant	131 Greenwich High Rd	020 8853 3020	£££££	2 am	Fish swim in the chandeliers. Get the idea?
Rivington Grill	178 Greenwich High Rd	020 8293 9270	£££	11 pm	Good for brekkie or dinner before a Picturehouse movie

Map 121 • Camberwell (West)

Kazakh Kyrgyz Restaurant	158 Camberwell Rd	020 7277 2228	££	1 am	Unsuspectingly tantalising Central Asian cuisine—belly dancer included.
New Dewaniam	225 Camberwell New Rd	020 7703 9318	£	12 am	Mouth-watering Indian takeaway for a tenner.
Su-Thai	16 Coldharbour Ln	020 7738 5585	££	10 pm	Reassuringly delicious Massaman curry & corn fritters.

Map 122 • Camberwell (East)

Angels & Gypsies	29 Camberwell Church St	020 7703 5984			Like some kind of Dali-Almodovar fantasy
Garavaggio's	47 Camberwell Church St	020 7207 1612	£	11 pm	Cheap Italian with impressive fare. Stands out from the rest.

Map 123 • Peckham

Bellenden Brasserie	168 Bellenden Rd	020 7252 9424	£££	11 pm	Too classy for us. We're too busy sniggering at "bell-end".

Map 124 • Peckham East (Queen's Road)

805 Bar Restaurant	805 Old Kent Rd	020 7639 0808	£££	12 am	West African oasis. In Peckham.

Map 126 • New Cross

Manzes	204 Deptford High St	020 8692 2375	£	5 pm	Who ate all the pies? You'll certainly want to.

Map 127 • Coldharbour Lane / Herne Hill (West)

Café Prov	2 Half Moon Ln	020 7978 9228	£££	10 pm	Local art (for sale) decorates this relaxed restaurant/bar/ cafe.
Ichiban Sushi	58 Atlantic Rd	020 7738 7006	£	11 pm	The bee's knees.
The Lounge	56 Atlantic Rd	020 7733 5229	£	10 pm	A local favourite for breakfast, recovery and hanging on weekends.
New Fujiyama	5 Vining St	020 7737 6583	£	10.30 pm	This place blows Wagamama's out of the water.

Map 128 • Denmark Hill / Herne Hill (East)

Lombok	17 Half Moon Ln	020 7733 7131	£££	10.30 pm	From Stir-fries to curries, a no-fuss pan-Asian standby.
Number 22	22 Half Moon Ln	020 7095 9922	££££	10.30 pm	Gorge yourself on Spanish wine, sherry and loads of brilliant tapas.

Map 129 • East Dulwich

The Palmerston	91 Lordship Ln	020 8693 1629	££££	10 pm	Gastropub that's a lot more gastro than pub.
Sea Cow	37 Lordship Ln	020 8693 3111	££	11 pm	Fishmonger meets chip shop with Billingsgate beauties.

Map 130 • Peckham Rye

The Rye	31 Peckham Rye	020 7639 5397	££	10 pm	A pocket of delicious East Dulwich swank [illegible]
Thai Corner Cafe	44 Northcross Rd	020 8299 4041	££*	11 pm	Tiny, laidback neighbourhood cafe.

Map 131 • Vauxhall / Albert Embankment

Thai Pavillion East	78 Kennington Rd	020 7582 6333	££££	12 am	Thai food you will crave in retro round room.

Map 132 • Battersea (West)

The Greyhound	136 Battersea High St	020 7978 7021	£££	12 am	Quietly excellent gastro-pub. Worth seeking out.
Ransom's Dock	35 Parkgate Rd	020 7223 1611	£££	11 pm	Friendly, stylish, likes wine and children.

Map 134 • South Lambeth

ar Estrella	115 Old South Lambeth Rd	020 7793 1051	£	12 am	Football on telly, tapas in tummy. The heart of Little Portugal.
anton Arms	177 S Lambeth Rd	020 7582 0965	£££		Recently acquired by Anchor & Hope folks. Bring on the yuppies.
lot Stuff	19 Wilcox Rd	020 7720 1480	£	10 pm	Hard to find. Slightly dingy. Mental Staff. Amazing food.

Key: £ : Under £10 / ££ : £10–£20 / £££ : £20–£30 / ££££ : £30–£40 / £££££: £40+
** : Does not accept credit cards./ † : Accepts only American Express / ††: Accepts only Visa and Mastercard*
Time listed refers to kitchen closing time on weekend nights

Map 135 • Oval

Adulis	44 Brixton Rd	020 7587 0055	£	11 pm	C'mon, it's yummmy and cheap. And we can't cook Eritrean.
The Bonnington Café	11 Vauxhall Grove	019 3257 1323	£*	10.30 pm	Cute as a vegan button.
Kebab and Hamburger Bar	32 Clapham Rd	020 7820 8846	£*	10 pm	Fancy a doner kebab? Go nowhere else.

Map 136 • Putney

Chakalaka	136 Upper Richmond Rd	020 8789 5696	££	10.30 pm	A truly zebra-fied exterior but fantastically authentic South African food.
La Mancha	32 Putney High St	020 8780 1022	££	11 pm	Awesome lobster
Ma Goa	242 Upper Richmond Rd	020 8780 1767	££	11 pm	Amazing regional Goan cuisine.
Moomba Bar & Kitchen	5 Lacy Rd	020 8785 9151	£££	12 am	Messiah of brunch.
Olé Restaurant and Bar	240 Upper Richmond Rd	020 8788 8009	££	11.30 pm	Paella fanatics get in line.
Talad Thai	320 Upper Richmond Rd	020 8789 8084	££	10.30 pm	Thai-ny, family-run restaurant with Thai supermarket, cooking classes and Thai regulars.
Wallace & Co	146 Upper Richmond Rd	020 8780 0052	££	11 pm	Ethics on a plate from TV's Gregg Wallace.

Map 137 • Wandsworth (West)

Miraj	123 Putney Bridge Rd	020 8875 0799	£	10 pm	Curry in a hurry? Cheap, tasty take away joint.
Yia Mas	40 Upper Richmond Rd	020 8871 4671	££	11 pm	Cosy, welcoming Greek/Cypriot place. No plate smashing.

Map 138 • Wandsworth (Central)

Brady's	513 Old York Rd	020 8877 9599	££	11 pm	Up-market fish and chip cafe and take-away.
Kathmandu Valley	5 West Hill	020 8871 0240	££	11.45 pm	Nepalese is the new black (read: curry).

Map 139 • Wandsworth (East)

The Fish Club	189 St John's Hill	020 7978 7115	££	10 pm	The thinking man's chippie.
Steam	55 E Hill	020 8704 4680	£££	10.30 pm	Walks past the bar and find yourself in bistro heaven.

Map 140 • Clapham Junction / Northcote Rd

Cafe Parisienne	225 Lavender Hill	020 7924 5523	£	5 pm	Massive sarnies and baked potatoes
I Sapori di Stefano Cavallini	146 Northcote Rd	020 7228 2017	££	11 pm	Totally authentic. Pasta made on site daily.

Map 141 • Battersea (South)

The Lavender	171 Lavender Hill	020 7978 5242	££	11 pm	Rustic European eclectic—stellar cassoulets

Map 142 • Clapham Old Town

Benny's	30 North St	020 7622 5868	£*	11.30pm	Marvel at Benny's chest hair, chat and fish and chips.
Mooli	36 Old Town	020 7627 1166	££	11 pm	Good twist on the Italian local.
Tom Ilic	123 Queenstown Rd	020 7622 0555	£££	10.30 pm	British fare that's the business—a result of hard-earned talent.
Trinity	4 The Polygon	020 7622 1199	£££	10.30 pm	How to do local dining really quite fantastically well.

Map 143 • Clapham High Street

Alba Pizzeria	3 Bedford Rd	020 7733 3636	££	11.30 pm	A necessary pit stop before a Clapham night out.
Café Wanda	153 Clapham High St	020 7738 8760	££	10.30 pm	Back away from the fantastic dessert counte real slow.
The Fish Club	57 Clapham High St	020 7720 5853	££	10 pm	Posh fish and chips, worth the extra clams.
Gastro	67 Venn St	020 7627 0222	££	12 am	Low-lit gallic bistro extraordinaire
The Pepper Tree	19 Clapham Common South Side	020 7622 1758	£*	11 pm	Speedy Thai with soul.
The Rapscallion	75 Venn St	020 7787 6555	££££	10 pm	Good fall-back. Wee bit dear.
San Marco Pizzeria	126 Clapham High St	020 7622 0452	££†	11.30 pm	Arguably the best pizza outside Italy—take that New York!

Tsunami	5 Voltaire Rd	020 7978 1610	££££	10.30 pm	The new Nobu. Unbelievable. Unfortunate name.

Map 144 • Stockwell / Brixton (West)

Franco Manca	4 Electric Lane	020 7738 3021	££	5 pm	Organic pizza perfection for around a fiver. Worth any wait.
Speedy Noodle	506 Brixton Rd	020 7326 4888	£*	1 am	Prime location and the cheapest, worst food in Brixton.
SW9 Bar Cafe	11 Dorrell Pl	020 7738 3116	£	9 pm	Great hangover curing breakfasts (and hangover causing booze).

Map 146 • Earlsfield

Carluccio's	537 Garratt Ln	020 8947 4651	££	11:30 pm	Sensational pasta dishes and optional curbside setting.

Map 147 • Balham (West)

The Bombay Bicycle Club	95 Nightingale Lane	020 8673 6217	££	10 pm	Award winning curries.
Chez Bruce	2 Bellevue Rd	020 8672 0114	££££	10.30 pm	Worth its fancy-pants (read Michelin) star.

Map 148 • Balham (East)

Dish Dash	11 Bedford Hill	020 8673 5555	££	11 pm	Tasty food. Tiny portions. Laid back vibe.
The Exhibit	12 Balham Station Rd	020 8772 6556	££	10pm	Cool, up-market venue. Friendly, laid back vibe.
Harrison's	15 Bedford Hill	020 8675 6900	££	10.30 pm	Great food if you can tolerate the 'look at me!' crowd.

Map 150 • Brixton

Asmara	386 Coldharbour Ln	020 7737 4144	££	11.15 pm	Disconcerting but delicious curry with pancakes to mop it up.
Franco Manca	4 Market Row	020 8747 4822	££		London's best pizza? Eclectic concoctions of sour dough goodness comes west.
Khan's	24 Brixton Water Lane	020 7326 4460	££	11 pm	Great curry, and BYO to boot. Have it!
The Lounge	56 Atlantic Rd	020 7733 5229	£	10pm	A local favourite for breakfast, recovery and hanging on weekends.
Negril	132 Brixton Hill	020 8674 8798	£	10 pm	Tasty Carribean with veg options (which are joy).
Opus Café	89 Acre Ln	0207 737 1414	£	6 pm	Cakes and coffee. Niceness.
Upstairs Bar and Restaurant	89 Acre Ln	020 7733 8855	££££	10.30 pm	A real find. Getting discovered. Sshhh.

Map 151 • Tooting Bec

Mirage	215 Upper Tooting Rd	020 8772 4422	£	10.30 pm	Better than Mirch Masala? We think so.
Masaledar Kitchen	121 Upper Tooting Rd	020 8767 7676	££	11 pm	Last word in top-notch Indian cuisine
Mirch Masala	213 Upper Tooting Rd	020 8672 7500	£	12 am	Cheap, no frills, award-winning curries. Sublime.
Spice Village	32 Upper Tooting Rd	020 8672 0710	£	11 pm	Go for grilled

Map 152 • Tooting Broadway

Jaffna House	90 Tooting High St	020 8672 7786	££	12 am	Mediocre curry fare beneath flourescent bulbs.
Radha Krishna Bhavan	86 Tooting High St	020 8682 0969	££	11.30 pm	Busy, buzzing, bhavan of South Indian curry.
Rick's Cafe	122 Mitcham Rd	020 8767 5219	£££	11 pm	Tooting's best kept culinary secret.
Sate Bello	8 Amen Corner	020 8767 5225	££	11 pm	A kiss on each cheek for every diner. Homely Italian.
Urban Coffee	74 Tooting High St	020 8682 9479	£*	10 pm	Nifty WiFi caff in the bowels of Tooting.

So are we still in the Recession? Who knows? Who cares? We're getting used to this boom and bust cycle but we've cut up all our credit cards. When it comes to retail, people will always spend whether money or no (that's how we got in this fine mess remember Stanley?), it's just that with little of the stuff about, people are more discerning about what they spend their hard earned cash/State Benefits on. And of course if we didn't spend we would never collectively crawl out of this endless dirge of gloom. As the well-observed slogan on the reusable eco-shopping bag from Modern Toss (available at **Magma, Map 12**) says, "Buy More Shit Or We're All Fucked". Indeed. But if the economic crisis is teaching us anything it's to be more picky about what we purchase and for retailers not just to deliver the goods but also all the extras that we, as polite English people, so foolishly see as just "extras". Primarily what I mean is, that intangible thing that contributes to a satisfying shopping experience and brings a customer back to the same store again and again: excellent service - helpfulness, genuine smiles and interest in the product and the customer. Beautiful packaging, loyalty cards, discounts, samples, invites to in-store events all help too. In an adverse way, consumers have never had more power than now to demand what they want or - as important - don't want. So just make sure you buy more cool shit as opposed to any old shit.

The British High Street is certainly changing and support for independent shops is growing. A leaning towards handmade items and crafts which support local designers and artisans--Columbia Road and Cheshire Street are hotspots for this kind of thing. Yes there are a lot of these shops cropping up that purely sell "beautiful things" like **Shelf (Map 91)**, **Constructive Lives (Map 25)**, **Of Cabbages And Kings (Map 64)**, and, (if it's a beauty of a decaying kind you're looking for) **Viktor Wynd's Shop of Horrors (Map 87)** to name a few (and we like them). But when it comes to fashion we also like to know that a little bit of love has been sprinkled into the making of an item. Special mention here must go to Amy Anderson of **Comfort Station (Map 91)** who produces the most thoughtful and whimsical pieces of jewellery and **Vivien of Holloway (Map 74)** who has built a real niche following but whose fabulous 1950s tailoring would make any gal feel like a doll. Both have gorgeous, well-fitted, unique shop spaces too.

For blokes, **Folk (Map 5)** are renowned for their limited collections, particularly shoes which are hand-stitched (hence the price tag).

Part of this trend is Pop-Up Shops which are installed for a few months at a time sometimes displaying the work of a single designer/company or else a co-operative of independent designers. Not only is this a thrifty way of setting up shop in these uncertain times, it also provides a showcase for new young things so always worth a look. These tend to appear around Carnaby Street and Spitalfields especially in the summer.

The Big Boys

When it comes to department stores, **Selfridges (Map 2)** is without a doubt the daddy--arguably (and the emphasis is on that word depending o your budget) you can just get everything yo need from here but if you're strapped, at least g and marvel at the window displays. **Harvey Nic (Map 37)** and **Harrods (Map 37)** are very muc for ladies who lunch, and the Knightsbridge se use them like corner shops--that's not to sa they don't have their uses. For a more persona touch, **Fenwick (Map 2)** and **Liberty (Map 10** are wonderful British institutions which take yo far from the madding crowd. If all these close quarters encounters get up your nose head t **Whiteleys (Map 30)** or the Behemoth that **Westfield Shopping Centre (Map 33)**.

Haute Et High Street

For flexing that plastic, Bond Street has alwa been the place to spend but Bruton Stree which branches off the main drag, is setti quite a precedent with **Matthew Williamso (Map 9)**, **Stella McCartney (Map 9)** and **Dian Von Furstenburg (Map 9)** all in residenc Always one to mix things up and throw us c track, **Marc Jacobs' (Map 9)** London store is be found on Mount Street--check out the Ma for Marc Jacobs range for affordable design garb--by which we mean £3 and upwards. Y really. If you want to feel like Alice down t rabbit hole, make a trip to **Dover Street Mark (Map 9)**, owned by Rei Kawakubo of Com Des Garçons--a real experience even if you not buying. Throwing down the gauntlet wh it comes to experiential retail is **LN-CC (M 86)**. For those of us in the real world, **Topsh**

(Map 3) is the grand kahuna of high street shopping--seventh heaven on three floors for fashionistas. For super-slick, sharp ready-to-wear you can't beat Spanish stores, **Zara (Map 2)** and **Mango (Map 3)** who both do high street with an edge and turnover is pretty quick to ensure their stock remains covetable. New contenders for higher end high-street include **Cos (Map 10)** and **Hoss Intropia (Map 10)**, and let's not forget our Stateside cousins who have sent ripples of excitement through the fash pack by opening flagship stores of **Anthropologie**, **Banana Republic**, and **Abercrombie & Fitch** all **(Map 10)** in the big smoke. There are also little shopping oases to be found in the capital. St Christopher's Place is hidden behind the hustle and bustle of Oxford Street and houses cool European brands like **Marimekko (Map 2)** alongside more familiar fare. Kingly Court (behind Carnaby Street--itself a great shopping spot for trend-led labels) has independent boutiques such as t-shirt shop **Super Superficial (Map 10)**. The area around Seven Dials in Covent Garden which includes Neal's Yard is eclectic with high-end boutiques like **Orla Kiely (Map 13)** and **Miss Lala's Boudoir (Map 13)** on Monmouth and skatewear at **Slam City Skates (Map 13)** and **Superdry (Map 13)** on Earlham. Edgy fashion abounds out East: head to **Good Hood (Map 84)** to start your shopping crawl or **No One (Map 91)** where they've got everything we want before we even know we want it.

Back To The Future

'intage' seems to be the term for anything over ve years old nowadays but London's vintage and secondhand) scene is thriving. Some of the est-known, best-loved shops include **Rellik Map 25)** in Portobello, **Annie's (Map 80)** in lington (a favourite of La Moss), and **Beyond etro (Map 91)** and **Absolute Vintage (Map 1)** in Shoreditch (famous hunting ground for ylists). If you want to hear what the young, ylish and clueless get up to head to **Rokit (Map 1)** and eavesdrop on the staff's mindnumbing nversations. For genuine thrift, the turnover goods in our charity shops is mind-boggling. **xfam Dalston (Map 86)** is renowned for being good rummage: it's hit and miss but then at's the nature of the thrifting beast. Most rdy shoppers will happily tread the city twice over for good charity shop finds but if you want some certainty of finding designer threads you can't beat the British Red Cross in both **Victoria (Map 19)** and **Chelsea (Map 45)** where you will discover the likes of Ralph Lauren, Armani and pairs of Manolos amongst the usual flotsam and jetsam. The **Notting Hill Housing Trust (Map 35)** is also a reliable source of local celebrities' cast-offs from like, yesterday. For all you true vintage fashion fiends who want to mingle with like-minded souls and find genuine vintage togs (i.e. pre-1980s) the **Frock Me! Vintage Fashion Fair (Map 45)** and **Anita's Vintage Fashion Fair (Map 135)** are unequalled for choice and variety. Wake up and smell the mould.

Keep On Running, Cycling, Skating Etc.

Lillywhite's (Map 10) is the obvious place to go for cheap sportswear--it has earned a bit of a bargain basement tag where once it was prestigious (the Lillywhites were instrumental in the game of cricket during the 19th century) but it doesn't stop the shoppers pouring in, and tourists buying their favourite London football team shirts. **Sweatshop (Map 17)** is a chain of stores but the original Teddington shop is frequented by world-class athletes as well as Sunday joggers. The staff really know their stuff (why is this so rare!?). An equally good indie chain is **Runners Need (Map 20)**. If it's sweatshop-made kit you're after head to **Niketown (Map 2)**, which is as scary as the name suggests. Though we're no Amsterdam, the economic shitstorm has inspired many Londoners to don skintight clothes and take to two wheels. If you're after a battered old charmer of a bike, **Recycling (Map 112)** does a fab job at selling secondhand wheels. If you've had your designer bike nicked, head down to Brick Lane at the weekend and buy it off some dodgy geezer. **Slam City Skates (Map 13)** is the only dedicated place for Southbank skaters to get their duds.

Home Sweet Home

John Lewis (Map 2) is a British standard (read: very sensible) and has been the store of choice for middle-class couples' wedding lists for decades. With fantastic staff (who all get a share of the profits) and well-made stuff, their maxim is "never knowingly undersold". **Twentytwentyone (Map 80)** is a designer's wet dream selling originals as well as new items. So impressive is their collection that they often lend out furniture to film companies who want the authentic look of an era on set. **SCP (Maps 30 & 84)** is perfect for unnecessary yet tasteful knick-knacks. The wonderfully named **Timorous Beasties (Map 6)** make wickedly amusing wallpapers--their most famous being a toile de jouy design for modern days (spot the alcopop-drinking chavs and the Gherkin in the background). **Labour and Wait (Map 91)** does the retro home stuff better than most. If you want personable, "Where can I find one of these?" type of service try **Russell's Hardware & DIY (Map 151)** in Tooting or **KTS The Corner (Map 86)** in Dalston.

Electricity For You And Me

Apple have done a very good job at monopolising our lives and getting everyone to 'Think Different,' so why you'd need to go anywhere other than the **Apple Store (Map 10)** we're not sure. However, traditionally, Tottenham Court Road is the hideout for the anally retentive Hi-Fi nut and the nerdoid pirate radio enthusiast a-like. The area positively thrums with electricity. In all cases it's best to shop around, play prices against each other and barter until you get the lowest price--often cash payment will get you well below the RRP. **Computer Exchange (Map 3)** is the one-stop shop for gaming, DVDs, computing and phones, which--as the name suggests--will part-exchange and knock money off for cash transactions. For audiovisual, **Richer Sounds (Map 106)** is a trusted chain, and if we're talking electronics in the purist sense, **Maplin (Map 3)** is geek central. Whether you'll get anyone who knows what they're talking about is another matter. Photography enthusiasts should check out the **London Camera Exchange (Map 24)** for old-school SLRs and digital cameras and **Red Dot Cameras** for Leicas **(Map 7)**.

Food For Thought

We like our food in London and the more diverse the better. Whether it's chowing down on burgers from Lucky Chip and Vietnamese baguettes from Banh Mi 11 down **Broadway Market (Map 89)** or fresh scallops and some raclette down **Borough Market (Map 106)** before moseying on down to **Maltby Street Market (Map 107)** for gelato, we're not afraid to say, "Please Sir, I want some more" (mainly because we're paying for it). **Whitecross Street (Map 7)** also has an impressive selection of foodie stalls. We have New York (and in particular, the Magnolia Bakery) to thank for the invasion of cupcake stores but the original and best is the **Hummingbird Bakery (Map 29)** which makes Red Velvet cupcakes that taste like little pieces of baked orgasm. Just try and restrain yourself from licking the last morsels of frosting from the paper. Nostalgia for old style sweetie shops can be bought at **Mrs. Kibble's Olde Sweet Shop (Map 10)** whether your fetish is for cola cubes, sherbet flying saucers or Wham bars. Numerous Italian delis can be found around the city selling cured meats, buffalo mozzarella, biscotti and everything else that Mama used to make - **Camisa & Son (Map 11)** is small but crammed full of delicacies, while **Spiazzo (Map 53)** i bigger and sparklier. Organic freaks can bypas the rather average Whole Foods chain and head to local independent places like **The Grocery (Map 91)** or **Mother Earth (Map 75)**. For th cheapest and best coffee-to-go in Soho try th **Algerian Coffee Stores (Map 11)**. Looking fo Unicum? Look no further than **Gerry's Spirit Shop (Map 11)** where you can find obscur liquors like Zubrowka Bison Grass Vodka an good quality Cachaça.

Art And Craft Supplies

Crafty types and closet Van Goghs can pick u supplies at **Cass Art (Map 80)** three-store flagship store in Islington. There's everythin here for aspiring Manga cartoonists ar weekend watercolourists alike, and lots fun bits and pieces for school holiday/rair day projects in the basement. Much of th high quality stock can be found at cut-pri throughout the year--stock up on Moleski note and sketchbooks which are frequen marked down. **The London Graphic Cent (Map 13)** has more design-led stock as well fine art material attracting architects and graph designers. Known for its greeting cards a stationary, **Paperchase (Map 3)** on Tottenha Court Road also has--true to its name-- astonishing array of handmade papers on top floor--from flocked designs to fibrous pape made with dried flowers. You've got to love **Blade Rubber (Map 4)** just for its name, and for keeping sketches, photos, and memories intact. **Wyvern Bindery (Map 6)** is one of few of its kind to offer book-making services.

Axes, Saxes, Drums, Strums…

Traditionally, Tin Pan Alley (real name: Denmark Street) has always been the hub of musical creativity in the city. Back in the day when rents were affordable, a community grew up around this little side street which went on to see Jimi Hendrix and The Beatles record in the basements, and a young Elton John sitting on the rooftops penning "Your Song". Nowadays you may spot Jack White trying out a Digitech Whammy or Jonny Greenwood looking for some new toy to replace his Marshall Shred Master. If we had to choose a couple, we'd buy Macaris for cheapness and **Wumjos (Map 12)** for friendliness. There are plenty of independent music stores to be found in London's boroughs, and often they are specialists, happy to have a natter about what exactly it is that you're looking for and what the weather's like. Try **Top Wind (Map 104)** for all your flute needs, **Duke of Uke (Map 91)** for banjo and ukulele-lovers, though the staff are a little arsey, and **Phil Parker (Map)** for all you jazz cats needing a hand with your brass. For the medieval troubadour in your life, **Hobgoblin (Map 3)** has its own luthier who makes lutes. Try **Ray Man (Map 71)** in Camden for unusual ethnic instruments and drone boxes. For the largest collection of sheet music in Europe, **Chappel of Bond Street (Map 11)** (now in Wardour Street but they've kept the name) is your destination. One thing though, will you instrument shop assistants please stop jamming while you're talking to us?

Music Non Stop

The slow, painful death of the CD can be seen in almost every indie music store in London, and it coincides with the financial doom and gloom that has befallen Virgin Records, Zavvi and Sanctuary (thankfully we still have one branch of **Fopp (Map 12)** left). Bizarrely, the death march of the traditional record shop has become a moonwalk: more and more boutique record shops are springing up selling new and used wax. The Berwick Street vinyl epicenter may have been drained of late, but other parts of London have become haunts for us of haunched posture and good taste. **Sister Ray (Map 11)** is forever teetering on the edge, but **Revival Records (Map 11)** is the long gone Reckless Records' offspring. If you find yourself on the Essex Road, have a gander at **Flashback (Map 83)** and **Haggle Vinyl (Map 83)**: you're sure to find something to please and appeal in the former and appall in the latter. The **Music & Video Exchange (Map 29, 71)** in Notting Hill was way ahead of its time and has been the swapshop of choice for years, it's still the king as far as we're concerned. When south of the river, do as Camberwellians do and drop in at **Rat Records (Map 121)**. To guarantee a withering look from a record shop lifer go and discuss the use of naivety in Legowelt's output at **Phonica (Map 10)** in Soho. Catch some indie shmucks at **Pure Groove (Map 15)** in Holloway, and many a muso's all-round fave, **Sounds of the Universe (Map 11)** is owned by the **Soul Jazz** label.

Antiques And Bric-A-Brac, Flea Markets And Stalls

There may have been a time, dear reader, when Markets sold fleas. And brics and bracs. Perhaps we used to know what these elusive words meant. Frankly, we numbskulls at NFT don't care about etymology unless it's secondhand and collectable. First stop on many shoppers" lists-both serious collectors and weekend browsers--are **Alfie's Antique Market (Map 76)** and **Gray's Antique Market (Map 2)**. Here you'll find art, antiques, jewellery, vintage clothing and rare books all housed under one roof.

Once the centre of the Britpop phenomenon in the '90s and a thriving mini-metropolis for vintage and antique stalls, Camden is now rather anaesthetised but packs of German and French kids on school trips still rifle through the emo and goth gear that overfloweth. There is some gold to be found in shops like **Episode (Map 71)** and **Rokit (Map 71)**, and **Aldo Liquidation (Map 71)** is good for a bargain (or practising your rugby tackle). Certainly the place still has atmosphere.

Well-known to scavengers, **Camden Passage (Map 80)** in Angel rather confusingly, is a welcome retreat from the mallrat-filled N1 centre across the road in Islington. The Mall and also Pierrepoint Arcade (tucked away behind the passage) offer a cornucopia of clothing, jewelry, military paraphernalia, homewares, prints, and a host of other bits and bobs. On Saturdays, market stalls set up in the street and surprises like original Givenchy earrings from 1978 (4 quid!) can be salvaged from amongst the knick-knacks. This is another brilliant little vintage bazaar continually threatened by chains and redevelopment. Go protest by buying any old crap.

Brick Lane (Map 91) also opens up on Sunday and in the summer there is a real carnival feel with fruit and veg, plumbing and DIY bits and pieces, electricals, toiletries, furniture (dentist's chair anyone?), clothes, DVDs lining the lane and spiling into Sclater Street. Watch your bags and all the silly haircuts. Brick Lane also has the added advantage of having many a watering hole and curry house where you can stop and people-watch if it all makes you want to go all 'Falling Down' on their asses. If that's not your thing, (Up)Market is held in the **Truman Brewery (Map 91)** every Sunday and showcases new designers as well as housing some vinyl, vintage and gourmet street food. **Spitalfields Market (Map 91)** has been tarted up to be a sanitized precinct of chain stores but there are still some unusual boutiques and independent shops.

The triumvirate of hipster markets consists of **Columbia Road Market (Map 91)**, **Broadway Market (Map 89)**, and Chatsworth Road Market (just north of Map 90). Also in the East is **Roman Road Market (Map 94)**. It's proper gorblimey, lor' love a duck cockerney territory but you may find yourself soaking up the atmosphere more than finding anything of real interest. If Lady Luck is stroking your inner thigh you get some great bargains Sarf of the river at **Deptford Market (Map 119)**.

Though certainly not as bountiful in treasure as the car boot sales of other parts of the country London does have some. The best in Zone 2 is definitely the **Battersea Car Boot Sale (Map 141)**, a sprawling mess that kicks off around midday is a godsend to all us alcoholics and narcoleptics.

Map 1 • Marylebone (West)

Green Valley	36 Upper Berkeley St	020 7402 7385	Essential Lebanese supermarket: get the manoushe.
Maroush Deli	45 Edgware Rd	020 7723 0773	Lebanese food emporium—fresh coffee, ice-creams and best houmous in town.
Phil Parker	106 Crawford St	020 7486 8206	Brass-o-rama.
Primark	499 Oxford St	020 7495 0420	Enter the scrum.
Spymaster	3 Portman Sq	020 7486 3885	Stab-proof vests, in house P.I., you know, the usual.
Totally Swedish	32 Crawford St	020 7224 9300	Salt liquorice and Plopp bars for scandiphiles.

Map 2 • Marylebone (East)

Browns South Molton Street	24 S Molton St	020 7514 0016	Sleep with someone rich, then bring them here.
The Button Queen	76 Marylebone Ln	020 7935 1505	Antique buttons galore for budding fashionistas.
Content Beauty/Wellbeing	14 Bulstrode Street	020 3075 1006	Exceptional selection of organic beauty products.
Daunt Books	83 Marylebone High St	020 7224 2295	Almost intimidatingly beautiful book shop.
Divertimenti	33 Maryelbone High St	020 7935 0689	Go and pretend you need a £500 coffee machine.
Duffer of St George	268 Oxford St	020 7836 3722	Rude tees.
Fenwick	63 New Bond St	020 7629 9161	A welcome escape from Oxford Street for those in the know.
French Sole	61 Marylebone Ln	020 7486 0021	Spendy but these pumps can withstand London's terrible pavements.
Gray's Antique Market	58 Davies St	020 7629 7034	A world of bygone beauty a skip away from Bond Street.
John Lewis	278 Oxford St	020 7629 7711	Where John Betjeman would have gone if the world explode
La Fromagerie	2 Moxon St	020 7935 0341	Blow your inheritance on some Abbaye De Trois Vaux
Marimekko	16 St Christopher's Pl	020 7486 6454	Retro prints from Jackie Kennedy's favourite Finn.
Monocle	2 George St	020 7486 8770	From the folks who brought us the magazine with the same name, a store geared towards travel
Niketown	236 Oxford St	020 7612 0800	Like a real town! Owned by Nike! But without sweatshops.
Noa Noa	14 Gees Ct	020 7495 8777	Desirable Boho Danish label.
Paul Smith	38 Marylebone High St	020 7935 5384	Kitsch and dolls from the fashion designer. Don't ask why.
Paul Smith Sale Shop	23 Avery Row	020 7493 1287	Cheap designer suits. Sweet.
Romanian Charity Shop	Lamb's Conduit St	020 8761 2277	Good quality clothes, good cause, warm feeling inside.
Selfridges & Co	400 Oxford St	080 0123 400	A Mecca for the shopping elite who want everything.

Skandium	86 Marylebone High St	020 7935 2077	Ikea for grown-ups.
VV Rouleaux	102 Marylebone Ln	020 7224 5179	Trimmings and ribbons like you've never seen.
The Widescreen Center	47 Dorset St	020 7935 2580	Telescopes, binoculars, projectors, screens, film cameras & virtual reality.
Zara	242 Oxford St	020 7318 2700	Spiffy suits and cute casualwear from the Balearic brand.

Map 3 • Fitzrovia

Beard Papa	143 Oxford St	020 7494 9020	Cream puffs for Japanophiles.
British Museum shop	Great Russell St	020 7323 1234	Have you lost your Elgin Marbles?
Chess & Bridge	369 Euston Rd	020 7388 2404	Chess fetishists won't be able to control themselves here.
Computer Exchange	32 Rathbone Pl	084 5345 1664	Good selection of secondhand DVDs, games and gadgets.
Harmony	103 Oxford St	020 7734 5969	Also known as Butt Plugs R Us.
Hobgoblin Shop	24 Rathbone Pl	020 7323 9040	Folky paradise; impressive/amusing collection of alternative instruments.
Mango	225 Oxford St	020 7434 3694	Let's go Mango!
Maplin	218 Tottenham Ct Rd	020 7323 4411	A whole world of technical geeketry to immerse yourself in.
Paperchase	213 Tottenham Ct Rd	020 7467 6200	More than meets the eye to this high street card shop.
R.D. Franks	5 Winsley St	020 7636 1244	Fashion book and magazine emporium.
Scandinavian Kitchen	61 Great Titchfield St	020 7580 7161	Smorgasbord!
Stargreen Box Office	20 Argyll St	020 7734 8932	Try here for tickets to sold-out gigs.
Topshop	216 Oxford St	020 7636 7700	Kate Moss still loves it. We do too.
Topshop	36 Great Castle Street	084 4848 7487	Clothing for the New Generation.
Urban Outfitters	200 Oxford St	020 7907 0800	Heaps of streetwear and crazy things for your house.

Map 4 • Bloomsbury (West)

ɜlade Rubber Stamps Ltd	12 Bury Pl	0845 873 7005	Scrapbooking materials plus traditional and made-to-order rubber stamps
'inema Bookshop	13 Great Russel St	020 7637 0206	Shrine to literary study of the moving image.
ɜosh! Comics	39 Great Russell St	020 7636 1011	A Japanese school boy's wet dream. Comics galore!
ames Smith & Sons	53 New Oxford St	020 7836 4731	Umbrella shop - because you might just need one.
.ondon Review Bookshop	14 Bury Pl	020 7269 9030	Big books, big name personal appearances—and cake!
Maplin	218 Tottenham Ct Rd	020 7323 4411	A whole world of technical geeketry to immerse yourself in.
'aperchase	213 Tottenham Ct Rd	020 7467 6200	More than meets the eye to this high street card shop.
;hepherds Bookbinders	76 Southampton Row	020 7831 1151	Like a Continental papeterie; beautiful specialty paper and bookbinding.
'ork Cameras	18 Bury Pl	020 7242 7182	New and second hand, specializing in Canon.

Map 5 • Bloomsbury (East)

ntoni & Alison	43 Rosebery Ave	020 7833 2002	Home of "bonkers" fashion duo.
ibas Hair & Beauty	72 Marchmont St	020 7837 9555	Lovely, friendly hair salon, excellent prices, 15% student discount.
runswick Center	Hunter St	020 7883 6066	Brutalist shopping centre pushing the utopian/dystopian envelope
he Flash Centre	68 Marchmont St	020 7837 5649	Studio lighting specialists.
olk	49 Lamb's Conduit St	020 7404 6458	Great clothes, even better shoes.
nternational Magic	89 Clerkenwell Rd	020 7405 7324	When you need some tricks up your sleeve.
oy	Brunswick Centre	020 7833 3307	Funky Urban Outfitters type stuff, but cheaper.
lagma Concept Store	117 Clarkenwell Rd	020 7242 9503	Funky book & novelty shop.
omething	58 Lamb's Conduit St	020 7430 1516	For when you're looking for a little sumthin-sumthin

Map 6 • Clerkenwell

he Black Tulip	28 Exmouth Market	020 7689 0068	Think all florists are the same?
obbin Bicycles	397 St John St	020 7837 3370	Making commuting fun - London's nicest cycling enthusiast.
rindisa Retail	Borough Market Floral Hall	020 7713 1600	Chorizo, salchichon, Serrano ham—famed importers Brindisa have it all. The Family Business.
: One Jewellery	41 Exmouth Market	020 7713 6185	Gorgeous sparkly fings.
ondon Tattoo	332 Goswell Rd	020 7833 5996	Was on the telly. Caused quite a buzz.
and R Meats	399 St John St	020 7837 1781	So meat-savvy they'll even know the best cut on you.
etro Imagining	32 Great Sutton St	020 7865 0000	Photo processing.
ttoo Shop	58 Exmouth Market	020 7278 9526	Tatts for all the family.
norous Beasties	46 Amwell St	020 7833 5010	Outlandish prints for the daringly tasteless home.
yvern Bindery	56 Clerkenwell Rd	020 7490 7899	Book binding for theses, portfolios and presentations. Repairs and restoration.

lap 7 • Barbican / City Road (South)

ead & Honey	205 Whitecross St	020 7253 4455	Streetwear for discerning Hoxtonites.

lap 9 • Mayfair / Green Park

C	35 Dover St	020 7409 0121	Not cheap but so, so chic.
ane Von Furstenberg	25 Bruton St	020 7499 0886	Forget the LBD, every girl needs a DVF.
ver Street Market	17 Dover St	020 7518 0680	Serious designer wear for people with serious money.

Marc Jacobs	24 Mount St	020 7399 1690	Never out of fashion.
Matthew Williamson	28 Bruton St	020 7629 6200	The boy who knows how to dress real girls.
Stella McCartney	30 Bruton St	020 7518 3100	Stella's star keeps rising despite initial doubts in Fahionland.

Map 10 • Piccadilly / Soho (West)

Abercrombie & Fitch	7 Burlington Gardens	084 4412 5750	Like GAP but more expensive.
American Apparel	3 Carnaby St	020 7297 9400	25% off all sexual harrassment lawsuits.
Anthropologie	158 Regent St	020 7529 9800	Go check out the innovative window dressing if nothing else.
Apple Store	235 Regent Street	020 7153 9000	Get your hardware here so you can buy NFT apps.
Arigato	48 Brewer St	020 7287 1722	Japanese food store and sushi bar. Lychee jelly sweets, anyone?
b store	24 Savile Row	020 7734 6846	Tell the bank you'll look REALLY cool in these shoes.
Banana Republic	224 Regent St	020 7758 3550	Your Stateside buddies don't need to ship over your clothes anymore.
Behave	48 Lexington Sreet	020 7734 6876	Hipster clothes.
Beyond Retro Soho	58 Great Marlborough St	020 7434 1406	Biggest, original, live-bands-on-Saturday vintage.
The Black Pearl	10 Kingly Ct	020 7439 0702	Because your earrings should rock as hard as you do.
Burlington Arcade	Burlington Arcade & Piccadilly		Welcoming shoppers since 1819.
Cos	222 Regent St	020 7478 0400	COS you can. See what I did there?
The European Bookshop	5 Warwick St	020 7734 5259	For when you get sick of English.
Fortnum And Mason	181 Piccadilly	020 7734 8040	The world's poshest marmalades.
Freggo	27 Swallow St	020 7287 9506	Argentinean ice cream for insomniacs. About freakin' time.
Hamley's	188 Regent St	087 1704 1977	World's biggest toy store. Terrifying just before Christmas.
Hatchard's	187 Piccadilly	020 7439 9921	Still musty, floors still creak, despite being owned by The Man.
Hoss Intropia	211 Regent St	020 7287 3569	High-end high street.
Lazy Oaf	19 Fouberts Place	020 7033 4291	Rockin good little design shop with the emphasis on illustration
Liberty	214 Regent St	020 7734 1234	Splendid wood-panelled department store. Beautiful and obscure scents and perfumes.
Lillywhites	24 Lower Regent St	087 0333 9600	Good if you know exactly what you're looking for.
Mrs Kibble's Olde Sweet Shoppe	57 Brewer St	020 7734 6633	Tooth-rottingly good sweet shop. Who needs incisors, anyway
Muji	41 Carnaby St	020 7287 7323	Japanese chain hits London—simple, minimalist goods but great quality.
Phonica	51 Poland St	020 7025 6070	Cutting edge vinyl/CD shop; alas, no Michael Bolton in stock.
Playlounge	19 Beak St	020 7287 7073	Toys for adults, no not those types of toys.
Richard James	29 Savile Row	020 7434 0605	Bespoke contemporary Savile Row tailoring.
Rigby & Peller	22 Conduit St	084 5076 5545	Furnishers of the Queen's basement.
SKK (Lighting)	34 Lexington St	020 7434 4095	Change your bedroom ambiance, light up your love life.
Stella McCartney	30 Bruton St	020 7518 3100	Stella's star keeps rising despite initial doubts in Fashionland.
Twinkled	1 Kingly Ct	020 7734 1978	Awesome selection of vintage clothes and accessories.
Twosee	21 Fouberts	020 7494 3813	Many exclusives at this quirky boutique, for those that care.
The Vintage Magazine Shop	39 Brewer St	020 7439 8525	Yellowing magazines and a million student classic posters.
Whole Foods Market	69 Brewer St	020 7434 3179	Overwhelming selection of organic exotica.

Map 11 • Soho (Central)

Algerian Coffee Store	52 Old Compton St	020 7437 2480	Pick up some Blue Mountain beans and a 95p cappu-to-go.
American Retro	35 Old Compton St	020 7734 3477	Random hipster Americana junk. Recommended.
Bang Bang	9 Berwick St	020 7494 2042	Intimate secondhand clothes shop.
Calumet Trading	175 Wardour St	020 7434 1848	Cameras and accessories.
Chappell of Bond Street	152 Wardour St	020 7432 4400	...Which is actually on Wardour Street.
Cheapo Cheapo Records	53 Rupert St	020 7437 8272	The name's no lie - Cheapo records and DVDs.
Cowling & Wilcox	26 Broadwick St	020 7734 9556	Good arts supplies shop to spend your Monet in (groan!).
Gerry's	74 Old Compton St	020 7734 2053	A veritable alcoholic's Utopia.
I Camisa & Son	61 Old Compton St	020 7437 7610	The best Italian deli out of Italy.
Paradiso Boudoir	60 Dean St	020 7287 6913	Sexier than most sex shops.
Revival Records	30 Berwick St	020 7437 4271	Sickly phoenix risen from the ashes of Reckless Records.
Sister Ray	34 Berwick St	020 7734 3297	Alternative vinyl, CDs and DVDs.
Snog	9 Brewer St	020 7494 3301	Healthy dessert!
Sounds of the Universe	7 Broadwick St	020 7734 3430	Blow your friends' minds with obscure African vinyl.
Vinyl Junkies	94 Berwick St	020 7439 2923	Get your fix, you grubby vinyl fiend.

Map 12 • Soho (East)

Angels	119 Shaftesbury Ave	020 7836 5678	Chock full of fancy dress outfits.
Fopp	1 Earlham St	020 7845 9770	May Fopp never, ever die again. Long live the music bargain!
Forbidden Planet	179 Shaftesbury Ave	020 7420 3666	Cult/film/TV memorabilia shop that will leave Star Wars fans salivating.
Harmony	167 Charing Cross Rd	020 7734 5969	Also known as Butt Plugs R Us.
Julienne & Porselli	9 West St	020 7836 2862	Before American Apparel...when only dancers wore dancewear...
Kokon to Zai	57 Greek St	020 7434 1316	Mad fashion laboratory providing competition for The Pinea Eye.
Macaris	92 Charing Cross Rd	020 7836 2856	Family-run instrument shop with historic roots.
Magma	16 Earlham St	020 7240 7571	Super-cool housewares and knick-knacks from the Magma gods.

Magma	8 Earlham St	020 7240 8498	The high priest of f'ing cool books.
Ray's Jazz	113 Charing Cross Rd	020 7437 5660	Convivial Shop/Cafe. Essential for Americana and, uh, jazz!
Rockers	5 Denmark St	020 7240 2610	Quiffs, picks, riffs and licks. Sick.
Turnkey	114 Charing Cross Rd	020 7419 9999	Every musical gadget you need for your next glitchtronica symphony.
Wunjo Guitars	20 Denmark St	020 7379 0737	Mind-bendingly friendly Scot selling lovely vintage gear…

Map 13 • Covent Garden

Artbox	29 Earlham St	020 7240 0097	Hello Kitty overload.
The Astrology Shop	78 Neal St	020 7497 1001	For people who believe that shit - and people who don't.
The Bead Shop	21 Tower St	020 7240 0931	Great resource for amateur beaders and professional designers
Ben's Cookies	13 The Piazza	020 7240 6123	Cookie chain good. Chips in dough yum.
Blackout II	51 Endell St	020 7240 5006	Vintage heaven.
Cath Kidston	28 Shelton St	020 7836 4803	Kitsch at its most chic, and vice-versa.
Coco de Mer	23 Monmouth St	020 7836 8882	High-class, kinky fun.
Cybercandy	3 Garrick St	084 5838 0958	For when a plain old Mars bar just won't cut it.
David and Goliath	4 The Market Pl	020 7240 3640	Droll, funky t-shirts and other fun stuff.
Hope and Greenwood	1 Russell St	020 7240 3314	Old style sweets.
Kiehls	29 Monmouth St	020 7240 2411	Kiehls UK Flagship store of New Yorks' famous apothecarists.
Libidex at Liberation	49 Shelton St	020 7836 5894	Caters for all your kinks. Yes, even that one.
The Loft	35 Monmouth St	020 7240 3807	Designer jumble sale.
London Graphic Centre	16 Shelton St	020 7759 4500	One stop shop for graphics geeks.
Miss Lala's Boudoir	18 Monmouth St	020 7836 6670	Dangerously hot underwear. Visit only if your purse is full.
Neal's Yard Dairy	17 Shorts Gardens	020 7240 5700	Follow your nose to very fine cheeses.
Nigel Hall	18 Floral St	020 7379 3600	Where to get business casualed well.
Octopus	54 Neal St	020 7836 2911	Makes the everyday so much more fun.
Orla Kiely	31 Monmouth St	020 7240 4022	Trademark cutesy prints from the Irish designer.
Pop Boutique	6 Monmouth St	020 7497 5262	Retrotastic!
Rokit	42 Shelton St	020 7836 6547	Vast array of vintage clothing.
Scoop	40 Shorts Gardens	020 7240 7086	Queues out the door for freshly made gelato. Fragola rocks.
Screenface	48 Monmouth St	020 7836 3955	Professional theatre make-up which can withstand the sweat of clubbing.
Slam City Skates	16 Neal's Yard	020 7240 0928	Rambunctious skate shop.
Stanford's	12 Long Acre	020 7836 1321	Treasure trove of maps, travel books and accessories.
Superdry	24 Earlham St (Thomas Neal Centre)	020 7240 9437	Super funky pseudo-Japanese urban wear. Friendly staff.
Tabio	66 Neal St	020 7836 3713	Only the Japanese could create such an array of socks.
Urban Outfitters	42 Earlham St	020 7759 6390	Heaps of streetwear and crazy things for your house.

Map 14 • Holborn / Temple

Konditor & Cook	46 Gray's Inn Rd	020 7404 6300	Unusual location to find K&C's famous Magic Cakes..
Topshop	60 The Strand	020 7839 4144	Clothing for the New Generation.

Map 15 • Blackfriars / Farringdon

Pure Groove Records	6 West Smithfield	020 7778 9278	Cool instore gigs/events and great selection of new indie releases.

Map 16 • Square Mile (West)

Church's Shoes	90 Cheapside	020 7606 1587	An English shoe institution.
Manucci	5 Cheapside	020 7248 1459	Feeling out of place? Get a suit here.
Space NK Apothecary	145 Cheapside	020 7726 2060	Skin care heaven.

Map 17 • Square Mile (East)

Paul A Young Fine Chocolates	20 Royal Exchange	020 7929 7007	"Everytime you go away…" you take a piece of chocolate.
Sweatshop (City branch at Cannon's Gym)	Cousin Lane	020 7626 4324	Ickle version of the athletes' favourite frequented by suits.

Map 18 • Tower Hill / Aldgate

A. Gold	42 Brushfield St	020 7247 2487	Perfect for impressive picnic supplies. But smells like a sock.
Montezuma's	51 Brushfield St	020 7539 9208	Chocolate you'd leave your boyfriend for.
Petticoat Lane Market	Middlesex St	N/A	No petticoats here love, but look for the FCUK stall
Precious	16 Artillery Passage	020 7377 6668	One of few independent boutiques left standing.
Sweaty Betty	5 Rood Lane	020 7929 1790	Clothes for you to stretch in, Gretchen…

Map 19 • Belgravia

British Red Cross Victoria	85 Ebury St	020 7730 2235	Green welly-brigade territory. Good range of mens' suits.
Moyses Flowers	Peter Jones - Sloane Sq	020 7881 6425	Tastefully delicate posies to enchant your beloved.
Mungo & Maud	79 Elizabeth St	020 7952 4570	Real dogs don't wear clothes! Chihuahuas do though…and pugs…

Map 20 • Victoria / Pimlico (West)

Capital Carboot Sale	Pimlico Academy, Lupus St	0845 0943 871	We love a rummage through other people's rubbish.
Grays of Westminster	40 Churton St	020 7828 4925	Charming period shop specializing in Nikon.
La Bella Sicilia	23 Warwick Way	020 7630 5914	Old-skool deli with cheery old owners and pasta aplenty.
Rippon Cheese Stores	26 Upper Tachbrook St	020 7931 0628	A world of cheese.
Runners Need	24 Palace Street	020 7630 5056	Place for all you joggers "who go round and round"
Topshop	18 Victoria St	020 7828 6139	Clothing for the New Generation.

Map 21 • Pimlico (East)

Black Rose	112 Belgrave Rd	020 8279 2014	Gothic. Very, very gothic.

Map 22 • Westminster

Haelen Centre	41 Broadway	020 8340 4258	All your hippy, wholemeal, organic needs under one roof.
National Map Centre	Caxton St	020 7222 2466	Nope, still can't find it.

Map 23 • St. James's

Richard Caplan	25 Bury St	020 7807 9990	New and used equipment specializing in Leica.

Map 24 • Trafalgar Square / The Strand

Austin Kaye	425 The Strand	020 7240 1888	Vintage watches. Don't expect e-bay prices.
Australia Shop	27 Maiden Ln	020 7836 2292	Relive the holiday (minus the sun. Or Brad the dive-instructor).
Gelato Mio	45 Villiers St	020 7930 5961	You scream, I scream, yeah, we get it.
The Italian Bookshop	5 Cecil Ct	020 7240 1634	"Of course, there is only one way to read Dante…"
London Camera Exchange	98 Strand	020 7379 0200	My lens is longer than yours.
Motor Books	13 Cecil Ct	020 7836 5376	The ultimate Dad shop.
Rohan	10 Henrietta St	020 7831 1059	Super-friendly fleece-clad staff wielding waterproofs.
Stanley Gibbons	399 Strand	020 7836 8444	World's leading stamp dealer attracts collectors, investors and the curious.

Map 25 • Kensal Town

Constructive Lives	312 Portobello Rd	020 8969 1399	Get your Trellick Tower mug here!
Honest Jon's	278 Portobello Rd	020 8969 9822	Obscure and rare Jazz, Funk, Reggae and Hip-Hop.
Rellik	8 Golborne Rd	020 8962 0089	Opposite the Trellik Tower - geddit? Specialises in Queen Viv (Westwood).
What Katie Did	281 Portobello Rd	0845 430 8743	Fabulous 1940s-inspired boudoir boutique for rib-crushing corsets, stockings and pointy bras.

Map 28 • Ladbroke Grove / Notting Hill (West)

Cowshed	119 Portland Rd	020 7078 1944	Express mani-pedis for women who have places to go etc.
The Cross	141 Portland Rd	020 7727 6760	The original London boutique…still going…
Gelato Mio	138 Holland Park Ave	020 7727 4117	Get ice-cream, head to park.
Jeroboams	96 Holland Park Ave	020 7727 9359	London's largest independent wine merchant.
Virginia	98 Portland Road	020 7727 9908	If money is no object, what you want is here.

Map 29 • Notting Hill Gate

& Clarke's Bread	124 Kensington Church St	020 7229 2190	All-butter brioche and honey loaves for Harvey Nics, Selfridges, and you.
Bodas	38 Ledbury Rd	020 7229 4464	Everyday underwear that gives M&S a run for its money.
The Grocer on Elgin	6 Elgin Crescent	020 7221 3844	Restaurant standard ready meals for lazy people.
The Hummingbird Bakery	133 Portobello Rd	020 7229 6446	Takeaway cupcakes reminiscent of New York's Magnolia Bakery.
James Knight of Mayfair	67 Notting Hill Gate	020 7221 6177	The Queen's fish at the Queen's prices.
Melt	59 Ledbury Rd	020 7727 5030	Posh chocs made before your bulging eyes.
Mr Christian's Delicatessen	11 Elgin Crescent	020 7229 0501	Great little deli with non-Portobello Rd prices.
Music & Video Exchange	38 Notting Hill Gate	020 7243 8574	Invented second hand record shops. Best in London.
Negozio Classica	283 Westbourne Grove	020 7034 0005	Half bar, half store selling high-end Italian kitchen goods.
Diane von Furstenberg	83 Ledbury Rd	020 7221 1120	High end wear for those who can afford it.
Portobello Road Market	223 Portobello Rd	n/a	Antiques, clothes, food, and more. A London institution.
R Garcia and Sons	248 Portobello Rd	020 7221 6119	Overwhelming selection of Spanish groceries.
Retro Man	34 Pembridge Rd	020 7792 1715	Vintage fixes for modern men. And men only.
Retro Woman	32 Pembridge Rd	020 7598 2233	Exclusive vintage ware that's worth it.
Rough Trade West	130 Talbot Rd	020 7229 8541	More character and better records than the soulless East Branch.
Travel Bookshop	13 Blenheim Cresent	020 7229 5260	I DARE you to ask them about Hugh Grant.

Map 30 • Bayswater

Al Saqi Books	26 Westbourne Grove	020 7229 8543	Specialist book shop for anything and everything Middle Eastern.
Planet Organic	42 Westbourne Grove	020 7727 2227	Organic heaven.
Porchester Gate Spa	Queensway & Porchester Rd	020 7793 3980	Proper old school art deco Turkish baths and spa for less than £25!
Whiteleys Shopping Centre	Queensway	020 7229 8844	Slightly more soulful than Smithfields.

Map 32 • Shepherd's Bush (West)

Nut Case	352 Uxbridge Rd	020 8743 0336	About time nuts got some respect.

Map 33 • Shepherd's Bush

Westfield Centre	Ariel Way	020 3371 2300	Very likable shopping center. Really.
Whole Foods Market	63 Kensington High St	020 7368 4500	Overwhelming selection of organic exotica.

Map 35 • Kensington

Ben's Cookies	12 Kensington High St	020 7376 0559	Chunky cookies in wonderous flavours. Hidden in High Street Ken Station.
Buttercup Cake Shop	16 St Albans Grove	020 7937 1473	No other pleasure on earth comes close to these cupcakes.
Homebase	195 Warwick Rd	084 5640 7062	So much stuff that you never knew you needed.
Notting Hill Housing Trust	57 Kensington Church St	020 7937 5274	There's gold in that 'Hill.
Trailfinders	194 Kensington High St	020 7938 3939	Personable one stop shop for travel bookings, advice and services.
Urban Outfitters	36 Kensington High St	020 7761 1001	Heaps of streetwear and crazy things for your house.
Whole Foods Market	63 Kensington High St	020 7368 4500	Overshelming selection of organic exotica.

Map 36 • South Kensington/Gloucester Rd

Partridges Deli	17 Gloucester Rd	020 7581 0535	Family run mega-deli to the queen.
Snog	32 Thurloe Pl	020 7584 4926	Crazy frozen yoghurt joint with interior mad enough to be in Tokyo.

Map 37 • Knightsbridge

Burberry	2 Brompton Road	020 3367 3000	Flagship store of the classic British brand.
Divertimenti	227 Brompton Rd	020 7581 8065	Go and pretend you need a £500 coffee machine.
Harrods	87 Brompton Rd	020 7730 1234	Arch conspiracy theorist Mr Al-Fayed's still classy department store.
Harvey Nichols	109 Knightsbridge	020 7235 5000	More 1999 than 2009, but still a great department store.
Rigby & Peller	2 Hans Rd	084 5076 5545	Sexy lingerie fit for a queen…for THE Queen?
Skandium	247 Brompton Rd	020 7584 2066	For lottery winners who can't shake their love of Ikea.
Space NK Apothecary	307 Brompton Rd	020 7589 8250	Skin care heaven.

Map 38 • Chiswick

As Nature Intended	201 Chiswick High Rd	020 8742 8838	Main store from orgainc food company. Pricey but worth the trek.
The Bread Shop	296 Chiswick High Rd	020 8747 8443	Bloomin' marvellous bread! Great selection and they even do spelt loaves.
Mortimer & Bennett Terrace	33 Turnham Green	020 8995 4145	Gourmet deli that is guaranteed to get you excited about pickled asparagus.
Eco-Age	213 Chiswick High Rd	020 8995 7611	Colin Firth's eco-friendly homeware store with recycled chairs and eco-paint.
Outsider Tart	83 Chiswick High Rd	020 7096 1609	Amazing cupcake selection to lure you away from Red Velvet.
Oxfam Books	90 Turnham Green Terrace	020 8995 6059	Fantastic fiction selection - the rich read too!
Something Nice	40 Turnham Green Terrace	020 8742 7135	Gifts you didn't even know you wanted. Great if you're stumped for pressies.
Theobroma Cacao	43 Turnham Green Terrace	020 8996 0431	Which translates as "Chocolate Thrombosis". Choccy penises? Leave it out!
Wheelers Garden Centre	Turnham Green Terrace	020 8747 9505	Last chance station for forgotten occasions next to Turnham Green tube.

Map 39 • Stamford Brook

Mac's Cameras	262 King St	020 8846 9853	Used and hard-to-find gear. Heaven for photography nerds.
Thai Smile	287 King St	020 8846 9960	Heaven for those who love Asian cooking. For the rest it's just intriguing.

Map 40 • Goldhawk Rd / Ravenscourt Park

Bushwacker Wholefoods	132 King St	020 8748 2061	Small and friendly organic and health food shop. Booja, Booja Ice-cream!!

Map 42 • Baron's Court

Curious Science	319 Lillie Road	020 7610 1175	Stock up on stuffed mutant cow heads and cases of eyeballs.

Map 43 • West Brompton / Fulham Broadway / Earls Court

Fulham Broadway Centre	Fulham Road	020 7385 6965	Shopping, cinema, retaurants and tube station all in one place.

Map 44 • Chelsea

Furniture Cave	533 Kings Rd	020 7352 2046	Swanky. Huge. Quintessentially Kings Road.
Richer Sounds	258 Fulham Rd	033 3900 0027	Chain selling all things electronic, technologic, an so forth.
The Shop At Bluebird	350 King's Rd	020 7351 3873	Spend a fortune here and become an "edgy" individual.

Map 45 • Chelsea (East)

British Red Cross Chelsea	69 Old Church St	084 5054 7101	Known locally as La Croix Rouge Boutique.
Frock Me! Vintage Fashion Fair	Chelsea Town Hall, Kings Rd	020 7254 4054	Held every couple of months, "pre-war" tearoom refreshes shopping casualties.
The Hummingbird Bakery	47 Old Brompton Rd	020 7584 0055	Notting Hill's big brother with seating to devour Red Velvets and lattes.
Kate Kuba	24 Duke of York Sq	020 7259 0011	What more could a woman want?! Shoes, shoes, shoes…
Nomad Books	781 Fulham Rd	020 7689 9988	Glorious little place with added coffee shop.
Sweaty Betty	125 King's Rd	020 7349 7597	Clothes for you to stretch in, Gretchen…

Map 46 • Sloane Square

Fresh Line	55 King's Rd	020 7881 0900	Home made cosmetics—fresh!
Patridges Deli	2 Duke of York St	020 7730 0651	Family run mega-deli to the queen.
Peter Jones	Sloan Sq	020 7730 3434	Upmarket department store. Argos of the 'daharlings' with cash to splash.
Rigby & Peller	13 Kings Rd	084 5076 5545	Sexy lingerie fit for a queen…the queen?
Space NK Apothecary	307 King's Rd	020 7351 7209	The Superdrug for the Sloane Square ladies who lunch.

Map 48 • Fulham

Hurlingham Books	91 Fulham High St	020 7736 4363	More stacked than Arnie was in the 70s.

Map 51 • Highgate

The Corner Shop	88 Highgate High St	020 8340 1118	Locals' favourite fending off the advance of Tesco's.
Dragonfly Wholefoods	24 Highgate High St	020 8347 6087	Great little organic food shop and juice bar.
Highgate Butchers	76 Highgate High St	020 8340 9817	Reassuringly expensive meat. Them cows must have lived like kings.
Hop N Pops	389 Archway Rd	020 8348 0624	Great selection for all budgets.
Le Chocolatier	78 Highgate High St	020 8348 1110	Essential at Easter—not just eggs but whole chocolate chickens.
Mind	329 Archway Rd	020 8341 1188	Great selection for skint book worms.
Oxfam	80 Highgate High St	020 8340 3888	Musty bookstore with some cracking titles.
Second Layer Records	323 Archway Rd	078 7805 1726	I was into Avant Rock before you were etc. etc.
Walter Castellazzo Design	84 Highgate High St	020 8340 3001	A lot of cool and ridiculously pricey things.
Wild Guitar	393 Archway Rd	020 8340 7766	Get your retro gear in this brilliant guitar shop.

Map 52 • Archway (North)

Archway Cycles	183 Archway Rd	020 8340 9696	Because tube fares will just keep going up.
Archway Video	220 Archway Rd	020 8340 2986	Local favourite with videos/DVDs for sale and rent.
The Green Room	192 Archway Rd	020 8340 7759	Amazing selection of weird things you probably don't need.
Pax Guns	166 Archway Rd	020 8340 3039	Errm… "best" gun shop in the area?
Wine of Course	216 Archway Rd	020 8347 9006	Impress the guests at your next dinner party.

Map 53 • Crouch End

Walter Purkis And Sons	17 The Broadway	020 8340 6281	Proof fish don't need their tasty batter skins.

Map 57 • Hampstead Heath

Daunt Books	51 S End Rd	020 7794 8206	A right daunty little shop.
Giocobazzi's Delicatessen	150 Fleet Rd	020 7267 7222	The taste of posh Italy.

Map 58 • Parliament Hill / Dartmouth Park

BABA	11 Swain's Ln	020 8442 9111	Quirky kitchenware and gifts.
Corks	9 Swain's Ln	020 8340 4781	Superb selection of interesting wines and beers.
Forks	7 Swain's Ln	020 8340 1695	Friendly, well-stocked deli. Fresh crepes in summer!

Map 59 • Tufnell Park

The Blue Carbuncle	130 Junction Rd	020 7272 6691	Uber-cool vintage clothes, cameras and collectibles.
The Hornsey Trust Charity Shop	124 Fortess Rd	020 7267 2338	Eccentric staff? Check. Affluent, moth-eaten cast offs? Check.
North London Adoption Centre	135 Junction Rd	020 7272 6048	Need a cat? Of course you do! Miau!

Map 60 • Archway

Second Chance	7 St John's Way	020 7281 5449	Heaps of rubbish and the occasional incredible find.
Super Persia	621 Holloway Rd	020 7272 2665	Very proud little shop specializing in Iranian sweets.

Map 61 • Holloway (North)

Michael's Fruiterers	56 7 Sisters Rd	020 7700 1334	Fruit n veg fest. Nowhere's fresher.

Map 62 • Finsbury Park

The Happening Bagel Bakery	284 Seven Sisters Rd	020 8809 1519	Another Haringey gem, with some delicious pastries too!

Map 64 • Stoke Newington

Ark	161 Stoke Newington High St	020 7275 9311	Cute little interiors and gift shop.
'he Beaucatcher Salon	44 Stoke Newington Church St	020 7923 2522	Hairdressers and community hub.
›elle Epoque Boulangerie	37 Newington Green	020 7249 2222	Fancy schmancy, delicious pastries.
›ridgewood & Neitzert	146 Stoke Newington Church St	020 7249 9398	Renowned string section repair, exchange and sales.
hurch Street Bookshop	142 Stoke Newington Church St	020 7241 5411	Great shack with out of print books and shite records.
Aetal Crumble	13 Stoke Newington Church St	020 7249 0487	Affordable, flippin' gorgeous, jewellery made on site.
Aind	11 Stoke Newington Church St	020 7812 9210	Great little chazza benefiting from middle-class donors.
)f Cabbages & Kings	34 Kersley Rd	020 7254 0060	Another of those crafty little shops that keep popping up.
ibbons and Taylor	157 Stoke Newington Church St	020 7254 4735	Long-standing vintage clothes shop—Stokey original.
osa Lingerie	3 Church Walk	020 7254 3467	The oldest knickers in Stokey.
oute 73 Kids	92 Stoke Newington Church St	020 7923 7873	Bus inspired toy shop.
'graffiti	172 Stoke Newington Church St	020 7254 7961	You've been framed.
acred Art	148 Albion Rd	020 7254 2223	(Needles + Ink + Skin) x Pain = Art.
he Spence Bakery	161 Stoke Newington Church St	020 7249 4927	Bread elevated to an art form.
toke Newington Farmers Market	Stoke Newington Church St & Stoke Newington High St	020 7502 7588	Overpriced, organic, natural, Hea…Zzzzzzzz.

Map 65 • West Hampstead

arty Party	206 Kilburn High Rd	020 7624 4295	Party Party Stuff Stuff!
rimark	54 Kilburn High Rd	020 7624 4664	Enter the scrum.

Map 67 • Belsize Park

elsize Village Delicatessen	39 Belsize Ln	020 7794 4258	For a truly international picnic basket.
otus and Frog	32 England's Ln	020 7586 3931	Quirky gifts for young and old.

Map 70 • Primrose Hill

udith Michael & Daughter	73 Regents Park Rd	020 7722 9000	Gorgeous vintage to help you lighten your purse.
icolas (off licence)	67 Regents Park Rd	020 7722 8576	A wide range of wines, including some cheap ones.
ress	3 Erskine Rd	020 7449 0081	Impressive array of brands for a boutique. Good sales.
imerose Hill Books	134 Regents Park Rd	020 7586 2022	Fabulously curated selection of new books.
rimrose Newsagent	91 Regents Park Rd	020 7722 0402	Newsagent, stationers, post office, drycleaners and internet cafe.
chard Dare	93 Regent's Park Rd	020 7722 9428	Quite lovely kitchen/cooking products.
hepherd Foods	59 Regents Park Rd	020 7586 4592	Highly priced but quaint local deli.
hikasuki	67 Gloucester Ave	020 7722 4442	Affordable vintage and modern design.
weet Pea	77 Gloucester Ave	020 7449 9292	Unusual handmade jewelry.
ann Rokka	123 Regents Park Rd	020 7722 3999	Wildly expensive "lifestyle store" in old Primrose hill train station.
eomans Grocers	152 Regent's Park Rd	020 7722 4281	Greengrocer that sells flowers and has a great juicebar.

Map 71 • Camden Town / Chalk Farm / Kentish Town (West)

Acumedic	101 Camden High St	020 7388 6704	Chinese medicine centre offering acupuncture AKA polite masochism.
Arckiv Vintage Eyewear	Chalk Farm Rd and Castlehaven Rd	077 9010 2204	Those film kids get their vintage eyewear here.
Aldo Sale Shop	231 Camden High St	020 7284 1982	If you find shoes that fit they're free. Not really.
Cyberdog	The Stables Market, Chalk Farm Rd	020 7482 2842	Enormous sci-fi set displaying PVC, neon, and leather clubbing gear.
Episode	26 Chalk Farm Rd	020 7485 9927	Unusual vintage store with comparatively low ringworm risk.
Escapade	45 Chalk Farm Rd	020 7485 7384	Dress up as Wonder Woman! Also caters for females.
Eye Contacts	10 Chalk Farm Rd	020 7482 1701	Opticians that sells uber-trendy spectacles.
Fresh & Wild, Camden	49 Parkway	020 7428 7575	Organic and wholefood oasis with eat-in possibilities.
Graham and Green	164 Regents Park Rd	020 7586 2960	Wonderfully dinky yet scarily pricey shop.
Metal Militia	258 Camden High St	020 7734 5720	Screeeeammm for me Camden High Street!!
Music & Video Exchange	208 Camden High St	020 7267 0123	Great secondhand music shop, seemingly staffed by grouches on Mogadon.
Proud Camden	Chalk Farm Rd	020 7482 3867	Stock up on contemporary photography.
Ray Man Music	54 Chalk Farm Rd	020 7692 6261	Wonderful shop full of exotic instruments. Bavarian noseflute, anyone?
Rokit	225 Camden High St	020 7267 3046	Second hand, sorry, vintage clothing store to the stars.
Sounds That Swing	46 Inverness St	020 7267 4682	"It ain't worth a thing..." rockabilly, psych and doo-wop.
Traid	154 Camden High St	020 7485 5253	Characterful recycled clothes. Touch of wank, but still we like.
Up The Video Junction	Middle Yard, Camden Lock Pl	077 9266 1294	Rare, out-of-print, cult DVDs.
Village Games	65 The West Yard	020 7485 0653	Huge selection of boardgames.
Whole Foods Market	49 Parkway	020 7428 7575	Overwhelming selection of organic exotica.

Map 72 • Kentish Town

Blustons	213 Kentish Town Rd	020 7485 3508	Clothes for grannies. Those under 70 need not enter.
Dots	132 St Pancras Way	020 7482 5424	Friendly music shop with free hash cakes...OK, just cookies.
Fish	161 Kentish Town Rd	020 7267 0139	Gift shop run by actress Sophie Thompson.
Phoenicia - Mediterranean Food Hall	186 Kentish Town Rd	020 7267 1267	Olives, just-roasted nuts, baclava, ice-cream bar. Meze heaven. Ditch Sainsburys.
Pro Percussion	205 Kentish Town Rd	020 7485 4434	BANG! BOOM! CRASH! For drummers young and old.

Map 73 • Holloway

Bumblebee Natural Foods	33 Brecknock Rd	020 7284 1314	Hot veggie lunches, lush cakes. Organic fruitopia over the roac
DOC Records	5 Cardwell Terrace, Cardwell Rd	020 7700 0081	Probably full of contagious diseases. Worth a rummage.

Map 74 • Holloway Road / Arsenal

21st Century Retro	162 Holloway Rd	020 7700 2354	Mothballs and tweed in this retro paradise.
Fettered Pleasures	90 Holloway Rd	020 7619 9333	Treat your man to something nice.
House of Harlot	90 Holloway Rd	020 7700 1441	Funky fetish fashion.

Map 75 • Highbury

Cabbies Delight Auto Parts	9 Green Lanes	020 7226 1692	21,000 car parts and 21 years experience.
La Fromagerie	30 Highbury Park	020 7359 7440	Blow your inheritance on some Abbaye De Trois Vaux.
Mother Earth	282 St Paul's Rd	020 7354 9897	Unfortunate New Age name, decent little shop.
Vivien of Holloway	294 Holloway Rd	020 7609 8754	Want to dress like Joan from Mad Men?

Map 76 • Edgeware Road / Marylebone (North)

Alfie's Antique Market	25 Church St	020 7723 6066	Kitsch oddball sanctuary for vintage treats.
Archive Secondhand Books & Music	83 Bell St	020 7402 8212	Old and unusual books.
Elvisly Yours	233 Baker St	020 7486 2005	With stalkers like these, it's no wonder Elvis is hiding.
London Beatles Store	231 Baker St	020 7935 4464	All you need is love, and no taste.
Lord's Cricket Shop	Lord's Cricket Ground, Lisson Grove	020 7616 8570	They won't even ask why you want a cricket bat.

Map 77 • Mornington Crescent / Regent's Park

Calumet Trading	93 Drummond St	020 7380 1144	Cameras and accessories.
Greens and Beans	131 Drummond St	020 7380 0857	Wheat grass, supplements and tofu.

Map 78 • Euston

All Ages Records	27 Pratt St	020 7267 0303	Truly independent punk & hardcore record shop. F*** the system!
Housmans Bookshop	5 Caledonian Rd	020 7837 4473	Bookshop for progressive peaceniks and radical revolutionaries.

Peyton & Byrne	Pancras Rd	020 7278 6707	Cupcake perfection.
Transformation	52 Eversholt St	020 7388 0627	The world's largest shop for transvestites and transsexuals. Seriously.

Map 79 • King's Cross

Cosmo Cornelio	182 Caledonian Rd	020 7278 3947	Old-skool, moustache trimming Italian barbers.
King's Cross Continental Stores	26 Caledonian Rd	020 7837 0201	1960s Italian deli still run by original Italian owners. Fab.

Map 80 • Angel / Upper St

A Ferrari Deli	48 Cross St	020 7226 1951	Yes, Mr Ferrari's grumpy. But he is 102.
After Noah	121 Upper St	020 7359 4281	Stuff your Nintendo Wiis—these are proper toys, retro-style.
Annie's Vintage Costume and Textiles	12 Camden Passage	020 7359 0796	Proper vintage—1900s to 1940s.
Camden Passage	Camden Passage	020 7359 0190	Thingamebobs, whatsits and doodahs aplenty.
Cass Art	66 Colebrooke Row	020 7354 2999	Large, neat-as-a-pin, extremely pleasing art supply shop.
Gill Wing Kitchen Shop	194 Upper St	020 7226 5392	Splendid array of kitchen gadgetry to keep foodies amused.
Monte's Deli	23 Canonbury Ln	020 7354 4335	Tasty, but look elsewhere if you need a hearty meal.
Palette London	21 Canonbury Ln	020 7288 7428	Islington's eclectic vintage shop—clothes, books, homeware
Paul A Young Fine Chocolates	33 Camden Passage	020 7424 5750	"Everytime you go away…" you take a piece of chocolate.
Raymond Roe Fishmonger	35 Chapel Market	020 7833 8656	Market stall with a sea's worth of fish.
Twentytwentyone	274 Upper St	020 7288 1996	Bauhaus to Boontje and beyond.

Map 81 • Canonbury

Get Stuffed	105 Essex Rd	020 7226 1364	Polar bear for the living room, anyone? Taxidermy emporium.
HG Lockey & Sons	8 Halton Cross St	020 7226 7044	For all your, er, coal and smokeless fuel needs.
Handmade and Found	109 Essex Rd	020 7359 3898	For something totally unique.
James Elliot Master Butcher	96 Essex Rd	020 7226 3658	So much choice they'd probably stock human if they could.
Planet Organic	64 Essex Rd	020 7288 9460	Organic heaven.
Raab's The Baker's	136 Essex Rd	020 7226 2830	Crusty white bloomers, chelsea buns. No paninis.
Sew Fantastic	107 Essex Rd	020 7226 2725	If you'd thought it up, you'd have opened it too.

Map 82 • De Beauvoir Town / Kingsland

2&4 Gallery	4 Southgate Rd	020 7254 5202	Independent shop selling furniture but coffee too.
North One Garden Centre	25 Englefield Rd	020 7923 3553	Dinky little garden centre catering for dinky little London gardens.

Map 83 • Angel (East) / City Rd (North)

Flashback	50 Essex Rd	020 7354 9356	Don't come in whistling Barbie Girl.
Haggle Vinyl	114 Essex Rd	020 7704 3101	Record shop that reminds you how little you know about music.
Past Caring	54 Essex Rd	N/A	Oddball collection of furniture, pictures and, if you're lucky, mannequins.

Map 84 • Hoxton

Good Hood	41 Coronet St	020 7729 3600	Like American Apparel before it got shit.
Sh!	57 Hoxton Sq	084 5868 9599	Dildo-tastic! Guys must come (ahem) accompanied by a galpal.

Map 85 • Stoke Newington (East)

Bargain Bookshop	153 Stoke Newington High St	020 7249 8983	Books! Bargains! AH!
Hamdys	167 Stoke Newington High St	020 7254 0681	Porn-free newsagents run by stubborn maverick.
Rouge	158 Stoke Newington High St	020 7275 0887	Cool Chinese housewares. Via Belgium of course.
Stoke Newington Bookshop	159 Stoke Newington High Street	020 7249 2808	Long-standing local stellar indie bookshop.

Map 86 • Dalston / Kingsland

Centre Supermarket	588 Kingsland Rd	N/A	Beers from all corners of the globe.
Dalston Mill Fabrics	69 Ridley Rd	020 7249 4129	Veritable treasure trove for budding Vivienne Westwoods and John Gallianos.
Oxfam	514 Kingsland Rd	020 7254 5318	Flagship charity shop. Go find treasures!
Party Party	9 Ridley Rd	020 7254 5168	Fancy dress and party supplies plus an outstanding cake decorating department.
Ridley Road Market	51 Ridley Rd	084 4357 4634	Absolutely mental market… bush meat, wonky haircuts you name it.
Sound 323 @ Cafe Oto	18 Ashwin St	077 0735 2638	Blisteringly avant record shack.

St Vincent's	484 Kingsland Rd	020 7249 3511	Christian charity shop. Jesus galore.
Turkish Food Centre	89 Ridley Rd	020 7254 6754	Olives and feta galore, bakery onsite, plus other fresh groceries.

Map 87 • Hackney Downs / Lower Clapton

Palm 2	152 Lower Clapton Rd	020 8533 1787	Legendarily friendly corner shop beloved of bloggers.
The Pet Shop	40 Amhurst Rd	020 8986 6862	Brillant local pet shop
Salvation Army Clapton	122 Lower Clapton Rd	020 8985 3902	Come all ye unfaithful…
Second Time Around	60 Lower Clapton Rd	020 985 5536	Buy back the old shit that got stolen last week.
Umit & Son	35 Lower Clapton Rd	020 8985 1766	Crazed film buff selling vintage porn, super 8 and crisps?!?

Map 88 • Haggerston / Queensbridge Rd

KTS The Corner	415 Kingsland Road	020 7249 3199	Helpful DIY store if you can't do it yourself.

Map 89 • London Fields / Hackney Central

Artvinyl	13 Broadway Market	020 7241 4129	The best vinyl and CD covers, printed on canvas.
Broadway Market	Broadway Market	N/A	Yummy mummies and Guardian-reading couples peruse.
Burberry Factory Shop	29 Chatham Pl	020 8985 3344	Ever wondered how Burberry became associated with chavs?
Candle Factory	184 Mare St	020 8986 6356	Well-made, well-priced candles.
Lazy Days	21 Mare St	078 1632 3848	Not far from Hackney Road where you'll find more furniture.
L'eau a la Bouche	49 Broadway Market	020 7923 0600	Cute French delicatessen shop.
Viktor Wynd's Shop of Horrors	11 Mare St	020 7998 3617	Macabre and marvellous shop and gallery

Map 90 • Homerton / Victoria Park North

Cheech Miller	227 Victoria Park Rd	020 8985 9900	Everything you need for the park: kites, frisbees, skateboards, unicycles.
The Ginger Pig	99 Lauriston Rd	020 8986 6911	Brilliant butcher bequeathing beef to the Borough.
Sublime	225 Victoria Park Rd	020 8986 7243	Boudoir-like boutique selling select and independent labels.
Work Shop	77 Lauriston Rd	020 8986 9585	Beautiful handmade pottery for home and kitchen by Caroline Bousfield Gregory.

Map 91 • Shoreditch / Brick Lane / Spitalfields

A Butcher of Distinction	91 Brick Ln	020 7770 6111	Distinct indeed, impeccable collection of preppy, fresh n' clean stylings.
Absolute Vintage	15 Hanbury St	020 7247 3883	If Imelda Marcos ran a misanthropic clothes shop.
Bangla City	86 Brick Ln	020 7456 1000	Breaks the rule saying you should avoid smelly supermarkets.
Bernstock Speirs	234 Brick Ln	020 7739 7385	Look no further if you're searching for a signature titfer.
Beyond Retro	112 Cheshire St	020 7613 3636	The Daddy of all jumble sales.
Blackmans	44 Cheshire St	078 5088 3505	Are plimsolls still cool on Brick Lane? Help!
Brick Lane	Brick Ln	N/A	Nathan Barleys still pissed off their face from the night before.
Brick Lane Market	91 Brick Ln	020 7770 6028	Great Sunday market with lots of food and cool clothes.
Caravan	3 Redchurch St	020 7033 3532	Quirky interiors shop with items new and old on offer.
A Child of The Jago	10 Great Eastern St	020 7377 8694	Slapdash assortment of otherworldly vintage.
Comfort Station	22 Cheshire St	020 7033 9099	Quirky and comforting collection of handmade jewellery.
Columbia Road Market	Columbia Rd	N/A	Get there early, nab outside tables for brekkie then shop.
Columbia Road Flower Market	Columbia Rd	N/A	A Sunday morning hot spot for plant lovers. After 2pm is prime bargain time.
Duke of Uke	22 Hanbury St	020 7247 7924	For all your many ukelele and banjo needs.
FairyGothMother	15 Lamb St	020 7377 0370	Not entirely "Goth"- a Dita Von Teese of a shop…
The Grocery	54 Kingsland Rd	020 7729 6855	Selling the good life to lower Kingsland Road.
Hurwundeki	98 Commercial St	020 7392 9194	Boutique-y empire slowly creeping across London.
Junky Styling	91 Brick Ln	020 7247 1883	Bespoke tailoring from old rags. But posher.
Labour And Wait	18 Cheshire St	020 7729 6253	Brilliant wee shop selling old and old looking goods.
The Laden Showrooms	103 Brick Ln	020 7247 2431	Eclectic bazaar of small labels scavenged by stylists and starlets.
Lapin & Me	14 Ezra Street	020 7739 4384	Cute shop selling toys for big kids and little kids.
Luna and Curious	198 Brick Ln	020 7033 4111	Curiouser and curiouser…lovely local artists' and designers' co-operative.
No One	1 Kingsland Rd	020 7613 5314	Sporty designer wear. Killer shades.
Nudge Records	20 Hanbury St	020 7655 4823	Notorious little shack owned by the Brothers Collishaw. Reggae/dub.
Prick Your Finger	260 Bethnal Green Rd	020 8981 2560	Haberdashery brought to you by whimsical St Martin's grads.
Present	140 Shoreditch High St	020 7033 0500	Fashionable designer menswear shop with a coffee bar.
Rough Trade East	91 Brick Ln	020 7392 7788	East London outpost of the absurdly cool Rough Trade Records.
Ryantown	126 Columbia Road	020 7613 1510	Home of the ever popular paper cutter Rob Ryan.
Second Tread	261 Hackney Rd	020 7033 9862	In every fashionista's little black book: seconds and ex-model shoes.
Shelf	40 Cheshire Street	020 7739 9444	Neat selection of craftsty stuff you don't need but want
Taj Stores	112 Brick Ln	020 7377 0061	Weird and wonderful Eastern food.
Tatty Devine	236 Brick Ln	020 7739 9191	Bonkers jewellery loved by celebs, fashionistas and hipsters.
Taylor Taylor	12 Cheshire St	020 7033 0330	Salon for the indulgent customer.

Taylor Taylor	137 Commercial St	020 7377 2737	French boudoir-style hairdressers with free cocktail bar. Feel like a princess.
Treacle	110 Columbia Rd	020 7729 0538	Dreamy cupcakes. Don't ask for coffee—this is a TEAshop!

Map 92 • Bethnal Green

AP Fitzpatrick	142 Cambridge Heath Rd	020 7790 0884	Art supplies and expert advice.
Paul Mark Hatton	65 Roman Rd	020 8981 7110	Pocket ashtray anyone? Fans include Jack Nicholson and Liv Tyler.

Map 94 • Bow

Pure	430 Roman Rd	020 7364 1717	The place to spend your wedge in E3.
Roman Road Market	Roman Rd	020 7377 8963	Big, colourful, cheap as chips—bargain tat hawked by lively east-end traders.
Sew Amazing	80 St Stephens Rd	020 8980 8898	Long established sewing machine shop. Repairs and recycling service provided.
South Molton Drugstore	583 Roman Rd	020 8981 5040	Branded cosmetics and toiletries at knock-down prices.

Map 97 • Stepney / Shadwell (East)

East End Thrift Store	Assembly Passage	020 7423 9700	Come on Thursday nights for the in-store parties.
John Lester Wigmakers	32 Globe Rd	020 7790 2278	Need a syrup?

Map 104 • South Bank / Waterloo / Lambeth North

The Bookshop Theatre	51 The Cut	020 7033 0599	Thesp-oriented but charming, including a tiny stage for performances.
Calder Bookshop - The Bookshop Theater	51 The Cut	020 76202900	Enduringly fashionable hub for the unfashionably literate.
I Knit London	106 Lower Marsh	020 7261 1338	The UK's only knitting shop with a licensed bar. Wool is cool.
Konditor & Cook	22 Cornwall Rd	020 7261 0456	Yummy scrummy choccies and cake.
Oasis	84 Lower Marsh	020 7401 7074	Friendly independent salon for massages, waxing, facials and fab pedicures.
Radio Days	87 Lower Marsh	020 7928 0800	Cave of vintage wonders.
ScooterCaffe	132 Lower Marsh	020 7620 1421	Scooter shop has superb coffee. Word spreads. Becomes café too.
Silverprint	12 Valentine Pl	020 7620 0844	Specialist dealer in photographic consumables.
Southbank Book Market	Under Waterloo Bridge	0871 663 2501	Fun little scribe's market in brillant surroundings.
Top Wind	2 Lower Marsh	020 7401 8787	Serious flute worship.
Waterloo Camping	37 The Cut	020 7928 4110	Eccentric army surplus/camping store, run by two friendly brothers.
What The Butler Wore	131 Lower Marsh	020 7261 1353	'60s, '70s vintage boutique—retro-glam party garments plus resident moggy, Binky.

Map 105 • Southwark / Bankside (West)

Elephant & Castle Market	Elephant & Castle	N/A	An anti-Portobello Road Market…slightly dodgy but dirt-cheap.

Map 106 • Bankside (East) / Borough / Newington

Borough Market	8 Southwark St	020 7407 1002	Go on an empty stomach and feast on samples.
Brindisa Retail	32 Exmouth Market	020 7713 1600	Chorizo, salchichon, Serrano ham—famed importers Brindisa have it all.The Family Business.
German Deli	8 Southwark St	020 7378 0000	Sauerkraut and sausages if you like that kinda stuff.
Paul Smith	13 Park St	020 7403 1678	Kitsch and dolls from the fashion designer. Don't ask why.
Richer Sounds	2 London Bridge Walk	033 3900 0021	The original store of this small chain offering low prices.
Vinopolis	1 Bank End	020 7940 8300	Wine tasting and buying megastore. Spitting optional.

Map 107 • Shad Thames

The Design Museum Shop	28 Shad Thames	020 7940 8754	Stuff you wish you'd thought of.
Fine Foods	218 Long Lane	020 7403 7513	Little, local Italian deli to coo over.
Long Lane Deli	218 Long Ln	020 7403 7513	A popular Italian delicatessen.
United Nude	124 Bermondsey St	020 7407 3758	Nope, we don't understand these shoes At All.

Map 111 • Rotherhithe (East) Surrey Quays

Decathlon	Surrey Quays Rd	020 7394 2000	The Daddy of sports & outdoors shops.

Map 112 • Kennington / Elephant and Castle

Pricebusters Hardware	311 Elephant & Castle	020 7703 8244	Impressively cheap, friendly staff and an amusing collection of

Recycling	Shopping Centre 110 Elephant Rd	020 7703 7001	bric-a-brac. They sell'em bikes, they fix'em bikes. Second hand.

Map 113 • Walworth

Mixed Blessings Caribbean Bakery	12 Camberwell Rd	020 7703 9433	Bread that's so good you'll need to queue.

Map 114 • Old Kent Road (West) / Burgess Park

Old Kent Road Food Centre	252 Old Kent Rd	020 7277 4368	Your basic nice grocery store.

Map 119 • Deptford (East)

Deptford Market	Deptford High St	N/A	Cheap, busy, eclectic: Proof that there IS life in Deptford.

Map 120 • Greenwich

Belle	20 College Approach	020 8465 5777	Plush retail experience with attentive staff.
Bullfrogs	22 Greenwich Church St	020 8305 2404	Strange name, decent shop. Independent boutique.
Cheeseboard	26 Royal Hill	020 8305 0401	Buy your cheese then head to Theatre of Wine…
Compendia	10 The Market	020 8293 6616	No, not bored games, good old fashioned board games
Emma Nissim	10 Greenwich Market	020 8853 3139	Eclectic collection of t-shirt designs, and silk scarves and ties.
Meet Bernard	23 Nelson Rd	020 8858 4047	Dapper gents outfitters.
Mr Humbug	Greenwich Market	020 7871 4944	Infinitesimal old-fashioned sweets to relive your childhood sugar buzzes.

Map 121 • Camberwell (West)

Butterfly Walk Shopping Centre	Denmark Hill	N/A	The usual attractions.
Rat Records	348 New Camberwell Rd	077 9542 4575	Ramshackle and friendly. There's bargains if you've got superhuman patience.

Map 123 • Peckham

Curious Science	5 Commercial Way	020 8961 3113	Stock up on stuffed mutant cow heads and cases of eyeballs.
Persepolis	30 Peckham High St	020 7639 8007	Can a deli change your life? Yes. Yes, it can.
Primark	51 Rye Ln	020 7639 9655	More of a chance of scoring that 'it' item at this branch.

Map 127 • Coldharbour Lane / Herne Hill (West)

Blackbird Bakery	208 Railton Rd	020 7095 8800	London needs more lovely independent bakeries (like this).

Map 128 • Denmark Hill / Herne Hill (East)

Tales on Moon Lane	25 Half Moon Ln	020 7274 5759	Cute children's bookshop (as if there were any other kind!).

Map 129 • East Dulwich

The Cheeseblock	69 Lordship Ln	020 8299 3636	Best cheese south of the river.

Map 130 • Peckham Rye

Hope And Greenwood	20 North Cross Rd	020 8613 1777	Twee but tasty old-style sweets.

Map 133 • Battersea (East)

London Recumbents	Battersea Park	020 7498 6543	Much more fun in theory than in practice.

Map 134 • South Lambeth

Lassco House & Garden	30 Wandsworth Rd	020 7394 2100	Homebase for the unique, antique, or eccentric.
New Covent Garden Market	New Covent Garden Market	020 7720 2211	Known as London's Larder. Nowhere near Covent Garden

Map 139 • Wandsworth (East)

Cake Boy	2 Kingfisher House, Battersea Reach	020 7978 5555	Cookery school and cake emporium extraordinaire.

Map 140 • Clapham Junction / Northcote Rd

Anita's Vintage Fashion Fair	Battersea Arts Centre, Lavender Hill	020 8325 5789	Hardcore collectors, designers, and students find inspiration amongst the rails.

Dub Vendor	274 Lavender Hill	020 7223 3757	Dub, reggae, ska, rocksteady, roots, dancehall record specialist.
EF Russ	101 Battersea Rise	020 7228 6319	Model specialist—trains, boats, planes and more.
Huttons	29 Northcote Rd	020 7223 5523	Eclectic mix of unusual clothes, furniture and gifts.
Kiehls	20 Northcote Rd	020 7350 2997	Can't beat face masks with algae extracts or pear-flavoured lipbalm.
QT Toys and Games	90 Northcote Rd	020 7223 8637	Toys for big and small kids. Cool gifts.
Party Superstores	268 Lavender Hill	020 7924 3210	The queues on Halloween will scare you to death.
Space NK Apothecary	46 Northcote Rd	020 7228 7563	Skin care heaven.
Sweaty Betty	136 Northcote Rd	020 7978 5444	Look like a total Betty, like, even when you're sweaty.
TK Maxx	St John's Rd & Barnard Rd	020 7228 8072	The best bargains in town.
Traid	28 St John's Rd	020 7924 3065	Characterful recycled clothes. Touch of wank, but still we like.
Vintage Market Place	Battersea Arts Centre	020 8325 5789	Hardcore collectors, designers, and students find inspiration amongst the rails.
Whole Foods Market	305 Lavender Hill	020 7585 1488	Overwhelming selection of organic exotica.

Map 141 • Battersea (South)

Avalon Comics	143 Lavender Hill	020 7924 3609	Proper geeky indie comic shop. Marvel-lous.
Battersea Car Boot Sale	401 Battersea Park Rd	079 4138 3588	Yeah! A huge, tumultous boot sale that starts mid afternoon!
Comet Miniatures	44 Lavender Hill	020 7228 3702	Get your Airfix fix. Model shop and sci-fi.

Map 142 • Clapham Old Town

Puppet Planet	787 Wandsworth Rd	020 7627 0111	Not great if you're pupaphobic but otherwise rather charming.

Map 143 • Clapham High Street

Apex Cycles	40 Clapham High St	020 7622 1334	Bikes fixed, bikes sold.
Esca	160 Clapham High St	020 7622 2288	Your Clapham Common picnic starts here.
M. Moen & Sons	24 The Pavement	020 7622 1624	Butcher for the bourgeoisie, incredibly good, massively expensive.
Paws	62 Clapham High St	020 7720 9962	Attendant, napping canines remind shoppers where the takings will go.
Today's Living Health Store	92 Clapham High St	020 7622 1772	Health foods, herbal remedies and other jiggery pokery.

Map 144 • Stockwell / Brixton (West)

A&C Co Continental Grocers	3 Atlantic Rd	020 7733 3766	Portuguese-owned institution, famous for pestos, chorizo and mamma's tortilla.
Lisa Stickley London	74 Landor Rd	020 7737 8067	Dotty 1940s-inspired handbags to tea-towels. Cath Kidston but better.
The Old Post Office Bakery	76 Landor Rd	020 7326 4408	Disused P.O turned artisan baker's. Local loaf? The Brixton Rye.

Map 146 • Earlsfield

The Earlsfield Bookshop	513 Garratt Ln	020 8946 3744	Dusty old secondhand book haven.

Map 147 • Balham (West)

Bon Vivant	59 Nightingale Ln	020 8675 6314	Great local deli.

Map 148 • Balham (East)

Moxon's	Westbury Parade	020 8675 2468	Fresh fish for foodies with deep pockets. Knowledgeable staff.

Map 149 • Clapham Park

MacFarlanes	48 Abbeville Rd	020 8673 5373	Gourmet goodness galore.

Map 150 • Brixton

Traid	2 Acre Ln	020 7326 4330	Characterful recycled clothes. Touch of wank, but still we like.

Map 151 • Tooting Bec

Russell's Hardware & DIY	46 Upper Tooting Rd	020 8767 7555	DIY treasure chest. Friendly, helpful owners.
Wandsworth Oasis HIV/AIDs Charity Shop	40 Trinity Rd	020 8767 7555	Thrift store treasure trove.

Map 152 • Tooting Broadway

Tooting Market	21 Tooting High St	020 8672 4760	Quaint indoor labyrinth worth nosing about.

NFT
NFT
WHAT IS THAT?!
HUH? OH, IT'S WWW.NOTFORTOURISTS.COM
NFT
NFT
BUT WHY?! WHY WOULD YOU USE ANYTHING OTHER THAN ME?
WELL, THE WEBSITE JUST OFFERS A FEW THINGS THAT YOU DON'T: DAILY CONTENT, FUN PHOTOS, SEARCHABLE DATABASE... COOL STUFF LIKE THAT.
DEVASTATED
OH... I SEE...

BUT I FIT IN YOUR POCKET. YOU CAN TAKE ME ANYWHERE.
SWOOP!
OH!
TUCK TUCK
OH PLEASE. THE WEBSITE COULD NEVER REPLACE YOU. I NEED YOU BOTH TO GET THE MOST OUT OF MY CITY!

A

Street Index

Street Index

B

Street Index

Street Index

Street Index

Street Index

Street Index

Street Index

E

Street Index

Street Index

Street Index

Street Index

H

Street Index

I

Street Index

J

K

L

Street Index

Street Index

M

Street Index

Street Index

Street Index

Street Index

Street Index

Street Index

S

Street Index

Street Index

Street Index

T

Street Index

Street Index

U

V

Y

Z

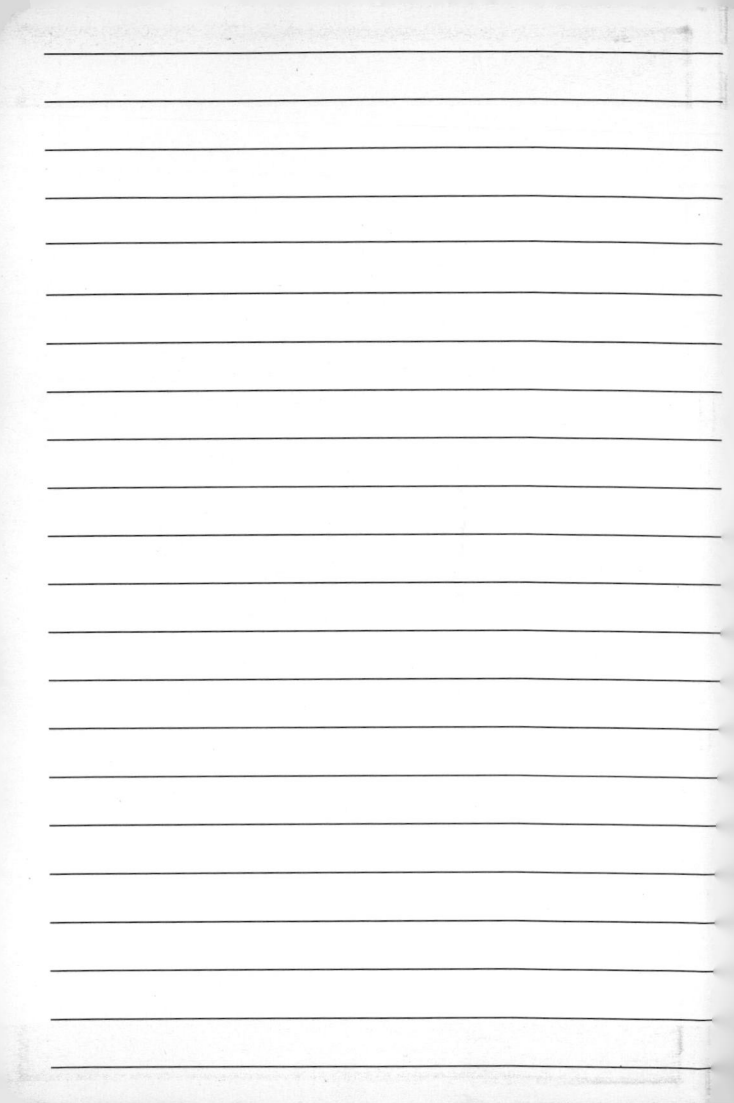